NORTH AMERICA

SOUTH AMERICA

SOUTHWEST ASIA & NORTH AFRICA

EUROPE

RUSSIA & THE EURASIAN REPUBLICS

Southeast Asia

Central America & the Caribbean

Sub-Saharan AFRICA

AUSTRALIA, THE PACIFIC REALM & ANTARCTICA

EUROPE

South Asia

South Asia

Southeast Asia

Central America & the Caribbean

NATIONAL GEOGRAPHIC LEARNING | CENGAGE Learning

SOUTHWEST ASIA & NORTH AFRICA

NORTH AMERICA

SOUTH AMERICA

NATIONAL GEOGRAPHIC

World Cultures and Geography

★ TEXAS

Acknowledgments

Grateful acknowledgment is given to the authors, artists, photographers, museums, publishers, and agents for permission to reprint copyrighted material. Every effort has been made to secure the appropriate permission. If any omissions have been made or if corrections are required, please contact the Publisher.

Photographic Credits

Front Cover: © Roger Ressmeyer/Corbis
Back Cover: © Neale Clark/Robert Harding World Imagery/Getty Images

Acknowledgments and credits continued on page R124.

Visit National Geographic Learning online at www.NGSP.com
Visit our corporate website at www.cengage.com

Printed in the USA
RR Donnelley
Willard, OH

ISBN: 978-12858-5819-7

15 16 17 18 19 20 21 22 23

10 9 8 7 6 5

Andrew J. Milson

Andrew Milson is a professor of social science education and geography at the University of Texas at Arlington. He taught middle school history and geography near Dallas, Texas. Andy conducts research on geographic education and the use of geospatial technologies in education. He has published more than 30 articles and is an elected member of the Executive Board of the National Council for Geographic Education. He serves as an associate editor of the *Journal of Geography*.

Peggy Altoff

Peggy Altoff's experience includes teaching middle school and high school students, supervising teachers, and serving as adjunct university staff. Peggy served as a state social studies specialist in Baltimore and as a K–12 facilitator in Colorado Springs. She was president of the National Council for the Social Studies (NCSS) in 2006–2007 and was on the task force for the new NCSS National Curriculum Standards.

Mark H. Bockenhauer

Mark Bockenhauer is a professor of geography at St. Norbert College and a former geographer-in-residence at the National Geographic Society. Mark has extensive experience in teacher professional development. He co-wrote *Our Fifty States* and the *World Atlas for Young Explorers, 3rd edition*—both for National Geographic. Mark is coordinator of the Wisconsin Geographic Alliance, and he served as president of the National Council for Geographic Education in 2007.

Janet Smith

Jan Smith is an associate professor of geography at Shippensburg University. Jan began her teaching career as a high school teacher in Virginia where she served as a teacher consultant for the Virginia Geographic Alliance for many years. Her primary research interest focuses on how children develop their spatial thinking skills. Jan served as president of the National Council for Geographic Education in 2008, and she is currently the coordinator for the Pennsylvania Geographic Alliance.

Michael W. Smith

Michael Smith is a professor in the Department of Curriculum, Instruction, and Technology in Education at Temple University. He became a college teacher after 11 years of teaching high school English. His research focuses on how experienced readers read and talk about texts, as well as what motivates adolescents' reading and writing. Michael has written many books and monographs, including the award-winning *"Reading Don't Fix No Chevys": Literacy in the Lives of Young Men*.

David W. Moore

David Moore is a professor of education at Arizona State University. He taught high school social studies and reading before entering college teaching. He currently teaches teacher preparation courses and conducts research in adolescent literacy. David has published numerous professional articles, book chapters, and books, including *Developing Readers and Writers in the Content Areas* and *Principled Practices for Adolescent Literacy*.

CONSULTANTS AND REVIEWERS

Teacher Reviewers

Texas Teacher Consultant

Merry Lobrecht
Social Studies Supervisor
Humble ISD, retired

Kayce Forbes
Deerpark Middle School
Austin, Texas

Michael Koren
Maple Dale School
Fox Point, Wisconsin

Patricia Lewis
Humble Middle School
Humble, Texas

Julie Mitchell
Lake Forest Middle School
Cleveland, Tennessee

Linda O'Connor
Northeast Independent
School District
San Antonio, Texas

Leah Perry
Exploris Middle School
Raleigh, North Carolina

Robert Poirier
North Andover Middle School
North Andover, Massachusetts

Heather Rountree
Bedford Heights Elementary
Bedford, Texas

Erin Stevens
Quabbin Regional
Middle/High School
Barre, Massachusetts

Beth Tipper
Crofton Middle School
Crofton, Maryland

Mary Trichel
Atascocita Middle School
Humble, Texas

Andrea Wallenbeck
Exploris Middle School
Raleigh, North Carolina

Reviewers of Religious Content

The following individuals reviewed the treatment of religious content in selected pages of the text.

Charles Haynes
First Amendment Center
Washington, D.C.

Shabbir Mansuri
Institute on Religion and
Civic Values
Fountain Valley, California

Raka Ray
Chair, Center for South Asia Studies
University of California
Berkeley, California

National Geographic Society

The National Geographic Society contributed significantly to *World Cultures and Geography.*
Our collaboration with each of the following has been a pleasure and a privilege: National
Geographic Maps, National Geographic Education Programs, National Geographic Missions
Programs, National Geographic Digital Motion, National Geographic Digital Studio, and
National Geographic Weekend. We thank the Society for its guidance and support.

Greg Anderson
Linguist
National Geographic Fellow

Greg Anderson records and preserves many different endangered languages. He is also the co-director of the Enduring Voices Project.

Katey Walter Anthony
Aquatic Ecologist and Biogeochemist
National Geographic Emerging Explorer

Katey Walter Anthony explores ways to use a greenhouse gas for energy.

Ken Banks
Mobile Technology Innovator
National Geographic Emerging Explorer

Ken Banks develops mobile technology to connect groups in remote areas.

Katy Croff Bell
Archaeological Oceanographer
National Geographic Emerging Explorer

Katy Croff Bell uses deep sea technology to explore the depths of the ocean and the Black Sea.

Christina Conlee
Archaeologist
National Geographic Grantee

Christina Conlee researches geoglyphs and Nasca lines etched into the earth in South America.

Alexandra Cousteau
Social Environmental Activist
National Geographic Emerging Explorer

Alexandra Cousteau works to educate people to protect water resources and oceans.

Thomas Taha Rassam (TH) Culhane
Urban Planner
National Geographic Emerging Explorer

T.H. Culhane works with residents of Cairo to install solar water heaters.

Jenny Daltry
Herpetologist
National Geographic Emerging Explorer

Jenny Daltry saves endangered species of reptiles and inspires local people to protect reptiles and their habitats.

Wade Davis
Anthropologist and Ethnobotanist
National Geographic Explorer-in-Residence

Wade Davis studies plants and people while living within many indigenous cultures around the world.

Sylvia Earle
Oceanographer
National Geographic Explorer-in-Residence

Sylvia Earle's research focuses on exploring and preserving marine ecosystems.

Grace Gobbo
Ethnobotanist
National Geographic Emerging Explorer

Grace Gobbo studies traditional medicine practices in Tanzania and plants native to the region.

Beverly Goodman
Geoarchaeologist
National Geographic Emerging Explorer

Beverly Goodman uses her skills to uncover past tsunamis and to help prevent disasters in the future.

David Harrison
Linguist
National Geographic Fellow

David Harrison studies and archives endangered languages and cultures. He is also the co-director of the Enduring Voices Project.

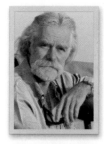

Dereck Joubert
Filmmaker and Conservationist
National Geographic Explorer-in-Residence

Dereck Joubert researches and films big cats and wildlife in Africa, sharing their stories with the world.

Kristofer Helgen
Zoologist
National Geographic Emerging Explorer

Kristofer Helgen discovers new species of mammals and researches animals from across the world.

Albert Lin
Research Scientist and Engineer
National Geographic Emerging Explorer

Albert Lin uses computer technologies to search for archeological sites without disturbing the land.

Fredrik Hiebert
Archaeologist
National Geographic Fellow

Fredrik Hiebert uncovers mysteries of the past and has traced ancient trade routes, including the Silk Road.

Elizabeth Kapu'uwailani Lindsey
Filmmaker and Anthropologist
National Geographic Fellow

Elizabeth Lindsey strives to preserve the Polynesian culture by using documentary films and education.

Zeb Hogan
Aquatic Ecologist
National Geographic Fellow

Zeb Hogan studies freshwater fish and educates people on how to save these fish species from extinction.

Sam Meacham
Cave Diver
National Geographic Grantee

Sam Meacham explores, preserves, and maps aquifers, caves, and other groundwater sources in Mexico.

Shafqat Hussain
Conservationist
National Geographic Emerging Explorer

Shafqat Hussain works with herders in Pakistan to protect the endangered snow leopard.

Kakenya Ntaiya
Educator and Activist
National Geographic Emerging Explorer

Kakenya Ntaiya established a school for girls in Kenya, and she continues to improve girls' education there.

© Sharon Farmer

Beverly Joubert
Filmmaker and Conservationist
National Geographic Explorer-in-Residence

Beverly Joubert has spent years filming and protecting big cats and other wildlife in Africa.

Johan Reinhard
Anthropologist
National Geographic Explorer-in-Residence

Johan Reinhard conducts field research in South America and investigates the cultural practices of Andes people.

Enric Sala
Marine Ecologist
National Geographic Explorer-in-Residence

Enric Sala dedicates his life to finding ways to reverse the damage humans have caused to the seas.

Beth Shapiro
Molecular Biologist
National Geographic Emerging Explorer

Beth Shapiro studies samples of ancient DNA to find out how species change over time.

Kira Salak
Writer/Adventurer
National Geographic Emerging Explorer

Kira Salak is an adventure traveler who writes about her explorations in exotic, often dangerous places.

Cid Simoes
Sustainable Agriculturalist
National Geographic Emerging Explorer

Cid Simoes teaches farmers in Brazil how to farm in economically efficient and ecologically sound ways.

Katsufumi Sato
Behavioral Ecologist
National Geographic Emerging Explorer

Katsufumi Soto uses technology to study animal behaviors with the goal of conserving their habitats.

José Urteaga
Marine Biologist and Conservationist
National Geographic Emerging Explorer

José Urteaga uses creative ideas to help save sea turtles from extinction.

Paola Segura
Sustainable Agriculturalist
National Geographic Emerging Explorer

Paola Segura teaches sustainable farming techniques to farmers in Brazil, conserving the rain forest.

Spencer Wells
Population Geneticist
National Geographic Explorer-in-Residence

Spencer Wells studies human migration patterns. He is the director of National Geographic's Genographic Project.

THE ESSENTIALS OF GEOGRAPHY

TECHTREK

myNGconnect.com

Digital Library
Unit 1 GeoVideo
Introduce the Essentials of Geography

Explorer Video Clip
Sylvia Earle, Oceanographer
National Geographic Explorer-in-Residence

NATIONAL GEOGRAPHIC PHOTO GALLERY

Photos of Earth's physical features
and physical environmental processes;
major cities of the world and images of
world cultures

Maps and Graphs
Interactive Map Tool

Interactive Whiteboard GeoActivities
• Draw the Stages of an Earthquake
• Build a Climograph
• Map the Spread of Buddhism

Archaeologists at work

TECHTREK

myNGconnect.com

Digital Library
Unit 2 GeoVideo
Introduce North America

Explorer Video Clip
Sam Meacham, Cave Diver
National Geographic Grantee

NATIONAL GEOGRAPHIC PHOTO GALLERY

Regional photos, including the Grand Canyon and Great Plains, Mexico City, Austin, Vancouver, and New York City; and historical images, portraits, and cultural festivals

Maps and Graphs
Interactive Map Tool

Interactive Whiteboard GeoActivities
• Compare Climates
• Illustrate the Rain Shadow Effect
• Create a Sketch Map of Tenochtitlán

Tourists at the Grand Canyon, Arizona

TECHTREK

myNGconnect.com

Mayan girl

Digital Library
Unit 3 GeoVideo
Introduce Central America & the Caribbean

Explorer Video Clip
José Urteaga, Marine Biologist
  and Conservationist
National Geographic Emerging Explorer

PHOTO GALLERY

Regional photos, including the rain forest,
  the Andes Mountains, and Montserrat

Music Clips
Audio clips of music from the region

Maps and Graphs
Outline Maps

Interactive Whiteboard GeoActivities
• Research Rain Forest Species
• Build a Time Line of Colonial Rule
• Analyze Push-Pull Factors

TECHTREK

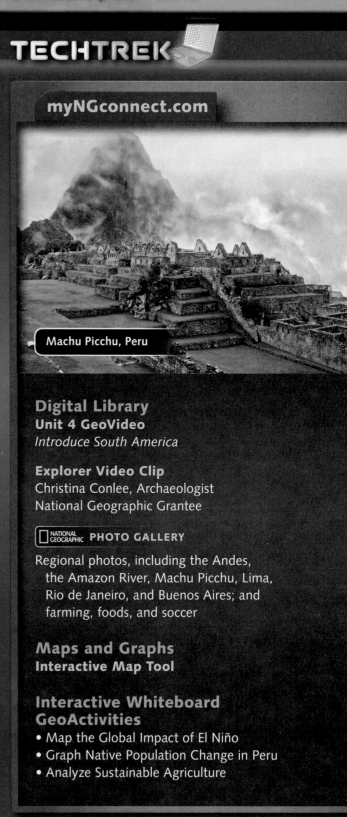

myNGconnect.com

Machu Picchu, Peru

Digital Library
Unit 4 GeoVideo
Introduce South America

Explorer Video Clip
Christina Conlee, Archaeologist
National Geographic Grantee

NATIONAL GEOGRAPHIC PHOTO GALLERY
Regional photos, including the Andes, the Amazon River, Machu Picchu, Lima, Rio de Janeiro, and Buenos Aires; and farming, foods, and soccer

Maps and Graphs
Interactive Map Tool

Interactive Whiteboard GeoActivities
• Map the Global Impact of El Niño
• Graph Native Population Change in Peru
• Analyze Sustainable Agriculture

UNIT 5 EUROPE

TECHTREK

myNGconnect.com

Digital Library
Unit 5 GeoVideo
Introduce Europe

Explorer Video Clip
Enric Sala, Marine Ecologist
National Geographic Explorer-in-Residence

PHOTO GALLERY

Regional photos, including Florence,
Paris, Amsterdam, and Budapest

Maps and Graphs
Interactive Map Tool

Interactive Whiteboard GeoActivities
• Map Europe's Land Regions
• Compare Greek and Roman Governments
• Analyze Causes and Effects of World War I

Louvre Museum, Paris, France

TECHTREK

myNGconnect.com

Digital Library
Unit 6 GeoVideo
Introduce Russia & the Eurasian Republics

Explorer Video Clip
Katey Walter Anthony, Aquatic Ecologist
National Geographic Emerging Explorer

NATIONAL GEOGRAPHIC PHOTO GALLERY

Regional photos, including St. Basil's Cathedral in Moscow, the Ural Mountains, Siberian tundra, and St. Petersburg

Music Clips
Audio clips of music from the region

Maps and Graphs
Interactive Map Tool

Interactive Whiteboard GeoActivities
• Analyze Central Asian Economies
• Graph Napoleon's March Through Russia
• Explore the Trans-Siberian Railroad

St. Basil's Cathedral, Moscow, Russia

UNIT 7 Sub-Saharan Africa

TECHTREK

myNGconnect.com

A musician and griot in Senegal

Digital Library
Unit 7 GeoVideo
Introduce Sub-Saharan Africa

Explorer Video Clip
Dereck and Beverly Joubert, Conservationists
National Geographic Explorers-in-Residence

NATIONAL GEOGRAPHIC PHOTO GALLERY

Regional photos, including Kenya's
savanna, Victoria Falls, Johannesburg,
and the Great Rift Valley

Music Clips
Audio clips of music from the region

Maps and Graphs
Interactive Map Tool

Interactive Whiteboard GeoActivities
• Compare Precipitation Across Regions
• Locate a Wildlife Reserve
• Research Vanishing Cultures

TECHTREK

myNGconnect.com

View from the world's tallest building, Dubai

Digital Library
Unit 8 GeoVideo
Introduce Southwest Asia & North Africa

Explorer Video Clip
Beverly Goodman, Geoarchaeologist
National Geographic Emerging Explorer

NATIONAL GEOGRAPHIC PHOTO GALLERY

Regional photos, including the Blue Mosque,
Hagia Sophia, and Topkapi Palace

Maps and Graphs
Outline Maps

Interactive Whiteboard GeoActivities
• Explore an Ancient Irrigation System
• Compare Major Rivers of the World
• Trace the Benefits of Education

TECHTREK

myNGconnect.com

Digital Library
Unit 9 GeoVideo
Introduce South Asia

Explorer Video Clip
Kira Salak, Writer/Adventurer
National Geographic Emerging Explorer

NATIONAL GEOGRAPHIC PHOTO GALLERY

Regional photos, including the Himalayas, the Ganges River, and the Taj Mahal; Hindu artifacts and cultural celebrations; snow leopards; and monsoon season

Music Clips
Audio clips of music from the region

Maps and Graphs
Interactive Map Tool

Interactive Whiteboard GeoActivities
• Draw a Mental Map of South Asia
• Build a Time Line of Colonialism in India
• Graph and Compare Internet Use

Climbers on Mount Everest

UNIT 10 East Asia

CHAPTER 19
East Asia Geography & History 524

CHAPTER 20
East Asia Today 560

TECHTREK

myNGconnect.com

Digital Library
Unit 10 GeoVideo
Introduce East Asia

Explorer Video Clip
Albert Lin, Research Scientist and Engineer
National Geographic Emerging Explorer

NATIONAL GEOGRAPHIC **PHOTO GALLERY**

Regional photos, including the Great Wall
of China, Mount Fuji, Tibet, cultural
artifacts, Samurai armor, factories, bullet
trains, and a Buddhist temple in Korea

Maps and Graphs
Interactive Map Tool

Interactive Whiteboard GeoActivities
• Follow the Chang Jiang
• Barter on the Silk Roads
• Explore the Forbidden City

Mount Fuji, Japan

UNIT 11
Southeast Asia

TECHTREK

myNGconnect.com

A floating market in Thailand

Digital Library
Unit 11 GeoVideo
Introduce Southeast Asia

Explorer Video Clip
Kristofer Helgen, Zoologist
National Geographic Emerging Explorer

NATIONAL GEOGRAPHIC PHOTO GALLERY

Regional photos, including the Mekong and Irrawaddy rivers, Angkor Wat, and Hanoi and Jakarta

Maps and Graphs
Interactive Map Tool

Interactive Whiteboard GeoActivities
• Investigate New Species
• Map the Spice Trade
• Analyze Remittances and GDP

UNIT 12
AUSTRALIA, THE PACIFIC REALM & ANTARCTICA

TECHTREK

myNGconnect.com

Opera House, Sydney, Australia

Digital Library
Unit 12 GeoVideo
Introduce Australia, the Pacific Realm & Antarctica

Explorer Video Clip
David Harrison and Greg Anderson, Linguists
National Geographic Fellows

NATIONAL GEOGRAPHIC PHOTO GALLERY

Regional photos, including the Great Barrier Reef and glaciers in Antarctica

Maps and Graphs
Interactive Map Tool

Interactive Whiteboard GeoActivities
• Research Indigenous Species
• Research and Report on Endangered Languages
• Build a Time Line of Indigenous Rights

SPECIAL FEATURES

National Geographic Explorers

Global Issues

Document-Based Questions

Compare Across Regions

Graphs

Charts and Tables

Infographics and Models

THE GREAT PYRAMID OF KHUFU, 2550 B.C.

NATIONAL GEOGRAPHIC **Atlas** A2–A39

Maps

NATIONAL GEOGRAPHIC
ATLAS

World Physical

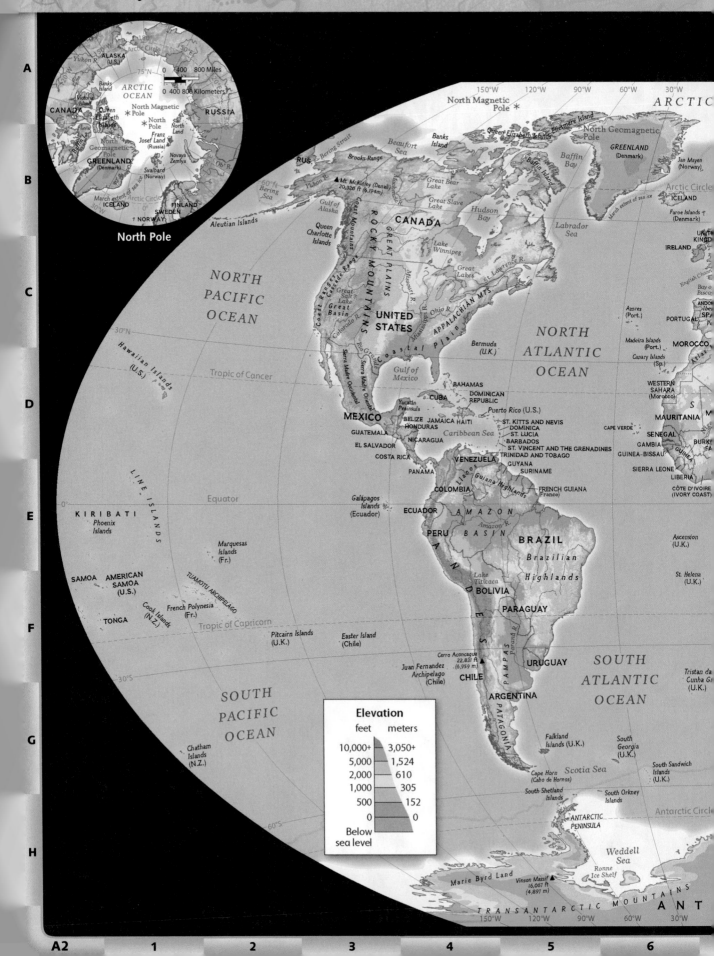

North Pole

ARCTIC OCEAN

ALASKA (U.S.)
Yukon R.
Banks Island
CANADA
Victoria Island
Queen Elizabeth Islands
Baffin Island
GREENLAND (Denmark)
North Geomagnetic Pole
ICELAND
NORWAY
SWEDEN
FINLAND
Svalbard (Norway)
Novaya Zemlya
Ob' R.
Franz Josef Land (Russia)
North Land
North Pole
North Magnetic Pole
Arctic Circle
RUSSIA
75°N
March extent of sea ice
30°W

0   400   800 Miles
0 400 800 Kilometers

Elevation

feet	meters
10,000+	3,050+
5,000	1,524
2,000	610
1,000	305
500	152
0	0
Below sea level	

North Magnetic Pole
North Geomagnetic Pole
ARCTIC
Queen Elizabeth Islands
Ellesmere Island
North Geomagnetic Pole
GREENLAND (Denmark)
Jan Mayen (Norway)
Arctic Circle
ICELAND
Faroe Islands (Denmark)
IRELAND
UNITED KINGDOM

Banks Island
Beaufort Sea
Brooks Range
Mt. McKinley (Denali) 20,320 ft (6,194m)
Gulf of Alaska
Aleutian Islands
Bering Strait
Bering Sea
Yukon R.
RUS.
Great Bear Lake
Great Slave Lake
Hudson Bay
Baffin Bay
Labrador Sea
CANADA
GREAT PLAINS
ROCKY MOUNTAINS
Lake Winnipeg
Great Lakes
Mackenzie R.
St. Lawrence R.
50°N

Queen Charlotte Islands
Coast Ranges
Cascade Range
Columbia R.
Great Salt Lake
Great Basin
Sierra Nevada
UNITED STATES
Missouri R.
Ohio R.
Mississippi R.
APPALACHIAN MTS.
Coastal Plain
English Channel
Bay of Biscay
Azores (Port.)
PORTUGAL
SPAIN
ANDORRA
Iberian
MOROCCO
Atlas

NORTH PACIFIC OCEAN
30°N
Hawaiian Islands (U.S.)
Tropic of Cancer
Sierra Madre Occidental
Sierra Madre Oriental
Rio Grande
Colorado R.
Gulf of Mexico
Bermuda (U.K.)
NORTH ATLANTIC OCEAN
Madeira Islands (Port.)
Canary Islands (Sp.)
WESTERN SAHARA (Morocco)
MAURITANIA

MEXICO
Yucatán Peninsula
BAHAMAS
CUBA
DOMINICAN REPUBLIC
Puerto Rico (U.S.)
BELIZE   JAMAICA HAITI
HONDURAS
GUATEMALA
EL SALVADOR
NICARAGUA
ST. KITTS AND NEVIS
DOMINICA
ST. LUCIA
BARBADOS
ST. VINCENT AND THE GRENADINES
TRINIDAD AND TOBAGO
Caribbean Sea
CAPE VERDE
SENEGAL
GAMBIA
GUINEA-BISSAU
GUINEA
SIERRA LEONE
LIBERIA
CÔTE D'IVOIRE (IVORY COAST)
BURKINA FASO
SUDAN
MALI

COSTA RICA
PANAMA
VENEZUELA
COLOMBIA
GUYANA
SURINAME
FRENCH GUIANA (France)
Guiana Highlands
Llanos
KIRIBATI
Phoenix Islands
Galápagos Islands (Ecuador)
Equator
ECUADOR
PERU
AMAZON BASIN
Amazon R.
BRAZIL
Ascension (U.K.)

LINE ISLANDS
Marquesas Islands (Fr.)
ANDES
Brazilian Highlands
St. Helena (U.K.)

SAMOA
AMERICAN SAMOA (U.S.)
TUAMOTU ARCHIPELAGO
French Polynesia (Fr.)
Lake Titicaca
BOLIVIA
PARAGUAY

TONGA
Cook Islands (N.Z.)
Tropic of Capricorn
Pitcairn Islands (U.K.)
Easter Island (Chile)
Paraná R.
PAMPAS
URUGUAY
SOUTH ATLANTIC OCEAN
Tristan da Cunha Group (U.K.)

30°S
Cerro Aconcagua 22,831 ft (6,959 m)
Juan Fernandez Archipelago (Chile)
CHILE
ARGENTINA

SOUTH PACIFIC OCEAN
Chatham Islands (N.Z.)
PATAGONIA
Falkland Islands (U.K.)
South Georgia (U.K.)
South Sandwich Islands (U.K.)

60°S
Cape Horn (Cabo de Hornos)
Scotia Sea
South Shetland Islands
South Orkney Islands
Antarctic Circle

ANTARCTIC PENINSULA
Weddell Sea
Marie Byrd Land
Vinson Massif 16,067 ft (4,897 m)
Ronne Ice Shelf
TRANSANTARCTIC MOUNTAINS
ANTARCTICA

150°W   120°W   90°W   60°W   30°W

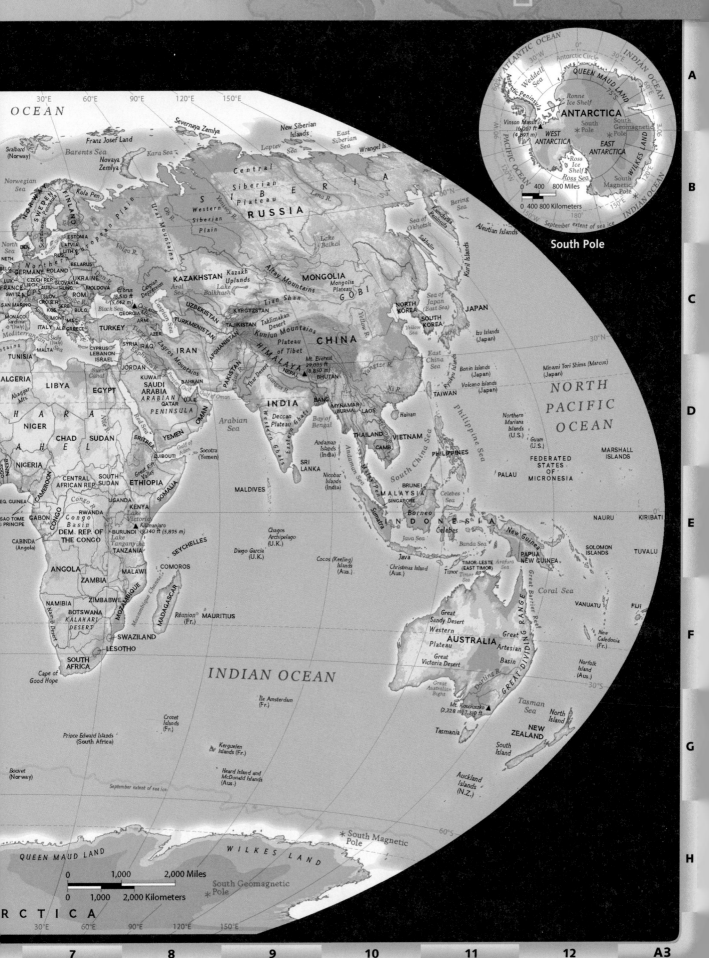

OCEAN

30°E 60°E 90°E 120°E 150°E

Svalbard (Norway)

Franz Josef Land

Severnaya Zemlya

New Siberian Islands

East Siberian Sea

Barents Sea

Novaya Zemlya

Kara Sea

Laptev Sea

Wrangel Is.

Norwegian Sea

NORWAY

SWEDEN

FINLAND

Kola Pen.

Scandinavian Peninsula

Northern European Plain

Central Siberian Plateau

S I B E R I A

Western Siberian Plain

Ob R.

Yenisey R.

Lena R.

Bering Sea

Kamchatka Peninsula

North Sea

DEN.

NETH.

BELG.

GERMANY

LUX.

POLAND

Volga R.

Ural Mountains

RUSSIA

Lake Baikal

Sea of Okhotsk

Aleutian Islands

Sakhalin

FRANCE

CZECH REP.

SWITZ.

LIECH.

SLOVAKIA

AUS.

HUNG.

MOLDOVA

UKRAINE

BELARUS

EST.

LATVIA

LITH.

RUS.

Caspian Depression

KAZAKHSTAN

Kazakh Uplands

Aral Sea

Lake Balkhash

Altay Mountains

MONGOLIA

Mongolia Plateau

GOBI

Kuril Islands

Sea of Japan (East Sea)

JAPAN

SAN MARINO

MONACO

Sardinia (Italy)

ITALY

SLOV.

CRO.

B.H.

SERB.

MNE.

KOS.

MAC.

ALB.

BULG.

ROM.

GEORGIA

ARM.

AZER.

Elbrus 18,510 ft (5,642 m)

Black Sea

Caspian Sea

UZBEKISTAN

KYRGYZSTAN

TAJIKISTAN

Taklimakan Desert

Tian Shan

CHINA

NORTH KOREA

SOUTH KOREA

Yellow Sea

Yellow R.

East China Sea

Izu Islands (Japan)

TUNISIA

MALTA

GREECE

TURKEY

CYPRUS

SYRIA

LEBANON

ISRAEL

IRAQ

Tigris R.

Euphrates R.

Zagros Mountains

IRAN

AFGHANISTAN

Kunlun Mountains

Plateau of Tibet

H I M A L A Y A

Mt. Everest 29,035 ft (8,850 m)

NEPAL

BHUTAN

Yangtze R.

Xi R.

TAIWAN

Bonin Islands (Japan)

Minami Tori Shima (Marcus) (Japan)

Volcano Islands (Japan)

Ryukyu Islands (Japan)

Mediterranean Sea

Sicily (Italy)

JORDAN

KUWAIT

BAHRAIN

QATAR

U.A.E.

SAUDI ARABIA

ARABIAN PENINSULA

Suez Canal

Red Sea

Persian Gulf

Gulf of Oman

OMAN

Thar Desert

PAKISTAN

Indus R.

INDIA

Ganges R.

BANG.

MYANMAR (BURMA)

LAOS

Hainan

South China Sea

Philippine Sea

NORTH PACIFIC OCEAN

Northern Mariana Islands (U.S.)

Guam (U.S.)

MARSHALL ISLANDS

ALGERIA

LIBYA

EGYPT

Ahaggar Mts.

S A H A R A

Arabian Sea

Western Ghats

Deccan Plateau

Eastern Ghats

Bay of Bengal

Andaman Islands (India)

Andaman Sea

Mekong R.

THAILAND

VIETNAM

CAMB.

PHILIPPINES

PALAU

FEDERATED STATES OF MICRONESIA

NIGER

CHAD

SUDAN

NIGERIA

S A H E L

YEMEN

Gulf of Aden

DJIBOUTI

Socotra (Yemen)

ERITREA

SRI LANKA

Nicobar Islands (India)

BRUNEI

MALAYSIA

SINGAPORE

Celebes Sea

NAURU

KIRIBATI

EQ. GUINEA

SAO TOME & PRINCIPE

GABON

CAMEROON

CENTRAL AFRICAN REP.

SOUTH SUDAN

ETHIOPIA

SOMALIA

UGANDA

KENYA

MALDIVES

Borneo

Celebes

Java Sea

I N D O N E S I A

Sumatra

New Guinea

SOLOMON ISLANDS

TUVALU

CONGO

DEM. REP. OF THE CONGO

Congo Basin

Congo R.

RWANDA

BURUNDI

Lake Victoria

Lake Tanganyika

TANZANIA

Kilimanjaro 19,340 ft (5,895 m)

Great Rift Valley

SEYCHELLES

Chagos Archipelago (U.K.)

Diego Garcia (U.K.)

Cocos (Keeling) Islands (Aus.)

Christmas Island (Aus.)

Java

Banda Sea

Timor

TIMOR-LESTE (EAST TIMOR)

Timor Sea

Arafura Sea

PAPUA NEW GUINEA

Coral Sea

Great Barrier Reef

VANUATU

New Caledonia (Fr.)

FIJI

CABINDA (Angola)

ANGOLA

ZAMBIA

MALAWI

COMOROS

MOZAMBIQUE

ZIMBABWE

NAMIBIA

BOTSWANA

Namib Desert

KALAHARI DESERT

MADAGASCAR

Mozambique Channel

Réunion (Fr.)

MAURITIUS

Great Sandy Desert

Western Plateau

Great Victoria Desert

AUSTRALIA

Great Artesian Basin

GREAT DIVIDING RANGE

Darling R.

Norfolk Island (Aus.)

SWAZILAND

LESOTHO

SOUTH AFRICA

Cape of Good Hope

INDIAN OCEAN

Île Amsterdam (Fr.)

Crozet Islands (Fr.)

Great Australian Bight

Mt. Kosciuszko (2,228 m) 7,310 ft

Tasman Sea

North Island

NEW ZEALAND

Prince Edward Islands (South Africa)

Kerguelen Islands (Fr.)

Tasmania

South Island

Bouvet (Norway)

Heard Island and McDonald Islands (Aus.)

Auckland Islands (N.Z.)

September extent of sea ice

60°S

South Magnetic Pole

QUEEN MAUD LAND

W I L K E S   L A N D

0   1,000   2,000 Miles

0   1,000   2,000 Kilometers

South Geomagnetic Pole

R C T I C A

30°E 60°E 90°E 120°E 150°E

7   8   9   10   11   12   A3

30°N

30°S

60°N

South Pole inset

ATLANTIC OCEAN

60°W

30°W

0°

30°E

INDIAN OCEAN

60°E

Antarctic Circle

Weddell Sea

Antarctic Peninsula

Ronne Ice Shelf

QUEEN MAUD LAND

ANTARCTICA

Vinson Massif 16,067 ft (4,897 m)

WEST ANTARCTICA

South Pole

South Geomagnetic Pole

EAST ANTARCTICA

PACIFIC OCEAN

120°W

90°W

Ross Ice Shelf

Ross Sea

South Magnetic Pole

WILKES LAND

INDIAN OCEAN

90°E

120°E

150°E

180°

0   400   800 Miles

0   400   800 Kilometers

September extent of sea ice

South Pole

30°E 60°E 90°E 120°E 150°E

A
B
C
D
E
F
G
H

World Political

North Pole

ARCTIC OCEAN
North Pole
Franz Josef Land (Russia)
Svalbard (Norway)
GREENLAND (Denmark)
Nuuk (Godthåb)
ICELAND
Reykjavik
NORWAY
SWEDEN
FINLAND
Murmansk
Arkhangel'sk
RUSSIA
Yellowknife
CANADA
ALASKA (U.S.)
Anchorage
Yukon R.
Arctic Circle

ARCTIC

Queen Elizabeth Islands
Ellesmere Island
GREENLAND (KALAALLIT NUNAAT) (Denmark)
Jan Mayen (Norway)
Banks Is.
Victoria Island
Baffin Island
Baffin Bay
Arctic Circle
Beaufort Sea
RUS.
ALASKA (U.S.)
Bering Strait
Bering Sea
Aleutian Islands
Gulf of Alaska
Queen Charlotte Islands
CANADA
Hudson Bay
Labrador Sea
Nuuk (Godthåb)
Reykjavik
ICELAND
Faroe Islands (Denmark)

NORTH PACIFIC OCEAN

UNITED STATES
Ottawa
Washington, D.C.
St.-Pierre & Miquelon (France)

UNITED KINGDOM
IRELAND
Dublin
London
English Channel
ANDORRA
SPAIN
PORTUGAL
Madrid
Lisbon
Azores (Port.)
NORTH ATLANTIC OCEAN

30°N
Tropic of Cancer
HAWAI'I (U.S.)
MEXICO
Gulf of Mexico
Mexico City
Nassau
BAHAMAS
Havana
CUBA
Madeira Islands (Port.)
Rabat
Canary Islands (Sp.)
MOROCCO
Ladyoune
WESTERN SAHARA (Morocco)

Belmopan
BELIZE
Guatemala City
GUATEMALA
San Salvador
EL SALVADOR
HONDURAS
Tegucigalpa
NICARAGUA
Managua
Kingston
JAMAICA
Port-au-Prince
HAITI
DOMINICAN REPUBLIC
Santo Domingo
PUERTO RICO (U.S.)
ST. KITTS AND NEVIS
DOMINICA
ST. LUCIA
BARBADOS
ST. VINCENT AND THE GRENADINES
TRINIDAD AND TOBAGO
Caribbean Sea
MAURITANIA
Nouakchott
MALI
CAPE VERDE
Praia
Dakar
Banjul
Bissau
GAMBIA
GUINEA-BISSAU
SENEGAL
Bamako
Conakry
Freetown
SIERRA LEONE
LIBERIA
Monrovia
Yamoussoukro
CÔTE D'IVOIRE (IVORY COAST)
BURKINA FASO
Ouagadougou
GUINEA
Accra

COSTA RICA
San José
Panama City
PANAMA
Caracas
VENEZUELA
Bogotá
COLOMBIA
Georgetown
Paramaribo
GUYANA
Cayenne
FRENCH GUIANA (France)
SURINAME

Equator
Galápagos Islands (Ecuador)
Quito
ECUADOR
PERU
Lima
BRAZIL
Ascension (U.K.)

KIRIBATI
Phoenix Islands
LINE ISLANDS
Marquesas Islands (Fr.)
La Paz
BOLIVIA
Sucre
Brasília
St. Helena (U.K.)

SAMOA
Apia
AMERICAN SAMOA (U.S.)
TUAMOTU ARCHIPELAGO
Tahiti
French Polynesia (Fr.)
Cook Islands (N.Z.)
TONGA
Nuku'alofa
Tropic of Capricorn
PARAGUAY
Asunción
São Paulo

Pitcairn Islands (U.K.)
Easter Island (Chile)
URUGUAY
Montevideo
Buenos Aires
SOUTH ATLANTIC OCEAN
Tristan da Cunha Group (U.K.)

Juan Fernandez Archipelago (Chile)
Santiago
CHILE
ARGENTINA
30°S

SOUTH PACIFIC OCEAN

Chatham Islands (N.Z.)
Falkland Islands (U.K.)
South Georgia (U.K.)
Scotia Sea
South Sandwich Islands (U.K.)
Prime Meridian
South Shetland Islands
South Orkney Islands
Antarctic Circle
60°S
Weddell Sea
ANTA

150°W   120°W   90°W   60°W   30°W

OCEAN

30°E 60°E 90°E 120°E 150°E

Svalbard (Norway)

Franz Josef Land

Severnaya Zemlya

New Siberian Islands

Barents Sea

Novaya Zemlya

Kara Sea

Laptev Sea

East Siberian Sea

Wrangel Is.

Norwegian Sea

North Sea

RUSSIA

60°N

Bering Sea

Aleutian Islands

NORWAY SWEDEN FINLAND

Oslo Helsinki

Stockholm Tallinn ESTONIA

DEN. LATVIA

Copenhagen LITH. RUS.

NETH. Minsk

IREL. GERMANY POLAND BELARUS

Amsterdam Berlin Warsaw

Pris LUX. CZECH SLOVAKIA UKRAINE

FRANCE SWITZ. LIECH. SLOV. HUNG. Kiev

SAN MARINO ITALY AUT. CRO. ROM.

MONACO Rome BULG.

Moscow

Astana

KAZAKHSTAN

Lake Balkhash

Ulaanbaatar

MONGOLIA

Lake Baikal

Sea of Okhotsk

Kuril Islands

Bishkek KYRGYZSTAN

UZBEKISTAN Tashkent

Beijing

NORTH KOREA Sea of Japan (East Sea)

JAPAN

ALB. GREECE Sofia

Istanbul

GEORGIA ARM. AZER. Baku

Tbilisi Yerevan

TURKMENISTAN TAJIKISTAN Dushanbe

Pyongyang SOUTH KOREA Tokyo

Seoul

Izu Islands (Japan)

Ashgabat

Black Sea Ankara TURKEY AZER.

Mediterranean Sea Valletta Athens

MALTA

Nicosia CYPRUS SYRIA Beirut Baghdad

LEBANON ISRAEL Damascus

Tehran

IRAN

AFGHANISTAN Kabul

Islamabad

Shanghai

CHINA

East China Sea

Yellow Sea

30°N

Taipei

Ryukyu Islands (Japan)

Bonin Islands (Japan)

Volcano Islands (Japan)

Minami Tori Shima (Marcus) (Japan)

TUNISIA

Algiers Tunis

Tripoli

Cairo

Jerusalem JORDAN IRAQ

Amman

Kuwait City KUWAIT

BAHRAIN Manama

PAKISTAN

Delhi New Delhi NEPAL Thimphu BHUTAN

Kathmandu

Dhaka BANG.

TAIWAN

North Pacific Ocean

NORTH PACIFIC OCEAN

ALGERIA

LIBYA

EGYPT

Riyadh QATAR Doha U.A.E.

Abu Dhabi

SAUDI ARABIA

OMAN Muscat

Mumbai (Bombay)

INDIA

Bay of Bengal

MYANMAR (BURMA)

Nay Pyi Taw

Hanoi

Haikou

LAOS VIETNAM

Haikou

Haiman

Manila

PHILIPPINES

Philippine Sea

Northern Mariana Islands (U.S.)

Guam (U.S.)

NIGER CHAD SUDAN

Niamey N'Djamena Khartoum

ERITREA

Asmara

YEMEN

Gulf of Aden

Arabian Sea

Socotra (Yemen)

DJIBOUTI Djibouti

Andaman Islands (India)

Yangon (Rangoon)

THAILAND Krung Thep (Bangkok)

CAMBODIA

South China Sea

Phnom Penh

BRUNEI Bandar Seri Begawan

MARSHALL ISLANDS

Majuro

Melekeok PALAU

FEDERATED STATES OF MICRONESIA

Palikir

NIGERIA Abuja

Porto-Novo

CAMEROON CENTRAL AFRICAN REP.

Bangui

SOUTH SUDAN Juba

ETHIOPIA

Addis Ababa

SOMALIA

SRI LANKA

Colombo

Sri Jayawardenepura Kotte

MALDIVES Male

Nicobar Islands (India)

Kuala Lumpur MALAYSIA

SINGAPORE

Celebes Sea

Sumatra

NAURU Yaren

TARAWA KIRIBATI

Tarawa (Bairiki)

SAO TOME AND PRINCIPE GABON CONGO

Libreville

Yaounde DEM. REP. OF THE CONGO

São Tomé

EQ. GUINEA Malabo

BENIN TOGO

UGANDA Kampala

RWANDA Kigali

Nairobi

KENYA

Mogadishu

INDONESIA

Jakarta

Java

Java Sea

CABINDA (Angola)

Brazzaville BURUNDI Bujumbura

Kinshasa

TANZANIA Dodoma

Dar es Salaam

Victoria SEYCHELLES

Chagos Archipelago (U.K.)

Diego Garcia (U.K.)

Cocos (Keeling) Islands (Aus.)

Christmas Island (Aus.)

Dili TIMOR-LESTE (EAST TIMOR)

Arafura Sea

Timor Sea

PAPUA NEW GUINEA

Port Moresby

SOLOMON ISLANDS

Honiara

TUVALU Funafuti

Luanda

ANGOLA ZAMBIA

Lusaka

MALAWI Lilongwe

Moroni COMOROS

Coral Sea

VANUATU Port-Vila

FIJI Suva

NAMIBIA ZIMBABWE

Harare MOZAMBIQUE

Windhoek BOTSWANA

Antananarivo MADAGASCAR

Réunion (Fr.) Port Louis

MAURITIUS

New Caledonia (Fr.)

Gaborone (Tshwane) Pretoria

Mbabane Lobamba Maputo

SWAZILAND

AUSTRALIA

Norfolk Island (Aus.)

Bloemfontein LESOTHO Maseru

SOUTH AFRICA

Cape Town

INDIAN OCEAN

Great Australian Bight

Canberra A.C.T.

30°S

Tasman Sea North Island

Île Amsterdam (Fr.)

Crozet Islands (Fr.)

Prince Edward Islands (South Africa)

Kerguelen Islands (Fr.)

Tasmania

NEW ZEALAND

South Island Wellington

Bouvet (Norway)

Heard Island and McDonald Islands (Aus.)

Auckland Islands (N.Z.)

60°S

0 1,000 2,000 Miles

0 1,000 2,000 Kilometers

RCTICA

30°E 60°E 90°E 120°E 150°E

South Pole

ATLANTIC OCEAN 30°W Antarctic Circle 30°E INDIAN OCEAN

60°W Weddell Sea 60°E

Antarctic Peninsula 75°S QUEEN MAUD LAND

Ronne Ice Shelf

Vinson Massif 16,067 ft (4,897 m) South Pole

ANTARCTICA

PACIFIC OCEAN 90°W 90°E

Ross Ice Shelf Ross Sea WILKES LAND

0 400 800 Miles

0 400 800 Kilometers

120°W 180° 150°E 120°E INDIAN OCEAN

A B C D E F G H

7 8 9 10 11 12 A5

NATIONAL GEOGRAPHIC
Endangered Species

CALIFORNIA CONDOR
Condors are threatened by pesticides and habitat loss. A captive breeding program has raised numbers in the wild from 22 in 1987 to more than 160 today.

It's About Habitat

Wild animals need space to live. That means room to roam, room to find food, and room to hide. Quality habitat also means clean water and clean air. However, as the human population grows, the places where people live tend to spread into quality habitat. As the habitat is lost the number of animals decreases. If too much of a species' habitat is lost, the animal is at risk of becoming extinct. The International Union for Conservation of Nature (IUCN) works to save habitat. By identifying the level of endangerment with simple categories, the IUCN helps target the habitats that need to be conserved and the species to be protected.

NORTH AMERICA

NORTH ATLANTIC OCEAN

PACIFIC OCEAN

CONSERVATION STATUS
- Critically Endangered
- Endangered
- Vulnerable

- Asian elephant
- Black rhino
- Blue whale
- California condor
- Giant armadillo
- Giant panda
- Hawksbill turtle
- Mountain gorilla
- Polar bear
- Snow leopard
- Tiger
- Whooping crane

SOUTH AMERICA

BLUE WHALE
Commercial whaling is no longer a danger, but climate change threatens the blue whale's food source, krill. Fewer than 5,000 individuals exist in the wild.

HAWKSBILL TURTLE
The Hawksbill's habitat is severely threatened, but a thriving trade in turtle products poses a greater danger.

POLAR BEAR
Climate change is the polar bear's biggest threat. They hunt on Arctic and sub-Arctic ice flows. As the ice melts, they lose access to their main food source, seals.

Populations in bil

6
4
2
0

Year 1820 1840 1860 1880 1900 1920 1940 1960 1980 2000 2020

60,000
40,000
20,000
0

Extinctions

Population

Extinction

Source: www.whole-systems.org/extinctions.html

ARCTIC OCEAN

EUROPE

ASIA

AFRICA

SOUTH ATLANTIC OCEAN

INDIAN OCEAN

AUSTRALIA

TIGER

With a territory that once ranged across Asia, tigers remain in only a few pockets of the continent, primarily Southeast Asia. There may be as few as 3,200 left in the wild.

GIANT PANDA

The giant panda faces an uncertain future. Though fiercely protected, its habitat is threatened by the roads, railroads, and pollution that are part of China's expanding economy.

BLACK RHINOCEROS

Black rhinos suffered a huge decline between 1970 and 1992 because of poaching. Although in severe danger, their numbers have been slowly rising.

THE WHOOPING CRANE *Success Story*

The whooping crane was near extinction, with only about 20 birds left in the wild. Thanks to intensive recovery efforts, the species now boasts a population of over 600, with more growth expected. The species is still endangered, but scientists believe the recovery is sustainable.

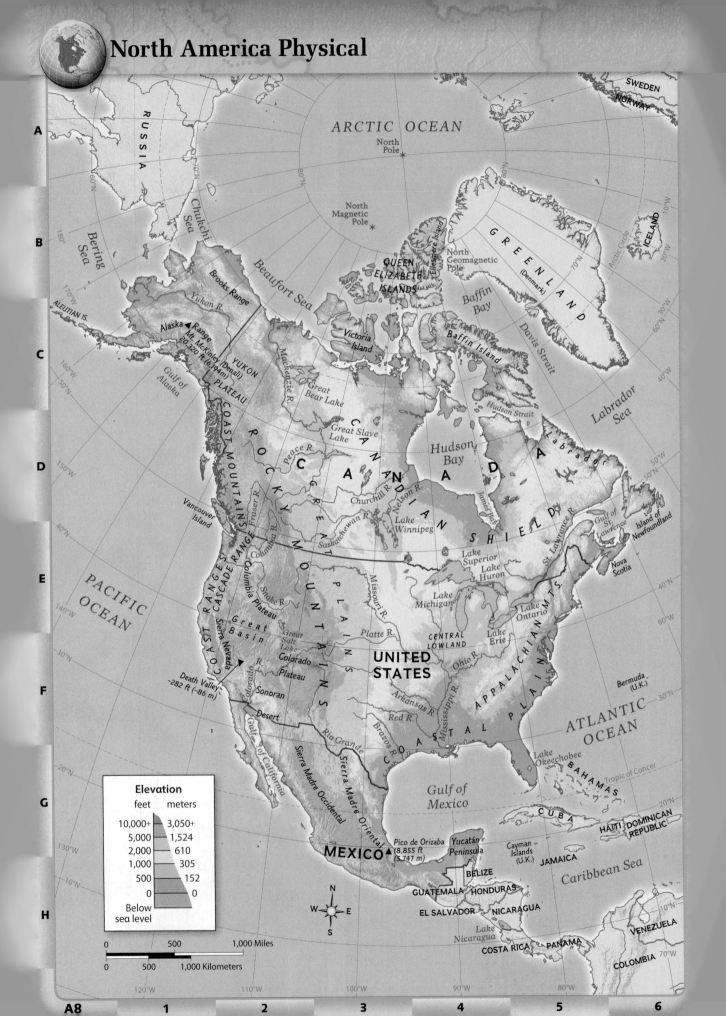

North America Physical

ARCTIC OCEAN

North Pole

SWEDEN

NORWAY

RUSSIA

Chukchi Sea

North Magnetic Pole

QUEEN ELIZABETH ISLANDS

Ellesmere Island

North Geomagnetic Pole

GREENLAND (Denmark)

ICELAND

Arctic Circle

Bering Sea

ALEUTIAN IS.

Brooks Range

Yukon R.

Beaufort Sea

Victoria Island

Baffin Island

Baffin Bay

Davis Strait

Alaska Range

Mt. McKinley (Denali) 20,320 ft (6,194m)

YUKON PLATEAU

Mackenzie R.

Great Bear Lake

Labrador Sea

Gulf of Alaska

COAST MOUNTAINS

Great Slave Lake

Peace R.

CANADIAN SHIELD

Hudson Strait

Labrador

Vancouver Island

ROCKY MOUNTAINS

Fraser R.

Columbia R.

Churchill R.

Nelson R.

Hudson Bay

James Bay

St. Lawrence R.

Gulf of St. Lawrence

Island of Newfoundland

PACIFIC OCEAN

CASCADE RANGE

COAST RANGES

Columbia Plateau

Snake R.

Great Basin

Sierra Nevada

Great Salt Lake

Colorado R.

Colorado Plateau

Saskatchewan R.

Lake Winnipeg

Lake Superior

Lake Huron

Lake Michigan

Lake Ontario

Lake Erie

GREAT PLAINS

Missouri R.

Platte R.

CENTRAL LOWLAND

APPALACHIAN MTS.

Nova Scotia

Death Valley -282 ft (-86 m)

Sonoran Desert

UNITED STATES

Ohio R.

Arkansas R.

Red R.

Mississippi R.

Bermuda (U.K.)

ATLANTIC OCEAN

Gulf of California

Rio Grande

Brazos R.

Sierra Madre Oriental

Sierra Madre Occidental

Gulf of Mexico

Lake Okeechobee

BAHAMAS

Tropic of Cancer

CUBA

HAITI DOMINICAN REPUBLIC

MEXICO

Pico de Orizaba 18,855 ft (5,747 m)

Yucatán Peninsula

Cayman Islands (U.K.)

JAMAICA

Caribbean Sea

BELIZE

GUATEMALA HONDURAS

EL SALVADOR NICARAGUA

Lake Nicaragua

COSTA RICA PANAMA

VENEZUELA

COLOMBIA

Elevation

feet	meters
10,000+	3,050+
5,000	1,524
2,000	610
1,000	305
500	152
0	0
Below sea level	

0   500   1,000 Miles

0   500   1,000 Kilometers

N
W E
S

A

B

C

D

E

F

G

H

Seattle
Olympia
WASHINGTON

Portland
Salem
OREGON

Columbia R.

Helena
MONTANA
Missouri R.

Bozeman

Yellowstone R.

NORTH DAKOTA
Bismarck

James R.

SOUTH DAKOTA
Pierre

Boise
IDAHO

Snake R.

WYOMING

Cheyenne

N. Platte R.

NEBRASKA

Sacramento

San Francisco

Carson City

NEVADA

Great Salt Lake

Salt Lake City

UTAH

Green R.

Colorado R.

Lake Powell

COLORADO

Denver

Colorado Springs

S. Platte R.

Platte R.

Arkansas R.

KANSAS

Wichita

CALIFORNIA

Las Vegas

Lake Mead

Los Angeles

San Diego

Salton Sea

PACIFIC OCEAN

ARIZONA

Phoenix

Gila R.

Rio Grande

Santa Fe

Albuquerque

NEW MEXICO

Canadian R.

Oklahoma City

OKLAHOMA

El Paso

Pecos R.

Red R.

TEXAS

Brazos R.

Austin

San Antonio

Rio Grande

Laredo

MEXICO

CANADA

RUSSIA

Chukchi Sea

ARCTIC OCEAN

Barrow

Beaufort Sea

Arctic Circle

ALASKA

CANADA

Anchorage

Bering Sea

Gulf of Alaska

Juneau

Aleutian Islands

0   300 Miles
0   300 Kilometers

A10

1   2   3   4   5   6

CANADA

MINNESOTA
Duluth
Minneapolis
St. Paul
WISCONSIN
Madison
Milwaukee

IOWA
Des Moines
Lincoln
Topeka
Jefferson City
St. Louis
MISSOURI

ILLINOIS
Springfield
Chicago

Lake Superior
MICHIGAN
Lansing
Detroit
Grand R.
Lake Michigan
Lake Huron
Lake Erie

INDIANA
Indianapolis
Columbus
Cincinnati
Louisville
Frankfort
KENTUCKY
Nashville
TENNESSEE
Memphis

OHIO
WEST VIRGINIA
Charleston
Ohio R.
Cumberland R.
Wabash R.

Lake Ontario
Buffalo
NEW YORK
Albany

St. Lawrence R.
MAINE
Augusta
VERMONT
NEW HAMPSHIRE
Montpelier
Concord
Boston
MASSACHUSETTS
Providence
Hartford RHODE
CONNECTICUT ISLAND
Hudson R.

PENNSYLVANIA
New York
Harrisburg
Trenton
NEW JERSEY
Philadelphia
Baltimore
Annapolis
Dover
DELAWARE
Washington, D.C.
MARYLAND
Long Island

VIRGINIA
Richmond
James R.
Virginia Beach
Roanoke R.
Raleigh
NORTH CAROLINA
Columbia
SOUTH CAROLINA
Savannah R.

ARKANSAS
Little Rock
Arkansas R.
Tennessee R.

ALABAMA
Montgomery
Alabama R.
GEORGIA
Atlanta

ATLANTIC OCEAN

Jackson
MISSISSIPPI
Mississippi R.
Baton Rouge
New Orleans
LOUISIANA
Houston

Tallahassee

FLORIDA
St. Johns R.
Lake Okeechobee
Miami
Florida Keys

Gulf of Mexico

BAHAMAS

Tropic of Cancer

N
W   E
S

0   150   300 Miles
0   150   300 Kilometers

MINNESOTA
Red River of the North
Mississippi R.
Missouri R.
Des Moines R.

INSET MAP

HAWAI'I
Honolulu
Hilo
0   100 Miles
0   100 Kilometers
160°W   158°W   156°W
22°N
20°N

90°W   80°W   70°W   50°N   40°N   30°N

A
B
C
D
E
F
G
H

7   8   9   10   11   12   A11

Central America & the Caribbean Physical

90°W

85°W

80°W

A

FLORIDA
(U.S.)

Grand Bahama
Island

Abaco
Island

B

A

Bimini
Islands

Eleuthera
Island

25°N

Gulf of Mexico

Straits of Florida

New
Providence

Andros Island

H

Cat
Island

Great Exuma

A

Tropic of Cancer

B

Great Bahama Bank

Long Island

M

W

C

U

B

A

YUCATÁN

Yucatan Channel

PENINSULA

Isle of
Youth

G

R

C

20°N

E

A

T

Cayman Islands
(U.K.)

M E X I C O

Grand
Cayman

E

R

D

M
E
X
I
C
O

BELIZE

JAMAICA

Usumacinta R.

Gulf of
Honduras

E

SIERRA MADRE

GUATEMALA

Motagua R.

C A R I B B

15°N

HONDURAS

EL SALVADOR

Coco R.

Mosquito Coast

F

NICARAGUA

Lake
Managua

Rio Grande
de Matagalpa

N

W   E

Lake
Nicaragua

S

10°N

G

PACIFIC

PANAMA CANAL

OCEAN

COSTA RICA

P A N A M A

H

Gulf of
Panama

0   100   200 Miles

Coiba
Island

COLO

0   100   200 Kilometers

90°W

85°W

80°W

1   2   3   4   5   6

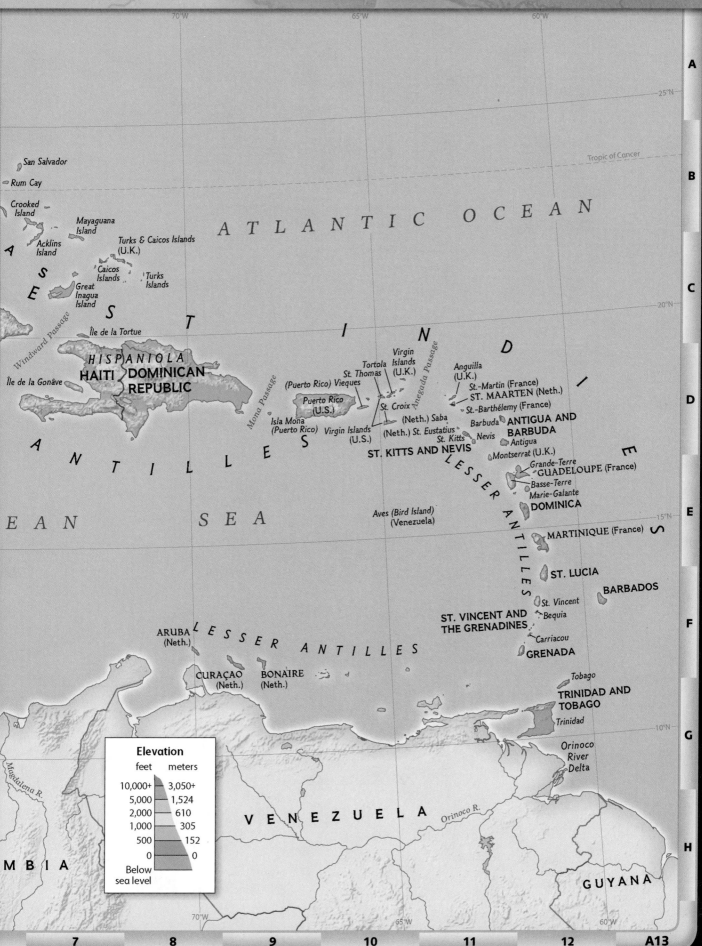

San Salvador

Rum Cay

Crooked
Island

Mayaguana
Island

Acklins
Island

Turks & Caicos Islands
(U.K.)

Caicos
Islands

Great
Inagua
Island

Turks
Islands

A S T

E S T

ATLANTIC OCEAN

Tropic of Cancer

Windward Passage

Île de la Tortue

HISPANIOLA

HAITI

DOMINICAN
REPUBLIC

Île de la Gonâve

A N T I L L E S

I N D I E S

Mona Passage

(Puerto Rico) Vieques

Puerto Rico
(U.S.)

Isla Mona
(Puerto Rico)

St. Thomas

Tortola

Virgin
Islands
(U.K.)

Anegada Passage

St. Croix

Virgin Islands
(U.S.)

(Neth.) Saba

(Neth.) St. Eustatius

St. Kitts

Anguilla
(U.K.)

St.-Martin (France)

ST. MAARTEN (Neth.)

St.-Barthélemy (France)

Barbuda

Nevis

ANTIGUA AND
BARBUDA

Antigua

ST. KITTS AND NEVIS

Montserrat (U.K.)

L E S S E R   A N T I L L E S

Grande-Terre
GUADELOUPE (France)

Basse-Terre

Marie-Galante

DOMINICA

E A N   S E A

Aves (Bird Island)
(Venezuela)

MARTINIQUE (France)

ST. LUCIA

BARBADOS

St. Vincent

Bequia

ST. VINCENT AND
THE GRENADINES

Carriacou

GRENADA

ARUBA
(Neth.)

L E S S E R   A N T I L L E S

CURAÇAO
(Neth.)

BONAIRE
(Neth.)

Tobago

TRINIDAD AND
TOBAGO

Trinidad

Orinoco
River
Delta

Magdalena R.

VENEZUELA

Orinoco R.

Elevation

feet	meters
10,000+	3,050+
5,000	1,524
2,000	610
1,000	305
500	152
0	0
Below sea level	

M B I A

GUYANA

70°W

65°W

60°W

25°N

20°N

15°N

10°N

A

B

C

D

E

F

G

H

7   8   9   10   11   12   A13

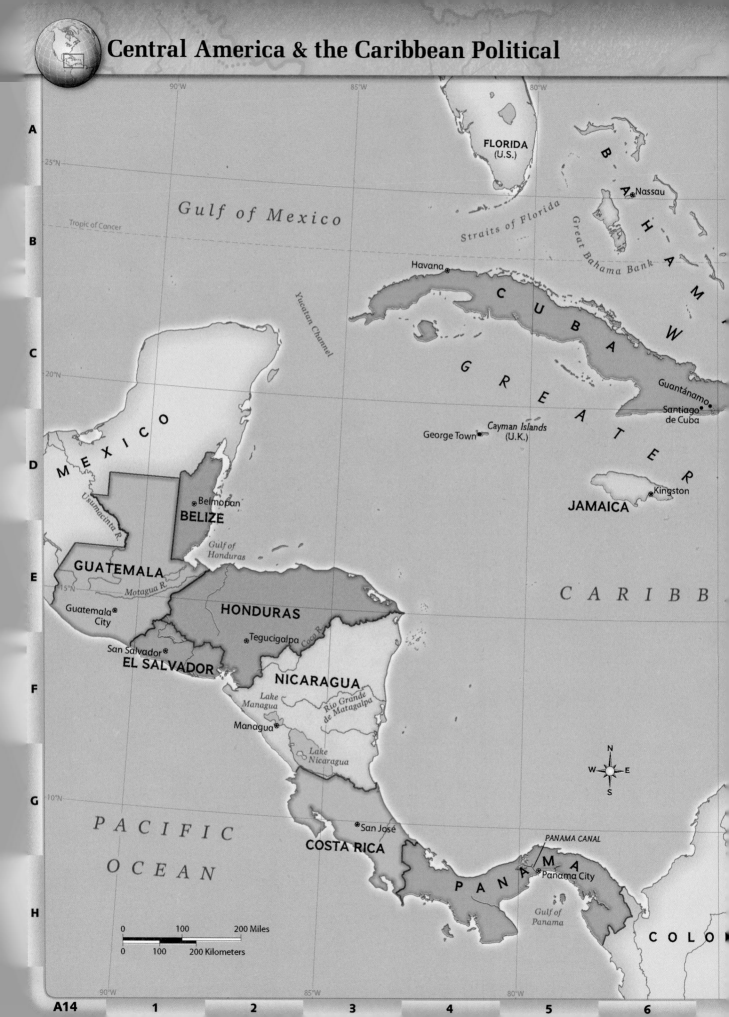

Central America & the Caribbean Political

A

25°N

B

Tropic of Cancer

ATLANTIC OCEAN

Turks & Caicos Islands
(U.K.)

Cockburn
Town

C

20°N

W
I
N
D
W
A
R
D

Windward Passage

HISPANIOLA

DOMINICAN
REPUBLIC

Virgin
Islands
(U.K.)

Anguilla
(U.K.)

The Valley

St.-Martin (France)
ST. MAARTEN (Neth.)

Charlotte Amalie

Port-au-Prince

HAITI

San Juan

Puerto Rico
(U.S.)

Road
Town

St.-Barthélemy (France)

D

Santo
Domingo

Mona Passage

(Neth.) Saba

(Neth.) St. Eustatius

Virgin Islands
(U.S.)

Basseterre

ST. KITTS AND NEVIS

ANTIGUA AND
BARBUDA

St. John's

Brades
Montserrat (U.K.)

GUADELOUPE (France)

Basse-Terre

A
N
T
I
L
L
E
S

L
E
S
S
E
R

A
N
T
I
L
L
E
S

E

15°N

Aves (Bird Island)
(Venezuela)

DOMINICA

Roseau

MARTINIQUE (France)

Fort-de-France

Castries

ST. LUCIA

BARBADOS

C
A
R
I
B
B
E
A
N

S
E
A

Kingstown

Bridgetown

ST. VINCENT AND
THE GRENADINES

F

ARUBA
(Neth.)

Oranjestad

L
E
S
S
E
R

A
N
T
I
L
L
E
S

St. George's GRENADA

Willemstad

CURAÇAO
(Neth.)

Kralendijk

BONAIRE
(Neth.)

TRINIDAD AND
TOBAGO

Port of Spain

G

10°N

Magdalena R.

Lake
Maracaibo

Orinoco
River
Delta

V E N E Z U E L A

Orinoco R.

H

M B I A

GUYANA

70°W   65°W   60°W

7   8   9   10   11   12   A15

South America Physical

HONDURAS

EL SALVADOR

NICARAGUA

COSTA RICA

PANAMA

Caribbean Sea

Lake Maracaibo

Orinoco R.

LLANOS

VENEZUELA

GUYANA

SURINAME

FRENCH GUIANA
(France)

GUIANA HIGHLANDS

COLOMBIA

Boundary claimed
by Suriname

Equator

GALÁPAGOS IS.
(ARCHIPIÉLAGO
DE COLÓN)
(Ecuador)

ECUADOR

Negro R.

A M A Z O N

Amazon R.

Marañón R.

Amazon R.

S e l v a s

A
N
D
E
S

P E R U

B A S I N

Purus R.

Madeira R.

Tapajós R.

Xingu R.

Araguaia R.

Tocantins R.

Ucayali R.

B R A Z I L

Campos

São Francisco R.

Lake
Titicaca

MATO GROSSO
PLATEAU

BRAZILIAN

BOLIVIA

Paraguay R.

Pantanal

HIGHLANDS

Atacama Desert

Paraná R.

PARAGUAY

Iguazú
Falls

Elevation

feet	meters
10,000+	3,050+
5,000	1,524
2,000	610
1,000	305
500	152
0	0
Below sea level	

Tropic of Capricorn

Ojos del Salado
22,615 ft
(6,893 m)

Gran Chaco

C
H
I
L
E

A
R
G
E
N
T
I
N
A

P
A
M
P
A
S

Cerro Aconcagua
22,831 ft
(6,959 m)

Paraná R.

Entre Ríos

Uruguay R.

URUGUAY

Río de
La Plata

Colorado R.

PACIFIC

OCEAN

ATLANTIC

OCEAN

Valdés
Peninsula

N
W   E
S

P
A
T
A
G
O
N
I
A

Gulf of
San Jorge

Laguna del Carbón
-344 ft (-105 m)

Strait of
Magellan

TIERRA
DEL FUEGO

FALKLAND ISLANDS
(ISLAS MALVINAS) (U.K.)
Administered by the United Kingdom
(claimed by Argentina)

South Georgia
(U.K.)

Cape Horn
(Cabo de Hornos)

Scotia Sea

0	500	1,000 Miles
0	500	1,000 Kilometers

ANTARCTICA

Antarctic Circle

South America Political

HONDURAS
EL SALVADOR
NICARAGUA
COSTA RICA
PANAMA

Caribbean Sea

Barranquilla
Maracaibo
Lake Maracaibo
Caracas

Medellín
Bogotá
Cali
COLOMBIA

Orinoco R.

VENEZUELA

GUYANA
Georgetown
SURINAME
Paramaribo
Cayenne
FRENCH GUIANA
(France)

Boundary claimed
by Suriname

Equator

GALÁPAGOS IS.
(ARCHIPIÉLAGO
DE COLÓN)
(Ecuador)

Quito
ECUADOR

Negro R.

Amazon R.

Manaus

Fortaleza

P E R U

Amazon R.
Marañón R.
Ucayali R.
Purus R.
Madeira R.
Tapajós R.
Xingu R.
Araguaia R.
Tocantins R.

B R A Z I L

Recife

Lima

Lake Titicaca
La Paz
Santa Cruz
BOLIVIA
Sucre

São Francisco R.

Brasília
Salvador (Bahia)

Belo Horizonte

Tropic of Capricorn

PARAGUAY

Paraguay R.
Paraná R.

São Paulo
Rio de Janeiro

Asunción

Curitiba

C H I L E

Córdoba

Santiago

A R G E N T I N A

Rosario
Paraná R.
Uruguay R.

Porto Alegre

URUGUAY

Buenos Aires
Montevideo
*Río de
La Plata*

PACIFIC
OCEAN

ATLANTIC
OCEAN

Colorado R.

N
W   E
S

Gulf of
San Jorge

Strait of
Magellan
TIERRA
DEL FUEGO

Stanley
FALKLAND ISLANDS
(ISLAS MALVINAS) (U.K.)
*Administered by the United Kingdom
(claimed by Argentina)*

South Georgia
(U.K.)

Scotia Sea

0   500   1,000 Miles
0   500   1,000 Kilometers

ANTARCTICA

Antarctic Circle

A17

Europe Physical

A18

20°E   30°E   40°E   50°E   60°E   70°E   80°E

70°N

Barents Sea

KOLA PENINSULA

White Sea

Pechora R.

Ob R.

60°N

FINLAND

Gulf of Bothnia

Northern Dvina R.

Irtysh R.

R   U   S   S   I   A

70°E

Lake Onega

E   U   R   O   P   E   A   N   P   L   A   I   N

Kama R.

Lake Ladoga

Gulf of Finland

50°N

ESTONIA

Volga R.

N

LATVIA

W   E

S

Ural R.

LITHUANIA

K   A   Z   A   K   H   S   T   A   N

BELARUS

Aral Sea

60°E

E

Vistula R.

Don R.

UZBEKISTAN

LAND

Volga R.

CARPATHIAN MOUNTAINS

U   K   R   A   I   N   E

Dniester R.

Dnieper R.

OVAKIA

MOLDOVA

Caspian Sea

40°N

ARY

TURKMENISTAN

ROMANIA

Sea of Azov

CRIMEA

SERBIA

Danube R.

Black Sea

GEORGIA

KOSOVO

Balkan Mountains

AZERBAIJAN

BULGARIA

ARMENIA

MACEDONIA

Bosporus

AZERB.

Sea of Marmara

ALBANIA

Dardanelles

T   U   R   K   E   Y

Aegean Sea

GREECE

I   R   A   N

Crete (Greece)

Rhodes (Greece)

CYPRUS

SYRIA

Euphrates R.

Tigris R.

IRAQ

50°E

30°N

LEBANON

40°E

A

B

C

D

E

F

G

H

Europe Political

A
B
C
D
E
F
G
H

1 2 3 4 5 6

ICELAND
Reykjavík

Norwegian Sea

Arctic Circle

Prime Meridian

Faroe Islands (Denmark)

Shetland Islands (U.K.)

NORWAY

SWEDEN

Oslo

Stockholm

Gotland (Sweden)

Baltic

Hebrides (U.K.)

Orkney Islands (U.K.)

SCOTLAND

NORTHERN IRELAND
Belfast

Edinburgh

North Sea

DENMARK
Copenhagen

IRELAND

Shannon R.

Dublin

UNITED KINGDOM

WALES
Cardiff

ENGLAND

London

Thames R.

NETHERLANDS
Amsterdam

Hamburg

Elbe R.

Berlin

GERMANY

Vistula R.

POL

English Channel

Channel Islands (U.K.)

Brussels
BELGIUM

Rhine R.

Frankfurt

Oder R.

Prague

CZECH REPUBLIC (CZECHIA)

LUXEMBOURG
Luxembourg

Seine R.

Paris

Danube R.

Munich

Vienna

Bratislava

SLOV

ATLANTIC OCEAN

Loire R.

FRANCE

LIECHTENSTEIN
Vaduz

SWITZERLAND
Bern

AUSTRIA

Budapest

HUNG

Bay of Biscay

Rhône R.

Milan

Po R.

SLOVENIA
Ljubljana

Zagreb

CROATIA

MONACO

SAN MARINO

BOSNIA AND HERZEGOVINA
Sarajevo

PORTUGAL

Douro R.

SPAIN

Ebro R.

Madrid

ANDORRA
Andorra

Corsica (France)

ITALY

Adriatic Sea

MONTENEGRO
Podgorica

Lisbon

Tagus R.

Barcelona

Rome

Guadiana R.

VATICAN CITY

Balearic Islands (Spain)

Sardinia (Italy)

Tyrrhenian Sea

GIBRALTAR (U.K.)

Mediterranean Sea

Sicily (Italy)

Ionian Sea

MOROCCO

ALGERIA

0   200   400 Miles
0   200   400 Kilometers

TUNISIA

MALTA
Valletta

Sea

60°N 30°W 20°W 10°W 70°W 10°E

30°W

50°N

20°W

40°N

30°N

10°W

0°

Russia & the Eurasian Republics Physical

ARCTIC

Norwegian Sea

SVALBARD
(Norway)

FRANZ JOSEF LAND

Barents
Sea

NOVAYA ZEMLYA

Kara Sea

Yamal Peninsula

Gyda
Peninsula

Kola
Peninsula

White Sea

UNITED
KINGDOM

North
Sea

DENMARK

GER.

Baltic Sea

POLAND

LITHUANIA

LATVIA

ESTONIA

BELARUS

Dnieper R.

Lake
Ladoga

Lake
Onega

Northern Dvina R.

Pechora R.

URAL MOUNTAINS

R

U

S

S

Yenisey R.

Ob R.

Pur R.

Taz R.

Ob R.

WEST

SIBERIAN

PLAIN

Irtysh R.

Kama R.

CENTRAL

RUSSIAN

UPLAND

Volga R.

UKRAINE

MOLDOVA

Sea of
Azov

Volga R.

Don R.

Ural R.

Tobol R.

Esil R.

Ertis R.

Western

Black Sea

Caucasus Mountains
Elbrus
18,510 ft.
(5,642 m)

Caspian Depression

THE
STEPPES

Kazakh
Uplands

KAZAKHSTAN

Lake
Balkhash

TURKEY

GEORGIA

ARMENIA

AZERBAIJAN

Caspian Sea

Aral
Sea

Syr Darya

Ile R.

IRAQ

KUWAIT

Euphrates R.

Tigris R.

IRAN

TURKMENISTAN

UZBEKISTAN

Amu Darya

KYRGYZSTAN

TAJIKISTAN

AFGHANISTAN

NORWAY

SWEDEN

FINLAND

Prime Meridian

Arctic Circle

10°W

0°

60°N

70°N

80°N

20°E

50°N

30°E

40°N

40°E

30°N

50°E

60°E

70°E

80°E

N
W   E
S

A
B
C
D
E
F
G
H

1   2   3   4   5   6

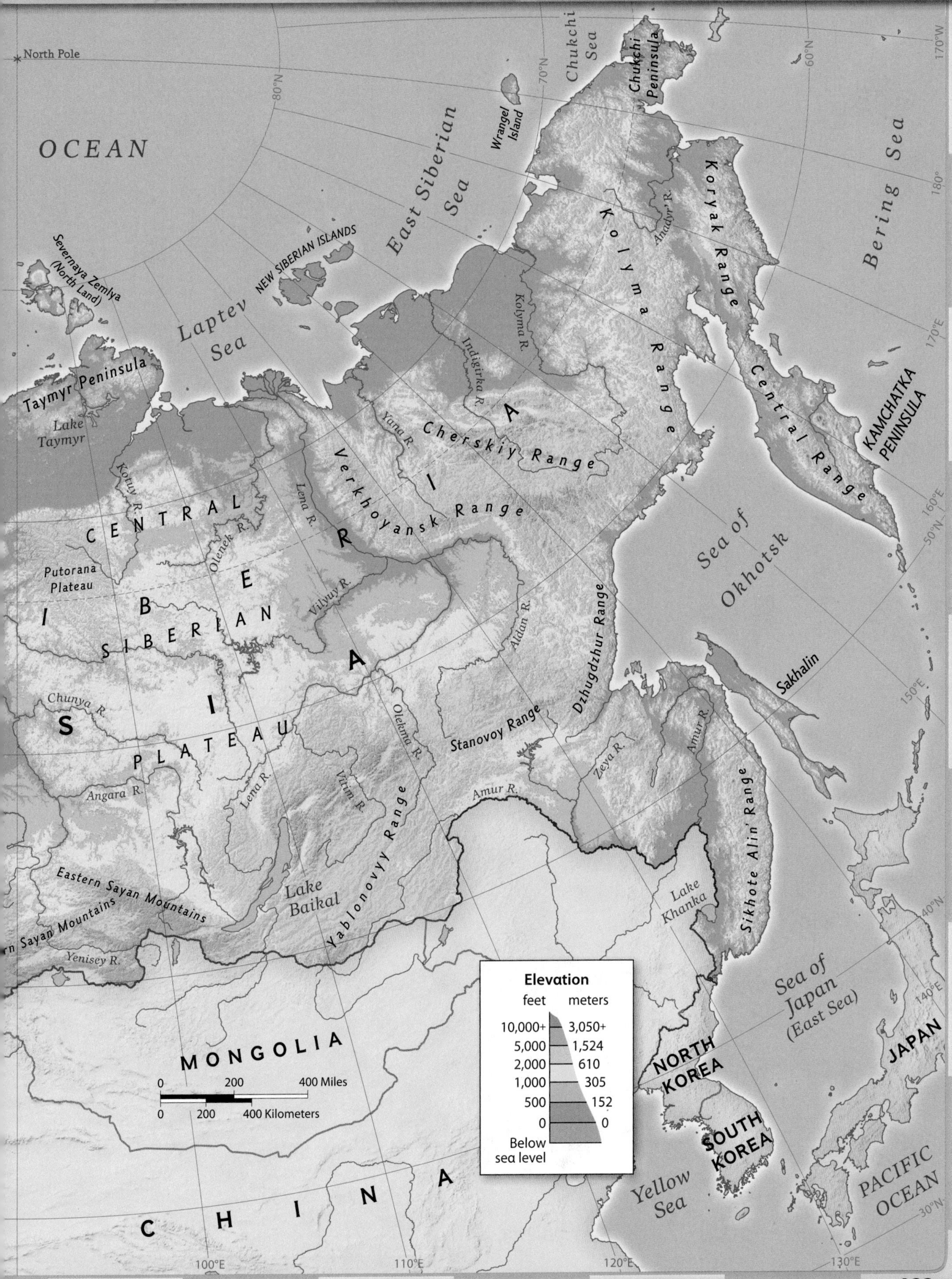

North Pole
OCEAN
Chukchi Sea
Chukchi Peninsula
Wrangel Island
East Siberian Sea
Bering Sea
Koryak Range
Anadyr' R.
Kolyma Range
Severnaya Zemlya (North Land)
NEW SIBERIAN ISLANDS
Laptev Sea
Kolyma R.
Indigirka R.
Taymyr Peninsula
Lake Taymyr
Central Range
KAMCHATKA PENINSULA
Yana R.
Cherskiy Range
Kotuy R.
Verkhoyansk Range
Lena R.
CENTRAL
Olenek R.
SIBERIA
Putorana Plateau
Sea of Okhotsk
Vilyuy R.
SIBERIAN
Aldan R.
Dzhugdzhur Range
Sakhalin
Chunya R.
Olekma R.
Stanovoy Range
PLATEAU
Zeya R.
Amur R.
Angara R.
Lena R.
Vitim R.
Yablonovyy Range
Sikhote Alin' Range
Eastern Sayan Mountains
Western Sayan Mountains
Lake Baikal
Lake Khanka
Yenisey R.
Elevation
feet meters
10,000+ 3,050+
5,000 1,524
2,000 610
1,000 305
500 152
0 0
Below sea level
MONGOLIA
0 200 400 Miles
0 200 400 Kilometers
NORTH KOREA
SOUTH KOREA
Sea of Japan (East Sea)
JAPAN
Yellow Sea
PACIFIC OCEAN
CHINA
80°N
70°N
60°N
50°N
40°N
30°N
170°W
180°
170°E
160°E
150°E
140°E
130°E
120°E
110°E
100°E
A
B
C
D
E
F
G
H
7
8
9
10
11
12

UNITED KINGDOM

Prime Meridian

ARCTIC

Norwegian Sea

SVALBARD
(Norway)

FRANZ JOSEF LAND

North Sea

DENMARK

N O R W A Y

Barents Sea

NOVAYA ZEMLYA

Kara Sea

GER.

S W E D E N

F I N L A N D

Murmansk

Baltic Sea

ESTONIA

St. Petersburg

Archangel

LITHUANIA

LATVIA

Kaliningrad

Northern Dvina R.

Pechora R.

Ob R.

Pur R.

Yenisey R.

POLAND

BELARUS

Dnieper R.

Lake Ladoga

Lake Onega

Rostov

Moscow

Volga R.

R

Nizhniy Novgorod

Kazan

Kama R.

U

Taz R.

MOLDOVA

UKRAINE

Saratov

Volgograd

Volga R.

Samara

Ufa

Yekaterinburg

Irtysh R.

Tobol R.

S

Ob R.

Sea of Azov

Don R.

Ural R.

Chelyabinsk

Esil R.

Omsk

Ertis R.

Novosibirsk

Black Sea

Sochi

GEORGIA

Tbilisi

ARMENIA

Yerevan

TURKEY

AZERBAIJAN

Baku

Caspian Sea

K A Z A K H S T A N

Astana

Qaraghandy

Lake Balkhash

Aral Sea

Ile R.

Euphrates R.

Tigris R.

IRAQ

UZBEKISTAN

TURKMENISTAN

Syr Darya

Tashkent

Almaty

Bishkek

KYRGYZSTAN

Ashgabat

Amu Darya

TAJIKISTAN

Dushanbe

IRAN

KUWAIT

AFGHANISTAN

ARCTIC Circle

10°W
0°
60°N
70°N
80°N
10°E
20°E
50°N
30°E
40°N
40°E
30°N
50°E
60°E
70°E
80°E

A
B
C
D
E
F
G
H

N
W E
S

OCEAN

North Pole

Severnaya Zemlya
(North Land)

NEW SIBERIAN ISLANDS

Wrangel
Island

East Siberian
Sea

Chukchi
Sea

Bering Sea

Anadyr' R.

Anadyr

Laptev
Sea

Kolyma R.

Indigirka R.

Lake
Taymyr

Kotuy R.

Yana R.

Olenek R.

Lena R.

Vilyuy R.

Yakutsk

Aldan R.

Magadan

Sea of
Okhotsk

S I A

Mirny

Olekma R.

Chunya R.

Sakhalin

Angara R.

S

Lena R.

Vitim R.

Zeya R.

Amur R.

Amur R.

Irkutsk

Lake
Baikal

Lake
Khanka

Madivostok

Sea of
Japan
(East Sea)

Yenisey R.

JAPAN

MONGOLIA

NORTH
KOREA

0   200   400 Miles

0   200   400 Kilometers

SOUTH
KOREA

PACIFIC
OCEAN

CHINA

Yellow
Sea

7   8   9   10   11   12   A25

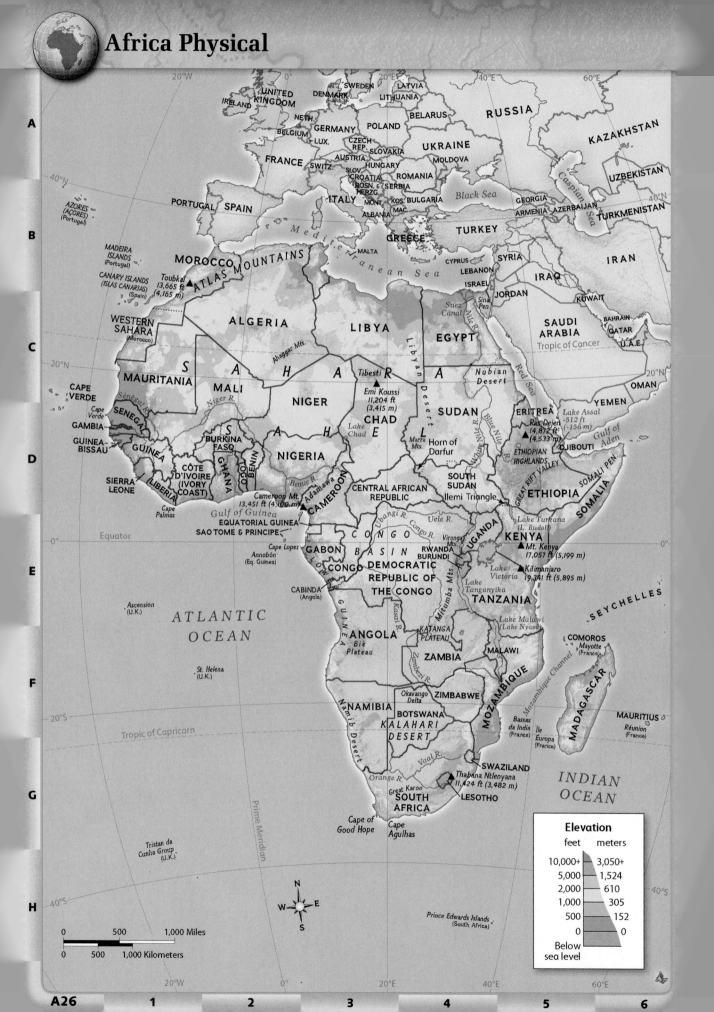

Africa Physical

Elevation

feet	meters
10,000+	3,050+
5,000	1,524
2,000	610
1,000	305
500	152
0	0
Below sea level	

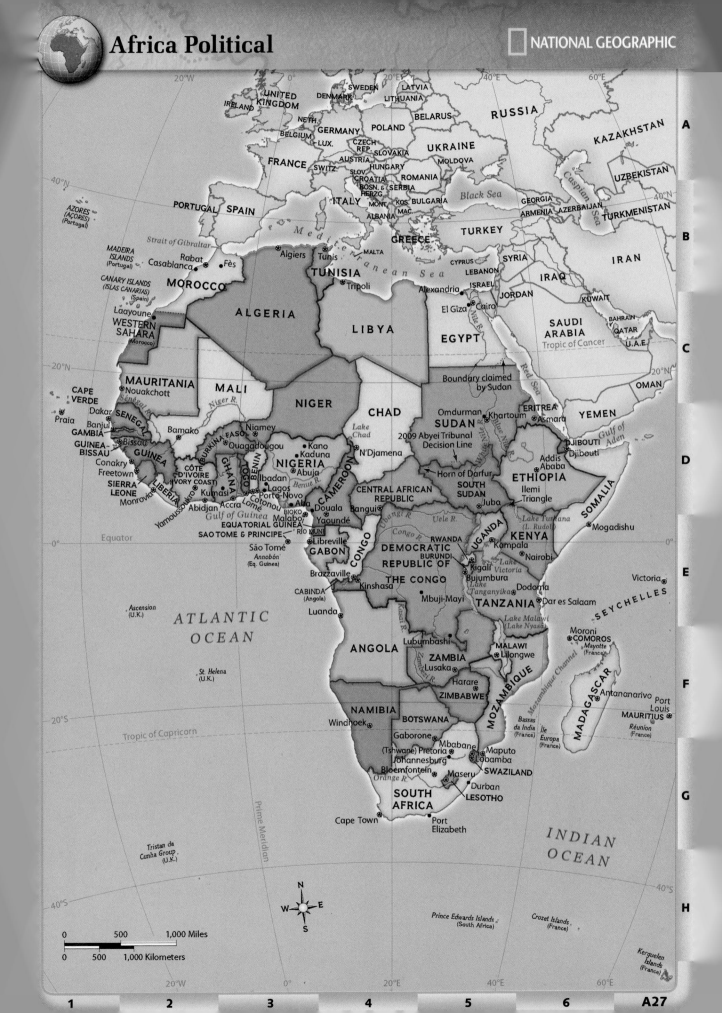

Africa Political

IRELAND
UNITED KINGDOM
SWEDEN
DENMARK
LATVIA
LITHUANIA
NETH.
GERMANY
BELGIUM
LUX.
POLAND
BELARUS
RUSSIA
KAZAKHSTAN
FRANCE
SWITZ.
CZECH REP.
SLOVAKIA
AUSTRIA
HUNGARY
UKRAINE
MOLDOVA
ROMANIA
UZBEKISTAN
SLOV.
CROATIA
BOSN. & HERZG.
SERBIA
BULGARIA
Black Sea
GEORGIA
ARMENIA AZERBAIJAN
TURKMENISTAN
ITALY
MONT.
ALBANIA
KOS. MAC.
GREECE
TURKEY
MALTA
CYPRUS
SYRIA
LEBANON
IRAQ
IRAN

AZORES (AÇORES) (Portugal)
PORTUGAL SPAIN
Strait of Gibraltar
Mediterranean Sea
Algiers
Tunis
Tripoli
Alexandria
ISRAEL
JORDAN
El Gîza Cairo
KUWAIT
SAUDI ARABIA
BAHRAIN
QATAR
U.A.E.

MADEIRA ISLANDS (Portugal)
Rabat
Casablanca
Fès
MOROCCO
TUNISIA
LIBYA
EGYPT
Tropic of Cancer
OMAN

CANARY ISLANDS (ISLAS CANARIAS) (Spain)
Laâyoune
WESTERN SAHARA (Morocco)
ALGERIA
Boundary claimed by Sudan
Red Sea
YEMEN

CAPE VERDE
Praia
Dakar
Nouakchott
MAURITANIA
MALI
NIGER
CHAD
Omdurman
Khartoum
Asmara
ERITREA
Gulf of Aden
SENEGAL
Senegal R.
Niger R.
Lake Chad
SUDAN
DJIBOUTI
Djibouti
GAMBIA
Banjul
Bamako
Niamey
Kano
N'Djamena
2009 Abyei Tribunal Decision Line
GUINEA-BISSAU
Bissau
BURKINA FASO
Ouagadougou
Kaduna
Horn of Darfur
Addis Ababa
Conakry
GUINEA
Kumasi
GHANA
BENIN
NIGERIA
Ibadan
Abuja
Benue R.
CENTRAL AFRICAN REPUBLIC
SOUTH SUDAN
ETHIOPIA
Ilemi Triangle
Freetown
SIERRA LEONE
Monrovia
LIBERIA
Yamoussoukro
Abidjan
CÔTE D'IVOIRE (VORY COAST)
TOGO
Lomé
Lagos
Porto-Novo
Cotonou
Accra
Aba
CAMEROON
Douala
Yaoundé
Bangui
Ubangi R.
Uele R.
Juba
SOMALIA
Lake Turkana (L. Rudolf)
Mogadishu
Gulf of Guinea
BIOKO
Malabo
EQUATORIAL GUINEA
SAO TOME & PRINCIPE
RÍO MUNI
Congo R.
UGANDA
KENYA
São Tomé
Annobón (Eq. Guinea)
Libreville
GABON
CONGO
DEMOCRATIC REPUBLIC OF THE CONGO
RWANDA
BURUNDI
Kigali
Kampala
Lake Victoria
Nairobi
Equator
Brazzaville
Kinshasa
Bujumbura
Lake Tanganyika
Dodoma
Victoria
CABINDA (Angola)
Mbuji-Mayi
TANZANIA
Dar es Salaam
SEYCHELLES
Luanda
Kasai R.
Kwanza R.

ATLANTIC OCEAN
Ascension (U.K.)
St. Helena (U.K.)
Lubumbashi
ANGOLA
ZAMBIA
Lusaka
Lake Malawi (Lake Nyasa)
MALAWI
Lilongwe
Moroni
COMOROS
Mayotte (France)
MADAGASCAR
Antananarivo
Port Louis
MAURITIUS
Réunion (France)

Zambezi R.
Harare
ZIMBABWE
MOZAMBIQUE
Mozambique Channel
Bassas da India (France)
Île Europa (France)

Tropic of Capricorn
NAMIBIA
Windhoek
BOTSWANA
Gaborone
(Tshwane) Pretoria
Mbabane
Maputo
Lobamba
SWAZILAND
Johannesburg
Bloemfontein
Maseru
LESOTHO
Durban
Orange R.

Prime Meridian
SOUTH AFRICA
Cape Town
Port Elizabeth
INDIAN OCEAN

Tristan da Cunha Group (U.K.)
N W E S
Prince Edwards Islands (South Africa)
Crozet Islands (France)
Kerguelen Islands (France)

0   500   1,000 Miles
0   500   1,000 Kilometers

Southwest Asia Physical

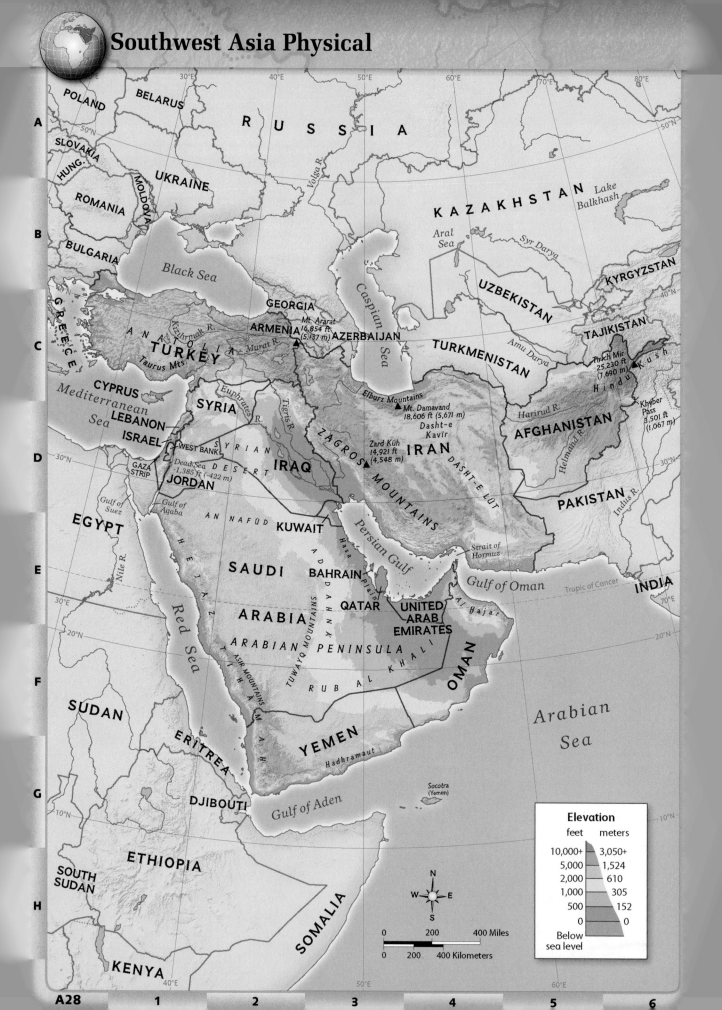

POLAND
BELARUS

R U S S I A

SLOVAKIA
HUNG.
UKRAINE
MOLDOVA
ROMANIA

KAZAKHSTAN
Lake Balkhash

BULGARIA

Black Sea

Aral Sea

Syr Darya

UZBEKISTAN

KYRGYZSTAN

GEORGIA

G R E E C E

A N A T O L I A
Kizilirmak R.
TURKEY
Murat R.
Taurus Mts.

Mt. Ararat
16,854 ft
(5,137 m)
ARMENIA
AZERBAIJAN

Caspian Sea

TURKMENISTAN

Amu Darya

TAJIKISTAN

Tirich Mir
25,230 ft
(7,690 m)
Hindu Kush

CYPRUS

Mediterranean Sea

LEBANON
ISRAEL

SYRIA
Euphrates R.
Tigris R.

WEST BANK
S Y R I A N
D E S E R T

Elburz Mountains
Mt. Damavand
18,606 ft (5,671 m)
Dasht-e Kavīr

Z A G R O S

Zard Kūh
14,921 ft
(4,548 m)

IRAN

DASHT-E LŪT

Harirud R.

AFGHANISTAN

Helmand R.

Khyber
Pass
3,501 ft
(1,067 m)

GAZA
STRIP
Dead Sea
-1,385 ft (-422 m)
JORDAN

IRAQ

M O U N T A I N S

Indus R.

PAKISTAN

EGYPT

Gulf of
Suez
Gulf of
Aqaba

A N   N A F Ū D

KUWAIT

Persian Gulf

Hasa Plain

Strait of
Hormuz

Nile R.

SAUDI

BAHRAIN

QATAR

Gulf of Oman

Tropic of Cancer

INDIA

Red Sea

H E J A Z

A D   D A H N Ā

UNITED
ARAB
EMIRATES

Al Hajar

ARABIA

A S I R   M O U N T A I N S

ARABIAN   PENINSULA

T U W A Y Q   M O U N T A I N S

R U B   A L   K H A L I

OMAN

Arabian
Sea

SUDAN

ERITREA

T   I   H   A   M   A

YEMEN

Hadramaut

Socotra
(Yemen)

DJIBOUTI

Gulf of Aden

ETHIOPIA

SOUTH
SUDAN

SOMALIA

KENYA

Elevation

feet	meters
10,000+	3,050+
5,000	1,524
2,000	610
1,000	305
500	152
0	0
Below sea level	

N
W   E
S

0   200   400 Miles
0   200   400 Kilometers

A B C D E F G H

1 2 3 4 5 6

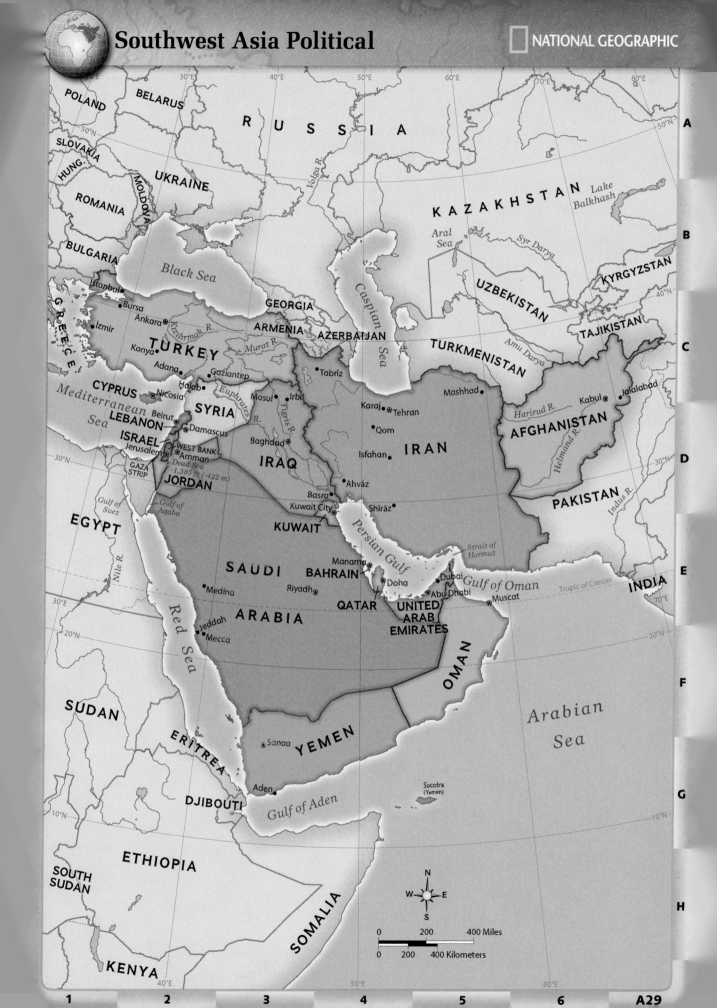

Southwest Asia Political

POLAND
BELARUS
SLOVAKIA
HUNG.
ROMANIA
MOLDOVA
UKRAINE
BULGARIA
GREECE

R U S S I A

KAZAKHSTAN
Lake
Balkhash

Aral
Sea

UZBEKISTAN
KYRGYZSTAN

Black Sea

Istanbul
Bursa
Ankara
Izmir
Konya
TURKEY
Adana
Gaziantep
Halab
CYPRUS
Nicosia
Beirut
LEBANON
Damascus
SYRIA
Mosul
Irbil
Baghdad
WEST BANK
Amman
JORDAN
Jerusalem
ISRAEL
GAZA
STRIP
Dead Sea
-1,385 ft (-422 m)

GEORGIA
ARMENIA
AZERBAIJAN
TURKMENISTAN

Kizilirmak R.
Murat R.
Euphrates R.
Tigris R.

Tabriz
Karaj
Tehran
Qom

Caspian
Sea

Amu Darya
Syr Darya

TAJIKISTAN

Mashhad
Harirud R.
Kabul
Jalalabad
AFGHANISTAN
Helmand R.
IRAN
Isfahan
Ahvaz
Shiraz
PAKISTAN
Indus R.

Mediterranean
Sea

IRAQ

Basra
Kuwait City
KUWAIT

EGYPT

Gulf of
Suez
Gulf of
Aqaba

Nile R.

Red Sea

Medina

Jeddah
Mecca

SAUDI

ARABIA

Riyadh

Manama
BAHRAIN
Doha
QATAR
UNITED
ARAB
EMIRATES

Persian Gulf

Strait of
Hormuz

Dubai
Abu Dhabi
Muscat

Gulf of Oman
Tropic of Cancer
INDIA

OMAN

Arabian

Sea

SUDAN

ERITREA

DJIBOUTI

Sanaa
YEMEN

Aden
Gulf of Aden

Socotra
(Yemen)

SOUTH
SUDAN

ETHIOPIA

SOMALIA

KENYA

N
W   E
S

0   200   400 Miles
0   200   400 Kilometers

A
B
C
D
E
F
G
H

1   2   3   4   5   6   A29

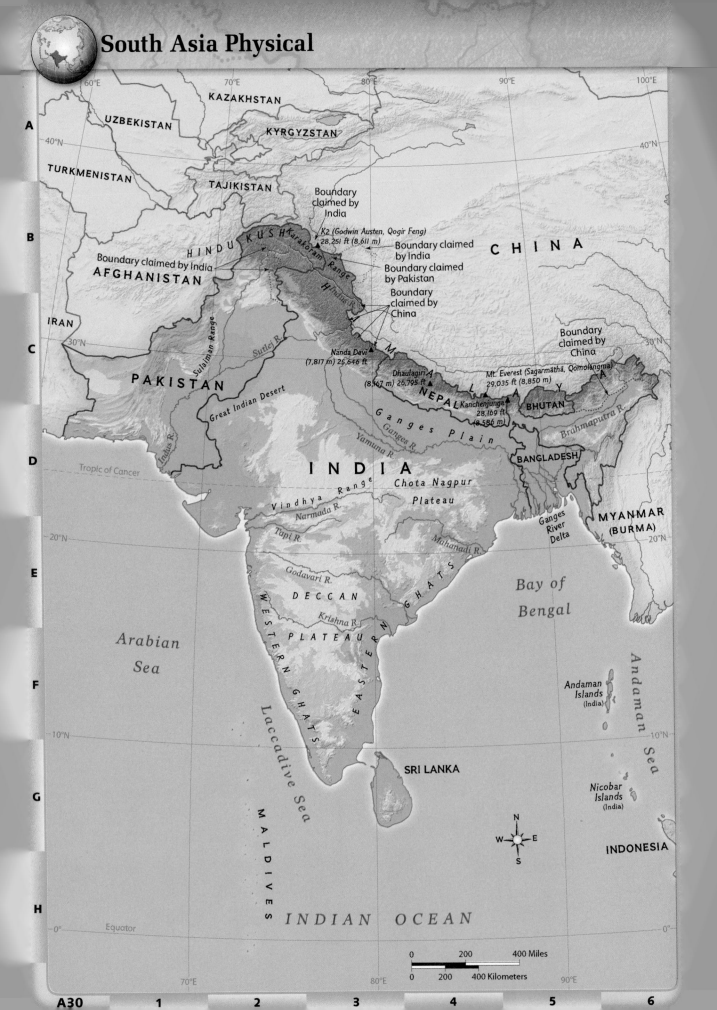

South Asia Physical

UZBEKISTAN

KAZAKHSTAN

KYRGYZSTAN

TURKMENISTAN

TAJIKISTAN

Boundary
claimed by
India

HINDU KUSH

K2 (Godwin Austen, Qogir Feng)
28,251 ft (8,611 m)

Boundary claimed
by India

CHINA

Boundary claimed by India

AFGHANISTAN

Karakoram Range

Boundary claimed
by Pakistan

Indus R.

Boundary
claimed by
China

Boundary
claimed by
China

IRAN

Nanda Devi
(7,817 m) 25,646 ft

M

Dhaulagiri
(8,167 m) 26,795 ft

PAKISTAN

Sutlej R.

A

L

Mt. Everest (Sagarmāthā, Qomolangma)
29,035 ft (8,850 m)

A

Y

Great Indian Desert

NEPAL

Kanchenjunga
28,169 ft
(8,586 m)

BHUTAN

Brahmaputra R.

Indus R.

Ganges Plain

Ganges R.

Yamuna R.

INDIA

BANGLADESH

Tropic of Cancer

Chota Nagpur
Plateau

MYANMAR
(BURMA)

Vindhya Range

Narmada R.

Tapi R.

Ganges
River
Delta

Godavari R.

DECCAN

Mahanadi R.

Bay of
Bengal

WESTERN GHATS

Krishna R.

PLATEAU

EASTERN GHATS

Arabian
Sea

Andaman Islands
(India)

Andaman Sea

Laccadive Sea

SRI LANKA

Nicobar
Islands
(India)

N

W   E

S

INDONESIA

M A L D I V E S

INDIAN OCEAN

Equator

| 0 | 200 | 400 Miles |
| 0 | 200 | 400 Kilometers |

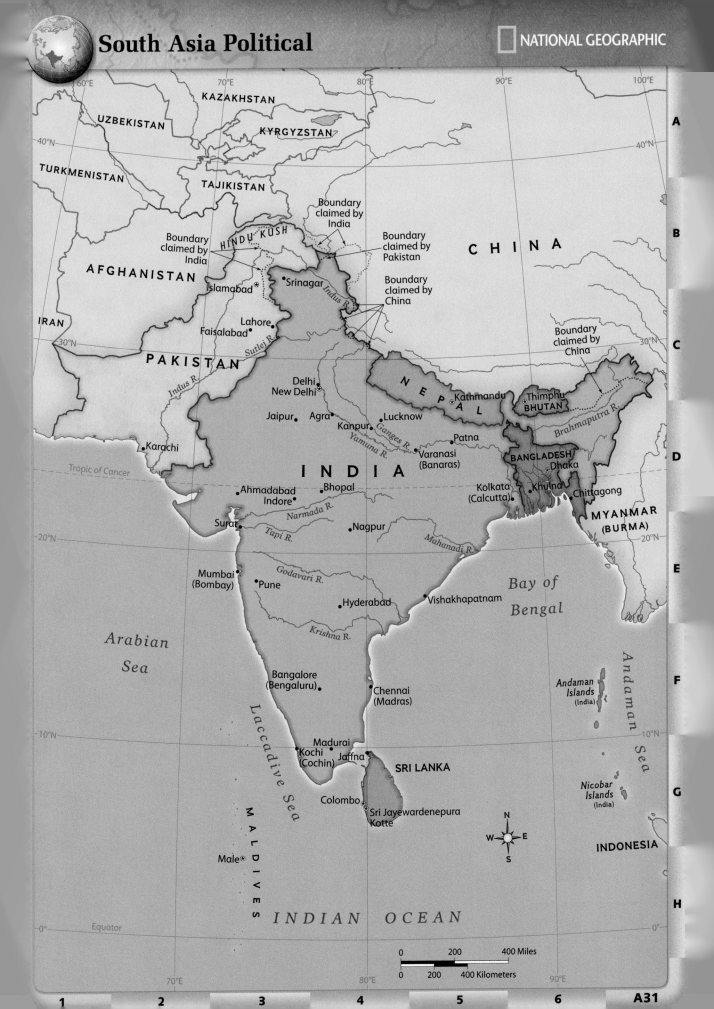

South Asia Political

KAZAKHSTAN

UZBEKISTAN

KYRGYZSTAN

TURKMENISTAN

TAJIKISTAN

Boundary claimed by India

Boundary claimed by India

HINDU KUSH

Boundary claimed by Pakistan

CHINA

AFGHANISTAN

Islamabad ⊛

Srinagar

Boundary claimed by China

IRAN

Lahore

Indus R.

Boundary claimed by China

Faisalabad

PAKISTAN

Sutlej R.

NEPAL

Kathmandu ⊛

Thimphu ⊛
BHUTAN

Indus R.

Delhi
New Delhi ⊛

Jaipur

Agra

Lucknow

Brahmaputra R.

Karachi

Kanpur

Ganges R.

Patna

Yamuna R.

Varanasi
(Banaras)

BANGLADESH

Dhaka ⊛

Tropic of Cancer

Ahmadabad
Indore

Bhopal

Kolkata
(Calcutta)

Khulna

Chittagong

Surat

INDIA

Narmada R.

Nagpur

Tapi R.

MYANMAR
(BURMA)

Mahanadi R.

Mumbai
(Bombay)

Godavari R.

Pune

Bay of
Bengal

Hyderabad

Vishakhapatnam

Arabian
Sea

Krishna R.

Andaman
Islands
(India)

Bangalore
(Bengaluru)

Chennai
(Madras)

Laccadive Sea

Madurai
Kochi
(Cochin)

Jaffna

SRI LANKA

Nicobar
Islands
(India)

M
A
L
D
I
V
E
S

Colombo ⊛

Sri Jayewardenepura
Kotte

N
W   E
S

INDONESIA

Male ⊛

INDIAN OCEAN

Equator

0   200   400 Miles

0   200   400 Kilometers

A31

East Asia Physical

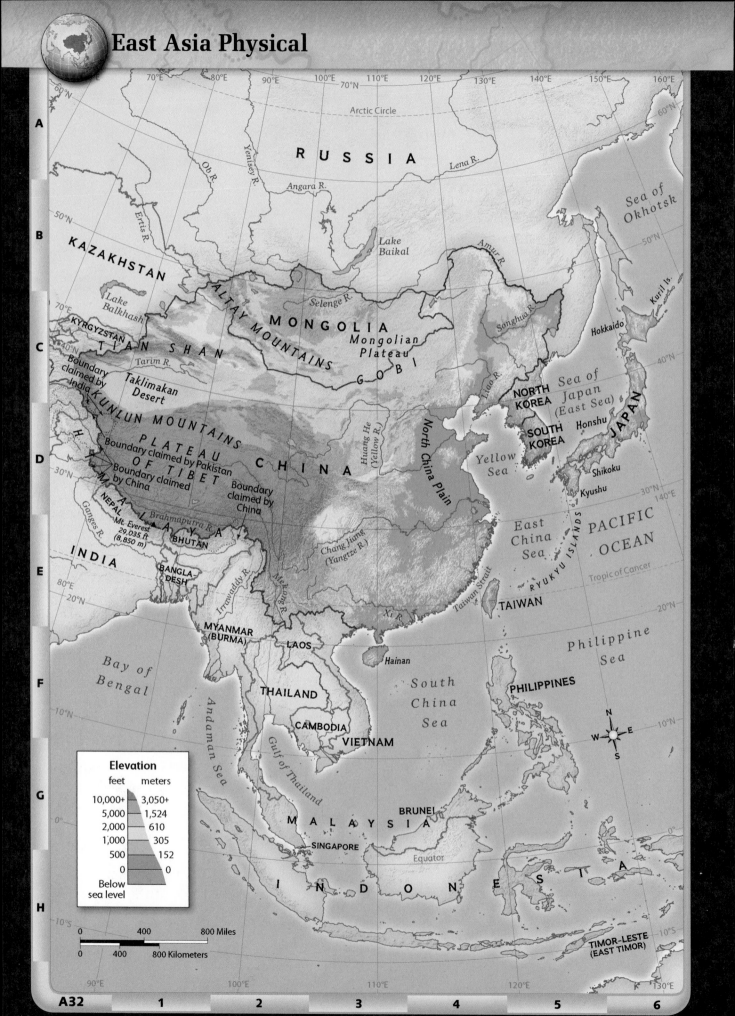

A32

Elevation

feet	meters
10,000+	3,050+
5,000	1,524
2,000	610
1,000	305
500	152
0	0
Below sea level	

0   400   800 Miles

0   400   800 Kilometers

RUSSIA

KAZAKHSTAN

KYRGYZSTAN

TIAN SHAN

ALTAY MOUNTAINS

MONGOLIA

Mongolian Plateau

GOBI

Lake Baikal

Selenge R.

Songhua R.

Amur R.

Lena R.

Angara R.

Ob R.

Yenisey R.

Ertis R.

Lake Balkhash

Tarim R.

Taklimakan Desert

KUNLUN MOUNTAINS

PLATEAU OF TIBET

Boundary claimed by India

Boundary claimed by Pakistan

Boundary claimed by China

Boundary claimed by China

CHINA

Huang He (Yellow R.)

North China Plain

Liao R.

NORTH KOREA

SOUTH KOREA

Sea of Japan (East Sea)

Sea of Okhotsk

Kuril Is.

Hokkaido

Honshu

JAPAN

Shikoku

Kyushu

Yellow Sea

East China Sea

RYUKYU ISLANDS

PACIFIC OCEAN

Tropic of Cancer

TAIWAN

Taiwan Strait

HIMALAYA

NEPAL

Mt. Everest 29,035 ft (8,850 m)

BHUTAN

Brahmaputra R.

Ganges R.

INDIA

BANGLA DESH

MYANMAR (BURMA)

Irrawaddy R.

Mekong R.

Chang Jiang (Yangtze R.)

Xi R.

Hainan

LAOS

THAILAND

CAMBODIA

VIETNAM

Andaman Sea

Bay of Bengal

Gulf of Thailand

South China Sea

Philippine Sea

PHILIPPINES

MALAYSIA

BRUNEI

SINGAPORE

Equator

INDONESIA

TIMOR-LESTE (EAST TIMOR)

Arctic Circle

N
W   E
S

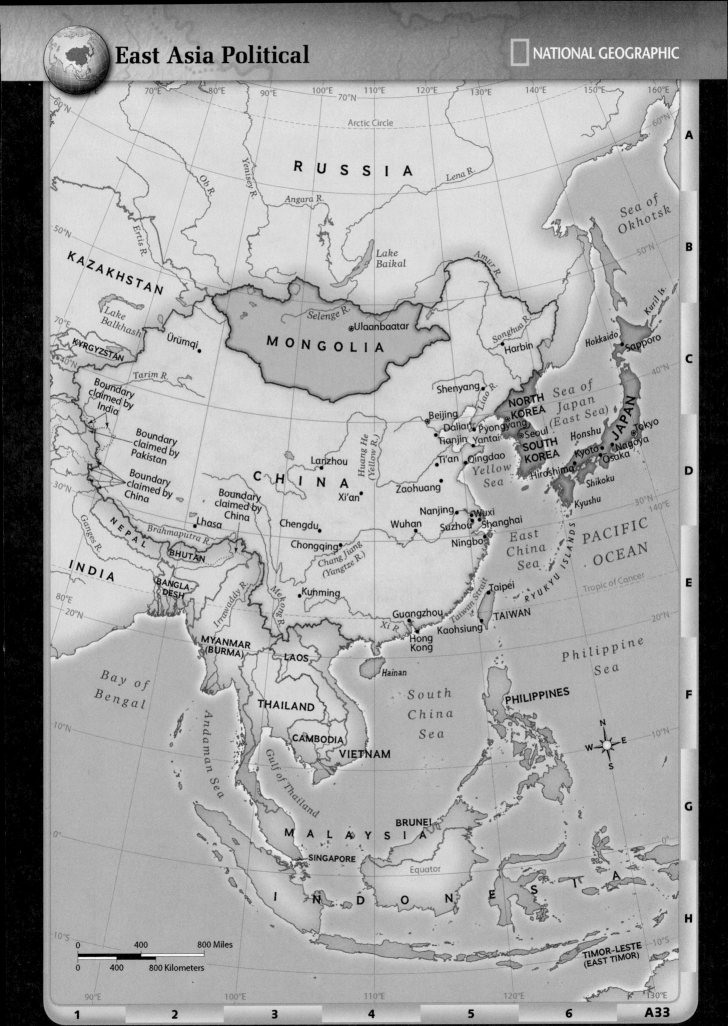

East Asia Political

Arctic Circle

RUSSIA

Ob R. *Yenisey R.* *Angara R.* *Lena R.* *Amur R.*

KAZAKHSTAN

Lake Baikal

Ertis R.

Lake Balkhash

KYRGYZSTAN

Ürümqi

Tarim R.

Boundary claimed by India

Boundary claimed by Pakistan

Boundary claimed by China

Selenge R.

MONGOLIA

⊛Ulaanbaatar

Songhua R.

Harbin

Liao R.

Shenyang

Sea of Okhotsk

Kuril Is.

Hokkaido

Sapporo

Sea of Japan (East Sea)

NORTH KOREA

⊛Pyongyang

Beijing⊛

Dalian

Tianjin Yantai

⊛Seoul

SOUTH KOREA

JAPAN

⊛Tokyo

Honshu

Kyoto Nagoya

Osaka

Lanzhou

CHINA

Huang He (Yellow R.)

Ti'an Qingdao

Hiroshima

Shikoku

Zaohuang

Yellow Sea

Kyushu

40°N

Boundary claimed by China

Xi'an

Lhasa

Chengdu

NEPAL

Brahmaputra R.

BHUTAN

Ganges R.

INDIA

BANGLA-DESH

Chongqing

Chang Jiang (Yangtze R.)

Nanjing Wuxi

Wuhan Suzhou Shanghai

Ningbo

East China Sea

RYUKYU ISLANDS

PACIFIC OCEAN

Tropic of Cancer

Kuhming

Irrawaddy R. *Mekong R.*

MYANMAR (BURMA)

LAOS

Guangzhou

Xi R.

Hong Kong

Kaohsiung

Taipei

TAIWAN

Taiwan Strait

Hainan

Bay of Bengal

Andaman Sea

THAILAND

South China Sea

PHILIPPINES

Philippine Sea

CAMBODIA

Gulf of Thailand

VIETNAM

N
W   E
S

BRUNEI

MALAYSIA

SINGAPORE

Equator

INDONESIA

TIMOR-LESTE (EAST TIMOR)

0   400   800 Miles
0   400   800 Kilometers

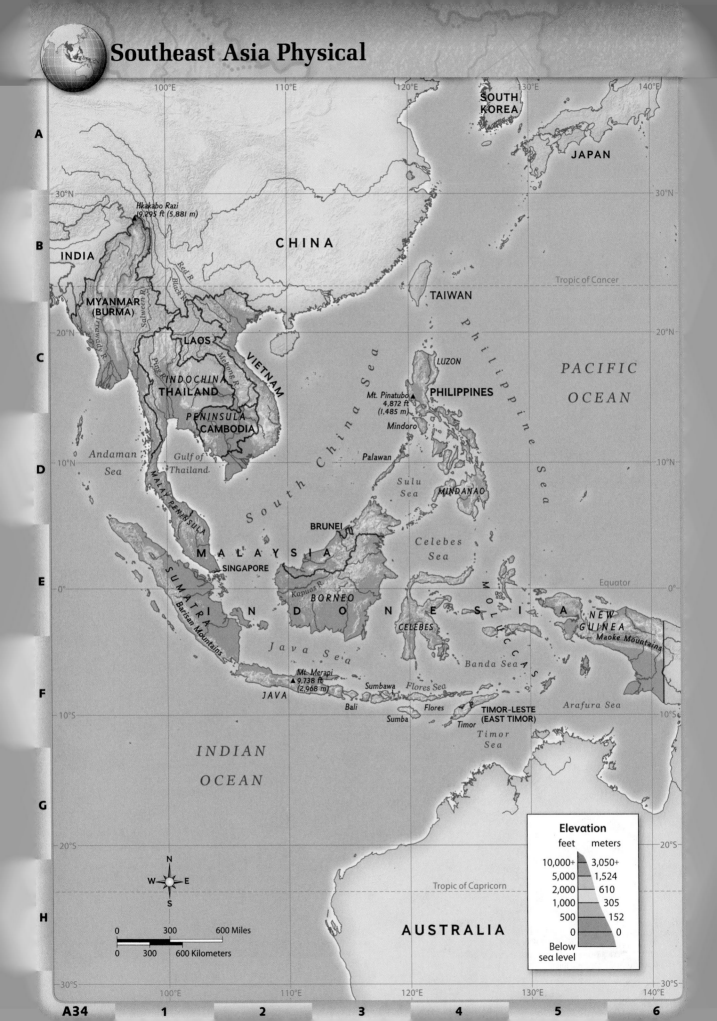

Southeast Asia Physical

A

B

C

D

E

F

G

H

INDIA

CHINA

SOUTH KOREA

JAPAN

Hkakabo Razi
19,295 ft (5,881 m)

MYANMAR (BURMA)

LAOS

VIETNAM

Tropic of Cancer

TAIWAN

Irrawady R.

Salween R.

Red R.

Black R.

INDOCHINA

THAILAND

Mekong R.

Ping R.

PENINSULA

CAMBODIA

Andaman Sea

Gulf of Thailand

MALAY PENINSULA

LUZON

PHILIPPINES

Mt. Pinatubo
4,872 ft
(1,485 m)

Mindoro

Palawan

Philippine Sea

PACIFIC OCEAN

South China Sea

Sulu Sea

MINDANAO

BRUNEI

Celebes Sea

MALAYSIA

SINGAPORE

SUMATRA

Barisan Mountains

Kapuas R.

BORNEO

INDONESIA

CELEBES

M O L U C C A S

Equator

NEW GUINEA

Maoke Mountains

Java Sea

Mt. Merapi
9,738 ft
(2,968 m)

JAVA

Bali

Sumbawa

Sumba

Flores Sea

Flores

Timor

Banda Sea

TIMOR-LESTE
(EAST TIMOR)

Timor Sea

Arafura Sea

INDIAN OCEAN

Tropic of Capricorn

AUSTRALIA

N
W   E
S

| 0 | 300 | 600 Miles |
| 0 | 300 | 600 Kilometers |

Elevation

feet	meters
10,000+	3,050+
5,000	1,524
2,000	610
1,000	305
500	152
0	0
Below sea level	

A34   1   2   3   4   5   6

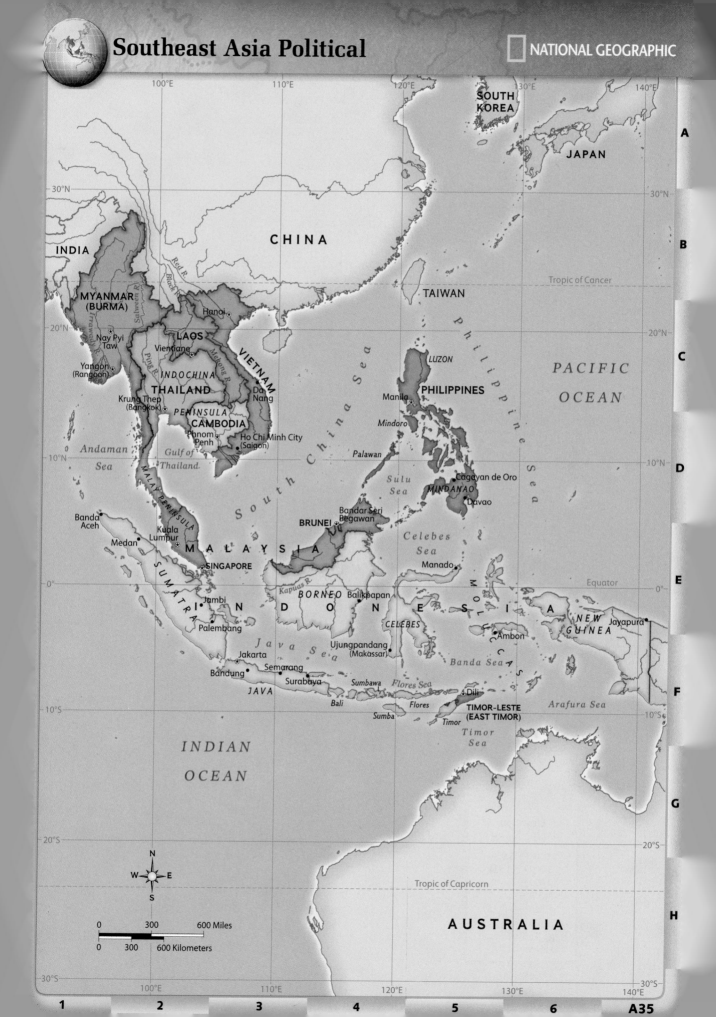

Southeast Asia Political

SOUTH KOREA

JAPAN

CHINA

INDIA

TAIWAN

MYANMAR (BURMA)

Hanoi

LAOS

Vientiane

Nay Pyi Taw

Yangon (Rangoon)

INDOCHINA

THAILAND

Krung Thep (Bangkok)

PENINSULA

CAMBODIA

Phnom Penh

Da Nang

VIETNAM

Ho Chi Minh City (Saigon)

Tropic of Cancer

PACIFIC OCEAN

LUZON

Manila

PHILIPPINES

Mindoro

Palawan

South China Sea

Philippine Sea

Sulu Sea

MINDANAO

Cagayan de Oro

Davao

Andaman Sea

Gulf of Thailand

Banda Aceh

Medan

Kuala Lumpur

MALAY PENINSULA

SINGAPORE

MALAYSIA

Bandar Seri Begawan

BRUNEI

Celebes Sea

Manado

SUMATRA

Jambi

Palembang

Kapuas R.

BORNEO

Balikpapan

INDONESIA

CELEBES

Ujungpandang (Makassar)

MOLUCCAS

NEW GUINEA

Jayapura

Equator

Jakarta

Bandung

Semarang

Surabaya

Java Sea

JAVA

Bali

Sumbawa

Flores

Sumba

Flores Sea

Timor

TIMOR-LESTE (EAST TIMOR)

Dili

Ambon

Banda Sea

Arafura Sea

Timor Sea

INDIAN OCEAN

Tropic of Capricorn

AUSTRALIA

Red R.

Black R.

Salween R.

Irrawaddy R.

Ping R.

Mekong R.

N

W E

S

0   300   600 Miles

0   300   600 Kilometers

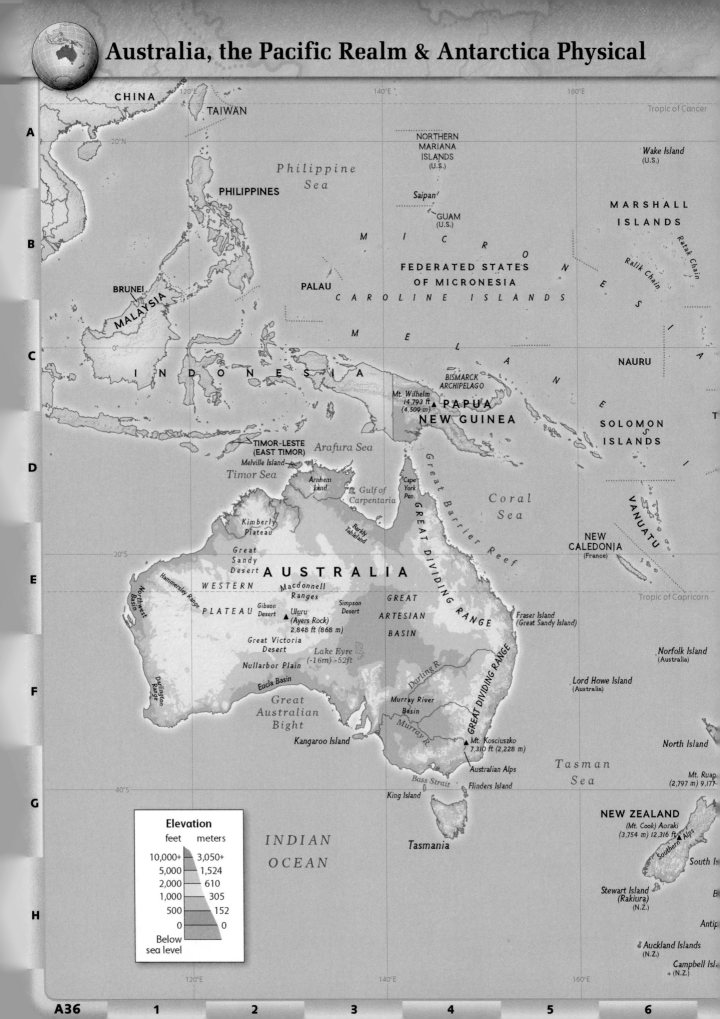

Australia, the Pacific Realm & Antarctica Physical

CHINA

TAIWAN

Tropic of Cancer

NORTHERN
MARIANA
ISLANDS
(U.S.)

Wake Island
(U.S.)

*Philippine
Sea*

PHILIPPINES

Saipan

MARSHALL
ISLANDS

GUAM
(U.S.)

M   I   C   R   O

Ralik Chain

Ratak Chain

BRUNEI

FEDERATED STATES
OF MICRONESIA

N   E   S

MALAYSIA

PALAU

CAROLINE   ISLANDS

I

0°

M   E   L   A

NAURU

A

I   N   D   O   N   E   S   I   A

BISMARCK
ARCHIPELAGO

N

Mt. Wilhelm
14,793 ft
(4,509 m)

PAPUA
NEW GUINEA

E

S   I

SOLOMON
ISLANDS

T

TIMOR-LESTE
(EAST TIMOR)

Arafura Sea

Melville Island

Timor Sea

Arnhem
Land

Cape
York
Pen.

*Coral
Sea*

VANUATU

Gulf of
Carpentaria

Kimberly
Plateau

Burketown
Tableland

GREAT BARRIER REEF

NEW
CALEDONIA
(France)

Great
Sandy
Desert

AUSTRALIA

Tropic of Capricorn

Hammersley Range

WESTERN

Macdonnell
Ranges

GREAT

Northwest
Basin

PLATEAU

Gibson
Desert

Uluru
(Ayers Rock)
2,848 ft (868 m)

Simpson
Desert

ARTESIAN

Fraser Island
(Great Sandy Island)

Norfolk Island
(Australia)

Great Victoria
Desert

Lake Eyre
(-16m) -52ft

BASIN

Nullarbor Plain

Lord Howe Island
(Australia)

Darlington Range

Eucla Basin

Darling R.

GREAT DIVIDING RANGE

*Great
Australian
Bight*

Murray River
Basin

Murray R.

Mt. Kosciuszko
7,310 ft (2,228 m)

*Tasman
Sea*

North Island

Mt. Ruap
(2,797 m) 9,177

Kangaroo Island

Australian Alps

Bass Strait

Flinders Island

King Island

NEW ZEALAND
(Mt. Cook) Aoraki
(3,754 m) 12,316 ft

*INDIAN
OCEAN*

Tasmania

Southern Alps

South Is

Stewart Island
(Rakiura)
(N.Z.)

B

Antip

Auckland Islands
(N.Z.)

Campbell Isl
(N.Z.)

Elevation

feet	meters
10,000+	3,050+
5,000	1,524
2,000	610
1,000	305
500	152
0	0
Below sea level	

1   2   3   4   5   6

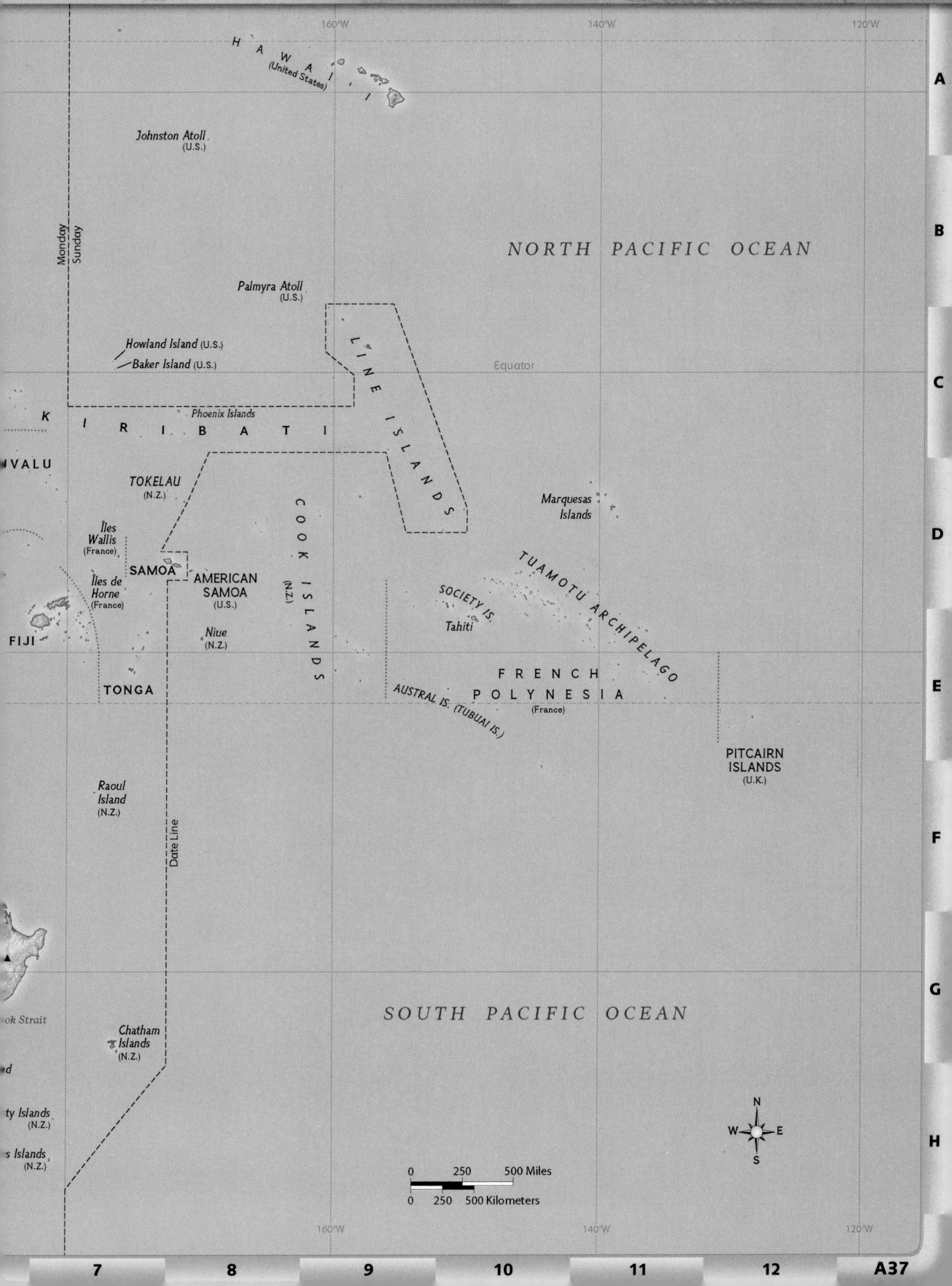

160°W   140°W   120°W

A

H A W A I I
(United States)

Johnston Atoll
(U.S.)

Monday Sunday

NORTH PACIFIC OCEAN

B

Palmyra Atoll
(U.S.)

Howland Island (U.S.)

Baker Island (U.S.)

Equator

C

K I R I B A T I

Phoenix Islands

L I N E I S L A N D S

VALU

TOKELAU
(N.Z.)

Marquesas
Islands

D

Îles
Wallis
(France)

SAMOA

AMERICAN
SAMOA
(U.S.)

Îles de
Horne
(France)

FIJI

Niue
(N.Z.)

C O O K I S L A N D S
(N.Z.)

SOCIETY IS.

Tahiti

T U A M O T U A R C H I P E L A G O

TONGA

AUSTRAL IS. (TUBUAI IS.)

FRENCH
POLYNESIA
(France)

E

Raoul
Island
(N.Z.)

Date Line

PITCAIRN
ISLANDS
(U.K.)

F

ok Strait

Chatham
Islands
(N.Z.)

SOUTH PACIFIC OCEAN

G

ty Islands
(N.Z.)

s Islands
(N.Z.)

N
W E
S

H

0 250 500 Miles
0 250 500 Kilometers

160°W   140°W   120°W

7   8   9   10   11   12   A37

CHINA

TAIWAN

120°E

140°E

160°E

Tropic of Cancer

20°N

A

Philippine Sea

NORTHERN
MARIANA
ISLANDS
(U.S.)
Saipan Capital Hill

Wake Island
(U.S.)

MARSHALL
ISLANDS

PHILIPPINES

(Agana) Hagâtña GUAM
(U.S.)

B

Melekeiok ⊛

Majuro

FEDERATED STATES

OF

PALAU

MICRONESIA

Palikir ⊛

BRUNEI

MALAYSIA

0°

NAURU
Yaren ⊛

Ta
(B

I N D O N E S I A

C

PAPUA
NEW GUINEA

SOLOMON
ISLANDS

T

TIMOR-LESTE
(EAST TIMOR)

Arafura Sea

Port
Moresby ⊛

Honiara ⊛

*Timor
Sea*

Darwin ★

Honiara ⊛

D

*Coral
Sea*

VANUATU

Gulf of
Carpentaria

Port
Vila

NORTHERN
TERRITORY

Great Barrier Reef

20°S

NEW
CALEDONIA
(France)

E

Tropic of Capricorn

QUEENSLAND

Nouméa ●

A U S T R A L I A

WESTERN
AUSTRALIA

*Lake
Eyre*

SOUTH
AUSTRALIA

Brisbane ★

Norfolk Island
(Australia)

Darling R.

NEW SOUTH
WALES

Lord Howe Island
(Australia)

F

Perth ★

*Great
Australian
Bight*

Adelaide ★

Murray R.

Sydney ★

Canberra,
AUSTRALIAN
CAPITAL TERRITORY

Aucklan

VICTORIA

*Tasman
Sea*

NEW
ZEALAND

Melbourne ★

40°S

Bass Strait

G

*INDIAN

OCEAN*

TASMANIA

Hobart ●

Chr

H

Antip

Auckland Islands
(N.Z.)

Campbell Isl
(N.Z.)

120°E

140°E

160°E

1   2   3   4   5   6

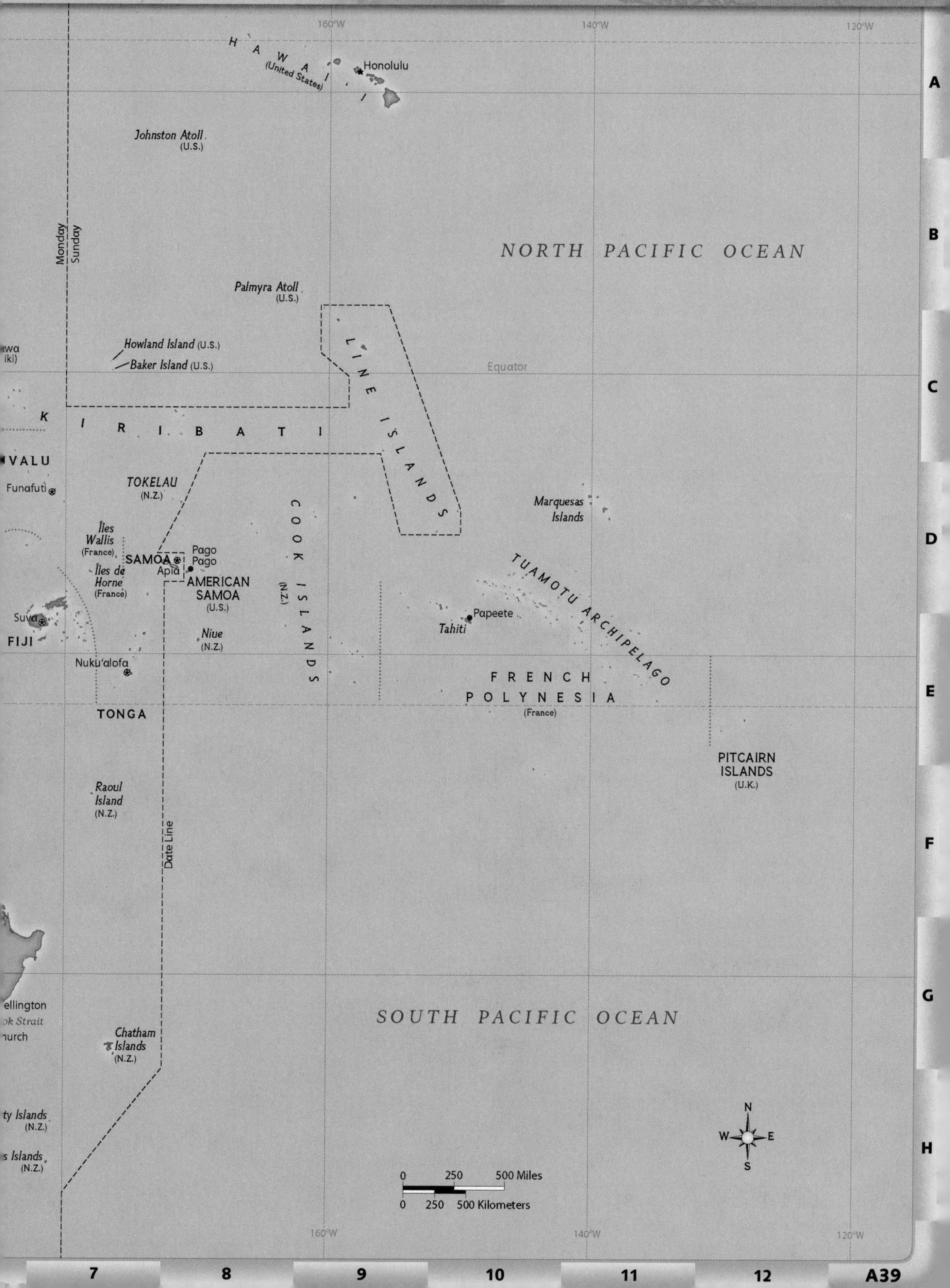

160°W   140°W   120°W

A

H A W A I' I
(United States)
★ Honolulu

Johnston Atoll
(U.S.)

B

NORTH   PACIFIC   OCEAN

Palmyra Atoll
(U.S.)

Monday
Sunday

Howland Island (U.S.)
Baker Island (U.S.)

Equator

C

kwa
iki)

K I R I B A T I

L
I
N
E

I
S
L
A
N
D
S

VALU

TOKELAU
(N.Z.)

Marquesas
Islands

Funafuti ⊛

D

Îles
Wallis
(France)

SAMOA ⊛
Apia

Pago
Pago

C
O
O
K

I
S
L
A
N
D
S
(N.Z.)

T
U
A
M
O
T
U

A
R
C
H
I
P
E
L
A
G
O

Îles de
Horne
(France)

AMERICAN
SAMOA
(U.S.)

Papeete

Suva ⊛

Niue
(N.Z.)

Tahiti

FIJI

Nuku'alofa
⊛

F R E N C H
P O L Y N E S I A
(France)

E

TONGA

PITCAIRN
ISLANDS
(U.K.)

Raoul
Island
(N.Z.)

Date Line

F

ellington
k Strait
urch

SOUTH   PACIFIC   OCEAN

G

Chatham
Islands
(N.Z.)

ty Islands
(N.Z.)

N
W ✦ E
S

H

s Islands
(N.Z.)

0   250   500 Miles

0   250   500 Kilometers

160°W   140°W   120°W

Inspiring people to care about the planet

-National Geographic Society Mission

For more than 100 years, National Geographic Society has sparked our curiosity about the world. NGS supports a network of explorers whose work in the field is vital to the planet. Some of them are shown below. Through education and exploration, the Society works to protect the physical environment and preserve the world's cultures.

Explorers at WORK

Oceanographer
NG Emerging Explorer Katy Croff Bell explores underwater archaeology.

Research Scientist
NG Emerging Explorer Albert Lin uses technology to study artifacts from Asian civilizations.

Archaeologist
NG Emerging Explorer Beverly Goodman researches the ways in which humans affect nature along coastlines.

Conservationist
NG Emerging Explorer Shafqat Hussain protects endangered snow leopards.

© Sharon Farmer

Educator
NG Emerging Explorer Kakenya Ntaiya works to improve girls' education in Kenya.

Filmmaker & Anthropologist
NG Fellow Elizabeth Kapu'uwailani Lindsey strives to preserve the Polynesian culture through documentary film.

Across the world, archaeologists, anthropologists, oceanographers, and linguists represent National Geographic Society in their work. Don't let their long titles confuse you—they are all scientists doing exciting work in the field. New information about Earth's physical features is uncovered every day.

These are some of the explorers at work for National Geographic Society.

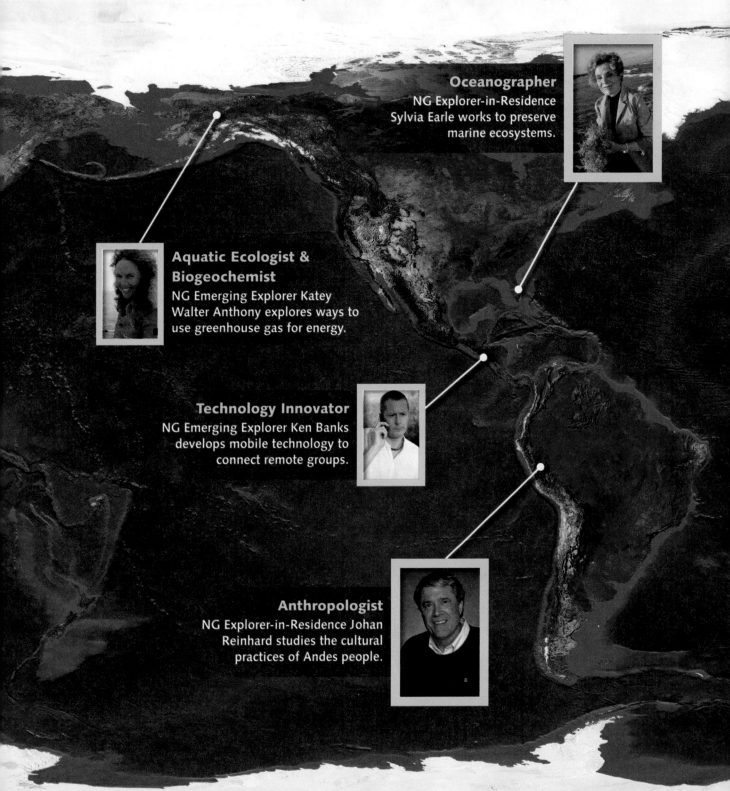

Oceanographer
NG Explorer-in-Residence Sylvia Earle works to preserve marine ecosystems.

Aquatic Ecologist & Biogeochemist
NG Emerging Explorer Katey Walter Anthony explores ways to use greenhouse gas for energy.

Technology Innovator
NG Emerging Explorer Ken Banks develops mobile technology to connect remote groups.

Anthropologist
NG Explorer-in-Residence Johan Reinhard studies the cultural practices of Andes people.

From the classroom to the world

Tools for EXPLO

National Geographic explorers all depend on tools for exploration. You can use the variety of tools provided with your program at myNGconnect.com to explore the world and its cultures.

my eEdition

Interactive Map Tool
A comprehensive online mapmaker at your fingertips

ORATION

Taj Mahal, India

Digital Library
GeoVideos, Explorer Video Clips, and
hundreds of photographs of the world's
physical geography and cultures

NATIONAL GEOGRAPHIC
GeoActivity

World Cultures and Geography
South Asia Geography & History, Section 1.1 Physical Geography

Draw a Mental Map of South Asia

Play a Mental Mapping game to find out
how much you remember about South
Asia's physical geography. The goal is to
get as many points as possible based on
what you remember.

◁ 1 of 6 ▷

SOUTH ASIA

COUNTRIES	LANDFORMS	BODIES OF WATER
Bangladesh	Deccan Plateau	Arabian Sea
Bhutan	Eastern Ghats	Bay of Bengal
India	Ganges Delta	Ganges River
Maldives	Himalayas	Indian Ocean
Nepal	Thar Desert	Indus River
Pakistan	Western Ghats	
Sri Lanka		

NATIONAL GEOGRAPHIC SCHOOL PUBLISHING

**Interactive Whiteboard
GeoActivities**

**Hands-on activities to learn more
about how the world works**

India's
Architecture

Magazine Maker CD-ROM

**Tool for creating student magazines
using program resources or
by uploading your own photos**

From the classroom to the world

The knowledge and skills that explorers need are described in the National Geography Standards, shown here. Keep them in mind as you study *World Cultures and Geography*.

HIGH

COMMUNICATE

1. How to use maps and other geographic representations, geospatial technologies, and spatial thinking to understand and communicate information

2. How to us mental maps to organize information about people, places, and environments in a spatial context

3. How to **ANALYZE** the spatial organization of people, places, and environments on Earth's surface

ANALYZE

4. The physical and human characteristics of places

EXPERIENCE

5. That people create regions to **INTERPRET** Earth's complexity

INTERPRET

6. How culture and **EXPERIENCE** influence people's perceptions of places and regions

7. The physical processes that shape the patterns of Earth's surface

8. The characteristics and spatial distribution of ecosystems and biomes on Earth's surface

9. The characteristics, distribution, and migration of human populations on Earth's surface

ER ORDER THINKING

10. The characteristics, distribution, and complexity of Earth's cultural mosaics

11. The **PATTERNS** and networks of economic interdependence on Earth's surface

12. The processes, patterns, and functions of human settlement

PATTERNS

13. How the forces of cooperation and conflict among people influence the division and control of Earth's surface

14. How human actions **MODIFY** the physical environment

15. How physical systems affect human systems

MODIFY

16. The changes that occur in the meaning, use, distribution, and importance of resources

17. How to **APPLY** geography to interpret the past

18. How to **APPLY** geography to interpret the present and plan for the future

APPLY

THE ESSENTIALS OF GEOGRAPHY

MEET THE EXPLORER

NATIONAL GEOGRAPHIC

Explorer-in-Residence Spencer Wells is director of the Genographic Project. He analyzes DNA samples to trace humankind's ancient migration patterns and learn where we really come from.

INVESTIGATE GEOGRAPHY

In 2002, NASA released its spectacular "blue marble" image of Earth. It is made from satellite observations gathered over several months, and then carefully combined. The image was inspired by a photo taken by astronauts during a 1972 space mission.

CONNECT WITH THE CULTURE

Culture is how people of a certain region live, behave, and think, but culture is not limited by geography. A busy urban area like New York City (shown here) attracts people from around the world, representing a vast variety of cultures. Those cultures can live together in a single place.

THINK LIKE A GEOGRAPHER

Scientists work to uncover the skeleton of an ancient whale in Wadi Al Hitan, Egypt. Fossils, like those shown here, reveal clues about the earth's past.

NATIONAL GEOGRAPHIC   CHAPTER 1

THE GEOGRAPHER'S
TOOLBOX

PREVIEW
THE CHAPTER

Essential Question How do geographers think about the world?

SECTION 1 • GEOGRAPHIC THINKING

KEY VOCABULARY

- spatial thinking
- geographic pattern
- Geographic Information System (GIS)
- absolute location
- Global Positioning System (GPS)
- relative location
- region
- continent
- terrace

ACADEMIC VOCABULARY
significant, categorize

Essential Question How do people use geography?

SECTION 2 • MAPS

KEY VOCABULARY

- globe
- map
- latitude
- equator
- longitude
- prime meridian
- hemisphere
- scale
- cartographer
- elevation
- relief
- projection

ACADEMIC VOCABULARY
distort, theme

TERMS & NAMES

- North Pole
- South Pole
- Northern Hemisphere
- Southern Hemisphere
- Western Hemisphere
- Eastern Hemisphere

TECHTREK FOR THIS CHAPTER

Student eEdition

Maps and Graphs

Interactive Whiteboard GeoActivities

Digital Library

Global Positioning System (GPS)

Go to **myNGconnect.com** for information on geographers' tools.

Scientists wear breathing aids while collecting gas samples from a spring in the Cueva (Cave) de Villa Luz in Mexico.

TECHTREK

myNGconnect.com For an online map
and photos of cities on water

Maps and Graphs

Digital Library

WESTERN HEMISPHERE

Vancouver, Canada

New York City, United States

Rio de Janeiro, Brazil

DENVER, COLORADO

CHICAGO, ILLINOIS

∧ **Critical Viewing** Denver, Colorado, is located in the foothills of the Rocky Mountains. Chicago, Illinois, is located on the shore of Lake Michigan—one of the five Great Lakes. How might these different locations affect the activities of people who live in these cities?

Main Idea Geographers study the location of places and the people who live there.

Geography is about more than the names of places on a map. It involves **spatial thinking**, or thinking about the space on Earth's surface, including where places are located and why they are there.

Ask Geographic Questions

Geographers use spatial thinking to ask questions, such as "Where is a place located? Why is this location **significant**, or important?"

Look at the photographs of Denver, Colorado, and Chicago, Illinois, above. Denver is near the Rocky Mountains, where gold was once discovered. Chicago is on Lake Michigan, which made it an important shipping center for many years.

Now find New York City on the map. It is on a protected bay. Why is New York's location significant? Like Chicago, it is near water, which is good for trade.

Study Geographic Patterns

By asking and answering many questions, geographers can find patterns. **Geographic patterns** are similarities among places. The location of large cities near water is one example of a geographic pattern.

Many geographers use computer-based **Geographic Information Systems (GIS)**. They create maps and analyze patterns using many layers of data.

Before You Move On

Summarize What do geographers study? How do they study it?

FORMATIVE ASSESSMENT

MAP LAB
 GeoJournal

1. **Location** Where is Rio de Janeiro located on the map? Use directional words in your answer.
2. **Make Inferences** Look at the other cities on the map. Where are most of them located? What pattern do you notice?
3. **Summarize** What are geographic patterns, and how do geographers find them?

1.2 Themes and Elements

TECHTREK
myNGconnect.com For photos
and Guided Writing

Digital
Library

Student
Resources

> **Main Idea** Geographers use themes and
> elements to understand the world.

Geographers divide their work into
physical geography (landforms, bodies of
water, the features of Earth's surface) and
human geography (cities, bridges, dams,
the things people make as part of their
culture).

The Five Themes of Geography

The five themes and six elements will help
you **categorize** , or group, information.

1. **Location** provides a way of locating
   places. **Absolute location** is the
   exact point where a place is located.
   Geographers use a satellite system
   called the **Global Positioning System
   (GPS)** to find absolute location. **Relative
   location** is where a place is in relation
   to other places. The Great Wall is
   located near Beijing in northern China.

2. **Place** includes the characteristics of a
   location. A famous place in the western
   United States is the Grand Canyon. It
   has steep rock walls that were carved
   over centuries by the Colorado River.

3. **Human-Environment Interaction**
   explains how people affect the
   environment and how the environment
   affects people. For example, people
   build dams to change the flow of rivers.

4. **Movement** explains how people, ideas,
   and animals move from one place
   to another. The spread of different
   religions around the world is an
   example of movement.

5. **Region** involves a group of places that
   have common characteristics. North
   America is a region that includes the
   United States, Mexico, and Canada.

Critical Viewing Tourists climb
the Great Wall of China, a human
geographic feature. What
physical land features can you
see in the photo?

The Great Wall runs through the Chinese countryside.

Six Essential Elements

Some geographers identify essential elements, or key ideas, to study physical processes and human systems.

1. **The World in Spatial Terms** Geographers use tools such as maps to study places on Earth's surface.

2. **Places and Regions** Geographers study the characteristics of places and regions.

3. **Physical Systems** Geographers examine Earth's physical processes, such as earthquakes and volcanoes.

4. **Human Systems** Geographers study how humans live and what systems they create, such as economic systems.

5. **Environment and Society** Geographers explore how humans change the environment and use resources.

6. **The Uses of Geography** Geographers interpret the past, analyze the present, and plan for the future.

Before You Move On

Make Inferences How do geographers use the themes and elements to better understand the world?

FORMATIVE ASSESSMENT

WRITING LAB GeoJournal

1. **Connect to Texas** Write a paragraph in which you use the five themes to describe your community. Explain which theme is the most important in making your community what it is today. Go to **Student Resources** for Guided Writing support.

2. **Categorize** Which theme and which element would you use to categorize information about forms of energy? Explain your answer.

3. **Compare and Contrast** Create a chart like the one below. Use the six essential elements to compare how your town or city relates to another one you know about.

ELEMENT	MY TOWN	OTHER TOWN
The World in Spatial Terms	North of the highway	South of the highway
Places and Regions		
Physical Systems		

1.3 World Regions

TECHTREK

myNGconnect.com For an online map
and photos of world regions

Maps and
Graphs

Digital
Library

Main Idea Geographers divide the world into
regions. Each region is shaped by shared physical
and human processes.

In 1413, a Chinese admiral and explorer,
Zheng He, sailed from China to Arabia.
When he arrived in Arabia, he saw people
dressed in ways he had never seen. Yet,
like him, these people wanted to trade.

Regions and Continents

Zheng He saw that regions of Earth have
similarities and differences. A **region** is a
group of places with common traits. The
places within a region are linked by trade,
culture, and other human activities. They
also share similar physical processes and
characteristics, such as climate.

A region often includes an entire
continent. A **continent** is a large landmass
on Earth's surface. Geographers have
identified seven continents: Africa, Asia,
Australia, Europe, North America, South
America, and Antarctica.

Geographers study the world's regions,
but they also take a global perspective
when they investigate Earth. They might,
for instance, study ocean currents around
the globe or how one region affects
another. Both ways of looking at the world
add to our understanding of it.

Before You Move On
Make Inferences Why do geographers study the
world by dividing it into regions?

Visual Vocabulary Chinese field workers
view the terraced landscape. A **terrace** is a
flat surface that is built into a hillside.

WORLD REGIONS

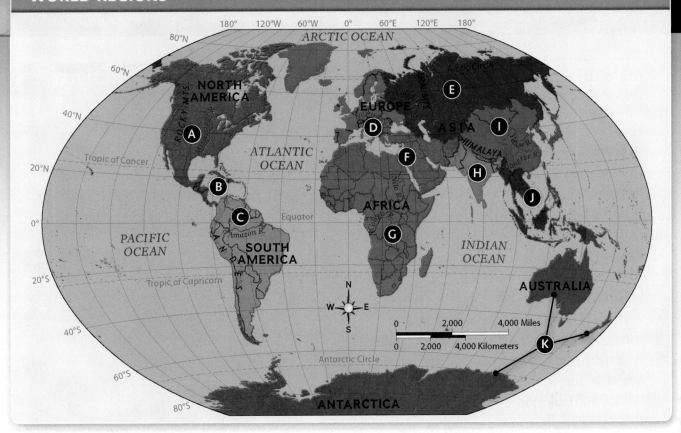

Regions in This Book

A **North America** contains the United States, Canada, and Mexico, along with the Great Lakes—the largest group of freshwater lakes.

B **Central America and the Caribbean** includes the islands of the Caribbean and the countries that connect North and South America.

C **South America** includes Brazil, a growing economic power, and the Amazon Rain Forest, the world's largest tropical rain forest.

D **Europe** includes 29 countries and has nearly 24,000 miles of coastline.

E **Russia and the Eurasian Republics** includes countries that were part of the former Union of Soviet Socialist Republics (U.S.S.R.).

F **Southwest Asia and North Africa** spans two continents—Africa and Asia.

G **Sub-Saharan Africa** includes Africa south of the Sahara, the world's largest desert.

H **South Asia** includes India, one of the world's fastest growing countries.

I **East Asia** includes China, the world's most populous country.

J **Southeast Asia** includes Indonesia, a country made up of over 17,000 islands.

K **Australia, the Pacific Realm, and Antarctica** includes the Pacific island nations north and east of Australia and New Zealand.

FORMATIVE ASSESSMENT
MAP LAB

GeoJournal

1. **Interpret Maps** Which regions span more than one continent?

2. **Region** Find your region on the map. Write one geographic question about the region and answer the question.

3. **Define** Start a geography and cultures Term Bank with words you will use routinely such as *region* or *physical processes*. Add images, notes, or clues to help you remember meanings. Work with a partner to simplify terms. For example, a simpler word for *modify* is *change*.

2.1 Elements of a Map

> **Main Idea** Globes and maps are two different tools used to study places on Earth.

Have you ever needed to figure out how to get to a friend's house? Imagine that the only resource you had was a globe. In order to see enough detail to find your friend's house, the globe would have to be enormous—much too big to carry around in your pocket!

Globes and Maps

A three-dimensional, or spherical, representation of Earth is called a **globe**. It is useful when you need to see Earth as a whole, but it is not helpful if you need to see a small section of Earth.

Now imagine taking a part of the globe and flattening it out. This two-dimensional, or flat, representation of Earth is called a **map**. Maps and globes are different representations of Earth, but they have similar features.

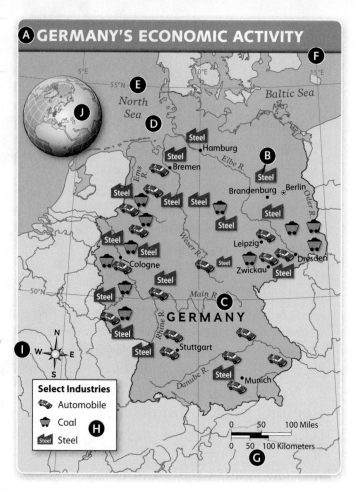

A GERMANY'S ECONOMIC ACTIVITY

Select Industries
- Automobile
- Coal
- Steel

Map and Globe Elements

A A **title** tells the subject of the map or globe.

B **Symbols** represent information such as natural resources and economic activities.

C **Labels** are the names of places, such as cities, countries, rivers, and mountains.

D **Colors** represent different kinds of information. For example, the color blue usually represents water.

E **Lines of latitude** are imaginary horizontal lines that measure the distance north or south of the equator.

F **Lines of longitude** are imaginary vertical lines that measure the distance east or west of the prime meridian.

G A **scale** shows how much distance on Earth is represented by distance on the map or globe. For example, a half inch on the map above represents 100 miles on Earth.

H A **legend**, or key, explains what the symbols and colors on the map or globe represent.

I A **compass rose** shows the directions north (N), south (S), east (E), and west (W).

J A **locator globe** shows the specific area of the world that is shown on a map. The locator globe on the map above shows where Germany is located.

Latitude

Lines of **latitude** are imaginary lines that run east to west, parallel to the equator. The **equator** is the center line of latitude. Distances north and south of the equator are measured in degrees (°). There are 90 degrees north of the equator and 90 degrees south. The equator is 0°. The latitude of Berlin, Germany, is 52° N, meaning that it is 52 degrees north of the equator.

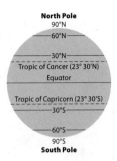

Longitude

Lines of **longitude** are imaginary lines that run north to south from the **North Pole** to the **South Pole**. They measure distance east or west of the prime meridian. The **prime meridian** runs through Greenwich, England. It is 0°. There are 180 degrees east of the prime meridian and 180 degrees west. The longitude of Berlin, Germany, is 13° E, meaning that it is 13 degrees east of the prime meridian.

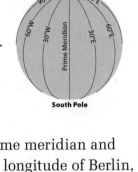

Remember that absolute location is the exact point where a place is located. This point includes a place's latitude and longitude. For example, the absolute location of Berlin, Germany, is 52° N, 13° E. You say this aloud as "fifty-two degrees North, thirteen degrees East."

Hemispheres

A **hemisphere** is half of Earth. The equator divides Earth into the **Northern Hemisphere** and the **Southern Hemisphere**. North America is entirely in the Northern Hemisphere. Most of South America is in the Southern Hemisphere.

The **Western Hemisphere** is west of the prime meridian. The **Eastern Hemisphere** is east of the prime meridian. South America is in the Western Hemisphere. Most of Africa is in the Eastern Hemisphere.

Before You Move On

Monitor Comprehension How are maps and globes different? How is each one used?

FORMATIVE ASSESSMENT

MAP LAB   GeoJournal

1. **Interpret Maps** What types of industry are located in Germany? What map elements did you use to find the answers?

2. **Make Inferences** What is the main industry in southern Germany? Why might this industry be located there?

3. **Identify** What is the difference between lines of latitude and lines of longitude?

4. **Location** Use a map or globe to find the absolute location of Munich, Germany.

2.2 Map Scale

> **Main Idea** Maps use different scales for different purposes.

On a walk through a city, such as Charlotte, North Carolina, you might use a highly-detailed map that shows only the downtown area. To drive up the Atlantic coast, however, you would use a map that covers a large area, including several states. These maps have different scales.

Interpreting a Scale

A map's **scale** shows how much distance on Earth is shown on the map. A large-scale map covers a small area but shows many details. A small-scale map covers a large area but includes few details.

A scale is usually shown in both inches and centimeters. One inch or centimeter on the map represents a much larger distance on Earth, such as a number of miles or kilometers.

To use a map scale, mark off the length of the scale several times on the edge of a sheet of paper. Then hold the paper between two points to see how many times the scale falls between them. Add up the distance.

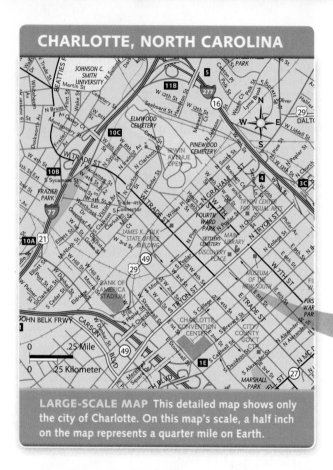

CHARLOTTE, NORTH CAROLINA

LARGE-SCALE MAP This detailed map shows only the city of Charlotte. On this map's scale, a half inch on the map represents a quarter mile on Earth.

Purposes of a Scale

The scale of a map should be appropriate for its purpose. For example, a tourist map of Washington, D.C., should be large-scale, showing every street name, monument, and museum.

Critical Viewing The Atlantic Ocean rolls in along the dunes on the Outer Banks of North Carolina. Which map labels the location of the Outer Banks?

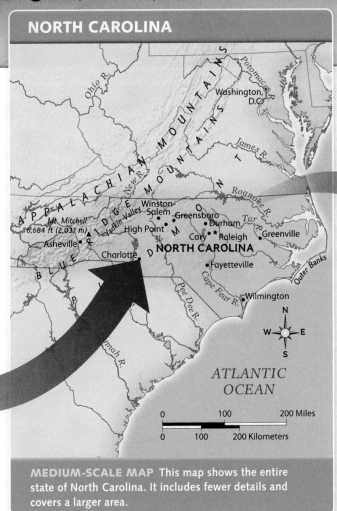

NORTH CAROLINA

MEDIUM-SCALE MAP This map shows the entire state of North Carolina. It includes fewer details and covers a larger area.

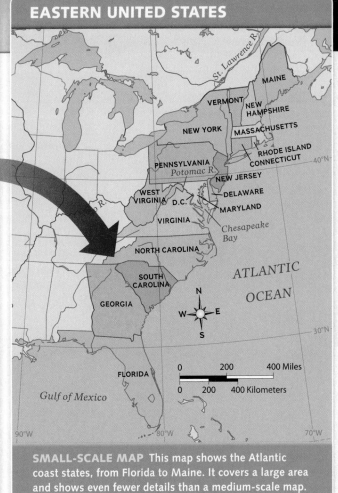

EASTERN UNITED STATES

SMALL-SCALE MAP This map shows the Atlantic coast states, from Florida to Maine. It covers a large area and shows even fewer details than a medium-scale map.

Maps of any scale show geographic patterns. The map of Washington, D.C., for instance, would show that many government buildings are in one area.

Before You Move On
Summarize What are the purposes of a small-scale map and a large-scale map?

FORMATIVE ASSESSMENT

MAP LAB

GeoJournal

1. **Interpret Maps** On the North Carolina map, approximately how many inches represent 200 miles? On the eastern United States map, how many miles does one inch represent?

2. **Pose and Answer Questions** What geographic pattern do you see in the location of cities in North Carolina? How might you explain this pattern?

3. **Connect to Texas** With a partner, use the maps on pages A8 and A9 to pose and answer geographic questions you learned about on page 13. Focus on the Texas region. Then answer: What scale of map would you need for more detail?

2.3 Political and Physical Maps

TECHTREK

myNGconnect.com For online political
and physical maps of world regions

 Maps and
Graphs

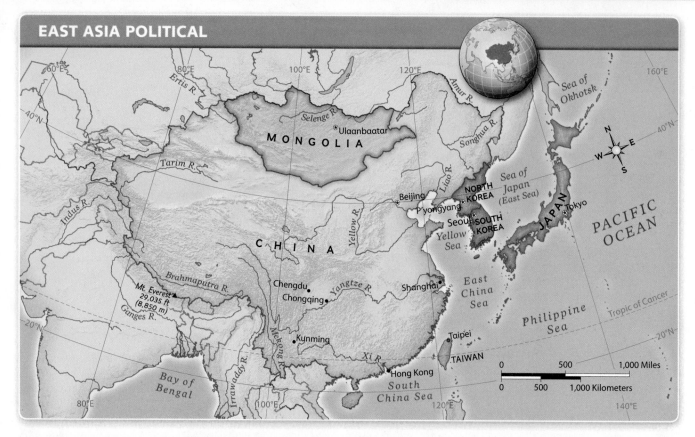

EAST ASIA POLITICAL

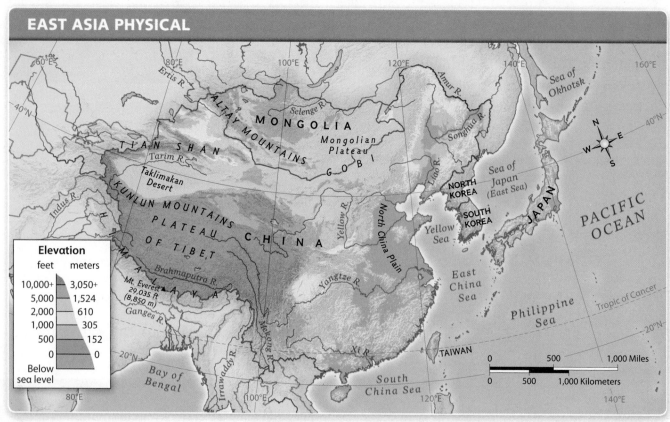

EAST ASIA PHYSICAL

Elevation	
feet	meters
10,000+	3,050+
5,000	1,524
2,000	610
1,000	305
500	152
0	0
Below sea level	

Main Idea Political maps show features that humans have created on Earth's surface. Physical maps show natural features.

The governor of a state needs a map that shows counties and cities. A mountain climber needs a map that shows cliffs, canyons, and ice fields. **Cartographers**, or mapmakers, create different kinds of maps for these different purposes.

Political Maps

A political map shows features that humans have created, such as countries, states, provinces, and cities. These features are labeled, and lines show boundaries, such as those between countries.

Physical Maps

A physical map shows natural features of physical geography. It includes landforms, such as mountains, plains, valleys, and deserts. It also includes oceans, lakes, rivers, and other bodies of water.

A physical map can also show elevation and relief. **Elevation** is the height of a physical feature above sea level. **Relief** is the change in elevation from one place to another. Maps show elevation by using color. The physical map at left uses seven colors for seven ranges of elevation.

Before You Move On
Monitor Comprehension How is a political map different from a physical map?

Critical Viewing The Sobaek Mountains cut diagonally across South Korea. Which map best indicates the location of these mountains?

FORMATIVE ASSESSMENT
MAP LAB
 GeoJournal

1. **Interpret Maps** What is the most mountainous country in East Asia? How did you find the answer?
2. **Human-Environment Interaction** Based on elevations shown on the map, what economic activity would you expect to find on the North China Plain?
3. **Draw Conclusions** What do the locations of Hong Kong, Shanghai, and Tokyo have in common? What conclusion can you draw about the location of cities around the world?

2.4 Map Projections

TECHTREK

myNGconnect.com For additional
maps in a variety of projections

 Maps and Graphs

Main Idea Cartographers use various projections to show Earth's curved surface on a flat map.

The world is a sphere, but maps are flat. As a result, maps **distort**, or change, shapes, areas, distances, and directions found in the real world. To reduce distortion, mapmakers use **projections**, or ways of showing Earth's curved surface on a flat map. Five common map projections are the azimuthal, Mercator, homolosine, Robinson, and Winkel Tripel. Each projection has strengths and weaknesses—each distorts in a different way.

When cartographers make maps, they need to choose a map projection. The type of projection depends on the map's purpose. Which elements are acceptable to distort? Which are not acceptable to distort? For example, if a cartographer is creating a navigation map, it is important that directions are not distorted. It may not matter, however, if some areas or shapes are distorted.

Before You Move On

Make Inferences How do cartographers decide which projection to use?

AZIMUTHAL PROJECTION

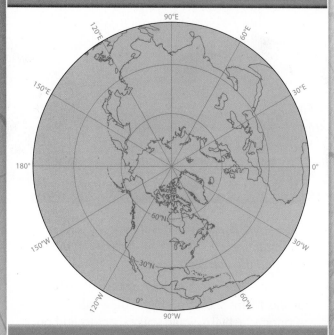

Mapmakers create the **azimuthal projection** by projecting part of the globe onto a flat surface. The projection shows directions accurately but distorts shapes. It is often used for the polar regions.

MERCATOR PROJECTION

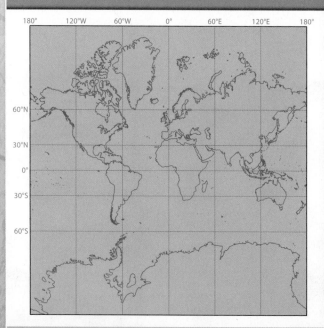

This **Mercator projection** shows much of Earth accurately, but it distorts the shape and area of land near the North and South Poles. This projection shows direction accurately, so it is good for navigation maps.

HOMOLOSINE PROJECTION

The **homolosine projection** resembles the flattened peel of an orange. It accurately shows the shape and area of landmasses by cutting up the oceans. However, it does not show distances accurately.

ROBINSON PROJECTION

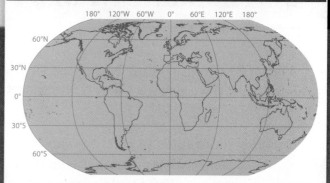

The **Robinson projection** combines the strengths of other projections. It shows the shape and area of the continents and oceans with reasonable accuracy. However, the North and South Poles are distorted.

WINKEL TRIPEL PROJECTION

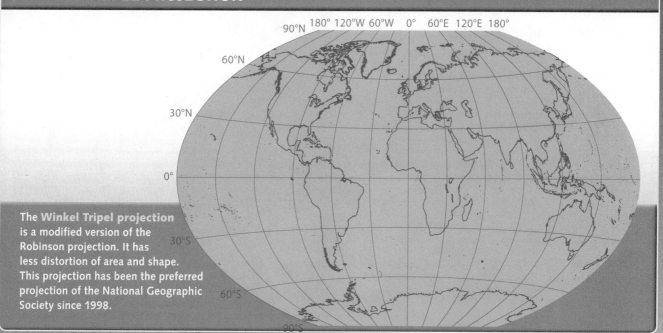

The **Winkel Tripel projection** is a modified version of the Robinson projection. It has less distortion of area and shape. This projection has been the preferred projection of the National Geographic Society since 1998.

FORMATIVE ASSESSMENT

MAP LAB

 GeoJournal

1. **Compare and Contrast** Locate Greenland on the Mercator projection and on the Robinson projection. What is similar and different in the two maps? Why?

2. **Location** What does the azimuthal projection show about the relative location of Alaska and Russia?

2.5 **Thematic Maps**

TECHTREK

myNGconnect.com For additional
examples of thematic maps

Maps and
Graphs

Main Idea Thematic maps focus on specific topics, such as the population density or economic activity in a region or country.

Suppose you wanted to create a map showing the location of sports fields in your community. You would create a thematic map, which is a map about a specific **theme**, or topic.

Types of Thematic Maps

Thematic maps are useful for showing a variety of geographic information, including economic activity, natural resources, and population density. Common types of thematic maps are the point symbol map, the dot density map, and the proportional symbol map.

Before You Move On

Make Inferences Look through this textbook and identify another example of a thematic map. Why did you choose this map?

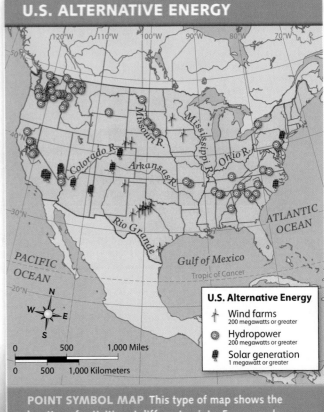

U.S. ALTERNATIVE ENERGY

U.S. Alternative Energy
- Wind farms
  200 megawatts or greater
- Hydropower
  200 megawatts or greater
- Solar generation
  1 megawatt or greater

POINT SYMBOL MAP This type of map shows the location of activities at different points. For example, this map has symbols that show some sources of wind, water, and solar energy in the United States.

> **Critical Viewing** Solar panels in the Nevada desert absorb light from the sun and turn it into energy. Why might Nevada be a good location for solar fields?

THAILAND'S POPULATION DENSITY

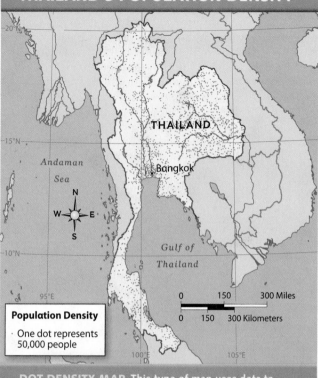

Population Density
· One dot represents 50,000 people

DOT DENSITY MAP This type of map uses dots to show how something is distributed in a country or region. Each dot represents an amount. For example, the dots on this map show population density in Thailand.

PHILIPPINES' EARTHQUAKES

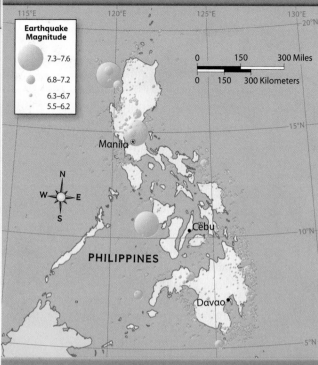

Earthquake Magnitude
7.3–7.6
6.8–7.2
6.3–6.7
5.5–6.2

PROPORTIONAL SYMBOL MAP This type of map uses symbols of different sizes to show the size of an event. For example, the size of the circles on this map shows the severity of earthquakes in the Philippines.

FORMATIVE ASSESSMENT

MAP LAB

GeoJournal

1. **Place** According to the map, which area of the United States has the most wind farms?

2. **Make Inferences** In the Philippines, where are people most at risk for severe earthquakes? What do these places have in common?

3. **Tap Prior Knowledge** To better understand the meaning of *theme*, think of ways you have heard it used such as *theme song*. Talk with a partner about themes or topics you know.

4. **Connect to Texas** Review the lesson on page R29. Then sketch a thematic map of your neighborhood to show stores, gas stations, and other economic activity. Title your map. Include a legend that explains any symbols you draw.

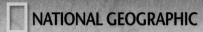

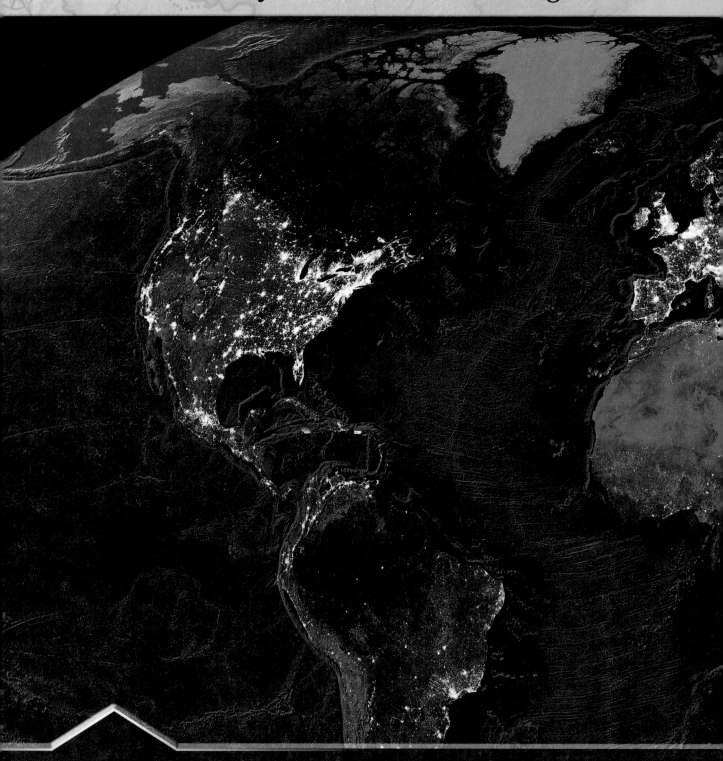

For more photos from
the National Geographic
Photo Gallery, go to
the **Digital Library** at
myNGconnect.com.

Mayan artifact

Golden Gate Bridge

Neuschwanstein Castle

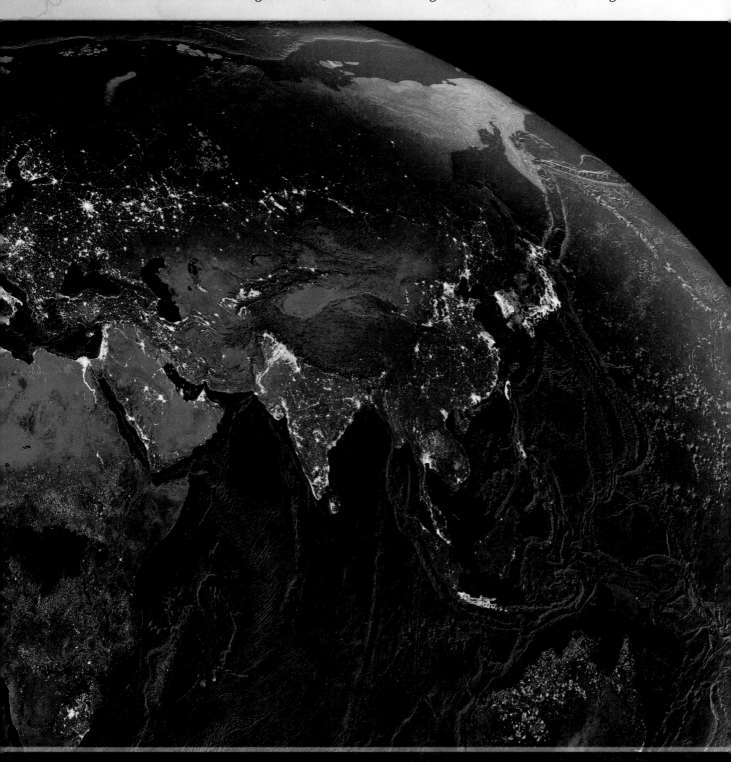

Archaeologist at work

Eastern Hemisphere, 1928

Tokyo, Japan, at night

Lima, Peru

VOCABULARY

For each pair of words, write one sentence that explains the connection between the two words.

1. absolute location; relative location

> The absolute location of Washington, D.C., is 39° N, 77° W; its relative location is on the Potomac River.

2. region; continent

3. latitude; longitude

4. relief; elevation

5. distort; projection

MAIN IDEAS

6. What are Geographic Information Systems? How do geographers use them? (Section 1.1)

7. How are the five themes of geography and the six essential elements similar? How are they different? (Section 1.2)

8. Why is the construction of a highway an example of human-environment interaction? (Section 1.2)

9. What are traits of a region? (Section 1.3)

10. How do latiitude and longitude help determine the absolute location of a place? (Section 2.1)

11. Is a map of the world a large-scale map or a small-scale map? Why? (Section 2.2)

12. How do physical maps show elevation and relief? (Section 2.3)

13. How do map projections distort Earth? (Section 2.4)

14. What type of thematic map would a cartographer use to show different types of agriculture in Africa? Explain your answer. (Section 2.5)

GEOGRAPHIC THINKING

ANALYZE THE ESSENTIAL QUESTION

How do geographers think about the world?

Critical Thinking: Describe Geographic Information

15. How do geographers use spatial thinking to make sense of space on Earth's surface?

16. How would you describe New York City using the five themes of geography?

17. What is an example of a physical process, and how can it affect a region?

INTERPRET MAPS

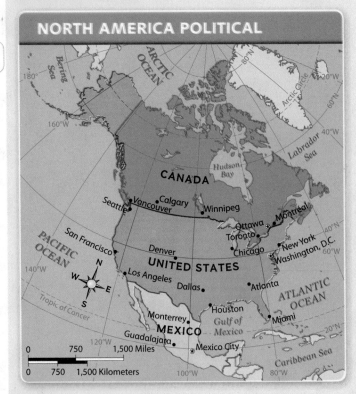

NORTH AMERICA POLITICAL

18. **Region** According to the map, what is the relative location of Canada's cities? Why do you think they are located there?

19. **Compare and Contrast** How does the relative location of Mexico's cities compare with the relative location of Canada's cities?

MAPS

ANALYZE THE ESSENTIAL QUESTION

How do people use geography?

Critical Thinking: Make Inferences

20. On a Mercator projection map, Greenland looks larger than South America. However, it is actually much smaller. How could this affect a person's understanding of land areas?

21. A geographer wants to show where economic activities are located. What kind of thematic map should the geographer use? Explain.

22. An explorer is the first to map a region that has hills, canyons, and flat areas. What type of map should the explorer create? Explain.

INTERPRET PRIMARY SOURCES

In 1953, Sir John Hunt led a group of climbers up Mount Everest, the highest mountain in the world. Read Hunt's description of climbing Everest and answer the questions.

> What makes Everest murderous is . . . its cold, its wind, and its climbing difficulties. . . . At 28,000 feet a given volume of air breathed contains only a third as much oxygen as at sea level. On the ground, even if a man were exercising violently, his lungs would need but 50 liters of air per minute. Near Everest's summit he struggles to suck in as much as 200 liters. Since he inhales his air cold and dry and exhales it warm and moist, the stress on his parched lungs and respiratory passages becomes appalling.
>
> —*National Geographic*, July 1954

23. **Find Details** What are the characteristics of the environment on Mount Everest?

24. **Differentiate** What tells you the excerpt above is a primary source and not a secondary source?

ACTIVE OPTIONS

Synthesize the Essential Questions by completing the activities below.

25. **Pose and Answer Geographic Questions** Choose a place in the world you would like to visit. List questions such as, "Why am I curious about it?" "What are its features?" "Where is it located?" "Why is its location significant?" Research and write your answers. Guess what places your classmates chose. Take turns sharing questions and answers. **Share facts about your place with the class.**

Research Tips
- Use print or online encyclopedias, or other reliable Web sites. Review the lesson on page R39.
- Set a period of time for finding answers to help you avoid getting distracted.
- Be sure to put others' writing into your own words.

TECHTREK myNGconnect.com For maps and photographs of the five themes of geography

26. **Create a Digital Presentation** Use software to create a presentation about what geographers do. Show how they organize and categorize what happens in both the natural world and the human world. To illustrate your presentation, select photographs from the **Digital Library** or from other sources. Find maps in the **Online World Atlas**. Use correct spelling and punctuation on your slides.

Geographers use five themes to study places and people.

· Location is an example of one theme. Geographers determine location several ways.

PHYSICAL & HUMAN GEOGRAPHY

PREVIEW THE CHAPTER

Essential Question How is the earth continually changing?

SECTION 1 • THE EARTH

KEY VOCABULARY

- solstice
- equinox
- tectonic plate
- continental drift
- plain
- plateau
- continental shelf
- butte
- erosion
- earthquake
- tsunami
- volcano
- evaporation
- condensation
- precipitation

ACADEMIC VOCABULARY
benefit, essential

TERMS & NAMES

- Ring of Fire

Essential Question What shapes the earth's varied environments?

SECTION 2 • PHYSICAL GEOGRAPHY

KEY VOCABULARY

- climate
- weather
- vegetation
- hurricane
- cyclone
- tornado
- raw material
- nonrenewable resource
- renewable resource
- habitat
- ecosystem
- marine life

ACADEMIC VOCABULARY
restore, impact

Essential Question How has geography influenced cultures around the world?

SECTION 3 • HUMAN GEOGRAPHY

KEY VOCABULARY

- culture
- civilization
- communal
- gaucho
- culture region
- kimono
- monotheistic religion
- polytheistic religion
- economy
- capital
- entrepreneurship
- free enterprise economy
- gross domestic product (GDP)
- government
- citizen
- democracy
- human rights

ACADEMIC VOCABULARY
symbol

TERMS & NAMES

- United Nations (UN)
- Universal Declaration of Human Rights

A special suit for collecting lava samples

Scientists observe a cloud of ash erupting from Italy's Mount Etna.

1.1 Earth's Rotation and Revolution

TECHTREK

myNGconnect.com For photos and a model of the four seasons

 Digital Library

 Student Resources

> **Main Idea** Earth's tilt, rotation, and revolution cause weather changes and the four seasons.

In the summer, people who live in the northern parts of Iceland, Norway, Sweden, and Finland have more than 20 hours of daylight. In the winter, these same people have more than 20 hours of darkness. These long days and nights result from Earth's tilt and revolution around the sun.

Revolution and Rotation

The solar system is formed by the sun, Earth, and seven other planets. Earth, which is the third planet from the sun, revolves around the sun at a speed of about 67,000 miles per hour. It takes one year for Earth to make one revolution.

At the same time, Earth rotates on its axis, an imaginary line that runs from the North Pole to the South Pole through the center. Each rotation takes almost one day.

> **Critical Viewing** Bathers in Iceland celebrate the summer solstice with a midnight swim in a hot spring. Based on the photo, what can you tell about the summer solstice in Iceland?

Earth tilts at an angle of about 23.5°. Because of this tilt, the Northern Hemisphere receives more direct sunlight for half the year, and temperatures are warmer. During these months, the Southern Hemisphere receives less direct sunlight, and temperatures are cooler.

As Earth continues around the sun, the Northern Hemisphere faces the sun less directly and temperatures are cooler. Meanwhile the Southern Hemisphere faces the sun more directly, and temperatures are warmer. This process creates the four seasons in both hemispheres.

Summer and Winter Solstices

The exact moment at which summer and winter start is called a **solstice**. June 20 or 21 is the summer solstice in the Northern Hemisphere. It is the longest day of the year. Six months later, on December 21 or 22, the Northern Hemisphere has its winter solstice. This is the shortest day of the year.

The Southern Hemisphere is exactly the opposite. June 20 or 21 is its winter solstice and December 21 or 22 is its summer solstice.

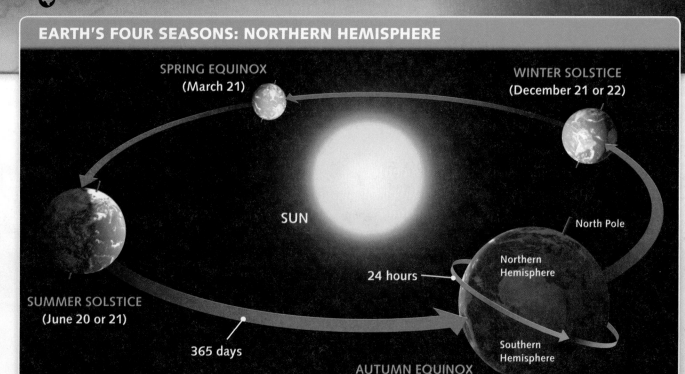

EARTH'S FOUR SEASONS: NORTHERN HEMISPHERE

SPRING EQUINOX
(March 21)

WINTER SOLSTICE
(December 21 or 22)

SUN

North Pole

Northern
Hemisphere

24 hours

SUMMER SOLSTICE
(June 20 or 21)

Southern
Hemisphere

365 days

AUTUMN EQUINOX
(September 23)

South Pole

Spring and Autumn Equinoxes

The beginning of spring and autumn is called an **equinox**. Twice a year, the sun's rays hit the equator directly, and day and night are the same length. In the Northern Hemisphere, the spring equinox occurs around March 21, and the autumn equinox occurs around September 23. The Southern Hemisphere is exactly the opposite.

Before You Move On

Monitor Comprehension How do Earth's tilt, rotation, and revolution cause the seasons?

FORMATIVE ASSESSMENT

VIEWING LAB GeoJournal

1. **Analyze Models** According to the model above, when do the sun's rays hit the Southern Hemisphere most directly? This is the beginning of which season?

2. **Analyze Visuals** What happens to the sun in Iceland on the day of the summer solstice? Why does this happen?

3. **Compare and Contrast** How are the spring equinox and the autumn equinox alike?

4. **Make Inferences** What happens to the length of days in the Northern Hemisphere after the spring equinox?

1.2 Earth's Complex Structure

TECHTREK

myNGconnect.com For photos and
diagrams that illustrate plate tectonics

 Digital
Library

 Student
Resources

Main Idea Physical processes within
Earth bring about changes on the surface.

If you could dig a tunnel to Earth's center,
you would travel through several layers.
Each layer would be under tremendous
pressure and give off intense heat.

Earth's Layers

On your journey, you would first pass
through the crust. This layer includes
landmasses and the ocean floor. It is
about 30 miles thick.

Next, you would come to the mantle,
which consists of molten, or melted, rocks
called magma. The mantle is about 1,800
miles thick and has two parts—the upper
mantle and the lower mantle.

Descending even deeper, you would
find yourself in the outer core, which
is about 1,400 miles thick. This layer is
mostly liquid, consisting of molten iron
and nickel.

At the very center is the inner core.
It is about 700 miles thick. It reaches a
temperature of 12,000° F—hotter than the
surface of the sun. The inner core is made
up of iron, which remains solid because
the pressure from all the layers above it is
so intense.

EARTH'S STRUCTURE

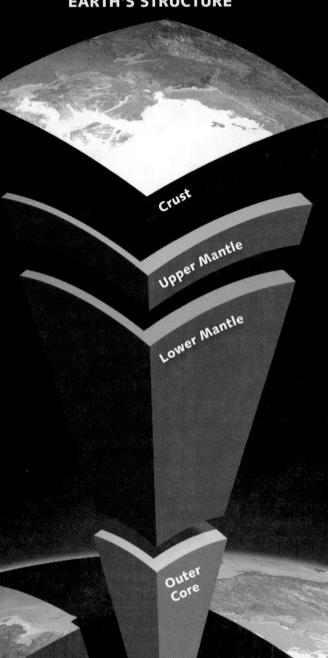

Crust

Upper Mantle

Lower Mantle

Outer Core

Inner Core

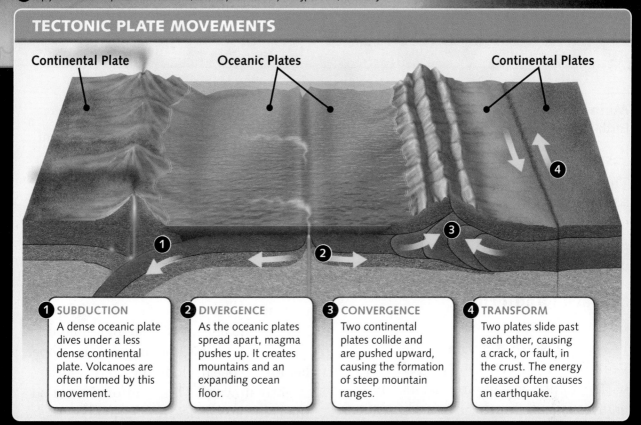

TECTONIC PLATE MOVEMENTS

Continental Plate   Oceanic Plates   Continental Plates

1 SUBDUCTION
A dense oceanic plate dives under a less dense continental plate. Volcanoes are often formed by this movement.

2 DIVERGENCE
As the oceanic plates spread apart, magma pushes up. It creates mountains and an expanding ocean floor.

3 CONVERGENCE
Two continental plates collide and are pushed upward, causing the formation of steep mountain ranges.

4 TRANSFORM
Two plates slide past each other, causing a crack, or fault, in the crust. The energy released often causes an earthquake.

Tectonic Plates

Earth's crust is divided into sections called tectonic plates. The plates float on Earth's mantle. They are constantly shifting and may move up to four inches a year.

The seven continents rest on these tectonic plates. As the plates have shifted over time, the continents have moved into their current positions. This slow movement of the continents is known as continental drift.

Tectonic plates move in four ways, as shown in the diagram above. The enormous force of the movements and collisions creates mountains and causes earthquakes and volcanoes.

Before You Move On
Make Inferences **How do the movements of tectonic plates change Earth's surface?**

FORMATIVE ASSESSMENT
VIEWING LAB  GeoJournal

1. **Pose and Answer Questions** With a partner, ask questions about information in the model above. Use the model to describe how earthquakes are caused. Then answer: Which movement can result in volcanoes?

2. **Place** The Himalaya Mountains formed by convergence when the Indian plate collided with the Eurasian plate. The Indian plate is still moving almost an inch north every year. How do you predict this will affect the Himalayas?

3. **Summarize** What is the main characteristic of each layer of Earth?

1.3 Earth's Landforms

TECHTREK

myNGconnect.com For photos and
a diagram of landforms

Digital
Library

Student
Resources

Main Idea Landforms are physical features on Earth's surface. They are continually reshaped by physical processes.

The Rocky Mountains rise more than 14,000 feet above sea level. The Grand Canyon is more than 5,000 feet deep. Both are landforms, or physical features on Earth's surface.

Surface Landforms

Landforms such as the Rocky Mountains in western North America and the Grand Canyon in Arizona provide a variety of physical environments. These environments support millions of plants and animals.

Several common landforms are found on Earth's surface. A mountain is a high, steep elevation. A hill also slopes upward but is less steep and rugged. In contrast, a **plain** is a level area. The Great Plains, for example, are flat landforms stretching from the Mississippi River to the Rocky Mountains. A **plateau** is a plain that sits high above sea level and usually has a cliff on all sides. A valley is a low-lying area that is surrounded by mountains.

Ocean Landforms

Earth's oceans also have landforms that are underwater. Mountains and valleys rise and fall along the ocean floor. Volcanoes erupt with hot magma, which hardens as it cools to form new crust.

The edge of a continent often extends out under the water. This land is called the **continental shelf**. Most of Earth's marine life lives at this level of the ocean. Beyond the continental shelf, the land develops a steep slope. Beyond the slope, before the ocean floor, the land slopes slightly upward. This landform is called the continental rise. It is formed by rocks and sediment carried by ocean currents. Together, these landforms are known as the continental margin.

> **Visual Vocabulary** A **butte** (BYOOT) is a hill or mountain with steep sides and a flat top. These buttes in Monument Valley, Arizona, are called "the Mittens."

THE CONTINENTAL MARGIN

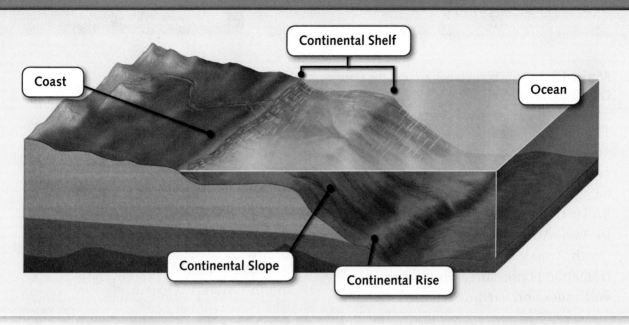

Coast

Continental Shelf

Ocean

Continental Slope

Continental Rise

The Changing Earth

Earth is always changing, and the changes affect plant and animal life. For example, a flood can cause severe erosion, which can ruin farmers' fields. **Erosion** is the process by which rocks and soil slowly break apart and are swept away.

Erosion also results from weathering, which is when air, water, wind, or ice slowly wear away rocks and soil. The buttes in Monument Valley, Arizona, were formed in this way over a span of millions of years.

Before You Move On

Summarize Describe how physical processes reshape Earth's landforms.

FORMATIVE ASSESSMENT

SPEAKING LAB GeoJournal

1. **Pose and Answer Questions** With a partner, pose questions about ocean landforms shown in the model. What aspects of the ocean are you most curious about?

2. **Turn and Talk** Make a list of landforms you often experience. Turn to a partner and talk about how one of them affects your life. Then research one Texas landform and develop an outline to talk about it with the class. Read lesson pages R9 and R10 for support.

1.4 The Ring of Fire

Main Idea Plate boundaries around the Pacific Ocean cause earthquakes and volcanic eruptions.

The **Ring of Fire** is a circle of volcanoes and earthquakes along the rim, or outer edge, of the Pacific Ocean. It exists because a large tectonic plate under the ocean slides against plates in Asia, Australia, South America, and North America. The movements create tremendous pressure, which causes volcanoes and earthquakes.

Earthquakes

An **earthquake** is a violent shaking of Earth's crust. Many earthquakes occur along faults, which are cracks in Earth's surface. Earthquakes are common in the Ring of Fire, but they also occur in other areas on Earth. One area runs from the land around the Mediterranean Sea through East Asia. Other earthquake zones include the middle of the Arctic Ocean and the Atlantic Ocean.

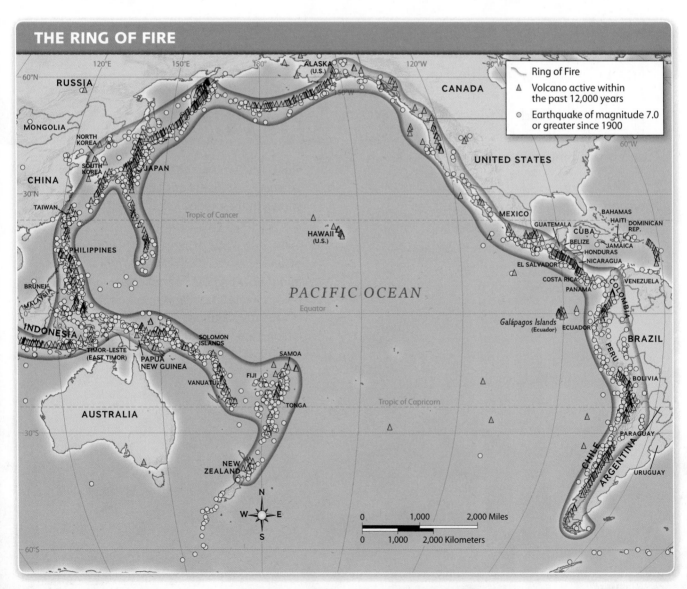

THE RING OF FIRE

Ring of Fire
△ Volcano active within the past 12,000 years
○ Earthquake of magnitude 7.0 or greater since 1900

Mount St. Helens, Washington

On May 18, 1980, Mount St. Helens erupted, blasting away one side of the mountain.

Earthquakes can cause buildings, bridges, and roads to collapse. For example, in 2010, an earthquake in Haiti killed more than 200,000 people. Many people who died were trapped under buildings that collapsed.

Earthquakes beneath the ocean can cause **tsunamis**, which are large, powerful ocean waves that can cause great destruction along the coast.

Volcanoes

The Ring of Fire contains more than 75 percent of the world's volcanoes. A **volcano** is a mountain that erupts in an explosion of molten rock, gases, and ash. Lava, which is molten rock, flows down the side of the mountain.

Volcanoes can cause severe damage. In 1883, Krakatoa in Indonesia spewed ash and rock fragments over an area of 300,000 square miles. It also triggered a tsunami that killed 36,000 people. Yet volcanoes can also **benefit**, or be useful to, plant and animal life. For example, mineral-rich lava turns into fertile soil.

Scientists have learned how to predict volcanic eruptions, and engineers can design buildings that survive earthquakes. As a result, more people can live safely.

Before You Move On

Monitor Comprehension What is the Ring of Fire and why is it significant?

FORMATIVE ASSESSMENT

WRITING LAB  GeoJournal

1. **Make Inferences** Why do so many buildings collapse during an earthquake?

2. **Human-Environment Interaction** How do earthquakes and volcanoes affect people? How have people tried to solve these problems? Copy and complete the chart.

DISASTER	PROBLEM	SOLUTION
earthquake		
volcano		

3. **Write an Action Plan** Imagine that you live along the Ring of Fire. With a partner, write an outline of an action plan to help people survive a serious earthquake.

SECTION 1.4 **41**

1.5 Waters of the Earth

TECHTREK

myNGconnect.com For photos of water
and a diagram of the hydrologic cycle

Digital
Library

Student
Resources

Main Idea Water is essential for all forms of life on Earth.

The Mississippi River begins as a small stream in northern Minnesota. More than 2,000 miles south, it pours more than 4.7 million gallons of water per second into the Gulf of Mexico. Water flowing in rivers like the Mississippi is **essential**, or necessary, for all forms of life.

Fresh Water

The Mississippi River contains fresh water. People use fresh water to drink, cook, bathe, and irrigate crops. Early civilizations developed along rivers such as the Nile River in Egypt because of the available fresh water.

Different bodies of fresh water exist for different geographic reasons. A river is a path of water that flows from a higher elevation to a lower elevation. Streams, brooks, and creeks are like rivers, but smaller. A lake is a large body of water that is surrounded by land.

Salt Water

Salt water contains salt and other minerals. It is a major source of the world's seafood supply and a means of transportation. Oceans are large bodies of salt water. Earth's four oceans are the Atlantic, the Pacific, the Indian, and the Arctic. Continuously moving flows of water, called currents, circulate through the oceans and affect climates on land.

Seas are smaller bodies of salt water. The Red Sea, for example, lies between the Arabian Peninsula and eastern Africa.

THE HYDROLOGIC CYCLE

The hydrologic cycle is the continual movement of water from Earth's surface into the air and back again.

2 CONDENSATION
During **condensation**, cooler temperatures in the atmosphere cause the water vapor to change into droplets that form clouds.

1 EVAPORATION
During **evaporation**, the sun heats the ocean, and water vapor rises up into the atmosphere.

Before You Move On
Monitor Comprehension How is water essential for all life on Earth?

6.03.C compare world regions using data from charts, models; 6.04.B explain the geographic factors responsible for patterns of population in places; 6.04.D locate major physical geographic features; 6.06.A describe effects of physical environmental processes

3 PRECIPITATION
The water droplets grow heavier and fall back to Earth in the form of **precipitation**, which is rain or snow.

4 RUNOFF
Precipitation soaks into the ground and runs into rivers, underground water reservoirs, and, eventually, the ocean.

WORLD'S LONGEST RIVERS

River	Location	Length (miles)
Nile	Africa	4,241
Amazon	South America	4,000
Chang Jiang (Yangtze)	Asia	3,964
Mississippi-Missouri	North America	3,710
Yenisey-Angara	Asia	3,440

Source: *National Geographic Atlas of the World*, 8th ed.

FORMATIVE ASSESSMENT
DATA LAB  GeoJournal

1. **Interpret Charts** According to the chart, which continent has two of the longest world rivers, and what are they? How do you think the two rivers have affected that continent?

2. **Interpret Models** How does the hydrologic cycle explain why rivers and lakes do not run out of water?

3. **Location** St. Louis, Missouri, is located just south of where the Missouri River flows into the Mississippi River. Why is this a good location for a major city?

2.1 Climate and Weather

TECHTREK
myNGconnect.com
For maps and photos of climate and weather

Maps and Graphs   Digital Library

> **Main Idea** Climate and weather are different, but they both influence life on Earth.

People who live in Sacramento, California, have mild winters. When they go skiing in the nearby Sierra Nevada Mountains, they wear parkas to protect themselves from the colder temperatures. They have adapted to a different climate.

Climate Elements

Climate is the average condition of the atmosphere over a long period of time. It includes average temperature, average precipitation, and the amount of change from one season to another. For example, Fairbanks, Alaska, has a cold climate. In the winter, the temperature can reach -8°F. Yet the temperature can rise to 90°F in the summer. The city goes through changes from one season to another.

Four factors that affect a region's climate are latitude, elevation, prevailing winds, and ocean currents. Places at high latitudes, such as Fairbanks, experience more change between winter and summer. Places close to the equator have nearly the same temperature throughout the year. Places at higher elevations have generally colder temperatures than places closer to sea level.

Prevailing winds are winds coming from one direction that blow most of the time. In Florida in the summer, the prevailing winds come from the south, making a warm climate even hotter.

Ocean currents also affect climate. The Gulf Stream is a current that carries warm water from the Caribbean Sea toward Europe. Air passing over the water becomes warm and helps create a mild winter climate in England and Ireland.

Critical Viewing Skiers head to the top of Clouds Rest in Yosemite National Park, California. What does the photo suggest about the weather at this location?

WESTERN UNITED STATES: CLIMATE

CANADA

PACIFIC OCEAN

UNITED STATES

MEXICO

Climate Regions
- Humid Temperate–No dry season
- Humid Temperate–Dry summer
- Unclassified highlands
- Dry–Semiarid
- Dry–Arid
- Humid Cold–No dry season

WESTERN UNITED STATES: WEATHER

- Wet, stormy weather
- Sunny, dry weather
- Cold front
- Warm front

CANADA

PACIFIC OCEAN

UNITED STATES

MEXICO

Weather Conditions

Weather is the condition of the atmosphere at a particular time. It includes the temperature, precipitation, and humidity for a particular day or week. Humidity is the amount of water vapor in the air. If a weather forecaster says the humidity is at 95 percent, he or she means that the air is holding a large amount of water vapor.

Weather changes because of air masses. An air mass is a large area of air that has the same temperature and humidity. The boundary between two air masses is called a front. If a forecaster talks about a warm, humid front, he or she usually means that thunderstorms are headed toward the area.

Before You Move On

Monitor Comprehension What is the difference between climate and weather?

FORMATIVE ASSESSMENT

MAP LAB GeoJournal

1. **Interpret Maps** Compare the weather map and the climate map of the western United States. How do you think ocean currents and mountains affect the climate and the weather?

2. **Make Inferences** How might the climate and weather of the western United States influence everyday life there?

3. **Place** The chart shows average temperatures and rainfall for Los Angeles, California. Ask and answer questions about the data.

Los Angeles, CA	January	July	November
Temperature (°F)	57.1	69.3	61.6
Rainfall (inches)	2.98	0.03	1.13

Source: National Drought Mitigation Center

2.2 World Climate Regions

myNGconnect.com For an online map and photos of world climate regions

Maps and Graphs

Digital Library

Main Idea Geographers identify climate regions to help them understand and categorize life on Earth.

A climate region is a group of places that have similar temperatures, precipitation levels, and changes in weather. Geographers have identified 5 climate regions that are broken down into 12 subcategories. Places that are located in the same subcategory often have similar vegetation, or plant life.

Before You Move On
Make Inferences **How might climate regions help geographers analyze life in a particular place?**

WORLD CLIMATE REGIONS

ARCTIC OCEAN

NORTH AMERICA

PACIFIC OCEAN

ATLANTIC OCEAN

SOUTH AMERICA

A Dry Climates have little to no rain or snow and both hot and cold temperatures. Plant life includes shrubs and cacti.

Saguaro Cactus, Sonoran Desert, Arizona

B Humid Temperate Climates have cool winters, warm summers, and ample rainfall. Plant life includes mixed forests with evergreens and leafy trees.

Mixed Forest, Great Smoky Mountains, North Carolina

C Humid Equatorial Climates are found near the equator. They have high temperatures and rainfall all or most of the year. Plant life includes tropical plants and rain forests or grasslands with trees.

Bromeliads, Amazon rain forest, Peru

D Tundra or **Ice Climates** are north of the Arctic Circle and south of the Antarctic Circle. They have long, cold winters and short summers. Plant life includes mosses or no vegetation.

Mosses, Disko Bay, Greenland

E Humid Cold Climates have cold winters, warm summers, rain, and snow. Plant life includes evergreen or deciduous (leafy) forests.

Natural Park, Eastern Siberia, Russia

TECHTREK

Go to myNGconnect.com to explore this map with the Interactive Map Tool.

EUROPE

ASIA

AFRICA

PACIFIC OCEAN

INDIAN OCEAN

AUSTRALIA

ANTARCTICA

N
W · E
S

FORMATIVE ASSESSMENT

MAP LAB | GeoJournal

1. **Interpret Maps** What is the most common climate in northern Africa? How might this climate affect population?

2. **Compare and Contrast** How does the climate of western Europe differ from that of eastern Europe?

3. **Human-Environment Interaction** What advantages would humid temperate climates have for farming? For logging?

Humid Equatorial
- No dry season
- Short dry season
- Long dry season

Dry
- Semiarid
- Arid

Humid Temperate
- No dry season
- Dry summer
- Dry winter

Humid Cold
- Dry winter
- No dry season

- Tundra or ice
- Unclassified highlands

2.3 Extreme Weather

Main Idea Extreme weather can cause great destruction, but scientists are lessening its effect.

On August 29, 2005, Hurricane Katrina raced toward New Orleans, Louisiana. The water level in the Gulf of Mexico rose 34 feet and flooded 80 percent of the city. Thousands of people lost their homes and many businesses were destroyed.

Wild Weather

Katrina is an example of extreme weather, which is weather so powerful it can deeply affect human lives. A **hurricane** such as Katrina is a strong storm with swirling winds and heavy rainfall. Winds rotate fiercely and can reach 200 miles per hour. A hurricane is a type of **cyclone**, which is a storm with rotating winds. In the Eastern Hemisphere, a cyclone is called a typhoon.

A **tornado** is a smaller storm than a cyclone, but it has even more powerful winds that can reach 300 miles per hour. A tornado follows an unpredictable path and can rip buildings from their foundations. Tornadoes occur all over the world, but most of them form in the United States, east of the Rocky Mountains.

Other types of extreme weather are not as dangerous as cyclones or tornadoes, but they still put people at risk. A flood occurs when water covers an area of land that is usually dry. Floods often occur after a cyclone. A blizzard is a heavy snowstorm with strong winds and very cold temperatures. A drought results when the amount of rainfall drops far below the average amount. It is sometimes accompanied by a heat wave, or unusually high temperatures over a period of time.

HOW A TORNADO FORMS

Air rises from the ground into the bottom of a thunderstorm cloud.

The air begins to rotate and extends to the ground in a funnel shape.

EXTREME WEATHER IN THE UNITED STATES

Extreme Weather in the Continental United States
- Tornado Alley
- Coastal areas most prone to hurricane landfall
- Areas most prone to blizzards
- Areas most prone to severe drought

0   250   500 Miles

0   250   500 Kilometers

Scientific Solutions

Scientists are working to lessen the effects of extreme weather on humans. For example, they can often predict the path of a hurricane. They have also worked with engineers to design levees, or walls to hold back floodwaters. Many residents of New Orleans believe that better levees might have limited the damage caused by flooding after Hurricane Katrina.

The ability to predict tornadoes has also improved. Today, the National Weather Service uses radar and satellite imagery, as well as a network of "spotters," to track big storms. Today's instant communications technology makes it possible to broadcast warnings before a storm strikes.

Before You Move On

Summarize How are scientists helping to lessen the impact of extreme weather?

FORMATIVE ASSESSMENT

VIEWING LAB   GeoJournal

1. **Analyze Visuals** What happens in each stage of tornado formation?

2. **Interpret Maps** According to the map, which state is at risk for all four types of extreme weather?

3. **Draw Conclusions** Even though scientists can predict when and where tornadoes may occur, why do these storms still catch people by surprise?

4. **Human-Environment Interaction** How might a severe drought affect people who live in the Great Plains area of the United States?

2.4 Natural Resources

Main Idea Natural resources are central to economic development and basic human needs.

What materials make up a pencil? Wood comes from trees. The material that you write with is a mineral called graphite. The pencil is made from natural resources, which are materials on Earth that people use to live and to meet their needs.

Earth's Resources

There are two kinds of natural resources. Biological resources are living things, such as livestock, plants, and trees. These resources are important to humans because they provide us with food, shelter, and clothing.

Mineral resources are nonliving resources buried within Earth, such as oil and coal. Some mineral resources are **raw materials**, or materials used to make products. Iron ore, for example, is a raw material used in making steel. The steel, in turn, is used to make skyscrapers and automobiles.

Categories of Resources

Geographers classify resources in two categories. **Nonrenewable resources** are resources that are limited and cannot be replaced. For example, oil comes from wells that are drilled into Earth's crust. Once a well runs dry, the oil is gone. Coal and natural gas are other examples of nonrenewable resources.

Renewable resources never run out, or a new supply develops over time. Wind, water, and solar power are all renewable. So are trees because a new supply can grow to replace those that have been cut down.

> **Critical Viewing** Pumpjacks pump oil at a field in California. Based on the photo, how does this action affect the land?

SELECTED NATURAL RESOURCES OF THE WORLD

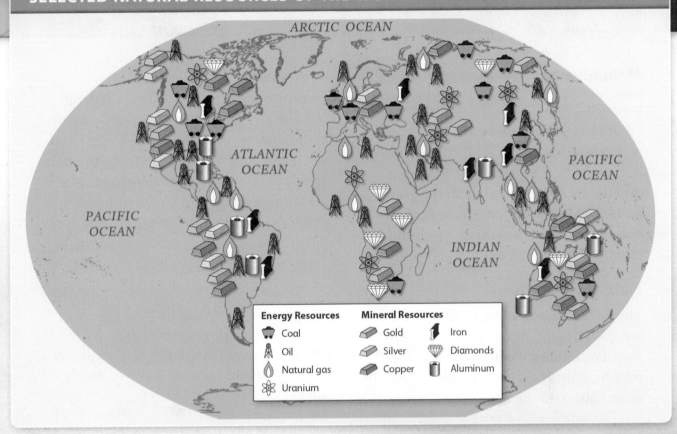

Energy Resources
- Coal
- Oil
- Natural gas
- Uranium

Mineral Resources
- Gold
- Silver
- Copper
- Iron
- Diamonds
- Aluminum

Natural resources are an important part of everyday life, yet countries with a large supply are not always wealthy. Nigeria, for example, is a major supplier of oil, but seven out of every ten Nigerians live in poverty. Japan is one of the wealthiest countries in the world—yet it must import oil from other countries.

Before You Move On
Monitor Comprehension Why are natural resources important?

FORMATIVE ASSESSMENT

MAP LAB
 GeoJournal

1. **Interpret Maps** Copper is in demand for electric wiring and other uses. What part of the world do you think benefits from the demand for copper? Why?

2. **Location** Where are supplies of oil found in the world? Is this a renewable or nonrenewable resource? Explain how you know.

3. **Describe Geographic Information** What are examples of a biological and a mineral resource? How are these examples different?

2.5 Habitat Preservation

TECHTREK

myNGconnect.com For photos of animal habitats

 Digital Library

> **Main Idea** Plants and animals depend on their natural habitats to survive.

At the beginning of the 20th century, millions of elephants roamed across Africa. Today the African elephant population is fewer than a half million. These elephants are an endangered species, which is a plant or an animal in danger of becoming extinct.

Natural Habitats

The African elephant is endangered for several reasons. One is the demand for their ivory tusks. Poachers, or people who hunt animals illegally, slaughtered elephants at a rapid rate in the early 1970s.

Another reason elephants are endangered is the loss of their **habitat**. A habitat is a plant or an animal's natural environment. African elephants' habitats are grasslands and forests. Unfortunately, much of this land is being turned into farms and villages to feed and house Africa's growing human population. Thousands of other plants and animals have lost their natural habitats in this way.

Another threat to habitats is pollution, or human activity that harms the environment. During the 1960s, for example, Lake Erie in the United States was a polluted habitat, and fish nearly disappeared from its waters.

Critical Viewing Elephants roam the Samburu National Reserve in Kenya. What can you tell about their natural habitat?

6.07.B analyze ways people have modified physical environment; 6.21.B analyze by drawing inferences; 6.21.C interpret information from visuals; 6.22.C express ideas orally based on experiences

Habitat Loss and Restoration

The loss of habitats can destroy an entire ecosystem. An **ecosystem** is a community of plants and animals and their habitat. Earth has many different ecosystems that interact with each other. The destruction of one ecosystem affects all the others. For example, many scientists believe the destruction of rain forest habitats has led to rapid changes in Earth's climate.

People around the world have taken steps to save ecosystems and preserve natural habitats. In 1973, for example, the United States passed the Endangered Species Act, which protects the habitats of endangered species. People have also **restored**, or brought back, habitats such as forests by planting trees.

Before You Move On
Monitor Comprehension How do plants and animals lose their natural habitats?

Tiny spruce trees grow in a cut forest near Olympic National Park in the state of Washington.

FORMATIVE ASSESSMENT
PHOTO LAB   GeoJournal

1. **Analyze Visuals** Farming is one of many ways humans change the environment. Why might an elephant's habitat in Kenya be desirable to people for farming?

2. **Describe** Based on the photo above, what steps are taken to restore forest habitats?

3. **Human-Environment Interaction** What is your natural habitat? What are your daily experiences with both the natural world and human-made world? What resources are around you? Use your experiences to describe your habitat orally to the class.

4. **Define** Add to the Term Bank you started on page 17. Include a list of terms you'll often read in this course. Practice with a partner to memorize the terms and their meanings so you can identify the words by sight.

2.6

SECTION **2** PHYSICAL GEOGRAPHY

NATIONAL GEOGRAPHIC

TECHTREK

myNGconnect.com For photos
of oceans and an Explorer Video Clip

 Maps and
Graphs

Digital
Library

Exploring the
World's Oceans
with Sylvia Earle

> **Main Idea** The oceans, a natural habitat for thousands of plant and
> animal species, face many challenges.

Life in the Ocean

As a child, Sylvia Earle loved oceans. This love continued
into her adult life. In over 50 years, Explorer-in-Residence
Sylvia Earle has led roughly 70 diving expeditions to
explore **marine life**, or the plants and animals of the ocean.
During these dives, she has seen the incredible variety of
ocean life—more than 30 major divisions of animals.

However, Earle has also seen the different ways people
have harmed the oceans. "Taking too much wildlife out
of the sea is one way," she claims. "Putting garbage, toxic
chemicals, and other wastes in is another." Earle has
witnessed a huge drop in the number of fish in the ocean.
She has also noted pollution's destructive **impact**, or effect,
on the oceans' coral reefs. These "rain forests of the sea"
house one-fourth of all marine life.

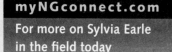

myNGconnect.com

For more on Sylvia Earle
in the field today

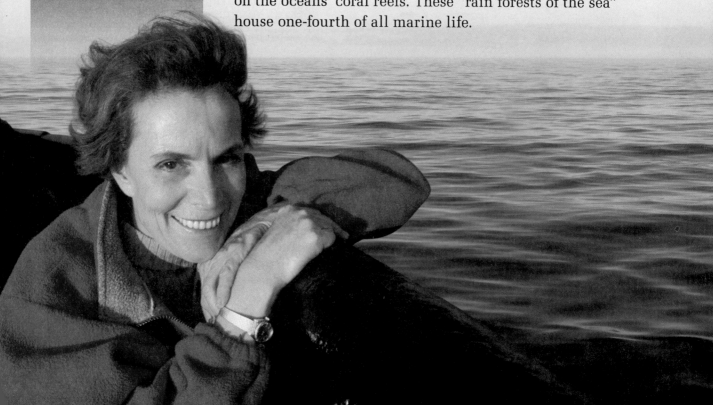

EARTH'S "HOPE SPOTS"

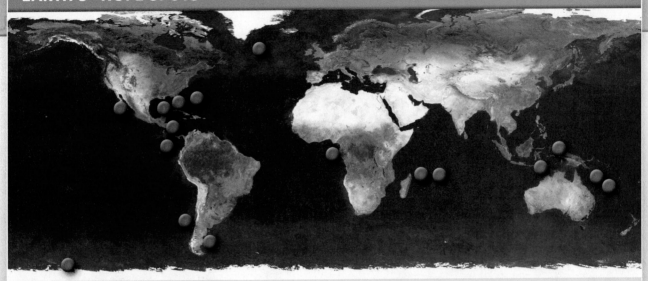

 Critical Viewing This satellite map of the world shows the location of 17 "hope spots," places that are important to the overall health of Earth's oceans. What patterns, if any, do you notice about the location of these spots?

Mission Blue

Many people believe human activity has no effect on the vast oceans. They also do not understand the impact oceans have on all forms of life. "The ocean is the cornerstone of our life support system," says Earle. "Take away life in the ocean and we don't have a planet that works."

Earle is trying to educate the public. In 2009, she launched Mission Blue, a program that seeks to heal and protect Earth's oceans. One of the program's goals is to establish marine protected areas (MPAs) in endangered hot spots, or "hope spots" as she calls them. These spots are ocean habitats that can recover and grow if human impact is limited.

Voice of the Ocean

Earle's efforts to save Earth's oceans have earned her many awards and honors, including the title "Hero for the Planet." She continues to work tirelessly to protect the world's oceans.

In 2010, the Gulf of Mexico was hit with the largest oil spill in U.S. history. Earle went before Congress to testify about the impact of the spill on the Gulf's natural resources. "I really come to speak for the ocean," she began.

Before You Move On

Summarize According to Sylvia Earle, what challenges do our oceans face?

FORMATIVE ASSESSMENT

READING LAB 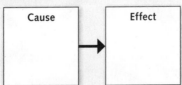 GeoJournal

1. **Monitor Comprehension** What does Sylvia Earle hope to accomplish through the Mission Blue program?

2. **Analyze Cause and Effect** How has human activity affected the world's oceans? Use a chart like the one below to list some of the causes and effects of these activities.

Cause		Effect
	→	

For more photos from
the National Geographic
Photo Gallery, go to
the **Digital Library** at
myNGconnect.com.

Grand Canyon

Kathmandu, Nepal

Japanese man with laptop

Critical Viewing A crab walks over sea urchins in a tidal pool at Slip Point in Clallam Bay, Washington. River outlets and tides create this plentiful and diverse coldwater habitat.

Maori carving

Polar bears

Woman and baby, Peru

Tornado

3.1 World Cultures

TECHTREK

myNGconnect.com For photos of cultures around the world

Digital Library

Main Idea The ways people speak, eat, work, play, and worship are all part of culture.

A Japanese tea ceremony is an old tradition. The host greets the guests and prepares the tea. The guests remain silent. Once the tea is poured, though, a lively conversation follows.

Expressions of Culture

The tea ceremony is an important part of Japan's culture. **Culture** is how people in a region live, behave, and think. Expressions of culture include language, religion, beliefs, and customs. Culture also includes the arts, such as music, dance, literature, theater, and film.

Culture is reflected in symbols that people recognize and respect. A **symbol** is an object that stands for something else. For example, the stars on the American flag are symbols for the 50 states.

Civilization and Culture

Culture is a main trait of civilizations. A **civilization** is a society that has a highly developed culture and technology. People in a civilization are not born knowing their culture. They learn it by watching and imitating others.

A civilization's culture affects people's lives. It guides how people meet their basic needs of food, clothing, and shelter. It also influences people's values and beliefs.

Visual Vocabulary Senegalese children gather around a **communal**, or shared, plate of food. Communal dishes are common in African cuisine.

Visual Vocabulary A **gaucho** (GOW cho), or cowboy, herds sheep in South America.

Visual Vocabulary Women dressed in **kimonos**, traditional Japanese clothing, bow at a fashion show. In Japan, it is customary to bow when meeting someone.

Culture Regions

Geographers study culture regions, areas that are unified by common cultural traits, or characteristics. For instance, some geographers group Mexico, Central America, the islands of the Caribbean, and South America in a culture region called Latin America. Many of the people in this region speak Spanish or Portuguese and practice the Roman Catholic religion. (The Roman Catholic church is the Christian church that recognizes the Pope in Rome, Italy, as its head.) Many also share a history of Spanish colonization.

Before You Move On
Monitor Comprehension What are some expressions of culture?

FORMATIVE ASSESSMENT

PHOTO LAB · GeoJournal

1. **Understand Culture** Each photo and caption shows an expression of culture in a different culture region. What is culture? What are examples of common traits that unify a culture region?

2. **Turn and Talk** What is one activity, such as playing music or dancing, that is important in your culture? Discuss with a partner and prepare a response to share with the class.

3.2 Religions and Belief Systems

TECHTREK
myNGconnect.com For an online
map and photos of world religions

Maps and Graphs

Digital Library

Main Idea Religions and belief systems are important parts of cultures around the world.

Religious institutions are basic to all societies. A religion is an organized system of beliefs and practices. Thousands of religions exist in the world. Most teach that one or more gods, or supreme powers, exist. Most religions teach a set of beliefs and a moral or ethical code. Major world religions include Christianity, Hinduism, Islam, Buddhism, Judaism, and Sikhism.

Elements of Religion

Religion is a powerful influence that helps people answer questions such as, "What is the purpose of life?" At the center of many religions is the belief in a deity. **Monotheistic religions** are those with a belief in one deity. Christianity, Islam, and Judaism are monotheistic religions. **Polytheistic religions**, such as Hinduism, have many deities.

In Judaism and Christianity, the Ten Commandments are a code of conduct telling what to do and not do in one's life.

Scriptures are sacred, or highly respected, texts that communicate the beliefs of a religion. The Bible is the sacred text for Christianity, the Koran is the sacred text for Islam, and the Torah is the sacred text for Judaism.

People celebrate holidays and observe special days to practice and honor their religious beliefs. In today's societies, Christmas, Easter, Yom Kippur, Ramadan, and Diwali are among major religious celebrations.

Origin and Spread of Religions

Several of the major world religions are based on the teachings of an individual. For example, Christianity grew from the teachings of Jesus Christ nearly 2,000 years

BUDDHISM

Founder Siddhartha Gautama, the Buddha
Followers 400 million
Basic Beliefs People reach enlightenment, or wisdom, by following the Eightfold Path and understanding the Four Noble Truths.

CHRISTIANITY

Founder Jesus of Nazareth **Followers** 2.3 billion
Basic Beliefs There is one God, and Jesus is the only Son of God. Jesus was crucified but was resurrected. Followers reach salvation by following the teachings of Jesus.

SIKHISM

Founder Guru Nanak
Followers 27 million
Basic Beliefs Sikhs believe in one God. One can achieve unity with God through service to humanity, meditation, and honest labor. Vaisakhi is a significant holiday during which Sikhs celebtate their history, community, and values. It is celebrated every April.

ISLAM

Founder The Prophet Muhammad
Followers 1.6 billion
Basic Beliefs There is one God. Followers must follow the Five Pillars of Islam in order to achieve salvation. The Hajj is the annual pilgrimage to Mecca. One of the Five Pillars states that Muslims must make the pilgrimage at least once in their lives.

6.15.B identify common traits that define cultures; 6.15.E analyze similarities, differences, among various societies; 6.16.A identify institutions basic to all societies, including religious; 6.16.B compare characteristics of institutions in societies; 6.19.B explain significance of religious holidays or observances

WORLD RELIGIONS

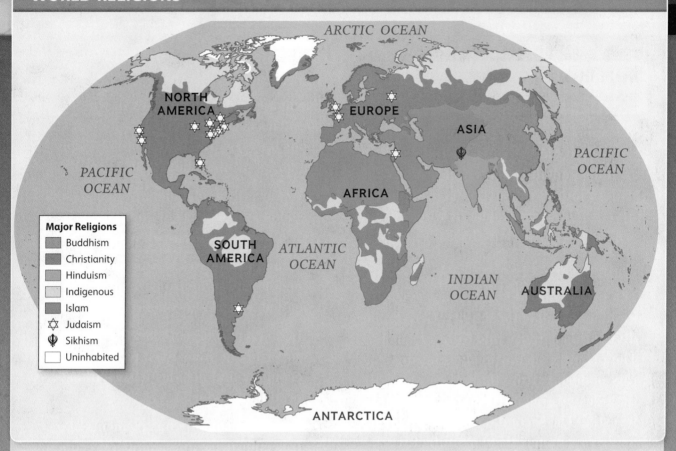

ago. Other religions, such as Hinduism, grew from the beliefs of ancient peoples.

Religions have grown and spread around the world. For example, Buddhism began in India, but it spread to Japan, China, Korea, and Southeast Asia through migration and trade. Religions have also spread due to the work of missionaries, people who convert others to follow their religion.

Before You Move On

Make Inferences How is religion an important part of culture?

JUDAISM

Founder Abraham   **Followers** 15 million
Basic Beliefs There is one God. People serve God by living according to his teachings. God handed down the Ten Commandments to guide human behavior.

HINDUISM

Founder Unknown   **Followers** 860 million
Basic Beliefs Souls continue to be reborn. The cycle of rebirth ends only when the soul achieves enlightenment, or freedom from earthly desires.

FORMATIVE ASSESSMENT

READING LAB GeoJournal

1. **Monitor Comprehension** What do religions of the world have in common?

2. **Compare and Contrast** How are Hinduism and Buddhism similar? How is the achievement of salvation different for Christianity and Islam?

3. **Region** What major religions are found in the area around the eastern Mediterranean Sea? Why do you think they are found in this region?

3.3 Economic Geography

TECHTREK

myNGconnect.com For an online
economic indicator chart

**Student
Resources**

Main Idea People produce, buy,
and sell goods in a variety of ways.

Singapore became a trading colony of
the British Empire in 1824. Today, it is
an independent country, but trade is
still an important part of its economy.
An economy is a system in which people
produce, sell, and buy things.

Economic Activity

The production of goods and services is
known as economic activity. Geographers
divide this activity into different sectors.
The primary sector involves taking
raw materials from the soil or water. It
includes mining, farming, fishing, and
forestry. The secondary sector involves
using raw materials to manufacture
products, such as cars. The tertiary, or
third, sector includes services, such as
banking and health care.

Factors of Production

Geographers study where economic
activity occurs and how this activity is
connected around the world. A country
is more likely to have a strong economy
if it has all four factors of production—
land, labor, capital, and entrepreneurship.
Land includes all the natural resources
used to produce goods and services. Labor
involves the size and education level of
the workforce. Capital is a country's
wealth and infrastructure. The fourth
factor, entrepreneurship, involves the
creativity and risk needed to develop new
goods and services.

Economic Systems

Economic systems are ways in which
countries organize the production of
goods and services. Four main systems
are found around the world:

- In a traditional economy, people trade
  goods and services without money.

- In a free enterprise economy, privately
  owned businesses create goods that
  people buy in markets. This is also
  called a market economy or capitalism.

- In a command economy, the
  government owns most parts of the
  economy and decides what will be
  produced and sold.

- A mixed economy has elements of a
  free enterprise and command economy.

Economic Indicators

The strength of a country's economy
can be measured by several indicators,
or signs. One is gross domestic product
(GDP). It is the total value of the goods
and services that a country produces.
The GDP per capita is the value of
products that a country produces per
person. Other indicators include income,
literacy rate, and life expectancy.

Economies fall in one of two categories.
Countries with high GDPs are more
developed countries. Most of their
economic activity is in the tertiary
sector. Countries with low GDPs are less
developed countries. Most of their activity
is in the primary or secondary sector.

Before You Move On
Summarize What are four ways in which countries
organize the production of goods and services?

6.03.C compare countries using data from charts; 6.05.A identify geographic factors responsible for location of economic activities; 6.08.A describe ways factors of production influence economies; 6.10.B describe levels of economic development using indicators; 6.21.B analyze by drawing conclusions, inferences; 6.21.C organize and interpret information from visuals, charts

ECONOMIC INDICATORS OF SELECTED COUNTRIES

Country	Population	GDP (in U.S. dollars)	GDP Per Capita (in U.S. dollars)	Life Expectancy	Literacy Rate (percent)
Afghanistan	31.1 million	33.5 billion	1,000	50	28.0
Brazil	201.0 million	2.3 trillion	12,000	73	88.6
China	1.3 billion	12.3 trillion	9,100	75	92.2
Ethiopia	90.8 million	103.1 billion	1,200	60	42.7
Germany	81.1 million	3.1 trillion	39,100	80	99.0
Haiti	9.9 million	12.9 billion	1,300	63	52.9
Mexico	116.2 million	1.7 trillion	15,300	77	86.1
Singapore	5.4 million	325.1 billion	60,900	85	92.5
United States	316.6 million	15.6 trillion	49,800	79	99.0

Sources: The World Bank; United Nations; CIA World Factbook; 2012, 2013 (est.)

Critical Viewing This shipping terminal in Singapore is busy all day and all night. Based on the photo and the chart, what type of country is Singapore—a more developed or a less developed country?

FORMATIVE ASSESSMENT

DATA LAB

 GeoJournal

1. **Interpret Charts** Which country has the largest population? the largest GDP per capita? What can you conclude about the relationship between the two?

2. **Make Inferences** Describe how a country's economy might be influenced when one or more of the factors of production is not present.

3. **Region** For your home region in Texas, what is an example of an economic activity from each of the three sectors?

4. **Turn and Talk** List the economic terms in the text with a partner. Talk about prior experiences you have had seeing, hearing, or using the words *market, indicator, labor,* or *command.*

3.4 Political Geography

Main Idea Countries around the world have different forms of government.

How is trash collection related to the protection of free speech? Both are responsibilities of government. A **government** is an organization that keeps order, sets rules, and provides services for a society. Political geographers study boundaries between different places, where different types of government exist, and how geography affects government.

Government and Citizens

Governments govern citizens. A **citizen** is a person who lives within the territory of a government and is granted certain rights and responsibilities by that government.

Governments are either limited or unlimited. A limited government does not have complete control over its citizens. The citizens have some individual rights and responsibilities. An unlimited government has complete control over every aspect of its citizens' lives.

Critical Viewing Voters in South Africa line up for miles to vote. How important to them is the right to vote? How can you tell?

Types of Government

In the modern world, five types of government are common. The major differences among them are in the power and rights that citizens have.

- In a **democracy**, citizens elect representatives to govern them. A legislature creates laws, an executive branch carries out laws, and a judicial branch interprets laws. Citizens have many rights, such as those in the Bill of Rights of the U.S. Constitution. The United States was the first modern country to establish a constitutional republic.

- In a monarchy, a king, queen, or emperor rules society. The ruler usually inherits, or is born into, the office. Citizens in an absolute monarchy, such as Saudi Arabia, have few or no rights. In a constitutional monarchy, such as the United Kingdom, the queen or king shares power with a government organized by a constitution.

- In a dictatorship, one person, the dictator, rises to power and rules society. The dictator controls all aspects of life, including education and the arts. Citizens have few or no rights. North Korea has been ruled by a dictator for more than a half century.

- In an oligarchy, a group of a few people rules society. The ruling group usually is wealthy or has military power, and citizens have few or no rights. The government of Myanmar (Burma) has been an oligarchy since 1988.

Critical Viewing Female soldiers march in a military parade in North Korea to celebrate the country's 60th anniversary. Based on the photo, what qualities are valued by North Korea's government?

- Communism is a type of command economy in which the government, controlled by the Communist Party, owns all the property. Citizens have few or no rights. Cuba has been a communist country since 1959.

Before You Move On

Summarize What are common types of government in the modern world?

FORMATIVE ASSESSMENT

READING LAB GeoJournal

1. **Monitor Comprehension** Which of the five types of government are limited governments? Which are unlimited governments?

2. **Categorize** Governments are organized to be ruled by one, by few, or by many. Create a chart for the five forms of government using this format:

Type of Government	Rule by One	Rule by Few	Rule by Many
democracy			✔

3. **Make Inferences** Look at the map of Russia in the National Geographic Atlas in the front of your textbook. How might Russia's geography affect the government's ability to rule?

3.5 Protecting Human Rights

TECHTREK
myNGconnect.com For more on the
Universal Declaration of Human Rights

Digital
Library

Global
Issues

Main Idea The Universal Declaration of Human Rights states how all people deserve to be treated.

KEY VOCABULARY

human rights, n., political, economic, and cultural rights that all people should have

Nesse Godin was 13 years old during World War II when the Nazis occupied her town in Lithuania. Because she and her family were Jewish, they were transferred to a concentration camp. Then Nesse was sent to different labor camps, where she worked digging ditches. In January 1945, she and other prisoners were forced to march in the cold weather with little food. Many prisoners died.

The Need for a Declaration

Nesse Godin survived the events of the Holocaust, but 6 million other people did not. At the end of World War II, people vowed to never let it happen again.

In 1945, 51 countries from around the world formed the United Nations (UN). The main goals of this organization were to keep peace, to develop friendly relationships among countries, and to protect people's **human rights**. On December 10, 1948, the UN General Assembly approved the commission's **Universal Declaration of Human Rights**.

The need for such a declaration has not diminished since the 1940s. Governments around the world have been, and continue to be, guilty of targeting particular groups of people and denying them their human rights.

The declaration has 30 articles, or sections. Article 1 states that all people should be treated with respect:

All human beings are born free and equal in dignity and rights. They are endowed with reason and conscience and should act towards one another in a spirit of brotherhood.

Twenty-one of the articles explain political rights, such as the right to equality before the law, the right to freedom from torture, and the right to take part in government. Six of the articles address people's economic and cultural rights, such as the right to work, the right to education, and the right to participate in the cultural life of the community.

The Impact of Human Rights

The declaration has had an impact, or effect, on people and governments. During the 1960s–1980s, countries around the world cooperated to pressure the Republic of South Africa to grant human rights to its non-white population. Many countries refused to trade with South Africa, and the country was barred from participating in the Olympic Games from 1964–1990.

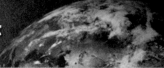

Inspiring people to care about the planet
National Geographic Society Mission

UNIVERSAL DECLARATION OF HUMAN RIGHTS

● ● ● ● ● ● ●

Article 26.1 | Article 25.2 | Article 24 | Article 18 | Article 5 | Article 4 | Article 1

No one shall be held in slavery or servitude ...

Motherhood and childhood are entitled to special care and assistance.

All human beings are born free ...

Everyone has the right to freedom of thought, conscience, and religion ...

No one shall be subjected to torture or to cruel, inhuman, or degrading treatment or punishment.

Everyone has the right to education.

Everyone has the right to rest and leisure ...

In 1994, South Africa finally gave in to the pressure and held elections in which all people could vote. The people elected Nelson Mandela, a leader of the African population, as president. This action showed the power of human rights.

Before You Move On
Monitor Comprehension According to the Universal Declaration of Human Rights, how do all people deserve to be treated?

FORMATIVE ASSESSMENT
WRITING LAB
 GeoJournal

1. **Form and Support Opinions** Choose one of the rights from the Universal Declaration of Human Rights that are listed above. In a paragraph, explain what this right means and why it is important.

2. **Write Reports** Select a news story in the newspaper or on television. In a short report, explain how the story shows the importance of protecting human rights.

Review

VOCABULARY

For each pair of vocabulary words, write one sentence that explains the connection between the two words.

1. solstice; equinox

> Summer begins at the solstice while spring begins at the equinox.

2. plateau; continental shelf
3. renewable resource; nonrenewable resource
4. habitat; restore
5. free enterprise economy; democracy

MAIN IDEAS

6. How does Earth's tilt affect the seasons? (Section 1.1)
7. What layers would you pass through on a journey to Earth's center? (Section 1.2)
8. How does erosion change Earth's surface? (Section 1.3)
9. How have scientists tried to lessen the impact of earthquakes and volcanoes? (Section 1.4)
10. In what ways is climate different from weather? (Section 2.1)
11. How is a humid equatorial climate different from a humid temperate climate? (Section 2.2)
12. What is an example of a renewable resource and a nonrenewable resource? (Section 2.4)
13. What are endangered species, and what factors threaten them? (Section 2.5)
14. What are four ways in which culture affects people's lives? (Section 3.1)
15. How is a free enterprise economy different from a command economy? (Section 3.3)
16. What are the common types of government in the modern world? (Section 3.4)

THE EARTH

ANALYZE THE ESSENTIAL QUESTION

How is the earth continually changing?

Critical Thinking: Make Inferences

17. What impact do the changing seasons have on how farmers grow food?
18. Why did early civilizations develop along rivers?
19. How does the hydrologic cycle return water to Earth?

PHYSICAL GEOGRAPHY

ANALYZE THE ESSENTIAL QUESTION

What shapes the earth's varied environments?

Critical Thinking: Draw Conclusions

20. How would plants in humid cold climates and humid equatorial climates differ?
21. What factors might prevent a country rich in natural resources from using them effectively?

INTERPRET CHARTS

U.S. AND WORLD ENDANGERED SPECIES			
Group	United States	Other Countries	Total Number
Mammals	71 species	255 species	326 species
Reptiles	13 species	66 species	79 species
Fish	74 species	11 species	85 species
Birds	76 species	184 species	260 species

Source: U.S. Fish and Wildlife Service

22. **Analyze Data** What percentage of endangered animals in the United States are mammals? What percentage in other countries are mammals?
23. **Human-Environment Interaction** What steps might wildlife conservationists take to reduce the number of endangered species?

HUMAN GEOGRAPHY

ANALYZE THE ESSENTIAL QUESTION

How has geography influenced cultures around the world?

Critical Thinking: Find Main Ideas and Details

24. What are some characteristics of American culture?

25. In what ways do different religions spread?

26. What is an example of each sector of economic activity?

27. What are two examples of different ways in which governments govern?

INTERPRET MAPS

CANADA'S BIOLOGICAL RESOURCES

Barley
Cattle
Corn
Fish
Forest products
Potatoes
Swine
Wheat

0   400   800 Miles

0   400   800 Kilometers

28. **Place** Are Canada's resources mostly in the north or the south? Why do you think this is the case?

ACTIVE OPTIONS

Synthesize the Essential Questions by completing the activities below.

29. **Write a Public Service Announcement (PSA)** Write a PSA about what to do during an extreme weather emergency in your community. Focus on one type of weather event that is common in your area. Explain the supplies that a household should have. Provide an escape route or hiding place. Also, explain how people should behave during the emergency. **Share your PSA with the class.**

   Writing Tips
   - Do research to find the advice of weather experts.
   - Take notes and organize your information to make it clear to readers.
   - Use a tone that is calm and shows that you are informed.

   Go to **Student Resources** for Guided Writing support.

TECHTREK   myNGconnect.com For photographs of elements of culture

30. **Compare Cultures with Visuals** Recall that culture includes traditions, the ways we communicate, and how we express ourselves. Choose a part of culture that interests you—a creative expression such as what people wear, their music, art, or their sports, cooking, or languages. Research photos from the **Digital Library** or print sources that show the same aspect of culture from societies around the world. Analyze the similarities and differences you see. Then describe common traits that define the cultures.

   Look around the classroom, school, or neighborhood and find words, ads, signs, or announcements. Take photos if you can to share with the class and explain what cultural meanings the printed words reveal.

Climate

In this unit, you learned that climate is the average condition of the atmosphere in a region over a long period of time. Climate is determined by the latitude of a location, as well as by ocean currents, air currents, and elevation.

Two important factors of climate are temperature and precipitation. These factors determine the length and timing of the growing season and influence the types of economic activities in a region. For instance, a country with year-round warm temperatures and precipitation probably has a better agricultural industry than a country with low temperatures and a short rainy season.

Compare

- Brazil
- Russia
- United States

CLIMATE MAPS AND CLIMOGRAPHS

A climate map provides an overview of the climate in a region. However, sometimes more specific information about a city or country is needed. Geographers use a special tool called a **climograph** (climate + graph) to graphically show a range of temperature and precipitation in a place over a period of time. A climograph includes a bar graph that shows the amount of precipitation for a location. Average monthly temperature is shown by a line connecting 12 points, one for each month of the year.

Climographs are useful in comparing the climates of two different locations. They help geographers and others better understand the effects of climate on human activities in those locations.

INTERPRET CLIMOGRAPHS

Look at the climographs for the cities of Belem, Brazil, and Omsk, Russia, on the opposite page. The months of the year are listed across the bottom of each climograph. A scale on the left vertical axis measures precipitation, or rainfall, in inches. A scale on the right vertical axis measures temperature in degrees Fahrenheit (°F).

The bars on the climographs show the rainfall for Belem, Brazil, and Omsk, Russia. The lines connecting the dots show the range of temperatures for each location.

Study the data in the climographs to analyze the climate in Belem and Omsk. Then answer the questions at right.

AVERAGE MONTHLY TEMPERATURE AND PRECIPITATION

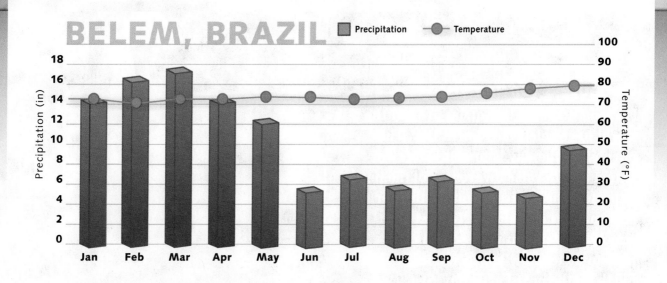

BELEM, BRAZIL

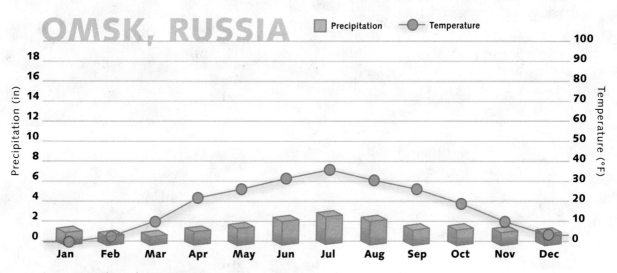

OMSK, RUSSIA

Source: National Drought Mitigation Center, University of Nebraska–Lincoln

RESEARCH LAB GeoJournal

1. **Interpret Graphs** How would you describe the range of temperatures in Belem? What is the average temperature in Omsk in January? In July?

2. **Make Inferences** Most crops need water and warm temperatures in order to grow. Based on this information, what can you tell about the growing season in each city?

Connect to Texas Research data for Seattle, Washington and a city in Texas. For each, find out the average temperature and rainfall for every month of the year. Record the data in a chart and then use it to build a climograph for each city. Pose and answer three questions with a partner to compare the graphs and analyze the data.

Active Options

TECHTREK
myNGconnect.com
For writing templates

Student
Resources

ACTIVITY 1

Goal: Extend your understanding of the environment.

Compose a Top Ten List

For over 40 years, countries around the world have celebrated Earth Day. The purpose of the day is to appreciate our planet and to raise awareness of the need to protect the environment. With your classmates, create a Top Ten list of actions students in your school can plan to do to show appreciation for Earth on the next Earth Day. See if you can get permission to post copies of your list around the school to share with other students.

A reforestation event in the Philippines

ACTIVITY 2

Goal: Learn about culture through religious architecture.

Create a Guide to Religious Architecture

Religious institutions have inspired some of the world's monumental architecture. Use the **Magazine Maker CD-ROM** to showcase examples of historic buildings constructed by different religions. Include the name of each structure, when it was built, its location, and interesting details about it. Then analyze why these buildings were built to last over time.

ACTIVITY 3

Goal: Learn about positive uses of technology.

Write about Technology

Explorer Spencer Wells uses technology to analyze DNA. Look back across the unit for examples of technology used by scientists, especially pages 28–29 and 49. Search NASA on the Internet to find out how satellites collect data about the earth. Then write a paragraph telling how you think satellite imagery could help all societies of the world.

6.03.B pose and answer questions about geographic distributions and patterns shown on models;
6.03.C compare regions and countries using data from models; 6.03.D create models depicting aspects
of countries and world regions; 6.04.D locate major physical or human geographic features of places or
regions; 6.22.D create visual material based on research

TEKS

TEKS PROJECT

Goal: Visualize and represent an aspect of physical or human geography.

Create a Model

Scientists, historians, and inventors create models to better imagine their ideas, to understand very large or very small objects, or to envision how something happens or has happened in the past.

A geographic model might demonstrate elevation, show a cross-section of a volcano, or show the process of erosion. Models can represent things created by people, such as the Great Wall of China or how terrace farming works.

Carry It Out Create a model to represent an aspect of physical or human geography. Draw or build part of Big Bend National Park to learn how it was formed. Then you can work with other students to pose and answer questions to compare it to canyons in Peru, France, or South Africa for example. Or simulate the collision and grinding of tectonic plates, or show the scale of a tsunami. For human geography, use a globe to locate and compare the most populated cities in each of the world's regions. Collect data from your research to pose and answer questions to find patterns or distributions.

- Choose your model subject. Set goals and a schedule for making your model.
- Research and take notes. Sketch your idea.
- Gather the materials you'll need or create your model using software.

Reflect On It How does your model and the data you researched allow you to compare countries and regions? Write a short paragraph to share, which includes examples of comparisons.

Water-carved canyons in Big Bend National Park, Texas, show eons of erosion activity.

EXPLORE NORTH AMERICA

WITH NATIONAL GEOGRAPHIC

MEET THE EXPLORER

NATIONAL GEOGRAPHIC

By analyzing ancient DNA, Emerging Explorer Beth Shapiro traces the decline of bison in North America. She has proved the decline was not caused by hunters but by an ice age 20,000 years ago.

INVESTIGATE GEOGRAPHY

Niagara Falls attracts millions of visitors every year. The waters also generate plenty of low-cost electricity. For nearly 50 years, the United States and Canada have shared Niagara's power production, along with a strong desire to preserve its unique setting.

STEP INTO HISTORY

The U.S. Capitol in Washington, D.C., houses the legislative branch of government in two chambers of Congress. It symbolizes a federal republic, a federation of states with elected representatives. Mexico has also practiced this form of government since 1824.

ONLINE WORLD ATLAS

Washington, D.C.
1,886 miles
Mexico City,
Mexico

Go to myNGconnect.com for maps of North America.

CONNECT WITH THE CULTURE

Tourists peer over the western rim of the Grand Canyon, in northwest Arizona. The Skywalk, completed in 2007, is owned and operated by the Hualapai tribe.

NORTH AMERICA
GEOGRAPHY & HISTORY

PREVIEW
THE CHAPTER

Essential Question What are the significant physical features of North America?

KEY VOCABULARY

- contiguous
- temperate
- glacier
- export
- drought
- commercial agriculture

- cordillera
- rain shadow effect
- dam
- peninsula
- subsistence farming

- aquifer
- cenote
- sustainable

ACADEMIC VOCABULARY

modify

TERMS & NAMES

- Great Plains
- Great Lakes
- Grand Canyon
- Mexican Plateau

Essential Question How did the United States and Canada develop as nations?

KEY VOCABULARY

- colonize
- plantation
- fortify
- missionary
- tax
- revolution
- constitution

- amendment
- pioneer
- industrialization
- transcontinental
- abolition
- secede
- civil war

- alliance
- neutrality
- dictator
- terrorism

ACADEMIC VOCABULARY

adapt, protest

TERMS & NAMES

- Declaration of Independence
- Bill of Rights
- Louisiana Purchase

- Manifest Destiny
- Trail of Tears
- Emancipation Proclamation

- Gettysburg Address
- Reconstruction
- Pearl Harbor
- Holocaust
- Cold War

Essential Question How have various cultures influenced Mexico's history?

KEY VOCABULARY

- civilization
- hieroglyphics
- empire
- tribute
- conquistador

- epidemic
- republic
- exile
- annexation
- reform

- land reform
- tyranny

ACADEMIC VOCABULARY

oppose

TERMS & NAMES

- Olmec
- Maya
- Aztec
- Hernán Cortés
- Montezuma

- Miguel Hidalgo
- Santa Anna
- Alamo
- Mexican Cession

- Gadsden Purchase

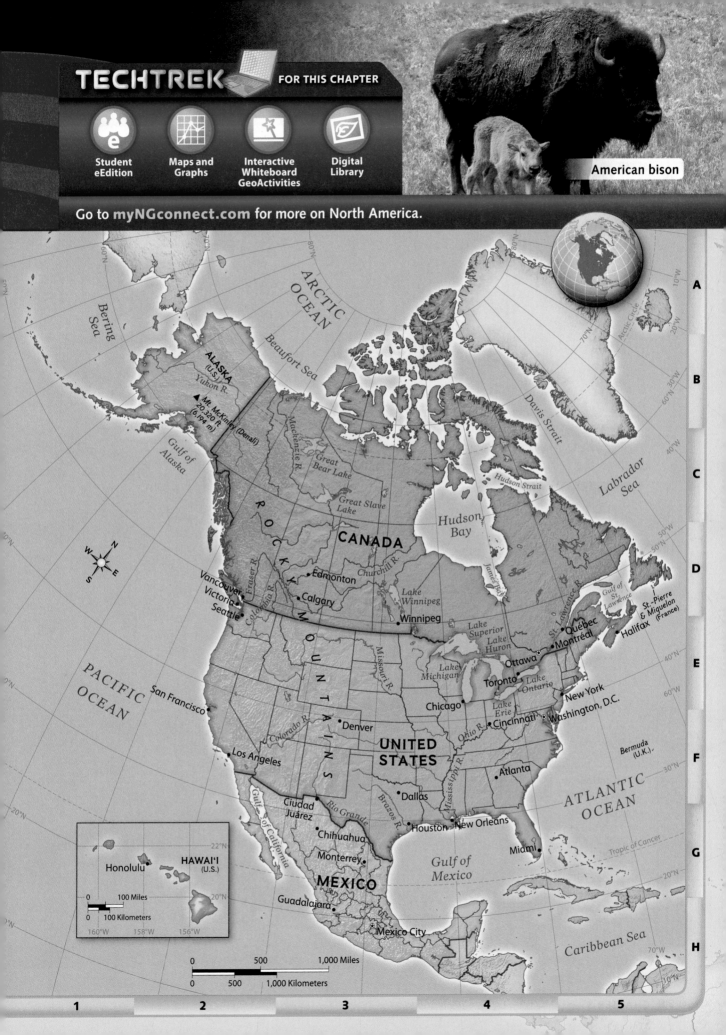

TECHTREK
FOR THIS CHAPTER

Student eEdition

Maps and Graphs

Interactive Whiteboard GeoActivities

Digital Library

Go to myNGconnect.com for more on North America.

American bison

ARCTIC OCEAN

Bering Sea

Beaufort Sea

ALASKA (U.S.)

Yukon R.

▲ Mt. McKinley (Denali) 20,320 ft (6,194 m)

Gulf of Alaska

Mackenzie R.

Great Bear Lake

Great Slave Lake

Hudson Strait

Davis Strait

Labrador Sea

CANADA

Hudson Bay

James Bay

PACIFIC OCEAN

Fraser R.

Columbia R.

Vancouver
Victoria
Seattle

Edmonton

Calgary

Churchill R.

Winnipeg

Lake Winnipeg

Lake Superior
Lake Huron

Lake Michigan

St. Lawrence R.

Gulf of St. Lawrence

St.-Pierre & Miquelon (France)

Québec
Montréal
Halifax

Ottawa

Toronto
Lake Ontario

Lake Erie

New York

Washington, D.C.

San Francisco

Los Angeles

Missouri R.

Denver

Colorado R.

UNITED STATES

Ohio R.

Cincinnati

Chicago

Mississippi R.

Atlanta

Bermuda (U.K.)

ATLANTIC OCEAN

Dallas

Brazos R.

Rio Grande

Ciudad Juárez

Chihuahua

Houston

New Orleans

Miami

Tropic of Cancer

Gulf of California

Monterrey

Gulf of Mexico

MEXICO

Guadalajara

Mexico City

Caribbean Sea

N
W E
S

HAWAI'I (U.S.)

Honolulu

0   100 Miles
0   100 Kilometers

22°N

20°N

160°W   158°W   156°W

0   500   1,000 Miles
0   500   1,000 Kilometers

A
B
C
D
E
F
G
H

1   2   3   4   5

70°N
60°N
50°N
40°N
30°N
20°N

160°W 140°W 120°W 100°W 80°W 70°W 60°W 50°W 40°W 30°W 20°W

Arctic Circle

60°N

Maps and Graphs

 Digital Library

TECHTREK

myNGconnect.com For online maps of North America and Visual Vocabulary

NORTH AMERICA PHYSICAL

Visual Vocabulary
glacier

Visual Vocabulary
Great Plains

Elevation

feet	meters
10,000+	3,050+
5,000	1,524
2,000	610
1,000	305
500	152
0	0
Below sea level	

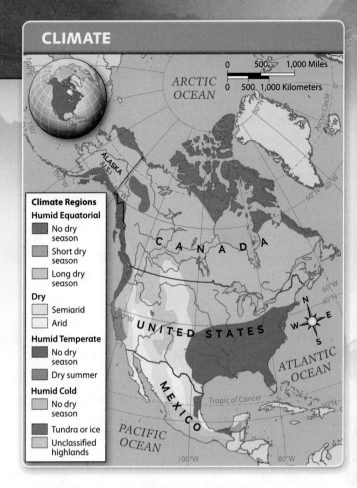

CLIMATE

ARCTIC OCEAN

ALASKA (U.S.)

CANADA

UNITED STATES

MEXICO

ATLANTIC OCEAN

PACIFIC OCEAN

Tropic of Cancer

0   500   1,000 Miles
0   500 1,000 Kilometers

Climate Regions

Humid Equatorial
- No dry season
- Short dry season
- Long dry season

Dry
- Semiarid
- Arid

Humid Temperate
- No dry season
- Dry summer

Humid Cold
- No dry season
- Tundra or ice
- Unclassified highlands

Main Idea North America has a wide variety of landforms, bodies of water, and climates.

North America stretches from the cold arctic of northern Canada to the warm tropics of Mexico. At the center lie the 48 **contiguous** United States, which means they are all connected in one block. The state of Alaska is in the northwest of the continent. The islands of the state of Hawaii are in the Pacific Ocean.

Highlands, Plains, and Plateaus

Land elevation in North America generally rises from east to west, though the east has some highlands, or areas of hills and mountains. East of the Rocky Mountains lie the **Great Plains**. Plains are flat areas of land, which make up most of the center of North America. Plains also appear near coasts. Plateaus—flat lands of high elevation—are located between mountains in the western United States and central Mexico.

Rivers and Lakes

Major cities developed along the region's numerous rivers, such as Cincinnati on the Ohio River, New Orleans on the Mississippi River, and Juárez (HWA rez) on the Rio Grande. The St. Lawrence River provides a waterway from the Atlantic Ocean to the **Great Lakes**. Combined, these five lakes form the largest body of fresh water in the world. Four of the lakes provide a physical boundary between the United States and Canada, just as the Rio Grande is a natural border between the United States and Mexico.

A Variety of Climates

This region includes **temperate**, or mild, climates as well as extremes of cold and heat. Parts of the far north are covered by **glaciers**, or large masses of ice and packed snow. Much of northern Mexico is warm and dry, and Mexico's tropical south has warm climates and rainfall all year.

Before You Move On
Monitor Comprehension Identify the region's major landforms, bodies of water, and climates.

FORMATIVE ASSESSMENT

MAP LAB GeoJournal

1. **Interpret Maps** According to the physical map, how might goods be moved from Lake Michigan to the Atlantic Ocean?

2. **Region** According to the climate map, what types of climate occur in both Mexico and Alaska?

SECTION **1** GEOGRAPHY

1.2 **The Great Plains**

TECHTREK

myNGconnect.com For a map and photos
of the Great Plains in North America

Maps and
Graphs

Digital
Library

Main Idea The Great Plains of the United States and Canada are a rich agricultural region with valuable energy resources.

The Great Plains region runs through the center of the continent. The crops grown there feed the population of North America with enough left to **export**, or send to other countries for aid or profit.

Farming on the Great Plains

The Great Plains are well suited to agriculture for two reasons. First, the soil is rich with nutrients, so it produces bountiful crops. Second, the climate on the Great Plains is temperate and the area usually has a plentiful amount of rain.

Some years, rainfall is below normal for a long period of time, causing **drought** that can kill crops. In the 1930s, for example, the region experienced a drought that lasted several years. Plowing of native prairie grasses that helped hold the soil contributed to soil erosion, and the Plains became known as the "Dust Bowl." The persistent winds in the area stirred up great clouds of dry soil, or dust. Today, these winds can be a source of power.

Much of the original prairie land has been replaced by fields of wheat, corn, and other grains. These crops are grown on huge farms where planting and harvesting are done by machine. Such large, highly productive farms are typical of **commercial agriculture**, or the business of producing crops to sell.

Rivers such as the Missouri and the Mississippi transport goods from the Great Plains to lowland areas. Grain from the Canadian plains is moved by rail to the Atlantic Ocean and by ship on the Great Lakes and St. Lawrence River.

Energy Resources

The Great Plains in the United States and Canada are home to major deposits of oil and natural gas. The main oil fields in the United States are found in the southern part of the Great Plains, from Kansas to Texas. Texas also has many offshore oil fields in the Gulf of Mexico.

> **Critical Viewing** A harvesting machine is used on this wheat farm in Manitoba, Canada. What power sources are in use on this farm?

6.06.C analyze effects of physical processes on humans; 6.07.B identify and analyze ways people have modified environment; 6.10.A give examples of agricultural industries; 6.21.B analyze by drawing inferences; 6.21.C interpret information from maps

AGRICULTURAL REGIONS AND GREAT PLAINS
United States and Canada

Legend:
- Fruits, vegetables & specialized crops
- Dairying
- Mixed livestock, cotton, tobacco & feed grains
- Corn
- Subtropical agriculture
- Mediterranean agriculture
- Commercial grain
- Livestock ranching

0   200   400 Miles
0   200   400 Kilometers

Commercial drilling in the Gulf of Mexico is risky. Oil deposits lie beneath layers of salt that can shift and cause an underwater earthquake. In 2010, human error caused an explosion of a large deepwater drilling structure, resulting in a major oil spill. The spill harmed wildlife and threatened the economy of the region.

Energy resources from the Great Plains are important to the United States, where more energy is used than is produced. High winds in the plains may be utilized as an alternative energy source.

Before You Move On

Summarize What makes the Great Plains an important area for agriculture and energy?

FORMATIVE ASSESSMENT

MAP LAB GeoJournal

1. **Interpret Maps** Look at the climate map in Section 1.1 and the map above. What reason can you suggest for the differences in climate across the Great Plains?

2. **Human-Environment Interaction** Identify two commercial activities that have modified the environment in the Great Plains.

3. **Make Inferences** Analyze the effect of drought on the environment and on people's lives. Explain what might have happened to the farmers in the "Dust Bowl" in the 1930s.

SECTION **1** GEOGRAPHY

TECHTREK

myNGconnect.com For a map and photos
of the western United States and Canada

Maps and
Graphs

Digital
Library

1.3 Western Mountains and Deserts

Main Idea The resources of the western United States and Canada are rich in some areas and limited in others.

Mountains and high plateaus cover much of the western United States and Canada. These landforms create natural barriers to western coastal regions and offer plentiful resources in some areas.

Landforms and Climate

The main landform in the western part of the region is the cordillera. A **cordillera** is a system of several mountain ranges that often run parallel to one another. In North America, the cordillera includes the Rocky Mountains and the Sierra Nevadas.

In the United States, the area between the Rocky Mountains and Sierra Nevada Mountains is the Great Basin. A basin is a depression in the surface of the land. The Great Basin is a desert, a dry, often sandy area with little rainfall or plant life.

The Great Basin is marked by smaller mountain ranges and canyons, which are deep, steep-sided valleys formed when rivers cut through soft rock. The best known canyon is the **Grand Canyon** in the southwestern United States. Formed over hundreds of millions of years, it is 277 miles in length and up to 18 miles wide.

The Great Basin is mostly dry. Warm, moist air flows east from the Pacific Ocean toward the mountains of the cordillera. As this warm air rises up the mountains, it cools and releases moisture on the mountains' western slopes. The air that eventually reaches the land east of the mountains is dry. This process is called the **rain shadow effect**.

Resources and Conservation

Varying climates contribute to a varied supply of resources. The Great Basin and the mountain ranges that surround it contain important mineral deposits.

> **Critical Viewing** A group of horses follows hikers in a Great Basin canyon. What effects of erosion can be seen in the photo?

6.03.B pose and answer questions about geographic distributions, maps; 6.04.B identify, explain geographic factors responsible for patterns of population; 6.07.B identify, analyze ways people have modified the environment; 6.08.B identify problems when natural resources are in short supply; 6.21.C interpret visuals and maps

Areas of southwestern Canada hold reserves of natural gas. This area's heavy rainfall and many lakes allow for the use of water power to provide electricity.

Water for human use is in short supply in the southwestern United States. The population there has grown rapidly in recent years, and the demand for water has increased in this already dry area. A **dam**, which is a barrier that controls the flow of water, can help solve the problem of water shortage. However, dams can also cause problems such as excess soil erosion. The Hoover Dam on the Colorado River makes use of water power to supply electricity, irrigation, and drinking water to parts of Arizona, Nevada, and southern California.

Before You Move On

Make Inferences What does the shortage of certain resources mean for the people who live in the West?

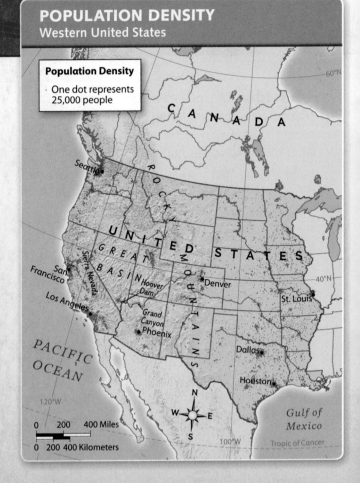

POPULATION DENSITY
Western United States

Population Density

· One dot represents 25,000 people

FORMATIVE ASSESSMENT

PHOTO LAB   GeoJournal

1. **Describe Geographic Information** Turn to a classmate and brainstorm words to describe the photo. What information in the lesson supports your description?

2. **Interpret Maps** Where is population density highest and lowest in this part of the region?

3. **Analyze Visuals** What physical features shown in the photo might explain the population distribution in this region?

1.4 Mexico's Mountains and Plateaus

TECHTREK
myNGconnect.com For a map and photos of Mexico's resources

Maps and Graphs

Digital Library

> **Main Idea** The mountains and plateaus of Mexico are important to the country's economy.

Central Mexico is made up mainly of mountains and plateaus. These landforms yield rich resources that contribute to Mexico's economy.

Landforms and Climate

Mexico includes two **peninsulas**, narrow strips of land that extend out into a body of water: the Baja (BAH hah) in western Mexico and the Yucatán (yoo kah TAHN) in the southeast. Mexico is shaped like an upside-down triangle with the mountains of the Sierra Madre running along each side. The **Mexican Plateau** lies between the two ranges of the Sierra Madres. Mexicans call the southern area of this plateau the Mesa Central, and the northern area the Mesa del Norte. A mesa—the Spanish word for "table"—is a high, flat plateau. Mexico's highest mountain, volcano Pico de Orizaba, rises at the southern edge of the plateau.

Mexico City, the capital, is on the Mesa Central. The city is home to more than 20 million people, almost 20 percent of the population of Mexico. Some areas of the Mesa Central have been subject to volcanic activity, which results in rich, volcanic soil. This soil helps to produce crops that are important to Mexico's economy, such as sugarcane, corn, and wheat.

Northern Mexico sits in the temperate zone, and the southern half lies in the tropics. On the high Mesa Central, climate is **modified**, or made less extreme, by a higher elevation. Temperatures there are cooler than along lower coastal areas.

Resources and Agriculture

Mexico's mountains hold resources such as copper, silver, and zinc. However, the richest resource is the oil found in and around the Gulf of Mexico. Over three million barrels are produced each day.

Agriculture is also important to the country. Farmers in the north grow cotton, wheat, and fruit, and also raise cattle. To the south, farms produce sugarcane, coffee, and tropical fruits. Many rural Mexicans live by **subsistence farming**, growing just enough food to feed their families. This type of farming occurs mostly in the southern highlands.

Before You Move On
Monitor Comprehension Why is the Mexican Plateau important to the country's economy?

> **Critical Viewing** At a height of more than 18,000 feet, Pico de Orizaba is the highest mountain in Mexico. What words would you use to describe this mountain?

6.04.A locate societies on maps and globes using latitude and longitude to determine absolute location;
6.04.D identify physical and human geographic features; 6.04.E draw sketch maps;
6.06.B identify location of nonrenewable natural resources; 6.21.C interpret information from maps

Volcano Pico de Orizaba, Mexico

MEXICO'S CITIES AND RESOURCES

Legend:
- Cattle
- Citrus fruit
- Coffee
- Corn
- Fish
- Sugarcane
- Wheat
- Copper
- Oil
- Silver
- Zinc

FORMATIVE ASSESSMENT

MAP LAB

GeoJournal

1. **Location** Use the map or a globe to find the absolute location of Mexico City. Study the cities on the map. Close the book and draw a sketch map of Mexico. Locate as many cities as you can remember. Then open the book and check the locations.

2. **Location** Based on the map, where are most of Mexico's oil reserves?

3. **Interpret Maps** Using directional words, describe where most cattle is raised in Mexico.

1.5

SECTION **1** GEOGRAPHY

■ **NATIONAL GEOGRAPHIC**

TECHTREK
myNGconnect.com For photos of the
Yucatán and an Explorer Video Clip

Digital
Library

Exploring the Yucatán
with Sam Meacham

> **Main Idea** Exploring untapped resources can help solve the problem of scarce water in dry areas of Mexico.

myNGconnect.com

For more on Sam
Meacham in the field
today

Sacred Wells

Mexico's Yucatán Peninsula has both wet and dry seasons. Because of the peninsula's physical geography, very little surface water is available. National Geographic Grantee Sam Meacham is helping to find ways to gain access to this valuable resource.

The peninsula is composed mostly of limestone. Water from rainfall seeps through pores, or openings, in the limestone and flows underground. The weight of this groundwater creates cracks underground. Over time, the cracks expand into caves. These underwater caves function as **aquifers**, or layers of rock beneath the earth that contain water. The Yucatán Peninsula has a dry surface, so the water contained in these aquifers is critical to the water supply.

Sometimes the surface rock collapses to reveal the underground pools. These exposed pools are called **cenotes** (se NO tayz)—Mayan for "sacred wells." Meacham's team explores the cenotes, which provide entry to underground rivers and underwater caves that contain substantial water resources. One cave that Sam's team explored has 112 miles of underwater passages.

Saving an Important Resource

Meacham's team is helping to reveal not only the importance of this groundwater, but also a potential threat to its safety. The Yucatán Peninsula is a popular tourist destination.

6.06.B identify location of renewable natural resources; 6.20.A give examples of scientific discoveries, role of scientists; 6.21.B analyze by summarizing, drawing inferences

Visitors come to enjoy the white sand beaches of the Caribbean coastline on the eastern side of the peninsula. While income from tourism is needed to build Mexico's economy, Meacham fears that high levels of tourism can be a threat to the aquifer. Tourist activities produce garbage and sewage. If this material is not disposed of properly, the water that collects in the cenotes can become polluted, and therefore unusable.

Meacham leads a nonprofit organization devoted to protecting the Yucatán aquifer. His work exploring and mapping underwater caves will provide access to scientists who want to study these reserves of water. Access to the water from this underground reserve can help Mexico's economy grow in a way that is **sustainable**, or based on preserving resources rather than using them up.

Before You Move On

Summarize How does Sam Meacham's work help preserve the water supply?

Critical Viewing This cenote is in the Yucatán. Would you find exploring cenotes appealing? Why or why not?

FORMATIVE ASSESSMENT
VIEWING LAB GeoJournal

1. **Analyze Visuals** Go to the **Digital Library** and watch the Explorer Video Clip. Take notes. Then talk about the images in the video and the value of Meacham's work.
2. **Make Inferences** Why is Meacham's work important for the Yucatán Peninsula?
3. **Human-Environment Interaction** What impact does human behavior have on the environment in the Yucatán?

2.1 Exploration and Colonization

TECHTREK

myNGconnect.com For a map and images of European colonies

 Maps and Graphs

 Digital Library

Main Idea European colonization of North America brought settlers from several countries and permanently changed life on the continent.

In the late 1400s, many Native American groups lived on the continent. Each group **adapted**, or adjusted, to the environment in which it lived. For example, Native Americans in the eastern woodlands hunted deer and farmed the land. In the West, the Lakota hunted the large herds of American bison, a type of buffalo that grazed on the Great Plains.

Europe Meets Native America

In 1492, Christopher Columbus sailed west from Spain and reached islands in the Caribbean Sea. This voyage was part of a period of European exploration of the Americas. Explorers wanted to find riches and claim new lands for their rulers.

The lives of Native Americans were permanently changed by the arrival of Europeans. Settlers carried diseases such as smallpox, which the native people could not fight. Disease killed a large percentage of certain Native American populations. The spread of settlements also pushed many Native American groups off their traditional lands.

By the late 1500s, European countries had begun to **colonize** the area, or build settlements and develop trade in lands that they controlled. Spain formed the colony of St. Augustine in present-day Florida. In the 1600s, the British settled Jamestown in Virginia and Plymouth in Massachusetts. New Sweden was established in what is now Delaware, and New France arose along the St. Lawrence River in what is now Quebec, Canada. These colonies were mostly small settlements. Most people farmed, traded furs, or did craft work.

The European powers began to compete for land. The British and French fought more than once over their colonies. In 1763, the British would eventually gain control of New France and become the major colonial power north of Mexico.

Slavery in the Colonies

Over time, the British colonies thrived. In the south, huge **plantations**, or large farms that grow crops for profit, needed more labor than farmers' families could provide. Thousands of Africans were forced into slavery and brought across the Atlantic to the colonies.

Cathedral Basilica of St. Augustine, Florida

1607
English establish colony in Jamestown, Virginia.

1550

1600

1565
Spain forms colony in St. Augustine, Florida.

1608
French establish colony in Quebec, Canada.

EUROPEAN COLONIES AND NATIVE AMERICAN GROUPS, c. 1650

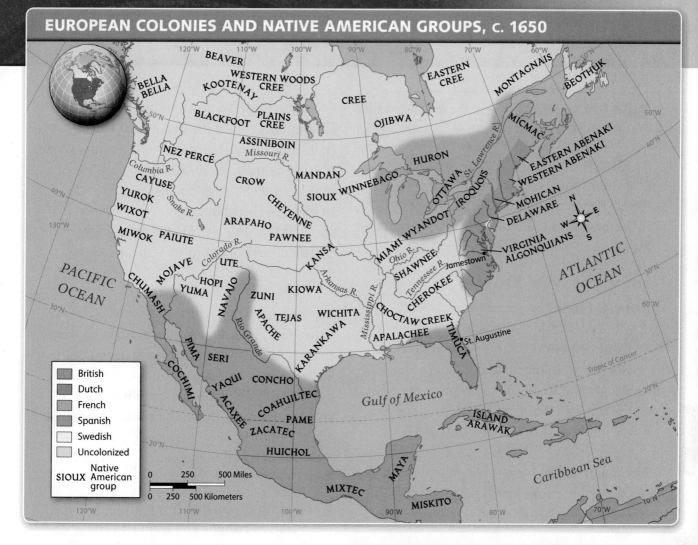

Map legend:
- British
- Dutch
- French
- Spanish
- Swedish
- Uncolonized
- SIOUX Native American group

0   250   500 Miles
0   250   500 Kilometers

As production of cotton increased on plantations in the South, the population of slaves in these states grew rapidly. The economy of the Southern colonies became more and more dependent on slave labor.

Before You Move On

Summarize How did European colonization change life in North America?

FORMATIVE ASSESSMENT

MAP LAB    GeoJournal

1. **Identify** According to the map, where were most of the European colonies located by 1650?

2. **Interpret Maps** In 1650, which Native American groups might have been most affected by Europeans? Why?

3. **Location** Why did British colonies in the South have the greatest number of slaves?

1620
English settlers set up colony in Plymouth, Massachusetts.

1650

1664
Dutch colony Beverwyck is renamed Albany, New York.

1730s
Swedish colony, present-day Wilmington, Delaware, becomes successful market town.

1700

British settlers arrive in Plymouth, Massachusetts.

2.2 Settling Quebec

TECHTREK
myNGconnect.com For a map and
images of New France

 Maps and
Graphs

 Digital
Library

Main Idea Conflict between the British and the French shaped the development of Canada.

As European colonies grew, the British and the French competed for land in North America. Their conflict had a major influence on the development of Canada as a nation.

Founding New France

In 1534, French explorer Jacques Cartier (kar tee AY) sailed into the Gulf of St. Lawrence and claimed the area as New France. Later he sailed down the St. Lawrence River as far as present-day Montreal. This exploration opened a profitable fur trade with Native Americans. French traders exchanged European goods for beaver pelts, which were used to make hats that were popular in Europe.

In the early 1600s, Samuel de Champlain (sham PLAYN) built Quebec (keh BEK), the first major settlement of New France. In 1672, Louis Jolliet and Jacques Marquette left New France to explore the Mississippi River. They learned that the river flowed through Spanish territory into the Gulf of Mexico.

Life in New France

Most people in New France were farmers. However, farming was more difficult there than in the British colonies farther south. The soil was not as productive, and the colder climate made the growing season shorter. As a result, New France never had a large population. By the early 1700s, New France had far fewer people than the British colonies in North America.

The French generally got along better with Native Americans than did the British. Certain French groups, such as *voyageurs* and missionaries, had positive contact with some Native Americans in New France.

> **Critical Viewing** Walls were built around Quebec City to **fortify**, or strengthen, the city. Why do you think these were needed?

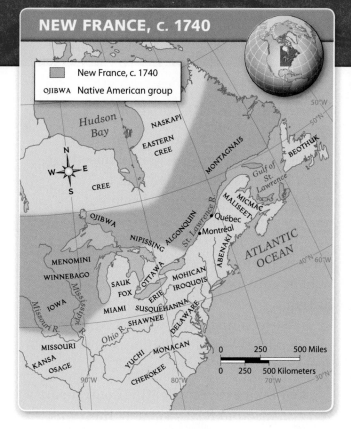

NEW FRANCE, C. 1740

New France, c. 1740

OJIBWA Native American group

French explorer Samuel de Champlain

Voyageurs were adventurous men who traveled the area to trade with Native Americans for furs. **Missionaries** were sent by the Roman Catholic Church to convince Native Americans to accept Christianity. This contact was often cooperative and usually peaceful.

The British Take Control

The British and French were rivals for power in the region. War erupted in 1754 over whether a specific area of the upper Ohio River belonged to Britain or France. A bigger issue at the time, though, was which culture—British or French—would gain a stronger hold in North America. With greater military and financial resources, the British conquered Quebec and in 1760 gained control of the rest of New France.

With tension growing in the American colonies, Britain needed loyalty from its French subjects in Quebec. In 1774, the British passed the Quebec Act, which strengthened elements of French culture.

The Quebec Act established a French system of law and allowed the mostly Catholic population freedom to practice their religion. After the American Revolution, some people loyal to Britain migrated to Quebec from the United States. As a result, Quebec today has both French and English influences.

Before You Move On

Make Inferences Why were there elements of French culture in Quebec after British conquest?

FORMATIVE ASSESSMENT

MAP LAB   GeoJournal

1. **Interpret Maps** Look at the map in Section 2.1. Where was New France in relation to the British colonies?

2. **Compare** Based on maps in 2.1 and 2.2, how did the two countries' colonies compare in size?

3. **Draw Conclusions** Why were the British able to defeat the French?

2.3 Revolution and Independence

TECHTREK
myNGconnect.com For a map and images of the events of the Revolution

Maps and Graphs

Digital Library

> **Main Idea** The American colonists fought for and won independence from Britain.

As the British colonies in America grew, conflicts arose between the colonists and the government of Britain about how to govern the new land.

Trouble in the Colonies

In the 1760s, the British government passed several laws taxing the colonists. A **tax** is a fee demanded by the government to pay for public services. These taxes angered the colonists, who had no representation in British government. The colonists **protested**, or objected to, British control. In 1773, in an event that came to be known as the Boston Tea Party, angry colonists dumped a shipment of tea from Britain into Boston Harbor because they felt the tea was unfairly taxed.

In response, Britain enacted measures meant to punish the colonies. These actions led some colonists to become more determined to govern themselves. Many were ready to overthrow the government and replace it with one of their own making. In other words, some colonists were ready for a **revolution**.

The American Revolution

On April 19, 1775, violence erupted in Lexington and Concord, Massachusetts, when British soldiers were sent to destroy military supplies of colonial rebel groups. One of these rebels was Paul Revere. He alerted the Minutemen, colonists who were standing ready to fight at only a minute's warning, that the British were coming. The trouble between Patriots—colonists who wanted American independence—and Britain was now an armed conflict.

Over the next year, fighting continued. In 1776, colonial leaders signed the **Declaration of Independence**, written by Thomas Jefferson and claiming rights for America as an independent country.

Benjamin Franklin, a colonial political leader, traveled to France to help convince the French government to support the Patriot cause against the British. France decided to loan money to the Patriots and to send troops and ships. Marquis de Lafayette, a French nobleman, became an officer in the Patriot army and helped General George Washington.

Liberty Bell rung for the first time on July 8, 1776

Tax stamp issued by the British government for use in the colonies

1760

1773 Colonists protest tea tax in the "Boston Tea Party."

1770

1765 British Parliament passes Stamp Act, creating a new tax; colonists protest.

1767 Parliament enacts new taxes, resulting in more protests.

General Washington led the Patriots to final victory at Yorktown, Virginia, where British troops surrendered in 1781. The two sides signed the Treaty of Paris in 1783, which was a formal agreement that resolved the issues between Britain and the United States. The Treaty of Paris recognized American independence. It also set the borders of the United States from the Atlantic Ocean to the Mississippi River and from Canada to the northern border of Florida. The American Revolution had created the United States of America.

Lasting Effects

The Revolution had worldwide impact. Assistance from the French had helped Americans win the war. However, France suffered economic trouble because of the aid it had provided, and this contributed to its own revolution. The American example also helped inspire revolutions in Haiti and Central America. Finally, the Revolution also affected Canada. Many who were still loyal to Britain moved to Canada, increasing British presence there.

Before You Move On

Summarize What factors contributed to the Americans' victory over the British?

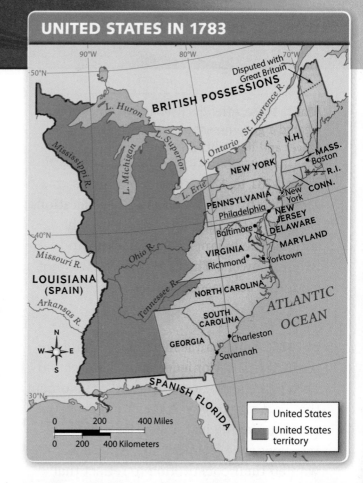

UNITED STATES IN 1783

Legend:
- United States
- United States territory

FORMATIVE ASSESSMENT

READING LAB · GeoJournal

1. **Make Inferences** Why was the Boston Tea Party an effective way to protest?
2. **Evaluate** What were the contributions of Patriots Paul Revere, Benjamin Franklin, and George Washington to the Revolution?
3. **Analyze Cause and Effect** In what ways did the Revolution influence other nations?

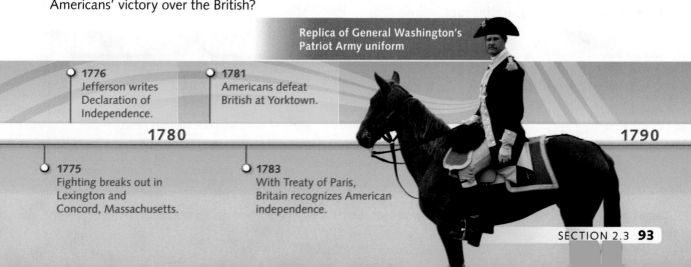

Replica of General Washington's Patriot Army uniform

1776 Jefferson writes Declaration of Independence.

1781 Americans defeat British at Yorktown.

1780

1790

1775 Fighting breaks out in Lexington and Concord, Massachusetts.

1783 With Treaty of Paris, Britain recognizes American independence.

2.4 U.S. Constitution

TECHTREK
myNGconnect.com For images and a diagram of the U.S. government

Digital Library

Student Resources

Main Idea After the Revolution, Americans created a government based on a balance of power and the rights of the people.

From 1781 to 1789, the United States was governed by the Articles of Confederation. However, this plan did not effectively address the balance between state and federal powers. The new country was not as united as it needed to be.

A New Plan

In 1789, American leaders met to improve the Articles of Confederation. They ended up writing a new **constitution**, a document that organizes a government and states its powers. Having just fought for and won independence from Britain, Americans wanted their constitution to reflect that spirit of independence. The document needed to grant certain freedoms to individuals and limit government control. Differing concerns of northern and southern states also had to be addressed.

Officially approved in 1789, the Constitution of the United States has become a model for other countries. It establishes a government based on five principles, shown in the graphic (right). The federal government consists of three branches, shown in the diagram below.

Bill of Rights

One reason the U.S. Constitution has lasted for so many years is that it can be changed, which makes it a living document. It allows for **amendments**, which are formal changes to a law.

The first ten amendments to the U.S. Constitution make up the **Bill of Rights**. The rights and freedoms it guarantees are summarized below.

1. Freedom of religion, speech, press, assembly, and petition
2. Right to bear arms
3. Freedom from quartering of troops
4. Freedom against unreasonable search and seizure
5. Freedom from self-incrimination (testifying against yourself) and right to due process
6. Right to a speedy trial and to confront accusers
7. Right to a trial by jury
8. Freedom from cruel and unusual punishment
9. Protection of rights not named in the Constitution
10. Powers not given to the federal government are given to states and people

Before You Move On

Make Inferences Why did Americans want to ensure that the U.S. Constitution limited the powers held by their own government?

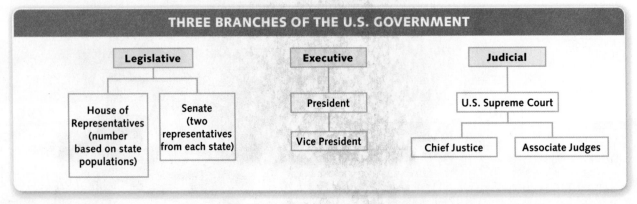

THREE BRANCHES OF THE U.S. GOVERNMENT

Legislative	Executive	Judicial
House of Representatives (number based on state populations) — Senate (two representatives from each state)	President → Vice President	U.S. Supreme Court — Chief Justice, Associate Judges

SEPARATION OF POWERS
Government power is divided among three separate branches.

CHECKS AND BALANCES
Each branch partly needs another branch to do its work.

THE U.S. GOVERNMENT
The Constitution is based on five principles, or basic ideas.

FEDERALISM
Specific powers are granted to the central government and state governments.

LIMITED GOVERNMENT
Individual rights and the powers of state governments limit the U.S. government.

DEMOCRACY
Government is based on the rights and the equality of every citizen.

The U.S. Constitution was written in Independence Hall in Pennsylvania.

FORMATIVE ASSESSMENT

SPEAKING LAB
GeoJournal

1. **Describe** Tell how the U.S. government is a limited government.

2. **Turn and Talk** Turn to a partner and come up with three questions to ask those who wrote the Constitution. Research answers to your questions if they are not in the lesson. Present your questions and answers orally to the class.

2.5 Expansion and Industrialization

TECHTREK
myNGconnect.com For a map and images of expansion and industrialization

 Maps and Graphs   Digital Library

Main Idea During the 1800s, the United States expanded its territory and industries.

The treaty that settled the Revolution expanded U.S. territory to include land east of the Mississippi River. In 1803, President Thomas Jefferson doubled the size of the country by making the **Louisiana Purchase.**

Settling the West

Some Americans expected that the United States would expand its territory all the way to the Pacific Ocean. Many believed it had the right to do so. This idea came to be known as **Manifest Destiny**.

In 1804, Army officers Meriwether Lewis and William Clark were hired to lead an exploration of the newly purchased land. The expedition set out from St. Louis and traveled to the Pacific Ocean and back. Its arrival at the Columbia River in Oregon ▶ was important because it helped establish a U.S. claim as far west as the Pacific Ocean.

Starting in the 1840s, thousands of Americans became **pioneers**, or settlers of new land. Their westward journey was marked by rough lands, deep rivers, the threat of disease, and even possible attack by Native Americans. The trails they used, such as the Sante Fe and Oregon Trails, still show deep ruts from wagon wheels.

Settlers' thirst for land also led to the forced removal of Native Americans. The Indian Removal Act of 1830 relocated tribes to the West. Some tribes in the southeast had highly developed farming and governments, and no interest in land to the West. If tribes refused to leave, U.S. troops forced them. The Cherokee, who tried to negotiate to keep their land, were eventually forced into a strenuous 116-day journey to Oklahoma. This route became known as the **Trail of Tears**.

> **Critical Viewing** Camps like this one were set up for workers along the construction of the transcontinental railroad. What would be the advantages and disadvantages of being a worker on this project?

6.02.A identify influence of individual achievement on historical societies; 6.05.A identify factors responsible for economic activity in regions; 6.07.B identify ways people have modified the environment; 6.21.B analyze by summarizing

RAILROADS AND PIONEER TRAILS

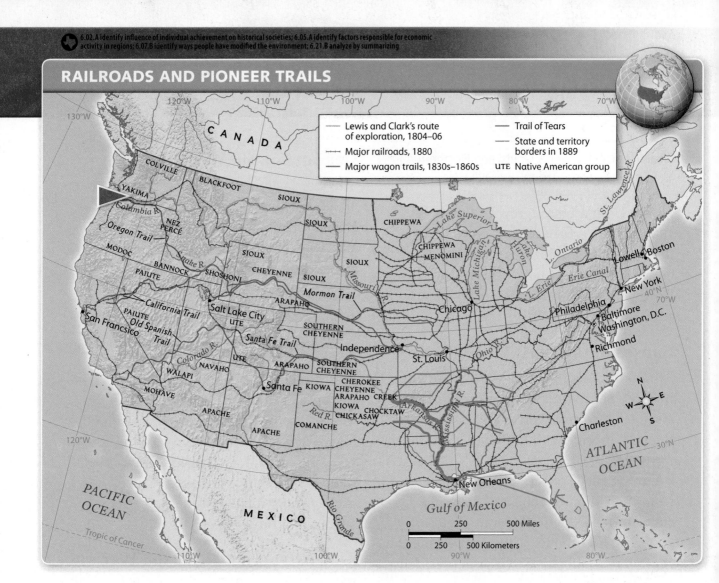

Legend:
- Lewis and Clark's route of exploration, 1804–06
- Major railroads, 1880
- Major wagon trails, 1830s–1860s
- Trail of Tears
- State and territory borders in 1889
- UTE Native American group

Industrialization

After independence, industry grew quickly in the east, especially textiles. By 1813, for example, the production of cloth was completely mechanized, or made by machines rather than by hand. The town of Lowell, Massachusetts, with its early textile mills, was the first U.S. town to be planned around an industry.

Industrialization—the shift to large-scale production—expanded throughout the 19th century. The construction of the Erie Canal in 1825 provided a water route from the Atlantic to the Great Lakes. As a result, New York City became a major American port. Railroads allowed goods and people to travel even greater distances, especially the **transcontinental** railroad.

Completed in 1869, this railroad crossed the entire continent. Movement to the West was faster and easier for Americans than it had ever been before.

Before You Move On

Monitor Comprehension In what ways did the United States expand its territory and industries during the 1800s?

FORMATIVE ASSESSMENT

READING LAB  GeoJournal

1. **Summarize** What is Manifest Destiny? What effect did it have on the United States?
2. **Location** How did the Indian Removal Act of 1830 affect tribes in the southeastern states?
3. **Make Inferences** How did the construction of canals and railroads benefit manufacturers?

2.6 Civil War and Reconstruction

TECHTREK

myNGconnect.com For a map and
images of the Civil War

Maps and
Graphs

Digital
Library

> **Main Idea** Differences between Northern
> and Southern states led to the Civil War.

As the United States grew in the early
1800s, a powerful division arose within
the country. Southerners wanted slavery to
be allowed in new territories in the West.
However, **abolition**, or the movement for
ending slavery, was growing in the North.

Causes of the Civil War

Abraham Lincoln was elected president
in 1860. Southerners, who depended on
slave labor to run their plantations, feared
the new president would try to end slavery
in the South. As a result, 11 Southern
states **seceded**, or formally withdrew,
from the Union in 1860 and 1861. These
states formed the Confederate States of
America. Richmond, Virginia, became the
capital and Jefferson Davis was president.

Lincoln declared the states in rebellion
and vowed to reunite the Union. Soon
after, Confederate troops fired upon Fort
Sumter, a federal fort located in South
Carolina. This event was the beginning of
the Civil War in the United States. A **civil
war** is war between opposing groups of
citizens in the same country.

Conduct of the War

The war lasted four years, from 1861 to
1865. The Confederates, led by General
Robert E. Lee, won many early battles.
However, the Union had a larger military,
a stronger economy, and more resources.

In the midst of the war, on January 1,
1863, the **Emancipation Proclamation**,
which freed all slaves in Confederate
territory, became effective. The same
year, Lincoln delivered the **Gettysburg
Address** to honor those who died there
in a key battle. These two events helped
to highlight a moral purpose to the
war—freedom and equality. Eventually,
the resources and economy of the North
proved too strong, and the Confederacy
surrendered in 1865.

Reconstruction After the War

Racial tensions, desperate poverty, and
hostility toward the U.S. government
lingered in the South after the war.
These problems presented challenges to
Reconstruction, the effort to rebuild and
reunite the states as one nation.

Although former slaves had been
granted new rights, many white Southerners did not allow them new freedoms.

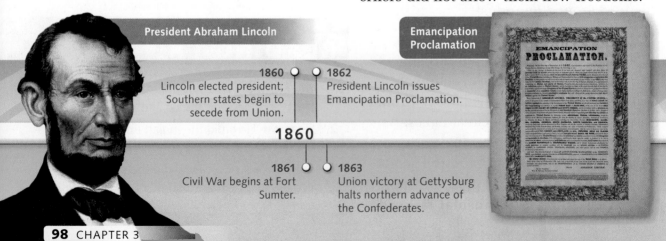

President Abraham Lincoln

**Emancipation
Proclamation**

1860
Lincoln elected president;
Southern states begin to
secede from Union.

1862
President Lincoln issues
Emancipation Proclamation.

1860

1861
Civil War begins at Fort
Sumter.

1863
Union victory at Gettysburg
halts northern advance of
the Confederates.

CIVIL WAR IN THE UNITED STATES

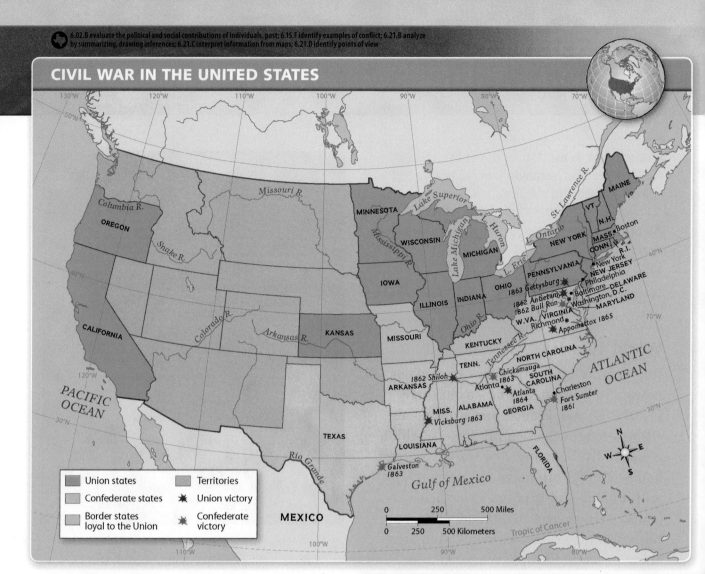

Legend:
- Union states
- Confederate states
- Border states loyal to the Union
- Territories
- ✸ Union victory
- ✸ Confederate victory

The government had to send federal troops to protect former slaves. By 1877, Reconstruction had abruptly ended. Almost a century passed before the federal government would again protect the civil rights of African Americans.

Before You Move On

Summarize What differences in point of view between Northern and Southern states led to the Civil War?

MAP LAB

 GeoJournal

1. **Interpret Maps** Based on the map, where were most battles fought?

2. **Make Inferences** Which side was most likely to suffer damage from the war? Why?

3. **Evaluate** What political action of President Lincoln made an important social contribution to the United States?

1864
Union captures Atlanta; Lincoln is re-elected president.

1865

April 11, 1865
Confederacy surrenders.
April 14, 1865
President Lincoln is shot.

1877
Reconstruction ends.

1870

A schoolroom where freed black slaves learned to read

2.7 World Conflict

Main Idea In the 20th and 21st centuries, the United States became increasingly involved in world affairs and conflicts.

As the United States grew in population and prosperity, so did its economic power. This new strength made it difficult for the country to remain uninvolved in world issues and conflicts.

World War I

Due to growing conflicts between major powers in Europe, war broke out there in 1914. Russia, France, and Britain—the Allies—fought the Central Powers, which were led by Germany. The United States had economic **alliances**, or partnerships, with France and Britain. Nevertheless, the country stood firm in its **neutrality**, or refusal to take sides, and worked to bring about peace in Europe. When German submarines sank the Lusitania, a ship carrying U.S. passengers, the United States could no longer remain neutral. In 1917, America joined the Allies and helped them win the war. The terms of the peace treaty signed after the war were thought by many Germans to be unfair.

World War II and the Cold War

After a period of prosperity following World War I, the U.S. stock market crashed in 1929. The crash set in motion a series of events that led to a worldwide economic downturn called the Great Depression. In 1933, Adolf Hitler rose to power with promises to restore Germany's political and economic strength. He became a **dictator**, a ruler with complete control, and he planned to conquer all of Europe.

Critical Viewing A woman works in an engine shop in 1942. Why would women be doing this kind of work at this time?

Hitler's invasion of Poland in 1939 started World War II. The United States again stayed neutral, until the Japanese bombed **Pearl Harbor**, a U.S. naval base in Hawaii, on December 7, 1941. The next day, the United States joined Britain, France, and the Soviet Union against the Axis Powers, led by Germany, Italy, and Japan.

After years of fighting, Germany surrendered in May, 1945, but Japan fought on. In August that year, U.S. planes dropped atomic bombs on Japan. Bombs hit Hiroshima on August 6, and Nagasaki on August 9. Both cities were completely destroyed, and as many as 140,000 civilians were killed. Japan surrendered on September 2, 1945.

FORMATIVE ASSESSMENT

WRITING LAB GeoJournal

1. **Find Main Idea and Details** What role did the United States play in World Wars I and II?

2. **Summarize** What ideas did the United States promote during the Cold War?

3. **Write a Paragraph** Write a short paragraph that describes U.S. involvement in world affairs in the 1900s and beyond. Go to **Student Resources** for Guided Writing support.

The war had a great human cost. The **Holocaust**—Hitler's organized murder of Jews and other groups—killed an estimated six million people. Overall, an estimated 50 million people were killed, primarily in Europe and the Soviet Union.

Even though the United States and the Soviet Union had been allies, the two countries had political differences. They engaged in a **Cold War**, a long period of political tension without fighting. The United States promoted global democracy and freedom, while the Soviet Union promoted communism, in which the state controls all parts of the economy. The Cold War ended in 1991 when the government of the Soviet Union broke apart.

Terrorism and Modern Conflict

As the 21st century approached, a new type of warfare was becoming more common: **terrorism**. Terrorists use violence to achieve political results.

On September 11, 2001, terrorists attacked the United States. They hijacked four passenger planes and crashed them into civilian and military targets, killing over 3,000 people. The United States invaded Afghanistan where the terrorist group originated. Until 2013, other major terrorist attacks on U.S. soil had been prevented. But on April 15, 2013, home-made terrorist bombs exploded during the Boston Marathon, killing and maiming bystanders.

Before You Move On

Summarize In what ways did the United States become increasingly involved in world conflict in the 20th and 21st centuries?

Rescue workers provide medical aid in New York City on September 11, 2001.

3.1 The Maya and the Aztecs

TECHTREK

myNGconnect.com For maps of the Maya and Aztecs and photos of artifacts

 Maps and Graphs   Digital Library

Main Idea The Mayan and Aztec civilizations made important cultural contributions to Mexico.

Present-day Mexico was settled several thousand years earlier than the United States. About 11,000 years ago, Native American groups lived in the Valley of Mexico, the area around modern Mexico City. They survived by hunting and gathering plants to eat. Around 7,000 years ago, the settlers began growing maize, or corn, which was a native grass. High yields from these crops allowed the population to grow.

The Maya

By about 1000 B.C., an organized society called the **Olmec** lived along the southern coast of the Gulf of Mexico. Their culture had a strong influence on later cultures in Mexico, such as the Maya. The **Maya** lived on the present-day Yucatán Peninsula in Mexico and in northern Central America.

Around 100 B.C., the Maya began to develop into a **civilization**, a society with highly developed culture, politics, and technology. Evidence the Maya left behind provides information about their culture, such as their system of writing.

The Maya used **hieroglyphics**, a system of writing that consisted mostly of pictures and symbols—or hieroglyphs—as characters. The recorded history they left behind in hieroglyphic paintings reveals a highly developed written language. The Maya also studied the sun, moon, stars, and planets, which allowed them to develop an accurate calendar. They used the calendar to mark dates that were important in their religion.

After about A.D. 900, Mayan civilization apparently declined. Historians do not fully understand why this happened. Possible theories include violent conflict between cities, overpopulation, or the overuse of land available for farming.

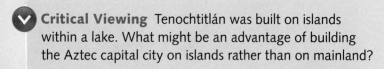

Critical Viewing Tenochtitlán was built on islands within a lake. What might be an advantage of building the Aztec capital city on islands rather than on mainland?

MAYAN CIVILIZATION
c. 900

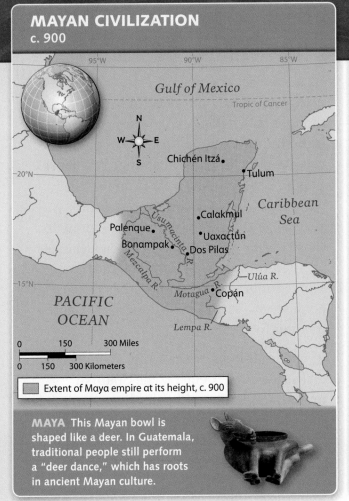

Extent of Maya empire at its height, c. 900

MAYA This Mayan bowl is shaped like a deer. In Guatemala, traditional people still perform a "deer dance," which has roots in ancient Mayan culture.

AZTEC EMPIRE
1520

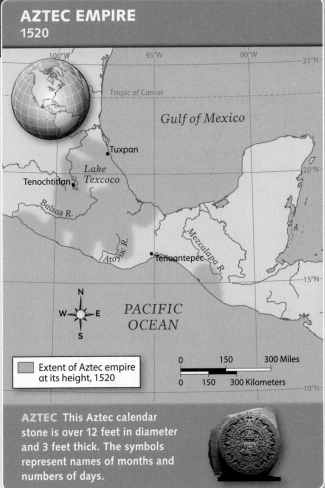

Extent of Aztec empire at its height, 1520

AZTEC This Aztec calendar stone is over 12 feet in diameter and 3 feet thick. The symbols represent names of months and numbers of days.

The Aztecs

After the Mayan decline, other native groups gained power in Mexico. The dominant group was the **Aztecs**, who settled in the area of modern Mexico City around A.D. 1325. The Aztec people built a city called Tenochtitlán (teh nohch teet LAHN) on islands in Lake Texcoco. They constructed human-made islands called *chinampas*, or "floating gardens," on the lake to give them more area to grow food.

The Aztecs built a broad **empire**—an extensive group of peoples governed by one ruler—through military conquest of neighboring lands. They gained further power by enslaving conquered people and using their labor to build more cities. Rulers also collected **tribute**, or fees, in the form of money, crops, or other goods.

The Aztec Empire continued to thrive until Spanish explorers arrived in the 1500s, which changed life in the region.

Before You Move On
Evaluate What cultural contributions did the Maya and the Aztecs make?

FORMATIVE ASSESSMENT
MAP LAB

 GeoJournal

1. **Interpret Maps** Use directional words to describe the location of the Maya and Aztecs.

2. **Make Inferences** What might account for so little overlap in the land areas of each group?

3. **Analyze Visuals** What does the circular shape of the Aztec calendar suggest about the Aztec idea of a year?

4. **Summarize** How was the Aztec Empire able to gain so much power?

3.2 The Conquistadors

TECHTREK

myNGconnect.com For images of
warriors and conquistadors

Digital
Library

> **Main Idea** The Spanish conquest of the
> Aztec Empire had a lasting effect on the
> native populations of Mexico.

After Columbus's voyages, Spain seized
control of many islands in the Caribbean
in the early 1500s. From there, Spanish
explorers continued to look for new lands.
In their travels, they heard tales of wealth
among the Aztecs and set out to obtain it.

The Conquest of Mexico

Late in 1518, **Hernán Cortés** landed in
Mexico with a force of about 500 soldiers.
Cortés was a **conquistador**, a Spanish
soldier-explorer. He was determined to
conquer more of the Americas. Cortés
quickly realized that the Aztecs were
widely hated by other native groups—and
that the rumors of Aztec wealth were true.

The Aztec ruler, **Montezuma**, welcomed
Cortés and his men to Mexico's capital,
Tenochtitlán. Within three years, however,
Cortés had killed Montezuma and captured
the city. He ordered the city burned and
built a new capital—Mexico City—on its
ashes. By 1525, Spanish control reached as
far south as Central America.

Frame of Reference

The meeting of Cortés and Montezuma was
historic, however historians only know
what Cortés and Spanish eyewitnesses
wrote about it. Years later, Spanish friars
recorded what Aztecs said about the
Spanish arrival, but these accounts also
included the Spanish frame of reference,
a view that may have softened or justified
Spanish actions.

An Aztec account of what Montezuma
thought of the conquistadors might help
us better understand how the Spanish
conquered a large civilization in so short
a time. The Spanish were outnumbered,
but they rode horses, and used guns,
swords, and armor—superior weapons to
those of the Aztecs. Cortés made alliances
with groups the Aztecs oppressed. Once
Montezuma was dead and other Aztec
nobles were killed, the Aztec armies fell
into confusion.

One of the biggest reasons for the Aztec
defeat was unexpected. The Spanish
unknowingly brought over diseases that
the natives had never encountered and
could not resist.

A copper engraving of
conquistador Hernán Cortés

Illnesses like measles and smallpox became epidemics. An **epidemic** is the outbreak of a disease that spreads widely. These diseases infected and killed huge numbers of the native population. The deaths weakened the Aztecs' ability to resist the Spanish conquest.

Results of the Conquest

From their base in Mexico, the Spanish armies conquered all of Central America. They went on to conquer most of South America, building their own vast empire. European diseases continued to wipe out native populations for many years.

Natives who survived were enslaved by the Spanish and forced to work on farms and in silver mines. Using slave labor, the Spanish mined vast wealth from the large amounts of silver in the mountains of Northern Mexico.

Spain's success and sudden wealth had another effect. It drove Spain's rivals in Europe to send explorers to the Americas in search of wealth. These European powers also created new empires there.

Before You Move On

Monitor Comprehension What did the Spanish conquest mean for the Aztecs and other native populations of Mexico?

An engraving of Aztec ruler Montezuma

FORMATIVE ASSESSMENT

VIEWING LAB

GeoJournal

1. **Compare and Contrast** Look at the engravings of Hernán Cortés and Montezuma. What similarities and differences do you notice? Copy the Venn Diagram and complete it with details from the images to compare and contrast the two leaders.

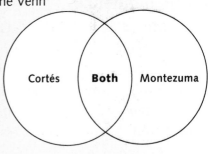

Cortés   **Both**   Montezuma

2. **Identify** What is one factor historians believe contributed to the Spanish conquest?

3. **Make Inferences** What frame of reference did the Spanish have that influenced their actions?

4. **Draw Conclusions** The Aztec Empire map on page 103 shows how far inland Cortés traveled to conquer the Aztec capital. Montezuma would have known Cortés was coming. What might have influenced Montezuma to welcome the Spanish instead of fighting them?

3.3 Mexican Independence

TECHTREK
myNGconnect.com For images of Mexican independence

Digital Library

> **Main Idea** Conflict between social classes in colonial Mexico led to a movement for Mexican independence from Spain.

Because of the conquistadors, Mexico became a major part of Spain's colonial empire. The empire included Central America and Spanish-held areas in the Caribbean and present-day United States.

Colonial Mexico

In the early 1800s, the society of colonial Mexico was divided into social classes. At the top were people born in Spain, called *peninsulares* (pen in soo LAH rayz). They held the highest offices in the government and the church. Next were *criollos* (kree OH yohz), people of Spanish background born in Mexico. Next came mestizos (mes TEET sohz), people of mixed Spanish and native heritage. Native Americans and slaves were the lowest class of society.

Independence

In 1810, **Miguel Hidalgo**, a Catholic priest, led a revolt against the *peninsulares.* He led an army of almost 100,000 men, including many mestizos. His army killed many *peninsulares* and *criollos* and captured several of Mexico's cities.

Government troops resisted Father Hidalgo's army, and in 1811, the troops defeated the priest's army and seized him. On July 30, 1811, they executed him, but his rebellion inspired others in Mexico to continue the fight.

José Morelos, a priest and revolutionary, took over leadership of the Mexican independence movement. In November 1813, he and his followers declared independence from Spain. They drafted a constitution that made Mexico a **republic**, a government of elected officials. The constitution also guaranteed freedom, equality, and security to Mexico's citizens. However, Spain refused to accept this constitution, and Spanish troops refused to surrender. For nearly two years they pursued Father Morales's army throughout southern Mexico. He was captured by Spanish troops and executed in 1815.

The Struggle Continues

Small groups of rebels continued to fight. In 1820, one leader united them—Colonel Augustín de Iturbide (ee toor BEE day). Early in 1821, he issued a plan that included Three Guarantees. First, Mexico would be independent of Spanish control.

Father Miguel Hidalgo

1800s
Colonial Mexico class system solidified

1800

1810
Miguel Hidalgo leads a revolt against the *peninsulares.*

1810

1811
Hidalgo is executed.

★ 6.01A trace characteristics of societies resulting from historical factors (colonization);
6.15.F identify examples of conflict and cooperation; 6.21.B analyze information by
summarizing, categorizing, drawing inferences, drawing conclusions

Second, *peninsulares* and *criollos* would be equal to each other under the law. Third, Roman Catholicism would be the only religion in the country.

Iturbide's army rapidly defeated Spanish troops in Mexico. In 1821, Spain signed a treaty granting independence to Mexico. In 1822, with a tremendous thirst for power, Iturbide crowned himself the emperor of Mexico. His reign was a disaster. Even though he had great success leading the rebels to defeat Spain, as emperor he could not unify the country. One of his generals, Antonio López de **Santa Anna**, rebelled against him. In 1823, Iturbide gave up his crown and was **exiled**, or forced to leave the country.

Santa Anna's new government wrote the Constitution of 1824. That year, the United States, Britain, and other countries recognized Mexico as an independent country. However, Spain continued to fight for control of Mexico. Santa Anna's troops finally defeated Spanish forces in 1830. That same year, Mexico's people elected Santa Anna as their president.

Before You Move On
Monitor Comprehension What were the classes of society in Mexico, top to bottom?

∧ **Critical Viewing** A crowd surrounds Colonel Iturbide before he crowns himself emperor.

FORMATIVE ASSESSMENT

READING LAB   GeoJournal

1. **Summarize** Organize information from the timeline and the visuals to write or tell a story that summarizes what happened in the early 1800s in Mexico. Give reasons for people's actions. How do you think their actions affected the lives of men and women who lived there?

2. **Draw Conclusions** How did the colonial structure, or class structure, lead to demands for independence?

1822	1824
Iturbide proclaims himself emperor of Mexico.	Mexico adopts a new constitution as a republic.

1820

1821 ○
Spain grants Mexico's independence.

○ 1823
Santa Anna and others force Iturbide out of power.

1830

Mexican general and political leader Antonio López de Santa Anna

3.4 The U.S.-Mexican War

> **Main Idea** As a result of the U.S.-Mexican War, Mexico lost some territory to the United States.

When Santa Anna became president of Mexico, the country included land from present-day Texas to California and north to Utah. This territory soon faced a crisis.

The Texas Revolution

To encourage new settlers in the area of Texas, Mexico offered land grants to Americans to set up colonies there, and they had begun arriving in 1821. The American population grew so quickly that in 1830 Mexico passed a law blocking further settlement. This move started a growing hostility between the Mexican government and the settlers in Texas.

In 1835, Texans began to rebel against Mexican forces. In response, President Santa Anna led a large army to Texas to end the rebellion. In 1836, in a battle that lasted 13 days, Mexican forces killed almost all of the approximately 200 Texan rebels defending a fort called the **Alamo**. Despite this defeat, Texans continued their fight for independence. The next month, under the leadership of General Sam Houston, the Texan army defeated Santa Anna's troops at the Battle of San Jacinto.

War with the United States

After winning independence from Mexico, Texans created the Republic of Texas. For nine years, the country struggled with debt, disputes with Mexico, and violence between settlers and Native Americans. In 1845, Texas joined the United States through **annexation**, or adding territory.

Texas and the United States claimed that the southern border was the Rio Grande, but Mexico said the border was the Nueces River, farther north. In early 1846, American troops were sent to occupy the disputed area between the two rivers. When Mexican and U.S. troops fought near the Rio Grande in May 1846, the United States declared war on Mexico.

Santa Anna's troops battled the U.S. army but were defeated after two years. As a result, in 1848 Mexico gave up the area from Texas to California. This land became known as the **Mexican Cession**. In 1853, Santa Anna sold further Mexican land to the United States in what came to be known as the **Gadsden Purchase.** In Mexico, many people **opposed**, or objected to, this decision.

General Sam Houston

The Alamo

1830 ○
Mexico blocks further American settlement of Texas, limits rights of Texans.

1845 ○
United States annexes Texas.

1820

1840

1836 ○
Texans revolt and win independence, but Mexico refuses to recognize it.

1846 ○
War between Mexico and United States begins.

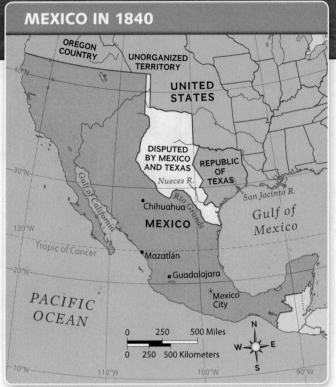

MEXICO IN 1840

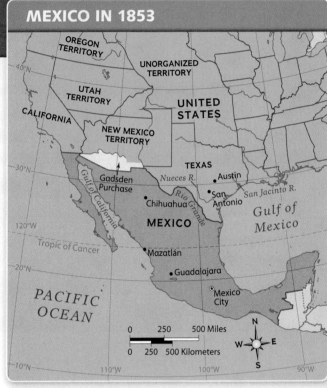

MEXICO IN 1853

La Reforma—The Reform

Due to growing opposition to Santa Anna and his policies, he was forced out of leadership in 1854. New leaders wanted to change Mexican society. In 1857, President Benito Juárez proposed major **reforms**, or changes, to promote social equality. Religious and military leaders refused to accept these reforms, and the country entered a long period of civil unrest and violence. Conflicts between those who wanted reform in Mexico and those who did not continued throughout the 1860s.

Before You Move On

Make Inferences Why would the Republic of Texas have agreed to become part of the United States after winning independence?

FORMATIVE ASSESSMENT

MAP LAB
GeoJournal

1. **Location** Find the Nueces River and the Rio Grande on the map. Describe the distance between the two rivers.

2. **Compare and Contrast** Based on the two maps, what territories did the United States gain after war with Mexico?

3. **Analyze Cause and Effect** How did the dispute over the border between Texas and Mexico lead to war?

Treaty of Guadalupe Hidalgo, with seals pressed in red wax

1848
War between Mexico and United States ends; United States gains Mexican Cession.

1853
In Gadsden Purchase, Mexico sells parts of modern Arizona and New Mexico to United States.

1858
Reformer Benito Juárez becomes president of Mexico.

1860

President Benito Juarez image on Mexican banknote

3.5 The Mexican Revolution

TECHTREK

myNGconnect.com For writing
templates

Student
Resources

The U.S.-Mexican War and the resulting civil conflict had weakened Mexico's economy and government. After Juárez's death, General Porfirio Díaz became dictator. Díaz's policies mainly benefited the wealthy.

The Mexican Revolution was partly a fight for land reform, in which large estates would be broken up and the land would be given to the poor. Emiliano Zapata and Pancho Villa led the struggle, which lasted from 1910 to 1920 and killed more than one million Mexicans.

General Porfirio Diaz

DOCUMENT 1

Plan of Ayala

Zapata issued the Plan of Ayala in 1911 to state goals for the revolution.

[W]e who undersign . . . declare solemnly . . . . . . to end the tyranny [harsh government] which oppresses us. . . .

[T]he pueblos [villages] or citizens who have the titles [to property being held by the government] . . . will immediately enter into possession of that real estate [property] . . . .

[T]he immense majority of Mexican [settlements] and citizens are owners of no more than the land they walk on [and] suffer . . . the horrors of poverty without being able to improve their social condition in any way.

CONSTRUCTED RESPONSE

1. What does the plan say about conditions in Mexico?

DOCUMENT 2

Constitution of 1917

One important goal of the constitution was to bring about changes in land ownership.

Article 27. Ownership of the lands and waters within the boundaries of the national territory is vested [included] originally in the Nation, which has . . . the right to transmit [give] title thereof to private persons . . . .

[N]ecessary measures shall be taken to divide up large landed estates; to develop small landed holdings [smaller farms] in operation; . . .

to encourage agriculture . . . and to prevent the destruction of natural resources. . . The rights of small landed holdings in operation [will be] respected at all times.

CONSTRUCTED RESPONSE

2. How might the division of large estates into small holdings change Mexico?

[T]HE IMMENSE MAJORITY OF MEXICAN . . . CITIZENS ARE OWNERS OF NO MORE THAN THE LAND THEY WALK ON.

— PLAN OF AYALA, 1911

Pancho Villa

DOCUMENT 3

Photo of Pancho Villa

Pancho Villa (VEE yuh), the son of a poor farm laborer, became a folk hero in Mexico. He gained popularity by stealing from the rich in order to give to the poor. Villa's knowledge of the physical geography of northern Mexico helped him avoid being captured.

CONSTRUCTED RESPONSE

3. What does this photo of Villa suggest about him as a leader?

FIND OUT MORE Where can you find secondary source material on the Mexican Revolution? Review page R38. Use a secondary source to locate and share one fact about Mexican society in the early 1900s.

FORMATIVE ASSESSMENT

WRITING LAB GeoJournal

DBQ Practice Think about the Plan of Ayala, the Constitution of 1917, and the photograph of Pancho Villa. What do these show about the conditions that led to the Mexican Revolution?

Step 1. Review the excerpts, the photo, and the biographical information about Villa.

Step 2. On your own paper, jot down notes about the main ideas expressed in each document.

Document 1: Plan of Ayala

Main Idea(s) _____

Document 2: Constitution of 1917

Main Idea(s) _____

Document 3: Photo of Pancho Villa

Main Idea(s) _____

Step 3. To construct a topic sentence, answer this question: What do the three documents show about conditions in Mexico?

Step 4. Write a detailed paragraph explaining how the conditions led to the Mexican Revolution. Use the documents to support your ideas. Use standard grammar, spelling, and punctuation. (See R24 for editing help.)

CHAPTER 3

Review

VOCABULARY

For each pair of vocabulary words, write one sentence that explains the connection between the two words.

1. temperate; glacier

> Many areas of North America have a temperate climate, but others are so cold they are covered by glaciers.

2. export; commercial agriculture
3. colonize; plantation
4. abolition; secede
5. civilization; hieroglyphics
6. empire; tribute

MAIN IDEAS

7. How does the geography of eastern and western North America differ? (Section 1.1)
8. What are important resources of the Great Plains? (Section 1.2)
9. What resources are available from Mexico's mountains and plateaus? (Section 1.4)
10. Why were European countries interested in settling North America? (Section 2.1)
11. Why has the U.S. Constitution been able to last so long? (Section 2.4)
12. What were the causes and results of the Civil War? (Section 2.5)
13. How did the United States change in the late 1800s? (Section 2.6)
14. What events led to U.S. involvement in three world conflicts? (Section 2.7)
15. What were the cultural achievements of the Maya? (Section 3.1)
16. Why were the Spanish able to conquer the Aztec Empire? (Section 3.2)

GEOGRAPHY

ANALYZE THE ESSENTIAL QUESTION

What are the significant physical features of North America?

Critical Thinking: Compare and Contrast

17. In what ways is the physical geography of Mexico different from that of the United States and Canada? In what ways is it similar?
18. What energy resources are found in all three countries of North America?
19. How are the western United States and the Yucatán similar in terms of resources?

U.S. & CANADIAN HISTORY

ANALYZE THE ESSENTIAL QUESTION

How did the United States and Canada develop as nations?

Critical Thinking: Make Inferences

20. How did Reconstruction attempt to address issues that resulted from the Civil War?
21. Which groups suffered as a result of U.S. expansion west? Which groups gained?
22. Why did the population of the United States grow faster than that of Canada?

INTERPRET CHARTS

SETTLING QUEBEC	
1534	Jacques Cartier claims St. Lawrence River Valley for France.
1608	Samuel de Champlain founds colony of Quebec for France.
1671	France claims the Great Lakes and the Mississippi River.
1759	British capture Quebec during Seven Years' War.

23. **Interpret Charts** What land and water claims did France make in the 1500s and 1600s?
24. **Make Inferences** What can you infer about the French explorations in the Americas?

6.18.B relate ways expressions of culture have been influenced by the past; 6.21.A use primary and secondary sources; 6.21.B analyze information by summarizing, drawing inferences, comparing, contrasting 6.21.C organize information (timelines); interpret information from charts, maps; 6.22.C express ideas orally based on research; 6.22.D create written and visual material based on research; 6.22.F use proper citations to avoid plagiarism

HISTORY OF MEXICO

ANALYZE THE ESSENTIAL QUESTION

How have various cultures influenced Mexico's history?

Critical Thinking: Summarize

25. Why did the Spanish place the capital of colonial Mexico where they did?

26. What are the social divisions that led to the Mexican Revolution?

27. How did this social class structure lead to Mexican independence from Spain?

INTERPRET MAPS

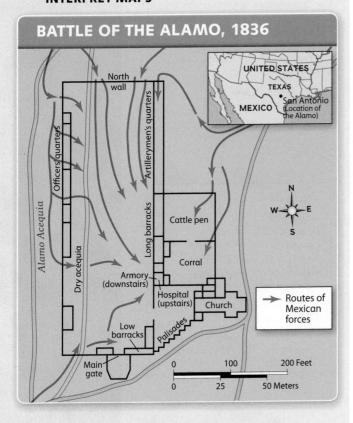

BATTLE OF THE ALAMO, 1836

28. **Interpret Maps** Which areas of the Alamo appear to have been avoided by Mexican forces?

29. **Make Inferences** Which part of the Alamo did Mexican forces not use as entry? Why might this be?

ACTIVE OPTIONS

Synthesize the Essential Questions by completing the activities below.

30. **Connect to Texas** How has today's culture been influenced by the past? Places, businesses, and sports teams can be named after a notable figure, such as Sam Houston. An artifact from daily life can become a cultural symbol, such as the cowboy boot. Describe two examples of cultural expressions around you that show influences of the past. Organize photos, illustrations, or music samples for an oral presentation. **Share your examples with the class.**

> **Writing Tips**
> - Describe the examples as if you were writing captions. Avoid repeating what is obvious in the images you show.
> - Be sure to explain how the past was an influence on your example.

31. **Conduct Internet Research** Choose a city in one of the three North American countries. First, look online for general information about the city's history. To research other sources, refer to lessons on R38 and R39 for support.

Locate primary sources (historic photos, for example) as well as secondary sources. Find out when and how the city was settled, and who (individuals and groups) contributed to its history. Construct a time line that shows the sequence of events in the city's history. Use photos, drawings, or other images to illustrate the time line. Be sure to give citations for your sources. (See page R4 for more information on how to avoid plagiarism.) Add your time line to a class exhibit on North America.

CHAPTER 4

NORTH AMERICA
TODAY

PREVIEW
THE CHAPTER

Essential Question What issues do the United States and Canada face today?

KEY VOCABULARY

- diversity
- indigenous
- immigrant
- tolerance
- mass media
- smartphone
- global
- mobile
- manufacturing
- fiber optic
- recession
- petroleum
- ethanol
- hybrid
- wind turbine
- naturalization
- due process

ACADEMIC VOCABULARY

dynamic

TERMS & NAMES

- Internet

Essential Question How has globalization affected Mexico?

KEY VOCABULARY

- descendant
- ancestry
- mural
- artifact
- globalization
- nationalize
- economic sector
- multi-party democracy

ACADEMIC VOCABULARY

reform

TERMS & NAMES

- North American Free Trade Agreement (NAFTA)
- Institutional Revolutionary Party (PRI)

TECHTREK FOR THIS CHAPTER

Student eEdition

Maps and Graphs

Interactive Whiteboard GeoActivities

Digital Library

Go to **myNGconnect.com** for more on North America.

New York City's Empire State Building stands out against the Hudson River in the background. Manhattan, a densely populated area of the city, is a major economic center in the global economy.

1.1 North America's Cultural Diversity

TECHTREK

myNGconnect.com For a chart of languages in North America

Student Resources

Main Idea The opportunities and freedoms offered in the United States and Canada have attracted a diverse population.

Diversity, or variety, is a major feature of U.S. and Canadian culture. Both countries have a diverse mix of races, languages, religions, and nationalities.

Diversity in the United States

Early cultures included indigenous, or native, tribes, European settlers, and Africans who had been forced onto the continent as slaves. After independence, immigrants came from many other parts of Europe seeking freedom and opportunity. An immigrant is a person who takes up permanent residence in another country.

Many historians describe immigration as a series of waves, starting in the 1600s with European colonists. From 1820 to 1870, a second wave brought more than seven million people, many from Ireland and Germany, fleeing poor conditions. Immigrants also came from China, seeking opportunity in the American West. Starting in 1880, a third wave, mostly from parts of southern and eastern Europe, brought 23.5 million more. Changes to U.S. immigration laws in the 1960s brought a fourth wave, many from Asia and the Caribbean. Today, most immigrants come from Mexico, China, the Philippines, and India.

Immigrants bring not only their culture, but also their skills and ambitions, and can play a major role in economic growth. In fact, many immigrants come here for that reason. In the United States they have the freedom to start a business.

Critical Viewing Street signs in Chicago's Chinatown are posted in two languages. In what way would signs like this be helpful to immigrants?

American culture has come to be defined by its diversity. Tolerance—acceptance of different views—is an important American value.

Diversity in Canada

Native groups such as the Inuit have been in Canada for thousands of years and are still there today. Historically, Canada has encouraged immigration in order to attract workers to help build its economy.

In the 1600s and 1700s, British and French colonies in Canada had attracted large numbers of immigrants from France, Ireland, and Britain. After World War II, many Europeans who had lost their homes moved to Canada. Immigrants from Asia and Latin America began to arrive in the late 1900s. However, most people in Canada today still have European roots.

Before You Move On

Summarize Why are the cultures of the United States and Canada so diverse?

6.01.A trace characteristics of societies resulting from historical factors (immigration);
6.03.C compare countries using data from charts; 6.15.C define a multicultural society,
consider positive qualities; 6.21.B analyze information by summarizing, comparing

SPEAKERS OF MAJOR LANGUAGES, UNITED STATES AND CANADA

Language	United States	Canada
Arabic	845,396	261,640
Chinese	2,600,150	1,102,065
English	228,699,523	17,882,775
French	1,305,503	6,817,655
German	1,109,216	450,570
Italian	753,992	455,040
Polish	593,598	211,175
Portuguese	731,282	219,275
Spanish	35,468,501	345,345
Tagalog (Filipino)	1,513,734	235,615

Sources: 2009 American Community Survey; Statistics Canada, Census of the Population, 2006

People gather in Times Square in New York for a New Year's celebration.

FORMATIVE ASSESSMENT

LANGUAGE LAB
GeoJournal

1. **Compare and Contrast** After English, what is the next major language spoken in the United States and in Canada?

2. **Place** What do the top two languages spoken in Canada suggest about its history?

3. **Summarize** What makes a society diverse, or multicultural? What waves of immigration brought new cultures to the United States? What have been the benefits?

TECHTREK
myNGconnect.com For photos
and a map on media culture

Maps and Graphs

Digital Library

Main Idea The movement of ideas through various media has shaped communication and cultures in the United States and Canada.

Mass media refers to communication that reaches large audiences. Traditionally this meant newspapers, radio, and television. Today, mass media also includes the rapid and nearly continuous flow of information through personal electronic devices.

Print Media to Electronic Media

During the 1800s, newspapers provided information that often influenced public opinion. By the 1920s, radio provided news and entertainment. It was the most important source of news during World War II. President Franklin Roosevelt used radio for his "fireside chats," in which he shared information about the war with the American public. By this time it was clear that mass media was a powerful tool.

In the 1950s, many U.S. households acquired their first television sets, and this medium surpassed radio in its popularity as a source for news and entertainment. In 1963 the entire nation viewed film footage of the assassination of President Kennedy. In the same decade television became an important medium for witnessing the Vietnam War and the protests against it.

In the 1990s, new media technologies exploded in popularity. Cell phones connected people around the world, even if they were on the move. The **Internet**, a communications network, gave people the power to access huge amounts of information from a variety of sources. It also allowed individuals to distribute their own media, such as blogs and videos, to a mass audience. With so much information available electronically, people rely less on print publications.

Critical Viewing Mobile media today combines communication and visual technology. Which details in the photo best illustrate American culture?

American Gothic
Grant Wood
Art Institute of Chicago

BROADBAND INTERNET ACCESS BY U.S. COUNTY
Percentage of Households with Minimum 4 Mbps Availability

MAP TIP A choropleth map is a thematic map that uses shading to represent different levels. Here the shading represents levels of Internet use in the United States.

0   200   400 Miles
0   200   400 Kilometers

Seattle
Minneapolis
Boston
Salt Lake City
San Francisco
Chicago
New York
Denver
Washington, D.C.
Los Angeles
St. Louis
Raleigh
Memphis
Atlanta
San Antonio
Miami

Over 95%
75%–95%
50%–74%
Under 50%

INSET MAP
ALASKA
Anchorage

INSET MAP
HAWAI'I

Global and Mobile Media Today

Today, texting, instant messaging, and social networking allow fast and easy communication among cultures around the world. Much of this is done with **smartphones**, which combine communication and software applications into one handheld device. Media technology encourages a culture that is **global**, or worldwide. Access to information is available from anywhere in the world. Media culture forms around shared ideas or interests, rather than physical location. Most technology is now **mobile**, which means it moves along with the people who use it. For many people, new media has entirely replaced traditional methods of communication.

Before You Move On

Make Predictions What future economic impact might technological innovations have in the United States and Canada?

FORMATIVE ASSESSMENT
MAP LAB

 GeoJournal

1. **Region** Based on what you know about population density in the United States, how would you describe the pattern of Internet access across the country?

2. **Compare and Contrast** How does high speed Internet access in your county compare to the rest of the country? Why might this be?

3. **Draw Conclusions** Evaluate the impact of improved communication technology. Explain the the influence you think it has on cultural change.

TECHTREK

myNGconnect.com For photos of
manufacturing and current events

Digital
Library

Main Idea The economies of the United States and Canada are changing due to new technology and worldwide trends.

The Canadian and U.S. economies differ in some ways. For example, businesses are less regulated in the United States. Canada's government plays a larger role in its economy by owning some businesses and providing health care for all citizens. The economies of both countries have changed dramatically over the past 150 years.

The Economy of the Past

In the early 1800s, most Americans and Canadians worked in industries in which people make a living directly from the land. Most people farmed, worked in mines, fished, or logged timber.

During the mid-1800s, the Industrial Revolution, which began in Europe, swept the United States and Canada. **Manufacturing**, or using machines to make raw materials into a usable product, became an important part

Critical Viewing Automated robot arms weld trucks in a Michigan assembly plant. What details in the photo illustrate this automation?

6.09.A compare ways societies organize production and distribution of goods and services;
6.09.B benefits of U.S. free enterprise system; 6.10.A define and give examples of service
industries; 6.17.C evaluate impact of improved communication technology among cultures;
6.20.A give examples of technological innovations; 6.21.B analyze by drawing inferences

 Visual Vocabulary **Fiber optics** is a method of sending light through glass fibers. Fiber optic cables can transmit digital code quickly across great distances.

of the economy. In vast factories, workers manufactured products such as iron and steel. The manufacturing industry led the economy from the 1870s until the 1950s.

During the 1950s, the service industry expanded. Workers in this industry provide a service rather than make a product. Jobs in areas such as health care, education, entertainment, banking, and retail are all part of the service industry.

The Information Economy

Both the U.S. and Canadian economies are free-enterprise economies, and they are **dynamic**—they change quickly. One reason for rapid change is the use of new computer and information technologies.

In 1974, a tiny company called MITS built the first personal computer, the Altair. It had limited memory but worked well. The only problem was that you had to build it yourself from a kit! Today, more than 8 out of every 10 U.S. and Canadian households have computers, and **fiber optics** uses digital technology to transmit voice, text, and visual messages. These types of advancements have shifted the economy in a new direction.

Today's technologies allow people to store, organize, and retrieve enormous amounts of financial information with a few mouse clicks. New technologies also can bring about more jobs in the communication and information industry. Faster communication across greater distances helps support a global economy, unlimited by physical distance.

Global Recession

To function well, a free-enterprise economy requires ethical, or fair and honest, behavior. The U.S. and other world economies experienced a **recession**, or a slowdown in growth, beginning in 2007, when reckless banking practices caused a crisis, and millions of people worldwide lost their jobs.

Before You Move On
Summarize Explain why it is important for economies to be dynamic and ethical.

FORMATIVE ASSESSMENT

READING LAB   GeoJournal

1. **Evaluate** What do you think is one benefit of the U.S. free enterprise system for the development of technology? Read about free enterprise on page R43.
2. **Identify** What is a service industry? Give examples of jobs in service industries.
3. **Compare** Use what you learned from page 62 and this lesson to compare the U.S. and Canadian economies.

1.4 Finding New Energy Sources

Main Idea The growing demand for nonrenewable fossil fuels for energy has led to exploration into renewable, alternative energy sources.

In April 2010, the *Deepwater Horizon* oil drilling rig in the Gulf of Mexico exploded. The explosion opened a hole in a well drilled in the seafloor. Oil gushed from that hole every day for nearly three months, leaking nearly 5 million barrels of oil. Before this accident, the worst U.S. oil disaster at sea was the grounding of the *Exxon Valdez* tanker in 1989. That disaster lost around 260,000 barrels of oil—a large amount, but far smaller than the amount of oil leaked after the explosion of the *Deepwater Horizon*.

KEY VOCABULARY

petroleum, n., the raw material used to create oil products

wind turbine, n., an engine powered by wind to generate electricity

ethanol, n., a fuel obtained from plants that can be used alone or blended with gasoline

hybrid, n., a vehicle that can run using either an electric motor or a gas-powered engine

Oil Supply and Demand

The United States runs on energy, and oil provides about a third of that energy. **Petroleum** is a nonrenewable resource, meaning that it will eventually run out. However, no one knows exactly how much petroleum might be left in reserves that lie deep beneath the earth's surface.

Experts try to predict when the United States will use up all of its own oil supply, and they don't all agree. However, they do agree that the demand for oil is growing, rapidly shrinking the supply of this nonrenewable resource. Some experts say that as early as 2020, there won't be enough oil in the United States for everyone who wants it.

Today, the United States depends on other countries for more than two-thirds of its oil. As demand rises and supply falls, the price of oil will rise. Rising oil prices can slow economic growth and drive countries into competition for oil.

Before You Move On

Summarize What are some of the effects of an increasing demand for oil in the United States?

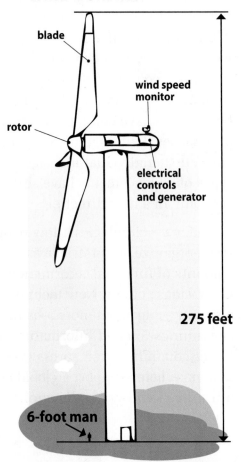

WIND TURBINE

blade

wind speed monitor

rotor

electrical controls and generator

275 feet

6-foot man

6.07.C describe ways technology influences human interaction with environment; 6.20.A give examples of technological innovations; 6.20.B explain how political decisions have affected the use of technology; 6.21.B analyze information by comparing, summarizing

Inspiring people to care about the planet
National Geographic Society Mission

Alternative Solutions

Energy sources other than oil include nuclear power, **ethanol**, solar power, and wind power. However, each has issues that make it less than ideal. Nuclear power plants take a long time to build and are very expensive. They also create radioactive waste. Making ethanol from grains means some agricultural production is used for fuel instead of food. Solar panels and wind turbines cannot always produce electricity on demand.

Auto manufacturers are now making more electric and **hybrid** vehicles. Hybrids use fuel cells to make energy. Scientists hope to use common gases like hydrogen and oxygen in these cells. If so, the supply of energy will be cheap and almost unlimited.

COMPARE ACROSS REGIONS

Innovation in Other Countries

Countries around the world are using a variety of energy innovations. For example, Brazil has been producing ethanol since the 1970s and is a leading producer of this fuel. Britain has banned conventional light bulbs in favor of bulbs with lower wattage, which use less energy. Nuclear power supplies more than 76 percent of France's electricity. Denmark's coal plants produce both electricity and hot water, making them more efficient. Some nations, such as Iceland and New Zealand, use geothermal energy, heat produced within the earth. These alternatives are some energy-efficient solutions and illustrate new ways of looking at energy production.

Visual Vocabulary A **wind turbine** is an engine that is powered by wind in order to generate electricity. A group of wind turbines placed together is a wind farm.

Before You Move On

Make Predictions How might future scientific discoveries affect energy use in the United States?

FORMATIVE ASSESSMENT

READING LAB GeoJournal

1. **Summarize** What issues prevent certain alternative energy sources from being used?

2. **Explain** How do you think political decisions in other countries have influenced their use of technology for energy innovations?

3. **Tap Prior Knowledge** Turn and talk with a partner about *nonrenewable* and how word meanings change when *non-* is added, as in *nonfiction* and *nonsense*.

1.5 Citizens' Rights and Responsibilities

TECHTREK

myNGconnect.com For photos
and a chart on citizens' rights

Digital
Library

Student
Resources

> **Main Idea** Citizens in the United States and Canada enjoy many rights and also have certain responsibilities.

The governments of the United States and Canada share many similarities. Leaders are elected by voters. Government power is shared by the national government and smaller units—states in the United States and provinces in Canada. Laws are made by a legislative body. Perhaps most importantly, all citizens in these countries have rights and responsibilities.

Government Structures

Both governments consist of three branches—the executive, the legislative, and the judicial—each with specific powers. The legislative, or law-making, branches are the U.S. Congress and the Canadian Parliament. In the United States, the head of the executive branch is the president, elected by the people. In Canada, by contrast, the chief executive is the prime minister, who is chosen by the party with the most seats in Parliament.

> **Critical Viewing** A young man registers to vote at the University of Texas. How does the sign on the table convey the importance of voting?

YOUR VOTE IS YOUR VOICE
HOOK THE VOTE
REGISTER TO VOTE HERE
BY MIDNIGHT TONIGHT!

6.13.A describe roles and responsibilities of citizens in various societies; 6.13.C compare role of U.S. citizens with citizens from various societies; 6.14.B explain relationships among rights, responsibilities, and duties in societies with representative governments; 6.21.B analyze by making generalizations; 6.22.C express ideas orally

CITIZENS' RIGHTS

UNITED STATES

Protection of rights not guaranteed by the Constitution

Right to bear arms

UNITED STATES & CANADA

Right to a **Right to trial by jury**
speedy trial **Right to vote**

Freedom of speech, religion, press, assembly Protection against unreasonable search

Right to have a lawyer

Right to be protected against discrimination on basis of race or gender

CANADA

Right to be educated in a minority language (French)

Rights and Responsibilities

In both countries, all citizens enjoy basic rights, such as the right to citizenship, equality, and fair treatment. People become citizens by being born in the country or by **naturalization**, the process that someone born in another country follows to become a citizen.

The Bill of Rights, which is the first ten amendments to the U.S. Constitution, and Canada's Charter of Rights guarantee basic freedoms. Among these are freedom of speech and religion, and certain legal rights. For example, citizens have the right to **due process**, or specific rules that authorities must follow. Canada's charter also identifies two official languages, English and French. Citizens in Canada have the right to be educated in either one.

The citizens of the United States and Canada enjoy a great deal of freedom. They can live where they wish and speak their own languages. They can express their opinions freely and practice any religion they choose. They can gather together and speak out against their government. Many people who live in these two countries immigrated from countries that did not allow these basic freedoms.

In both countries, citizens with rights also have responsibilities. The right to vote brings with it the responsibility to cast a vote fairly, through formal elections. Legal rights bring about the responsibility to obey laws and to serve on a jury, which is a group of fellow citizens who listen to both sides of a legal matter and decide whether laws were broken.

Some responsibilities are not identified in any document, but are just as important as those required by law. For example, citizens are expected to treat each other fairly. The United States and Canada are home to a wide variety of races, religions, and customs. Citizens in diverse societies like these have the responsibility to accept one another's differences.

Before You Move On

Make Inferences Why is responsibility an important part of having rights and freedoms?

FORMATIVE ASSESSMENT

SPEAKING LAB GeoJournal

1. **Make Generalizations** Based on the graphic above, which document, the Bill of Rights or Canada's Charter of Rights, provides stronger protection for rights? How?

2. **Express Ideas Through Speech** Write and deliver a speech that describes the citizen responsibility you believe is most important. Explain why you think so and give an example.

2.1 Daily Life in Mexico

TECHTREK
myNGconnect.com For photos
of Mexico's daily life

Digital
Library

> **Main Idea** Life in Mexico today reflects a blend of traditional and modern elements and Native American and Spanish cultures.

Much of Mexican life is modern, but many Mexican people hold a deep respect for the past. Mexican culture blends contributions from the Native American and Spanish cultures that shaped its history.

A Blending of Cultures

Native people of Mexico had created successful empires before the Spanish conquest in 1521. **Descendants**, or future generations, of these indigenous people still make up a large part of Mexico's population. The largest population group is the mestizos, who are Mexicans of mixed **ancestry**, or heritage. This ancestry can include native, European (particularly Spanish), and African family roots. Mixed ancestry is a source of pride among mestizos in Mexico.

Former Foreign Ministry building; now a monument

Church built during Spanish colonial rule

Ruins from ancient Aztec city

The Plaza of Three Cultures in Mexico City represents three elements of Mexican culture: Aztec, Spanish, and mestizo.

The blend of cultures is seen in the many languages and religions of Mexico. While nine out of ten Mexicans speak only Spanish, the country's official language, the rest speak one of more than 50 Native American languages. Similarly, more than 80 percent of Mexico's people follow the traditional Roman Catholic religion. However, many Native Americans practice traditional religions, and many Mexican customs show the blending of cultures. For example, a celebration called the Day of the Dead, which honors one's ancestors, mixes native and Catholic traditions.

Many Mexican artists have blended native and European culture. Diego Rivera and David Alfaro Siqueiros (sih KAY rohs) used European style to paint **murals**, or large paintings on walls, that highlight Native American culture in Mexico.

Modern and Traditional Life

Today, life in Mexico is a balance of the traditional and modern. Once largely rural, Mexico is now an urban nation. More than three-quarters of its people live in cities. The capital, Mexico City, is one of the world's largest cities, and is home to one-fifth of Mexico's population.

Mexico embraces past and present. The country has preserved sites that include Aztec and Mayan art and **artifacts**, or tools and other ornaments that show something about how a culture lived. The National Palace in Mexico City, built to house colonial viceroys, is still used as a government building. Mexico also has bold, modern architecture, such as the Lighthouse of Commerce in Monterrey.

Mexican cooking continues to include staple foods of its indigenous people: corn, beans, and squash. Corn is ground to make *tortillas*, a flat bread served with many meals. Traditional foods now must fit into a more modern lifestyle. Families used to share a large midday meal, but shorter lunch hours and long commutes for modern workers make it difficult to keep up this tradition.

Some Mexican people follow traditional practices as a way of life. This is especially true among rural people. For example, *vaqueros*, or cowboys, still work on some ranches in northern Mexico, using their traditional skills.

Before You Move On
Summarize In what ways is Mexican culture a blend of influences?

FORMATIVE ASSESSMENT

READING LAB  GeoJournal

1. **Discuss** What aspects of life in Mexico today trace back to the Spanish conquest and colonization, which you read about on pages 104–107? Listen for words such as *adapt*, *oppose*, *resist*, and *traditions* in the discussion.

2. **Place** In what ways does the Plaza of Three Cultures represent Mexican culture?

3. **Make Inferences** Why might the mixed cultural heritage of the *mestizos* be a source of pride in Mexico?

> **Critical Viewing** A quinceañera (keen sin NYAR ah) is a traditional celebration of a girl's 15th birthday. It is both a religious and a social event. What details in the photo remind you of other ceremonies?

2.2 The Impact of Globalization

TECHTREK

myNGconnect.com For photos and a
graph of Mexico's Gross Domestic Product

 Maps and Graphs

 Digital Library

Main Idea Mexico has a developing economy that faces challenges as a result of global trends.

As parts of Mexico are modernizing, the country's economy is growing. However, **globalization**, the development of a world economy based on free trade and the use of labor from other countries, has presented economic challenges.

A Drive for Growth

For much of the 20th century, some major industries in Mexico were **nationalized**, or placed under government control. All income from a nationalized industry goes to the government. The profitable oil industry, for example, was nationalized in 1932. For periods of time during the 1900s, the government also controlled Mexico's banking, transportation, and telecommunications systems.

In the 1980s, in an effort to improve the country's economy, Mexico released some control of these industries to private and foreign investors. Another factor of Mexico's economic growth was the adoption of the **North American Free Trade Agreement (NAFTA)** in 1994, which removed many barriers to trade. Since then, Mexican trade with the rest of North America—mostly with the United States—has increased nearly 300 percent. However, NAFTA's critics say the agreement unfairly favors commercial agriculture over small-scale farmers.

Three Economic Sectors

Economic activity in Mexico takes place in three **economic sectors**, or subdivisions of the economy: agriculture, manufacturing, and service. The agricultural sector includes large-scale production for export.

Critical Viewing This worker cleans molds that are used to make shoe soles in a factory in Leon, Mexico. What skills would be required of factory workers?

6.08.A describe ways factors of production influence economies; 6.09.A compare ways societies organize production and distribution of goods and services; 6.10.A define and give examples of agricultural, manufacturing, service industries 6.10.B describe levels of economic development using indicators; 6.21.C interpret information from graphs

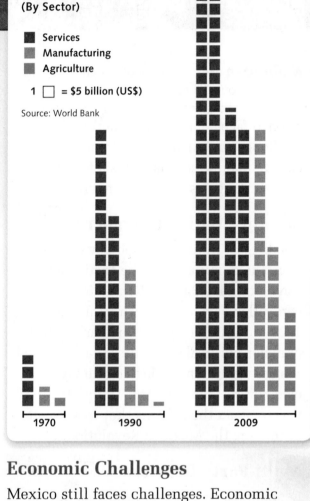

MEXICO'S GDP
(By Sector)

■ Services
■ Manufacturing
■ Agriculture

1 □ = $5 billion (US$)

Source: World Bank

1970   1990   2009

Major exports include tropical fruits, coffee, sugarcane, and cotton. Silver is also an important mineral resource for Mexico's export income in this sector. Export income also comes from oil sold on world markets.

Manufacturing in Mexico includes automobiles, food processing, and metal products. Heavy foreign investment followed the adoption of NAFTA, which increased manufacturing activity. This investment led to more *maquiladoras*, foreign-owned factories where parts made elsewhere are put together into finished goods and then exported worldwide.

The dollar amount provided to the GDP (Gross Domestic Product) by service industries increased by a factor of more than 25 between 1970 and 2009. This sector includes services such as banking and transportation. Mexico's warm climate and cultural treasures attract tourists from around the globe, making tourism another big part of the service economy.

Economic Challenges

Mexico still faces challenges. Economic growth hasn't happened for most poor people. Many Mexicans have difficulty finding work and migrate to the United States. Some Mexican-owned businesses have transferred jobs to countries where workers are paid less.

Before You Move On

Make Inferences In what ways has globalization affected Mexico's economy?

FORMATIVE ASSESSMENT

DATA LAB   GeoJournal

1. **Analyze Data** Based on the graph, which economic sector has grown the most?

2. **Synthesize** How might NAFTA account for the growth in agriculture between 1990 and 2009?

3. **Region** Why is tourism important to Mexico?

2.3 Reaching Toward Democracy

TECHTREK
myNGconnect.com For a graph and photos on democracy in Mexico

Maps and Graphs

Digital Library

Main Idea Mexico has made progress toward democracy but still faces serious obstacles.

Mexico faces not only economic challenges but also political ones. The country's political history is a factor in today's struggles toward democracy.

Stability Without Democracy

The biggest limit on democracy came from the dominance of the **Institutional Revolutionary Party (PRI)**, which controlled Mexico's government from 1929 to 2000. The PRI formed as a result of major political instability that included the assassination of Mexico's newly elected president in 1928. The party's goal was to enact the reforms that were fought for during the Mexican Revolution.

Multi-Party Democracy

Economic and political problems during the 1990s weakened the PRI's hold on power in the Mexican states. In 1994, the Zapatista Liberation Army staged a violent rebellion in response to new economic policies that were harmful to poor, indigenous people. This rebel group seized control of several Mexican states.

In 1996, the government enacted election **reforms**, or changes aimed at correcting problems. These reforms made voting more fair and made it easier for parties other than the PRI to run candidates. Elections between candidates from the PRI and other parties were closer each year. In 2000, the election of Vicente Fox of the National Action Party (PAN) broke 71 years of PRI rule.

Fox was appealing to many Mexican people. He promised to improve the economy, clean up government corruption, and resolve disputes with rebellious political groups, particularly the Zapatistas. The results of Fox's presidency were complex. He had raised the expectations of many Mexican people who were suffering economically. However, the PRI still controlled Congress. Therefore, Fox's reform efforts moved slowly and many Mexicans who originally supported Fox were disappointed.

> **Critical Viewing** Felipe Calderón greets supporters after being declared winner of the 2006 presidential election. How would you describe the emotions of the crowd?

Perhaps the most important result of Fox's presidency was that it brought about **multi-party democracy**, a political system in which elections include candidates from more than one party. Presidents in Mexico serve only one six-year term, so the 2006 election included two new candidates: Felipe Calderón of the PAN and López Obrador from the leftist party of the Democratic Revolution, which had become another important political voice in Mexican politics. Calderón was declared winner, but with less than a one percent lead over Obrador. This election further proved that multi-party democracy was in place in Mexico.

Challenges Ahead

One of the obstacles to Mexico's democracy comes from the illegal drug trade, which is controlled by several drug cartels. The activities of the cartels brought about heavy violence in the early 2000s, especially along the U.S.-Mexico border. In 2009, President Calderón sent troops to the area to control the violence, but the cartels still challenge the authority of Mexico's government. Democracy is also challenged by the Zapatistas' ongoing control in several Mexican states.

A positive trend in Mexico is its increasing literacy rate. By the start of the 21st century, nearly 90 percent of Mexico's population was literate, or able to read and write. A high literacy rate is one factor that helps a society be more productive and contribute to the country's economy. It is also an important element of a democracy, because people need to be informed to take part in decision-making.

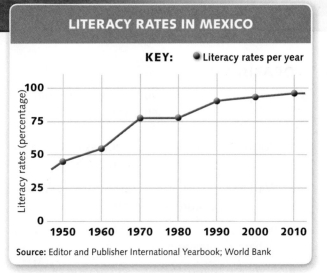

LITERACY RATES IN MEXICO

KEY: ● Literacy rates per year

Literacy rates (percentage)

Source: Editor and Publisher International Yearbook; World Bank

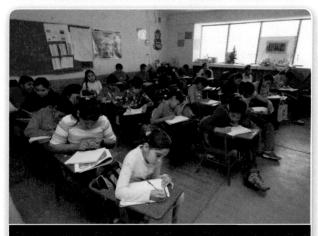

Many children in rural Mexico speak a regional dialect and must learn Spanish in school.

Before You Move On

Monitor Comprehension How has the Mexican government become more democratic?

FORMATIVE ASSESSMENT

READING LAB GeoJournal

1. **Identify Problems and Solutions** What problems does Mexico's government now face? How might it solve them? Explain your answer.

2. **Interpret Graphs** During which 10-year period did Mexico's literacy rate increase the most? When did it increase the least?

3. **Draw Conclusions** How might Mexico's growing literacy rate help achieve democracy?

VOCABULARY

On your paper, write the vocabulary word that completes the following sentences.

1. North America's _____ shows in its mix of races, languages, and religions.

2. With new media able to reach people all over the world, culture has become _____.

3. A _____ occurs when the economy shows a sharp decline in business activity.

4. A vehicle that runs on a combination of electric and gas power is called a _____.

5. Some Mexican artists create _____ that show the country's native cultures.

6. When an industry is _____, it is placed under government control.

MAIN IDEAS

7. How did the United States and Canada become so diverse? (Section 1.1)

8. How has mobile technology affected cultures in the United States and Canada? (Section 1.2)

9. How did the information age transform the U.S. and Canadian economies? (Section 1.3)

10. Why are researchers looking at alternative sources of energy? (Section 1.4)

11. How do immigrants from other lands gain the rights and responsibilities of American and Canadian citizenship? (Section 1.5)

12. What are two examples of the continuing influence of Spanish culture on Mexico? (Section 2.1)

13. What economic success has Mexico seen in recent decades? (Section 2.2)

14. Why is it important for a country struggling toward democracy to have more than one political party? (Section 2.3)

FOCUS ON UNITED STATES & CANADA

ANALYZE THE ESSENTIAL QUESTION

What issues do the United States and Canada face today?

Focus Skill: Identify Problems and Solutions

15. What do you think is the single biggest challenge facing the United States? Why do you think so?

16. What do you think is the single biggest challenge facing Canada? Why do you think so?

17. Choose one of the challenges you identified in the previous two questions. What do you think the country should do about that challenge? Why would those steps help?

INTERPRET TABLES

UNITED STATES TRADE BALANCE ($ BILLIONS)			
	2006	2007	2008
Total	-760.4	-701.4	-696.0
With main trading partners			
Canada	−71.8	−68.2	−78.3
China	−234.1	−258.5	−268.0
Germany	−89.1	−94.2	−43.0
Japan	−89.7	−84.3	−74.1
Mexico	−64.5	−74.8	−64.7

Source: 2010 Statistical Abstract of the United States, Table 1264 and Table 1271

18. **Analyze Data** A negative trade balance means that a country imports more than it exports. What trend do you see in the overall trade balance from 2006 to 2008?

19. **Synthesize** If the United States eliminated its trade deficit with Canada and Mexico, would that have much effect on the overall trade balance? Why or why not?

FOCUS ON MEXICO

ANALYZE THE ESSENTIAL QUESTION

How has globalization affected Mexico?

Focus Skill: Summarize

20. How has the balance of rural and urban populations shifted in Mexico?

21. What factors have contributed to economic growth in Mexico?

22. What challenges come along with economic growth in Mexico?

23. What qualities will help Mexico become a successful democracy and take part in the global economy?

INTERPRET MAPS

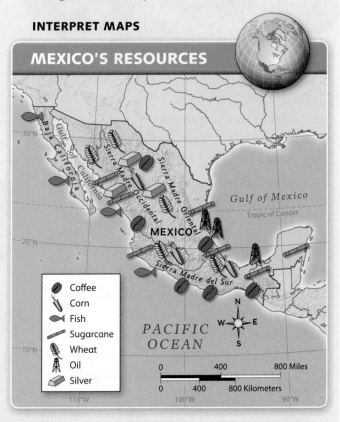

MEXICO'S RESOURCES

Legend:
- Coffee
- Corn
- Fish
- Sugarcane
- Wheat
- Oil
- Silver

PACIFIC OCEAN

Gulf of Mexico

Tropic of Cancer

MEXICO

Baja California

Gulf of California

Sierra Madre Occidental

Sierra Madre Oriental

Sierra Madre del Sur

0   400   800 Miles

0   400   800 Kilometers

110°W   100°W   90°W

30°N   20°N   10°N

24. **Interpret Maps** Which natural resource is found only in the mountains? Which resource besides fish and oil is found on coastal plains?

25. **Synthesize** Which resources on the map are important to Mexico's success in the global economy? Explain why.

ACTIVE OPTIONS

Synthesize the Essential Questions by completing the activities below.

26. **Write a Speech** Suppose you are president of the United States preparing to visit either Mexico or Canada. In a speech to that country's people, you want to emphasize the cooperation and good relations between your two countries. Choose one of those countries and then write and deliver a two-minute speech that a president might deliver. Use vocabulary that includes geographic, economic, and cultural terms. **After all the speeches are delivered, discuss the ideas that were presented.**

Writing Tips
- Vary the sentence types you use to keep listeners interested.
- Use examples to show how the two countries cooperate.
- State your goals for good future relations.

27. **Create an Economic Sectors Model** All societies have economic institutions that oversee activities such as the producing and selling of goods. Agriculture, manufacturing, and service industries create products and work with wholesale and retail industries to get their goods into the marketplace.

Work with a partner and start by writing definitions of each industry. Use the Economics Handbook (page R41) and put definitions in your own words. Then review the unit for examples of each industry. For instance, the map legend on page 81 shows examples of agriculture. Draw a model to show how economic industries and activities interconnect. Use connecting words (*first, next, then,* or *finally*) to describe how your model works.

Becoming a Citizen

TECHTREK
myNGconnect.com For graphs of
U.S. naturalizations

 Maps and
Graphs

Naturalization is the process by which someone who was not born in a country can become a citizen of that country. Every country spells out in detail who can or cannot become a citizen and what steps must be taken as part of the naturalization process.

Requirements for naturalization in most countries include specific guidelines in several areas: residency (the amount of time spent living in the country); language proficiency (the ability to speak the country's official language); cultural and historical knowledge of the country (usually a written test); and character, or the kind of person you are (usually determined by a background check).

Compare

- China
- Cuba
- Ethiopia
- India
- Iran
- Mexico
- Ukraine
- United States

NATURALIZATION AND CITIZENSHIP

Most countries require a person who wishes to become a citizen to first gain permanent residency status before even applying for naturalization. A permanent resident is allowed to live and work in a country, but legally is still a citizen of the home country. The years of permanent residency a country requires may be fewer for a person who has served or is willing to serve in that country's military.

People applying for U.S. citizenship are tested in English to prove their language proficiency. They must also pass a test on U.S. history, government, and the rights and responsibilities of citizens. Those responsibilities or duties include serving on juries, obeying laws, and voting in elections.

In the United States, citizens can participate in their democracy. They join a political party. They express ideas and opinions to elected officials or community groups to influence the political process. Citizens can also run for office.

To become naturalized, an applicant must give up loyalty to other nations, defend the Constitution, and obey laws. The final step in obtaining citizenship in the United States and in many other countries is a naturalization ceremony, in which new citizens take an oath to live by their new country's laws and customs.

Review the lesson with a partner to build background knowledge on citizenship. Review page R32 in the Skills Handbook before interpreting the graphs and data on the facing page.

6.13.A describe roles and responsibilities of United States citizens; 6.13.B explain how opportunities for citizens to participate in and influence the political process vary among societies; 6.13.C compare role of U.S. citizens with roles of citizens from various societies; 6.14.A identify and explain the duty of civic participation; 6.21.C organize and interpret information on graphs; 6.21.F use math skills to interpret social studies information (graphs); 6.22.D create written material

U.S. NATURALIZATION*

BY THE NUMBERS

899,162
Number of applications filed for U.S. naturalization, 2012

65,874
Number of denied applications for U.S. naturalization, 2012

$680
U.S. naturalization application filing fee

40
Median age at naturalization, 2010–2012

7
Median years as permanent resident, 2012

22%
Percentage of naturalized citizens with a Bachelor's degree, 2010

$51,926
Median household income of naturalized citizens, 2011

U.S. MILITARY NATURALIZATIONS

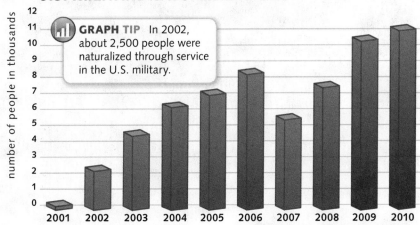

GRAPH TIP In 2002, about 2,500 people were naturalized through service in the U.S. military.

U.S. NATURALIZATIONS

Country of origin
● Mexico   ● India   ● China   ● Cuba

GRAPH TIP In 2000, nearly 200,000 people from Mexico became naturalized U.S. citizens. In 2001, the number decreased to just over 100,000 people.

*Sources: U.S. Department of Homeland Security; Congressional Research Service

---

FORMATIVE ASSESSMENT

RESEARCH LAB GeoJournal

1. **Draw Conclusions** Why would a country require knowledge about its history, government, and culture to gain citizenship?

2. **Research Databases** Choose two countries highlighted on the map, one with a representative government, one nonrepresentative. Research the roles of citizens in each country. Then compare their roles with those of U.S. citizens.

3. **Interpret Graphs** What is similar about the number of U.S. naturalizations from all four countries from 2000 to 2001? What about from 2007 to 2008?

Research and Create Graphs Create a line graph similar to the one above. Research the Homeland Security online database (Table 21, Yearbook of Immigration Statistics) to find out the number of people from Ethiopia, Iran, and Ukraine who became U.S. naturalized citizens over the most recent four-year period. With a partner, pose and answer questions about data patterns for the countries. Describe how the data changed over the four years and give possible reasons why.

Active Options

ACTIVITY 1

Goal: Evaluate important physical structures.

Write Seven Wonders List

Since ancient times, people have made "Seven Wonders" lists of magnificent structures around the world, such as the Great Pyramids in Egypt or the Statue of Zeus in Greece.

Create such a list for the continent of North America. Review the photos in the **Digital Library** and use the research links to help you decide which structures belong on the list. Your list can include both natural structures and structures built by humans. For each item on your list, write the reasons why the structure deserves to be named as one of the Seven Wonders of North America.

Mount Rushmore in South Dakota

ACTIVITY 2

Goal: Research a national park.

Conduct a Walk in the Park

The U.S. National Park Service protects about 400 parks, and Parks Canada protects over 40 national parks. Choose a national park in North America from the list below or from another source. Do research and use the **Magazine Maker CD-ROM** to create a "show and tell" route through the park to show what makes it so important and worth preserving.

National Parks
- Denali, AK
- Everglades, FL
- Big Bend, TX
- Yosemite, CA
- Zion, UT
- Yellowstone, WY, MT, ID
- Glacier, British Columbia, Canada
- Prince Edward Island, Canada

ACTIVITY 3

Goal: Learn about the roles of scientists.

Explore the Explorers

Find out more about National Geographic Explorers Beth Shapiro and Sam Meacham. How did they become interested in their work? What are their current projects? How does what they do help societies around the world? With a group, design a visual profile of one of the scientists, using words and images to show the importance of the scientist's work.

6.08.A describe ways in which the factors of production (entrepreneurs) influence economies; 6.09.A compare ways in which various societies organize the production and distribution of goods and services; 6.09.B compare and contrast among free enterprise, socialist, and communist economies in various contemporary societies, including the benefits of the U.S. free enterprise system; 6.09.C understand the importance of morality and ethics in maintaining a functional free enterprise system; 6.10.C identify and describe the effects of government regulation and taxation on economic development and business planning; 6.16.A identify institutions basic to all societies (economic)

TEKS

TEKS PROJECT

Goal: Understand economic systems and the benefits of free enterprise.

Plot a Product's Path

Every society has an economic system. In a free enterprise system, people can choose what they buy. Entrepreneurs can start companies and compete to create the most appealing products. By contrast, a collective economic system, such as socialism or communism, does not allow the same kind of free choice. The state controls how goods and services are bought and sold.

In free enterprise systems, the government usually acts to protect buyers and to ensure that businesses are ethical and abide by laws. This regulation, if too excessive, can prevent ideas from developing into products. In the same way, too many taxes can prevent businesses from making enough profit to keep going. However, a benefit of the U.S. free enterprise system is that entrepreneurs have a voice in it and can share ideas.

The Challenge Form a team and choose a product to run through a free enterprise system and a communist economic system. Review what you learned in the unit (*see* Section 1.3) and refer to pages R41 and R43 as well. Draw parallel diagrams, plotting the product's path, from its creation to its purchase. Who plans the business and then develops the product in each system? How is the quality of materials needed for the product decided? Who sets the price? Who can buy it? Where? Use your diagrams to compare and contrast the systems.

Reflect On It Tell what you learned by comparing the production and distribution of goods. Then share your ideas about the advantages of free enterprise.

Austin, Texas, is host to international festivals in which entrepreneurs share ideas.

Explore Central America & the Caribbean with NATIONAL GEOGRAPHIC

MEET THE EXPLORER

NATIONAL GEOGRAPHIC

Emerging Explorer Ken Banks created a communication tool for farmers in El Salvador. They can discuss crop pricing and remain competitive using an inexpensive cell phone.

INVESTIGATE GEOGRAPHY

Central America was once entirely covered by rain forests. Farmers have cleared many of these hot, tropical areas for cattle ranching and sugar plantations. The remaining rain forests still contain many plants and tropical birds, including this toucan.

STEP INTO HISTORY

Toussaint L'Ouverture led a slave revolt in Santo Domingo, later called Haiti, and laid the groundwork for its independence in 1804. The former slave was a brilliant general, defeating the powerful French army.

Washington, D.C.
1,556 miles
San Juan, Puerto Rico

Go to myNGconnect.com for maps of Central America and the Caribbean.

CONNECT WITH THE CULTURE

Brightly colored, handwoven Guatemalan textiles, like the young girl wears in this photo, reflect the country's traditional Mayan roots.

CHAPTER 5

Central America & the Caribbean
GEOGRAPHY & HISTORY

PREVIEW THE CHAPTER

Essential Question How has physical geography been a positive or negative influence on the economy of the region?

SECTION 1 • GEOGRAPHY

KEY VOCABULARY
- isthmus
- coastal plain
- rain forest
- archipelago
- tectonic plate
- seismic
- ecosystem
- deforestation
- fertile
- tourism
- canopy
- extinction
- poacher

ACADEMIC VOCABULARY
critical

TERMS & NAMES
- Caribbean Sea

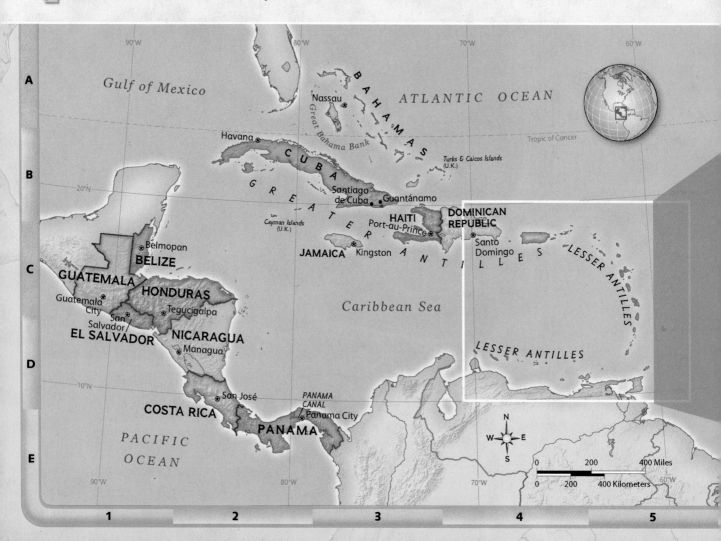

TECHTREK

 FOR THIS CHAPTER

 Student eEdition

 Maps and Graphs

Interactive Whiteboard GeoActivities

 Digital Library

lemur frog, Costa Rica

Go to **myNGconnect.com** for more on Central America and the Caribbean.

Essential Question How have economic resources influenced the history of the region?

KEY VOCABULARY

- cash crop
- scarcity
- triangular trade
- multitude
- staple
- viceroy
- province
- harbor
- dictator
- commonwealth

ACADEMIC VOCABULARY

exploit

TERMS & NAMES

- Columbian Exchange
- Toussaint L'Ouverture

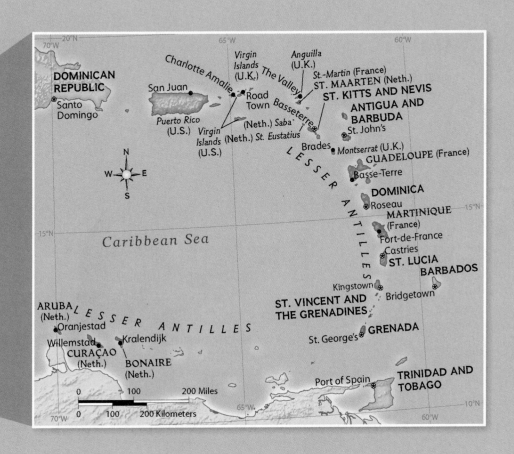

1.1 Physical Geography

CENTRAL AMERICA AND THE CARIBBEAN PHYSICAL

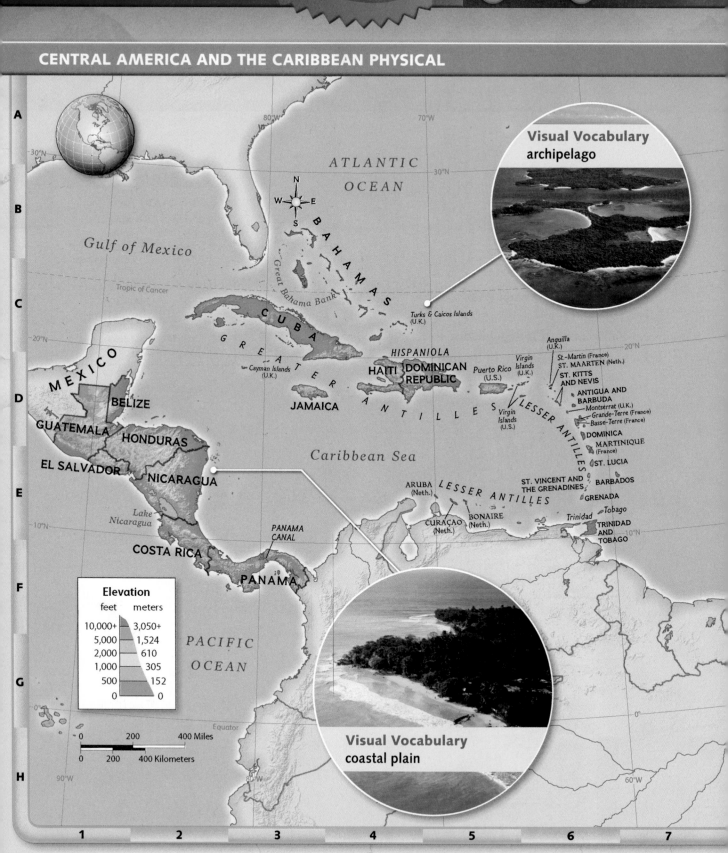

Visual Vocabulary
archipelago

Visual Vocabulary
coastal plain

ATLANTIC OCEAN

Gulf of Mexico

Tropic of Cancer

BAHAMAS
Great Bahama Bank

CUBA

GREATER ANTILLES

Turks & Caicos Islands (U.K.)

Cayman Islands (U.K.)

HISPANIOLA

HAITI   DOMINICAN REPUBLIC

JAMAICA

Puerto Rico (U.S.)

Virgin Islands (U.K.)

Virgin Islands (U.S.)

Anguilla (U.K.)
St.-Martin (France)
ST. MAARTEN (Neth.)
ST. KITTS AND NEVIS
ANTIGUA AND BARBUDA
Montserrat (U.K.)
Grande-Terre (France)
Basse-Terre (France)
DOMINICA
MARTINIQUE (France)
ST. LUCIA

LESSER ANTILLES

MEXICO

BELIZE

GUATEMALA

HONDURAS

EL SALVADOR

NICARAGUA

Lake Nicaragua

COSTA RICA

PANAMA

PANAMA CANAL

Caribbean Sea

ARUBA (Neth.)

CURAÇAO (Neth.)

BONAIRE (Neth.)

LESSER ANTILLES

ST. VINCENT AND THE GRENADINES

BARBADOS

GRENADA

Tobago

Trinidad

TRINIDAD AND TOBAGO

PACIFIC OCEAN

Equator

Elevation

feet	meters
10,000+	3,050+
5,000	1,524
2,000	610
1,000	305
500	152
0	0

0   200   400 Miles
0   200   400 Kilometers

CLIMATE

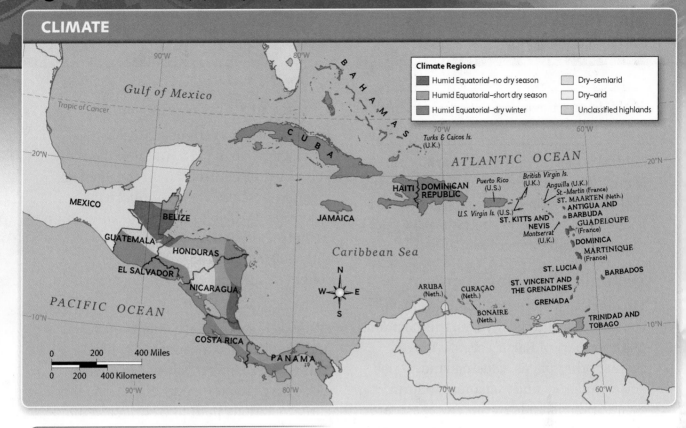

Climate Regions
- Humid Equatorial–no dry season
- Humid Equatorial–short dry season
- Humid Equatorial–dry winter
- Dry–semiarid
- Dry–arid
- Unclassified highlands

Main Idea Mountains, coastal plains, and rain forests are the main landforms that support the region's economy.

Central America and the Caribbean islands are located between the continents of North America and South America. The physical geography of the region supports the agriculture and tourism that are so valuable to the region's economy.

Central America

Central America is an **isthmus**, a narrow strip connecting two large land areas. A range of volcanic mountains spreads across the seven countries of the region. The climate in the mountains is cool and the rich volcanic soil is ideal for growing coffee beans, an important export. The **coastal plains**, which are the lowlands next to the seacoast, and the tropical **rain forests**— heavily wooded forests that may receive more than 100 inches of rain per year— provide resources that boost the economy.

The Caribbean Islands

The Caribbean islands curve in an **archipelago**, or chain of islands, between the Atlantic Ocean and the **Caribbean Sea**. Sugarcane, grown on coastal plains, is the leading crop. The climate is mild in winter and hot in summer, and attracts visitors year-round.

Before You Move On

Summarize In what ways do the main landforms of the region support the economy?

FORMATIVE ASSESSMENT

MAP LAB
GeoJournal

1. **Location** Based on the physical map, where are the mountainous regions of Central America located?

2. **Interpret Maps** What is the climate like on the Central American and Caribbean coasts?

3. **Turn and Talk** Discuss with a classmate the differences in climate in the mountains and on the coastal plains. Where would you like to live?

1.2 Earthquakes and Volcanoes

TECHTREK

myNGconnect.com For a map of plates
and photos of volcanoes and earthquakes

 Maps and
Graphs

Digital
Library

Main Idea Earthquakes and volcanoes affect daily life and economic activities in the region.

Central America and many Caribbean islands were underwater millions of years ago. The formation of the mountains and islands in this region shows how physical geography can change over time.

Tectonic Plate Movements

This region sits on the Caribbean Plate. For tens of millions of years, this **tectonic plate**—a part of Earth's crust—moved against other plates, causing land to rise and mountains and volcanoes to form. Some of the islands in the Caribbean are really just the tips of ancient volcanoes created by tectonic plate movement.

The location of the islands on these plates is significant. Today, plates slowly continue to move, crashing into or sliding over or under each other. This movement causes earthquake, or **seismic**, activity and volcanic eruptions. An eruption in Montserrat in 1996 caused two-thirds of the population to flee their homes.

Impact of Earthquakes

In 2010, Haiti experienced its most destructive earthquake in more than 200 years, measuring 7.0 on the moment magnitude scale. The earthquake caused extensive damage to many of Haiti's cities, including its capital, Port-au-Prince. More than 200,000 people were killed and roughly a million were left homeless.

The earthquake also destroyed **critical** systems, the extremely important services and supplies that a community needs. Many Haitians were left without water, gas, electricity, transportation, or medical care. Donations poured in from around the world in an international effort to help Haiti recover and rebuild.

Before You Move On

Summarize What causes earthquakes and volcanoes in this region, and what are some of the effects?

> **Critical Viewing** This courthouse was buried in a landslide caused by a volcano on Montserrat. What does this photo suggest about volcanoes?

PLATES AND VOLCANOES

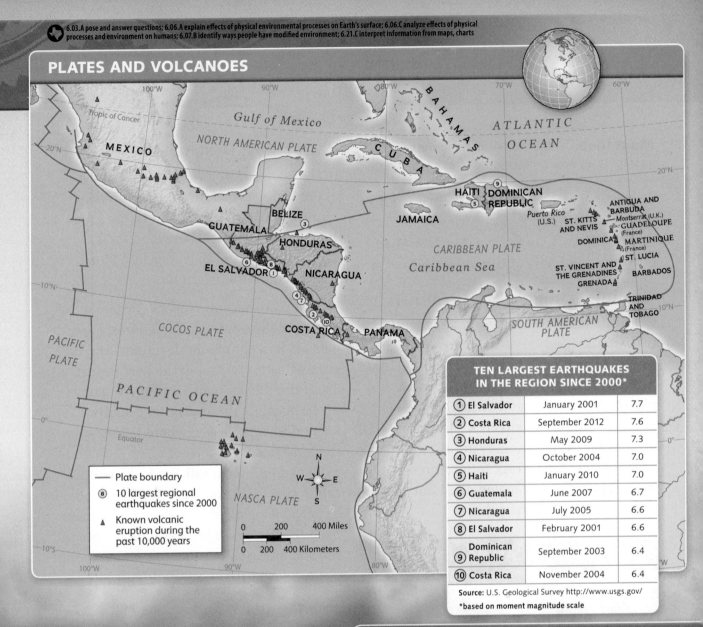

TEN LARGEST EARTHQUAKES IN THE REGION SINCE 2000*		
① El Salvador	January 2001	7.7
② Costa Rica	September 2012	7.6
③ Honduras	May 2009	7.3
④ Nicaragua	October 2004	7.0
⑤ Haiti	January 2010	7.0
⑥ Guatemala	June 2007	6.7
⑦ Nicaragua	July 2005	6.6
⑧ El Salvador	February 2001	6.6
⑨ Dominican Republic	September 2003	6.4
⑩ Costa Rica	November 2004	6.4

Source: U.S. Geological Survey http://www.usgs.gov/

*based on moment magnitude scale

FORMATIVE ASSESSMENT

MAP LAB

GeoJournal

1. **Interpret Maps** What is significant about Central America's location near where the Caribbean Plate and the Cocos Plate meet?

2. **Location** According to the map, where do the most and the fewest volcanic eruptions happen in Central America? Use the chart to pose and answer questions with a partner about earthquakes in the region.

3. **Make Inferences** Why are land masses clustered around the edges of the Caribbean Plate?

4. **Analyze** What effects have the region's physical processes had on the people who live there and their environment?

1.3 Rain Forests of Central America

TECHTREK
myNGconnect.com For an online
map and photos of the rain forest

 Maps and
Graphs

 Digital
Library

> **Main Idea** Central American rain forests are an important economic resource for the region.

Central America's rain forests cover a large portion of the region. Countries in the region are working to save rain forests and grow economically at the same time.

The Importance of Rain Forests

Central American rain forests have tall trees with broad leaves, and grow in tropical areas with heavy rainfall. A rain forest is an individual **ecosystem**, a place where plants and animals rely on the environment to survive. Many rare species make their homes in rain forests. The quetzal (ket SAHL), for example, is the national symbol of Guatemala. It makes a nest in rain forest trees.

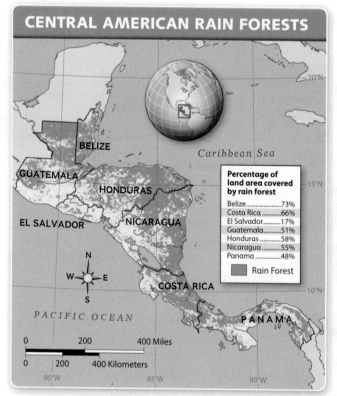

CENTRAL AMERICAN RAIN FORESTS

BELIZE
Caribbean Sea
GUATEMALA
HONDURAS
EL SALVADOR
NICARAGUA

Percentage of land area covered by rain forest

Belize.....................73%
Costa Rica.............66%
El Salvador...........17%
Guatemala............51%
Honduras.............58%
Nicaragua.............55%
Panama.................48%

◼ Rain Forest

COSTA RICA
PACIFIC OCEAN
PANAMA

0   200   400 Miles
0   200   400 Kilometers

90°W   85°W   80°W

20°N
15°N
10°N

Rain Forest Destruction

In the 1500s, rain forests covered most of Central America. They thrived for hundreds of years until the 1900s. From 1990 to 2005, Nicaragua, Honduras, Guatemala, and El Salvador lost 14 to 30 percent of their rain forest land.

There are several reasons for forest loss, or **deforestation**. Many forests are cleared for commercial farmland and for grazing cattle to supply the beef industry. Trees provide valuable timber, or wood for building. Rain forests are usually located in rural areas, where people use the land to survive. Trees are cut down for firewood and for small farms. However, rain forest soil is not very **fertile**, or able to produce plentiful crops. Rural farmers need to clear more land after nutrients in the soil are used up. The forests are being cleared faster than they can regrow.

The Future

Many countries encourage rain forest tourism. **Tourism**—the travel industry—brings income to the region and provides jobs so rural people do not need to depend on rain forest land for farming. Certain farming methods can also prevent further damage to rain forests. Shade coffee, for example, grows under the protection of trees. This crop can grow on the same soil as other crops, such as beans. This practice preserves soil quality.

Before You Move On

Make Inferences How do Central America's rain forests contribute to the economy?

Visual Vocabulary Canopy refers to the tops of trees that create a roof over the rain forest. Many visitors take rain forest canopy tours.

Critical Viewing A tourist ziplines through the rain forest in Honduras. A cable is strung at an angle between two points, and the rider uses a pulley to "zip" from the top of the line to the bottom. What would you see by exploring the canopy of the rain forest that would be different from exploring at ground level?

FORMATIVE ASSESSMENT

DATA LAB
GeoJournal

1. **Analyze Data** Based on the percentages of land covered by rain forest, in which country would you expect rain forest tourism to be most important? Explain your response.

2. **Create Graphs** Using data shown on the map in this lesson, make a bar graph showing the percentage of forested land in Central American countries. Which method of showing the data do you find the most clear, and why?

SECTION **1** GEOGRAPHY

1.4

NATIONAL GEOGRAPHIC

TECHTREK

myNGconnect.com For photos
and an Explorer Video Clip

Digital
Library

Saving Sea Turtles

with José Urteaga

> **Main Idea** People can save their region's valuable resources by revisiting traditional ideas and finding new economic solutions.

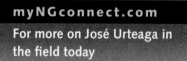

myNGconnect.com

For more on José Urteaga in the field today

Identifying the Problem

In the early 1980s, sea turtles in Nicaragua began to disappear. Their decline in population was unusual, considering that they had outlived dinosaurs. For more than 100 million years, sea turtles migrated to Nicaragua's beaches to lay eggs, sometimes hatching 600,000 babies at a time. Emerging Explorer José Urteaga (uhr tay AH gah) is a young marine biologist who decided to find out why sea turtles were disappearing so fast that they were close to **extinction**, or dying out completely.

Urteaga discovered that **poachers**, people who hunt or fish illegally, were stealing sea turtle eggs from beach nests. Poor people in Nicaragua live on less than $1 a day, but a poacher can earn as much as $5 selling just 12 eggs a day, because of the great demand for the eggs. Sea turtle eggs are highly valued in Nicaraguan culture. Turtle meat and turtle eggs are traditional foods of the country. People also use sea turtle shells to make jewelry.

Finding a Solution

Urteaga knew that to save the turtle eggs, he had to help poor people earn money in other ways. He also had to encourage people to see their culture in a new way. Starting in 2002, he put together a team that worked with poachers, celebrities, young people, and conservation groups.

First, he convinced poachers to sell their turtle eggs to him so he could hatch them. Then he taught poachers how to make a living by farming, raising bees, guiding tourists, and making crafts. Urteaga even hired former poachers to patrol the beaches and protect the nests. He started hatcheries, places designed for hatching eggs, to make sure new generations of turtles would survive.

To inspire cultural change, Urteaga focused his message on young people. He launched a huge media campaign to reach this audience.

The campaign included sold-out rock concerts to raise awareness as well as celebrities stating, "I don't eat turtle eggs." His school programs teach children how important it is to protect the species. Children also have the opportunity to work with the hatcheries. In 2008, young people celebrated the first release of hatched baby turtles in their town's hatchery by wearing t-shirts showing a tiny turtle breaking out of its egg. Urteaga's goal is to end the demand for turtle eggs and save sea turtles from extinction by educating a new generation.

By 2010, thanks to Urteaga and his team, almost 90 percent of sea turtle nests became protected. Urteaga is committed to continue saving sea turtles by "motivat[ing] people through their brains and their hearts."

Before You Move On

Monitor Comprehension What actions are helping to change how people view Nicaragua's sea turtles?

Critical Viewing Baby sea turtles head to the sea. What difficulties might they meet along the way?

FORMATIVE ASSESSMENT

VIEWING LAB  GeoJournal

1. **Pose and Answer Questions** Write three questions about the efforts to save the sea turtles. Go to the **Digital Library** to watch the Explorer Video Clip. Then work with a partner to answer each other's questions.

2. **Analyze Visuals** What did you find to be the most powerful image in the video?

3. **Make Predictions** Urteaga's work has had a cultural and environmental impact. Predict future impacts from future scientific work. Describe economic changes that could result from scientific discoveries.

NATIONAL GEOGRAPHIC

Photo Gallery • Orange Cup Coral

For more photos from the National Geographic Photo Gallery, go to the **Digital Library** at myNGconnect.com.

Waterfall in Costa Rica

Satiny parrot snake

Vegetable market, Guatemala

⌄ Critical Viewing A cluster of orange cup coral clings to a support piling on Bonaire Island, West Indies. This type of coral catches its food with sticky tentacles, preying primarily on shrimp and small fish.

Bucket orchid

Musician with steel drum

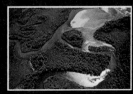
Coiba Island, Panama

Red-legged honeycreeper

2.1 **Trade Across Continents**

TECHTREK

myNGconnect.com For a trade map on global trade

 Maps and Graphs

> **Main Idea** European exploration of the Americas led to new trade routes among the world's continents.

Shortly after Columbus landed in the Caribbean in 1492, the Spanish began to make use of the region's rich resources. Their actions were the first steps toward global trade.

Farming for Profit

Spanish settlers in the Caribbean grew **cash crops**, or crops for profit. Land on the islands was well suited for growing certain raw materials that were in short supply in Europe. For example, sugarcane grew well on the islands, and could be sold in Europe where there was a **scarcity**, or shortage. Spanish settlers **exploited**, or took advantage of, the labor of the native people for the heavy work on their farms.

The native people were also weakened by sickness. They could not fight the diseases, like smallpox and malaria, that settlers brought with them from Europe. As large numbers of native people died from disease, Spanish settlers had to look elsewhere for the workers they needed to farm their cash crops. So, after minerals and raw materials arrived in Spain, manufactured goods went to Africa to pay for slaves, beginning more than 300 years of slavery in the Americas.

New Trade Changes the World

Beginning in the 1500s, goods were exchanged in what became known as **triangular trade**—trade among three continents: the Americas, Europe, and Africa. The new trade established economic patterns that continue today.

Visual Vocabulary A **cash crop** is a crop grown for profit. Tomatoes, native to the Americas, were an important cash crop for Caribbean farmers to sell to Europe.

TRIANGULAR TRADE

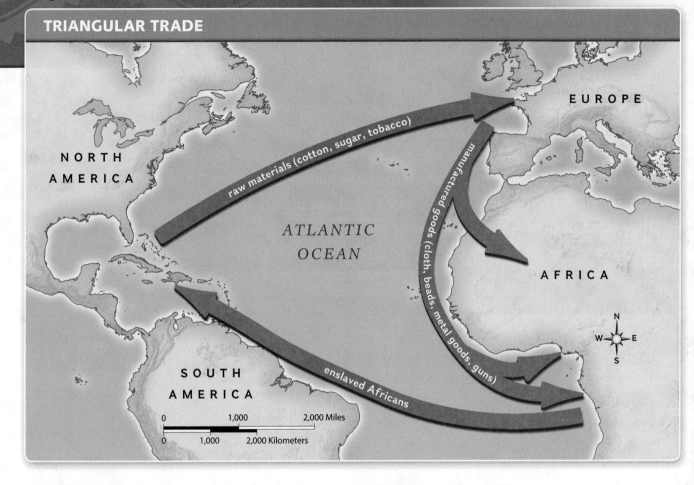

ATLANTIC OCEAN

NORTH AMERICA

EUROPE

AFRICA

SOUTH AMERICA

raw materials (cotton, sugar, tobacco)

manufactured goods (cloth, beads, metal goods, guns)

enslaved Africans

0   1,000   2,000 Miles

0   1,000   2,000 Kilometers

Triangular trade soon brought about competition among European countries for the resources of the region. Spain was gaining great wealth from its settlements in the Americas, causing other European countries to join the race for profit. Portugal, France, and Britain began competing with Spain for control over trade and colonization of the Americas.

Before You Move On

Monitor Comprehension In what ways did European exploration lead to new trade routes?

FORMATIVE ASSESSMENT

READING LAB   GeoJournal

1. **Summarize** Explain how Europe's scarcity of sugar led to international trade. What was the effect on people in the Caribbean?

2. **Make Inferences** What role did native people play in the Caribbean economy?

3. **Movement** Trace the pattern of the triangular trade from the Caribbean to Europe to Africa. Describe the pattern of the trade using directional words. Use the scale to estimate the distance from Africa to the Caribbean.

2.2 The Columbian Exchange

TECHTREK

myNGconnect.com For photos and Guided Writing.

📖 Student Resources 📨 Digital Library

Triangular trade between Europe, the Americas, and Africa brought about the exchange of plants, animals, and even diseases. This worldwide exchange has become known as the "**Columbian Exchange**," named for Christopher Columbus. The basic elements of everyday life—from what people ate to whether they lived or died—changed forever on several continents.

DOCUMENT 1

The diagram at right illustrates crops and diseases exchanged among continents.

CONSTRUCTED RESPONSE

1. Based on the diagram, which crops from Europe became important to the economy of the Caribbean? In which direction did disease travel in the **Columbian Exchange**?

The Columbian Exchange

DOCUMENT 2

Columbus's Journal

Columbus kept a journal detailing his arrival in the Caribbean in 1492. This excerpt describes the first trades made with Native Americans.

CONSTRUCTED RESPONSE

2. Explain what can be inferred from Columbus's statement "I was very attentive to them, and strove to learn if they had any gold."

Saturday, October 13, 1492

At daybreak great **multitudes** [numbers] of men came to the shore. . . loaded with balls of cotton, parrots, javelins, and other things. . . These they exchanged for whatever we chose to give them. I was very attentive to them, and strove [tried] to learn if they had any gold. . . [They] readily bartered [traded] for any article we saw fit to give them. . . such as broken platters and fragments of glass.

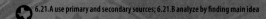
THEY CAME LOADED WITH BALLS OF COTTON, PARROTS, JAVELINS, AND OTHER THINGS. . . . THESE THEY EXCHANGED FOR WHATEVER WE CHOSE TO GIVE THEM.

— CHRISTOPHER COLUMBUS

Columbus and his crew arrive in the Caribbean.

DOCUMENT 3

The Historian's Viewpoint

Alfred Crosby is the historian who invented the phrase "Columbian Exchange." Below is an excerpt from an essay he wrote on the global impact of the Columbian Exchange.

What is the significance of the Columbian Exchange [?]. . . What is the staple [main food] of the Bantu of southern Africa? Maize [corn], an American food. What is the staple of Kansas and Argentina? Wheat, an Old World [European] food. . .

How many of the six billion of us are dependent for our nourishment on crops and meat animals that didn't cross the great oceans until after 1492?

CONSTRUCTED RESPONSE

3. What point is Alfred Crosby trying to make about the main foods of southern Africa, Kansas, and Argentina?

FORMATIVE ASSESSMENT

WRITING LAB  GeoJournal

DBQ Practice Look at the illustration, and reread the diary entry and the passage from Crosby's essay. What do these documents tell you about the Columbian Exchange?

Step 1. Review what you know about how trade developed between continents.

Step 2. Take notes about the main ideas in Documents 1, 2, and 3.

Document 1: Diagram of the Columbian Exchange

Main Idea(s) _____

Document 2: Quotation from Columbus

Main Idea(s) _____

Document 3: Excerpt from Alfred Crosby essay

Main Idea(s) _____

Step 3. Construct a topic sentence that answers this question: How did the Columbian Exchange change the world's food supply?

Step 4. Write a detailed paragraph that explains the effect of the Columbian Exchange on the food supply of Europe and the Americas. Go to **Student Resources** for Guided Writing support.

2.3 Paths Toward Independence

TECHTREK

myNGconnect.com For an online map of European colonies in the region

Maps and Graphs

Main Idea Ideas of freedom led to fights for independence in 19th-century Central America and the Caribbean.

The Columbian Exchange led to increased competition for global trade among European countries. By the 1780s, Europe had colonized nearly all of Central America and the Caribbean. Forced labor and other harsh practices used by European settlers stirred thoughts of independence among native groups, who wanted to regain control of their lands.

Haiti Leads the Way

In 1791, Haiti (then Saint-Domingue) had become the leading producer of sugarcane in the Caribbean. A small number of wealthy French colonists there used about a half million slaves. Their labor provided the backbone of this economy. As demand for sugar grew, more slaves were brought to Haiti from Africa. By 1791, slaves far outnumbered white planters.

Two years earlier, a revolution, or an overthrow of the government, had taken place in France. By August of 1791, the conflict spread to Haiti. As European planters, free people of color, and the English and French armies fought, Haitian slaves began a rebellion.

In 1794, the French government abolished slavery, but it kept control of the island. **Toussaint L'Ouverture** (too SAN loh ver CHOOR), a former slave, began a movement for independence. L'Ouverture's army struggled with the French for power until 1803, when he died in prison. Soon after his death, his army won victory over the French military. Haiti declared itself independent on January 1, 1804.

Calls for Freedom Spread

Spanish colonies in the Americas were ruled by Spanish **viceroys**—governors who represented the Spanish king and queen. Viceroys controlled the land's resources, such as gold, silver, and crops, and native labor. Most of the region fell under official control of the Spanish viceroy in Mexico City.

In 1821, Mexico seized control of much of present-day Central America. In 1823, it broke from Mexican control and became the United Provinces of Central America. **Provinces** are smaller parts of a larger nation. However, internal conflict renewed calls for independence. Over the next 20 years, each province—Guatemala, Honduras, El Salvador, Nicaragua, and Costa Rica—would declare independence.

INDEPENDENCE IN CENTRAL AMERICA AND THE CARIBBEAN

Toussaint L'Ouverture, leader of slave rebellion in Haiti

1820s–40s
Guatemala, Honduras, El Salvador, Nicaragua, Costa Rica, Dominican Republic

1800

1850

1804
Haiti

1823
Central America becomes United Provinces of Central America.

Juan Pablo Duarte, father of independence in the Dominican Republic

EUROPEAN COLONIAL CLAIMS

Legend:
- Viceroyalty of New Spain, c. 1700
- Viceroyalty of New Granada, c. 1700
- British territory
- Dutch territory
- French territory
- — Present-day boundary

Gulf of Mexico

ATLANTIC OCEAN

BAHAMAS

Tropic of Cancer

CUBA

20°N

MEXICO

BELIZE

JAMAICA

HAITI | DOMINICAN REPUBLIC

Puerto Rico

ANTIGUA AND BARBUDA (British)

Guadeloupe (French)

GUATEMALA | HONDURAS

ST. KITTS AND NEVIS (British)

DOMINICA (French)

Martinique (French)

EL SALVADOR

NICARAGUA

Caribbean Sea

ST. LUCIA (British)

BARBADOS (British)

GRENADA (French)

ST. VINCENT AND THE GRENADINES (French)

TRINIDAD AND TOBAGO (British)

PACIFIC OCEAN

10°N

COSTA RICA

PANAMA

0   300   600 Miles

0   300   600 Kilometers

100°W   90°W   80°W   70°W   60°W

Caribbean Independence

As you've learned, Haiti was the first Caribbean island to become independent. The United States and Europe wanted to keep control of the islands' many resources. As a result, most of the islands would not be independent until the 1900s.

In fact, several islands became independent as recently as the second half of the 20th century, as the time line shows. Today, some islands remain connected to the European countries that settled them. For example, Bermuda continues to be a British territory, and Aruba is still part of the Netherlands.

Before You Move On

Make Inferences How might the Spanish desire to control resources have brought about the fights for independence?

FORMATIVE ASSESSMENT

MAP LAB

GeoJournal

1. **Location** With your finger, trace the outline of the Viceroyalty of New Spain shown on the map. What present-day countries are included in this area?

2. **Interpret Maps** Find Panama on the map. Which viceroyalty did it belong to? Why do you think Panama could be considered more like South America than Central America?

3. **Make Inferences** What fact about Toussaint L'Ouverture might explain his commitment to gaining independence for slaves in Haiti?

4. **Interpret Time Lines** Between which years was there the biggest gap in Central American and Caribbean countries declaring independence?

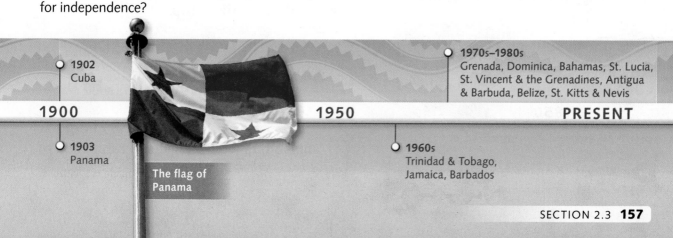

1902 Cuba

1970s–1980s
Grenada, Dominica, Bahamas, St. Lucia, St. Vincent & the Grenadines, Antigua & Barbuda, Belize, St. Kitts & Nevis

1900   1950   PRESENT

1903 Panama

1960s
Trinidad & Tobago, Jamaica, Barbados

The flag of Panama

2.4 Comparing Cuba and Puerto Rico

TECHTREK

myNGconnect.com For resource
maps and photos of Cuba and Puerto Rico

Maps and Graphs   Digital Library

Main Idea Cuba and Puerto Rico took very different economic paths in the 20th century.

In a quest for silver, gold, and other riches, Spain settled the Caribbean islands of Cuba and Puerto Rico as colonies. The islands had ideal conditions for growing sugarcane, and both had good natural **harbors**, or places where ships could land protected from the open sea.

Cuba's Path to the 21st Century

Spain ruled Cuba as a colony from 1511 to 1898. The Spanish built the city of Havana, where European ships carrying cargo such as silver and corn stopped before crossing the Atlantic. Spanish colonists also built sugarcane plantations.

However, native Cubans wanted to control their own resources and political destiny. During the 1800s, they staged several failed rebellions. They finally won independence from Spain in 1898, after the United States defeated Spain in the Spanish-American War. The U.S. military continued to occupy Cuba and control much of the country's economy. Over the next 50 years, Cuba's government was controlled by a series of leaders. Many of them were corrupt, or dishonest, and led with complete control as **dictators**.

In 1959, a revolutionary leader named Fidel Castro overthrew Cuba's dictator. Castro's military took control of the government, seized all land and personal property, and established communism in Cuba. Castro took over U.S.-owned businesses and built ties with the Soviet Union, an enemy of the United States. The United States eventually cut economic and political ties with Cuba.

Until the early 1990s, the government in Cuba controlled all economic activity. In 1993, to improve Cuba's economy, the government started to allow citizens to open their own businesses.

Commonwealth of Puerto Rico

Like Cuba, Puerto Rico was a Spanish colony from the 1500s until 1898. During this time the Spanish mined gold and built huge sugarcane plantations. Spanish control made most native Puerto Ricans poor, so they tried to rebel against Spain.

During the Spanish-American War, the United States sent troops to Puerto Rico. The island's location was important to U.S. military and economic interests. After Spain surrendered to the United States in 1898, the Treaty of Paris made the island a U.S. territory. In 1917, Puerto Ricans were granted U.S. citizenship.

CUBA

PUERTO RICO

1850

1898 Treaty of Paris grants Cuban independence; U.S. continues to occupy.

1898 Treaty of Paris grants control of Puerto Rico from Spain to U.S.

1900

1901 U.S sets up naval base at Guantánamo Bay, Cuba.

1917 Puerto Ricans are made U.S. citizens.

CUBA'S ECONOMIC RESOURCES

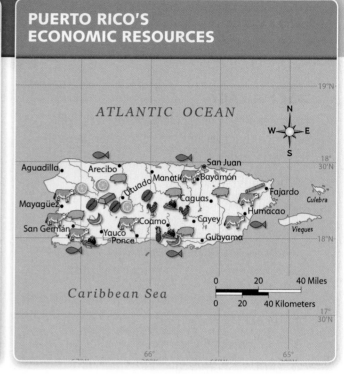

Economic products and resources

Bananas — Fish — Sugarcane
Cattle — Pineapples — Swine
Citrus fruit — Potatoes — Tobacco
Coffee — Poultry — Vegetables
Copper — Rice

PUERTO RICO'S ECONOMIC RESOURCES

For many years, Puerto Ricans worked for more freedom from the United States. In 1952, Puerto Rico became a U.S. **commonwealth**, a nation that governs itself but is part of a larger country.

Unlike Cubans, Puerto Ricans have political freedom. Like the United States, Puerto Rico benefits from a free-enterprise economy. The government has done what it can to help Puerto Ricans start new businesses, and shift the economy away from farming toward manufacturing. Thousands of Puerto Ricans work in factories that make high-tech products. Many also work in the tourist industry.

Before You Move On

Summarize How did differences in the governments of Cuba and Puerto Rico affect economic opportunities in the two countries?

FORMATIVE ASSESSMENT

MAP LAB
GeoJournal

1. **Interpret Maps** Which resource is most of the land used for in Cuba? in Puerto Rico?

2. **Region** Look at the climate map in Section 1.1 and the maps above. Why would the economic resources be similar in both countries?

3. **Make Inferences** Why would the United States have wanted control over Cuba and Puerto Rico after the Spanish-American War?

4. **Interpret Time Lines** Which events show each country's connection to the United States?

Fidel Castro

1925
Communist Party of Cuba is formed.

1959
Castro seizes power; Cuba becomes a Communist country.

Sila Calderón

1950

PRESENT

1920s
Nationalist Party in Puerto Rico argues for Independence from United States.

1952
Puerto Rico becomes U.S. Commonwealth.

2000
Puerto Rico elects its first woman govenor, Sila Calderón.

VOCABULARY

For each pair of vocabulary words, write one sentence that explains the connection between the two words.

1. isthmus; archipelago

> An isthmus is one strip of land connected to two larger land areas, but an archipelago is a group of islands.

2. seismic; tectonic plate
3. rain forest; ecosystem
4. deforestation; fertile
5. cash crops; scarcity
6. province; viceroy
7. harbor; commonwealth

MAIN IDEAS

8. What feature of Central America makes the soil fertile? (Section 1.1)
9. How do earthquakes and volcanoes affect Central America and the Caribbean? (Section 1.2)
10. What are some causes of rain forest deforestation? (Section 1.3)
11. In what way will creating new jobs help save Nicaragua's sea turtles? (Section 1.4)
12. How did Columbus's landing in the Caribbean lead to international trade? (Section 2.1)
13. How did the Columbian Exchange affect the Europeans and the native peoples of the Caribbean? (Section 2.2)
14. What actions by the Spanish led Central American and Caribbean countries to seek independence? (Section 2.3)
15. How did the economies of Cuba and Puerto Rico develop after independence from Spain? (Section 2.4)

GEOGRAPHY

ANALYZE THE ESSENTIAL QUESTION

How has physical geography been a positive or negative influence on the economy of the region?

Critical Thinking: Compare and Contrast

16. What physical features do Central America and the Caribbean have in common?
17. What is similar about how the Central American and the Caribbean land masses were created?
18. What is the difference in climate in the mountains and coastal plains? How does this difference affect farming?

INTERPRET MAPS

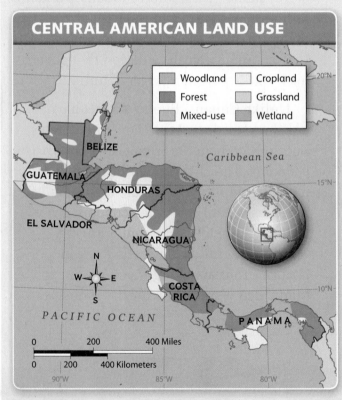

CENTRAL AMERICAN LAND USE

Woodland · Cropland · Forest · Grassland · Mixed-use · Wetland

19. **Interpret Maps** How is most land used in Central America?
20. **Draw Conclusions** Locate the wetland areas on the map. What conclusion can you draw about where wetlands are located in Central America?

HISTORY

ANALYZE THE ESSENTIAL QUESTION

How have economic resources influenced the history of the region?

Critical Thinking: Analyze Cause and Effect

21. How did volcanoes contribute to the success of farming in the region?

22. What did the Spanish hope to gain through control of the region?

23. What effect did outside control of Caribbean islands have on their independence?

24. What political effect did Fidel Castro and his military have on Cuba?

25. Why has manufacturing become a greater part of Puerto Rico's economy than agriculture?

INTERPRET CHARTS

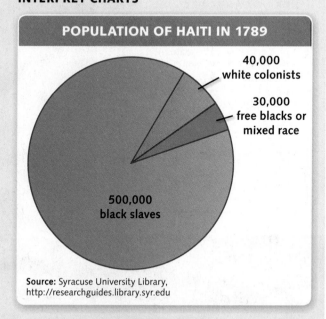

POPULATION OF HAITI IN 1789

40,000 white colonists

30,000 free blacks or mixed race

500,000 black slaves

Source: Syracuse University Library, http://researchguides.library.syr.edu

26. **Analyze Data** How many more black slaves were there than white colonists in Haiti in 1789?

27. **Make Inferences** How does the racial makeup of the population in Haiti in 1789 help to explain why a rebellion started?

ACTIVE OPTIONS

Synthesize the Essential Questions by completing the activities below.

28. **Create a Three-Point Speech** In a small group, discuss Cuba's economic record as a non-free-market system and the benefits of free enterprise for Puerto Rico. Look up the meanings of *morality* and *ethics*. Then talk about the conduct needed to keep a free-enterprise system working well, including the importance of competition, and the importance of fairness and keeping agreements. Summarize your ideas into three points. **Present them orally to the class.**

> **Teamwork Tips**
> - Listen closely to others' ideas and take notes. Ask for clarification, if you need it.
> - Share your own ideas about the two countries. Answer others' questions.
> - Work together to summarize ideas into points. Agree on three.

29. **Create a Chart** Make a chart showing comparisons among three countries in the region. Be sure one of your countries is in Central America and one is in the Caribbean. Use online sources to gather data on economic resources and current leaders. Combine your charts to create a class database for the region. Then conduct a geography panel to interpret the data, taking turns to pose and answer questions.

	(Central American country)	(Caribbean country)	(Your choice)
Population			
Square Miles of Land			

CHAPTER 6

Central America & the Caribbean TODAY

PREVIEW THE CHAPTER

Essential Question How do trade and globalization affect the cultures of the region today?

SECTION 1 • CULTURE

KEY VOCABULARY

- tourism
- intersection
- fuse
- canal
- terrain
- lock

ACADEMIC VOCABULARY

distinct, eliminate

TERMS & NAMES

- Taino
- Calypso
- Panama Canal Zone

Essential Question How is the region trying to improve the standard of living?

SECTION 2 • GOVERNMENT & ECONOMICS

KEY VOCABULARY

- infrastructure
- reserve
- policy
- marketing
- standard of living
- food security
- global warming
- malnutrition
- surplus
- migrate
- remittance
- habitat
- ecotourism

ACADEMIC VOCABULARY

displace

TERMS & NAMES

- Human Development Index
- Port-au-Prince

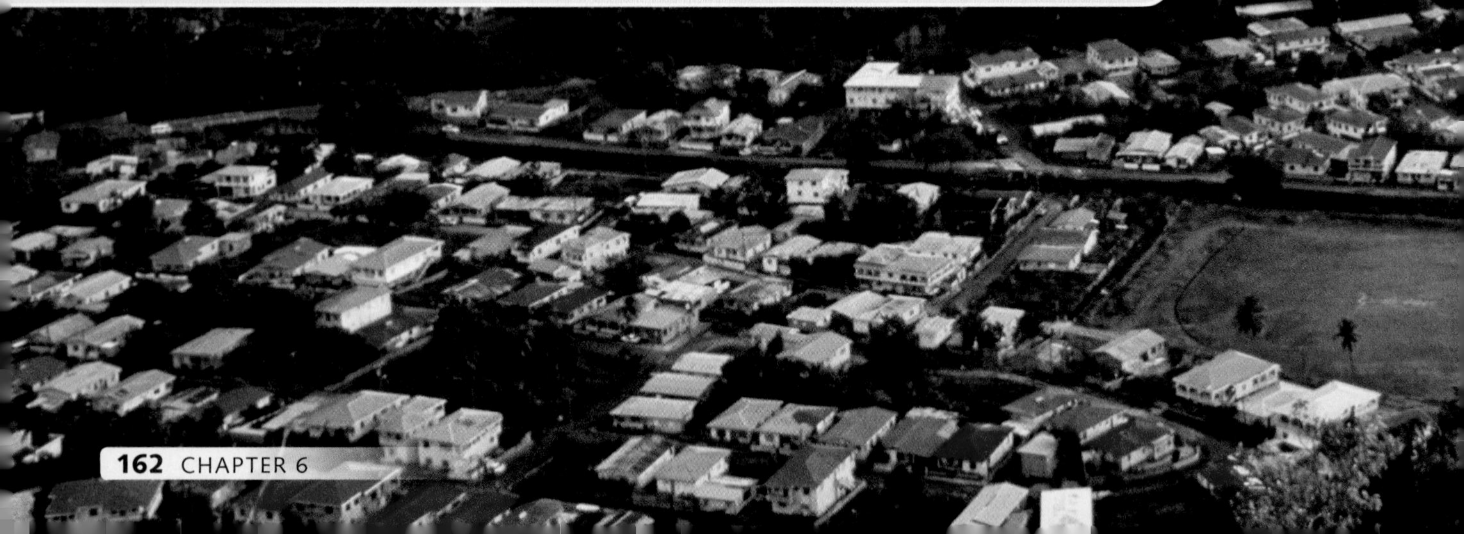

TECHTREK FOR THIS CHAPTER

Student eEdition

Maps and Graphs

Interactive Whiteboard GeoActivities

Digital Library

Go to **myNGconnect.com** for more on Central America and the Caribbean.

Agriculture and tourism drive the economy in Souffriere, a small town on the island of St. Lucia in the Caribbean Sea.

1.1 The Impact of Tourism

TECHTREK

myNGconnect.com For a chart and photos of of tourism in the region

Student Resources

Digital Library

Main Idea Tourists who visit Central America and the Caribbean have a major effect on income and resources of the region.

Tourism, or the business of travel, is an important source of income for Central America and the Caribbean. However, with more than 20 million tourists each year, the environment can be damaged.

Diversity Attracts People

For centuries, this region has been an **intersection** of cultures, a meeting point for traders and settlers from many countries. Rich resources attracted European groups, including the English, French, and Dutch. The slave trade brought African culture to the region. The blend of cultures is part of the region's appeal.

Since the 1980s, global air travel and advertising have made tourism an important industry. Visitors usually stay in one of the many island resorts, or on cruise ships that sail around the islands. This "overnight tourism," though, can have long-term negative effects.

Efforts to Improve

Overnight tourists use a great deal of electricity and consume vast amounts of water and food. This causes shortages for the local people. Large resorts and cruise ships release pollution into the air and water, which threatens marine life.

Organizations such as the United Nations seek to increase environmental protections. However, because the tourism industry is such a large part of the region's economy, local governments are sometimes resistant to new limitations. Many travelers and businesses are making efforts to offset the damage.

Cruise lines are beginning to use recyclable materials and conserve fuel in an effort to continue business without further harming the environment. Some travelers even contribute to programs that plant trees in the region.

Before You Move On

Monitor Comprehension In what ways does tourism affect the region's income and resources?

> **Critical Viewing** These pyramids in Guatemala are temples where ancient Mayans worshipped. What aspects of these ruins might make them appealing to tourists?

TOURISM IN CENTRAL AMERICA AND THE CARIBBEAN

Country	International Tourist Arrivals* (number of people)	Receipts from Tourism ** (US $billions)	Percentage of Total Receipts from Tourism ** (percent)
Bahamas	5,003,967	$2.2	64.6
Barbados	1,272,772	$1.2	56.6
Belize	1,082,268	$0.3	35.0
Dominican Republic	4,239,686	$4.0	34.0
El Salvador	966,416	$0.8	20.9
Guatemala	1,181,526	$1.1	12.1
Honduras	1,056,642	$0.6	8.5
Nicaragua	734,971	$0.3	9.4
Panama	1,004,207	$1.2	12.6
St. Lucia	802,240	$0.3	66.0

* Source: Association of Caribbean States
** Source: World Bank Online

This adventure tour in Martinique is led by local guides.

FORMATIVE ASSESSMENT

DATA LAB   GeoJournal

1. **Interpret Charts** Which country in the region received the most money from tourism? Which ones received the least?

2. **Analyze Data** Which country depends most on money received from tourism?

3. **Identify Solutions** What can travelers and the tourism industry do to cause less harm to the environment in this region?

1.2 Caribbean Food and Music

TECHTREK

myNGconnect.com For a music
clip and photos and Guided Writing

 Digital
Library

📖 Student
Resources

> **Main Idea** Caribbean food and music blend influences from indigenous cultures and other world cultures.

Worldwide trade and global communication have spread Caribbean culture traits to the world. At the same time, other cultures continue to influence the food and music in the region.

Caribbean Food

Since the Columbian Exchange, new influences continued to add to the region's diet. Foods from the native **Taino** (TY noh) and from Europe, Africa, and Asia have **fused**, or blended, into a rich cooking tradition.

The basic foods in the Greater Antilles include rice, beans, yams, peppers, plantains (similar to bananas), and avocados. Poultry and fish are also local foods. Caribbean cooks use blends of spices to flavor their foods. For example, Jamaican jerk is a **distinct**, or easily recognized, blend of strong spices used for grilling meat. Freed African slaves living in the Jamaican mountains developed the spice blend in order to preserve meat. Today, many Jamaican families follow the tradition of sharing a large lunch on Sundays. Foods served might include jerk chicken, fish, fried plantains, and a popular dish of rice and black-eyed peas.

In the past, islanders ate healthy diets based on fruits and vegetables, mixed with meat or fish. When open trade was firmly established in the 1990s, fast food restaurants arrived in the region, adding modern foods to the islanders' diet.

This pepper shrimp is a very spicy dish popular in Jamaica.

Caribbean Music

Native cultures used wind instruments and drums in their music. European colonists brought stringed instruments to the islands. Island cultures blended European and African instruments and rhythms to make their own musical styles.

Calypso began on the island of Trinidad as a type of folk music. It uses simple rhythms and local language to tell stories. *Soca*, developed in the 1970s, is a mixture of calypso and East Indian music. Popular Afro-Cuban styles made it to New York in the 1940s, where they combined with jazz to create *salsa*. Some other well-known Caribbean styles are Dominican Republic *merengue* (meh RENG gay) and Jamaican *ska* and *reggae* (REG ay).

Before You Move On

Monitor Comprehension What foods and styles of music have blended to become part of culture in the Caribbean Islands?

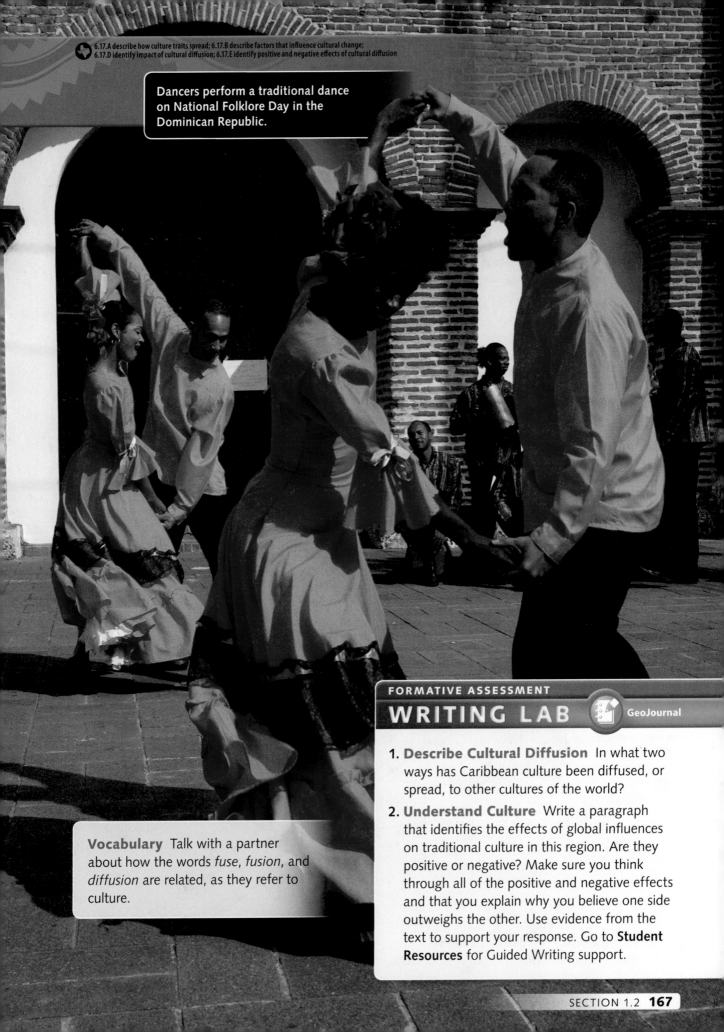

Dancers perform a traditional dance on National Folklore Day in the Dominican Republic.

Vocabulary Talk with a partner about how the words *fuse*, *fusion*, and *diffusion* are related, as they refer to culture.

FORMATIVE ASSESSMENT

WRITING LAB · GeoJournal

1. **Describe Cultural Diffusion** In what two ways has Caribbean culture been diffused, or spread, to other cultures of the world?

2. **Understand Culture** Write a paragraph that identifies the effects of global influences on traditional culture in this region. Are they positive or negative? Make sure you think through all of the positive and negative effects and that you explain why you believe one side outweighs the other. Use evidence from the text to support your response. Go to **Student Resources** for Guided Writing support.

1.3 The Panama Canal

TECHTREK

myNGconnect.com For photos
and an illustration of the Panama Canal

Digital
Library

Student
Resources

Main Idea The Panama Canal provides a water route connecting the Atlantic and Pacific oceans.

As early as the 1500s, Spanish explorers wanted to create an artificial water route, or **canal**, through the Central American isthmus. A canal would significantly reduce the time it took for ships to travel from Europe to the Pacific.

Connecting Two Oceans

Trade routes from the Atlantic to the Pacific required a difficult journey across land or a long water passage around the tip of South America. In 1855, the United States completed the first railroad across Panama. Goods and people could now travel across the isthmus by rail. However, the idea for a canal remained.

Building the Canal

Panama declared independence from Colombia in 1903. Then the government signed a treaty that gave the United States control of the **Panama Canal Zone**, the area where the canal would be built.

Many obstacles had to be overcome in building the canal. To try to keep builders healthy, doctors worked to **eliminate**, or get rid of, mosquitoes that caused serious diseases. The **terrain**, or physical land features, of Panama also posed challenges. As many as 40,000 workers at a time made plans, cleared brush, drained swamps, and drilled through rocks. The canal took 100 steam engines and 10 years to finish, from 1904 to 1914—and more than 20,000 workers died in the process.

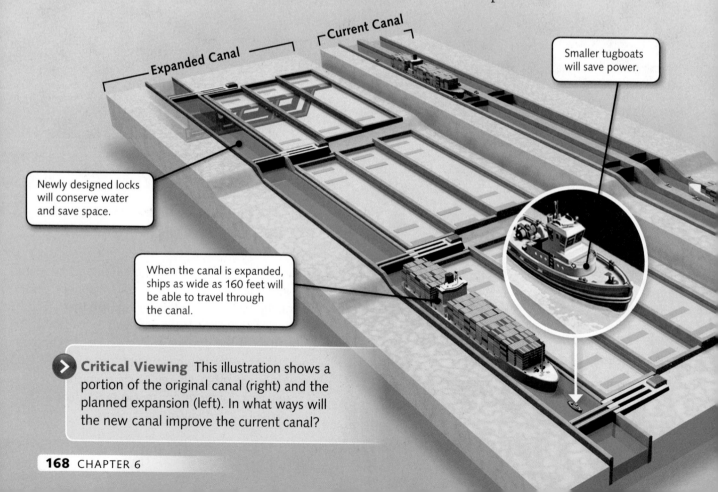

Expanded Canal

Current Canal

Smaller tugboats will save power.

Newly designed locks will conserve water and save space.

When the canal is expanded, ships as wide as 160 feet will be able to travel through the canal.

> **Critical Viewing** This illustration shows a portion of the original canal (right) and the planned expansion (left). In what ways will the new canal improve the current canal?

PANAMA CANAL MILESTONES

1855 The United States completes a railroad across Panama.

1881 A French company attempts to build a canal across Panama.

1889 The French company's plan for a canal collapses.

1903 Panama declares independence from Colombia; canal rights are granted to the United States.

1914 The Panama Canal is opened to water traffic.

1977 Treaty with the United States grants ownership of the Canal Zone to Panama.

1999 Panama is granted complete control of the canal.

2015 Expansion of the canal is scheduled for completion.

PANAMA CANAL

Visual Vocabulary **Locks** are devices that help to equalize the water levels of the waterways being connected. These locks in the Panama Canal are the first step down to the Pacific Ocean.

Canal Connects the World

The Panama Canal's slogan, "The Land Divided, the World United," reflects the importance of this water passage. Before its completion, a ship traveling from New York to San Francisco had to travel 14,000 miles. The canal's 51-mile length shortened the travel distance by almost half, to approximately 6,000 miles.

As technologies advanced, larger ships were built. In 2006, Panama voted to expand the canal so it could accommodate these ships and the increased trade that caused traffic jams. The project is scheduled for completion in 2015.

Before You Move On

Make Inferences What made building a water route connecting the Atlantic to the Pacific important?

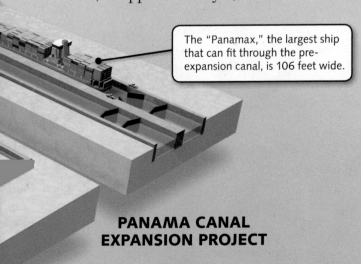

The "Panamax," the largest ship that can fit through the pre-expansion canal, is 106 feet wide.

PANAMA CANAL EXPANSION PROJECT

FORMATIVE ASSESSMENT

VIEWING LAB GeoJournal

1. **Location** Look at the locator map above that shows the position of the Panama Canal. Why do you think builders picked that spot instead of a different one?

2. **Analyze Visuals** Based on the illustration, how will the expansion of the Panama Canal save money?

3. **Summarize** Based on the milestones, how long did the United States control the canal?

2.1 Comparing Costa Rica and Nicaragua

Main Idea Costa Rica and Nicaragua both work to build a more stable economy, despite different political conditions.

During the 20th century, Costa Rica and Nicaragua (nik uh RAHG wah) had very different histories. As a result, Costa Rica became a strong and stable democracy, while Nicaragua became the poorest country in Central America.

Different Political Paths

Costa Rica has enjoyed peace for over 60 years. In fact, since 1949 the country has never had an army. Costa Rica's capital city of San José is home to several global human rights organizations. Without political conflict to interfere, Costa Rica has had the opportunity to create a stable economy. Tourism is the country's greatest source of income. This industry provides jobs to more than 50 percent of the working population.

Unlike Costa Rica, Nicaragua has had an unstable government since its independence from Spain in 1821. This instability included dictatorships and civil wars that lasted through the 1990s. In addition, the country was hit by a major hurricane in 1998. It destroyed Nicaragua's **infrastructure**, the basic systems a society needs, such as roads, bridges, and electricity. Thousands were left without homes, jobs, or medical care.

Unstable conditions make the fight against poverty more difficult. Nicaragua entered the 21st century facing challenges. It needed to build its economy and develop social programs to help poor people, who make up about a fourth of the population.

> **Visual Vocabulary** A **reserve** is land set aside for farming. Members of the Miraflor Nature Reserve in Nicaragua can set up farms on the land there.

6.01.B analyze historical background, past conflicts and current conditions; 6.03.C compare countries using data from charts; 6.05.C explain impact of geographic factors on economic development, domestic, foreign policies; 6.08.A describe ways factors of production influence societies; 6.09.A compare ways countries organize production and distribution; 6.10.B describe levels of economic development using indicators

COMPARING ECONOMIC DEVELOPMENT INDICATORS

	Costa Rica	Nicaragua
Life Expectancy at Birth	79 years	74 years
Adult Literacy Rate aged 15 and above	94.9%	67.5%
Per Capita Income (U.S. Dollars)	$7,640	$1,510
Population Below the Poverty Line	24.8%	42%

Source: CIA World Factbook, World Bank; 2011, 2012 (est.)

Economic Challenges

Costa Rica's economy has grown over the past 20 years. However, the poverty rate has remained between 15 and 20 percent. Changes in government **policy**—official guidelines and procedures—might account for this lack of improvement.

In the 1980s, after years of heavy spending and borrowing, the country was running out of money. Over the next decades, various policies were enacted to address this economic crisis. The government restricted its spending and raised taxes. Funding was reduced for social programs, many of which were created to help poor people. In 2007, in an effort to bring about economic growth, Costa Rica joined other Central American countries in a free trade agreement with the United States. The agreement went into effect in Costa Rica in 2009.

Nicaragua joined the same free trade agreement. In 2012, the Nicaraguan economy grew by 4%, just behind Costa Rica's. However, rural poverty in Nicaragua is still a problem. Rural businesses have used **marketing** to promote their products, and new roads have helped for transporting goods. Yet many Nicaraguans continue to migrate to Costa Rica for seasonal work, such as for the coffee and banana harvests.

Before You Move On

Summarize In what ways have both countries built a more stable economy?

FORMATIVE ASSESSMENT

DATA LAB GeoJournal

1. **Analyze Data** Study the chart. Complete this sentence: As the literacy rate increases, the poverty rate _____.

2. **Place** Based on the chart, which country seems to have a better standard of living, or quality of life? How can you tell?

3. **Compare and Contrast** Write a paragraph to describe levels of economic development for each country, as well as the political and geographic factors that have influenced each economy. Include domestic or foreign policies.

2.2 **Challenges in Haiti**

Main Idea Haiti faces many great challenges in its efforts to build a strong economy and decrease poverty.

In the 1700s, the French colony of Saint-Domingue (san do MANG yuh), which is today's Haiti, was the richest in the Caribbean. Today, Haiti is the poorest country in the Western Hemisphere with 80 percent of its people living in poverty.

Poverty's Historical Roots

Haiti gained independence from France in 1804. Because most of Haiti's citizens had been slaves, they did not have any money or means of income. European nations feared slave revolts in their colonies in the Caribbean, and so did not support Haiti financially when it became an independent nation. In the 20th century, political conflict and outbreaks of disease kept tourists away, making it difficult for Haiti to grow economically.

> **Critical Viewing** Members of a Chinese emergency rescue team work in Port-au-Prince two days after the 2010 earthquake. Based on the photo, how might past building practices have contributed to the extent of the devastation?

21st Century Haiti

The **Human Development Index** (HDI) is used by geographers to compare quality of life in different countries. HDI combines measures of the health, education, and **standard of living**—the level of goods, services, and material comforts—of people in a country. People in countries with a low HDI, such as Haiti, are often less healthy, less educated, and poorer than people in countries with a high HDI, such as the United States.

Politics in 21st century Haiti have been marked by instability and corruption. Due to violence between political groups, U.S. forces were sent in 2004 to Haiti's capital city, **Port-au-Prince**, to maintain security. Over the next few years, further efforts toward peace in Haiti were unsuccessful.

Adding to Haiti's challenges, a massive earthquake struck in January of 2010. Port-au-Prince and the surrounding area were nearly destroyed. Over 1.5 million people were **displaced**, or forced from their homes. Damage to the airport and to seaports made it difficult to receive immediate help from other countries.

As Haiti tried to recover, organizations from around the world began donating money and supplies such as food and medicine. Some countries also sent emergency rescue workers. Many nations and global organizations excused Haiti from paying back billions of dollars in loans, so they could rebuild at home.

Before You Move On

Summarize What factors contribute to the difficulties Haiti faces in overcoming poverty?

RESPONDING TO THE EARTHQUAKE

1.5 million
Number of Haitians displaced from their homes and living in temporary housing after the earthquake

28,000
Number of displaced Haitians that had moved into new homes six months after the earthquake

1,340
Number of tent cities and camps still being used six months after the earthquake

Source: 2010 United Press International

The day after the earthquake, Haitians set up this tent city amid the rubble. In this aerial photo, the colorful squares in the center are the roofs of tents used as temporary shelters.

FORMATIVE ASSESSMENT
DATA LAB GeoJournal

1. **Analyze Data** How many displaced Haitians were in new homes six months after the earthquake? How many were still homeless?

2. **Make Inferences** What factors might explain this difference in numbers?

3. **Draw Conclusions** What do the photos show about how Haitians and the international community responded after the earthquake?

2.3 Feeding Central America

TECHTREK

myNGconnect.com For photos on food security in Central America

 Digital Library

 Global Issues

Main Idea Food supply in Central America is affected by natural disasters and human activities.

Food security, or easy access to enough food, is an important issue around the world. Understanding the causes of shortages can help local governments and global organizations take the right steps toward improving food security in Central America.

Impact on Food Supply

Natural disasters have a major impact on the food supply. Many countries struck by Hurricane Mitch in 1998—El Salvador, Guatemala, Honduras, and Nicaragua—barely had time to recover before major flooding hit Central America in 2008. Disasters can destroy a country's major crops, such as bananas in Honduras. The 2010 earthquake in Haiti made it difficult for Haitians to gain access to nutritious meals and safe water.

In some countries, such as Guatemala and Nicaragua, the rainy season doesn't always provide enough water for the crops that make up the food supply. Even one dry season can greatly reduce food production.

Human activity can also threaten the food supply. Many countries have not managed their natural resources well. Lack of water for irrigation, declining soil quality from growing the same crop year after year, and deforestation all have led to food shortages.

Today, climate change adds a new threat to the food supply. Climate scientists predict that **global warming** will cause more extreme weather patterns, leading to flooding in some areas and drought in others. Many Central Americans survive mainly on corn and beans, but drought has dried up these crops in many areas.

Before You Move On

Summarize How do nature and human activities affect the food supply in Central America?

KEY VOCABULARY

food security, n., easy access to enough food

global warming, n., an increase in temperature around the world

malnutrition, n., a lack of healthy food in the diet, which leads to physical harm

surplus, n., amount beyond what is needed

SOME MAJOR CROPS IN SELECTED CENTRAL AMERICAN COUNTRIES

EL SALVADOR

GUATEMALA

HAITI

HONDURAS

NICARAGUA

- eggs
- beans
- maize
- bananas
- avocados
- mangoes
- plantains
- oranges
- rice
- nuts

Fresh mangoes from Haiti

6.03.C compare countries using data from graphs; 6.05.A identify geographic factors for economic activities;
6.06.C analyze effects of physical processes on humans; 6.08.C explain impact of scarcity of resources;
6.23.A identify a problem, evaluate solution

Inspiring people to care about the planet
National Geographic Society Mission

Childhood Hunger

Childhood **malnutrition**, or the lack of healthy food in the diet, is one of the most serious effects of food shortages in Central America. In some countries, many pregnant women do not get the nutrition they need. As a result, some babies are very small at birth. Poor nutrition continues throughout childhood and can slow down a child's healthy growth.

In Guatemala, 23 percent of children under five are underweight and almost half are small for their age because they don't get proper nutrients in their diet. Many poor families spend their whole day trying to grow or buy enough food to get to the next day. There is no time to tend to health issues or for children to go to school. In these conditions, cycles of malnutrition are difficult to break.

Solutions For the Future

Most experts believe that the best way to improve food security in Central America is to increase each country's own crop production. Growth in agriculture means larger food supplies and lower food prices. It can also mean higher incomes for farmers both large and small.

Land quality is a determining factor in a country's ability to increase crop production. Honduras and Guatemala have large areas of good quality land for farming. In most years, much of Guatemala and the coastal areas of Nicaragua and Honduras typically experience enough rainfall for their crops to thrive.

Areas with low amounts of quality soil or inadequate rainfall, such as El Salvador and southern Honduras, benefit from programs that provide fertilizer and irrigation methods to help rural farmers.

Education is another way to improve food security in Central America. The United Nations recommends rural people be educated in productive farming methods. Programs have been designed to teach rural farmers in Central America how to keep soil healthy, and how to grow crops and sell the **surplus**, or extra.

In emergency situations such as the earthquake in Haiti, a country can benefit from the aid of foreign countries. However, when a poor country can improve its food supply by learning how to increase its own crop production, it can achieve long-term food security without outside aid.

Before You Move On

Make Inferences How does education provide a long-term solution to the problem of food security in Central America?

FORMATIVE ASSESSMENT
READING LAB GeoJournal

1. **Location** What geographic features and conditions of Central America contribute to food shortages in the region?

2. **Summarize** Why is it hard for a poor family to break out of the cycle of malnutrition?

3. **Turn and Talk** What kinds of programs would help improve food security in one country in the region? Turn to a classmate and use information from the lesson to develop some specific ideas.

2.4 Migration and the Caribbean

TECHTREK

myNGconnect.com For photos and a
graphic of migration and the Caribbean

Digital
Library

Main Idea Many Caribbean people migrate
to other countries to find economic opportunites
and help support their familes back home.

People **migrate**, or move from one place
to another, because of push-pull factors.
Push factors make people move away from
an area because of difficulties like war
or drought. Pull factors draw people to a
place because it offers more security and
better job opportunities.

Migration Within the Caribbean

Today, it is hard to make a living on
many Caribbean islands. The collapse
of major businesses, including the sugar
industry, has pushed workers out of rural
areas into cities to find work. As a result
of this internal migration, or migration
within a country or region, two-thirds of
the population now lives in cities such as
Santo Domingo in the Dominican Republic
or San Juan, Puerto Rico.

Many of these cities have become
overcrowded. Urban unemployment is
high in the Caribbean. Migrants seeking
better jobs and a higher standard of living
have been forced to travel to other islands
within the Caribbean region.

By the 1990s, the tourism industry had
expanded dramatically across the region.
The demand for workers pulled many
people to islands with large or growing
tourist industries, such as Aruba, the
Bahamas, and the Virgin Islands.

Migration Out of the Caribbean

At the same time, push-pull factors played
a part in workers leaving to go the United
States, Canada, Europe, and other places.
For example, political conflict in Cuba
and Haiti pushed people to migrate to
the United States.

Critical Viewing Santo Domingo in the Dominican Republic,
the oldest city founded by Europeans in the Western Hemisphere,
has a growing population. Based on the photo, what economic
opportunities might exist in Santo Domingo?

Remittances

Most migrants who find work in another country send money back to their families in the form of **remittances**, money sent to a person in another place. Remittances have become a significant part of the economy of some Caribbean countries. For example, Jamaica receives more than $79 million each year in official aid, or money from other governments or organizations. However, the island receives 27 times that figure (see chart at right) in remittances. These remittances are sent from relatives in other countries, such as the United States, Canada, and France.

Before You Move On

Summarize How are people who migrate out of the Caribbean able to help support their families back home?

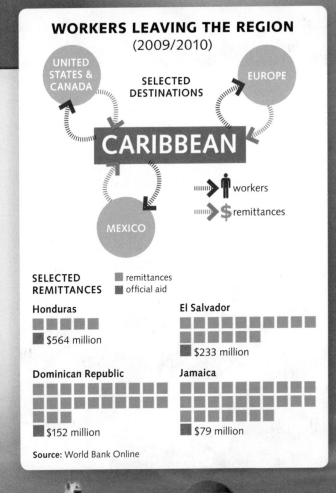

WORKERS LEAVING THE REGION
(2009/2010)

UNITED STATES & CANADA — EUROPE

SELECTED DESTINATIONS

CARIBBEAN

MEXICO

workers
remittances

SELECTED REMITTANCES

remittances
official aid

Honduras
$564 million

El Salvador
$233 million

Dominican Republic
$152 million

Jamaica
$79 million

Source: World Bank Online

FORMATIVE ASSESSMENT

DATA LAB

 GeoJournal

1. **Analyze Visuals** Based on the graphic, what leaves the Caribbean? What comes back in?

2. **Analyze Data** What brings more money into countries in this region, official aid or remittances? How does the graphic show this?

3. **Movement** Explain ways in which migration has influenced the region. Use *remittance* in your response and be sure its meaning is clear and correct.

2.5 Conserving the Rain Forest

TECHTREK

myNGconnect.com For photos of
ecotourism in Central America and the Caribbean

Digital
Library

Main Idea Ecotourism provides a new opportunity for this region to protect rain forest habitats and fight poverty.

The rain forests and other natural resources of Central America and the Caribbean are a draw for large numbers of travelers every year. Tourism, however, can damage or even permanently destroy these valuable resources.

Rain Forest Habitats

A rain forest is an important animal **habitat**, a natural home or environment for certain species. Plants in the rain forest provide nourishment for the animal population and replenish the air with oxygen. Some animal and plant species in the rain forest are not known to exist anywhere else.

The features of the rain forest that attract visitors are the very same features that are threatened by excessive tourism. If a species loses its habitat, or the habitat is altered in any way, that species may face extinction. Conserving the resources of the rain forest is an important step towards protecting species that live there.

quetzal

three-toed sloth

Visual Vocabulary A **habitat** is a place where certain species have what they need to live. The rain forest canopy is an important animal habitat.

Rain Forest Ecotourism

Ecotourism is a way of visiting natural areas that conserves the resources of the region. The purpose of ecotourism is to allow a visitor to experience an environment in its most natural form. A rain forest ecotourist might explore from the ground on a guided hike or a birdwatching tour. Another ecotourist might explore from above by taking a tour of the rain forest canopy, home to a great variety of animal species.

This method of travel not only protects plants and animals of the rain forest, but also improves the lives of the local people. Ecotourism helps stop deforestation and soil destruction by providing alternative jobs to poor farmers who live off rain forest land. Local people can work in hotels, or as tour guides or rangers.

Ecotourism helps to preserve the environment by allowing a country to profit from and sustain its resources in their natural form. Housing for ecotourists is designed to have very little effect on the environment. For example, the construction of the Lapa Rios Resort in Costa Rica caused the loss of only one tree.

However, even ecotourists can have a negative impact. If too many ecotourists visit a single location, they can interfere with the habitat there. International conservation organizations have become involved in ecotourism. They have begun to point travelers to destinations that are working to preserve the natural resources of the region.

Before You Move On

Summarize How does ecotourism help protect against deforestation?

blue jeans frog

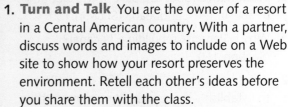

FORMATIVE ASSESSMENT
SPEAKING LAB GeoJournal

1. **Turn and Talk** You are the owner of a resort in a Central American country. With a partner, discuss words and images to include on a Web site to show how your resort preserves the environment. Retell each other's ideas before you share them with the class.

2. **Compare and Contrast** In what way is the focus of ecotourists different from that of other tourists? Provide an example.

3. **Make Predictions** What new technology or scientific discovery might help the rain forest environment in the future? Collaborate with a partner to describe in detail a technology or discovery and its possible impact.

VOCABULARY

For each pair of vocabulary words, write one sentence that explains the connection between the two words.

1. tourism; intersection

> The Caribbean was once an intersection of cultures, which makes it a popular area for tourism today.

2. canal; terrain
3. lock; canal
4. infrastructure; policy
5. food security; global warming
6. malnutrition; food security
7. migrate; remittance
8. ecotourism; habitat

MAIN IDEAS

9. What technological advances helped bring tourists to Central America and the Caribbean? (Section 1.1)

10. What native foods are part of the diet of people in the Caribbean? (Section 1.2)

11. Why is Panama rebuilding its canal? (Section 1.3)

12. What has made it possible for Costa Rica to establish a more stable government than Nicaragua? (Section 2.1)

13. What were the most important needs of the people in Haiti after the earthquake of 2010? (Section 2.2)

14. What is one way to improve food security in Central America? (Section 2.3)

15. Why are remittances so important to many countries in the region? (Section 2.4)

16. In what ways does ecotourism protect the resources of the rain forest? (Section 2.5)

CULTURE

ANALYZE THE ESSENTIAL QUESTION

How do trade and globalization affect the cultures of the region today?

Critical Thinking: Analyze Cause and Effect

17. What characteristics of Caribbean culture attract tourists today?

18. How might global communication continue to affect cultures in the region?

19. How did Caribbean music become a blend of several different styles?

20. How will an increase in ships passing through the Panama Canal help the region?

INTERPRET MAPS

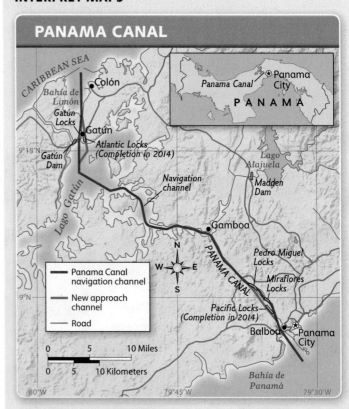

PANAMA CANAL

21. **Interpret Maps** What is the length of the Panama Canal in miles and in kilometers?

22. **Analyze Visuals** Will the new locks replace or add to the old ones? How can you tell?

GOVERNMENT & ECONOMICS

ANALYZE THE ESSENTIAL QUESTION

How is the region trying to improve the standard of living?

Critical Thinking: Compare and Contrast

23. What challenges does Nicaragua face in fighting poverty that Costa Rica does not?

24. Why was it helpful for Haiti to be excused from paying back some of its foreign debt?

25. Why is improving land quality and education a better way to ensure food security than providing foreign aid?

Critical Thinking: Make Inferences

26. Assume that the price of sugar and bananas has fallen and the production costs are high due to global competition. How might this affect migration in the region?

27. What economic opportunities does ecotourism provide for poor people?

INTERPRET CHARTS

POPULATION AND POVERTY IN CENTRAL AMERICA		
Country	Population in Millions	Percent Living Below Poverty Line
Benchmark: United States	316.6	15.1
Guatemala	14.3	54.0
Costa Rica	4.6	24.8
Honduras	8.4	60.0
Dominican Republic	10.2	34.4

Sources: CIA World Factbook

28. **Analyze Data** Which Central American country has the lowest percentage of people living in poverty?

29. **Make Inferences** From which country or countries do you think more people might migrate? Why do you think so?

ACTIVE OPTIONS

Synthesize the Essential Questions by completing the activities below.

30. **Locate and Use Resources** What are the different cultures of the Caribbean? What are the experiences of people living in this multicultural region? Research and write answers to these questions using primary and secondary resources, such as interviews, articles, or memoirs. **Share your findings with the class.**

> **Research Tips**
> - A print or electronic encyclopedia can provide information on cultures. (See pages R38–39.)
> - Search for first-person accounts or other writings by and about individuals who live or have lived on one of the islands. Use proper citations for your sources. (See page R4.)

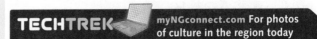
TECHTREK myNGconnect.com For photos of culture in the region today

31. **Organize a Culture Fest** Team up with classmates to demonstrate how living in the Caribbean islands, where unique natural habitats, diverse cultures, and economic struggles might affect the way artists and musicians express themselves. How do day-to-day issues influence creative works? Find examples of Caribbean cultural expressions—music, art, dance, literature, for example—to show and describe in a presentation. Use photos from the **Digital Library** and other sources. Invite other classes in your school to your festival presentation.

Canals as Transportation

Waterways can often be effective routes for moving people and goods from one place to another. However, natural waterways such as rivers and lakes don't always connect to each other, so water traffic comes to a stop. From ancient times to today, people have built canals to connect natural waterways for transportation and to gain access to water.

Sometimes the bodies of water being joined by a canal have different water levels. In that case, the canal will require the use of locks, which are devices that help to equalize the water levels of the waterways being connected. The Dutch (Netherlands) are believed to be the first to make use of locks, as early as the 1300s.

Compare

- China
- Egypt
- France
- Netherlands
- Panama
- Scotland
- Sweden
- United States

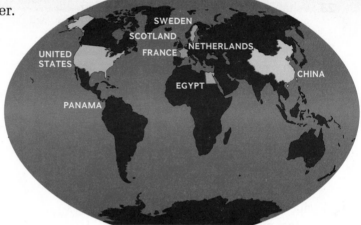

ECONOMIC IMPACT OF CANALS

Early Middle Eastern civilizations are believed to have built canals for irrigation and drinking water, and the Romans built them to transport their military throughout Europe. Later, canals played an important role in Europe and the United States during the Industrial Revolution. These waterways provided cheaper, faster ways to move goods to new markets and to bring raw materials to factories, which helped the economy to grow.

Eventually, railroads took over much of the work of the canals. In fact, it is not uncommon to find a railroad running alongside certain canals. However, some cities today still use canals for transportation, and some of those canals have become popular tourist attractions.

IMPORTANT CANALS

In the United States, the Erie Canal provides a 363-mile water route from the Atlantic Ocean to the Great Lakes.

Like the Erie Canal, the Panama Canal (Central America) and the Suez Canal (Egypt) are important shipping routes. Use the visuals on the opposite page to compare these two major canals.

Other canals around the world serve the same important function:

- Caledonian Canal (Scotland)
- Canal du Midi (France)
- Göta Canal (Sweden)
- Grand Canal (China)
- Amsterdam-Rhine Canal (Netherlands)

COMPARE TWO IMPORTANT CANALS

PANAMA CANAL

PANAMA CANAL

1904
year building began

1914
year the canal opened

PACIFIC — Connects → **ATLANTIC**

Approximate Distance

SAVED
7,900 miles

San Francisco → New York

Locks

— 52 miles —

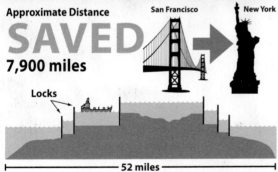

SUEZ CANAL

SUEZ CANAL

1859
year building began

1869
year the canal opened

MEDITERRANEAN SEA — Connects → **RED SEA**

Approximate Distance

SAVED
5,530 miles

London → Persian Gulf

— 101 miles —

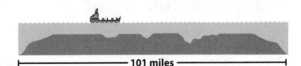

Source: www.britannica.com

RESEARCH LAB GeoJournal

1. **Summarize** How have canals been used from ancient times to today?

2. **Compare** Based on the visual, which canal saves more miles between major cities?

Research and Create Charts Choose two of the canals from the list on the opposite page. Do research and create a chart to compare data about the two canals. Based on the information you find, you may want to match the categories in your chart with those shown on the visual above.

Active Options

ACTIVITY 1

Goal: Research and prepare a speech.

TALK ABOUT BATS

Countries of Central America and the Caribbean are home to many species of bats. Over 70 species live on the small island of Barro Colorado in Panama. Research bats in the region. As you outline your talk, incorporate a main idea, and ideas that support it, to explain the unique features of bats that help them function in their habitats. (See lessons on pages R3 and R10.)

big-eared bat

ACTIVITY 2

Goal: Learn about a new technology.

WRITE A FEATURE ARTICLE

National Geographic Emerging Explorer Ken Banks created software to allow rural groups to communicate even if they don't have Internet access. Rural farmers can get up-to-date information on crop prices—without access to phone or wireless connections—and stay competitive. Use the Internet to find out more about this mobile technology. Then use **Magazine Maker CD-ROM** to write a feature article that explains the ways this technology can be used to help societies.

ACTIVITY 3

Goal: Extend your knowledge of the geography of the Caribbean.

CREATE A SKETCH MAP

The Caribbean is famous as the setting for pirate activity through the ages. Create a sketch map of the region that shows places where pirate activity took place. Write captions that describe some famous pirates and explain their routes around the islands.

6.15.D analyze the experiences and evaluate the contributions of diverse groups to multicultural societies;
6.17.D identify and define the impact of cultural diffusion on individuals and world societies; 6.17.E identify
examples of positive and negative effects of cultural diffusion; 6.21.D identify different points of view about an
issue or topic; 6.23.B use a decision-making process

TEKS

TEKS PROJECT

Goal: Follow a process for making decisions.

Make a Documentary Decision

Suppose your film company would like to interview Caribbean musicians and record their experiences in a documentary that asks: What impact has the spread of their music had on their lives? How have contemporary issues influenced their music?

Explore the Concept To decide on the focus of the film, brainstorm and follow a decision-making process with collaborators around the world. Hold a teleconference using communications equipment so that people in different locations can meet at the same time. Discuss who should take part—musicians, film producers, a script-writer, and others. Will you all be speaking the same language? If not, what languages might be spoken? What are polite greetings in those languages? Each class member selects a role.

Carry It Out During the teleconference, answer these questions:

What cultural contributions have the Caribbean musicians made? Which musicians or styles do we want to feature?

Share information and raise issues in a conversational way. (Use synonyms or describe what you mean to help those listening better understand you.)

Narrow the options for who or what the documentary will be about and what it will show. Based on the best option, make a decision about the focus of your film. Give it a title.

Reflect On It As a group, create a flow chart to show the steps taken to make the decision.

Musicians and dancers celebrate Caribbean culture in an annual street parade in London.

EXPLORE
SOUTH AMERICA
WITH NATIONAL GEOGRAPHIC

MEET THE EXPLORERS

NATIONAL GEOGRAPHIC

Husband-and-wife team and Emerging Explorers Cid Simoes and Paola Segura work to teach farmers in Brazil to conserve their land while growing sustainable, profitable crops.

CONNECT WITH THE CULTURE

Since 1940, this stadium, the Estádio do Pacaembu in São Paulo, Brazil, has hosted important soccer matches, including several FIFA World Cup matches in 1950. Soccer helps to unify Brazil. It has won five World Cup championships, more than any other country.

INVESTIGATE GEOGRAPHY

The Amazon River and its tributaries border eight countries and supply one-fifth of the world's river flow. The rain forests found along its winding course are the largest on Earth and home to millions of plants and animals—many found nowhere else.

Go to myNGconnect.com for maps of South America.

Washington, D.C.

2,377 miles

Bogotá, Colombia

STEP INTO HISTORY

The buildings, temples, and plazas of Machu Picchu, built at the height of the Inca Empire in the 1400s, stand high in a tropical mountain forest in Peru.

CHAPTER 7

SOUTH AMERICA GEOGRAPHY & HISTORY

PREVIEW THE CHAPTER

Essential Question How does elevation influence climate in South America?

SECTION 1 • GEOGRAPHY

KEY VOCABULARY

- vegetation
- grasslands
- adapt
- subsistence farming
- tributary
- biodiversity
- current
- rain shadow
- transpiration
- greenhouse gas

ACADEMIC VOCABULARY

saturate, acknowledge

TERMS & NAMES

- Andes Mountains
- Amazon River Basin
- Llanos
- Angel Falls
- Pampas
- Atacama Desert
- El Niño

Essential Question How did mountains, plateaus, and rivers shape the region's history?

SECTION 2 • HISTORY

KEY VOCABULARY

- descendant
- kinship
- terraced
- suspension bridge
- artifact
- geoglyph
- excavate
- lowland
- nomad
- hunter-gatherer
- slash-and-burn
- treaty
- convert
- monopoly
- rebellion
- exile
- liberate

ACADEMIC VOCABULARY

utilize, transform, transition

TERMS & NAMES

- Machu Picchu
- Guaraní
- Tupinambá
- Yanomami
- Treaty of Tordesillas
- Francisco Pizarro
- Atahualpa

110°W
0°
10°S
20°S
30°S
120°W
40°S

TECHTREK
FOR THIS CHAPTER

Student eEdition

Maps and Graphs

Interactive Whiteboard GeoActivities

Digital Library

Go to **myNGconnect.com** for more on South America.

jaguar

Caribbean Sea

Caracas

Orinoco R.

VENEZUELA

GUYANA

Georgetown

Paramaribo

Cayenne

Bogotá

COLOMBIA

FRENCH GUIANA (France)

Boundary claimed by Suriname

Equator

GALÁPAGOS IS. (Ecuador) (ARCHIPIÉLAGO DE COLÓN)

Quito

ECUADOR

Negro R.

SURINAME

A   N   D   E   S

A   M   A   Z   O   N

Amazon R.

A   M   A   Z   O   N

B   A   S   I   N

Amazon R.

Madeira R.

BRAZIL

P   E   R   U

Tocantins R.

Araguaia R.

Lima

Lake Titicaca

La Paz

BOLIVIA

Sucre

Brasília

PACIFIC OCEAN

Paraguay R.

PARAGUAY

Rio de Janeiro

São Paulo

Tropic of Capricorn

Asunción

Paraná R.

Cerro Aconcagua 22,831 ft (6,959 m)

Santiago

URUGUAY

Buenos Aires

Montevideo

ATLANTIC OCEAN

C   H   I   L   E

A   R   G   E   N   T   I   N   A

N
W   E
S

0   500   1,000 Miles
0   500   1,000 Kilometers

Stanley

FALKLAND ISLANDS (U.K.) (ISLAS MALVINAS)
Administered by the United Kingdom (claimed by Argentina)

South Georgia (U.K.)

10°N

90°W   80°W   70°W   60°W   50°W   40°W   30°W   20°W

100°W

10°N

0°

10°S

20°S

30°S

40°S

50°S

A

B

C

D

E

F

G

H

2   3   4   5   6

TECHTREK

myNGconnect.com For online maps
of South America and Visual Vocabulary

Maps and
Graphs

Digital
Library

SOUTH AMERICA PHYSICAL

Elevation

feet	meters
10,000+	3,050+
5,000	1,524
2,000	610
1,000	305
500	152
0	0
Below sea level	

Caribbean Sea

GALÁPAGOS IS. (Ecuador)
(ARCHIPIÉLAGO
DE COLÓN)

LLANOS
Orinoco R.
GUYANA
VENEZUELA
SURINAME
GUIANA HIGHLANDS
FRENCH GUIANA
(France)
COLOMBIA
ECUADOR
Negro R.
Equator
A M A Z O N
Amazon R.
B A S I N
Amazon R.
Madeira R.
P E R U
A N D E S
Lake
Titicaca
BOLIVIA
BRAZIL
Araguaia R.
Tocantins R.
BRAZILIAN
Campos
MATO GROSSO
PLATEAU
HIGHLANDS
Atacama Desert
Tropic of Capricorn
PARAGUAY
Gran Chaco
Paraguay R.
ATLANTIC
OCEAN
Paraná R.
Entre Ríos
URUGUAY
Cerro Aconcagua
22,831 ft
(6,959 m)
C H I L E
A R G E N T I N A
PAMPAS
P A T A G O N I A

Visual Vocabulary
Andes Mountains

Visual Vocabulary
Pampas

PACIFIC
OCEAN

N
W   E
S

Laguna del Carbón
-344 ft (-105 m)

FALKLAND ISLANDS (U.K.)
(ISLAS MALVINAS)
Administered by the United Kingdom
(claimed by Argentina)

TIERRA
DEL FUEGO

Cape Horn
(Cabo de Hornos)

Scotia Sea

South Georgia
(U.K.)

0	500	1,000 Miles
0	500	1,000 Kilometers

> **Main Idea** South America contains diverse physical features.

South America's physical features vary widely. The continent contains the dramatic Andes Mountains, the massive Amazon River Basin, and wide open grasslands and plains.

High Mountains, Large Basin

The **Andes Mountains** are a string of mountain ranges that stretch about 5,500 miles along the western side of the continent. Many of the mountains in the Andes rise higher than 20,000 feet above sea level. The climate in the Andes is generally cool and dry. Because of low temperatures and high elevation, few types of **vegetation**, or plants, grow here.

The **Amazon River Basin** is the largest river basin on Earth. It covers nearly 2,700,000 square miles in the north-central part of South America—nearly the width of the continent. The river drains this basin, flowing from the Andes to the Atlantic Ocean. The climate is warm and wet. Many different species of plants and animals thrive in the Amazon Basin.

Northern Grasslands, Southern Plains

The northern part of South America has a warm climate, and it contains both low and high elevations. Cattle ranching dominates the **Llanos,** or **grasslands**— wide open areas used for grazing and crops. The Guiana Highlands in the north boast unusual plants and animals. The highest waterfall in the world—**Angel Falls**—is located in Venezuela.

CLIMATE

Humid Equatorial
- No dry season
- Short dry season
- Long dry season

Dry
- Semiarid
- Arid

Humid Temperate
- No dry season
- Dry winter
- Dry summer

- Tundra & ice
- Unclassified highlands

In much of the southern part of the continent, the climate is mild and the elevation is low. The rich soil of the grassy plain in Argentina called the **Pampas** is ideal for growing alfalfa, corn, and wheat.

Before You Move On

Monitor Comprehension What are the main physical features in South America?

FORMATIVE ASSESSMENT

MAP LAB
GeoJournal

1. **Location** According to the physical map, what is the elevation of Cerro (or Mount) Aconcagua, and where is it located?

2. **Interpret Maps** Look at the two maps. What is the difference in climate between the Andes and the Amazon Basin? Which climate supports more diverse vegetation?

3. **Draw Conclusions** Based on climate and elevation, which area of South America is best for growing crops and why?

1.2 Life at Different Elevations

TECHTREK

myNGconnect.com For online maps and photos of different altitude zones

 Maps and Graphs   Digital Library

Main Idea Elevation and climate affect where people live and how they use the land.

The people of South America must **adapt**, or modify, their economic activities to fit the different elevations and climates of the region. Life can vary greatly from one part of South America to another.

Elevation and Climate

People, animals, and plants adapt to a range of climates across the continent. More people live in the mild climates of the plains and grasslands than live in the extreme climates of high mountains and tropical rain forests. The low-elevation plains, such as the Llanos, the Pampas, and the Coastal Plain, are moderate, both in temperature and rainfall.

SOUTH AMERICAN ALTITUDE ZONES

Altitude Zone	Climate	Elevation Range	Crops
Tierra Caliente	hot; adequate to extreme rainfall	0 to 2,500 feet	bananas, peppers, sugarcane, cacao
Tierra Templada	warm; adequate rainfall	2,500 to 6,000 feet	corn, beans, wheat, coffee, vegetables
Tierra Fría	cool; some rainfall	6,000 to 12,000 feet	wheat, barley, potatoes
Tierra Helada	cold; little rainfall	12,000 to 15,000 feet	no substantial crops

Source: H.J. deBlij, *The World Today: Concepts and Regions in Geography.* Hoboken, NJ: John Wiley & Sons, 2009.

Critical Viewing At an elevation of 11,800 feet, La Paz, Bolivia, is the world's highest capital city. What details in this photo show how people have adapted to living in a high-elevation urban environment?

POPULATION DENSITY

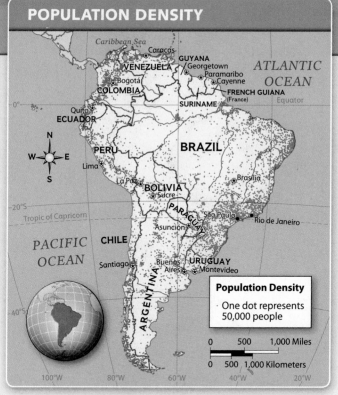

Population Density

· One dot represents 50,000 people

RESOURCES

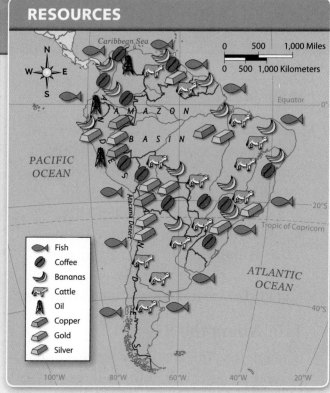

Fish
Coffee
Bananas
Cattle
Oil
Copper
Gold
Silver

They are located in the *tierra templada* (tee EHR ah tem PLAH dah) elevation zone. The cool, dry elevations of the Andes are called *tierra fría* (FREE ah), or cold land.

Further up in the Andes, a very high and cold elevation range is called *tierra helada* (he LAH dah), or frozen land. At the other extreme, the hot and humid Amazon River Basin is *tierra caliente* (kay YEN tay), or hot land.

Using the Land

Elevation and climate determine how people use the land. Rain is scarce at high elevations in the mountains and highlands of the continent. Some farmers in the Andes herd animals and grow only enough food for their families. This is called **subsistence farming**. However, others have become part of the global economy, selling wool to European and other manufacturers.

On the plains, higher rainfall provides opportunities for ranching and profitable, large-scale farming. Crops produced at these lower elevations in the region include tropical fruits, sugarcane, coffee, corn, wheat, and soybeans.

Before You Move On

Make Inferences Why do people settle in areas with moderate climates and low elevations?

FORMATIVE ASSESSMENT

DATA LAB GeoJournal

1. **Interpret Charts** According to the chart, in what altitude zone do potatoes grow? Which altitude zone experiences the most rainfall?

2. **Draw Conclusions** Based on the chart, why do no substantial crops grow in the *tierra helada* zone?

3. **Human-Environment Interaction** According to the population density map, where do most people in South America live? Use the resources map to help you explain why those areas have the most population.

1.3 The Amazon River

TECHTREK

myNGconnect.com For an online map
and photos of river basin life

Maps and
Graphs

Digital
Library

Main Idea The Amazon River supports
life in its vast rain forest.

The Amazon River begins high in the
Andes Mountains of Peru. It flows east
for 4,000 miles across the continent
and empties into the Atlantic. This
massive river system has more than
1,000 **tributaries**, or small rivers that
drain into a larger river. Seven of these
tributaries are more than 1,000 miles long.

Life Along the River

Though the Amazon River is the world's
second longest river, it is the largest river
in the world by volume. The Amazon
creates the largest river basin—2,700,000
square miles—and includes the world's
largest tropical rain forest. The Amazon
rain forest is home to thousands of plant
and animal species and millions of insect
species. The variety of species in an
ecosystem is called its **biodiversity**.

Annual flooding of the river from
melting snow and rain in the Andes
usually occurs between June and October.
The floodwaters deposit rich nutrients,
or substances that support life, in the
lowland forest soils. These nutrients
support the biodiversity of the rain forest.

Today, a growing population puts
pressure on rain forest lands through
mining, logging, farming, and land
development. Conservationists suggest that
setting limits on development will help
protect the Amazon rain forest.

Before You Move On

Summarize In what ways does the Amazon River
support life in its rain forest?

AMAZON RIVER AND ITS TRIBUTARIES

Source	Andes Mountains
Length	4,000 miles
Basin	2.7 million square miles
Directional Flow	East-northeasterly
Number of Tributaries	More than 1,000
Three Notable Tributaries	1 Madeira (2,082 miles long) 2 Tocantins (1,677 miles long) 3 Negro (1,400 miles long)

Source: Encyclopædia Britannica

Visual Vocabulary A **tributary** is a small river that drains into a larger river. The Purus River is a tributary that runs through continuous forest on its way to the Amazon.

Legend
- Amazon River drainage area
- Areas prone to flooding
- Rain forest
- Shoreline or river
- Area where the country border and a river coincide
- ⊛ Capital city
- ◉ Administrative capital city
- • Other city

ATLANTIC OCEAN

VENEZUELA
GUIANA HIGHLANDS
GUYANA
SURINAME
FRENCH GUIANA (France)
Georgetown
Paramaribo
Cayenne
Boa Vista
Angel Falls (total drop 3,212 ft 979 m)
Orinoco R.
Boundary claimed by Suriname
Macapá
Mouths of the Amazon
Marajó Island
Belém
AMAZON
Negro R.
Balbina Reservoir
Amazon R.
Santarém
Manaus
Solimões R. (Amazon R.)
Juruá R.
BASIN
Madeira R.
Tapajós R.
Xingu R.
Tucuruí Reservoir
Marabá
BRAZIL
Purus R.
Teles Pires R.
Araguaia R.
Tocantins R.
Porto Velho
Rio Branco
Juruena R.
Guaporé R.
Lake Titicaca
La Paz
BOLIVIA
Santa Cruz
Sucre
PARAGUAY
Paraguay R.

FORMATIVE ASSESSMENT
MAP LAB
GeoJournal

1. **Location** Locate the Purus River and Marañón rivers on the map. Use the map legend to describe the land that surrounds each river.
2. **Interpret Maps** What are three cities located on the Amazon River? Which tributary flows into Manaus?
3. **Monitor Comprehension** How is the biodiversity of the Amazon River and rain forest threatened by a growing population?

1.4 Cold and Warm Currents

Main Idea Wind currents and ocean currents influence climate across South America in powerful and unpredictable ways.

Like elevation, wind currents and ocean currents influence climate too. **Currents** are the continuous movement of air or water in the same direction. As you read about these currents, follow their patterns on the maps at right.

Currents and Climate

Cold wind and ocean currents flow from the high latitudes near the South Pole toward the equator, making the west coast of South America generally cool and dry. Warm wind and ocean currents flow in the other direction, from the equator toward the South Pole, and create a warm and humid climate on the east coast.

The Peru Current brings cold waters to the Pacific coast in the west. It flows along the southern coast of Chile and northward along the coast of Peru. The Peru Current carries nutrient-rich waters from deep in the Pacific Ocean, so fish thrive off the coasts of Chile, Peru, and Ecuador.

On the eastern side of the continent, the Brazil Current brings warm waters from the Atlantic. The coasts and inland areas of Brazil and Argentina receive warm, humid wind currents and, in some areas, plenty of rainfall. This rainfall nourishes crops and vegetation. The plains of the Pampas benefit from the Brazil Current.

These moist wind currents do not reach the **Atacama Desert**, located on the western side of the Andes. This desert lies in a **rain shadow**, a dry region on one side of a mountain range. In South America, the Andes prevent moist Atlantic winds from reaching west of the mountains. Instead, moisture condenses into rain on the eastern side of the Andes. So, even though it lies along one of the world's largest bodies of water, the Atacama Desert is one of the driest places in the world. On average, only a half inch of rain falls each year.

Critical Viewing Vicunas live in the Atacama Desert in Chile. From what you can see in the photo, how would you describe their habitat?

Critical Viewing This lush sugarcane plantation in Argentina contrasts with the dry Atacama Desert. What details in the photo tell you that this plantation does not lie in a rain shadow?

WIND CURRENTS

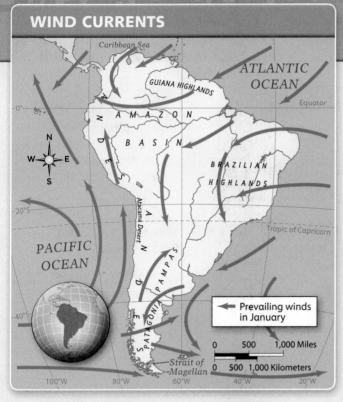

OCEAN CURRENTS

El Niños on the Pacific Coast

El Niños influence climate on the western coast of South America. An **El Niño** (ehl NEEN yoh) happens when the usual wind and ocean currents reverse. This reversal brings warm air currents and water currents that produce high rainfall in coastal areas. El Niños occur in Peru because of its location in the current system and on the Pacific coast.

El Niños do not occur every year, but they do happen somewhat regularly, at least once every 12 years. They are difficult to predict and their results can be devastating. Heavy rains **saturate**, or soak, coastal areas. These rains cause severe flooding and wipe out habitats. They can also cause damage to crops, canals, bridges, and roads. Scientists try to predict when an El Niño is likely to arrive. This helps prepare local populations to deal with the impacts of heavy rainfall.

Before You Move On

Monitor Comprehension How do wind and ocean currents influence climate in South America?

FORMATIVE ASSESSMENT

MAP LAB

 GeoJournal

1. **Interpret Maps** Locate the Atacama Desert on the wind currents map. Do wind currents from the Pacific flow over the desert? How might this contribute to its lack of rain?

2. **Describe Geographic Information** Scientists use complex maps like these to predict weather patterns and climate changes. In what ways is the information on these maps similar, and in what ways is it different?

1.5 Rain Forests and Climate Change

TECHTREK

myNGconnect.com For a graph on deforestation and photos of the rain forest

 Maps and Graphs

 Digital Library

Main Idea The health of the Amazon rain forest can influence climate change across the globe.

Climate change and global warming are topics that are often in the news. In order to understand how these topics are connected to rain forests, it helps to understand the scientific processes that keep rain forests healthy.

Rain forests are complex ecosystems. As you have read, thousands of different animals, birds, and insects live in the Amazon rain forest. Many unusual plants grow there, too. Some of these plants are used to fight deadly diseases like malaria and cancer.

How Rain Forests Work

Through a process called **transpiration**, plants and trees release water vapor into the air. As the water vapor rises, it cools, forming thick clouds that then produce rain. The warm air and moist soil support the growth of vegetation. In fact, trees grow so high and thick that sometimes sunlight does not reach the forest floor.

The plants in the Amazon rain forest perform an important function. They absorb greenhouse gases from Earth's atmosphere. A **greenhouse gas** is a gas that traps heat energy, warming the earth. Burning fossil fuels such as coal and oil produces greenhouse gases like carbon dioxide.

Too much carbon dioxide in the air causes the atmosphere to warm because it reflects heat energy back to Earth. Rain forest plants and trees naturally absorb this carbon dioxide from the air. In this way, rain forests help clean Earth's air.

Before You Move On

Summarize Why are rain forests important?

KEY VOCABULARY

transpiration, n., the process by which plants release water vapor into the air

greenhouse gas, n., a gas that absorbs heat energy and reflects it back to Earth

ACADEMIC VOCABULARY

acknowledge, v., to recognize

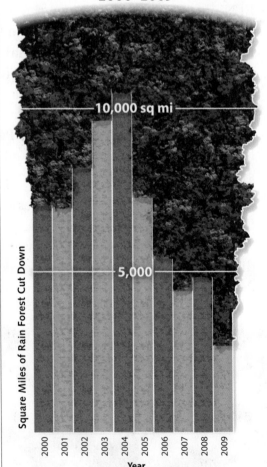

DEFORESTATION IN BRAZIL, 2000–2009

Square Miles of Rain Forest Cut Down

10,000 sq mi

5,000

2000 2001 2002 2003 2004 2005 2006 2007 2008 2009

Year

Source: National Institute for Space Research, Brazil, 2010

Inspiring people to care about the planet
National Geographic Society Mission

Changes in the Rain Forest

Since the mid-20th century, large sections of the Amazon rain forest have been cut down. In *National Geographic*, journalist Scott Wallace reported that 20 percent of the rain forest has been lost in the last 40 years. (January 2007)

Widespread deforestation threatens the biodiversity of the Amazon. As more of the rain forest is lost, fewer trees and plants remain to produce moisture and cloud cover and to remove greenhouse gases from the air. These changes are having a global impact.

COMPARE ACROSS REGIONS

A Global Climate Challenge

Changes in the Amazon rain forest are party responsible for changes in climate identified by scientists. Climate change is a gradual shift in Earth's climate due to natural causes. In its history, Earth has undergone many climate changes.

Global warming, on the other hand, is a term used by some scientists to describe the rapid warming of Earth's surface observed over the last century. They argue that the heavy use of fuels that release carbon dioxide contributes to rising temperatures. Since the beginning of the 20th century, the average temperature of the globe has risen 1.4°F. While that number might seem small, scientists **acknowledge**, or recognize, that a change of even one or two degrees is cause for concern. Rapid changes in average temperature can destroy habitats and change ecosystems.

Deforestation is underway in the Amazon rain forest near Rondonia State, Brazil.

Protecting the Amazon and other rain forests around the world is critical to the health of the planet. Many countries in South America are working to protect the Amazon rain forest. Across the Atlantic, countries in the African rain forest of the Congo River Basin face similar challenges. Leaders of Cameroon, Democratic Republic of Congo, Guinea, and Ghana are cooperating to manage sustainable forestry operations and to protect easily-damaged wildlife habitats.

Before You Move On
Monitor Comprehension What problems threaten the health of the Amazon rain forest?

FORMATIVE ASSESSMENT

READING LAB  GeoJournal

1. **Summarize** What is the difference between climate change and global warming?
2. **Describe** In what ways do rain forests clean Earth's air?
3. **Interpret Graphs** According to the graph, what has been the general trend in deforestation since 2004? What do you think caused this trend?

2.1 The Inca

TECHTREK

myNGconnect.com For an online empire map and photos of Inca civilization

Maps and Graphs

Digital Library

Main Idea The Inca ruled a vast empire in a difficult, mountainous environment.

The Inca Empire in South America stretched along the Pacific coast. The empire included parts of present-day Colombia, Ecuador, Peru, Bolivia, Chile, and Argentina. From 1438 until the Spanish conquest in the 1530s, the Inca Empire was one of South America's largest and most advanced civilizations.

Workings of the Empire

The Inca built the capital of their empire in Cuzco, in what is now Peru. Inca government and society were highly organized. The emperor—called the Sapa Inca—was considered a **descendant**, or a relative of, the sun god, Inti. At its high point, the empire included 80 provinces and about 12 million people.

Within Inca society, families were organized into groups based on **kinship**, or blood relationship, and common land ownership. Inca married within their kinship groups. They also worked together and shared land and resources. The leader of each family worked for the empire for a few months of the year as builders, farmers, craftsmen, or foot soldiers.

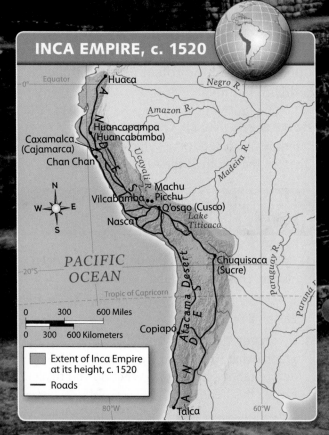

INCA EMPIRE, c. 1520

Equator
Huaca
Negro R.
Amazon R.
Huancapampa (Huancabamba)
Caxamalca (Cajamarca)
Chan Chan
Ucayali R.
Madeira R.
Machu Picchu
Vilcabamba
Q'osqo (Cusco)
Nasca
Lake Titicaca
PACIFIC OCEAN
Chuquisaca (Sucre)
Paraguay R.
Tropic of Capricorn
Atacama Desert
Paraná R.
0   300   600 Miles
0   300   600 Kilometers
Copiapó
A N D E S
Extent of Inca Empire at its height, c. 1520
— Roads
80°W   60°W
Talca

> **Critical Viewing** The ancient ruins of Machu Picchu are located in Peru, at an elevation of 7,710 feet. Based on what is shown in the photo, what do you think might have been the challenges of building a city at high elevations?

6.02.A identify and describe influence of group achievements on past societies; 6.05.B identify geographic factors for controlling territory; 6.07.A identify and analyze ways people adapted to their environment; 6.07.B ways people have modified environment; 6.07.C describe ways technology influences interactions with environment; 6.18.A explain relationship between societies and their architecture

Achievements of the Inca

The Inca **utilized**, or made practical use of, their advanced engineering skills to adapt to the mountainous environment. For example, the Inca farmed on **terraced** fields, or flat fields cut into slopes or mountainsides. They also built irrigation canals to water their crops because the climate was arid.

The Inca adapted to their mountainous surroundings in other ways. They built suspension bridges using vines and wood. A **suspension bridge** is a bridge used to cross canyons or water. The Inca also built a system of roads that helped keep the empire unified.

Another example of the Inca's engineering skills is **Machu Picchu** (MAH choo PEE choo), built in the 1400s. The Inca built this complex city on a mountain by constructing giant walls, terraces, sloping ramps, and steep stairways.

 **Visual Vocabulary Suspension bridges** are bridges used to cross canyons or water. This rebuilt suspension bridge in Peru is modeled after the bridges the Inca built.

Some archaeologists believe it served as a royal estate. Today it is a UNESCO World Heritage Site because of its historical and archaeological significance.

By the 1530s, the empire faced internal problems that included a weak economy and civil war. A much smaller but better-equipped Spanish force conquered the Inca in 1532. Today, the descendants of the Inca, the Quechua, live in the Andes of Peru, Ecuador, and Bolivia.

Before You Move On
Make Inferences In what ways did the Inca maintain control of their empire?

FORMATIVE ASSESSMENT

PHOTO LAB GeoJournal

1. **Analyze Visuals** Machu Picchu is shown here and on pages 186–187. How important do you think architecture was to the Inca? Explain.

2. **Analyze** How and why did the Inca adapt to their physical environment?

3. **Describe** As a group, what influence do you think Inca achievements had on other societies?

4. **Make Inferences** How did the technology of the suspension bridge and irrigation canals change how the Inca interacted with their environment?

2.2

SECTION 2 HISTORY

NATIONAL GEOGRAPHIC

TECHTREK
myNGconnect.com For photos of an
Explorer at work and an Explorer Video Clip

Digital
Library

Exploring
Nasca Culture
with Christina Conlee

Main Idea Artifacts and other archaeological discoveries provide insight into the Nasca culture.

myNGconnect.com
For more on Christina Conlee in the field today

Archaeologists study how people lived in the past. They examine **artifacts**, or objects left behind by past cultures. NG Expeditions Council Grantee Christina Conlee is an archaeologist who studies the Nasca of Peru. The Nasca lived on a desert plateau in southern Peru nearly 2,000 years ago. They left behind beautiful ceramic artifacts as well as the Nasca lines, which are a series of **geoglyphs**, or large, geometric designs and animal shapes drawn on the ground. The Nasca were one of the first complex societies in South America.

A Surprising Find

In 2004, Conlee and her team were **excavating**, or carefully uncovering, what they thought was a house in La Tiza, Peru. She was surprised to unearth, instead, an ancient burial site. Between 2004 and 2006, Conlee and her team excavated nine burial sites. Artifacts collected at the sites included elaborate ceramics and copper objects. Conlee believes that the kinds of artifacts she found belonged to individuals with a high social rank in the community.

Some of the artifacts uncovered were not typical of traditional Nasca ceramics. The presence of copper objects, shell ornaments, and more elaborate tomb paintings suggested a different population group. Were they local Nasca or people from another culture?

Ancient Migrations

Conlee was determined to find the answer. Through chemical analysis she performed on the bones, Conlee determined that the remains did indeed belong to the Nasca. However, her analysis also proved that some remains belonged to a group of Nasca rivals called the Wari.

The Wari were more powerful than the Nasca. Conlee believes when they moved into Nasca areas, they may have caused some Nasca to move away. Ultimately, the migration of the Wari may even have led to the end of Nasca culture. Conlee's studies and discoveries continue to reveal new insights about Nasca culture and their migration patterns.

Before You Move On
Make Inferences What did archaeological discoveries reveal about ancient Nasca culture?

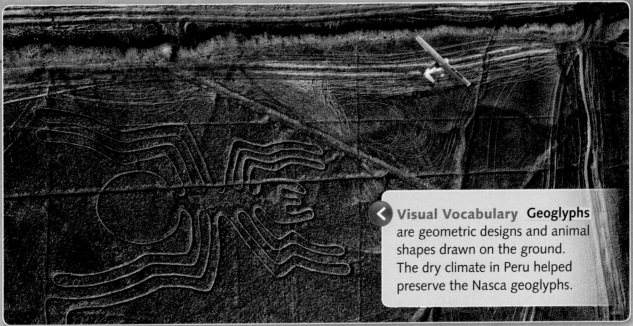

Visual Vocabulary Geoglyphs are geometric designs and animal shapes drawn on the ground. The dry climate in Peru helped preserve the Nasca geoglyphs.

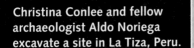
Christina Conlee and fellow archaeologist Aldo Noriega excavate a site in La Tiza, Peru.

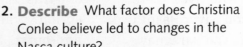
FORMATIVE ASSESSMENT
VIEWING LAB
GeoJournal

1. **Analyze Visuals** Go to the **Digital Library** for an Explorer Video Clip about high-altitude archaeologist Johan Reinhard. What type of discoveries has he made?

2. **Describe** What factor does Christina Conlee believe led to changes in the Nasca culture?

National Geographic Explorer-in-Residence Johan Reinhard

2.3 People of the Lowlands

TECHTREK

myNGconnect.com For an online map and photos of the Yanomami

Maps and Graphs   Digital Library

Main Idea People have lived in the lowlands of South America for thousands of years.

People who lived in South America began to settle in low-lying areas of the continent more than five thousand years ago. The development of agriculture and a stable food supply allowed for larger groups of people to live there together.

Lowland River Basins

The **lowland**, or low-lying, areas of South America include several fertile river basins. The lowlands include the Orinoco River and surrounding grasslands, the Amazon River Basin, and the Paraguay River Basin.

These rivers and basins contained abundant animal life and vegetation to support ancient people who lived there. For example, the Amazon River Basin was an ample source of fish. The Paraguay Basin, which includes Gran Chaco, a floodplain, provided fertile soils for growing food.

Developing Agriculture

At first, lowland people lived as **nomads**, or people who move from place to place. As **hunter-gatherers**, or people who hunted animals and gathered plants and fruits for food, they moved to different locations as food became scarce.

As early as 3000 B.C., people began to farm the land and build villages in the lowlands. Establishing a stable food supply encouraged different groups to settle in villages rather than continue to move from place to place.

The **Guaraní** (GWAH rah NEE) people lived in the eastern and central lowlands on the Paraguay and Paraná Rivers. Before planting crops, the Guaraní cleared the land by cutting down and burning existing forest and vegetation. This agricultural technique is called **slash-and-burn**. Typically, Guaraní women grew corn and root vegetables such as sweet potatoes and cassava. In addition to farming, Guaraní men hunted and fished.

SLASH-AND-BURN AGRICULTURE

1 Slash Wooded areas and jungles are too thick to plant crops. Farmers slash, or cut down, trees.

2 Burn Fallen trees and foliage are burned to clear the land. Ash produced by the fires is used as fertilizer.

3 Fertilize and Plant Cleared land is fertilized with ash. Crops such as corn and sweet potatoes are planted.

Another group, the **Tupinambá** (too pee NAAM baa), settled near the mouth of the Amazon and southward along the Atlantic coast. They also cultivated crops using slash-and-burn agriculture. Because they lived in the Amazon River Basin and near the ocean, the Tupinambá also fished and hunted river mammals and turtles.

The Yanomami

Today, indigenous groups continue to live in rain forests throughout the Amazon River Basin. The **Yanomami** (yaa noh MAA mee) are still hunter-gatherers who use the slash-and-burn technique to clear the land for farming. They live in villages but migrate to different areas to meet agricultural needs. Many have moved to the north-central lowlands, where they have found more fertile land.

Before You Move On
Make Inferences How did the physical features of the lowlands shape the lives of the people who lived there?

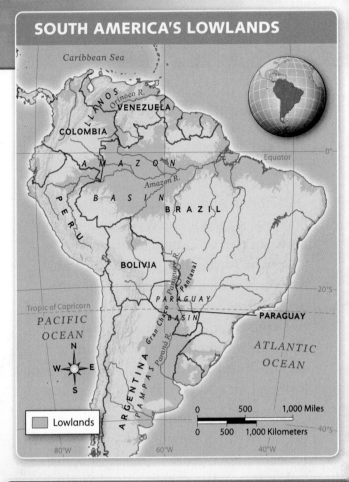

SOUTH AMERICA'S LOWLANDS

Lowlands

4 Migrate Groups move on to new locations after soil on cleared lands becomes less productive.

FORMATIVE ASSESSMENT

SPEAKING LAB GeoJournal

1. **Turn and Talk** Turn to a partner and explain the process of slash-and-burn agriculture in the lowlands. Refer to images in the lesson for details if you need to.

2. **Create Charts** With a partner, make a chart comparing nomadic and settled lifestyles. Discuss the characteristics of each and its advantages. Challenge yourselves to use social studies terms when you share information.

	NOMADIC	SETTLED
Movement	1. Move frequently	
Food Sources	2.	

3. **Location** In what parts of the continent did the Guaraní and Tupinambá live? Where do the Yanomami live? Use the text to help you locate these areas on the map.

TECHTREK

myNGconnect.com For an online map
of Spanish settlement and photos of artifacts

Maps and
Graphs

Digital
Library

> **Main Idea** The arrival of the Spanish in the
> 1500s shaped the history and culture of the South
> American continent.

In 1494, in order to avoid conflicts over
exploration and settlement, Spain and
Portugal signed a **treaty**, or an agreement
between two or more countries. The
Treaty of Tordesillas (tor duh SEE uhs)
drew a line on a map that divided the
newly discovered lands between the
two countries. The treaty divided South
America into two parts. The Spanish
claimed lands west of the line, and
Portugal claimed lands east of the line.

The Treaty of Tordesillas set the stage
for the Spanish conquest of most of South
America. Four years later, Christopher
Columbus, sailing on behalf of Spain,
landed on South America's northern coast.

The Spanish Conquest

As they had in Mexico, Spanish
conquistadors arrived in South America
determined to expand Spain's empire
and search for resources such as gold and
silver. In 1533, **Francisco Pizarro**, with
a small army of men, overthrew the Inca
emperor, **Atahualpa** (AH tah WAHL pah).
Pizarro founded the city of Lima, Peru,
which became the center

Critical Viewing *The Spaniard and the
Inca Chief* by James McConnell. What
stories does this painting tell about the
Spanish and the Inca?

of the Spanish government and empire
in South America. Other conquistadors
explored and conquered Colombia, on
the northern coast, and most of Chile, on
the western coast. (See the map opposite.)
The Spanish conquest of South America
permanently **transformed**, or changed,
much of the continent and its people.

This gold mask is one example of the wealth
the Spanish sought in South America.

1498–1500
Columbus's third voyage
reaches northern coast of
South America.

1400

1450

Gold statues discovered in the
mountains of Argentina illustrate
the extent of the Inca Empire.

1438–1533
Inca Empire rules
vast area of
South America.

1494
Spain and Portugal
sign the Treaty of
Tordesillas.

Impact on Native Populations

Deadly diseases that traveled with the Spanish to South America wiped out entire villages and native populations. Because these groups had no resistance to diseases such as smallpox, measles, and influenza, many died quickly.

The Spanish enslaved natives and forced them to work on plantations and ranches and in mines. Large numbers of enslaved native people died from the effects of harsh labor conditions.

Missionaries who arrived after the 1550s viewed South America as an opportunity to spread Christianity. The goal was to **convert**, or persuade native populations to change their religious beliefs. Some conversions were forced. Many native people began to practice the Catholic faith, and some blended aspects of Christianity with their own religious practices.

Before You Move On

Summarize What impact did the Spanish have on the history and culture of South America?

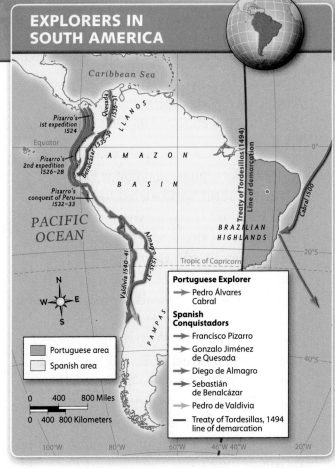

EXPLORERS IN SOUTH AMERICA

Portuguese Explorer
→ Pedro Álvares Cabral

Spanish Conquistadors
→ Francisco Pizarro
→ Gonzalo Jiménez de Quesada
→ Diego de Almagro
→ Sebastián de Benalcázar
→ Pedro de Valdivia
— Treaty of Tordesillas, 1494 line of demarcation

Portuguese area
Spanish area

0   400   800 Miles
0   400 800 Kilometers

FORMATIVE ASSESSMENT

MAP LAB

 GeoJournal

1. **Movement** According to the map, where were Spanish conquistadors most active in the 1520s and 1530s? Who made multiple expeditions?

2. **Evaluate** Locate the line of demarcation on the map. How would you describe the impact of that line on South America?

3. **Interpret Time Lines** About how many years passed between the signing of the Treaty of Tordesillas and the overthrow of the Inca?

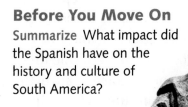

Pedro Álvares Cabral, Portuguese navigator, lands on eastern coast of South America in 1500.

1500

1532
Spanish conquer Inca Empire.

1541
Spanish establish Santiago, Chile.

1550

1524
Pizarro reaches northwestern coast of South America.

1535
Spanish establish Lima, Peru, as center of empire in South America.

TECHTREK

myNGconnect.com For an online map of Portuguese settlement in South America

Maps and Graphs

Main Idea Portuguese colonization and the arrival of slaves from Africa influenced the history of Brazil.

In 1500, Portuguese navigator Pedro Álvares Cabral was headed to India with his fleet when he went off course. He landed on the southeastern coast of present-day Brazil. Cabral realized the area lay within the land allowed Portugal by the Treaty of Tordesillas and claimed it.

Sugar and Slaves

Portuguese interest in Brazil was limited until the 1530s. Unlike the Spanish in Peru, the Portuguese did not conquer the native population and quickly take over the land. Instead, Portuguese colonization of Brazil took place over several decades.

Portuguese settlers discovered that these new lands contained natural resources valued in European markets. First, the Portuguese exported brazilwood, which was sought for its red color used to dye fabric. Then colonists realized that sugarcane, which grew abundantly in Brazil, was a more valuable crop. They built plantations and began exporting sugarcane and sugar products to Europe. The Portuguese tried enslaving natives to work the sugar plantations, but overwork

⌃ **Critical Viewing** This 1819 painting shows slaves working on a plantation in Brazil. What details do you notice?

and disease killed many of them. The Portuguese then turned to another source for labor: Africa.

Because of their earlier exploration, the Portuguese knew about the slave markets in Africa. By the mid-1500s, the Portuguese and other European countries were exporting African slaves across the Atlantic to South America and the Caribbean. The Portuguese were able to create a **monopoly**, or complete control, of the slave trade. A continuous trade in slaves began in Brazil in 1560 and lasted well into the 19th century.

1532
Portuguese begin growing sugarcane in Brazil.

1550

1560
Portuguese import African slaves to work sugar plantations.

1695
Gold is discovered in the present-day state of Minas Gerais.

1650

This lighthouse still stands on the site of a colonial trading port in Salvador, Brazil.

6.01.A trace characteristics of societies that resulted from historical events such as colonization;
6.02.B evaluate economic and cultural contributions of groups, past; 6.21.B analyze by summarizing;
6.21.C interpret information from maps, timelines

PORTUGUESE CLAIMS IN BRAZIL

Portuguese Wealth

Brazil's abundant natural resources, combined with the African slave labor to extract them, made the Portuguese wealthy. As valuable natural resources like gold and diamonds were discovered, Portuguese demand for slave labor increased. Slaves were brought in to work on sugar and coffee plantations and in gold and diamond mines. Portuguese slave traders imported more than five million slaves from Africa to Brazil.

The Portuguese successfully put down **rebellions**, or revolts, against their rule until the early 1800s. Brazil finally declared independence from Portugal in 1822, but not everyone was free. Even though the slave trade had ended in 1850, slavery continued in Brazil for several decades until it was abolished in 1888.

Before You Move On

Monitor Comprehension What influence did the slave trade have on Brazil's history?

1826 Jean Baptiste-Debret depicts slaves carrying sacks of coffee in Brazil.

FORMATIVE ASSESSMENT
READING LAB   GeoJournal

1. **Movement** Why did the Portuguese import slaves from Africa?

2. **Summarize** In what way did slaves contribute to Portuguese wealth?

3. **Interpret Maps** According to the map, where in South America did the Portuguese settle? What is the pattern of their settlement?

4. **Interpret Time Lines** How long did slavery exist in Brazil? What year did slavery end? Use the time line to form your answer.

1840s
Coffee becomes Brazil's top export.

1750

1850

1725
Diamonds are discovered in Minas Gerais.

1822
Brazil declares its independence from Portugal.

1888
The Golden Law abolishes slavery in Brazil.

2.6 Simón Bolívar on Independence

TECHTREK
myNGconnect.com For paintings of
revolutionary leaders and Guided Writing

 Digital
Library

 Student
eEdition

 Student
Resources

Most of South America was ruled by the Spanish for more than 300 years. Making the transition, or change, from colonial rule to independence was difficult. Simón Bolívar led the revolution against the Spanish. Bolívar was born in 1783 to a wealthy family in Caracas, Venezuela. Both of his parents died when he was a child. After their death, his uncle made sure that he received an education and sent Bolívar to Europe. There, Bolívar learned new ideas about freedom and government. In 1810, he joined the independence movement in Venezuela. Present-day Bolivia was named in his honor.

DOCUMENT 1

The Letter from Jamaica (1815)

Bolívar wrote this letter in Jamaica while living in **exile**, or a state of absence from one's home country, during Venezuela's struggle for independence. Here he describes the need for revolution and independence from Spain.

> The hatred we feel for the Peninsula [Spain] is greater than the sea separating us from it; it would be easier to bring the two continents together than to reconcile [unite] the spirits and minds of the two countries.

CONSTRUCTED RESPONSE

1. What sea is Simón Bolívar referring to in this passage?

2. What two countries in particular is Bolívar discussing?

3. How would you describe the overall tone of Bolívar's words in this passage?

DOCUMENT 2

The Angostura Address (1819)

After returning from exile in Jamaica, Bolívar delivered this speech in Venezuela in 1819.

> The continuation of power in the same individual has frequently led to the demise [downfall] of democratic government. . . . A just zeal [enthusiasm for a cause] is the guarantee of republican freedom, and our citizens should properly fear that the same ruler who has long ruled them will wish to rule them forever.

CONSTRUCTED RESPONSE

4. According to Bolívar, what should citizens fear most in a ruler?

5. What does Bolívar argue leads to the "demise of democratic government"?

6. How does a "just zeal" guarantee freedom, according to Bolívar?

A JUST ZEAL IS THE GUARANTEE OF REPUBLICAN FREEDOM.
— SIMÓN BOLÍVAR

Source: Tito Salas, *Retrato Ecuestre del Libertador*, 1936.

DOCUMENT 3

Simón Bolívar, "The Liberator"

To **liberate** means to set someone or something free. Simón Bolívar earned the name "the Liberator" for his brave efforts against the Spanish during the struggle for independence. Bolívar is also often referred to as the "George Washington of South America."

CONSTRUCTED RESPONSE

7. In 1936, the Venezuelan government commissioned artist Tito Salas to paint this work for the National Pantheon, a monument built to honor national heroes. What details did Salas include to present Bolívar as a liberator?

FIND OUT MORE How would you find out whose ideas Bolívar studied to learn about freedom and government? What primary sources might inform you? What secondary sources?

FORMATIVE ASSESSMENT

WRITING LAB GeoJournal

DBQ Practice By the early 1800s, many countries in South America began to press for independence from Spain. In what ways did Bolívar lead Venezuela's fight for independence?

Step 1. Review the colonial period of South America in Sections 2.4 and 2.5.

Step 2. On your own paper, take notes about the main ideas expressed in each document in this lesson.

> Document 1: The Letter from Jamaica
> Main Idea(s) _____
>
> Document 2: The Angostura Address
> Main Idea(s) _____
>
> Document 3: Painting of Bolívar
> Main Idea(s) _____

Step 3. Construct a topic sentence that answers this question: Why did Bolívar want to liberate South America from Spanish rule?

Step 4. Write a detailed paragraph that explains why Bolívar wanted self-rule and freedom for South America. Go to **Student Resources** for Guided Writing support.

VOCABULARY

On your paper, write the vocabulary word that completes each of the following sentences.

1. People who lived in the South American lowlands practiced _____ agriculture.

2. The Portuguese had a _____ on the slave trade.

3. Archaeologists _____ artifacts to learn about past cultures.

4. Over 1,000 _____ feed into the Amazon River.

5. A _____ is an agreement between two or more countries.

MAIN IDEAS

6. What are two extreme physical features on the South American continent? (Section 1.1)

7. What two factors help determine where people settle in South America? (Section 1.2)

8. In what ways does the Amazon River nourish the rain forest? (Section 1.3)

9. What unpredictable weather event impacts Peru and what are its effects? (Section 1.4)

10. How do rain forests protect the health of the planet? (Section 1.5)

11. How did the Inca adapt to their mountain environment? (Section 2.1)

12. In what ways have archaeologists contributed to an understanding of Nasca culture? (Section 2.2)

13. What natural resources helped the people of the lowlands thrive? (Section 2.3)

14. How did the arrival of the Spanish impact native populations? (Section 2.4)

15. In what ways did slave labor benefit the colonial Portuguese economy? (Section 2.5)

16. Why was Simón Bolívar called "the Liberator"? (Section 2.6)

GEOGRAPHY

ANALYZE THE ESSENTIAL QUESTION

How does elevation influence climate in South America?

Critical Thinking: Compare and Contrast

17. Compare and contrast climate and elevation in the Andes and the Amazon River Basin.

18. Compare and contrast these two altitude zones: *tierra templada* and *tierra fría*.

19. Compare the ways in which currents and landforms influence climate in Chile.

INTERPRET MAPS

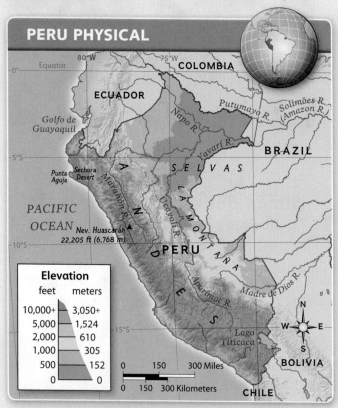

PERU PHYSICAL

20. **Identify** What major mountain range lies in Peru, and what map element can help you determine its location?

21. **Describe Geographic Information** Where does Peru's largest area of lowlands lie in relation to the equator? Use the word "latitude" in your answer.

HISTORY

ANALYZE THE ESSENTIAL QUESTION

How did mountains, plateaus, and rivers shape the region's history?

Critical Thinking: Draw Conclusions

22. In what ways does Machu Picchu demonstrate the Inca's engineering skills?

23. Describe what archaeological evidence left behind on the desert plateau reveals about migration patterns of the Nasca culture.

24. How did people of the lowlands change from a nomadic to a settled way of life, and what role did the region's abundant rivers play in that change?

25. Which mountain resources in South America encouraged Spanish exploration, conquest, and colonization?

INTERPRET PRIMARY SOURCES

Portuguese historian Pero de Magalhães Gândavo wrote *The Histories of Brazil* in 1576. Read his description of the valuable resources found in Brazil, and then answer the questions below.

> Certain Indians arrived in the Captaincy of Porto Seguro. . . giving news of the existence of green stones in a mountain range many leagues inland; and they were emeralds. . . and there were many other mountains of blue earth in which they [Indians] assured them there was much gold.

26. **Identify** According to this passage, what important minerals were found inland?

27. **Make Inferences** Based on your reading, how did the discovery of valuable resources in Brazil influence decisions about importing slaves from Africa?

ACTIVE OPTIONS

Synthesize the Essential Questions by completing the activities below.

28. **Write Journal Entries** Describe South America from the perspective of a traveler in the region. Research two countries. In your journal, write two entries on each country: one on climate and elevation, and another on physical features, such as mountains and rivers. Use the following tips to help you write your journal entries. **Share your journal entries with a classmate or friend.**

> **Writing Tips**
> • Take notes before you begin to write.
> • Write an outline to help you organize details for the two countries you select.
> • Include as many details as possible.
> • Write in first-person narrative.

29. **Create Charts** Work in a group to make a four-column comparison chart that compares Brazil, Argentina, Venezuela, and Ecuador. Use online sources to gather the data. Compare your group's data with data found by other groups. What sources did you find most useful in your research?

	Brazil	Argentina	Venezuela	Ecuador
Climate				
Elevation				
Major Cities				
Main Crops				
Year of Independence				

SOUTH AMERICA TODAY

PREVIEW THE CHAPTER

Essential Question In what ways is South America culturally diverse?

KEY VOCABULARY

- mestizo
- roots
- language family
- topography
- immigrate
- cuisine

ACADEMIC VOCABULARY
predominant

TERMS & NAMES

- Aymara
- Quechua
- Guaraní
- Mundurukú
- Creole
- Candomblé

Essential Question How is modern South America building its economies?

KEY VOCABULARY

- prosperous
- coup
- soybean
- fertilizer
- temperate
- Mediterranean climate
- export revenue
- profitable

ACADEMIC VOCABULARY
ruthless, diversify, erratic

TERMS & NAMES

- Dry Pampas
- Wet Pampas

Essential Question How has Brazil become an economic power?

KEY VOCABULARY

- steel
- ethanol
- biofuel
- megacity
- slum
- infrastructure
- venue

ACADEMIC VOCABULARY
foremost, impact

TERMS & NAMES

- São Paulo
- Rio de Janeiro

TECHTREK

FOR THIS CHAPTER

Student eEdition

Maps and Graphs

Interactive Whiteboard GeoActivities

Digital Library

Go to **myNGconnect.com** for more on South America.

This cathedral in Brazil's capital city reflects the country's efforts to modernize.

SECTION **1** CULTURE

TECHTREK
myNGconnect.com For photos of
indigenous cultures in South America

Digital
Library

1.1 Indigenous Cultures

> **Main Idea** Indigenous cultures in South America maintain traditions in a modern world.

Indigenous groups have lived in South America for thousands of years. Their descendants still live and work in the region today.

European Contact

As you have learned, the arrival of the Spanish, the Portuguese, and other Europeans during the colonial period changed life for the indigenous people in South America. Unfamiliar diseases and warfare with Europeans killed many native people and substantially reduced their populations.

European contact also introduced a new population group: the mestizo. Many people in South America are **mestizo**, or of mixed European and native ancestry. Some mestizos also have African **roots**, or cultural origins, because of the large numbers of slaves who were imported in the colonial period.

> **Critical Viewing** Potato farmers work near the Aymara community of San Jose, Peru. Based on what you see in the photo, what is farming like for the Aymara?

Maintaining Traditions

The Aymara, Quechua, and Guaraní are the three largest indigenous groups in South America today. The **Aymara** (eye MAHR uh) live in the Andes of Peru and Bolivia. Today, the Aymara continue some of the traditions of their ancestors, such as speaking their native language, also called Aymara. The Aymara also continue to herd llamas and alpacas and grow crops such as potatoes and quinoa (KEEN wah), a grain that grows well in the mountains.

The **Quechua** (KEHCH wah) live in the Andes of Peru, Ecuador, and Bolivia. Like the Aymara, many Quechua farmers live in isolated mountain villages, far away from modern cities and lifestyles. Their religious practices are a blend of Catholicism and native beliefs. The Quechua have maintained traditions such as weaving and speaking their native language, Quechua.

The **Guaraní** (gwah rah NEE) live in Paraguay and are the main indigenous group in that country. Most people in Paraguay trace their roots to both Guaraní and Spanish ancestors. The Guaraní culture is represented in Paraguay's folk art and the Guaraní language.

The **Mundurukú** (moon doo ROO koo), another important native group, live in Brazil. Their ancestors farmed, hunted, and fished in the rain forest. Although they live in relative isolation, one way the Mundurukú adapt to the modern world is by selling forest products such as latex, a liquid substance harvested from native rubber trees.

INDIGENOUS POPULATIONS OF SOUTH AMERICA

Country	National Population	Indigenous Population	Indigenous Percentage
Argentina	33,900,000	372,996	1.10
Bolivia	8,200,000	4,142,187	50.51
Brazil	155,300,000	254,453	0.16
Chile	14,000,000	989,745	7.07
Colombia	35,600,000	620,052	1.74
Ecuador	10,600,000	2,634,494	24.85
French Guiana	104,000	4,100	3.94
Guyana	806,000	45,500	5.65
Paraguay	4,800,000	94,456	1.97
Peru	22,900,000	8,793,295	38.40
Suriname	437,000	14,600	3.34
Venezuela	21,300,000	315,815	1.48

Source: International Union for Conservation of Nature, 2007

Before You Move On

Monitor Comprehension What traditions do indigenous groups maintain today?

FORMATIVE ASSESSMENT

DATA LAB
 GeoJournal

1. **Analyze Data** According to the chart, in what countries do the highest and lowest numbers of indigenous people live? In what ways might low percentages impact indigenous populations?

2. **Make Inferences** Based on the chart and text, what percentage of people in Paraguay are indigenous? What other way might they identify themselves?

3. **Explain** What does "mestizo" mean? In what way does this cultural group reflect South America's colonial past?

TECHTREK

my NG connect.com For a map
of indigenous languages

Maps and
Graphs

1.2 Language Diversity

Main Idea South America has a rich diversity of languages.

As you know, South America is a land of varied cultures. It is also a land of diverse languages. The various languages that South Americans speak come from at least 50 **language families**, or groups of related languages.

European Influences

The **predominant**, or main, languages in South America are Spanish and Portuguese. Other European languages spoken include French and Italian. Spanish, Portuguese, French, and Italian are Romance languages, or languages that come from Latin. During the 1800s, the land extending from Mexico through South America became known as Latin America. The widespread presence of the Romance languages helped to define Latin America as a culture region.

European presence in South America also brought about the development of Creole. **Creole** is a language that results when two other languages are combined together. During the colonial period, plantation workers created a common language that was a blend of European and non-European languages. In this way, groups who spoke different first languages found a way to communicate. Some people living on the Atlantic and Caribbean coasts of South America still speak Creole today.

Although European influence on languages in South America is strong, indigenous languages continue to thrive.

INDIGENOUS LANGUAGES

Language Families
- Arawakan
- Chibcha
- Cariban
- Macro-Gê
- Quechua-Aymara
- Ticuna
- Tukanoan
- Tupi-Guaraní
- Yanomami
- Other indigenous language

The large number of indigenous groups on the continent is one reason why more than 500 languages are spoken today. A second reason is because of the physical features, or **topography**, of the land and the density of its jungles. The mountain ranges and rain forests isolated indigenous groups and kept their languages separate from European languages.

Indigenous Languages

In some countries, indigenous languages hold official status because of their widespread use. For example, along with Spanish, Quechua is considered an official language in Peru. In Paraguay, where Guaraní and Spanish are both official languages, more people speak and understand Guaraní than Spanish.

6.04.E draw sketch maps; 6.04.F locate major world countries; 6.15.B identify and describe traits that define cultures; 6.17.A identify and describe factors that influence cultural change; 6.17.D identify and define impact of cultural diffusion on individuals and world societies 6.21.B analyze by drawing conclusions, summarizing; 6.21.C interpret information from maps

Critical Viewing Spanish is the official language of Colombia, but more than 80 indigenous languages are also spoken there. In what ways might language be an important part of this celebration?

Unlike Quecha and Guaraní, however, some indigenous languages in South America are spoken only by small groups of people in remote parts of the continent. Several of these languages—such as Kallawaya in Bolivia, Sáliva in Colombia, and Maka in Paraguay—are endangered, or in danger of vanishing completely.

National Geographic's Enduring Voices Project is working toward preserving these and other endangered languages. Enduring Voices works in language-diverse places, such as South America, to document and record indigenous languages. As this project captures the sounds and words of these languages, it is also helping to preserve the histories, songs, and stories of the cultures that speak them.

Before You Move On
Summarize What factors have contributed to South America's language diversity?

FORMATIVE ASSESSMENT

LANGUAGE LAB  GeoJournal

1. **Identify and Describe** Language is a culture trait. Tell how new languages spread and combined in South America. Then describe geographic factors that have preserved indigenous languages.

2. **Draw Conclusions** Why might people who speak endangered languages be willing to work with the Enduring Voices Project?

3. **Interpret Maps** Based on the map, which indigenous language families are represented along the Tocantins River?

4. **Draw a Sketch Map** Identify the location of the region's countries by drawing them on a sketch map. Talk with a partner about how geography and culture might have played a role in establishing political borders.

1.3 Daily Life

> **Main Idea** South Americans' daily activities reflect aspects of their varied cultures.

Like most people around the world, South Americans' daily lives revolve around how they worship and celebrate, how they learn and play, and what they eat.

Religious Practices

As you have read, Roman Catholicism became the main religion in South America during the colonial period. Spanish and Portuguese colonists were Roman Catholic, and they converted many native people to Catholicism. Roughly 80 percent of South Americans are Roman Catholic, with Brazil having the world's largest Catholic population.

After the Spanish and Portuguese, other Europeans **immigrated**, or moved permanently, to South America. Some of them were Protestants, or Christians who separated from the Catholic church. Today, most Protestants in the region live in Chile and the Guianas and in parts of Brazil, Bolivia, and Ecuador.

Other religious practices exist alongside Christianity in South America. In Brazil, a local religion called **Candomblé** combines African spiritual practices with Catholicism. The annual Carnival festival in Brazil mixes Roman Catholic practices with traditional African celebrations.

School and Sports

Every country in South America provides public education. However, some children struggle to receive adequate schooling. These children may live in rural areas with few schools and may not attend school regularly. Other children may leave school at an early age to help earn money for their families. Though some barriers to education exist, the majority of people on the continent are able to read and write.

Critical Viewing A teacher conducts class in Peru. How would you describe the students, their classroom, and what they are doing?

6.15.B identify and describe common traits that define cultures; 6.16.A identify institutions basic to all
societies (religious, educational); 6.18.B relate ways past has influenced expressions of culture; 6.22.C express
ideas orally based on experiences; 6.22.D create written material based on research

Playing *futbol*—known in the United States as soccer—or watching a favorite team compete is a popular pastime in South America. Brazilian soccer teams frequently compete in, and often win, the World Cup, a global soccer tournament that occurs once every four years.

Regional Food

South American **cuisine**, or the food that is characteristic of a particular place, varies in different parts of the continent. In coastal countries like Chile, seafood is often a main ingredient, such as in a stew called *paila marina* (pie yuh mah REE nah). In Uruguay and Argentina, where there is a good deal of grazing land, beef is often served. In the mountains of Peru, llamas provide a good source of meat. Stews with black beans, or *feijoadas* (fay ho AH daz), rice, and vegetables are common throughout South America.

Before You Move On

Monitor Comprehension What daily activities reflect the various cultural elements of South America?

 Critical Viewing This market is located in Santiago, Chile. Based on this photo, what kind of food can you infer might be important in Chilean cuisine?

FORMATIVE ASSESSMENT

WRITING LAB GeoJournal

Connect to Texas Suppose you are living in a South American country for a short time. Write a blog or online journal entry describing your experiences. Describe traits of culture that are common to your home life in Texas.

Step 1 Outline your blog entry. Write a topic sentence for each paragraph you plan to write.

Step 2 Use online sources to research your country of choice. Include aspects of culture mentioned in the text.

Step 3 Look for photos that might illustrate different aspects of daily life in that country.

Step 4 Read aloud your entry or post it for your classmates.

2.1 Comparing Governments

Main Idea The governments of South America are moving toward democracy and strengthening their economies.

In the early 1800s, movements for independence in countries across South America brought an end to colonial rule. However, in many countries, real power remained in the hands of a few wealthy families. South American governments have gone through many changes since independence. Argentina, Peru, and Chile provide three examples of the challenges South American governments have struggled to overcome.

Argentina

Argentina has faced economic and political challenges. After independence in 1816, dictators held power for several decades. In the 1850s, the country adopted a new constitution and entered into a **prosperous**, or economically strong, period that lasted until the late 1920s. In 1930, military officers staged a **coup**, or takeover, of the government. After another coup in 1943, Colonel Juan Domingo Perón gained support among workers.

In 1946, Perón was elected president. He raised wages for workers and established social and economic programs. Many of Perón's reforms were expensive, and corruption weakened his administration. In the 1950s, he was overthrown by military leaders who were dissatisfied with his leadership.

For decades, Argentina sought to move forward. Since the 1980s, democratically elected presidents have faced serious

economic crises. Today, though, Argentina's constitutional government is stable, and, since recovering from a serious financial crisis in the early 2000s, its economy is one of the strongest in South America.

Peru

Peru gained independence in 1821. For most of its history, Peru's government has shifted between democratically elected presidents and military rule. Many leaders—even those elected democratically—have favored wealthy landowners over ordinary citizens. Political instability made economic and social progress difficult in Peru.

In 2001, Peruvians elected their first Quechua president, Alejandro Toledo. Toledo had the support of the Quechua people and a large majority of Peru's poor population. His election demonstrated that Peru's government could represent all of its citizens.

Critical Viewing President Alejandro Toledo greets children in Peru. What does this photo lead you to think about Toledo's approach to leadership?

Chile

Chile declared independence in 1818. Since then, Chile has mostly been a representative democracy. Like many other countries in South America, though, Chile has experienced rule by a dictator. In 1973, Salvador Allende's government was overthrown by the military. General Augusto Pinochet (peen oh SHAY) acted as a dictator in Chile for nearly two decades, from 1973 to 1990. Pinochet was **ruthless**, or cruel, and no one was allowed to disagree with his policies.

Chile returned to democratic rule in 1990. In 2006, the people of Chile elected its first female president, Michelle Bachelet Jeria. Bachelet's election was especially meaningful. Her father was

killed during Pinochet's rule, and she and her mother were both imprisoned and exiled because they opposed Pinochet. As president, Bachelet helped ease poverty, expanded social reforms, and used profits from copper exports to create new employment opportunities.

Before You Move On
Summarize In what ways are Argentina, Peru, and Chile alike and different in their movement toward democracy and strong economies?

FORMATIVE ASSESSMENT

SPEAKING LAB  GeoJournal

1. **Turn and Talk** Turn to two other classmates and compare the governments of Argentina, Peru, and Chile since independence. What are their challenges? Take notes during your discussion. Ask each of your partners a question and respond to their questions in turn.

2. **Describe** What did Michelle Bachelet achieve to improve life in Chile? Discuss why her election was significant. How might it influence other contemporary societies?

Michelle Bachelet Jeria arrives at the presidential palace after her inauguration in Chile in 2006.

2.2 The Pampas Economy

Main Idea The Pampas is a fertile region that contributes to the economic success of Argentina.

The wide, grassy Pampas is South America's major crop-growing region. The Pampas is also the grazing ground for another valuable export—cattle.

An Agricultural Heart

The Pampas is a large plain that stretches across central Argentina from the Atlantic Ocean to the foothills of the Andes Mountains. The Pampas covers about 295,000 square miles in the northern half of the country, nearly one-quarter of Argentina's land area.

During the colonial period in the 1800s, the Spanish imported horses and cattle to the region. Spanish and mestizo cowboys, called gauchos, herded cattle and sheep on the Pampas, a practice continued by modern gauchos.

Cattle grazing takes place in the region's dry zone, or the **Dry Pampas**, located in the west. The humid zone, or the **Wet Pampas**, is in the east. Agriculture abounds in the Wet Pampas, where nearly 40 inches of rain falls on average each year. Together, the cattle industry and agriculture contribute greatly to the region's economic prosperity.

In the 1980s, a new crop became profitable in Argentina: **soybeans**, a type of bean grown for food and also for industrial products such as plastics, inks, and adhesives. Soybeans grow quickly and unlike crops such as wheat and corn, do not need as much **fertilizer**, a substance added to soil to enrich it. In response to demand, Argentines increased soybean production. Low production costs and high prices in global markets make soybeans a valuable crop in Argentina.

Critical Viewing This gaucho is tending sheep on the Pampas in Argentina. Based on the photo, how would you describe the work of a gaucho?

6.05.A identify and describe geographic factors responsible for economic activities; 6.10.A give examples of agriculture; 6.21.B analyze by summarizing; 6.21.C interpret information from maps

1 DRY PAMPAS Argentines are among the world's top consumers of beef. Beef consumption per capita in Argentina is 119 pounds per year compared to 82 pounds per year in the United States.

2 SOYBEANS These soybeans are grown in the Wet Pampas. Soybeans are used to make vegetable oil and livestock feed. Soybeans can also be cooked and eaten, and are a good source of protein.

3 WET PAMPAS This patchwork of crops is in the Wet Pampas, Argentina's main agricultural area. Soybeans, wheat, corn, flax, and alfalfa are some of the crops grown here.

ARGENTINA'S LAND USE

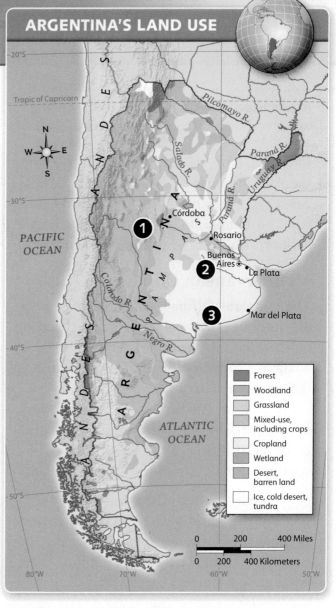

Legend:
- Forest
- Woodland
- Grassland
- Mixed-use, including crops
- Cropland
- Wetland
- Desert, barren land
- Ice, cold desert, tundra

Before You Move On

Summarize How does the rich soil of the Pampas contribute to Argentina's economy?

FORMATIVE ASSESSMENT
READING LAB   GeoJournal

1. **Monitor Comprehension** What crop has become an important export in Argentina, and why is it profitable?

2. **Interpret Maps** How might Argentina's coastal location benefit its agriculture industry?

3. **Turn and Talk** Do you have prior knowledge of or experience with what is shown in the photos? Take turns in a small group telling stories using the photos, key vocabulary, and asking and answering questions for more information.

2.3 Chile's Food Production

TECHTREK

myNGconnect.com For a map of
Mediterranean climates and photos of agriculture

Maps and
Graphs

Digital
Library

Main Idea The mild climate in central Chile
supports abundant agricultural exports.

Chile is a long, narrow country. It borders
the Pacific Ocean and stretches more than
2,600 miles north and south. Central Chile
enjoys a **temperate** , or mild, climate that
supports an extensive agriculture industry.

Mediterranean Climates

The temperate climate along the coasts
of southern Europe and northern Africa
on the Mediterranean Sea is called
a **Mediterranean climate** . This climate is
defined by hot, dry summers and mild,
rainy winters. Mediterranean climates are
found in southern Australia, southern and
central California in the United States,
southern South Africa, and central Chile.

One reason such widely scattered
parts of the world have similar climates
is because of latitude. Remember that
latitude measures distance from the
equator in degrees. Places with

Mediterranean climates have similar
latitudes either north or south of the
equator. Generally, these latitudes measure
between 30°S–40°S or 30°N–40°N. In
addition to similar latitudes, places with
Mediterranean climates lie on western
coasts and have similar precipitation
patterns because of their coastal positions.

Chile's Agricultural Bounty

Because of Chile's location on the western
coast of South America at nearly 30°S,
farmers in central Chile can grow a
rich mix of crops. Fruits such as grapes,
peaches, and apples are grown for export
in Chile's fertile valleys.

Two crops in particular show
how Chile takes full advantage of its
Mediterranean climate: grapes and olives.
A thriving wine industry depends on
the many varieties of grapes that grow in
Chile's vineyards. Chile has also become a
major exporter of olives and specialty

Critical Viewing Chile exports 40 percent of its
fruit to the United States. What details in this photo
tell you these peaches are imported from Chile?

WORLD MEDITERRANEAN CLIMATES

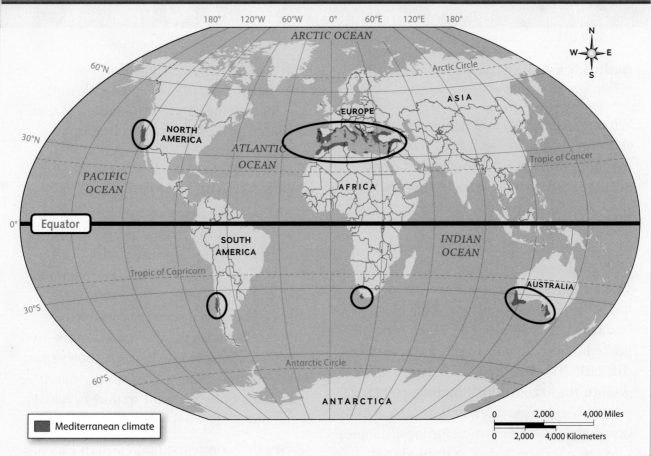

Mediterranean climate

olive oils. Chilean wine and olive oil exports increased dramatically in the 1990s and early 2000s. Both wine and olive products are exports traditionally dominated by Mediterranean countries such as Italy, France, and Greece.

While agricultural production is a source of growth for Chile's economy, copper remains its most valuable export. The growth of agricultural exports since the late 1980s helped Chile **diversify**, or vary, its economy. Diverse economies depend on multiple industries—such as mining and agriculture—and tend to be stronger and more competitive.

Before You Move On

Summarize What main agricultural exports are supported by Chile's Mediterranean climate?

FORMATIVE ASSESSMENT

MAP LAB

GeoJournal

1. **Interpret Maps** Look at the grid on the map of Mediterranean climates. Which Mediterranean climates are located south of the equator? At what latitude do they lie?

2. **Location** According to the map, where is the largest Mediterranean climate region located? Based on your reading, what might the weather be like during the winter months in that region?

3. **Summarize** Summarize the characteristics of a Mediterranean climate. Use the chart below to organize your summary.

MEDITERRANEAN CLIMATES	
1.	
2.	

2.4 Products of Peru

TECHTREK

myNGconnect.com For photos of
agricultural products of Peru

 Digital
Library

Main Idea Agriculture and mining industries in Peru are helping the economy to grow.

What do asparagus and gold have in common? They are both products of the mountains of Peru. Agriculture and mining are key industries in this country.

High Mountain Agriculture

The Andes Mountains in Peru feature high peaks and low, steep valleys. The valleys are fertile in some areas, but often not suitable for agriculture. **Erratic**, or inconsistent, rainfall and rugged terrain make large-scale farming in the mountains difficult. The few crops that do grow well in these conditions include potatoes, wheat, corn, vegetables, and quinoa. These crops are generally grown for local people and are not exported. The limited cash crops grown for export include sugarcane, wheat, coffee, and asparagus, a vegetable valued in international markets.

Other economic activities in the Peruvian mountains include cattle and alpaca ranching. By far, though, the most profitable economic activity in Peru is mining.

Peru's Mining Economy

Peru is a leading exporter of metals and minerals such as silver, zinc, lead, copper, tin, and gold. These products are used in many industries worldwide. For example, copper is made into wire for electrical and telephone systems. Lead is used for automobile batteries, and gold is made into jewelry and electronic parts. Exports of metals and minerals alone supply nearly two-thirds of Peru's total **export revenue**, or the money earned from exports.

Two developments helped Peru increase export revenues from mining so that it became more profitable than agriculture. The first was new government policies on mine ownership, which began in

> **Critical Viewing** This Peruvian farmer uses traditional methods to plow a field. What can you infer about the challenges of this type of farming?

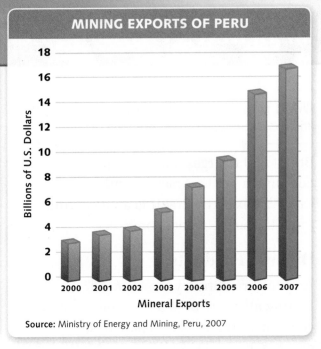

MINING EXPORTS OF PERU

Billions of U.S. Dollars

Mineral Exports

Source: Ministry of Energy and Mining, Peru, 2007

^ Critical Viewing Copper is made into electrical wire and into tubes and pipes used for plumbing. Based on the photo, what can you infer about the importance of this export?

the early 1990s. These domestic policies brought about private ownership of the mines. This shift allowed for investment in needed improvements, which led to a rapid growth of the mining industry in Peru. Existing mines became more **profitable**, or financially successful, and new mines opened. Today the Yanacocha gold mine, which opened in Peru in 1993, is the largest gold mine in South America.

Peru's mining revenues also increased because of an upward trend in world prices for silver, gold, and other metals and minerals since the late 1990s. For 2012, the country's mining revenues reached $25 billion and were estimated to continue to increase to $30 billion by the end of 2013.

Before You Move On

Monitor Comprehension What exports have helped Peru's economy to grow?

FORMATIVE ASSESSMENT

DATA LAB   GeoJournal

1. **Interpret Graphs** Calculate the difference in mining revenues between 2000 and 2007, measured in dollars. What accounts for that difference?

2. **Summarize** What governmental policy change in the 1990s led to a growth of the mining industry?

3. **Human-Environment Interaction** With a group, list all the ways you can think of that metals from Peru might be part of your daily life.

3.1 Brazil's Growing Economy

TECHTREK

myNGconnect.com For an online map of Brazil's resources and photos of economic activity

 Maps and Graphs

 Digital Library

> **Main Idea** Brazil is a leading industrial country and has a strong, diverse economy.

Brazil is the largest and most populous country in South America with many different exports. Brazil is an emerging force in the global economy.

Diverse Products

Agriculture, forestry, ranching, and fishing all contribute to the country's economy. Brazil exports bananas, oranges, mangoes, cacao beans, soybeans, rice, cashew nuts, and pineapples. It is the **foremost**, or leading, global coffee producer and grows one-third of the world's total number of coffee beans. Brazil is also one of the leading exporters of sugarcane and raw sugar.

Forests in Brazil contain many raw materials, including timber, or wood prepared for use in construction. Wood from Brazilian forests is also used to make pulp for paper products. Mahogany, a rain forest hardwood, is a valuable export used to make fine furniture.

Cattle ranching is a big business in Brazil. Export products from cattle include leather and beef. Today, Brazil exports more beef than the United States, Australia, and Argentina.

> **Critical Viewing** Sugarcane has sharp leaves that scratch and cut. Based on what you see in the photo, what protective gear is this cutter wearing?

Brazil's coastline stretches more than 4,600 miles along the Atlantic Ocean. New technology, facilities, and processes will allow Brazil to develop its commercial fishing industry.

Mining and Manufacturing

Mining contributes to Brazil's growing economy. Brazil is a top producer and exporter of iron ore, bauxite (aluminum ore), gold, copper, and diamonds. Oil wells dot Brazil's coast.

In addition to its mineral production, Brazil's manufacturing industry is central to the country's economic strength. Brazil manufactures **steel**, a strong metal made from iron and other metals. Brazilian steel is used in automobiles, transportation equipment, and aircraft. Brazil also manufactures computers and electronic equipment.

Fuel of the Future

Brazil has produced and exported sugarcane and sugar since the 1500s. For several decades, the country has been developing its sugar-based ethanol industry. **Ethanol** is a liquid removed from sugarcane or corn. It is mixed with gasoline to make an alternative fuel called a **biofuel**. Cars that run on biofuels use less gasoline. Because they are made from agricultural products, biofuels are a renewable source of energy. Today, Brazil is poised to be a global leader in the production of biofuel.

Before You Move On
Summarize What factors enable Brazil to develop a diverse economy?

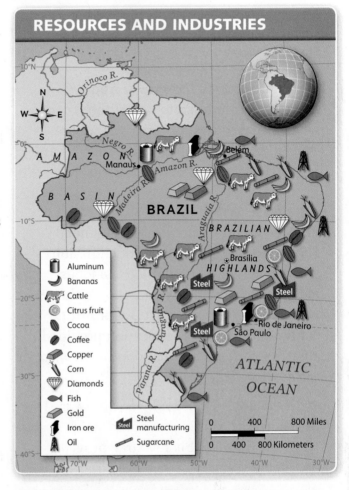

RESOURCES AND INDUSTRIES

Legend:
- Aluminum
- Bananas
- Cattle
- Citrus fruit
- Cocoa
- Coffee
- Copper
- Corn
- Diamonds
- Fish
- Gold
- Iron ore
- Oil
- Steel — Steel manufacturing
- Sugarcane

0   400   800 Miles
0   400   800 Kilometers

FORMATIVE ASSESSMENT

MAP LAB   GeoJournal

1. **Interpret Maps** Study the map. What are two resources that provide fuel for Brazil? Where are these resources found?

2. **Draw Conclusions** Where are most cattle resources located in Brazil? Why might cattle not be concentrated in the Amazon Basin?

3. **Human-Environment Interaction** In what ways have Brazilians used natural resources to build a strong economy?

4. **Form and Support Opinions** What part of Brazil's economy do you think will be the most important in the future? Why?

3.2 São Paulo

TECHTREK

myNGconnect.com For a graph
and photos of São Paulo, Brazil

Maps and
Graphs

Digital
Library

> **Main Idea** São Paulo is the largest city in the
> Southern Hemisphere and a major contributor to
> Brazil's economy.

São Paulo, Brazil, has grown from a quiet mission town to one of the world's **megacities**, or cities with more than 10 million people. It is a cultural and industrial center of South America.

Early Growth

Portuguese missionary priests founded São Paulo in 1554. They built a mission and school, which remained the focus of the town for many years. São Paulo was also a point of departure for military expeditions. Its hilltop location provided a natural defense and panoramic views of the surrounding area.

In the late 1600s, gold was discovered in the nearby mountains of the state of Minas Gerais. This resource proved extremely valuable, and by the mid-1700s, Brazil was producing nearly half of the world's supply of gold. Roughly 50 years later, gold deposits were mostly depleted. However, coffee production soon replaced gold mining as the main economic activity. By the mid-1800s, coffee had become a significant export crop. Wealth gained from coffee production transformed São Paulo and contributed to its rapid growth in industry and population.

In just 20 years between 1880 and 1900, the population of São Paulo jumped from 35,000 to 240,000. Some of the population growth came from rural to urban migration. However, much of the city's growth was the result of immigration from Asia and Europe.

The Modern City

In the mid-1900s, São Paulo became the industrial center of Brazil. By the 1950s, the automotive industry was well

6.03.B answer questions about geographic distributions; 6.04.B identify, explain geographic factors responsible for population patterns; 6.21.B analyze by summarizing; 6.21.C interpret information from graphs; 6.22.A use social studies terminology correctly

developed. Jobs in the industry attracted workers from other parts of Brazil and other South American countries. São Paulo continues to manufacture and export one million cars each year.

In addition to manufacturing industries, tourism has contributed to the city's economic growth. Today, São Paulo attracts people from countries all over the world. Visitors to São Paulo enjoy the city's museums, its shopping district, its diverse collection of restaurants, and a bustling nightlife.

One result of the rapid expansion of São Paulo's economy is the explosive population growth since 1950. Many people who migrated there made their homes in **slums**, or overcrowded and

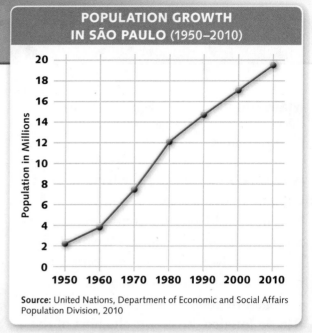

POPULATION GROWTH IN SÃO PAULO (1950–2010)

Population in Millions

Source: United Nations, Department of Economic and Social Affairs Population Division, 2010

poverty-stricken urban areas. Slums, or *favelas*, as they are called in Brazil, developed on the outskirts of the city. Slums are not unique to São Paulo, but are characteristic of large cities that experience rapid population growth.

Before You Move On
Summarize What industries are most important in São Paulo today?

These young people are part of a fashion event staged at a São Paulo train platform.

FORMATIVE ASSESSMENT

DATA LAB

 GeoJournal

1. **Interpret Graphs** According to the graph, during what two decades did São Paulo experience the most rapid rate of growth? What accounts for that increase?

2. **Analyze Data** Using the data in the graph, how much larger in millions of people was São Paulo in 2010 than 1950? Describe population growth in São Paulo since the 1990s.

3. **Movement** Explain how migration has influenced São Paulo. What were some pull factors in the city's history? Be sure the meaning of *pull factor* is clear in your response.

3.3 Impact of the Olympics

TECHTREK

myNGconnect.com For photos of
Olympic preparations and Guided Writing

Digital
Library

Student
Resources

Main Idea Brazil is working hard to maximize the economic and social impact of the 2016 Olympic Games.

Athens, Greece, hosted the first modern Olympics in 1896. Since that time, the International Olympic Committee (IOC) has decided which countries would host the games. Not once had the committee chosen a city in South America. That changed in 2009 when the IOC selected **Rio de Janeiro**, Brazil, as the host of the 2016 Olympics.

Preparing the City

Rio has previous experience hosting international sports events. In 2007, Brazil hosted the Pan-American Games, which are similar to the Olympics but open only to countries in the Western Hemisphere. At that time, Brazil's government made improvements to the **infrastructure**, or the basic systems that a society needs, such as roads, bridges, and sewers. However, more improvements are needed to host the Olympics. Thirty-four competition **venues**, or locations for organized events, need to be built or updated. Efficient transportation to and from the venues is also important.

The Olympic Games last only a few weeks. However, many in Rio de Janeiro hope that one **impact**, or effect, will be long-term improvements in the health of their city. Overcrowded and often dangerous favelas surround Rio. As part of its Olympic preparations, the city plans to tear down and rebuild in these locations. Areas that were once slums will become paved neighborhoods with running water, electricity, and gas—all of which are missing in the existing favelas.

Critical Viewing Brazilian soccer star Pélé (far right) celebrates winning the bid with the Rio Olympic committee. Based on this photo, what can you say about the committee's reaction?

Hosting the Games

Benefits come to countries that host the Olympic Games. First, constructing buildings such as stadiums and the Olympic Village (where athletes stay) creates jobs. Ideally, these structures will still be used long after the games are over. Businesses such as hotels and restaurants benefit, too. Athletes and tourists from around the world flood a host city and spend money on lodging, food, and other goods. Billions more watch the Olympics on television. With such wide exposure, Rio de Janeiro hopes to earn a reputation as a thriving and world-class city.

Before You Move On

Make Predictions In what ways might the 2016 Olympics change Rio?

FORMATIVE ASSESSMENT

PHOTO LAB   GeoJournal

1. **Analyze Visuals** Look at the photo of Rio de Janeiro. As a tourist visiting Rio, what impression might you have of the city?

2. **Location** Locate the major urban centers of São Paulo and Rio on the map on page 189, or on a globe, and describe their locations. Based on what you have learned about both cities, what factors may have influenced the IOC's decision to choose Rio to host the 2016 games?

3. **Form and Support Opinions** Consider what you learned from the text and photos. Write two or three sentences that explain whether or not you consider Rio a good choice for the 2016 Games. Support your opinion with facts and details. Go to **Student Resources** for Guided Writing support.

The Christ the Redeemer statue atop Corcovado Mountain overlooks Rio de Janeiro.

VOCABULARY

For each pair of vocabulary words, write one sentence that explains the connection between the two words.

1. venue; infrastructure

Olympic hosts often build new infrastructure such as roads and new competition venues for the events.

2. export revenue; profitable

3. Mediterranean climate; temperate

4. soybean; fertilizer

5. megacity; slum

6. steel; ethanol

MAIN IDEAS

7. What are the three largest indigenous groups in South America? (Section 1.1)

8. Why are so many different languages spoken in South America? (Section 1.2)

9. In what ways has religion shaped the daily lives of South Americans? (Section 1.3)

10. What governmental changes have occurred in Argentina, Peru, and Chile since independence? (Section 2.1)

11. How does the Pampas region contribute to Argentina's economy? (Section 2.2)

12. What are the main characteristics of the Mediterranean climate in Chile? (Section 2.3)

13. What are Peru's most profitable exports? Why? (Section 2.4)

14. What exports and industries shape Brazil's economy? (Section 3.1)

15. In what way has population growth put pressure on São Paulo? (Section 3.2)

16. How is Rio de Janeiro preparing to host the 2016 Olympic Games? (Section 3.3)

CULTURE

ANALYZE THE ESSENTIAL QUESTION

In what ways is South America culturally diverse?

Critical Thinking: Summarize

17. In what ways do governments in South America recognize indigenous languages?

18. How did the majority of South Americans become Roman Catholic?

GOVERNMENT & ECONOMICS

ANALYZE THE ESSENTIAL QUESTION

How is modern South America building its economies?

Critical Thinking: Find Main Ideas

19. What industry has contributed to Peru's economic growth?

20. How does Chile's Mediterranean climate influence its economy?

INTERPRET GRAPHS

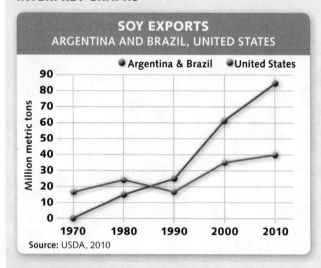

SOY EXPORTS
ARGENTINA AND BRAZIL, UNITED STATES

● Argentina & Brazil   ● United States

Million metric tons

Source: USDA, 2010

21. **Analyze Data** According to the graph, about when did Argentina and Brazil surpass the United States as soy exporters?

22. **Make Generalizations** Look at the graph. What decade represents the most rapid period of growth for soy exports overall?

FOCUS ON BRAZIL

ANALYZE THE ESSENTIAL QUESTION

How has Brazil become an economic power?

Critical Thinking: Make Generalizations

23. What factors point to Brazil's current and future economic strength?

24. In what ways does São Paulo reflect Brazil's economic potential?

INTERPRET MAPS

25. **Location** According to the map, where are most cities located in Brazil? How would you explain this?

26. **Make Inferences** Locate Brasília, the current capital of Brazil, and Rio de Janeiro, its former capital. What might the transfer of capital city from Rio de Janeiro to Brasília in 1960 predict about future development in Brazil?

ACTIVE OPTIONS

Synthesize the Essential Questions by completing the activities below.

27. **Create a Culture Poster** Introduce a country in South America by creating a poster. Use the **Digital Library** to choose photos or draw your own pictures to show its cultural diversity. Include different people and words in their languages, as well as their foods, sports, and celebrations. Research and write short captions for the images. **Present your poster to the class.**

> **Presentation Tips**
> - Write notes for presenting your poster. Ask for help in pronouncing words.
> - Explain why you chose the country or start with an interesting fact about its culture.
> - Point to an image and tell your listeners what it shows.

28. **Conduct Internet Research** Work in a team to research two facts each about the economies of Brazil, Argentina, Colombia, and Peru. Create a chart like the one below. Then find two facts about each country's culture and create another chart. Use online sources. Turn your facts into questions and quiz other teams in a game.

Brazil	Fact 1: _____
	Fact 2: _____
Argentina	Fact 1: _____
	Fact 2: _____
Colombia	Fact 1: _____
	Fact 2: _____
Peru	Fact 1: _____
	Fact 2: _____

Sports and the Olympics

TECHTREK
myNGconnect.com For Guided Writing

Student Resources

As you have learned, the 2016 Olympics will be held in Rio de Janeiro, Brazil, which will mark the first time Brazil has hosted the games. In 2008, China hosted its first Olympic Games. Nearly 11,000 athletes from 204 countries competed in Beijing. Spectators around the world were awed by competing athletes who broke 40 world records and 130 Olympic records.

In any Olympics, the medal count draws the interest of many people. The top medal winners at the 2008 Games were the United States (110), China (100), and Russia (72). Exploring different factors that help determine high medal counts reveals patterns as well as surprises.

Compare

- Australia
- Brazil
- China
- Jamaica
- United States

POPULATION AND ECONOMICS

Countries that win medals generally have populations of at least one million. According to 2008 population statistics, the most populous country represented at the games was China, followed by India and the United States. However, high populations do not guarantee high medal counts. China and the United States won many medals at the 2008 Olympics, but India won just three. Other, less populous countries won more, including two of the least populous countries at the games, Slovenia and Jamaica.

Population is not the only factor in determining a high medal count. How strong a country is economically matters as well. The Gross Domestic Product (GDP), or the measure of the total value of goods and services provided in a country, is one indicator of the economic health of a country. Countries with higher GDPs have more resources for training and supporting athletes for international competitions. At the Beijing Games, the highest ranking GDPs, measured in U.S. billions of dollars, belonged to the United States, Japan, and China. However, countries with low GDPs were competitive with countries with higher GDPs. Zimbabwe, with one of the lowest GDPs, won four medals.

HOME ADVANTAGE

One advantage for hosting the Olympic Games has been, historically, a higher medal yield. Host countries tend to win 30 to 40 percent more medals than in the previous Olympic cycle. At the Beijing Games, China won 100 medals. Four years earlier at the Summer Games held in Athens, Greece, China had won only 63 medals.

OLYMPIC SNAPSHOT
(Beijing Olympics, Summer 2008)

KEY = Total Medal Count = Population (millions) $ = GDP (billions)

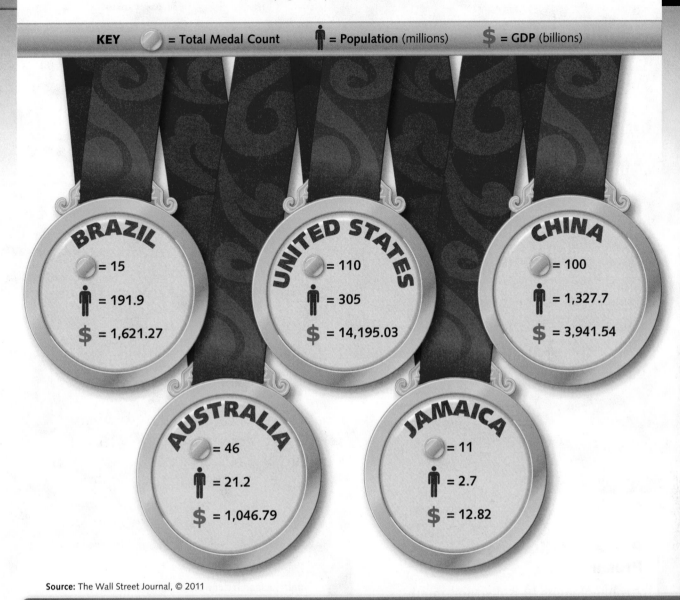

BRAZIL
- = 15
- = 191.9
- $ = 1,621.27

UNITED STATES
- = 110
- = 305
- $ = 14,195.03

CHINA
- = 100
- = 1,327.7
- $ = 3,941.54

AUSTRALIA
- = 46
- = 21.2
- $ = 1,046.79

JAMAICA
- = 11
- = 2.7
- $ = 12.82

Source: The Wall Street Journal, © 2011

FORMATIVE ASSESSMENT
RESEARCH LAB GeoJournal

1. **Explain** Which three countries have the highest GDPs and populations? How does Australia compare to these countries?

2. **Identify** Of the countries listed above, which has the lowest GDP? How does its medal count compare with Brazil's?

3. **Make Predictions** How many medals did Brazil win in 2008? Based on historical patterns of "home advantage," how many medals can you guess Brazil might win at the 2016 Games?

Research and Draw Conclusions Select two countries, each from a different part of the world. Research their performances at one of these Summer Olympic Games: Athens (2004), Sydney (2000), or Atlanta (1996). Compare your findings to the Olympic snapshot of the 2008 Beijing games above. In what ways do your countries compare to the top medal winners? What surprises did you find?

Active Options

TECHTREK
myNGconnect.com For photos of Amazon rain forest life

 Digital Library

ACTIVITY 1

Goal: Extend your understanding of life in the Amazon rain forest.

Create a Photo Gallery

The Amazon rain forest is home to thousands of species of birds, land animals, and fish. Thousands of types of trees, plants, and insects live there, too. Do research and choose several examples of different Amazon plants, insects, and animals that interest you. Use the Magazine Maker CD-ROM to create a photo gallery of the plants, animals, and insects you selected. Write a description of each photo. Invite your friends to visit your virtual gallery.

Spider monkey, Amazon rain forest, Peru

ACTIVITY 2

Goal: Learn more about South American history and culture.

Prepare a Multimedia Presentation

Archaeologists have learned much about different cultures in South America. National Geographic grant recipient Christina Conlee explores artifacts left behind by the Nasca culture. Use online sources to find information about them. Then select your favorite artifact and create a multimedia presentation about it. Include at least one photo of the artifact in your presentation. Write a label that describes the artifact. Create a title for your presentation.

ACTIVITY 3

Goal: Research daily life in Latin America.

Write a Feature Article

The culture region called Latin America includes Mexico, Central America, the islands of the Caribbean, and South America. Because of years of Spanish colonial influence, Latin America is united by common cultural practices. Using online sources, write a feature article about aspects of daily life that unite Latin America as a culture region. Focus on food, sports, festivals, religion, and traditional dress.

6.20.A give examples of scientific discoveries and technological innovations, including the roles of scientists and inventors, that have transcended the boundaries of societies and have shaped the world; 6.20.B explain how resources, belief systems, economic factors, and political decisions have affected the use of technology; 6.20.C make predictions about future social, political, economic, cultural, and environmental impacts that may result from future scientific discoveries and technological innovations; 6.22.D create written and visual material based on research

TEKS

TEKS PROJECT

Goal: Make predictions about the impact of future discoveries and innovations.

Create Innovation Awards

Scientists, inventors, artists, engineers—these people help improve the lives of others by solving problems or creating new ways of doing things. Throughout history, some societies have supported new ideas and made discoveries and advances. Why do some societies make advances while others do not? Belief systems or lack of government support might get in the way of new technologies. New ideas in science may take years to prove they are worthwhile. In what other ways might the use of new discoveries or technologies be affected?

Predict Now think about ways technology can affect societies. With a partner, predict how a *future* discovery or innovation could have a positive impact on:

- a social problem such as hunger or inequality
- an economic need such as more jobs
- an environmental concern such as loss of habitat or pollution
- cultural expressions such as new forms of literature or music
- a political situation such as a border dispute

Carry It Out Share your predictions. As a class, choose one prediction from each of the categories to receive an innovation award. Then form five groups. Each group will name and design one of the awards. In your group, make drawings or a model of the award—or create the actual award. Conduct research if you need to and be as innovative as possible within the time you have.

Write a brief description of the future innovation and organize a class awards ceremony.

An innovative sculpture for experiencing light and color, called Exxopolis, has visitors in Houston.

UNIT 5

EXPLORE EUROPE WITH NATIONAL GEOGRAPHIC

NATIONAL GEOGRAPHIC

Some archaeological sites are underwater. Emerging Explorer Katy Croff Bell works with archaeologists in the Mediterranean and Black seas to help them figure out where to look for submerged secrets.

The Alps are the highest and most extensive mountain range in Europe. They stretch across central Europe and are concentrated in France, Germany, Italy, Switzerland, and Austria. This is the Lauterbrunnen Valley in Oberland, Switzerland.

The Colosseum in Rome is one of the Roman Empire's greatest architectural and engineering achievements. The arena, completed in A.D. 80, seated nearly 50,000 spectators who watched gladiator games, performances, and even mock naval battles.

London,
United Kingdom

3,673 miles

Washington, D.C.

Go to myNGconnect.com for maps of Europe.

CONNECT WITH THE CULTURE

Architect I.M. Pei's modern pyramid serves as an entrance into the Louvre in Paris, France. The museum holds some of the world's greatest art treasures.

EUROPE
GEOGRAPHY & HISTORY

PREVIEW
THE CHAPTER

Essential Question How did Europe's physical geography encourage interaction with other regions?

KEY VOCABULARY
- peninsula
- uplands
- polder
- bay
- fjord
- canal
- waterway
- ecosystem
- marine reserve

ACADEMIC VOCABULARY
navigable, erosion

TERMS & NAMES
- Northern European Plain
- Alps
- Danube River
- Rhine River

Essential Question How did European thought shape Western civilization?

KEY VOCABULARY
- democracy
- city-state
- golden age
- philosopher
- republic
- patrician
- plebeian
- barbarian
- aqueduct
- feudal system
- serf
- perspective
- indulgence

ACADEMIC VOCABULARY
aristocrat, veto

TERMS & NAMES
- Acropolis
- Alexander the Great
- Julius Caesar
- Augustus
- Christianity
- Middle Ages
- Crusades
- Renaissance
- Johannes Gutenberg
- Martin Luther
- Reformation
- Counter-Reformation

Essential Question How did Europe develop and extend its influence around the world?

KEY VOCABULARY
- navigation
- colony
- textile
- factory system
- radical
- guillotine
- natural rights
- apartheid
- nationalism
- trench
- reparations
- concentration camp

ACADEMIC VOCABULARY
convert, alliance

TERMS & NAMES
- Industrial Revolution
- Enlightenment
- John Locke
- Reign of Terror
- Napoleon Bonaparte
- Treaty of Versailles
- Great Depression
- Adolf Hitler
- Holocaust
- Iron Curtain
- Cold War
- Berlin Wall

TECHTREK
FOR THIS CHAPTER

Student eEdition

Maps and Graphs

Interactive Whiteboard GeoActivities

Digital Library

Go to myNGconnect.com for more on Europe.

Chestnut horses

ATLANTIC OCEAN

Reykjavik
ICELAND

Arctic Circle

Jan Mayen (Norway)
70°N

Barents Sea

Prime Meridian

Norwegian Sea

NORWAY

SWEDEN

FINLAND

Gulf of Bothnia

Faroe Islands (Denmark)
Shetland Islands (U.K.)

Orkney Islands (U.K.)

Hebrides (U.K.)

Oslo

Stockholm

Helsinki

Tallinn

ESTONIA

Volga R.

NORTHERN IRELAND

SCOTLAND

Edinburgh

North Sea

Gotland (Sweden)

Baltic Sea

Riga

LATVIA

LITHUANIA

Vilnius

Minsk

BELARUS

Don R.

Belfast

IRELAND

Shannon R.

UNITED KINGDOM

Dublin

DENMARK

Copenhagen

Kaliningrad

WALES

ENGLAND

Cardiff

Thames R.

London

NETHERLANDS

Amsterdam

Elbe R.

Berlin

Vistula R.

Warsaw

POLAND

Oder R.

Kiev

UKRAINE

Dnieper R.

English Channel

Channel Islands (U.K.)

BELGIUM

Brussels

GERMANY

Frankfurt

Prague

CZECH REPUBLIC (CZECHIA)

Kraków

LUXEMBOURG

Paris

Rhine R.

Seine R.

Loire R.

LIECHTENSTEIN

Danube R.

Vienna

SLOVAKIA

Bratislava

CARPATHIAN MOUNTAINS

MOLDOVA

Chisinau

Sea of Azov

FRANCE

Bay of Biscay

Bern

SWITZERLAND

Mt. Blanc (4,810 m) 15,781 ft

AUSTRIA

SLOVENIA

Ljubljana

Budapest

HUNGARY

Zagreb

CROATIA

Belgrade

ROMANIA

Bucharest

Black Sea

Rhône R.

Po R.

PYRENEES

Douro R.

ANDORRA

SAN MARINO

MONACO

ITALY

BOSNIA AND HERZEGOVINA

Sarajevo

Danube R.

SERBIA

Prishtina

KOSOVO

BULGARIA

Sofia

PORTUGAL

SPAIN

Madrid

Tagus R.

MONTENEGRO

Podgorica

Rome

VATICAN CITY

Corsica (France)

Adriatic Sea

Skopje

Titana

MACEDONIA

ALBANIA

Lisbon

GIBRALTAR (U.K.)

Balearic Islands (Spain)

Sardinia (Italy)

Tyrrhenian Sea

Ionian Sea

GREECE

Athens

Aegean Sea

Sicily (Italy)

Rhodes (Greece)

MALTA

Valletta

Mediterranean Sea

Crete (Greece)

0   200   400 Miles
0   200   400 Kilometers

30°W 20°W 10°W 0° 10°E 20°E 30°E 40°E 50°E 60°E

60°N

50°N

40°N

30°N

1   2   3   4   5

A B C D E F G H

TECHTREK

myNGconnect.com For online maps of Europe and Visual Vocabulary

Maps and Graphs

Digital Library

EUROPE PHYSICAL

Elevation

feet	meters
10,000+	3,050+
5,000	1,524
2,000	610
1,000	305
500	152
0	0
Below sea level	

Visual Vocabulary
uplands

Visual Vocabulary
peninsula

> **Main Idea** Europe is made up of several peninsulas with varied land regions and climates.

Europe is a "peninsula of peninsulas." A **peninsula** is a body of land surrounded on three sides by water.

A Peninsula of Peninsulas

Europe forms the western peninsula of Eurasia, the landmass that includes Europe and Asia. In addition, Europe contains several smaller peninsulas, including the Italian, Scandinavian, and Iberian. Europe also consists of significant islands, including Great Britain, Ireland, Greenland, Iceland, Sicily, and Corsica.

Four land regions form Europe. The Western Uplands are made up of **uplands**, or hills, mountains, and plateaus, that stretch from the Scandinavian Peninsula to Spain and Portugal. The **Northern European Plain** is made up of lowlands that reach across northern Europe. The Central Uplands are hills, mountains, and plateaus at the center of Europe. The Alpine region consists of the **Alps** and several other mountain ranges.

Varied Climates

Most of Europe lies within the humid temperate climate region. The North Atlantic Drift, an ocean current of warm water, keeps temperatures relatively mild. Winds also affect climate. The sirocco (shuh RAH koh) sometimes blows over the Mediterranean Sea and brings wet weather to southern Europe at different seasons. The mistral is a cold wind that sometimes blows through France and brings cold, dry weather to the country.

CLIMATE

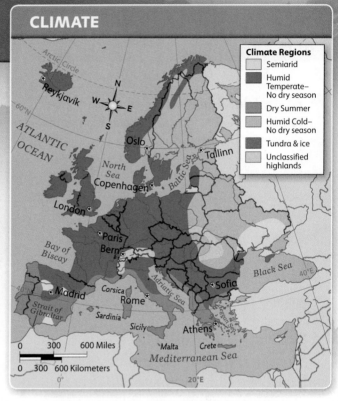

In general, a Mediterranean climate brings mild, rainy winters and hot, dry summers and supports a long growing season. Hardy plants grow best in this climate. In contrast, Eastern Europe has a humid continental climate with long, cold winters. Iceland, Greenland, and northern Scandinavia have a polar climate and a limited growing season.

Before You Move On

Monitor Comprehension What are the main land regions and climates in Europe?

FORMATIVE ASSESSMENT

MAP LAB

GeoJournal

1. **Interpret Maps** Study both maps in this lesson. Which climate regions are found on the Scandinavian Peninsula? Based on the climate, where do you think most of the peninsula's population is concentrated?

2. **Compare and Contrast** Use both maps to determine what places in Europe have the coldest climates. What geographic characteristics do these places have in common?

SECTION 1 GEOGRAPHY

1.2 A Long Coastline

TECHTREK

myNGconnect.com For an online map and
photos of Europe's coastal features and ports

 Maps and Graphs

 Digital Library

Main Idea Europe's long coastline helped to promote trade, industry, exploration, and settlement on the continent.

Europe has more than 24,000 miles of coastline. If you walked 25 miles a day along the continent's coasts, it would take more than four years to walk the entire distance. These extensive coastlines provided early Europeans with great access to oceans and seas.

Trade and Industry

Europe's water access has benefited the continent in many ways. These benefits include the growth of trade and the development of industry.

Trade has been central to Europe's growth. The civilizations of ancient Greece and Rome flourished largely because of trade. Early sailors traveled to nearly every port on the roughly 2,500-mile-long Mediterranean Sea. They brought back from other lands goods and ideas, such as grains, olive oil, and new religions, that greatly influenced European culture.

Europe also developed several industries that depend on oceans and seas, including a fishing industry. In fact, Europeans have fished along their coastlines for thousands of years.

In lowland areas such as the Netherlands, the people created a way to drain water from the sea in order to increase their farming industry. They built dikes, or giant walls, to hold back the sea in order to create **polders**. Most of the low-lying land of a polder, which once was part of the seabed, was transformed into farms. Today, the Netherlands has about 3,000 polders.

Critical Viewing A boat docks at a harbor in Gdansk (guh DANTSK), Poland, on the Baltic Sea. What do you notice about the harbor?

6.03.A pose and answer geographic questions; 6.04.B identify geographic factors responsible for patterns of population; 6.04.D identify physical and human geographic features; 6.05.A identify and explain factors responsible for location of economic activities; 6.07.B identify ways people have modified the environment; 6.21.B analyze by identifying cause-effect relationships, summarizing

EUROPE'S MAJOR LANDFORMS AND RIVERS

MAP TIP

This map shows Europe's landforms and rivers, but it also includes country borders within the continent. You can use the map in Section 1.1 to identify the countries.

Exploration and Settlement

The location of the continent near large bodies of water also encouraged exploration. In the 1400s, explorers helped European rulers obtain raw materials, spread religious beliefs, and build empires.

Over time, people settled around the ports where the ships docked. Towns often grew up near **bays**, which are bodies of water surrounded on three sides by land. Some of the towns, including Hamburg, Germany, became large cities as trade and industry expanded. In contrast, the deep and narrow bays of Norway, called **fjords** (fee ORDZ), did not encourage settlement.

Before You Move On

Summarize In what ways has Europe benefited from its long coastline?

MAP LAB

 GeoJournal

1. **Pose and Answer** Use the map above and those in Section 1.1 to pose and answer three questions with a partner about the location of countries, cities, or geographic features in relation to one another.

2. **Analyze Cause and Effect** Complete the chart by writing one effect for each cause.

CAUSE	EFFECT
Trade was conducted on Europe's oceans and seas.	Goods and ideas spread.
Industry developed on the coasts.	
Cities grew along the coasts.	

1.3 Mountains, Rivers, and Plains

TECHTREK

myNGconnect.com For an online map and photos of Europe's landforms and natural resources

Maps and Graphs   Digital Library

> **Main Idea** The landforms and resources in Europe support many economic activities.

As you have already learned, Europe consists of four main land regions. A great variety of landforms lie within these regions, including mountains and a vast plain. Many important rivers also cross the continent.

Mountain Chains

Europe's Alpine region contains several mountain chains. The Alps stretch from Austria and Italy to Switzerland, Germany, and France. The Pyrenees are located to the west of the Alps and separate Spain and France. South of the Alps lie the Apennines, which run along the Italian Peninsula. The Carpathians extend through Poland, Romania, and Ukraine.

All of these mountain chains provide natural resources for industries, including forests, which supply wood, and mineral resources, such as iron ore. The valleys between the mountains contain fertile land for growing crops.

Rivers and Plains

Europe has a wealth of rivers. Many are **navigable**, which means that boats and ships can travel easily on them. The **Danube River** is an important transportation route. The river starts in Germany and passes along or through ten countries before emptying into the Black Sea. The **Rhine River** is another vital body of water used to transport goods deep inland. The river originates in Switzerland, winds through Germany, and flows into the North Sea.

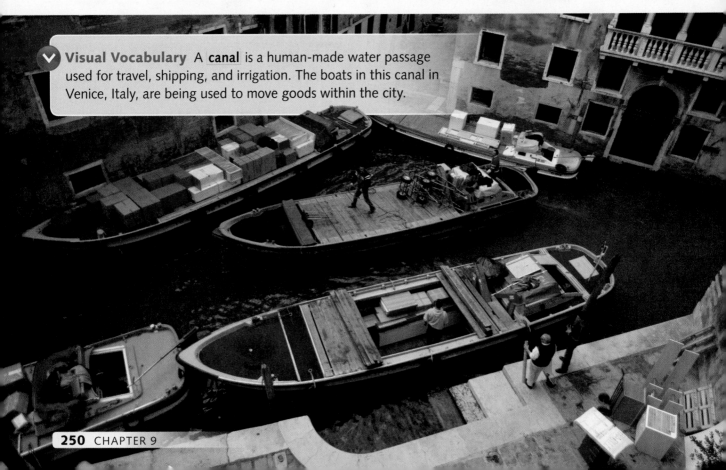

> **Visual Vocabulary** A **canal** is a human-made water passage used for travel, shipping, and irrigation. The boats in this canal in Venice, Italy, are being used to move goods within the city.

LAND USE AND NATURAL RESOURCES

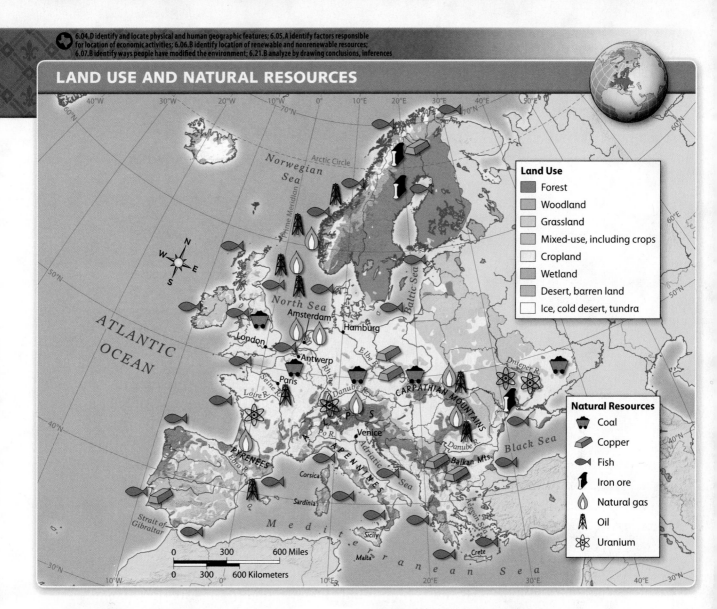

Land Use

- Forest
- Woodland
- Grassland
- Mixed-use, including crops
- Cropland
- Wetland
- Desert, barren land
- Ice, cold desert, tundra

Natural Resources

- Coal
- Copper
- Fish
- Iron ore
- Natural gas
- Oil
- Uranium

For centuries, Europeans have built canals. When linked together, canals and rivers form **waterways**, or navigable routes of travel and transport. The small country of the Netherlands has more than 3,000 miles of rivers and canals.

Many of the rivers in Europe cross the Northern European Plain. This vast lowland region stretches across France, Belgium, Germany, and Poland all the way to Russia. The fertile soil on the plain makes it ideal for growing crops, and thousands of farms are sprinkled throughout the region. The plain also contains some of the largest and most heavily populated cities, or urban centers, in Europe, including Paris, France.

Before You Move On

Summarize What economic activities are supported by Europe's landforms and resources?

FORMATIVE ASSESSMENT

MAP LAB

GeoJournal

1. **Interpret Maps** What natural resources are found in the Carpathian Mountains? What geographic challenges might workers deal with when they extract these resources?

2. **Draw Conclusions** Find the Danube River on the map. What natural resources are found along the river? What role might the Danube play in handling these resources?

3. **Make Inferences** What natural resources are found in the North Sea? What impact might they have on the countries bordering the sea?

1.4

SECTION ① GEOGRAPHY

NATIONAL GEOGRAPHIC

TECHTREK

myNGconnect.com For a map, photos, and an Explorer Video Clip

Maps and Graphs

Digital Library

Protecting the
Mediterranean
with Enric Sala

Main Idea Human activities have harmed the Mediterranean Sea's natural environment.

Under the Sea

On June 4, 2010, National Geographic Explorer-in-Residence Enric Sala began an expedition: exploring the underwater world of the Mediterranean Sea. He wanted to find out how human activities have affected the sea's ecosystem.

myNGconnect.com

For more on Enric Sala in the field today

An ecosystem is a community of living organisms and their natural environment. Three human activities have had an impact on the Mediterranean's ecosystem. One is overfishing, which occurs when people catch fish at a faster rate than the fish can reproduce. Another is pollution. The third is overdevelopment, which has occurred as coastal populations have grown. (See the chart on the next page.) Growing populations have added to the Mediterranean's pollution and the erosion, or wearing away, of its coastline.

Critical Viewing Sala swims with a sea turtle. What equipment is he using during this underwater exploration?

MEDITERRANEAN EUROPE

Sala's work was inspired by Jacques Cousteau, the French underwater explorer. When he became an explorer himself, Sala sailed with Cousteau's son, Pierre-Yves Cousteau. They compared the condition of the Mediterranean Sea now with its condition 65 years earlier and found that the sea has been damaged. Sala concluded, "We have lost most of the large fish and the red coral because of centuries of exploitation [misuse]."

Marine Reserves

In spite of the harm that has been done, Sala sees signs of hope. During their Mediterranean expedition, he and Cousteau visited the Scandola Natural Reserve, near Italy. Scandola is a marine reserve, or protected area where people are prohibited from fishing, swimming, or anchoring their boats. As a result, marine life is thriving at the reserve. "This marine reserve," Sala said, "has restored the richness that Jacques Cousteau showed us 65 years ago."

Before You Move On

Monitor Comprehension **What can be done to protect the Mediterranean Sea from the human**

POPULATION OF MEDITERRANEAN CITIES (IN MILLIONS)		
City	1960	2011
Athens, Greece	2.2	3.8
Barcelona, Spain	1.9	5.4
Istanbul, Turkey	1.74	11.0
Marseille, France	0.8	1.4
Rome, Italy	2.33	3.3

Source: UN, 2013

FORMATIVE ASSESSMENT

DATA LAB

 GeoJournal

1. **Interpret Charts** Which city, by 2011, had undergone the most growth and which the least? Based on the text, what can you infer about the impact on the coastline in each case?

2. **Identify Problems and Solutions** Use the problem solving process on page R20. With a partner, come up with options for preserving Mediterranean fish populations.

3. **Turn and Talk** Take notes as you listen closely to Sala's video clip in the **Digital Library**. With a partner, determine the "bad news" and good news in his message.

For more photos from the National Geographic Photo Gallery, go to the **Digital Library** at myNGconnect.com.

The Carnival in Venice

Ancient Roman aqueduct

Musicians in Krakow, Poland

Critical Viewing These rocky pinnacles, or pointed formations, took shape thousands of years ago on a hill in Scotland called the Storr. The largest of the formations shown here is known as the Old Man of Storr.

Italy's Amalfi Coast

French pastries on display

The Parthenon in Athens

Armor from the 1600s

2.1 Roots of Democracy

TECHTREK
myNGconnect.com For an online
map of ancient Greek city-states

Maps and
Graphs

> **Main Idea** The ideas out of which democracy grew first took root in ancient Athens.

The rulers of Athens laid the groundwork for **democracy**, a government in which people can influence law and vote for representatives. Democracy was one of the great achievements of Greek civilization.

The Greek City-States

Greece lies on both the Balkan and Peloponnesus (pehl uh puh NEE suhs) peninsulas. The two are connected by an isthmus, or narrow strip of land. People first arrived in Greece around 50,000 B.C. Early civilizations developed between 1900 B.C. and 1400 B.C.

Around 800 B.C., several Greek city-states started to thrive. A **city-state** is an independent community that includes a city and its surrounding territory. The mountains on the peninsulas made transportation and communication difficult. As a result, each city-state developed independently. The two largest and most important Greek city-states were Athens and Sparta.

Each city-state established its own community and government. The earliest form of government in the city-states was a monarchy, in which a king or queen rules. Over time, a group of upper-class noblemen called **aristocrats** began to act as advisors to the king. In some city-states, the aristocrats set up a ruling council that served as the government. This council was a form of oligarchy (AHL ih gahr kee), in which a small group rules.

Around 650 B.C., tyrants in many of the city-states seized power away from the councils, took control of the government, and re-established one-person rule. Today, any harsh ruler may be called a tyrant. However, not all tyrants in ancient Greece were bad leaders. Some were fair and had the support of the Greek people.

Democracy in Athens

Around 600 B.C. in Athens, a statesman named Solon controlled the government of the city-state. He established assemblies in which all the wealthy people of Athens—not just the aristocrats—made the laws.

Then in 508 B.C., a leader named Cleisthenes (KLIHS thuh neez) increased the people's power even more. He established a direct democracy. Under this government, all citizens voted directly for laws. However, only Athenian adult males were citizens and had the right to vote.

Athens and Sparta

Democracy developed in Athens but not in all city-states. Sparta, Athens' rival, had an oligarchy ruled by a small group of warriors. They supervised a military training system for Spartan boys.

In 490 B.C., Athens and Sparta joined together to defeat the invading army of the Persian Empire under King Darius I. After that, however, the two city-states became fierce enemies.

Before You Move On

Summarize What ancient Greek ideas served as the roots of modern democracy?

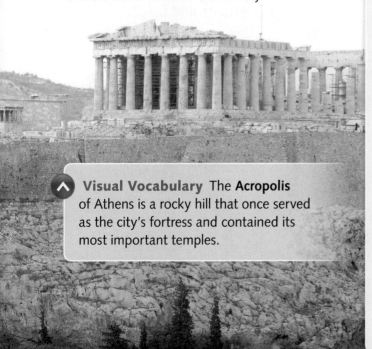

Visual Vocabulary The **Acropolis** of Athens is a rocky hill that once served as the city's fortress and contained its most important temples.

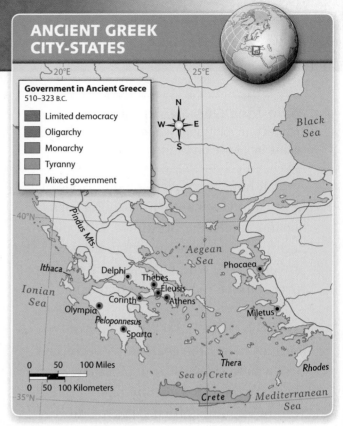

ANCIENT GREEK CITY-STATES

Government in Ancient Greece
510–323 B.C.

- Limited democracy
- Oligarchy
- Monarchy
- Tyranny
- Mixed government

Black Sea
Aegean Sea
Ionian Sea
Ithaca
Delphi
Thebes
Eleusis
Corinth
Athens
Olympia
Peloponnesus
Sparta
Phocaea
Miletus
Thera
Rhodes
Sea of Crete
Crete
Mediterranean Sea
Pindus Mts.

0   50   100 Miles
0 50 100 Kilometers

FORMATIVE ASSESSMENT

READING LAB GeoJournal

Vocabulary Use the Greek roots in the chart to form a word in English that completes each of the following sentences:

a. The form of government that represents the people is called _____ (use your own paper) _____.

b. People empowered to enforce a city's laws are the _____ (use your own paper) _____.

c. The ruler of a kingdom is also called a _____ (use your own paper) _____.

SELECTED ENGLISH WORDS FORMED FROM GREEK ROOTS		
Greek Root	**Meaning**	**English Word**
demos	people	democracy
polis	city-state	policy
aristo	best	aristocracy
monos	one	monarchy
oligo	few	oligarchy

TECHTREK

myNGconnect.com For an online
map and photos of Classical Greece

 Maps and
Graphs

 Digital
Library

Main Idea Greek ideas about democracy, architecture, philosophy, and science have had a lasting influence on Western culture.

As you have learned, democracy began in ancient Greece. In 461 B.C., Pericles became the leader of Athens. His rule began a **golden age**, a period of wealth and power during which democracy developed further and Greek culture flourished.

Golden Age of Greece

Pericles had three goals for Greece. The first was to strengthen democracy. He accomplished this goal by paying citizens who held public office. This meant that even people who were not wealthy could afford to serve in government.

The leader's second goal was to expand the empire. Pericles built a strong navy and used it to increase Athens' power over the other Greek city-states.

Pericles' third goal was to make Athens more beautiful. He began rebuilding the city, including the Acropolis. Many of Athens' temples had been destroyed during the war with Persia. Pericles constructed a new temple called the Parthenon, dedicated to the goddess Athena for whom Athens was named.

Greek Achievements

The golden age of Greece was a period of extraordinary achievements. Greek architects designed temples and theaters with graceful columns. **Philosophers**, people who examine questions about the universe, searched for the truth. Socrates (SAHK ruh teez) and his student, Plato (PLAY toh), were leading philosophers.

In the sciences, the mathematician Euclid (YOO klihd) developed the principles of geometry. The physician Hippocrates (heh PAH kruh teez) changed the practice of medicine by insisting that illnesses originated in the human body and were not caused by evil spirits.

Greek Culture Spreads

Greece's golden age ended around 431 B.C., when war broke out between Athens and Sparta. The conflict, known as the Peloponnesian War, lasted 27 years and weakened both Athens and Sparta.

Statue of the goddess Athena

1900–1400 B.C.
Early Greek
civilizations
develop.

1900 B.C.

Early Greek
gold lion's head

1000 B.C.

800 B.C.
Greek city-states
begin to thrive.

750 B.C.

ALEXANDER'S EMPIRE, 330 B.C.

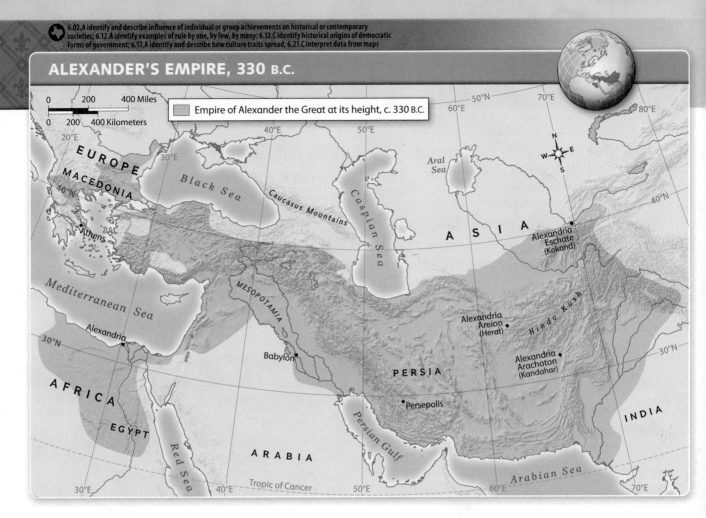

Empire of Alexander the Great at its height, c. 330 B.C.

Around 340 B.C., King Philip II of Macedonia took advantage of the weakened city-states and conquered Greece. In 334 B.C., Philip's son, **Alexander the Great**, became king and began to extend his father's empire. Alexander loved Greek culture and spread its ideas throughout the lands he conquered. Alexander died in 323 B.C. at the age of 33. The Greek ideas about democracy, science, and philosophy that he helped spread shaped the modern world.

Before You Move On

Monitor Comprehension What Greek ideas have had a lasting influence on Western culture?

FORMATIVE ASSESSMENT

MAP LAB GeoJournal

1. **Location** Across which continents did Alexander's empire spread? What empires did Alexander's armies conquer?
2. **Categorize** Look back at Greek history, beginning on page 256. Give examples of government rule by one, by few, and by many.

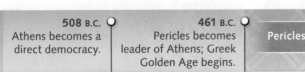

508 B.C.
Athens becomes a direct democracy.

461 B.C.
Pericles becomes leader of Athens; Greek Golden Age begins.

Pericles

340 B.C.
Philip II of Macedonia conquers Greece.

500 B.C.

250 B.C.

490 B.C.
Greeks defeat the Persian Empire.

431 B.C.
Peloponnesian War between Athens and Sparta begins.

334 B.C.
Alexander the Great begins to extend his father's empire.

2.3 The Republic of Rome

> **Main Idea** The Roman Republic created a form of government that Europe and the West would later follow.

Around 1000 B.C., the peninsula of Italy was dotted with hundreds of small villages. According to an ancient legend, two brothers named Romulus and Remus founded Rome in 753 B.C. The brothers were said to be the children of a god and to have been raised by a wolf.

The Beginnings of Rome

Archaeologists actually believe that people known as the Latins founded Rome around 800 B.C. They came from a region of Italy called Latium and lived on Rome's seven steep hills, which provided protection from enemy attack. The Tiber River, which flows through Rome, provided water for farming and a route for trade. Over time, Rome developed into a wealthy city-state.

▼ **Critical Viewing** The Roman Forum contained the ancient city's most important buildings, including the Senate. In what ways does this photo reflect Rome's former glory?

A Republic Forms

Around 600 B.C., the Etruscans, a people from northern Italy, conquered Rome. One Etruscan king named Tarquin was a brutal tyrant. In 509 B.C., the Romans rebelled against him, and Roman leaders began to create a republic. A **republic** is a form of government in which the people elect officials who govern according to law.

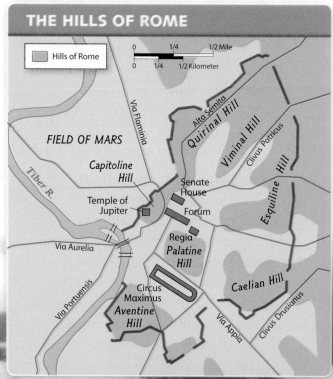

THE HILLS OF ROME

Hills of Rome

0   1/4   1/2 Mile
0   1/4   1/2 Kilometer

FIELD OF MARS
Via Flaminia
Alta Semita
Quirinal Hill
Viminal Hill
Clivus Patricus
Capitoline Hill
Senate House
Esquiline Hill
Tiber R.
Temple of Jupiter
Forum
Via Aurelia
Regia
Palatine Hill
Caelian Hill
Via Portuensis
Circus Maximus
Aventine Hill
Via Appia
Clivus Drusianus

6.02.A identify and describe influence of individual or group achievements on historical or contemporary societies;
6.02.B evaluate political contributions, groups; 6.12.B compare ways societies organize government;
6.21.B analyze by comparing, contrasting; 6.21.C interpret information from charts

GOVERNMENT OF THE ROMAN REPUBLIC

EXECUTIVE

- Two consuls
- Elected to one-year term
- Led the government and controlled the army

LEGISLATIVE

Senate
- 300 members made up of patricians
- Not elected; selected by the consuls to serve for life
- Made the laws and advised consuls

Assembly
- Made up of plebeians
- Elected tribunes as representatives
- Made the laws and selected consuls

JUDICIAL

- Eight judges
- Governed provinces
- Served for one year

Legal Code
- Twelve Tables
- Established rights and responsibilities of Roman citizens

Two main classes of people lived in Rome at this time. The **patricians** were mostly wealthy landowners. The **plebeians** were mostly farmers. At first, only the patricians could take part in government. They controlled the Senate and made laws.

In 490 B.C., plebeians gained the right to form an assembly and elect legislative representatives called tribunes. The assembly made laws and elected the consuls, the two executive officials who led the government for a year at a time. One consul could **veto**, or reject, a decision made by the other consul.

The judicial branch was made up of eight judges who served for one year. These judges oversaw the lower courts and governed the provinces.

Around 450 B.C., the government published the Twelve Tables. These were bronze tablets that set down the rights and responsibilities of Roman citizens. At this time, only adult male landowners born in Rome were citizens. Roman women were citizens but could not vote or hold office.

The Roman Way

Citizens of Rome believed in values that were known as the Roman Way. These values included showing self-control, working hard, doing one's duty, and pledging loyalty to Rome. The Roman Way helped to unite all Roman citizens.

The Romans applied these values as the Republic began to conquer new lands and expand. During the second century B.C., Rome defeated the empire of Carthage in northern Africa. By 100 B.C., Rome controlled most of the lands around the Mediterranean. About this time, tensions began to grow between patricians and plebeians. These tensions triggered a war between the two groups. The war set the stage for the end of the Roman Republic—and the birth of the Roman Empire.

Before You Move On

Summarize What were the Romans' political contributions to later Western societies?

FORMATIVE ASSESSMENT

DATA LAB GeoJournal

1. **Interpret Charts** According to the chart, members of the Senate were selected by the consuls. However, the assembly elected the consuls. In what way did this arrangement help to control the Senate's power?

2. **Turn and Talk** Study the chart and consider what you know about the U.S. government. Then, with a partner, compare and contrast the two systems of government.

2.4 The Roman Empire

TECHTREK

myNGconnect.com For an online map of the
Roman Empire and photos of Roman architecture

Maps and
Graphs

Digital
Library

Main Idea The Roman Empire was one of the largest in history and left a legacy in technology and language.

As you have read, tensions grew between the patricians and plebeians not long after Rome defeated Carthage. The Roman soldiers had brought back great wealth from the conquered territory. They used their wealth to buy large plots of farmland. Small farmers could not compete with them, and the gap between rich and poor widened. In 88 B.C., war erupted between the patricians and plebeians.

Creation of the Empire

After years of war, a general named **Julius Caesar** rose to power and became the sole ruler of Rome in 46 B.C. Caesar started projects to help the poor and tried to re-establish order in Rome, but he developed powerful enemies. In 44 B.C., a small group of senators stabbed him to death.

Octavian, Caesar's nephew, fought in the long, internal war for power that followed Caesar's death. Octavian won, but the war put an end to the Roman Republic. Calling himself **Augustus**, which means "honored one," Octavian became the ruler of the Roman Empire in 27 B.C. His rule began a period called the *Pax Romana*, which is Latin for "Roman peace."

Rome's Decline

For about 500 years, the Roman Empire was the most powerful in the world and extended over three continents. Around A.D. 235, however, Rome had a series of poor rulers. In addition, German tribes, whom the Romans called **barbarians**, began invading the empire from the north.

In 330, Emperor Constantine moved the capital of the weakened empire from Rome to Byzantium, in present-day Turkey, and renamed the city Constantinople. He also made Christianity lawful throughout the empire. **Christianity**, which is based on Jesus' life and teachings as described in the Bible, began in the Roman Empire.

In 395, the empire was divided into an Eastern Empire and a Western Empire with two different emperors. In 476, invaders overthrew the last Roman emperor and ended the Western Empire.

Rome's Legacy

The Western Empire fell, but Rome left the world a great legacy, or heritage. For example, Roman engineers built a network of roads that connected the empire. Many of the roads are still in use.

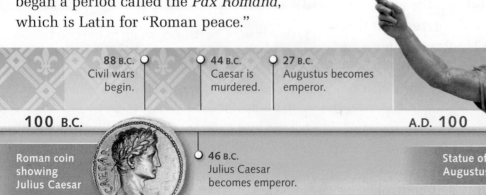

88 B.C.	44 B.C.	27 B.C.
Civil wars begin.	Caesar is murdered.	Augustus becomes emperor.

100 B.C.

A.D. **100**

Roman coin showing Julius Caesar

46 B.C. Julius Caesar becomes emperor.

Statue of Augustus

THE ROMAN EMPIRE AT ITS HEIGHT, A.D. 200

[Map labels:]

JUTLAND

BRITAIN
Londinium

BELGIUM
GERMANY

ATLANTIC OCEAN

E U R O P E

Don R.

Caspian Sea

50°N

GAUL
Lugdunum

A L P S

Potaissa

CRIMEA
Panticapaeum

CAUCASUS MTS.

DACIA

Black Sea

40°N

Narbo
Pyrenees
Massilia

Po R.
Apennines
Ravenna
Salonae
ILLYRIA

Danube R.
Balkan Mts.
THRACE

Sinope
Amisus

ARMENIA

SPAIN
Tarraco

Ebro R.

Corsica

Rome ITALY

Byzantium

CAPPADOCIA

Tigris R.

A S I A

Gades

Sardinia

Brundisium
MACEDONIA

Thessalonica

Pergamum
Ephesus

Tarsus
Antioch

SYRIA

Euphrates R.

New Carthage

Carthage
Sicily
Syracuse

Athens
ACHAEA

Cyprus

Damascus

30°N

MAURETANIA
NUMIDIA

Malta

Crete

Mediterranean Sea
Cyrene

JUDAEA
Aelana

LIBYA

Alexandria

EGYPT

A F R I C A

Nile R.

Red Sea

Tropic of Cancer

Expansion of the Roman Empire

Roman Republic in 264 B.C.

Roman Empire at its height, c. A.D. 200

0   200   400 Miles

0   200   400 Kilometers

N E W S

0°   10°E   20°E   30°E   40°E

The engineers also developed the arch and used it to construct buildings and **aqueducts**, which carried water to parts of the empire. Latin, the language of Rome, became the basis for Romance languages, such as Spanish and Italian. Many English words have Latin roots.

Before You Move On

Summarize Describe the Roman Empire's rise, fall, and legacy.

FORMATIVE ASSESSMENT

MAP LAB   GeoJournal

1. **Interpret Maps** According to the map, over which continents did the Roman Empire extend? What challenges might the size of the empire have presented to its rulers?

2. **Location** Find Byzantium on the map. Why do you think Constantine chose this location to become the capital of the Eastern Empire?

A.D. 395
Empire is divided into an Eastern Empire and a Western Empire.

Painting of German invader

A.D. 300

A.D. 500

A.D. 330
Constantine moves the capital from Rome to Byzantium.

A.D. 476
Rome falls to invaders.

2.5 Middle Ages and Christianity

TECHTREK

myNGconnect.com For portrayals of the Crusades in fine art

Digital Library

> **Main Idea** The Roman Catholic Church and the feudal system influenced Western Europe during the Middle Ages.

After the fall of the Roman Empire, Western Europe entered a period known as the **Middle Ages**, which lasted from about 500 to 1500. During this period, Western Europe consisted of numerous kingdoms. Castles, like those on the Rhine River in Germany, served as defensive fortresses. The Roman Catholic Church helped unite people during the Middle Ages, and the feudal system provided a social structure.

The Roman Catholic Church

In 1054, Christianity officially divided into two parts: the Roman Catholic Church in Western Europe and the Eastern Orthodox Church in Eastern Europe. The Roman Catholic Church was the center of life for most people in Western Europe. It cared for the sick, provided education, and helped preserve books and learning.

The Church also played a leading role in government. It collected taxes, made its own laws, and waged wars. In 1096, the Church began a series of **Crusades**. These were military expeditions undertaken to take back holy lands in Southwest Asia from Muslim control. The Crusades cost many lives and ended in 1291.

The Feudal System

The many kingdoms of Western Europe were often at war. From about 400 to 800, a German group called the Franks stopped the fighting and unified most of Western Europe. Their most important leader was Charlemagne (SHAHR luh mayn).

When Charlemagne died in 814, warfare between the kingdoms returned and Western Europe again became divided. To provide security for each kingdom, the feudal system developed. The **feudal system** was a social structure that was organized like a pyramid. At the top was a king who owned vast territory. Beneath the king were lords, powerful noblemen who owned land. The lords gave pieces of their land to vassals, who pledged their loyalty and service to the lord. Some vassals also served as knights, who were warriors on horseback.

Each lord lived on an estate called a manor, which functioned as a small village. **Serfs**, who farmed the lord's land in return for shelter and protection, were at the bottom of the pyramid. Serf families dwelt in small huts on the manor and gave most of the crops they grew to their lord.

The Growth of Towns

In time, the growth of towns helped end the feudal system. Trade and businesses developed, and people began to leave the manors. A deadly disease called the bubonic plague, which swept through Europe in 1347, also weakened the feudal system. The plague killed millions and greatly reduced the workforce in the towns. Desperate for workers, employers offered higher wages. As a result, farmers left the country to seek the higher-paying jobs in the towns.

Before You Move On
Summarize In what ways did the Roman Catholic Church and the feudal system influence Western Europe during the Middle Ages?

MANOR IN THE MIDDLE AGES

This model shows a simplified view of a feudal manor. Rolling fields and farmland lay outside its walls.

The church was the center of life on the manor.

The lord lived in relative safety and ease in his castle.

Serfs lived in tiny huts with dirt floors.

Guards protected the manor from rival lords.

FORMATIVE ASSESSMENT
VIEWING LAB GeoJournal

1. **Interpret Visuals** What details in the model suggest the measures taken to protect those who lived in the manor?

2. **Make Inferences** Notice the position of the church in the manor. Why might it have been positioned near the lord's castle?

3. **Compare and Contrast** Based on the model and what you have read, in what ways did life probably differ for lords and serfs?

2.6 Renaissance and Reformation

> **Main Idea** Both the Renaissance and the Reformation brought great change to Europe.

You have learned that the growth of towns in Western Europe helped put an end to the feudal system. The Roman Catholic Church also began to lose some of its power at this time. As these key structures of the Middle Ages weakened, the **Renaissance** began to take hold. The Renaissance was a rebirth of art and learning that started in Italy in the 1300s and had spread through Europe by 1500.

The Renaissance

Several other factors led to the Renaissance. Increased trade in the growing towns brought some Italian merchants great wealth. This wealth allowed them to buy the artists' work.

As you have learned, the Western part of the Roman Empire fell in 476. The Eastern part continued and became known as the Byzantine Empire. The fall of this empire in 1453 also advanced the Renaissance. Scholars from the empire came to Italy, bringing with them ancient writings of the Greeks and Romans. Studies of these works encouraged humanism, which focuses on human rather than religious values. In addition,

a German inventor named **Johannes Gutenberg** developed a printing press in 1450 that printed many books in a short amount of time. Soon, more people in Europe had access to knowledge—including the new humanist ideas.

The result was an explosion of ideas expressed in art, architecture, and literature. Artists such as Leonardo da Vinci, Michelangelo (my kuhl AN juh loh), and Raphael (rah fee ELL) used **perspective** to make a painting look as if it had three dimensions. Architects used elements of ancient Greek and Roman design to create churches and buildings. Writers wrote in the everyday spoken language of their region. For example, Dante Alighieri (ah lah GYER ee) wrote *The Divine Comedy* in Italian, not Latin, which was the written language of Church scholars.

The Reformation

Meanwhile, some people began looking more critically at the Church. **Martin Luther**, a monk in Germany, was shocked by the corrupt practices of some priests. To raise funds, they often sold **indulgences**, which relaxed the penalty for sin.

Gutenberg's printing press

1300s
Renaissance begins in Italy.

1300

1308
Dante starts writing *The Divine Comedy* in Italian.

Portrait of Dante

1400

1450s
Johannes Gutenberg develops the printing press.

Critical Viewing *The School of Athens* by Italian artist Raphael uses perspective. The Renaissance painting also portrays ancient Greek philosophers and scientists, celebrating their ideas.

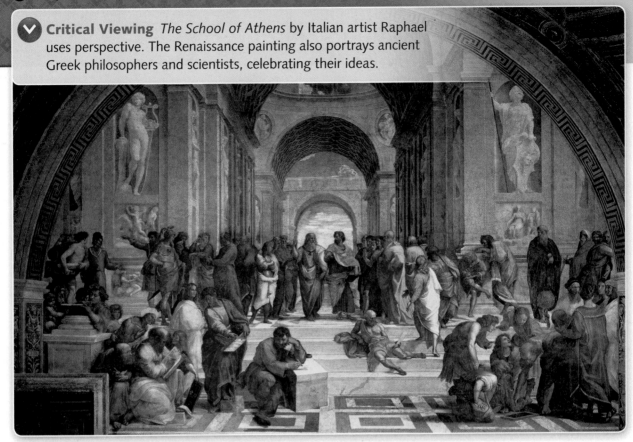

In 1517, Luther wrote the 95 Theses, in which he objected to such practices, and nailed them to a church door. Luther's actions started the **Reformation**, the movement to reform Christianity. Over time, people founded Protestant churches. The term comes from the word *protest*.

In response, the Church began a reform movement called the **Counter-Reformation** and placed more emphasis on faith and religious behavior. Nonetheless, the conflict between Catholics and Protestants would continue for the next 300 years.

Before You Move On

Monitor Comprehension What changes did the Renaissance and Reformation bring to European culture and society?

FORMATIVE ASSESSMENT

READING LAB GeoJournal

1. **Summarize** What was the Renaissance?
2. **Evaluate** What was Gutenberg's contribution to culture and society?
3. **Make Inferences** Explain why access to knowledge changed European societies' relationship to their art and literature.

Michelangelo's *David*

○ 1504
Michelangelo completes the sculpture *David*.

○ 1517
Martin Luther nails his 95 Theses to the door of a church in Wittenberg, Germany.

1500

1600

○ 1497
Leonardo da Vinci finishes painting *The Last Supper*.

In this illustration, Martin Luther posts the 95 Theses.

3.1 Exploration and Colonization

TECHTREK

myNGconnect.com For an online map of European colonization in Africa, Asia, and the Americas

Maps and Graphs

Main Idea To expand trade, Europeans explored Africa, Asia, and the Americas and established colonies on all three continents.

Around 1415, Prince Henry of Portugal decided that he would send explorers to Africa to establish new trade routes. Henry, who became known as Prince Henry the Navigator, founded a **navigation** school. The school taught sailors about mapmaking and shipbuilding and marked the beginning of the Age of Exploration.

European Exploration

Portugal was the first of many European countries to sponsor voyages of exploration. Europeans wanted to find gold and establish trade with Asia to obtain spices, silk, and gems. They also wanted people in other lands to **convert**, or change their religion, to Christianity.

The voyages were filled with danger. Explorers often sailed for months in ships that were small and not always able to withstand strong storms at sea. The men also faced disease and attacks by native peoples. Furthermore, the explorers were traveling to unknown lands. Mapmakers often marked unexplored places with the phrase "Here be dragons."

Nonetheless, Portuguese explorers such as Bartolomeu Dias and Vasco da Gama sailed along the coast of Africa in the late 1400s to open up trade with Asia. Italian explorer Christopher Columbus uncovered a "new world"—the continents of North America and South America—in 1492. In the 1530s, Jacques Cartier (kahr TYAY) explored parts of North America for France. An Englishman, Sir Francis Drake, sailed around the world in 1577.

> **Critical Viewing** In this painting, Columbus and his crew land in North America as Native Americans arrive to meet the explorers in their canoes. What qualities must explorers have had to undertake their voyages?

EARLY COLONIZATION OF AFRICA, ASIA, AND THE AMERICAS

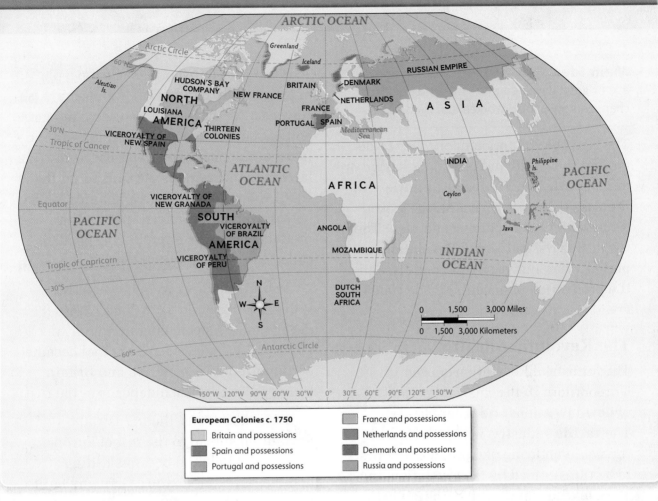

European Colonies c. 1750

- Britain and possessions
- Spain and possessions
- Portugal and possessions
- France and possessions
- Netherlands and possessions
- Denmark and possessions
- Russia and possessions

Establishing Colonies

In addition to trade, Europeans used the voyages of exploration to claim lands for their own countries. When explorers landed in a new place, they declared it a colony. A **colony** is an area controlled by a distant country. As you have learned, Spanish explorers claimed colonies in Mexico and South America. The French and the English also established colonies in North America. By 1650, European countries controlled parts of Africa and Asia as well.

European exploration and colonization resulted in a sharing of goods and ideas known as the Columbian Exchange. From the Americas, Europeans obtained new foods, such as potatoes, corn, and tomatoes. Europeans introduced wheat and barley to the Americas. They also introduced diseases like smallpox. The diseases killed millions of native peoples.

Before You Move On

Monitor Comprehension What inspired Europeans to undertake voyages of exploration, and what did they gain as a result?

FORMATIVE ASSESSMENT

MAP LAB  GeoJournal

1. **Interpret Maps** According to the map, where in Asia did France establish a large colony? Why was this location beneficial geographically?

2. **Identify Problems and Solutions** Study the map. Who was Spain's main rival for colonies in South America? What problems might have arisen from their rivalry?

SECTION 3 EMERGING EUROPE

3.2 The Industrial Revolution

TECHTREK

myNGconnect.com For an online map and images of the Industrial Revolution

Maps and Graphs

Digital Library

Main Idea The Industrial Revolution was an age of great developments in technology that changed how people worked and lived.

The Age of Exploration opened up trade around the world and brought great wealth to many western European countries. To increase this wealth, businesses looked for new ways to expand production. The result was the **Industrial Revolution**, a period when industry grew rapidly, and the production of machine-made goods greatly increased.

The Revolution Begins

The Industrial Revolution started in Great Britain in the 1700s as a result of new inventions and technologies. The **textile** industry, which deals with the manufacturing of cloth, was the first to be transformed by the revolution. In 1769, textile manufacturers began using machines that were run using water from a stream. Then, around 1770, James Hargreaves invented the spinning jenny. This machine allowed workers to make cotton and wool yarn at a much faster rate.

Before these inventions, most people made cloth by hand in their homes. However, the new machines were too large and expensive to use in small houses. Instead, the machines were placed in factories, and workers manufactured the goods there. In these early factories, each person worked on a small part of the product. This way of producing goods is called the **factory system**.

At first, factories were powered by water. Then around 1776, James Watt developed the steam engine, which was powered by coal. As a result, coal became an important raw material, and Britain benefited from its rich deposits of the fuel.

In the late 1700s, the Industrial Revolution spread to the rest of Europe. France and Belgium became leading manufacturers of textiles. Germany built factories for processing iron. Railroad systems developed in the 1800s. In 1825, George Stephenson built the first railroad in England. By 1850, thousands of miles of tracks crossed Europe.

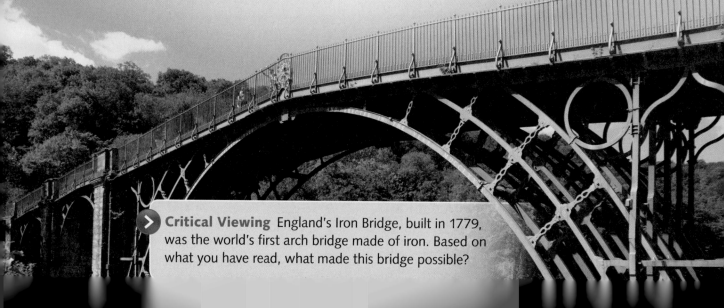

Critical Viewing England's Iron Bridge, built in 1779, was the world's first arch bridge made of iron. Based on what you have read, what made this bridge possible?

INDUSTRIES IN EUROPE, 1840–1890

Legend:
- Coal
- Iron ore
- Textiles
- Railroad
- International boundary

Impact of the Revolution

The Industrial Revolution had a tremendous impact on how people worked and lived. Cities grew rapidly because people migrated there for factory jobs. Standards of living rose, and a prosperous middle class grew.

However, factory workers often faced harsh conditions. Laborers worked as many as 16 hours a day. Child labor was common. Boys and girls as young as five years of age worked in factories and mines. Some were chained to their machines.

Many workers lived in small, crowded houses in neighborhoods where open sewers were common. Diseases spread quickly in these cramped buildings.

Over time, the workers' quality of life improved as sewer systems were created and other public health acts were passed.

Before You Move On
Summarize In what ways did the Industrial Revolution change how people lived and worked?

FORMATIVE ASSESSMENT
MAP LAB
GeoJournal

1. **Interpret Maps** Where in Europe were most of the industries concentrated? What does this suggest about the economies of countries in other parts of Europe?

2. **Human-Environment Interaction** Which industry was the most widespread in Europe? Why was this such an important industry?

3. **Evaluate** Based on the map, which countries probably imported the fewest raw materials?

3.3 The French Revolution

TECHTREK

myNGconnect.com For images
of the French Revolution

Digital
Library

> **Main Idea** The late 1700s in France was a period of economic and political unrest, which led to the French Revolution and the rise of Napoleon.

By the summer of 1789, the French people had not yet benefited from the Industrial Revolution. Harvests were poor, and prices skyrocketed. On July 14, mobs attacked the Bastille, Paris's ancient prison. This action sparked the French Revolution.

Roots of the Revolution

For years, France's lower and middle classes had suffered injustices. French society was composed of three large groups, called the Three Estates. The First Estate was made up of clergy. The Second Estate was made up of the nobility, or aristocrats. The Third Estate included everyone else, from merchants to peasants. The Third Estate paid most of the taxes but had no voice in government.

The people of the Third Estate began to call for change. Many of them were influenced by the **Enlightenment**. This movement stressed the rights of the individual. The ideas of Enlightenment thinkers like Voltaire and **John Locke** had helped inspire the American Revolution in 1776. The American Revolution, in part, inspired the revolution in France.

The Revolution Begins

In May 1789, the Third Estate demanded reforms, but the king of France, Louis XVI, refused. In response, the Third Estate formed the National Assembly. On August 26, 1789, the assembly issued the *Declaration of the Rights of Man and of the Citizen*. This document guaranteed liberty, equality, and property to citizens. The assembly tried to form a new government in which Louis would share power with an elected legislature. However, he again refused to cooperate.

French citizens stormed the Bastille because they thought it held guns and gunpowder.

The guillotine was considered an efficient and painless method of execution.

1785

1790

1795

1789
Mobs attack
the Bastille.

1792
Jacobins seize
power.

1793
King Louis XVI and Marie
Antoinette are executed;
Reign of Terror begins.

1794
Robespierre is
executed, and the
Reign of Terror ends.

6.02.A identify influence of individual or group achievements on historical societies; 6.15.F identify and explain examples of conflict; 6.21.D identify different points of view; 6.22.C express ideas orally based on research

The Radicals Take Over

Finally, in 1792, the Jacobins, a group of **radicals**, or extremists, seized power and formed the National Convention. The following year, the group executed Louis XVI and Marie Antoinette, his queen.

The violence soon got worse. Jacobin leader Maximilien Robespierre led a **Reign of Terror**. The Jacobins used a machine called the **guillotine** (GHEE uh teen) to cut off the heads of an estimated 40,000 people. In July 1794, the French finally turned on Robespierre and executed him.

 Critical Viewing Marie Antoinette, shown here, was often accused of reckless spending. What details in this painting support this accusation?

Napoleon's Rise

After five years of violence, the French were exhausted. France was at war with Prussia, Austria, and Britain, and the government was not ruling effectively.

A young general, **Napoleon Bonaparte**, saw his chance and overthrew the government. Over the next five years, Napoleon increased his powers. He then declared himself Emperor Napoleon I and set about conquering other European powers and building an empire. Britain and Prussia finally defeated him in 1815.

Before You Move On

Summarize What led to the French Revolution and the rise of Napoleon?

FORMATIVE ASSESSMENT

SPEAKING LAB   GeoJournal

Express Ideas Through Speech Get together in a group and do research to prepare a panel discussion in which you will present the viewpoints of various figures from this section.

Step 1 Decide who each person in your group will be. You might choose from King Louis XVI, Marie Antoinette, Maximilien Robespierre, and Napoleon or be a member of the Third Estate.

Step 2 Come up with a few questions that your panel will discuss. The questions should focus on the French Revolution, the Reign of Terror, and Napoleon's rise.

Step 3 Present the panel discussion. As you answer questions or ask others to explain or clarify what they have said, stay in character.

1804
Napoleon names himself Emperor.

1800   **1805**   **1810**

1799
Napoleon overthrows the French government.

Statue of Napoleon on horseback

1815
Napoleon is defeated.

SECTION 3 DOCUMENT-BASED QUESTION

TECHTREK
myNGconnect.com For photos of
the documents and Guided Writing

Digital
Library

Student
Resources

3.4 Declarations of Rights

As you have learned, thinkers like John Locke and Voltaire led the Enlightenment. They asserted that people have natural rights, or rights that people possess at birth, such as life, liberty, and property. Two key documents describe these rights: the American Declaration of Independence and the French *Declaration of the Rights of Man and of the Citizen*. In 1993, Nelson Mandela of South Africa received the Nobel Peace Prize. In his speech at the ceremony, he explained that the rights detailed in the declarations are still important.

DOCUMENT 1

from the **Declaration of Independence** (July 4, 1776)

> We hold these truths to be self-evident, that all men are created equal, that they are endowed [provided] by their Creator with certain unalienable [guaranteed] Rights, that among these are Life, Liberty, and the pursuit of Happiness; that, to secure these rights, Governments are instituted among Men, deriving their just powers from the consent of the governed.

This painting illustrates the signing of the Declaration of Independence.

CONSTRUCTED RESPONSE

1. What rights are citizens guaranteed?

DOCUMENT 2

from the **Declaration of the Rights of Man and of the Citizen** (August 26, 1789)

> The representatives of the French people, organized as a National Assembly, . . . have determined to set forth in a solemn declaration the natural, unalienable, and sacred rights of man. Articles:
>
> 1. Men are born and remain free and equal in rights. Social distinctions [classes] may be founded only upon the general good.
>
> 2. The aim of all political association is the preservation of the natural . . . rights of man. These rights are liberty, property, security, and resistance to oppression.

CONSTRUCTED RESPONSE

2. Think about what you learned in Section 3.3 about the roots of the French Revolution. In what ways might the ideas in this document have inspired the French people to revolt?

6.02.A identify and describe the influence of individual or group achievements on historical or contemporary societies; 6.02.B evaluate the social, political contributions of individuals; 6.21A locate and use primary and secondary sources; 6.21.B analyze by finding main ideas; 6.22.D create written material

MEN ARE BORN AND REMAIN FREE AND EQUAL IN RIGHTS.

— DECLARATION OF THE RIGHTS OF MAN AND OF THE CITIZEN

Mandela and fellow Nobel recipient, F. W. de Klerk, were elected co-presidents of South Africa in 1994.

DOCUMENT 3

from **Nobel Lecture** by Nelson Mandela (December 10, 1993)

Nelson Mandela helped lead the struggle to end **apartheid** (uh PAHRT hyt) in South Africa. This system had denied black South Africans their rights. In recognition of his efforts, Mandela received the Nobel Peace Prize. The following excerpt is from his acceptance speech.

> *The value of our shared reward will and must be measured by the joyful peace which will triumph, because [of] the humanity that bonds both black and white into one human race. . . .*
>
> *Thus shall we live, because we will have created a society which recognizes that all people are born equal, with each entitled in equal measure to life, liberty, prosperity, human rights, and good governance.*

CONSTRUCTED RESPONSE

3. How do the rights Mandela discusses reflect those described in Documents 1 and 2?

FIND OUT MORE Locate the full text of Nelson Mandela's Nobel Lecture. Tell where you found it. Then use a secondary source to learn more about why Mandela was awarded the Nobel Prize.

FORMATIVE ASSESSMENT

WRITING LAB GeoJournal

DBQ Practice Think about the ideas in the Declaration of Independence and the *Declaration of the Rights of Man and of the Citizen*. How did these ideas influence Nelson Mandela?

Step 1. Review your answers to Constructed Response questions 1, 2, and 3.

Step 2. On your own paper, jot down notes about the main ideas expressed in each document.

Document 1: Declaration of Independence

Main Idea(s) _____

Document 2: Declaration of the Rights of Man and of the Citizen

Main Idea(s) _____

Document 3: Nobel Lecture

Main Idea(s) _____

Step 3. Use your notes to construct a topic sentence that answers this question: How did the Declaration of Independence and the *Declaration of the Rights of Man and of the Citizen* influence Nelson Mandela?

Step 4. Write a paragraph that explains specific phrases and ideas in the Declaration of Independence and the *Declaration of the Rights of Man and of the Citizen*. Go to **Student Resources** for Guided Writing support.

3.5 Nationalism and World War I

TECHTREK
myNGconnect.com For an online
map of Europe before World War I

Maps and
Graphs

Main Idea Nationalism, new alliances, and growing tensions in Europe led to World War I.

After the French Revolution, the French people developed powerful feelings of nationalism. **Nationalism** is a strong sense of loyalty to one's country. During the 1800s, nationalism swept through Europe.

Italy and Germany Unify

Nationalism led to unification efforts in Italy and Germany. In 1800, the Italian Peninsula was made up of separate city-states. In 1870, the states came together to form a unified Italy. Germany was also composed of many different states in the early 1800s. Beginning in 1865, Prussia, the most powerful German state, led the way to unification. Driven by nationalist feelings, Prussia fought to take control of other German states away from their non-German rulers. In 1871, the states came together as a united German Empire.

Growing Tensions in Europe

By 1900, tensions had begun to grow among European powers. Nationalism had united some countries from within. However, nationalism also created fierce competition among rival countries.

Mainly, the countries competed for raw materials and colonies in Africa and Asia. To strengthen their position, Britain, France, and Russia formed an **alliance**, or agreement to work toward a common goal, called the Triple Entente. The German Empire and Austria-Hungary formed an alliance known as the Central Powers.

These alliances were tested in June 1914, when Archduke Franz Ferdinand of Austria-Hungary was assassinated in Serbia by a nationalist from Bosnia-Herzegovina. The assassin belonged to a group that was unhappy with Austrian rule of Bosnia-Herzegovina and wanted to unite with Serbia. Immediately after the assassination, Austria-Hungary declared war on Serbia. Then, because Serbia was a Russian ally, Russia declared war on Austria-Hungary. Within weeks, much of Europe had been drawn into war.

A Brutal War

The Great War, as it was called, dragged on for four brutal years. Both sides fought from **trenches**, or long ditches that protected soldiers from the enemy's gunfire. Both sides also used deadly technology, including machine guns, airplanes, tanks, and poison gas. German U-boats, or submarines, sank British ships.

1870
Italy
unifies.

Prussian prime minister
Otto von Bismarck oversaw
German unification.

Illustration of
Archduke Ferdinand's
assassination

1870

1885

1900

1871
German states
unite to form the
German Empire.

1914
Archduke Ferdinand
is assassinated;
World War I begins.

In 1917, Germany seemed to gain an advantage when the Communist Party seized control of Russia's government and economy and made peace with Germany. That same year, the United States entered the war on the side of France and Britain. The fresh American troops helped turn the tide against Germany. In 1918, Germany surrendered to France, Britain, and the United States. By the time the war ended, ten million soldiers had died. About seven million civilians also lost their lives.

Impact of the War

In 1919, Germany signed the **Treaty of Versailles**. Under this peace treaty, Germany was forced to pay several billion dollars in damages and accept full blame for the war. Many of Germany's territories were taken away, and new countries were formed, including Austria, Hungary, Czechoslovakia, Yugoslavia, and Turkey. The treaty angered and humiliated the German people and did little to ease tensions in Europe. These tensions would help lead the way to another world war in a little more than 20 years.

EUROPE BEFORE WORLD WAR I 1914

Triple Entente
Neutral countries that joined the Triple Entente
Central Powers
Neutral countries that joined the Central Powers
Countries that remained neutral

Before You Move On

Monitor Comprehension In what ways did nationalism, new alliances, and growing tensions in Europe lead to World War I?

FORMATIVE ASSESSMENT

MAP LAB

GeoJournal

1. **Region** According to the map, which empires ruled much of Europe in 1914?

2. **Explain** What were the reasons for cooperation and for conflict among European societies in this period? Give an example of each.

Poster illustrating the alliance of Britain, France, and Russia in 1915

Leaders who signed the treaty

1917 United States enters the war.
1919 Treaty of Versailles is signed.

1915

1918 World War I ends.

1930

French prime minister Georges Clemenceau

American president Woodrow Wilson

British prime minister David Lloyd George

3.6 World War II and the Cold War

TECHTREK
myNGconnect.com For an
online map of post-war Europe

**Maps and
Graphs**

> **Main Idea** After World War II was fought to defeat the Axis Powers, the Cold War developed between the democratic United States and the Communist Soviet Union.

At the end of World War I, Germany lost its military power. As you have read, the Treaty of Versailles also placed full blame for the war on Germany and forced it to pay **reparations**, or money to cover the losses suffered by the victors. The Great Depression, which began in 1929, further damaged Germany's economy. The **Great Depression** was a severe downturn in the world's economy. During this crisis, **Adolf Hitler** rose to power in Germany.

World War II

Hitler became the leader of the National Socialist German Workers' Party, or the Nazis. In 1936, Hitler made an alliance with Italy. Germany also formed an alliance with Japan, where the military had seized power. Germany, Italy, and Japan formed the Axis Powers.

Germany's invasion of Poland in 1939 started World War II. Two of Poland's allies, Great Britain and France, declared war on Germany soon after the invasion. Germany responded by conquering Poland and then quickly took over most of Europe, including France.

In 1941, Japan attacked the United States at Pearl Harbor, Hawaii. As a result, the United States abandoned its neutrality and entered the war on the side of Britain and the Soviet Union. Together, they were known as the Allies. Over time, many other countries took sides and joined either the Allies or the Axis Powers.

After more than five years of war, Germany surrendered on May 8, 1945. Allied troops were stunned to find the Nazi **concentration camps** where six million Jews and other victims had been murdered. This mass slaughter was called the **Holocaust**. Japan continued to fight until the United States dropped atomic bombs on Hiroshima and Nagasaki. Japan surrendered on September 2, 1945.

The Cold War

After World War II, the Soviet Union established Communist governments in Eastern Europe. Germany was divided into Communist East Germany and democratic West Germany. The imaginary boundary that separated Eastern and Western Europe was called the **Iron Curtain**. The division marked the beginning of the **Cold War**, a period of great tension between the United States and the Soviet Union.

To defend against possible attack, both sides forged military alliances. Western Europe and the United States formed NATO (North Atlantic Treaty Organization), while Communist Eastern Europe formed the Warsaw Pact. The two never directly waged war against each other during the course of the Cold War.

In the 1980s, many eastern European countries overthrew their Communist governments. In 1991, the Soviet Union itself collapsed. The Cold War ended, and democracy replaced communism throughout Eastern Europe.

Before You Move On

Make Inferences In what ways did World War II help lead to the Cold War?

6.03.A pose and answer geographic questions; 6.11.A identify examples of limited and unlimited governments; 6.15.F give examples of conflict among societies; 6.21.C interpret information from visuals, maps

POST-WORLD WAR II EUROPE, 1950

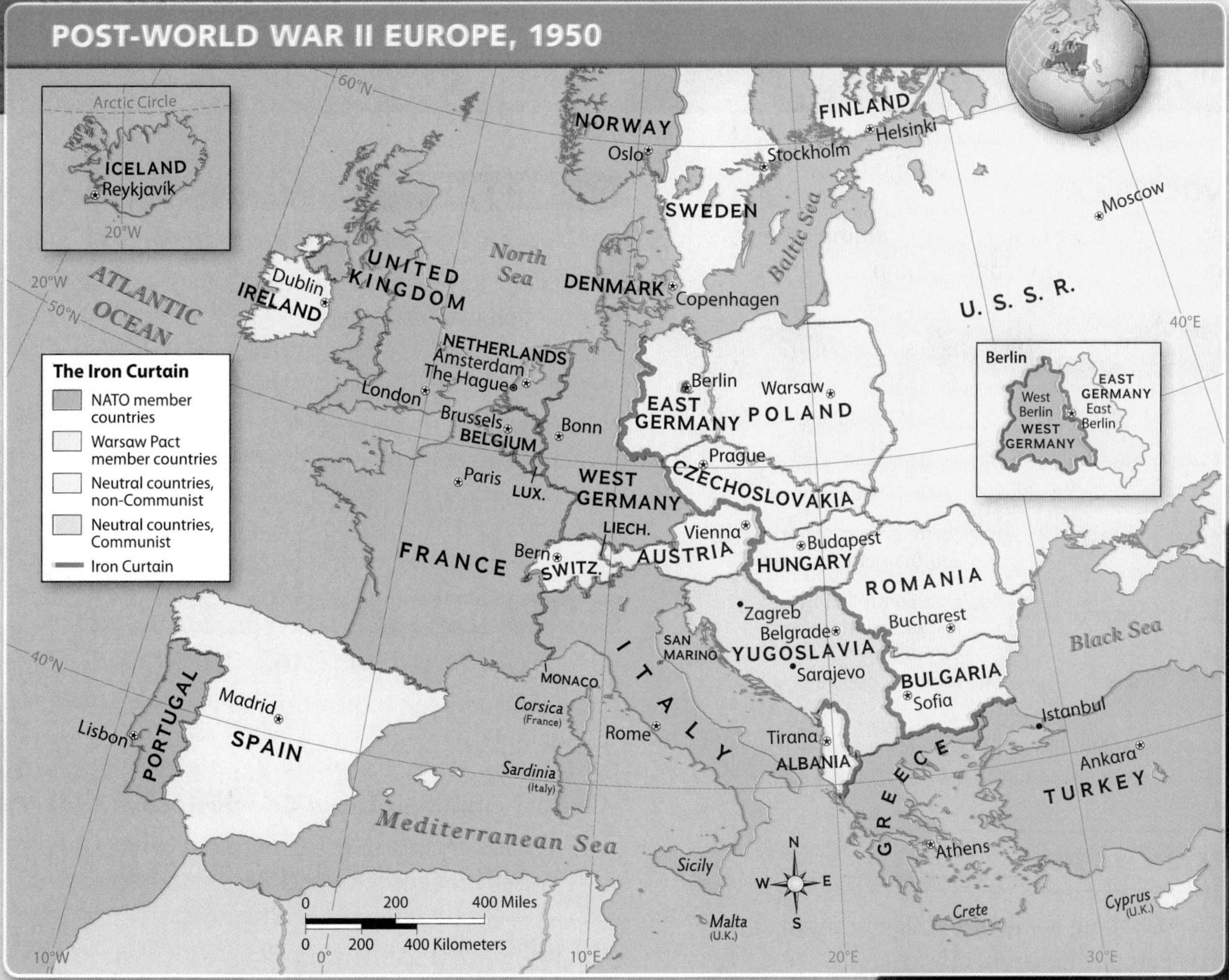

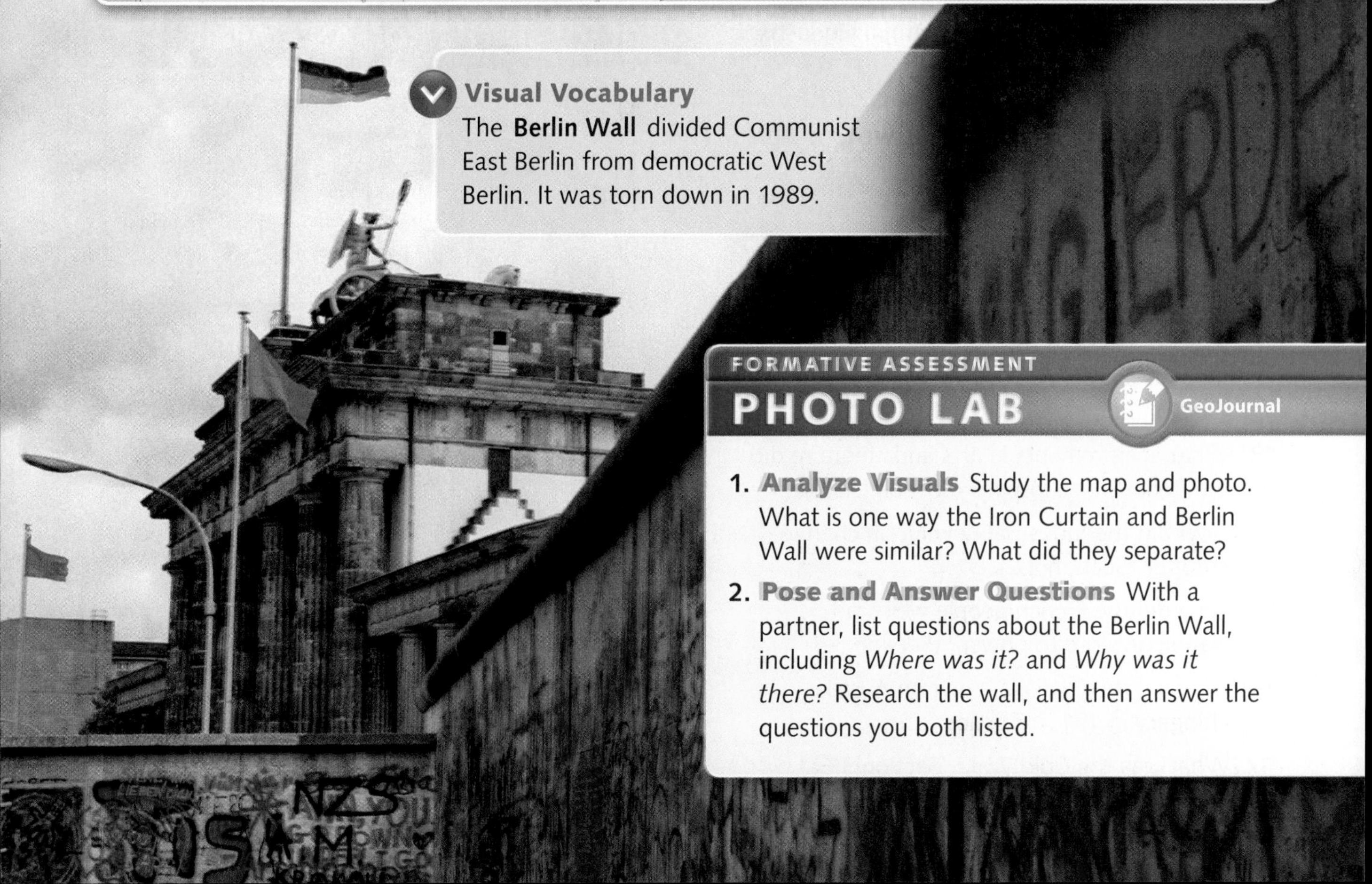

Arctic Circle
ICELAND
Reykjavík
20°W
60°N
NORWAY
Oslo
FINLAND
Helsinki
Stockholm
SWEDEN
Moscow
Baltic Sea
North Sea
UNITED KINGDOM
IRELAND
Dublin
ATLANTIC OCEAN
20°W
50°N
DENMARK
Copenhagen
U. S. S. R.
40°E
The Iron Curtain
NATO member countries
Warsaw Pact member countries
Neutral countries, non-Communist
Neutral countries, Communist
Iron Curtain
NETHERLANDS
Amsterdam
The Hague
London
Brussels
BELGIUM
Bonn
Berlin
EAST GERMANY
Warsaw
POLAND
Berlin
West Berlin
WEST GERMANY
EAST GERMANY
East Berlin
Prague
CZECHOSLOVAKIA
Paris
LUX.
WEST GERMANY
LIECH.
Vienna
AUSTRIA
Budapest
HUNGARY
ROMANIA
FRANCE
Bern
SWITZ.
Zagreb
Belgrade
YUGOSLAVIA
Sarajevo
Bucharest
Black Sea
SAN MARINO
40°N
MONACO
BULGARIA
Sofia
Madrid
SPAIN
PORTUGAL
Lisbon
Corsica (France)
Rome
ITALY
Tirana
ALBANIA
Istanbul
Ankara
TURKEY
GREECE
Sardinia (Italy)
Mediterranean Sea
Athens
Sicily
N
W
E
S
0
200
400 Miles
0
200
400 Kilometers
Malta (U.K.)
Crete
Cyprus (U.K.)
10°W
0°
10°E
20°E
30°E

Visual Vocabulary

The **Berlin Wall** divided Communist East Berlin from democratic West Berlin. It was torn down in 1989.

FORMATIVE ASSESSMENT

PHOTO LAB

GeoJournal

1. **Analyze Visuals** Study the map and photo. What is one way the Iron Curtain and Berlin Wall were similar? What did they separate?
2. **Pose and Answer Questions** With a partner, list questions about the Berlin Wall, including *Where was it?* and *Why was it there?* Research the wall, and then answer the questions you both listed.

CHAPTER 9
Review

VOCABULARY

Match each word in the first column with its definition in the second column.

WORD	DEFINITION
1. ecosystem	a. sold to relax penalty for sin
2. democracy	b. strong sense of loyalty to one's country
3. plebeians	c. community of living organisms and their environment
4. indulgence	d. area controlled by a distant country
5. colony	e. common people
6. nationalism	f. government of the people

MAIN IDEAS

7. What are some of the significant islands in Europe? (Section 1.2)

8. Where is much of Europe's farming industry located? (Section 1.3)

9. What events led to the development of democracy in ancient Greece? (Section 2.1)

10. How were plebeians represented in the Roman Republic? (Section 2.3)

11. In what way did the Roman Empire influence language? Why? (Section 2.4)

12. In what ways did the Roman Catholic Church serve as a unifying force in Western Europe? (Section 2.5)

13. What achievements in arts and literature did the Renaissance inspire? (Section 2.6)

14. How did the Industrial Revolution change Europe? (Section 3.2)

15. Why did the French people welcome Napoleon's rise to power? (Section 3.3)

16. Why did Russia declare war on Austria-Hungary in 1914? (Section 3.5)

17. What was the Cold War? (Section 3.6)

GEOGRAPHY

ANALYZE THE ESSENTIAL QUESTION

How did Europe's physical geography encourage interaction with other regions?

Critical Thinking: Evaluate

18. In what ways do rivers like the Danube make trade easier within Europe?

19. Why has trade been central to Europe's growth throughout its history?

EARLY HISTORY

ANALYZE THE ESSENTIAL QUESTION

How did European thought shape Western civilization?

Critical Thinking: Draw Conclusions

20. What elements of the democracy practiced in ancient Greece did the United States adopt?

INTERPRET MAPS

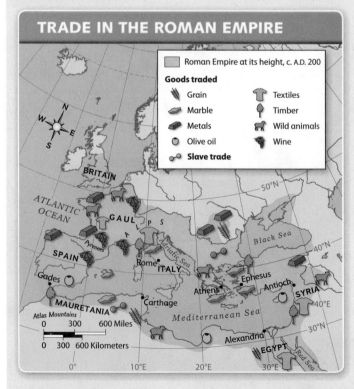

TRADE IN THE ROMAN EMPIRE

21. **Movement** From what part of the Empire did Rome obtain its grains? its textiles?

EMERGING EUROPE

ANALYZE THE ESSENTIAL QUESTION

How did Europe develop and extend its influence around the world?

Critical Thinking: Make Inferences

22. In what way did improvements in navigation and shipbuilding lead Europe to establish colonies in other parts of the world?

23. Why did the Industrial Revolution make European leaders eager to establish colonies in the Americas and Asia?

24. What are some of the positive effects of nationalism? What are some negative effects?

INTERPRET TABLES

MILES OF RAILWAY TRACK IN SELECTED EUROPEAN COUNTRIES (1840–1880)			
	1840	**1860**	**1880**
Austria-Hungary	144	4,543	18,507
Belgium	334	1,730	4,112
France	496	9,167	23,089
Germany	469	11,089	33,838
Great Britain	2,390	14,603	25,060
Italy	20	2,404	9,290
Netherlands	17	335	1,846
Spain	0	1,917	7,490

Source: Modern History Sourcebook

25. **Analyze Data** How much railway track did the Germans build between 1840 and 1880? What might account for this increase?

26. **Draw Conclusions** France and Spain are almost the same size. Note the difference in the extent of the railway system in each one in 1880. What does this suggest about the level of industrialization in each country?

ACTIVE OPTIONS

Synthesize the Essential Questions by completing the activities below.

27. **Write Tour Notes** Suppose that you are going to lead a group of tourists on a trip on one of Europe's rivers. Select and research the river. You might choose the Danube, Rhine, Tiber, Rhone, Thames, or Seine. Then write notes for a guided tour of the river. Start by describing its location, size, and appearance. Next, point out important sites along the river and explain their historical significance. Finally, discuss the river's uses today. **Gather photos of the river and conduct the tour with your group of "tourists."**

> **Writing Tips**
> - Use language that appeals to the senses to help your tourists see and experience the river.
> - Include stories about the sites and historical events to hold your audience's interest.

28. **Create a Slide Show** Why might a government or a society's cultural institutions build buildings to last a long time? How do buildings express ideas? Use the **Digital Library** or other online sources to find five examples of European buildings that help answer the questions. Prepare a slide show. Write captions or notes for your presentation, including the identity of each building, its location, and when it was built.

BUILDING	FACTS ABOUT IT
1.	
2.	
3.	

EUROPE TODAY

PREVIEW THE CHAPTER

Essential Question How is the diversity of Europe reflected in its cultural achievements?

KEY VOCABULARY

- dialect
- heritage
- perspective
- abstract
- troubadour
- opera
- genre
- epic poem
- novel
- staple
- cuisine

ACADEMIC VOCABULARY
cosmopolitan

TERMS & NAMES

- Romantic period
- impressionism
- Baroque period
- Classical period

Essential Question What are the costs and benefits of European unification?

KEY VOCABULARY

- tariff
- currency
- euro
- sovereignty
- eurozone
- consumer
- democratization
- privatization
- demographics
- aging population

ACADEMIC VOCABULARY
exchange, assimilate

TERMS & NAMES

- Common Market
- European Union (EU)
- Orange Revolution

TECHTREK

FOR THIS CHAPTER

Student eEdition

Maps and Graphs

Interactive Whiteboard GeoActivities

Digital Library

Go to **myNGconnect.com** for more on Europe.

Buildings with traditional red-tiled roofs line this square in Prague in the Czech Republic.

1.1 Languages and Cultures

TECHTREK

myNGconnect.com For photos
reflecting European culture

 Digital
Library

Main Idea Europe has a great variety of languages, cultures, and cities.

Europe has more than a half billion people, yet they live in an area that is one-half the size of the United States. In addition, the continent of Europe contains more than 40 countries. The result is a great diversity, or wide variety, of languages and cultures.

European Languages

Many of the languages spoken in Europe today fall into three language groups: Romance, Germanic, and Slavic. The Romance languages include French, Spanish, and Italian. The Germanic languages are spoken mostly in northern Europe and include German, Dutch, and English. Most people in Eastern Europe speak Slavic languages, such as Russian, Polish, and Bulgarian.

Some countries in Europe have more than one official language. Belgium, for example, has three: Dutch, French, and German. Even in countries with only one official language, people may speak different dialects. A **dialect** is a regional variety of a language. In Italy, for instance, people in Rome speak a dialect of Italian that differs from that in other cities.

Cultural Traditions

Because Europe is composed of many different countries and ethnic groups, it has a rich cultural **heritage**, or tradition. Europe's cultural diversity is reflected in its religions and celebrations.

Christianity is the dominant religion in Europe. Today, about 45 percent of the continent's total population is Catholic. Protestantism is most common in Northern Europe.

Critical Viewing In this photo of the Palio, a centuries-old cultural tradition is honored as these horses race in Italy. What details in the photo convey the excitement of the race?

In recent years, Islam has become the fastest-growing religion in Europe. Immigrants from Turkey, North Africa, and Southwest Asia move to Europe and bring their Muslim faith with them.

Many of the holidays celebrated in Europe are rooted in religion. However, Europeans enjoy other kinds of festivals as well. One of the most colorful is the Palio, a horse race held each summer in Siena, Italy. In this race, which dates back to the Middle Ages, ten riders from ten of the city's neighborhoods compete.

City Life

More than 70 percent of Europeans live in urban areas. In Belgium, over 95 percent of the people live in or near its cities. Most of Europe's cities are **cosmopolitan**, which means that they bring together many different cultures and influences. London is an example of a cosmopolitan city. Its restaurants and shops reflect the South Asian, Caribbean, and East Asian origins of some of its newer citizens.

Many European cities date back hundreds of years. As a result, they developed in ways very different from American cities. These cities are often smaller in area than those in the United States and have narrow, winding streets. Most people live in apartments rather than individual houses. For recreation, city dwellers visit their many parks. They also tend to use public transportation more often than most Americans.

Before You Move On

Make Inferences What might be some of the advantages and disadvantages of Europe's great variety of languages and cultures?

FORMATIVE ASSESSMENT

READING LAB GeoJournal

1. **Define** What is a multicultural society? How is Europe's society diverse?

2. **Explain** Look up Easter, Ramadan, and Yom Kippur in the World Religions Handbook (R51). Explain why these religious observances would be significant in Europe.

3. **Turn and Talk** Get together with a partner and discuss cultural festivals and holidays you celebrate. Take notes on your discussion to share with the rest of the class.

1.2 Art and Music

Main Idea European art and music have developed over thousands of years.

Throughout the centuries, European art and music have changed to reflect different styles and beliefs.

European Art

European art grew out of the artistic achievements of ancient Greece and Rome. Greek and Roman gods and goddesses were frequent subjects of the artists from these cultures, but they were portrayed to represent realistic human forms.

Much of the art of the Middle Ages reflected the influence of Christianity. The religious subjects were often presented as two-dimensional figures. During the Renaissance, artists used **perspective** to give their work greater depth. Although religious subjects were common, artists also painted portraits of people.

In the **Romantic period** of the early 1800s, artists moved away from religious themes to paint landscapes and other natural scenes that would convey emotion. **Impressionism** emerged in the late 1800s. Impressionist artists, such as Claude Monet, used light and color to capture a moment. By 1900, artists wanted to create a new form of art. These modern artists often worked in an **abstract** style, which emphasized form and color over realism.

Critical Viewing The *Mona Lisa*, by Italian Renaissance artist Leonardo da Vinci, is probably the most famous portrait of all time. What about this painting might account for its popularity?

Critical Viewing This painting, *Impression, Sunrise,* by French artist Claude Monet, gave the impressionist movement its name. What kind of mood is conveyed in this painting?

Most opera houses contain a stage, an orchestra pit, and several levels of balconies. The ceiling of the Paris Opéra, shown here, was painted by Russian-born artist Marc Chagall.

European Music

Music has been composed for religious ceremonies since the Middle Ages. It has also been used to entertain or express universal themes—emotions and ideas people understand, no matter who they are or when they live.

In the Middle Ages, **troubadours** sang about bravery and love. During the Renaissance, new instruments, such as the violin, were played by nobles and street musicians alike. The **Baroque period**, from about 1600 to 1750, was famous for complex musical patterns and for **opera**, in which highly trained singers act out stories. The **Classical** and Romantic periods followed. Ludwig van Beethoven (BAY toh vuhn) of Germany wrote huge symphonies in the early 1800s

that expressed the intensity of human feelings. Then in the late 1800s, French composers, like French artists, created a more impressionistic style.

Before You Move On

Monitor Comprehension What styles and beliefs have influenced European art and music?

FORMATIVE ASSESSMENT

LISTENING LAB GeoJournal

1. **Analyze Audios** Listen to the music clip of Beethoven's Fifth Symphony in the **Digital Library**. Describe the music's mood.

2. **Make Generalizations** Explain the relationship between a society and the art or music it creates. Then connect a period described in this lesson to events or ideas from the same time in European history. Review Chapter 9.

1.3 Europe's Literary Heritage

TECHTREK

myNGconnect.com For photos of
European writers and Guided Writing

Digital
Library

Student
Resources

> **Main Idea** European literature has reflected
> new ways of thinking over the centuries.

Plays by the English playwright William
Shakespeare (1564–1616) are performed
almost every day. European writers such
as Shakespeare have influenced literature
for centuries. They wrote in many
different **genres**, or forms of literature,
including poetry, plays, and novels.

Literary Origins

European literature began with the ancient
Greeks and Romans. Around 800 B.C., the
Greek poet Homer wrote the epic poems
The Iliad and *The Odyssey*. An **epic poem**
is a long poem that tells the adventures
of a hero who is important to a particular
nation or culture. Around 20 B.C., the
Roman poet Virgil wrote *The Aeneid*, an
epic poem about the founding of Rome.

One of the greatest writers of the late
Middle Ages and early Renaissance was
the Italian poet Dante (1265–1321). He
wrote *The Divine Comedy*, an epic poem
of over 14,000 lines that deals with the
religious beliefs and politics of his time.

Many later works of the Renaissance
focused on human behavior. Shakespeare
explored this theme in plays such as
Hamlet. Spanish writer Miguel de
Cervantes (1547–1616) wrote what is
considered the first modern novel, *Don
Quixote* (kee HO tee). A **novel** is a long
work of fiction, containing characters and
a plot. The printing press, which Johannes
Gutenberg developed in the 1450s, helped
spread the popularity of these books.

The 1700s and 1800s

In the mid-1700s, Enlightenment ideas
about reason and government inspired the
movement toward democracy. These ideas,
in turn, led French and English writers of
the time, such as Voltaire and John Locke,
to explore the rights of the individual.

In the 1800s, writers of the Romantic
period continued this exploration, with
an emphasis on emotion and nature. For
example, German author Johann Wolfgang
von Goethe (GHER tuh) (1749–1832) wrote
The Sorrows of Young Werther, a novel
about a sensitive young artist.

Other writers of the 1800s took a much
more realistic look at life. In novels such
as *Sense and Sensibility*, British writer
Jane Austen (1775–1817) used humor
to examine women's role in society.

Critical Viewing Inspired by tales of
knights, Don Quixote (right) goes to
battle evil with his servant Sancho Panza
(left). What details in this painting suggest
that Cervantes' novel is a comedy?

6.02.A identify and describe influence of individual achievements on societies; 6.18.A explain relationships between societies and their literature; 6.18.B relate ways contemporary expression of culture have been influenced by the past; 6.18.C describe ways issues influence creative expressions; 6.18.D identify examples of literature that convey universal themes; 6.22.D create written material based on research; 6.22.E use standard grammar, spelling, and punctuation

Critical Viewing Austen's novels typically end with marriage, such as the one shown in this scene from a film adaptation of *Sense and Sensibility*. Tell what an English wedding was like in the early 1800s, based on the photo.

Another British writer, Charles Dickens (1812–1870), commented on social issues, including poverty, in such novels as *Oliver Twist*. Norwegian playwright Henrik Ibsen (1828–1906) wrote plays, such as *A Doll's House*, which criticized the traditional role of husbands and wives at that time.

Modern Literature

The two world wars had a great impact on the modern literature of the 20th century. Writers at this time reflected the sense that life was uncertain and unpredictable. Some experimented. For example, English writer Virginia Woolf (1882–1941) and Irish writer James Joyce (also 1882–1941) focused on the thought processes of characters in their novels. French novelist Marcel Proust completed *Remembrance of Things Past*, which observed daily sensory experiences and memory. Romanian playwright Eugene Ionesco (1909–1994) used ridiculous situations to comment on what he saw as the emptiness of life.

Writers worldwide have been influenced by these authors.

Before You Move On

Summarize What new ways of thinking has European literature reflected over the centuries?

FORMATIVE ASSESSMENT

WRITING LAB  GeoJournal

Write a Report Think about themes in Europe's literary heritage that go beyond Europe's boundaries and could appeal to people everywhere and in any period. Write a report describing how a society's issues, beliefs, or events can influence literature. Use one writer's work from the lesson as an example.

Step 1 Research to learn more about the writer and the period in which he or she lived.

Step 2 Did issues or events of the time influence the writer? Did the writer's achievements influence societies? Explain these influences.

Step 3 Refer to pages R4, R10, and R24 to draft your report. Use proper citations. Swap with a classmate to check one another's grammar, spelling, and punctuation.

1.4 Cuisines of Europe

TECHTREK
myNGconnect.com For photos
of traditional European foods

Digital
Library

Main Idea Landforms and climate have influenced the cooking traditions of Europe.

Throughout most of Europe, foods such as meat, bread, and cheese are **staples**, or basic parts of people's diets. However, the **cuisine**, or cooking traditions, of most European countries is largely determined by the landforms and climate of a particular region.

Foods of Western Europe

The hot, dry climate in the Mediterranean countries of Spain, France, Italy, and Greece is ideal for growing olives, tomatoes, and garlic. As a result, these are key ingredients in their cuisines. Fish from the bodies of water surrounding the countries is also an important menu item.

The cuisines of France and Italy have influenced cooking throughout the world and are especially known for their sauces. French sauces are typically made of milk or cheese, while those of Italy are often tomato based.

People in western European countries with cooler climates often eat more filling fare. In Germany, Great Britain, and Ireland, potatoes grow well and are popular side dishes. In contrast with the light sauces of France and Italy, German cooks often serve heavier gravies.

In Scandinavian countries such as Sweden and Norway, the people often eat herring and other fish. Scandinavians also enjoy deer meat provided by the herding culture of these northern countries.

> **Critical Viewing** The French often enjoy long, relaxed meals with friends and family. What attitude toward life and food does this traditional way of eating suggest?

Foods of Eastern Europe

Eastern Europe's cold climate results in a shorter growing season than that of Western Europe. In Russia, root vegetables such as turnips and beets are well adapted to the country's climate. A soup called *borscht*, which is made from beets, is a traditional offering on cold winter nights.

The fertile soil of Hungary allows Hungarian farmers to grow grains and potatoes. These crops are used to make a variety of breads and dumplings. A meat stew called *goulash* is Hungary's national dish. It is made with beef, potatoes, and vegetables, and seasoned with paprika. Paprika is a red spice that was brought to Hungary by the Turks in the 1500s.

Bread like this round loaf is the traditional centerpiece at a Ukrainian wedding.

Like Hungary, Ukraine has fertile soil and fields of wheat and other grains. The country is known for its bread. On special occasions, cooks prepare breads decorated with ornaments made of dough.

Before You Move On

Summarize How have landforms and climate influenced European cooking traditions?

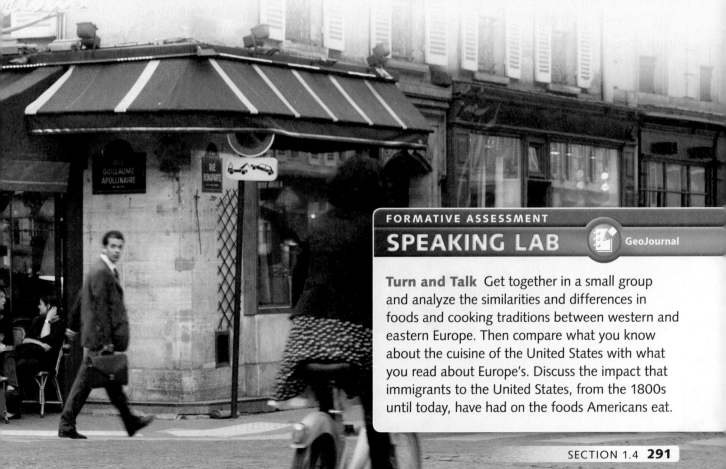

FORMATIVE ASSESSMENT

SPEAKING LAB   GeoJournal

Turn and Talk Get together in a small group and analyze the similarities and differences in foods and cooking traditions between western and eastern Europe. Then compare what you know about the cuisine of the United States with what you read about Europe's. Discuss the impact that immigrants to the United States, from the 1800s until today, have had on the foods Americans eat.

SECTION **2** GOVERNMENT & ECONOMICS

TECHTREK

myNGconnect.com For an online map
of the European Union

Maps and
Graphs

2.1 The European Union

> **Main Idea** The European Union was formed
> to unite Europe and benefit it economically.

In 1948, the United States established
a program called the Marshall Plan to
help Europe rebuild after World War II.
To manage the U.S. aid money, European
countries formed the Organization for
European Economic Cooperation in 1948.
As a result, European countries discovered
that they could rebuild their countries
faster when they worked together.

The Common Market

In 1957, some European countries sought
even closer economic ties. They formed
the European Economic Community (EEC),
which became known as the **Common
Market**. The first countries to join were
Belgium, France, Italy, Luxembourg, the
Netherlands, and West Germany. Several
more countries joined during the 1980s.

The Common Market pledged to create
"an ever closer union among the European
peoples." However, it was primarily
formed to create a single market among
the member nations. A single market is
one in which a group of countries trades
across its borders without restrictions or
tariffs. A **tariff** is a tax paid on imports
and exports.

A United Europe

In 1992, the countries of the Common
Market sought to extend their economic
organization throughout Europe. They
met in Maastricht in the Netherlands and
signed the Treaty of Maastricht, which
created the **European Union (EU)**. By 2010,
the EU had 27 member nations with a total
of more than 500 million people. When
considered as a single economy, the EU is
the largest in the world.

European Union flag

> **Critical Viewing** The EU flag, seen here in front of the
> organization's Parliament building in Strasbourg, France, is
> also the flag of Europe. The flag's circle of stars represents
> European unity. Why is this a fitting symbol for the EU?

EUROPEAN UNION

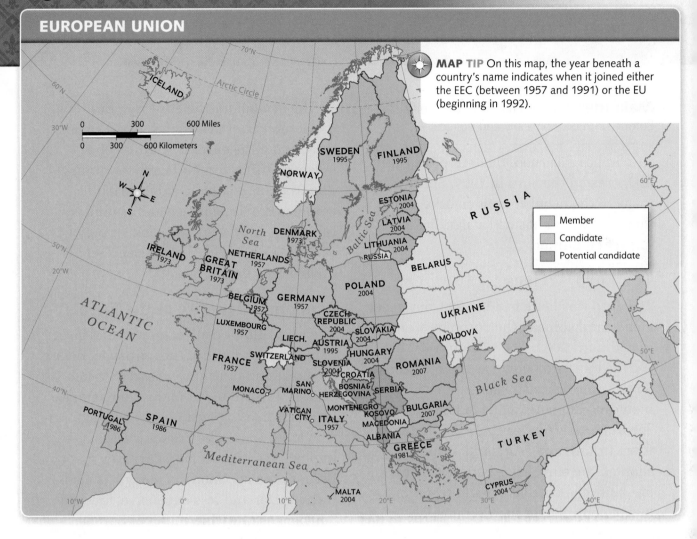

MAP TIP On this map, the year beneath a country's name indicates when it joined either the EEC (between 1957 and 1991) or the EU (beginning in 1992).

Legend:
- Member
- Candidate
- Potential candidate

The EU has a government with an executive, a legislative, and a judicial branch. These branches propose, pass, and enforce the organization's policies and legislation. The EU also has agencies that direct economic policies. Through these agencies, the EU has eliminated tariffs among most member nations and founded a European bank. In 1999, the EU created a common **currency**, or form of money, called the **euro**. By 2011, 17 member nations had adopted this currency.

One of the requirements for joining the EU is having a stable democracy that respects human rights. Some countries that have applied for membership, such as Turkey, are still under review. However, other European countries, including Norway, have chosen not to join. Norway does not want to give up its **sovereignty**, or control over its own affairs.

Before You Move On
Monitor Comprehension How has the European Union helped unite Europe?

FORMATIVE ASSESSMENT

MAP LAB

GeoJournal

1. **Interpret Maps** Organize the map's information into a list. Put member countries in order by date. Then list the candidate and potential candidate countries.

2. **Draw Conclusions** Based on the map, in what area are most of the members who joined in later years located? What political situation might have prevented them from joining earlier?

2.2 The Impact of the Euro

TECHTREK

myNGconnect.com For photos of the euro

Digital Library

> **Main Idea** The euro has helped to unify Europe both economically and politically.

As you have learned, the European Union (EU) created the euro in 1999. Since then, many of the member nations have adopted the euro, which has had a significant impact on Europe.

The Euro Arrives

The euro was launched in 1999, but paper money and coins of the currency were not issued until 2002. The 17 countries that use the euro are known as the **eurozone**. Some countries that belong to the EU, including Romania, hope to join the eurozone soon. Other countries, including Great Britain and Denmark, have not adopted the euro. They believe that giving up their own currency might result in a loss of control over their economies.

The symbol for the euro is €. Euro paper money, or banknotes, is the same throughout the eurozone. Euro coins, however, differ from country to country. The front, or common, side of each coin has the same image and a number indicating its value. The back, or national, side shows a design that was chosen by the member nation.

Economic Benefits of the Euro

The euro allows people, money, and goods to move freely within the eurozone. Before the creation of the euro, when a French citizen traveled to Germany, for example, he or she had to pay a fee to **exchange**, or convert, francs—the French currency—into marks—the German currency. Because the common currency has made travel easier and less expensive, tourism has increased within much of Europe.

The prices of fruit in this Italian market are in euros.

A single currency means lower fees for conducting business. As a result, trade has increased among European nations by an estimated 10 percent since 2002. The currency has also made costs easier to compare for companies within the eurozone. As a result, companies can import the least expensive products and then pass along the savings to **consumers**, the people who buy the goods.

Political Benefits of the Euro

In 2010, the unity of the eurozone was tested. Greece and Ireland—countries in the eurozone—were deeply in debt. To help them manage their debt, the other eurozone nations loaned the two countries money. In return, Greece and Ireland had to raise taxes and reduce spending. By cooperating, the eurozone was able to help two of its member nations.

1-EURO COIN OF THREE EUROZONE COUNTRIES

Front   Back

AUSTRIA
Mozart, Austrian composer

GERMANY
Eagle, German symbol

IRELAND
Harp, Irish symbol

Before You Move On

Summarize In what ways has the euro helped Europe unify economically and politically?

FORMATIVE ASSESSMENT

VIEWING LAB GeoJournal

1. **Compare and Contrast** Study the euros in the diagram. Note that the front of the coin is the same for all three countries shown. What elements appear on the front of each euro? What does each element represent?

2. **Make Inferences** Why might the countries have wanted their own design on the euro?

3. **Conduct Internet Research** Go online to find out what impact helping Greece and Ireland has had on the euro and the eurozone. Share your findings with the class.

2.3 Democracy in Eastern Europe

Main Idea Eastern European countries have faced many challenges in their transition to democracy.

After World War II, many eastern European countries came under the control of the Soviet Union. The citizens of these countries lacked democratic freedoms and had a low standard of living. In 1981, Poland rebelled peacefully against its Communist government. By the late 1980s, similar rebellions had spread throughout Eastern Europe. Finally, in 1991, Russia and several other republics declared their independence, and the Soviet Union collapsed.

The Road to Democracy

Since gaining their independence, Poland, Hungary, and the Czech Republic developed stable democratic governments In other countries, **democratization**, or the process of becoming a democracy, has been more difficult to achieve. In 1991, civil war broke out among ethnic groups in Yugoslavia. Over time, the country divided into several new democratic countries, including Serbia and Croatia.

Ukraine has also had setbacks. In 2004, the Ukrainian people staged the **Orange Revolution** and peacefully removed their prime minister, Viktor Yanukovych.

Critical Viewing Polish citizens shop and relax in a spacious mall in Warsaw. What does the shopping complex in this photo suggest about Poland's economy?

Many believed that he was corrupt and was being controlled by Russia. However, their new leader, Viktor Yushchenko, disappointed the Ukrainians. Some believed he had become anti-democratic and blamed him for their weakened economy. In 2010, the voters brought Yanukovych back to power.

Rebuilding Economies

The former Communist countries of Eastern Europe also began to rebuild their economies. They changed from government-controlled economies to market economies. They accomplished this goal through **privatization**. That means that government-owned businesses became privately owned.

Eastern European countries have had mixed results since making the adjustment to a market economy. Poland has had the greatest success. It has a fast-growing economy and exports goods throughout Europe. Other countries have been slower to establish new businesses and become competitive. They have also experienced rises in prices and unemployment.

The leaders of many eastern European countries wish to integrate with the rest of Europe. They want to join the European Union and NATO, a military alliance of democratic states in Europe and North America. While some citizens of eastern European countries believe that they were more secure under Communist leaders, others—particularly young people— disagree. They favor democracy and feel that this form of government can better help them solve their countries' problems.

Before You Move On

Summarize What challenges have eastern European countries faced in their transition to democracy and a market economy?

FORMATIVE ASSESSMENT
READING LAB GeoJournal

1. **Summarize** Describe Poland's story, from 1981 to today. Why do you think the standard of living there has improved?

2. **Research and Compare** Look again at the map on page 279 showing Eastern European countries under communism. Read about communism on page R41 and R48. How did these countries organize the production of goods and services under communism? How do you think those goods and services were sent to stores or supplied to citizens? Compare how their economies today are organized as free enterprise economies.

2.4 Changing Demographics

TECHTREK

myNGconnect.com For an online graph of Europe's changing demographics

Maps and Graphs

Global Issues

Main Idea New immigrants are changing Europe.

Every May, people from Germany, Denmark, Hungary, Bulgaria, and other European countries come together to celebrate Europe's diversity on Europe Day. The celebrations reflect Europe's changing **demographics**, the characteristics or the profile of a human population. The population has become more diverse as people from Africa and Asia have immigrated to Europe.

Reasons for Immigration

For years, Europe has had an **aging population**. In other words, the average age of people on the continent has been rising. This trend has had a number of causes. For one thing, Europeans have been living longer because of better medical care. For another, most families are having fewer children. So today, senior citizens form a higher percentage of Europe's total population.

The trend created a need for more workers to replace the many senior citizens who were retiring. Workers were also needed to keep the economy strong and pay taxes to support education and health care. As a result, immigrants came to Europe to take the newly available jobs. They left their home countries for economic reasons—to work and send money back to relatives. Or they left for political reasons—to escape conflict or an unjust government. Some came after the fall of communism in Eastern Europe in the 1980s and 1990s. Now membership within the European Union has made it easier for many to migrate within Europe.

Before You Move On

Summarize In what way did Europe's aging population create a need for immigrants?

KEY VOCABULARY

demographics, n., the characteristics of a human population, such as age, income, and education

aging population, n., a trend that occurs as the average age of a population rises

ACADEMIC VOCABULARY

assimilate, v., to be absorbed into a society's culture

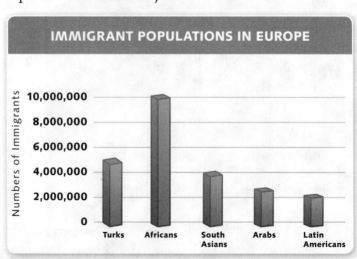

IMMIGRANT POPULATIONS IN EUROPE

Source: UN Statistics, 2008

Inspiring people to care about the planet
National Geographic Society Mission

New Citizenship Roles

Immigrants who leave a country in which they have had no voice in government or the political process, and become citizens of a representative government, must learn new citizenship roles. They have the opportunity to vote in free, multi-party elections, for example, and the right to speak out against government policies. They also have responsibilities, which for citizens in Western Europe are similar to those of the United States.

Challenges of Immigration

The global economic crisis and resulting unemployment in Europe led a number of young people from Spain and Portugal, for example, to emigrate to Brazil for jobs. Brazil needed workers in construction, engineering, and architecture to prepare for the 2014 World Cup of soccer and the 2016 Olympic Games. This reversed a migration trend.

The mix of different cultures has also created problems. Many immigrants are Muslims, with cultural and religious practices that differ from those of their Christian neighbors. Some Europeans would like to see the Muslim immigrants **assimilate**, or be absorbed into their society's culture. They believe the immigrants should adopt European traditions and values. Others believe a more multicultural approach is better. This approach encourages tolerance and embraces all cultures.

COMPARE ACROSS REGIONS

Australia's Skilled Immigrants

Like Europe, Australia has an aging population. Many in the Australian government believe that immigration can help change that trend. As a result, each year the government identifies gaps in the country's workforce. It then determines the number of skilled immigrants who can come to Australia. Between 2010 and 2011, more than 127,000 immigrants arrived as part of this skilled migration program. Many came from Great Britain, India, and China.

Of course, Europe receives many more immigrants than Australia each year. Italy alone took in more than 558,000 immigrants in 2010. Many Europeans appreciate the cultural enrichment that immigrants bring to their countries. However, some believe that Europe, like Australia, should set immigration limits.

Before You Move On
Monitor Comprehension What are the ways in which new immigrants are changing Europe?

FORMATIVE ASSESSMENT

READING LAB GeoJournal

1. **Compare** Explain how opportunities are different for immigrants coming from a non-representative government to a democratic one.
2. **Make Inferences** Think about the opposing points of view on assimilation. Why might some immigrants resist assimilation?
3. **Identify Problems and Solutions** What has Australia done to solve some of the problems posed by immigration?

VOCABULARY

Match each word in the first column with its meaning in the second column.

WORD	DEFINITION
1. abstract	a. tax on imports and exports
2. dialect	b. control over one's own affairs
3. sovereignty	c. art style emphasizing form and color
4. tariff	d. absorb into another culture
5. privatization	e. privately owned businesses
6. assimilate	f. regional language

MAIN IDEAS

7. Why are there so many different dialects in Europe? (Section 1.1)

8. What is the fastest-growing religion in Europe? Why might that be so? (Section 1.1)

9. During the Romantic period, what themes did artists use in their paintings? (Section 1.2)

10. Why do you think the ancient Greeks and Romans celebrated historic events in epic poems? (Section 1.3)

11. How does the soup called *borscht* reflect Russia's geography? (Section 1.4)

12. What is one of the requirements for joining the European Union? (Section 2.1)

13. In what way has the euro helped increase trade among European nations? (Section 2.2)

14. Why did the Ukrainian people stage the Orange Revolution? (Section 2.3)

15. What factors have led people from other parts of the world to immigrate to Europe? (Section 2.4)

CULTURE

ANALYZE THE ESSENTIAL QUESTION

How is the diversity of Europe reflected in its cultural achievements?

Critical Thinking: Draw Conclusions

16. In what ways do the many dialects in Europe show its great diversity?

17. What aspects of ancient Greek and Roman art inspired Renaissance artists?

18. Why did pasta with tomato sauce develop in Italy rather than Russia?

INTERPRET MAPS

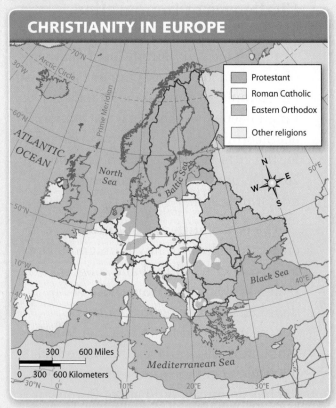

CHRISTIANITY IN EUROPE

19. **Region** Where do most Protestants live in Europe? Where do most Catholics live?

20. **Make Inferences** Find the countries on the map in which a relatively small part of the population belongs to a different Christian denomination. What challenges might the people in the minority religion face?

GOVERNMENT & ECONOMICS

ANALYZE THE ESSENTIAL QUESTION

What are the costs and benefits of European unification?

Critical Thinking: Analyze Cause and Effect

21. In what way did the Marshall Plan help bring about the formation of the European Union?

22. What was the response of the eurozone countries when Greece and Ireland became deeply in debt in 2010?

23. What was the impact of the fall of communism on Eastern Europe? What was the impact on Western Europe?

24. What problems are caused by illegal immigration to Europe?

INTERPRET CHARTS

COST OF A TEN-MINUTE PHONE CALL TO THE U.S. IN EUROS (€)*		
Country	1997	2012
Belgium	7.50	2.17
Czech Republic	3.09	2.34
Denmark	7.41	2.72
Ireland	4.61	1.96
Spain	6.17	1.66
France	6.78	1.96
United Kingdom	3.50	2.19

* 1997 prices have been converted to euros
Source: Eurostat

25. **Analyze Data** According to the chart, how did the cost of making a telephone call change between 1997 and 2012?

26. **Analyze Cause and Effect** What move made by the European Union might have brought about the change in the cost of a telephone call?

ACTIVE OPTIONS

Synthesize the Essential Questions by completing the activities below.

27. **Write a Dialogue** Why join the European Union? Why not join? Research the benefits and drawbacks for Iceland. For each point of view, include a main idea and supporting ideas from your research. Then, with a partner, write a dialogue in which two citizens of Iceland discuss whether to join or not. **Perform your dialogue for the class**.

> **Writing Tips**
> - Create characters who have equally valid points of view.
> - Include what's at stake for the speakers, to show why they care.
> - Vary sentence types. Include questions and short and long responses.

TECHTREK   myNGconnect.com For photos of Europe and European art

28. **Identify Lasting Art** The *Mona Lisa* on page 286 is an example of a work of art that has appealed to people from many cultures across time. Find another example from the **NG Photo Gallery** of other print or online sources you think has a similar appeal. Research the artwork and organize an oral presentation in which you show and describe the work, tell its theme or message, such as the power of nature or what it means to be human, and explain why people can relate to it.

After your presentation, take part in a Q & A. Before you respond to a question, restate it or summarize it. Ask for clarification, if you need to. Give information about the artwork such as who made it, when or why, and provide details that will interest your listeners.

World Languages

TECHTREK
myNGconnect.com For an online graph about world languages

Maps and Graphs

In this unit, you learned about the diversity of languages in Europe. Every culture in the world uses language to communicate. Scholars estimate that there are about 7,000 languages spoken today.

Most countries name one or more languages as official languages. An official language is the one used by a country's government. For example, French is the official language of France, and English and French are the official languages of Canada. Most countries have groups of people whose first language differs from the official language. It is estimated that at least half of the people in the world speak one or more languages in addition to their first language.

Compare

- Africa
- Americas
- Asia
- Europe
- Australia & Oceania

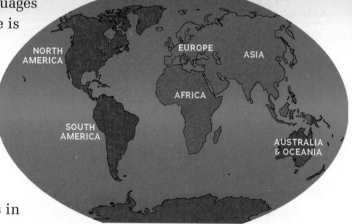

LIVING LANGUAGES

Although there are thousands of world languages, many are not widely spoken. In addition, sometimes the distinction, or difference, between a language and a dialect is not clear.

The following are the ten most widely spoken languages in the world in order of their ranking. Each is spoken as a native language by at least 100 million people. Some are official languages in widely different regions of the world. Some of the languages appear in only one region of the world.

1. Mandarin Chinese
2. Spanish
3. English
4. Hindi/Urdu
5. Arabic
6. Bengali
7. Portuguese
8. Russian
9. Japanese
10. German

DYING LANGUAGES

Some languages are spoken by so few people that they are in danger of dying out. In fact, linguists, or people who study languages, estimate that one language dies every two weeks.

Languages die for different reasons. Some simply disappear with the death of the last speaker. Others fade more slowly as a dominant language replaces it. A few linguists are trying to document some of these languages to preserve the history and culture of the people who spoke them.

The graph at right shows the number of languages spoken on the world's continents, as well the names of a few of the languages spoken. Note that "Americas" consists of the number of languages spoken on the North American and South American continents. Compare the data in the graph and use it to answer the questions.

NUMBER OF LANGUAGES SPOKEN BY CONTINENT

Source: *Ethnologue*, 16th Edition, 2009

2,110

2,322

▷ Hola
▷ Guten tag
Hello
▷ Kia ora   ▷ Hujambo
▷ Ohayou

EUROPE

AFRICA

ASIA

AMERICAS

AUSTRALIA & OCEANIA

1,250

993

234

SARDINIAN
Norwegian
BOSNIAN greek
Scottish Gaelic
Irish russian DUTCH
BELARUSIAN
ITALIAN Latvian
french Danish
Czech LATIN
POLISH

SWAHILI
Tswana
Arabic Lingala
BERBER
kongo somali Kirundi
setswana
Kanuri
Rwanda-Rundi
BAMBARA
Tsonga
LUO Shona
OROMO
Tigrinya
Zulu
VENDA PEDI
HAUSA
FRENCH SOTHO
FULA
CHICHEWA
Sango SWAZI
Ibibio
UMBUNDU
Afrikaans
Xhosa Spanish
GBE
Malagasy
TSHILUBA
yoruba
PORTUGUESE
Gikuyu Twi
igbo
Sesotho Ndebele
Kiswahili
Malinke English
LUHYA

ARABIC
Lao
TAGALOG hindi
PERSIAN xiang
Bengali
PASHTU Thai
tibetan
VIETNAMESE
NYAW
Zhuang URDU
cantonese
HLAI Jingpho
Korean
Kashmiri DOGRI
MONGOLIAN
WU
NICOBARESE KUY
INDONESIAN
javanese
TAMIL MIN
punjabi CHAM
GAN
TURKMEN
TETUM Saraiki
burmese MON
TATAR
ARAMAIC bodo
Kurdish KAREN
Gondi Hmong
Filipino azeri
Dzongkha
HEBREW Mandarin
Mizo
Japanese
Ainu Sundanese
CEBUANO
KAZAKH

french
English
xinca KEKCHI
CREE
PAPIAMENTO
CREOLE ojibwe
ALEUT navajo
quiche
Oneida DANISH
tagish HOPI
Spanish ZUNI
QUECHUA
Aymara
nahua HINDI
Sranan Tongo
MAM
INUIT mayan
Haida
PORTUGUESE
DUTCH

ULITHIAN
Takuu
NAURUAN
Aranda Nukuoro
ANUTA PILENI
Mae
POHNPEIAN Rapa
pitcairnese
TRUKESE
palauan
Kapingamarangi
bislama yapese
CAROLINIAN
SAMOAN
HINDUSTANI
Chamorro French
Tahitian English
TUVALUAN
niuean Tok Pisin
Sonsoralese
Marshallese
Maori
I-KIRIBATI Tongan
Hiri Motu
FIJIAN

FORMATIVE ASSESSMENT

RESEARCH LAB GeoJournal

1. **Compare and Contrast** On which continent are the most languages spoken? the fewest? What do these numbers suggest about the cultural unity of each continent?

2. **Analyze Data** Study the graph and the list of languages with the most native speakers. How many of the total languages in Europe are among those spoken most in the world?

Research and Create Charts Research to find out more about the people who speak Hindi and Portuguese. Create a chart for each language showing approximately how many people speak it and where it is spoken. Which language has more native speakers? Which language is an official language in more places? What might account for this?

Active Options

TECHTREK

myNGconnect.com For photos of Renaissance art, nuclear power plants in Europe, and music clips

Digital Library

ACTIVITY 1

Goal: Extend your understanding of Renaissance art.

Write a Renaissance Arts Magazine

The Renaissance was a period of great artistic activity in Europe. Choose a city in Europe that was influenced by the Renaissance between 1400 and 1600. With a group, plan and publish a magazine showcasing that city's artistic achievements. Use the Magazine Maker CD-ROM to find photos and information on the following:

- art
- architecture
- literature
- fashion

Brunelleschi's dome atop the Cathedral of Florence in Italy

ACTIVITY 2

Goal: Research the use of nuclear power in Europe.

Create a Pro-and-Con Chart

Some European countries are planning to build nuclear plants, while others have chosen to close existing plants. Use the library or Internet research to create a pro-and-con chart that explains some of the advantages and disadvantages of nuclear power. Be prepared to present your chart and explain the issues.

ACTIVITY 3

Goal: Learn about European culture through its music.

Put Together a Playlist

Get together in a group and create a playlist of music from Europe— traditional, classical, or the music of today. Choose examples that express universal themes, or ideas and situations most everyone understands. Share your list and explain the themes. Tell where the music is from and whether it shows influences from other cultures.

identify and describe the influence individual and group achievements on societies; 6.02.B evaluate the social, political, economic, and cultural contributions of individuals and groups, past and present; 6.14.A explain duty of civic participation; 6.14.B explain relationships among rights, responsibilities, and duties; 6.20.A give examples of the roles of scientists and inventors that have shaped the world; 6.22.D create visual and written material based on research

TEKS

TEKS PROJECT

Goal: Identify and describe contributions and achievements of individuals or groups.

Create a Hall of Fame

If you've ever visited a Hall of Fame, you know it displays images and stories about notable men and women. To create your own Hall of Fame, collaborate with a group to choose your inductees.

Creatives? Who inspires you to write, compose, design, or experiment? Who makes positive things happen? Think of inventors, scientists, artists, musicians.

Local or Global? What groups or individuals have improved the well-being and quality of life for others? Who tackles large global problems such as world hunger, or works quietly with others at the local food pantry? Think of a group of "unsung heroes."

Citizens? Who has shown you the importance of civic participation? Discuss the rights, responsibilities, and duties of citizens, and think about who sets a good example.

Carry It Out List your inductees and decide how to honor them. Write biographical sketches to explain why they are extraordinary, and draw or print portraits to post. Invite other classes to tour your Hall of Fame.

Reflect On It What accomplishment or contribution to society would *you* like to be known for some day? What Hall of Fame would you wish to be inducted into? You could be "famous" among a small group or among a worldwide group— people whose ideas and actions achieve large and small things.

Voluntario. Bénévole. Swayamsevak. Kujitolea. Dobrovolník. The word for *Volunteer* could be printed on T shirts the world over for groups who help others.

UNIT 5 **305**

Explore
Russia & THE EURASIAN REPUBLICS
WITH NATIONAL GEOGRAPHIC

MEET THE EXPLORER

NATIONAL GEOGRAPHIC

Tracing ancient trade routes, NG Fellow Fredrik Hiebert excavated a 4,000-year-old Silk Road city in Turkmenistan. He also searches for underwater settlements in the Black Sea.

INVESTIGATE GEOGRAPHY

North of the Arctic Circle in Russia, reindeer herded by a nomadic clan charge across the tundra. Many groups in the Arctic rely heavily on the reindeer. The animals, also known as caribou, provide food, clothing, and shelter, as well as transportation.

CONNECT WITH THE CULTURE

A young Mongolian Kazak family stands in front of a yurt, a shelter used by nomads. Kazaks are a nomadic, animal-herding people. Yurts allow them to live in harsh climates and give them the freedom to move and graze their animals in traditional tribal communities.

4,859 miles

Moscow, Russia

Washington, D.C.

Go to myNGconnect.com for maps of Russia and the Eurasian Republics.

STEP INTO HISTORY

Saint Basil's Cathedral in Red Square, Moscow, Russia, was built between 1554 and 1560. The cathedral has nine chapels, each topped with an onion-shaped dome.

CHAPTER 11

Russia & THE EURASIAN REPUBLICS

GEOGRAPHY & HISTORY

PREVIEW THE CHAPTER

Essential Question How have size and extreme climates shaped Russia and the Eurasian republics?

KEY VOCABULARY

- landmass
- steppe
- permafrost
- tundra
- taiga
- nonrenewable fossil fuel
- peat
- hydroelectric power

- methane
- greenhouse gas
- semiarid
- arid
- pesticide

ACADEMIC VOCABULARY
isolate, remote

TERMS & NAMES

- Ural Mountains
- North Atlantic Drift
- Siberia
- Black Sea
- Caspian Sea
- Aral Sea

Essential Question How has geographic isolation influenced the region's history?

KEY VOCABULARY

- state
- tribute
- czar
- reign
- secular
- invader
- scorched earth policy
- serf

- strike
- communism
- socialism
- collective farm
- propaganda

ACADEMIC VOCABULARY
expand, promote

TERMS & NAMES

- Slav
- Kievan Rus
- Genghis Khan
- Mongol Empire
- Silk Roads
- Peter the Great
- Catherine the Great
- Nazi Germany

- Industrial Revolution
- V. I. Lenin
- Bolshevik
- Russian Revolution
- Soviet Union
- Cold War
- Mikhail Gorbachev

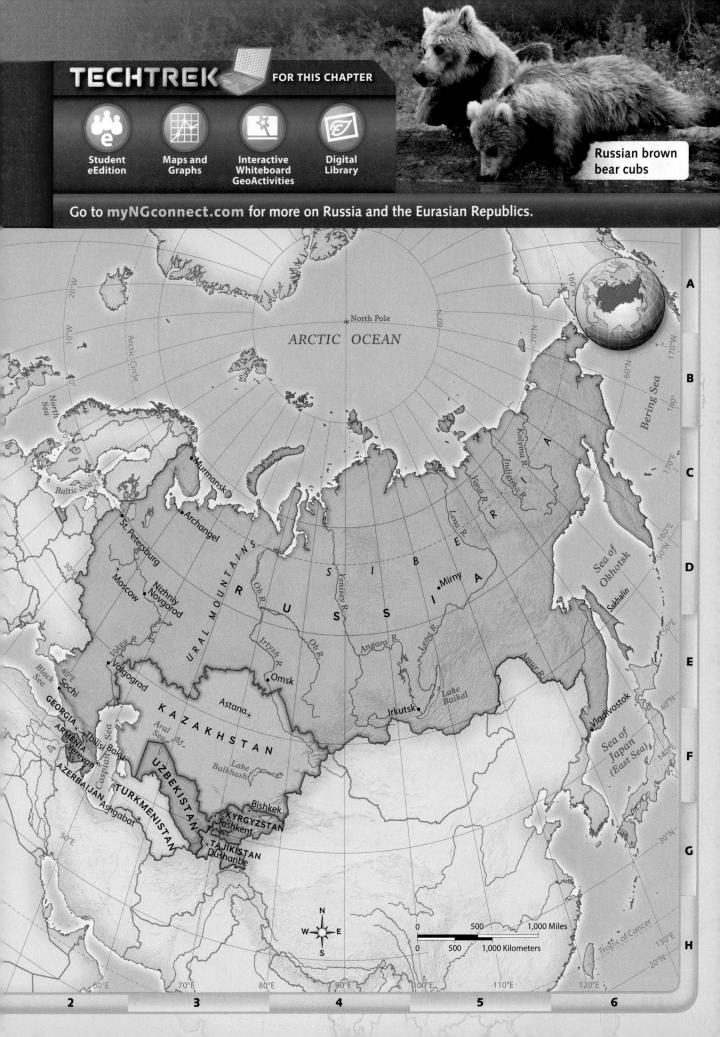

TECHTREK FOR THIS CHAPTER

Student eEdition

Maps and Graphs

Interactive Whiteboard GeoActivities

Digital Library

Go to **myNGconnect.com** for more on Russia and the Eurasian Republics.

Russian brown bear cubs

A
B
C
D
E
F
G
H

ARCTIC OCEAN

North Pole

Bering Sea

Murmansk

Archangel

Baltic Sea

North Sea

St. Petersburg

Moscow

Nizhniy Novgorod

Volga R.

Volgograd

Sochi

Black Sea

GEORGIA
Tbilisi
ARMENIA
Yerevan
Baku
AZERBAIJAN
Ashgabat
TURKMENISTAN

Caspian Sea

Aral Sea

KAZAKHSTAN

Astana

Omsk

Ob R.

Irtysh R.

Lake Balkhash

UZBEKISTAN

Bishkek

KYRGYZSTAN

Tashkent

TAJIKISTAN
Dushanbe

URAL MOUNTAINS

R U S S I A

S I B E R I A

Ob R.

Yenisey R.

Angara R.

Lena R.

Lena R.

Irkutsk

Lake Baikal

Amur R.

Mirny

Yana R.

Kolyma R.

Indigirka R.

Sea of Okhotsk

Sakhalin

Vladivostok

Sea of Japan (East Sea)

Tropic of Cancer

Arctic Circle

N
W   E
S

500   1,000 Miles
0
500   1,000 Kilometers
0

1   2   3   4   5   6

SECTION ① GEOGRAPHY

1.1 **Physical Geography**

TECHTREK

myNGconnect.com For maps of Russia and the Eurasian republics and Visual Vocabulary

 Maps and Graphs

 Digital Library

RUSSIA AND THE EURASIAN REPUBLICS PHYSICAL

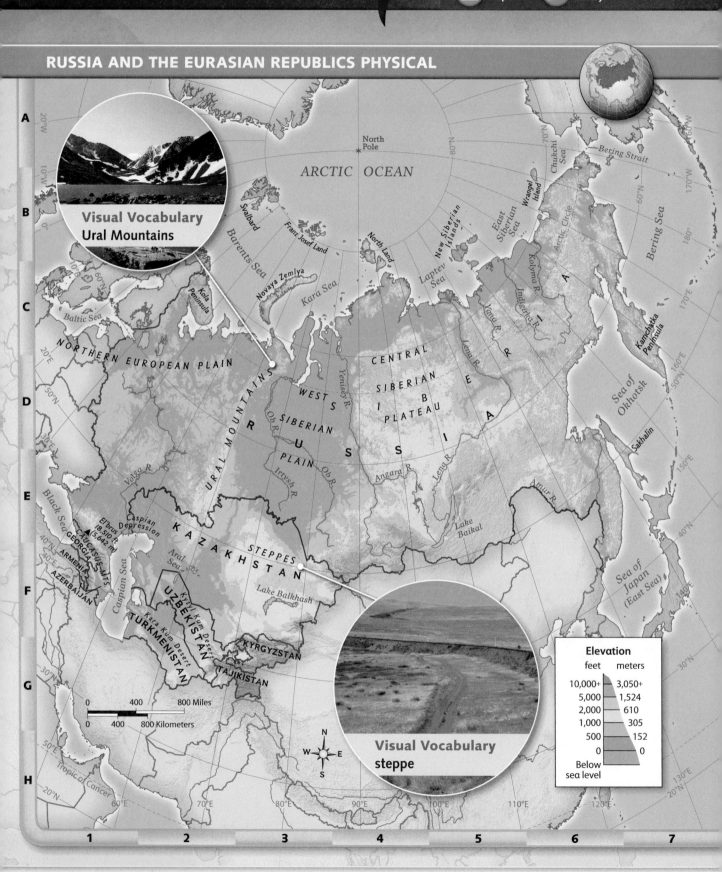

Visual Vocabulary
Ural Mountains

ARCTIC OCEAN

North Pole

Svalbard
Franz Josef Land
North Land
New Siberian Islands
East Siberian Sea
Wrangel Island
Chukchi Sea
Bering Strait
Bering Sea
Arctic Circle

Barents Sea
Novaya Zemlya
Kara Sea
Laptev Sea
Kolyma R.
Indigirka R.
Jana R.

Baltic Sea
Kola Peninsula

NORTHERN EUROPEAN PLAIN

CENTRAL SIBERIAN PLATEAU

WEST SIBERIAN PLAIN

Yenisey R.
Ob R.
Irtysh R.
Volga R.
Ob R.

U R A L   M O U N T A I N S

R U S S I A

Lena R.
Angara R.
Lena R.
Amur R.

Kamchatka Peninsula
Sea of Okhotsk
Sakhalin

El'brus 18,510 ft (5,642 m)
Caspian Depression
Caspian Sea
Black Sea
CAUCASUS MTS.
GEORGIA
ARMENIA
AZERBAIJAN
TURKMENISTAN
Kara Kum Desert
Kyzyl Kum Desert
UZBEKISTAN
Aral Sea

K A Z A K H S T A N
STEPPES
Lake Balkhash
KYRGYZSTAN
TAJIKISTAN

Lake Baikal

Sea of Japan (East Sea)

0   400   800 Miles
0   400   800 Kilometers

N W E S

Tropic of Cancer

Visual Vocabulary
steppe

Elevation

feet	meters
10,000+	3,050+
5,000	1,524
2,000	610
1,000	305
500	152
0	0
Below sea level	

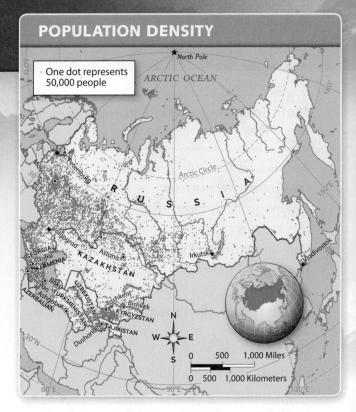

POPULATION DENSITY

One dot represents 50,000 people

> **Main Idea** Russia and the Eurasian republics cover a huge area and contain a variety of geographic features.

Russia and the Eurasian republics take up about one-sixth of the land surface of the entire earth. The region's geographic features have limited its population.

Huge Landmass

Russia is the largest country in the world in total area. Its **landmass**, or continuous extent of land, stretches almost 6,000 miles from east to west. The Eurasian republics lie south of Russia. The republics in the Caucasus Mountains are Armenia, Azerbaijan (ahz ur by JAHN), and Georgia. Those in Central Asia include Kazakhstan (kah zahk STAHN), Kyrgyzstan (kihr gih STAN), Tajikistan (tah jik ih STAN), Turkmenistan (turk MEN ih stan), and Uzbekistan (ooz BEK ih stan).

Plains, or large areas of level ground, cover much of the region. The relatively low **Ural Mountains** separate the Northern European Plain from the West Siberian Plain. In much of southwestern Russia and northern Kazakhstan, the very large plains are called **steppes**. Much of this land is good for agriculture and grazing.

Natural Barriers

Russia has oceans on its northern and eastern borders and mountainous areas along much of its southern border. These natural barriers separate Russia from its neighbors. The deserts and mountains of Central Asia keep republics such as Kyrgyzstan and Tajikistan **isolated**, or cut off from other countries.

Because so much of Russia's coastline lies to the north of the Arctic Circle, few ports stay open to ships and trade all year long. Murmansk, located far to the north on Kola Peninsula, is one such port. An ocean current called the **North Atlantic Drift** warms the waters around Murmansk and keeps them ice-free most of the time.

Before You Move On

Monitor Comprehension What are some of the key geographic features of this region?

FORMATIVE ASSESSMENT

MAP LAB

GeoJournal

1. **Place** Find the Ural Mountains on the physical map. What is the elevation of the mountains? Locate the steppes. How does its elevation compare with that of the Ural Mountains?

2. **Interpret Maps** Use the population density map to determine how density differs west and far east of the Urals. Then study the physical map. What physical features might contribute to the population distribution?

1.2 **Land of Extreme Climates**

TECHTREK

myNGconnect.com For a climate
map and photos of extreme climates

Maps and
Graphs

Digital
Library

> **Main Idea** The extreme climates of this region have an impact on where and how people live.

About half the land in Russia is so cold that it has **permafrost**, or permanently frozen ground, beneath it. Yet parts of Russia can also reach 100°F in summer, and large areas of Central Asia are desert. Because of these extremes, most of the population lives in the western part of the region, where the climate is not as harsh.

Cold, Dark Winters

Latitude is an important factor in the climate of a region. The northern boundary of Russia is a coastal plain along the Arctic Ocean, with no natural barriers to keep out arctic winds. The high northern latitudes of Moscow and areas to its north help bring this region long, dark, snowy winters. St. Petersburg, for example, has a latitude of almost 60° N. For about one month each winter, there is has hardly any daylight in the city.

Climate and Vegetation

Climate affects the types of vegetation that grow in different areas. **Tundra**, or flat land found in arctic and subarctic regions, exists in **Siberia**, which lies in central and eastern Russia. Here, only small plants can grow. Permafrost prevents most trees from growing because their roots can't spread deep under the ground.

> **Critical Viewing** Snow and ice cover the ground throughout much of the long winter in the arctic city of Noril'sk. Based on the photo, what challenges might people encounter in the city's wintry weather?

CLIMATE

Climate Regions

- Dry–Semiarid
- Dry–Arid
- Humid Temperate–No dry season
- Humid Cold–No dry season
- Humid Cold–Dry winter
- Cold Polar–Tundra & ice
- Unclassified Highlands

Just south of the tundra is the **taiga** (TY guh), or forest area. Mostly small evergreens like pines grow here. This area provides valuable timber resources.

Extremes in temperature and moisture make it hard for some areas to be used for agriculture. Much of the northern territory has short summers and, as a result, short growing seasons. The semiarid and desert areas are limited to herding and grazing. Farming is concentrated in the fertile soils of the western plains and steppes, along the **Black Sea**, the **Caspian Sea**, and in some river valleys.

Before You Move On

Summarize In what ways do this region's extreme climates affect the people who live there?

FORMATIVE ASSESSMENT
MAP LAB
GeoJournal

1. **Location** What is the climate like in the northeastern part of Russia? How does latitude affect the climate in this region?

2. **Interpret Maps** What areas in the region have arid or semiarid climates? What areas have a humid cold climate with dry winters?

3. **Pose and Answer Questions** Study the map and then create another climate question to ask a partner.

4. **Human-Environment Interaction** Look at the population map in Section 1.1 and then compare it with the climate map on this page. In what ways might climate determine where people live in the region?

1.3 Natural Resources

TECHTREK

myNGconnect.com For a resource map and photos of resources

Maps and Graphs

Digital Library

Main Idea Russia and the Eurasian republics have plentiful natural resources, but many of them are in remote locations.

This region is among the world's richest in natural resources. These resources are important for the countries' economies.

Energy Resources

Russia and the Eurasian republics have plentiful energy resources, especially oil and natural gas. Russia is also a leading coal producer. These resources are **nonrenewable fossil fuels**. They cannot reproduce quickly enough to keep pace with their use. Russia also has large amounts of **peat**, which is very old decayed plant material. Peat is burned like coal. In addition, some rivers provide **hydroelectric power**. Power production plants use the force of the rivers' water to generate electricity.

Mineral Resources

The region contains large quantities of mineral resources that provide raw materials for factories and support industrial development. These resources include metallic ores, such as iron and aluminum, along with gold, copper, platinum, uranium, cobalt, manganese, and chrome.

Almost 20 percent of the world's reserves of iron ore are located in the region, with Russia and Kazakhstan among the main sources of this mineral. Iron ore is used to produce iron and steel, which are used in the construction of roads, railways, and buildings.

In 2010, huge reserves of minerals were found in nearby Afghanistan. Soon, this country might compete with Russia and the republics as a major producer of iron, copper, and other metals.

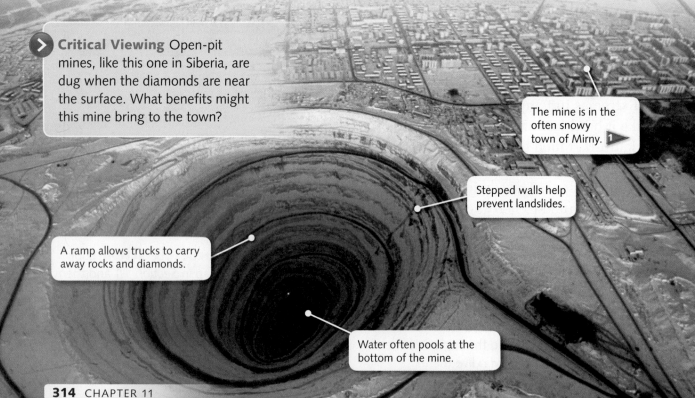

Critical Viewing Open-pit mines, like this one in Siberia, are dug when the diamonds are near the surface. What benefits might this mine bring to the town?

The mine is in the often snowy town of Mirny.

Stepped walls help prevent landslides.

A ramp allows trucks to carry away rocks and diamonds.

Water often pools at the bottom of the mine.

NATURAL RESOURCES

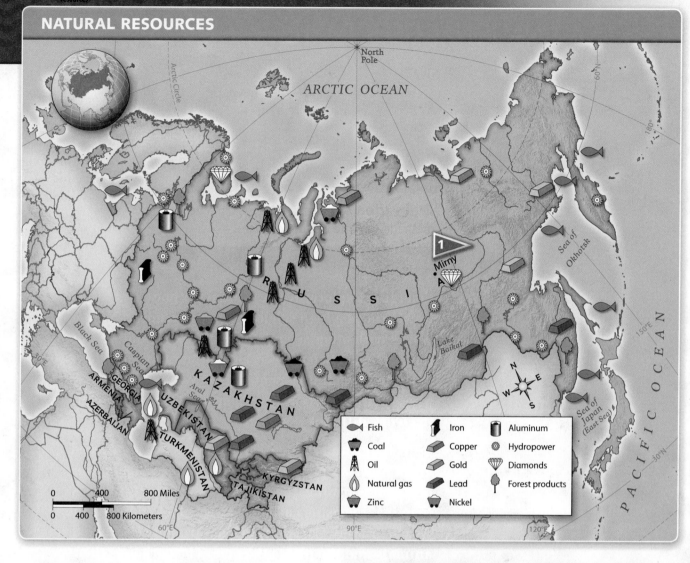

Map Legend:
- Fish
- Coal
- Oil
- Natural gas
- Zinc
- Iron
- Copper
- Gold
- Lead
- Nickel
- Aluminum
- Hydropower
- Diamonds
- Forest products

The Challenge of Location

Much of the region's resources are in **remote**, or hard to reach, locations. For example, Siberia contains oil fields, hydroelectric power sources, and minerals, such as nickel and gold. Many of these resources are located in the far-eastern, and coldest, parts of Siberia. The permafrost there makes it difficult to drill or mine for the natural resources and transport them to market. As a result, the resources in these areas of Siberia remain largely untouched.

Before You Move On

Summarize What are some important natural resources of Russia and the Eurasian republics, and why are some of them hard to reach?

FORMATIVE ASSESSMENT

DATA LAB GeoJournal

Create a Database With a group, gather data to compare the mineral resources of the United States with those of Russia. List minerals on the map and research goods made from them. Then each group chooses one mineral to research the quantities mined in the two regions. Finally to compare regions, combine your research data into a class database.

MINERALS	GOODS
Iron	steel, medicine, magnets, auto parts, paper clips
Aluminum	kitchen utensils, drink cans, foil, airplane and car parts

SECTION **1** GEOGRAPHY

NATIONAL GEOGRAPHIC

1.4

TECHTREK
myNGconnect.com For photos of the explorer's work and an Explorer Video Clip

Digital Library

Exploring
Siberian Lakes
with Katey Walter Anthony

Main Idea As permafrost thaws in Siberia, it releases methane gas into the atmosphere.

Expedition to Siberia

Emerging Explorer Katey Walter Anthony first went to Siberia as a high school exchange student. Now she works with other scientists from Alaska and Russia at the Northeast Science Station in Cherskiy, Siberia, to study how climate change is affecting the area—and possibly the entire world. Siberia's frigid climate makes the work difficult.

Anthony and some other scientists are concerned about Siberia's permafrost. They believe that because of global warming, the permafrost below its lakes is thawing, releasing carbon that was locked inside the frozen ground. Carbon is formed from dead prehistoric animals and the plants they ate. The carbon is then turned into methane, a colorless, odorless natural gas that can have a negative impact on the environment.

Anthony checks for methane on a frozen lake.

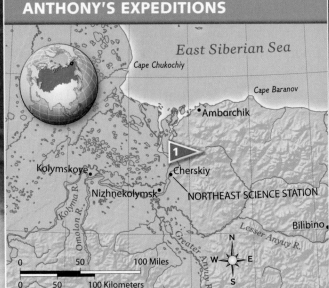

ANTHONY'S EXPEDITIONS

East Siberian Sea

Cape Chukochiy

Cape Baranov

Ambarchik

Kolymskoye

Cherskiy

Nizhnekolymsk

NORTHEAST SCIENCE STATION

Kolyma R.

Omolon R.

Bilibino

Lesser Anyuy R.

Greater Anyuy R.

0   50   100 Miles

0   50   100 Kilometers

N
W   E
S

PROCESS OF METHANE RELEASE

3 Methane is released into the atmosphere.

2 Methane is released into the lake as the permafrost thaws.

1 Organic matter is trapped in the permafrost.

frozen lake

soil

sediments

permafrost

METHANE RELEASE Warming temperatures thaw the permafrost and release methane gas. The methane heats the air as it is released into the atmosphere as a greenhouse gas.

Methane and Climate Change

Methane is a greenhouse gas, a gas that traps the sun's heat over the earth. Anthony explains, "It's 25 times more powerful than carbon dioxide on 100-year time scales" and could have the most powerful effect of all on global warming. Siberian lakes could release about ten times as much methane as is in the atmosphere now. Some experts believe this could cause temperatures across the world to rise higher and faster.

To check for methane, Anthony chops holes into the ice on the lakes to collect gas samples that she brings back to the lab. Sometimes she wants to know right away what gases might be present, so she lights a match. If a giant flame shoots up, she knows she's found methane.

Before You Move On

Monitor Comprehension What impact does methane have on the atmosphere?

FORMATIVE ASSESSMENT

VIEWING LAB GeoJournal

1. **Analyze Visuals** Go to the **Digital Library** to view the video clip on Emerging Explorer Katey Walter Anthony. How might her work in Siberia be applied to other places in the world?

2. **Pose and Answer Questions** With a partner, study the model and pose questions about it. Then answer: What does the methane have to pass through to enter the atmosphere? Why does the gas penetrate this material so easily?

3. **Analyze Cause and Effect** List some causes and effects of methane release using a chart like the one below.

CAUSES	EFFECTS

1.5 Central Asian Landscapes

TECHTREK

myNGconnect.com For online maps and photos of Central Asia

Maps and Graphs

Digital Library

Main Idea Human activities have led to the shrinking of the Aral Sea, which has damaged the surrounding landscape.

As you have learned, methane gas is threatening Siberia's environment. Central Asia's landscape has also been damaged. Human activities have nearly destroyed one of its most important bodies of water.

Adapting to Dry Conditions

Central Asia includes landforms such as deserts, mountains, forests, and steppes. Though the area doesn't experience the extreme cold of northern Russia, there are places in northern Kazakhstan that can reach 0°F in winter. In general, summers are hot and longer than in the northern parts of the region. Central Asia's temperatures vary so widely in part because it is not protected by a large body of water, which would help to keep temperatures moderate.

Large parts of Central Asia are **semiarid** or **arid**, meaning there is little or no rainfall. These dry lands are best suited for livestock grazing. Because of irrigation in some river valleys, however, farmers have also been able to grow crops such as cotton.

The Shrinking Aral Sea

Major efforts to grow cotton led to the shrinking of the **Aral Sea** in Kazakhstan and Uzbekistan. The body of water is actually a salt-water lake. The rivers that fed the lake were redirected into canals for irrigation. The Aral Sea was once the fourth largest lake in the world, but now it is only a fraction of the size it was in 1960.

Pollution contributed to problems in the Aral Sea. Fertilizer and **pesticides**, which are chemicals that kill harmful insects and weeds, ran into it. As the lake shrank, salt and pesticides destroyed the habitat of many plants and animals and threatened human health. The lake's once-thriving fishing industry was also damaged. One resident of the area said, "My father and grandfather were fishermen in this town, but as you can see, the boats are now sitting in the middle of a desert."

In 2005, Kazakhstan, with the help of the World Bank, built a dam to save the North Aral Sea. That part has increased in size, and fishing has returned to the area. However, the southern part of the lake, in Uzbekistan, is almost completely gone.

Before You Move On
Monitor Comprehension What human activities caused the Aral Sea to shrink, and what damage to the landscape has occurred as a result?

> **Critical Viewing** Camels walk past a stranded ship on land where the Aral Sea used to be. What does this picture suggest about the Aral Sea?

North Aral Sea, 1973

Aral Sea, 1973

This satellite image shows what the Aral Sea looked like in 1973. At this time, the North and South Aral seas were full of water.

North Aral Sea, 2009

Aral Sea, 2009

This satellite image shows what the Aral Sea looked like in 2009. The photo reveals that efforts to save the North Aral Sea have worked.

FORMATIVE ASSESSMENT
PHOTO LAB  GeoJournal

1. **Analyze Visuals** Study the photos above of the Aral Sea. How much time passed between the photo on the left and the photo on the right? What happened during that time period?

2. **Identify** What details in the photo below tell you that this part of the Aral Sea has been devastated for a long time?

3. **Human-Environment Interaction** Why did people redirect the Aral Sea? What steps have been taken to fix what happened as a result?

TECHTREK

myNGconnect.com For an online map
of the Silk Roads and photos of artifacts

Maps and Graphs   Digital Library

> **Main Idea** Settlers and conquerors from Europe and Asia shaped the early history of Russia and the Eurasian republics.

Settlement of Russia by different groups dates back to around 1200 B.C. At that time, a people called the Cimmerians lived north of the Black Sea in what is now southern Ukraine. Over hundreds of years, many other groups ruled this region.

Kievan Rus

The people whose culture had the most lasting influence on early Russia were the **Slavs** (slahvz). Some historians think they were farmers near the Black Sea around 700 B.C. or earlier. Others think they came from Poland around the A.D. 400s. By the A.D. 800s, the Slavs had built towns near rivers in Ukraine and western Russia.

In 862, Vikings from Scandinavia called the Varangian Russes (vahr ANG ee ehn ROOS ehz) took control of the Slavic town of Novgorod. Russia's name may have come from this tribe. About 20 years later, a Varangian prince captured Kiev (KEE ehf). He established a **state**, or defined territory with its own government, that came to be known as **Kievan Rus**.

Mongol Rule and Trade

By the late 1100s, Kiev's power had declined. Struggles for control within the ruling family weakened the state.

In the early 1200s, **Genghis Khan** (JEHNG gihs KAHN) established the **Mongol Empire** in Central Asia. In 1240, his grandson, Batu Khan, extended the empire by taking over Kievan Rus and much of Russia.

Russian princes had to declare their loyalty and pay **tribute**, or taxes, to the Mongol ruler, the khan. Mongols selected one of the princes to serve as grand prince and represent Russian interests.

The empire isolated Russia from European influence for more than 200 years. However, Mongol rule kept Russia and Central Asia open to the East. The **Silk Roads**, ancient trade routes, carried goods and new ideas throughout the Mongol Empire. As you can see on the map on the next page, the Silk Roads connected Southwest Asia and Central Asia with China. Goods traded included gold, jade, and silk. Merv, in Turkmenistan, and Samarkand, in Uzbekistan, were important stops on the Silk Roads.

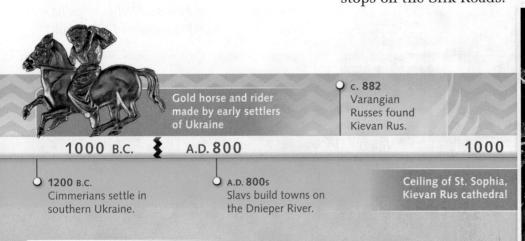

Gold horse and rider made by early settlers of Ukraine

c. 882 Varangian Russes found Kievan Rus.

1000 B.C.   A.D. 800   1000

1200 B.C. Cimmerians settle in southern Ukraine.

A.D. 800s Slavs build towns on the Dnieper River.

Ceiling of St. Sophia, Kievan Rus cathedral

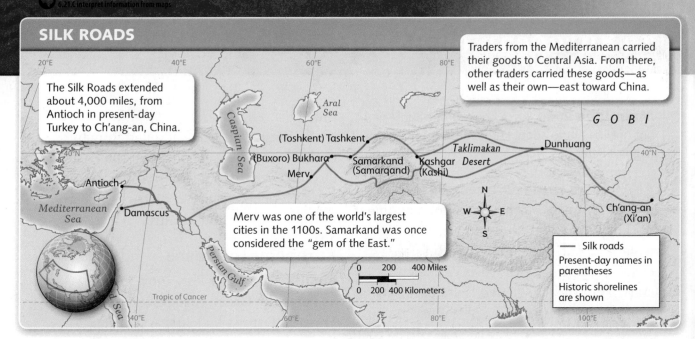

SILK ROADS

The Silk Roads extended about 4,000 miles, from Antioch in present-day Turkey to Ch'ang-an, China.

Traders from the Mediterranean carried their goods to Central Asia. From there, other traders carried these goods—as well as their own—east toward China.

Merv was one of the world's largest cities in the 1100s. Samarkand was once considered the "gem of the East."

— Silk roads

Present-day names in parentheses

Historic shorelines are shown

The Rise of Moscow

Around 1330, the Mongols allowed Grand Prince Ivan I of Moscow to collect tribute for them. Ivan kept some of the money for himself and used it to buy land and **expand** his territory. Moscow became stronger as Mongol rule weakened.

In 1380, Grand Prince Dmitry defeated the Mongols in battle. In 1480, Ivan III—also called Ivan the Great—refused to pay tribute to the Mongols, and they never demanded it again. This action ended Mongol rule in Russia. Ivan the Great's grandson, Ivan IV, expanded Russia and made it into an empire. He became Russia's first **czar** (zahr), or emperor.

Before You Move On
Summarize How did settlers and conquerors shape the early history of Russia?

FORMATIVE ASSESSMENT

MAP LAB
GeoJournal

1. **Place** Why do you think the main route of the Silk Roads split in two between the cities of Kashgar and Dunhuang?

2. **Interpret Maps** Study the map. Why was Samarkand an important stop on the routes?

3. **Analyze Cause and Effect** What actions strengthened Moscow and what resulted from its rise? Use a chart like the one below to list the causes and effects.

CAUSES	EFFECTS

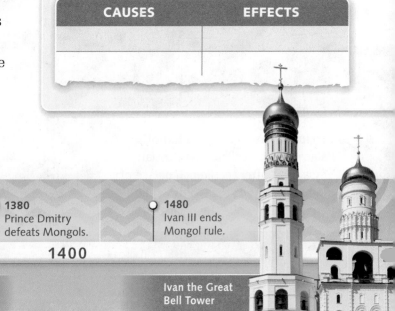

1237–1240 Mongols conquer Russia.

1380 Prince Dmitry defeats Mongols.

1480 Ivan III ends Mongol rule.

1200

1400

Mongol emperor Genghis Khan

Ivan the Great Bell Tower

2.2 European or Asian?

TECHTREK

myNGconnect.com For an online map
and photos of historic buildings

 Maps and Graphs

 Digital Library

Main Idea Russia lies in both Europe and Asia but only began to adopt European ideas under the reign of Peter the Great.

As you have already learned, Russia was isolated from Western Europe for a couple of centuries under Mongol rule. This isolation continued under the Russian czars, beginning with Ivan IV. Then, starting in the 1600s, two czars began to bring a European influence to Russia.

Spanning Europe and Asia

Geographically, Russia extends across the landmass of Europe and Asia, which is often called Eurasia. The Ural Mountains separate the continents. Many of the Russian people live in the European area west of the mountains.

In spite of lying partly in Europe, Russia did not develop a European culture. In the late 900s, Christianity became the main religion in Russia. However, while Western Europe adopted Roman Catholicism, Russia embraced the Eastern Orthodox branch of Christianity. The Russian people came to distrust western European ideas and culture.

European Influence

Finally, Czar Peter Romanov, known as **Peter the Great**, recognized that Western Europe had surpassed Russia both economically and militarily. Peter, who ruled from 1682 to 1725, decided to modernize Russia. As a result, he became the first Russian czar to travel to Western Europe. From his travels, he brought back European ideas about how government and business should be run. He also introduced a Western style of architecture. Many buildings in St. Petersburg, including the Peterhof Palace shown below, reflect this style.

> **Critical Viewing** The Peterhof Palace is often called "the Russian Versailles," after the French palace of King Louis XIV. What words would you use to describe the palace?

6.02.B evaluate contributions of individuals, past; 6.04.F identify location of major world countries;
6.05.B identify geographic factors that influence ability to control territory; 6.17.A describe how culture
traits spread; 6.21.C interpret information from maps

Catherine the Great, empress from 1762 to 1796, also introduced European ideas to Russia, focusing on the arts and education. Western forms of entertainment, such as opera, became popular during her **reign**, or rule. In addition, Catherine founded many new schools and supported the idea of educating women. She also built hospitals and **promoted**, or encouraged, vaccinating against smallpox. Planners redesigned cities, and European architecture replaced older Russian styles.

The empress attempted to create a more **secular** country, one in which the church was less powerful. In fact, Catherine wanted to pass laws that would allow citizens to practice the religion of their choice. However, her attempt at reform was unsuccessful.

Before You Move On
Summarize What European ideas did Russia adopt under Peter the Great?

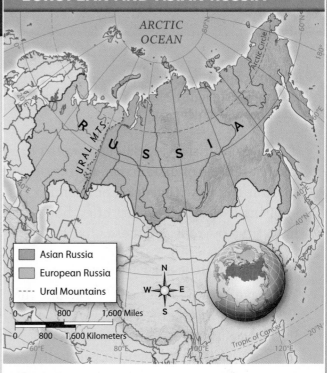

EUROPEAN AND ASIAN RUSSIA

ARCTIC OCEAN

RUSSIA

URAL MTS.

Legend:
- Asian Russia
- European Russia
- ---- Ural Mountains

0   800   1,600 Miles
0 800 1,600 Kilometers

 MAP TIP Map projections sometimes distort, or bend, the area shown. The Mollweide projection here makes Europe look somewhat mashed together but it is helpful in showing vast expanses of polar regions in small spaces.

FORMATIVE ASSESSMENT
READING LAB GeoJournal

1. **Interpret Maps** In which continent does most of Russia lie?

2. **Location** What aspects of Russia's geography played a part in its isolationism?

3. **Describe** How were culture traits spread during Peter and Catherine's rule?

4. **Evaluate** What contributions did both Peter and Catherine make to social, cultural, and economic life in Russia?

2.3 Defending Against Invaders

TECHTREK

myNGconnect.com For an online
map and photos of historical figures

 Maps and
Graphs

 Digital
Library

> **Main Idea** For centuries, Russia used its geographic strengths—location, size, isolation, and climate—to defend against invaders.

Throughout history, Russians adapted to the challenges of distance and climate in their country. **Invaders**, or enemies entering by force, however, often had a hard time overcoming these challenges.

Russia Builds an Empire

You have learned that Ivan IV became the first czar of Russia in 1547. Ivan began building Russia's empire by conquering territory from the Mongols. Eventually, Russia expanded across Siberia to the Pacific Ocean.

As Russia continued to grow under Peter the Great and Catherine the Great, the country was often forced to defend its empire against invaders. Enemies from Europe had to cope with Russia's vast expanse and harsh climate. They were rarely successful at invading the country. Two famous examples are the failed invasions of Napoleon and Hitler.

Napoleon Invades Russia

Napoleon I became emperor of France in 1804, and his empire included much of Europe. Angered that Britain had defeated him in battle, he came up with a plan to limit Britain's trade with European countries. Czar Alexander I refused to go along with the plan. Alexander thought reducing trade with Britain would be bad for Russia's economy.

In revenge, Napoleon invaded Russia in the summer of 1812. The Russians followed a **scorched earth policy**, where troops retreat in front of the advancing army and destroy crops and other resources that might supply the enemy. When Napoleon arrived in Moscow, the city was nearly deserted. The Russians had burned it to destroy any supplies that might have helped the French troops.

By mid-October, Napoleon started his retreat. He knew the harsh Russian winter was coming. Soon, snow and extreme cold began to weaken the French army. Russian troops attacked the army as it fled. Of the roughly 420,000 troops that set out for Moscow, only about 10,000 survived.

Ivan IV stands before St. Basil's, which he had constructed.

1500

1547
Ivan IV is crowned first czar.

1600

1604–1613
Civil war and invasions

1613
Romanov rule begins. The family, which included Peter the Great and Catherine the Great, ruled until 1917.

1700

1703
St. Petersburg is founded.

Picture of Nicholas II, the last of the Romanovs

6.01.A trace characteristics of societies that resulted from factors such as invasion; 6.05.B identify geographic factors that influence control of territory; 6.21.B analyze by comparing; 6.21.C interpret information from maps; 6.21.F use math skills to interpret social studies information

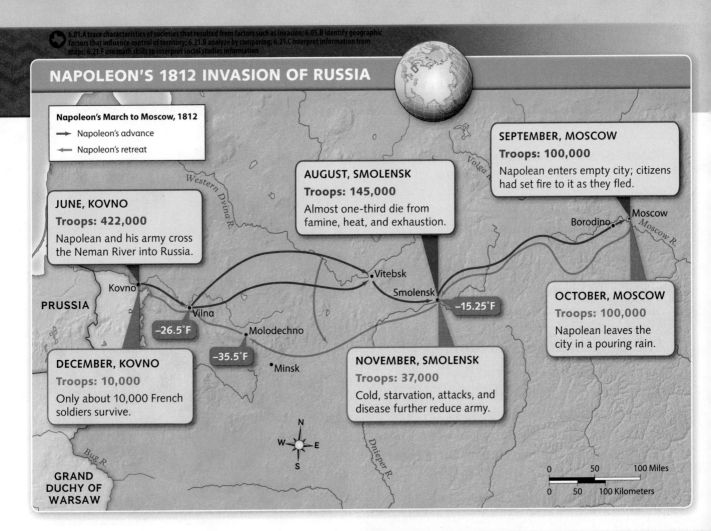

NAPOLEON'S 1812 INVASION OF RUSSIA

Napoleon's March to Moscow, 1812
→ Napoleon's advance
← Napoleon's retreat

JUNE, KOVNO
Troops: 422,000
Napolean and his army cross the Neman River into Russia.

AUGUST, SMOLENSK
Troops: 145,000
Almost one-third die from famine, heat, and exhaustion.

SEPTEMBER, MOSCOW
Troops: 100,000
Napolean enters empty city; citizens had set fire to it as they fled.

OCTOBER, MOSCOW
Troops: 100,000
Napolean leaves the city in a pouring rain.

DECEMBER, KOVNO
Troops: 10,000
Only about 10,000 French soldiers survive.

NOVEMBER, SMOLENSK
Troops: 37,000
Cold, starvation, attacks, and disease further reduce army.

PRUSSIA
GRAND DUCHY OF WARSAW

Kovno
Vilna
−26.5°F
−35.5°F
Molodechno
Minsk
Vitebsk
Smolensk
−15.25°F
Borodino
Moscow
Western Dvina R.
Volga R.
Moscow R.
Dnieper R.
Bug R.

0   50   100 Miles
0   50   100 Kilometers

Hitler Invades Russia

History repeated itself when Adolf Hitler sent troops from **Nazi Germany** to invade Russia during World War II. Frigid winter weather resulted in the deaths of many Nazi soldiers. Hitler was unable to take Moscow in 1941, or Stalingrad in 1943. Of the 300,000 Nazi troops that fought at Stalingrad, only about 5,000 came home.

Before You Move On
Monitor Comprehension What role did Russia's geography play in defeating Napoleon and Hitler?

FORMATIVE ASSESSMENT

MAP LAB
GeoJournal

1. **Movement** Using the map, figure out how far Napoleon's army had to travel to get to Moscow from Kovno.

2. **Interpret Maps** What does the map tell you about the weather as the French troops retreated from Moscow?

3. **Compare and Contrast** In what ways were Nazi Germany's experiences in Russia similar to those of Napoleon?

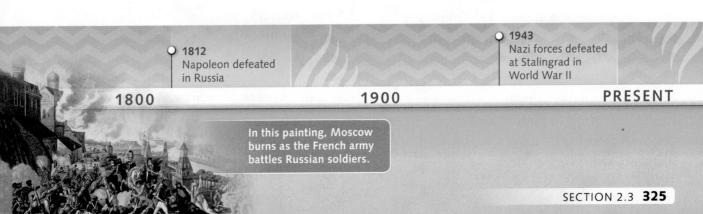

1812
Napoleon defeated in Russia

1943
Nazi forces defeated at Stalingrad in World War II

1800   1900   PRESENT

In this painting, Moscow burns as the French army battles Russian soldiers.

2.4 Serfdom to Industrialization

TECHTREK

myNGconnect.com For an online map of Russia's resources and industries

Maps and Graphs

> **Main Idea** Both peasants and industrial workers led difficult lives, but they played important roles in Russia's history.

For centuries, most Russian workers were peasants. They worked the land for wealthy landlords. The peasants were free to leave the estate as long as they paid their debts after the harvest.

The Beginning of Serfdom

Ivan IV, also known as Ivan the Terrible, changed this system in the 1500s. He murdered many nobles and gave their lands to people who supported him. These people needed the peasants to farm their estates, so Ivan passed laws that tied the peasants to the land as **serfs**. Serfs had their own houses and a small plot of land to farm, but they had to pay the landlord rent. Serfs could not leave the estate without permission and had few rights.

In 1861, Czar Alexander II freed the serfs. He wanted these workers to be free to work in industry and help modernize Russia. As a result, he ended their legal ties to their landlords. Serfs could then become industrial workers for wages.

Industrial Revolution in Russia

Under Peter the Great, early industries, such as shipbuilding and metalworking, had begun. Yet the **Industrial Revolution** didn't really begin in Russia until the 1890s. By 1913, it had become the fifth largest industrial nation in the world. As in other countries, however, the change from rural work to factory work was difficult. Most industrial workers and peasants were very poor.

Critical Viewing Serfs clear the land of large stones in this illustration. Based on the illustration, what can you conclude about the type of work serfs performed?

Many peasants starved because of poor harvests, and city factory workers were unhappy with their working conditions. Frequent worker **strikes**, or work stoppages, and protests gave way to political unrest. Revolutionary activist and politician **V. I. Lenin** led a political group called the **Bolsheviks**. They wanted workers to take over industry and the government. In February 1917 the Bolsheviks began the **Russian Revolution** and overthrew the czar. Lenin became leader of the new government.

Before You Move On

Summarize What roles did serfs and industrial workers play in Russian history?

RESOURCES AND INDUSTRIES IN WESTERN RUSSIA, 1900

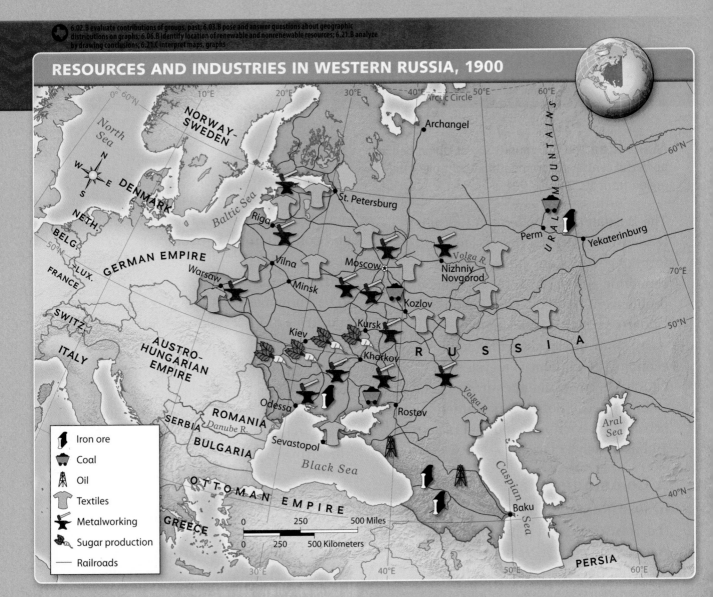

Legend:
- Iron ore
- Coal
- Oil
- Textiles
- Metalworking
- Sugar production
- Railroads

GROWTH OF KEY INDUSTRIES IN RUSSIA, 1890–1900

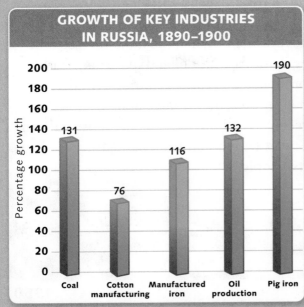

Percentage growth:
- Coal: 131
- Cotton manufacturing: 76
- Manufactured iron: 116
- Oil production: 132
- Pig iron: 190

Source: Peter Stearns, *The Industrial Revolution in World History*, 1998

FORMATIVE ASSESSMENT

DATA LAB

GeoJournal

1. **Pose and Answer Questions** With a partner, ask questions about the graph data. Then answer: Which industry grew the least between 1890 and 1900? The most? Why do you think the industries grew at those rates?

2. **Draw Conclusions** Based on the graph, the map, and the text, what conclusions can you draw about the Industrial Revolution in Russia?

3. **Movement** Examine the map shown above. Why do you think several railroad lines ran through Moscow?

2.5 The Soviet Union

> **Main Idea** The Communist Soviet Union had a powerful central government that controlled the region from 1922 until 1991.

The Bolsheviks, who led the Russian Revolution, believed that a Communist form of government and a socialist economic system were the answers to the problems of the Industrial Revolution. Under **communism**, a single political party controls the government and economy. **Socialism** is a system in which the government controls economic resources. The Bolsheviks wanted to end private ownership of land and resources and establish a classless society.

A Communist State

In 1922, Russia, Ukraine, Belarus, and the Transcaucasian republics of Armenia, Azerbaijan, and Georgia formed the Union of Soviet Socialist Republics (U.S.S.R.), also known as the **Soviet Union**. Later, other republics came under the control of the Soviet Union and the central Communist government in Moscow.

From 1927 to 1953, the Soviet people lived under the total command of Josef Stalin. Stalin's government isolated its citizens from contact with the West.

The Cold War

After World War II, the Soviet Union and the United States were the two most powerful countries in the world. Tension and conflict arose between the two because of their very different political and economic systems. The conflict came to be known as the **Cold War** because the countries did not fight each other directly.

The Cold War led the United States and Soviet Union to develop nuclear weapons. The United States went to war in Korea and Vietnam during the 1950s and 1960s to try to prevent communism from spreading to these countries. The Cold War also resulted in a "space race." The Soviet Union won the race in 1957 when it launched its Sputnik satellite into space.

A Controlled Economy

The Soviet Union also became an industrial leader and a world power, second only to the United States. The government owned most businesses and agriculture. On **collective farms**, workers produced a certain amount of food—determined by the government—and received a share of surplus crops. Still, the Soviet Union had trouble feeding all of its people.

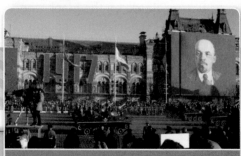

A banner of Lenin overlooks Red Square as Soviet Russia celebrates the anniversary of the 1917 Russian Revolution.

1922 Soviet Union forms.

1941–1945 Soviet Union fights Germany in World War II.

1925

1950

1924 Stalin becomes Soviet leader.

1945 Cold War begins.

Visual Vocabulary The Soviet Union used propaganda, like this poster, to promote Communist ideas. **Propaganda** is information designed to influence people's opinions.

Quality of life was poor, too. People had guaranteed jobs, but their standard of living was much lower than that in Western countries. For example, they had little access to consumer goods. President **Mikhail Gorbachev** (mih KYL GAWR buh chawf) tried to reform and improve the economy. However, a movement toward adopting democratic forms of government was spreading across Eastern Europe. In 1991, the Soviet Union collapsed, and its republics gained their independence.

Before You Move On

Monitor Comprehension In what ways did the Communist government of the Soviet Union control its republics?

FORMATIVE ASSESSMENT

VIEWING LAB GeoJournal

1. **Analyze Visuals** In the propaganda poster, the figure in the back is holding a flag with Stalin's picture on it. What are other figures holding? What might each figure represent?

2. **Draw Conclusions** How might the space race have increased tensions of the Cold War?

3. **Make Inferences** Review communism and socialism on pages R41, R46, and R48. Why do you think the Soviet Union's collective economic system struggled to feed the people and provide a high quality of life, despite better rights for workers?

1957
Soviets launch
Sputnik satellite.

U.S. president
**Ronald Reagan
and Gorbachev**

1985
Gorbachev begins reform programs
and works with President Reagan
to end Cold War.

1975

PRESENT

1961
Soviets send first
person into space.

1991
Soviet Union
collapses.

VOCABULARY

On your paper, write the vocabulary word that completes each of the following sentences.

1. _____ under the tundra keeps trees from growing there.

2. Some rivers provide _____, using the power of water to generate electricity.

3. _____ is information designed to influence people's opinions.

4. Czar Alexander I freed the _____ in 1861.

5. _____ is a form of socialism in which a single party controls the government and economy.

MAIN IDEAS

6. What natural barriers separate Russia and the republics from their neighbors? What impact do the barriers have on these countries? (Section 1.1)

7. Why are Russian winters cold and dark in some places? (Section 1.2)

8. What are the two main types of natural resources in this region? (Section 1.3)

9. What does Katey Walter Anthony hope to learn by studying the presence of methane in Siberian lakes? (Section 1.4)

10. What type of agriculture is suited to the dry climate of Central Asia? (Section 1.5)

11. How was Kievan Rus founded? (Section 2.1)

12. What western European influences did Peter the Great and Catherine the Great introduce to Russia? (Section 2.2)

13. What factors helped defeat the Nazis in Russia? (Section 2.3)

14. In what ways were serfs different from peasants in Russia? (Section 2.4)

15. What methods did the government of the Soviet Union use to control the country's economy? (Section 2.5)

GEOGRAPHY

ANALYZE THE ESSENTIAL QUESTION

How have size and extreme climates shaped Russia and the Eurasian republics?

Critical Thinking: Analyze Cause and Effect

16. Why does Russia have few ice-free ports?

17. What impact do Russia's size and extreme climate have on its use of natural resources?

18. In what way did the climate in Central Asia contribute to the shrinking of the Aral Sea?

INTERPRET MAPS

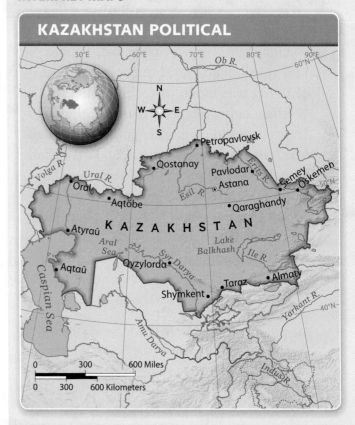

KAZAKHSTAN POLITICAL

19. **Location** Which two cities are best located to take advantage of energy resources in the Caspian Sea?

20. **Make Inferences** Why do you think Kazakhstan moved its capital from Almaty to Astana in 1997?

HISTORY

ANALYZE THE ESSENTIAL QUESTION

How has geographic isolation influenced the region's history?

Critical Thinking: Make Inferences

21. What effect did the Mongols have on Russia's relationship with Europe?

22. During Napoleon's invasion of Russia, what impact might distance have had on the army's horses and supplies?

23. In what way might physical geography have prevented the Industrial Revolution from starting in Russia as early as it started in western European countries?

INTERPRET TABLES

TIME INDUSTRIAL LABORERS NEEDED TO WORK TO BUY SELECTED GOODS, 1986		
	Moscow	United States
Loaf of bread	11 min*	18 min
Liter of milk	20 min	4 min
Grapefruit	112 min	6 min
Chicken	189 min	18 min
Bus fare (2 miles)	3 min*	7 min
Postage stamp	3 min	2 min
Pair of jeans	56 hrs	4 hrs
Washing machine	177 hrs	48 hrs

* price supports by government

Source: Radio Free Europe, published in the *New York Times*, June 28, 1987

24. **Compare and Contrast** What type of food must have had the biggest price difference? What food was probably more expensive in the United States than in Moscow?

25. **Make Generalizations** Based on the chart, what do you think life was like for industrial laborers in the Soviet Union in 1986?

ACTIVE OPTIONS

Synthesize the Essential Questions by completing the activities below.

26. **Write an Email** Schools sometimes conduct exchange programs with schools in other countries. Given what you know about the geography, history, and culture of Russia, decide which area of Russia you would like to visit. Write an email to a classmate recommending a particular location in Russia using the tips below. **Send the email to a classmate and ask for feedback on the information provided.**

> **Writing Tips**
> - Organize your ideas under two or three main headings before you begin writing.
> - Use a clear, straightforward style to present specific, useful, and interesting details in your email.
> - Make sure you explain why you offer the advice that you do.

Go to **Student Resources** for Guided Writing support.

27. **Gather and Share Information** Work in a group to gather two new facts about Russia and each of the republics. Use online sources to help you find the facts. Then create a chart to record your facts and share them in an oral presentation. Compare your findings with those of other groups.

Russia	Fact 1: _____
	Fact 2: _____
Armenia	Fact 1: _____
	Fact 2: _____
Azerbaijan	Fact 1: _____
	Fact 2: _____

CHAPTER 12

Russia & THE EURASIAN REPUBLICS
TODAY

PREVIEW THE CHAPTER

Essential Question What features, such as size and climate, have influenced Russian culture?

KEY VOCABULARY

- culture
- nomad
- yurt
- terrain
- gauge
- port
- diplomacy

ACADEMIC VOCABULARY

enlist

TERMS & NAMES

- Trans-Siberian Railroad
- Hermitage Museum

Essential Question How have Russia and the Eurasian republics dealt with recent political, economic, and environmental challenges?

KEY VOCABULARY

- perestroika
- glasnost
- coup
- federal system
- proportional representation
- revenue
- pipeline
- radioactive
- fallout
- half-life
- contaminate

ACADEMIC VOCABULARY

autonomy, vulnerable

TERMS & NAMES

- Russification
- Kremlin
- Chernobyl

TECHTREK

FOR THIS CHAPTER

Student eEdition

Maps and Graphs

Interactive Whiteboard GeoActivities

Digital Library

Go to **myNGconnect.com** for more on Russia and the Eurasian Republics.

Uzbek women and girls from a mountain village wear a *rumol*, a traditional head scarf.

1.1 Climate and Culture

TECHTREK

myNGconnect.com For photos reflecting climate and culture in Russia and the republics

Digital Library

Main Idea The variety of climates in Russia and the Eurasian republics has a major impact on the region's cultures.

Culture refers to a group's unique way of life. Cultural traits include food—what people eat and how they obtain it—shelter, clothing, religion, and language. The first three traits are influenced by climate.

Enduring the Cold in Siberia

About 30 different native peoples live in the tundra and taiga of Siberia in Russia. These include the Yakut, Nenets, Evenki, Chukchi, and Inuit (IHN yoo iht). All of these people have similar cultures but different languages.

People living in these cold climates, with their long winters and short, hot summers, traditionally dress in clothes made from reindeer fur. Some people, such as the Nenets, still live as **nomads**, moving from place to place according to the seasons in search of food. This way of life is changing, however, and today many native people live in towns or cities.

Herding in Central Asia

Like the Nenets in Siberia, some herders in Kazakhstan and other parts of Central Asia also continue to lead nomadic lives. In the region's dry climate, this traditional culture focuses on herding sheep, camels, cattle, and horses. Animals provide food and milk as well as hides and wool for clothing and tents. Although herding continues to be important in this region, many herders now live in rural villages in houses made of mud bricks that have been baked by the sun.

Farming in the Steppes

On the steppes of Russia and parts of Central Asia, the rich soil and moderate climate—cold winters and warm summers—are suited to agriculture. A peasant farming culture developed in this climate. In this culture, people grew grain crops, especially wheat, and raised livestock. They lived in settled villages. Later they worked for landlords on large estates and became serfs.

> **Critical Viewing** A Nenet boy studies for school in the frozen tundra of northwest Siberia. What impact might the intense cold reflected in this photo have on everyday activities?

6.06.C analyze effects of environment on humans; 6.07.A identify and analyze ways people have adapted; 6.15.A identify and describe common traits that define cultures; 6.15.B identify and describe common traits that unify a culture region; 6.21.B analyze by summarizing; 6.21.C interpret information from visuals; 6.22.A use social studies terminology correctly

ADAPTING TO CLIMATE

Cold

Dry

Moderate

SIBERIA Many native people of Siberia center their culture around reindeer. The warm, durable clothing worn by this family is made from reindeer skin. Reindeer meat and fat also provide nutritious food.

CENTRAL ASIA The animals the Kazakhs of Central Asia raise provide almost everything the herders need to live. Felt, or wool fibers pressed together, is used to make hats and traditional tents called yurts.

STEPPES Life for farmers on the steppes revolves around the seasonal growing cycle. Farmers often use simple tools to grow their crops. Animals help with the work and provide meat and milk.

Today, large corporations or individuals own the farms. Farmers still grow wheat as in the past, and they grow other grain crops as well, including maize, or corn, and barley. Many of these grain products are exported to other countries. Beets and potatoes are also common crops, along with sunflowers, which are grown to make oil used in cooking.

Before You Move On
Summarize What impact have the variety of climates in Russia and the Eurasian republics had on the region's cultures?

FORMATIVE ASSESSMENT
PHOTO LAB GeoJournal

1. **Analyze Visuals** The Central Asian yurt shown above is movable. Why might this be an important consideration for nomadic herders?

2. **Compare and Contrast** Study the photos. Analyze what people of Siberia and Central Asia do to adapt to their climate and explain why.

3. **Summarize** Describe some of the common traits that define culture in each of these regions: Siberia, Central Asia, and the steppes. Be sure the meanings of *culture* and *common traits* are used correctly in your response.

1.2 Trans-Siberian Railroad

TECHTREK

myNGconnect.com For an online map of the
Trans-Siberian Railroad and photos of sites on its routes

Maps and Graphs

Digital Library

Main Idea The Trans-Siberian Railroad links the western and eastern parts of Russia.

The **Trans-Siberian Railroad** is the world's longest continuous railroad, spanning about 6,000 miles and crossing eight time zones. *Trans-Siberian* means "across Siberia." The railroad links Moscow with eastern Russia. It also carries people and goods to East Asia and Europe.

Building the Railroad

Russia began to build the railroad in 1891. It was designed to connect Moscow with Vladivostok (vlah duh VAWH stock), a busy port on the Pacific Ocean. At that time, no reliable form of transportation linked this far eastern port with the European part of Russia.

Laborers began at both ends of the route and worked their way toward the center, but the climate and **terrain**, or physical features of the land, made progress very difficult. Workers had to lay tracks across long stretches of permafrost, and the route went through mountains, forests, rivers, and lakes. Materials—including explosives used to blast through rocks and cliffs— had to be brought thousands of miles to the work sites.

The construction project required many workers. As a result, thousands of Russian peasants, convicts, and soldiers were **enlisted**, or selected, to labor on the railroad. They were given only picks and shovels to do their difficult work. Human workers and horses hauled the heavy materials. The laborers worked long hours in extreme heat in the summer and extreme cold in the winter. They also had to deal with attacks by thieves and, occasionally, tigers. The main route, running from Moscow to Vladivostok, was finally completed in 1916.

Critical Viewing A Trans-Siberian Railroad train runs along the banks of Lake Baikal in Siberia. In this photo, the conductor looks out of the train as it curves around the lake. What challenges did the workers probably face while building this part of the railroad?

ROUTES OF THE TRANS-SIBERIAN RAILROAD

Map showing the routes of the Trans-Siberian Railroad across Russia, with cities including Murmansk, St. Petersburg, Moscow, Minsk, Kaliningrad, Brest, Kharkiv, Volgograd, Sochi, Samara, Ufa, Nizhniy Novgorod, Yekaterinburg, Chelyabinsk, Omsk, Astana (KAZAKHSTAN), Novosibirsk, Irkutsk, Lake Baikal, Ulaanbaatar (MONGOLIA), Beijing (CHINA), Harbin, Vladivostok, Sovetskaya Gavan', Yakutsk, Magadan, Anadyr. Labels: ARCTIC OCEAN, Arctic Circle, RUSSIA, Sea of Okhotsk, PACIFIC OCEAN, Black Sea, Caspian Sea, URAL MOUNTAINS.

Legend:
— Trans-Siberian rail routes
— Other railways

Scale: 0 — 400 — 800 Miles; 0 — 400 — 800 Kilometers

Effects of the Railroad

The railroad transformed Siberia and its traditional culture. Between 1891 and 1914, more than five million people immigrated to Siberia. New towns and cities grew up along the train's route. Soviet leaders began to industrialize Siberia and mine its plentiful raw materials. During World War II, the railroad moved Soviet troops and materials across Russia.

The Railroad Today

Today, the railroad operates several more routes and has replaced all of the old steam engines with electric trains that carry passengers and freight. The railroad also plays an important role in the world economy. Container cargo, or goods packed in large steel boxes, travels from China and other parts of East Asia to Europe. One challenge is that the **gauge**, or width of the tracks, in Russia is wider than in Europe or China. As a result, containers need to be transferred to different trains at the borders. Still, shipping containers by land across Russia is much faster—and cheaper—than shipping by sea.

Before You Move On
Monitor Comprehension In what ways has the Trans-Siberian Railroad helped to link Russia?

FORMATIVE ASSESSMENT

MAP LAB GeoJournal

1. **Interpret Maps** Use the map scale to determine the distance from Novosibirsk to Irkutsk on the Trans-Siberian Railroad.

2. **Movement** Trace the Trans-Siberian Railroad route to China. What benefit does it offer to manufacturers of consumer goods in China?

3. **Make Inferences** Why are there many tunnels and bridges along the route of the Trans-Siberian Railroad?

1.3 St. Petersburg Today

TECHTREK
myNGconnect.com For photos of St. Petersburg

Digital Library

> **Main Idea** St. Petersburg is Russia's second largest city and a center of culture, industry, and trade.

St. Petersburg is located in northwest Russia on the Neva River. The river flows into the Gulf of Finland, which is at the most eastern part of the Baltic Sea. Because of its far northern location—at a latitude of about 60°N—St. Petersburg has long winter nights. In fact, for about one month a year, there's barely any daylight. For about three weeks in summer, the sky never gets completely dark. Special music and dance events are held during these "White Nights" to take advantage of the long days.

Window to the West

St. Petersburg originally sat on isolated swampland, making it a poor place on which to build. Nevertheless, Peter the Great chose the site in 1703 to gain a **port**, or harbor, on the Baltic Sea for trade. He also wanted to create a modern city—for the times—that would resemble those in Western Europe and become Russia's "window to the West." Peter got his wish. He had St. Petersburg filled with islands, canals, and bridges like those in the western European cities of Amsterdam and Venice. He also built wide boulevards like those in Paris and London.

FAST FACTS ON ST. PETERSBURG	
Population	4.6 million people
Land Area	550 square miles
Location	Average temperature in January: 21°F Average temperature in July: 65°F Latitude: 59° 57'N; longitude: 30° 19'E
Date Founded	1703

St. Petersburg's historic architecture also reflects western European influences. Many of the buildings from the 1700s still survive, including the Winter Palace, **Hermitage Museum**, and summer palaces of several czars. St. Petersburg is also filled with many beautiful and historic Russian Orthodox churches and cathedrals in Western and Eastern style.

The city is Russia's cultural center. St. Petersburg boasts world-famous museums and ballet companies, such as the Kirov. It also contains many universities and theaters and the country's oldest music academy. In addition, St. Petersburg offers a variety of contemporary music, including jazz and rock.

A Vibrant Economy

Manufacturing and construction are important industries in St. Petersburg. The city is also a center for trade and distribution of goods to and from Europe.

Above all, the local economy depends on tourism. More than three million visitors came to see the city's attractions in 2003 on its 300th anniversary. Many historic buildings that had been damaged during World War II were restored in time for the celebration. Vladimir Putin, Russia's president in 2003, is from St. Petersburg. He wanted the city to become a center of **diplomacy**, a place where international affairs could be conducted. Like Peter the Great, Putin wanted Russia to be more connected to the West.

Before You Move On

Summarize In what ways is St. Petersburg a center of culture, industry, and trade?

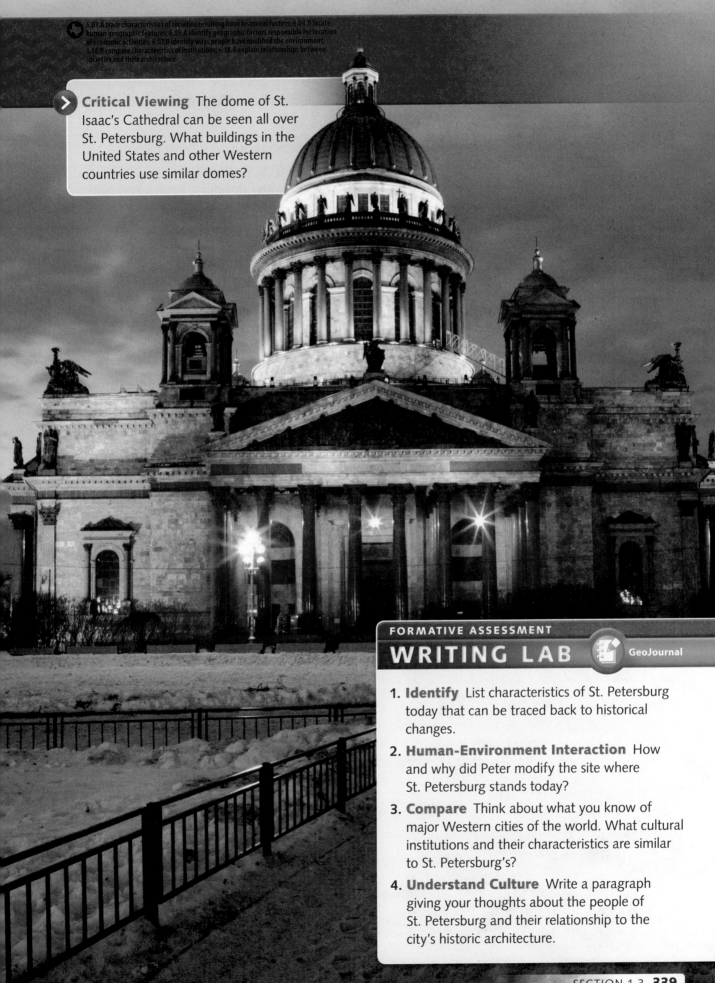

6.01.A trace characteristics of societies resulting from historical factors; 6.04.D locate human geographic features; 6.05.A identify geographic factors responsible for location of economic activities; 6.07.B identify ways people have modified the environment; 6.16.B compare characteristics of institutions; 6.18.A explain relationships between societies and their architecture

> **Critical Viewing** The dome of St. Isaac's Cathedral can be seen all over St. Petersburg. What buildings in the United States and other Western countries use similar domes?

FORMATIVE ASSESSMENT

WRITING LAB   GeoJournal

1. **Identify** List characteristics of St. Petersburg today that can be traced back to historical changes.

2. **Human-Environment Interaction** How and why did Peter modify the site where St. Petersburg stands today?

3. **Compare** Think about what you know of major Western cities of the world. What cultural institutions and their characteristics are similar to St. Petersburg's?

4. **Understand Culture** Write a paragraph giving your thoughts about the people of St. Petersburg and their relationship to the city's historic architecture.

2.1 The Soviet Collapse

TECHTREK

myNGconnect.com For photos
of the Soviet Union

Digital
Library

Main Idea Economic problems and people's desire for independence caused the Soviet Union to collapse in 1991.

As you have learned, the Soviet Union formed in 1922. During the 1970s and 1980s, the economy of the huge region slowed. Soviet money had almost no value outside the country. Stores had little food on their shelves and few goods to buy. In addition, people in the Eurasian republics had long resented the Soviet policy of **Russification**. Under this policy, the Soviet Union moved Russians into the republics and put them in charge. They also forced local people to learn the Russian language.

Gorbachev Brings Reform

In 1985, Mikhail Gorbachev became head of the Soviet Communist Party and began to introduce reforms. He promoted a movement known as **perestroika** (pehr ih STROY kuh), which means "restructuring." Gorbachev wanted to restructure the economy. Less government control, he believed, would make the economy more effective.

After the economy had failed to improve by 1990, the government presented a new plan to change the economy in 500 days. According to this plan, the republics would have greater control over their economies, and state ownership of businesses would decline.

Gorbachev also introduced the policy of **glasnost** (GLAHS nuhst), or "openness," which encouraged people to speak openly about the government. This freedom of expression went beyond what Gorbachev had intended, however. People started to criticize and protest against the central government, and they began to demand even more freedom.

Critical Viewing Food shortages in the Soviet Union resulted in empty shelves, as you can see in this 1990 photo of a Moscow grocery store. What impact do you think seeing stores like this had on the Soviet people?

The Soviet Union Falls

After the collapse of the Berlin Wall in Germany in November 1989, the Communists no longer had control over Eastern Europe. People in many of the Soviet republics also wanted freedom from the central Communist government. Weakened by the economy, the government could no longer manage its vast empire. By the fall of 1990, all of the republics had declared their **autonomy**, or determination to govern themselves.

In August 1991, conservative Communists who opposed Gorbachev's political and economic reforms attempted a coup against him. A **coup** (KOO) is a sudden overthrow of the government by force. The coup failed, but Gorbachev knew he had lost power. On December 25, 1991, he resigned as president, and the Soviet Union dissolved. All of the republics became independent countries.

Life After Independence

Some groups within the newly independent republics and Russia's own borders sought independence for themselves. In Azerbaijan, Armenians continue to fight over a part of the country where most of the people are ethnic Armenians. Within Russia, the Muslim republic of Chechnya (CHEHCH nee uh) has struggled to gain full independence.

The economic transition has been difficult as well. Less government control in Russia has led to a large gap between rich and poor, higher prices, unemployment, and an increase in corruption and organized crime. Some of the Eurasian republics still have centrally controlled economies and governments.

Before You Move On

Make Inferences In what ways did attempts to reform the Soviet economy and political system contribute to the collapse of the Soviet Union?

FORMATIVE ASSESSMENT

SPEAKING LAB GeoJournal

1. **Turn and Talk** With a partner, discuss the causes and effects of the Soviet Union's collapse. Organize your ideas in a chart.

2. **Describe** What was the economic situation when the Soviet government had too much power—and then not enough? Talk about reasons for limiting government.

3. **Compare** Review free enterprise on page R43. Discuss the differences between a free-enterprise economy and the Soviet economy. What are the benefits of the U.S. free-enterprise system?

2.2 Russia's Government

TECHTREK

myNGconnect.com For current
events on Russia and photos of its leaders

Connect
to NG

Digital
Library

Main Idea Russia's central government consists of three branches and, together with the president, holds most of the power.

Following the collapse of the Soviet Union, Russia adopted a new constitution. This set up a **federal system**, with a strong central government and local government units. The United States also has a federal system. Russia's government is more democratic than that of the former Soviet Union. Everyone 18 years and older can vote, and there are several political parties. However, the central government and the president hold most of the power.

Presidential Power

In Russia, the president is the head of the executive branch and the most powerful government leader. Vladimir Putin served as president from 2000–2008. In 2008, Dmitry Medvedev (med VYED if) was elected president. He served one term.

Medvedev appointed Putin prime minister, so Putin was not far from power. In March 2012, Putin was reelected president. Opposition candidates and their parties in Russia are not strong, but there were protests to Putin's election.

Legislators and Judges

There are two houses in the legislative branch. The lower house is the State Duma. Members are elected based on **proportional representation**. Under this system, a political party gets the same percentage of seats as the percentage of votes it received. A party must receive at least seven percent of the vote to get seats. Putin's party, the United Russia Party, holds about 64 percent of the seats.

The upper house of the legislative branch is the Federation Council. Executive and legislative leaders in each of the local government units appoint the members of this house. The State Duma is the more powerful legislative house. All bills must first be considered in the State Duma, even those proposed by the upper house.

> **Critical Viewing** The **Kremlin** is a historic complex of palaces and churches in the heart of Moscow. What feature in the photo suggests that the Kremlin once served as the city's fortress?

COMPARE RUSSIAN AND U.S. GOVERNMENTS

Russia	Government Branches	United States
• President, elected to a six-year term Prime Minister, appointed • Government Ministers, appointed	Executive	• President and Vice President, both elected to a four-year term • Cabinet, appointed

• Federal Assembly:
  – Federation Council (166 members), appointed to a four-year term
  – State Duma (450 members), elected to a five-year term
	Legislative	• Congress:
		  – Senate (100 members), elected to a six-year term
		  – House of Representatives (435 members), elected to a two-year term

• Constitutional Court Judges, appointed for life	Judicial	• Supreme Court Judges, appointed for life

The highest court in Russia is the Constitutional Court. The Federation Council appoints these judges based on the president's recommendations. The judges are appointed for life. In general, the judicial branch in Russia is more **vulnerable**, or open, to political pressure than in most Western democracies. That means that officials in the executive and legislative branches are sometimes able to influence the judges.

Central Control

The central government in Moscow still tries to control most levels of government. Those in power generally choose the people they want to be elected.

In 2000, then-president Putin reduced the number of local government units in Russia from 89 to 7 to increase central control of them. The president already exercised some power over these units because he nominated their governors.

Before You Move On

Summarize What branches make up the central government, and in what ways do the government and the president exercise their power?

FORMATIVE ASSESSMENT

DATA LAB
 GeoJournal

1. **Identify** Based on the chart, which officials in the Russian executive branch probably serve a role similar to that of the Cabinet members in the U.S. government?

2. **Compare and Contrast** Study the chart. In what way is the legislative branch in Russia similar to that in the United States? In what way is it different?

3. **Express Ideas Through Speech** Is the government in Russia more or less democratic than that in the United States? Think about which officials are elected or appointed and how power is handled. Discuss with a partner.

2.3 Unlocking Energy Riches

 TECHTREK

myNGconnect.com For an online map and photos of the region's energy pipelines

Maps and Graphs

Digital Library

Main Idea Oil and natural gas enrich the economies of Russia and several countries around the Caspian Sea.

In addition to reforming its government, Russia has worked to develop its economy. Oil and natural gas are its greatest sources of wealth. In fact, the country is the largest exporter of oil and natural gas in the world. These resources account for about two-thirds of the value of all Russia's exports and one-third of its **revenue**, or income.

Siberian Boom Towns

About 70 percent of Russian oil comes from western Siberia. Since the end of the Soviet Union, the region has been booming, or growing rapidly. Workers from western Russia and Central Asia come to Siberia for good-paying jobs. They earn enough to buy apartments in cities such as Surgut. New suburbs have developed, and many people enjoy a higher standard of living. Oil wealth has also helped fund new airports, museums, and schools.

Caspian Sea Riches

Some experts believe that the Caspian Sea may actually have more energy reserves than the Persian Gulf. Russia would like to control the energy from the Caspian. Russia, Turkmenistan, and Kazakhstan signed an agreement to build a pipeline to transport natural gas from the Caspian through Kazakhstan into Russia. From there, Russia exports the gas to Europe. But Russia's state-owned pipeline network does not control all of the region's exports.

New pipelines carry gas from Turkmenistan to China and Iran. Kazakhstan also uses tanker and rail transport, reducing its dependency on Russia.

> **Visual Vocabulary** Oil workers seal a pipeline in Kazakhstan. A **pipeline** is a series of connected pipes used to transport liquids or gases.

OIL AND NATURAL GAS PIPELINES

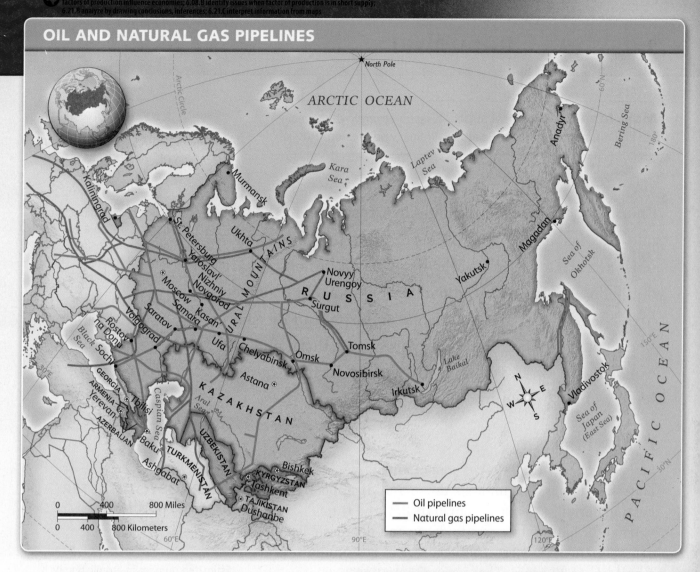

Oil pipelines
Natural gas pipelines

Azerbaijan has large reserves of both oil and natural gas. It used to send the fuel through pipelines to Russia. Now it makes more money by trading mainly with the United States and by piping the fuel directly through Georgia and Turkey. By so doing, Azerbaijan does not have to share export profits with Russia.

For now, Russia gains a great deal of wealth from its exports of natural gas and oil. However, by relying too heavily on energy exports, the country risks using up these natural resources.

Before You Move On

Monitor Comprehension In what ways have oil and natural gas enriched Russia and countries around the Caspian Sea?

FORMATIVE ASSESSMENT

MAP LAB
GeoJournal

1. **Movement** About how far does natural gas travel by pipeline from Surgut in western Siberia to St. Petersburg in Russia? Why do you think pipelines might be a good way to transport the gas over long distances?

2. **Pose and Answer Questions** Come up with your own question about the information shown on the map. Then challenge a partner to answer your question.

3. **Draw Conclusions** What would Russia gain by controlling the energy from the Caspian Sea?

4. **Make Inferences** Why are countries in Central Asia developing pipelines to transport oil and natural gas directly to China and Iran?

2.4 After Chernobyl

TECHTREK

myNGconnect.com For photos
of the Chernobyl disaster and Guided Writing

Digital
Library

Student
Resources

Main Idea The Chernobyl nuclear disaster severely damaged the environment in parts of Belarus, Ukraine, and western Russia.

On April 26, 1986, a nuclear reactor at a power plant in Chernobyl exploded and caught fire, resulting in the worst nuclear disaster in history. **Chernobyl** is in the country of Ukraine. At the time of the disaster, Ukraine was part of the Soviet Union. A **radioactive** cloud about 3,280 feet high spread over parts of Ukraine, Belarus, and Russia. Winds carried the **fallout** into parts of northern and central Europe. These radioactive materials have caused harm to humans, animals, and plants.

Health Effects

Scientists know that it takes some radioactive materials a long time to break down and disappear. Each material has a particular **half-life**, the time needed for half of its atoms to decay and decrease. For example, the highly radioactive element cesium has a half-life of 30 years. That means that after 30 years, half of its atoms will still be radioactive.

Thirty people died within three months of the accident, most from being exposed to huge amounts of radioactive material. Over time, thousands of the people who helped clean up the disaster have developed health problems. Some of the children born to exposed parents carry the effects in their genes. In addition, radioactive iodine got into the milk of cows that grazed on **contaminated**, or infected, grass after the accident. This caused an increase in thyroid cancer, especially in children. Millions of people are still living on contaminated land. Officials cannot yet predict the long-term effects on people's health.

Before You Move On

Summarize What are some of the health problems that occurred as a result of the Chernobyl nuclear disaster?

KEY VOCABULARY

radioactive, adj., giving off energy caused by the breakdown of atoms

fallout, n., radioactive particles from a nuclear explosion that fall through the atmosphere

half-life, n., the time needed for half the atoms in a radioactive substance to decay and decrease

contaminated, adj., unfit for use because of the presence of unsafe elements

CHERNOBYL DISASTER BY THE NUMBERS

400
Estimated number of atomic bombs it would take to equal the accident

4,000
Estimated number of people who may die from cancers caused by radiation exposure from the accident

600,000
Estimated number of people who received significant radiation exposure, including evacuees, residents, and those who helped clean up after the accident

5 million
Estimated number of people still living on contaminated areas in Ukraine, Belarus, and Russia

Source: UN Chernobyl Forum, 2006

6.07.C describe ways technology influences human interaction with environments; 6.09.A compare ways societies organize production and distribution of goods and services; 6.21.B analyze by comparing, contrasting, summarizing, making predictions 6.21.D identify different points of view; 6.21.E identify frame of reference

Inspiring people to care about the planet
National Geographic Society Mission

Environmental Damage

Belarus was hardest hit because of the direction the wind blew just after the accident. About 23 percent of the country was contaminated, including agricultural and forest land. In Ukraine, 7 percent of the land and 40 percent of its forests were contaminated. In Russia, the area bordering with Belarus was most affected.

Radiation is expected to remain in the soil for many years. Plants that grow in the region's forests are contaminated and so are the animals that feed on them. Many reindeer herds had to be killed shortly after the accident because they were so infected by the radiation.

The fallout has especially contaminated the fish in the rivers and lakes of Ukraine because these waters flow down from the site of the disaster. Some radiation that has gotten into groundwater sources will last for hundreds of years.

Few humans live in the 18-mile fenced area around the Chernobyl reactor now.

As a result, the people know that the plants are technologically more advanced and safer than the one in Ukraine. The French scientists and engineers who built them learned the lesson of Chernobyl.

Before You Move On
Monitor Comprehension What has been learned from the Chernobyl disaster?

COMPARE ACROSS REGIONS

France's Nuclear Program

In spite of what happened at Chernobyl, many countries have continued to develop nuclear energy. France, for example, has more than 55 nuclear plants that generate more than 75 percent of its electricity. Many of the French people welcome a new nuclear plant in their town because it brings jobs and prosperity to the area.

The French are aware of the dangers of nuclear energy plants, but they have little fear. Many of the plants offer tours, and advertisements help reinforce the idea that nuclear energy is a fact of life in France.

FORMATIVE ASSESSMENT

READING LAB  GeoJournal

1. **Summarize** What damage did the Chernobyl disaster cause to the environment?

2. **Make Predictions** In what ways do you think the disaster will continue to affect people in Ukraine, Belarus, and Russia?

3. **Identify Point of View** Suppose two new nuclear plant sites are proposed, one for a location in Russia and one in France. In each place, what might be the reaction of those who live near the sites? Write two sentences comparing their views. Then explain what is different about their frames of reference. Review page R8 and go to **Student Resources** for Guided Writing support.

VOCABULARY

For each pair of vocabulary words, write one sentence that explains the connection between the two words.

1. nomad; yurt

> For centuries, nomads in Central Asia have traditionally lived in felt tents called yurts.

2. perestroika; glasnost

3. federal system; proportional representation

4. radioactive; contaminated

5. fallout; half-life

MAIN IDEAS

6. Describe some of the different types of climate in Russia and the Eurasian republics. (Section 1.1)

7. In what ways has Russia benefited from the Trans-Siberian Railroad? (Section 1.2)

8. Why is St. Petersburg called Russia's "window to the West"? (Section 1.3)

9. How did installing Russian officials in the republics help bring about the collapse of the Soviet Union? (Section 2.1)

10. In what way did Gorbachev's changes to the government contribute to the fall of the Soviet Union? (Section 2.1)

11. Which branch of Russia's central government has the most power? Which branch has the least power? (Section 2.2)

12. Why is western Siberia said to be "booming"? (Section 2.3)

13. What was the impact of the Chernobyl nuclear disaster on Ukraine, Belarus, and Russia? (Section 2.4)

CULTURE

ANALYZE THE ESSENTIAL QUESTION

What factors, such as size and climate, have influenced Russian culture?

Critical Thinking: Make Inferences

14. What impact does climate have on nomadic herders in Siberia and Central Asia?

15. Why was it difficult to build the Trans-Siberian Railroad across Russia?

16. At what time of year might tourists prefer to visit St. Petersburg? Why?

INTERPRET MAPS

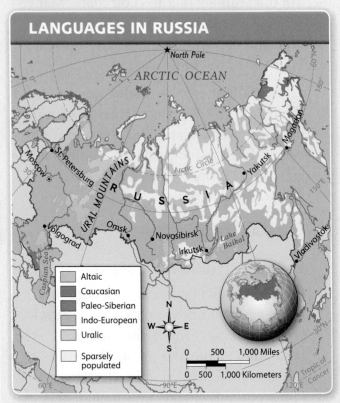

LANGUAGES IN RUSSIA

17. **Region** What are the two major language families in Russia?

18. **Compare and Contrast** What do the languages spoken west and east of the Ural Mountains have in common? In what ways do they differ?

GOVERNMENT & ECONOMICS

ANALYZE THE ESSENTIAL QUESTION

How have Russia and the Eurasian republics dealt with recent political, economic, and environmental challenges?

Critical Thinking: Make Generalizations

19. What impact did the collapse of the Soviet Union have on Russia's role in the region?

20. Why did Russia's central government reduce the number of local government units?

21. In what ways do Russia's location and power help the country control energy resources in the region?

22. Why was Russia less affected by the Chernobyl nuclear disaster than Ukraine and Belarus?

INTERPRET TABLES

NATURAL GAS RESERVES		
Country	Amount (cu m)*	World Rank
Russia	47.5 trillion	1
Iran	33 trillion	2
Qatar	25.2 trillion	3
Turkmenistan	24.3 trillion	4
Saudi Arabia	8.0 trillion	5
United States	7.7 trillion	6
United Arab Emirates	6.0 trillion	7

Source: CIA World Factbook, 2012 (est.) / *cu m = cubic meters

23. **Analyze Data** According to the table, about how much more natural gas reserves does Russia have than the United States?

24. **Evaluate** Which two world regions appear to have most of the world's natural gas reserves, based on the table?

25. **Movement** By what major means are reserves exported to other countries within and outside the Russia and the Eurasian Republics?

ACTIVE OPTIONS

Synthesize the Essential Questions by completing the activities below.

26. **Write Journal Entries** Write several journal entries from the point of view of a worker on the Trans-Siberian Railroad. Describe the difficulties of the work and the obstacles you encounter. Use the writing tips below to help you write your entries. **When you have finished, trade your entries with a partner and compare them.**

> **Writing Tips**
> - Include details on where you worked, the tools you used, and the conditions you endured.
> - Describe any unexpected experiences, such as an encounter with thieves or wild animals along the tracks.
> - Express your feelings about having been enlisted to carry out the work.

27. **Create Charts** Research data to compare countries in the region. Identify the size, largest cities, and major religions of each country. Include Kazakhstan, Kyrgyzstan, Tajikistan, Turkmenistan, and Uzbekistan in your chart. Discuss major similarities and differences. As you study countries in new regions, expand your chart into a class database for comparing and interpreting data across regions.

COMPARE COUNTRIES			
Country	Size	Major Cities	Major Religions
Russia			
Armenia			
Azerbaijan			
Georgia			

Natural Resources and Energy

TECHTREK

myNGconnect.com For an online
graph on energy sources

Maps and
Graphs

In this unit, you learned that Russia and many of the Eurasian republics have plentiful supplies of natural gas and oil. In fact, Russia has the world's largest supply of natural gas. Russia's Asian neighbor, China, is the world's biggest producer of coal. These energy sources are in great demand from countries all over the world.

The choices people make about energy are critical to a healthy planet. As you have learned, some energy sources pollute the environment as they burn. Many scientists believe that the carbon dioxide those sources give off contributes to an overall global temperature increase. To ease these problems, they would like to reduce the use of fossil fuels and develop nonfossil energy sources.

Compare

- Brazil
- China
- Mexico
- Russia
- United States

FOSSIL FUELS

Fossil fuels are formed by buried plants and animals that have been dead for millions of years. This type of fuel is found in deposits beneath the earth's surface and must be burned to release its energy. These fuels supply about 85 percent of the world's energy. Fossil fuels include coal, oil, and natural gas.

These energy sources are classified as nonrenewable because they take millions of years to form and supplies are being used up faster than new ones can redevelop. Although natural gas is relatively clean—meaning that it doesn't create much pollution—fossil fuels, especially coal, tend to be dirty and release a great deal of harmful carbon dioxide into the air.

NONFOSSIL FUELS

Nonfossil fuels are alternative sources of energy and include the following: hydroelectric power from water, nuclear power, wind power, solar energy from the sun, and biofuels made from vegetable oil.

Many of these energy sources are renewable because they can be quickly replenished. Some countries use significant amounts of nuclear energy and hydroelectric power. However, the other nonfossil fuels make up only two percent of the world's energy.

Russia and China use both fossil and nonfossil fuels. The graphs on the next page show the energy consumption in both countries. Compare the data in the graphs and use it to answer the questions.

ENERGY CONSUMPTION PER COUNTRY

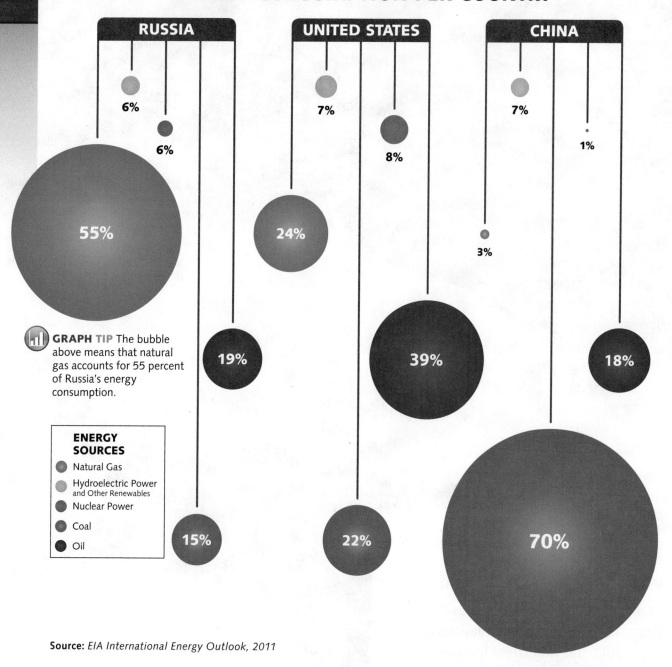

RUSSIA

6%

6%

55%

GRAPH TIP The bubble above means that natural gas accounts for 55 percent of Russia's energy consumption.

19%

ENERGY SOURCES
- Natural Gas
- Hydroelectric Power and Other Renewables
- Nuclear Power
- Coal
- Oil

15%

UNITED STATES

7%

8%

24%

39%

22%

CHINA

7%

1%

3%

18%

70%

Source: *EIA International Energy Outlook, 2011*

FORMATIVE ASSESSMENT

RESEARCH LAB GeoJournal

1. **Explain** What is the main source of energy in each country? Why might that be the case?

2. **Analyze Data** What is the energy consumption of nonfossil fuels in each country? What does this suggest about the development of alternative energy in Russia and China?

Research and Make Comparisons Research energy consumption in Brazil and Mexico to compare the data with consumption in Russia and China. Which country uses more nonfossil and renewable energy sources? What might this statistic suggest about its pollution levels?

Active Options

TECHTREK

myNGconnect.com For photos of natural and cultural sites in Russia and the Eurasian republics and other UNESCO World Heritage sites

Digital
Library

ACTIVITY 1

Goal: Extend your understanding of animals native to Russia and the Eurasian republics.

Design a Poster for Native Animals

Russia is home to both land and sea animals. Some of these animals, including those listed on the right, have been over-hunted or are considered undesirable neighbors. Research one of these animals and use the information to design a poster that will help viewers appreciate it. Consider the animal's habitat, surviving population, and efforts made to protect it.

- Blue whale
- Brown bear
- Gray wolf
- Polar bear
- Siberian tiger

Polar bears

ACTIVITY 2

Goal: Research the natural and cultural heritage of Russia and the Eurasian republics.

Write a World Heritage Guide

The United Nations Educational, Scientific and Cultural Organization (UNESCO) has identified hundreds of sites that form part of the world's natural and cultural heritage. A variety of these World Heritage sites are located in the Russia Federation and the Eurasian republics. Prepare a guide for students visiting the area. Choose five to ten UNESCO World Heritage sites in the region. Provide information for each site. If desired, use the **Magazine Maker CD-ROM** as a template.

ACTIVITY 3

Goal: Learn about Russian culture through the country's folk tales.

Hold a Russian Folk Tale Festival

Folk tales, such as "The Old Man and the Bear" and "Baba Yaga," are an age-old part of the Russian culture. With a group, find some Russian folk tales online and read them. Decide which ones you will present in the festival. Then decide how you will present the tales. You may each choose to retell a story, or you may decide as a group to act out one or more of the tales.

6.03.A pose and answer geographic questions including: Where is it located? Why is it there? What is significant about its location? How is its location related to the location of other people, places, and environments?; 6.03.B pose and answer questions about geographic distributions and patterns for various world regions and countries shown on databases; 6.03.C compare various world regions and countries using data from databases; 6.03.D create databases depicting aspects of various world regions and countries; 6.21.B analyze information by categorizing.

TEKS

TEKS PROJECT

Goal: Create an analysis tool for comparing countries or regions.

Create a Database

You've learned that geographers ask how a location is related to the location of other places or environments, or why it is significant. With location data, geographers look for patterns and make connections about why things are where they are, or why people live in a place, or move to or from it. Geographers rely on databases that have compiled information from the past and present, from all over the world.

Create a database that organizes information about countries or regions of the world. Make your categories the same so you can easily compare them. As your focus, choose an aspect of world geography or culture that interests you; for example, technological wonders, animal habitats, amazing landforms, religions, or what sports are played.

Team up with others who have similar interests and choose one topic for a database. Think about the best way to organize your information. What categories will you put at the top of the columns? Will you create an electronic spreadsheet or a large hand-drawn grid posted on a wall? (Refer to the lesson on page R36 in your book if you need to.)

Carry It Out Gather data from research or information in your textbook. Fill in data and then analyze it to compare what you've learned about the geography or culture of countries and world regions. Choose a day for a class "Crunch It," in which teams pose and answer questions about data and challenge one another to search and find information.

Reflect On It What did you notice about how collecting data can change how you think about a topic?

Most nations of the world have an accessible online database about their geography, government, and culture.

EXPLORE SUB-SAHARAN AFRICA
WITH NATIONAL GEOGRAPHIC

MEET THE EXPLORER

NATIONAL GEOGRAPHIC

Emerging Explorer Kakenya Ntaiya, educator and activist (shown at center), founded the first primary school for girls in her village. Her work provides African girls with an education and an opportunity to develop leadership skills.

INVESTIGATE GEOGRAPHY

Giraffe mothers and their young run in Serengeti National Park, Tanzania. The Serengeti, connected to the Masai Mara National Park in neighboring Kenya, is the only place in Africa where large animal herds, including gnu, zebras, and gazelles, still make vast land migrations.

STEP INTO HISTORY

This ancient Dogon village was built into the sandstone cliffs of Mali, West Africa. Today, most Dogon people are farmers, and practice the tradtional religion of their ancestors. Much of their social organization and cultural practices relates to this belief system.

Washington, D.C.

8,106 miles

Pretoria (Tshawne),
South Africa

Go to **myNGconnect.com** for maps of Sub-Saharan Africa.

CONNECT WITH THE CULTURE

Musicians and griots—storytellers—
perform on the beach outside Dakar,
Senegal. The instrument is a kora. It has
21 strings and is similar to a lute.

CHAPTER 13

SUB-SAHARAN AFRICA
GEOGRAPHY & HISTORY

PREVIEW
THE CHAPTER

Essential Question How has the varied geography of Sub-Saharan Africa affected people's lives?

SECTION 1 • GEOGRAPHY

KEY VOCABULARY

- basin
- savanna
- desertification
- rift valley
- pride
- interior
- deforestation
- transition zone
- highlands
- rain forest
- hydroelectric power
- landlocked
- escarpment
- habitat
- poaching
- nocturnal
- ecotourism

ACADEMIC VOCABULARY
dormant

TERMS & NAMES

- Sahel
- Kalahari
- Great Rift Valley
- Kilimanjaro
- Congo River
- Great Escarpment
- Zambezi River
- Okavango Delta

Essential Question How did trade networks and migration influence the development of African civilization?

SECTION 2 • HISTORY

KEY VOCABULARY

- agricultural revolution
- first language
- caravan
- *lingua franca*
- trans-Saharan
- alluvial
- city-state
- trans-Atlantic slave trade
- malnutrition
- imperialism
- colonialism
- missionary

ACADEMIC VOCABULARY
incentive

TERMS & NAMES

- Bantu
- Swahili
- Timbuktu
- Kongo
- Great Zimbabwe
- Middle Passage
- Berlin Conference
- Pan-Africanism
- Jomo Kenyatta
- Kwame Nkrumah

30°W

30°N

30°N

20°N

CAPE VERDE
Praia

10°N

0°

10°S

10°S

20°S

30°S

30°W

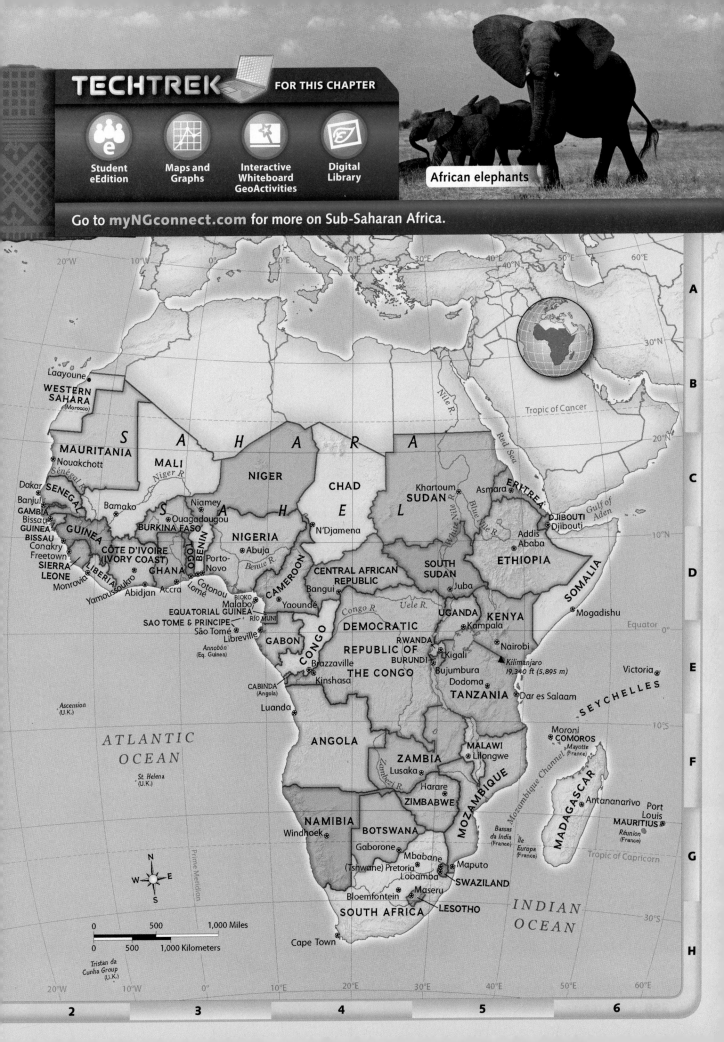

20°W   10°W   0°   10°E   20°E   30°E   40°E   50°E   60°E

30°N

Tropic of Cancer

20°N

10°N

Equator 0°

10°S

Tropic of Capricorn

30°S

A **B** **C** **D** **E** **F** **G** **H**

2 **3** **4** **5** **6**

Laayoune

WESTERN SAHARA (Morocco)

MAURITANIA

Nouakchott

MALI

Dakar
SENEGAL
Banjul
GAMBIA
Bissau
GUINEA-BISSAU
Conakry
GUINEA
Freetown
SIERRA LEONE
Monrovia
LIBERIA

Bamako

S A H A R A

Niger R.

Niamey
Ouagadougou
BURKINA FASO

NIGER

CHAD

S A H E L

NIGERIA

Abuja

CÔTE D'IVOIRE (IVORY COAST)
Yamoussoukro
GHANA
Abidjan
Accra
TOGO
BENIN
Porto-Novo
Lomé
Cotonou
BIOKO
Malabo
EQUATORIAL GUINEA
RÍO MUNI
SAO TOME & PRINCIPE
São Tomé
Libreville
Annobón (Eq. Guinea)
GABON

Benue R.
CAMEROON
Yaoundé

N'Djamena

CENTRAL AFRICAN REPUBLIC
Bangui

Congo R.

Uele R.

CONGO
Brazzaville
DEMOCRATIC REPUBLIC OF THE CONGO
Kinshasa
CABINDA (Angola)

Luanda

SUDAN
Khartoum

White Nile R.
Blue Nile R.

Nile R.

Red Sea

ERITREA
Asmara

DJIBOUTI
Djibouti

Gulf of Aden

Addis Ababa
ETHIOPIA

SOUTH SUDAN
Juba

SOMALIA
Mogadishu

UGANDA
Kampala

RWANDA
Kigali
BURUNDI
Bujumbura

KENYA
Nairobi

Kilimanjaro 19,340 ft (5,895 m)

Victoria

SEYCHELLES

TANZANIA
Dodoma
Dar es Salaam

ATLANTIC OCEAN

Ascension (U.K.)

St. Helena (U.K.)

ANGOLA

ZAMBIA
Lusaka
Zambezi R.

MALAWI
Lilongwe

MOZAMBIQUE

Moroni
COMOROS
Mayotte (France)

Mozambique Channel

MADAGASCAR
Antananarivo
Port Louis
MAURITIUS
Réunion (France)

Harare
ZIMBABWE

NAMIBIA
Windhoek

BOTSWANA
Gaborone

Mbabane
(Tshwane) Pretoria
Maputo
Lobamba
SWAZILAND

Bloemfontein
Maseru
LESOTHO

SOUTH AFRICA

Cape Town

Bassas da India (France)
Île Europa (France)

INDIAN OCEAN

Prime Meridian

N W E S

0   500   1,000 Miles
0   500   1,000 Kilometers

Tristan da Cunha Group (U.K.)

1.1 **Physical Geography**

TECHTREK

myNGconnect.com For an online map
of Sub-Saharan Africa and Visual Vocabulary

Maps and Graphs   Digital Library

SUB-SAHARAN AFRICA PHYSICAL

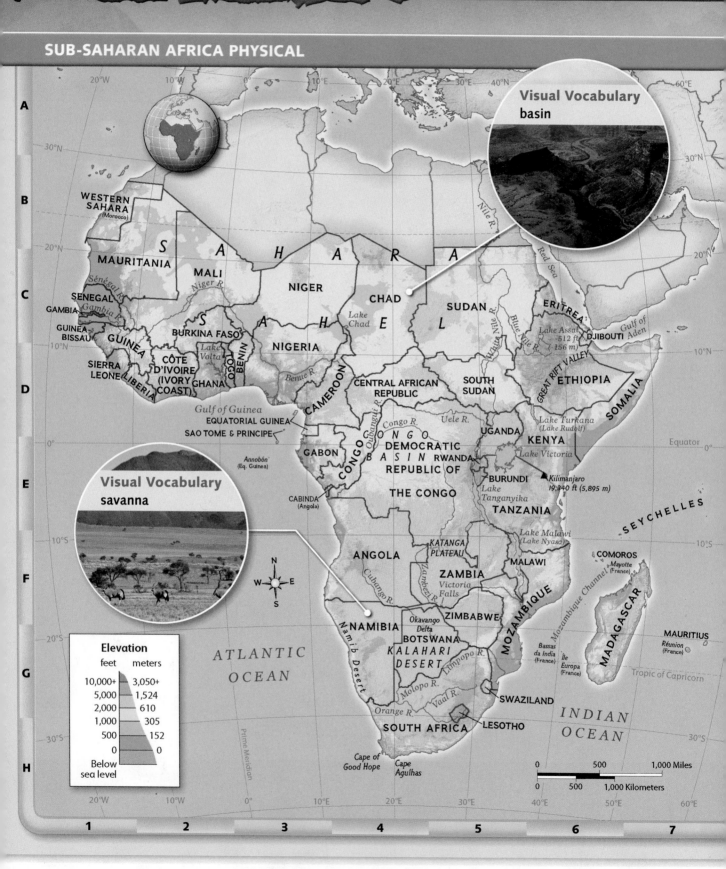

Main Idea Sub-Saharan Africa is divided into four parts, each with varied geographic features.

Sub-Saharan Africa lies south of the Sahara desert. The region extends from Senegal in western Africa to Ethiopia and Somalia in eastern Africa, and southward to the tip of the continent. Sub-Saharan Africa includes the island nation of Madagascar (ma duh GAS kahr).

Africa's Continental Drift

As you have learned, the continents once belonged to one supercontinent called Pangaea. The movement of Earth's tectonic plates caused the continents to drift apart, and Africa became a separate continent. Plate tectonics also caused the formation of certain physical features on the African continent. Lakes, basins, and valleys were all formed as the plates moved. A **basin** is a region drained by a river system.

Landforms and Water

Sub-Saharan Africa is divided into four parts: west, central, east, and south. West Africa includes savannas and much of the Sahel. The **Sahel** (saa HEL) is a semiarid grassland that separates the Sahara in the north from the tropical grasslands, or **savannas**, in the south. In the Sahel, one climate gradually changes to another. Parts of the Sahel, for example, are changing to desert. This process, called **desertification**, means there is less fertile land to grow food. Desertification is caused by many factors including climate change and overpopulation.

Central Africa's primary landform is rain forest, especially in the Congo Basin. In East Africa, **rift valleys**—deep valleys that formed when Earth's crust separated and broke apart—stretch from the Red Sea southward through Mozambique. Southern Africa features great plateaus and another major desert, the **Kalahari**. The Kalahari has limited surface water, but supports a variety of plants and wildlife.

Access to fresh water is an issue for sub-Saharan Africans due to limited water resources and poor sanitation. The situation is improving, however. For example, between 1990 and 2010, the percentage of people in Namibia with access to clean water increased from 57 percent to 93 percent as the government and individual communities began working together to solve the problem.

Before You Move On
Monitor Comprehension What are the main geographic features of sub-Saharan Africa's four parts?

FORMATIVE ASSESSMENT

MAP LAB GeoJournal

1. **Human-Environment Interaction** According to the map, the approximate width of the Sahara is 3,000 miles from east to west. Why is the Sahara considered a natural boundary?

2. **Location** Use the map to point out two sources of fresh water in sub-Saharan Africa.

3. **Describe Geographic Information** Describe the causes of desertification and the problem it poses for sub-Saharan farming.

1.2 East Africa and the Rift Valley

TECHTREK

myNGconnect.com For online maps of East Africa and photos of the Great Rift Valley

 Maps and Graphs   Digital Library

> **Main Idea** East Africa is best known for the Great Rift Valley and the deep lakes found there.

East Africa is easy to spot on a map—it is shaped like a rhinoceros horn. In fact, the region is known as the Horn of Africa. The "horn" is formed by the countries of Somalia, Djibouti (ji BOO tee), Eritrea, and Ethiopia. Other countries in East Africa are Sudan, Kenya, Uganda, Rwanda, Burundi, and Tanzania.

The Great Rift Valley

The most important physical feature of East Africa is the **Great Rift Valley**. This valley is part of a chain of valleys that stretch from southwest Asia to southern Africa. In some places the valley is 60 miles wide. Valley walls often rise more than 6,000 feet in height.

This chain of valleys was formed by tectonic plates that separated and created deep cracks, or rifts, in the earth's crust. The rift valleys have been forming for about 20 million years and continue to develop today.

Plate movements also created the freshwater lakes in the Great Rift Valley. As low spots and rifts developed, they slowly filled with rainwater to create lakes. West of Tanzania is Lake Tanganyika (TANG guhn YEE kuh). At 4,700 feet deep, it is the second deepest freshwater lake in the world.

Plateaus and Savannas

East Africa sits mostly on plateaus. As the climate map shows, the two most substantial elevated areas are in Ethiopia and Kenya. The higher elevations of these areas means the temperatures are cooler, even though much of the area is on or near the equator.

In addition to the rift valleys and lakes, plate movements created volcanoes. Both **Kilimanjaro** (19,340 feet) in Tanzania and Mount Kenya (17,058 feet) in Kenya are **dormant**, or inactive, volcanoes. The volcanic soil around these mountains is fertile, meaning crops grow well.

> **Visual Vocabulary** A **pride**, or group, of lions moves through tall savanna grass in Kenya. A pride averages about 15 members.

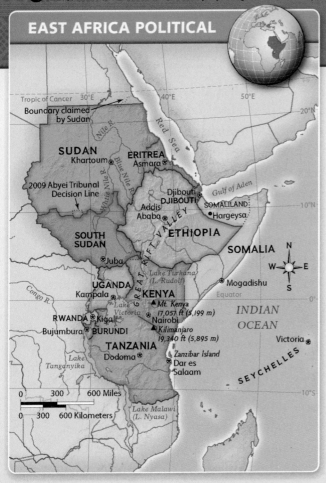

EAST AFRICA POLITICAL

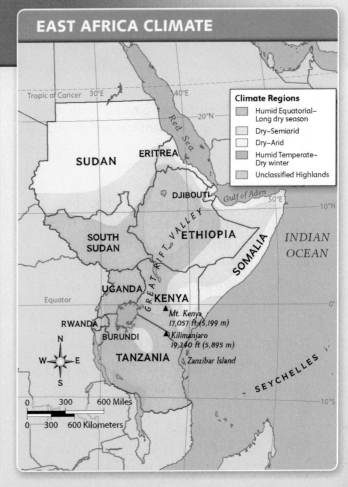

EAST AFRICA CLIMATE

Both Tanzania and Kenya have vast savannas where wildlife such as lions, giraffes, and elephants roam freely or in protected reserves.

Before You Move On

Summarize Describe the physical characteristics of the Great Rift Valley.

FORMATIVE ASSESSMENT

MAP LAB   GeoJournal

1. **Location** Using the maps, locate three sources of freshwater in East Africa.

2. **Interpret Maps** Based on the climate map, which countries have the largest variety of climate regions in East Africa? How does that information add to your understanding of this region?

3. **Make Inferences** How might climate, elevation, and access to water determine where people live in East Africa?

1.3 West Africa's Steppes

TECHTREK

myNGconnect.com For an online map and photos of desertification

 Maps and Graphs

 Digital Library

> **Main Idea** West Africa's physical geography includes steppes and highlands as well as tropical coast and dry desert.

West Africa runs from the Atlantic coast south of the Sahara, eastward to the continent's **interior**, or area away from the coast. This part of Africa supports several different ways of life, depending on the landforms and climates found in each area.

Steppes and Highlands

Semiarid steppes, or grasslands, define part of West Africa. As you know, the grassland between the Sahara desert and the tropical savannas is the Sahel. The Sahel runs through the middle of West Africa. The area has a short rainy season and, as a result, is very dry.

The growing population in West Africa has increased the demand for food crops. To create more cropland, West Africans have had to cut down forests, a practice called **deforestation**. Deforestation in West Africa has left the arid soil unprotected.

Soil has eroded, or washed away, because of overuse. These conditions, along with climate change, contribute to desertification, an ongoing problem in sub-Saharan Africa.

Highlands, which are areas of higher mountainous land, are also found in West Africa. The Adamawa Highlands are on Nigeria's eastern border. The Futa Jallon Highlands rise in Senegal on its border with Guinea. This series of sandstone plateaus is marked by rugged canyons.

Tropical Coast, Dry Desert

Coastal countries differ from interior countries in West Africa. Countries on the coast have more people and more cities than those in the interior. Coastal countries often have tropical climates. Some cities on the Gulf of Guinea get more than 80 inches of rain per year, and the coast of Côte d'Ivoire can get more than 10 feet per year. In contrast, the northern desert areas of Niger, an interior country, get less than 10 inches of rain per year.

> **Visual Vocabulary** A **transition zone** is an area between two geographic regions that has characteristics of both. The Sahel (shown here in Mali) is a transition zone between the Sahara in the north and the savannas in the south.

The largest cities in West Africa are located near or on the Atlantic coast. Such coastal cities have many advantages. Adequate rainfall, fishing, and trade all make it easier for West African coastal cities to support growing populations.

The interior countries of West Africa are mostly covered by desert. Deforestation and desertification, along with the lack of water, make farming in the poor soil a constant struggle. About 80 percent of people in Chad make their living from subsistence farming and raising livestock. In 2003, Chad began exporting oil. This new economic resource may improve Chad's economy and make money available for improved farming technology. Besides oil, the country exports cotton and gum arabic, a tree sap used globally in glues, medicines, soft drinks, and candy.

Before You Move On
Monitor Comprehension In what ways are West Africa's steppes different from the coasts?

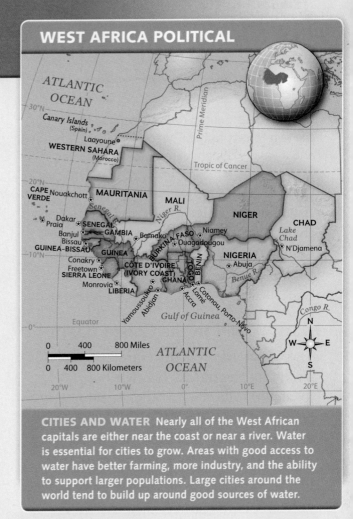

WEST AFRICA POLITICAL

CITIES AND WATER Nearly all of the West African capitals are either near the coast or near a river. Water is essential for cities to grow. Areas with good access to water have better farming, more industry, and the ability to support larger populations. Large cities around the world tend to build up around good sources of water.

FORMATIVE ASSESSMENT
PHOTO LAB
GeoJournal

1. **Analyze Visuals** Based on the photo, what characteristics of the Sahel in Mali make it a transition zone?

2. **Location** What does the photo suggest about the challenges of living in this transition zone?

3. **Interpret Maps** What makes the capital of Nigeria different from other capitals in West Africa?

1.4 Rain Forests and Resources

TECHTREK

myNGconnect.com For a land use map and photos of wildlife

 Maps and Graphs

 Digital Library

Main Idea Central Africa is defined by the rain forests of the Congo River Basin and a variety of natural resources.

Central Africa is bordered by the Adamawa Highlands of West Africa and the Great Rift Valley of East Africa. On the north and south, Central Africa lies between the plateaus of the Sahel and Southern Africa.

Rain Forest in the Congo Basin

The Congo Basin is the main geographic feature of Central Africa. The basin is located on the equator and surrounded by higher elevations. Within the basin is a **rain forest**, which is a forest with warm temperatures, plentiful rain, high humidity, and thick vegetation.

The rain forest in Central Africa is second in the world in size only to the South American rain forest. Vegetation grows so thick that sometimes sunlight does not reach the ground. The plants also make ground movement difficult, so most people live on the edges of the rain forest.

Spectacular wildlife also thrives in the rain forest. The okapi, related to the giraffe, lives in the Congo Basin. Some other rain forest animals include gorillas similar to the one shown here, leopards, and rhinoceroses.

The **Congo River** is a major waterway in Central Africa. Like the Amazon River of South America, the Congo is located in an equatorial area and flows into the Atlantic Ocean. Several large rivers in Central Africa feed into the Congo River, including the Ubangi, the Aruwimi, and the Lomami rivers.

Resources of Central Africa

Central Africa includes the Central African Republic, Congo, Cameroon, São Tomé (sow too MAY) and Príncipe, Equatorial Guinea, and Gabon.

> **Critical Viewing** A western lowland gorilla walks in the forest in Democratic Republic of the Congo. Why might the rain forest be able to support so many plants and animals?

CENTRAL AFRICA'S LAND USE

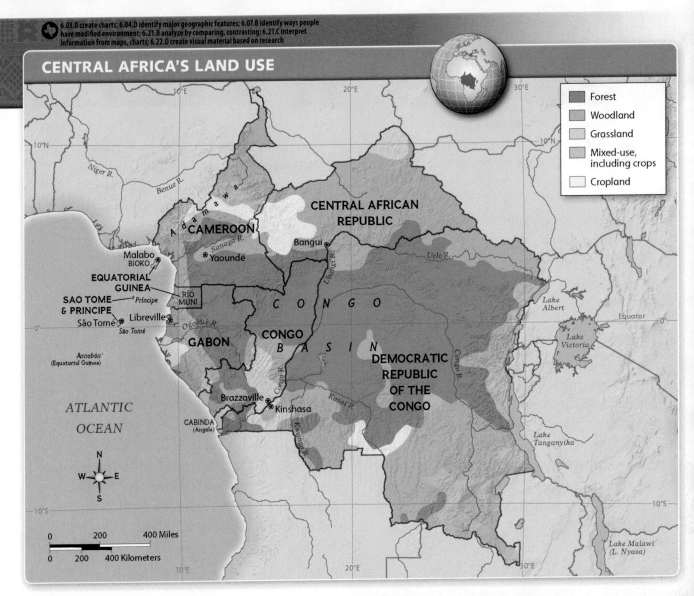

Legend:
- Forest
- Woodland
- Grassland
- Mixed-use, including crops
- Cropland

However, the largest, most populous country in Central Africa is the Democratic Republic of the Congo (DRC). The capital of the DRC is Kinshasa.

The DRC has a wealth of natural resources, including copper, forests, diamonds, and the Congo River itself. The river provides **hydroelectric power**, or electricity produced by a water source such as a river. The river is forced through turbines, or engines, and produces electricity for the DRC and other countries.

Before You Move On

Monitor Comprehension Describe the rain forest and natural resources found in Central Africa.

FORMATIVE ASSESSMENT

MAP LAB
GeoJournal

1. **Interpret Maps** How does the latitude of the Congo Basin help explain its climate and vegetation?

2. **Conduct Internet Research** Use the Internet to research the Amazon River Basin of South America. On a chart like the one below, compare and contrast the Congo River Basin and Amazon River Basin.

	LOCATION	SIZE	RAINFALL
Congo River Basin			
Amazon River Basin			

1.5 Southern Plateaus and Basins

TECHTREK

myNGconnect.com For online
maps and photos of Southern Africa

 Maps and
Graphs

 Digital
Library

Main Idea Southern Africa's physical geography offers opportunities for economic development.

Southern Africa has fertile farmland, valuable natural resources, and abundant wildlife. The income from exporting natural resources gives Southern Africa the highest standard of living in sub-Saharan Africa.

Basins and Plateaus

The Congo Basin extends into the Southern African countries of Angola and Zambia. From there, the land rises to a large plateau that spans most of Southern Africa. Six of the area's countries are **landlocked**, or have no direct access to a coast. Another major African basin, the Kalahari in Southern Africa, includes the Kalahari Desert. However, the basin also has areas rich with wildlife.

The plateau of Southern Africa is defined by the **Great Escarpment**. An **escarpment** is a steep slope. The Great Escarpment is the steep slope from the plateau down to the coastal plains of Southern Africa. The Great Escarpment is most dramatic in the countries of South Africa and Lesotho. It also extends northeast into Zimbabwe and northwest into Namibia and Angola.

The **Zambezi River** in Southern Africa collects water from the entire south-central part of Africa. The Zambezi flows through Angola, Zambia, along Zimbabwe's border, and through Mozambique (mo zam BEEK) to the Indian Ocean. The Kariba Dam on the Zambezi provides hydroelectric power. In fact, the countries of Zambia and Zimbabwe get most of their electricity from the dam.

Critical Viewing Miners near Johannesburg, South Africa, work deep underground to extract resources. Based on the photo, what are some of the dangers that miners might face?

6.02.B evaluate economic contributions of groups; 6.05.A identify geographic factors responsible for economic activities;
6.07.B identify ways people have modified environment; 6.08.A describe ways factors of production influence economies;
6.10.B describe levels of economic activity using indicators; 6.21.C interpret information from maps

SOUTHERN AFRICA
Gross Domestic Product Per Capita, 2012

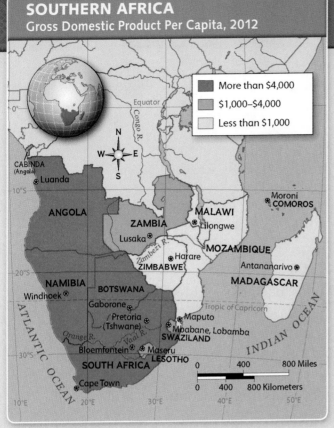

More than $4,000
$1,000–$4,000
Less than $1,000

SOUTHERN AFRICA
Natural Resources

Coal   Corn
Gold   Wheat
Copper   Tobacco
Uranium   Sugarcane
Diamonds   Sheep
Tea   Fish

Mining and Farming

A zone of mineral deposits winds through Zambia, Zimbabwe, and South Africa. Copper, gold, and diamonds are mined in this zone, and destined for jewelry and industrial uses. In fact, South Africa is one of the world's largest gold producers. Many people migrate there to work in the mines even though the work can be dangerous.

Southern Africa's temperate climate supports a variety of crops. For example, South Africa has many vineyards that thrive on its plateau, and Zimbabwe has tea plantations on its eastern escarpment. Angola produced nearly 20 percent of the world's coffee until 1975 when a civil war began. When the war ended in 2002, coffee production started again. Fruits, such as bananas, pineapples, and apples, are grown throughout Southern Africa. Corn, wheat, and other grains can also be found across the area.

South Africa, Botswana, and Namibia have the highest Gross Domestic Product in Southern Africa. Other countries are working to overcome factors that have weakened their economies, such as civil war and disease. For them, economic success is a goal for the future.

Before You Move On
Monitor Comprehension In what ways do the area's resources and crops support its economy?

FORMATIVE ASSESSMENT

MAP LAB
GeoJournal

1. **Compare and Contrast** According to the Gross Domestic Product map, which countries have the highest GDP? The lowest GDP?

2. **Interpret Maps** In what ways might South Africa's natural resources contribute to differences on the GDP map?

3. **Evaluate** What contributions have farmers and miners made to Southern Africa?

SECTION **1** GEOGRAPHY

■ **NATIONAL GEOGRAPHIC**

1.6

TECHTREK

myNGconnect.com For an online map, photos, and an Explorer Video Clip

Maps and Graphs   Digital Library

Exploring
Africa's Wildlife
with Dereck and Beverly Joubert

> **Main Idea** Humans are working to protect endangered African big cats and their homes.

Big Cats in Africa

Big cats, such as lions, cheetahs and leopards, are a vital part of African wildlife. Since the 1940s, the number of lions in Africa has been reduced from about 450,000 to 20,000—and humans caused most of this reduction. Hunting, movement into big cat **habitats** (natural homes), and **poaching** (illegal hunting) all contribute to fewer big cats in the wild.

Working to Protect Habitats

"It seems like we were explorers from birth, wandering the wild Earth with a passion," said Dereck Joubert. The Jouberts, who are National Geographic Explorers-in-Residence, learned about wildlife on game reserves in Southern Africa. Today, they live in Botswana. "On our first trip to Botswana and the **Okavango** (oh kuh VAANG oh) **Delta**, in 1981, we felt we had come home," the Jouberts noted.

That same year, the Jouberts joined the Chobe Lion Research Institute in Botswana. They began an intensive study of lions,

myNGconnect.com

For more on Dereck and Beverly Joubert in the field today

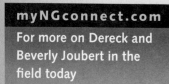

6.02.B evaluate the economic contributions of individuals; 6.20.A give examples of roles of scientists who have transcended boundaries of societies and shaped the world; 6.21.C interpret information on maps

AFRICAN WILDLIFE RESERVES

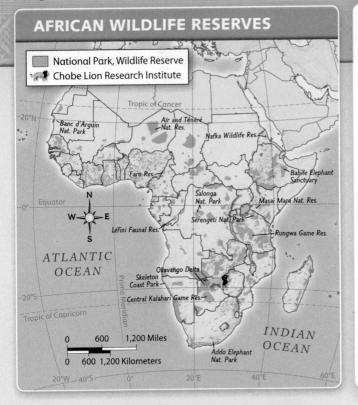

- National Park, Wildlife Reserve
- Chobe Lion Research Institute

Tropic of Cancer

20°N

Banc d'Arguin Nat. Park

Aïr and Ténéré Nat. Res.

Nafka Wildlife Res.

Faro Res.

Babile Elephant Sanctuary

Salonga Nat. Park

Masai Mara Nat. Res.

Equator

0°

Serengeti Nat. Park

Léfini Faunal Res.

Rungwa Game Res.

ATLANTIC OCEAN

Okavango Delta

Skeleton Coast Park

20°S

Central Kalahari Game Res.

Tropic of Capricorn

20°S

INDIAN OCEAN

0   600   1,200 Miles

0   600 1,200 Kilometers

Addo Elephant Nat. Park

20°W   40°S   0°   20°E   40°E   60°E

BIG CATS BY THE NUMBERS

5
Distance in miles from which a lion's roar can be heard

12
Average life span of a male lion in the wild

23
Distance in feet a cheetah can cover in one stride

70
A cheetah's top speed in miles per hour

550
Weight in pounds of a fully grown male lion

Source: Smithsonian National Zoo, National Geographic Society

which included adopting a **nocturnal**, or night-based, lifestyle. They worked during the night in the African wilderness for months at a time. Since leaving the Chobe Institute, the Jouberts have worked on their own in many different filmmaking, photography, and conservation projects.

The Jouberts have a mission: conserving big cat habitats. Protecting habitats also protects the biodiversity, or variety of life, in the habitat. The Jouberts' projects draw attention to the plight of big cats in Africa. Their knowledge of how big cats live helps other conservationists to develop habitat protection programs.

The Jouberts also support **ecotourism**, which is tourism that is focused on wildlife protection and responsible use of land and resources. Ecotourism teaches visitors about conservation issues. For the Jouberts, teaching is an essential part of their work. Ultimately, they believe that "We are part of a global community of lions and leopards, buffalo, dung beetles, snakes, trees, and ice caps, not somehow apart from it all."

Before You Move On
Summarize What are some ways of protecting African big cats?

FORMATIVE ASSESSMENT

READING LAB GeoJournal

1. **Make Inferences** Using what you know about sub-Saharan geography, what might explain the lack of wildlife reserves in the north?

2. **Draw Conclusions** The Jouberts have helped save the big cats. How have they also helped the economy of sub-Saharan Africa?

2.1 Bantu Migrations

TECHTREK

myNGconnect.com For a map of the Bantu migrations and photos of Bantu culture

 Maps and Graphs

 Digital Library

Main Idea Bantu-speaking people migrated from West Africa and influenced the language and culture of the African continent.

As you have read, sub-Saharan Africa's varied physical features support a variety of crops today. About 10,000 years ago an agricultural revolution began in Central Africa. During the **agricultural revolution**, humans began to grow crops instead of gathering plants. Sometime after the agricultural revolution, around 2000 B.C., one of the greatest migrations in human history began—the **Bantu** migration. By A.D. 1000, Bantu peoples had spread from their Central African homeland south and east across sub-Saharan Africa.

The Bantu People

People migrate for economic, political, religious, social, and environmental reasons. When groups of people move, cultures blend, new languages form, technology spreads—and sometimes conflict occurs.

Historians and anthropologists are not certain why the Bantu chose to migrate when and where they did. Whatever the reason, the Bantu people began to move and carried their cultural traits and skills along with them.

The Bantu had knowledge of iron working, and their use of iron weapons gave them an advantage over other tribal groups. As the Bantu people moved, they forced other groups to move or become absorbed into Bantu culture.

The many different groups that became part of Bantu culture kept much of their own culture as well. As a result, the nearly 85 million people who trace their history to the Bantu migrations share a very diverse culture today.

> **Critical Viewing** Bantu descendants pick tea in South Africa. One possible reason for the Bantu migration was to find better farmland. What does this photo suggest about farming methods in South Africa today?

Bantu Languages

Today, people whose ancestors were Bantu exist in more than 400 ethnic groups, including the Zulu, the Swahili, and the Kikuyu. Original Bantu languages have evolved into more than 450 languages.

Swahili (also known as Kiswahwali) is one of the best-known of the surviving Bantu languages. For more than 5 million people, Swahili is the language they learn as children, or their **first language**. For 30 million other people, Swahili is their second language. Swahili is spoken mainly in East Africa and can be heard in several different forms, or dialects.

Swahili is heavily influenced by the Arabic language. Arab traders from northern Africa and Bantu-speaking people of eastern Africa met and exchanged goods over many centuries. Over time, Swahili became the language used to conduct trade.

Beginning in the early 19th century, Arab trade **caravans**—groups of merchants traveling together for safety—traveled farther into the interior of Africa, spreading Swahili to more people. Eventually, Swahili would be used by some Europeans who colonized parts of Africa where the language was spoken.

Today, many areas in Africa have two groups of people with different first languages. In these areas, Swahili is frequently spoken by both groups as a way to communicate. As a result, Swahili is the **lingua franca** (LEEN gwa FRAWN kah), or common language between multiple groups of people.

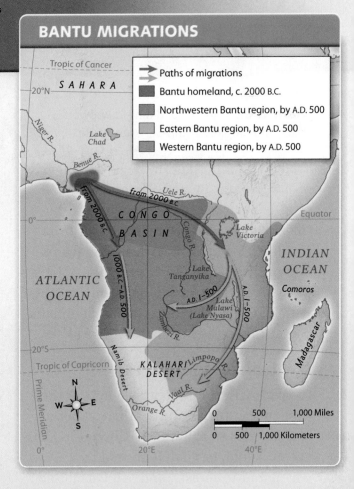

BANTU MIGRATIONS

Paths of migrations
Bantu homeland, c. 2000 B.C.
Northwestern Bantu region, by A.D. 500
Eastern Bantu region, by A.D. 500
Western Bantu region, by A.D. 500

Before You Move On

Summarize How did the Bantu influence the culture and language of the African continent?

FORMATIVE ASSESSMENT

MAP LAB   GeoJournal

1. **Interpret Maps** What landform in Africa might have influenced the Bantu people to migrate south instead of north?

2. **Movement** Based on the map, over what period of time did the Bantu migration take place?

3. **Draw Conclusions** How was the migration of the Bantu people supported by their use of metal-working technology?

4. **Make Inferences** Why might it be important for an area to have a *lingua franca*, or common language?

2.2 Early States and Trade

TECHTREK

myNGconnect.com For an online map of the African empires and and photos of Great Zimbabwe

 Maps and Graphs

 Digital Library

Main Idea Trade helped develop powerful states and empires in sub-Saharan Africa.

Trade was important in the development of sub-Saharan Africa. The promise of valuable trade goods brought Arab traders to a transportation corridor from North Africa to West Africa. This **trans-Saharan** trade, or trade across the Sahara, introduced Africans to the Islamic religion, which spread from the Arabian peninsula beginning in the 8th century A.D.

West African Empires

In West Africa, a number of empires arose over the centuries and all thrived because of the gold and salt trade. **Alluvial** (a LOO vee ahl) gold, or gold deposited by a river, was found in forests, and salt was found in deserts. These goods were traded in the savanna between the forest and desert, where the empire of Ghana began.

Ghana gained wealth and power by taxing the gold and salt trade, controlling West Africa from A.D. 700 to the 1200s. Ghana declined, and the kingdom of Mali, led by King Sundiata, overtook Ghana. His great-nephew, Mansa Musa, continued to control trade, spread Islam, and make the city of **Timbuktu** a center of education.

Another empire that traded gold and salt was Songhai. Brought to its height by Askia Muhammad, Songhai prospered from the 900s to the 1400s. South of Songhai, the kingdom of Benin lasted from the 1200s to the 1800s. Benin actively traded with European countries such as Portugal and the Netherlands.

East African Empires and States

The powerful East African empire of Aksum was located in present-day Ethiopia. Aksum flourished between A.D. 300 and 600. Adulis, its main port, was located on the Red Sea and served as a center of trade. Many **city-states** (independent states made up of a city and the territories depending on it), such as Mogadishu, formed on the coast of East Africa as trading grew.

Other African States

Powerful states also arose in Central and Southern Africa. In Central Africa, the state of **Kongo** (different from the modern country of Congo) was founded in 1390. Kongo became known for its highly-organized government. Soon after its founding, the Portuguese arrived and became involved in many aspects of the state, including politics, trade, and religion.

Aksum Coins

300

600

900

A.D. 300
East African empire of Aksum begins growing to its height in present-day Ethiopia.

A.D. 700
Ghana becomes center of gold and salt trade in West Africa.

Modern vendor cuts a slab of salt to sell in a Mali market.

SUB-SAHARAN AFRICAN EMPIRES

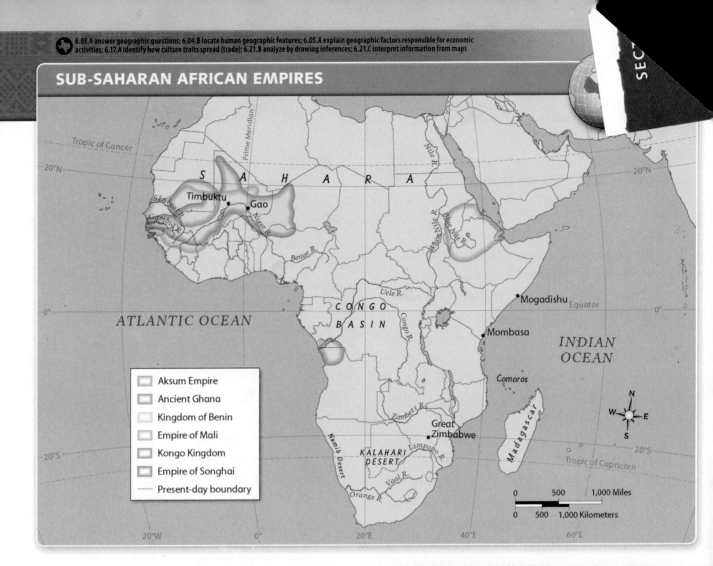

Between 1200 and 1450, the Shona people in Southern Africa built a walled city out of stone, called **Great Zimbabwe** (zim BAH bwe). *Zimbabwe* is a Shona word meaning "stone houses." The Shona traded gold, copper, and iron with places as far away as China and India.

Before You Move On
Summarize In what ways did trade help develop the early states and kingdoms in Africa?

FORMATIVE ASSESSMENT

MAP LAB
GeoJournal

1. **Place** Locate the city-state of Mogadishu on the map. Why would its location be beneficial for trade?

2. **Interpret Maps** Based on the map and the time line, which empire was oldest?

3. **Make Inferences** What might explain why the West African empires of Ghana, Mali, and Songhai overlapped?

1200

1300s ○
Mali empire in West Africa at its height

○ **1591**
Songhai empire comes to an end.

1500

Mansa Musa ruled Mali for about 25 years.

1800

2.3 Impact of the Slave Trade

Main Idea The European slave trade involved millions of people and had lasting effects on Africa and the Americas.

Slavery existed in Africa for many years before European contact. For example, African tribal groups turned male war captives into slaves. Women and children were often incorporated into families, and the children of some slaves could be born free. When Islam came to Africa beginning in the A.D. 700s, some Muslims began to capture and sell Africans to North Africa and Southwest Asia.

European Slave Trade Begins

The Portuguese were the first Europeans to explore the African coast in the 1400s. The **trans-Atlantic slave trade**, or trading of slaves across the Atlantic Ocean, started around 1500. Enslaved people were brought to African coastal cities and held captive until sold. The Portuguese, Spanish, Dutch, French, and English all purchased slaves at African coastal ports.

After purchase, enslaved Africans were crowded onto large ships headed for European colonies in the Americas. This trip across the Atlantic Ocean, known as the **Middle Passage**, could take several months. About 2 million people died in the Middle Passage, many due to **malnutrition** (inadequate food or nourishment) or disease.

Once slaves arrived in the Americas, they were sold at auction, often to go to work on large farms called plantations. Sugar, tobacco, and cotton were some of the major plantation crops. European demand for these crops increased and the plantations got bigger. As the plantations grew, so did the demand for slave labor.

The **incentive**, or motivating reason, for slavery was profit. Europeans bought enslaved people in order to have a cheap and captive labor source. The plantation owners made more money because they did not have to pay the slaves.

> **Critical Viewing** This is a European ship used to transport enslaved Africans. What does this illustration suggest about conditions on the ships for enslaved Africans?

THE MIDDLE PASSAGE		
	LEFT FROM AFRICA	ARRIVED IN THE AMERICAS
1500–1600	277,506	199,285
1601–1700	1,875,631	1,522,677
1701–1800	6,494,619	5,609,869
1801–1867	3,873,580	3,370,825
TOTAL	12,521,336	10,702,656

Source: http://slavevoyages.org/tast/assessment/estimates.faces

Consequences of the Slave Trade

The trans-Atlantic slave trade lasted from the 1500s to the mid-1800s. Historians estimate that more than 12 million Africans were enslaved and shipped to the Western Hemisphere. The majority of slaves were sent to Brazil and the Caribbean.

People forced into slavery were generally young because they had a better chance of surviving the Middle Passage. Also, when they arrived at their destination, it was expected that young people would be able to work longer and harder in the fields.

Many Africans taken were male, and many were potential leaders in their community. Families were often torn apart. These losses weakened many African communities and completely destroyed others.

Millions of people in North America, the Caribbean, and South America are descendents of enslaved Africans. These people have shaped cultures in those regions by sharing their languages, customs, and traditions. The impact of the slave trade has lasted for centuries.

3.25 feet

The journey across the Atlantic could take up to 90 days depending on the weather. Enslaved Africans were packed onto ships and chained below deck. They were only taken above deck for brief periods. Unable to stand up or move, many Africans died where they sat.

Before You Move On

Summarize How did the European slave trade develop and how did it change cultures?

FORMATIVE ASSESSMENT

DATA LAB GeoJournal

1. **Interpret Charts** Based on the chart, how many people died during the Middle Passage?

2. **Analyze Data** During which time period did the greatest number of enslaved Africans die?

3. **Movement** How did the forced movement of Africans affect communities around the world?

4. **Write Reports** Research one of the following topics and then write a short report on how each affected sub-Saharan Africa: sugar plantations, the triangular trade, or slave ports. Go to **Student Resources** for Guided Writing support.

2.4 Colonization to Independence

TECHTREK

myNGconnect.com For online maps
of colonialism and photos of African leaders

Maps and
Graphs

Digital
Library

> **Main Idea** European powers colonized and ruled large parts of Africa until Africans began independence movements in the mid-1900s.

As you have learned, the Portuguese began exploring the African coast in the 1400s. By the 1500s, many European nations were seeking to control large parts of Africa.

Imperialism and Colonialism

Imperialism is the practice of extending a nation's influence by controlling other territories. European imperialism in Africa began when Europeans started trading with slave merchants on the coast. Little by little, Europeans moved into African lands in search of profitable resources. Eventually, several European countries conquered African lands and established colonies. The practice of directly controlling and settling foreign territories is known as **colonialism**.

By the mid-1800s, European powers began to fight over their African colonies. They wanted more natural resources to fuel industrialization, or the transition to large-scale industries, in Europe. Because of advanced European weapons, there was little the Africans could do to stop them.

Scramble for Africa

In 1884, Europeans held the **Berlin Conference** to settle their disputes about colonial claims in Africa. No Africans were invited to attend. Europeans at the conference divided Africa among themselves. By 1910, France, Germany, Belgium, Portugal, Italy, Spain, and Great Britain had established themselves as colonial powers in all parts of Africa.

Many Europeans believed that African culture and religion were inferior to those of Europe. They wanted to change African traditions. Europeans sent **missionaries** —people sent by a church to spread their religion among native populations—to convert Africans to Christianity.

African Independence

In the early 1900s, **Pan-Africanism**, a movement to unify African people, grew among African leaders in London and other cities around the world. By the 1950s and 1960s, this nationalist movement had brought together many African leaders. **Jomo Kenyatta** (JOH moh ken YAA taa) of Kenya and **Kwame Nkrumah** (KWAA may en KROO mah) of Ghana helped to gain independence for their people.

A caravel ship used in trade voyages

1500

1600

1700

1500s
European imperialism
in Africa begins.

1642
The Dutch take possession of
Portuguese forts in West Africa.

EUROPEAN COLONIES, 1938

Legend:
- Belgian
- British
- French
- British & French
- Italian
- Portuguese
- Spanish
- Independent countries
- —— 1938 boundaries

RÍO DE ORO
CAPE VERDE (Port.)
GAMBIA (Br.)
PORT. GUINEA
SIERRA LEONE
LIBERIA
FRENCH WEST AFRICA
GOLD COAST
NIGERIA
CAMEROONS
SPANISH GUINEA
SAO TOME AND PRINCIPE (Port.)
Gulf of Guinea
FRENCH EQUATORIAL AFRICA
CABINDA (Port.)
ANGLO-EGYPTIAN SUDAN
ERITREA
FRENCH SOMALILAND
BRITISH SOMALILAND
ETHIOPIA
ITALIAN EAST AFRICA
SOMALIA
UGANDA
KENYA
BELGIAN CONGO
RUANDA URUNDI
TANGANYIKA
ZANZIBAR (Br.)
INDIAN OCEAN
SEYCHELLES (Br.)
Comoros (Fr.)
ATLANTIC OCEAN
ANGOLA
NORTHERN RHODESIA
SOUTHERN RHODESIA
NYASALAND
MOZAMBIQUE
MAURITIUS (Br.)
MADAGASCAR
Réunion (Fr.)
SOUTH WEST AFRICA
BECHUANALAND
SWAZILAND
UNION OF SOUTH AFRICA
BASUTOLAND
Tropic of Cancer
Prime Meridian
Equator
Tropic of Capricorn

0 600 1,200 Miles
0 600 1,200 Kilometers

AFRICAN NATIONS, 2013

WESTERN SAHARA (Morocco)
CAPE VERDE
MAURITANIA
MALI
NIGER
CHAD
SUDAN
ERITREA
DJIBOUTI
SENEGAL
GAMBIA
GUINEA-BISSAU
GUINEA
SIERRA LEONE
LIBERIA
BURKINA FASO
CÔTE D'IVOIRE
GHANA
TOGO
BENIN
NIGERIA
CAMEROON
CENTRAL AFRICAN REP.
SOUTH SUDAN
ETHIOPIA
SOMALIA
EQUATORIAL GUINEA
SAO TOME & PRINCIPE
GABON
CONGO
DEM. REP. OF THE CONGO
RWANDA
BURUNDI
UGANDA
KENYA
TANZANIA
SEYCHELLES
ATLANTIC OCEAN
ANGOLA
ZAMBIA
MALAWI
COMOROS
ZIMBABWE
MOZAMBIQUE
MADAGASCAR
Réunion (France)
MAURITIUS
NAMIBIA
BOTSWANA
SOUTH AFRICA
SWAZILAND
LESOTHO
INDIAN OCEAN
Tropic of Cancer
Prime Meridian
Equator
Tropic of Capricorn

0 600 1,200 Miles
0 600 1,200 Kilometers

In 1963 the Organization of African Unity (OAU) was founded to promote Pan-Africanism. The OAU is known today as the African Union (AU). It continues to promote African unity and cooperation, but also functions as an economic group similar to the European Union.

Before You Move On

Make Inferences What action by Africans helped bring colonialism to an end?

FORMATIVE ASSESSMENT

MAP LAB
GeoJournal

1. **Location** Which modern countries made up the colony of French Equatorial Africa?

2. **Interpret Maps** Identify the locations of Mali and Sudan. Describe the changes to Africa's internal borders from 1938 to today.

3. **Analyze Cause and Effect** Why did European countries colonize Africa? Trace some of the effects of colonization on African societies today.

This political cartoon (1892) suggests that Europe now controls the African continent.

2002
African Union replaces OAU.

1800

1884
Berlin Conference divides Africa.

1900

1963
Organization of African Unity (OAU) is founded.

2000

Jomo Kenyatta

For more photos from
the National Geographic
Photo Gallery, go to
the **Digital Library** at
myNGconnect.com.

Mountain gorilla, Africa

Nigerian camel caravan

South African women

These circular ponds contain a mixture of water and salty earth. The mud is moved to evaporation areas where salt is left behind. The color of the salt depends on where the mud came from.

Students in Botswana

African lions

Victoria Falls, Zimbabwe

Zulu village, South Africa

CHAPTER 13

Review

VOCABULARY

For each pair of vocabulary words, write one sentence that explains the connection between the two words.

1. savanna; Sahel

The Sahel runs south of the Sahara and north of the savannas, forming a border between the two.

2. ecotourism; habitats
3. Swahili; *lingua franca*
4. Middle Passage; trans-Atlantic slave trade
5. imperialism; Pan-Africanism

MAIN IDEAS

6. What are the four regions of sub-Saharan Africa? (Section 1.1)
7. Which large landform in East Africa was created by the separation of tectonic plates? (Section 1.2)
8. Which region of West Africa supports more population, and why? (Section 1.3)
9. What is the major river in Central Africa, and what effect does it have on the region? (Section 1.4)
10. What are the two main types of landforms that make up Southern Africa? (Section 1.5)
11. What factors threaten the big cats of Africa? (Section 1.6)
12. From what African region did the Bantu people begin their migration? (Section 2.1)
13. How did gold and salt help Ghana develop as a kingdom? (Section 2.2)
14. What were some effects of slavery on communities in Africa? (Section 2.3)
15. What reasons did Europeans have for wanting to colonize Africa? (Section 2.4)

380 CHAPTER 13

GEOGRAPHY

ANALYZE THE ESSENTIAL QUESTION

How has the varied geography of sub-Saharan Africa affected people's lives?

Critical Thinking: Draw Conclusions

16. What might be some ways for Africans to combat the challenges of desertification?
17. How does not having access to a coastal port impact a country?
18. What advantages or challenges does physical geography create for economic development in Central Africa?

INTERPRET TABLES

IMPACT OF CHANGES IN LAND				
Change	Environment	Human Health	Safety Issues	Politics & Economics
Desertification	Loss of habitat; decline in variety of plant and animal life; increased soil erosion	Malnutrition, hunger	Wars over arable land and limited water resources	Poverty; decreased political and economic influence; population movement
Deforestation	Decline in variety of plant and animal life; loss of habitat; reduced resources	Loss of potential new medical products	Increased landslides and flooding	Loss of forest products; loss of indigenous communities; loss of tourism opportunities
Soil Erosion	Loss of soil and habitat; loss of farmland	Loss of food and water; hunger, malnutrition	Risk of flooding and landslides	Loss of property; reduced farm development

Source: http://www.eoearth.org/article/Global_Environment_Outlook_(GEO-4):_Chapter_3#Introduction

19. **Summarize** How does desertification lead to loss of habitat?
20. **Form and Support Opinions** Think about the causes of desertification, deforestation, and soil erosion. Which one do you think would be easiest to solve? Explain.

HISTORY

ANALYZE THE ESSENTIAL QUESTION

How did trade networks and migration influence the development of African civilization?

Critical Thinking: Analyze Cause and Effect

21. How can the effects of the Bantu migration be seen in Africa today?

22. In what ways did trade networks help build African kingdoms?

INTERPRET MAPS

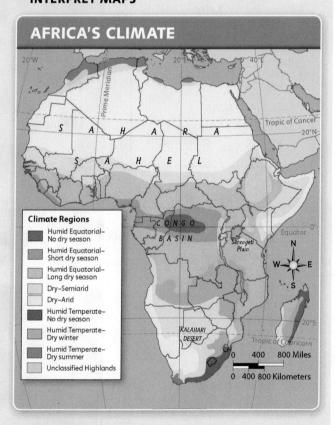

AFRICA'S CLIMATE

23. **Location** What climate zone covers most of the Sahara?

24. **Region** Think about the four areas of sub-Saharan Africa: West, East, Central, and Southern. What area has the largest number of different climate zones?

25. **Make Inferences** What is the relationship between the climate zones and the rain forests of the Congo Basin?

ACTIVE OPTIONS

Synthesize the Essential Questions by completing the activities below.

26. **Create Time Lines** Review this chapter for information on the history of sub-Saharan African countries. Then use a computer or pen and paper to create a time line similar to those found in this book. **Post the time line in your classroom so others can add more entries.**

> **Time Line Tips**
> - Take notes before you begin.
> - Include important dates for a time line.
> - Include important rulers and events.
> - Find at least one photo that represents your country.

27. **Create a Thematic Map** Create a natural resources map. Use maps in this chapter and other online sources to gather information about natural resources in sub-Saharan Africa. Add them to an outline map similar to the one below. Use a map key to show the resources.

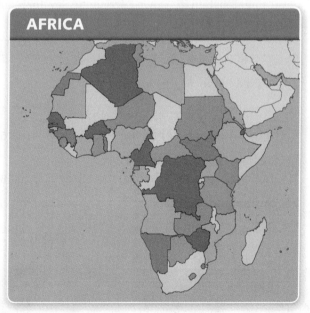

AFRICA

CHAPTER 14

SUB-SAHARAN AFRICA TODAY

PREVIEW THE CHAPTER

Essential Question What historical and geographic factors have influenced the cultures of sub-Saharan Africa?

SECTION 1 • CULTURE

KEY VOCABULARY

- ethnic group
- transportation corridor
- griot
- oral tradition
- reserve
- domestic policy
- modernization
- literacy rate
- ethnobotanist
- medicinal plant

ACADEMIC VOCABULARY

evident

TERMS & NAMES

- African Union
- Youssou N'Dour
- Nairobi
- Jomo Kenyatta

Essential Question How have conflict and government instability slowed economic development in sub-Saharan Africa?

SECTION 2 • GOVERNMENT & ECONOMICS

KEY VOCABULARY

- mineral
- commodity
- coup
- famine
- erosion
- legume
- microcredit
- epidemic
- pandemic
- vaccine
- infectious
- refugee
- clan
- failed state
- segregation
- apartheid
- homeland

ACADEMIC VOCABULARY

concentrated

TERMS & NAMES

- Lost Boys of Sudan
- African National Congress
- Nelson Mandela
- Steve Biko

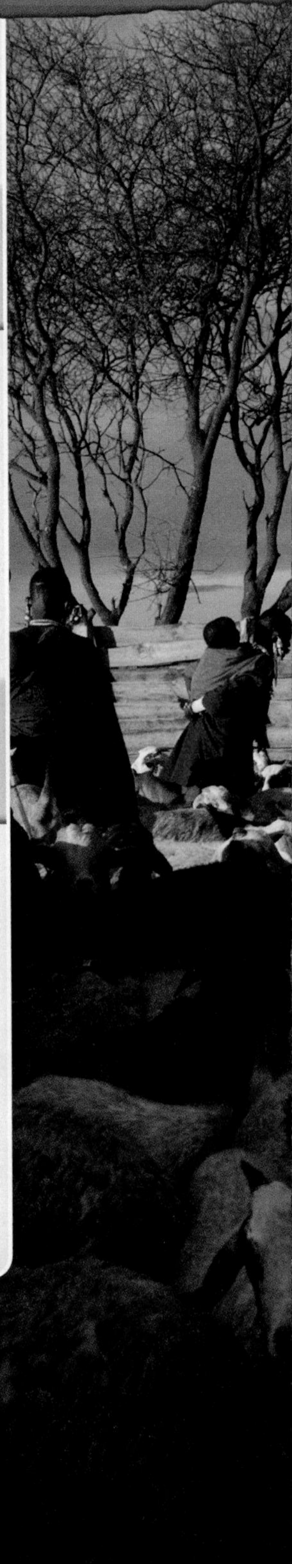

TECHTREK FOR THIS CHAPTER

Student eEdition

Maps and Graphs

Interactive Whiteboard GeoActivities

Digital Library

Go to myNGconnect.com for more on sub-Saharan Africa.

Traditional Masai in Tanzania herd a flock of goats into a pen.

1.1 Africa's Borders and Cultures

TECHTREK

myNGconnect.com For a language map and photos of African culture

 Maps and Graphs

 Digital Library

Main Idea European powers created new colonial borders that ignored the existing borders of traditional African cultures.

Africa is a continent of diverse cultures and countries. Today, about two thirds of Africans live in rural villages that have varied customs and languages. About 1,000 languages are spoken in Africa by different **ethnic groups**, which are groups of people who share a common culture, language, and sometimes racial heritage. Many Africans identify themselves first as members of a tribe rather than a country.

The Impact of Colonialism

Before Europeans arrived, borders between African cultural groups developed by agreement or conflict. Natural features such as oceans, lakes, mountain ranges, and rivers often defined borders. Natural borders were easier to control than borders set by groups of people. Borders along bodies of water also provided **transportation corridors**, or routes to easily move people and goods from place to place.

When Europeans colonized the continent, they routinely ignored the borders of African cultural groups. Instead, colonial borders were set to address the European need for resources. To do so, some sub-Saharan African cultural groups were divided, forced to share territory with rivals, or both.

As African countries began to gain independence in the 1900s, they did not change their colonial borders. As a result, few sub-Saharan African countries share one common culture.

Conflict and Cooperation

Cultural differences across Africa have often led to civil wars over political control, territory, and resources. Somalia's ethnic groups, for example, have never united to form a single nation. Military dictatorships often have been necessary to impose order.

> **Critical Viewing** Fishermen sun-dry fish caught in a lake near their village in Malawi. What can you infer about this fishing culture from the photo?

COOPERATIVE INTERNATIONAL ORGANIZATIONS IN AFRICA

Organization	Purpose
African Union	Peace-keeping; oppose colonization; promote unity; cooperate for economic development
Economic Community of West African States (ECOWAS)	Promote economy, industry, transportation, energy resources, agriculture, and natural resources
Southern African Development Community	Support local economy, transportation networks, and political interaction
Economic Community of Central African States (ECCAS)	Promote industry, transportation, communication, energy, natural resources, economy, tourism, education
East African Community (EAC)	Improve cooperation in transport and communication, industry, security, immigration, and economic matters

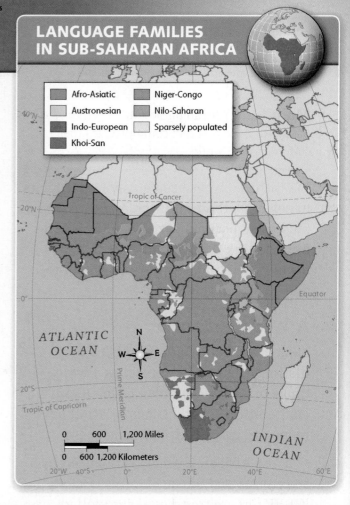

LANGUAGE FAMILIES IN SUB-SAHARAN AFRICA

Legend:
- Afro-Asiatic
- Austronesian
- Indo-European
- Khoi-San
- Niger-Congo
- Nilo-Saharan
- Sparsely populated

To address these challenges, African countries have developed organizations (see chart above) such as the **African Union** and the East African Community (EAC). These organizations promote cooperation and economic progress within and between countries.

Before You Move On

Summarize How were colonial borders different from sub-Saharan Africa's traditional borders?

FORMATIVE ASSESSMENT

MAP LAB

GeoJournal

1. **Interpret Maps** Locate country borders near areas with the Nilo-Saharan language group. What can you infer about the location of language groups and the borders that were created during colonization?

2. **Human-Environment Interaction** On the map, identify the oceans that surround Africa. How do natural features such as rivers, lakes, and oceans help countries control territory and methods of transportation?

3. **Make Generalizations** How did colonization lead to conflict between present-day cultures in Africa?

4. **Synthesize** What is one goal that is shared by the organizations shown in the chart?

1.2 African Music Goes Global

TECHTREK

myNGconnect.com For audio clips
of African music and photos of musicians

Digital
Library

Magazine
Maker

Main Idea African music connects the people to their past and communicates their cultures to the world.

Music has always been a way for Africans to celebrate their cultures. Today, African music has become part of many cultures. Experts link African music to the development of jazz, blues, rock-and-roll, and gospel in the United States.

A Wealth of Music

Each area of sub-Saharan Africa has distinctive music that reaches a wide range of audiences. Advancements in communication and transportation have helped to spread African music.

West African music is influenced by the stories and music of griots. **Griots** (GREE oh) are traditional storytellers. For centuries, they orally passed on the histories of West African cultures. Because they were not written down, these histories are part of the **oral tradition**, the practice of orally passing stories from one generation to the next.

Griots accompany their songs with harps, lutes, and drums. Their influence is **evident**, or clearly present, in West African music today.

Much West African music is a fusion, or blend, of griot music and other African music with global music. Mbalax (uhm BALAKS), for example, is a blend of griot percussion and songs with Afro-Cuban influences. **Youssou N'Dour** is a contemporary griot who plays mbalax music. His popularity has helped spread the music out of West Africa to audiences around the world.

In South Africa, music sometimes focused on politics. One example is protest music. Miriam Makeba and a number of other South African musicians left South Africa to protest government policies in the 1970s and 1980s—gaining global audiences for their music.

Before You Move On
Summarize What are some examples of how African music connects the people to their past and communicates their culture to the world?

South African singer Lira performs in Soweto, South Africa.

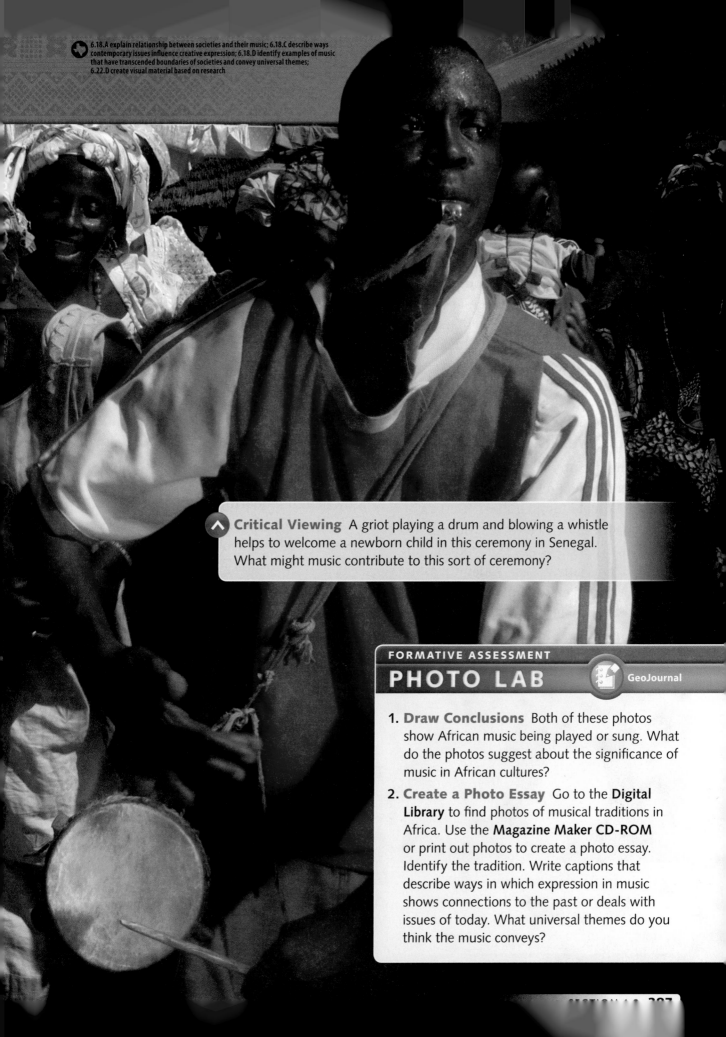

6.18.A explain relationship between societies and their music; 6.18.C describe ways contemporary issues influence creative expression; 6.18.D identify examples of music that have transcended boundaries of societies and convey universal themes; 6.22.D create visual material based on research

Critical Viewing A griot playing a drum and blowing a whistle helps to welcome a newborn child in this ceremony in Senegal. What might music contribute to this sort of ceremony?

FORMATIVE ASSESSMENT

PHOTO LAB
GeoJournal

1. **Draw Conclusions** Both of these photos show African music being played or sung. What do the photos suggest about the significance of music in African cultures?

2. **Create a Photo Essay** Go to the **Digital Library** to find photos of musical traditions in Africa. Use the **Magazine Maker CD-ROM** or print out photos to create a photo essay. Identify the tradition. Write captions that describe ways in which expression in music shows connections to the past or deals with issues of today. What universal themes do you think the music conveys?

1.3 Kenya Modernizes

TECHTREK

myNGconnect.com For an online
map and photos of Kenya

 Maps and
Graphs

 Digital
Library

Main Idea Kenya is modernizing its economy
and improving its standard of living.

Kenya's geographic features range from
beaches, savannas, deserts, and farmland
to snow-capped mountains such as
Mount Kenya, for which the country
is named. Large mammals such as the
African elephant, giraffes, and lions
roam Kenya's **reserves**, land set aside for
the protection of animals. The diverse
geography and wildlife are key to Kenya's
economic future.

Cultural Diversity

You can hear many languages and see an
array of traditional clothing on a busy
street in **Nairobi** (ny ROE bee), Kenya's
capital. More than 40 ethnic groups live
in Kenya. The largest are the Kikuyu
(ki KOO yoo), Luhya, Luo, Kalenjin, and
Kamba. This diversity makes Kenya a
multicultural society.

Critical Viewing Students work at
Kibagare Good News Centre School in
Nairobi, Kenya. What details in the photo
remind you of a day in your classroom?

As you've learned, cultural diversity
has sometimes led to rivalry and conflict
in Africa. Even so, diverse groups have
been able to work toward common goals.

For example, the people of Kenya united
in their struggle for independence from
British rule. After independence in 1963,
Jomo Kenyatta, a Kikuyu, became Kenya's
first elected leader. To help all Kenyans
pull together, he appointed members from
different ethnic groups as his advisors.

Modernization

Kenyatta and other leaders encouraged
domestic policies, or government plans
within a country, that led to economic
growth and modernization. **Modernization**
is the development of policies and actions
designed to bring a country up to world
standards in technology and other areas.

Education is an important factor in
modernization for Kenya. Most children
there attend free elementary schools. The
adult **literacy rate**, or percentage of people
who can read, soared from 32 percent in
1970 to 85 percent in 2003.

Nairobi, Kenya

KENYA'S PARKS AND RESERVES

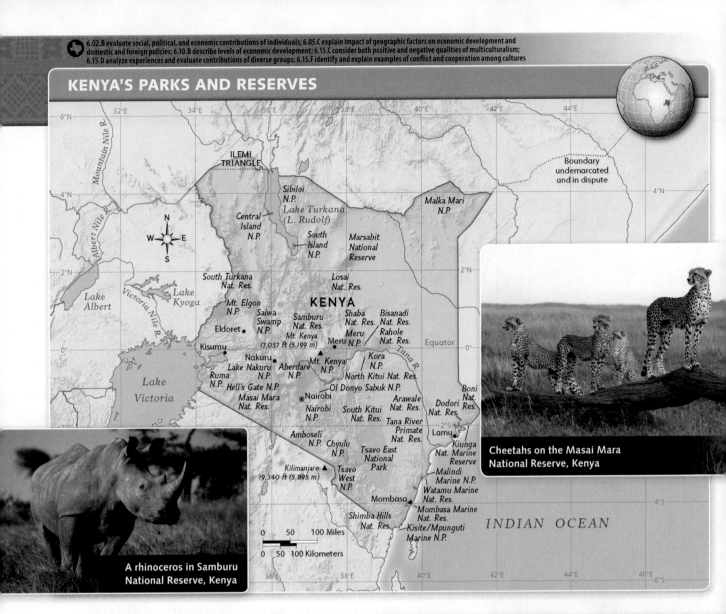

A rhinoceros in Samburu National Reserve, Kenya

Cheetahs on the Masai Mara National Reserve, Kenya

Kenya's modernization is also evident in its growing tourist industry. The scenic beauty and unique wildlife found in Kenya's national parks and reserves attracts tourists. The government is determined to protect the parks and reserves because of the jobs and money they bring into the country.

In 2000, Kenya, Uganda and Tanzania formed the East African Community. Today Rwanda and Burundi are also EAC members. All five countries work together to encourage entrepreneurship and trade in the region.

Before You Move On

Summarize What steps has Kenya taken to modernize?

FORMATIVE ASSESSMENT

MAP LAB

 GeoJournal

1. **Interpret Maps** What does the number of national parks and reserves shown on the map indicate about their importance in Kenya?

2. **Place** In what ways are the national parks and reserves shown on the map part of the economic modernization of Kenya?

3. **Form and Support Opinions** What makes Kenya diverse? Explain an advantage or disadvantage of diversity in Kenya. Support your opinion with details from the map and from what you have read about Kenya.

4. **Turn and Talk** Think about Jomo Kenyatta's decision to include different ethnic groups in his council. Talk to a partner and discuss effective ways of bringing people together.

SECTION **1** GEOGRAPHY

NATIONAL GEOGRAPHIC

TECHTREK

myNGconnect.com For photos of Explorers at work and an Explorer Video Clip

Digital Library

Exploring
Traditional Cultures
with Grace Gobbo and Wade Davis

> **Main Idea** Preserving indigenous cultures and traditional ways of life benefits modern societies around the world.

Cures in the Forest

When Emerging Explorer Grace Gobbo walks through a Tanzanian rain forest, she sees more than trees, flowers, and vines. She sees possible cures. As an **ethnobotanist**, she studies the relationship between cultures and plants.

Tanzanians have relied on traditional healers for centuries. Gobbo interviewed more than 80 traditional healers who rely on **medicinal plants**, or plants used to treat illnesses. Scientific research has confirmed that many of the plants these healers use do help treat illnesses. In fact, large drug companies are now using the same plants in many medicines.

However, many of the forests where these plants grow are at risk from logging and clear-cut farming. By teaching the value of medicinal plants, Gobbo hopes to inspire people to preserve their forests and maintain their traditional healing methods. "Nothing was written down," she explains. "The knowledge is literally dying out with the elders."

myNGconnect.com

For more on Grace Gobbo and Wade Davis in the field today

AFRICAN PLANTS AND USES

Plant Latin name	Location	Medicinal Use
Tulbaghia violacea	Southern Africa	lowers blood pressure
Catharanthus roseus	Madagascar	treats rheumatism (joint or muscle disorder)
Peltophorum africanum	Southern Africa	relieves stomach problems
Strychnos madagascariensis	Southern Africa	relieves stomach problems
Harpagophytum procumbens	Southern Africa and Madagascar	reduces swelling
Sutherlandia frutescens	Southern Africa	treats cancer
Agapanthus praecox	Southern Africa	treats heart disease and chest pain

Preserving Culture

Like Gobbo, National Geographic Explorer-in-Residence Wade Davis is an ethnobotanist who has studied the use of native plants around the world. His current focus, however, is indigenous cultures around the globe—the customs and practices of people in their daily lives. Davis has lived among 15 cultural groups in the Americas, Asia, Africa, and the Arctic.

Davis has proposed that there is a cultural web of life, just as there is a biological connection between all forms of life. He believes that every culture is connected and that all indigenous cultures have contributed to the cultural web. Davis hopes to preserve this cultural diversity, just as Gobbo works to protect medicinal plants and knowledge of traditional healing in Tanzania.

Davis believes that the development of modern industry and technology has contributed to a decline in the number of indigenous cultures. As a result, the entire cultural web suffers from the loss of each culture. Davis further believes that, like the world's plants and animals, human cultures should be protected so that they can continue to contribute to humanity.

Before You Move On

Monitor Comprehension Why are Gobbo and Davis working to preserve traditional cultures?

FORMATIVE ASSESSMENT

VIEWING LAB GeoJournal

1. **Analyze Visuals** Go to the **Digital Library** to watch the Explorer Video Clip of Wade Davis. How are his contributions similar to and different from those of Grace Gobbo?

2. **Summarize** According to Wade Davis, why is preserving indigenous cultures important for humanity?

3. **Interpret Reports** Go to National Geographic Current Events and search and choose a report on ethnobotany. Organize information from the report. What is the main idea? Does it have a point of view? Share your findings with the class.

National Geographic Explorer-in-Residence Wade Davis

2.1 Prized Mineral Resources

TECHTREK

myNGconnect.com For an online map
and photos of mining in sub-Saharan Africa

 Maps and
Graphs

Digital
Library

> **Main Idea** Sub-Saharan Africa has mineral
> resources that could improve life for its people.

The mineral resources of sub-Saharan
Africa have the potential to lift the
economies of sub-Saharan countries.
However, careful management is needed to
maximize benefits for the African people.

Mineral Riches

Sub-Saharan Africa has large deposits
of gold, diamonds, and other **minerals**,
which are inorganic solid substances
formed through geological processes.
Many of these minerals are exported to
Europe, North America, and Asia where
they are used to make automotive and
electronic products.

Many sub-Saharan countries use
mineral resources as **commodities**, which
are materials or goods that can be bought,
sold, or traded. These commodities can
bring in enormous wealth, but economic
progress has been slow. Over time,
government corruption has taken much of
the profits from mineral mining.

SELECTED OIL AND DIAMOND EXPORTS SUB-SAHARAN AFRICA, 2005–2006

Oil		
Country	World Rank	Percentage of Country's Total Exports
Nigeria	6	91.9
Angola	12	96.6
Equatorial Guinea	21	92.7
Democratic Republic of the Congo	22	89.6
Sudan	29	88.0
Chad	37	94.6

Diamonds		
Country	World Rank	Percentage of Country's Total Exports
South Africa	5	6.9
Botswana	9	83.5
Namibia	14	43.5
Angola	16	2.4
Democratic Republic of the Congo	17	41.5
Central African Republic	32	36.8

Source: The World Bank

> **Critical Viewing** Gold miners dig
> in the Chudja mine near the village of
> Kobu in northeastern Congo. What
> does the photo suggest about
> working conditions in the mines?

SUB-SAHARAN AFRICA'S RESOURCES

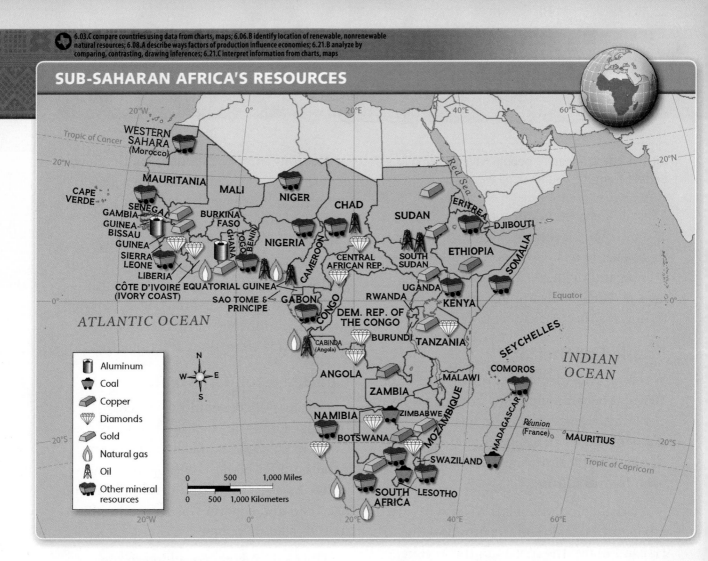

Economic Improvement

Today, unstable governments continue to challenge many sub-Saharan countries. For example, the Central African Republic has significant diamond resources as the chart shows, but a lack of infrastructure, smuggling, and political unrest have limited the development of its diamond mining industry. As a result, the country remains one of the poorest in the world.

Some countries such as South Africa, Namibia, and Tanzania have successfully used their mineral profits to build their economies. In Botswana, the government is a partner in the country's largest diamond mining company. It has invested the profits in education, infrastructure, and health care. Countries with resources that follow Botswana's example can improve the stability of their economies and improve the lives of their citizens.

Before You Move On

Monitor Comprehension In what ways do sub-Saharan countries' mineral resources improve life for their people?

FORMATIVE ASSESSMENT

MAP LAB   GeoJournal

1. **Place** Based on the map, what mineral resources can be found in Tanzania?

2. **Compare and Contrast** Compare the resources of two countries on the map. From their resources, what can you infer about their economies?

3. **Pose and Answer Questions** Use the chart to pose questions with a partner about distributions of exports from different countries. Then answer: What would happen to Angola's economy if its oil exports were disrupted?

2.2 Nigeria and Oil

Main Idea Nigeria's people have received little benefit from the country's oil wealth.

Nigeria has a population of more than 150 million people, the largest in Africa. Its coastline has major ports, and its river system and delta are among the world's largest. Nigeria also produces more oil than any other African country.

Ethnic Conflict

When oil was discovered in Nigeria in the 1950s, it became the focus of the country's economy. However, Nigeria has faced many obstacles in attempting to use its oil riches. The most difficult challenge has been ethnic conflict.

British colonialism left Nigeria divided among three major ethnic groups—the Hausa-Fulani, the Igbo, and the Yoruba. There were also 250 smaller groups and at least two major religions. When Nigeria gained independence in 1960, these groups struggled for control.

Not long after independence, the new government was overthrown in a **coup**, or an illegal takeover by force. In a series of coups, rival ethnic groups replaced existing governments—often putting military leaders in charge. After Muslims in the north adopted *sharia*, or Islamic law, Christians in the area began moving south. This movement further divided the country, this time along religious lines.

Challenges of Oil Wealth

In the early 1970s, world oil prices increased and the Nigerian economy grew. Cities expanded and farmers left their rural land for better paying jobs in the cities. As a result, agricultural production declined and Nigeria was forced to import food to feed its people.

The oil industry has added to the ethnic tension. Different groups struggle to control the oil and its profits. Conflict and corruption have prevented Nigerians from

> **Critical Viewing** Fishermen cast a net near an oil refinery in the Niger River delta. Think about the oil industry and the simple fishing shown in the photo. In what ways are they connected?

sharing in the oil wealth. Most people living in the Niger River delta, where oil production is **concentrated** , or centered, live in poverty.

The delta region is also heavily polluted from oil spills. People in the delta have protested against the pollution and demanded that more of the oil profits be used to improve the area.

Nigeria's Progress

Between 2007 and 2011, Nigeria made economic gains. Its leaders received favorable loans to repay the country's debt to other countries. Officials began putting in place economic reforms designed to improve Nigeria's infrastructure. Maintaining these improvements while resolving ethnic conflicts will be a challenge for Nigeria's future.

Before You Move On

Summarize Why have Nigeria's people benefited so little from the country's oil wealth?

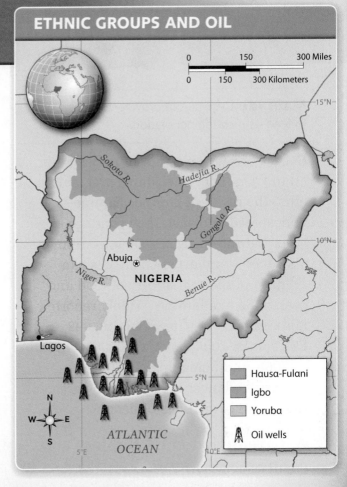

ETHNIC GROUPS AND OIL

Hausa-Fulani
Igbo
Yoruba
Oil wells

FORMATIVE ASSESSMENT

MAP LAB
GeoJournal

1. **Location** What ethnic group appears to have the most access to the country's oil industry?

2. **Interpret Maps** Identify the delta region on the map. What are some possible consequences of polluting this region?

3. **Analyze Cause and Effect** Use a chart similar to the one below to list effects related to Nigeria's oil industry.

CAUSE	EFFECTS
Nigeria's oil industry	1.
	2.
	3.

2.3 Agriculture and Food Supply

Main Idea Africa is improving its ability to feed its growing population.

Images of African children in need are all too common. Their hunger is real and often the result of famine. **Famine** is a widespread and sustained shortage of food. Natural disasters, such as droughts and floods, and armed conflicts can all disrupt the availability of food and contribute to a famine. Widely reported famines occurred in Sudan in 1998, Ethiopia in 2000, 2002, and 2003, Niger in 2005, and Somalia in 2011. Famine is a constant danger in Africa and threatens the health of millions of people.

A Threatened Food Supply

Population growth has been rapid in some parts of Africa, but food production has not increased as rapidly. The average African eats 10 percent fewer calories today than he or she did 20 years ago. The number of undernourished people in sub-Saharan Africa increased from about 90 million in 1970 to 214 million in 2012. Many African children suffer from malnutrition, which is a lack of nutrients essential to good health. Because of hunger and malnutrition, African children typically have shorter life expectancies than other children around the world.

⊼ **Critical Viewing** Women harvest cotton in Mali. Based on the photo, how would you describe this Mali cotton farm?

❯ **Visual Vocabulary** **Erosion** is the wearing away of Earth's surface by natural forces. The grid-like structures in the photo are fences made from branches. The fences keep sand from eroding onto land used for crops and grazing.

African food crops include corn, yams, and sorghum, which is a type of grain. Before colonization, Africans grew these crops with the goal of feeding everyone. After colonization, European settlers took the most fertile land, and farming shifted from food crops to cash crops for export. Cash crops such as coffee and cotton are grown because they can be sold for more money than food crops. The income from cash crops allows farmers to purchase more, but less food is grown to feed the African people.

Since independence, some land has been returned to Africans. However, African land can be easily overworked and overgrazed, exhausting the soil. Farmers also struggle with droughts, soil erosion, and desertification.

New and Better Farming

Africans are working to improve agricultural practices. For example, farmers are moving animals from place to place to avoid overgrazing. They are also growing different crops on the same plot to avoid exhausting the soil. More **legumes**, which are peas or beans, are being planted. These add to the food supply and release helpful nutrients into the soil. Farmers are also enriching the soil by using fertilizer with animal and plant waste instead of chemicals.

Microcredit, or small loans, has helped poor farmers invest in land, tools, and seeds. Relief agencies have begun to provide free seeds and tools to farmers. Scientists hope to develop seeds that are more productive and drought resistant. These seeds could help farmers grow more food crops for their own use as well as cash crops for export. If successful, these efforts will feed Africans, extend life expectancies, and improve economies.

Before You Move On

Summarize What is Africa doing to improve its agriculture?

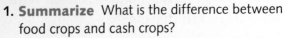

FORMATIVE ASSESSMENT

WRITING LAB GeoJournal

1. **Summarize** What is the difference between food crops and cash crops?

2. **Analyze Cause and Effect** What is the relationship between reduced food production and life expectancy?

3. **Write Comparisons** Write a paragraph comparing African food crops and cash crops. Describe why is it important for African farmers to balance growing food crops with cash crops. Then work in groups and share your paragraphs. Go to **Student Resources** for Guided Writing support.

2.4 Improving Public Health

> **Main Idea** National governments and international agencies are committed to improving health care in Africa by reducing the impact of diseases.

KEY VOCABULARY

epidemic, n., an outbreak of disease affecting a large number of people within a community at the same time

pandemic, n., an outbreak of disease occurring over a wide geographic area

vaccine, n., treatments to increase immunity to a particular disease

infectious, adj., capable of spreading rapidly to others

Nearly one million people die of malaria each year, and 9 out of 10 of them are in Africa. Eighty-five percent of the victims are children under the age of five. Malaria is one of many chronic diseases that plague the continent.

Climate, Poverty, and Disease

In 2012, 52 years was the estimated average life expectancy for sub-Saharan Africans. That is almost 30 years shorter than the average in North America. One cause is the deadly toll taken by diseases such as malaria, sleeping sickness, and yellow fever.

Only 15 percent of the world's people live in Africa, but 90 percent of tropical disease cases occur there. The organisms that cause disease thrive in its tropical climates, as do the insects that carry the diseases.

For example, malaria is carried by a mosquito and causes flu-like symptoms. Severe forms can cause brain and nerve damage and death. Malaria probably began in ancient times as an **epidemic**—an outbreak limited to a particular community. Later, it became a **pandemic**, meaning it spread over a large area, in this case, across much of the world. Malaria can be prevented by draining or treating water where insects breed and by sleeping under mosquito nets treated with chemicals to kill insects.

In addition to the tropical climate, poverty contributes to the spread of disease. Poor Africans may lack mosquito nets, screened windows, and technology for draining insect breeding grounds. Poverty also raises the rates of other infections because of overcrowding, poor sanitation, and contaminated water.

Before You Move On

Summarize What are some factors that contribute to the spread of disease in Africa?

Students in Ethiopia read before school under the protection of a mosquito net.

Inspiring people to care about the planet
National Geographic Society Mission

COMPARE ACROSS REGIONS

The Fight Against Disease

The fight against diseases such as malaria, HIV/AIDs, and yellow fever has become a global commitment. Many agencies offer medication to treat diseases and vaccines to prevent them. **Vaccines** are treatments designed to increase immunity, or resistance, to a particular disease. Scientists are trying to find new vaccines and cures for **infectious** diseases, or diseases that can spread rapidly.

Eliminating malaria is a global goal for the 21st century. Worldwide, there are an estimated 250 million cases every year. A non-governmental organization (NGO) called Malaria No More works to fight malaria in Africa. An NGO is a nonprofit volunteer group founded by citizens. Malaria No More hands out mosquito nets to protect people.

The World Health Organization (WHO) battles malaria around the world. The group's Mekong Malaria Program in Southeast Asia works with governments and NGOs to monitor disease outbreaks and treatment programs in the region.

A major source of funding for malaria treatment programs is the Bill and Melinda Gates Foundation. The foundation funds research for a vaccine and more effective anti-malarial drugs for people who have already been infected.

All of these programs reflect a renewed commitment on the part of national governments, private foundations, and NGOs to fight malaria and other diseases around the world.

MALARIA BY THE NUMBERS

50
Countries worldwide on track to reduce cases by 75% by 2015

60
Number of seconds between each death of an African child due to malaria

109
Countries worldwide reporting malaria cases in 2012

2,414
Estimated number of people worldwide who die every day from malaria

801,000
Estimated number of Africans who die every year from malaria

Source: World Health Organization, United Nations Children's Fund

Before You Move On

Monitor Comprehension What are the main tools in the global fight against disease?

FORMATIVE ASSESSMENT

READING LAB GeoJournal

1. **Analyze Cause and Effect** What is one cause of the short life expectancy among sub-Saharan Africans?

2. **Make Predictions** How might development of a vaccine against malaria affect the life expectancy in Africa?

3. **Make Inferences** How might you expect malaria to impact the economies of countries with large numbers of cases?

4. **Make Generalizations** Evaluate the contributions foundations and governments and non-government organizations make to improve the quality of life for societies.

2.5 Sudan and Somalia

Main Idea Civil wars involving ethnic and religious groups in Sudan and Somalia have limited progress in these countries.

For years, Sudan and Somalia have been plagued by war, famine, and disease. Many people survived conflict only to die of starvation. In both countries, climate, history, and culture all combined to help create this difficult situation.

As you've learned, colonial rule in Africa left countries divided among different ethnic and religious groups. Sudan and Somalia also face a geographic division: The Sahel runs through both of these countries, dividing them between northern Africa and sub-Saharan Africa.

Conflict in Sudan

Sudan is mostly desert in the north. Nomadic Muslim herders of Arabic descent live there. The south is swamp and savanna that was settled by farmers of African descent. Northerners are mainly Muslim, while southerners practice mainly Christianity or indigenous religions. Both north and south include a mix of ethnic groups.

These differences have resulted in human rights abuses. Since Sudan's independence in 1956, the government has oppressed Christians in the country. In Darfur, the government created a largely Arab militia in 2003. The militia attacked government protestors, but also attacked militia members' personal enemies. Almost 400,000 people were killed, and about 2.5 million people became **refugees**, or people who flee a place to find safety.

Neighboring countries such as Chad set up refugee camps for people fleeing Sudan. One camp housed more than 250,000 people in 2010. The camps have no permanent shelter or sewer system, often suffer food shortages, and rely on the host countries and relief agencies for help.

The refugees included a group known as the **Lost Boys of Sudan**. These young men were orphaned by the civil war and stuck together to escape the violence. They traveled to Ethiopia, then back to Sudan, and then to camps in Kenya. In 2001, the United States took in more than 3,500 of these young men. Many attended high school and college in the United States.

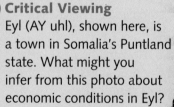
> **Critical Viewing**
> Eyl (AY uhl), shown here, is a town in Somalia's Puntland state. What might you infer from this photo about economic conditions in Eyl?

6.01.B analyze background to evaluate relationship between past conflicts and current conditions;
6.11.D review record of human rights abuses of limited and unlimited governments;
6.15.F identify and explain examples of conflict; 6.21.C interpret information from maps

SUDAN POLITICAL

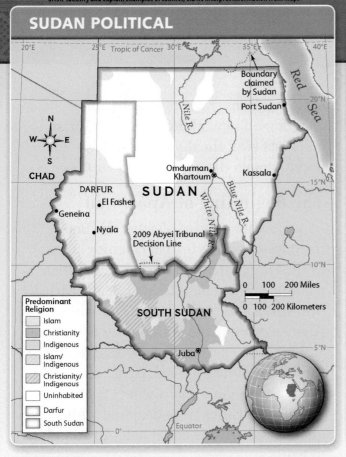

Predominant Religion
- Islam
- Christianity
- Indigenous
- Islam/ Indigenous
- Christianity/ Indigenous
- Uninhabited
- Darfur
- South Sudan

SOMALIA POLITICAL

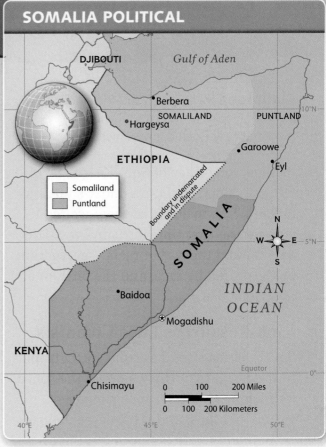

- Somaliland
- Puntland

Somalia

Somalians have suffered through conflict among five major **clans**, or large, family-based units with loyalty to the group. Even within the clan, sub-clans may clash. As a result, Somalians have never united to form a single nation.

In 1991, clan-based groups overthrew a crumbling military government and battles raged between rival clans. This conflict disrupted farms that were already threatened by flood and drought. With no central government, some clans turned to piracy, which continues today. They attack and rob foreign ships or hold the ships and their crews for ransom.

Somalia is considered by many to be a **failed state**, a country in which government, economic institutions, and civil order have broken down. The regions of Somaliland and Puntland have claimed

independence but have not received international recognition. In the 21st century, forces from the United Nations and the African Union have been trying to keep peace in the region.

Before You Move On

Summarize How have conflicts limited progress in Sudan and Somalia?

FORMATIVE ASSESSMENT

MAP LAB
GeoJournal

1. **Interpret Maps** Using the map of Sudan, describe the geographic distribution of the main religions.

2. **Region** Using the map of Somalia, describe how it is divided. Based on your description, what challenges might Somalia face?

3. **Draw Conclusions** What is a failed state, and why might Sudan and Somalia both be considered failed states?

2.6 Ending Apartheid

> **Main Idea** In 1994, South Africa moved from a minority, racist government to a democratically elected government.

In 1994, long lines of South Africans of all races stood for hours under a blazing hot sun. The majority of them waited to vote for the first time in their lives. This day marked the end of racial **segregation**, or separation by race, and the birth of a new democracy.

Rich Resources Lure Colonists

South Africa stretches from warm tropics in the north to chilly waters in the south. Its geography and climate support a variety of crops, and it has large deposits of diamonds, gold, and other minerals.

In the 19th century, both Dutch and British colonists laid claim to these lands. The Dutch settlers, known as Boers or Afrikaners, formed their own republics. Boers had enslaved Africans and imported other people as laborers from Asia. Both the British and the Boers seized lands from Zulus, Xhosa, and other Africans. Even more Africans were forced to work for Boer and British colonists after the discovery of large gold and diamond deposits around 1870.

The Beginning of Apartheid

In 1902, after a series of wars, the Boer territories became British colonies known as the Union of South Africa. The British colonial government divided South Africa into white and black areas. Only white Africans could vote. Most of the land, and all of the best land, was reserved for the white minority. Black Africans were left with the land that was less useful or productive. Cities were declared white, and black Africans could enter them only to work.

> **Critical Viewing** A crowd in South Africa celebrates at a soccer match. What can you infer from the photo about how a sporting event might help bring people together?

In 1948, new laws created **apartheid** (uh PART hite), or the legal separation of races. In addition to being divided by race, South Africans could only own land in areas assigned to them. Black South Africans were required to carry identification papers at all times.

In 1970, the government made all black South Africans citizens of a homeland instead of citizens of South Africa. **Homelands** were supposed to be self-governing areas, but the national government actually controlled them. The homelands separated the races even more.

The End of Apartheid

In the early 20th century, black Africans formed the **African National Congress** (ANC) to protest their treatment. Later, South Africa outlawed the ANC and imprisoned its leaders, including **Nelson Mandela**. In 1977, **Stephen Biko**, president of a student protest organization, was arrested and beaten to death. He and Mandela became symbols for the protest movement in South Africa.

In 1989, a new white president, F. W. de Klerk, began to change apartheid laws. He legalized the ANC and released its leaders, including Mandela. In 1994, voting rights were extended to all South Africans, and the people elected Mandela president.

Decades of apartheid left South Africa far from racial equality. The government has worked to give black South Africans access to better jobs and farmland, but a large economic gap remains between most blacks and whites in the country. In 2002, the government took control of the country's

Nelson Mandela gestures at a rally shortly after his release from prison. Internationally respected, he dedicated most of his life to racial equality. He died at age 95 in 2013.

mineral resources, in part to make sure that black South Africans profited fairly. South Africa's ability to harness its resources has allowed it to develop the most prosperous economy in Africa.

Before You Move On

Summarize How did South Africa change from minority rule to a more democratically elected government?

FORMATIVE ASSESSMENT

READING LAB *GeoJournal*

1. **Monitor Comprehension** What was apartheid and how did it begin?

2. **Movement** In what ways did colonization and apartheid remove Africans from their homes?

3. **Compare and Contrast** Give an example of how the government under apartheid limited peoples' rights and an example of how the government expanded rights after apartheid.

VOCABULARY

For each pair of vocabulary words, write one sentence that explains the connection between the two words.

1. ethnic group; transportation corridor

> *Bodies of waters can act as transportation corridors between different African ethnic groups.*

2. griot; oral tradition
3. ethnobotanist; medicinal plant
4. commodity; mineral
5. famine; erosion
6. epidemic; pandemic

MAIN IDEAS

7. What factors were ignored when the colonial boundaries of African countries were drawn? (Section 1.1)

8. How has Africa's music influenced music in the United States? (Section 1.2)

9. What challenges has Kenya faced in modernizing its economy? (Section 1.3)

10. How are Grace Gobbo and Wade Davis helping to preserve traditional cultures? (Section 1.4)

11. What circumstances have kept Africans from profiting from mineral resources? (Section 2.1)

12. How has population growth made it harder for Africa to feed its people? (Section 2.3)

13. What is being done to reduce the spread of malaria in Africa? (Section 2.4)

14. What are some of the causes of the conflict in Sudan and Somalia? (Section 2.5)

15. How has life improved in South Africa since the end of apartheid? (Section 2.6)

CULTURE

ANALYZE THE ESSENTIAL QUESTION

What historical and geographic factors have influenced the cultures of sub-Saharan Africa?

Critical Thinking: Draw Conclusions

16. Without the influence of colonialism, would African countries be as ethnically diverse as they are today? Why or why not?

17. In what ways have sub-Saharan Africa's geography, climate, and resources helped to shape the lifestyles of its people?

INTERPRET MAPS

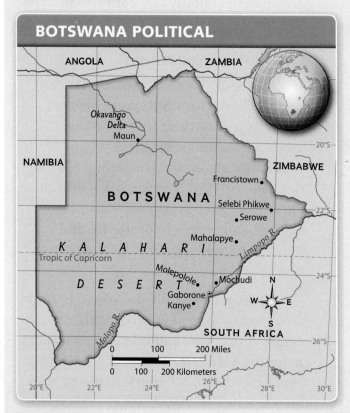

BOTSWANA POLITICAL

18. **Location** Which city can be found near 22°S latitude and 28°E longitude?

19. **Human-Environment Interaction** What type of geographic feature defines the irregular shape of Botswana's southern border?

GOVERNMENT & ECONOMICS

ANALYZE THE ESSENTIAL QUESTION

How have conflict and government instability slowed economic development in sub-Saharan Africa?

Critical Thinking: Analyze Cause and Effect

20. Describe some specific natural resources that have helped sub-Saharan African countries develop economically.

21. How did colonialism slow down Africa's economic development?

22. What effects did apartheid have on racial equality in South Africa?

INTERPRET GRAPHS

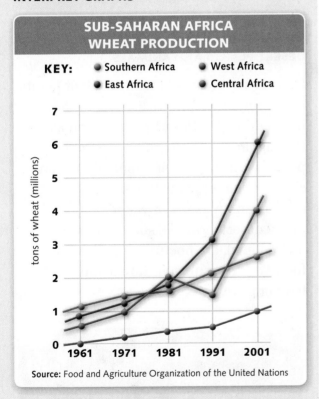

SUB-SAHARAN AFRICA WHEAT PRODUCTION

KEY:
● Southern Africa
● East Africa
● West Africa
● Central Africa

y-axis: tons of wheat (millions) — 0 to 7
x-axis: 1961 1971 1981 1991 2001

Source: Food and Agriculture Organization of the United Nations

23. **Analyze Data** In which region of Africa did food production increase the most?

24. **Evaluate** What additional information is needed in order to determine growth in food production per capita?

ACTIVE OPTIONS

Synthesize the Essential Questions by completing the activities below.

25. **Gather Information** Suppose it is 2001 and a group of Lost Boys from Sudan are coming to your school. With a group, talk about ways to welcome them. List words and daily routines they would need to know. Conduct research about their language. **Share your ideas orally with the class.**

> **Collaboration Tips**
> • Listen, take notes, and ask others to clarify what they say; respond to their questions as well.
> • Retell what you've heard to confirm your understanding.
> • Agree in advance on how you will explain your ideas to the class.

26. **Create a Chart** Make a three-column chart showing comparisons among three countries in sub-Saharan Africa. Be sure each country comes from a different area (West, East, Central, or Southern). Use online sources to gather the data for the categories shown below. Based on the data, which country has the most people? The fewest?

	Ghana (West Africa)	Uganda (East Africa)	Lesotho (South Africa)
Year Country Gained Independence			
Population			
Square Miles of Land			
Main Economic Resources			

Deserts of the World

Deserts make up about one fifth of the land on Earth. Geologically speaking, deserts as we know them are relatively young—forming within the last 65 million years. Deserts are dry lands that can lose more water through evaporation than they get from precipitation. Rainfall in deserts is usually less than 10 inches a year. Limited rainfall, low humidity, often high daytime temperatures, and winds all contribute to the desert's dryness.

Deserts sometimes cover large areas and extend beyond country borders. For example, the Sonoran Desert crosses the border between Mexico and the United States. The Kalahari Desert covers parts of three countries—Botswana, Namibia, and South Africa.

Compare

- Botswana
- China
- Mexico
- Mongolia
- Namibia
- South Africa
- United States

PHYSICAL CHARACTERISTICS

Many people think of a desert as a hot, sandy wasteland with no water and no life. In fact, there is an amazing diversity among deserts. Some are hot and sandy, but some have rainy seasons and can get very cold. While about one fourth of deserts are made of sand, the rest are composed of dirt, clay, rock, ice, and other materials. For example, Antarctica is a desert. Deserts can be flat or hilly, below sea level or in mountains.

DESERT PLANTS AND ANIMALS

Deserts are home to a wide array of plants and animals that have adapted to the harsh climates. Desert plants, such as the saguaro cactus (below), can go long periods without water. Some plants have shallow root systems that cover a large area to gather as much water as possible. Many desert animals, such as the elf owl (below), are nocturnal, hunting for food after the sun goes down and the temperatures drop.

Namib Desert, Namibia

Elf owl in a saguaro cactus, Sonoran Desert, United States

SELECTED DESERTS OF THE WORLD

Gobi Desert

Sonoran Desert

Kalahari Desert

SONORAN

KALAHARI

GOBI

Location:
United States, Mexico

Approximate size:
100,000 square miles

Average yearly rainfall:
4–12 inches

Interesting animal species:
Gila monster

Examples of temperature ranges:
120°F (summer)
32°F (winter)

Location:
Botswana, South Africa, Namibia

Approximate size:
220,000 square miles

Average yearly rainfall:
3–7.5 inches

Interesting animal species:
Meerkat

Examples of temperature ranges:
113°F (summer)
7°F (winter)

Location:
China, Mongolia

Approximate size:
500,000 square miles

Average yearly rainfall:
2–8 inches

Interesting animal species:
Bactrian Camels

Examples of temperature ranges:
113°F (summer)
-40°F (winter)

Source: World Wildlife Fund; worldatlas.com; gobidesert.org; Arizona-Sonoran Desert Museum

FORMATIVE ASSESSMENT

RESEARCH LAB GeoJournal

1. **Analyze Data** Which desert has the widest range in temperatures?

2. **Compare and Contrast** How do the deserts compare in size?

Research and Create Charts Locate the Patagonian and Sahara deserts on a map. Do research to compare the deserts and use a chart like the one above to present your findings. Adjust the categories depending on the information you want to compare.

Active Options

TECHTREK

myNGconnect.com For photos of endangered species and writing templates

 Digital Library

Student eEdition

ACTIVITY 1

Goal: Extend your understanding of endangered animals.

Write a Briefing

Do research and prepare a written briefing about one of the endangered Sub-Saharan animals listed below. A briefing is a short summary of important information about a topic. Use research links or current events at Connect to NG to find reports or articles. Organize information from one or two them. What are the latest and most important findings? Give your audience facts about the animal and about efforts to protect it.

- African elephant
- addax
- black rhinoceros
- mandrill (shown at right)
- pygmy hippopotamus
- lowland gorilla

mandrill

ACTIVITY 2

Goal: Research sub-Saharan Africa's culture.

Keep a Culture Journal

Congratulations! You have won a seven-day, all-expenses-paid tour to one of these countries: Kenya, Tanzania, South Africa, Botswana, Zimbabwe, or Zambia. The only condition is that you keep a daily journal describing what you see and do. Choose your country and begin your tour. Use the **Magazine Maker CD-ROM** to share your journal with friends back home.

ACTIVITY 3

Goal: Review sub-Saharan Africa with a game.

Play a Capital Game

With a group, look at a map and choose 25 countries in sub-Saharan Africa. Write the name of each country on a small card. On another small card, write the capital of each country. Now you're ready to play. Each player draws a country card and tries to identify the capital. If the player misses, the card is put at the bottom of the pile, and it is the next player's turn. If the player names the capital correctly, he or she keeps the card and it is the next player's turn. The one with the most cards wins. Vary the game by choosing a capital card and trying to name the country.

6.10.C identify and describe the effects of government regulation and taxation on economic development and business planning; 6.22.D create written material based on research; 6.23.A use a problem-solving process

TEKS

TEKS PROJECT

Goal: Use a problem solving process.

Solve an Economic Problem

Because new ideas affect cultures, and events of all kinds take place, the economics of a society constantly change. Some things work well; sometimes problems arise. This is true for all societies, past and present.

In this unit you read about the impact of globalization, border disputes, and problems of food supply. Developing countries sometimes face the problem of too much government regulation. Depending on the country, taxes keep bridges, tunnels, and highways safe; they pay for the military, help fund public schools, and pay salaries for police and firefighters. But too many taxes or too much government control in a country that is struggling to develop economically can have a negative impact on business activities and planning.

Investigate With classmates, draw names of the countries of Sub-Saharan Africa. Your goal is to get to know a country well and explore how different groups, within the country or outside it, might solve one of its problems.

Apply the Process Use the problem-solving process on page R20. Follow these steps: identify a problem, gather information, list and consider options, consider advantages and disadvantages, choose a solution, describe how the country could put it to work, and predict the outcome of the solution. Join other classmates who have identified a problem similar to the one you chose.

Reflect On It Present your solutions to the class and evaluate the possible effectiveness of solutions. Describe any effects of government regulation or taxation you learned about.

Woman shopping at a market in Garoua, Cameroon, Africa

Explore
SOUTHWEST ASIA
& NORTH AFRICA
with NATIONAL GEOGRAPHIC

MEET THE EXPLORER

NATIONAL GEOGRAPHIC

Emerging Explorer and urban planner Thomas Taha Rassam (TH) Culhane works in Cairo's poorest neighborhoods. He installs rooftop solar water heaters and household biogas systems using environmentally friendly technology.

INVESTIGATE GEOGRAPHY

The Ramses temple, on the Nile River, was carved thousands of years ago in Egypt. Ancient Egypt was an oasis in the desert of northeastern Africa. Egypt depended on annual flooding of the river to support its society.

STEP INTO HISTORY

Jerusalem is home to the Dome of the Rock (shown here), an Islamic and Jewish holy place. It also contains many sites of importance to Christianity, including the Church of the Holy Sepulchre.

5,810 miles

Washington, D.C.

Cairo,
Egypt

Go to **myNGconnect.com** for maps of Southwest Asia and North Africa.

CONNECT WITH THE CULTURE

From the top of the world's tallest building, the Burj Khalifa in Dubai, dense development reflects the recent construction boom in the United Arab Emirates.

411

CHAPTER 15

SOUTHWEST ASIA & NORTH AFRICA GEOGRAPHY & HISTORY

PREVIEW THE CHAPTER

Essential Question How have climate and location influenced the region in the past and today?

KEY VOCABULARY

- arid
- desertification
- alluvial plain
- silt

- irrigation
- petroleum
- nonrenewable
- fault

- oasis
- qanat

ACADEMIC VOCABULARY
reliable

TERMS & NAMES

- Sahara Desert
- Nile River

- Fertile Crescent
- Rub Al Khali

- North Anatolian Fault

Essential Question How did civilizations develop in Southwest Asia and North Africa?

KEY VOCABULARY

- cultural hearth
- agricultural revolution
- domesticate
- city-state
- cuneiform

- monotheistic
- messiah
- pilgrimage
- diffusion
- adherent

- sultan
- religious tolerance

ACADEMIC VOCABULARY
extent

TERMS & NAMES

- Ur
- Hammurabi
- Nebuchadnezzar
- Judaism
- Christianity

- Islam
- Hebrew Bible
- Christian Bible
- Qur'an
- Diaspora

- Constantine
- Ottoman Empire
- Byzantine Empire
- Osman
- Suleyman I

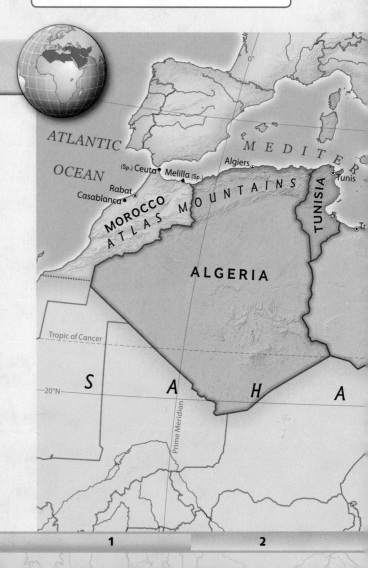

ATLANTIC OCEAN

MEDITER

(Sp.) Ceuta Melilla (Sp.)

Algiers

Tunis

Rabat
Casablanca

MOROCCO

ATLAS MOUNTAINS

TUNISIA

Tr

ALGERIA

Tropic of Cancer

S   A   H   A

20°N

Prime Meridian

TECHTREK

FOR THIS CHAPTER

Student eEdition

Maps and Graphs

Interactive Whiteboard GeoActivities

Digital Library

Arabian camel

Go to **myNGconnect.com** for more on Southwest Asia and North Africa.

Essential Question How did an advanced civilization develop in Egypt?

SECTION 3 • FOCUS ON EGYPT

KEY VOCABULARY

- floodplain
- hydroelectric power
- hieroglyphics
- dynasty
- pyramid
- pharaoh
- deity
- papyrus
- tomb
- sarcophagus

ACADEMIC VOCABULARY
regulate

TERMS & NAMES

- Aswan High Dam
- Hatshepsut
- Ramses II
- Re
- Isis
- Giza
- Great Pyramid of Khufu

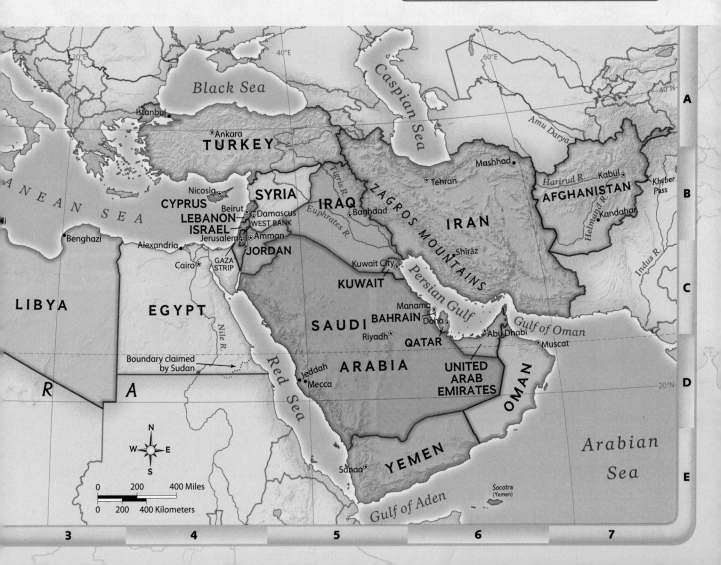

1.1 **Physical Geography**

TECHTREK

myNGconnect.com For online maps of Southwest Asia and North Africa and Visual Vocabulary

 Maps and Graphs

 Digital Library

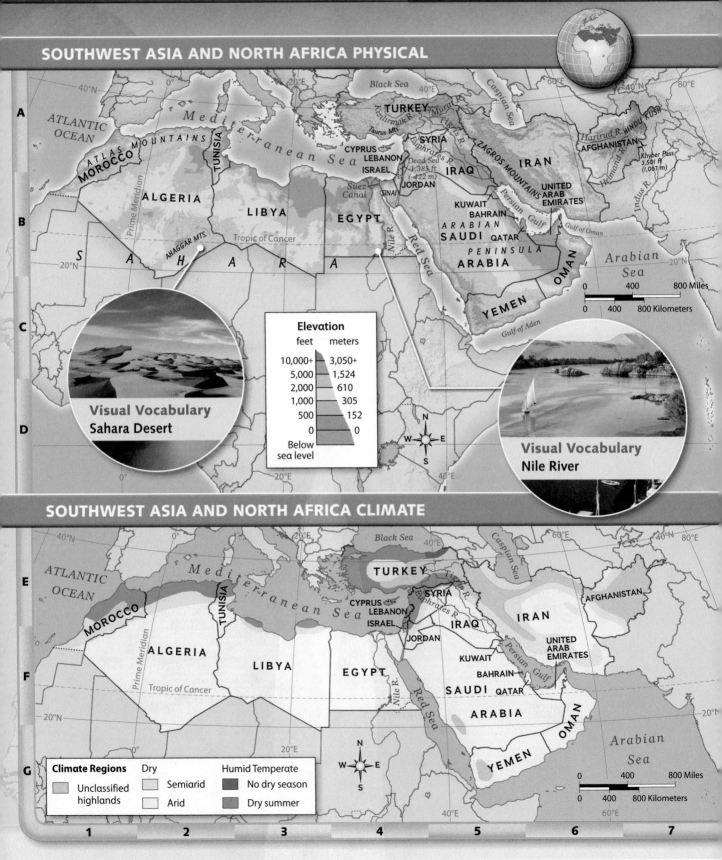

SOUTHWEST ASIA AND NORTH AFRICA PHYSICAL

ATLANTIC OCEAN

Mediterranean Sea

Black Sea

TURKEY

Kizilirmak R.

Taurus Mts.

Murat R.

Caspian Sea

ATLAS MOUNTAINS

MOROCCO

TUNISIA

CYPRUS
LEBANON
ISRAEL

SYRIA

Euphrates R.

Tigris R.

ZAGROS MOUNTAINS

IRAN

AFGHANISTAN

Harirud R. HINDU KUSH

Khyber Pass
3,501 ft
(1,067 m)

Helmand R.

Indus R.

ALGERIA

LIBYA

Dead Sea
1,385 ft
(−422 m)

JORDAN

Suez
Canal

SINAI

IRAQ

KUWAIT

BAHRAIN

UNITED
ARAB
EMIRATES

Prime Meridian

Tropic of Cancer

AHAGGAR MTS.

S   A   H   A   R   A

EGYPT

Nile R.

Red Sea

ARABIAN
SAUDI

QATAR

PENINSULA

ARABIA

Persian Gulf

Gulf of Oman

OMAN

*Arabian
Sea*

YEMEN

Gulf of Aden

40°N

0°

20°E

40°E

60°E

40°N

80°E

20°N

20°N

0   400   800 Miles
0   400   800 Kilometers

Visual Vocabulary
Sahara Desert

Elevation

feet	meters
10,000+	3,050+
5,000	1,524
2,000	610
1,000	305
500	152
0	0
Below sea level	

N
W   E
S

Visual Vocabulary
Nile River

0°   20°E   40°E

SOUTHWEST ASIA AND NORTH AFRICA CLIMATE

ATLANTIC OCEAN

Mediterranean Sea

Black Sea

TURKEY

Tigris R.

Caspian Sea

MOROCCO

TUNISIA

CYPRUS
LEBANON
ISRAEL

SYRIA

Euphrates R.

IRAQ

IRAN

AFGHANISTAN

ALGERIA

LIBYA

JORDAN

KUWAIT

BAHRAIN

UNITED
ARAB
EMIRATES

Prime Meridian

Tropic of Cancer

EGYPT

Nile R.

Red Sea

SAUDI

QATAR

Persian Gulf

ARABIA

OMAN

*Arabian
Sea*

YEMEN

40°N

0°

20°E

40°E

60°E

40°N

80°E

20°N

20°N

N
W   E
S

0   400   800 Miles
0   400   800 Kilometers

Climate Regions	Dry	Humid Temperate
Unclassified highlands	Semiarid	No dry season
	Arid	Dry summer

0°   20°E   40°E   60°E

1   2   3   4   5   6   7

6.03.C compare countries using data from maps; 6.04.D identify and locate geographic features;
6.04.E draw sketch maps, regions; 6.04.F identify location of major countries;
6.06.A describe and explain effects of physical processes; 6.06.C analyze effects of physical processes on humans;
6.07.C describe ways technology influences interaction with environment

Main Idea The expansive region of Southwest Asia and North Africa is hot, and water in the region is sometimes scarce.

Southwest Asia and North Africa span parts of the Asian and African continents. Two notable physical features located in this region are the world's longest river and its largest desert. Changes in climate in some places led to new patterns of migration and settlement.

Physical Features and Climate

Much of Southwest Asia and North Africa is made up of vast, barren deserts. This desert area is **arid**, or very dry, with extremely high daytime temperatures. For example, most of the **Sahara Desert** and Arabian Peninsula receive fewer than four inches of rain per year. Daytime temperatures can climb to 130°F.

The region includes several different mountain ranges. The Atlas Mountains are located at the tip of northwest Africa. The Zagros Mountains in Iran stretch along the Persian Gulf, and the Taurus Mountains in Turkey border the Mediterranean Sea. The climate in these mountains is semi-arid and temperatures can fall below 0°F.

Three important rivers have historically supported life in this region, and they continue to do so today. The **Nile River** flows through Egypt, and the Tigris and Euphrates rivers flow through Syria and Iraq. Water is scarce in most of this region, except near rivers and coasts. Cultures have developed and grown along these waterways. Many of the world's oldest cities are located here.

Desert Transformation

Today, the Sahara stretches 3,500 miles across North Africa from the Red Sea to the Atlantic Ocean. However, this broad area of the continent has not always been desert. The Sahara's climate has changed dramatically over time. Nearly 10,000 years ago, the world's largest desert was tropical grassland.

Around 5300 B.C., seasonal rains that watered the Sahara began shifting southward. Over time, the Sahara became a desert. The gradual transition from fertile to less productive land is called **desertification**. The drier climate prompted people living in the Sahara to migrate out of the desert. They settled in the Nile River Valley, where they found a **reliable**, or dependable, water source.

Before You Move On
Monitor Comprehension In what ways have heat and water resources defined this region?

FORMATIVE ASSESSMENT
MAP LAB  GeoJournal

1. **Location** Draw a sketch map to identify the location of the region's countries. Include the four seas, three gulfs, and three rivers. Based on the land and climate, predict how people may have adapted to the geography or used technology to live in this region.

2. **Make Inferences** Based on the climate map, compare the climates of Lebanon and Yemen. Which country can you infer receives more rainfall?

3. **Describe Geographic Information** How did the climate of the Sahara change over time, and what caused the change?

1.2 Tigris and Euphrates Rivers

TECHTREK

myNGconnect.com For an online map
and photos of the Tigris and Euphrates rivers

 Maps and
Graphs

 Digital
Library

Main Idea The Tigris and Euphrates rivers have supported life for thousands of years.

One of the world's earliest civilizations began between two rivers in a desert. The ancient name for this area is Mesopotamia, which means "land between the rivers."

Two Rivers

As you have read, the climate of this region is hot and dry. However, the area surrounding and extending from the Tigris and Euphrates rivers is known as the **Fertile Crescent.** This fertile area arcs from the Mediterranean Sea to the Persian Gulf. Its rivers and floodplains were an ideal location for early agriculture.

The source of both the Tigris and Euphrates rivers is in the mountains of Turkey. The rivers flow through parts of Turkey, Syria, and Iraq. They join at Al Qurnah, Iraq, before emptying into the Persian Gulf.

Though the Tigris and the Euphrates flow in similar directions, each river has distinct features. As the longest river in southwestern Asia, the Euphrates River is about 1,740 miles long—about 600 miles shorter than the Mississippi River in the United States. After leaving eastern Turkey, the Euphrates flows southeast through Syria and across Iraq, and is fed by two major tributaries. Over its journey, the flow of the river slows down. As the Euphrates winds through hot desert land, much of its water evaporates.

The Tigris River is also a long river, about 1,180 miles in length. After leaving Turkey, it flows southeast through Iraq. Fed by several fast-moving tributaries, the Tigris carries more water than the Euphrates. The speed and unpredictable flow of the Tigris sometimes cause major floods. Though floods can be destructive, they have also enabled development of agriculture along the rivers.

◀ **Critical Viewing** This man tends sheep along the Euphrates River in Syria. From the photo, how would you describe the climate and landscape of this river valley?

6.03.B pose and answer questions about patterns on charts, maps; 6.04.B identify, explain factors responsible for patterns of population; 6.04.D identify physical features; 6.06.A explain effects of physical processes; 6.06.C analyze effects of physical processes on humans; 6.07.A analyze how people adapt to environment; 6.07.B analyze ways people modify environment; 6.07.C describe ways technology influences human interaction with environment

TIGRIS AND EUPHRATES RIVERS

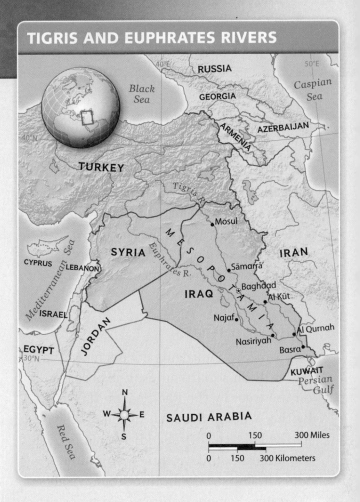

Fertile Land

The land between the rivers is an **alluvial plain**, which is a flat area of land located next to a stream or river that floods. Regular flooding deposits **silt**, or fine particles of soil, along the riverbanks. This silt makes the soil fertile.

Historically, farmers have relied on the natural flooding of the rivers to water their crops. However, farmers have also used irrigation. **Irrigation** is the process of redirecting water to crops using channels and ditches. When irrigated, crops in dry areas can grow over a wider area.

The Tigris and Euphrates rivers continue to support life. For example, most of Iraq's population lives between the two rivers and Iraq's capital, Baghdad, lies on the Tigris River. Frequent flooding used to overrun the city, but today Baghdad uses dams and embankments, or walls, to help control floods and regulate irrigation.

Before You Move On

Summarize In what ways are the Tigris and Euphrates rivers important to this region?

FORMATIVE ASSESSMENT
MAP LAB
GeoJournal

1. **Human-Environment Interaction** Explain the effects of flooding on the land in the Fertile Crescent. What effect has this process had on the people who live there?

2. **Pose and Answer Questions** What do you notice about where most cities are located in Iraq? How and why have people modified the environment in the region? With a partner, create a chart like the one below to pose and answer additional questions. Tell where you found your answers.

FERTILE CRESCENT

Question	Answer

SECTION 1 GEOGRAPHY

TECHTREK
myNGconnect.com For an online map
and photos of the Arabian deserts

1.3 The Arabian Peninsula

Main Idea The Arabian Peninsula is primarily desert and provides a large percentage of the world's petroleum.

Though the Arabian Peninsula is nearly surrounded by water, it is mostly desert. This peninsula's geologic history, or the way Earth developed over millions of years, provides the basis of its economic activity today.

Sand and Heat

The Arabian Peninsula covers more than one million square miles. It is bordered on the west by the Red Sea, on the south by the Arabian Sea, and in the northeast by the Persian Gulf. Saudi Arabia is the largest country on the peninsula. Kuwait, Oman, Qatar, the United Arab Emirates, Yemen, Bahrain, and parts of Jordan and Iraq are also on the peninsula. Temperatures in this area often rise to 130°F, and very little rain falls.

Several deserts lie on the Arabian Peninsula. The Syrian Desert is located in the northern and central part of the peninsula. Another desert, the **Rub al Khali,** covers 250,000 square miles of southern Saudi Arabia—almost the size of the state of Texas. Its name, Rub al Khali, means "empty quarter." Except for small groups of nomads, almost no one lives in the Rub al Khali.

The coasts of the peninsula contrast with its desert interior. The western part of the peninsula along the Red Sea features mountain peaks, some as high as 9,000 feet. Fertile soil along the coasts even allows for some farming. For example, date palms, which can tolerate salty soils, grow abundantly along the Persian Gulf's coastal salt flats. Salt flats are soils with high concentrations of salt. Sand and gravel cover most of this area but a valuable resource lies under it.

> **Critical Viewing** The Matrah district in the Muscat Sultanate of Oman sits on the Gulf of Oman. Based on the photo, how would you describe the district?

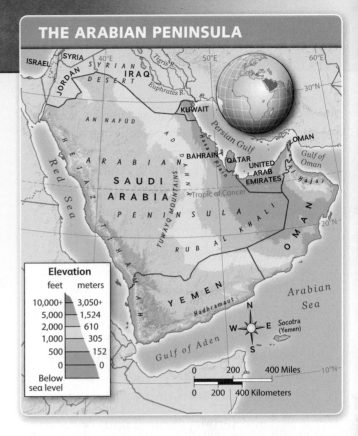

THE ARABIAN PENINSULA

Oil

Large **petroleum**, or unrefined oil, reserves lie underneath the Arabian Peninsula. Petroleum develops from tiny animals and plants that died millions of years ago. Over time, heat and pressure change these organic materials into a new substance that moves through rock layers and collects in large deposits. Once extracted from the ground, petroleum can be refined into gasoline, diesel fuel, and other products.

Because it takes so long to form, petroleum is a **nonrenewable** natural resource. As you have read, a nonrenewable resource is a resource that cannot reproduce quickly enough to keep pace with its use.

Twenty-five percent of the world's known petroleum reserves are on the Arabian Peninsula. In fact, petroleum production is the most important industry on the peninsula. Most of the countries in the world depend on petroleum in one

form or another for their energy needs. This dependence links the countries on the Arabian Peninsula to the rest of the world in critical ways.

Before You Move On

Summarize What role does the Arabian Peninsula play in the production of the world's petroleum?

FORMATIVE ASSESSMENT

PHOTO LAB   GeoJournal

1. **Analyze Visuals** Look at the photo and read the caption. Then locate approximately where this district lies on the map. Based on the photo and the map, how would you describe the physical features of this area? Consider elevation in your response.

2. **Make Inferences** Based on the photo and the text, what can you infer about patterns of settlement on the Arabian Peninsula?

3. **Human-Environment Interaction** In what ways does climate impact agriculture on the Arabian Peninsula?

1.4 Anatolian and Iranian Plateaus

TECHTREK
myNGconnect.com For an online
map and photos of Turkey and Iran

Maps and
Graphs

Digital
Library

> **Main Idea** The Anatolian and Iranian plateaus have a long history as a crossroads of trade.

Humans have lived on the Anatolian and Iranian plateaus for thousands of years. Though these plateaus are located in different parts of this region, they share characteristics and patterns of settlement.

Plateaus and Mountains

Most of Turkey sits on a peninsula called Anatolia. The Anatolian Plateau 1 is located in the central part of this peninsula. The Iranian Plateau 2 is located in the center of present-day Iran.

Seismic activity formed both plateaus. The **North Anatolian Fault** runs east to west just south of the Black Sea. Activity along this **fault**, or fracture in Earth's crust, has caused many earthquakes. Scientists believe the North Anatolian Fault may have triggered a huge, long-lasting flood about 7,500 years ago, creating the Black Sea. Tectonic shifts also shaped the Iranian Plateau. When the

Arabian and Eurasian plates pushed into each other, the Zagros Mountains formed.

The high mountains on each plateau help create a rain shadow. A rain shadow is a dry area on one side of a mountain range. Moisture from surrounding seas rises and condenses, but rain and snow fall only as the air rises up the side facing the moist winds. Land on the other side, sheltered from winds by the mountains, receives little precipitation.

Trade and Settlement

The dryness of the plateaus has meant sparse settlement. However, the climate did not discourage travelers and traders. **Oases**, or fertile places in dry areas where water is found, dot the plateaus. Across the centuries, these oases were stops for trade caravans.

Throughout history, traders have crossed the Anatolian peninsula on their way between Europe and East Asia. Traders to and from ancient Greece

> **Critical Viewing** The Zagros Mountains border the Iranian Plateau. Based on what you see in the photo, what might be some challenges of living on this plateau?

ANATOLIAN AND IRANIAN PLATEAUS

MAP TIP The dark blue lines on this map show the boundaries of the tectonic plates on which these continents lie. The plates themselves are labeled in purple. The red lines indicate country boundaries. The North Anatolian Fault lies on the boundary between the Eurasian and the Anatolian plates.

(Map of Anatolian and Iranian Plateaus region showing Black Sea, Caspian Sea, Mediterranean Sea, Red Sea, Persian Gulf, Gulf of Oman, countries including Turkey, Syria, Lebanon, Israel, Jordan, Iraq, Iran, Afghanistan, Egypt, Saudi Arabia, Kuwait, Bahrain, Qatar, United Arab Emirates, Oman, and Cyprus. Physical features include Caucasus Mountains, Taurus Mts, Zagros Mountains, Elburz Mountains, Mt. Ararat 16,854 ft (5,137 m), Mt. Damavand 18,606 ft (5,671 m), Zard Küh 14,921 ft (4,548 m), Anatolian Plate, Arabian Plate, African Plate, Eurasian Plate, Indian Plate, North Anatolian Fault, Dasht-e Kavir, Dasht-e Lut, Khuzestan Plain, Bosporus, Sea of Marmara, Tigris R., Euphrates R., Nile R., Amu Darya, Indus R.)

Legend:
— Tectonic plate boundary
— Country boundary

Scale: 0 – 200 – 400 Miles / 0 – 200 – 400 Kilometers

traveled along the Mediterranean coast. Some people moved inland, across the Taurus Mountains, and settled on the Anatolian Plateau. These settlements became stops on important trade routes.

Early human settlement took place on the Iranian Plateau, too. About 2,500 years ago, people invented a system to bring water into their arid lands. They built **qanats** (kuh NOTZ), or underground tunnels, to carry mountain waters to dry plains. This technology is still used today in Iran's capital, Tehran.

Before You Move On

Monitor Comprehension In what way does the location of the Anatolian and Iranian plateaus make them an important crossroads?

FORMATIVE ASSESSMENT

MAP LAB
GeoJournal

1. **Interpret Maps** Locate the tectonic plate boundaries on the map. Which plates does the North Anatolian Fault border? On which plates do Turkey and Iran lie?

2. **Draw Conclusions** Locate the Zagros Mountains on the map. What conclusions can you draw about how these mountains formed?

3. **Place** What climate effect do the surrounding mountain ranges have on the Anatolian and Iranian plateaus?

4. **Explain** Over time, how did trade influence settlement on the plateaus?

TECHTREK

my N G c o n n e c t . c o m For an online map and
photos of Mesopotamian artifacts

Maps and
Graphs

Digital
Library

Main Idea Mesopotamia's early civilization
contributed much to other cultures.

Mesopotamia is known as an
early **cultural hearth**, or center of
civilization from which ideas and
technology spread to other cultures. The
emergence of farming there more than
10,000 years ago allowed for advanced
societies to grow.

Agriculture Develops

As you have learned, the Fertile Crescent
extends from the Persian Gulf to the
eastern shore of the Mediterranean Sea.
About 9500 B.C., people in this fertile
land began to shift from gathering food
to growing food. This shift is called
the **agricultural revolution**. This
revolution enabled groups of people to
settle in one place and eventually develop
advanced civilizations.

In addition to farming, Mesopotamians
began to **domesticate** animals, or keep
them as a source of animal labor and
food. Farming villages grew into bigger
settlements and then cities. Eventually,
these cities unified into the world's
first **city-states**,
or independent
political units.

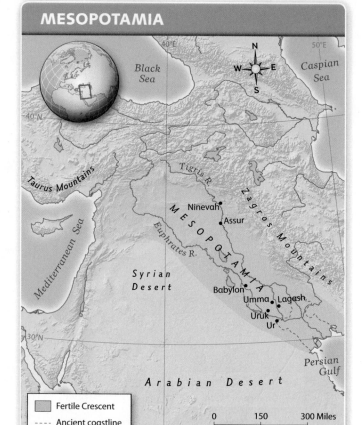

MESOPOTAMIA

Black Sea

Caspian Sea

Taurus Mountains

Mediterranean Sea

Tigris R.

Zagros Mountains

Ninevah

Assur

Euphrates R.

M E S O P O T A M I A

Syrian Desert

Babylon

Umma Lagash

Uruk

Ur

Persian Gulf

A r a b i a n   D e s e r t

Fertile Crescent

---- Ancient coastline
(about 5000 B.C.)

0   150   300 Miles

0   150   300 Kilometers

Sumer

The first Sumerian city-states formed
around 3500 B.C. Sumer was an ancient
Mesopotamian region in what is now
southeastern Iraq. Located in the lower
valley of the Tigris and Euphrates
rivers, **Ur** was one of the most important
Sumerian city-states. Between 2800
and 1850 B.C., Ur was a center of trade.

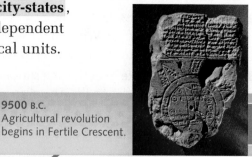

9500 B.C.
Agricultural revolution
begins in Fertile Crescent.

Ancient Mesopotamian
map with cuneiform text

1900 B.C.
Amorites conquer
Mesopotamia.

9500 B.C.   3500 B.C.   2500 B.C.

3500 B.C.
City-states begin
to develop in
Sumer.

Golden helmet from Ur, a
Mesopotamian city-state

Its location on the Euphrates River helped it become a major port. Sea-traders from Ur connected Mesopotamia with people as far away as the Indus Valley in South Asia.

Sumerians made many significant cultural contributions. They used advanced mathematics and invented the first wheeled vehicles and the first codes of law. Sumerians also used written language to record their knowledge. Sumerian writing, called **cuneiform** (kyoo NEE uh form), is the earliest known form of writing. Clay tablets carved with cuneiform provide scientists with many details about daily life and culture in Sumer.

Babylonia

Around 1900 B.C., the Amorites, a nomadic group from Arabia, conquered Mesopotamia. The Amorites adopted much of Sumerian culture and continued using cuneiform. Eventually, the conquered lands became known as Babylonia. The Babylonian Empire included all of southern Mesopotamia. During the 1700s B.C., King **Hammurabi** developed a code of law known as Hammurabi's Code.

After Hammurabi's death, outside invaders weakened the Babylonian Empire. Nearly 1,000 years after Hammurabi's rule, another strong ruler emerged. **Nebuchadnezzar** (nehb buh kuhd NEHZ uhr) was Babylonia's king from 605 to 562 B.C. His ambitious projects included rebuilding the port at Ur on the Persian Gulf and the creation of the Ishtar Gate in Babylon, the empire's capital. The Persians captured Babylonia in 539 B.C. Then, in 331 B.C., Alexander the Great from Macedonia conquered the Persians and Babylonia was never independent again.

Before You Move On

Summarize In what ways did Mesopotamia's early civilizations contribute to other cultures?

FORMATIVE ASSESSMENT

SPEAKING LAB GeoJournal

1. **Express Ideas Through Speech** What was the impact of the agricultural revolution? Work with a partner to develop an oral presentation that describes the agricultural revolution and how it impacted human development.

2. **Conduct Internet Research** Go online to research the cultural contributions of Mesopotamian civilizations. Discuss your findings with a partner.

○ **1750 B.C.**
Babylonian Empire begins decline.

Detail from Ishtar Gate of ancient Babylonia

○ **331 B.C.**
Alexander the Great takes over Babylonia.

1500 B.C.

500 B.C.

○ **1792 B.C.**
Hammurabi becomes king of Babylonia.

Sculpture of Hammurabi

○ **539 B.C.**
Persians conquer Babylonia.

2.2 Birthplace of Three Religions

TECHTREK
myNGconnect.com For a map
of the birthplace of three religions

Maps and
Graphs

Main Idea Three of the world's most influential religions began in Southwest Asia.

Judaism, **Christianity**, and **Islam** all began in Southwest Asia. All three religions are monotheistic, meaning that they worship one God.

Judaism

The Jewish people trace their ancestry to Abraham, who lived in southern Mesopotamia around 1800 B.C. According to the Hebrew Bible, God told Abraham to move his people to Canaan—where Lebanon and Israel are located today. Over hundreds of years, the descendants of Abraham developed a distinct religion, Judaism. In 1000 B.C., King David made Jerusalem the capital of the Kingdom of Israel. Jews built and rebuilt the sacred First and Second Temples there. Jerusalem remains the holiest city for Jews today.

The Jewish belief in one God was new. At the time, most people believed in many gods. The establishment of monotheism marked a shift in religious practices. The **Hebrew Bible** is the sacred text of Judaism. It contains Jewish history and teaches how to lead a moral life.

Christianity

Christianity also developed as a monotheistic religion. Among Jewish teachings was the expectation of a Messiah, a leader or savior. Jews believe the Messiah has yet to come. Christians, however, believe the Messiah was a Jew named Jesus. Born in Nazareth 2, Jesus began to preach in Galilee sometime around A.D. 30. Jesus drew many followers as he preached. Roman leaders who resented his popularity sentenced Jesus to death and he died in Jerusalem.

According to Christian literature, Jesus rose from the dead and told his followers to spread his message. The sacred book of Christianity is the **Christian Bible**, which includes the Old Testament, containing the Hebrew Bible, and the New Testament. The New Testament is about the life and teachings of Jesus.

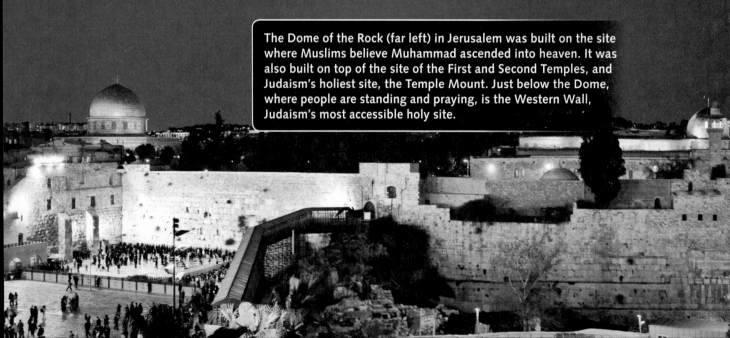

The Dome of the Rock (far left) in Jerusalem was built on the site where Muslims believe Muhammad ascended into heaven. It was also built on top of the site of the First and Second Temples, and Judaism's holiest site, the Temple Mount. Just below the Dome, where people are standing and praying, is the Western Wall, Judaism's most accessible holy site.

Islam

Another monotheistic religion that developed in this region was Islam. According to its followers, called Muslims, in the early 600s, a man from Mecca ▶3 named Muhammad received revelations from Allah, the Arabic name for God. Muslims recognize Abraham, Jesus, and others as God's messengers, or prophets. For Muslims, Muhammad is the last prophet.

The holy book of Islam is the **Qur'an**, which contains the revelations Muhammad received until his death. Muslims fulfill religious duties known as the Five Pillars of Islam. One of these duties includes a **pilgrimage**, or journey, to Mecca, in Saudi Arabia, at least once in a lifetime.

Before You Move On
Monitor Comprehension **What characteristics do these three religions share?**

BIRTHPLACE OF THREE RELIGIONS
Judaism, Christianity, and Islam

Map labels: 30°E, 40°E, Mediterranean Sea, PHOENICIA, Damascus, Nazareth, Sea of Galilee, Jordan R., Jerusalem, Jericho, PHILISTIA, Dead Sea, Alexandria, JUDAH, Giza, 30°N, EGYPT, Mt. Sinai 7,497 ft (2,285 m), Nile R., ARABIAN PENINSULA, Red Sea, Medina, Tropic of Cancer, Mecca

0   100   200 Miles
0   100   200 Kilometers

▲ **Critical Viewing** The Church of the Holy Sepulchre in Jerusalem was built on the site where Christians believe Jesus was buried. What details in the photo convey the religious nature of this setting?

FORMATIVE ASSESSMENT

READING LAB   GeoJournal

1. **Turn and Talk** With a partner, reread passages and talk about why religious institutions are basic to societies.

2. **Location** Describe Jerusalem's relative location. Then answer, *Why is it there? What is significant about its location to each of the three religions?*

3. **Understand Culture** Read more about these religions on pages R52–R54. Then conduct research to evaluate the importance of either Moses or Abraham to each religion. Prepare a brief oral report, being sure to include main ideas and important supporting ideas from your research.

2.3 Diffusion of Religions

> **Main Idea** Religions spread around the world through migration, missionaries, and trade.

In the years since becoming established as major religions, Judaism, Christianity, and Islam have spread thousands of miles from their birthplaces in Southwest Asia. The **diffusion**, or spread, of each religion happened in different ways.

Migration, Missionaries, Trade

Judaism spread through the migration of the Jewish people. In A.D. 135, the Romans killed, enslaved, or exiled most of the Jewish population. While many Jews began to move from their homeland due to persecution, or discrimination because of their beliefs, a small group of Jews maintained a continuous presence. By the 1200s, migrants had traveled as far as Eastern Europe. The spread of Jews around the world is called the **Diaspora**. As Jews in Europe faced increased persecution in the late 19th century, growing numbers returned to their ancient homeland. In 1948, the Jewish people established modern Israel there. Today, about 15 million Jews live throughout the world.

After the Roman Emperor **Constantine** legalized Christianity in 313, it became the official religion of the Roman Empire. As the empire expanded, so did Christianity. During the Middle Ages, European kings promoted Christianity in conquered lands. Beginning in the 1500s, predominantly Christian and European countries began to colonize the Americas, Africa, and other regions. Christian missionaries spread their faith. Today, Christianity has about 2.3 billion **adherents**, or followers.

Islam spread through the expansion of Muslim rule and through trade. By the 1500s, Islam had moved from the Arabian Peninsula throughout North Africa, Southwest Asia, Southeast Europe, and parts of India. Muslim traders spread Islam as they traveled and exchanged goods. Today, Islam has about 1.6 billion followers, more than any religion except for Christianity.

Before You Move On
Summarize Compare and contrast the ways in which Judaism, Christianity, and Islam spread.

1 Trade The Great Mosque (above) in Kairouan, Tunisia, was founded in 670. Kairouan was an important stop for desert trade caravans. The Great Mosque continues to be an important holy site for Muslims today.

2 Migration In 1845, 37 Jewish immigrants from Germany founded the Temple Emanu-el synagogue in New York City. As the congregation grew, it constructed new buildings, including this one, built in 1928. Temple Emanu-el is the largest synagogue in the world.

SELECTED EXAMPLES OF RELIGIOUS DIFFUSION

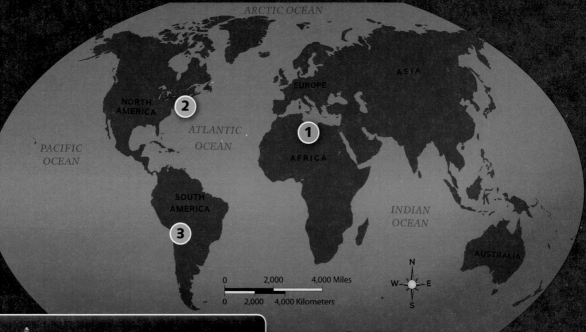

3 Missionaries Catholic missionaries arrived in present-day Bolivia in the 1540s to convert the Inca to Christianity. This cathedral in Sucre, Bolivia, was built in 1559. Christianity is the main religion in Bolivia and most of South America today.

FORMATIVE ASSESSMENT

VIEWING LAB   GeoJournal

1. **Movement** Identify each location indicated on the map. What can you infer about how and where each religion spread?

2. **Evaluate** How does the religious community at Temple Emanu-el reflect the Diaspora?

3. **Explain** How did Christianity reach the Americas? How might colonization account for the number of Christian adherents today?

TECHTREK

myNGconnect.com For an online map of the
Ottoman Empire and photos of Ottoman architecture

Maps and
Graphs

Digital
Library

Main Idea The Ottoman Empire was a powerful empire in Southwest Asia and North Africa that lasted more than five centuries.

The heart of the **Ottoman Empire** was located in what is present-day Turkey. As you have learned, Turkey is on the Anatolian Plateau, through which several trade routes crossed. Many groups had tried to control this area, including the Hittites, the Greeks, the Persians, and the Romans, who took control in A.D. 30.

The Birth of the Ottoman Empire

When the Roman Empire split in 395, this area became part of the **Byzantine Empire**, the eastern part of the Roman Empire. The Byzantines ruled parts of Anatolia and Southeast Europe for 1,000 years. Turks from Central Asia began to invade and conquer parts of the Byzantine Empire in the 1300s. These Turks became known as Ottomans, after **Osman,** the name of their first leader.

In 1453, the Ottomans defeated the Byzantine Empire. They captured the city of Constantinople, renamed it Istanbul, and made it the capital of the empire. Istanbul became an important center of trade and wealth under Ottoman rule.

The Empire at Its Height

The Ottoman Empire expanded its reach of power in the mid-1500s. Under the rule of **Suleyman I**, the Ottoman Empire stretched from present-day Hungary in Europe to the Persian Gulf and Red Sea in Asia. After Suleyman's reign, the empire continued to grow. It reached its farthest **extent**, or degree of spread, in the late 1600s.

> **Critical Viewing** Topkapi Palace in Istanbul served as a palace for Ottoman sultans from the mid-1400s to the early 1900s. Based on the photo, how might you describe this palace?

THE OTTOMAN EMPIRE, 1683

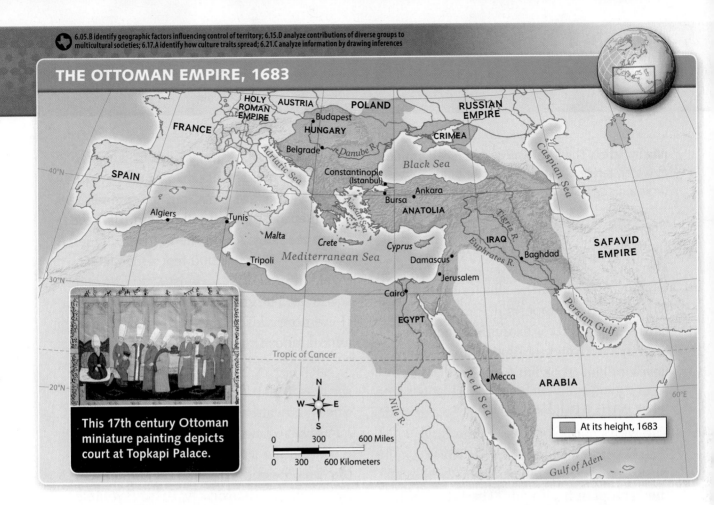

This 17th century Ottoman miniature painting depicts court at Topkapi Palace.

At its height, 1683

Most Ottoman wealth was gained through trade and taxation. The busiest trade routes in the region ran through the empire. The Ottomans controlled trade on rivers, as well as ports on important seas such as the Black Sea and the Mediterranean Sea. When the empire conquered other lands, Ottoman **sultans**, or leaders, appointed officials to collect taxes from their new subjects. Taxes were a major source of wealth in the Ottoman empire.

Because it covered such a vast area, the Ottoman Empire was composed of many different ethnic groups, including Turks, Greeks, Slavs, Arabs, and Armenians. The Ottomans were Muslim and they spread Islam throughout the empire. They were known for their **religious tolerance**. Existing religious groups maintained their own practices and communities within the empire.

Internal conflicts and wars with European countries began to weaken the empire by the late 1600s. The empire lasted into the 1900s, but after World War I, it lost most of its remaining territory. In 1923, Turkey, the last remnant of the Ottoman Empire, became a republic.

Before You Move On

Make Inferences How did the Ottoman Empire grow so powerful and last so long?

FORMATIVE ASSESSMENT
MAP LAB
GeoJournal

1. **Region** According to the map, which bodies of water did the Ottoman Empire control at its height? How did such control benefit the empire economically?

2. **Describe Geographic Information** Look at the map. Where is the capital of the Ottoman Empire? Why might that be a good location for the capital?

3.1 The Nile River Valley

TECHTREK

myNGconnect.com For an online map
and photos of the Nile River Valley

Maps and
Graphs

Digital
Library

Main Idea The Nile River has provided a source of water, fertile plains, and transportation for thousands of years.

The Nile is the longest river in the world, flowing through Africa for 4,132 miles. The United States at its widest point is still nearly 1,500 miles shorter than the Nile. The river supports life along its banks. In Egypt, for example, the Nile's regular flooding has allowed for the development of agriculture in its valley.

The Nile and Its Valley

The Nile's main sources are the Blue Nile River and the White Nile River. The Blue Nile originates from Lake Tana in the Ethiopian highlands. The White Nile originates from Lake Victoria, which lies in Tanzania, Uganda, and part of Kenya.

Unlike most rivers, which flow east, west, or south, the Nile flows north. This happens because the southern sources of the river are higher in elevation than the mouth of the river on the Mediterranean Sea. Lake Tana is 6,000 feet above sea level, and Lake Victoria is 3,720 feet above sea level. The river drops in elevation as it flows northward through Sudan and Egypt and empties into the Mediterranean.

Each spring, snows melt at the river's sources, causing predictable flooding. The floodwaters deposit rich and fertile silt along the river's floodplain. A **floodplain** is the low-lying land next to rivers formed by sediment deposited by flooding. Historically, these favorable farming conditions supported permanent settlements and the development of an advanced civilization. The ebb and flow of the river allowed farmers to plan around its flood cycles.

Critical Viewing Palm trees grow along the Nile at Armana. How does this photo fit with the written description of the Nile River Valley?

NILE RIVER VALLEY

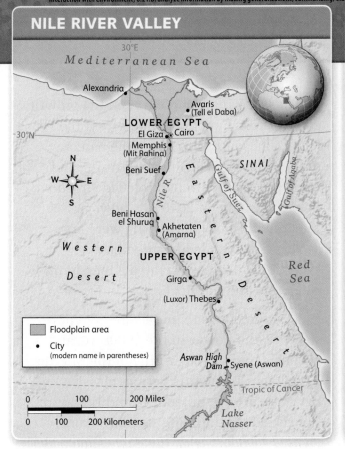

This satellite image captures the Nile River in Egypt at night. The majority of Egypt's population lives along the Nile.

The Nile Valley Today

Use of the Nile River has changed since the 1960s, when construction of a major dam began. In 1970, the **Aswan High Dam** was completed. One reason for its creation was to generate **hydroelectric power**, a form of energy created using flowing water. The Aswan High Dam provides about 15 percent of Egypt's electric power. Another reason the dam was built was to **regulate**, or control, the flooding of the Nile. Such irrigation allows for crops to be grown year-round because farmers are no longer dependent on the natural flooding cycle.

Today, the Nile River Valley is a densely populated area. In fact, about 95 percent of Egyptians live along the Nile. Surrounded by desert, the river continues to support life and agriculture along its banks.

Before You Move On

Summarize In what ways is the Nile River important to life in the region?

FORMATIVE ASSESSMENT

PHOTO LAB — GeoJournal

1. **Analyze Visuals** Based on the photo of the Nile River, what details demonstrate characteristics of a floodplain?

2. **Make Generalizations** Look at the satellite image above. What generalization can you make about settlement in the Nile Valley?

3. **Interpret Maps** What advantage might cities located along the Nile River have?

4. **Human-Environment Interaction** How and why did people modify, or change, the environment of the Nile region in 1970?

3.2 Egypt's Ancient Civilization

TECHTREK
myNGconnect.com For photos
of ancient Egyptian artifacts

Digital
Library

> **Main Idea** Egypt's ancient civilization developed significantly during four main time periods.

As you have read, as the Sahara became a desert, people who lived there began to migrate to the Nile River Valley in search of a reliable source of water. They brought with them skills in pottery, metalworking, and agriculture. By around 3000 B.C., a writing system based on pictures called **hieroglyphics** (HY ruh GLIHF ihks) had developed. For the next several thousand years, ancient Egyptian civilization thrived along the Nile River.

Old and Middle Kingdoms

Ancient Egyptian civilization is divided into four main periods, shown on the time line below. Around 3000 B.C., the kingdoms in Egypt unified under King Menes. His rule began the first **dynasty**, or series of rulers in the same family. Many dynasties followed. In the Early Dynastic period, agriculture and trade developed along the Nile. Egyptians began to build stone monuments called **pyramids**.

The Old Kingdom continued the growth of dynasties. Egypt expanded from the Nile Delta southward along the banks of the Nile. More advanced farming and trade practices enriched the Old Kingdom. Between 2150 and 2040 B.C., however, the annual floods of the Nile were not as strong, which led to a decrease in crops. This decrease created a long-term economic and political crisis in Egypt.

Menuhotep II's reign restored Egypt to stability and power in the 1900s B.C. and is considered the beginning of the Middle Kingdom. During this period, classic Egyptian arts, architecture, and literature flourished. In the 1600s B.C., however, Hyksos invaders from the East weakened and took over the Middle Kingdom.

New Kingdom

Egyptians rebelled against the Hyksos and the defeat of the Hyksos ushered in the New Kingdom—ancient Egypt's greatest period of power and wealth. Its boundaries extended into the desert, to the Red Sea and along the eastern coast of the Mediterranean Sea.

During this period, Egyptians began to call their kings **pharaohs**. One New Kingdom pharaoh was **Hatshepsut** (hat SHEHP soot), a female pharaoh.

3200 B.C. Migration to Nile River Valley	The Great Sphinx at Giza lies near King Khafre's pyramid.	**2575–2150** B.C. Old Kingdom	**1975–1640** B.C. Middle Kingdom

3000 B.C.   **2500** B.C.   **2000** B.C.

2950–2575 B.C.
Early Dynastic Period

Egyptian
hieroglyphics

During her reign, Egypt's economy was strengthened through trade. Another New Kingdom pharaoh, **Ramses II**, expanded Egypt's empire through conquest.

The New Kingdom began to decline about 1075 B.C. In 525 B.C., the Persian Empire conquered Egypt. In 332 B.C., Alexander the Great liberated Egypt from Persian rule. Alexander was a Macedonian king who overthrew many empires, including the Persians. Eventually, Egypt became a province of the Roman Empire.

Egyptian Legacies

Ancient Egyptians made important contributions to culture, knowledge, and technology. Ancient Egyptian religion emphasized the belief in an afterlife, and was built around worship of **deities**, or gods. Two important deities were the sun god, **Re**, and the goddess, **Isis**.

Ancient Egyptians invented a paper-like material called **papyrus**. They used engineering skills to build cities and pyramids, and their mathematical and scientific observations endure today.

Before You Move On

Summarize In what ways did ancient Egypt's civilization develop over its four main time periods?

Critical Viewing Artifacts like this statue from the tomb of Tutankhamen show how ancient Egyptians buried their royalty. What details from the photo indicate that King Tut is royalty?

FORMATIVE ASSESSMENT

READING LAB GeoJournal

1. **Summarize** Ancient Egypt is frequently described as "the gift of the Nile." Based on your reading, summarize the details that might lead to this description.

2. **Movement** When and why did migration to the Nile River Valley occur?

3. **Interpret Time Lines** Based on the text and the time line, what explains the gaps in years between the Old, Middle, and New Kingdoms?

1539–1075 B.C.
New Kingdom

Painting of the Egyptian goddess Isis

30 B.C.
Egypt becomes province of Roman Empire.

1500 B.C.   **1000 B.C.**   **500 B.C.**

332 B.C.
Alexander the Great conquers Egypt.

3.3 The Great Pyramids

TECHTREK
myNGconnect.com For online photos of the Egyptian pyramids

Digital Library

> **Main Idea** The ancient Egyptians built great tombs for their pharaohs.

The pyramids are among the enduring legacies of ancient Egypt. Archaeologists and engineers still marvel at how the Egyptians built the pyramids without modern machines and technology.

Royal Tombs

Egyptian pyramids were built for two reasons. One purpose of the pyramids was to provide individual **tombs**, or burial places, for royalty. Secondly, kings and pharaohs demonstrated their power by having huge pyramids built for them. Ten pyramids were built at **Giza** alone.

Pyramids were holy sites, meant to transport the pharaohs to the afterlife. Ancient Egyptians believed the dead could enjoy earthly possessions, so they filled burial chambers with clothes, food, and furniture for that purpose.

The Great Pyramid of Khufu

Built around 2550 B.C., the largest pyramid is the **Great Pyramid of Khufu,** which took 20 years to build. Initially, the pyramid stood 481 feet high. Over time, erosion has worn away the limestone and granite surface that had covered the outside of the pyramid. As a result, today the Great Pyramid is only 449 feet tall.

Critical Viewing Khufu's Great Pyramid (far right) is the oldest and tallest. It stands with the pyramids for Khafre (middle) and Menkaure (far left). What details in the photo convey the sizes of the pyramids?

6.03.A answer geographic questions, How is its location related to location of other places, environments;
6.04.D locate major human geographic features; 6.20.A give examples of technological innovations;
6.20.B explain how belief systems have affected use of technology; 6.21.C interpret information from databases, visuals

The interior of the Great Pyramid has three separate burial chambers and several passageways. Because the Great Pyramid was looted, or burglarized, by thieves seeking valuable artifacts, only Khufu's **sarcophagus**, or coffin, remains in his burial chamber.

Before You Move On

Summarize For what purposes did ancient Egyptians build the pyramids?

THE GREAT PYRAMID OF KHUFU, 2550 B.C.

3 KING'S CHAMBER
Khufu was buried in this chamber, which lies nearly at the exact center of the pyramid.

2 GRAND GALLERY
The Grand Gallery leads to the King's chamber.

4 QUEEN'S CHAMBER
Though it is called the Queen's Chamber, none of Khufu's wives were buried there. Egyptologists believe Khufu wanted more than one burial option.

1 ENTRANCE
Pyramid-builders tried to guard against robberies by constructing heavy walls to seal off entrances. However, most pyramids were looted by other Egyptians and many treasures disappeared.

5 UNFINISHED CHAMBER
The Unfinished Chamber lies underground, beneath the Great Pyramid.

VOCABULARY

For each pair of vocabulary words, write one sentence that explains the connection between the two words.

1. pharaoh; tomb

> Pyramids were built as tombs for the pharaohs.

2. hieroglyphics; papyrus
3. petroleum; nonrenewable
4. agricultural revolution; domesticate
5. desertification; arid

MAIN IDEAS

6. Describe the climate in Southwest Asia and North Africa. (Section 1.1)
7. In what ways are the Tigris and Euphrates rivers important to the region? (Section 1.2)
8. What natural resource on the Arabian Peninsula contributes most to the economy? (Section 1.3)
9. What characteristics do the Anatolian and Iranian plateaus share? (Section 1.4)
10. Why did Mesopotamia become a cultural hearth? (Section 2.1)
11. What core belief do Judaism, Christianity, and Islam share? (Section 2.2)
12. How did Judaism, Christianity, and Islam spread? (Section 2.3)
13. In what ways did the Ottoman Empire gain wealth and power? (Section 2.4)
14. How did the Nile River help early civilizations form? (Section 3.1)
15. What contributions did ancient Egyptians make to human knowledge? (Section 3.2)
16. For what purpose did ancient Egyptians build the pyramids? (Section 3.3)

GEOGRAPHY

ANALYZE THE ESSENTIAL QUESTION

How have climate and location influenced the region in the past and today?

Critical Thinking: Analyze Cause and Effect

17. When the Sahara changed from grassland to desert, how did people living there respond?
18. In what ways did the flooding of rivers influence development in the region?

HISTORY

ANALYZE THE ESSENTIAL QUESTION

How did civilizations develop in Southwest Asia and North Africa?

Critical Thinking: Summarize

19. Summarize the ways in which European countries spread Christianity.
20. What circumstances and events led to the end of the Ottoman Empire?

INTERPRET TABLES

RELIGION IN SOUTHWEST ASIA AND NORTH AFRICA				
	Christianity	Islam	Judaism	Other
Egypt	10.0%	90.0%	—	—
Israel	2.1%	16.8%	75.5%	5.6%
Jordan	6.0%	92.0%	—	2.0%
Lebanon	39.0%	59.7%	—	1.3%
Morocco	1.1%	98.7%	2.0%	—
Saudi Arabia	—	100.0%	—	—
Turkey	—	99.8%	—	0.2%

Source: CIA World Factbook, 2010

21. **Compare and Contrast** What country has the largest percentage of Christians?
22. **Make Inferences** Why does Israel have the largest Jewish population?

FOCUS ON EGYPT

ANALYZE THE ESSENTIAL QUESTION

How did an advanced civilization develop in Egypt?

Critical Thinking: Draw Conclusions

23. In what ways does the Nile River support life along its banks today?

24. Why is ancient Egypt referred to as "the gift of the Nile"?

25. In what ways do the pyramids demonstrate the advanced architectural and engineering skills of the ancient Egyptians?

INTERPRET MAPS

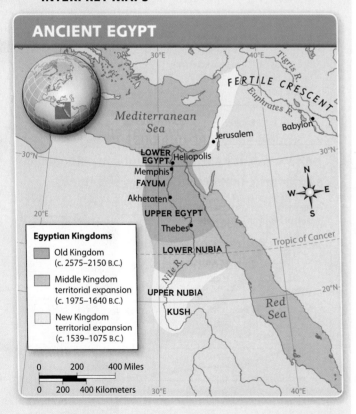

ANCIENT EGYPT

Egyptian Kingdoms
- Old Kingdom (c. 2575–2150 B.C.)
- Middle Kingdom territorial expansion (c. 1975–1640 B.C.)
- New Kingdom territorial expansion (c. 1539–1075 B.C.)

26. **Location** At its height, how far did ancient Egyptian kingdoms extend? Use the map scale to determine the north-south extent of the kingdoms.

27. **Explain** Which of Egypt's ancient kingdoms reached the furthest south? Based on what you know, what explains this expansion?

ACTIVE OPTIONS

Synthesize the Essential Questions by completing the activities below.

28. **Write about Ancient Culture** Use secondary sources, from your library or online, to write about one of the following: Nebuchadnezzar, Alexander the Great, Jesus, or a female pharaoh. Or choose an individual whose contributions to past societies you would like to evaluate and describe.

> **Writing Tips**
> - As you take notes from research, focus on main ideas and any ideas that support them.
> - Start with a hook to interest your reader, and be sure the individual's most important contributions are clear.

29. **Research Archaeological Sites** Many important artifacts from ancient civilizations have been found in Southwest Asia and North Africa. Conduct research, and prepare a chart that highlights two important archaeological sites in the region. Use online sources to gather your data. Organize your research with a chart similar to the one below.

	SITE #1	SITE #2
name and location of site		
date of discovery		
ancient civilization		
important artifacts found there		
what artifacts reveal about their civilization		

CHAPTER 16

SOUTHWEST ASIA & NORTH AFRICA TODAY

PREVIEW THE CHAPTER

Essential Question How have resources and migration shaped culture in Southwest Asia and North Africa?

SECTION 1 • CULTURE

KEY VOCABULARY

- migration
- guest worker
- strait
- mosque
- breakwater
- tsunami
- sheikh
- emirate

ACADEMIC VOCABULARY

sprawl, interact

TERMS & NAMES

- Bedouin
- Tuareg
- Bosporus Strait
- Grand Bazaar
- Hagia Sophia
- Blue Mosque
- Dubai
- United Arab Emirates

Essential Question What forces have affected the development of modern countries in the region?

SECTION 2 • GOVERNMENT & ECONOMICS

KEY VOCABULARY

- hereditary
- suffrage
- reserve
- petrochemical
- self-rule
- intifada
- coalition
- totalitarian
- extremist
- terrorist
- literate
- vocational

ACADEMIC VOCABULARY

distribute, disregard

TERMS & NAMES

- Knesset
- Jerusalem
- Palestine Liberation Organization (PLO)
- Shi'ite
- Sunni
- Kurd
- Saddam Hussein
- Taliban
- al-Qaeda

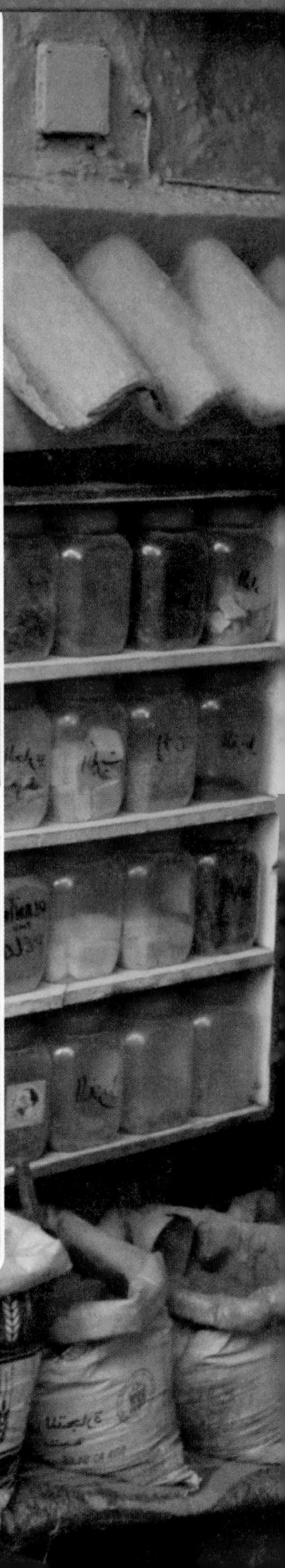

TECHTREK FOR THIS CHAPTER

Student eEdition

Maps and Graphs

Interactive Whiteboard GeoActivities

Digital Library

Go to **myNGconnect.com** for more on Southwest Asia and North Africa.

Women visit a souk, or market, in Morocco.

1.1 Migration and Trade

TECHTREK

myNGconnect.com For photos
of the Tuareg and Bedouin

Digital
Library

Main Idea Trade and migration continue to define Southwest Asia and North Africa.

Migration, or the movement from one place to another, is a familiar process in Southwest Asia and North Africa. Three kinds of migration mark this region: movement for herding, movement for trade, and movement for job opportunities.

Nomadic Herders

The **Bedouin** (BEHD u ihn) are a nomadic, Arabic-speaking people who live in the deserts of Saudi Arabia, Iraq, Syria, Israel, and Jordan. Most Bedouin trace their ancestry to the Arabian Peninsula. Strongly independent, Bedouin often identify themselves first as Bedouin rather than as citizens of a country.

The Bedouin move from place to place as they herd camels, sheep, goats, or cattle. Their migration patterns depend on the season and the needs of their herds.

Salt Traders

As you have learned, the Sahara is a vast, hot desert and a difficult physical barrier to cross. However, for those who overcame the difficulties, trade across the Sahara could be very profitable. One group of traders, the **Tuareg** (TWAH rehg), historically dominated the trans-Saharan caravan trade—especially the salt trade. The Tuareg are a semi-nomadic people who live in various North African countries, including Algeria and Libya.

Critical Viewing A Tuareg nomad leads a camel caravan across the Sahara. What details in this photo illustrate what the climate is like?

Each winter, Tuareg traders travel in small caravans across a wide expanse of barren sand dunes in the Sahara. Caravans stop at oases along the way for rest and water. At these oases, the Tuareg trade goats for salt and millet, a grain, for dates, which are dried fruits of the date palm. After returning home, the Tuareg sell the salt and dates at markets for a profit.

This desert highway is located in the western Sahara.

Guest Workers

Today's migration is prompted by a variety of different factors. Resource-rich countries such as Saudi Arabia draw millions of **guest workers**, or temporary laborers who migrate to work in another country. Companies employ guest workers to fill labor needs and shortages. Guest workers, seeking better wages than they might make in their home countries, work in industries such as oil, mining, and construction. In some cities, such as Dubai in the United Arab Emirates, guest workers represent a large percentage of the total population.

Before You Move On
Summarize How would you describe the different types of migration in the region?

FORMATIVE ASSESSMENT
PHOTO LAB   GeoJournal

1. **Analyze Visuals** Based on the photo, how would you describe a caravan? What do people use to protect themselves in this environment?

2. **Compare and Contrast** Based on the photos of the caravan and the highway, compare and contrast modern and traditional methods of movement in this region. What might be benefits and drawbacks of both methods?

3. **Movement** What factors draw guest workers to this region today?

1.2 Istanbul: Bridging East and West

TECHTREK
myNGconnect.com For a map of the Bosporus Strait and photos of Istanbul

Maps and Graphs

Digital Library

Main Idea For centuries, Istanbul has been a thriving city at the crossroads of Europe and Asia.

As the only city in the world located on two continents, Istanbul ▶ is a cultural bridge between Europe and Asia. Istanbul has had several names. It began as the ancient city of Byzantium and became Constantinople in 330. When the Ottomans claimed the city as their new capital in 1453, Constantinople became known as Istanbul. Though it is no longer a capital, Istanbul is the cultural and industrial center of Turkey.

Center of Trade and Culture

Istanbul sits on both sides of the **Bosporus Strait.** A **strait** is a narrow passage of water that connects larger bodies of water. The Bosporus Strait connects the Black Sea with the Sea of Marmara, the Aegean Sea, and, ultimately, the Mediterranean Sea. The Bosporus Strait is an important waterway that links Asia with Europe and North Africa.

Istanbul's location made this city an important center of trade for thousands of years. The **Grand Bazaar** stands as a reminder of Istanbul's history as a commerical hub. It has 5,000 shops and has been important for trade since the mid-1400s.

Istanbul is home to world-famous architecture. The Byzantines built the **Hagia Sophia** in the 500s as a Christian cathedral. In 1453, the building was converted into a **mosque**, or a Muslim place of worship. Another historical building is the **Blue Mosque**. Built in the early 1600s, it features six minarets, or tall, slender towers. The high ceilings of the Blue Mosque are decorated with more than 20,000 blue tiles that give the mosque its name.

People and cultures from all over the region converge in Istanbul. Most residents are Muslim Turks, but Istanbul is also home to many other ethnic and religious groups. Historically, diverse groups have practiced their own religions in this Muslim city.

Rapid Growth

Today, more than 13 million people live in Istanbul, a hilly city that **sprawls**, or spreads out, for more than 90 square miles. Since the 1950s, rapid population growth has created a housing shortage. Many homes were built quickly and are not earthquake-safe, a real danger for a city that sits on the very active North Anatolian Fault.

Critical Viewing This café is located near the Grand Bazaar. What details do you notice about how this tea is prepared and served?

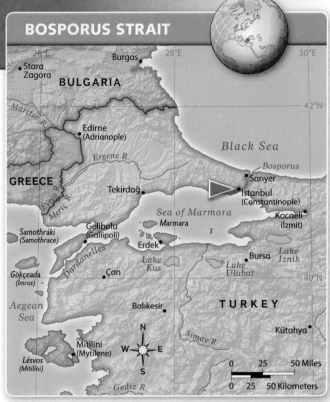

BOSPORUS STRAIT

Determined to keep pace with growth, city leaders are modernizing infrastructure and services. For example, one major building project is the construction of a tunnel under the Bosporus Strait for high-speed commuter trains. Once completed, this modern— and earthquake-safe—tunnel will help transport 1.5 million people back and forth across the Bosporus every day.

Before You Move On
Make Inferences In what ways has Istanbul connected Europe and Asia?

FORMATIVE ASSESSMENT
WRITING LAB GeoJournal

Write Reports Work with a partner to research and write a short report on Istanbul.

Step 1 Make a three-column chart with the labels Location, Trade, and Culture.

Step 2 Together, fill in the columns with details from the reading. Go to **myNGconnect.com** to add details and information to your chart.

Step 3 Use the chart to help you write a two-paragraph report that describes the city as a hub of trade and culture, both historically and today.

Critical Viewing The Hagia Sophia (left) and the Blue Mosque (right) are located in Istanbul. How would you describe the city's architecture?

1.3

SECTION **1** GEOGRAPHY
NATIONAL GEOGRAPHIC

TECHTREK
myNGconnect.com For photos of
Goodman at work and an Explorer Video Clip

Digital
Library

Exploring
Ancient Israel
with Beverly Goodman

> **Main Idea** Underwater exploration reveals clues about
> historical events in ancient Israel.

"Coastlines are the most dynamic natural environments
on earth," says National Geographic Emerging Explorer
Beverly Goodman. Goodman uses archaeology, geology, and
anthropology to study how nature and people **interact**, or
affect one another, on constantly changing coastlines.

Herod's Harbor

In 2003, Beverly Goodman and a team of archaeologists were
in Caesarea (say suh REE ah), Israel, to explore the ruins of
the harbor built by Herod the Great, King of Judea, at the end
of the first century B.C. Caesarea was a major port of trade
between the Roman Empire and Asia. It was located on the
coast of the Mediterranean Sea, in present-day Israel.

The harbor at Caesarea was one of the first
harbors constructed on the open sea and had
no peninsula or other natural protection.
Instead, Herod's builders used concrete
blocks to construct two huge **breakwaters**,
or barriers, to protect the harbor. It was a
gigantic structure, but for some reason it was
heavily damaged and today lies in ruins on
the seafloor.

myNGconnect.com

**For more on Beverly
Goodman in the
field today**

> **Critical Viewing** Caesarea was an important port city on the Mediterranean coast. How might the surrounding physical features make it difficult to preserve the ruins?

An Ancient Tsunami

Initially, Goodman focused her work on understanding the construction of the ancient harbor. However, while diving, Goodman's team found layers of pottery, stone, and shells. This discovery would not have been unusual, except that the layer of shells was more than three feet thick. Goodman and her team determined that all the shells were deposited by a single, rapid, violent event. The discovery proved that a tsunami struck and destroyed the harbor sometime in the first or second century. A **tsunami** is a giant wave caused by an earthquake, volcano, or landslide.

Goodman is making similar excavations throughout the Mediterranean. She hopes to determine a pattern of tsunami activity across the region. Her findings may help the increasing number of people living on coasts anticipate tsunamis in the future.

Before You Move On

Monitor Comprehension In what way has underwater exploration led to an increased understanding of events in ancient Israel?

FORMATIVE ASSESSMENT

VIEWING LAB GeoJournal

1. **Analyze Visuals** Watch the Explorer Video Clip and consider this question: What did you find interesting about Beverly Goodman's work?

2. **Pose and Answer Questions** After viewing the video clip, write two questions about what you saw. Ask a partner to answer your questions, and answer your partner's questions.

3. **Make Predictions** In what way might future scientific discoveries affect aspects of culture in the region? Share your ideas with a partner.

Now an archaeological park open to visitors, Caesarea is located about 60 miles northwest of Jerusalem.

1.4 Dubai: Desert City

TECHTREK

myNGconnect.com For photos
of Dubai's sand islands

 Digital
Library

> **Main Idea** Dubai is a multicultural and rapidly developing city on the Persian Gulf.

In 1959, the **sheikh**, or Arab leader, of **Dubai** decided to turn a small fishing village into a modern city in the desert. Today, Dubai is one of the fastest growing cities in the world.

Built on Sand

As both a city and a state, Dubai is one of seven **emirates**, or states, that make up the **United Arab Emirates** (UAE). The emirates are located on the Persian Gulf between Qatar, Saudi Arabia, and Oman. The UAE's location on the Persian Gulf makes it a prime trading center in this oil-rich part of the world.

Compared to other cities in the region, Dubai is a new city. Islands created out of sand from the Persian Gulf provide homes for wealthy residents and hotels for tourists. The Palm Jumeirah, the island

Critical Viewing The Palm Jumeirah is an island built out of sand from the Persian Gulf. In what ways might Dubai's sand islands extend its shoreline?

featured below, is shaped like a palm tree. Just as Dubai extended its shoreline, it has also grown its skyline. In 2009, the tallest building in the world (shown at right) opened to tourists and businesses.

Multicultural City

Dubai attracts tourists, investors, and workers from more than 150 countries. International business and tourism drive its economic growth. Businesses have moved here because they do not have to pay corporate taxes or income taxes. Dubai also has a well-developed international banking system. The global economic crisis hit Dubai and slowed its high growth rate. By 2013, tourism was helping its recovery.

Only about one in eight residents of Dubai are citizens of the United Arab Emirates. Guest workers from South Asian countries such as India represent more than 60 percent of the population. The official language of the emirate is Arabic, but people also speak Hindi, Urdu, English, and Bengali.

Because of its multicultural population, Dubai also shows a degree of religious tolerance. Located on the Arabian Peninsula, where the population is mostly Muslim, this city's Islamic mosques, Christian churches, and Hindu temples accommodate people of different faiths. Religious and ethnic conflicts among its residents are rare.

Before You Move On

Understand Culture Evaluate the contributions of Dubai's diverse groups to its multicultural society.

POPULATION OF DUBAI*

	Male	Female	Total
Employed Citizens	30,725	11,053	41,778
Employed Non-Citizens	1,183,914	126,556	1,310,470
Total Employed Persons	1,214,639	137,609	1,352,248

*Aged 15 and older

Source: Dubai Statistics Centre—Labor Force Survey, 2009

< **Critical Viewing** The Burj Khalifa stands 2,716.5 feet high and is the tallest building in the world. Based on what you can see in this photo, in what ways does the city contrast with its desert surroundings?

FORMATIVE ASSESSMENT

DATA LAB
GeoJournal

1. **Analyze Data** Look at the chart. Compare the total numbers of employed non-citizens with employed citizens in Dubai. What do you think explains the difference in numbers?

2. **Draw Conclusions** The total population of Dubai, employed and non-employed, is 1,570,923. What conclusions can you draw when you compare this number to the total number of employed citizens?

2.1 Comparing Governments

> **Main Idea** Countries in Southwest Asia and North Africa have varied types of governments.

Many governments in Southwest Asia and North Africa are monarchies. Other countries have established representative democracies. These varying governments must coexist as neighbors in the same region.

Monarchies

Saudi Arabia is a monarchy ruled by a king. The position of king is **hereditary**, or passed on through family. The Council of Ministers helps the king govern but power rests with the monarch. Ministers, many of whom are from the royal family, are appointed by the king and can be dismissed at any time. Saudi kings govern by Islamic law and the country has no formal constitution. Opposition to those in power is not tolerated and political parties are banned. Only males at least 21 years of age have **suffrage**, or the right to vote. Woman cannot vote. However, no national elections have yet been held.

Like Saudi Arabia, a hereditary monarch rules Jordan. Unlike Saudi Arabia, however, Jordan is a constitutional monarchy. In this form of government, monarchs must follow the constitution of the country and their power is not absolute. Jordan's legislative branch includes two parts: the National Assembly and the Chamber of Deputies. Monarchs appoint the members of the National Assembly but citizens elect the members of the Chamber of Deputies. All Jordanians 18 years of age and older can vote.

Democracies

While countries such as Saudi Arabia and Jordan are monarchies, other countries in the region are democracies. Israel and Turkey are two examples.

Israel is a parliamentary democracy. In this type of democracy, instead of voting for individuals, citizens cast ballots for a particular party. Based on election results, each party is assigned a number of seats in the **Knesset** (kuh NEH set), or the Israeli parliament. The Knesset then elects a president and a prime minister. Israel does not have a formal constitution, but instead has a set of basic laws passed by the Knesset as its foundation.

After the end of Ottoman rule in 1923, Turkey became a republic. A republic is a form of democratic government in which representatives elected by the people hold power. Although it was established as a republic, only one party existed in Turkey for about 25 years. Since the 1950s, though, Turkey has been a multiparty republic. In 2007, voters in Turkey approved a constitutional amendment to establish direct presidential elections.

Regional Unrest

Some governments in the region are technically democracies but have had a history of suppressing fair elections and limiting citizens' rights. Beginning in 2010, economic crises in these countries fueled political revolt.

In January 2011, several uprisings led to shifts in leadership. In Tunisia, President Ben Ali stepped down after days of protest by Tunisians. Encouraged by Tunisia's success, protesters in Egypt gathered in Cairo, demanding that President Hosni Mubarak (moo BAR uhk) step down. On February 11, he resigned the office he had held for 30 years. Libyans, watching the events in Egypt, ousted their leader, Colonel Mu'ammar al-Qadhafi (kuh DAH fee). Since these uprisings, known as the Arab Spring, protests in Syria evolved by 2013 into a civil war between the government, an unlimited regime, and those who opposed it. The same year, Egypt's military overturned its new government, and violence erupted.

Before You Move On

Summarize Explain examples of conflict between groups in the region.

> **Critical Viewing** Many Egyptians celebrated the resignation of Hosni Mubarak in Cairo's Tahir Square (shown below) on February 11, 2011. What details in the photo convey the importance of the moment?

FORMATIVE ASSESSMENT

SPEAKING LAB GeoJournal

1. **Turn and Talk** In a small group, describe the limited and unlimited governments in the region to confirm your understanding. What are some differences between the region's monarchies and democracies?

2. **Conduct Internet Research** Go online and research the heads of state for five countries in this region. Summarize how the leaders came to power. Be prepared to share your findings with the class.

2.2 Oil and Wealth

TECHTREK

myNGconnect.com For an online map
and photos of oil-rich countries in the region

Maps and Graphs   Digital Library

Main Idea Oil-producing countries in Southwest Asia and North Africa possess important sources of energy and wealth.

Petroleum, or oil in its unrefined form, was discovered in the region in the 1900s. In fact, most of the world's known petroleum deposits are concentrated in Southwest Asia and North Africa. Much of the world, including the United States, depends on the region for this important energy source.

An Oil-Rich Region

By extracting and exporting oil, several countries have grown wealthy. Among those countries, Saudi Arabia, Iran, Iraq, Kuwait, and the United Arab Emirates possess more than half of the world's known petroleum **reserves**, or future supply. About 20 percent of the world's known oil reserves are located in Saudi Arabia alone.

Even when oil prices drop, the major oil-exporters rank among the world's wealthiest countries. Some countries, such as Saudi Arabia, have used this wealth to build modern ports, airports, highways, and industrial plants. A few countries, including Kuwait and the UAE, have built industries that manufacture modern plastics and **petrochemicals**, or products made from petroleum.

Jobs in oil-rich countries have attracted guest workers. Some guest workers fill oil-producing and construction jobs. Others work in service industries or as domestic workers. Guest workers fill jobs that tend to be low-paying and temporary. In Saudi Arabia, guest workers comprise about 80 percent of the labor force; in Kuwait, they represent about 60 percent.

Critical Viewing This oil tanker is anchored in the Persian Gulf. What can you infer from the photo about the size of ships used to export oil?

OIL IN SOUTHWEST ASIA AND NORTH AFRICA

Daily Oil Production
Thousand barrels per day
- Less than 10
- 10 to 100
- 100 to 1,500
- 1,500 to 3,000
- 3,000 to 5,000
- More than 5,000
- Oil fields

Oil Wealth and the Income Gap

Like oil itself, oil wealth is not evenly **distributed**, or spread out, within the region, or even within individual countries. Oil-rich countries include large areas of desert and remote villages. People who live in these underdeveloped rural areas tend not to benefit from oil wealth. Many rural residents have migrated to cities in the region seeking better economic opportunities.

However, the income gap is widening even within large, modern cities. For example, Riyadh, Saudia Arabia, is a rapidly-expanding city of more than four million people. Although it is the capital of one of the wealthiest countries in the world, housing is expensive. Many young Saudis are unemployed, and poverty is an increasing problem.

Before You Move On

Monitor Comprehension In what ways has wealth gained from oil benefited and changed countries in the region?

OIL RESERVES / PRODUCTION, TOP FIVE OIL-PRODUCING COUNTRIES

	Saudi Arabia	Iran	Iraq	Kuwait	UAE
Barrels of Reserves	266.7 billion	137.6 billion	115 billion	104 billion	97.8 billion
Barrels Produced Per Day	9.764 million	4.172 million	2.399 million	2.494 million	2.798 million

Source: CIA World Factbook, 2009 estimates

FORMATIVE ASSESSMENT

MAP LAB  GeoJournal

1. **Location** Look at the map. Near what geographic feature are most oil fields located? How might this feature benefit the countries as exporters?

2. **Interpret Maps** Of the top five oil-producing countries, which are located on the Arabian Peninsula? What other oil-producing countries are located there?

3. **Analyze Data** Which country in this region is second to Saudi Arabia in terms of oil production and reserves? According to the map, which countries produce less than 100,000 barrels per day?

2.3 Tensions in Southwest Asia

> **Main Idea** Israelis and Palestinians have struggled over issues of land, self-rule, and security for many years.

Current tensions in Southwest Asia have a long history. Complicated matters of land, security, and **self-rule**, or the government of a country by its own people, are critical issues for both Israelis and Palestinians.

Founding Modern Israel

After World War I, many territories once ruled by the Ottomans became spheres of European rule. The area of present-day Jordan, Israel, the West Bank, and the Gaza Strip was placed under British control and named the British Mandate. Many Jews immigrated there, joining already established Jewish communities. An increased Jewish presence caused resentment among Palestinian Arabs.

The experience of the Holocaust during World War II prompted the United Nations (UN) to create a state for the Jewish people. In 1947, the UN voted to divide the British Mandate into two states: Arab and Jewish. Surrounding Arab countries and the Palestinian Arabs rejected the state offered by the UN. The Jews accepted the UN plan and in 1948 declared Israel an independent state.

Immediately, six Arab countries—Egypt, Iraq, Jordan, Syria, Saudi Arabia, and Lebanon—declared war against Israel. Before the war, many Palestinian Arabs fled to neighboring countries or to Arab towns in the West Bank. Israel won the war, and Egypt and Jordan took control of much of what the UN had proposed for an Arab state.

Israeli and Palestinian leaders meet to negotiate peace in 1993.

A series of Arab-Israeli wars followed for the next several decades. During these wars, the Arab states threatened or attacked Israel, and Israel defended itself. During the 1960s, Palestinian leaders created the **Palestine Liberation Organization (PLO).** At the time, the PLO wanted to create a Palestinian state in place of Israel.

Israelis and Palestinians Today

In 1987, Palestinians launched an intifada, or mass uprising. Palestinians protested—sometimes violently—against Israeli control of the Gaza Strip and the West Bank. In the 1990s, leaders of Israel, Arab countries, and the Palestinians began peace talks. Israel agreed to give the Palestinians self-rule in the Gaza Strip and the West Bank. Palestinians agreed to recognize Israel's right to exist and to renounce terrorism and violence. However, Palestinian terrorism against Israelis increased. Israel withdrew completely from the Gaza Strip and turned over control of much of the West Bank to the Palestinians.

Efforts toward peace stalled, however. Israelis and Palestinians could not agree on several issues—especially **Jerusalem.** Israel's capital is Jerusalem, but Palestinians also want to establish East Jerusalem as their capital. Tensions over the collapse of the peace process led to a second intifada in 2000. In response to the violence, in 2002, Israel began building a security barrier along the boundary between Israel and the West Bank. Permits are required to pass through the checkpoints along the barrier, which divides many workers from their workplaces and people from basic services. In ten years, the barrier had reduced, but not ended, violence.

ISRAEL POLITICAL

MAP TIP
Palestinians have self-rule in the Gaza Strip and limited rule in the West Bank. The permanent status of these areas is undecided.

Palestinians still desire a state. Israelis still desire security. World leaders are helping work toward a peaceful solution but progress is slow.

Before You Move On
Make Inferences What issues divide Israelis and Palestinians?

FORMATIVE ASSESSMENT

MAP LAB
GeoJournal

1. **Interpret Maps** Locate Israel on the map. Explain the significance of its location.

2. **Make Inferences** Find the Gaza Strip and the West Bank on the map. How might the location of these territories present challenges for Palestinian self-rule?

3. **Movement** In what ways is movement restricted among people who live in Israel and the West Bank?

2.4 Iraq's Problems and Promise

Main Idea Internal division and wars have caused great problems for Iraq, but a move toward democracy promises a better future.

For much of its modern history, Iraq has been torn by war and ruled by foreign rulers or dictators. In recent years, however, democracy—and with it, hope for the future—has begun to take root.

Religious and Ethnic Divisions

Internal divisions have a long history in Iraq. When the Ottoman Empire ended after World War I, Great Britain established a monarchy in Iraq and defined the country's borders. The new territory brought together two distinct Arabic groups, **Shi'ite** (SHEE eyt) and **Sunni** (SOO nee) Muslims.

These two Muslim groups have been divided since the death of Muhammad, Islam's founder, in 632. The Shi'ites believe that the leaders of Islam should be descendants of Muhammad. The Sunnis believe that Islam's leaders should be chosen from those most qualified. About 75 percent of the world's Muslims are Sunni. However, Shi'ites represent about 60 percent of Iraq's population.

Iraq's newly established borders also included members of an ethnic group called the Kurds. The **Kurds** are Sunni Muslims but have a history, language, and culture that differs from their Arabic neighbors. Kurds represent 15 to 20 percent of Iraq's population. Because they are a minority ethnic group, the Kurds have at different times in their history experienced serious discrimination.

War-Torn Nation

Iraq waged war in the 1980s with neighboring Iran partly as a result of the Sunni-Shi'ite divide. The largely Shi'ite Iran had overthrown its monarch in 1979 and established an Islamic government. Iraqi president **Saddam Hussein** was a Sunni Muslim who rose to power that same year. He feared that the Iranian Shi'ites would persuade the Shi'ites in Iraq to overthrow his government. The two countries fought for eight years, and the war ended with no clear winner.

In 1990, Iraq invaded Kuwait. Hussein claimed that Kuwait had been stealing Iraqi oil. In late 1990 and early 1991, the United States formed a **coalition**, or alliance, with other countries. Coalition countries drove Iraqi forces from Kuwait.

Move Toward Democracy

In 2003, another coalition of countries invaded Iraq. The coalition believed that Iraq was concealing weapons of mass destruction. Although none were found, the coalition removed Hussein from power. Many Iraqis were relieved. As a **totalitarian** dictator, Hussein had demanded complete obedience and ruled through terror.

In 2005, free elections were held in Iraq and legislators drafted a democratic constitution. Violence still occurs, but Iraqis are working to stabilize and rebuild their country.

Before You Move On

Summarize What factors do you think make Iraq's future look promising?

6.01.B evaluate relationship between past conflict and current conditions; 6.15.F identify and explain examples of conflict; 6.17.A evaluate impact of improved communications technology among cultures; 6.20.C make predictions about future cultural impacts from technological innovations; 6.21.B analyze by identifying cause-effect relationships, making predictions; 6.21.C interpret information from maps

IRAQ'S RELIGIOUS AND ETHNIC DIVISIONS

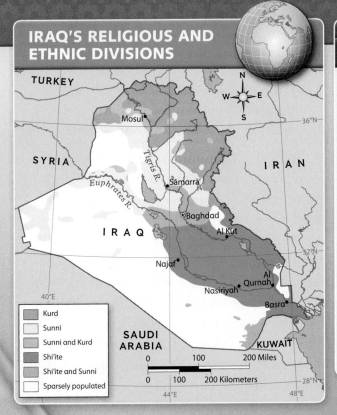

TURKEY

SYRIA

IRAN

Mosul

Tigris R.

Euphrates R.

Sāmarrā'

Baghdad

Al Kut

IRAQ

Najaf

Nasiriyah

Al Qurnah

Basra

SAUDI ARABIA

KUWAIT

36°N

40°E

44°E

48°E

28°N

Legend:
- Kurd
- Sunni
- Sunni and Kurd
- Shi'ite
- Shi'ite and Sunni
- Sparsely populated

0   100   200 Miles

0   100   200 Kilometers

FORMATIVE ASSESSMENT

MAP LAB

GeoJournal

1. **Interpret Maps** Locate the Tigris River. Which groups live along the river north of Baghdad? Which groups live along the river south of Baghdad? Which cities are located on the Tigris River?

2. **Analyze Cause and Effect** Locate Iraq's Shi'ite population and Iraq's neighbor, Iran. How did the establishment of a Shi'ite government in Iran lead to the Iran-Iraq war?

3. **Make Predictions** Iraqis get their news from television and several daily newspapers. Internet use is not as widespread, but about 80% of the population has mobile phones. Do you think technology can play a role in bringing cultures together? If so, how? If not, explain.

Critical Viewing Iraqi women hold up ink-stained fingers indicating participation in provincial elections. What details in the photo suggest their feelings of pride?

2.5 Afghanistan: Moving Forward

TECHTREK
myNGconnect.com For a
map of Afghanistan

 **Maps and
Graphs**

> **Main Idea** Afghanistan struggles to define itself and move forward in the modern political world.

Afghanistan is one of the world's poorest countries. After decades of war and upheaval, the country is trying to build a stable central government.

Afghanistan Divided

The physical features and ethnic diversity of Afghanistan complicate efforts to unify the country. First, Afghanistan is landlocked and its mountains and deserts make travel in the country difficult. Second, about 80 percent of Afghanistan's population is rural. Widely scattered, isolated villages focus on local, rather than national, affairs. Third, Afghanistan's population includes several ethnic groups. Rural Afghans identify with their ethnic groups rather than as citizens of

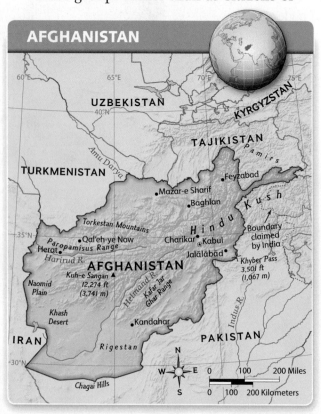

AFGHANISTAN

Afghanistan. Of Afghanistan's ethnic groups, Pashtun are most numerous, followed by Tajik, Hazara, and Uzbek.

In 1978, a Communist political party took power. This new government **disregarded**, or ignored, local ethnic and religious customs and forced policies of modernization. The speed and extent of change triggered rebellions throughout the country. Afghan leaders asked another communist government, the Soviet Union, for help. In 1979, the Soviets invaded Afghanistan. Islamic forces known as mujahedeen (moo ja heh DEEN) fought the Soviets for ten years.

After the Soviet Union withdrew from Afghanistan in 1989, the Afghan government fell, civil war tore the country apart, and locally armed leaders took control of much of the country. A group of Pashtuns known as the **Taliban** brought these local leaders under control and in 1996 seized the capital, Kabul.

The Impact of Extremism

The Taliban are **extremists**, or people who hold rigid religious or political views. The Taliban immediately imposed their own brand of Islamic law. They destroyed non-Islamic works of art and enforced strict dress and behavior codes. The Taliban forbade women to work, go to school, or leave the house without a male relative.

Because of Taliban rule, Afghanistan became attractive to other extremist groups, including a group called **al-Qaeda**. On September 11, 2001, 19 al-Qaeda **terrorists**, or people who use violence to achieve political results, hijacked four U.S.

airplanes. They flew the planes into the towers of the World Trade Center in New York City and the Pentagon in Washington D.C. A plane headed for the White House crashed in a Pennsylvania field. In response, the United States and its allies bombed terrorist camps in Afghanistan. The Taliban were removed from power and a new government was established, but violent conflict continued.

Today, Afghanistan remains divided, but efforts to unify the country through elections continue. Most Afghan leaders believe that with political stability, economic development will follow.

Before You Move On

Evaluate What is the relationship between past conflicts and the current situation in Afghanistan?

FORMATIVE ASSESSMENT

READING LAB   GeoJournal

1. **Summarize** What factors have complicated efforts to unify Afghanistan?

2. **Turn and Talk** On pages 66–67, you read about human rights. How do you think Taliban rule failed to protect the rights of Afghanistan citizens?

3. **Movement** On the map, notice how much of Afghanistan is covered by mountains. How might Afghanistan's physical features influence settlement patterns?

Critical Viewing Afghan girls collect water outside Kabul, Afghanistan's capital. From what you can infer from the photo, in what ways is Kabul a modern city, and in what ways is it still developing?

2.6 Building Schools

TECHTREK

myNGconnect.com For photos and research links on building schools

 Digital Library   Global Issues

> **Main Idea** Building schools in Afghanistan and other developing countries is critical to the future.

KEY VOCABULARY

literate, adj., able to read and write

vocational, adj., related to a job or profession

For more than 30 years, Afghanistan has endured armed conflict, invasion, and instability. As a result, more than half of Afghan children do not attend school. Building schools in this country and in other parts of the developing world is a key part of improving children's lives and futures.

Building Schools

According to the United Nations Children's Emergency Fund (UNICEF), only 28 percent of all Afghans are literate, or able to read and write. Lack of schools is one reason for low literacy rates in the war-torn country.

As you have read, when Taliban rulers took power in Afghanistan in the 1990s, they imposed their own form of Islamic law. Under Taliban rule, Afghan children, especially girls, had little or no access to education. In early 2002, just after the Taliban was pushed out, fewer than one million children in Afghanistan attended school. None of these students were girls.

Recognizing an immediate humanitarian need, multiple agencies worked with tribal leaders, military officials, and teachers in Afghanistan to build and re-open schools for Afghan children. By 2010, seven million students in Afghanistan attended school. Of these students, 37 percent were girls. New or re-built schools have been established in rural areas of Afghanistan and neighboring Pakistan, and literacy levels are climbing. In addition to teaching children to read and write, these schools offer health education and provide **vocational**, or job skills, training.

Before You Move On

Summarize What factors motivated agencies to build or re-open schools in Afghanistan?

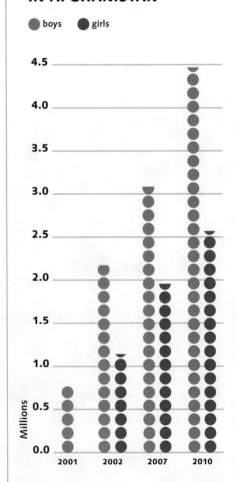

SCHOOL ATTENDANCE* IN AFGHANISTAN

● boys   ● girls

*Equivalent of Grades 1–6

Source: Ministry of Education, Afghanistan, 2010; UNESCO Institute for Statistics, 2010

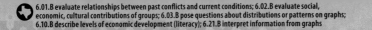

Inspiring people to care about the planet
National Geographic Society Mission

Educating Girls

One challenge facing developing countries such as Afghanistan is that many girls do not attend school or they leave school at an early age. For example, on average, girls in Afghanistan attend school four fewer years than boys. Limited attendance at school results in lower rates of literacy.

Research shows that girls and women equipped with education can bring about positive change in their families and in their communities. Worldwide, a higher level of education for mothers is linked to better infant and child health. In addition, the number of years a girl spends in school is linked to her level of earnings as an adult. When women and girls earn income in the developing world, they usually invest 90 percent of that income back into their families.

COMPARE ACROSS REGIONS

Schools for Africa

As one of the agencies working in Afghanistan, UNICEF recognizes the importance of building schools in war-torn and developing countries. Through its Schools for Africa program, UNICEF also partners with communities and local governments to build schools, improve classrooms, and increase access to education and opportunities for more than eight million children in at least 11 African countries.

One of these countries is Niger. Like Afghanistan, Niger is an extremely poor country. Only 38 percent of school-aged children attend school. Also like Afghanistan, school attendance rates

 Critical Viewing Based on your school experiences and the past conflicts you read about, tell why this Afghan school's learning environment is important.

for girls are lower than for boys. Because of a lack of education, many girls marry and have children at a young age and tend to remain in poverty.

Schools for Africa is active in other sub-Saharan countries, including Malawi, Angola, and Rwanda. Through partnership with local residents, Schools for Africa aims to improve children's lives.

Before You Move On
Summarize In what ways does educating girls help strengthen communities?

FORMATIVE ASSESSMENT
READING LAB GeoJournal

1. **Evaluate** What social contributions have UNICEF and Schools for Africa made? How might these groups also be important economically and culturally?

2. **Make Generalizations** What activities by governments and educational institutions are needed to keep literacy rates high and keep citizens informed?

VOCABULARY

For each pair of vocabulary words, write one sentence that explains the connection between the two words.

1. guest worker; migration

> Modern migration in the region includes guest workers from many countries.

2. breakwater; tsunami
3. petrochemical; reserve
4. sheikh; emirate
5. terrorist; extremist
6. literate; vocational

MAIN IDEAS

7. In what ways have migration and trade shaped this region? (Section 1.1)
8. What factors make Istanbul a center of commerce? (Section 1.2)
9. How might underwater exploration of ancient sites help people living on coasts today? (Section 1.3)
10. What factors have encouraged the rapid economic growth of Dubai? (Section 1.4)
11. What are characterstics of two systems of government in the region? (Section 2.1)
12. What important resources do countries in this region possess? (Section 2.2)
13. What issues have led to violence among Israelis and Palestinians? (Section 2.3)
14. What challenges does Iraq face at home and internationally? (Section 2.4)
15. In what ways do ethnic and geographic factors divide Afghanistan? (Section 2.5)
16. Why is building schools in Afghanistan an important goal? (Section 2.6)

CULTURE

ANALYZE THE ESSENTIAL QUESTION

How have resources and migration shaped culture in Southwest Asia and North Africa?

Critical Thinking: Make Generalizations

17. In what ways has migration defined the population and culture of Dubai?
18. What factors have made Istanbul the cultural center of Turkey?
19. What characteristics do different patterns of migration in the region share?

INTERPRET GRAPHS

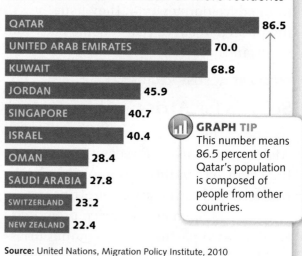

INTERNATIONAL MIGRANTS IN SELECTED COUNTRIES, 2010

Percentage of total population, countries with one million or more residents

Country	Percentage
QATAR	86.5
UNITED ARAB EMIRATES	70.0
KUWAIT	68.8
JORDAN	45.9
SINGAPORE	40.7
ISRAEL	40.4
OMAN	28.4
SAUDI ARABIA	27.8
SWITZERLAND	23.2
NEW ZEALAND	22.4

GRAPH TIP This number means 86.5 percent of Qatar's population is composed of people from other countries.

Source: United Nations, Migration Policy Institute, 2010

20. **Explain** Of the countries selected for this graph, which of them are located on the Arabian Peninsula? What factors draw international migrants to countries located on the Arabian Peninsula?
21. **Make Inferences** Based on what you know, why might the United Arab Emirates have more international migrants than Israel?

GOVERNMENT & ECONOMICS

ANALYZE THE ESSENTIAL QUESTION

What forces have affected the development of modern countries in the region?

Critical Thinking: Evaluate

22. In what ways has conflict over land caused problems in Israel?

23. What are some ways in which Afghanistan is moving forward in the modern world?

24. What impact did the discovery of petroleum have on the culture of oil-rich countries?

INTERPRET MAPS

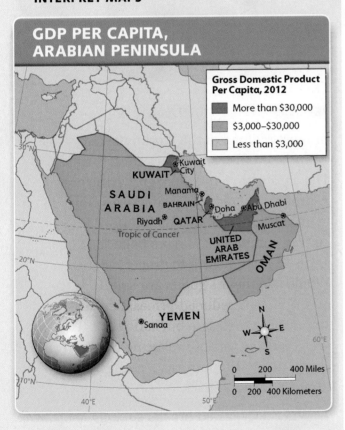

GDP PER CAPITA, ARABIAN PENINSULA

Gross Domestic Product Per Capita, 2012
- More than $30,000
- $3,000–$30,000
- Less than $3,000

25. **Make Inferences** What can you infer from the map about the economic significance of the oil industry?

26. **Compare** Compare the GDP per capita of Kuwait and Yemen. Based on what you know, what might explain the difference?

ACTIVE OPTIONS

Synthesize the Essential Questions by completing the activities below.

27. **Write Discussion Questions** Explore the geographic, cultural, and historical factors that have shaped the region by writing discussion questions for a roundtable. As a group, choose three countries in this region and write discussion questions about each country. Elect a roundtable host, and decide which questions the host will ask. **Present your roundtable in class. Be prepared to answer questions from your audience.**

> **Writing Tips**
> - Research your country selection thoroughly.
> - Write questions that require more than a "yes" or "no" or one-word answer.

Go to **Student Resources** for Guided Writing support.

28. **Understand Culture** Countries in this region have rich cultures. Working with a partner, choose two countries and do research to answer this question: Which cultural traits do these countries share, and which are unique to each country? Use online sources to gather your information. Use a Venn diagram to organize the information you find. Share your diagrams with other groups.

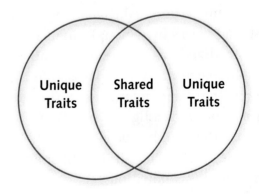

Unique Traits | Shared Traits | Unique Traits

The World's Bread

In Egypt, *baladi* and *pita* are breads eaten almost every day. All over the world, bread is a staple, or main food. Most cultures have one or more traditional forms of bread. Bread comes in a variety of shapes and sizes. It can be made from the ground flour of grains such as wheat, barley, rye, oats, or flaxseed.

Two main categories of bread are leavened and unleavened. Leavened breads are made with yeast, a microorganism used to make bread dough rise. Sandwich bread is an example of leavened bread. Unleavened breads—like many flatbreads eaten around the world—are made without yeast.

Compare

- Egypt
- France
- India
- Mexico
- Peru
- Russia
- United States

REGIONAL GRAINS, LOCAL BREADS

Types of bread vary around the world. Bread can be made from locally grown grains, or even vegetables. Flour made from barley is used to make Egyptian flatbreads. In Peru, potatoes provide a base for potato rolls. Both cornmeal and flour are used to make two different kinds of tortillas in Mexico and other Latin American countries.

How much processing goes into flours for bread varies by region. In highly industrialized countries such as the United States, wheat is processed to remove the rough outer layer of the wheat grain to produce a light, white flour. Because the bran has been removed, processed flours contain less fiber and are considered less nutritious.

PROCESS AND DISTRIBUTION

In most regions of the world, making large quantities of bread follows these stages: The agriculture industry grows the grains. A processing plant manufactures flour from the grains and sells the flour to baking companies. Bakers bake the bread and sell it wholesale to grocery stores. **Wholesale** means goods are sold in large quantities for reduced prices. Grocery stores buy wholesale but sell retail. They are **retail** industries, meaning they sell goods in small quantities or single units directly to customers.

Whether yeasted breads such as baguettes in France or unleavened flatbreads such as a naan bread in India, bread has fed people for centuries. Compare the regional breads on the opposite page.

BREAD AROUND THE WORLD

The price of bread to consumers varies around the world. Some governments subsidize the price, or pay to reduce the cost, in order to make bread affordable to its poorest citizens. Elsewhere, grain prices directly sway the market. The prices per loaf shown here are estimates.

35¢

Potato rolls
(Peru)

When wheat prices soared in 2008, the Peruvian government promoted bread made from locally grown potatoes.

$1.37

White bread
(United States)

Many Americans have switched to whole wheat loaves for health reasons, but heavily processed white bread is still popular with consumers.

89¢

Brown bread
(Russia)

The Russian governnment hopes increased wheat plantings will continue to lower the cost of this staple.

1¢

Pita (Egypt)

A hollow, leavened flatbread, pita is the foundation of many meals. The Egyptian government subsidizes the price.

$1.50

Baguette (France)

An icon of French cuisine, the price of baguettes has increased steadily. In 2002, a loaf cost about 70 cents.

Source: *National Geographic* October; 2008; U.S. Bureau of Labor Statistics, 2013

FORMATIVE ASSESSMENT
RESEARCH LAB GeoJournal

1. **Create a Flow Chart** In a flow chart, show the industries involved in making and selling breads. Define each industry and give an example for each (agricultural, manufacturing, wholesale, and retail) that you know of from your daily life.

2. **Make Inferences** Why do you think some breads are more expensive than others?

Research and Create Charts Research the breads of Mexico and India. Learn about different flours used to make breads in those countries, and determine whether their governments subsidize the price. Identify breads made both for everyday use and for special holidays or festivals. Create a chart organizing your information.

Active Options

ACTIVITY 1

Goal: Extend your understanding of trade in the region.

Draw a Map

For 2,000 years, the Silk Roads connected
Asia, Europe, and Africa and were major
routes for trade and cultural exchange.
Do research and draw a map that shows
the path of the Silk Roads as they crossed
Southwest Asia and North
Africa. Include major
cities and any other
relevant detail.

Caravan crossing
the Silk Roads, as
detailed on a 14th
century Spanish map

ACTIVITY 2

Goal: Research ancient Egyptian culture.

Write Field Notes

Conduct online research to take a virtual
tour of the Valley of the Kings. Take notes
on what you observe, and keep a written
log of all the stops you make. Use the
Magazine Maker CD-ROM to record in
each log entry what you see. Include any
visuals that might let others see what you
are experiencing.

ACTIVITY 3

Goal: Learn more about recycling.

Make a Decision

National Geographic Emerging Explorer
Thomas Taha (TH) Rassam-Culhane
helps people in Egypt and around the
world think creatively about how to
recycle used materials. With a small
group, research online to learn new
ways to reuse materials. Then follow
the process on page R19 to decide
on a recycling project to propose to
your school.

6.03.D create maps of world regions; 6.18.A explain relationships between societies and their art, music, and literature; 6.18.D identify examples of art, music, and literature that convey universal themes; 6.22.D create written and visual material based on research; 6.23.B use a decision-making process

TEKS

TEKS PROJECT

Goal: Understand culture and relationships among societies and their arts.

Create a Culture Time Capsule

In the mid 20th century, ancient scrolls and texts were discovered in caves near the Dead Sea and in the Egyptian desert. The dry climate conditions in both places helped preserve these writings for 1,500 years or more. Like time capsules, the discoveries allowed people in the future to learn about times past.

Imagine a future people who cannot understand your language but who might envision your daily life through drawings, objects, photographs, or a scrapbook. Create a time capsule to show your day-to-day life. You might invent a code, too, by making drawings for simple English words.

This gold bracelet with its lapis lazuli stone may have been worn by the pharoah Ramses II.

Team Up and Talk With a group, discuss these topics, explaining your thoughts:

• What would your time capsule choices "say" about your society? What people hope for is often revealed in the arts they create, whether in a song, game, or film. Share some examples that come to mind.

• What printed and electronic works might have appeal beyond your culture? Think about tragic and comic situations and emotions people have, everywhere, past and present. Listen to your classmate's examples and ask for explanations about those you are unfamiliar with.

Collect the Contents Together form an idea for a culture time capsule, including its contents and how you will store the materials. You might create individual scrapbooks or take photos of life around you over the course of a week. Consider scanning images and items to create a virtual time capsule, which you can project for a school presentation.

Put It Together Make or gather what you have decided to include in your capsule. Get in touch with the International Time Capsule Society of Oglethorpe University in Atlanta, Georgia, which keeps a database of time capsules.

Explore South Asia

with NATIONAL GEOGRAPHIC

MEET THE EXPLORER

NATIONAL GEOGRAPHIC

Emerging Explorer Shafqat Hussain created Project Snow Leopard to save the endangered snow leopard species and boost the local economy in the mountain regions of Pakistan.

INVESTIGATE GEOGRAPHY

Mount Everest, on the border of Nepal and China, is the ultimate climbing challenge. In 2006, 70-year-old Takao Arayama became the oldest to climb it. In 2010, 13-year-old Jordan Romero became the youngest. At 29,035 feet, Everest is the tallest mountain in the world.

STEP INTO HISTORY

The Taj Mahal, a UNESCO World Heritage site, has attracted visitors to India since it was built in the 1600s. The white marble masterpiece was built by Emperor Shah Jahan as a memorial to his wife. The project took 20,000 workers 22 years to complete.

7,486 miles

New Delhi, India

Washington, D.C.

Go to myNGconnect.com for maps of South Asia.

CONNECT WITH THE CULTURE

These women are participating in a wedding in Rajasthan, India. Weddings in South Asia are elaborate celebrations that may last for several days and include hundreds of guests.

467

South Asia
GEOGRAPHY & HISTORY

PREVIEW THE CHAPTER

Essential Question How do South Asia's water systems affect how people in the region live?

SECTION 1 • GEOGRAPHY

KEY VOCABULARY

- subcontinent
- plate
- delta
- elevation
- subsistence farmer
- monsoon
- evaporation
- drought
- arable
- famine
- sustainable
- conservation
- ecosystem
- pollution
- sanitation
- aquifer

ACADEMIC VOCABULARY
collide, reverse

TERMS & NAMES

- Himalaya Mountains
- Deccan Plateau
- Indus River
- Ganges Delta

Essential Question How have physical features, religion, and empires shaped South Asia's borders?

SECTION 2 • HISTORY

KEY VOCABULARY

- isolation
- cultural hearth
- caste system
- empire
- tolerance
- deity
- reincarnation
- colonialism
- civil disobedience
- mythology
- symbol

ACADEMIC VOCABULARY
isolation, displace

TERMS & NAMES

- Harappan
- Aryans
- Sanskrit
- Asoka
- Taj Mahal
- Hinduism
- Buddhism
- Jainism
- Sikhism
- Islam
- Vedas
- Mohandas Gandhi
- Partition
- Bhagavad Gita

TECHTREK

FOR THIS CHAPTER

Student
eEdition

Maps and
Graphs

Interactive
Whiteboard
GeoActivities

Digital
Library

Go to **myNGconnect.com** for more on South Asia.

snow leopard

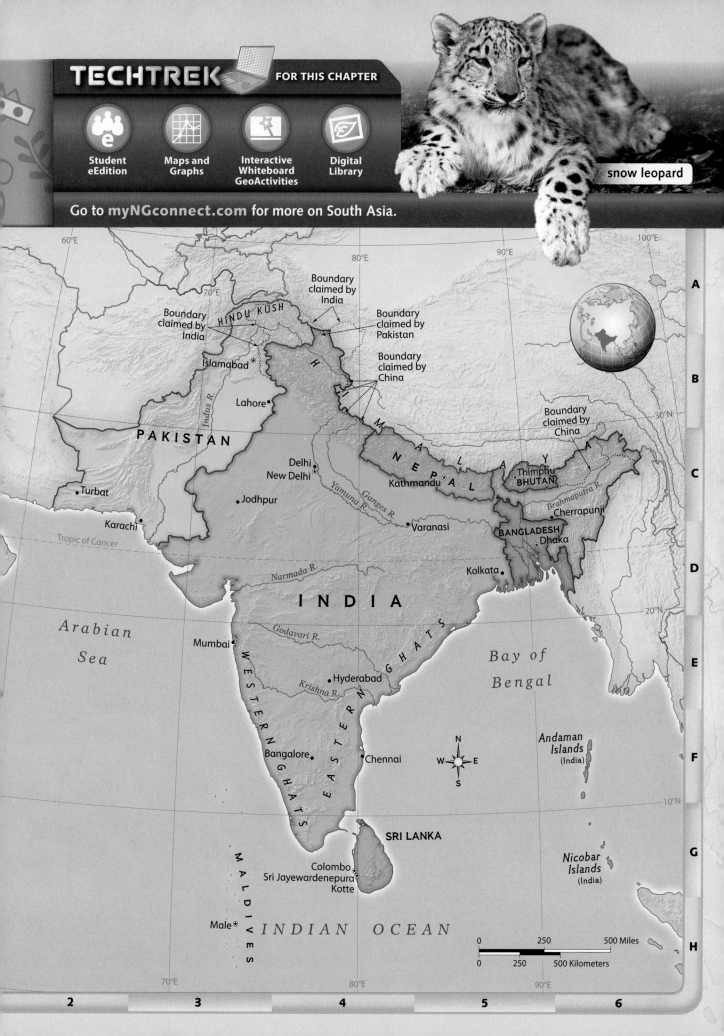

Boundary
claimed by
India

HINDU KUSH

Boundary
claimed by
India

Boundary
claimed by
Pakistan

Boundary
claimed by
China

Boundary
claimed by
China

Islamabad ✳

H
I
M
A
L
A
Y
A

Lahore •

PAKISTAN

NEPAL

Thimphu ✳
BHUTAN

Indus R.

Delhi •
New Delhi ✳

Kathmandu ✳

• Turbat

Jodhpur •

Yamuna R.

Ganges R.

Brahmaputra R.

• Cherrapunji

Karachi •

Varanasi •

BANGLADESH
Dhaka •

Tropic of Cancer

Narmada R.

Kolkata •

INDIA

Arabian
Sea

Godavari R.

Mumbai •

Bay of
Bengal

Hyderabad •

Krishna R.

W
E
S
T
E
R
N
G
H
A
T
S

E
A
S
T
E
R
N
G
H
A
T
S

Andaman
Islands
(India)

Bangalore •

Chennai •

N
W   E
S

SRI LANKA

M
A
L
D
I
V
E
S

Colombo •
Sri Jayewardenepura
Kotte

Nicobar
Islands
(India)

Male ✳

INDIAN   OCEAN

0   250   500 Miles

0   250   500 Kilometers

SOUTH ASIA PHYSICAL

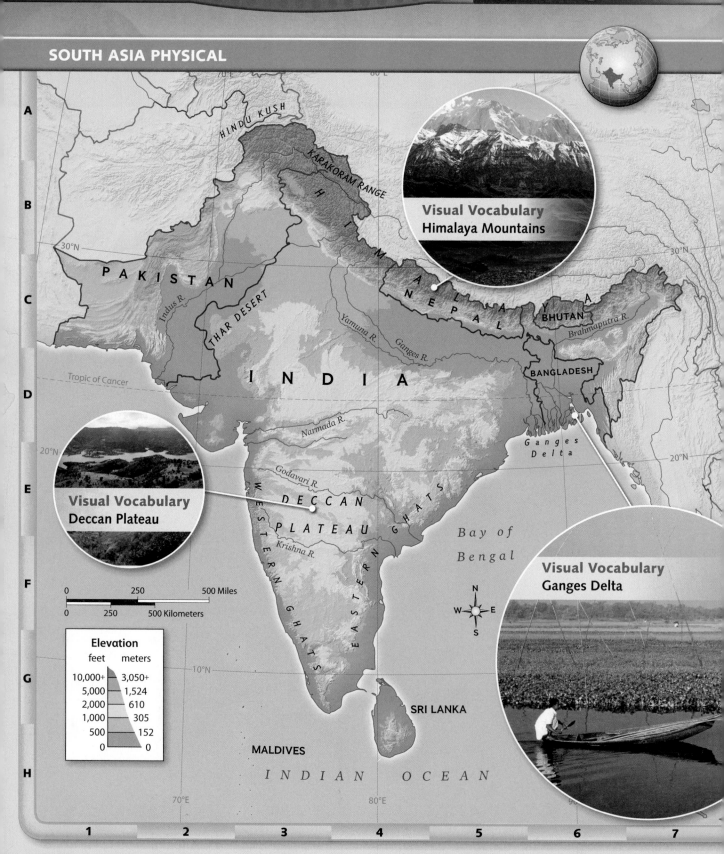

Visual Vocabulary
Himalaya Mountains

Visual Vocabulary
Deccan Plateau

Visual Vocabulary
Ganges Delta

HINDU KUSH

KARAKORAM RANGE

H I M A L A Y A

PAKISTAN

Indus R.

THAR DESERT

NEPAL

BHUTAN

Brahmaputra R.

Yamuna R.

Ganges R.

BANGLADESH

I N D I A

Tropic of Cancer

Narmada R.

Ganges Delta

Godavari R.

D E C C A N
P L A T E A U

WESTERN GHATS

EASTERN GHATS

Krishna R.

Bay of
Bengal

N
W   E
S

SRI LANKA

MALDIVES

I N D I A N   O C E A N

30°N

20°N

10°N

70°E

80°E

30°N

20°N

Scale

0	250	500 Miles
0	250	500 Kilometers

Elevation

feet	meters
10,000+	3,050+
5,000	1,524
2,000	610
1,000	305
500	152
0	0

CLIMATE

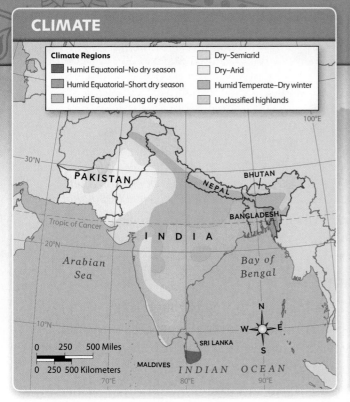

Climate Regions

- Humid Equatorial–No dry season
- Humid Equatorial–Short dry season
- Humid Equatorial–Long dry season
- Dry–Semiarid
- Dry–Arid
- Humid Temperate–Dry winter
- Unclassified highlands

PAKISTAN
NEPAL
BHUTAN
BANGLADESH
I N D I A
Tropic of Cancer
Arabian Sea
Bay of Bengal
SRI LANKA
MALDIVES
INDIAN OCEAN

0 250 500 Miles
0 250 500 Kilometers

POPULATION DENSITY

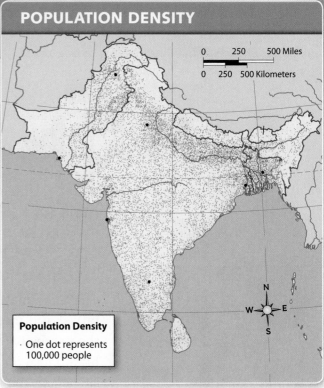

0 250 500 Miles
0 250 500 Kilometers

Population Density
· One dot represents 100,000 people

Main Idea The key physical features of South Asia include mountains, rivers, and a delta.

On a map, South Asia looks like a diamond-shaped chunk of land that was shoved into Asia. At the center of this diamond is the Indian **subcontinent**, a separate region of the Asian continent.

Continental Collision

South Asia is a separate **plate**, a rigid section of the earth's crust that can move independently. The plate is still moving. As a result, the **Himalaya Mountains** are being pushed higher. They are the highest mountain range in the world. The Himalayas were formed about 50 million years ago when the Indian plate **collided** with the Eurasian plate. This movement produced the world's tallest mountain, Mount Everest in Nepal. The Himalayas separate South Asia from the rest of Asia. Rainwater and snowmelt from these mountains form South Asia's rivers.

Major River Systems

Much of South Asia's water drains into the Ganges River and the **Indus River**. These river systems provide drinking water and nourish farmland, and are considered holy by Hindus. In Bangladesh, the Brahmaputra River joins the Ganges, forming the low, fertile **Ganges Delta**. A **delta** is an area where a river deposits sediment as it empties into a body of water.

Before You Move On
Summarize What are some key physical features of South Asia?

FORMATIVE ASSESSMENT

MAP LAB

GeoJournal

1. **Location** Where is the Ganges River located?
2. **Identify** What is the climate like in northeast India near Dhaka and Kolkata?
3. **Draw Conclusions** The population in northeastern South Asia is very dense. What physical features might account for this?

SECTION **1** GEOGRAPHY

NATIONAL GEOGRAPHIC

1.2

TECHTREK

myNGconnect.com For a map of the
Snowman Trek and an Explorer Video Clip

Maps and Graphs

Digital Library

Exploring the Himalayas
with Kira Salak

> **Main Idea** South Asia's mountain systems create unique challenges for its people.

myNGconnect.com

For more on Kira Salak in the field today

The Snowman Trek

The Snowman Trek involves hiking through some of the tallest and most isolated mountains in the world. Most of the passes between the mountain peaks are over 16,000 feet high. I eased comfortably into the first few days of the Trek, absorbing the beauty of the environment. On the third day we were introduced to the extreme **elevation**—the height above sea level—that we would experience the rest of the climb. It was nine hours, all uphill, to 11,800 feet.

We came to our first high mountain pass at Nyile La (roughly 16,000 feet). **1** This marked the first test for altitude sickness, a condition caused by a reduced level of oxygen in the air. As we climbed, the clouds parted to reveal many snow-topped peaks—the "rooftop of the world."

Life in the Mountains

Later, we hiked to one of the most isolated villages, Thanza, **2** with an elevation of 13,700 feet. Only about 300 people live there. Most are **subsistence farmers**. They grow food for their families, but nothing to sell to anyone else. Food consists of a high-altitude rice, with meat and cheese from yaks, which are long-haired Tibetan oxen. Homes are built from what can be found. Walls are made from stone, and shingles from wood. Clay is the mortar that holds it together.

BHUTAN: THE SNOWMAN TREK

Legend:
- ⊛ National capital
- • Town
- ⌒ River
- ⟩⟨ Pass
- —— International boundary
- ━━ Snowman trek

Elevation

feet	meters
10,000+	3,050+
5,000	1,524
2,000	610
1,000	305
500	152
0	0

CHINA

INDIA

Places on map: Thanza, Nyile La, Gasa, Nikka Chhu, Bumtang Tang, Lhuntshi, Tashi Yangtse, Punakha, Dur Village, Tongsa, Thimphu, Paro, Chukha, Tashigang, Mongar, Phuntsholing, Sarbhang, Geylegphug, Dewangiri

HIMALAYA

BLACK MTS.

BHUTAN

Rivers: Sankosh R., Wong Chu R., Amo R., Mangde R., Bumthang R., Kuru R., Manas R.

0 — 25 — 50 Miles
0 — 25 — 50 Kilometers

As we left Thanza, all signs of human presence vanished. Even our trail disappeared from underfoot. When we were done with the Trek and arrived in Nikka Chhu village ▶3 we calculated that we'd each taken half a million steps and walked at least 216 miles.

Before You Move On

Monitor Comprehension What key challenges do people living in South Asia's mountain systems face?

FORMATIVE ASSESSMENT

MAP LAB GeoJournal

1. **Place** Based on the map and description of Bhutan, why do you think people built most of their towns where they did?

2. **Create Charts** Make a chart like this one. What geographic factors explain the differences between your life and life in Bhutan?

NECESSITIES	MY LIFE	BHUTAN
shelter		
access to water		
access to food		
level of fitness required		

1.3 Living with Monsoons

TECHTREK

myNGconnect.com For online
monsoon maps and photos of monsoons

 Maps and
Graphs

 Digital
Library

Main Idea Seasonal monsoons provide water for crops and bring fresh soil to farmland.

Monsoons are seasonal winds that bring intense rainfall during part of the year. These powerful wind patterns are an important feature of South Asia's climate.

Summer: Wet Monsoons

From May to early October, winds blow northward from the Indian Ocean and bring heavy rain. Certain areas receive 100 inches of rain per year. During very wet years, these areas might receive over 300 inches.

The summer monsoon rains irrigate crops and fill reservoirs. The rains can also cause deadly floods and landslides. Despite these annual downpours, people forge ahead with their daily activities. They adapt by finding ways to save crops and navigate flooded streets.

Winter: Dry Monsoons

From November to April, the winter monsoons **reverse** direction and blow southward. The air from this direction is usually dry. The dry monsoons do not produce as much rain as the wet monsoons do.

In fact, a very dry monsoon season can destroy crops, which threatens farmers' livelihoods and the economic well-being of the region. Because of this, people must carefully manage water they stored during the wet monsoons. They use this water to drink and to irrigate their crops. By the following June, after months of hot, dry weather, the heavy rain is welcome.

Before You Move On

Make Inferences How do seasonal monsoons affect the region's economic development?

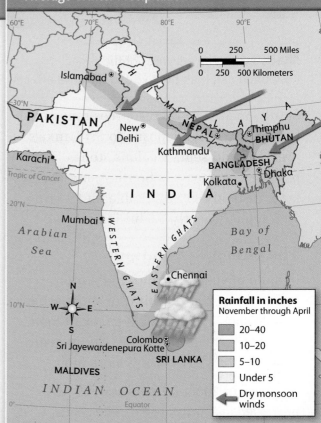

SUMMER MONSOON
Average Summer Precipitation

Rainfall in inches
May through October

- Over 40
- 20–40
- 10–20
- 5–10
- Under 5
- Wet monsoon winds

WINTER MONSOON
Average Winter Precipitation

Rainfall in inches
November through April

- 20–40
- 10–20
- 5–10
- Under 5
- Dry monsoon winds

WET MONSOONS The wet monsoon winds pick up moisture from the Indian Ocean as they flow northwest. This moisture turns into heavy rain when it crashes into the mountains of the Indian subcontinent. The rain saturates the land and swells the rivers. This provides nourishment for crops, animals, and people alike.

DRY MONSOONS The dry monsoons begin in the northeast and pick up moisture from the land as they move southwest. This is **evaporation**, the process of a liquid becoming a gas. If the wet monsoons do not produce enough rainfall, the dry monsoons can lead to a **drought**, or prolonged period without rain.

< Critical Viewing These children don't seem bothered by their flooded schoolyard. What does this photo suggest about the children's life during monsoon season?

FORMATIVE ASSESSMENT
MAP LAB
 GeoJournal

1. **Location** Locate Kolkata on the summer monsoon map. Why do you think Kolkata receives so much rain in the summer?

2. **Compare** Find Kolkata on the winter monsoon map. Does the city receive more or less rainfall in the winter? Why is there a difference in rainfall from summer to winter?

3. **Human-Environment Interaction** What might life be like for the people in Kolkata in summer? In winter?

1.4 Resources and Land Use

Main Idea The advances of the Green Revolution had both positive and negative effects.

South Asia's natural resources range from India's huge coal deposits to Sri Lanka's precious and semi-precious stones. The big story, however, is South Asia's **arable** land, or land that is suitable for farming, which feeds nearly 1.5 billion people.

The Green Revolution

In spite of vast farmland, India often suffered terrible **famines**, or times when people starved because of a lack of food. During the 1950s and 1960s, India made slow progress in growing more food.

Then, in 1966, farmers started using new seeds to grow wheat. The seeds dramatically increased crop yield, or the amount of food grown on a unit of land. India's wheat production shot up from 10.3 million metric tons in 1960 to 20 million metric tons in 1970. Farmers also increased production of rice, fruits, sugarcane, and vegetables. This rapid and significant rise in food production was known as the Green Revolution.

However, the high-yield seeds required more fertilizer, irrigation, and pesticides, which are chemicals that kill diseases and insects. Fertilizers, pesticides, and irrigation cost money. As a result, the Green Revolution benefited mostly wealthy farmers. The Green Revolution also had negative effects on the environment. Rain washed fertilizers and pesticides into rivers, causing pollution.

Sustainable Agriculture

Today, South Asian governments and farmers are adapting to the physical environment. They use new technologies and methods that are **sustainable**, or capable of being continued without long-term damage to the environment. More farmers are using natural fertilizers, such as manure, to enrich soils. They are also using crop rotation, in which they change by season the crops grown on a plot of land. These methods help to grow more food and also protect the environment.

Before You Move On
Summarize What have been the positive and negative effects of the farming methods used during the Green Revolution?

Visual Vocabulary Arable refers to land that is suitable for farming. This field is designed to let water soak into the ground. In India, more than 50 percent of the land is arable.

LAND USE AND NATURAL RESOURCES

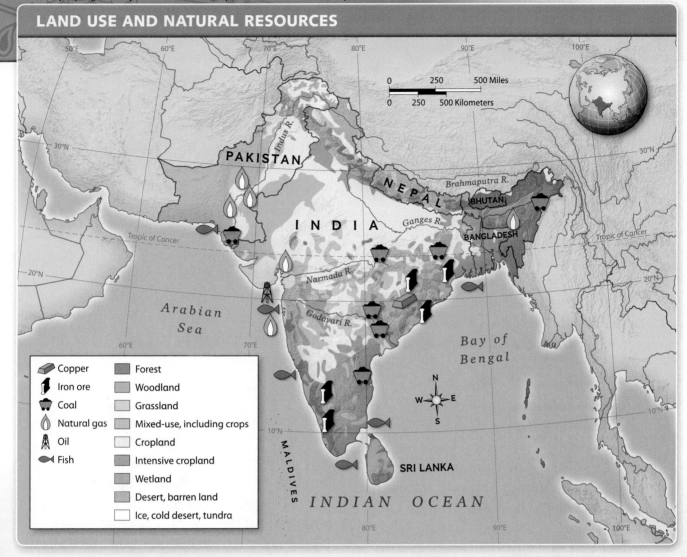

Legend:
- Copper
- Iron ore
- Coal
- Natural gas
- Oil
- Fish
- Forest
- Woodland
- Grassland
- Mixed-use, including crops
- Cropland
- Intensive cropland
- Wetland
- Desert, barren land
- Ice, cold desert, tundra

GRAIN PRODUCTION AND POPULATION (1950–2012)

	Food Grain Production (millions of metric tons)	Wheat Production (millions of metric tons)	Population (millions)
1950	50.8	6.4	361
1960	82.0	10.3	439
1970	108.4	20.0	548
1980	129.6	31.8	683
1990	176.4	49.8	846
2000	201.6	76.3	1,000
2012	257.4	94.0	1,220

Sources: CIA Factbook; Indian National Science Academy

FORMATIVE ASSESSMENT

MAP LAB

GeoJournal

1. **Location** What types of land use are most common around the main rivers in South Asia?

2. **Compare** Look at the physical map in Section 1.1 and compare it with the land use map on this page. Why do you think there are fewer natural resources in the northeast?

3. **Interpret Charts** How much wheat per person did India produce in 1950? In 2012? What happened to the amount of wheat grown?

4. **Human-Environment Interaction** How do physical features, climate, and land use in South Asia affect humans in the region?

1.5 Conservation

TECHTREK

myNGconnect.com For an online
population map and an Explorer Video Clip

Maps and
Graphs

Digital
Library

Main Idea People have contributed to the problems affecting the Ganges River.

Humans have a powerful impact on the land and the way it is used. One way they can protect the earth is through **conservation**, which is the protection of the environment. In South Asia, this includes protecting tigers in India and Bangladesh and preserving marine ecosystems in the Maldives. An **ecosystem** is a group of interacting organisms and their natural environment.

Conserving the Ganges

In India, conservation of the rivers is a national issue. The Ganges River is a valuable natural resource. It is also considered sacred by Hindus, India's main religious group. However, a growing population and poor waste disposal have led to the contamination of the Ganges.

One source of pollution in the Ganges is raw sewage, including household wastes. Varanasi has three sewage plants that process 100 million liters of sewage a day. However, the city produces up to 300 million liters a day.

Another source of pollution comes from industry. In industrial centers such as Kanpur, big leather-producing tanneries flush waste containing arsenic, chromium, and mercury into the Ganges. Chromium can cause cancer, and mercury can damage the nervous system.

These pollutants also damage the river habitat, which threatens animals such as the river dolphin. Parts of the Ganges are so polluted that scientists refer to them as "dead." They can no longer support plant or animal life.

Cleaning Up Pollution

Local non-governmental organizations (NGOs) are helping to reverse the damage. NGOs are nonprofit volunteer groups founded by citizens. For example, Rakesh Jaiswal founded EcoFriends to raise awareness of the condition of the Ganges at Kanpur. Jaiswal is hopeful that one day the Ganges will be clean again.

Before You Move On
Monitor Comprehension What are the main sources of pollution in the Ganges River?

Critical Viewing Pollution clogs the Ganges River. In what ways might pollution of the Ganges affect human life along its banks?

6.03.B pose questions about geographic distributions; 6.04.B identify geographic factors responsible for patterns of population; 6.07.B identify ways people have modified environment; 6.21.B analyze information by drawing inferences; 6.21.C organize and interpret information from visuals, maps

POPULATION OF THE GANGES RIVER BASIN

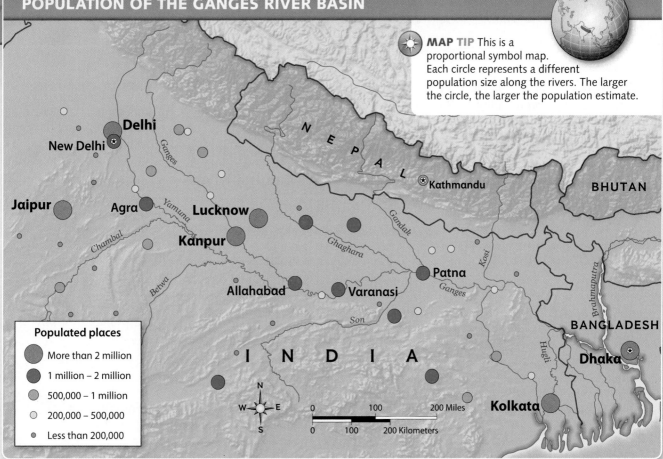

MAP TIP This is a proportional symbol map. Each circle represents a different population size along the rivers. The larger the circle, the larger the population estimate.

Delhi
New Delhi
NEPAL
Kathmandu
BHUTAN
Jaipur
Agra
Ganges
Yamuna
Lucknow
Kanpur
Chambal
Gandak
Ghaghara
Kosi
Betwa
Allahabad
Varanasi
Patna
Ganges
Brahmaputra
Son
BANGLADESH
Hugli
Dhaka
INDIA
Kolkata

Populated places
- More than 2 million
- 1 million – 2 million
- 500,000 – 1 million
- 200,000 – 500,000
- Less than 200,000

0   100   200 Miles
0   100   200 Kilometers

FORMATIVE ASSESSMENT

VIEWING LAB

GeoJournal

1. **Analyze Visuals** Go to the **Digital Library** to watch the video clip about pollution. What most interested you?

2. **Pose Questions** Draw this chart on your own paper. Write down three things you learned from the video clip and pose three questions you have after watching the clip.

National Geographic Emerging Explorer Alexandra Cousteau with Rakesh Jaiswal

WHAT I LEARNED	QUESTIONS I STILL HAVE
1. Kanpur is the 7th most polluted city in the world	
2.	

3. **Make Inferences** What connections can you make between the condition of the Ganges and population?

1.6 South Asia's Water Crisis

TECHTREK
myNGconnect.com For data
on South Asia's water crisis

Global
Issues

Main Idea South Asia faces a water crisis because of pollution, water scarcity, and flooding.

Several times a week, 12-year-old Somnath Dantoso drops a magnet attached to a fishing line into the Yamuna River. The river flows through New Delhi, India's capital city. He hauls rupees (India's coin money) out of the water, but he also hauls out garbage. The Yamuna is choking on **pollution**. It is loaded with food, tires, chemicals, sewage, and other waste. In fact, more than half of New Delhi's garbage ends up in the river. South Asia is facing a major water crisis.

Polluted Water and Disease

Many other rivers in India are polluted. Water pollution is just as bad in other parts of South Asia. In Pakistan, 38.5 million people do not have safe drinking water. More than 50 million people lack proper **sanitation**, such as sewers to carry away dirty water. Rivers in many of Nepal's cities are so polluted that people cannot use them for drinking water.

In Bangladesh, millions of wells have arsenic, a poison, in the water. Experts believe that 20,000 Bangladeshis may die every year from drinking poisoned water. One United Nations scientist said that it could be "the largest mass poisoning of a population in history."

The pollution has severe consequences for the health of South Asians. Contaminated water kills 500,000 infants a year in South Asia and Southeast Asia. It can cause cancer and other deadly diseases.

Before You Move On

Monitor Comprehension How does water pollution affect South Asia?

KEY VOCABULARY

pollution, n., making the environment dirty, foul, unclean, or contaminated

sanitation, n., measures such as sewers to protect public health

aquifer, n., a bed or layer beneath the surface of the earth that contains water

POLLUTION BY THE NUMBERS

55
Percentage of New Delhi's people who are connected to the city's sewage system

80
Percentage of Yamuna River's pollution resulting from raw sewage

500
Millions of dollars that the Indian government has spent trying to clean up the Yamuna River

855
Length in miles of the Yamuna from the Himalayas to the Ganges

1,815
Estimated growth of India's population every hour, 2012

Sources: Daniel Pepper, "India's Rivers Are Drowning in Pollution," *Fortune*, June 4, 2007; Rakesh Jaiswal, "India in Peril," *Smithsonian*, October 31, 2007.

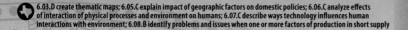
6.03.D create thematic maps; 6.05.C explain impact of geographic factors on domestic policies; 6.06.C analyze effects of interaction of physical processes and environment on humans; 6.07.C describe ways technology influences human interactions with environment; 6.08.B identify problems and issues when one or more factors of production in short supply

Inspiring people to care about the planet
National Geographic Society Mission

Scarce Water and Drought

Water is growing scarce for the 1.5 billion people in South Asia. Because of increasing population and climate change, the region has had severe droughts recently. Elizabeth Kolbert wrote in *National Geographic* magazine:

> Since higher temperatures lead to increased evaporation, even areas that continue to receive the same amount of overall precipitation will become more prone to drought. (April 2009)

Bangladesh has already experienced severe drought. One reason is that upstream dams in India have reduced water flow into Bangladesh's rivers. In addition, the country's exploding population has taken millions of gallons of water from **aquifers**. Less water means less food, resulting in widespread hunger.

Water scarcity is also caused by shrinking glaciers in the Himalayas, which supply water to rivers and lakes in Asia. The glaciers used to build up in winter and then melt in spring, supplying water to rivers and lakes in Asia. While some areas will have droughts, others will have more flooding. Kolbert added that warmer air temperatures may increase the severity of annual summer monsoons.

The people of South Asia are taking steps to clean up the region's rivers and lakes. Citizens are calling for companies to stop polluting and are pushing their governments to take action.

COMPARE ACROSS REGIONS

Watershed Solutions

A **watershed** is the geographic area from which rivers and streams drain to supply water. Instead of investing in sewage treatment only, in 2011 China's government had programs to give people who live upstream incentives, or rewards, not to pollute the watershed.

Watershed programs don't require power to run like sewage treatment pumps and filters. This fact played a positive role in disaster relief for Hurricane Sandy in 2012. During the storm when the power went out, clean drinking water still flowed to New York City. That was because city's government had given incentives to farmers and communities in the watershed area to protect it from pollution.

Before You Move On

Summarize What is causing water scarcity in South Asia?

FORMATIVE ASSESSMENT

READING LAB GeoJournal

1. **Identify** What problems arise when water is in short supply?

2. **Make Generalizations** What are different societies doing to address water problems?

3. **Create Thematic Maps** Choose a country in South Asia and research its watersheds. Draw a map to show one or more watersheds and calculate an estimated number of square miles for each.

> **Main Idea** South Asia's ancient civilizations developed around the region's river systems.

The physical geography of a place often influences its history. Good farmland and the geographic **isolation** (separation) of South Asia made the Indus and Ganges river valleys **cultural hearths**, or centers of civilization from which ideas spread. Mountains and oceans provided natural boundaries that limited invasions. Fertile soil along the rivers provided arable farmland. Two major civilizations that thrived here were the Harappans and the Aryans.

Harappan Civilization

The first urban civilization in South Asia was the **Harappan** (huh RA puhn) civilization. It developed along the Indus River in what is now Pakistan. The land was fertile and good for farming. As a result, people formed farming villages that grew into cities. The two greatest cities of this civilization were Mohenjo-Daro and Harappa. These cities were well planned and laid out in a grid pattern of straight streets. The cities also had brick houses, indoor plumbing, and a sewer system. These cities provide early examples of organized city planning that helped to support cultural growth.

The Harappan people developed advanced technologies and a system of measurement using weights and bricks that were a standard size. Among the ruins of these cities, archeologists have found stone seals with images of animals and script. Based on this evidence, scholars believe the Harappans may have developed a system of writing, but the scripts have not yet been translated.

After a period of prosperity, the Harappan civilization started to decline between 2000 and 1700 B.C. Historians believe some possible causes include the change of the Indus River's course, floods, earthquakes, and invaders.

Aryan Migration

Many historians believe a group of nomadic herders called the **Aryans** (AIR ee uhnz) migrated from Central Asia into the Indus Valley around 2000 B.C. From there, they moved into northern India, and eventually migrated further south. Their language, **Sanskrit**, became the basis of many modern languages in South Asia. The Aryans recorded religious teachings in Sanskrit in sacred texts called the Vedas. The early religion of the Aryans established the beginnings of Hinduism, the major religion of India today.

2600–2500 B.C.
Emergence of the Harappan, or Indus Valley, civilization

2000–1700 B.C.
Decline of the Harappan civilization

3000 B.C.   **2500 B.C.**   **2000 B.C.**

2500 B.C. A sculpture fragment of a priest-king from the site of Mohenjo-Daro

2000 B.C.
Beginning of Aryan migration into the Indus Valley

ANCIENT RIVER VALLEY CIVILIZATIONS

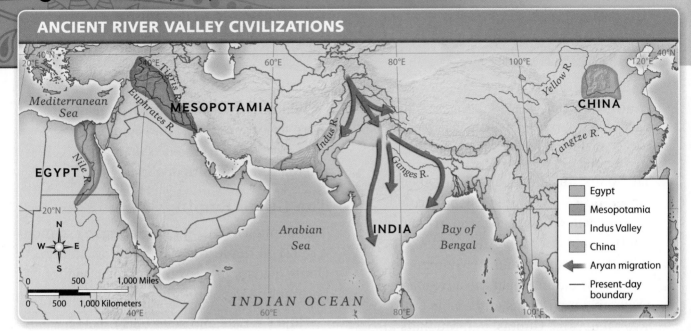

Legend:
- Egypt
- Mesopotamia
- Indus Valley
- China
- ← Aryan migration
- — Present-day boundary

Aryan society was organized into different social groups, or varnas, based on ancestries, family ties, and a person's occupation. Their social structure became known as the **caste system**. The caste system was made of four groups:

Brahmans: priests and scholars
Kshatriyas: rulers and warriors
Vaisyas: merchants and professionals
Sudras: artisans, laborers, and servants

Over the centuries, the caste system grew into thousands of subgroups. While its past influence made it an important part of South Asian culture, the caste system is slowly becoming less prominent as the region modernizes.

Before You Move On

Monitor Comprehension Where did South Asia's ancient civilizations develop?

FORMATIVE ASSESSMENT

LANGUAGE LAB — GeoJournal

1. **Compare** Read aloud the Sanskrit words in the chart. Compare them to the English words.

SELECTED INDO-EUROPEAN LANGUAGES

Sanskrit	pitar	matar	dvi
English	father	mother	two
Greek	patéras	matros	dyo
Latin	pater	mater	duo
Spanish	padre	madre	dos

2. **Draw Conclusions** A language family is a group of languages that come from a common ancestor. After looking at the chart, what can you conclude about languages in the same language family?

3. **Interpret Time Lines** During what period of time were the Vedas written?

1500–1200 B.C.
Vedas written

1500 B.C.

1500 B.C.
Aryan migration into northern India

1500 B.C. Pages from the Vedas, sacred text in Sanskrit

500 B.C.

TECHTREK

myNGconnect.com For an online map on
empires and photos of artifacts and architecture

Maps and Graphs

Digital Library

> **Main Idea** Three South Asian empires made significant cultural contributions in religion, science, and the arts.

The Mauryan, Gupta, and Mughal empires (an **empire** is the land or people ruled by one leader) dominated the history of South Asia between 321 B.C. and A.D. 1858. Like the Harappan and Aryan empires, these later empires had the advantage of protective mountains and arable land. The Mauryans, Guptas, and Mughals also helped spread three major religions in the region—Buddhism, Hinduism, and Islam.

The Mauryan Empire

The Mauryan (MOWR yuhn) Empire was founded in the Ganges River valley in 321 B.C. The Mauryans built an efficient and organized government, which allowed them to run the empire. They also had a standing, or permanent, army.

The leader **Asoka** ruled for nearly 40 years and brought the empire to its height around 250 B.C. As the Mauryan empire grew and flourished, Asoka turned away from conquest in favor of more peaceful policies. He studied Buddhist nonviolent teachings and built many stupas, which are Buddhist religious structures.

Buddhism began in India, but gained more followers in east and southeast Asia as it spread. After Asoka's death, the Mauryan Empire declined.

The Gupta Empire

The Gupta (GUP tuh) Empire began around A.D. 321 in the fertile Ganges River valley. Gupta leaders practiced Hinduism, which became the major religion of South Asia.

Gupta artists and scientists created lasting cultural contributions. Advances in metal working, literature, mathematics (including the development of the decimal), and astronomy were part of this legacy. Eventually, invasions weakened the Guptas and by A.D. 540, their reign was over.

The Mughal Empire

One thousand years later, the Mughal (MOO guhl) Empire was established in 1526 by Babur. Mughal rulers practiced Islam and came from Central Asia. Islam became a unifying force in South Asia and grew into a large religious minority.

Akbar the Great came to power in 1556 and ruled for 49 years. Akbar expanded the empire and practiced religious **tolerance**, or respect for others' beliefs.

321 B.C.–185 B.C.
Mauryan Empire

Asoka's Pillar, c. 273 B.C., inscribed with his laws. The lion is a symbol of India.

A.D. 321–A.D. 540
Gupta Empire

Gold coin from Gupta Empire, c. A.D. 321

500 B.C.   **A.D. 1**   **A.D. 500**

c. 250 B.C.
Height of the Mauryan Empire

400
Height of the Gupta Empire

321 B.C.
Chandragupta Maurya founds the Mauryan Empire.

321
Chandra Gupta I founds the Gupta Empire.

EMPIRES OF SOUTH ASIA

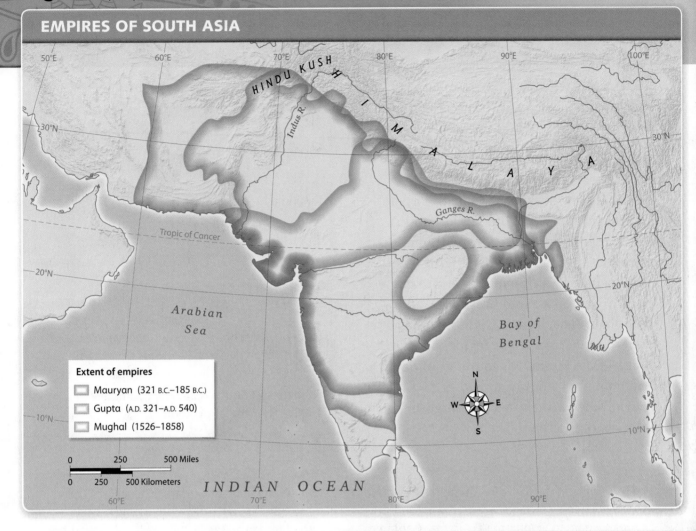

Extent of empires
- Mauryan (321 B.C.–185 B.C.)
- Gupta (A.D. 321–A.D. 540)
- Mughal (1526–1858)

0   250   500 Miles
0   250   500 Kilometers

Mughal leaders developed a large empire through military conquest. Cultural contributions of Mughal artists included the architecture of the **Taj Mahal** and detailed paintings called miniatures. The empire came to an end in 1858 when the British took control of the territory.

Before You Move On
Monitor Comprehension What cultural contributions did the three empires make?

FORMATIVE ASSESSMENT
MAP LAB
 GeoJournal

1. **Movement** What physical features influenced the empires' ability to control their territory?
2. **Make Generalizations** Based on the map and what you know about arable lands, what geographic features were vital for the success of these empires?

1526–1858
Mughal Empire

Taj Mahal, 1600s, built as a tomb for Shah Jahan's wife

1000   1500   PRESENT

1700 Height of the Mughal Empire

1526 Babur founds the Mughal Empire.

2.3 Religion in South Asia

TECHTREK
myNGconnect.com For an online map
and data on South Asian religions

Maps and
Graphs

Main Idea Religion was an important part of South Asia's history. It is still important to the culture today.

Religion is an important part of South Asia's history because it shaped borders and cultures. Two of the world's main religions—**Hinduism** and **Buddhism**—were founded in India along with two other religions, **Jainism** and **Sikhism**. Buddhism spread into East Asia and Southeast Asia. Today, Buddhism has more followers in those regions than in South Asia. **Islam** was founded in Saudi Arabia, but it quickly spread to South Asia. Today, it is the second-largest religion in the region.

SIKHISM Sikhism began in India in the late A.D. 1400s. Sikhs believe in one god, truthful living, and equality of humankind. Today, most Sikhs live in the Indian state of Punjab.

Followers in South Asia: Approximately 1 percent of the population

JAINISM Jainism developed in the 7th century B.C. Jains believe in *ahimsa*, or nonviolence towards all living things. Most Jains live in northwestern India.

Followers in South Asia: Approximately 1 percent of the population

BUDDHISM Buddhism was founded in India around 525 B.C. by a prince named Siddhartha Gautama. Gautama left his royal life to find a solution to human suffering. After six years, he discovered and began teaching the Four Noble Truths: 1) Suffering is a part of life; 2) Selfishness is a cause of suffering; 3) It is possible to move beyond suffering; and 4) There is a path that leads to this point.

People who followed Gautama's teachings called him the Buddha, or "Enlightened One." They recorded his teachings in a set of books called the *Tripitaka*, or "Three Baskets." During the next few centuries, Buddhism spread throughout Asia. In South Asia, it is the main religion of Bhutan and Sri Lanka. You can learn more about Buddhism in the chapters on East Asia.

Followers in South Asia: Approximately 2 percent of the population

HINDUISM Hinduism began as a blend of native beliefs and the religion of the Aryan people. It has developed over thousands of years. Today it is the main religion in India and Nepal. Hindus worship many deities, or supreme beings, but they believe that every deity is a part of one universal spirit, called Brahman.

Hindus also believe in reincarnation, or the rebirth of the soul. After death, a person's soul is reborn into another physical life. The kind of life is

determined by the soul's *karma*, or actions during a previous life. If the soul has lived a good life, it is reborn into a better life. If the soul has lived an evil life, it is reborn into a worse life. This process continues until the soul lives a perfect life.

These beliefs and others are recorded in many different texts. The most important are the **Vedas**, the *Puranas*, the *Ramayana*, and the *Mahabharata*.

Followers in South Asia: Approximately 63 percent of the population

6.03.B pose and answer questions about geographic distributions; 6.03.C compare countries using data from maps; 6.03.D create graphs depicting aspects of regions; 6.16.B compare characteristics of institutions (religious) in contemporary societies; 6.21.C organize data from maps; interpret data from graphs

SOUTH ASIA'S RELIGIONS

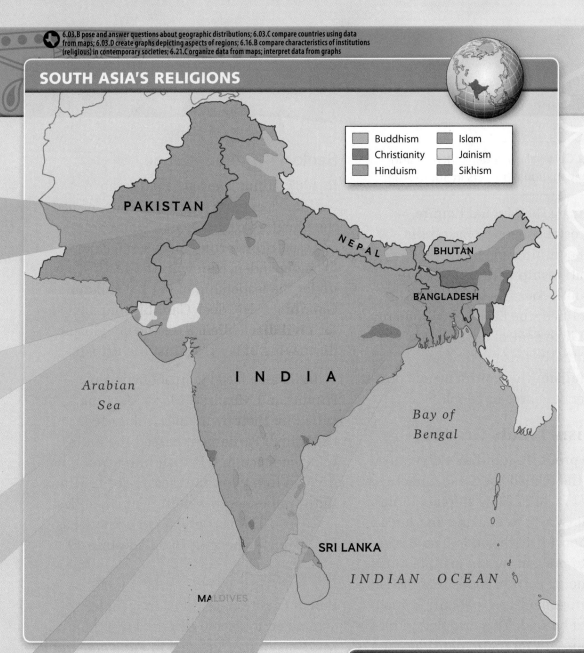

	Buddhism		Islam
	Christianity		Jainism
	Hinduism		Sikhism

PAKISTAN

NEPAL

BHUTAN

BANGLADESH

INDIA

Arabian
Sea

Bay of
Bengal

SRI LANKA

INDIAN OCEAN

MALDIVES

ISLAM Islam arrived with Muslim traders and armies in the early A.D. 700s. Today it is the main religion of Pakistan and Bangladesh. It is also the largest minority religion in India. You can learn more about Islam in the chapters on Southwest Asia.

Followers in South Asia: Approximately 30 percent of the population

Before You Move On

Summarize Why is religion important to South Asia's history?

FORMATIVE ASSESSMENT

DATA LAB
GeoJournal

1. **Create Graphs** Using the map and data in this section, make a circle graph that shows the percentages of followers of the religions in South Asia. How does the graph help you understand the distribution of religions across South Asia?

2. **Pose and Answer Questions** With a partner, ask and answer three questions about South Asia's religions.

3. **Location** In which two South Asian countries is Islam the dominant religion? What South Asian country separates these two Islamic countries from each other?

> **Main Idea** Colonialism, independence, and conflict set new national borders in South Asia.

In 1600, during the Mughal Empire, the British established the East India Company, beginning an extensive trading relationship with countries in East and South Asia. As the Mughal Empire declined, the East India Company was able to take control over parts of India. Eventually, this power grew into **colonialism**, the control by one power over a dependent area or people.

Colonialism Limits Growth

In order to profit from India's rich natural resources, the British used trade practices that favored Britain. They shipped India's raw materials back to England and forced India to import British goods. The British also tried to prevent Indian manufacturers from producing certain goods that British manufacturers made, so that only British goods could be sold. This crippled India's economic growth for more than 100 years.

In 1857, Indians unsuccessfully rebelled against British control. The East India Company was disbanded in 1858, but the British established direct rule over India called the *raj*. British colonization had a lasting impact on the region's borders.

Seeking Independence

In 1885, Hindus formed the Indian National Congress (INC). Muslims formed the Muslim League in 1906. Both groups opposed British rule. India's movement for independence grew in the 1930s under the leadership of lawyer **Mohandas Gandhi** (GAHN dee). Gandhi campaigned for **civil disobedience**, or the nonviolent disobeying of laws, against the British.

India also faced conflict between Hindus and Muslims. Many Muslims called for their own land. In July 1947, the British Parliament passed the India Independence Act. British India would be divided into two countries: majority-Hindu India and majority-Muslim Pakistan, East and West. The part of Pakistan known as East Pakistan became Bangladesh in 1971.

Partition Creates Boundaries

Before **Partition**, or division, people scrambled to decide where to live. Many Muslims in India moved to Pakistan, and many Pakistani Hindus migrated to India. For hundreds of thousands of Indians, the movement was not peaceful. In August of 1947 they were **displaced** (forced to leave their homes) or even killed in the religious conflicts that followed.

Silk textiles are a thriving industry in South Asia.

1850

1900

1857
First Indian revolt for Independence

1885
Indian National Congress Party leads India's movement for independence.

1906
Muslim League leads India's Muslims in movement for their own nation.

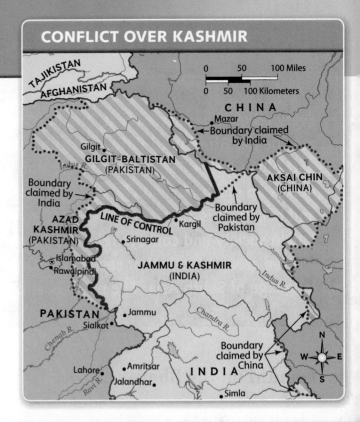

CONFLICT OVER KASHMIR

In 1948, Gandhi was assassinated. The boundaries set by Partition have strained relations in South Asia to the present.

Conflict Over Kashmir

Partition established the present-day borders of South Asia. After Partition, India and Pakistan began a violent conflict over a region known as Kashmir. Both India and Pakistan believed the region belonged to them.

In 1949, a cease-fire was called, and Kashmir was divided. India maintains control over the portion called Jammu and Kashmir; Pakistan controls the portion known as Gilgit-Baltistan. However, Indian and Pakistani soldiers stand guard along the disputed border, and tension remains at a high level.

Part of the continuing conflict centers around the control of water for drinking and irrigation. Many rivers, including the Indus, begin in Kashmir, and maintaining control of the water is important to both countries. In fact, both countries have threatened to use nuclear weapons to resolve the dispute.

Before You Move On

Summarize What impact did British rule in India have on borders in South Asia?

FORMATIVE ASSESSMENT

MAP LAB

GeoJournal

1. **Interpret Maps and Time Lines** On this map, striped areas represent conflict between two countries. Which three countries disagree about their borders? Based on the time line, when was Kashmir divided?

2. **Location** How does the presence of rivers factor into the cause of the conflict in Kashmir?

3. **Turn and Talk** What physical features of this region might make it hard to control borders? Turn to your classmate and identify details from this map, or other physical maps in the chapter, that might help answer this question. Take notes to share with the class.

○ **1947**
India gains independence. Partition occurs.

1950

Mohandas Gandhi

PRESENT

○ **1930**
Gandhi continues his civil disobedience campaigns.

○ **1949**
Kashmir divided between India and Pakistan

2.5 Gandhi and the Bhagavad Gita

TECHTREK

myNGconnect.com For photos of Hindu art and Guided Writing

 Digital Library

 Student Resources

Every religion has sacred text, and in Hinduism the most important may be the **Bhagavad Gita** (bah guh vahd GEE tah). It is a poem, part of the larger *Mahabharata* (muh hah BAH ruh tuh), which makes up much of Hindu mythology, or set of stories, traditions, and beliefs. It is an example of literature that has spread beyond Indian society and conveys religious themes. The Bhagavad Gita was written around the first or second century A.D. in Sanskrit, an ancient language of South Asia. The poem is still loved by millions of Hindus.

DOCUMENT 1

Gandhi on the Bhagavad Gita

When disappointments stare me in the face, and when I see not one ray of light . . . I turn to the Bhagavad Gita and find a verse to comfort me, and I immediately begin to smile in the midst of overwhelming sorrow. My life has been full of external tragedies, and if they have not left any visible and indelible [permanent] effect on me, I owe it to the teaching of the Bhagavad Gita.

Gandhi with his granddaughters

CONSTRUCTED RESPONSE

1. Think about what you learned in Section 2.4. What specific "external tragedies" might Gandhi be referring to?

DOCUMENT 2

from the Bhagavad Gita
translated by Ranchor Prime

The Bhagavad Gita includes a conversation between the deity Krishna and a young warrior, Arjuna. Krishna explains to Arjuna his responsibilities as a warrior. Gandhi especially liked this passage:

One without self-control cannot have a clear intelligence or a steady mind. An unsteady mind finds no peace, and without peace where is joy? As a strong wind sweeps away a boat on the water, so the mind dwelling on even one of the senses carries away the intelligence.

CONSTRUCTED RESPONSE

2. According to this passage, humans should not allow emotions to overcome logic. Think about what you have learned about how Hinduism unifies its followers. Explain how this work of literature transcends, or goes past, the boundaries of societies to express a universal theme.

6.02.B evaluate social, political, and cultural contributions of individuals, past; 6.18.D identify examples of literature that have transcended boundaries of society and convey universal themes; 6.21.A locate secondary sources, use primary and secondary sources to acquire information

WHEN DISAPPOINTMENT STARES ME IN THE FACE AND ALL ALONE I SEE NOT ONE RAY OF LIGHT, I GO BACK TO THE BHAGAVAD GITA.

— GANDHI

DOCUMENT 3

Vishnu, Preserver of the Universe

Hindus believe Krishna, the narrator of the Bhagavad Gita, is a human form of Vishnu, a Hindu deity. Every element in this image of Vishnu is a **symbol** (something that stands for another thing) of an idea in Hinduism. For example, the crown symbolizes Vishnu's highest authority.

CONSTRUCTED RESPONSE

3. The lotus flower in his left hand shows that Vishnu is spiritually perfect. How does this symbol reflect the qualities described in Documents 1 and 2?

Find Out More

Quotations are primary sources. Books and articles that tell where or when a quotation was made are secondary sources. Locate and use a secondary source on Gandhi's life. Identify the source and share two interesting facts from it.

FORMATIVE ASSESSMENT

WRITING LAB GeoJournal

DBQ Practice Think about the Bhagavad Gita and the picture of Vishnu. Why would these ideas and symbols be important to Gandhi and what he wanted for Hindus?

Step 1. Review Gandhi's influence on history on page 487 and the ideas of Hinduism on page 485.

Step 2. On your own paper, jot down notes about the main ideas expressed in each document.

Document 1: Quotation from Gandhi
Main Idea(s) _____

Document 2: Excerpt from the Bhagavad Gita
Main Idea(s) _____

Document 3: Image of Vishnu
Main Idea(s) _____

Step 3. Construct a topic sentence that answers this question: Which ideas and symbols from the Bhagavad Gita and the image of Vishnu would be important to Gandhi?

Step 4. Write a detailed paragraph that explains why each idea or symbol in your topic sentence was important to Gandhi and the history of India. Go to **Student Resources** for Guided Writing support.

Review

VOCABULARY

For each pair of vocabulary words, write one sentence that explains the connection between the two words.

1. subcontinent; plate

> The Indian subcontinent is on a different plate than the rest of Asia.

2. evaporation; drought

3. arable; sustainable

4. conservation; ecosystem

5. deity; reincarnation

6. mythology; symbol

MAIN IDEAS

7. How were the Himalaya Mountains formed? (Section 1.1)

8. How do people living at high elevations in Bhutan feed themselves? (Section 1.2)

9. What are the two kinds of monsoons in India, and what are the effects of each? (Section 1.3)

10. What were two results of the Green Revolution in India during the 1960s? (Section 1.4)

11. What factors contributed to the pollution of the Ganges River? (Section 1.5)

12. What are the consequences of water pollution in South Asia? (Section 1.6)

13. How did Hinduism develop in India? (Sections 2.1, 2.3)

14. What events led to India's independence from Britain? (Section 2.4)

15. How did Islam spread to India? (Section 2.3)

GEOGRAPHY

ANALYZE THE ESSENTIAL QUESTION

How do South Asia's water systems affect how people in the region live?

Critical Thinking: Analyze Cause and Effect

16. What is the geographic connection between snowmelt in the Himalayas and South Asia's extensive river systems?

17. What are the effects of the wet and dry monsoon seasons on India's farmers?

18. What geographic factors make the Ganges Delta one of the primary agricultural regions of the Indian subcontinent?

INTERPRET CHARTS

THE GREEN REVOLUTION AND INDIAN VILLAGES (1955–1986)				
	1955	**1965**	**1975**	**1986**
Percentage of farmland irrigated	60	80	100	100
Use of farm machinery per village	none	none	4 tractors	9 tractors
Population per village	876	*N/A	N/A	1,076
Average size of farms	4.8 acres	N/A	5.7 acres	N/A

*Not available
Source: Brace, Steve. *India*. Des Plaines, IL: Heinemann Library, 1999, p. 29

19. **Make Generalizations** What happened to the amount of land irrigated in the average Indian village between 1955 and 1975?

20. **Summarize** What was the trend in the use of farm machinery? What do you think explains this trend?

6.03.B answer questions about geographic distributions shown on databases; 6.03.C compare countries using databases; 6.04.F identify location of major countries; 6.12.B compare ways societies organize government; 6.21.B summarizing, generalizations, inferences, cause-effect; 6.22.B incorporate main and supporting ideas in verbal communication; 6.22.C express ideas orally based on research

HISTORY

ANALYZE THE ESSENTIAL QUESTION

How have physical features, religion, and empires shaped South Asia's borders?

Critical Thinking: Summarize

21. How did the Mauryan and Mughal empires bring religious diversity to India?

22. How did the Aryan migrations help to create cultural unity in the Indian subcontinent?

23. What religious differences led to boundaries between India and Pakistan?

INTERPRET MAPS

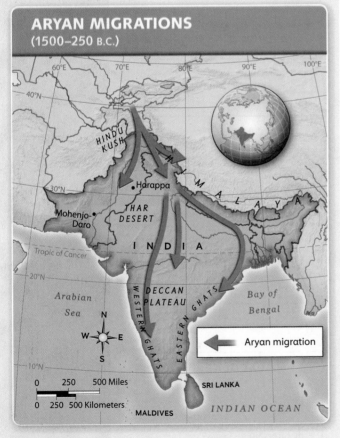

ARYAN MIGRATIONS
(1500–250 B.C.)

24. **Movement** What physical barrier did the Aryans have to cross to migrate into India?

25. **Make Inferences** Why might the Aryans' path of migration have avoided the western region of India?

ACTIVE OPTIONS

Synthesize the Essential Questions by completing the activities below.

26. **Write a Speech** Research village life in South Asia today. Write a brief speech to persuade a village government to adopt sustainable agriculture. (See page 476.) To be persuasive, include a main idea and ideas to support it, and include the benefits of this farming method. Use key vocabulary and show that you know its meaning. **Share your speech with the class.**

> **Writing Tips**
> - Use a convincing fact from your research.
> - Support your opinion with examples.
> - End with a strong conclusion that summarizes your position.

27. **Create Charts** Make a three-column chart showing comparisons among India, Pakistan, and Bangladesh. Use online databases to gather the data. With a partner, take turns stating a brief comparison for each category, giving details from your research notes and prior knowledge.

	India	Pakistan	Bangladesh
Year country was formed			
Capital city			
Square miles of land			
Main crops			
Form of Government			
Religion of majority of population			

CHAPTER 18

South Asia
TODAY

PREVIEW THE CHAPTER

Essential Question How is diversity reflected in South Asia's cultures?

KEY VOCABULARY
- karma
- pilgrimage
- henna
- sari
- literacy rate
- shalwar-kameez
- cricket
- popular culture

ACADEMIC VOCABULARY
discrimination

TERMS & NAMES
- Krishna
- Bollywood

Essential Question Why has India experienced an economic boom?

KEY VOCABULARY
- democracy
- federal republic
- infrastructure
- outsourcing
- developed nations
- developing nations
- microlending
- modernization

ACADEMIC VOCABULARY
accommodate, establish

TERMS & NAMES
- Parliament
- Golden Quadrilateral

Essential Question What are some effects of South Asia's rapid changes?

KEY VOCABULARY
- slum
- push-pull factors
- military dictatorship
- overpopulation
- cyclone

ACADEMIC VOCABULARY
deny

TERMS & NAMES
- Mohammed Ali Jinnah
- Benazir Bhutto

TECHTREK  FOR THIS CHAPTER

 Student eEdition

 Maps and Graphs

 Interactive Whiteboard GeoActivities

 Digital Library

Go to **myNGconnect.com** for more on South Asia.

A woman speaks on her mobile phone while riding on a bicycle rickshaw in Delhi, India.

495

1.1 Hinduism Today

TECHTREK
myNGconnect.com For photos of Hindu deities

Digital Library

Main Idea Hinduism unifies its followers through a wide variety of religious beliefs.

Approximately 63 percent of South Asians identify themselves as Hindus. In India, the majority is even larger. Hindus make up over 80 percent of the population, more than 930 million people. Hinduism in India is more than a religion—it is a way of life shared by a diverse population.

 Critical Viewing This tenth-century painting shows Krishna as the protector of cows. What details in the painting tell you that cows are valued by Hindus?

Basic Beliefs

Hindus believe that everything in the universe is part of one spiritual force called Brahman. To become one with Brahman, every soul must go through reincarnation, in which it is reborn into different forms of life. A soul's **karma**, or actions during a life, determines the soul's form in the next life. If a soul has good karma, it will be reborn into a higher state, such as a human. If the soul has bad karma, it will be reborn into a lower state, such as a plant.

These beliefs are recorded in sacred texts called the Vedas, which date back to Aryan civilization. Hindu texts, such as the *Mahabharata* and the *Ramayana*, teach Hindu beliefs in the form of epic poems. As you've learned, the Bhagavad Gita is part of the *Mahabharata*.

Hindu Deities and Sacred Spaces

According to Hindus, there are many gods and goddesses, but all come from Brahman. The three most important deities are Brahma, the creator of the universe; Vishnu, the preserver of the universe; and Shiva, the destroyer of the universe. **Krishna**, an avatar of Vishnu, is a popular Hindu deity. He is often pictured playing his flute.

Hindus believe that the Ganges River is sacred. Millions of Hindus make **pilgrimages**, or religious journeys, to the city of Varanasi to worship on the *ghats*, or stone steps and platforms along the river. Hindus also believe that bathing in the water gives them better karma.

The Caste System

In addition to Hinduism, the Aryan migration into India also brought the caste system. This system divided society into different social groups, or varnas, based on a person's occupation. As you have learned, there were four original varnas in the caste system: the *Brahmans* (priests and scholars); the *Kshatriyas* (rulers and warriors); the *Vaisyas* (merchants and professionals); and the *Sudras* (artisans, laborers, and servants).

Eventually, an unofficial fifth group was created to include those outside the varna system. These "Untouchables" performed the lowest jobs in Indian society, such as tanning animal skins and collecting garbage. Today, this group prefers to call itself *Dalit*.

The rules of the caste system were very strict. People could not marry out of their caste or even eat with people of a higher caste. It was nearly impossible to move into a different caste. In the last 50 years, however, these rules have become less rigid. India's constitution now forbids **discrimination**, or unfair treatment, against members of any caste and many groups have formed to struggle against such discrimination.

Before You Move On

Monitor Comprehension What religious beliefs unite Hindus?

Critical Viewing How is this Hindu temple similar to other religious buildings you have seen?

FORMATIVE ASSESSMENT

READING LAB GeoJournal

1. **Summarize** Name and describe the three most important Hindu deities.

2. **Compare and Contrast** Think about other world religions that you've learned about. How are they similar to or different from Hinduism? Copy the graphic organizer and use it to compare and contrast religions.

3. **Write a Response** Why is Hinduism so important to India? How would you describe Hinduism's connection to society and culture in India? Write two to three sentences explaining Hinduism's importance.

1.2 Changing Traditions

TECHTREK
myNGconnect.com For photos of
South Asian traditions

Digital
Library

Main Idea In South Asia, traditions blend with modern practices.

Many groups have helped shape South Asia's culture, from the Aryans to the British. Some aspects of the region's culture are very old and some are modern. These photographs show the ancient cultural traditions practiced by people in South Asia today.

Traditional Decoration

Since ancient times, Indian women and girls have decorated their hands with fancy patterns for special occasions, such as weddings or festivals. They use a reddish powder called **henna** to create the intricate designs (shown at right). Each design has a special meaning: A flower can mean happiness; a square might mean honesty; and a triangle might represent creativity.

Before You Move On

Make Inferences How do traditions blend with modern practices in South Asia?

> **Critical Viewing** What traditional and modern elements can you identify in this photo?

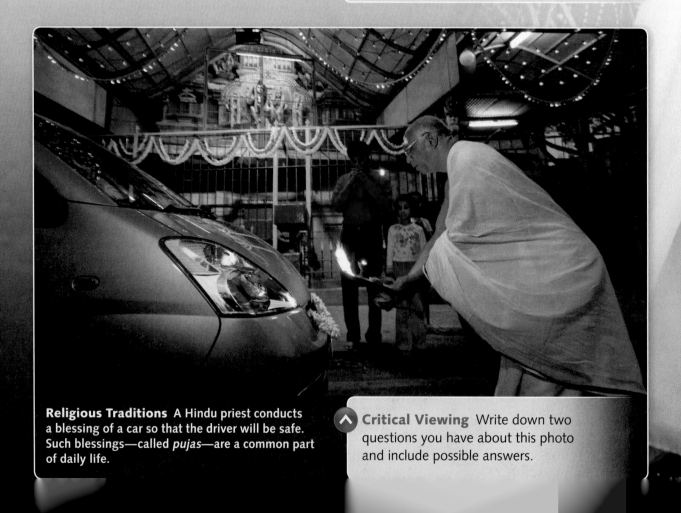

Religious Traditions A Hindu priest conducts a blessing of a car so that the driver will be safe. Such blessings—called *pujas*—are a common part of daily life.

∧ **Critical Viewing** Write down two questions you have about this photo and include possible answers.

6.15.B identify and describe common traits that define cultures; 6.18.B relate ways contemporary expressions of culture have been influence by the past; 6.21.B analyze by drawing inferences; 6.22.C express ideas orally based on experiences

Visual Vocabulary A **sari** is a traditional Indian garment for women worn wrapped around the body. Many saris are silk.

Visual Vocabulary **Henna** is a reddish powder used to create designs on skin. Henna is used for special occasions.

FORMATIVE ASSESSMENT

PHOTO LAB

GeoJournal

1. **Create a Photo Essay** Choose more photos of traditions from the **Digital Library**. Paste them on paper or use the **Magazine Maker CD-ROM** to create a photo essay. Write Visual Vocabulary captions for the photos to explain the traditions and how they are part of modern life. Share your essay. Use your experiences of traditions to talk about what you see in the images.

2. **Make Inferences** Many South Asians wear Western-style clothing. Why might wearing saris continue to be popular today?

1.3 Daily Life

TECHTREK

myNGconnect.com For photos of
daily life in South Asia and Visual Vocabulary

Digital
Library

Main Idea Some aspects of culture in South Asia show how tradition is important in everyday life.

Modern practices have spread to many parts of South Asia. However, people continue to observe early traditions.

Schools

Most countries in South Asia offer some level of free public education like the public schools in the United States. India's schools require attendance until age 14. In Bhutan, formal eduation has only been in place since 1950. However, education is definitely a shared value in the region. Schools are set up wherever there is space: mountain huts, river boats, desert tents, and even train platforms.

The **literacy rate** (the percentage of people who can read and write) for 15-to-24-year-olds ranges from 74 percent in Bangladesh to 96 percent in the Maldives. Rising literacy rates indicate that the region is developing.

Clothing

South Asia's climate extremes determine what people wear. For example, Bhutanese herders wear coats and yak-hair hats to protect themselves from the cold, while Sri Lankan fishermen dress lightly because of the heat.

Many men and women wear a **shalwar-kameez** (see photo opposite), a long shirt with loose-fitting pants. Once considered a traditional form of Muslim dress, the shalwar-kameez is now worn by Muslims and Hindus alike. Some women wear a sari, a single piece of cloth (often silk) wrapped to form a long dress. Western clothes are increasingly popular too.

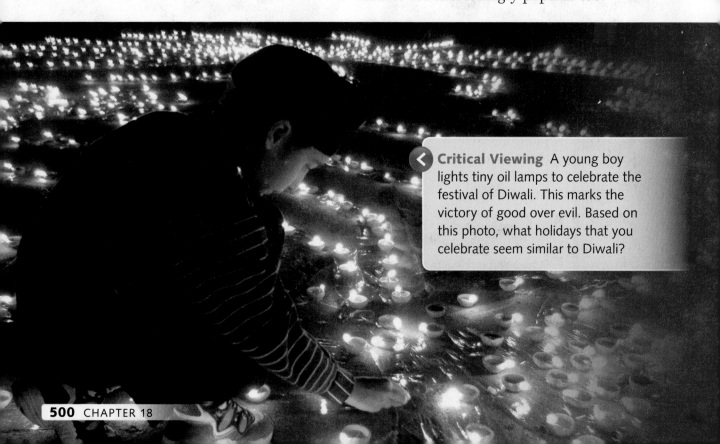

Critical Viewing A young boy lights tiny oil lamps to celebrate the festival of Diwali. This marks the victory of good over evil. Based on this photo, what holidays that you celebrate seem similar to Diwali?

6.10.B describe levels of economic development using indicators (literacy); 6.15.B identify and describe common traits that define cultures; 6.15.E analyze similarities and differences among world societies; 6.19.B explain significance of religious holidays and observances; 6.21.B analyze by comparing, summarizing; 6.22.D create written material based on research

Visual Vocabulary
shalwar-kameez

Visual Vocabulary cricket

Food

South Asia's cuisine—the food commonly served in a region—is richly spiced and often vegetarian. Cows are sacred to Hindus, so many Indians do not eat meat. Pakistan and India serve curry dishes with potatoes, eggplant, and okra. In Bhutan, yaks provide meat and milk, which is used to make butter and cheese. Each region prepares its own mixture of spices, or *masala*, to use in sauces. Rice is often the center of a meal, especially in Bangladesh and eastern and southern India. *Chapati*, a flat wheat bread, is common in northern India. *Dal*, a blended stew of peas, beans, or lentils, is a frequent side dish.

hockey, golf, and soccer are also popular. India has professional cricket and soccer leagues that draw many enthusiastic fans.

Before You Move On

Summarize What are three ways in which tradition is part of everyday life in South Asia?

Rice, potatoes, and wheat are staples of South Asian cuisine.

Sports

Traditional sports like kabaddi (described as a combination of wrestling and rugby) have existed in India for nearly 4,000 years. Western sports such as **cricket** (a team game similar to baseball), field

---

FORMATIVE ASSESSMENT

WRITING LAB — GeoJournal

1. **Connect to Texas** Create a culture diagram to compare cultures. Start with what you have read about daily life and traditions in South Asia. Fill in these categories: School, Clothing, Food, and Sports. Then write a detailed paragraph that describes the same categories of daily life in Texas. Exchange your paragraph with a partner to analyze the similarities and differences between cultures.

   Schools | Clothing
   — My Culture —
   Food | Sports

2. **Research** Diwali is a five-day festival of lights. Do online research and write about Diwali and two other Hindu festivals to explain their significance.

1.4 Popular Culture

TECHTREK

myNGconnect.com
For samples of Indian music

Digital
Library

Main Idea Music and movies help unify the diverse peoples and cultures of South Asia.

Music and movies are a lively part of South Asia's popular culture, which consists of the arts, music, and other elements of everyday life in a region.

Unifying a Culture

South Asia has a long musical history, ranging from religious music to blockbuster movie soundtracks. Traditional music echoes in today's spectacles of Bollywood movies. With wide availability and appeal, music and movies foster the development of a common culture.

Music

Young people in South Asia listen to Bollywood music, Indian rock, and Western pop. Many also enjoy Bhangra, a form of folk dance and music from the Punjab region of India and Pakistan. Some modern Indian musicians are fusing Indian and Western styles to create a new sound that keeps Indian musical traditions alive.

Critical Viewing Young people in New Delhi dance to a wide variety of music. What influences of Western popular culture do you see in the photograph?

The musician on the left plays traditional music near the Ganges River at Varanasi. The DJ on the right plays music in Mumbai. Classical Indian music is based on religious themes and can be heard in both traditional and contemporary music.

Movies

India's film industry began in Bombay (Mumbai) and is called **"Bollywood"** after its American counterpart, Hollywood. Many Bollywood movies have themes based on Hindu stories, feature musical numbers, and use the Hindi language. India produces more feature films than any other country in the world, and their international audience is growing.

The southern city of Chennai has its own film industry that produces films in the Tamil language. This film center is called "Kollywood" after the Kodambakkam district of Chennai.

Before You Move On

Make Inferences How do music and movies unify people of South Asia?

Cast members from the 2008 hit movie *Slumdog Millionaire* pose at the Academy Awards. Movies like *Slumdog Millionaire* showed that films about India are often popular in Western culture.

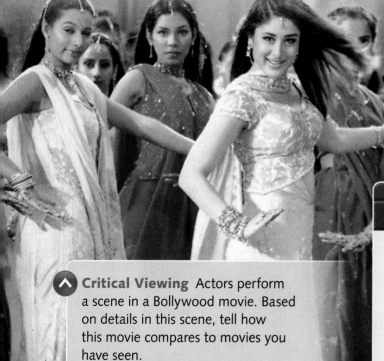

Critical Viewing Actors perform a scene in a Bollywood movie. Based on details in this scene, tell how this movie compares to movies you have seen.

FORMATIVE ASSESSMENT

SPEAKING LAB GeoJournal

Turn and Talk Do music and movies bring people together in the United States? Think about your answer, and then collaborate with a group to develop a response that can be presented orally. Your first sentence will answer the question. Each person in the group adds one sentence for support. Work together to vary the sentence types for an interesting presentation.

2.1 The Largest Democracy

> **Main Idea** The democratic government of India faces many challenges in governing more than one billion citizens.

In 2009, 64-year-old Meira Kumar became the Speaker of the lower house of India's **Parliament**. She was the first woman elected to this position— a milestone for the world's largest democracy. India's Parliament is the legislative branch of the government. It has two houses like the U.S. Congress.

Governing One Billion People

India has passed many milestones since its independence. One of the first was crafting a new constitution in 1949 to create a **democracy**, or a government in which citizens make decisions either directly or indirectly through elected representatives. India's constitution established a **federal republic**, which is a democratic form of government in which voters elect representatives and the central government shares power with the states. The United States is also a federal republic.

India's government has three branches: the legislative, the executive, and the judicial. The legislative branch has two houses, the *Lok Sabha* (similar to the U.S. House of Representatives) and the *Rajya Sabha* (similar to the U.S. Senate). Members of the *Lok Sabha* are elected every five years, and those of the *Rajya Sabha* serve six-year terms.

Parliament and the states' legislatures elect the president. The president appoints justices to the Supreme Court. However, the leader with the most power is the prime minister, who is head of the political party with the most members in the *Lok Sabha*. The prime minister heads the Council of Ministers, who operate the government.

India's Politics Today

In 2009, India held its national elections. Voting took place in phases over a one-month period and brought Meira Kumar into the headlines. Kumar promised to work toward a "casteless" society in India.

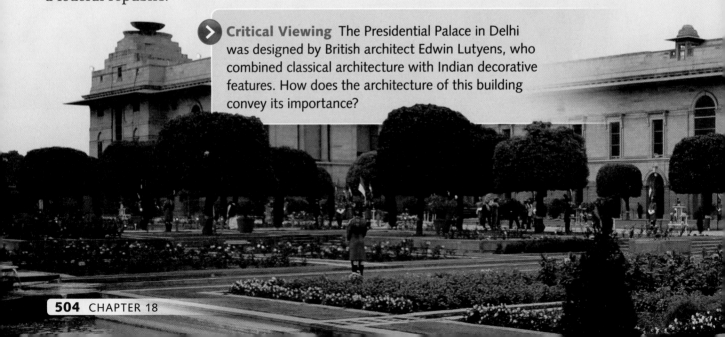

> **Critical Viewing** The Presidential Palace in Delhi was designed by British architect Edwin Lutyens, who combined classical architecture with Indian decorative features. How does the architecture of this building convey its importance?

INDIA'S GOVERNMENTAL STRUCTURE

LEGISLATIVE (Parliament)

Rajya Sabha
Upper House:
House of States
(250 members)

Lok Sabha
Lower House:
House of the People
(545 members)

EXECUTIVE

President

Prime Minister

Council of Ministers

JUDICIAL

Supreme Court
- Chief Justice
- 25 associate justices

The Indian government is tackling major challenges, such as India's fast-growing population. By 2030, India is expected to pass China as the world's most populous nation. The government is already working to improve its infrastructure in order to **accommodate,** or make room for, that growth. **Infrastructure** includes the basic systems that a society needs, such as roads, bridges, and sewers. You will read about one of India's

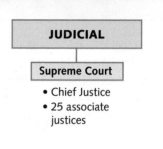

massive road projects, the Golden Quadrilateral, later in this chapter. In addition, because of the shortage of fossil fuels in India, the government is increasing its investment in nuclear power to produce electricity.

Another challenge for the government is reaching an agreement with Pakistan over control of largely Muslim Kashmir. This is a goal most observers believe is important to the region's future.

Before You Move On

Make Inferences What is a major challenge facing India in governing its citizens?

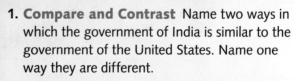

FORMATIVE ASSESSMENT

READING LAB GeoJournal

1. **Compare and Contrast** Name two ways in which the government of India is similar to the government of the United States. Name one way they are different.

2. **Analyze Visuals** How is India's government organized?

3. **Make Inferences** Review India's caste system on page 497. Describe how the election of Meira Kumar, the first woman Speaker of *Lok Sabha* and a member of the *Dalit* caste, is influential for India society today.

2.2 Economic Growth

TECHTREK

myNGconnect.com For photos of
economic growth and current events

Digital
Library

> **Main Idea** Many factors have contributed
> to India's rapid economic growth.

If you have a computer problem and
call for technical help, your call may be
answered in the southern Indian city
of Bangalore. Bangalore is the leading
center of India's telecommunications
industry. Companies there handle support
services for U.S. computer and software
companies. **Outsourcing**, the shifting of
jobs to workers outside of a company, has
been a big part of India's economic growth.

A Growing Economy

The value of the goods and services
produced in a country divided by the
number of people in that country is called
the per capita Gross Domestic Product
(GDP). Countries with a high per capita
GDP are known as **developed nations**,
and countries with a low per capita GDP
are called **developing nations**. Developed
nations have healthier, more educated
people, consume more goods and services,
use more energy, and employ more people
in manufacturing and service industries
than developing nations. Developing
nations have a lower standard of living
and less developed infrastructure.

Most South Asian countries are
developing nations. But some economists
see India as an emerging market, with a
high growth rate and goods and services
that compete in global trade. India's GDP
was growing quickly until the global
financial crisis. Between 2008 and
2013, the country's economy slowed.
Nevertheless its estimated middle class
of more than 300 million people nearly
matches the entire U.S. population.

Critical Viewing This busy call center
is in Bangalore, India. What appears to
be the main activity in this call center?

Factors Affecting Growth

The teaching of English—the language of international commerce—is a legacy of British colonialism that has worked in India's favor. A common language, a stable democratic government, and improvements in infrastructure have encouraged foreign investment.

What does India's growth mean to the average person? With nearly 70 percent of the people trying to exist on only two dollars a day, it means slow but improving access to more consumer goods and more opportunities. **Microlending**, the practice of making small loans to people starting their own businesses, is one way that the country's growing prosperity reaches even its poorest citizens.

Before You Move On

Monitor Comprehension What economic factors contributed to rapid growth in India?

COMPARISON OF SELECTED CONSUMER GOODS, SOUTH ASIA AND THE UNITED STATES

	Televisions	Cell Phone Subscriptions	Personal Computers	Total Number of Automobiles
	(per thousand people)			
Bangladesh	85	566	22	185,000
Bhutan	33	656	16	29,189
India	83	720	33	13,673,611
Maldives	40	530	152	3,917
Nepal	10	438	5	93,266
Pakistan	56	616	5	2,331,900
Sri Lanka	142	871	35	410,282
U.S.A.	893	1059	755	134,880,000

Between 2003 and 2011   Source: Encyclopedia Britannica

FORMATIVE ASSESSMENT
DATA LAB
 GeoJournal

1. **Compare** Explain per capita GDP. What is the difference between a developed nation and a developing nation?

2. **Describe** What is India's level of economic development?

3. **Make Inferences** How do you think labor, one of the factors of production, has influenced India's economy?

2.3 The Golden Quadrilateral

Main Idea India is modernizing its roadways to support its economic growth.

In the mid-1990s, India's prime minister complained, "Our roads don't have a few potholes. Our potholes have a few roads." Since then, the country has invested large amounts of money to improve its roads.

A Road to the 21st Century

In 1998, the prime minister announced that India would build a 3,633-mile superhighway called the **Golden Quadrilateral** (GQ) to connect four major cities: Delhi, Mumbai, Chennai, and Kolkata. The GQ is an example of India's efforts to improve its infrastructure. **Modernization** efforts like the GQ bring countries up to present standards in technology and other areas.

The GQ will help spread economic growth from India's bustling cities to its thousands of poor villages.

When India gained independence in 1947, drivers shared unpaved roads with cattle and slow-moving tractors. In 1998, the government **established** (put into place) the National Highways Authority to build thousands of miles of new roads, including the Golden Quadrilateral, at a cost of more than $30 billion. It is the largest public works project in the country's history. With the GQ's advanced technology, road sensors will automatically notify crews when it needs repairing. Providing faster and more reliable transportation is one step toward modernizing India's infrastructure and preparing for a profitable future.

Critical Viewing Traffic backs up in Bangalore at a GQ construction site. Based on details in the photograph, what challenges do you think a company might face when building a road in a heavily populated area?

6.03.B pose and answer questions about geographic distribution, graphs; 6.03.C compare countries using data from graphs; 6.03.D create graphs; 6.07.B analyze ways people have modified environment; 6.20.C predict social, economic, cultural impacts from scientific discoveries and technological innovations; 6.22.C express ideas orally based on experiences

The Impact of the GQ

India's investment in the GQ has already had a tremendous impact on its economy—and on people's lives. For example, farmers who could sell their crops only in nearby towns can now use the GQ to carry their products to Chennai and sell them for higher prices.

With better roads, manufacturers can set up factories and businesses in new locations because resources and goods can be transported more reliably than in the past. This means more jobs outside of crowded major cities. With better employment opportunities, and better roads, more Indians can purchase cars and trucks.

Before You Move On

Monitor Comprehension How have improvements in infrastructure helped India's economic growth?

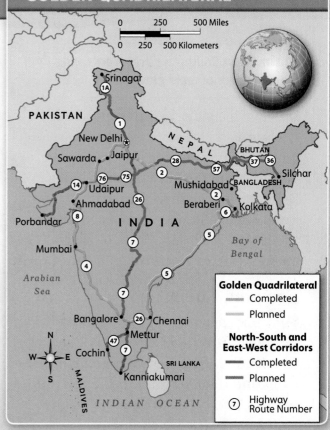

INDIA'S HIGHWAYS AND THE GOLDEN QUADRILATERAL

Golden Quadrilateral
- Completed
- Planned

North-South and East-West Corridors
- Completed
- Planned

⑦ Highway Route Number

SALES OF PASSENGER VEHICLES IN INDIA AND THE UNITED STATES

India   United States

Numbers in Hundred Thousands

2002   2007

Source: U.S. Bureau of Transportation Statistics; Society of Indian Automobile Manufacturers

SPEAKING LAB GeoJournal

1. **Connect to Texas** Based on your experience of roads and highways in Texas, what technological innovations, such as road sensors, could bring about improvements? Think about safety, maintenance, traffic, and mass transportation. Organize your ideas and share them with the class.

2. **Make Predictions** Describe a future technological innovation that could impact the economic or cultural life where you live. What improvements in society could new scientific discoveries make?

3. **Create Graphs** Draw a graph with this data for 2012: sales of passenger vehicles in India, 2.5 million; in the United States, 14.5 million. With a partner, pose and answer questions, comparing your graph with the one here.

3.1 The Impact of Urbanization

Main Idea South Asia's cities are facing the challenges of rapid growth.

Dharavi is a slum in Mumbai, India. A **slum** is an area in a city that has crowded, unclean housing, poor sanitation, and bad living conditions. Residents of Dharavi often walked a mile to get water, but now some have their own water taps. It's a small sign of progress in an area where improvement comes slowly.

Growing Cities

Since independence, cities in India have exploded in population. In 1951, about 62 million Indians lived in urban areas—cities and their surrounding communities. In 2001, nearly 300 million people lived in cities. Thirty-five cities have more than a million residents. People have flocked to India's cities because of a number of push-pull factors. **Push-pull factors** are the reasons why people migrate. "Push" factors cause people to leave a place, and "pull" factors draw them to another place.

One key factor pushing people to leave the countryside is poverty. Factors pulling people to cities include job opportunities and better education.

India's cities have gradually divided into small wealthy sections and vast slums. The slums have very poor infrastructure and lack clean water and electricity. Education and health-care services are inadequate. Permits to build new structures are hard to get. City centers are also jammed with growing numbers of automobiles, creating traffic congestion and adding to air pollution—which causes thousands of deaths each year. Despite these problems, the jobs and educational opportunities in the cities do help some people to improve their lives.

Pakistan faces similar issues. There, nearly 36 percent of Pakistan's population live in cities. The city of Karachi (kuh RAH chee) is approaching 13 million people—about 6 percent of Pakistan's entire population.

Critical Viewing Slums of Mumbai stand amidst new construction. What does this photo suggest about the differences between the way wealthy and poor people live?

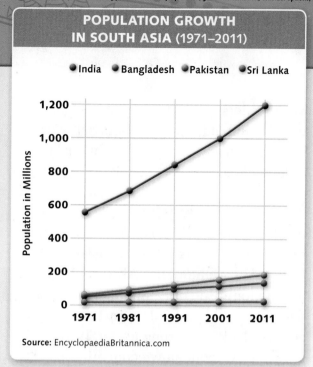

POPULATION GROWTH IN SOUTH ASIA (1971–2011)

● India ● Bangladesh ● Pakistan ● Sri Lanka

Population in Millions

1,200 / 1,000 / 800 / 600 / 400 / 200 / 0

1971 1981 1991 2001 2011

Source: EncyclopaediaBritannica.com

Critical Viewing This crowded city street is in Karachi, Pakistan. What can you infer about life in a Pakistani city from this photo?

Pakistan's Solutions

As in India, people are leaving rural areas in Pakistan and moving to the cities. With urban populations increasing at a rate of 3 percent per year, Pakistan's infrastructure has trouble keeping up. This leads to overcrowding in slums.

One solution to overcrowding has been the development of "secondary" cities around major urban centers. For example, Gujranwala is a secondary city to Lahore.

Secondary cities provide rural migrants with an affordable place to settle and find employment. The secondary cities also relieve strain on big cities such as Lahore. They do this by slowing the flow of people into the main city. Other South Asian cities, particularly in Bangladesh and Sri Lanka, face similar pressures.

Before You Move On

Monitor Comprehension What problems do the slums have in South Asia's cities?

DATA LAB  GeoJournal

1. **Analyze Data** About how much did Bangladesh's population grow from 1971 to 2011? Use a database to compare the population of each country today.

2. **Explain** How has human migration affected cities in India and Pakistan?

3. **Analyze** Use a problem-solving process to address overcrowding and slums. State the problem, research it, list and evaluate options. Choose one option and write a paragraph to explain why your solution would be effective.

3.2 Pakistan's Changing Government

TECHTREK

myNGconnect.com For an online political map

 Maps and Graphs

Main Idea Pakistan's government has alternated between democracy and military dictatorships.

Pakistan was created in 1947 as an Islamic country. Since then, it has alternated between civilian governments and **military dictatorships**, in which the army runs the government and **denies,** or refuses to recognize, citizens' rights. The changes in Pakistan's government have limited social and economic progress in the country.

A Lack of National Unity

One cause of Pakistan's changes in government has been a lack of unity. The country is divided into four provinces: Punjab, Sindh, Balochistan, and the North-West Frontier Province. Each province has its own tribal groups and languages. No leader has been able to pull the provinces together to form a unified nation.

The lack of unity was a problem from the start. In 1947, the country had two parts. West Pakistan was west of India. East Pakistan was east of India, more than 1,000 miles away from West Pakistan.

Most leaders came from West Pakistan, which troubled the people of East Pakistan. In 1971, East Pakistan declared independence and became Bangladesh.

Military Dictatorships

Another cause of Pakistan's changes in government has been inconsistent leadership. **Mohammed Ali Jinnah**, who led the founding of Pakistan, believed in democracy. When he died in 1948, the country lacked a strong leader. Pakistanis grew angry about slow economic development, and unrest between different groups of Pakistanis increased. In 1958, the military took over the government and established a military dictatorship.

After a civil war in 1971, Zulfikar Bhutto was elected to lead Pakistan. He promised to take steps to end poverty. However, in 1977, the military took control of Pakistan again, and Bhutto was executed in 1979.

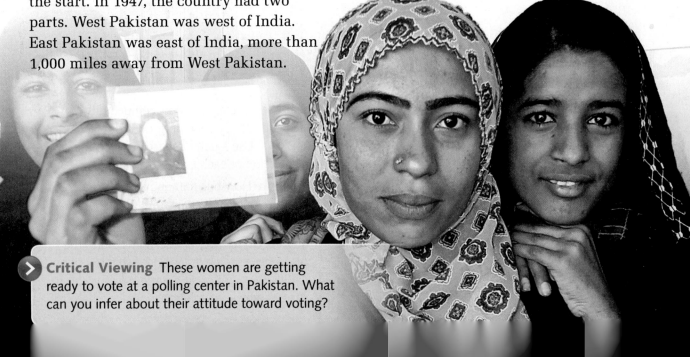

> **Critical Viewing** These women are getting ready to vote at a polling center in Pakistan. What can you infer about their attitude toward voting?

Benazir Bhutto's Election

Elections were held again in 1988 after the death of the military leader. Pakistanis elected Bhutto's daughter, **Benazir Bhutto**, as prime minister. Her opponents accused her of corruption. She denied the charges, but there were many threats on her life, and she fled Pakistan in 1999.

With the military in power again, Pakistan experienced moments of prosperity. Yet it also continued to deny people's rights. In 2007, the military promised elections, and Benazir Bhutto returned to Pakistan. However, she was assassinated later that year. Bhutto's husband, Asif Ali Zardari, was elected president in 2008.

Continuing Challenges

Pakistan's relationship with its larger neighbor, India, continues to be strained, particularly over the region of Kashmir. The two countries are frequently at a stand-off over the area. Violence regularly erupts, and war is a very real threat. Difficulty controlling the border with its eastern neighbor, Afghanistan, also continues to put a great deal of pressure on Pakistan's government.

Pakistan's internal problems show that successful countries need strong leaders who can bring different groups together. They also demonstrate the importance of having an effective government that makes sure the country's constitution is enforced, guaranteeing rights to all of its citizens.

Before You Move On

Make Inferences Explain why the military has taken power in Pakistan at various times.

PAKISTAN POLITICAL

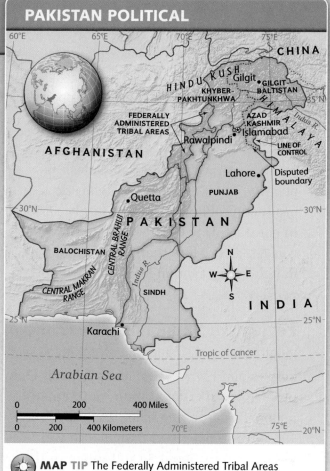

MAP TIP The Federally Administered Tribal Areas are seven areas along the border with Afghanistan that are inhabited by mainly Pashtun tribes. These areas are loosely governed by regulations put in place by the British *raj*.

FORMATIVE ASSESSMENT

READING LAB GeoJournal

1. **Analyze Cause and Effect** What circumstances have caused Pakistan to alternate between democratic governments and military governments?

2. **Location** Find the five major cities in Pakistan on the map. How might geographic factors explain their location?

3. **Make Inferences** Why would it be difficult to govern the four provinces of Pakistan?

4. **Evaluate** Why has it been difficult for Pakistan to move forward as a country?

3.3 Fighting Poverty in Bangladesh

Main Idea Bangladesh is one of the poorest countries in the world, but it is making progress toward improving its economy.

The biggest problem in Bangladesh is poverty. In 2009, the gross domestic product (GDP) per capita was only $1,500. In contrast, U.S. GDP per capita that year was $46,000. More than eight out of ten Bangladeshis live on less than two dollars per day.

Poverty in Bangladesh

Economists identify three problems that help explain why Bangladesh is poor. One problem is **overpopulation**, or too many people living in one place. In 2010, over 156 million people in Bangladesh were living on only about 55,600 square miles of land. That is roughly equivalent to half of the U.S. population living in an area the size of the state of Illinois.

The second problem facing Bangladesh is natural disasters. Rivers like the Ganges surge over their banks during summer monsoons. Many **cyclones**—the name for hurricanes in South Asia—also hit Bangladesh. Floods and cyclones destroy crops, adding to the problems of an uneven food supply and poverty.

Lack of education is a third problem. Only 48 percent of Bangladeshis can read and write. In contrast, 99 percent of Americans can read and write. In addition, about 8 million Bangladeshi children work in factories and at other jobs. Because they work for wages, they are not able to go to school.

Toward a Brighter Future

When Bangladesh became an independent nation in 1971, it had a military government like Pakistan's. Since 1991, though, it has had a democratically elected government. The government has improved the economy by encouraging exports and building new industries.

It is not easy to find products to export. Bangladeshi farmers grow rice, wheat, tea, and sugarcane, but those crops must feed the country's large population, and there is usually nothing left over to export. However, the country does export huge amounts of jute. Jute is a strong fiber used in making ropes, carpets, types of paper, and other products.

Critical Viewing Garments are a major export in Bangladesh. What conditions shown in this photo of a factory help explain why the garment industry has been successful?

6.06.B identify location of natural resources; 6.06.C analyze effects of physical processes on humans;
6.10.A give examples of manufacturing industries; 6.10.B describe levels of economic development using indicators;
6.21.B analyze information by summarizing, making generalizations, inferences; 6.21.C interpret information from maps

BANGLADESH RESOURCES AND INDUSTRIES

MAP TIP In the legend below, resources and industries are divided into three categories.

Crops
- Potatoes
- Rice
- Rice and jute
- Sugarcane
- Tea
- Tobacco
- Wheat

Major Industries
- Garments
- Cement
- Steel
- Paper

Natural Resources
- Natural gas
- Fish
- Shrimp

Bay of Bengal

Bangladesh has also built several industries. New factories produce paper, cement, and steel. (Locate them on the resources map above.)

Garment manufacturing—shown in the photo at left—has been particularly successful. In fact, garments are the country's largest export. Most of the employees in the garment industry are women, and today the clothing they produce is sold in countries around the world. This economic progress gives hope for a brighter future for Bangladesh.

Before You Move On

Summarize What are two strategies that Bangladesh has used to develop its economy?

FORMATIVE ASSESSMENT

MAP LAB

GeoJournal

1. **Human-Environment Interaction** What natural resource appears most frequently on the map? How would this natural resource contribute to building industries in Bangladesh?

2. **Write a Paragraph** Pick one resource on the map. Write a paragraph that explains where that resource is located in Bangladesh and why it might be important to Bangladesh's economy. Share your paragraph with classmates.

3. **Make Inferences** How has a lack of education interfered with economic development in Bangladesh?

4. **Make Generalizations** Why do you think that the garment industry has grown so quickly in Bangladesh?

VOCABULARY

For each pair of vocabulary words, write one sentence that explains the connection between the two words.

1. pilgrimage; karma

Hindus believe that a pilgrimage to the Ganges River will give them good karma.

2. shalwar-kameez; sari
3. democracy; federal republic
4. infrastructure; modernization
5. developed nations; developing nations

MAIN IDEAS

6. In what ways does Hinduism unify South Asia? (Section 1.1)
7. For what purpose do Indian women use henna? (Section 1.2)
8. How do foods differ from region to region in South Asia? (Section 1.3)
9. How do music and movies foster a common culture in South Asia? (Section 1.4)
10. Name two challenges facing the government of India today. (Section 2.1)
11. How has outsourcing contributed to rapid growth? (Section 2.2)
12. What is the Golden Quadrilateral, and what cities will it connect? (Section 2.3)
13. What problems are caused by rapid growth in South Asia's cities? (Section 3.1)
14. What are two causes of Pakistan's many changes in government? (Section 3.2)
15. What three factors have contributed to poverty in Bangladesh? (Section 3.3)

CULTURE

ANALYZE THE ESSENTIAL QUESTION

How is diversity reflected in South Asia's cultures?

Critical Thinking: Draw Conclusions

16. What is one basic belief of Hinduism? How does it influence Indian culture?
17. Why do you think established traditions have continued in South Asia today?
18. In what ways is South Asian food similar to and different from American food?
19. How does South Asia's music reflect the region's diversity?

INTERPRET MAPS

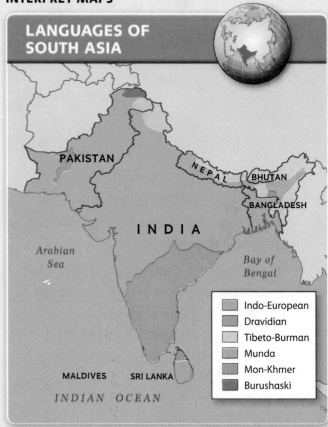

LANGUAGES OF SOUTH ASIA

PAKISTAN
NEPAL
BHUTAN
BANGLADESH
INDIA
Arabian Sea
Bay of Bengal
MALDIVES   SRI LANKA
INDIAN OCEAN

- Indo-European
- Dravidian
- Tibeto-Burman
- Munda
- Mon-Khmer
- Burushaski

20. **Region** According to the map, what is the major language family in South Asia?
21. **Make Inferences** Why might there be so many different language families in South Asia?

6.03.D create databases for regions or countries; 6.10.B describe economic development using indicators;
6.21.B analyze information by drawing conclusions, making generalizations, identifying cause-effect relationships;
6.21.C interpret information from maps, charts; 6.22.E use standard grammar, spelling, sentence structure, and punctuation.

FOCUS ON INDIA

ANALYZE THE ESSENTIAL QUESTION

Why has India experienced an economic boom?

Critical Thinking: Make Generalizations

22. In what ways is India's government similar to and different from the U.S. government?

23. If India's economy keeps expanding, what effect might that have on the other countries of South Asia?

24. How will the Golden Quadrilateral help to build India's economy?

GOVERNMENT & ECONOMICS

ANALYZE THE ESSENTIAL QUESTION

What are some effects of South Asia's rapid changes?

Critical Thinking: Analyze Cause and Effect

25. How do Pakistan's secondary cities help relieve strain on the major cities?

26. How has Pakistan's unstable government affected its citizens?

INTERPRET CHARTS

LITERACY RATE AND GDP PER CAPITA IN BANGLADESH (1981–2011)				
	1981	1991	2001	2011
Adult Literacy Rate (% people)	29%	35%	47%	57%
GDP Per Capita ($)	$319	$514	$664	$747

Source: The World Bank

27. **Analyze Data** What is the relationship between Bangladesh's adult literacy rate and GDP per capita?

28. **Evaluate** How would you explain the relationship between these two economic indicators? Why might GDP per capita affect the literacy rate?

ACTIVE OPTIONS

Synthesize the Essential Questions by completing the activities below.

29. **Write in Two Styles** Describe what you know about popular culture in India. Write informally as if speaking or texting to a friend. Then rewrite your description in formal language. Swap with a partner to check and correct grammar, spelling, and punctuation. Fix run-on or incomplete sentences. Be sure your subjects and verbs agree. **Share the two versions with the class**.

> **Writing Tips**
> • Review the lesson on page R24. Make a list of correct sentence structures to refer to.
> • Work with your partner to improve vocabulary and vary your sentence types before you share your examples aloud.

TECHTREK myNGconnect.com For photos of South Asia

30. **Create a Culture Database** Work with a partner or small group to organize a visual database for the region or for individual countries of your choice. A database charts information so you can search and find it, using key words, or tags. Gather images from the **Digital Library** or other sources. What is the subject of each? What words would you use if you were searching for such an image?

Photo	How It Represents South Asia
Subject:	
Subject:	

Economic Growth

Many factors—geography and climate, natural resources, the freedom of the markets to compete, and government policies—play a complex part in whether a country's economy can grow.

A government might control all or a large part of how goods and services are created and then how they are sold or provided to citizens. Some monarchies, totalitarian regimes, and societies that have communist and socialist economies are like that. Or a country might have a free-market economy in which the government has a smaller role such as to protect consumers. When India and Hungary became more free-market based in the 1990s, their economic growth increased.

Compare

- India
- Hungary
- Vietnam
- South Africa

INDIA

Think about the factors of production: 1) natural resources, 2) labor or workers, 3) capital (factories, computers, tractors, for example), and 4) people who start new businesses, such as entrepreneurs. Factors of production are needed to produce goods and services. They influence economic systems.

One factor, labor, means having enough skilled workers. India's large labor force has had to become skilled in industry and technology for India to become a fast-growing world market.

India also has had to increase its capital—the buildings, machinery, and materials needed for growth. In 2013, India was in the top ten countries with the largest GDP. However, its GNI, Gross National Income per capita (per person), remained low.

HUNGARY

Under communism, Hungary's economy was controlled by the government. Entrepreneurs could not start their own businesses. New businesses that can freely compete are one benefit of a free enterprise system. Another is freely buying and selling capital and at fair prices. Both of these factors encourage growth.

Today, with a free-market system, Hungary's economy is one of the most prosperous in Eastern Europe. The country has had a high literacy rate, and it has lower percentage of people living in poverty than in the United States. But like India and many other nations, Hungary suffered a slowdown because of the global economic crisis, which began in 2007–2008.

ECONOMIC INDICATORS FOR INDIA AND HUNGARY

(Data Comparison)

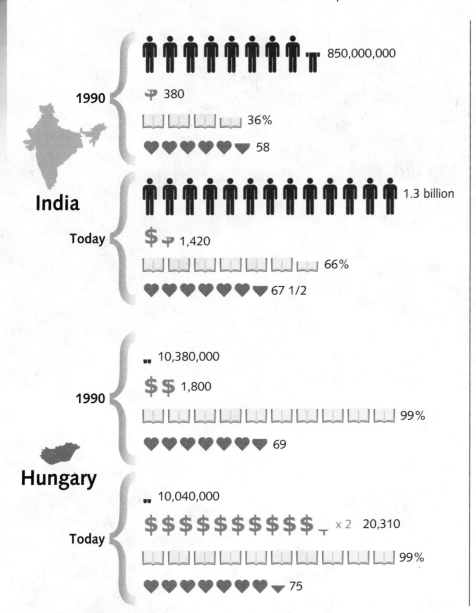

India

1990
850,000,000
₱ 380
36%
58

Today
1.3 billion
$ ₱ 1,420
66%
67 1/2

Hungary

1990
10,380,000
$ $ 1,800
99%
69

Today
10,040,000
$ $ $ $ $ $ $ $ $ × 2   20,310
99%
75

KEY

👤 **Population**
100,000,000 people

$ **GNI**
$1,000

📖 **Adult Literacy Rate**
10%

❤ **Life Expectancy**
10 years

U.S. Benchmark
Population: 313,914,040
GNI: $48,620
Adult Literacy Rate: 98%
Life Expectancy: 79 years

Sources: World Bank, Encyclopedia Brittanica, CIA World Factbook

FORMATIVE ASSESSMENT

RESEARCH LAB   GeoJournal

1. **Analyze Data** Which measurement increased the most in both countries?

2. **Turn and Talk** With a partner, use key vocabulary and information in the graph to describe the level of economic development today for India and Hungary compared with the United States. Then describe the benefits of the U.S. free enterprise system.

3. **Compare Countries** What economic system did Hungary have before the 1990s? How did the distribution of goods and services in that system differ from that of the United States?

4. **Describe** Which factors of production have influenced the economy of India? What problems do you think arise when one or more of the factors of production is in short supply?

Active Options

ACTIVITY 1

Goal: Extend your understanding of endangered animals.

Write About Endangered Species

National Geographic explorer Shafqat Hussain created Project Snow Leopard to protect the endangered snow leopard species in South Asia. With a partner, research one of the following endangered animals from the region:

- Bengal tiger
- Indian rhinoceros
- Ganges River dolphin
- Indus River dolphin
- Indian elephant
- Lion-tailed macaque

Create a presentation that tells about the animal, why the animal is endangered, and why it is important to protect the animal. Present your findings to the class. **Go to Student Resources** for Guided Writing support.

snow leopard

ACTIVITY 2

Goal: Research South Asia's culture.

Create *South Asia Today* Magazine

You and your classmates are on the staff of the magazine *South Asia Today*. Work together and use the **Magazine Maker CD-ROM** to create next month's issue. Go to the **Digital Library** to find images and information on:

- clothing
- festivals
- food
- movies
- music
- schools
- shopping
- sports

ACTIVITY 3

Goal: Review South Asia with a game.

Host a Geography Bee

Write a question about South Asia and its answer on a card. Your teacher will collect the questions and ask them to the class. Stand to answer the question. The last person standing wins!

6.13.A describe roles and responsibilities of citizens in various societies; 6.13.B explain opportunities to participate in political process; 6.13.C compare roles of citizens; 6.22.C express ideas orally based on research; 6.22.D create written and visual material based on research

TEKS

TEKS PROJECT

Goal: Conduct interviews to compare citizenship roles among societies.

Conduct Interviews

Successful interviews include questions that provide insight or a new way of thinking about a topic. Your mission for this project is to determine *what* questions to ask others about citizenship, *who* to ask to gain new insight, and *how* to conduct the interviews and organize the results.

Phase 1: The Questions Form small groups. To get started, read the questions below and come up with additional questions. Think of examples to help explain, so that interviewees might better understand what you want to know.

Would you describe the responsibilities you had as a citizen in another country? How did citizens take part in the political process? What duties did you have? As a U.S. citizen, how is your role different?

Phase 2: The Interviews Work with adults, teachers, and school administrators to prepare list of people to interview, proper ways to invite them, and how and where to schedule the interviews. You might be able to conduct "video calls" at your school. For the interviews, plan to use recording software and take hand-written notes. Practice interviewing, including how to clarify when speaking and how to rephrase a question to get detailed information.

Schedule and conduct the interviews. Change your questions if you need to.

Phase 3: The Analysis Listen to the recordings and read your notes. What conclusions can you draw about citizenship? What did you find out that surprised you? Provide short biographies about those who participated and add important stories they shared. Share your presentation with the class or school.

This American tutor is with students in Bangalore, India. Interview international workers who have deep experience of citizenship roles in different countries.

Explore East Asia
with NATIONAL GEOGRAPHIC

MEET THE EXPLORER

NATIONAL GEOGRAPHIC

Using advanced tools such as satellite imagery and remote sensors, Emerging Explorer Albert Yu-Min Lin searches for the tomb of Genghis Khan. His search leaves the land undisturbed and respects Mongolian beliefs and tradition.

INVESTIGATE GEOGRAPHY

The upper levels of a temple overlook snowcapped Mount Fuji in central Japan. Mount Fuji is a volcano that has been dormant for over 300 years. A shrine on its peak (12,388 feet) attracts thousands of climbers every summer.

CONNECT WITH THE CULTURE

With a population of over 1.3 billion, China is the world's most populous country. A large and growing population creates challenges, such as polluting auto traffic and overcrowded public transportation. Bicycle use helps to ease the problem.

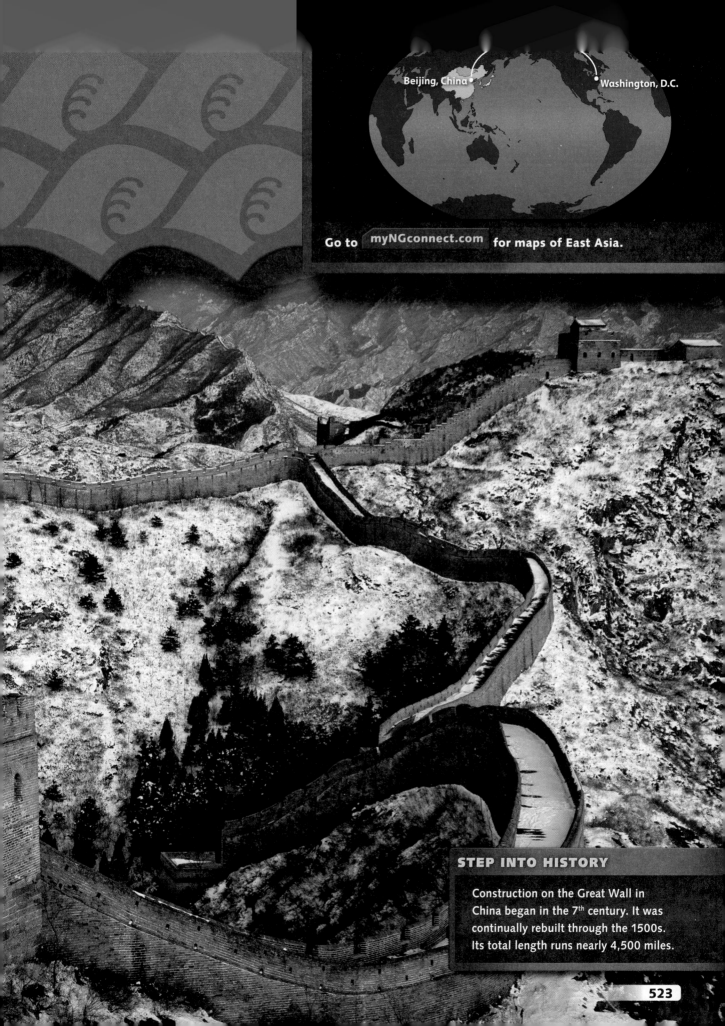

Go to **myNGconnect.com** for maps of East Asia.

Beijing, China

Washington, D.C.

STEP INTO HISTORY

Construction on the Great Wall in China began in the 7ᵗʰ century. It was continually rebuilt through the 1500s. Its total length runs nearly 4,500 miles.

CHAPTER 19

East Asia
GEOGRAPHY & HISTORY

PREVIEW THE CHAPTER

Essential Question How did geographic factors affect population distribution?

KEY VOCABULARY

- mainland
- basin
- alluvium
- loess
- archipelago
- eruption
- typhoon
- demilitarized zone (DMZ)
- steppe
- semiarid
- ger
- animal-borne
- carapace

ACADEMIC VOCABULARY
erode, refuge

TERMS & NAMES

- Kunlun Mountains
- Tibetan Plateau
- Chang Jiang
- Huang He
- North China Plain
- Ring of Fire
- Kanto Plain
- Gobi desert

Essential Question What influences, beliefs, and encounters helped shape China?

KEY VOCABULARY

- dynasty
- dynastic cycle
- empire
- terra cotta
- ethical system
- moral
- caravan
- maritime
- tribute
- expedition
- occupy
- collective farm
- elite

ACADEMIC VOCABULARY
ban, barter

TERMS & NAMES

- Shang
- Zhou
- Qin
- Shi Huangdi
- Great Wall of China
- Han
- Silk Roads
- Confucianism
- Zheng He
- Jiang Jieshi
- Mao Zedong
- Cultural Revolution

Essential Question What factors had an impact on the histories of Japan and Korea?

KEY VOCABULARY

- samurai
- shogun
- competitive
- zaibatsu
- rivalry
- celadon
- retreat
- armistice

ACADEMIC VOCABULARY
dissolve, seize

TERMS & NAMES

- Silla
- Koguryo
- Paekche
- Koryo
- Choson
- 38th parallel
- Cold War

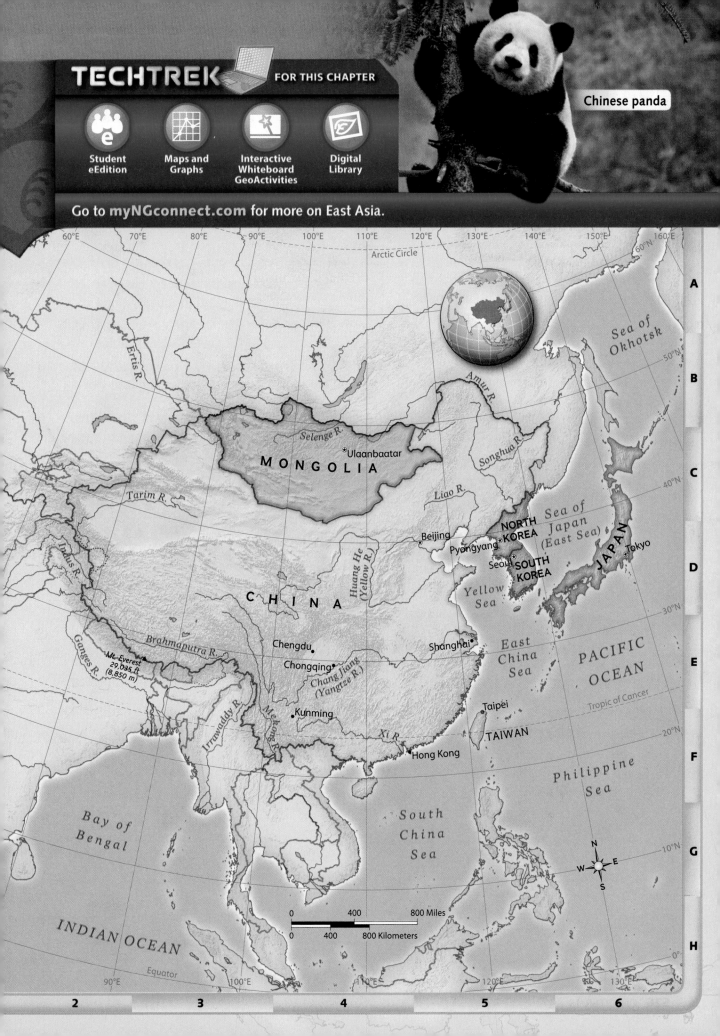

TECHTREK
FOR THIS CHAPTER

Student eEdition

Maps and Graphs

Interactive Whiteboard GeoActivities

Digital Library

Chinese panda

Go to myNGconnect.com for more on East Asia.

Arctic Circle

Sea of Okhotsk

Ertis R.

Selenge R.

MONGOLIA ∗Ulaanbaatar

Amur R.

Songhua R.

Tarim R.

Liao R.

Beijing•

NORTH KOREA ∗Pyongyang

Sea of Japan (East Sea)

JAPAN •Tokyo

CHINA

Huang He (Yellow R.)

Seoul∗ **SOUTH KOREA**

Yellow Sea

Indus R.

Ganges R.

Brahmaputra R.

Mt. Everest 29,035 ft (8,850 m)

Chengdu•

Chongqing•

Chang Jiang (Yangtze R.)

Mekong R.

Irrawaddy R.

Kunming•

Xi R.

Shanghai•

East China Sea

PACIFIC OCEAN

Tropic of Cancer

Taipei•

TAIWAN

Hong Kong•

Bay of Bengal

South China Sea

Philippine Sea

INDIAN OCEAN

Equator

0   400   800 Miles

0   400   800 Kilometers

N
W   E
S

EAST ASIA PHYSICAL

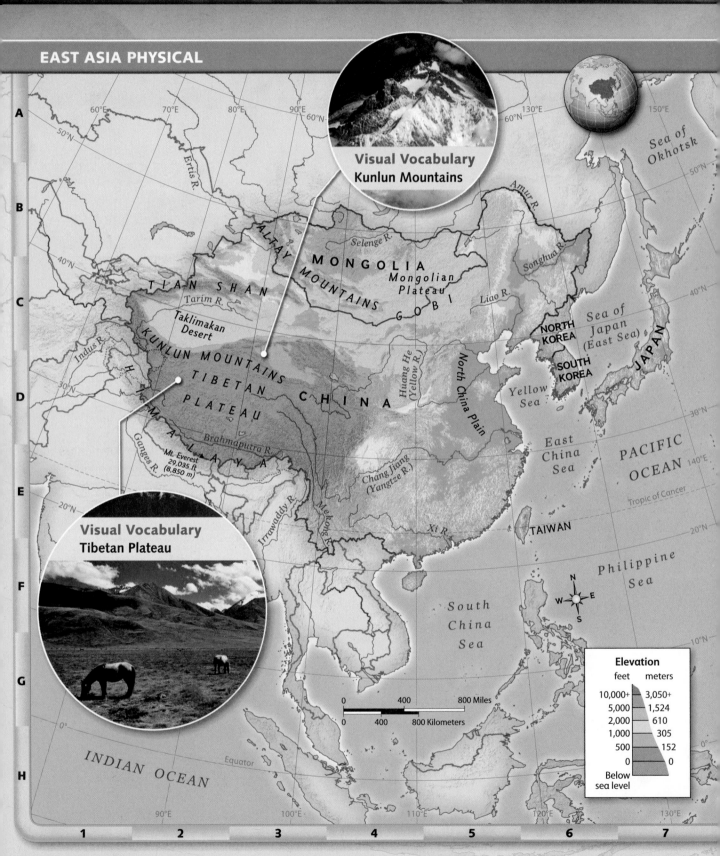

Visual Vocabulary
Kunlun Mountains

Visual Vocabulary
Tibetan Plateau

Sea of Okhotsk

ALTAY MOUNTAINS

TIAN SHAN

Ertis R.

Selenge R.

MONGOLIA

Mongolian Plateau

GOBI

Amur R.

Songhua R.

Liao R.

Tarim R.

Taklimakan Desert

KUNLUN MOUNTAINS

TIBETAN PLATEAU

CHINA

Huang He (Yellow R.)

North China Plain

NORTH KOREA

SOUTH KOREA

JAPAN

Sea of Japan (East Sea)

Yellow Sea

Indus R.

HIMALAYA

Ganges R.

Brahmaputra R.

Mt. Everest 29,035 ft (8,850 m)

Chang Jiang (Yangtze R.)

Irrawaddy R.

Mekong R.

Xi R.

East China Sea

TAIWAN

PACIFIC OCEAN

Tropic of Cancer

South China Sea

Philippine Sea

INDIAN OCEAN

Equator

0   400   800 Miles
0   400   800 Kilometers

Elevation

feet	meters
10,000+	3,050+
5,000	1,524
2,000	610
1,000	305
500	152
0	0
Below sea level	

CLIMATE

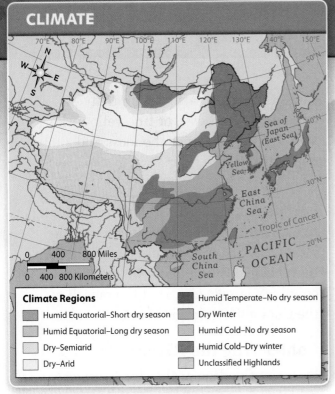

Climate Regions

Humid Temperate–No dry season

Humid Equatorial–Short dry season

Dry Winter

Humid Equatorial–Long dry season

Humid Cold–No dry season

Dry–Semiarid

Humid Cold–Dry winter

Dry–Arid

Unclassified Highlands

POPULATION DENSITY

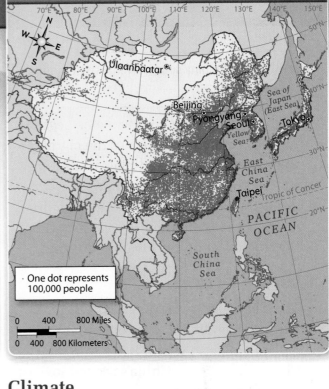

· One dot represents 100,000 people

Main Idea East Asia's landforms, bodies of water, and climate influence where people live.

East Asia includes China and Mongolia, which stretch across the **mainland**, or continental landmass, of Asia. The region also contains the island countries of Japan and Taiwan as well as North Korea and South Korea on the Korean Peninsula.

Landforms and Water

High mountains and plateaus, such as the **Kunlun Mountains** and **Tibetan Plateau**, cover much of East Asia. The Gobi desert covers parts of Mongolia and China.

Major rivers, such as the **Chang Jiang** (chahng jyahng) in China, flow through East Asia. River **basins**, the low areas drained by these rivers, support large populations. Many East Asians also live near coastal areas and on low-lying plains near the Pacific Ocean. People throughout the region depend on the Pacific for fish, trade, and transportation.

Climate

East Asia's climate ranges from tropical, in parts of China, South Korea, and Japan, to desert, in much of Mongolia. Monsoons greatly influence the region's climate. These seasonal winds bring hot, rainy summers and cool, dry winters to some parts of East Asia.

Before You Move On

Summarize In what ways do landforms, bodies of water, and climate help determine where people live in East Asia?

FORMATIVE ASSESSMENT

MAP LAB GeoJournal

1. **Interpret Maps** Use the physical map to locate the Tibetan Plateau on the population density and climate maps. Why do you think few people live on the plateau?

2. **Compare and Contrast** Compare the climate of inland East Asia with that of its coastal areas. What role might climate play in the population distribution of these areas?

1.2 China's Rivers and Plains

TECHTREK

myNGconnect.com For an online
map and photos of China's rivers and cities

 Maps and Graphs   Digital Library

Main Idea China's main river systems support large populations.

China's two largest river systems begin in the melting snow and ice of the country's western mountains and plateaus. As the waters flow down, they **erode**, or wear away, the land and deposit alluvium in river basins. **Alluvium** is soil carried by flowing water and is ideal for farming.

River Systems

The Chang Jiang, or Yangtze, is China's longest river. It passes through the Sichuan (sheesh whan) Basin and the Chang Jiang Plain. China's second longest river, the **Huang He** (hwahng huh), flows through the **North China Plain**. The Huang He is often called the Yellow River because it flows through an arid region that contains **loess** (less), or fine yellowish soil. The wind carries the loess and deposits it in the river.

China's river valleys and fertile plains provide rich agricultural land for growing rice and wheat. They also support many cities. The capital, Beijing (bay ghing), is in the North China Plain. Shanghai, the country's largest city, is at the mouth of the Chang Jiang on the East China Sea.

Controlling the Rivers

Frequent flooding of the rivers leaves behind deposits of fertile soil. Over the centuries, however, the flooding has also caused millions of deaths. Chinese engineers have built barriers such as dams and levees to hold the water back.

To connect China's major rivers, which flow from west to east, the ancient Chinese built a structure called the Grand Canal, which flows from north to south.

> **Critical Viewing** Boats on a branch of the Chang Jiang sail past skyscrapers in Shanghai. Based on the photo, how do the people in the city use the river?

CHINA'S RIVERS AND CITIES

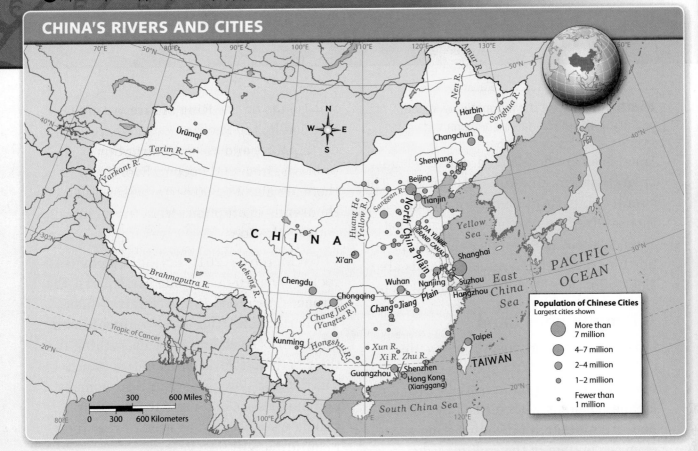

Population of Chinese Cities
Largest cities shown

- More than 7 million
- 4–7 million
- 2–4 million
- 1–2 million
- Fewer than 1 million

The roughly 1,100-mile-long canal—the longest in the world—links Beijing in the North China Plain to Hangzhou, just south of Shanghai. Barges travel along the canal, carrying bulk goods such as coal and gravel.

Before You Move On

Monitor Comprehension In what ways do China's rivers support large populations?

FORMATIVE ASSESSMENT

MAP LAB  GeoJournal

1. **Location** Study the map. How does the Grand Canal promote the transport of goods in China?

2. **Evaluate** Use the map above and the physical map in Section 1.1 to identify the landform where many of China's large cities are located. Why do you think the cities developed there?

1.3 The Island Arc of Japan

TECHTREK

myNGconnect.com For an online
earthquake map and photos of Japan

 Maps and
Graphs

 Digital
Library

Main Idea Japan is a mountainous island country with limited natural resources.

Japan is a closely related group of islands, or **archipelago** (ahr kuh PEH luh goh). The country consists of four main islands and thousands of smaller ones in an arc that extends about 1,400 miles in length. From north to south, the four main islands are Hokkaido, Honshu, Shikoku, and Kyushu.

A Mountainous Land

Mountains cover almost three-fourths of Japan and run like a spine down the middle of the four main islands. The Japanese islands were formed by the top part of a mountain range thrusting up from the bottom of the Pacific Ocean.

Japan is on the **Ring of Fire**, an area rimmed by the Pacific Ocean where earthquakes and volcanic **eruptions**, or blasts, frequently occur. Every year there are about 1,500 earthquakes and thousands of eruptions from the country's active volcanoes.

On March 11, 2011, northern Japan was rocked by a 9.0-magnitude earthquake, the strongest recorded in the country's history. The earthquake triggered a tsunami, with huge waves sweeping away everything in their path and devastating entire towns. The disaster destroyed countless homes and businesses, and more than 19,000 people were counted as dead or missing. Rebuilding will take years.

> **Critical Viewing** A tsunami wave washes over a street in the town of Miyako. What details in the photo help convey the size of the wave?

6.04.A locate societies on maps and globes using latitude and longitude; 6.04.B identify
and explain geographic factors for patterns of population; 6.04.D identify and locate
physical features; 6.06.A describe and explain effect of physical processes on Earth's crust;
6.08.B identify problems when factor of production in short supply; 6.08.C explain impact of
relative scarcity on economic interdependence

The tsunami severely damaged several nuclear power plants. By 2013, it was clear that actions taken to protect the public had prevented radiation exposure. But concerns about contaminated water still exist. Robots, instead of human workers, gather contamination data.

A Crowded Country

Because so much of Japan is covered with mountains and forests, the people crowd on its plains. About 80 percent of Japan's nearly 130 million people live on the plains of Honshu.

The **Kanto Plain** lies to the east of the Japanese Alps, which cross the central part of Honshu. The flat land of the Kanto Plain is good for agriculture and industry. Tokyo, Japan's capital and largest city, is located there.

Limited Natural Resources

Japan's most important natural resource is fish, caught in the Pacific Ocean and Sea of Japan. The country's fishing industry is one of the largest in the world. The seas are also essential to trade, which is vital to Japan's economy.

Because Japan has only small quantities of mineral resources, the country must import raw materials such as iron ore and lead. Japan also imports most of its energy resources, including petroleum and coal. Japan uses these imports in its industries and then exports finished products, such as automobiles and electronics.

Before You Move On

Summarize How do Japan's mountains and limited natural resources affect life in Japan?

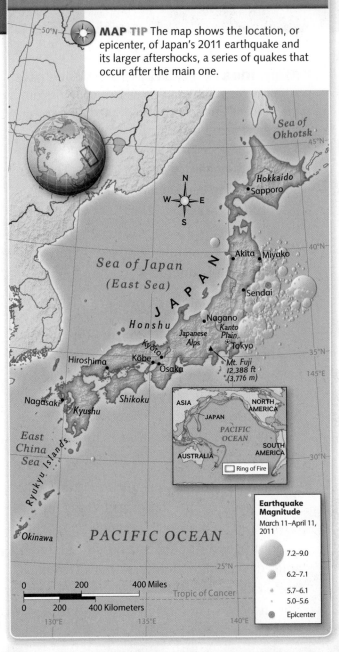

EARTHQUAKE 2011

MAP TIP The map shows the location, or epicenter, of Japan's 2011 earthquake and its larger aftershocks, a series of quakes that occur after the main one.

Earthquake Magnitude
March 11–April 11, 2011

- 7.2–9.0
- 6.2–7.1
- 5.7–6.1
- 5.0–5.6
- Epicenter

FORMATIVE ASSESSMENT

MAP LAB

 GeoJournal

1. **Location** Use the map or a globe to find the absolute location of Tokyo. Then locate the epicenter of the earthquake. About how far apart in miles are the two locations?

2. **Explain** What is the connection between scarcity, or limited resources, and the economic interdependence between Japan and other countries?

1.4 The Korean Peninsula

TECHTREK
myNGconnect.com For an online
map of Korea and Guided Writing

Maps and Graphs   Student Resources

Main Idea North Korea and South Korea have a similar geography, but these two countries on the Korean Peninsula remain divided.

The Korean Peninsula was divided into two countries after World War II. The two countries are the Democratic People's Republic of Korea, or North Korea, and the Republic of Korea, or South Korea. North Korea has a Communist government, while South Korea is democratic.

Geography and Climate

Like Japan, the Korean Peninsula is largely mountainous, with coastal plains and river valleys where most of the people live. With a population of about 50 million, South Korea has more than twice as many people as North Korea and is much more densely populated.

In South Korea, the southern and western plains are important areas for farming. The country's climate supports agriculture, with hot, humid summers and cold, dry winters. South Korea's two main industrial cities—Seoul, the capital, and Busan—are also located on the plains.

North Korea is more mountainous than South Korea. As a result, North Korea has less agricultural land than its neighbor. In general, North Korea's climate is colder and wetter than South Korea's, but **typhoons**, or hurricanes, can bring heavy rain and flooding to both countries.

Natural Resources and Industries

South Korea's natural resources include iron ore, copper, and coal. However, because these resources are limited, South Korea imports much of the raw materials it needs for industrial production. South Korea has a highly industrialized economy. Shipbuilding and steel are among the country's major industries, along with the manufacture of electronics and automobiles.

North Korea's natural resources include coal, magnesite, and iron ore. Unlike South Korea, many of North Korea's industries produce military equipment.

> **Critical Viewing** Steel is a major industry in South Korea. What details in the photo suggest that this plant in Busan is thriving?

LAND USE AND NATURAL RESOURCES

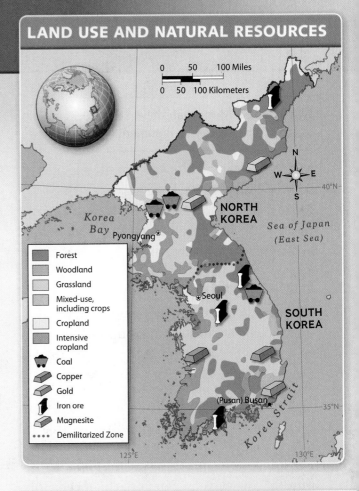

A Divided Land

From 1950 to 1953, the two Koreas fought in a conflict known as the Korean War. North Korea initiated the war by invading South Korea with the goal of taking over the peninsula. At the end of the war, the two countries remained divided. You will learn more about the Korean War in Section 3.

After the war, a **demilitarized zone (DMZ)**, or neutral area, was created between North Korea and South Korea. The DMZ is about 150 miles long and 2.5 miles wide. Soldiers still patrol the land, which has become a wilderness.

Over time, the isolation of the DMZ has created a **refuge**, or safe place, for large numbers of wildlife. Animal species, such as rare cranes, tigers, and bears live there. Scientists once thought that these animals had died out on the Korean Peninsula.

Before You Move On
Monitor Comprehension In what ways are North Korea and South Korea alike and different?

FORMATIVE ASSESSMENT
WRITING LAB GeoJournal

Compare and Contrast Write a paragraph in which you compare and contrast North Korea and South Korea. Use a Venn diagram like the one below to organize information about each country's geography, climate, natural resources, and industries. Exchange your finished paragraph with a partner and discuss your ideas. Go to **Student Resources** for Guided Writing.

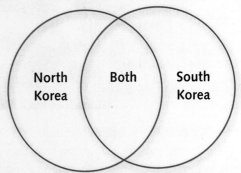

1.5 Mongolia's Desert Landscape

TECHTREK

myNGconnect.com For an online
physical map of Mongolia and photos of gers

 Maps and Graphs   Digital Library

> **Main Idea** Mongolians have adapted
> to life in a harsh, dry environment.

Mongolia is a landlocked country located
between northern China and eastern
Russia. The **Gobi desert**, the largest desert
in Asia, covers much of southern Mongolia
and extends into China.

High and Dry

Mountains, plateaus, **steppes**, or dry
grassland, and desert make up the physical
geography of Mongolia. All of the country's
land is 1,700 feet or more above sea level.

Most of the **semiarid**, or somewhat dry,
land gets fewer than 20 inches of rain, and
much of it falls in July and August. In the
Gobi desert, only about seven inches of
rain fall every year. Some parts of the Gobi
receive no rain at all. *Gobi*
means "place without water."
The extreme dryness and
strong winds that sometimes
blow through the desert
result in blinding
dust storms.

Summers in Mongolia are generally
short and hot, while winters are long and
cold. In the Gobi desert, temperatures can
reach 113°F in the summer and -40°F in
the winter. In addition, temperatures can
rise and fall in the desert by as much as 60
degrees within the same day.

People and Environment

In Mongolia's harsh environment, not
much livable space is available. Nearly
half of the country's roughly three million
people live in urban areas. About one-
third of the population lives in the capital
city of Ulaanbaatar (oo lahn BAH tawr).

Less than one percent of the land in
Mongolia is arable. As a result, most of the
people in rural areas are livestock herders.
Many lead a nomadic life. They move from
place to place with their sheep or
goats, looking for good pastureland.
Some herders live in **gers**. In Central
Asia, these tents are called yurts.

> **Visual Vocabulary** In this photo, a nomadic Mongolian
> woman stands outside her ger on the Gobi desert.
> A **ger** is a portable tent made of felt.

MONGOLIA PHYSICAL

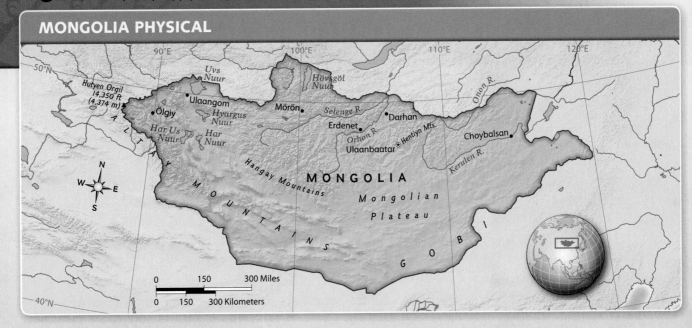

Preserving the Desert

As you have seen, the Mongolian people have learned to adapt to their desert environment. They also want to preserve it. The Gobi is expanding by a process called desertification, in which fertile land changes to desert. Much of this expansion is a result of human activities, including allowing livestock to overgraze pastureland. The Mongolians are trying to stop the process by reducing the number of livestock that graze the pastureland and by cutting down fewer trees.

Parts of the Gobi desert have also been turned into nature reserves and national parks. One of the parks in the southern part of the Gobi contains land of great interest to paleontologists, scientists who study prehistoric life. The area is one of the richest sources for dinosaur fossils in the world. In fact, the first dinosaur eggs were discovered here in the 1920s. The Gobi's harsh climate and remote location have helped protect and preserve the fossils for millions of centuries.

Before You Move On

Monitor Comprehension How have Mongolians adapted to their harsh, dry environment?

FORMATIVE ASSESSMENT

MAP LAB
GeoJournal

1. **Region** Study the physical map of Mongolia. What does the map tell you about sources of water in the country?

2. **Explain** Compare the map on this page with the climate and population maps in Section 1.1. In what ways do climate and land features explain the population density of Mongolia?

3. **Draw Conclusions** Why do you think most of Mongolia's cities are located in the north?

SECTION **1** GEOGRAPHY

1.6

■ **NATIONAL GEOGRAPHIC**

TECHTREK

myNGconnect.com For photos of an
Explorer's work and an Explorer Video Clip

Digital
Library

Tracking Aquatic
Wildlife
with Katsufumi Sato

> **Main Idea** Animal-borne recorders help scientists study how animals behave and learn how to protect them.

Tracking Technology

Since the 1990s, scientists have been attaching electronic data recorders to animals to gather information about everything from how fast the animal moves to how much it eats. These recorders are **animal-borne**, which means that the devices are carried by the animals themselves. Many of the recorders include cameras that take photos and videos of what the animal sees under natural conditions.

Emerging Explorer Katsufumi Sato is continually looking for ways to improve the technology, noting "We always work to perfect the instruments . . . and find better ways to attach and retrieve them." For example, when he first started studying sea turtles, he used a harness to attach the recorder. However, the harness slowed the turtle down as it swam. Eventually, Sato figured out how to glue the instrument to the turtle's **carapace**, or shell, to make it lighter and less awkward for the animal to carry.

myNGconnect.com

For more on Katsufumi
Sato in the field today

Unexpected Findings

Sato tracks sea creatures of all kinds. One of his research subjects is the cormorant, a large seabird that dives underwater to catch fish in its bill. For years, Japanese fishermen have been convinced that cormorants steal some of the fish in their nets. As a result, the fishermen have hunted and killed the birds. By attaching tiny animal-borne recorders to the birds, Sato hopes to learn the exact amount and type of fish the birds actually eat. The cormorants may not be as destructive as the fishermen believe.

Sato has also studied the loggerhead sea turtle. Many scientists thought that these turtles were dying because they ate the plastic bags that litter the ocean, mistaking them for jellyfish. The scientists believed that the turtles swallowed the bags and died of suffocation or starvation. However, animal-borne cameras proved that the turtles actually swim away from the plastic bags, recognizing that they are not food. This finding told scientists that they need to continue researching to learn what is really causing the turtles' declining numbers.

In another surprising study, Sato discovered that king penguins regulate how much air they inhale before a dive. They inhale more air before a deep dive and less air before a shallower dive. This behavior suggests that the penguins may be capable of planning their actions.

Before You Move On

Make Inferences How might animal-borne recorders be used to save animals?

Critical Viewing King penguins, similar to those Sato studied, gather on a bay north of Antarctica. What data might one of Sato's devices record about the penguins in this environment?

2.1 Early Dynasties

TECHTREK
myNGconnect.com For photos
of ancient Chinese artifacts

Digital
Library

> **Main Idea** Powerful families ruled and shaped ancient China for about 2,000 years.

In the 2100s B.C., farming settlements developed along the Huang He in eastern China. Over time, some of these settlements grew into cities and marked the beginning of an early civilization. Because Chinese culture developed from this early society, China is said to have the world's longest continuous civilization.

Shang and Zhou Dynasties

Around 1766 B.C., kings from the **Shang** family took over some of the cities along the Huang He. The Shang established a **dynasty**, a series of rulers from the same family. Eventually, the Shang ruled much of the area along the North China Plain.

Shang society was largely agricultural, but the leaders also built large walled cities. The society was structured, with nobles at the top and peasants at the bottom. The Shang used horse-drawn chariots to defend themselves against invaders. They also developed a system of writing, which helped unify their lands.

The **Zhou** (joh) people often fought with the Shang. Around 1050 B.C., they defeated the Shang and established their own dynasty. Throughout much of their long rule—longer than any other dynasty in Chinese history—the Zhou rulers waged war against invaders from the north and west. The Zhou also fought among themselves. Zhou kings had placed lords in charge of different parts of the region. These lords battled each other to acquire more land. The continual warfare led to great disorder in Chinese society.

Chinese rulers believed that the length of their dynasty was determined by the gods worshiped in ancient China. The pattern in the rise and fall of dynasties came to be known as the **dynastic cycle**, which is shown on the next page.

The Qin Dynasty

The **Qin** (chihn) Dynasty gained control of China in 221 B.C. *China* is thought to come from the name of this dynasty. Qin ruler **Shi Huangdi** (shee hwahng dee) strengthened the central government and expanded the lands under his control. He brought these lands together to form an **empire**, a group of states ruled by a single strong ruler, and became China's first emperor. Shi Huangdi unified his empire by building a system of roads and standardizing the Chinese currency.

1766 B.C.
The Shang establish a dynasty on the North China Plain.

1600 B.C.

Shang Dynasty oracle bone used to pose questions to the gods

Bronze vessel from the Zhou Dynasty

900 B.C.

1050 B.C.
The Zhou Dynasty begins its long rule.

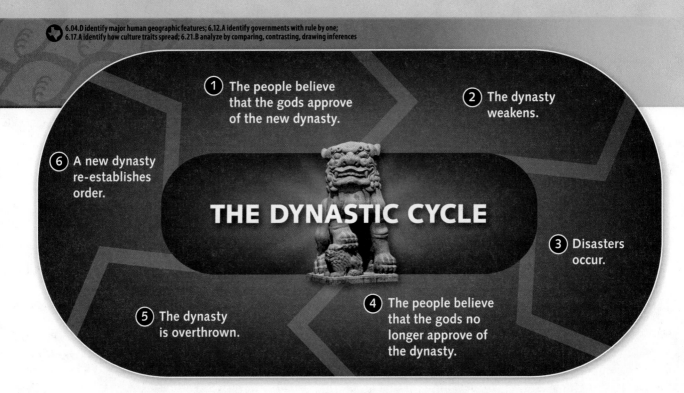

① The people believe that the gods approve of the new dynasty.

② The dynasty weakens.

⑥ A new dynasty re-establishes order.

THE DYNASTIC CYCLE

③ Disasters occur.

⑤ The dynasty is overthrown.

④ The people believe that the gods no longer approve of the dynasty.

Shi Huangdi also began construction on the **Great Wall of China** to protect against invaders from the north. Thousands were forced to labor on the huge project. Later rulers continued to expand the wall until it stretched about 4,500 miles.

Qin rule ended four years after Shi Huangdi's death in 210 B.C. Archaeologists discovered thousands of terra cotta, or baked clay, warriors buried near his tomb in 1974. Experts believe these life-sized statues were created to guard his tomb.

The Han Dynasty

The **Han** Dynasty came to power in China in 206 B.C. and lasted until A.D. 220. Han leaders expanded the empire and

established a strong central government. During this time, China began to trade with Europe and Central Asia along routes known as the **Silk Roads**. The goods and ideas traded helped create a prosperous civilization and an advanced culture in China. Many Chinese still call themselves "the people of the Han." You will learn more about the Silk Roads in Section 2.3.

Before You Move On
Monitor Comprehension How were the ancient Chinese dynasties alike, and how did they differ?

FORMATIVE ASSESSMENT
READING LAB  GeoJournal

1. **Make Inferences** The Qin Dynasty ended shortly after the death of Shi Huangdi. What does that fact suggest about the ruler that followed him?

2. **Form and Support Opinions** Which dynasty do you think had the greatest impact on Chinese society? Explain your reasons.

3. **Evaluate** Why did the Chinese people probably accept the overthrow of an old dynasty and the rise of a new one?

○ 221 B.C.
The Qin Dynasty forms an empire.

200 B.C.

206 B.C. ○
The Han Dynasty expands the Chinese Empire.

A terra cotta warrior found in Shi Huangdi's tomb

For more photos from the National Geographic Photo Gallery, go to the **Digital Library** at myNGconnect.com.

Great Wall of China

Tea farm, China

Tibet's Zar Gama Pass

Critical Viewing More than 8,000 life-size terra cotta, or baked clay, soldiers were found in Xi'an, China, in 1974. The soldiers had been buried next to the tomb of Emperor Shi Huangdi around 210 B.C.

2.2 **Confucianism**

TECHTREK

myNGconnect.com For photos of Confucian temples

Digital Library

This Confucian temple in Qufu, China—Confucius' birthplace in 551 B.C.—was built shortly after the teacher's death.

Main Idea The teachings of Confucius have influenced Chinese society for more than 2,000 years.

As you have read, the Chinese people endured long periods of conflict and disorder during the Zhou Dynasty. Confucius, a Chinese scholar and teacher born during that period, wanted to bring peace to his country. He developed ideas about the proper conduct of rulers and subjects and taught these ideas to others. His teachings form the basis of an ethical system called **Confucianism**. An **ethical system** teaches **moral**, or right, behavior. For more than 2,000 years, Confucius' teachings guided Chinese thought.

Teachings

Confucius' teachings are based on five relationships: father and son; elder brother and younger brother; husband and wife; friend and friend; and ruler and subject. Confucius taught that if these relationships were conducted respectfully, peace would be restored to society. The teachings below illustrate Confucius' emphasis on the importance of social relationships and study.

Don't worry if people don't recognize your merits; worry that you may not recognize theirs. (Analects 1.16)

To study without thinking is futile [useless]. To think without studying is dangerous. (Analects 2.15)

What you do not wish for yourself, do not do to others. (Analects 15.24)

Legacy

Confucius died believing that he had been a failure. In his lifetime, his teachings did not change Chinese society. However, his students wrote down his teachings and gathered them into a book called the *Analects* for future generations to read. In time, Han Dynasty rulers adopted Confucius' teachings and used them to select government officials based on their accomplishments rather than wealth.

Confucianism continued to influence Chinese society until the Communist Party seized power in 1949. The Communists **banned**, or outlawed, Confucianism because they considered it a religion. The government ended its ban in 1977. Since then, Confucianism has regained much of its influence. It is taught in schools, and many leaders have rediscovered Confucius' wisdom. Some officials have begun to use the teachings to guide their work and behavior.

Before You Move On

Understand Culture What are the basic teachings of Confucianism?

FORMATIVE ASSESSMENT

PHOTO LAB GeoJournal

1. **Analyze Visuals** What mood do you think the temple in the photo is meant to inspire?

2. **Describe** What influence did Confucius and his teachings have on Chinese society?

3. **Analyze Primary Sources** Reread the third sample of Confucius' teachings. What values does this teaching reflect?

4. **Explain** Why is Confucianism a philosophy and not a religion?

2.3 Silk Roads and Trade

TECHTREK
myNGconnect.com For an online map
of the Silk Roads and photos of trade items

 Maps and
Graphs

 Digital
Library

Main Idea Goods were traded and ideas spread on the Silk Roads, which connected China with much of the world.

You have learned that the Silk Roads were a series of trade routes that began during the Han Dynasty. The routes connected China with Europe, India, Central Asia, and North Africa. The Silk Roads got their name from the trade of silk cloth, which was made only in China at that time.

Trade Routes

The main overland route began in the city of Chang'an, the capital of ancient China. The route split in two to go around the Taklimakan Desert. It divided again to avoid the highest peaks of the Hindu Kush. Trade routes stretched west to Central Asia and Africa and south to India. Most of the overland traders traveled with **caravans**, or groups, with camels—which were well suited to the difficult terrain and dry climate.

The Silk Roads also included **maritime**, or sea, routes. From Nanjing, traders carrying Chinese goods traveled to Japan. From the ancient cities of Antioch and Tyre, trade continued to Rome.

Goods and Ideas

The overland roads covered about 4,000 miles, but few traders traveled the routes from end to end. Most Chinese traders were forbidden to go beyond their country's borders. As a result, they mainly exchanged their silk, jade, and spices with Central Asian nomads and traders from India. These, in turn, traded with merchants from the Mediterranean. Market towns sprang up along the routes, and some became major cities.

> **Critical Viewing** Camels can travel for long periods without water. Why do you think that ability might have been useful on the Silk Roads?

TRADE ROUTES OF THE SILK ROADS

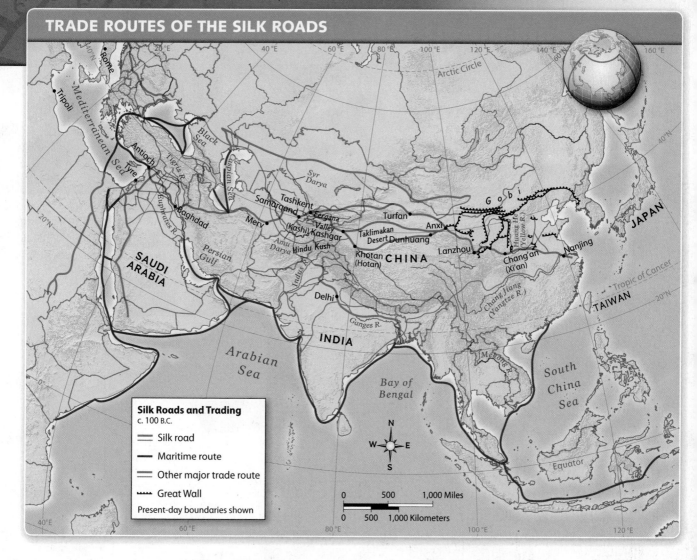

Silk Roads and Trading
c. 100 B.C.

— Silk road
— Maritime route
— Other major trade route
···· Great Wall

Present-day boundaries shown

0   500   1,000 Miles
0   500   1,000 Kilometers

Traders carried a variety of goods. Indian traders sold gems and sweet-smelling woods such as cedar. European goods included glass, pearls, and wool. Since there was not a single currency used by all the traders, they **bartered**, or exchanged goods without using money. For example, in exchange for their silk, Chinese traders might have received purple dyes from Mediterranean traders.

Government officials and missionaries also traveled on the routes. Their ideas spread along with the traders' goods. For instance, the Silk Roads helped spread Buddhism from India, where it began, to China and eventually to Korea and Japan.

Before You Move On

Monitor Comprehension How did the Silk Roads promote the exchange of goods and ideas?

FORMATIVE ASSESSMENT

MAP LAB  GeoJournal

1. **Movement** Based on the map, what route might traders have taken from Dunhuang, China, to Delhi, India?

2. **Make Inferences** Study the map. Explain why Kashgar developed into a thriving city.

3. **Create Thematic Maps** Use the map and the information in the text to draw a thematic map showing the activity on the Silk Roads. Use symbols to represent different goods and ideas.

2.4 Exploration and Isolation

Main Idea Zheng He made seven voyages of exploration that were intended to impress foreigners with China's wealth and power.

China dominated East Asia during the Ming Dynasty, which began in 1368. Ming emperor Yongle (yung lu) decided that he wanted to show the world China's wealth and power and take control of maritime trade. He also wanted other countries to pay him tribute, money demonstrating their recognition of his power.

Zheng He

To carry out this mission, Yongle ordered Admiral **Zheng He** (jung huh) to lead seven expeditions, or voyages, between 1405 and 1433. Zheng He's fleet was much larger than those of European explorers such as Christopher Columbus, who would set out almost 100 years later. Zheng He commanded thousands of men and sailed with hundreds of treasure ships designed to carry huge stores of trade goods.

Shortly after Zheng He's last expedition, China withdrew into isolation. This isolation continued until the 1800s, when European powers began controlling China's economy.

Before You Move On
Summarize In what ways did Zheng He's expeditions demonstrate China's wealth and power?

> **Critical Viewing** This illustration compares Zheng He's large ship with that of a European explorer. What impression might Zheng's ship have made when it arrived in a foreign port?

5 1417–1419
Zheng's treasure fleet visited the Arabian Peninsula and, for the first time, Africa. In Aden, the sultan presented exotic gifts such as zebras, lions, and ostriches.

6 1421–1422
Zheng He's fleet returned foreign ambassadors to their native countries after stays of several years in China.

7 1431–1433
The last voyage marked the end of China's age of exploration. Historians believe that Zheng died on the return trip and was buried at sea.

SAUDI ARABIA

Jeddah · Mecca

Red Sea

Arabian Peninsula

YEMEN

Sanaa ★

Aden

Mukalla

SUDAN

SOMALIA

KENYA

Mogadishu
Baraawe

AFRICA

Nairobi ★

Malindi

Pate I.
Lamu

Mombasa

Swahili coast

TANZANIA

4 1413–1415
As a result of the voyage, an estimated 18 countries sent tribute and foreign ambassadors to China.

3 1409–1411
During this voyage, Zheng He conducted a land battle in Sri Lanka. The voyage was also marked by Zheng's offering of gifts to a Buddhist temple.

2 1407–1409
The fleet returned foreign ambassadors from Sumatra, India, and elsewhere who had traveled to China on the first voyage.

1 1405–1407
In July, the fleet with 317 ships and 27,870 men left Nanjing with silks, porcelain, and spices for trade.

ZHENG HE'S VOYAGES, 1405-1433

This map shows the main and subsidiary, or secondary, routes of Zheng He's seven expeditions. Note that the map labels include place names from the 1400s as well as present-day names.

— Main route
- - - Subsidiary route
○ Major trading center
4 Destination

Present-day boundaries shown
Scale varies in this perspective.

IRAN
4 Hormuz
Persian Gulf
OMAN
Dhofar
Arabian Sea
Malabar Coast
1
2
3
Kozhikode (Calicut)
Cochin
Quilon
Jaffna
SRI LANKA
CEYLON
Colombo
Galle
Dondra Head
MALDIVES
INDIAN OCEAN
EQUATOR
INDIA
BANGLADESH
Bay of Bengal
Chittagong
Andaman Islands (India)
Nicobar Islands (India)
Banda Aceh
Semudera
Sumatra
Palembang
ASIA
YUNNAN
Kunyang
THAILAND
SIAM
Ayutthaya
CAMBODIA
VIETNAM
Kelantan
MALAYSIA
Pahang
Malacca
INDONESIA
Java
Surabaya
CHINA
Great Wall
Beijing
Grand Canal
Dalian
MING EMPIRE
JIANGSU
Origin of all 7 voyages
Nanjing
Yangtze
FUJIAN
Changle
Quanzhou
Xiamen
East China Sea
Hainan
CHAMPA
Qui Nhon
TAIWAN
South China Sea
Strait of Malacca

FORMATIVE ASSESSMENT
MAP LAB
GeoJournal

1. **Compare Maps** This map represents Zheng He's expeditions as they might appear on a globe. Compare this perspective with that of other maps you have seen in this book. How are the two perspectives similar? How are they different?

2. **Draw Conclusions** Based on the text and map captions, how would you describe Zheng He's influence on Chinese society in the early 1400s?

2.5 **Communist Revolution**

TECHTREK
myNGconnect.com For an online
map and photos of Communist China

Maps and
Graphs

Digital
Library

Main Idea The Chinese Communist Party under Mao Zedong significantly changed life in the People's Republic of China.

As you have read, China fell under the control of European powers in the 1800s. The Chinese Nationalist Party wanted to end this foreign control and modernize China. The party overthrew the ruling government and established the Republic of China in 1912. Over time, the Chinese people began to turn to the Communist Party, which arose in Shanghai in 1921. Many young people in particular believed that the Communists would be better able to modernize China. The Nationalists and Communists began a long struggle for power. By 1930, the two groups were locked in a bloody civil war.

Civil War

In 1933, Nationalist leader **Jiang Jieshi** (jee ahng jee shee) gathered a large army and attacked the Communists in their mountain base in Jiangxi (jee ahng shee) Province. Knowing they were outnumbered, the Communists fled to their base in Shaanxi (shahn shee) Province. Between 1934 and 1935, **Mao Zedong** (MOW dzuh dahng) led about 100,000 Communists over rough terrain on a series of marches that came to be known as the Long March. Tens of thousands of Communists died during the marches.

In 1937, the Japanese invaded China and **occupied**, or took possession of, parts of the country. The Nationalists and Communists set aside their differences to fight their common enemy. The two groups remained united against Japan throughout World War II. After the war, the Nationalists and Communists started fighting again. On October 1, 1949, the Communists declared victory and established the People's Republic of China on the mainland. The Nationalists fled and established a government in Taiwan, an island off the coast of the mainland.

Chairman Mao

As Chairman of the Communist Party, Mao became the leader of China and established a totalitarian dictatorship. The government seized farmland and forced the peasants to work on **collective farms**. Between 200 and 300 families lived and worked on each collective farm, which was strictly supervised by the government. The government also took over all businesses and industries. By 1957, industrial output had greatly increased.

○ **1912**
Nationalists establish
the Republic of China.

1920

○ **1921**
Communist Party is
founded in China.

○ **1934–1935**
Communists undertake
the Long March.

○ **1937–1945**
Communists and
Nationalists unite to
fight against Japan.

1940

Statue celebrating heroes of
the Communist revolution

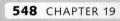

6.01.B analyze historical background to evaluate relationship between past conflicts and current conditions; 6.09.D examine record of collective non-free market economic systems; 6.15.F identify and explain examples of conflict; 6.21.C interpret information from maps, timelines

THE LONG MARCH

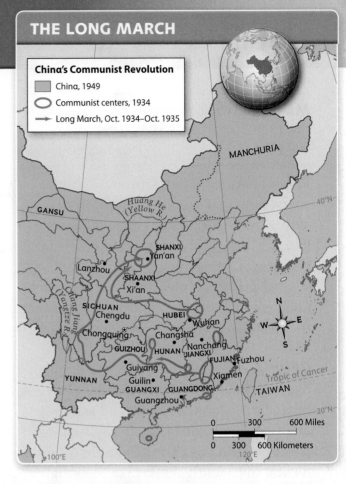

China's Communist Revolution

◻ China, 1949
⬭ Communist centers, 1934
➝ Long March, Oct. 1934–Oct. 1935

Encouraged by this initial success, Mao set a plan in motion the following year called the Great Leap Forward to make China's economy grow even faster. The plan failed. The government's poor management of China's industries slowed economic growth, and crop failures severely reduced agricultural yields. After an estimated 20 million people had died of hunger, Mao ended the plan in 1961.

Five years later, Mao began a new plan called the **Cultural Revolution** to remove what he considered anti-Communist elements from China. To help carry out the plan, young people belonging to military groups known as the Red Guards attacked anyone whom they considered **elite**, or superior. They particularly targeted teachers and intellectuals. Thousands of people were killed in the violence.

After Mao died in 1976, the situation slowly began to change in China. Today, the country is still Communist, but reforms begun in the 1980s have resulted in great economic growth and improved the lives of many Chinese people.

Before You Move On
Summarize What happened in China as a result of Communist control under Mao Zedong?

FORMATIVE ASSESSMENT

MAP LAB
GeoJournal

1. **Movement** Trace the route on the map from Jiangxi to Shaanxi Province. What directions did the route follow?

2. **Describe** Use the map on this page and the physical map in Section 1.1 to describe the terrain encountered by those who marched from Jiangxi to Shaanxi Province.

3. **Interpret Time Lines** For how many years did Mao Zedong rule China?

Mao Zedong

1958–1961
Mao begins the Great Leap Forward.

1960

1949
Communists establish the People's Republic of China with Mao Zedong as their leader.

1966
The Cultural Revolution begins.

1976
Mao dies.

1980s
Reforms begin that eventually lead to great economic growth.

1980

3.1 Japanese Samurai

TECHTREK
myNGconnect.com For photos and fine art of samurai culture

Digital
Library

> **Main Idea** Samurai were part of a feudal system that continued in Japan for about 700 years.

Emperors ruled Japan for hundreds of years, but in the 1000s, they began to lose authority. Landowning lords who belonged to wealthy families expanded their estates and grew increasingly powerful. They formed private armies and hired warriors known as **samurai** (SAM uh ry) to protect their estates.

Samurai Code and Culture

Samurai means "one who serves." The relationship between lords and samurai was part of a Japanese feudal system similar to the one that arose in Europe during the Middle Ages. Like the knights of the Middle Ages, the samurai developed a code of behavior based on the values of honor, bravery, and loyalty to their lords.

The samurai were not only skilled warriors but also developed their own culture. They wrote poetry and created fine ink paintings. The samurai values of loyalty and hard work and the warriors' artistic interests influenced Japanese society, art, and literature.

Shogun Rule

Powerful families battled each other for control of Japan during the 1100s. In 1192, a lord from the powerful Minamoto family won and received the title of **shogun**, or "military ruler," from the emperor. The shogun came to hold the true power in Japan. The Minamoto established a dynasty of shoguns that ruled Japan until the 1300s. After the Minamoto lost power,

rival families fought for control. Japan became divided into many warring states and experienced a long period of disorder.

Finally, in 1603, a shogun named Tokugawa Ieyasu (ee yeh yah soo) defeated his rivals. He united Japan and moved the capital from Kyoto to Edo, which is present-day Tokyo. The Tokugawa shoguns restored peace. However, they also isolated Japan from the rest of the world. In 1868, this isolation ended when the Japanese people persuaded the shogun to resign. Imperial rule was restored, and the new emperor put an end to the samurai class.

Before You Move On
Monitor Comprehension What role did the samurai play in Japan's feudal system?

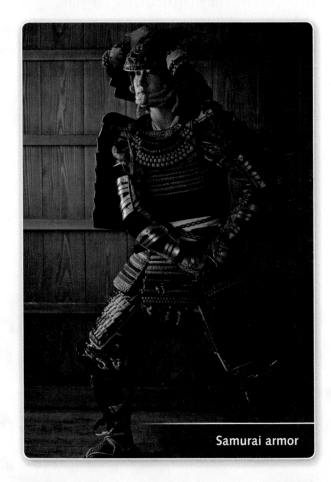
Samurai armor

6.02.B evaluate the social and political contributions of groups, past; 6.12.A identify and give examples of rule by one; 6.21.B analyze by comparing, contrasting; 6.21.C analyze information from visuals; 6.22.D create written material

Critical Viewing This painting shows samurai on horseback during a battle. What details in the painting illustrate the samurai's skill and bravery?

FORMATIVE ASSESSMENT
PHOTO LAB
GeoJournal

1. **Analyze Visuals** Study the photo of samurai armor. What words would you use to describe the warrior's equipment?

2. **Compare and Contrast** Compare the samurai in the photo and in the painting. Which details are similar? Which are different?

3. **Write Reports** Think about another group of warriors that you know about from history, comics, or movies such as *Star Wars*. In what way does their code compare with that of the samurai? Write a report comparing the two.

3.2 Japan Industrializes

> **Main Idea** Japan transformed itself into an industrialized economy beginning in 1868.

As you have learned, the emperor was restored to power in Japan in 1868. The restoration came about because many of the Japanese people wanted to end Japan's isolation. They wanted to make the country **competitive** with, or able to challenge, the newly industrialized Western nations. After the last of the Tokugawa shoguns resigned, a new era called *Meiji* (may jee), meaning "enlightened rule," began.

Building on Western Models

For hundreds of years, Japan's economy had been based on agriculture and fishing. The Meiji government looked to Western nations as models for a new industrial economy. Many foreign experts came to Japan to instruct the Japanese in English, engineering, and science. British advisers helped the Japanese government design railroad and communication systems and set up new industries.

At first, the government invested directly in coal and zinc mines and large-scale industries, especially those needed to build a modern military force. These industries included shipyards and weapons factories. The government also developed factories to produce textiles and silk. The government planned to export these goods so the country could acquire raw materials. Japan turned to China and Korea as sources for these raw materials and as potential markets for the finished products. By the 1880s, however, the government could not afford to continue

This woodblock print by the Meiji-era artist known as Hiroshige III illustrates a Tokyo railway station and train built in 1872 with the help of Western advisers and engineers.

this level of investment in the country's industries and sold the industries to private investors.

Large Businesses Develop

Over time, business in Japan became concentrated in several large, family-controlled organizations called **zaibatsu** (zeye BAHT sue). Each zaibatsu owned a number of different businesses, such as manufacturing, transportation, banking, insurance, trade, and real estate.

6.01.A trace characteristics of societies resulting from historical factors; 6.05.C explain impact of geographic factors on domestic and foreign policies; 6.10.C identify and describe effects of government regulation on economic development; 6.21.B analyze information by drawing inferences, identifying cause-effect relationships, summarizing

1. **Monitor Comprehension** In what way did the Japanese government change its regulation of businesses in the 1880s? How do you think the change affected the economy?

2. **Analyze Cause and Effect** What impact do you suppose industrialization had on Japan's economy and people?

3. **Make Inferences** Based on what you know of Japan's geography, how do you think Japan's need for raw materials affected its policies with other countries at that time? Why were weapons factories built?

Some of the zaibatsu were rooted in the shogun era. For example, the Mitsui family had been successful textile merchants under the Tokugawa shoguns. This family expanded first into banking and, in time, owned more than 270 companies.

Other zaibatsu began during the Meiji era. Mitsubishi, for instance, started as a large shipping firm. The family eventually established financial services and real estate businesses and industries such as oil, steel, and shipbuilding.

The zaibatsu were largely **dissolved**, or broken up, after World War II ended in 1945. Businesses owned by the zaibatsu were **seized**, or taken control of, and reorganized into smaller holdings.

However, the value the zaibatsu placed on hard work and thoroughness continues to influence Japanese industry today.

Before You Move On

Summarize What did Japan do to transform into an industrialized economy beginning in 1868?

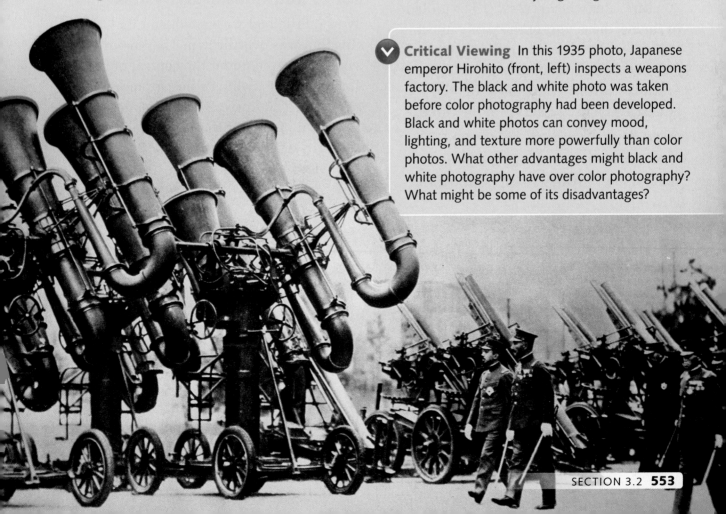

Critical Viewing In this 1935 photo, Japanese emperor Hirohito (front, left) inspects a weapons factory. The black and white photo was taken before color photography had been developed. Black and white photos can convey mood, lighting, and texture more powerfully than color photos. What other advantages might black and white photography have over color photography? What might be some of its disadvantages?

3.3 Korea's Early History

TECHTREK

myNGconnect.com For an online
map and images of Korea's early history

Maps and
Graphs

Digital
Library

> **Main Idea** A series of kingdoms and dynasties arose in Korea, developing a distinct culture.

In Section 2, you learned about the early dynasties that came to power in China. In 108 B.C., China's Han Dynasty expanded into Korea and took control of an area in the northwest. At that time, the Korean people belonged to scattered tribes. Eventually, groups of tribes united and formed three kingdoms on the peninsula: **Silla** (SIHL uh), **Koguryo** (koh gur YOO), and **Paekche** (PAHK CHAY).

The Three Kingdoms

Silla, the first kingdom to form, arose around 57 B.C. in the southeastern part of the peninsula. Koguryo emerged about 20 years later when several tribes united in the northern part of the peninsula and parts of eastern Manchuria in China. Paekche formed around 18 B.C. in the southwest. At first, Koguryo was the largest and most powerful of the three.

The three kingdoms were rivals and often invaded each other's territory. In spite of their **rivalry**, or opposition, the kingdoms had similar cultures, and their people spoke the same language. The kingdoms produced items such as leather goods, tools, and woolen clothing, which they exported to China. In return, the kingdoms received porcelain, paper, silk, and weapons. The kingdoms also absorbed some ideas from China, including its writing system, Confucianism, and Buddhism. Eventually, Buddhism spread from the Korean kingdoms to Japan.

In A.D. 660, the Tang Dynasty in China joined with Silla to defeat the other two kingdoms. Shortly after, Silla succeeded in driving out the Chinese. By 668, the Silla kingdom ruled the entire peninsula.

Koryo and Choson Dynasties

By 935, Silla had weakened, and its kingdom was overthrown. The Korean Peninsula came under the control of the **Koryo** Dynasty, which ruled for more than 450 years. The Koryo Dynasty modeled its government after that of China. Like the early kingdoms, Koryo was strongly influenced by Confucianism.

Silla crown

Hunting scene in
Koguryo wall painting

108 B.C.
Chinese Empire
expands into Korea.

37 B.C.
Koguryo develops
in the north.

100 B.C.

1 B.C.

57 B.C.
Silla arises in the southeastern
part of the peninsula.

18 B.C.
Paekche forms in
the southwest.

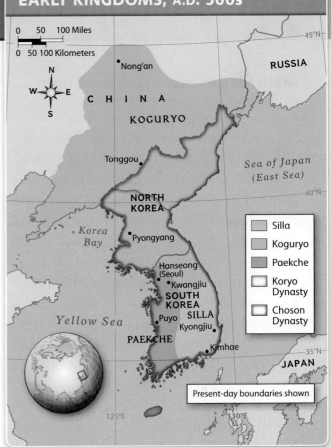

EARLY KINGDOMS, A.D. 500s

Present-day boundaries shown

A distinctly Korean culture developed during the Koryo period. Artists created **celadon** pottery, with its characteristic green glaze. They also carved all of the Buddhist scriptures onto more than 80,000 wooden blocks for printing. The blocks are called the Tripitaka Koreana. Invading Mongols destroyed the blocks in 1232, but a new set was re-created within 20 years. The temple of Haeinsa in South Korea is home to the set today and has been named a UNESCO World Heritage Site.

In 1392, the Koryo Dynasty was defeated and replaced by the **Choson** Dynasty, which lasted for 518 years. During this time, Korea continued to adopt elements of Chinese culture. Korean culture also flourished at this time, with developments in architecture, science, and technology. The Choson Dynasty ended in 1910 when Korea came under the control of Japan. Japanese occupation continued until 1945, when World War II ended.

Before You Move On
Summarize How were the Korean dynasties similar and different?

A monk holds a block of the Tripitaka Koreana.

FORMATIVE ASSESSMENT
MAP LAB
GeoJournal

1. **Interpret Maps** On the map, use your finger to trace the outline of the Koguryo Kingdom. What parts of present-day countries did the kingdom consist of?

2. **Draw Conclusions** Remember that Silla conquered Koguryo and Paekche in 668. How would the size of Silla at its greatest extent have compared with that of the Koryo and Choson dynasties, as shown on the map?

A.D. 500

A.D. 668
Silla controls the entire peninsula.

A.D. 935
Koryo Dynasty overthrows Silla.

Celadon pillow

A.D. **1392**
Choson Dynasty begins.

1500

SECTION 3 HISTORY OF JAPAN & KOREA

3.4 The Korean War

TECHTREK
myNGconnect.com For an online
map and photos of the Korean War

Maps and
Graphs

Digital
Library

> **Main Idea** After three years of war, North Korea and South Korea remained divided.

When the Japanese occupation ended in 1945, the Korean Peninsula was divided along the 38° North latitude line—usually referred to as the **38th parallel**. The United States held the land south of that line, and the Soviet Union occupied the land to the north. The United States and the Soviet Union came to be locked in a **Cold War**. This means that they did not fight one another directly in battle. Instead, they supported opposing groups in wars that took place in other parts of the world. One such war occurred in Korea.

Fighting Begins

In 1947, the United Nations called for free elections that would create one government for Korea. The elections were held, but the Soviet Union stepped in and established a Communist government in the north. The following year, Communist North Korea and democratic South Korea were created, with the 38th parallel serving as the border.

On June 25, 1950, North Korea attacked South Korea. The United Nations called for an international force to come to South Korea's aid. The United States supplied most of the troops and placed them under the command of General Douglas MacArthur, who had been an important military leader during World War II.

The fighting wore on for several years. At one point, the North Koreans pushed deep into South Korea and captured most of the peninsula. Then the UN forces made a surprise landing at Inchon and took back the South Korean capital of Seoul. As the North Koreans **retreated**, or drew back, the UN forces pushed north and captured the North Korean capital of Pyongyang. The course of the war shifted from one side to the other through 1952, but in the end, little territory was gained or lost.

Impact of the War

As many as four million soldiers and civilians were killed in the war. Much of the Korean Peninsula was damaged by bombs dropped by jet aircraft.

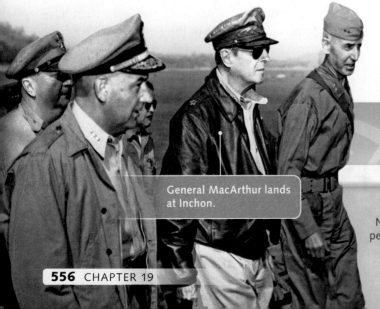
General MacArthur lands at Inchon.

JUNE 1950
North Korea invades South Korea.

OCTOBER 1950
UN forces capture Pyongyang.

1950

SEPTEMBER 1950
North Korea captures most of the peninsula; MacArthur's forces land at Inchon and take back Seoul.

Korean civilians particularly suffered during the war. Half of all industries and a third of all homes were destroyed. In addition, many people died of starvation.

The War Ends

In 1953, the UN forces and North Korea signed an **armistice**, or agreement to stop fighting, but a treaty was never signed. An area set near the 38th parallel, called the demilitarized zone (DMZ), still divides the two countries today. Since 1953, North Korean troops have guarded one side of the zone, while South Korean and American troops have guarded the other.

Today, Communist North Korea is largely isolated from the rest of the world, while South Korea is a democracy with a global, market economy. Over the years, the two countries have discussed the possibility of uniting. However, political differences and the threat of North Korea's nuclear arms program have made this unification increasingly unlikely.

Before You Move On

Make Inferences What, if anything, did the Korean War accomplish?

THE KOREAN WAR

→ North Korean offensive
→ South Korean offensive

RUSSIA
CHINA

0   50   100 Miles
0   50   100 Kilometers

Limit of South Korean advance Nov. 24, 1950

Sea of Japan (East Sea) — 40°N

Korea Bay

NORTH KOREA

Pyongyang ✹

Demarcation Line and Demilitarized Zone July 27, 1953

38th Parallel

N / W E / S

(Incheon) Inchon ⊙ ⊙ Seoul

SOUTH KOREA

Yellow Sea

Limit of North Korean advance Sept. 15, 1950

Busan (Pusan) — 35°N

JAPAN

125°E   130°E

FORMATIVE ASSESSMENT

MAP LAB

GeoJournal

1. **Movement** Study the map. Which country's forces moved further into enemy territory?

2. **Interpret Maps** Based on the map, why do you think it was easy for Chinese forces to rapidly come to North Korea's aid?

3. **Analyze Time Lines** Based on the time line captions, how would you characterize the course of the war?

Statues of American soldiers in the Korean War Veterans War Memorial in Washington, D.C.

JULY 1953
An armistice is signed, but North and South Korea remain divided.

1952   1954

JANUARY 1951
Chinese forces occupy Seoul.

MARCH 1951
UN forces retake Seoul.

South Korean soldiers patrol the DMZ.

VOCABULARY

On your own paper, write the vocabulary word that completes each of the following sentences.

1. _____ is yellow silt that blows from the Gobi desert onto the Huang He.

2. Tropical hurricanes called _____ bring heavy rains to North Korea.

3. The rise and fall of dynasties in China followed a pattern known as the _____.

4. Confucianism is considered an _____, which teaches right behavior.

5. Japanese warriors known as _____ were similar to the knights of the European Middle Ages.

MAIN IDEAS

6. Where do most East Asians live? Why? (Section 1.1)

7. What purpose does the Grand Canal in China serve? (Section 1.2)

8. What are the main natural resources of North Korea and South Korea? (Section 1.4)

9. What steps has Mongolia taken toward preserving the Gobi desert? (Section 1.5)

10. Who was Shi Huangdi and what were his accomplishments? (Section 2.1)

11. Why did the Chinese people embrace Confucianism? (Section 2.2)

12. What were the Silk Roads? (Section 2.3)

13. In what ways did Mao Zedong control life in China? (Section 2.5)

14. What qualities were valued under the samurai code of behavior? (Section 3.1)

15. Why did Japan begin to industrialize after 1868? (Section 3.2)

16. What happened at the conclusion of the Korean War? (Section 3.4)

GEOGRAPHY

ANALYZE THE ESSENTIAL QUESTION

How did geographic factors affect population distribution?

Critical Thinking: Analyze Cause and Effect

17. Why is eastern China more densely populated than western China?

18. Why do many of Japan's people live on the island of Honshu?

19. How has Mongolia's harsh environment affected the ways people live and work?

INTERPRET TABLES

RIVERS IN CHINA	
River	Length (miles)
Chang Jiang	3,900
Huang He	3,395
Xi Jiang	1,250
Yalu	490

Source: CIA World Factbook

20. **Analyze Data** About how many times bigger is the Chang Jiang than the Yalu?

21. **Draw Conclusions** Based on the table, what conclusions can you draw about rivers in China?

CHINA'S HISTORY

ANALYZE THE ESSENTIAL QUESTION

What influences, beliefs, and encounters helped shape China?

Critical Thinking: Make Generalizations

22. What impact has Confucianism had on Chinese government and society?

23. What did China gain from its trade on the Silk Roads and its voyages of exploration?

6.03.C compare countries using data; 6.21.B analyze by identifying cause-effect relationships, making generalizations, predictions, inferences; 6.21.C interpret information from maps; 6.21.D identify different points of view; 6.22.C express ideas orally; 6.22.B incorporate main and supporting ideas; 6.22.D create written and visual material based on research

INTERPRET MAPS

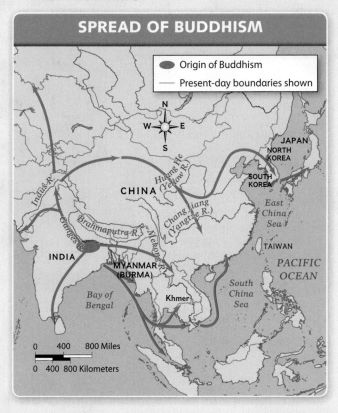

SPREAD OF BUDDHISM

24. **Interpret Maps** Study the map. Why do you think Buddhism spread to China before it came to Korea and Japan?

25. **Make Predictions** What other region shown on the map was most likely influenced by Buddhism?

HISTORY OF JAPAN & KOREA

ANALYZE THE ESSENTIAL QUESTION

What factors had an impact on the histories of Japan and Korea?

Critical Thinking: Make Inferences

26. Why do you think Japan's rulers chose to isolate the country once they had restored peace in the early 1600s?

27. In what ways has China influenced Korea throughout its history?

ACTIVE OPTIONS

Synthesize the Essential Questions by completing the activities below.

28. **Write a Speech** Choose a historical figure from the chapter who particularly interests you and write a speech from the figure's point of view. Research the person. Include main ideas and supporting ideas when you outline your speech. Use the tips below to help you write it. **Deliver your speech to the class.**

> **Writing Tips**
> • Describe some of the historical figure's beliefs and accomplishments.
> • Include brief stories from the person's life to hold your audience's interest.
> • Use a tone that will help convey the person's personality. For example, for Shi Huangdi, you might use a boastful tone. For Confucius, you would probably use a more modest tone.

29. **Create a Poster** Choose two countries of East Asia and compare and contrast their geography, history, and situation today. Use online sources to help you gather your data. Then organize your ideas in a Venn diagram like the one below. Finally, create your poster, using photos to illustrate your ideas.

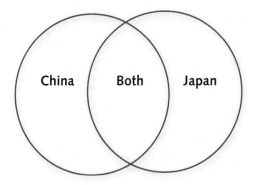

CHAPTER 20

East Asia TODAY

PREVIEW THE CHAPTER

Essential Question How do traditions and modernization create a unique way of life in East Asia?

SECTION 1 • CULTURE

KEY VOCABULARY

- meditation
- animism
- polytheism
- monotheism
- porcelain
- movable type
- multinational corporation
- economic globalization
- anime
- manga
- bullet train
- magnetic levitation

ACADEMIC VOCABULARY

aerodynamic

TERMS & NAMES

- Daoism
- Shinto
- Special Economic Zone

Essential Question What problems does East Asia face today, and what are its opportunities?

SECTION 2 • GOVERNMENT & ECONOMICS

KEY VOCABULARY

- entrepreneur
- gross domestic product (GDP)
- one-child policy
- fertility rate
- gorge
- reservoir
- martial law
- pagoda
- capital
- free trade
- drought
- famine

ACADEMIC VOCABULARY

comply, controversy

TERMS & NAMES

- Three Gorges Dam
- Lost Decade

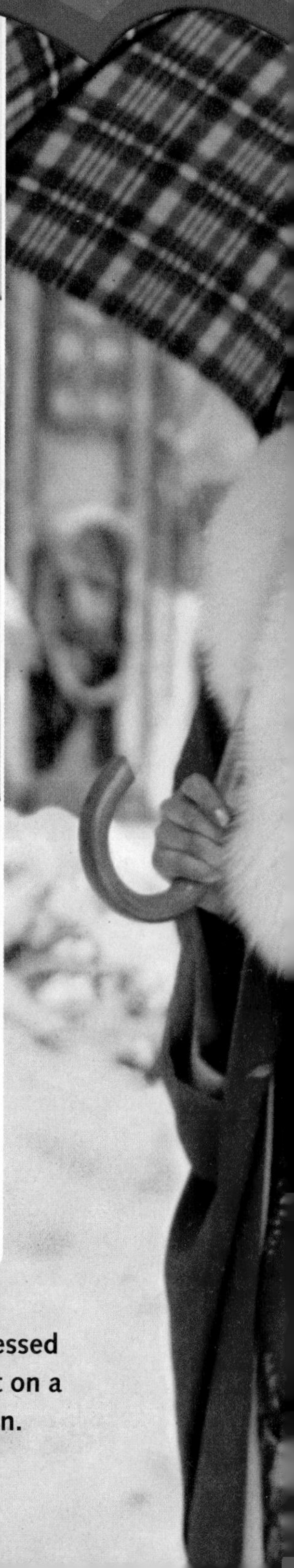

Young Japanese women dressed in traditional kimonos meet on a snowy day in Nagano, Japan.

TECHTREK

FOR THIS CHAPTER

Student eEdition

Maps and Graphs

Interactive Whiteboard GeoActivities

Digital Library

Go to **myNGconnect.com** for more on East Asia.

TECHTREK

myNGconnect.com For online graphs of religions in East Asia and photos of Buddhism

 Maps and Graphs

 Digital Library

Main Idea Buddhism and other religions spread throughout East Asia.

As you have learned, Buddhism began in India, but it came to have a far greater influence in East Asia. Missionaries traveling on the Silk Roads during the Han Dynasty first brought Buddhist teachings to China. Over time, Buddhism blended with other religious traditions throughout East Asia.

Blending Beliefs

Before Buddhism spread to East Asia, many people in the region practiced Confucianism and **Daoism**. Like Confucianism, Daoism is an ethical system. It stresses the harmony between people and nature. As Buddhism gained popularity, many East Asians combined elements of all three traditions.

Buddhism focuses on helping people end their physical and mental suffering by teaching them to give up worldly possessions. According to Buddhist teachings, one way to achieve this goal is through meditation. **Meditation** is the practice of using concentration to quiet and control one's thoughts.

In Mongolia, Buddhism mixed with **animism**, a belief that everything has a soul, including objects in nature. The native religion of Japan, **Shinto**, is similar to animism. The followers of this religion worship the spirits of their ancestors. They believe that these spirits exist in natural forces, including trees, rocks, and rivers.

> **Critical Viewing**
> Prayer flags flutter in the wind at a Buddhist temple in China. How might this temple's setting aid meditation?

Absorbing New Beliefs

People who practice animism and Shinto worship many different gods. Belief in more than one god is called **polytheism** (PAHL ee thee ihz uhm). Eventually, religions that teach belief in one god, such as Christianity and Islam, came to East Asia. Belief in one god is called **monotheism** (MAHN uh thee ihz uhm). Muslim traders in northwestern China helped spread Islam in the 700s. Today, it is the dominant religion in that part of China. Christian missionaries began to come to East Asia in the 1600s to spread their religion. Today, about 30 percent of South Koreans are Christians.

Throughout East Asia's history, governments supported different religions and philosophies. Han rulers, for example, promoted the ideas of Confucianism as a model for government and society. When Communist leaders came to power in China and North Korea, they banned the practice of religion, emphasizing Communist philosophy instead. Since the 1970s, however, there has been more religious tolerance in China.

Before You Move On

Understand Culture How were religions spread and absorbed in East Asia?

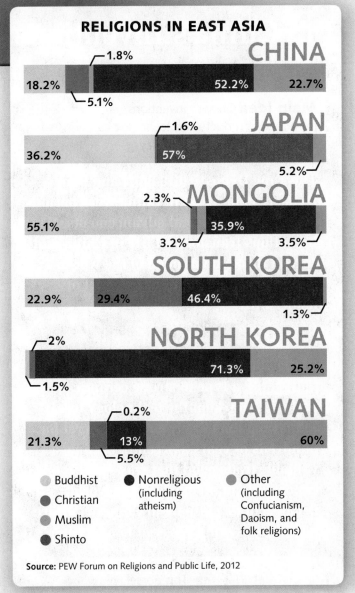

RELIGIONS IN EAST ASIA

CHINA — 18.2%, 1.8%, 5.1%, 52.2%, 22.7%

JAPAN — 36.2%, 1.6%, 57%, 5.2%

MONGOLIA — 55.1%, 2.3%, 3.2%, 35.9%, 3.5%

SOUTH KOREA — 22.9%, 29.4%, 46.4%, 1.3%

NORTH KOREA — 2%, 1.5%, 71.3%, 25.2%

TAIWAN — 21.3%, 0.2%, 5.5%, 13%, 60%

- Buddhist
- Christian
- Muslim
- Shinto
- Nonreligious (including atheism)
- Other (including Confucianism, Daoism, and folk religions)

Source: PEW Forum on Religions and Public Life, 2012

FORMATIVE ASSESSMENT

DATA LAB  GeoJournal

1. **Interpret Graphs** On the graph, notice the high percentages of "Other" in China, Mongolia, and Taiwan. What probably accounts for the numbers in this category?

2. **Analyze Data** Why do so many people in China consider themselves nonreligious?

3. **Draw Conclusions** As you have learned, many East Asians combine and practice more than one religion. What impact do you think religious diffusion has had on people?

1.2 China's Inventions

TECHTREK
myNGconnect.com For photos
of Chinese inventions

Digital
Library

Main Idea Chinese inventions introduced products and technologies that continue to be used today.

The Tang Dynasty (618–907) and Song Dynasty (960–1279) in China were periods of great technological advancements. New inventions transformed life in China and spread throughout much of the world. Many of these inventions are part of modern life.

Porcelain and Gunpowder

In the 700s, the Chinese developed porcelain, a type of strong ceramic pottery. They kept the technology used in making it a closely guarded secret for hundreds of years. Porcelain became a valuable trade good that was—and is— exported to many parts of the world. Because of its close tie to Chinese culture porcelain is often referred to as "china."

Critical Viewing This porcelain teapot was made during the Song Dynasty. Why do you think porcelain became so desirable?

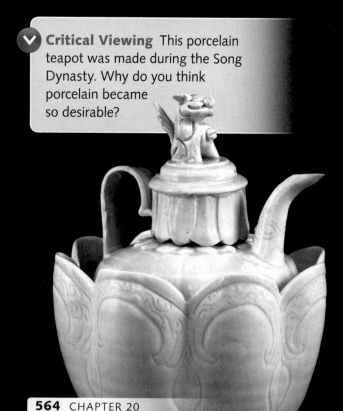

During the 800s, the Chinese invented a very different product: gunpowder. Gunpowder was first used for fireworks. Within 300 years, however, the Chinese were using it to shoot weapons. Fireworks, meanwhile, became a popular feature of Chinese celebrations because they were believed to frighten away evil spirits. Today, China is the world's largest manufacturer and exporter of fireworks.

Printing and Paper Money

The Chinese invented paper around A.D. 100. By the 700s, they began printing books using wooden blocks upon which text had been carved. Before block printing, people had reproduced books by copying each one by hand.

In the 1040s, the Chinese advanced printing further with the invention of movable type. Using this technique, individual characters carved on clay or metal blocks were placed in a frame to form a page of text. The blocks could be moved around to create many different pages. The Chinese used their printed books to spread the teachings of Confucius and Buddha.

The first paper money appeared in China in the 800s, but it did not become widely used until the 1020s. During the Song Dynasty, paper currency replaced the heavy metal coins that merchants and buyers previously carried. Paper money made trade easier and greatly expanded China's economy. However, people did not trust the new currency at first. After all, unlike the coins formerly used in trade, the paper itself had no value.

Magnetic Compass

Like paper, the compass was another early Chinese invention, dating from the 200s B.C. The compass from this period was used to position buildings and furniture in ways believed to bring good luck to the owners. By the 1100s, the Chinese had developed a magnetic compass for navigation by floating a magnetized needle in a bowl of water. They had learned that the needle always pointed in the north-south direction. With this floating compass, the Chinese explorer Zheng He traveled throughout Asia and Africa, demonstrating China's power and spreading its inventions.

Before You Move On
Make Inferences **In what ways have Chinese inventions influenced today's society?**

FORMATIVE ASSESSMENT

SPEAKING LAB GeoJournal

Turn and Talk In your opinion, which of the inventions described in this lesson has had the greatest impact on society? Get together with a partner to discuss why you think so. Make drawings or find images of other Chinese inventions to support your understanding of these technologies and their influences today. Organize your ideas in a paragraph and be prepared to share it aloud.

Critical Viewing Fireworks mark the opening of the 2008 Summer Olympics in Beijing. What aspects of this photo help explain why fireworks are so popular today?

SECTION 1 CULTURE

TECHTREK

myNGconnect.com For photos
reflecting Shanghai's growth

Digital
Library

1.3 Shanghai's Rapid Growth

MAOCHANG

豪康茶商館

淘進正宗

正宗苏帮面

昌

验配中心

> **Critical Viewing** People crowd Nanjing
> Road, a busy shopping district in Shanghai.
> What details in this photo suggest that
> Shanghai is a thriving center of business?

> **Main Idea** Shanghai's growth has resulted in a building and population boom.

Shanghai's location near the mouth of the Chang Jiang has attracted settlers since ancient times. Over the centuries, it became an important port city and busy trade center. Today, with a population of around 20 million, Shanghai has grown into China's largest city. It is also the country's center for finance and business.

Factors Fueling Growth

Shanghai's rapid growth began in the 1990s, when economic reforms led to new investments in the city. The economy of much of China is controlled by the central government. In 1990, however, the government allowed an area in Shanghai called Pudong to become a **Special Economic Zone**. This is an area that has the ability to develop a market economy with no government control of business.

As a result, Shanghai began to attract multinational corporations. A **multinational corporation** is a large company that is based in one country but establishes offices, branches, or plants in several others. Shanghai now hosts hundreds of multinational corporations. They have contributed to bringing economic globalization to China. **Economic globalization** occurs when economic activities are conducted across national borders.

Building and Population Boom

To make room for these corporations, the city witnessed a building boom in the 2000s. Thousands of new skyscrapers were constructed. One of the most important is the Shanghai World Financial Center, which opened in Pudong in 2008. It is the tallest building in China and home to the Shanghai Stock Exchange.

As Shanghai's economy has grown, so has its population. Since the 1990s, about four million people from China's rural areas have come to Shanghai seeking jobs. They now make up about 25 percent of the workforce. The city center became so crowded that about a half million households were relocated to the suburbs. The exploding growth in population also resulted in higher levels of pollution.

To address these problems, city planners are building several new towns around Shanghai's urban center. Each one will house about 500,000 people. To protect its environment, Shanghai has also funded efforts to use buses and taxis that run on cleaner fuel and has moved most of its factories out of the city center.

Before You Move On

Monitor Comprehension What factors fueled Shanghai's growth, and what happened in the city as a result?

FORMATIVE ASSESSMENT

READING LAB GeoJournal

1. **Make Inferences** What economic reasons might have led Chinese leaders to allow Pudong to become a Special Economic Zone?

2. **Analyze Causes and Effects** What have been some of the effects of Shanghai's rapid economic and population growth?

3. **Make Predictions** Describe what you think Shanghai might be like ten years from now.

NATIONAL GEOGRAPHIC
Photo Gallery · Shanghai's Skyscrapers

For more photos from the National Geographic Photo Gallery, go to the **Digital Library** at myNGconnect.com.

Bullet train passes Mt. Fuji

Toy factory, China

Silla palace, South Korea

▼ **Critical Viewing** The Oriental Pearl Tower and other skyscrapers line the banks of the Huangpu River in Shanghai. The Oriental Pearl, which is a television tower, features the revolving restaurant shown in the photo.

Japanese Kabuki drama

Buddhist monastery, Tibet

Japanese tea ceremony

Celebration in Taiwan

1.4 Japanese Anime

TECHTREK
myNGconnect.com For images
of Japanese anime and manga

Digital
Library

Main Idea Anime reflects both Western and Japanese cultural influences and has become popular around the world.

Anime is a style of animation, or cartoon, developed in Japan. The characters and settings in this art form are either drawn by hand or computer-generated. Anime is closely related to manga, or Japanese comic books. Manga stories are told using a series of panels. Many anime films are based on the art and stories in popular manga. In fact, an anime film may even use manga panels to introduce a story.

▲ **Critical Viewing** The artist in the top photo is drawing a panel, like that shown at bottom, for an anime film. What skills are probably needed to create anime?

Beginnings

Although anime films were produced in the early 1900s, the style and techniques used today didn't develop until the 1960s. Around that time, manga artist and animator Osamu Tezuka began to adapt some of the techniques used by Walt Disney in his own films. For example, Disney cartoons such as *Bambi* inspired Tezuka to draw characters with large eyes, which became a typical anime feature.

Anime uses elements from Western-style cartoons, but it also draws on Japanese culture. Ancient Japanese myths, Shinto, and Buddhism have all influenced many of the cartoons. For example, Shinto nature spirits populate the world depicted in *Spirited Away*, an anime film made in 2001 by director Hayao Miyazaki.

Popularity

Anime was a popular art form in Japan from the beginning, but Western audiences did not embrace it until the 1980s. Since then, anime has continued to gain fans—and respect—around the world.

One reason for anime's popularity is its broad range of subjects. Anime is used to tell stories in many different forms, including fantasy and science fiction. As a result, it appeals to all ages and both genders. Anime is also big business. In Japan, the art form and products related to anime earn more than $5 billion a year.

Before You Move On
Summarize In what ways does anime reflect Western and Japanese cultural influences, and why is it so popular?

This image shows a scene from Miyazaki's *Castle in the Sky*. Retell the scene based on information in the picture.

Lighting and colors convey an exciting mood.

The boy and girl have round, expressive eyes like many anime characters.

The camera angle in this scene shows perspective and depth.

FORMATIVE ASSESSMENT
PHOTO LAB
GeoJournal

1. **Analyze Primary Sources** Examine the anime image above. Who might be the intended audience for the film? What details in the image support your ideas?

2. **Turn and Talk** Discuss animated films you have seen and compare what you know about how they were made.

1.5 **Bullet Trains**

TECHTREK
myNGconnect.com For an online map
and photos of high-speed trains in East Asia

 Maps and
Graphs

 Digital
Library

Main Idea Bullet trains and other high-speed rail services have transformed travel in much of East Asia.

Japan pioneered the use of high-speed rail in 1964, with trains that traveled at speeds of more than 125 miles per hour (mph). They earned the nickname **bullet trains** because of their appearance and speed. Each train has a rounded nose like that of an airplane and a sleek, **aerodynamic** design. This means that the train moves with little resistance from the wind. The technology has spread, and now bullet trains connect cities in countries throughout East Asia.

> **Critical Viewing** A Japanese bullet train arrives in a station in Tokyo. Based on the photo, how would you describe the location of the station?

High-Speed Rail Spreads

The first bullet trains linked Tokyo with Osaka and allowed people to travel the 320-mile route in four hours instead of six. Today, the system connects Tokyo with all major cities on the main island of Honshu. Additional lines are being built on Kyushu as well. The trains on these lines travel at speeds up to 186 mph. The newer trains are also quieter and more energy efficient.

By the 2000s, bullet trains were running throughout much of East Asia. In 2004, South Korea established a high-speed rail system, connecting Seoul with major industrial cities and ports. In 2007, a high-speed rail system began in Taiwan and connected Taipei with cities in the southwestern part of the country.

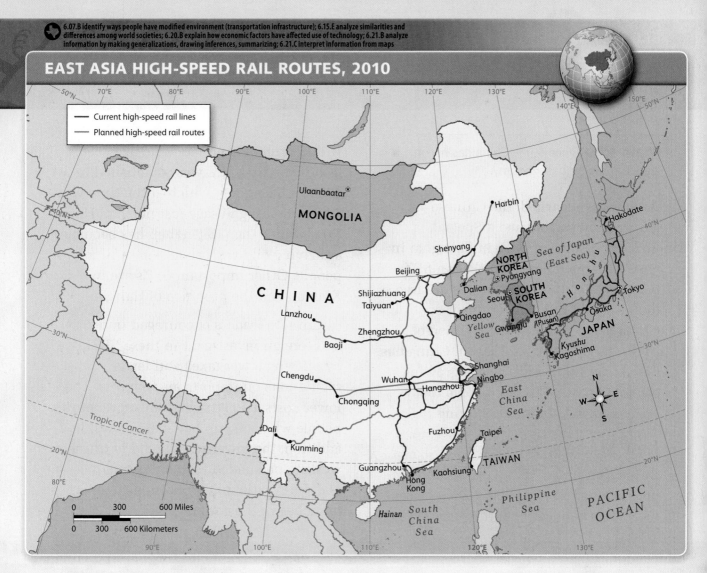

EAST ASIA HIGH-SPEED RAIL ROUTES, 2010

6.07.B identify ways people have modified environment (transportation infrastructure); 6.15.E analyze similarities and differences among world societies; 6.20.B explain how economic factors have affected use of technology; 6.21.B analyze information by making generalizations, drawing inferences, summarizing; 6.21.C interpret information from maps

Legend:
— Current high-speed rail lines
— Planned high-speed rail routes

The Chinese began developing high-speed rail in the 1990s. By 2009, China operated the fastest trains in the world, with speeds up to 245 mph. China has also taken advantage of another high-speed train technology: the magnetic levitation train, or Maglev for short. A **magnetic levitation** train rides on a cushion of air over tracks laid with many powerful magnets. Today, Maglev trains run between the Shanghai airport and Pudong, while achieving a top speed of 268 mph.

Benefits

The greatest benefit of high-speed trains may be the time passengers save by riding them. However, the trains have also given an economic boost to once-remote rural locations that are now linked to cities and towns. In addition, bullet trains produce less pollution than traditional trains. In fact, the Maglev is almost pollution-free.

Before You Move On

Summarize In what ways have high-speed rail services transformed travel in East Asia?

FORMATIVE ASSESSMENT

MAP LAB  GeoJournal

1. **Movement** On the map, study the rail routes in Japan. What generalization can you make about the routes?

2. **Region** According to the map, in what part of the country are most of China's routes concentrated? Why do you think that is so?

3. **Make Inferences** Why might people prefer to travel from one city to another on a bullet train rather than on a plane or by car?

2.1 China's Economy Today

TECHTREK

myNGconnect.com For online graphs
of China's GDP and photos of Chinese industry

Maps and Graphs

Digital Library

Main Idea Since 1979, China has become a leader in the global economy.

As you have learned, the Chinese government established a Special Economic Zone, or SEZ, in Shanghai in 1990. You may remember that an SEZ is an area in which businesses are free to develop without government control. China began to allow the creation of SEZs in the early 1980s. As a result, China has had one of the world's fastest growing economies, and Chinese people today enjoy a higher standard of living.

New Strategy for Growth

China limited its SEZs to cities and provinces along the Pacific Coast because its leaders believed that this location would promote and facilitate overseas trade. The first SEZ was established in 1980 in Shenzhen, which at the time was a small fishing village just north of Hong Kong. Since then, Shenzhen has become a thriving city with about ten million people. Other important SEZs are in Xiamen and the province of Hainan.

Chinese leaders encouraged trade and foreign investment in these SEZs by offering lower taxes and fewer regulations on imports and exports. The lower costs also attracted **entrepreneurs**, people who start up new businesses. In addition, the lower wages paid to Chinese workers persuaded regional companies and multinational corporations to open branches in the country.

Critical Viewing Chinese workers build electric bikes for domestic use and for export. What words would you use to describe the bikes in this photo?

6.03.C compare countries using data from graphs; 6.08.A describe ways factors of production influence economies (entrepreneurs); 6.10.A give examples of agricultural, service, and manufacturing industries; 6.10.B describe levels of development using economic indicators; 6.10.C identify the effects of government regulation on economic development and business planning; 6.21.B analyze by summarizing, drawing conclusions, inferences; 6.21.C interpret information from graphs

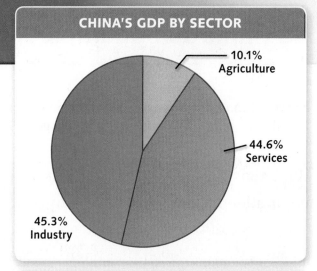

CHINA'S GDP BY SECTOR

10.1% Agriculture

44.6% Services

45.3% Industry

China's strategies have worked. In 2013, China had the world's third largest economy after the United States and the European Union. Economists measure the size of a country's economy based on **gross domestic product (GDP)**, the total value of all the goods and services produced in a country in a given year. China's GDP increases about ten percent per year.

A Diverse Economy

China's growing economy is powered by industry, services, and agriculture. The country's main industries include mining and iron and steel manufacturing. Globally, China is most known for its exports of clothing and textiles, electronics, and toys. China exports more than any other single country in the world. About 20 percent of its exports go to the United States.

Inside China's borders, service industries provide activities such as banking, insurance, trade, communication, education, health care, recreation, and transportation. As China welcomes more and more visitors, tourism is also becoming a large part of its economy.

Agriculture contributes little to China's GDP, but it employs 35 percent of the country's workers. Only about 15 percent of Chinese land is arable, but the country produces most of the food it needs for its large population.

Before You Move On

Summarize What steps has China taken to grow and diversify its economy?

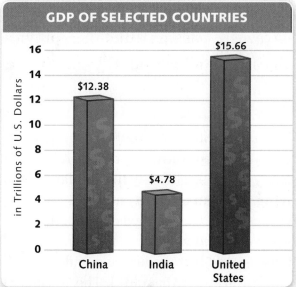

GDP OF SELECTED COUNTRIES

in Trillions of U.S. Dollars

China $12.38

India $4.78

United States $15.66

Source: CIA World Factbook 2010, 2012

FORMATIVE ASSESSMENT

DATA LAB — GeoJournal

1. **Draw Conclusions** According to the pie chart, how much of China's GDP is supplied by agriculture? Since 35 percent of the Chinese people work in agriculture, what conclusions can you draw about their earnings?

2. **Analyze Data** Study the bar graph and compare China's GDP with that of India. What do these numbers suggest about the relative rate of each country's GDP growth?

3. **Make Inferences** Based on what you have read, why are Chinese-made consumer goods sold at low prices in countries such as the United States?

2.2 China's Population Policy

TECHTREK
myNGconnect.com For an online
population pyramid of China

Student
Resources

Global
Issues

Main Idea China's one-child policy has slowed the population growth rate, but it is also bringing great change to Chinese society.

KEY VOCABULARY

one-child policy, n., law that restricts urban Chinese families to one child

fertility rate, n., average number of children born per woman

ACADEMIC VOCABULARY

comply, v., follow or obey

With about 1.3 billion people, China has the largest population in the world. For many years, Communist leaders encouraged the country's population to grow because they believed that having more people—and workers—would strengthen China's economy. In time, however, it became difficult to provide food, housing, education, and jobs for the country's citizens.

Slowing Population Growth

To curb their rapidly growing population, the government introduced the **one-child policy** in 1979. This law limited families living in urban areas to one child. Those who **complied** , or followed, the policy were rewarded with more food, improved housing, and better education and job opportunities for that child. Those who did not comply had to pay large fines. As a result, the rate of population growth declined to about 0.65 percent per year by 2010, which is about half of what it was in 1979. There are some exceptions to the policy. For example, minority populations and rural families may have two or more children. In 2013, the policy made world news as it seemed clear the government was about to loosen restrictions.

Before You Move On

Monitor Comprehension What policies did China put in place to decrease population growth?

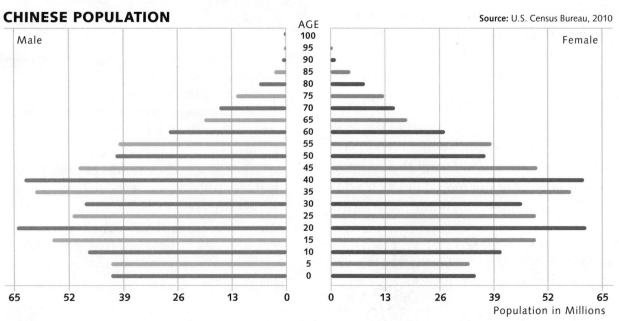

CHINESE POPULATION

Source: U.S. Census Bureau, 2010

Population in Millions

Inspiring people to care about the planet
National Geographic Society Mission

Effects of China's Policy

In general, China's one-child policy has worked. The **fertility rate**, or the average number of children born per woman, dropped from about six in the 1950s to about two by 1995. The Chinese government claimed that, since it was put in place, the policy has helped reduce the number of births in China by 400 million. According to the government, the policy has also improved the standard of living for many Chinese people.

With fewer children being born, the elderly will soon outnumber young people in China. Traditionally, daughters and daughters-in-law have taken care of elderly parents. However, in recent times when no adult child can do so, the seniors must turn to retirement funds or charity for support. In response, the Chinese government has begun to create community services to help the elderly who live alone.

Three generations of a familly pass a poster promoting population control.

India's Population Growth

Like China, India has a huge population. With about 1.2 billion people, India is second only to China in population— for now. Scientists predict that India's population will exceed China's by 2030. In contrast with China, about 50 percent of India's population is under the age of 25. While this statistic guarantees that India will have a large workforce, the young population will also put a strain on the country's schools and other resources.

In spite of this growth, India does not enforce strict population policies. Instead, the country encourages the advancement and education of its women. India's leaders believe that educated women are more likely to have smaller families. The government also offers cash bonuses to women in rural areas who wait to start a family and agree to have fewer children.

Before You Move On
Summarize What have been the effects of China's one-child policy?

FORMATIVE ASSESSMENT
READING LAB  GeoJournal

1. **Make Generalizations** Based on what you read, what is the connection between overpopulation and standard of living?

2. **Interpret Graphs** Study the population pyramid. If these numbers hold, which groups will be the largest in 20 years? What impact might this situation have on China's economy?

3. **Form and Support Opinions** In your opinion, which country's policies have a better chance of working, China's or India's? Why?

SECTION **2** GOVERNMENT & ECONOMICS

TECHTREK

myNGconnect.com For photos of the
Three Gorges Dam and Guided Writing

Student
Resources

Digital
Library

2.3 China's Three Gorges Dam

Main Idea The Three Gorges Dam in China is the largest dam in the world and has both benefits and drawbacks.

The **Three Gorges Dam** on the Chang Jiang River is nearly 1.3 miles wide and 600 feet high. The dam was built to prevent flooding along the eastern part of the river between the cities of Chongqing and Wuhan. It was also designed to generate hydroelectric power, promote economic development in the region, and ease navigation along the Chang Jiang.

Building a Giant Dam

Geographic factors determined where the dam would be built. The Three Gorges is an area where the Chang Jiang is very narrow—only about 350 feet wide as the river flows between steep cliffs. The area is named for this geographic feature. A **gorge** is a deep, narrow passage surrounded by steep cliffs. When snows melt in the spring or heavy rains fall during summer monsoons, the river can rise very quickly in the narrow area. Over the years, this seasonal rise has caused major flooding and millions of deaths.

As work on the dam began in 1994, a large artificial lake called a **reservoir** formed behind it to store the water being held back. This reservoir is about 500 feet deep, and it is longer than Lake Superior in the United States, the largest natural body of fresh water in the world. During dry periods, the dam will slowly release water from the reservoir. This raises the level of the river downstream to allow large ships to travel to China's interior.

Work on the dam was completed in 2006, but it did not become fully operational until 2011. The dam is a major engineering achievement. However, it has stirred **controversy**, or debate, both within China and abroad.

⌄ Critical Viewing The Three Gorges Dam has been called China's Great Wall across the Chang Jiang. Based on this photo, what feelings might the dam inspire in the Chinese people?

6.04.D identify and locate major physical and human geographic features; 6.06.C analyze effects of interaction of processes and environment on humans; 6.07.B identify and analyze ways people have modified the environment; 6.07.C describe ways technology influences interactions with environment; 6.21.D identify different points of view about an issue

Benefits and Drawbacks

The Chinese government expects to reap great benefits from the dam, which has already prevented serious flooding along the Chang Jiang. Improving conditions for commercial shipping along the river should increase economic development in the region. In addition, the government predicts that the hydroelectric power created by the dam will provide about 10 percent of China's total energy.

Critics, however, claim that the drawbacks of the dam, which cost an estimated $25 billion, outweigh the benefits. To create the reservoir, a large expanse of land had to be cleared. About 1.5 million people were displaced from their cities and villages, and more than 1,000 historic and cultural sites are now under water. The critics also fear that the dam may cause landslides and destroy the habitat of endangered animals. Many argue that building several smaller dams and using newer technology for producing energy would have been a better solution.

Before You Move On

Summarize Why did China build the Three Gorges Dam?

THREE GORGES DAM

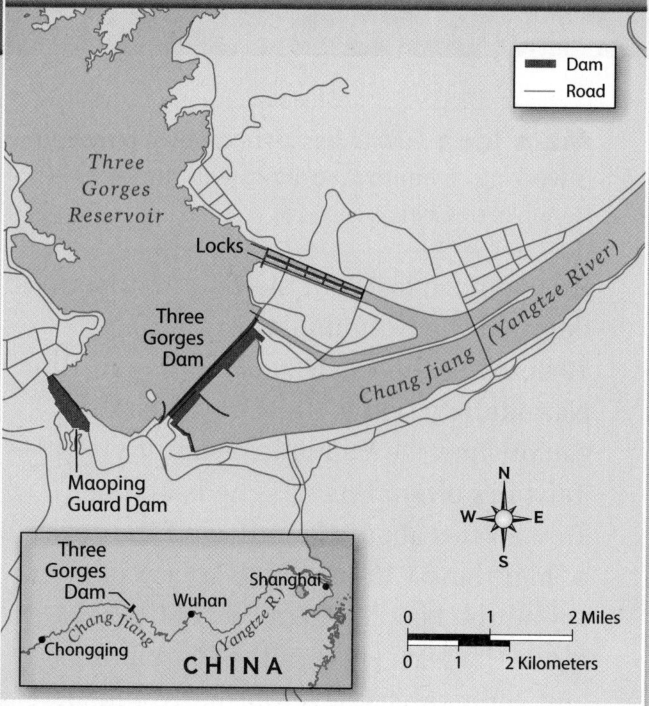

Dam
Road
Three Gorges Reservoir
Locks
Three Gorges Dam
Chang Jiang (Yangtze River)
Maoping Guard Dam
N
W
E
S
0
1
2 Miles
0
1
2 Kilometers
Three Gorges Dam
Wuhan
Shanghai
Chang Jiang
(Yangtze R.)
Chongqing
CHINA

MAP TIP
The smaller map shows where the Three Gorges Dam is located on the Chang Jiang. Notice that the dam is west of Shanghai in eastern China.

FORMATIVE ASSESSMENT

WRITING LAB

GeoJournal

Form and Support Opinions Do you think that building the Three Gorges Dam was a good idea? Use a chart like the one below to list the dam's benefits and drawbacks. Then write a brief paragraph in which you state and support your opinion with evidence. You may want to do additional research to learn more about the dam. Go to **Student Resources** for Guided Writing Support.

BENEFITS	DRAWBACKS
1.	
2.	

TECHTREK
myNGconnect.com For an
online map and photos of Taiwan

Maps and
Graphs

Digital
Library

> **Main Idea** Taiwan has a strong economy and is working to improve relations with the People's Republic of China.

As you have learned, the Communists defeated the Nationalists in China in 1949. After their defeat, about two million Nationalists fled to Taiwan where they established the Republic of China, Taiwan's official name. The island of Taiwan lies about 100 miles off the coast of mainland China, which is officially called the People's Republic of China. Since the war between the Communists and Nationalists never formally ended, there are still tensions between Taiwan and China.

A Democratic Government

In 1949, the Nationalists placed Taiwan under **martial law**—a government maintained by military power—which continued into the 1980s. During their long, one-party rule, Nationalist leaders claimed that they had authority over all of China, including the mainland.

Beginning in 1987, more political parties were allowed to take part in elections, and martial law was lifted. As a result, people on the island experienced more democratic freedom. However, Taiwan's political status, or legal position, has remained uncertain.

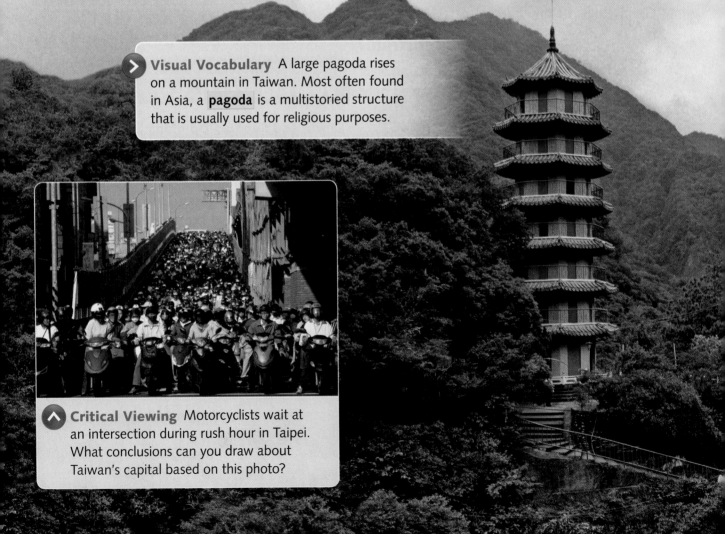

> **Visual Vocabulary** A large pagoda rises on a mountain in Taiwan. Most often found in Asia, a **pagoda** is a multistoried structure that is usually used for religious purposes.

Critical Viewing Motorcyclists wait at an intersection during rush hour in Taipei. What conclusions can you draw about Taiwan's capital based on this photo?

During the Cold War, many countries regarded Taiwan as the legitimate government of China. Today, these countries recognize the government of the People's Republic of China in Beijing but unofficially treat Taiwan as an independent state. Mainland China considers Taiwan one of its provinces. It has chosen not to challenge Taiwan, however, as long as it does not declare its independence.

A Strong Economy

During the 1960s and 1970s, Taiwan began to develop a market economy. Today, it has the 20th largest economy in the world with a gross domestic product (GDP) of about $900 billion.

Exports have fueled the growth of Taiwan's GDP. Important exports include electronics and machinery. Because Taiwan depends so much on exports, its economy declines when world demand for its goods decreases. Farming in Taiwan is limited because about two-thirds of the island is covered in mountains.

Taiwan wants to strengthen economic ties with mainland China, its leading export and import partner. Chinese investors have been able to invest directly in businesses in Taiwan, and Taiwanese financial firms have opened on mainland China. This improved economic cooperation may also lead to better diplomatic relations between the two.

Before You Move On

Monitor Comprehension What steps has Taiwan taken to improve its government, economy, and relations with China?

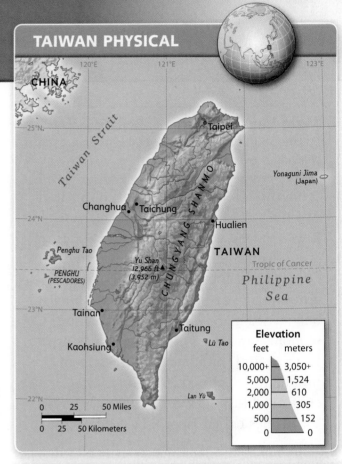

TAIWAN PHYSICAL

Elevation

feet	meters
10,000+	3,050+
5,000	1,524
2,000	610
1,000	305
500	152
0	0

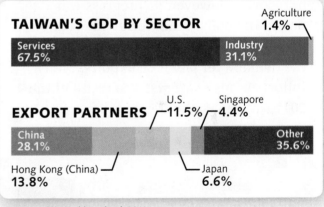

TAIWAN'S GDP BY SECTOR

Agriculture 1.4%

Services 67.5%	Industry 31.1%

EXPORT PARTNERS

U.S. 11.5% — Singapore 4.4%

China 28.1% — Hong Kong (China) 13.8% — Japan 6.6% — Other 35.6%

Source: CIA World Factbook 2010

FORMATIVE ASSESSMENT

DATA LAB

GeoJournal

1. **Analyze** What happened historically that resulted in different economic systems for Taiwan and China?

2. **Interpret Graphs** Based on the Export Partners graph, where are most of Taiwan's partners located? Why do you think this is so?

3. **Draw Conclusions** As you have read, much of Taiwan's economy depends on its exports. Which sector of the GDP probably provides most of those exports?

2.5 Japan's Economic Future

Maps and Graphs

Digital Library

Main Idea Japan is a major world economy but the country has faced several economic challenges over two decades.

From the 1960s until the late 1980s, Japan had the strongest economy in East Asia. It was second only to the United States in gross domestic product (GDP) worldwide. However, by 1990, the country's economic growth had begun to slow down. Many businesses had borrowed huge amounts of money and were deeply in debt. With little **capital**, or money for investment, production declined. The situation continued throughout the 1990s, a period sometimes called Japan's **Lost Decade**.

In the 2000s, Japan's economy began to recover. However, its progress was halted in 2008 by the worldwide economic downturn, which led to a decrease in the demand for Japanese exports. Many industries also suffered as a result of the 2011 earthquake and tsunami.

Economy Today

Japan is highly competitive and thriving free-market economy. Workers are well educated, and women make up nearly half of its labor force, although their jobs are not equal to those of men.

Because Japan has few natural resources, the country must import most of the raw materials needed for its many industries. Japan's economy depends heavily on exported goods produced by these industries, including cars, computers, and other electronics.

Japan is still among the world's top five exporters. However, it has been less aggressive than many other Asian countries in promoting free trade with its neighbors. **Free trade** is trade that does not impose tariffs, or taxes on imports. These taxes can make Japan's exports more expensive than those of other Asian countries with free-trade agreements.

> **Critical Viewing** A technician inspects flat-screen televisions in a factory in Osaka. How do the televisions in this photo compare with those made in America?

6.06.C analyze effects of interaction of physical processes and environment on humans; 6.08.A describe ways factors of production influence economies (entrepreneurs); 6.08.C explain impact of relative scarcity of resources on trade, economic interdependence; 6.09.A compare ways societies organize production and distribution of goods; 6.10.C identify effects of government taxation on economic development; 6.20.A give examples of technological innovations; 6.20.B explain how belief systems, economic factors, and political decisions affect use of technology

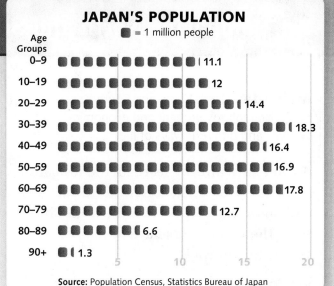

JAPAN'S POPULATION

= 1 million people

Age Groups	Population (millions)
0–9	11.1
10–19	12
20–29	14.4
30–39	18.3
40–49	16.4
50–59	16.9
60–69	17.8
70–79	12.7
80–89	6.6
90+	1.3

Source: Population Census, Statistics Bureau of Japan

Japan and Technology

For many years, Japan led the world in efficient systems of manufacturing, especially for autos and electronics, as proven by Toyota and Sony, two giant Japanese corporations. The country's belief in hard work and in making things well is part of the culture, which also embraces new technologies. In recent years, Japan has slipped from its higher ranking in global innovation. Some say a new entrepreneurial spirit is needed.

Today, Japan's government has decided to invest more in entrepreneurs. These men and women come up with new products or services, from social networks that help society to online games. For example, they might invent technologies that solve Japan's energy needs. New companies will face challenges, though. In addition to competition from other countries, Japan's population is expected shrink by the year 2050, possibly leading to a shortage of workers. This may have a harmful effect on the country's economy.

Japan's economy also faced challenges following the 2011 earthquake and tsunami. After the disaster, manufacturing fell sharply and power supplies decreased when several of Japan's nuclear power plants became permanently disabled. The cost of repairing the damage caused by the natural disaster was estimated at about $300 billion. Some analysts feared that the disaster could put a halt to Japan's economic recovery.

Before You Move On

Summarize What three events have hurt the Japanese economy?

FORMATIVE ASSESSMENT

DATA LAB GeoJournal

1. **Make Generalizations** Based on what you have read, describe ways in which aging workers and entrepreneurs could play a role in Japan's economic future.

2. **Summarize** Explain the impact that the lack of natural resources has had on Japan's trade with other nations.

3. **Understand Culture** Explain how Japan's cultural beliefs and political decisions have affected, and will affect, the use of technology.

2.6 Comparing North and South Korea

TECHTREK

myNGconnect.com For photos of the two Koreas

Digital Library

> **Main Idea** North Korea and South Korea have different government and economic systems and different ways of life.

As you have already learned, the Korean Peninsula was divided into North Korea and South Korea after World War II. Since then, these neighbors have developed in very different ways.

North Korea

North Korea, which is officially called the Democratic People's Republic of Korea, has a Communist government that follows a policy of self-reliance. This means that the country depends mostly on its own efforts and abilities. The policy has kept North Korea isolated from most other countries.

The North Korean government controls most of the country's economy. The country's isolation policy has restricted trade, but it does conduct a limited amount of commerce, particularly with China. Much of its industry is devoted to the production of military equipment.

Only about 18 percent of North Korea's land is arable, and the climate does not support a long growing season. In the 1990s, floods and **drought**, a long period of extremely dry weather, greatly decreased food production. The resulting **famine**, or extreme food shortage, is believed to have caused as many as three million deaths.

South Korea

South Korea, which is officially called the Republic of Korea, was ruled largely by repressive military leaders until 1987.

Since then, the country has developed into a successful democracy, with free elections and multiple political parties.

Unlike North Korea, South Korea did not isolate itself from the rest of the world. It accepted grants and loans from countries such as the United States and Japan. As a result, South Korea's market economy grew quickly beginning in the 1960s. Today, it is one of the largest economies in the world.

South Korea's economy depends heavily on manufacturing. Shipbuilding has long been a major industry. In fact, South Korea is the world's leading builder of ships. The country also produces automobiles and electronics. Like Japan, South Korea has few natural resources and relies largely on the goods it exports to fuel its economy.

Reunification

North Korea and South Korea have had a tense relationship since the end of the Korean War in 1953. In the early 2000s, meetings between the countries' leaders suggested that relations were improving. Attempts were made to encourage interaction between the two countries. However, North Korea's development of nuclear weapons and its military attack on a South Korean island in 2010 stirred up hostilities once again. Since then, there has been little hope that the two countries would reunite soon.

Before You Move On

Make Inferences What impact have the different governments and economic systems in North Korea and South Korea had on their people?

6.06.C analyze effects of interaction of physical processes and environment on humans;
6.09.A compare ways societies organize production and distribution of goods and services;
6.09.D examine record of collective non-free market economic systems; 6.16.B compare
characteristics of institutions; 6.12.C interpret information from visuals

Critical Viewing This photo shows a street in Seoul, South Korea's capital. What does the photo suggest about the city?

This photo shows an empty street in the North Korean city of Kaesong. For the most part, only government officials own cars, which are considered symbols of status and power.

FORMATIVE ASSESSMENT

PHOTO LAB

GeoJournal

Turn and Talk Work with a small group to discuss the photos of North Korea and South Korea. What do they suggest about differences in daily life? Reread passages to find reasons for the differences. Ask and answer questions, and listen for key vocabulary and comparing words in your discussion.

For more photos from
the National Geographic
Photo Gallery, go to
the **Digital Library** at
myNGconnect.com.

Capsule hotel, Japan

Japanese rice cakes

Hong Kong street market

Shinto torii gate

Kabuki theater actor

Crowded subway, Japan

The Bund, Shanghai

VOCABULARY

For each pair of vocabulary words, write one sentence that explains the connection between the two words.

1. monotheism; polytheism

> *Belief in one god is called monotheism, while belief in more than one god is called polytheism.*

2. anime; manga

3. gorge; reservoir

4. free trade; capital

5. famine; drought

MAIN IDEAS

6. What are East Asia's religious traditions and in what manner did they arise in the region? (Section 1.1)

7. How did the Chinese use the inventions of movable type and paper money? (Section 1.2)

8. What factors helped Shanghai become China's largest city? (Section 1.3)

9. Why did Japan develop a high-speed rail system in the 1960s? (Section 1.5)

10. Where did China encourage most economic growth after 1979? (Section 2.1)

11. What did China hope to accomplish with its one-child population policy? (Section 2.2)

12. Why are some people critical of the Three Gorges Dam? (Section 2.3)

13. What is Taiwan's relationship with China? (Section 2.4)

14. In what way is Japan's population related to its economic future? (Section 2.5)

15. How do the governments and economic systems of North Korea and South Korea differ? (Section 2.6)

CULTURE

ANALYZE THE ESSENTIAL QUESTION

How do traditions and modernization create a unique way of life in East Asia?

Critical Thinking: Draw Conclusions

16. Why did many East Asians blend new religious ideas with traditional beliefs?

17. Why did China allow an area of Shanghai to become a Special Economic Zone?

18. In what ways does high-speed rail travel promote economic development in East Asia?

INTERPRET MAPS

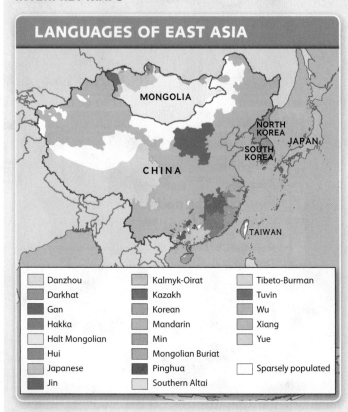

LANGUAGES OF EAST ASIA

Legend:
- Danzhou
- Darkhat
- Gan
- Hakka
- Halt Mongolian
- Hui
- Japanese
- Jin
- Kalmyk-Oirat
- Kazakh
- Korean
- Mandarin
- Min
- Mongolian Buriat
- Pinghua
- Southern Altai
- Tibeto-Burman
- Tuvin
- Wu
- Xiang
- Yue
- Sparsely populated

19. **Region** Which language is spoken in much of China? What might be the disadvantages for those who don't speak the language?

20. **Compare and Contrast** Which East Asian countries are most united by a common language? What does this fact suggest about the people of these countries?

GOVERNMENT & ECONOMICS

ANALYZE THE ESSENTIAL QUESTION

What problems does East Asia face today, and what are its opportunities?

Critical Thinking: Compare and Contrast

21. Compare the economic opportunities in China's coastal cities and rural areas. Which area provides greater opportunities? Why?

22. In what ways are the economies of Japan, South Korea, and Taiwan similar?

23. What do North Korea and South Korea have in common? Do you think these similarities might help the two countries unite some day? Explain why or why not.

INTERPRET CHARTS

LIFE IN THE TWO KOREAS		
	North Korea	South Korea
GDP (valued at U.S. prices)	$40 billion	$1.611 trillion
agriculture	23%	3%
industry	48%	39%
services	29%	58%
GDP per person	$1,800	$32,400
Life expectancy at birth	69.5 years	79.5 years
Infant mortality	25 deaths/ 1,000 live births	4 deaths/ 1,000 live births
Literacy	99%	97.9%

Sources: CIA World Factbook 2013

24. **Draw Conclusions** Based on the statistics in the chart under GDP per person, what conclusions can you draw about the standard of living in North Korea and South Korea?

25. **Make Inferences** Study the statistics on infant mortality. What do these numbers suggest about health care in each country?

ACTIVE OPTIONS

Synthesize the Essential Questions by completing the activities below.

26. **Create a Web Page** Make a home page for a Web site about East Asia today. Write a short introduction to the region and include links to each country. Use visuals, including photos, maps, charts, and graphs, that illustrate East Asia's culture and economic endeavors. Use the tips below to help you prepare your Web page. **Display your Web page and invite your classmates to "click" on the links. Be prepared to summarize what your viewers would find on each link.**

> **Writing Tips**
> - Use bullet points to summarize cultural and economic topics in East Asia today.
> - Provide labels for your links that will capture your audience's attention.
> - Include captions with your visuals that are brief and informative.

27. **Design an Anime Storyboard** Get together in a small group to design a storyboard for a scene in an anime film. First, brainstorm to come up with ideas for the scene's characters and plot. You can do online research to learn more about anime. Then sketch and write dialogue for each panel of the scene. Use a chart like the one below to organize your ideas.

PANEL 1	PANEL 2	PANEL 3
Characters:	Characters:	Characters:
Action:	Action:	Action:
Dialogue:	Dialogue:	Dialogue:

Mobile Access

TECHTREK

myNGconnect.com For an online graph

Maps and Graphs

Perhaps no other manufactured product since the personal computer has had so broad a global impact as the mobile phone and its cousin the smart phone. These devices play a part in economics, politics, civic participation, and the spread of culture—in activities that go far beyond taking photos, texting, or checking email.

In developing countries not so long ago, people had little to no access to global information. Today, those who cannot afford computers for Internet connections buy smart phones instead, which are less expensive. In addition, in countries where the government controls communication, people can sometimes find access to unbiased news and other information through mobile media.

Compare

- Argentina
- Bangladesh
- Brazil
- China
- India
- Mongolia
- Nepal
- South Korea
- United States
- Venezuela

CHINA AND MEDIA

China has the largest world population, and it has the most mobile phone subscribers. The BBC reported in 2013 that 464 million Chinese, or 44% of the population, used smartphone or wireless devices for Internet access. (In 2002, the percentage was 4.6%.) China's communist government, however, controls and censors media.

Chinese artist Ai Weiwei (EYE way way) used a blog to gather the names of children who died in poorly constructed schools during the 2008 earthquake in Sichuan province. The government had built the schools. It blocked the artist's Internet access on his computer. So he and others used cell phones. The 9,000 names they gathered became part of "Remembering," an artwork mounted on a long wall—9,000 backpacks, one for each child who died.

OTHER USES AND BENEFITS

Brazil's mobile phone and Internet usage tripled from 2007 to 2012. Mobile phone and smartphone use is on the rise not only in South America, East Asia, and South Asia but in countries in remote regions. In 2013, there were reportedly 4.5 billion mobile phones in the developing world. Developing countries are using resources to install mobile networks. This helps small businesses quickly keep up with market news using phones. Some studies show that cell phone use can increase a country's GDP.

Thousands of uses have been developed through mobile apps. These software applications are downloaded for banking, games, movies, social media, music, car rentals, and finding businesses, as well as for education, health information, government information, and public safety weather alerts.

6.03.C compare countries, regions using data; 6.11.C identify reasons for limiting power of government; 6.17.B describe factors that influence cultural change; 6.17.C evaluate impact of improved communication technology among cultures; 6.18.C describe ways contemporary issues influence creative expression; 6.20.B explain how resources, belief systems, economic factors, and political decisions affect use of technology; 6.21.C organize information from databases; 6.22.D create written material based on research

Hundreds of Chinese customers in Beijing line up overnight in 2012 to purchase a new release of the iPhone.

FORMATIVE ASSESSMENT

RESEARCH LAB GeoJournal

1. **Make Generalizations** Ai Weiwei used his mobile phone for creative expression in response to a political and social issue. In what ways do you think mobile access affects culture and cultural change?

2. **Draw Conclusions** What connection can you make between unlimited government and control of media access?

3. **Evaluate** What impact do you think improved communication technology has among different cultures?

4. **Research Data** Choose two countries from different regions from the list on page 590. Find out about their mobile access or mobile phone use. Use the World Factbook database online or other sources recommended by your teacher or librarian to write a paragraph that answers this question: How do you think resources and economic factors, as well as beliefs and political ideas, affect the use of technology?

Active Options

ACTIVITY 1

Goal: Learn about the importance
of cherry blossoms in Japan.

Celebrate the Cherry Blossom

Every year, the Japanese people hold
festivals to celebrate the cherry blossom.
In Japanese culture, the beauty of the
blossoms and the brief duration of their
bloom symbolize the fleeting nature of life.
The blossoms are often used in manga and
anime. Research to learn more about the
importance of cherry blossoms in
Japan. Then choose one of the
following ways to celebrate
the flower:

- Write a haiku in
  honor of the cherry
  blossom. A haiku is
  a three-line poem
  with five syllables
  in the first line,
  seven in the second
  line, and five in the
  third line. The poem
  does not rhyme.

- Sketch or paint a
  cherry blossom.
- Find and display
  examples of
  cherry blossoms in
  Japanese art.
- Research and report
  on three other
  places outside
  Japan that hold
  cherry blossom
  festivals.

**Anime illustration
of cherry blossoms**

ACTIVITY 2

Goal: Extend your knowledge of China's culture.

Create a Chinese Culture Magazine

Learn more about China's rich cultural
heritage. Get together in a small group
to design a magazine page on one part
of Chinese culture. You might focus on
the country's art, music, food, or martial
arts. Research your topic and use the
Magazine Maker CD-ROM to create
your page. Combine the pages created by
different groups into a magazine.

ACTIVITY 3

Goal: Make predictions based on prior knowledge.

I Predict!

What's the next stage for bullet trains
or mobile phones? Predict discoveries
in science and technology that could
affect culture or politics. How might
technology improve health? Explain the
basis for your predictions.

6.15. A identify traits that define cultures; 6.18. A explain relationships between societies and their architecture, art; 6.18.D identify examples of art, architecture that transcend boundaries; 6.20.B predict future impacts from scientific discoveries or technological innovations; 6.22.D create written and visual material based on research

TEKS

TEKS PROJECT

Goal: Understand relationships among societies and their arts.

Organize a World Expo

A world's fair or exposition ("expo," for short) is one place you might see new forms of energy put to use or unusual architecture built with materials that do not harm the planet. It's an awe-inspiring display of advances in science, technology, and the arts.

Expos have been around since the 19th century as a way to showcase cultures. Today, cultural influences can spread in seconds, thanks to high-speed communication technology.

How to Begin? To organize an expo, start with *what* and *where*. Choose an expo theme focused on arts and culture, and sketch a floor plan for exhibits organized by region. Then join with others to swap ideas. Discuss how food, art, fashion, music, literature, or traditions can blend to create something new. Be both creative and practical. Are there common ideas to narrow to a single theme and layout? Write a description of your expo goals.

Make It Global Email students in other countries and ask them for ideas about what they would show in their country's exhibit. Survey adults in your school and family members to help compile a list of contacts. Use your expo description for inviting others to join in.

Pull It Together For each country's exhibit, create a model, assemble objects, or create a collage of visual ideas using photos and drawings. How much can your team accomplish in the time you have? Scale back your vision so you can meet your deadline. Make videos of the expo presentations and edit them to post on your school's Web site.

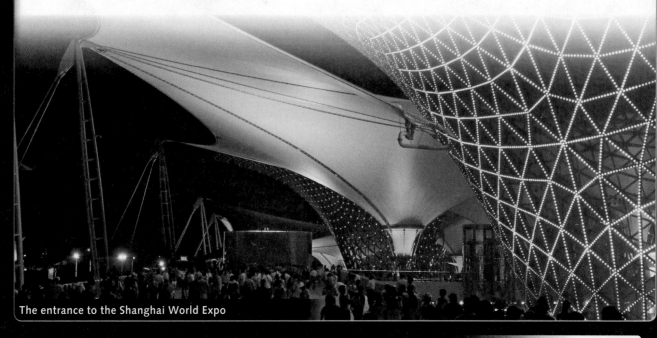

The entrance to the Shanghai World Expo

explore
Southeast Asia
with NATIONAL GEOGRAPHIC

MEET THE EXPLORER

NATIONAL GEOGRAPHIC

Emerging Explorer Jenny Daltry searches for unknown species of snakes, frogs, and crocodiles in unexplored corners of South Asia and Southeast Asia. Her work helps conserve these animals' habitats. Here, she inspects the fangs of a snake.

INVESTIGATE GEOGRAPHY

Mount Merapi is a volcanic mountain peak located near the center of the densely populated island of Java, Indonesia. It is the most active of the country's volcanoes. Its ash creates fertile soil, luring farmers in spite of the dangers.

STEP INTO HISTORY

A Buddhist monk prays at a statue in the Angkor Wat temple complex, Cambodia. Angkor Wat was originally built as a Hindu worship center in the 12th century. It remains the largest religious structure in the world.

Go to myNGconnect.com for maps of Southeast Asia.

8,563 miles

Washington, D.C.

Manila, Philippines

CONNECT WITH THE CULTURE

The busy floating market in Damnern Saduak, Thailand has been attracting buyers since 1872. Hats, shown here, along with fruits, vegetables, flowers, and other food, are available.

Southeast Asia
GEOGRAPHY & HISTORY

PREVIEW THE CHAPTER

Essential Question What are the geographic conditions that divide Southeast Asia into many different parts?

KEY VOCABULARY
- land bridge
- landlocked
- typhoon
- tsunami
- subsistence fishing
- ecologist
- bauxite
- biodiversity
- dynamic
- dormant
- zoologist
- wallaby

ACADEMIC VOCABULARY
enhance

TERMS & NAMES
- Ring of Fire
- Mekong River
- Chao Phraya River
- Irrawaddy River
- Malay Peninsula
- Foja Mountains

Essential Question How have physical barriers in Southeast Asia influenced its history?

KEY VOCABULARY
- complex
- bas-relief
- monopoly
- colonialism
- fossil
- commerce
- launch
- resistance

ACADEMIC VOCABULARY
transform

TERMS & NAMES
- Khmer Empire
- Angkor Wat
- Borobudur
- Dutch East India Company
- Manila
- Emilio Aguinaldo
- Ho Chi Minh

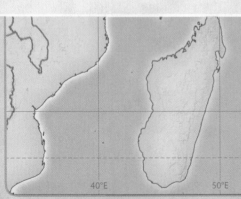

TECHTREK FOR THIS CHAPTER

Student eEdition

Maps and Graphs

Interactive Whiteboard GeoActivities

Digital Library

Go to **myNGconnect.com** for more on Southeast Asia.

| | 2 | 3 | 4 | 5 | 6 |

- 30°N
- Tropic of Cancer
- MYANMAR (BURMA)
- Nay Pyi Taw
- Yangon (Rangoon)
- Hanoi
- LAOS
- Vientiane
- THAILAND
- Krung Thep (Bangkok)
- VIETNAM
- CAMBODIA
- Phnom Penh
- Ho Chi Minh City (Saigon)
- Andaman Sea
- Gulf of Thailand
- South China Sea
- Manila
- PHILIPPINES
- PACIFIC OCEAN
- Philippine Sea
- Sulu Sea
- Bandar Seri Begawan
- BRUNEI
- Celebes Sea
- Strait of Malacca
- Kuala Lumpur
- MALAYSIA
- SINGAPORE
- SUMATRA
- Kapuas R.
- BORNEO
- INDONESIA
- CELEBES
- NEW GUINEA
- Equator
- Java Sea
- Jakarta
- JAVA
- Banda Sea
- Dili
- TIMOR-LESTE (EAST TIMOR)
- Timor Sea
- Arafura Sea
- INDIAN OCEAN
- Tropic of Capricorn

Red R.
Black R.
Mekong R.
Ping R.
Irrawaddy R.
Salween R.

0 300 600 Miles
0 300 600 Kilometers

N W E S

SOUTHEAST ASIA PHYSICAL

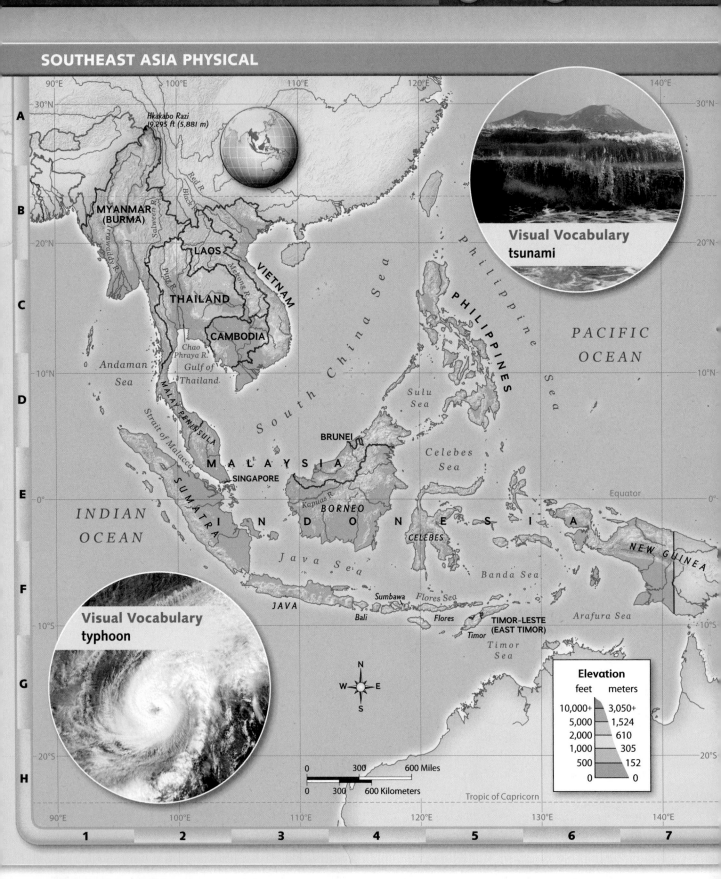

Hkakabo Razi
19,295 ft (5,881 m)

MYANMAR (BURMA)

Irrawaddy R.

Salween R.

Red R.

Black R.

LAOS

Ping R.

Mekong R.

VIETNAM

THAILAND

Chao Phraya R.

CAMBODIA

Andaman Sea

Gulf of Thailand

MALAY PENINSULA

Strait of Malacca

SUMATRA

INDIAN OCEAN

MALAYSIA

SINGAPORE

Kapuas R.

BORNEO

INDONESIA

CELEBES

Java Sea

JAVA

Bali

Sumbawa

Flores

Flores Sea

Timor

TIMOR-LESTE (EAST TIMOR)

Timor Sea

South China Sea

BRUNEI

Sulu Sea

Celebes Sea

PHILIPPINES

Philippine Sea

PACIFIC OCEAN

Banda Sea

Arafura Sea

NEW GUINEA

Equator

Tropic of Capricorn

Visual Vocabulary
tsunami

Visual Vocabulary
typhoon

0   300   600 Miles
0   300   600 Kilometers

Elevation

feet	meters
10,000+	3,050+
5,000	1,524
2,000	610
1,000	305
500	152
0	0

Main Idea Southeast Asia is a mountainous region with both mainland and island countries.

Southeast Asia has two kinds of countries: mainland and island. Indonesia and the Philippines are islands that were once connected by **land bridges**, strips of land connecting two land masses. Glaciers that melted over 6,000 years ago caused the sea level to rise, which separated these land masses. Malaysia is unique in that it includes land on the Asian continent as well as the island of Borneo.

Mainland Countries

The region's mainland countries are part of the Asian continent and include Myanmar, Thailand, Cambodia, Vietnam, and Laos. This cluster is linked by a long coastline. Only Laos is **landlocked**, or surrounded by land on all sides. Elevation is generally higher in the northern and eastern coast of mainland Southeast Asia. Mountains hold the source of several of the region's major rivers, which people rely on for transportation, food, drinking water, and irrigation.

The people of Myanmar, Laos, Vietnam, and Cambodia live mostly in small villages in the mountains or near waterways. However, many of the region's river deltas are densely populated. Bangkok, the country's most developed and densely populated city, is in the delta of the Chao Phraya River. Sediment deposits from this and other rivers created the fertile soil of Thailand's Central Plain, which is ideal for growing rice.

Southeast Asia generally has a tropical climate, although temperatures vary based on elevation and distance from the ocean. Mainland countries receive rainfall from May to September, the wet monsoon season. **Typhoons**, fierce tropical storms with heavy rains and high winds, often strike during this time. The rest of the year is the dry monsoon season.

Island Countries

Southeast Asia's island countries include Indonesia and the Philippines. They sit on the **Ring of Fire**, a volcanic zone around the Pacific Ocean where the plates that make up the earth's crust meet. Both countries have many active volcanoes. Undersea earthquakes can cause a **tsunami** (soo NAH mee), a giant ocean wave with enormous power. In 2004, an earthquake-caused tsunami near Sumatra killed at least 225,000 people. Its effects were felt as far away as East Africa.

Before You Move On

Monitor Comprehension How did islands form in the region?

FORMATIVE ASSESSMENT

MAP LAB

 GeoJournal

1. **Categorize** Use the map and text to explain the differences between the two types of countries that make up Southeast Asia.

2. **Make Inferences** Find Laos on the map. What difficulties might it face as a result of being landlocked? What might be a benefit?

3. **Human-Enviroment Interaction** Why are the region's river deltas densely populated?

1.2 Parallel Rivers

TECHTREK

myNGconnect.com For a map and
photos of Southeast Asia's rivers

 Maps and
Graphs

 Digital
Library

> **Main Idea** River systems in Southeast Asia support life in many ways.

Three parallel rivers run through mainland Southeast Asia: the Mekong (may KONG), the Chao Phraya (chow PRY uh), and the Irrawaddy. They begin in the highlands and flow south through valleys between mountains. As they approach the sea, they divide into a triangular shape made up of smaller streams. These river deltas are composed of silt, or fertile soil the rivers carried from upstream.

The Mekong River

At 2,600 miles, the **Mekong River** ▶ is the longest in Southeast Asia. It runs through the middle of the mainland and forms part of the borders of Myanmar, Laos, and Thailand. The mouth of the river, where it empties into the South China Sea, is in Vietnam near Ho Chi Minh City.

The Mekong Delta covers nearly 25,000 square miles, about the size of West Virginia. The densely populated delta is a rich rice-growing region. Some countries in the region are working to harness the river's power to produce hydroelectricity.

The Chao Phraya River

The **Chao Phraya River** ▶ is the most important river in Thailand. It is used to irrigate rice fields and serves as a major transportation route through the country. The capital city of Bangkok is located along its banks.

The Irrawaddy River

The **Irrawaddy River** ▶ is about half as long as the Mekong. It also supports rice farming and is used as a transportation network. As a result of the soil carried by the river and dumped at its mouth, the delta is growing by about 165 feet a year.

> **Visual Vocabulary** An **ecologist** is a scientist who studies the relationship between organisms and their environments. National Geographic Fellow Zeb Hogan is an aquatic ecologist working here in the waters of the Mekong River.

6.04.B identify factors responsible for patterns of population; 6.04.D identify and locate physical features;
6.07.B identify ways people have modified the environment; 6.15.F identify examples of cooperation among
cultures; 6.21.B analyze by summarizing, drawing inferences; 6.21.C interpret information from maps

RIVERS AND POPULATION DENSITY

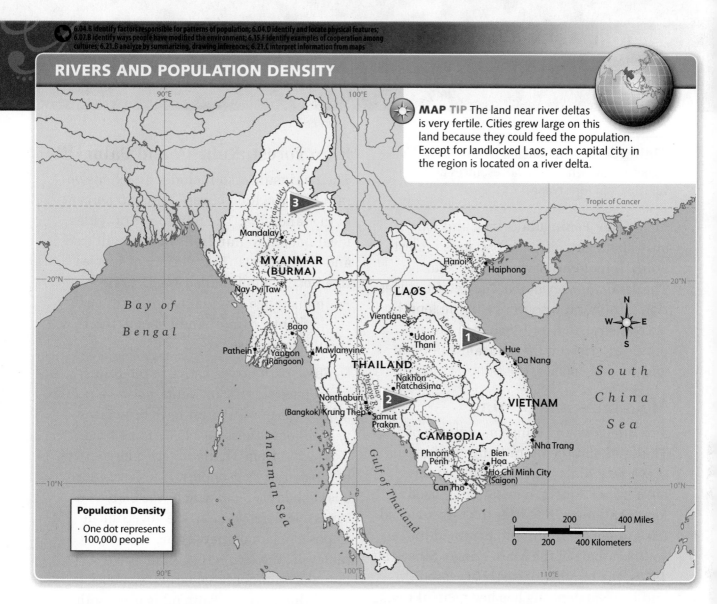

MAP TIP The land near river deltas is very fertile. Cities grew large on this land because they could feed the population. Except for landlocked Laos, each capital city in the region is located on a river delta.

Population Density
· One dot represents 100,000 people

In the rainy season, the Irrawaddy can rise more than 30 feet. Ports must have two areas for docking, one for each season. Farmers have adapted by storing water during the rainy season and releasing it onto their fields in the dry season.

Challenges of the Rivers

The rivers of Southeast Asia are used by many people for **subsistence fishing**, catching just enough fish to live on. Countries in the region must work together to control the threat of overfishing. **Ecologist** Zeb Hogan is part of a program that buys live fish from local fishermen for study. Efforts like this can protect endangered fish while still allowing local people to make a living.

Dams built along the rivers help control water levels, but they also sometimes interfere with transportation and disrupt river environments.

Before You Move On
Summarize What do river systems provide to support life in the region?

FORMATIVE ASSESSMENT
READING LAB  GeoJournal

1. **Monitor Comprehension** How are dams a threat to the region's rivers?
2. **Make Inferences** Why is water level a challenge for people who depend on the rivers?
3. **Region** Trace the course of the Mekong River on the map. What countries share this river?

SECTION **1** GEOGRAPHY

1.3 The Malay Peninsula

TECHTREK

myNGconnect.com For maps and
photos of the Malay Peninsula

 Maps and Graphs

 Digital Library

Main Idea The mountains of the Malay Peninsula are rich in mineral resources and valuable rain forest land.

The **Malay Peninsula** is long and narrow, only about 200 miles across at its widest point. It includes parts of Malaysia, Thailand, and Myanmar. Mountain ranges rich in mineral resources run the length of the peninsula, and lush rain forest provides a habitat for thousands of plant and animal species.

Mountains and Mining

The Bilaukataung Range mountains of Thailand and the Main Range mountains of western Malaysia have traditionally been mined for tin, a metal often used in food containers. **Bauxite**, the raw material used to make aluminum, is mined in the southern part of the Main Range. Since the 1970s, the number of easily accessed tin and bauxite deposits has been shrinking, causing a steady decline in mining.

Rain Forest, Rubber, and Palm Oil

The peninsula also includes an extensive rain forest, which covers about 40 percent of the land area. The rain forest provides ideal habitat to hundreds of different trees and other plants. This variety of species in an ecosytem is called **biodiversity**. Animals range from large creatures such as elephants, rhinos, and tigers to the very small deer mouse.

Some of the trees native to the rain forest have significant value, and as a result large areas of rain forest have been cleared to plant only those species. At one time, teak wood from Thailand was a large part of the country's economy. However, after a landslide in 1989, which was blamed on excessive deforestation, the government imposed a ban on harvesting teak. In Malaysia, the rain forest is cut down to make room for large farms of rubber and palm oil trees. Palm oil is used with machinery, to make soap, and for cooking.

Critical Viewing This land in Malaysia is being prepared for a palm oil farm. What can you infer was present before the land was cleared?

Villlage on a hillside in Cameron Highlands, Malaysia

MALAY PENINSULA PHYSICAL

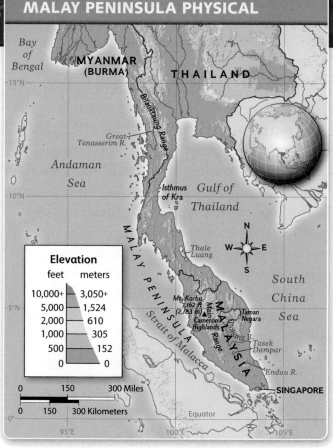

Bay of Bengal

MYANMAR (BURMA)

THAILAND

15°N

Bilauktaung Range

Great Tenasserim R.

Andaman Sea

10°N

Isthmus of Kra

Gulf of Thailand

MALAY PENINSULA

N W E S

Thale Luang

South China Sea

Strait of Malacca

Mt. Korbu 7,162 ft (2,183 m)

Cameron Highlands

Main Range

MALAYSIA

Taman Negara

Pahang R.

Tasek Dampar

5°N

Endau R.

SINGAPORE

Equator

0°

95°E   100°E   105°E

Elevation

feet	meters
10,000+	3,050+
5,000	1,524
2,000	610
1,000	305
500	152
0	0

0   150   300 Miles

0   150   300 Kilometers

CLIMATE

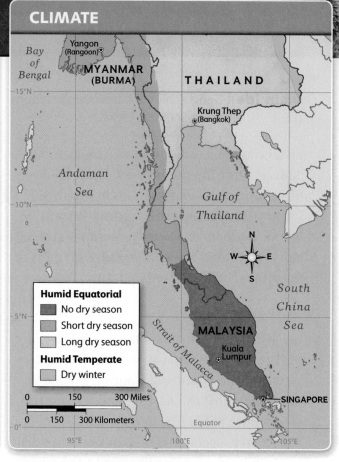

Bay of Bengal

Yangon (Rangoon)

MYANMAR (BURMA)

THAILAND

15°N

Krung Thep (Bangkok)

Andaman Sea

10°N

Gulf of Thailand

N W E S

South China Sea

Strait of Malacca

MALAYSIA

Kuala Lumpur

5°N

SINGAPORE

Equator

0°

95°E   100°E   105°E

Humid Equatorial
- No dry season
- Short dry season
- Long dry season

Humid Temperate
- Dry winter

0   150   300 Miles

0   150   300 Kilometers

Critics claim that after depleting its mineral resources, Malaysia is now destroying its forests. To clear the land, farmers first cut the trees and then burn anything leftover. Fertilizers are then applied, permanently changing the soil and making it impossible for the rain forest to regrow quickly.

The environmental damage has an economic impact. Rain forest tourism has become important to the peninsula's economy. Consequently, like Thailand's policy on teak, the governments are working on domestic policies to balance land development and rain forest conservation.

Before You Move On

Summarize How do environmental concerns conflict with the production of palm oil?

MAP LAB

 GeoJournal

1. **Region** According to the map, which country has all four of the climates shown?

2. **Make Generalizations** Look at the physical map. Which type of land makes up most of the Malay Peninsula?

3. **Make Inferences** What effect might tourism have on decisions Myanmar and Malaysia make about how they use their land?

SECTION 1 GEOGRAPHY

1.4 Island Nations

TECHTREK

myNGconnect.com For maps and photos
of the island nations of Southeast Asia

 Maps and
Graphs

 Digital
Library

Main Idea Geographic conditions on the islands affect settlement in Southeast Asia.

Five countries of Southeast Asia are islands or groups of islands: Indonesia, Singapore, Brunei, East Timor, and the Philippines. A part of Malyasia is on the island of Borneo. Mountains and water barriers among the islands have given rise to isolated cultures with distinct features.

Volcanic Activity

Located where the Eurasian, Indian, Philippine, and Australian plates come together, the islands of Southeast Asia are in a **dynamic**, or continuously changing, geographic zone. These plates are constantly—yet slowly—moving into and over each other. Most islands in the region were formed by the crashing together of these plates. The collisions gradually formed small land masses with high volcanic mountains that slope downward toward coastal plains.

Although many of the volcanoes above ground are no longer active, some that are **dormant**, or inactive for long periods of time, can suddenly erupt. For example, Mount Sinabung on Sumatra in Indonesia had been quiet for 400 years before erupting in 2010. Although many farmers stayed with their farms, tens of thousands of people fled. Volcanic eruptions can destroy villages, but the ash also creates the fertile, nutrient-rich soil that allows for successful farming. The humid climate of the islands **enhances**, or improves, the quality of agriculture. As a result, many crops can be cultivated year-round.

Indonesia

Indonesia is the giant of the region in both land area and population. It is nearly three times the size of Myanmar, the next largest. In population, Indonesia is more than three times as large as the Philippines, and it has more volcanoes than any other country in the world.

> **Critical Viewing** This village sits less than two miles from Mount Batur, an active volcano in Indonesia. What might be some advantages and disadvantages of living in this location?

TECTONIC PLATES AND VOLCANOES

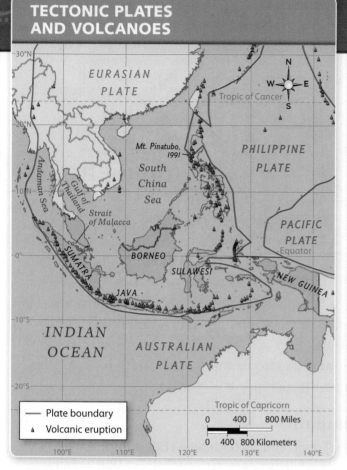

Plate boundary
Volcanic eruption

POPULATION DENSITY

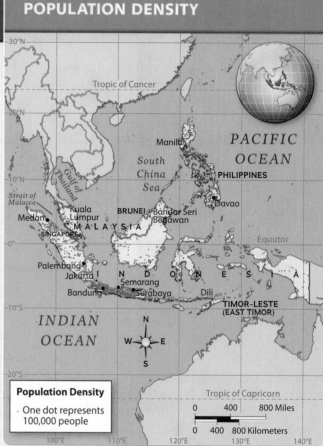

Population Density

· One dot represents 100,000 people

Indonesia is made up of thousands of islands. The five largest islands in size are Sumatra, Java, Borneo, Sulawesi, and New Guinea. Though Java is the smallest of the five, it is the most populous, with more than half of Indonesia's 250 million people. Four of Indonesia's five largest cities are on Java, including the capital, Jakarta. With the exception of the largest cities, most urban areas are more like large towns, each with its own local culture.

The Philippines

Settlement patterns in the Philippines are similar to those in Indonesia. The greatest concentration of people is on lowland plains, which provide soil made fertile by volcanic eruptions. Like Indonesia, the Philippines has an extremely large capital city. This city, Manila, has more than 11 million people.

The Philippines also has many small rural settlements that subsist on fishing or rice farming. Houses near the ocean are built on columns made of timber to allow for changing tides and boat traffic.

Before You Move On

Summarize In what ways has geography of the island nations affected life in Southeast Asia?

MAP LAB
GeoJournal

1. **Place** Based on the map of tectonic plates, which large island seems to be unaffected by active volcanoes or earthquakes? Why might this be?

2. **Compare** Based on the Population Density map, how does the population density of Borneo compare to that of Java? What might be the cause of this difference in population?

TECHTREK

myNGconnect.com For a map of New
Guinea, photos, and an Explorer Video Clip

 Maps and
Graphs

 Digital
Library

Discovering ● New
Species

with Kristofer Helgen

Main Idea The unexplored Foja Mountains of Indonesia may be home to unidentified plant and animal species.

Undiscovered Species

Today knowledge of animal and plant life is extensive and well documented. However, National Geographic Emerging Explorer Kristofer Helgen is a **zoologist**, a scientist who studies animals, and he knows there are hundreds of species that have yet to be discovered.

The Foja Mountains

The **Foja Mountains** of Indonesia have wildlife not found in any other region. The area is also largely unexplored. Helgen described the Foja (FOY ya) Mountains as "one of the few places in the world with no villages, no roads, no human population at all." Human presence is not part of life in this rain forest. "The animals there just don't know people," he said. "That's a very, very rare thing in this day and age."

In 2005, Helgen took part in a research trip to this remote area. The team included Helgen, who studies mammals, and other experts on plants, butterflies, reptiles, and birds.

The researchers found 20 new frog species, 5 new kinds of butterfly, and several new plant species. Helgen himself found new rat and mouse species. He also discovered a unique type of **wallaby**, a small relative of the kangaroo, which he hopes to name as a new species.

myNGconnect.com

For more on Kristofer Helgen in the field today

New species of blossom bat

Canopy of the Foja Mountain rain forest

"Pinocchio" frog, a new species of tree frog

New species of wallaby may be smallest ever

Scientific Opportunity

The research conducted in the Foja Mountains provides a chance for scientists to learn more about the diversity of animal and plant life. Because they have not been explored, the mountains also offer new scientists an opportunity to become trained in the discovery of new species. Students can join experienced scientists in future trips to the region. They will learn about working in the field even as they help make new discoveries.

Before You Move On

Make Inferences Why might there be many undiscovered species of plants and animals in the Foja Mountains?

FORMATIVE ASSESSMENT

VIEWING LAB  GeoJournal

1. **Analyze Visuals** Go to the **Digital Library** and view the Explorer Video Clip about Kristofer Helgen. How would you describe the land?

2. **Place** What in the video explains why scientists are excited about this area?

3. **Make Inferences** How do you think animals that have never encountered humans would behave the first time they see a person? Why?

4. **Create Charts** Make a chart listing the kinds of new species that might be found in a place like the Foja Mountains. Remember that the region is home to a rain forest.

PLANTS	ANIMALS

TECHTREK

myNGconnect.com For photos of ancient Southeast Asian kingdoms

Digital Library

> **Main Idea** The development of Southeast Asia was influenced by nearby powers because of its important location for trade.

The location of Southeast Asia between the Pacific and Indian Oceans meant its surrounding waterways were on important trade routes. Two powerful civilizations, China to the north and India to the west, heavily infuenced the cultural direction of the region. The impact came through military force and invasion, as well as through trade.

Mainland Empires

Chinese culture first came to Southeast Asia in 111 B.C., when the Chinese invaded and conquered part of what today is Vietnam.

India had already established trade before the Chinese arrived. This trade had a strong influence on the area's religious practices.

By the A.D. 700s, Buddhist and Hindu empires were competing for influence and power in other parts of the region. The largest and longest lasting was the **Khmer Empire** of Cambodia. Centered along the Mekong River valley, the Khmer (kuh MAYR) Empire covered much of Southeast Asia and lasted from the A.D. 800s to the 1430s.

At the peak of the empire's success in the 1100s, its ruler, King Suryavarman II, built the massive Hindu temple **Angkor Wat** in the capital city.

Angkor Wat, Cambodia

111 B.C.
China conquers Vietnam; Buddhism reaches Southeast Asia.

c. A.D. 780–850
Sailendra rulers of Java build Borobudur temple.

c. A.D. 890
Khmer Empire sets capital at Angkor.

100 B.C.   **A.D. 600**   **800**

A.D. 600s–c. 1100
Srivijaya Empire of Sumatra

Borobudur temple, Java, Indonesia

This religious **complex**, or set of interconnected buildings, was dedicated to the Hindu god Vishnu and served as a tomb for the king. Beautiful **bas-reliefs**, or sculptures that slightly project from a flat background, cover the walls with scenes from Hindu stories. Eventually forces from modern-day Thailand conquered the city and the complex fell into ruin.

In A.D. 939 the people of Vietnam broke from China and established the independent kingdom of Dai Viet. Though influenced by Chinese culture, Vietnam had its own cultural traits. For instance, women in Vietnam had higher social standing than women in China. Eventually Dai Viet grew weak and was reconquered by China in 1407.

Island Empires

Modern Indonesia was also home to powerful empires. The earliest was Srivijaya (sree vi JY ah), which arose on southern Sumatra in the A.D. 600s. This kingdom controlled the Strait of Malacca and was therefore able to control trade from South Asia to China. It was known throughout Asia as a center of trade and also as a center of Buddhist study. The empire declined around A.D. 1100.

A second Indonesian power was the Sailendra dynasty, which arose in Java and flourished from about A.D. 780 to 850. Sailendran rulers built another famous temple complex, **Borobudur.** Each of the temple's three levels symbolizes a step toward enlightenment, the ultimate spiritual goal of Buddhism.

Borobudur is an example of important art and architecture of early Buddhism. Like Angkor Wat, it is massive, and it is a World Heritage Site. This means it has "outstanding universal value" according to UNESCO, and is worth protecting.

Before You Move On
Summarize How did Chinese and Indian empires influence life in the region?

FORMATIVE ASSESSMENT

VIEWING LAB
GeoJournal

1. **Interpret Time Lines** Based on the time line, how long was Vietnam able to maintain its independence from China?
2. **Make Generalizations** Look at the photos. With a partner, talk about why Borobudur and Angkor Wat were built to last. Explain why you think so.
3. **Understand Culture** Why do you think these temples were important to the ancient societies that built them? Support your ideas with information from the photos and text.

A.D. 939
Vietnam gains independence from China; Dai Viet kingdom begins.

A.D. 1113–1150
Reign of Khmer king Suryavarman II, who built Angkor Wat

A.D. 1407
China conquers Vietnam again.

1000   1200   1400

Angkor Wat bas-relief sculpture

A.D. 1290s–c. 1500
Majapahit empire in Java

2.2 Trade and Colonialism

Main Idea The development of the spice trade in Southeast Asia led to colonization of the region.

As you have learned, trade with India and China brought the influence of these cultures to Southeast Asia. European influence arrived in the 1500s, as merchants hoped to establish a spice trade **monopoly**, or complete control of the market. Spices found in the region, such as cinnamon, nutmeg, and black pepper, could be sold for a high profit in Europe. Traders from Spain and Portugal came first, but the Netherlands' **Dutch East India Company** dominated the region for many years. This success established a strong Dutch influence in Indonesia.

European Control

From the 1600s to the 1800s, Europeans tried to gain an economic hold on Southeast Asia. By 1850, through a combination of alliances, favorable trade agreements, and even military force, the majority of the region was ruled by European powers. (See the time line below.) Only Thailand and parts of the Philippines were independent. Britain, France, Spain, and the Netherlands controlled the rest.

The economic motives that led European powers to Southeast Asia changed the region. Increased production and an ongoing demand for goods strengthened the region's economy. However, trade and wealth, once in the hands of indigenous kingdoms, were now held by distant economic powers. **Colonialism**—one country ruling and developing trade in another country for its own benefit—continued in Southeast Asia well into the 20th century.

Before You Move On
Monitor Comprehension How did development of the spice trade lead to colonization?

SPAIN

1521
Ferdinand Magellan lands at the Philippines and claims them for Spain.

1565
Spain makes first settlement on the Philippine islands.

1571
Spain captures site of Manila.

1830s
Spain opens Manila to trade.

1892
Filipinos begin movement aimed at independence from Spain.

1898
United States defeats Spain in the Spanish-American War and wins control of Philippines.

NETHERLANDS

1619
Dutch East India Company makes base at Batavia (modern Jakarta).

1641
The Netherlands captures Malacca from Portugal and becomes a major power in spice trade.

1824
The Netherlands and Britain reach agreement on control of Java and Sumatra (to Dutch) and Singapore and Malacca (to British).

1825–1839
The Netherlands fights to put down revolts on Java.

1860
The Netherlands and Portugal sign treaty to divide Timor between them.

GREAT BRITAIN

1781
Britain captures Sumatra from Dutch.

1786–1809
Britain gains control of Malaya trade.

1819
Britain founds Singapore, which becomes a major port city.

1824–1826
Britain controls western Burma.

1886
Britain completes control of Burma in Third Burmese War.

1888
Britain wins southern Burma.

1888
Britain gains control of northern Borneo.

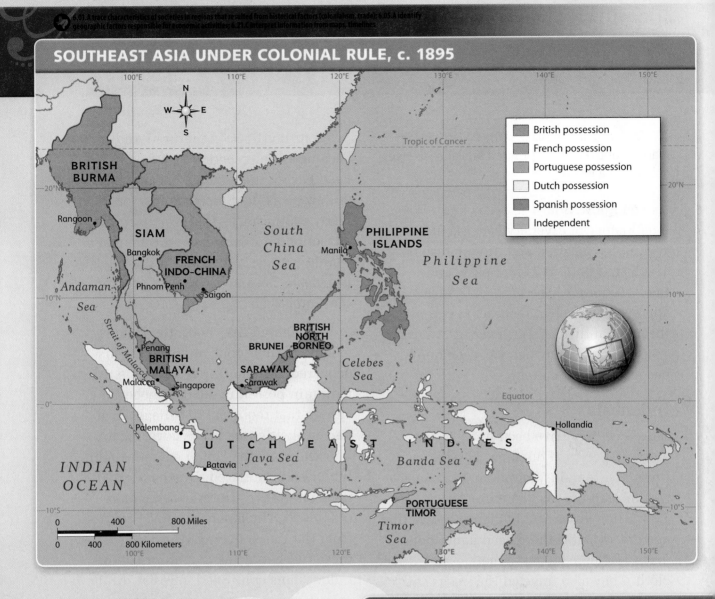

SOUTHEAST ASIA UNDER COLONIAL RULE, c. 1895

Legend:
- British possession
- French possession
- Portuguese possession
- Dutch possession
- Spanish possession
- Independent

BRITISH BURMA

Rangoon

SIAM

Bangkok

FRENCH INDO-CHINA

Phnom Penh

Saigon

Andaman Sea

Strait of Malacca

Penang

BRITISH MALAYA

Malacca

Singapore

South China Sea

Manila

PHILIPPINE ISLANDS

Philippine Sea

Tropic of Cancer

BRUNEI

BRITISH NORTH BORNEO

SARAWAK

Sarawak

Celebes Sea

Palembang

D U T C H   E A S T   I N D I E S

Java Sea

Batavia

Banda Sea

Hollandia

Equator

INDIAN OCEAN

PORTUGUESE TIMOR

Timor Sea

0 400 800 Miles
0 400 800 Kilometers

FRANCE

1644
France forms French East India Company.

1789
French East India Company disbanded during French Revolution.

1858
France captures Saigon, Vietnam.

1863
France seizes Cambodia.

1887
France creates Indo-Chinese Union (Cambodia, Vietnam).

1896
France and Britain agree to allow Siam to remain independent to separate their colonies.

MAP LAB

 GeoJournal

1. **Region** Based on the map, which European countries held the most territory in the region around 1895?

2. **Movement** Think about the importance of waterways in influencing trade in this region. Which European country was in the best position to control trade? Support your answer with evidence from the map.

3. **Interpret Time Lines** Based on the dates and events, what do you think was the attitude of the people of Southeast Asia toward European control? Why do you think so?

SECTION **2** HISTORY

TECHTREK

myNGconnect.com For photos
of Indonesia and the Philippines

Digital
Library

2.3 Indonesia and the Philippines

Main Idea Indonesia and the Philippines are island countries that have faced similar challenges in becoming independent.

As you know, Southeast Asia has a long history of diversity because of its geographic location and unique resources. The island nations of Indonesia and the Philippines have been influenced and even controlled by other cultures throughout history. However, after long struggles for independence, each one has become its own nation.

Indonesia

Indonesia may have been home to the earliest species of humans. **Fossils**, or preserved remains, found on Java suggest that human life existed there as early as 1.7 million years ago. Evidence shows that ancient societies there used hand tools, made implements out of metals, and wove cloth. They also traveled the sea as early as 2500 B.C., possibly to trade with other areas of Asia and beyond.

As its civilization matured, Indonesia became an intersection for trade in the East. Part of the country became known to Europe as the Spice Islands, for the many exotic spices that were a strong attraction for explorers and traders. For example, trade in nutmeg, a spice native to Indonesia, became extremely profitable for the Dutch who had settled there.

Throughout the 1800s, the Dutch expanded their control. Some revolts occurred, but the Dutch were able to maintain power. In 1830, they began a system that required all villages to give part of their crops to the government for export. As the Dutch gained wealth, Indonesians suffered. During the 1900s their resistance efforts became more organized. The Japanese seized control from the Dutch during World War II. As these two countries fought for control, Indonesians continued to resist. At the same time, a strong sense of national identity was developing. The country finally won independence in 1949.

nutmeg

mace

Mace (shown here) is a spice that covers nutmeg in its raw form. Both nutmeg and mace are highly valued for their distinct flavor.

⌃ Critical Viewing Emilio Aguinaldo (front, center) and members of the assembly of the First Philippine Republic, 1899. In early photography, subjects were required to sit for long periods to capture an image. How might this explain the expressions on these men's faces?

The Philippines

When the Spanish seized control of **Manila** in 1571, they made it the capital of their new colony. Manila was and still is the economic, political, and cultural center of the Philippines. Trade with China led many Chinese people to settle in Manila. They became the major force in **commerce**, or the business of trading goods and services.

In the 1800s, Spain's economic power began to fade and Manila became open to trade with more countries. This allowed some Filipinos to gain wealth and influence they had not known before.

Emilio Aguinaldo was a key leader in the movement for Filipino independence. He fought alongside the United States when it defeated Spain in the Spanish-American War in 1898, and thought the islands would become independent. However, after the war, the United States kept the islands as its own colony.

In late 1941, during World War II, Japan attacked the United States at Pearl Harbor, then attacked the Philippines. The outnumbered U.S. forces stationed on the islands were forced to leave. Later in the war, the United States took back control and remained in power until 1946, when the Philippines were granted independence. Today, it is a stable democracy.

Before You Move On

Summarize What challenges did Indonesia and the Philippines face in gaining independence?

FORMATIVE ASSESSMENT

READING LAB GeoJournal

1. **Location** Why was Southeast Asia so important to Europeans?
2. **Make Inferences** Why were Indonesians able to develop a strong national identity?
3. **Draw Conclusions** Was trade or conquest more important in shaping these countries? Why?

2.4 The Vietnam War

TECHTREK
myNGconnect.com For photos
of the war in Vietnam and Guided Wrting

 **Digital
Library**

 **Student
Resources**

In 1954 Vietnam was divided into two parts, North and South. President **Ho Chi Minh** of North Vietnam established a Communist government. War erupted in 1959 when he sent aid to overthrow the government in South Vietnam and create one country. The United States supported South Vietnam—it feared that defeat by the North would spread communism to other countries. U.S. forces fought there from 1964 to 1973. In 1975, South Vietnam surrendered. The reunited country became the Socialist Republic of Vietnam.

DOCUMENT 1

President Lyndon Johnson on U.S. Policy

In 1965, Johnson explained reasons for the involvement of the United States in the fighting in Vietnam:

> We are . . . there to strengthen world order. Around the globe . . . are people whose well-being rests, in part, on the belief that they can count on us if they are attacked. To leave Viet-Nam . . . would shake the confidence of all these people in the value of an American commitment. . . . Let no one think for a moment that retreat from Viet-Nam would bring an end to conflict. The battle would be renewed in one country and then another. The central lesson of our time is that the appetite of aggression is never satisfied.

CONSTRUCTED RESPONSE

1. How are Johnson's two reasons for fighting the Vietnam War related?

DOCUMENT 2

Letter from Ho Chi Minh

In 1967, Johnson sent Ho Chi Minh a letter suggesting that the two sides begin peace talks. Here is Ho Chi Minh's response:

> The Vietnamese people have never done any harm to the United States. But . . . the United States Government has constantly intervened in Viet-Nam, it has launched [started] and intensified the war of aggression in South Viet-Nam for the purpose of prolonging the division of Viet-Nam and of transforming [remaking] South Viet-Nam into an American neo-colony and an American military base. . . .
>
> The Vietnamese people . . . are determined to continue their resistance [opposition] until they have won real independence.

CONSTRUCTED RESPONSE

2. How does Ho Chi Minh respond to the suggestion of peace talks?

6.15.F identify examples of conflict; 6.21.A use primary sources; 6.21.B analyze by finding main ideas; 6.21.C interpret information from visuals; 6.21.D identify different points of view

THE VIETNAMESE PEOPLE . . . ARE DETERMINED TO CONTINUE THEIR RESISTANCE UNTIL THEY HAVE WON REAL INDEPENDENCE.

— HO CHI MINH

DOCUMENT 3

Photo of Warfare

The physical geography and climate of Vietnam presented challenges to soldiers. These challenges might be especially great for soldiers who were not native to the region and were not accustomed to heavy rains and dense plant life of the jungle.

CONSTRUCTED RESPONSE

3. What does the photo suggest about the conditions the soldiers faced in the war in Vietnam?

FORMATIVE ASSESSMENT

WRITING LAB GeoJournal

DBQ Practice Think about how North Vietnam compares in size and power to the United States. What factors might have allowed North Vietnam a chance to win the war?

Step 1. Think about Johnson's determination to fight in Vietnam, Ho Chi Minh's statements, and what the photo shows about the war in Vietnam.

Step 2. On your own paper, jot down notes about the main idea expressed in each document.

> Document 1: Excerpt: Johnson's Speech
> Main Idea(s) _____
> Document 2: Excerpt: Ho Chi Minh's Letter
> Main Idea(s) _____
> Document 3: Photo of Warfare
> Main Idea(s) _____

Step 3. Construct a topic sentence that answers this question: What factors might have affected North Vietnam's ability to fight and win a war against South Vietnam and the United States?

Step 4. Write a detailed paragraph that answers the question above, using evidence from the documents. Go to **Student Resources** for Guided Writing support.

VOCABULARY

Use the following vocabulary words in a sentence that shows understanding of each term's meaning.

1. landlocked

> *All countries in Southeast Asia have some coastline except Laos, making it the region's only landlocked country.*

2. subsistence fishing

3. dynamic

4. dormant

5. commerce

6. launch

MAIN IDEAS

7. How does the climate of the two parts of Southeast Asia differ? (Section 1.1)

8. Why are the upper reaches of the region's rivers less populated? (Section 1.2)

9. Where do you think most people live on mainland Malaysia? Why? (Section 1.3)

10. How do Manila and Java show that population in the Philippines and Indonesia tends to cluster? (Section 1.4)

11. What has allowed some species in the region to have gone undiscovered? (Section 1.5)

12. Why did trade play such a great role in the development of island kingdoms? (Section 2.1)

13. Which region of the world practiced colonialism in Southeast Asia and why? (Section 2.2)

14. What struggles did Indonesia and the Philippines face in developing their own culture? (Section 2.3)

15. What were North Vietnam and South Vietnam fighting about? (Section 2.4)

GEOGRAPHY

ANALYZE THE ESSENTIAL QUESTION

What are the geographic conditions that divide Southeast Asia into many different parts?

Focus Skill: Analyze Cause and Effect

16. Why are rivers and seas so important in this region?

17. Why are island countries like Indonesia and the Philippines good for farming?

18. In what way has Laos's lack of a coastline impacted its ability to engage in international trade?

INTERPRET MAPS

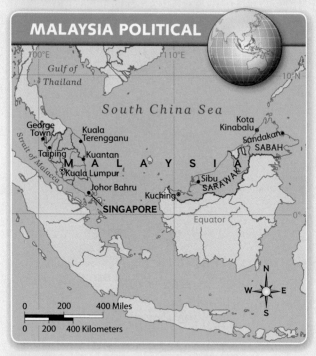

19. **Summarize** What is the advantage of the location of the mainland portion of Malaysia?

20. **Make Inferences** Look at the locator map. In what ways has Malaysia's location helped it establish trading partners?

HISTORY

ANALYZE THE ESSENTIAL QUESTION

How have physical barriers in Southeast Asia influenced its history?

Focus Skill: Draw Conclusions

21. Why do you think one great empire never arose to unite all of Southeast Asia?

22. Which other cultural regions do you think had the most influence on Southeast Asia? Explain your reasons.

23. What made it difficult for Europeans to establish complete control of the countries in this region?

INTERPRET MAPS

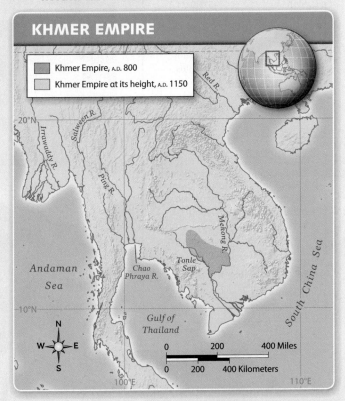

KHMER EMPIRE

- Khmer Empire, A.D. 800
- Khmer Empire at its height, A.D. 1150

24. **Region** How much of Southeast Asia did the Khmer Empire control at its greatest point? In what year was that the case?

25. **Make Inferences** The kingdom of Dai Viet existed along the South China Sea. What factors would have allowed it to remain independent of the Khmer Empire?

ACTIVE OPTIONS

Synthesize the Essential Questions by completing the activities below.

26. **Write a Press Release** You work for an art museum that is staging an exhibition of art and objects from Angkor Wat. Research and write a 3- or 4-paragraph press release to announce the exhibition, telling who, what, where, when, and why it is important. Because a release is distributed to news sources, it's critical that it have no spelling or grammatical errors. Exchange press releases with a partner to check one another's work. **Read your press release aloud.**

> **Writing Tips**
> - Name the museum and give the date and times of the exhibition.
> - Open with an exciting fact.
> - Clearly explain what kinds of art and objects the exhibition includes. Use vivid language.
> - Use standard grammar, spelling, and punctuation.

27. **Create a Time Line** Use information in the lessons and online research to gather facts about five key dates in the history of two countries in the region. Organize the information to construct a parallel time line, one for each country. How does the parallel time line help you compare the countries?

	COUNTRY 1	COUNTRY 2
Event 1		
Event 2		
Event 3		
Event 4		
Event 5		

CHAPTER 22

Southeast Asia TODAY

PREVIEW THE CHAPTER

Essential Question How have local traditions and outside influences shaped cultures in Southeast Asia?

SECTION 1 • CULTURE

KEY VOCABULARY

- prehistoric
- ritual
- attribute
- wat
- monk
- metropolitan area
- dialect
- adapt
- language diffusion
- poach
- restore
- domesticate

ACADEMIC VOCABULARY

predominant

TERMS & NAMES

- Java
- Sumatra
- Bali
- Cardamom Mountains

Essential Question How are Southeast Asia's governments trying to unify their countries?

SECTION 2 • GOVERNMENT & ECONOMICS

KEY VOCABULARY

- fragmented country
- remittance
- relocate
- trend
- port
- industrialize
- multinational corporation
- emergence
- reliable

ACADEMIC VOCABULARY

potential

TERMS & NAMES

- Madura
- inner islands
- outer islands
- Malaysia

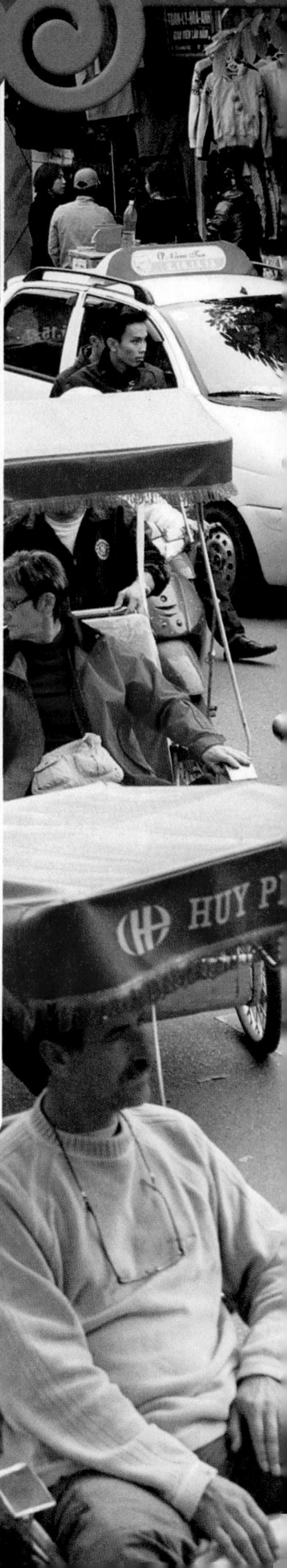

Go to **myNGconnect.com** for more on Southeast Asia.

Tourists and locals use rickshaws and motorbikes to get around in Hanoi, Vietnam.

1.1 **Religious Traditions**

TECHTREK

myNGconnect.com For photos
of religious traditions in Southeast Asia

**Digital
Library**

> **Main Idea** Religions in Southeast Asia have been shaped by both local traditions and outside influences.

Religious practices in Southeast Asia today blend many influences from several centuries. The **predominant**, or most common, belief systems have shifted in many parts of the region.

Traditional Religion

The traditional religion in Southeast Asia is animism, the belief that spirits exist in animals, plants, objects, and places. These spirits are believed to influence people's lives. Many historians think that animism began in **prehistoric** times before there were written histories. Animists perform **rituals**—formal regularly repeated actions—to please spirits so they bring good fortune to their human families or villages. Many small, tribal groups in the region still practice forms of animism.

Outside Influences

Other cultures entering Southeast Asia through trade or conquest brought their traditions with them. The Chinese brought Buddhism when they conquered Vietnam in 111 B.C. They also introduced a philosophy, or system of thought, called Confucianism, which became an important part of Vietnam's local religions. Beginning in the A.D. 100s, traders from India spread Buddhism and Hinduism across the region. By the 400s, Buddhism had taken hold on **Java** and later spread to **Sumatra**. In the 1100s, Cambodians built Angkor Wat to worship a Hindu god.

Arab traders carried Islam to Southeast Asia during the 1300s, where it spread from Malaysia to parts of Indonesia. Later, Europeans spread Christianity. Spain brought Roman Catholicism to the Philippines in the 1500s. The French introduced it to the mainland in the 1700s.

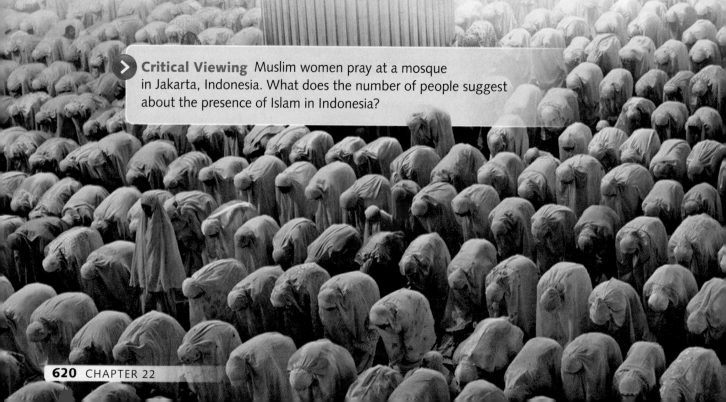

> **Critical Viewing** Muslim women pray at a mosque in Jakarta, Indonesia. What does the number of people suggest about the presence of Islam in Indonesia?

Children attend a prayer service in a Catholic school in Makassar, Indonesia.

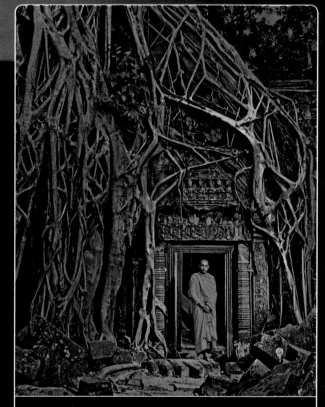

Forest roots devour ruins at Ta Prohm, a Buddhist temple at Angkor, Cambodia.

Religion Today

Over the centuries, the predominant religion of a country sometimes shifted depending on the beliefs of the ruling power. Today, Southeast Asia has a mix of religions. Buddhism is most prominent in mainland countries. Around 95 percent of the people in Thailand are Buddhists, and many Buddhist holy days are national holidays. Buddhism is also predominant in Myanmar. Islam is the main religion of Indonesia, which is the most populous Muslim country in the world. In Malaysia, about three out of five people are Muslim. Most people living in the Philippines and East Timor continue to practice Roman Catholicism, introduced by Europeans.

While some religions dominate each country, the region as a whole has religious diversity. For example, **Bali**, an island in Indonesia, is largely Hindu.

Islam has many followers in the southern Philippines. Diversity is also found in many of the ancient, local traditions that are still practiced in each country today.

Before You Move On

Monitor Comprehension Which religions were brought to the region by outside cultures?

FORMATIVE ASSESSMENT

PHOTO LAB   GeoJournal

1. **Interpret** What do the photos show about religion in Southeast Asia?

2. **Understand Culture** Describe the factors that influenced changes in the number of religions in the region. What brought about the spread of culture from other places?

3. **Turn and Talk** Ask questions with a partner to confirm your understanding of the region's religions. Then discuss how religious ideas and philosophical ideas are connected to culture.

1.2 Thailand Today

TECHTREK

myNGconnect.com For photos of modern Thailand

Digital Library

Main Idea Thai culture today reflects traditional foundations and modern influences.

Modern Thai culture includes regional traditions and other global infuences that blend into a unique Thai identity.

Classical Architecture

One **attribute**, or specific quality, of Thai culture is its remarkable architecture. Traditional buildings have steeply slanted roofs designed to shed the heavy monsoon rains. Many are built on legs to keep them high off the ground during the monsoon floods. The most important buildings in Thai architecture are **wats**, or Buddhist temples, influenced by designs from India, the Khmer empire, and China.

Buddhist Monks

As you have learned, Buddhism is the dominant religion in Thailand. Almost every village has a wat with a community of **monks**, men who devote themselves to religious work. Buddhist monks wear orange or yellow robes, live simply, and focus on religious practices such as meditation and other rituals.

Most young men traditionally became monks for at least three months during one rainy season. However, as more and more young people migrate away from rural communities and attend non-religious schools, young men are making shorter commitments to religious life, or sometimes none at all.

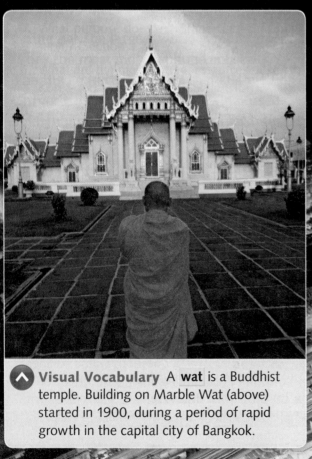

The Chao Phraya River cuts through downtown Bangkok at dusk.

Visual Vocabulary A **wat** is a Buddhist temple. Building on Marble Wat (above) started in 1900, during a period of rapid growth in the capital city of Bangkok.

Modern Influences

About four out of five young men and women now work in cities, especially Bangkok's large **metropolitan area**, the populated location that includes the city limits and surrounding area. Many still identify with their villages even though they mostly live and work in cities.

Urban life has also changed people's clothing, food, and entertainment. Most people in Thailand now wear Western-style clothing. Many urban women buy prepared food at local stores on their way home from work instead of cooking. Most homes now have televisions and other modern conveniences.

Young people in urban areas also turn to the Internet as a source of news, entertainment, and communication.

Before You Move On

Monitor Comprehension How has cultural diffusion changed the lives of men, women, and young people in Thai culture today?

∧ Critical Viewing Suvarnabhumi Airport in Bangkok opened in 2006. Based on the photo, what can you say about the design for the airport?

FORMATIVE ASSESSMENT

PHOTO LAB GeoJournal

1. **Make Inferences** What does the large photo show about life in modern Thailand?

2. **Understand Culture** What does each photo reveal about Thai culture? Use details from the photos to explain your answer.

3. **Analyze** How did traditional architecture help people adapt to their environment in Thailand?

1.3 Regional Languages

> **Main Idea** Geographically isolated cultures and large historic migrations have created a diversity of languages in the region.

As you have learned, language is an important part of any culture. People use language to express their ideas, values, and history. Like religion, language can bring people together or it can divide them. The people of Southeast Asia speak hundreds of different languages.

Native Languages

Each country in the region has a dominant native language. Generally the name of this language reflects the name of the country or its largest ethnic group. The dominant language is the official language used by government, business, education, and the media. In countries such as Indonesia and Malaysia, a common language has helped unify geographically fragmented areas. In Myanmar, the diversity of minority languages has made unifying the country more difficult.

Many people in Southeast Asia speak a **dialect**, a regional variation of a main language. Speakers of different dialects often belong to small groups that live in isolated communities. Some of these dialects exist only in oral form, and many dialects and ethnic languages are in danger of disappearing. People learn the official language as a way to **adapt**, or adjust to common practices, especially as cultures become more globally connected. When older speakers of an isolated language die, that language may disappear, resulting in a loss of traditional culture.

Critical Viewing Many people in rural villages in Vietnam speak a native language or a dialect of a main language. How might speaking a dialect influence this woman's business?

Language Migration

The region's location has historically attracted diverse people to trade. This movement led to **language diffusion**, or the spread of languages from their original homes. Traders had to find a common language in order to communicate. Malay served this purpose for early traders from Arab countries and different parts of China. Today, English is often used as the common language.

Immigrants also brought their languages to Southeast Asia. For example, Chinese is the dominant language in Singapore. Many speakers of Chinese dialects live in Malaysia and Brunei and in major cities throughout the region. Immigrants from India brought various Indian languages to Malaysia, Singapore, and Myanmar.

6.01.A trace characteristics of societies resulting from historical factors; 6.17.A identify how culture traits spread;
6.17.B identify and describe factors that influence cultural change; 6.17.D identify the impact of cultural diffusion
on societies; 6.21.B analyze by summarizing, drawing conclusions; 6.21.C interpret information from charts

SPOKEN LANGUAGES IN SELECTED SOUTHEAST ASIAN COUNTRIES

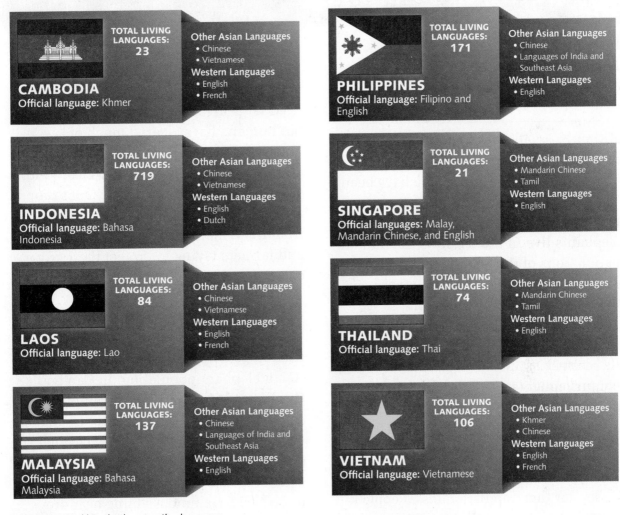

CAMBODIA
Official language: Khmer
TOTAL LIVING LANGUAGES: 23
Other Asian Languages
• Chinese
• Vietnamese
Western Languages
• English
• French

PHILIPPINES
Official language: Filipino and English
TOTAL LIVING LANGUAGES: 171
Other Asian Languages
• Chinese
• Languages of India and Southeast Asia
Western Languages
• English

INDONESIA
Official language: Bahasa Indonesia
TOTAL LIVING LANGUAGES: 719
Other Asian Languages
• Chinese
• Vietnamese
Western Languages
• English
• Dutch

SINGAPORE
Official languages: Malay, Mandarin Chinese, and English
TOTAL LIVING LANGUAGES: 21
Other Asian Languages
• Mandarin Chinese
• Tamil
Western Languages
• English

LAOS
Official language: Lao
TOTAL LIVING LANGUAGES: 84
Other Asian Languages
• Chinese
• Vietnamese
Western Languages
• English
• French

THAILAND
Official language: Thai
TOTAL LIVING LANGUAGES: 74
Other Asian Languages
• Mandarin Chinese
• Tamil
Western Languages
• English

MALAYSIA
Official language: Bahasa Malaysia
TOTAL LIVING LANGUAGES: 137
Other Asian Languages
• Chinese
• Languages of India and Southeast Asia
Western Languages
• English

VIETNAM
Official language: Vietnamese
TOTAL LIVING LANGUAGES: 106
Other Asian Languages
• Khmer
• Chinese
Western Languages
• English
• French

Sources: CIA World Factbook, www.ethnologue.com

European countries began establishing colonies in Southeast Asia in the 1500s. As the British, Dutch, French, and Spanish gained control of various countries, they used their languages to rule and do business. The United States controlled the Philippines for a time after Spanish rule and made English common there. As the countries of Southeast Asia gained independence in the 20th century, their governments chose dominant native languages to be the official languages. However, many people still speak a Western language as a second language.

Before You Move On

Summarize In what ways is language use changing as cultures become more connected?

FORMATIVE ASSESSMENT

LANGUAGE LAB  GeoJournal

1. **Movement** According to the chart, what East Asian language is most widespread in these Southeast Asian countries?

2. **Draw Conclusions** Based on the chart, what Western language is a Southeast Asian business person most likely to learn? Explain.

3. **Identify Problems and Solutions** What might a country do to save endangered languages spoken by its people?

1.4 Saving the Elephant

Main Idea Some countries in Southeast Asia are working to protect the endangered Asian elephant.

Although smaller than their African cousins, Asian elephants are huge and awe-inspiring creatures. Some have been trained to use their enormous strength for the benefit of people. However, most elephants live in the wild. As the human populations of the region increase, their growing numbers increasingly threaten the Asian elephant population.

Asian Elephants

As recently as 1900, it is estimated 80,000 Asian elephants may have been living in the wild. Today, their population is thought to range from 30,000 to 50,000.

Human behavior, such as **poaching**, or illegal hunting of a wild animal, is one reason for that population loss. People kill male Asian elephants for their ivory tusks. Ivory is highly valued for its beauty and hard texture. An international agreement banned trade in ivory in 1989, but it still continues illegally.

A bigger problem for Asian elephants is their loss of habitat. These huge animals need large areas of rain forest to find food, but humans have cleared much of the land for alternative uses, such as logging and iron mining. Land is also cleared for growing crops such as coffee. Once crops are planted, some elephants wander in from the remaining forests to eat them, and farmers trying to protect their crops sometimes kill those raiding elephants.

Protecting Elephants

Many countries in Southeast Asia have tried to **restore**, or bring back, the wild Asian elephant population. In Cambodia's **Cardamom Mountains**, for example, many conservationists have begun to use modern technology, such as electric fences that run off solar power, to keep elephants confined to protected places. Other methods are more basic. Hammocks hung near crops make the elephants think humans are in the fields, so they stay away.

> **Critical Viewing** Asian elephants look for food in Sumatra. Based on the photo, how would you describe their habitat?

Visual Vocabulary Many elephants are **domesticated**, or trained to work with humans. Domesticated elephants can provide service or entertainment.

ASIAN ELEPHANTS BY THE NUMBERS

11+
Height in feet

12,000+
Weight in pounds

300
Pounds of food (plants, grain) consumed in one day

80,000
Population estimate, wild, beginning of 20th century

30,000+
Population estimate, wild

16,000
Population in captivity (protected)

Sources: World Wildlife Federation, Fauna & Flora International, U.S. Fish & Wildlife Service, 2013

The results have been dramatic. The elephant-human interaction that leads to population loss was reduced so much that from 2005 to 2010, no elephants were killed anywhere in Cambodia. These efforts can lead to long-term protection of this endangered species.

Before You Move On
Monitor Comprehension What efforts have been made to protect the wild Asian elephant in Southeast Asia?

FORMATIVE ASSESSMENT
READING LAB GeoJournal

1. **Region** Which country has successfully reduced elephant killings?
2. **Interpret Charts** How has the population of Asian elephants changed over time?
3. **Human-Environment Interaction** What human activities threaten Asian elephants? Why are they a threat?

2.1 Governing Fragmented Countries

Main Idea Geographic and ethnic divisions make it difficult for some countries in Southeast Asia to become unified.

In Southeast Asia, Indonesia, Malaysia, and the Philippines face challenges in forming unified countries. All three are **fragmented countries**, or countries that are physically divided into separate parts, such as a chain of islands. The three countries also have diverse ethnic groups.

Indonesia

Indonesia's 17,000 islands span across 3,200 miles and are more different than they are similar. Java, for example, is densely populated and urbanized. Sumatra, on the other hand, is rural and contains large plantations. The country includes more than 300 ethnic groups and more than 700 languages are spoken.

To meet the complex challenges of fragmentation, Indonesia's government has tried to create a sense of nationhood. The country's motto, a saying that guides them, is "Diversity in unity." However, unity is not always easy to achieve. For example, there is conflict between the majority Malays and minority Chinese, and groups in northern Sumatra and Borneo have recently tried to gain independence. The government has focused on improving people's standard of living so that these groups will see the advantages of staying part of Indonesia.

Critical Viewing Perdana Putra is the Malaysian prime minister's palace. What other buildings that you have seen have onion domes similar to these?

6.05.C explain geographic factors on economic development and domestic policies of societies;
6.16.B compare characteristics of institutions in various societies (government); 6.23.A use a
problem-solving process to evaluate the effectiveness of a solution

Malaysia

Malaysia includes both mainland and island areas. The mainland section is on the Malay Peninsula, and the island section is part of the island of Borneo. The challenge to Malaysia's government is to unify two parts of a country that are separated by several hundred miles of ocean. About half the total population is Malay, and their numbers dominate mainland Malaysia. The country also has sizable Chinese and Indian minorities, and these groups have generally achieved economic success. However, government policies have typically favored Malays, which has created tension between the two groups.

The Malaysian government has tried to achieve unity in several ways. Foremost is emphasis on economic growth. The country has made strong progress toward becoming a developed nation. This economic growth has helped ease some of the tensions among ethnic groups.

The Philippines

Like Indonesia, the Philippines consists of thousands of islands, most of which are less than a square mile in size. Its wide variety of ethnicities includes Malays, Chinese, Japanese, Arab, and Spanish. Many Americans have immigrated to the country as well. The country has blended these groups into its own Filipino culture. The widespread use of Filipino, one of the country's official languages, helps to form the national identity. The other official language, English, is also widely spoken.

Filipino teacher, Leonora Jusay, gives a lesson to the 59 students in her class. Education is underfunded but school is widely attended.

Although the Philippine economy has grown, nearly a third of all people are poor. Due to a lack of jobs, a few million people have left the Philippines to find work in other countries. They send a share of their earnings back to the Philippines as **remittances** to help their families at home.

Before You Move On

Make Inferences Why would geographic and ethnic divisions make it difficult for a country to come together?

FORMATIVE ASSESSMENT

READING LAB GeoJournal

Identify Problems and Solutions With a partner or group, discuss what you read about the causes of fragmentation in Indonesia, Malaysia, and the Philippines. What could the governments do to improve unity? Use the problem solving process on page R20. Focus on how the governments could implement a solution to fragmentation and measure its success. Present your ideas to the class.

SECTION (2) GOVERNMENT & ECONOMICS

2.2 Migration Within Indonesia

TECHTREK

myNGconnect.com For photos
and a graph of Indonesia's population

Student
Resources

Digital
Library

Main Idea Efforts to bring unity to Indonesia's islands through relocation have had mixed results.

Indonesia is the fourth most populous country in the world. However, the majority of the people live on just a few of Indonesia's many islands. Living on the remote islands isolates citizens from the greater population, and the country remains fragmented.

Relocation Policy

The Dutch, who had colonized the area, recognized the problem of unifying the vast chain of islands. In the 1800s, they began **relocating**, or moving, individuals and families from Java, **Madura**, and Bali—called the **inner islands**—to the surrounding and less-central islands, the **outer islands**. After Indonesia won independence in 1949, the Indonesian government continued relocating people.

Currently, more than half of Indonesia's people live on the island of Java—an island with a small percentage of the country's total land area. The government hopes that continuing to spread out the Javanese people will help to unify the country. Indonesians native to Java speak the official language, and their presence on the outer islands can help spread the official language to those places where it is infrequently heard. A common language can help unify a fragmented country.

Effects of Internal Migration

So far, however, the practice of moving people among the islands has had unintended results. New arrivals came into conflict with native people, altering their way of life. Modern farming practices clashed with traditional land use and sometimes damaged the environment.

> **Critical Viewing** The outer islands, where this farmer works in a rice field, are less populated than the inner islands. What can you infer from the photo about life on the outer islands?

Critical Viewing Indonesians return to Jakarta after visiting their homes on other islands. What does the photo suggest about the movement from rural to urban areas like Jakarta?

INDONESIA: ISLAND POPULATIONS

INNER ISLANDS:
Java + Madura + Bali

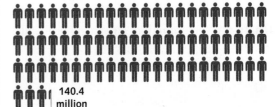

140.4 million

OUTER ISLANDS:
Sumatra

50.6 million

Sulawesi

 17.3 million

Borneo

 13.7 million

Flores + Sumba + Timor

  4.6 million

Lombok + Sumbawa

  4.4 million

New Guinea

  3.6 million

Moluccas

  2.5 million

 equals 2 million people

Source: *Europa World Year Book*, 2012; populations for 2010

The government hoped the new settlers could build successful farms, but many had trouble supporting themselves. Some ended up abandoning their new homes to return to the inner islands. As a result, Java and Bali remain crowded, making the government's relocation program ineffective. Crowding on Java and Bali grew even worse due to other **trends**, or changes over time. Indonesians living on the outer islands migrated there to flee rural poverty and find work on busier islands. Decades after the program began, Java and Bali are far more densely populated than Indonesia's other islands.

Before You Move On

Summarize How have government policies and economic factors determined migration within Indonesia?

FORMATIVE ASSESSMENT

DATA LAB
GeoJournal

1. **Interpret Graphs** With a partner, pose and answer questions about the region. Then answer: Which is the most populous outer island? Which is the least populous?

2. **Place** Look at the map of Indonesia on page 598. Compare the sizes of the islands to the population figures here. Which outer island has the highest population density? Why?

3. **Make Inferences** Explain the impact the scarcity of resources might have on how the Indonesian islands rely on one another.

2.3 Singapore's Growth

TECHTREK
myNGconnect.com For photos of Singapore and Guided Writing

Digital Library   Student Resources

Main Idea Singapore has grown economically due to its geographic location and economic policies.

The British established the modern port of Singapore in the early 1800s in an effort to compete with the Dutch in trade. Located just off the southern tip of the Malay Peninsula, the island has a perfect location near the shipping routes that link the Indian and Pacific oceans. This location gave it the **potential**, or possibility, of becoming a great **port**, a place where ships can exchange cargo. Today, the tiny island country is one of the world's busiest ports—and a strong economic power.

Building Success

In 1963, Malaysia gained independence from Britain. Singapore was part of this new country. However, conflict arose between the majority Chinese population of Singapore and the Malays of the rest of Malaysia. In 1965, to reduce the tension, the government offered Singapore its independence, and Singapore took it.

Singapore thrived because of its prime location. It served as the main transit point for sending raw materials such as timber, rubber, rice, and petroleum from Southeast Asia to other parts of the world. Manufactured goods from the United States and Europe came into the port and were shipped to other ports in Southeast Asia. Cars and machinery were shipped into the city from the west to be distributed around the region.

Prime Minister Lee Kuan Yew led Singapore from 1959 to 1990. He emphasized the country's role as an important port and led the drive to **industrialize**, or develop manufacturing. However, the government strictly controlled life in Singapore. Streets were kept clean, and there was very little crime.

Before You Move On

Monitor Comprehension What geographic assets have helped Singapore be part of the global economy?

KEY VOCABULARY

port, n., a place where ships can exchange cargo

industrialize, v., to develop manufacturing

multinational corporation, n., large business that has operations in many different countries

ACADEMIC VOCABULARY

potential, n., possibility or promise

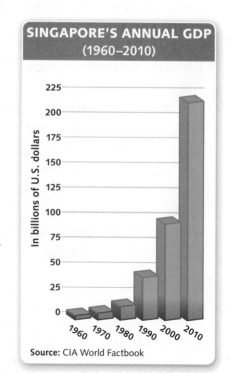

SINGAPORE'S ANNUAL GDP
(1960–2010)

In billions of U.S. dollars

225
200
175
150
125
100
75
50
25
0

1960 1970 1980 1990 2000 2010

Source: CIA World Factbook

6.05.A explain geographic factors responsible for location of economic activities; 6.05.C explain impact of geographic factors on foreign policy;
6.10.B describe levels of economic development using indicators; 6.10.C identify and describe effects of government taxation on economic
development; 6.16.B compare characteristics of institutions; 6.16.C analyze efforts institutions use to sustain themselves (education)

 Inspiring people to care about the planet
National Geographic Society Mission

Keeping Pace

When the British handed Hong Kong back to China in 1999, some Hong Kong business owners worried that Chinese rule would limit their freedom and prosperity. Singapore welcomed them, which boosted its economic growth. Singapore today has a stable free-market economy that relies on electronics exports and service businesses. It has one of the world's highest per capita GDP and is home to many **multinational corporations**.

To attract foreign investment, Singapore offers low tax rates and other economic incentives. Singapore's leaders invest heavily in infrastructure improvements to gain countrywide access to the most current technologies available. Telecommunications and other technologies rely on educated, highly skilled workers, so the country emphasizes improving the level of education in the workforce.

GLOBALIZATION ISSUES

Trustworthy companies can face problems when they manufacture overseas in cities or economic zones that are relatively new to free enterprise. Companies lose profits when there is counterfeiting or violations of product secrecy. Product safety is also a risk. China is the world's largest toy maker and exporter. In 2007 and 2010, millions of toys were recalled when toxins, choking hazards, or other dangers were found in them. These problems occur in many countries.

The U.S. Food and Drug Administration regularly reports contaminations in U.S.

^ **Critical Viewing** This late-night street scene shows the business district in Singapore. Which details in the photo are typical of a prosperous city?

food products. Companies that make or sell tainted products recall them and fix the problem, following ethical or fair behavior, which is based on morality, or good conduct. These practices are important for a free-enterprise system to function well.

Before You Move On

Summarize What issues might Singapore face as a major exporter of electronics products?

FORMATIVE ASSESSMENT

WRITING LAB GeoJournal

1. **Make Inferences** Describe how you think the government's position on taxation has affected economic development.

2. **Write Analyses** How has Singapore been affected by globalization? How has its economy been affected by other countries? Go to **Student Resources** for Guided Writing support.

2.4 Malaysia and New Media

TECHTREK

myNGconnect.com For graphs and photos of communication in Malaysia

 Maps and Graphs

 Digital Library

Main Idea Access to new media sources is changing the strict control on information formerly held by the government in Malaysia.

Since gaining independence in 1963, **Malaysia** has enjoyed prosperity and calm. The government has concentrated on building the economy. However, as in nearby Singapore, Malaysia has limited the freedoms its people can enjoy.

Controlling Information

One of these limits is government control of access to information. Freedom of the press is limited. Newspapers must obtain licenses from the government to operate, and the government can cancel those licenses at any time. Similar laws place restrictions on companies that want to run radio or television stations. Also, the government withholds information from media.

Tough laws punish media outlets that criticize the government. Members of the ruling party own many major newspapers. Even independently owned newspapers usually do not criticize the government.

New Media

The restrictions on the flow of information may be starting to loosen. Nearly two-thirds of Malaysians can now connect to the Internet. New media, like the Internet, give people access to new sources of information that the government may have more difficulty controlling.

Officially the government promises limitless Internet use. However, interference is not uncommon. Many Web site operators focusing on Malaysian news have been arrested multiple times for government criticism. Other journalists have been targeted as well.

> **Critical Viewing** A young woman uses her laptop in a public space in Malaysia. In what ways does the photo show both government control and freedom?

6.13.B explain how opportunities for citizens to participate in and influence political process vary among societies;
6.17.C evaluate the impact of improved communication technology among cultures; 6.20.B explain how political decisions have
affected use of technology; 6.20.C make predictions about future impacts that may result from technological innovations

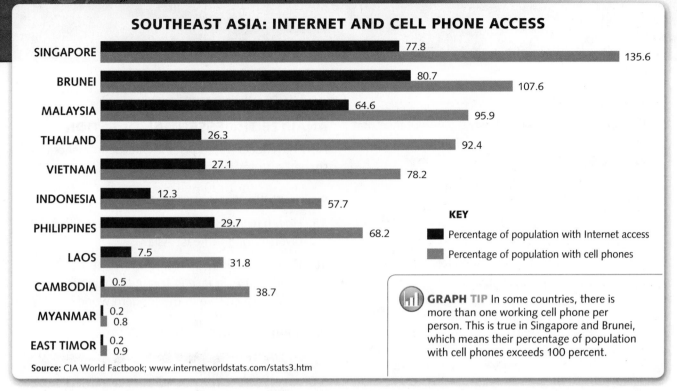

SOUTHEAST ASIA: INTERNET AND CELL PHONE ACCESS

Country	Internet	Cell phones
SINGAPORE	77.8	135.6
BRUNEI	80.7	107.6
MALAYSIA	64.6	95.9
THAILAND	26.3	92.4
VIETNAM	27.1	78.2
INDONESIA	12.3	57.7
PHILIPPINES	29.7	68.2
LAOS	7.5	31.8
CAMBODIA	0.5	38.7
MYANMAR	0.2	0.8
EAST TIMOR	0.2	0.9

KEY
■ Percentage of population with Internet access
■ Percentage of population with cell phones

GRAPH TIP In some countries, there is more than one working cell phone per person. This is true in Singapore and Brunei, which means their percentage of population with cell phones exceeds 100 percent.

Source: CIA World Factbook; www.internetworldstats.com/stats3.htm

In other instances, police raided Web site headquarters and seized computers in order to find specific people who wrote articles critical of the government.

Many Malaysians believed that until the **emergence**, or arrival, of the Internet the government controlled and manipulated information available to citizens. During elections in 2008, Web sites became the leading source of news for people in the country.

Web sites were outside of government control. They also were completely open to opinions and ideas from anyone in the country. Any citizen could file stories or post videos to the sites. Because of such openness, Web sites may have influenced the 2008 elections. As a result of that vote, the ruling party lost 58 seats in the national legislature. It was the worst result for the party in more than 40 years.

New media technologies give people access to information that is difficult for people in power to control. Poll results found that older citizens trust newspapers and television news and are less likely to embrace additional sources of media. However, among voters in their twenties and thirties, only a small minority trusted traditional media, while more than 60 percent said online news sources were **reliable**, or trustworthy.

Before You Move On
Summarize How has access to new media changed the strict government control of information in Malaysia?

FORMATIVE ASSESSMENT
DATA LAB

GeoJournal

1. **Analyze Data** How do percentages for Internet access and cell phone use in Malaysia compare to those of other countries in the region?

2. **Evaluate** What has been the impact of improved communication technology on Malaysian society?

3. **Make Predictions** What do the poll results suggest about the way traditional media will be accepted in the future? Why?

VOCABULARY

For each vocabulary word, write one sentence that explains its meaning and relates it to the content of the chapter.

1. prehistoric

> Many religions in Southeast Asia are prehistoric, meaning they existed before history was written down.

2. metropolitan area
3. dialect
4. domesticate
5. relocate
6. multinational corporation

MAIN IDEAS

7. How has colonial history shaped religion in the region? (Section 1.1)
8. How does modern Thailand reflect both tradition and external influences? (Section 1.2)
9. In what way has globalization changed language use in Southeast Asia? (Section 1.3)
10. What methods can help protect the wild Asian elephant population in Southeast Asia? (Section 1.4)
11. How has fragmentation been a problem for Indonesia, Malaysia, and the Philippines? (Section 2.1)
12. What have been the results of Indonesia's policy of moving people to new areas? (Section 2.2)
13. How has Singapore built its economy? (Sections 2.3)
14. How have new media changed politics in Malaysia? (Section 2.4)

CULTURE

ANALYZE THE ESSENTIAL QUESTION

How have local traditions and outside influences shaped cultures in Southeast Asia?

Focus Skill: Make Generalizations

15. How have outside influences increased the diversity of Southeast Asia?
16. What difficulties do the countries of Southeast Asia face in trying to maintain traditional culture in the modern world?

INTERPRET TABLES

PERCENTAGES OF ETHNIC GROUPS IN SELECTED SOUTHEAST ASIAN COUNTRIES		
Indonesia	Javanese: 41% Sundanese: 15% Madurese: 3%	Minangkabau: 3% Other: 38.4%
Laos	Lao: 55% Khmou: 11%	Hmong: 8% Other: 26%
Malaysia	Malay: 50% Chinese: 24%	Indian: 7% Other: 19%
Philippines	Tagalog: 28% Cebuano: 13% Ilocano: 9%	Bisaya/Binisaya: 8% Hiligaynon Ilonggo: 8% Other: 35%
Singapore	Chinese: 77% Malay: 14%	Indian: 8% Other: 1%
Thailand	Thai: 75% Chinese: 14%	Other: 11%
Vietnam	Kinh (Viet): 86%	Other : 14%

Source: CIA World Factbook

17. **Analyze Data** Which three countries have a single dominant ethnic group? What is the group in each case?
18. **Make Generalizations** Would you expect countries with one dominant ethnic group to have a single official national language? Why or why not?

GOVERNMENT & ECONOMICS

ANALYZE THE ESSENTIAL QUESTION

How are Southeast Asia's governments trying to unify their countries?

Focus Skill: Summarize

19. What economic and political concerns led Indonesia to adopt a policy of moving people from the inner islands to the outer islands?

20. Why did Singapore split from Malaysia and become independent?

21. How is the policy of Malaysia's government to limit freedom of the press related to the issue of fragmentation?

INTERPRET MAPS

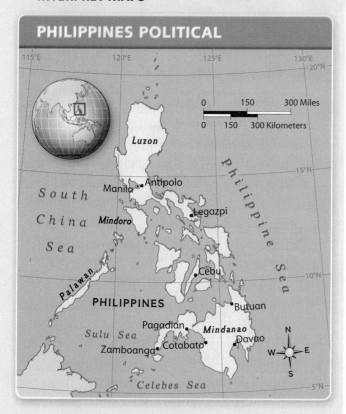

PHILIPPINES POLITICAL

22. **Interpret Maps** Why is it appropriate to call the Philippines a fragmented country?

23. **Draw Conclusions** What transportation improvements might the government invest in to help unify the country? Explain.

ACTIVE OPTIONS

Synthesize the Essential Questions by completing the activities below.

24. **Write a Culture Article** Introduce a friend to Southeast Asia today by writing an article about one country in the region. How do religious practices and regional languages shape culture in that country? Describe traditional art and music or the creative expressions of people who live there today. **Share your article with your friend.**

> **Writing Tips**
> - Research and take notes about the culture of your country.
> - Write in your own words to avoid plagiarism, which is copying the words and ideas of others. Cite your sources. (See page R4.)
> - Include details about the country's religions, art, music, or other aspects of culture.
> - Be sure you have an interesting introduction, smooth transitions between paragraphs, and a conclusion that summarizes your article.

25. **Create Graphs** Use online research to make a bar graph showing the per capita gross domestic product (GDP) of Cambodia, Malaysia, and the Philippines. Write a paragraph explaining which countries' economies might be affected by fragmentation. Use the example below as a guide for your graph.

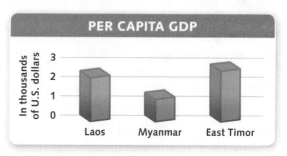

PER CAPITA GDP

Endangered species of both plants and animals can be found in every region of the world. A species is endangered when it runs the risk of becoming extinct, or disappearing completely from the world. Over time, various species have not survived. In fact, historically there have been five mass extinctions, in which a large number of existing species died out.

Today, the rate of extinction for plant and animal species has become hundreds of times faster than what scientists have observed through the fossil record. Many scientists believe the earth is currently in the midst of a sixth mass extinction. Those same scientists believe the main cause to be the destruction of habitat.

Compare Ranges of Endangered Big Cats

- Asiatic Lion
- Cheetah
- Iberian Lynx
- Jaguar
- Tiger

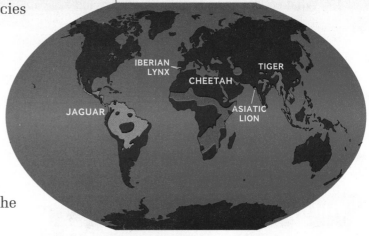

CAUSES OF EXTINCTION

Mining, logging, and clearing of forests for grazing cattle and growing crops all greatly change the natural landscape, or habitat, on which most species depend. Other development, such as the building of dams, highways, and housing, can increasingly divide animal populations into smaller, less diverse pockets. Some groups, like the big cats shown at right, face additional threats from hunters fearful of the animals' ability to harm people and livestock.

Climate change also can seriously stress a species' population and push it to extinction. For example, climate change can alter the amount of rain that falls, which affects plant growth and changes the food available in the habitat. When that happens quickly, species have difficulty adapting.

CONSERVATION

Species and their ecosystems contribute much to the health and well being of humans. A diversity of plants and animals, and the habitats in which they are found, provide fertile soils, medicines, clean air and water, fibers, building materials, and food.

The International Union for Conservation of Animals (IUCN) is one organization trying to help countries around the world find solutions for balancing human needs and environmental challenges. To help target the habitats and animals in need of support, the IUCN maintains a database called the "Red List of Endangered Species." The list identifies animal species as near threatened, vulnerable, endangered, and critically endangered, as shown on the diagram at right.

ENDANGERED BIG CATS

Source: The IUCN Red List of Threatened Species™

JAGUAR Hunting of jaguars has declined with protection, but habitat is becoming increasingly fragmented.

ASIATIC LION Once thought to be down to fewer than 20, the Asiatic lion is now protected in its only remaining habitat, the Gir Forest, India.

IBERIAN LYNX Recent surveys suggest only two remaining breeding populations remain in Spain. The lynx may be extinct in Portugal.

CHEETAH Declining prey species and fragmented habitat have kept cheetahs vulnerable.

TIGER Although fiercely protected and a stronghold in Southeast Asia, tigers have lost 93 percent of their historic range.

CONSERVATION STATUS
- Critically Endangered
- Endangered
- Vulnerable
- Near Threatened

Jaguar diagram years: 2008, 2002, 1996, 1990, 1988, 1986, 1994, 1988, 1996, 2002, 2008

Asiatic Lion diagram years: 2008, 2002, 1996, 1994, 1988, 1986, 1988, 1994, 1996, 2002, 2008

Tiger diagram years: 1986, 1988, 1994, 1996, 2002, 2008

FORMATIVE ASSESSMENT

RESEARCH LAB GeoJournal

1. **Analyze Data** Look at the diagram for the Asiatic lion. What happened between 2002 and 2008? How can you explain this?

2. **Draw Conclusions** Look at the diagram for the jaguar and the Iberian lynx. Think about where these cats live and the population density in those ranges. Why might this help explain why their levels of endangerment have changed?

Research and Compare Use the IUCN Red List of Threatened Species™ to research and compare the levels of endangerment within an animal group such as antelopes, seals, bats, bears, big apes, dolphins or otters. Identify the region and how humans are affecting the populations. What is being done to conserve the species? Create a table to describe your findings.

Active Options

ACTIVITY 1

Goal: Learn about unusual and healthy food.

Make a Recommendation

Southeast Asia is home to a rich variety of plants that includes a wide assortment of fruits. Several of the more exotic fruits are listed below. With a partner, use the list below and online sources to research fruit from the region. Recommend three fruits that your classmates might want to try. Show what the fruits look like and give reasons for recommending those three.

- ciku
- dragon fruit
- durian
- jackfruit
- langsat
- longan
- mangosteen
- rambutan
- salak
- sapodilla
- soursap
- star apple

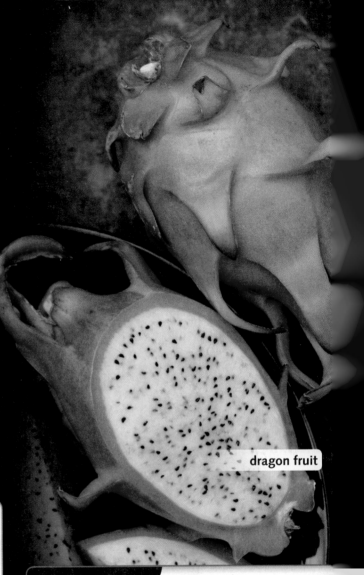

dragon fruit

ACTIVITY 2

Goal: Research a Southeast Asian city.

Culture Search

On a map or globe, locate each of the capital cities below, giving its coordinates. Then research one of the cities to learn what aspects of its cultural life interest you. Use the **Magazine Maker CD-ROM** to organize and illustrate your findings. Include places in the city you'd like to visit and facts to interest your readers.

- Bangkok, Thailand
- Kuala Lumpur, Malaysia
- Phnom Penh, Cambodia
- Singapore, Singapore

ACTIVITY 3

Goal: Extend knowledge of Southeast Asian wildlife through research and drama.

Set the Stage

Some of the world's oldest rain forests are in Southeast Asia. With a group, compose a one-act play set deep in the rain forest. Focus the drama on the region's rain forest issues, and include in your play one of the animals found there, such as the Komodo dragon, flying snake, or orangutan. Perform the play for the class.

6.03.C compare regions and countries using geographic tools; 6.04.D locate physical and human geography; 6.16.B compare characteristics of institutions; 6.22.D create visual material based on research

TEKS

TEKS PROJECT

Goal: Compare and connect world cultures.

Make Global Connections

Imagine walking into a vast room in which the walls and ceiling are covered with images from around the world, and beams of light connect the images across the space. Blue light, for instance, relates to government; green for geography; red for culture; and so on. Touch one of the beams and you learn how images are connected. The countries might have similar constitutions, exports, languages, landforms, or climate—hundreds of connections. Then watch as the beams split and send new colors to and from images, showing how cultures have blended and culture traits have spread, whether through shared knowledge, the arts, historical events, migration, or just simply travel. You've entered a web of global connections.

Make Comparisons Compare the physical world different societies live in. Compare aspects of human geography. Compare the characteristics of institutions from one society to the next. With a group, choose six world societies and six aspects of societies to compare. Collect the data. Use the **Digital Library** and other image resources to find images that show the societies and aspects you have chosen.

Make Connections Create your own web. Post your images and find ways to show and explain the connections. Then connect your societies with those of other groups. As a class, brainstorm an ideal or futuristic way to show relationships.

Reflect On It Discuss the question: How can the world appreciate and maintain distinct cultures and yet find common ways to communicate and work together?

Try creating your web with computer software that shows three dimensions, as in this image of the world.

UNIT 12

EXPLORE
AUSTRALIA,
THE PACIFIC REALM & ANTARCTICA
WITH NATIONAL GEOGRAPHIC

MEET THE EXPLORER

NATIONAL GEOGRAPHIC

National Geographic Fellow Elizabeth Lindsey helps conserve knowledge and traditions of Polynesian cultures. Her work focuses on such elements as Micronesian chants and traditional navigation methods that do not use any instruments.

STEP INTO HISTORY

Easter Island, a UNESCO World Heritage site, is located 2,200 miles west of Chile. It is known for its enormous stone statues, standing from 10 to 40 feet tall. More than 600 statues remain on the island.

CONNECT WITH THE CULTURE

The opera house in Sydney, New South Wales, Australia, is one of the most famous buildings in the world. Sydney, now one of the largest ports in the South Pacific, began as a convict settlement in the 18th century.

Washington, D.C.

9,762 miles

Canberra, Australia

Go to myNGconnect.com **for maps of Australia, the Pacific Realm, and Antarctica.**

INVESTIGATE GEOGRAPHY

Adélie penguins jump off of a rock ledge in Armstrong Reef, western Antarctica. They will feed heavily in the food-rich waters of the southern Pacific Ocean.

CHAPTER 23

AUSTRALIA, THE PACIFIC REALM & ANTARCTICA GEOGRAPHY & HISTORY

PREVIEW THE CHAPTER

Essential Question How did geographic isolation influence the development of this region?

SECTION 1 • GEOGRAPHY

KEY VOCABULARY

- coral reef
- atoll
- indigenous
- marsupial
- invasive species
- extinct
- feral
- hotspot
- coral island
- marine
- exoskeleton

ACADEMIC VOCABULARY

preserve

TERMS & NAMES

- Southern Hemisphere
- Southern Alps
- South Pole
- New Guinea
- Kingman Reef
- Great Barrier Reef

Essential Question How did geographic isolation shape the history of Australia and the Pacific Realm?

SECTION 2 • HISTORY

KEY VOCABULARY

- land bridge
- clan
- pictograph
- seafarer
- outrigger canoe
- navigation
- convict
- assisted migration
- generation
- linguist

ACADEMIC VOCABULARY

transport, convey

TERMS & NAMES

- Aborigine
- James Cook
- New South Wales
- Commonwealth of Australia
- Enduring Voices Project

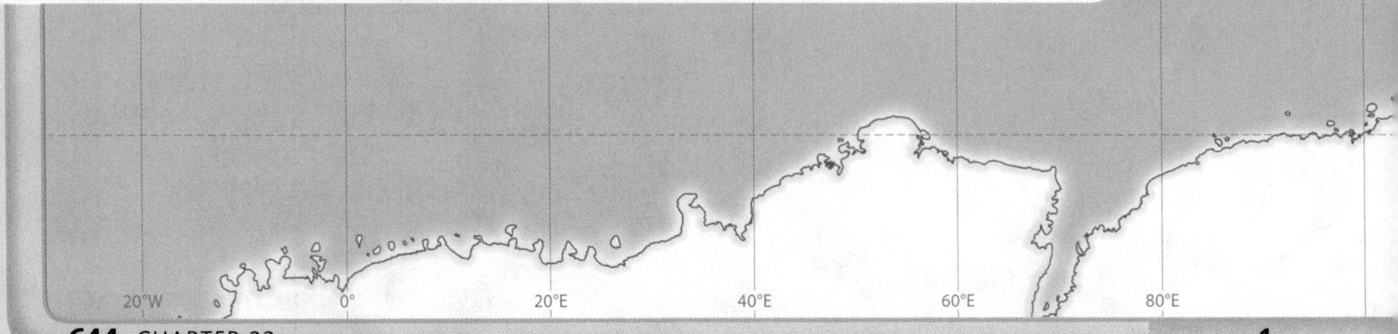

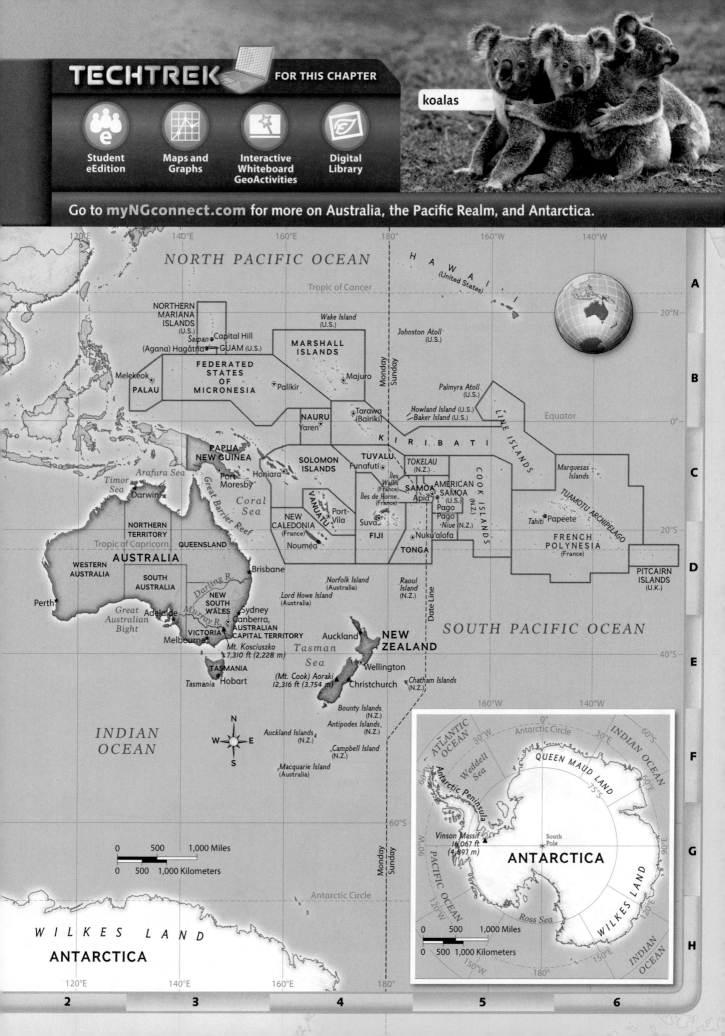

TECHTREK FOR THIS CHAPTER

Student eEdition

Maps and Graphs

Interactive Whiteboard GeoActivities

Digital Library

Go to myNGconnect.com for more on Australia, the Pacific Realm, and Antarctica.

koalas

NORTH PACIFIC OCEAN

HAWAI'I (United States)

Tropic of Cancer

NORTHERN MARIANA ISLANDS (U.S.)

Saipan • Capital Hill
(Agana) Hagåtña • GUAM (U.S.)

Wake Island (U.S.)

Johnston Atoll (U.S.)

MARSHALL ISLANDS

Majuro

Monday / Sunday

Palmyra Atoll (U.S.)

Melekeok • PALAU

FEDERATED STATES OF MICRONESIA

Palikir

Howland Island (U.S.)
Baker Island (U.S.)

Equator

NAURU
Yaren

Tarawa (Bairiki)

KIRIBATI

LINE ISLANDS

PAPUA NEW GUINEA

Arafura Sea

Port Moresby

Honiara

SOLOMON ISLANDS

TUVALU
Funafuti

TOKELAU (N.Z.)

Marquesas Islands

Timor Sea

Darwin

Coral Sea

Great Barrier Reef

VANUATU

Port-Vila

Îles Wallis (France)

Îles de Horne (France)

SAMOA
Apia

AMERICAN SAMOA (U.S.)
Pago Pago

COOK ISLANDS (N.Z.)

TUAMOTU ARCHIPELAGO

NORTHERN TERRITORY

Tropic of Capricorn

QUEENSLAND

NEW CALEDONIA (France)

Nouméa

Suva

FIJI

Niue (N.Z.)

Nuku'alofa

Tahiti • Papeete

FRENCH POLYNESIA (France)

WESTERN AUSTRALIA

AUSTRALIA

SOUTH AUSTRALIA

Brisbane

TONGA

Perth

Darling R.

NEW SOUTH WALES

Norfolk Island (Australia)

Raoul Island (N.Z.)

SOUTH PACIFIC OCEAN

PITCAIRN ISLANDS (U.K.)

Great Australian Bight

Adelaide

Murray R.

Sydney
Canberra, AUSTRALIAN CAPITAL TERRITORY

Lord Howe Island (Australia)

Auckland

VICTORIA

Melbourne

Mt. Kosciuszko 7,310 ft (2,228 m)

NEW ZEALAND

Date Line

TASMANIA

Tasman Sea

(Mt. Cook) Aoraki 12,316 ft (3,754 m)

Wellington

Tasmania • Hobart

Christchurch

Chatham Islands (N.Z.)

INDIAN OCEAN

N W E S

Bounty Islands (N.Z.)

Antipodes Islands (N.Z.)

Auckland Islands (N.Z.)

Campbell Island (N.Z.)

Macquarie Island (Australia)

0 500 1,000 Miles
0 500 1,000 Kilometers

Monday / Sunday

Antarctic Circle

WILKES LAND

ANTARCTICA

ANTARCTICA inset

ATLANTIC OCEAN

Antarctic Circle

INDIAN OCEAN

Weddell Sea

QUEEN MAUD LAND

Antarctic Peninsula

PACIFIC OCEAN

Vinson Massif 16,067 ft (4,897 m)

South Pole

ANTARCTICA

WILKES LAND

Ross Sea

INDIAN OCEAN

0 500 1,000 Miles
0 500 1,000 Kilometers

SECTION 1 GEOGRAPHY

1.1 Physical Geography

TECHTREK

myNGconnect.com For maps of Australia, the Pacific Realm, and Antarctica and Visual Vocabulary

 Maps and Graphs

 Digital Library

AUSTRALIA, THE PACIFIC REALM, AND ANTARCTICA PHYSICAL

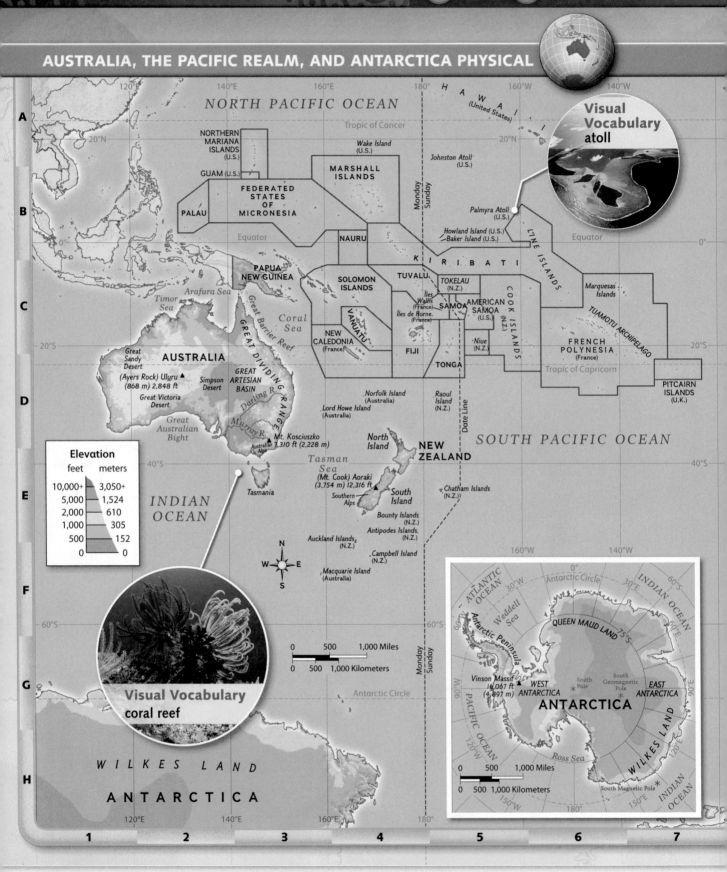

Visual Vocabulary
atoll

Visual Vocabulary
coral reef

Elevation

feet	meters
10,000+	3,050+
5,000	1,524
2,000	610
1,000	305
500	152
0	0

NORTH PACIFIC OCEAN

Tropic of Cancer

HAWAII (United States)

NORTHERN MARIANA ISLANDS (U.S.)

Wake Island (U.S.)

Johnston Atoll (U.S.)

GUAM (U.S.)

MARSHALL ISLANDS

FEDERATED STATES OF MICRONESIA

PALAU

Palmyra Atoll (U.S.)

NAURU

Howland Island (U.S.)
Baker Island (U.S.)

Equator

K I R I B A T I

LINE ISLANDS

PAPUA NEW GUINEA

SOLOMON ISLANDS

TUVALU

TOKELAU (N.Z.)

Marquesas Islands

Arafura Sea

Timor Sea

Coral Sea

VANUATU

Îles Wallis (France)
Îles de Horne (France)

SAMOA

AMERICAN SAMOA (U.S.)

COOK ISLANDS (N.Z.)

TUAMOTU ARCHIPELAGO

Great Barrier Reef

NEW CALEDONIA (France)

FIJI

Niue (N.Z.)

FRENCH POLYNESIA (France)

Tropic of Capricorn

AUSTRALIA

Great Sandy Desert

(Ayers Rock) Uluru ▲ (868 m) 2,848 ft

Simpson Desert

GREAT ARTESIAN BASIN

GREAT DIVIDING RANGE

Darling R.

TONGA

Norfolk Island (Australia)

Raoul Island (N.Z.)

PITCAIRN ISLANDS (U.K.)

Great Victoria Desert

Lord Howe Island (Australia)

Murray R.

Mt. Kosciuszko ▲ 7,310 ft (2,228 m)

Australian Alps

North Island

NEW ZEALAND

SOUTH PACIFIC OCEAN

Great Australian Bight

Tasman Sea

(Mt. Cook) Aoraki (3,754 m) 12,316 ft ▲

South Island

Chatham Islands (N.Z.)

Tasmania

Southern Alps

INDIAN OCEAN

Bounty Islands (N.Z.)

Antipodes Islands (N.Z.)

Auckland Islands (N.Z.)

Campbell Island (N.Z.)

Macquarie Island (Australia)

Date Line

Monday Sunday

N
W E
S

0 500 1,000 Miles
0 500 1,000 Kilometers

WILKES LAND

ANTARCTICA

ATLANTIC OCEAN

Weddell Sea

Antarctic Circle

INDIAN OCEAN

QUEEN MAUD LAND

Antarctic Peninsula

Vinson Massif ▲ 16,067 ft (4,897 m)

WEST ANTARCTICA

South Pole

South Geomagnetic Pole

EAST ANTARCTICA

ANTARCTICA

PACIFIC OCEAN

WILKES LAND

Ross Sea

South Magnetic Pole

INDIAN OCEAN

0 500 1,000 Miles
0 500 1,000 Kilometers

Main Idea This region lies in the Pacific Ocean and is geographically isolated from other parts of the world.

Australia, much of the Pacific Realm, and Antarctica are located in the **Southern Hemisphere**. The region is spread across a vast ocean area.

Australia

Australia is the only country in the world that is also a continent. Australia is sometimes called the "island continent" because it is surrounded by water. However, the climate is mostly dry. In fact, nearly 20 percent of the land mass of Australia is classified as desert. Few people live in the inland parts of the continent. Instead, most people live along the coasts where rainfall is plentiful.

The Pacific Realm and Antarctica

The Pacific Realm is a large area of the Pacific Ocean made up of thousands of small islands and coral reefs. **Coral reefs** are rock-like structures built by layers of coral organisms. Coral reefs thrive in warm ocean waters between latitudes of 30°N and 30°S. **Atolls**—ring-shaped reefs, islands, or chains of islands made of coral—also dot this area of the Pacific.

New Zealand, located southeast of Australia, is made up of two major islands, North Island and South Island. New Zealand's mountain range, the **Southern Alps,** includes peaks that rise more than 12,000 feet.

Antarctica is centered on the **South Pole,** the southernmost point of Earth's axis. A thick layer of ice covers almost all

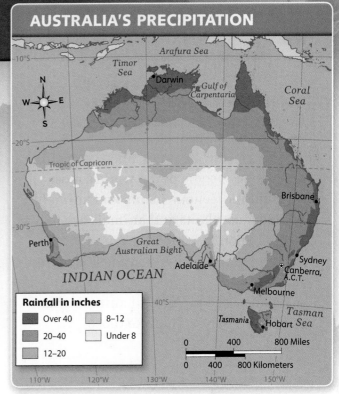

AUSTRALIA'S PRECIPITATION

Rainfall in inches
- Over 40
- 20–40
- 12–20
- 8–12
- Under 8

the continent's mountains, valleys, and islands. Antarctica has the coldest climate on Earth and is the continent with the highest average elevation.

Before You Move On
Monitor Comprehension How is this region isolated from other parts of the world?

FORMATIVE ASSESSMENT

MAP LAB
GeoJournal

1. **Human-Environment Interaction** Based on the precipitation map, which part of Australia might produce few crops and why?

2. **Interpret Maps** Between what latitudes do the Pacific islands lie? Explain how their location is ideal for the formation of coral reefs.

3. **Compare and Contrast** Examine the physical map of the region. In what ways are Australia and Antarctica similar and different? Use a chart like this one to answer the question.

SIMILARITIES	DIFFERENCES

1.2 Indigenous Plants and Animals

TECHTREK

myNGconnect.com For photos of
the region's indigenous plants and animals

Digital
Library

> **Main Idea** Many plants and animals are
> found exclusively in this region.

Australia, New Zealand, and the Pacific
islands have some of the world's most
unusual indigenous plants and animals.
Indigenous plants and animals are native
to the region in which they are found.
Because of the region's physical isolation,
these species developed with little outside
influence. The plants and animals that
developed here are unlike those
found elsewhere.

Cassowaries grow as high as five feet tall
and can be aggressive.

Plant Species

Thousands of wildflowers, shrubs, and
trees are native to the region. Among
them are eucalyptus (YOO kuh LIHP tuhs)
trees, whose leaves produce a fragrant
oil used in medicines. These leaves are
the only food that Australia's much-loved
koalas eat. Another common plant is the
acacia, with more than 700 varieties found
in Australia. Most acacia have brightly
colored flowers.

Native Animals

Animals native to this region include
marsupials (mar SOO pee uhlz), which
are mammals whose females carry
their babies in a pouch. Four types of
marsupials live in this region. Kangaroos
are the biggest marsupials. Other
marsupials include koalas, wallabies,
wombats, and Tasmanian devils.

Other indigenous mammals of
Australia and **New Guinea** include the
platypus and the echidna (ih KID neh).
These mammals are the only mammals
that lay eggs. The platypus and the
echidna have beaks, another bird-like
feature not typically found in mammals.

The region is home to many kinds of
birds, including New Zealand's kiwi and
kakapo, which do not fly. The cassowary
(KAS eh ware ee) and emu, also flightless,
stand five to six feet tall. Australia's
kookaburra, a large kingfisher, is famous
for its call, which sounds like laughter.

Before You Move On
Summarize What plant and animal
species are indigenous to the region?

Critical Viewing Eucalyptus trees grow rapidly and some even reach 300 feet in height. Based on the photo, how would you describe a koala's habitat?

FORMATIVE ASSESSMENT
PHOTO LAB
GeoJournal

1. **Analyze Visuals** Look at the photos. Write two sentences that describe the physical features of the cassowary and the koala. What are some other birds and animals with similar physical features?

2. **Make Inferences** Based on the photos and text, why might protecting the health of eucalyptus trees and other unique plant species be important?

1.3 Biological Hitchhikers

Main Idea The introduction of non-native plant and animal species has changed the natural habitats of Australia and New Zealand.

Plants and animals, and their habitats, developed as they did because of the physical isolation of the region. The introduction of new plants and animals to Australia and New Zealand has had negative consequences.

Invasive Species

Many non-native species were introduced to these countries on purpose—before people understood what problems might occur. New species also have arrived by accident. Planes and ships delivering produce and packages bring in hidden plant and animal "hitchhikers" that then invade natural habitats. Non-native plants and animals that disturb the habitats

^ **Visual Vocabulary** Invasive species are non-native plants and animals that disturb the habitats of native life forms. These rabbits in Australia are an invasive species.

of native life forms are called **invasive species**. Because of invasive species, some native plants and animals have become **extinct**, meaning no more living members of that group exist. In fact, 19 different species of small mammals have become extinct in Australia since the introduction of non-native mammals such as cats, foxes, and rabbits.

Dingoes, Rabbits, and Other Pests

Dingoes have lived in Australia for many years, but they were not indigenous to the island continent. Sea travelers from Asia brought dingoes with them about 3,000 years ago. Some dingoes escaped, became

< **Critical Viewing** Dingoes are hunters. Based on the photo, what other animals do dingoes look like?

EUROPEAN RABBITS IN AUSTRALIA, 1870–2000

MAP TIP
Use the legend to identify where and when rabbits spread in Australia. Each color represents a different decade. The red lines show the boundaries of territories.

Arafura Sea

Timor Sea

•Darwin

Gulf of Carpentaria

Coral Sea

NORTHERN TERRITORY

QUEENSLAND

Tropic of Capricorn

WESTERN AUSTRALIA

INDIAN OCEAN

Brisbane.★

SOUTH AUSTRALIA

NEW SOUTH WALES

Perth★

Great Australian Bight

Sydney
Canberra, ★
AUSTRALIAN
CAPITAL
TERRITORY

N
W E
S

Adelaide★

VICTORIA
Melbourne

INDIAN OCEAN

Invasive Species in Australia
Spread of the European rabbit by year

1870		1910
1880		1980
1890		2000
1900		

Geelong
Site of first European rabbit
release on the mainland

Bass Strait

Tasman Sea

0   250   500 Miles
0   250   500 Kilometers

TASMANIA
European rabbits abundant
as early as 1827

★Hobart

---

wild, and preyed on native kangaroos and wallabies. Today, dingoes continue to threaten native animals and livestock.

When Europeans began to settle in Australia in the 1800s, they brought along rabbits, which quickly became **feral**, or wild, and spread across the continent. Feral rabbits have caused serious damage to crops and grazing lands. In the 1950s, the Australian government tried to wipe out feral rabbits but was not successful.

Non-native plants have also done damage. In fact, in New Zealand, more types of invasive plants thrive in the wild than do native plants. One climbing plant called "old man's beard" has spread widely since the 1940s. It smothers native foliage, and can even bring down large trees.

Before You Move On

Summarize In what ways have invasive species impacted Australia and New Zealand?

FORMATIVE ASSESSMENT

MAP LAB

GeoJournal

1. **Interpret Maps** Look at the map. In what direction have rabbits moved across Australia? By what decade was the island of Tasmania overrun with rabbits?

2. **Interpret Maps** Based on the map, where were rabbits first released in Australia? Using the map scale, determine approximately how far rabbits spread between the years 1870 and 2000.

3. **Movement** What are invasive species? In what ways do human migrations encourage their spread?

1.4 The Pacific Islands

TECHTREK
myNGconnect.com **For photos**
of the Pacific islands

 Digital
Library

> **Main Idea** Physical processes helped form the Pacific islands over a long period of time.

Northeast of Australia and New Zealand, the Pacific islands are a group of 20,000 to 30,000 islands scattered across millions of square miles of the Pacific Ocean. These islands were formed by geologic changes over thousands of years.

High Islands, Low Islands

Geographers divide the Pacific islands into two main categories: high islands and low islands. High islands are formed by volcanic activity. As tectonic plates move over **hotspots**, or unusually hot parts of Earth's mantle, magma rises up through the plates and produces a volcanic eruption. Cooled molten material forms underwater volcanic cones. This process repeats, and over time, these volcanic cones emerge above water as islands.

Low islands also form over long periods of time. They tend to be smaller than high islands and sit only a few feet above sea level. Low islands are **coral islands**, which are islands created by a gradual buildup of the skeletons of corals and other tiny marine animals. Coral islands often sit on top of coral reefs. Many coral reefs form around the base of high volcanic islands. Over time these reefs become atolls.

Climate, Agriculture, and Fishing

The climate in the Pacific islands is tropical and warm throughout the year. Most islands have a wet season and a dry season, but precipitation on the islands varies. Warm ocean air cools at higher elevations on high, mountainous islands and produces rain. High islands receive plentiful rainfall. Pineapples, sugarcane, and mangoes grow well in their rich

PACIFIC ISLAND FORMATION

HIGH ISLAND FORMATION

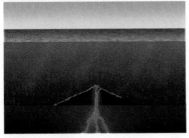

1 Magma rises from deep inside Earth's mantle.

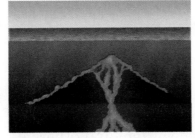

2 Cooled molten material forms underwater volcanic cones.

3 Volcanic cones emerge from the water as high islands.

LOW ISLAND FORMATION

1 Coral reefs form on the outer edges of high islands.

2 High islands appear to sink as erosion wears them away.

3 Over time, only the surrounding coral reef remains.

volcanic soil. Low islands, with no landforms to "catch" moisture, receive less rainfall. Though they are surrounded by ocean, drought is common on low islands. As a result, people on low islands depend less on agriculture and more on fishing.

Before You Move On

Monitor Comprehension How did the two types of Pacific islands form?

FORMATIVE ASSESSMENT

VIEWING LAB   GeoJournal

1. **Sequence Events** Describe the sequence of events in high and low island formation. Use the correct meanings of *atoll* and *coral reef* in your answer.

2. **Analyze Visuals** Based on the model and the text, in what way is molten material involved in island formation?

3. **Compare** The country of Iceland was formed by volcanic activity, similar to the process shown in the model. List island countries you have studied from different world regions. Draw simple models to compare how they were formed.

◀ **Critical Viewing Kingman Reef** lies under an atoll in the Line Islands and is one of the few unspoiled coral reefs remaining in the world. What details do you notice about life on this reef?

1.5 Saving the Reefs

TECHTREK

myNGconnect.com For photos
of Australia's Great Barrier Reef

Digital
Library

Global
Issues

Main Idea The Great Barrier Reef is a marine
ecosystem that is threatened by human activities.

KEY VOCABULARY

marine, adj., sea-based

exoskeleton, n., a hard,
external covering that
provides protection

ACADEMIC VOCABULARY

preserve, v., to protect

Each year, many people visit Australia's **Great Barrier
Reef**. In order to protect this ecosystem and others like
it around the world, Australia and other countries are
balancing tourism with preservation.

The Great Barrier Reef

The Great Barrier Reef is the world's largest coral reef.
Locate the Reef on the map on page 646. As you know, a
coral reef is a complex **marine**, or sea-based, ecosystem.
Small marine animals called corals secrete, or produce
and discharge, calcium carbonate. This hardens into
an **exoskeleton**, or a hard, external covering that
provides protection. Over time, colonies of these corals
form coral reefs that support marine life, from small
fish to predators such as sharks.

The Great Barrier Reef stretches 1,250 miles and
consists of around 2,900 separate reefs. It is home to one
of the most diverse collections of plants and animals
on Earth. Around 2,000 species of fish, 350 corals, and
4,000 mollusks, or soft-bodied marine animals with
exterior shells, live here. In recent years, scientists have
discovered hundreds of new animal species. Because
of the diversity and extent of life on the reef, it is
sometimes called "the rain forest of the sea."

The Australian government made the Great Barrier
Reef a national park in 1975. By doing so, it reduced the
potential negative impact of tourism through controls
on tourist activities in the park. Visitors to the Great
Barrier Reef can scuba dive, snorkel, view coral reefs
from glass-bottomed boats, and swim with dolphins.

Before You Move On

Summarize What kinds of marine life does the
Great Barrier Reef support?

**GREAT BARRIER REEF
BY THE NUMBERS**

1.99 million

Number of annual
tourists, 2012

72°–84°F

Ideal water temperature
range for corals

10,000

Average age of corals in years

2,900

Number of coral reefs that
make up the Great Barrier
Reef system

900

Number of islands in the
Great Barrier Reef system

600

Species of starfish and sea urchins
on the Great Barrier Reef

30

Species of whales and dolphins
observed on the Great Barrier Reef

Sources: Great Barrier Reef Marine
Park Authority, 2012

Inspiring people to care about the planet
National Geographic Society Mission

Science at Work

Today, the Great Barrier Reef's survival is threatened. The reef's ecosystem depends on a specific temperature range for reef-building corals to thrive. These corals depend on algae, small oxygen-producing organisms, for nourishment. Even small increases in water temperatures of 1°–2°F can prompt the algae to leave the corals, resulting in the corals' death. This process is called "coral bleaching" because it causes the corals to turn white.

In addition to increased water temperatures, pollution and overfishing have also caused problems for corals and other marine life on the reef. In fact, if steps toward preservation are not taken, scientists estimate that corals on the Great Barrier Reef could be extinct by 2050.

Experts are working to **preserve**, or protect, the reef. One group of scientists is trying to identify all the different species living in the reefs. Another group is focused on the effects of rising water temperatures on corals and reef life. A deeper understanding of the reef could lead to new methods of saving it.

COMPARE ACROSS REGIONS

Reef Preservation

Like the Great Barrier Reef, the Belize Barrier Reef—the second largest reef system in the world—attracts thousands of tourists each year. Belize is a small country in Central America that borders the Caribbean Sea. Mangrove trees, an important part of the reef's habitat, have been cut down. Sand and coral from the

^ Critical Viewing White tip sharks like this one live on the Great Barrier Reef. How might their survival depend on the protection of the reef?

ocean floor have also been disturbed, causing the loss of sea life. As tourism has grown, the reef has also been overfished.

As in Australia, local communities in Belize are actively preserving their reef. For the reef to be saved, the Belize government must work more closely with the tourism industry to control human activities in this fragile part of the world.

Before You Move On
Monitor Comprehension How do increasing water temperatures threaten coral reefs?

FORMATIVE ASSESSMENT
READING LAB GeoJournal

1. **Summarize** In what ways have human beings contributed to the problems facing coral reefs?
2. **Make Inferences** What might Belize learn from Australia about reef preservation?
3. **Draw Conclusions** The Great Barrier Reef Marine Park keeps track of numbers of tourists to the reef. Why might it be doing this?

SECTION **2** HISTORY

TECHTREK

myNGconnect.com For photos of
indigenous people and Australian rock art

Digital
Library

2.1 Indigenous Populations

Main Idea The languages and culture of Australia's indigenous people developed in isolation on the continent.

About 50,000 years ago, humans migrated to present-day Australia from Asia. They may have arrived by sea, or by **land bridge**, a narrow and temporary link between two land masses. The **Aborigines** (AB uh RIHJ uh neez) were Australia's first developed human culture. Most scientists believe this culture dates from 30,000 B.C.

Populating the Continent

Australia's Aborigines are considered the oldest continuous human culture in the world. In fact, the phrase *ab origine* means "from the beginning." Because of Australia's isolated location, Aboriginal culture and languages developed apart from other human groups. Over time, more than 200 different languages developed. These languages were unlike any others in the world.

Like other prehistoric peoples, Aborigines were nomadic hunters and gatherers. To adapt to the continent's dry climate, they conserved water and carried it with them as they moved. They lived in distinct groups of larger **clans**, or family units. Each clan had a strong attachment to the land on which it hunted and gathered food. In addition to providing a source of food, the land held spiritual meaning for the Aborigines.

Critical Viewing Uluru (oo LOO roo) is located in Australia's Northern Territory. Based on what you see in the photo, what aspects of Uluru might inspire Aborigines to view it as sacred?

> **Visual Vocabulary** Pictographs are painted pictures used to communicate. Not all pictographs are ancient. This one at Kakadu National Park in the Northern Territory is dated 1866.

Aborigines have considered the huge, red rock called Uluru, pictured at left, a sacred site for thousands of years. Rock art painted on cave walls at Uluru and other sites reveals much about Aborigines' beliefs. Some **pictographs** depict elements from the natural world while others portray religious ceremonies and important historical events.

Conflicts with Europeans

By 1788, when Europeans arrived in Australia, between 500,000 and one million Aborigines lived on the continent. Though Aborigines had established complex societies, most European settlers viewed their way of life as uncivilized.

Conflicts arose when Europeans seized Aborigines' lands. Separated from their land, Aborigines were not able to hunt, and many fell into poverty. Many died of disease because they did not have immunity or resistance to European illnesses. By 1921, they totaled only about 62,000. Today, Aborigines represent less than 3 percent of Australia's population, or 548,370 citizens.

Before You Move On
Summarize In what ways did Australia's location determine the way Aboriginal languages and culture developed?

FORMATIVE ASSESSMENT

PHOTO LAB GeoJournal

1. **Analyze Visuals** Based on the photo of rock art, what can you infer about how Aborigines used their surroundings to record events?

2. **Understand Culture** Locate Uluru on the map on page 659. What sacred sites in Texas, or in other parts of the world, have become tourist destinations, like Uluru? What might be the reasons for this?

3. **Movement** In what ways did conflicts over land cause problems for Aborigines?

2.2 Seagoing Societies

TECHTREK
myNGconnect.com For a
map and photos of the Pacific islands

 Maps and
Graphs

Digital
Library

Main Idea The first people to inhabit the Pacific Realm developed specific skills to adapt to life on the islands.

Several thousand years ago, ancient seafarers, or sea travelers, set sail from Southeast Asia, southern China, and Taiwan. They traveled over wide expanses of ocean and settled on islands in the Pacific Ocean.

Living on the Ocean

The islanders built canoes with attached floats, called **outrigger canoes**. These early settlers were experts at **navigation**, or the process of determining location and routes, as they traveled between islands. Seafarers used the patterns of stars to map their course. They also studied the flight patterns of birds, which indicated where land was located. Seafarers created stick charts, an early form of maps, from sticks, shells, and twine. Shells on the charts indicated islands and different shapes of sticks represented ocean currents.

△ **Critical Viewing** This stick chart is a type of map used by Pacific seafarers. How does this map differ from maps you use?

Over time, different cultures developed. On larger islands, inhabitants practiced advanced farming methods. On smaller islands, people supported themselves through fishing. Mountainous land on some islands kept groups of people isolated from one another and cultures developed independently. However, on

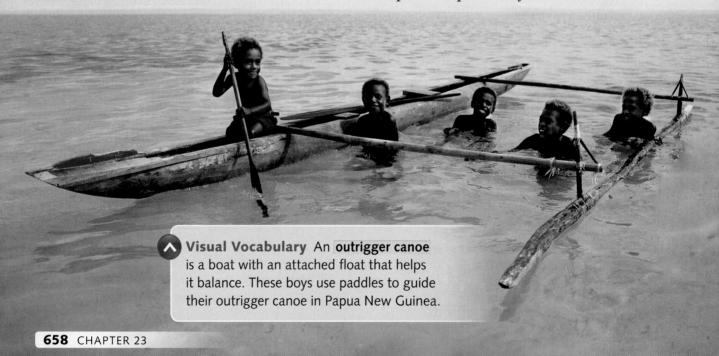

△ **Visual Vocabulary** An **outrigger canoe** is a boat with an attached float that helps it balance. These boys use paddles to guide their outrigger canoe in Papua New Guinea.

PACIFIC ISLANDS

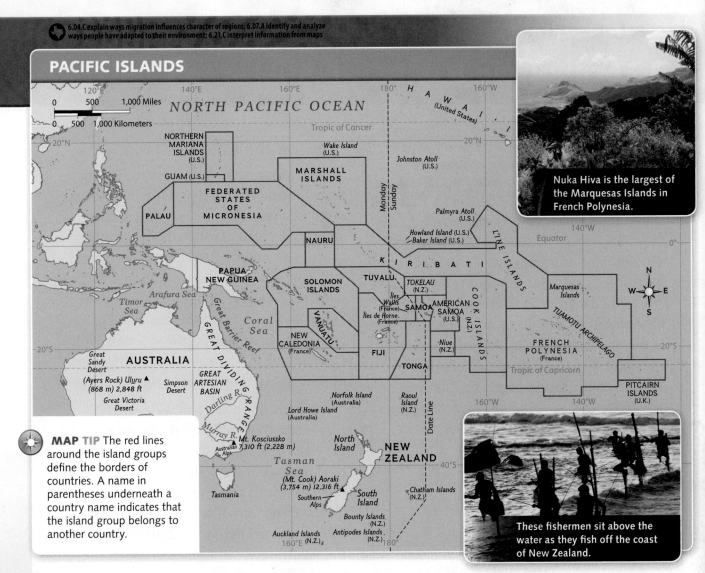

Nuka Hiva is the largest of the Marquesas Islands in French Polynesia.

MAP TIP The red lines around the island groups define the borders of countries. A name in parentheses underneath a country name indicates that the island group belongs to another country.

These fishermen sit above the water as they fish off the coast of New Zealand.

islands with few land barriers, people shared a similar language and culture. Sometimes groups of people moved from one island to another. In the 1100s, for example, the Maori people migrated from eastern Pacific islands to the North Island of New Zealand.

Western Influence

For the most part, seafaring societies remained isolated from Western contact. A few Europeans explored the Pacific islands as early as the 1500s, but most islanders did not encounter Europeans until the 1700s. Some Europeans traveled to this region in search of wealth or to spread Christianity. Other Europeans, such as British navigator **James Cook**, charted new territories.

During multiple voyages in the 1770s, Cook mapped islands in the Pacific, including New Zealand. In fact, the Cook Islands, which lie northeast of New Zealand, are named for James Cook.

Before You Move On
Summarize In what ways did the first people in the Pacific Realm adapt to the islands?

FORMATIVE ASSESSMENT
MAP LAB
GeoJournal

1. **Interpret Maps** The Pacific islands cover a broad expanse of ocean. In what way are the Pacific islands represented on this map?
2. **Identify** In the 1800s, most Pacific islands became colonies of Western countries. Based on the map, which islands remain possessions of other countries? How can you tell?

2.3 From Convicts to Colonists

TECHTREK
myNGconnect.com For images
of colonization in Australia

Digital
Library

Main Idea Convicts and other immigrants to Australia led the development of a new country.

Seventeen years after James Cook explored Australia's coast, British ships sailed for Australia. From 1788 to 1868, the British government sent **convicts**, or prisoners, to overseas colonies in order to decrease overcrowding in British prisons. When the American colonies established independence in 1776, the government needed a new place to send convicts. British colonization began in Australia as a way for the government to **transport**, or ship, its convicts to prisons overseas.

Photograph of a replica of James Cook's ship *Endeavour*

Settling the Colonies

Most transported convicts were young, healthy, and unmarried. Only 20 percent were women. Those who were married sometimes brought their families with them. The majority of convicts came from the working classes in England and Ireland. The government used convicts' skills and relied on their labor to build the colonies, including **New South Wales**. Convicts built roads, bridges, buildings, and farms as they served their sentences.

Though these settlers were British prisoners, they had certain freedoms. For example, many were allowed to live in their own homes and run their own businesses. At the end of their prison terms, freed convicts often remained in the colonies. Their contributions helped the Australian colonies to grow.

In 1831, the British set up a program for **assisted migration**. This program encouraged people to move to Australia by giving them financial help. Twenty years later, gold was discovered in Australia. This discovery drew many settlers to the continent including immigrants from China and the surrounding Pacific islands. An increased population and more available workers led to the growth

1788
Convict transportation begins; British establish colony at New South Wales.

1750

1800

1770
James Cook explores Australian coast.

1787
First Fleet sets sail for Australia.

1831
British policy of assisted migration begins.

★ 6.01.A trace characteristics of societies resulting from historical factors, colonization;
6.04.C explain ways human migration influences the character of places, regions;
6.21.B analyze by summarizing 6.21.C interpret information from timelines

of industries, such as manufacturing and mining. As more of the continent was explored, some settlers began sheep farming. Wool became an important product and export.

Australia's population quickly grew from 400,000 in 1850 to more than one million by 1860. Population growth and European settlement pushed Aborigines off lands that had belonged to their ancestors for many years.

Becoming A Country

In the 1890s, many Australians began to think that the colonies would benefit by becoming a single country. Colonists wrote a constitution and submitted it to the British government. In 1901, Great Britain approved the constitution, and the **Commonwealth of Australia** came into being. Though Australians now had their own government, they were still part of the British Empire. Today, Australia remains part of the British Commonwealth. Australia recognizes the British monarch as its head of state, but it is an independent country.

Before You Move On

Make Inferences In what ways did convicts lead the development of Australia?

 Critical Viewing Thomas Gosse painted *Founding of the Settlement of Port Jackson at Botany Bay in New South Wales* in 1799. What does his painting lead you to think about the settlement of Port Jackson?

FORMATIVE ASSESSMENT

READING LAB GeoJournal

1. **Summarize** According to your reading, why did the British begin to colonize Australia? What discovery in the 1800s attracted more immigrants to the continent?

2. **Movement** What migration patterns to and within the continent shaped Australia's history?

3. **Interpret Time Lines** Examine the time line. How many years did Great Britain transport convicts to Australia? Based on your reading, what other way did the British encourage migration to the continent?

Australian flag, designed in 1901

1851
Gold is discovered in Australia.

1868
Convict transportation is abolished.

1901
Australian colonies become Commonwealth of Australia.

1850

1900

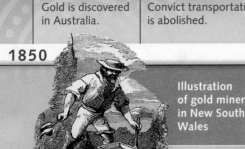

Illustration of gold miner in New South Wales

1890s
Australian colonies begin effort to become a single nation.

2.4

SECTION **2** HISTORY

NATIONAL GEOGRAPHIC

TECHTREK

myNGconnect.com For photos from
Enduring Voices and an Explorer Video Clip

Digital
Library

Exploring
Vanishing Languages

with David Harrison and Greg Anderson

> **Main Idea** Many languages spoken by indigenous people
> are endangered but efforts are underway to revitalize them.

The Importance of Language

Nearly 7,000 languages are spoken in the world today.
Language is a vital part of a people's identity. Each
one tells a great deal about the people who speak it.
Language **conveys**, or communicates, what is important to
a culture and helps pass along history, stories, and songs
from one generation to the next. A **generation** is a group
of individuals who are born and live about the same time.
Older generations share knowledge, like language, with
younger generations.

Today, many languages are disappearing. Languages
spoken by indigenous people are especially threatened.
Many languages have no written form and are spoken only
by a small group of people. As the children of these people
are exposed to other languages, they often stop speaking
their native language. Older members of the group are then
the only ones left who remember the language. With no
written record, the indigenous language disappears.

myNGconnect.com

For more on David
Harrison and Greg
Anderson in the
field today

David Harrison and Greg Anderson work
with Charlie Mangulda in Australia.

 Critical Viewing Harrison and Anderson interview Felix Andi in Papua New Guinea. Based on what you see here, what kinds of technology help linguists document endangered languages?

By 2100, more than half the world's languages may no longer exist. Some experts believe that on average a language is lost every two weeks. As these languages vanish, a wealth of information about history and culture goes with them. Because indigenous people often use language to share knowledge about native plants and animals, when their languages vanish, information about the natural world also disappears.

The Enduring Voices Project

National Geographic Fellows David Harrison and Greg Anderson are **linguists**, or language scientists. They founded National Geographic's **Enduring Voices Project** to study and document languages at risk. They work in many regions of the world. In 2010, in the foothills of the Himalayas in India, Harrison and Anderson documented a language previously unknown to researchers. Australia and Papua New Guinea are also among the places they identify as language hotspots because so many languages there are endangered. Over 800 languages are spoken in Papua New Guinea alone.

Harrison and Anderson use a variety of methods in their work. One is to interview the remaining speakers of the languages and make video and sound recordings. In addition to documenting the sounds and meanings of words, Harrison and Anderson gather valuable information about each group's history and culture. By studying these languages, they are also recording knowledge about the cultures.

Another method these linguists use is language revitalization. This involves supporting community-led efforts to bring vanishing languages back to life by teaching them to younger generations. Harrison and Anderson believe that educating young people is key to the survival of their languages.

Before You Move On
Summarize Why are many languages spoken by indigenous people endangered?

FORMATIVE ASSESSMENT

LANGUAGE LAB GeoJournal

1. **Understand Culture** Why is it important to revitalize indigenous languages?

2. **Make Inferences** Some words from indigenous languages have been adopted into English, such as *dingo* and *kangaroo*. Why might this be? Think about the special features of these animals before you answer.

3. **Analyze Visuals** Watch the Explorer Video Clip. Name at least two things you learned about the Enduring Voices Project. Then pose two questions you might ask David Harrison and Greg Anderson.

VOCABULARY

For each pair of vocabulary words, write one sentence that explains the connection between the two words.

1. indigenous; marsupial

> The kangaroo, which is indigenous to Australia, is a marsupial.

2. invasive species; extinct
3. coral reef; atoll
4. seafarer; outrigger canoe
5. convict; assisted migration
6. linguist; generation

MAIN IDEAS

7. In what ways are Australia, the Pacific Realm, and Antarctica similar? (Section 1.1)
8. Why does the region have so many plants and animals unlike anywhere else in the world? (Section 1.2)
9. How were invasive species introduced in the region? (Section 1.3)
10. What two geologic processes created the Pacific islands? (Section 1.4)
11. In what ways are coral reefs around the world endangered? (Section 1.5)
12. How did migration and location shape the history of the Aborigines? (Section 2.1)
13. Why might Western influences be limited in the Pacific islands? (Section 2.2)
14. What groups helped develop the continent of Australia? (Section 2.3)
15. What steps are linguists taking to preserve vanishing languages? (Section 2.4)

GEOGRAPHY

ANALYZE THE ESSENTIAL QUESTION

How did geographic isolation influence the development of this region?

Critical Thinking: Summarize

16. Why is Australia called an "island continent"?
17. How did indigenous plants and animals develop in this region?
18. In what ways do invasive species threaten the indigenous plants and animals in the region?
19. What physical features make some Pacific islands better suited for farming than others?

INTERPRET MAPS

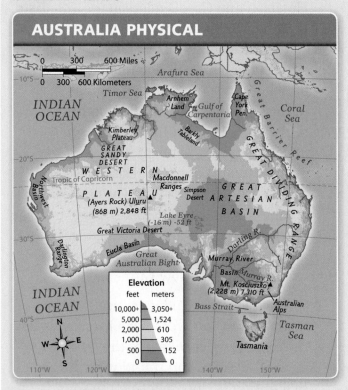

20. **Identify** What are the names of Australia's deserts? In what part of the continent do they lie?
21. **Location** In what sea is the Great Barrier Reef located? How is the name of the sea related to the reef?

HISTORY

ANALYZE THE ESSENTIAL QUESTION

How did geographic isolation shape the history of Australia and the Pacific Realm?

Critical Thinking: Draw Conclusions

22. In what ways did conflicts over land impact Aborigines in Australia?

23. What methods did ancient seafarers use to deal with the challenges of life on isolated islands in the Pacific Ocean?

24. Why might the British government have chosen Australia as a place to transport convicts?

25. On mountainous Pacific islands, how did physical features play a role in the establishment of multiple languages?

INTERPRET TABLES

COMPARING LANGUAGE USE IN AUSTRALIA AND PAPUA NEW GUINEA		
	Australia	Papua New Guinea
Percentage of people speaking English	78.5	2.0
Number of indigenous languages spoken	145	860

Sources: CIA World Factbook, 2010; Australian Government of Foreign Affairs and Trade 2010; BBC, 2010

26. **Compare and Contrast** Based on this table, in which country does the majority of the population speak English?

27. **Make Generalizations** Based on this table and what you have read, in which country—Australia or Papua New Guinea—did European settlers have a larger influence on indigenous populations?

ACTIVE OPTIONS

Synthesize the Essential Questions by completing the activites below.

28. **Write a Letter** Imagine that you are a settler in 1851 who has arrived in Australia to search for gold. Write a letter to a family member back in England, describing what you observed when you arrived. Explain whether you think this person should join you. **Send your letter to a friend and ask if it painted a clear picture of Australia.**

> **Writing Tips**
> • Address your letter to a particular person.
> • Draw on what you have read about Australia to describe what the country is like.

Go to **Student Resources** for Guided Writing support.

TECHTREK   myNGconnect.com
For photos of the region

29. **Create a Visual Presentation** Use the **Digital Library** or other online sources to create a visual presentation of this region. Choose a photo to go with each of the following statements. Describe your photos with additional research you conduct.

> • Australia is home to many unusual plants and animals.
> • Thousands of living creatures inhabit the Great Barrier Reef.
> • Some Pacific islanders still practice a traditional way of life.
> • Researchers work to revitalize endangered indigenous languages.

CHAPTER 24

AUSTRALIA, THE PACIFIC REALM & ANTARCTICA TODAY

PREVIEW THE CHAPTER

Essential Question How are Australia, the Pacific Realm, and Antarctica becoming connected to the rest of the world?

SECTION 1 • CULTURE

KEY VOCABULARY

- urban
- salinization
- immigration
- labor force
- oral tradition
- emigrate
- ice shelf
- scientific station

ACADEMIC VOCABULARY

deplete, maintain

TERMS & NAMES

- Sydney
- Polynesian Triangle
- Cook Islands
- Charles Wilkes
- Richard Byrd
- Antarctic Treaty

Essential Question What new economic patterns are emerging in the region?

SECTION 2 • GOVERNMENT & ECONOMICS

KEY VOCABULARY

- alliance
- free trade agreement
- reserve
- assimilation
- adventure tourism
- glacier
- crevasse
- renewable energy
- geothermal energy

ACADEMIC VOCABULARY

reclaim, lucrative

TERMS & NAMES

- Papua New Guinea
- Samoa
- Asia-Pacific Economic Cooperation (APEC)

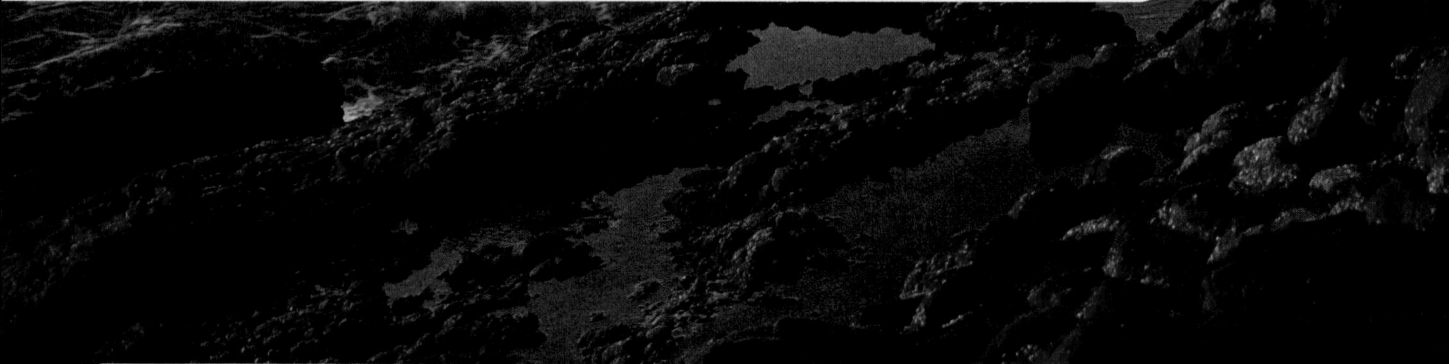

TECHTREK FOR THIS CHAPTER

Student eEdition

Maps and Graphs

Interactive Whiteboard GeoActivities

Digital Library

Go to **myNGconnect.com** for more on Australia, the Pacific Realm, and Antarctica.

Surfers study the waves at Piha, on the western coast of North Island, New Zealand.

667

1.1 From Ranch to City

TECHTREK

myNGconnect.com For a map and photos of
ranches and cities in Australia

Maps and Graphs

Digital Library

> **Main Idea** Most Australians live in coastal cities, and many have migrated from rural areas.

Today, Australia is one of the world's most **urban** countries—most people live in cities or nearby suburbs. Lately, even farmers and ranchers whose families have lived in rural areas for generations are choosing to relocate. Economic pressures in farming and ranching communities are pushing people toward cities.

A Dry Climate Turns Drier

Much of Australia's climate is arid. About 60 percent of the continent receives fewer than 10 inches of rain per year. The dry climate of Australia's interior makes farming and ranching difficult. Farmers have mainly depended on irrigation, rather than rainfall, to water their crops. Sheep and cattle ranchers, whose livestock graze in dry areas, also depend on irrigation.

However, irrigation comes with problems of its own. Years of continuous irrigation have helped cause **salinization**, which occurs when salt accumulates in soil. Too much irrigation into normally dry land raises the natural water table and causes salts to rise to the surface. Crops cannot grow in this salty soil. Low rainfall and high evaporation rates make soil in the interior of Australia prone to salinization.

In 2002, the longest drought in Australia's history began. Increased demands **depleted**, or drained, major irrigation sources such as the Murray and Darling rivers in New South Wales. The drought caused severe water shortages and the amount of water allowed for irrigation was greatly reduced. Farmers could not water their crops and ranchers sold entire herds of sheep and cattle at auction.

> **Critical Viewing** Ranchers in New South Wales herd sheep for auction. What can you infer about the conditions in which these ranchers work?

The Pull to the Cities

In Australia's interior, few alternatives to farming and ranching exist. Faced with the combination of drought and poor soil, farmers and ranchers have had to make hard choices. Many are moving to the cities on the coasts.

Families are also drawn to urban areas because of more plentiful goods and services, including better schools for their children. Today, nearly 75 percent of the population lives in one of five coastal cities: **Sydney,** Melbourne, Brisbane, Perth, and Adelaide.

Before You Move On
Summarize Why do most Australians live in or near cities?

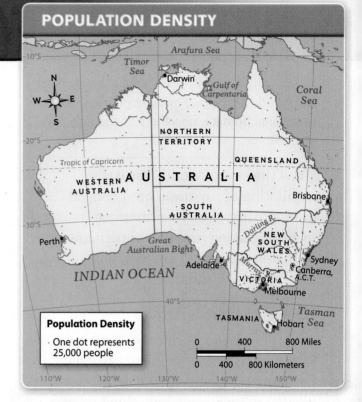

POPULATION DENSITY

Population Density
One dot represents 25,000 people

Critical Viewing Sydney is located on Australia's southeastern coast. Based on what you see in the photo, what might Sydney offer that might not be available in Australia's interior?

FORMATIVE ASSESSMENT
MAP LAB
GeoJournal

1. **Location** Use the map to identify the locations of Australia's five largest cities. Which of those cities is most isolated?

2. **Interpret Maps** Locate South Australia and New South Wales on the map. In which state do more people live? What advantage might New South Wales have over South Australia, in terms of access to fresh water?

1.2 Immigration to Australia

TECHTREK
myNGconnect.com For photos
of Australia's immigrant communities

Digital
Library

Main Idea Australia includes people who have come from a wide variety of countries and cultures.

Since the end of World War II, the population of Australia has changed dramatically. A marked increase in **immigration**, or moving permanently from one country to another, has diversified the country.

Postwar Immigration

After World War II, refugees from war-torn Europe sought new lands to call home. At the same time, the Australian government wanted to increase population and expand its available **labor force**, or the number of people available to work. The government loosened immigration restrictions, increasing the number of immigrants permitted entry. Both Australia and its new settlers benefited from the decision.

Between 1950 and 1960, Australia's labor force increased by 60 percent due to immigration. New arrivals found jobs in postwar construction projects and other industries. Immigrants from Poland, Germany, Hungary, Greece, Italy, and other European countries changed the ethnic makeup of Australian cities. Some immigrants did not speak English and introduced their native languages to Australia. Many immigrants opened businesses that sold food and goods from their native countries.

> **Critical Viewing** Young men carry a colorful dragon in this traditional Chinese New Year's parade in Sydney, Australia. From what you can see in the photo, in what ways does this parade maintain cultural traditions?

6.01.A trace characteristics of societies resulting from historical factors (immigration);
6.04.C explain ways migration influences places and regions; 6.15.D analyze experiences
of diverse groups, multicultural societies; 6.21.F use mathematical skills to interpret graphs

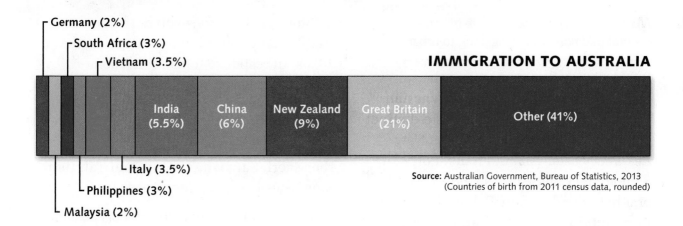

IMMIGRATION TO AUSTRALIA

Germany (2%)

South Africa (3%)

Vietnam (3.5%)

India (5.5%)

China (6%)

New Zealand (9%)

Great Britain (21%)

Other (41%)

Italy (3.5%)

Philippines (3%)

Malaysia (2%)

Source: Australian Government, Bureau of Statistics, 2013
(Countries of birth from 2011 census data, rounded)

Australia's Diversity

In the 1970s, new groups began to immigrate to Australia. For example, many refugees from the war in Vietnam fled by boat to the continent. Over the next few decades, immigrants from other Asian countries, including Japan, China, and India, relocated to Australia in search of job opportunities. Currently, about 33 percent of Australia's population is of Asian descent.

Many immigrants from New Zealand, the Pacific islands, Canada, and the United States have also moved to Australia since the 1970s. Unlike the early years of settlement, fewer of those who resettle in Australia each year come from Great Britain. Today, nearly one-quarter of Australians were born in other countries. English remains the official language, but more than 100 languages are spoken, including Chinese, Greek, and Italian.

Diversity is especially reflected in Australia's cities. Nearly 40 percent of new immigrants now settle in Sydney.

As Australia's largest city, Sydney is an attractive point of entry into the country. Melbourne, Australia's second largest city, boasts the largest Greek population in the world outside Greece. Brisbane and Perth receive large numbers of immigrants from Asia and Pacific island countries.

Before You Move On

Monitor Comprehension In what ways has immigration to Australia changed over the years?

FORMATIVE ASSESSMENT

DATA LAB — GeoJournal

1. **Movement** What percentage of immigrants to Australia arrived from the Asian countries included on the graph? Which two Asian countries represent the largest percentage of immigrants to Australia and why?

2. **Understand Culture** What contributions have diverse groups had on Australia's society? In a paragraph, analyze the experiences of two groups.

3. **Explain** What world events in the 20th century prompted different waves of immigration to Australia? What were different groups of immigrants seeking?

1.3 Polynesian Cultures

TECHTREK

my NGconnect.com For photos
of Polynesian culture today

 Digital
Library

> **Main Idea** Polynesian people maintain their cultural traditions while migrating to urban areas.

Polynesia spans a vast area in the South Pacific known as the **Polynesian Triangle**. This triangle captures a distinct Polynesian culture that includes New Zealand, Easter Island, French Polynesia, Samoa, the Cook Islands, and hundreds of other islands. Many Polynesians try to **maintain**, or preserve and carry on, their traditional cultures.

Traditional Polynesia

Historically, maintaining cultural practices was one function of the Polynesian family. Several generations of a single family lived together. Older members of the family taught younger members the arts of canoe-building, fishing, and navigation.

Polynesians have maintained traditional cultural practices and beliefs through the **oral tradition**, or passing stories by word of mouth from generation to generation. Polynesian stories explain how the universe was created and celebrate the connection between humans and the natural world.

Storytelling also involves the use of traditional Polynesian languages. In the 1970s, in response to fears that some languages were disappearing, many Polynesian schools established language programs that taught only traditional languages. Today, knowledge and use of the Maori, Samoan, Tongan, and Tahitian languages is more widespread.

In addition to storytelling, Polynesians have rich traditions in dance, music, and visual art forms such as woodcarving and basket-weaving. These art forms have provided ways for Polynesians to maintain and pass on their cultures. Dance, music, and visual arts are important elements of traditional Polynesian festivals, such as the Festival of Pacific Arts, held every four years in a different Polynesian country.

Polynesia Today

Like Australia, Polynesia has become increasingly urban since the 1960s. A lack of economic opportunities has pushed some Polynesians to migrate from rural villages to urban areas. Cities that have grown because of rural migration include Apia in Samoa, Pago Pago in American Samoa, and Nuku'alofa in Tonga.

Many Polynesians have **emigrated**, or left their home country, to live in other countries, including New Zealand and the United States. Between 1970 and 2000, emigration from Samoa to New Zealand doubled. Samoans emigrated to seek jobs and educational opportunities.

The **Cook Islands** provide examples of both rural to urban migration and emigration from Polynesia. Because of economic pressures, Cook Islanders have migrated from the countryside to the cities. Today, nearly 75 percent of Cook Islanders live in cities. Many others have emigrated to New Zealand to seek better economic futures.

Before You Move On
Summarize In what ways have Polynesian people maintained cultural traditions?

FORMATIVE ASSESSMENT
PHOTO LAB GeoJournal

1. **Analyze Visuals** Based on the photo, describe the vegetation and the island's physical features.

2. **Understand Culture** How have cultural expressions in Polynesia been influenced by the past?

3. **Movement** How has migration influenced the region?

4. **Explain** What are different ways in which Polynesians migrate? What are different reasons for migration? Organize your ideas:

POLYNESIAN CULTURES	
Form of Migration	Reasons Why

Men on Olosega Island in American Samoa harvest leaves of the panandus plant, which will be dried and woven into mats.

1.4 Human Footprint in Antarctica

TECHTREK
myNGconnect.com For an
online map and photos of Antarctica

Maps and Graphs

Digital Library

Main Idea People all over the world have been interested in Antarctica for hundreds of years.

Antarctica lies on the South Pole and has one of the most extreme climates on Earth. No humans live there permanently, but people have left their "footprint" through exploration and research.

Early Explorations

As early as 1773, Captain James Cook, a British naval captain, began looking for a southern continent. Ice blocked his southward journey. In 1820, British and Russian explorers were the first to report sighting land. American **Charles Wilkes** surveyed a 1,500-mile stretch of coastline in the late 1830s. His observations confirmed that Antarctica is a continent. Later explorers investigated Antarctica's thick sheets of ice and the ranges of the Transantarctic Mountains. They also explored the continent's coastal **ice shelves**, or floating sheets of ice that are attached to a landmass.

Twentieth century explorers made further discoveries. One dramatic event involved the race to the South Pole. In 1911, Robert Falcon Scott, from Great Britain, and Roald Amundsen, from Norway, each led expeditions to the South Pole. Amundsen's team reached the South Pole first. Though Scott's expedition

> **Critical Viewing** Researchers return to their station at the South Pole in Antarctica. Based on what you can see here, what preparations do people make in order to work in this extreme environment?

also reached the South Pole, none of its members survived the months-long journey back to base camp.

From 1929 through the 1940s, National Geographic supported American naval officer **Richard Byrd** as he explored the continent, both on land and by air. He studied its ice, rocks, and minerals and made observations about Earth's magnetism. Byrd's team also photographed Antarctica's coastline and discovered 26 new islands.

An International Treaty

By 1958, scientists from several different countries had built more than 50 **scientific stations**, or places to carry out research. Seven of these countries claimed sections of Antarctica as their own. However, some countries, including the United States, did not recognize the claims as legal. Then in 1959, 12 countries signed the **Antarctic Treaty.** According to the treaty, the continent can be used only for peaceful purposes. Any scientific discoveries must be shared internationally.

Today, Antarctica continues to serve as a center of research and global cooperation. One study, called the International Polar Year 2007–2008,

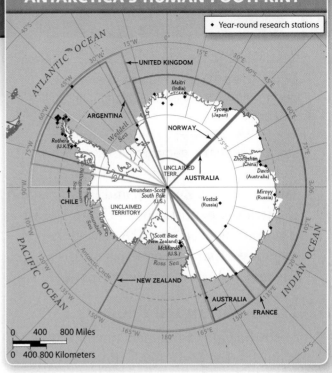

ANTARCTICA'S HUMAN FOOTPRINT

◆ Year-round research stations

involved scientists from more than 60 countries. Working together on more than 200 research projects, scientists collected data on thinning ice sheets in order to determine their effect on global sea levels. Studying changes in Antarctica helps scientists understand changes in other parts of the world.

Before You Move On

Make Inferences What benefit to contemporary societies was achieved by the group forming the Antarctic Treaty?

FORMATIVE ASSESSMENT

MAP LAB   GeoJournal

1. **Location** According to the map, which oceans surround Antarctica? From what central point do international claims originate?

2. **Interpret Maps** Based on the map, what country claims the largest area of Antarctica? What might explain the sizes of the South American and Australian claims?

3. **Explain** Why can no single country claim Antarctica as its own?

2.1 New Trade Patterns

TECHTREK

myNGconnect.com For a map and
photos of exported goods from the region

 Maps and
Graphs

 Digital
Library

Main Idea Trade is a source of economic growth for Australia, New Zealand, and the Pacific Realm.

For many years, geographic isolation and other factors made it difficult for Australia, New Zealand, and Pacific island countries to export goods to countries in other parts of the world. As the global economy expands, countries in this region are developing new trade partners.

Trade Within the Region

Australia gained independence from Great Britain in the early 1900s. It continued to rely on Great Britain as its sole trading partner for several decades afterward. By the late 1900s, however, Australia began to increase trade with other countries.

As the largest and most populous country in this region, Australia serves as an economic and trade anchor, or hub, for surrounding countries. Australia, New Zealand, Papua New Guinea, and the other countries in the Pacific Realm have built trade partnerships with one another.

These trade partnerships benefit the entire region economically. For example, **Papua New Guinea** exports gold and coffee to Australia. **Samoa** exports cocoa beans to New Zealand. Regional economic development has strengthened ties among countries and has given the region a stronger global presence.

New Global Partnerships

This region's increased participation in the world economy is due in part to an organization called the **Asia-Pacific Economic Cooperation (APEC)**. Founded in 1989, APEC's goal is to strengthen economic ties and trade **alliances**, or partnerships, among its members. Three member countries—Australia, New Zealand, and Papua New Guinea—are located in this region. Other APEC member countries border the Pacific Ocean, including China, Japan, Mexico, the United States, Chile, and Peru. APEC alliances help these countries compete in the global economy.

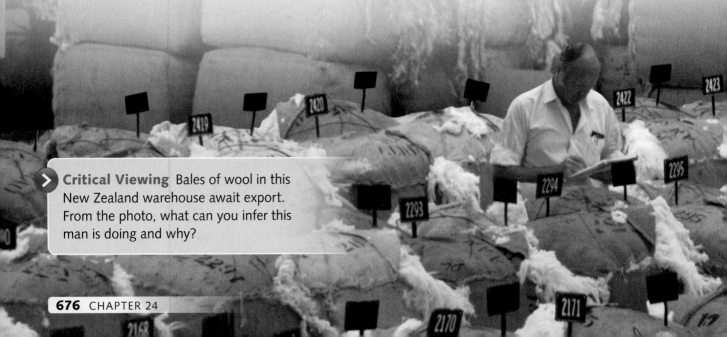

> **Critical Viewing** Bales of wool in this New Zealand warehouse await export. From the photo, what can you infer this man is doing and why?

APEC MEMBER COUNTRIES

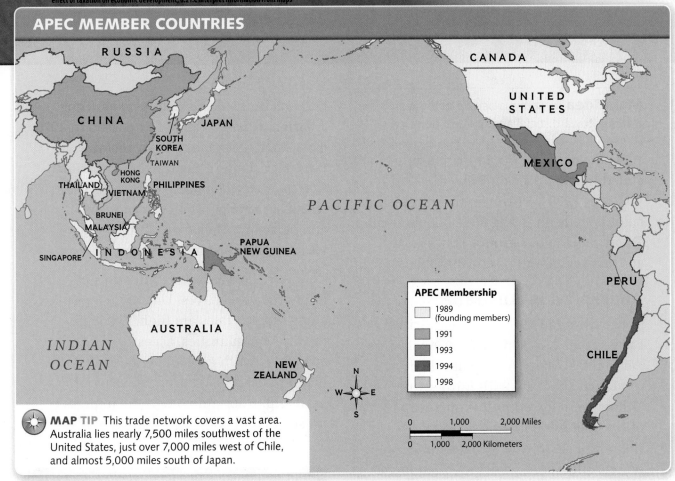

APEC Membership
- 1989 (founding members)
- 1991
- 1993
- 1994
- 1998

0   1,000   2,000 Miles
0   1,000   2,000 Kilometers

MAP TIP This trade network covers a vast area. Australia lies nearly 7,500 miles southwest of the United States, just over 7,000 miles west of Chile, and almost 5,000 miles south of Japan.

One of APEC's main achievements has been to establish free trade agreements among member countries. **Free trade agreements** are treaties between two or more countries that encourage trade by limiting tariffs, or taxes, on that trade. Since 1989, APEC has helped form more than 30 free trade agreements.

Before You Move On

Monitor Comprehension In what ways have trade alliances helped this region become competitive in the global economy?

FORMATIVE ASSESSMENT

MAP LAB

GeoJournal

1. **Interpret Maps** Of the founding APEC member countries represented on the map, which are located in North America? Which APEC countries are located in Asia?

2. **Make Inferences** According to the map, when did Australia, New Zealand, and Papua New Guinea join APEC? Based on your reading, in what ways might APEC membership benefit their economies?

3. **Evaluate** In what ways might limiting tariffs on trade between countries help strengthen trade alliances?

2.2 Rights for Indigenous People

TECHTREK

myNGconnect.com For current
events in the region

⊞ Maps and
Graphs

☑ Digital
Library

> **Main Idea** Indigenous people in the region are working toward social and political equality.

As you have read, direct British rule ended in Australia and New Zealand in the early 1900s. However, the effects of colonial rule on indigenous people remain. Today, indigenous groups continue to address social and political problems.

Aborigines in Australia

In the 18th and 19th centuries, British settlers took lands away from Australia's Aborigines. Many Aborigines died in violent conflicts with Europeans. Others were forced to live on **reserves**, or land set aside for native people. Colonial British rulers enacted laws and policies that promoted, and often forced, assimilation. **Assimilation** is a process in which a minority group is pressured to give up its cultural practices and be absorbed into another society's culture.

One way in which the British tried to force Aborigines to assimilate was by separating Aboriginal children from their parents. Children were placed in mission schools and homes. This practice took place from the early 1900s until the 1960s. An estimated 100,000 children were separated from their families, most of them permanently. They are referred to as the "Stolen Generation."

In the 1960s, the Aborigines' struggle to gain basic civil rights intensified. By 1962, Aborigines were able to vote in national elections for the first time. Five years later, they were finally included as citizens in the Australian census. The Aboriginal Land Rights Act passed in 1976 gave Aborigines the right to **reclaim**, or take back, land in the Northern Territory that had once belonged to their ancestors. In 2008, the Australian government apologized for the years of unjust treatment toward the Aborigines.

Today, Aborigines are still working to improve their lives. Unemployment and illiteracy rates are high. Especially in rural communities, access to adequate health care and education is unpredictable. After many years of hardship, Aborigines continue to press for social and political equality.

⌃ **Critical Viewing** Lowitja O'Donoghue, a member of the Stolen Generation, and Australia's Prime Minister Kevin Rudd meet in 2008. What does the photo lead you to think about indigenous peoples' reaction to the government's apology?

Maori in New Zealand

The Maori (MOW ree) are the indigenous people of New Zealand. They arrived from Polynesia in the 1300s and were New Zealand's only inhabitants until the British arrived in the late 1700s. Like the Aborigines in Australia, the Maori struggled with the British for control of their land. Although the 1840 Treaty of Waitangi (WY tahng ee) granted the Maori legal and land rights, it was largely ignored for more than 100 years. The Maori people have organized politically, and, like Australia's Aborigines, have had some success achieving civil rights and reclaiming lands.

Before You Move On

Make Inferences In what ways are indigenous people in the region regaining social and political equality?

FORMATIVE ASSESSMENT

READING LAB   GeoJournal

1. **Summarize** What is assimilation, and how did the British try to force this process on Aborigines in Australia?

2. **Make Inferences** In 1967, the Australian government counted Aborigines in the national census for the first time. What can you infer about how this inclusion might help Aborigines gain social and political equality?

3. **Compare** In what ways were the experiences of the Maori and the Aborigines similar?

Critical Viewing Maori protesters gather in New Zealand to demand that the Treaty of Waitangi be followed. What can you infer about the strategy these protesters are using?

2.3 Adventure Tourism

> **Main Idea** Tourism that involves physical
> activity and adventure is a major industry
> in the region.

Australia, the Pacific Realm, and
Antarctica are frequent destinations for
adventure tourism. **Adventure tourism**
takes travelers to remote areas and
involves active enjoyment of the
physical environment.

Adventure Activities

New Zealand and Australia are popular
destinations for adventure tourists. In
New Zealand, rock climbing, mountain
biking, and cave exploration are a few of
the ways people enjoy the rugged terrain.
Adventurers explore New Zealand's
interior rivers and lakes by rafting,
kayaking, and canoeing. Whale-watching
expeditions provide opportunities to see
the many different species that inhabit the
waters off New Zealand's coast.

People seeking active enjoyment of
unusual physical environments also travel
to Australia—particularly to its Great
Barrier Reef, which draws millions of
tourists every year. In 2009, more than
two million people visited this natural
wonder. Activities on the Great Barrier
Reef include snorkeling, scuba diving,
fishing, and exploring reef waters in glass-
bottomed boats.

In Antarctica, hikers trek across
glaciers, which are large masses of ice
and packed snow. Expert guides help
hikers cross dramatic **crevasses**, or deep,
open cracks in glaciers. Visitors to
Antarctica can also observe emperor

penguins, leopard seals, and other
Antarctic birds and animals in their
natural habitat.

Economic Benefits

In recent years, adventure tourism has
become a **lucrative**, or profitable, industry.
People work as expert adventure guides
and as drivers on tours. Others find jobs
in hotels, stores, airports, and restaurants
or on cruise ships that regularly carry
thousands of people to the region.

In the Pacific islands, even those
not directly involved with adventure
tourism often benefit from it. Some local
residents make a living creating and
selling traditional baskets, mats, and
masks. Other islanders earn income
by entertaining guests with traditional
feasts. Some critics worry that tourism as
an industry might devalue, or trivialize,
islanders' cultures and ways of life.
However, those who support the industry
focus on the opportunity to bring more
income into their economies.

Before You Move On

Monitor Comprehension In what ways is this
region an ideal destination for adventure tourism?

FORMATIVE ASSESSMENT

PHOTO LAB GeoJournal

1. **Human-Environment Interaction** Review
   each photo. In what ways do adventure tourists
   interact with the environment in this region?

2. **Define** Tell how adventure tourism is a
   service industry. With a partner, discuss and
   list the jobs needed to run adventure tourism
   businesses.

Visual Vocabulary A **crevasse** is a deep, open crack in a glacier. With the help of a guide, this group is crossing a crevasse on Franz Josef Glacier, South Island, New Zealand.

Critical Viewing Paramotoring, a form of motorized flying, is popular on South Island. *Parachute* and *motor* combine to make the word. What might a paramotorist see when flying over this terrain?

Scuba divers use an underwater platform to work on diving skills in the waters of Australia's Great Barrier Reef.

2.4 New Zealand Today

TECHTREK

myNGconnect.com For a map
and photos of New Zealand today

 Maps and
Graphs

Digital
Library

Main Idea New Zealand protects its culture and environment while developing new uses for natural resources.

For some countries, the desire to improve their economies sometimes means choosing between commercial uses of the land and protecting their cultures and natural environments. New Zealand has been able to balance these concerns.

Preserving Maori Culture

As you have read, the Maori were New Zealand's first inhabitants. During the British colonial period, many Maori groups lost ancestral lands. Reclaiming

△ **Critical Viewing** This sculpture in Auckland City is a modern representation of a traditional Maori entry gate. Based on the photo, in what ways does New Zealand balance tradition with modernity?

lands that once belonged to their ancestors continues to be a key issue for the Maori. In addition to protecting land for future generations, the Maori people are embracing traditional customs in order to preserve their culture. They have renewed a focus on traditional arts and ceremonies as well as their native language. Maori-speaking elders and parents worked with the New Zealand government to establish language immersion schools for Maori children. These schools use the Maori language exclusively throughout the school day. In 1987, the government made the Maori language one of New Zealand's official languages.

Energy for the Future

New Zealand has also made a special effort to preserve its natural heritage. The government has established many national parks and wildlife preserves. In fact, nearly 30 percent of the land is protected by the government.

Another way New Zealand protects its environment is by producing energy from solar, water, and wind sources. This kind of energy is not depleted by its use and is called **renewable energy**. One-third of energy consumed in New Zealand comes from renewable sources and that percentage is expected to increase.

One source of renewable energy in New Zealand is geothermal energy. **Geothermal energy** is heat energy from within the earth that can be turned into electricity. Geothermal reservoirs of hot water and steam are common in New Zealand because the country lies in an active volcanic zone. Geothermal energy is low-cost and non-polluting and provides around 13 percent of New Zealand's electricity needs.

New Zealand is considered an environment-friendly country because of its foward-thinking development of renewable energy sources. Through the establishment of wind farms, geothermal plants, and hydroelectric power stations, New Zealand is forging a new path for sustainable energy production.

Before You Move On
Summarize In what ways is New Zealand preserving its culture and its environment?

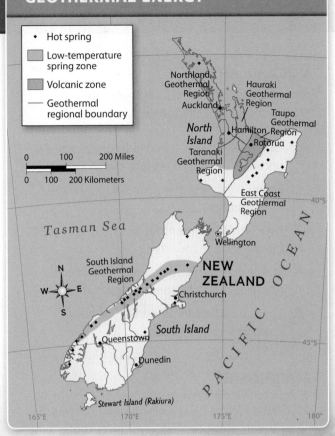

GEOTHERMAL ENERGY

- Hot spring
- Low-temperature spring zone
- Volcanic zone
- Geothermal regional boundary

FORMATIVE ASSESSMENT

MAP LAB

GeoJournal

1. **Interpret Maps** Geothermal energy zones are categorized by temperature. In what zone is the Taupo Geothermal Region? Based on the map, how might geothermal sites on South Island be described?

2. **Make Predictions** Most people live on New Zealand's North Island. What cities might benefit most from future development of geothermal energy plants?

Critical Viewing This geothermal pool is located near Rotorua. What can you infer from the photo about the temperature of the water?

VOCABULARY

On your paper, write the vocabulary word that completes each of the following sentences.

1. One reason farmers move to urban areas is because _____ is ruining the soil.

2. Polynesians pass along stories and history through their _____.

3. APEC member countries have _____ with other member countries.

4. In Antarctica, many different countries have set up _____ to conduct research.

5. _____ provides 10 percent of New Zealand's energy needs.

MAIN IDEAS

6. What factors have caused many Australian farmers and ranchers to move to urban areas? (Section 1.1)

7. In what ways have populations of immigrants to Australia changed over the years? (Section 1.2)

8. What cultural traditions are Polynesians preserving? (Section 1.3)

9. What does the Antarctic Treaty state about the use of Antarctica? (Section 1.4)

10. In what way have Australia and the Pacific islands strengthened their presence in the global economy? (Section 2.1)

11. What are many indigenous people trying to reclaim? (Section 2.2)

12. In what ways does adventure tourism highlight the region's diverse physical features? (Sections 2.3)

13. Name three things the New Zealand government has done to protect traditional culture and preserve the environment. (Section 2.4)

CULTURE

ANALYZE THE ESSENTIAL QUESTION

How are Australia, the Pacific Realm, and Antarctica becoming more connected to the rest of the world?

Critical Thinking: Make Inferences

14. In what ways might Australia's long drought impact trade with other countries?

15. What characteristics attract immigrants from around the world to Australia?

16. How might rural life change as a result of current migration patterns?

INTERPRET MAPS

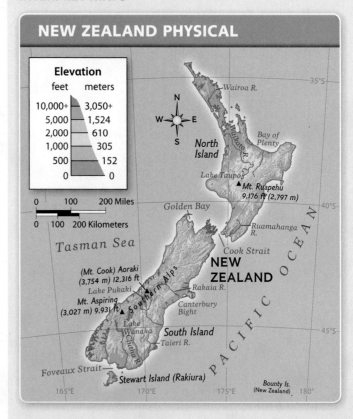

NEW ZEALAND PHYSICAL

17. **Place** What two main islands make up New Zealand? Which island has higher elevations?

18. **Region** Unlike Australia, New Zealand does not have extensive deserts. Instead, what physical feature can you infer from the map legend covers much of New Zealand?

6.03.B pose and answer questions about geographic distributions, on charts; 6.03.C compare various countries using data from charts; 6.03.D create charts depicting aspects of countries; 6.05.A identify and explain geographic factors responsible for economic activities; 6.21.B analyze by drawing conclusions, inferences; 6.21.C interpret information from maps, graphs

GOVERNMENT & ECONOMICS

ANALYZE THE ESSENTIAL QUESTION

What new economic patterns are emerging in the region?

Critical Thinking: Draw Conclusions

19. How might new trade partnerships among different countries benefit the entire region?

20. What energy sources in New Zealand might represent the energy of the future?

21. In what ways might adventure tourism benefit countries in the region economically?

INTERPRET GRAPHS

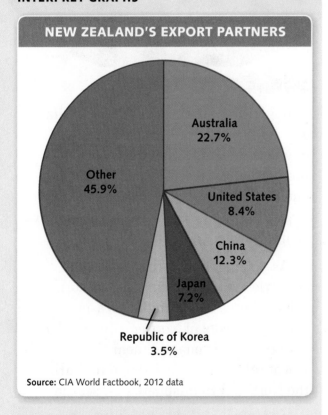

NEW ZEALAND'S EXPORT PARTNERS

Australia 22.7%

Other 45.9%

United States 8.4%

China 12.3%

Japan 7.2%

Republic of Korea 3.5%

Source: CIA World Factbook, 2012 data

22. Analyze Data What percentage of New Zealand's exports go to Australia? How does that number compare with Japan?

23. Identify Of the export partners shown on the pie chart, which are APEC members? Why might Australia represent nearly one-quarter of New Zealand's exports?

ACTIVE OPTIONS

Synthesize the Essential Questions by completing the activities below.

24. **Write a Travelogue** Imagine that you are a magazine writer trying to persuade your readers to visit one of the places you learned about in this chapter. Write two paragraphs that describe the features of the place and why it is a good choice for a vacation. **Share your paragraphs with a partner or a friend.**

> **Writing Tips**
> • Describe how your readers might travel to the location, and how long the trip might take.
> • Include specific details about important places travelers should make a point to visit.
> • Highlight at least one lesser-known attraction.

Go to **Student Resources** for Guided Writing support.

25. **Create Charts** Make a chart like the one below to compare information about three Pacific islands. Use online sources to gather the data. Then, with a partner, create three questions to ask other students.

	PAPUA NEW GUINEA	SAMOA	FRENCH POLYNESIA
Population			
Urban Population			
Square miles of land			
Exports			
Imports			

Pastures and Crops

myNGconnect.com For research
links about land use

Maps and
Graphs

Student
Resources

Australia's grasslands have been used for many years to support both ranching and agriculture. Countries with large, open grasslands use them for similar purposes, including grazing livestock and growing a variety of crops.

Decisions about land use are influenced by many factors, such as climate, crop yield, and sustainability. In most countries, mixed use of grasslands is more common than devoting land solely to ranching or agriculture. Comparing two countries, Australia and Argentina, reveals similarities in how these two countries use grasslands.

Compare

- Argentina
- Australia
- China
- India
- New Zealand
- Ukraine
- United States

GRAZING

Grasslands provide grazing, or feeding, grounds for ranch livestock. Cattle, horses, and sheep are the most common ranch livestock. Other livestock on ranches around the world include goats, alpacas, emus, ostriches, bison, deer, and elk.

Ranching industries have been in place in Australia and Argentina since the 1880s. Cattle were not native to either continent. European settlers imported cattle during the colonial periods.

Australia and Argentina are top beef producers today. Australia's beef industry is export-oriented, while much of Argentina's beef is consumed domestically. Each country faces challenges with its beef industry. Drought on pasture lands in Australia prompted ranchers to reduce herds. In Argentina, beef producers struggle with government policies that limit how much beef can be exported.

GROWING

Though their climates differ, Australia and Argentina are both top exporters of wheat. Most of Australia's wheat production is located in the southern and southwestern parts of the country. Argentina's fertile Pampas is a productive center of wheat cultivation.

As you can see on the map, both countries are located in the Southern Hemisphere. Their growing season occurs opposite of Northern Hemisphere countries. This enables them to make wheat sales on the global market during the Northern Hemisphere's off-season.

Around the world, demand for food production is increasing as the population climbs. In order to increase grain production, both Australia and Argentina are beginning to use marginal, or less desirable, lands to plant more wheat and other crops.

6.03.B pose and answer questions about geographic distributions; 6.03.C compare various countries using data from databases, charts, graphs, maps; 6.04.F identify locations of world countries; 6.05.A identify and explain geographic factors responsible for economic activities; 6.10.C identify effects of government regulation; 6.20.C make predictions about future impacts from scientific discoveries or technological innovations; 6.21.C organize and interpret information from outlines; 6.22.B incorporate main and supporting idea in written communication

Grassland Use Around the World

Major Crops and Livestock of Selected Countries

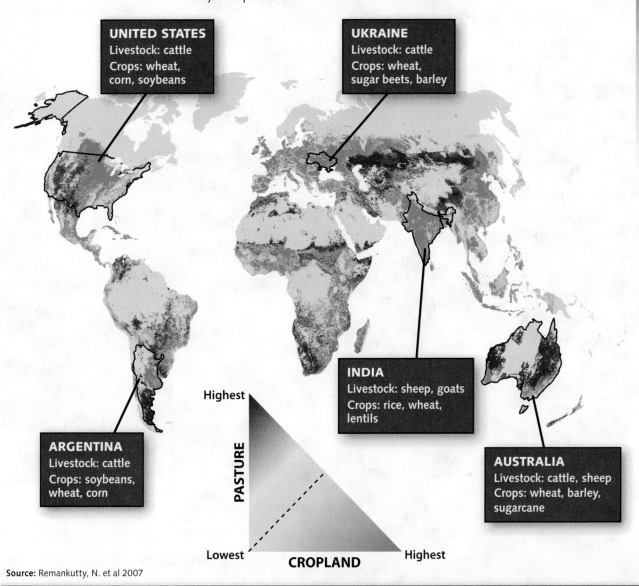

UNITED STATES
Livestock: cattle
Crops: wheat, corn, soybeans

UKRAINE
Livestock: cattle
Crops: wheat, sugar beets, barley

ARGENTINA
Livestock: cattle
Crops: soybeans, wheat, corn

INDIA
Livestock: sheep, goats
Crops: rice, wheat, lentils

AUSTRALIA
Livestock: cattle, sheep
Crops: wheat, barley, sugarcane

Highest

PASTURE

Lowest   CROPLAND   Highest

Source: Remankutty, N. et al 2007

FORMATIVE ASSESSMENT

RESEARCH LAB GeoJournal

1. **Identify** Look at the map. What crop do all five countries shown above grow?

2. **Compare and Contrast** Find India and Australia on the map. Which country devotes more land use to crops, and which country devotes more to grazing? What climate factors might account for these choices?

3. **Make Inferences** Which country do you think produces more beef, Australia or Ukraine? Why do you think so?

Research and Write a Report Research grassland use in China and New Zealand. Use data from databases, or charts and graphs, to compare countries. Then, analyzing the text and your research, think about what affects food production, grassland environments, and the economies of countries that rely on grasslands. Outline your report, incorporating main and supporting ideas. Then predict future scientific discoveries or technologies that could make a positive impact.

Active Options

TECHTREK

myNGconnect.com For photos of animal life in the region

 Digital Library   Magazine Maker

ACTIVITY 1

Goal: Extend your knowledge about Antarctica.

Prepare a Guidebook

You are leading a group going on a seven-day summer cruise to Antarctica. Do research and use the Magazine Maker to prepare a guidebook for your group that gives some facts about the continent and describes what visitors might expect to see on the cruise. Include examples of marine life and sea birds that inhabit the waters surrounding Antarctica.

leopard seal

ACTIVITY 2

Goal: Research indigenous animal species in Australia.

Write a Report

The Tasmanian devil and the Australian dingo are animals found only in Australia. Research one of these animals online. Write a report that details its habitat, what it eats, and what threats it might face. Include photos of your animal from the **Digital Library** with your written report.

ACTIVITY 3

Goal: Learn more about constellations in the Southern Hemisphere.

Identify the Stars

National Geographic Fellow Elizabeth Kapu'uwailani Lindsey studies the traditions of Pacific island seafarers who relied on their knowledge of the stars, waves, and birds to guide them. Many of the stars they observed in the Southern Hemisphere are not visible in the night skies in North America. Conduct research and identify five constellations of stars visible only in the Southern Hemisphere. Explain what shape each constellation forms and how that shape relates to its name.

REFERENCE HANDBOOK

The lessons of the *Skills Handbook* teach, in depth, the social studies skills strand of the **Texas Essential Knowledge and Skills.** The lessons also serve as a "go to" resource. Check out the handbook lessons when you apply skills to chapter content, activities, and projects.

The *Economics and Government Handbook* also supports terms and concepts taught in chapter content. From the lessons of the *World Religions Handbook*, you'll learn more about the origins and beliefs of major religions. The Religious Understanding Day assessment activity on page R58 focuses on holidays and observances.

GEO

Skills Handbook

In these lessons, you'll learn how to integrate social studies skills into your studies. You'll learn the language of skills, too—how to analyze, interpret, and evaluate—for taking part in everyday classroom communication.

Find the Main Idea

Every book, paragraph, or passage has a **main idea**, which is the sentence or sentences that state the subject of the text. A main idea can sometimes be unstated. In that case, details, or supporting ideas, in the text provide clues about the main idea. To find a main idea and details, follow the steps at right.

6.21.B analyze information by finding the main idea; 6.22.B incorporate main and supporting ideas in verbal and written communication

Step 1 Look for a stated main idea in the first and last sentences of the paragraph. If no main idea is obvious, look for ideas that offer clues about the unstated main idea.

Step 2 If you found the main idea in the first sentence, supporting details usually follow it. If the main idea is in the last sentence, ideas that support it usually come before.

GUIDED MODEL

Habitat Loss and Restoration

Ⓐ The loss of habitats can destroy an entire ecosystem. An ecosystem is a community of plants and animals and their habitat. **Ⓑ** <u>Earth has many different ecosystems that interact with each other.</u> **Ⓑ** <u>The destruction of one affects all the other ecosystems.</u> **Ⓑ** <u>For example, many scientists believe the destruction of rain forest habitats has led to global climate change.</u>

TIP When an author doesn't directly state the main idea of a passage, ask yourself, "What do the details of the passage have in common?" Find the connection between the details, put it into your own words, and you have the unstated main idea.

Step 1 Look for a stated main idea.

Read the first and last sentences in the paragraph. Do they state the main idea? If the main idea is not obvious, look for clues. Some details explain the main idea. Other details give examples of the main idea.

MAIN IDEA Ⓐ The loss of habitats can destroy an entire ecosystem. In this example, the stated main idea is the first sentence of the paragraph.

Step 2 Once you have figured out the main idea, locate ideas that support it.

In the example at left, supporting ideas follow the main idea.

DETAIL Ⓑ Earth has ecosystems that interact with each other.

DETAIL Ⓑ The destruction of one affects all the other ecosystems.

DETAIL Ⓑ Many scientists believe the destruction of rain forest habitats has led to global climate change.

When doing research for oral or written work, find the main and supporting ideas in your sources and include them, either in quotations or in your own words.

APPLY THE SKILL

Turn to page 258, "Classical Greece." Read the "Golden Age of Greece" passage. Identify the main idea and details. Record them in a web like the one at right.

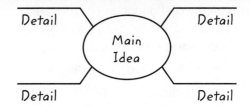

Take Notes and Cite Sources

6.21.B analyze information by finding the main idea, summarizing;
6.22.F use proper citations to avoid plagiarism

Taking notes while you listen, read, and research helps you understand and remember important facts, ideas, and details. When you take notes for writing a report or preparing a presentation, **citing sources** helps you avoid **plagiarism**, which is presenting another's work as if it is your own.

Step 1 Read the title to learn the topic.

Step 2 Find the main and supporting ideas. Summarize them in your own words.

Step 3 Search for key words and write down the words and their definitions.

Step 4 Cite the source. Give credit to the author or artist.

GUIDED MODEL

(A) Economic Indicators

(B) A country's economic strength can be measured by several indicators. One is **(C) gross domestic product** (GDP), or the total value of the goods and services that a country produces. **(C)** Other indicators include **GDP** per capita (or per person), income, basic literacy rate, and life expectancy.

(B) Economies are also placed in one of three categories. Countries with high GDPs, such as the United States, are **(C) more developed countries**. Countries with lower GDPs are **(C) less developed countries**.

TIP When writing a paper or report, use your own words as much as possible. Credit any words or phrases you copy and give credit for ideas that are not yours. Even visual material you copy or download, such as photos, illustrations, or charts, must have a citation.

Step 1 Read the title to learn the topic.
TITLE **(A)** Economic Indicators

Step 2 Find the main and supporting ideas and summarize them in your own words.
(B) Summary: *You can measure a country's economic strength using indicators, such as GDP, GDP per capita, income, basic literacy rate, and life expectancy. Countries can be placed in categories, such as as more developed, less developed, and newly industrialized.*

Step 3 Search for key words and write down the words and their definitions.
SAMPLE KEY WORD: (C) Gross domestic product is the total value of the goods and services a country produces.

Step 4 Cite the source. Write a citation for the information.
What book or Web site is the material from? Keep track of your sources. When you write a report, include citations either within the paragraphs or at the end in a bibliography, which lists all the sources you used.

APPLY THE SKILL

A bibliography citation for an encyclopedia should be formatted like this: Title of the article. Name of the encyclopedia. Year.

Your notes would include:

"Capitalism." Britannica Online Encyclopedia. Retrieved from http://www.britannica.com/EBchecked/topic/93927/capitalism

Select a book and Web site, and follow these formats to write the citations.

For a book: Author's last name, first name. Title of the work. Name of the publisher. Year it was published.

For a Web site: Author (if given). Year or date of the piece (if given). Title. The Web address.

Summarize

When you **summarize**, you restate text in your own words and shorten it. A summary includes only the most important information and details. You can summarize a spoken message or passage, or a chapter you've read, or a whole book. To summarize, follow the steps shown at right.

🌀 6.21.B analyze information by summarizing, finding the main idea

Step 1 Read the text looking for the most important information. Watch for topic sentences that provide the main ideas.

Step 2 Restate each main idea in your own words.

Step 3 Write your summary of the text using your own words and including only the most important information.

GUIDED MODEL

Foods of Eastern Europe

Ⓐ Eastern Europe's cold climate causes a shorter growing season than that in Western Europe. In Russia, root vegetables such as turnips and beets are well adapted to the country's climate. A soup called borscht made from beets is a traditional dish on winter nights.

Ⓑ The fertile soil of Hungary allows Hungarian farmers to grow grains and potatoes. These crops are used to make a variety of breads. A meat stew called goulash is Hungary's national dish. It is made with beef, potatoes, and vegetables and seasoned with a spice called paprika.

TIP When listening to a speaker, take notes and afterwards find the main ideas in your notes to retell in a summary what you heard.

Step 1 Read the text looking for the most important information. Watch for topic sentences that provide the main ideas.
TOPIC SENTENCE Ⓐ Eastern Europe's cold climate causes a shorter growing season than that in Western Europe.
TOPIC SENTENCE Ⓑ The fertile soil of Hungary allows Hungarian farmers to grow grains and potatoes.

Step 2 Restate each main idea in your own words.
RESTATED Ⓐ The climate of Eastern Europe is cold, so it has a shorter growing season than Western Europe.
RESTATED Ⓑ Hungarian farmers grow grains and potatoes.

Step 3 Write your summary of the text using your own words and including only the most important information.
SUMMARY: Eastern Europe has a cold climate, so it has a shorter growing season than Western Europe. Certain crops grow well there, such as potatoes and grains in Hungary.

APPLY THE SKILL

Turn to *Europe Today*, page 184, "Languages and Cultures." Read the "Cultural Traditions" passage. Identify the main ideas and important information, and restate them in your own words. Then write a summary of the passage using the topic sentence shown here.

Cultural Traditions
Europe's cultural traditions reflect the region's ethnic diversity. _____
_____
_____

Sequence Events

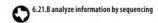

6.21.B analyze information by sequencing

When you **sequence events**, you put them in order based on when they occurred in time. Thinking about events in time order helps you understand how they relate to each other. To sequence events, follow the steps shown at right.

Step 1 Look for time clue words and phrases such as names of months and days, or words such as *before, after, finally, a year later,* or *lasted* that help you sequence events.

Step 2 Look for dates in the text and match them to events.

GUIDED MODEL

Greek Culture Spreads

Greece's golden age ended around **B** 431 B.C., when war broke out between Athens and Sparta. The conflict, known as the Peloponnesian War, **A** lasted 27 years. The war weakened both Athens and Sparta.

Around **B** 340 B.C., King Philip II of Macedonia took advantage of their weakness and conquered Greece. In **B** 334 B.C., Philip's son, Alexander the Great, began to extend the Macedonian Empire. Alexander's love of Greece led him to spread its culture throughout his empire. Alexander died in **B** 323 B.C. at the age of 33.

TIP A **time line** is a visual tool that can be useful for sequencing events. Time lines often move from left to right, listing events from the earliest to the latest.

Step 1 Look for time clue words and phrases.
TIME CLUES **A** lasted 27 years

Step 2 Look for specific dates in the text.

Be sure to read the text carefully because the dates in a paragraph may not always be listed in time order. Always match an event with its date. A chart like the one below can be a useful way to sequence dates and events.

SAMPLE DATE **B** 431 B.C., when Greece's golden age ends and the Peloponnesian War begins

DATE IN TEXT	EVENT
431 B.C.	Greece's golden age ends; Peloponnesian War breaks out between Athens and Sparta.
340 B.C.	King Philip of Macedonia conquers Greece.
334 B.C.	Alexander the Great starts extending the Macedonian Empire.
323 B.C.	Alexander the Great dies.

APPLY THE SKILL

Turn to *Europe Geography & History*, Section 2.3, "The Republic of Rome." Read the "A Republic Forms" passage. Identify the dates and events that occurred on each date. Use a time line like the one below to sequence the events.

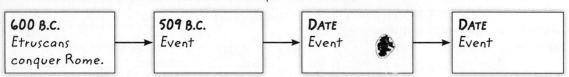

| 600 B.C. Etruscans conquer Rome. | → | 509 B.C. Event | → | DATE Event | → | DATE Event |

Categorize

When you **categorize**, you sort things into groups, or categories. Almost everything can be categorized, including objects, ideas, people, and information. Categorizing is important because it helps you recognize data patterns and trends. To categorize, follow the steps shown at right.

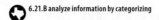 6.21.B analyze information by categorizing

Step 1 Read the title and text and ask yourself what the passage is about to determine how the information can be categorized.

Step 2 Look for clue words to help you categorize information.

Step 3 Decide what the categories will be.

Step 4 Sort the information from the passage into the categories.

GUIDED MODEL

A Political and Physical Maps

Cartographers, or mapmakers, create **B** <u>different kinds of maps for many</u> **B** <u>different purposes</u>.

A <u>A political map shows features that humans have created</u>, such as countries, states, and cities. These features are labeled, and lines show boundaries, such as country borders.

A <u>A physical map shows features of physical geography</u>. It includes landforms, such as mountains, plains, deserts, and bodies of water. A physical map also shows elevation and relief. Elevation is the height of a physical feature above sea level. Relief is the change in elevation from one place to another.

TIP Every day, we put information into categories, such as healthy food versus junk food or fiction versus nonfiction. Knowing how information is categorized helps you understand how things are related and organize ideas.

Step 1 Read the title and text and ask yourself what the passage is about to determine how the information can be categorized.

THE PASSAGE IS ABOUT A the features of two types of maps.

Step 2 Look for clue words to help you categorize information.

CLUE WORDS B *different kinds of maps, different purposes*

Step 3 Decide what the categories will be.

THE CATEGORIES political maps and physical maps

Step 4 Sort the information into the categories.

Use a chart like the one below to help you organize the information.

TYPE OF MAP	PURPOSES
Political	Shows man-made features, such as countries, states, cities, and boundaries
Physical	Shows features of physical geography, such as mountains, plains, deserts, and bodies of water; also shows elevation and relief

APPLY THE SKILL

Turn to *Europe Today*, Section 1.2, "Art and Music." Read the section carefully. Determine how categorizing can help you understand and organize the information about European art. Then create a chart like the one at right and categorize the information.

EUROPEAN ART	
PERIOD	**CHARACTERISTICS**
Middle Ages	religious subjects; two-dimensional
Romantic Period	landscapes, nature, conveys emotion

Identify Points of View

6.21.D identify different points of view; 6.21.E identify elements of frame of reference that influenced participants in an event

When you read about a past issue or current topic, think about the viewpoint presented. Are there other viewpoints to consider? What could influence an individual's point of view? You can **identify points of view** by following these steps.

Step 1 Identify the issue, topic, or event.

Step 2 Look for ideas or viewpoints individuals or groups have.

Step 3 Ask yourself what other opinions or points of view might be possible.

Step 4 Think about different situations, or the frame of reference, that could influence point of view.

GUIDED MODEL

A New Media in Malaysia

Once the Internet became available, many Malaysians realized their government had been changing and blocking out information in the news. Access to online information may have affected the national elections of 2008. B Some older voters still trusted newspapers and television reports from their role in independence efforts in the 1960s. But younger voters believed online news was more reliable. The ruling party did not do well in the voting results.

TIP A person's **frame of reference** is shaped by circumstances that influence his or her point of view. When trying to identify frame of reference, think about what might be at stake for the individuals involved, such as loss of work, loss of profit, loss of control over what people believe, or loss of life, freedom, or human rights.

Step 1 Identify the issue, topic, or event.

This passage is about A Internet access and the 2008 elections in Malaysia.

Step 2 Look for ideas or different viewpoints individuals or groups have.

VIEWPOINTS B *Older and younger Malaysians did not agree on which media sources could be trusted during the elections.*

Step 3 Ask what other opinions or points of view might be possible.

People make up the government. One view might have been that criticism of the government creates unrest. A different view would counter that censorship and distortion allow unfair decisions or hide violations of human rights.

Step 4 Think about different situations that could form a person's frame of reference

FRAME OF REFERENCE *Older voters may have known the influence of newspapers, television, and radio, which helped the country gain independence. For younger voters with a different frame of reference, old media was government controlled, but in new media many ideas could be freely expressed.*

APPLY THE SKILL

Turn to pages 556 and 557 and read about the Korean War. Think about the different points of view of the countries involved. What might have influenced the United States to take part?

Country	Point of View

Express Ideas Through Speech

6.22.C express ideas orally based on research and experiences

When you **express ideas through speech**, use effective language to say what you think. The purpose of your speech may be to narrate events, explain information, or convince your audience of your point of view. You can express ideas through speech by following the steps at right.

Step 1 Determine the topic you will be presenting and the purpose of your speech. Do research to gather information using a wide variety of reliable sources.

Step 2 Organize your ideas and create speaking notes and any visual aids you may need.

Step 3 Practice techniques to help you speak clearly and appropriately.

GUIDED MODEL

A Major Periods of European Literature

B Ancient Greeks and Romans (focus on journeys, heroes, and adventures)
• Iliad and Odyssey (Homer)
—epic poems, recited
Middle Ages (focus on religious beliefs and politics of the time)
• Divine Comedy (Dante)
Renaissance (focus on human experiences)
• plays of Shakespeare
• Don Quixote (Cervantes)
—first modern novel

TIP Connecting words, such as *also, and, however,* or *on the other hand,* will help you avoid repeating "uh" or "ah" between sentences. Use synonyms or describe what you mean when, in the moment, you can't remember the word you wanted to say. Vary your volume and speaking to add interest. Gestures, posture, facial expressions, and eye contact will help you engage your audience.

Step 1 Determine the topic and purpose of your speech and do research to gather the information you need.

A The topic of this student's speech is the history of European literature. The purpose is to explain the main periods of European literature.

Step 2 Organize your ideas and create speaking notes and any visual aids you may need.

Notes and visual aids will help you stay on topic, remember your points, and emphasize your message.

B Well-organized notes will help you if you lose your place while speaking or forget a point you wanted to make. Keep your notes simple— just list headings and key points and important people and events.

Step 3 Practice techniques to help you speak clearly and appropriately.

Speak honestly and use words appropriate to your audience. Practice using non-verbal cues (such as using body movements or pantomime) to convey your meaning. Emphasize connecting words with your voice and vary the types of sentences you use.

APPLY THE SKILL

Option 1

Select a topic from the book, research it, and prepare notes for an oral presentation. Be sure your audience understands the purpose of your speech and why you have chosen the topic. Include surprising details from your research.

Option 2

Select an event you took part in and describe your experience. Organize your ideas into speaking notes. Prepare a strong opening and closing statement. Throughout, vary your sentences to include short ones, complex ones, or even questions.

Write Outlines

Before you write a report or article, **writing an outline** is a useful way to organize information from your sources. A good outline lists the most important ideas and supporting details in order, either chronologically or by level of importance. To write an outline, follow the steps shown at right.

6.22.B incorporate main and supporting ideas in written communication based on research;
6.21.C organize information from outlines; 6.22.D create written material (outlines)

Step 1 Give your outline a title.

Step 2 Determine and record the main ideas in logical order using Roman numerals.

Step 3 Determine and record the ideas that support and explain the main ideas.

Step 4 Determine and record specific details below the appropriate supporting ideas.

GUIDED MODEL

Ⓐ <u>Earth's Water</u>
Ⓑ I. Fresh Water
　Ⓒ A. Sources
　　Ⓓ 1. Rivers, water flowing downward
　　　2. Lakes, large inland bodies of water
　　　3. Streams, brooks, and creeks
　　B. Uses
　　　1. Drinking and cooking
　　　2. Irrigating crops
II. Salt Water
　A. Oceans
　　1. Large bodies of salt water
　　2. Atlantic, Pacific, Indian, Arctic
　　3. Ocean currents and their effects
　B. Seas
　　1. Small bodies of salt water enclosed partly or completely by land
　　2. Red, Caspian, Arabian

Step 1 Give your outline a title.
Ⓐ If you are writing an outline to organize information for a report or comparison, the outline title will probably become the title of your paper.

Step 2 Determine and record the topics in logical order using Roman numerals.
Ⓑ Each topic will probably make up at least one paragraph in your paper.

Step 3 Determine and record the main ideas that support and explain each topic.
Ⓒ Label these using indented capital letters below the topics. Not all topics need the same number of main ideas.

Step 4 Determine and record specific details below the appropriate main ideas.
Ⓓ Label these details using more deeply indented numerals below the main ideas. Not every main idea will have the same number of details.

TIP Outline an author's essay or article to understand the structures writers use to interest or persuade their readers. Look at the beginning and ending and note how they are related. Look at the middle material and see how it supports the purpose or main topic of the writing.

APPLY THE SKILL

Turn to *Europe Geography and History*, page 268, "Exploration and Colonization." Then organize the information from the passage in an outline like the one shown at right. Use your outline to write a report.

<u>European Exploration</u>
I. Portuguese explorations
　A. Reasons
　　1. Find gold
　　2. Establish trade

Write Journal Entries

When you **write journal entries** in response to something you have read, you record your reactions, make notes, ask and answer questions, and respond to new information in an informal written format. To use written journal entries to respond to a question or writing prompt, follow these steps.

6.22.D create written material (journal entries)

Step 1 Use what you have learned and read about the topic to answer the question.

Step 2 Respond and react in a personal way to the question.

Step 3 Record any related questions, comments, or notes you might have.

GUIDED MODEL

QUESTION:

What challenges might immigrants moving to Europe face today?

JOURNAL ENTRY:

A Some immigrants may feel pressure to assimilate into European society and fear they will lose their identity and culture. Those belonging to non-Christian religions may feel discriminated against simply for having different religious beliefs.

B When my family moved, I hated that students at my new school had to wear a uniform. I refused to wear the jacket for the first week and got in trouble. I felt angry that I wasn't allowed to dress the way I wanted. I think I know a little bit about how the immigrants living in Europe feel.

C NOTE: Look up countries in Europe with large immigrant populations on the CIA World Factbook Web site.

Step 1 Use what you have learned and read about the topic to answer the question.

A The journal writer answers the question using facts from the book and his or her prior knowledge.

Step 2 Respond and react in a personal way to the question.

B The journal writer relates to the topic on a personal level and provides insight into the question based on personal experience.

Step 3 Record any related questions, comments, or notes you might have.

C The journal writer writes himself or herself a note to look up more information about the topic online.

TIP Journals can be used to record the steps in a research project (such as your observations during an experiment). You can also use a journal to write your thoughts and questions as you read a book or carry out a project.

APPLY THE SKILL

Turn to *Europe Today*, Section 1.1, "Languages and Cultures." Then write a journal entry to respond to the following question: What is life like for Europeans who live in cities today? The beginning of a sample entry is shown at right.

Most Europeans today live in cities that reflect the cultures and ethnic origins of immigrant populations.

Pose and Answer Questions

6.03.A pose and answer geographic questions; 6.03.B pose and answer questions about distributions and patterns

As you read, **pose questions** to learn more about a subject, to understand characteristics of regions or countries, or to discover geographic patterns. **Answer questions** by looking at maps or other visual tools, and by researching information in texts or databases. To pose and answer questions, follow these steps.

Step 1 Put what you want to know in the form of questions.

Step 2 Break down broad concepts or topics by asking *who, what, when, where, why,* **and** *how.*

Step 3 Research answers to your questions using text, charts, graphs, maps, models, or databases.

GUIDED MODEL

A Region's Risk

In Australia, New Zealand, and Antarctica, travelers trek to remote places to observe wildlife or experience unusual physical environments.

A In New Zealand, activities include rock climbing, mountain climbing, exploring caves, and rafting and kayaking trips. In Australia, millions go to the Great Barrier Reef to snorkel and scuba dive, or they visit dramatic landscapes across the country. Tourists hike the rugged, icy terrain of Antarctica's glaciers.

B The adventure tourism industry creates jobs and brings in money for local economies. But the risks are high, and people worry whether there is enough regulation of tour companies to ensure tourists' safety.

TIP Pose and answer questions with a partner or group. Trade lists of questions and share answers. Tell how and where you found your answers and discuss answers that do not agree.

Step 1 Put what you want to know in the form of questions.

A *I chose New Zealand for my questions because it interests me.*

Questions: What are the remote places people go to? Where are New Zealand's natural wonders located?

Step 2 Break down broad concepts or topics by asking *who, what, where, when, why,* **or** *how.*

B Safety: Who is in charge of being sure adventure tourists are safe? Why is safety a problem? What is being done?

Step 3 Research answers to your questions by using resources, such as text, charts, graphs, maps, models, and databases.

I looked up images of New Zealand's wild places, located them on a map, and researched what the government and others are doing to improve safety.

Answers: Places and natural wonders include caves, geysers, nature reserves, Tongariro National Park, and the geologic formation called The Pinnacles.

Safety: The government now requires a safety audit before companies can run tours. Tour groups are working to improve a record of accidents and injuries.

APPLY THE SKILL

Turn to *Human & Physical Geography*, page 34, "Earth's Rotation and Revolution." Read "Revolution and Rotation" and pose questions about the information. Record your questions in a chart like the one at right. Use the text and diagram to answer your questions.

MY QUESTIONS	ANSWERS
What process creates the four seasons?	the rotation and tilt of Earth

Make Predictions

When you **make predictions,** you think about the events described in a passage or selection, use your prior knowledge, and guess or predict what will happen next. Making predictions as you read can help you understand and remember what you have read. To make predictions, follow these steps.

6.21.B analyze information by making predictions

Step 1 Preview the passage or selection to anticipate what it is about.

Step 2 Use your personal knowledge. Ask yourself what you know about the topic.

Step 3 As you read, make predictions about what will happen next.

Step 4 Confirm or revise your predictions as you continue to read.

GUIDED MODEL

Ⓐ European Music

European music began in ancient Greece and Rome. Musicians played on Ⓒ simple instruments. During the Ⓑ Middle Ages, music was used in religious ceremonies. Also, singers called troubadours sang about knights and love. These songs influenced Ⓑ Renaissance music, when the Ⓒ violin was introduced.

The new instruments helped inspire the complex music of the Ⓑ Baroque period (1600–1750). Opera, which tells a story through words and music, was born then. The Ⓑ Classical and Romantic periods followed the Baroque and continued until about 1910.

TIP Use a prediction chart to take notes as you read. A prediction chart allows you to record predictions, state whether they were correct, and explain why.

Step 1 Preview the passage or selection to anticipate what it is about.

Ⓐ *The title tells me that this passage is about European music. By skimming ahead, I see the names of many different types of music,* Ⓑ *musical periods, and* Ⓒ *words relating to instruments.*

Step 2 Use your personal knowledge.

I know that the Romantic period in art took place in the early 1800s. I have listened to Baroque music before.

Step 3 As you read, make predictions about what will happen next.

I predict that this text will describe how music evolved in Europe.

Step 4 Confirm or revise your predictions as you continue to read.

My prediction was correct. The passage describes how music evolved from the Middle Ages to the present.

PREDICTION	CORRECT?	EVIDENCE
This passage will explain music I am familiar with.	Yes	It describes what opera is and when it developed.

APPLY THE SKILL

Turn to *Human & Physical Geography,* Section 1.2, "Earth's Complex Structure." Read the "Earth's Layers" text. Then use a prediction chart like the one shown at right to record and analyze your predictions.

PREDICTION	CORRECT?	EVIDENCE
This passage will describe the high temperatures deep within the earth.		

Compare and Contrast

When you **compare** two or more things, you examine the similarities and differences between them. When you **contrast** things, you focus on only their differences. To compare and contrast, follow the steps shown at right.

🔘 6.21.B analyze information by comparing, contrasting

Step 1 Determine what the subject of the passage or paragraph is.

Step 2 Identify two or more ideas, examples, or features relating to the subject that can be compared and contrasted.

Step 3 Search for clue words that indicate similarities (comparing) and differences (contrasting).

GUIDED MODEL

🅐 Varied Climates

Most of Europe lies within the humid temperate climate region. The North Atlantic Drift, an ocean current of warm water, keeps temperatures relatively warm. Winds also affect climate. The sirocco sometimes blows over the Mediterranean Sea and brings humid weather to southern Europe at different seasons. The mistral is a cold wind in winter that blows through France, bringing cold, dry weather.

🅒 In general, 🅑 a Mediterranean climate brings cool, wet winters and hot, dry summers. This climate supports a long growing season. 🅒 In contrast, 🅑 Eastern Europe has long, cold winters. Greenland, northern Scandinavia, and Iceland have polar climates and a limited growing season.

Step 1 Determine what the subject of the passage or paragraph is.
SUBJECT 🅐 the climates of Europe

Step 2 Identify features of the subjects that can be compared and contrasted.
FEATURE 🅑 climates of southern and eastern European countries

Step 3 Search the passage for clue words that indicate similarities and differences.
Those sentences will help you compare. Then look for clue words that indicate how the two aspects are different. Those sentences will help you contrast.
CLUE WORDS 🅒 in general (comparing); in contrast (contrasting)

TIP A Y-Chart and a Venn diagram, shown below, are useful graphic organizers for comparing and contrasting two topics. In a Y-Chart, list unique information on the branches and shared characteristics in the straight section. In a Venn diagram, list unique characteristics in the left and right sides and common characteristics in the overlapping area.

APPLY THE SKILL

Turn to *Human & Physical Geography*, Section 2.4, "Natural Resources." Read the "Categories of Resources" passage. Compare and contrast renewable resources and nonrenewable resources using a Y-Chart or Venn diagram.

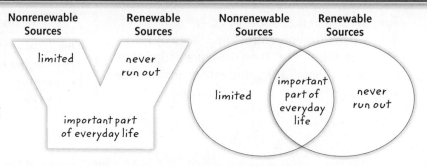

Analyze Cause and Effect

A **cause** is an event or action that makes something else happen. The **effect** is an event that happens as a result of the cause. Analyzing cause-and-effect relationships can help you understand how events are related. To analyze cause and effect, follow the steps shown at right.

Step 1 Determine the cause of an event. Look for signal words that show cause, such as *because, due to, since,* and *therefore*.

Step 2 Determine the effect that results from the cause. Look for signal words such as *led to, consequently,* and *as a result*.

Step 3 Look for a chain of causes and effects. An effect may be the cause of another action or event.

GUIDED MODEL

Rome's Decline

For about 500 years, the Roman Empire was the most powerful in the world and extended over three continents. **A** Beginning around A.D. 235, however, Rome had a series of poor rulers. **A** In addition, German tribes began invading the empire.

B As a result, in 312, Emperor Constantine moved the capital from Rome to Byzantium, in present-day Turkey, and renamed the city Constantinople. In 395, the empire was divided into an Eastern Empire and a Western Empire with two different emperors. **C** Because Rome had been severely weakened, invaders overthrew the last Roman emperor and ended the Western Empire in 476.

Step 1 Determine the cause.

Ask yourself why the event took place. Notice that an event may have more than one cause.

CAUSE(S)

A Beginning around A.D. 235, Rome had a series of poor rulers.

A German tribes began invading the empire.

Step 2 Determine the effect.

Ask yourself what happened as a result of the event or events.

EFFECT B As a result, in 312, Emperor Constantine moved the capital from Rome to Byzantium.

Step 3 Look for a chain of causes and effects.

An effect may cause another event.

CAUSE/EFFECT C Because Rome had been severely weakened, invaders overthrew the last Roman emperor and ended the Western Empire in 476.

TIP Test whether events have a cause-and-effect relationship by using this construction: "Because [insert cause], [insert effect] happened." If the construction does not work, one event did not lead to the other.

APPLY THE SKILL

Turn to *Human & Physical Geography*, Section 3.5, "Protecting Human Rights." Read "The Impact of Human Rights" passage. Identify a cause-and effect-relationship in the passage. Record the cause(s) and effect(s) in a graphic organizer like the one at right.

CAUSE	EFFECT
Declaration of Human Rights was developed	World pressured South Africa to grant human rights to non-whites

Make Inferences

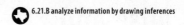

6.21.B analyze information by drawing inferences

Inferences are conclusions or interpretations a reader makes from information that a writer does not state directly. When you make inferences, you use common sense and your own experiences to figure out what the writer means. To make inferences, follow the steps shown at right.

Step 1 Read the text looking for facts and ideas.

Step 2 Think about what the writer does not say but wants you to understand.

Step 3 Reread the text and use what you know to make an inference.

GUIDED MODEL

Aryan Migration

Many historians believe a group of nomadic herders called the Aryans migrated from Central Asia into the Indus Valley around 2000 B.C. From there, they moved into northern India. **A** <u>Their language, Sanskrit, became the basis of many modern languages in South Asia.</u> The Aryans recorded religious teachings in Sanskrit in sacred texts called the Vedas. **B** <u>The Aryans established the beginnings of Hinduism, the major religion of India today.</u>

TIP Use a two-column chart to keep track of inferences. In the left column, write details, quotations, examples, statistics, and other facts. In the right column, write the inference that you draw from each fact. Note that an inference can be based on one fact or several facts.

Step 1 Read the text looking for facts and ideas.

You must know the facts before you can make inferences. Ask yourself, "What facts does the writer state directly in this text?"

FACT A The Aryan language, Sanskrit, became the basis of many modern languages in South Asia.

FACT B The early religion of the Aryans established the beginnings of Hinduism, the major religion of India today.

Step 2 Think about what the writer does not say but wants you to understand.

Ask yourself:
- *How do these facts connect with what I already know?*
- *How does this information help me better understand Hinduism?*

Step 3 Reread the text and use what you know to make an inference.

INFERENCE A Many modern languages have ancient origins.

INFERENCE B Modern religions are influenced by ancient religions.

APPLY THE SKILL

Turn to *Europe Geography & History*, Section 1.2, "A Long Coastline." Read the "Exploration and Settlement" text. Then make two inferences about how Europe's location near large bodies of water affected its people. Use a two-column chart like the one at right to record the facts you found and the inferences you made.

FACTS	INFERENCES

Draw Conclusions

When you **draw conclusions**, you make a judgment based on what you have read. You analyze the facts, make inferences, and use your own experiences to form your judgment. To draw a conclusion, follow the steps shown at right.

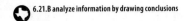 6.21.B analyze information by drawing conclusions

Step 1 Read the passage to identify the facts.

Step 2 Make inferences based on the facts.

Step 3 Use the inferences you have made and your own experiences and common sense to draw a conclusion.

GUIDED MODEL

A The euro was launched in 1999, but paper money and coins of the currency were not issued until 2002. **A** As of early 2011, 17 of the 27 European Union (EU) nations had adopted the euro. The countries using the euro are known as the eurozone. **A** Some EU countries, including Romania and Bulgaria, hope to join the eurozone soon. Other countries, including Great Britain and Sweden, have not adopted the euro. They believe that giving up their own currency might result in a loss of control over their economies.

TIP Use a diagram to organize the facts you have identified, the inferences you have made, and your conclusion. A diagram can help you clarify your thinking.

Step 1 Read the passage to identify the facts.

FACTS **A** The euro was introduced to Europe in 1999. By 2011, 17 out of 27 EU nations used it. Some countries hope to join the eurozone. Others, including Great Britain and Sweden, have not adopted the euro because they think it would result in a loss of control over their economies.

Step 2 Make inferences based on the facts.

INFERENCES *I see that most of the EU countries have adopted the euro, and at least two more want to adopt it. However, some countries have chosen not to adopt the currency. That must mean that there are both advantages and disadvantages to using the euro.*

Step 3 Use the inferences you have made and your own experience and common sense to draw a conclusion.

CONCLUSION: *In the future, more European countries will probably adopt the euro and become part of the eurozone. However, other countries will not adopt the euro because there are disadvantages to doing so.*

APPLY THE SKILL

Turn to *Human & Physical Geography*, Section 2.3, "Extreme Weather." Read the "Scientific Solutions" passage and draw conclusions about the solutions scientists have come up with to combat the dangers of extreme weather. Write a few sentences summarizing your conclusion. A sample sentence is shown at right.

Scientists are making great progress in predicting extreme weather _____

_____

_____

Make Generalizations

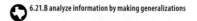

6.21.B analyze information by making generalizations

Generalizations are broad statements that apply to a set of ideas, a group of people, or a series of events. You make generalizations based on information you have read or heard. You can also draw on personal experiences. To make generalizations, follow the steps shown at right.

Step 1 Look for the overall theme or message of the selection.

Step 2 Find information in the passage that supports the theme.

Step 3 Draw on your personal knowledge.

Step 4 Make a generalization about the topic and put it into sentence form.

GUIDED MODEL

Life in the Ocean

Dr. Sylvia Earle has led more than 60 diving expeditions to explore marine life. During these dives, she has seen the incredible variety of ocean life— **B** "More than 30 major divisions of animals are known, from sponges and jellies to many kinds of beautiful worms and mollusks."

A Dr. Earle has also seen how people have harmed the oceans. **B** "Taking too much wildlife out of the sea is one way," she claims. "Putting garbage, toxic chemicals, and other wastes in is another." Dr. Earle has witnessed a huge drop in the number of fish in the sea. She has also noted pollution's impact on coral reefs.

TIP You can also make generalizations about information from multiple sources. Determine what information the sources have in common. Then form a generalization that all of the sources would support.

Step 1 Look for the overall theme.

COMMON THEME A Humans harm the diverse marine life in the oceans.

Step 2 Find information that supports the theme.

SUPPORTING INFORMATION B Dr. Sylvia Earle, an ocean expert, states that people harm ocean life by taking too much wildlife out of the sea and putting garbage, toxic chemicals, and other wastes into it. Dr. Earle has witnessed a huge drop in the number of fish in the sea and pollution's impact on coral reefs.

Step 3 Draw on your personal knowledge.

I know that living in polluted water is bad for living things. I watched a television program on how toxic waste in the oceans has caused the extinction of some species.

Step 4 Make a generalization about the topic and put it into sentence form.

GENERALIZATION *If we don't stop polluting the waters and taking too much wildlife from the oceans, many species could become extinct.*

APPLY THE SKILL

Turn to *Europe Geography & History*, Section 2.5, "Middle Ages and Christianity." Read "The Feudal System" passage. Then make generalizations about the feudal system's role in Europe, like the one at right, using the information in the passage and what you may already know.

> *The feudal system provided security for Europeans during the Middle Ages.*

Use a Decision-Making Process

6.23.B use a decision-making process

A **decision-making process** helps you organize the steps to take for reaching a decision. It also helps you sort out your options and figure out what the consequences might be of your decision.

Step 1 Gather information about the situation that needs a decision.

Step 2 List options, prioritize them, and focus on the strongest.

Step 3 Think about who or what would be affected by the options and in what ways.

Step 4 Decide what to do.

GUIDED MODEL

You Are There

A Your community needs a wildlife bridge to help bears, elk, and a long list of animals follow their migration patterns without getting hit by cars and trucks.

You join a committee. **B** From highway crews, you get the number of animals hurt or killed each year. Insurance companies provide vehicle damage costs. **A** Where's the best location for a wildlife structure? **C** You come up with a list, **D** find out who owns the property, and how traffic would be affected during construction. There could be four locations. **C** Now scientists who study wildlife join you to narrow the choices.

The committee reviews all the data **E** and chooses. The property owners agree. Now—you've got to get costs and raise the funds!

Step 1 Gather information about the situation that needs a decision.

> **SITUATION** **A** Wildlife bridge location needs to be decided.

> **INFORMATION** **B** Data includes number of animals, damage to vehicles, and where animals cross.

Step 2 List options, prioritize them, and focus on the strongest.

> **OPTIONS** **C** Locations (options) are listed, which narrow to four.

Step 3 Think about who or what would be affected by the options and in what ways.

> **PREDICT** **D** What will be the impact on property and effects on people's lives (traffic)?

Step 4 Decide what to do.

> **DECIDE** **E** Committee decides on actions to take after getting expert advice.

TIP Following steps in a process can prevent too much work pursuing too many options. Use a timer when evaluating options. Rate them and then go back and see which ones have the highest ratings. Spend your energy on those.

APPLY THE SKILL

Turn to page 578, "China's Three Gorges Dam" and write a "You Are There" piece as if you lived in a city along the river where flooding is a problem. You become part of the decision-making team for whether or not to build a dam. Describe the steps taken to reach the decision.

DECISION	STEPS TAKEN
	1. Figure out the information needed.

SKILLS HANDBOOK

Use a Problem-Solving Process

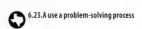 6.23.A use a problem-solving process

You have probably used a pro's and con's chart to help you evaluate a situation. In a **problem-solving process**, this is one of the steps—to consider the advantages or disadvantages of a possible solution to a problem.

Step 1 Gather information about the problem you have identified.

Step 2 List possible solutions.

Step 3 Consider the advantages and disadvantages of each option.

Step 4 Choose a solution. Later evaluate how effective it was.

GUIDED MODEL

Impact of the Revolution

The Industrial Revolution had a tremendous impact on how people worked and lived. Cities grew rapidly because people migrated to them for factory jobs. Standards of living rose, and a prosperous middle class grew.

A However, factory workers often faced harsh conditions. **B** Laborers worked as many as 14 hours a day. Child labor was common. Children as young as ten years old worked in factories and mines.

B Many workers lived in small, crowded houses in neighborhoods where open sewers were common. Diseases spread quickly in these buildings. **C** Over time, the workers' quality of life improved as public health acts were passed to provide sewage systems and larger buildings.

Step 1 Gather information about the problem you have identified.

PROBLEM A Factory workers faced harsh conditions during the Industrial Revolution.

CAUSES B long work hours, child labor, crowded lodgings, open sewers

Step 2 List possible solutions.

SOLUTIONS C Larger buildings for workers to live in were built, and sewage systems for improved sanitation were installed. Other: Improve conditions in the factories as well as at home.

Step 3 Consider the advantages and disadvantages of each option.

Those who were choosing solutions may have realized healthier workers are better for everyone in the long run.

Step 4 Choose a solution. Later evaluate how effective it was.

SUCCESS? Yes. Laws regulated working and living conditions, which are now much cleaner and safer. Sewers reduced disease. Children are not permitted to work in factories.

TIP Ideas that take care of a problem right away may only work temporarily, creating other problems later. Other solutions may last longer but take too much time to make happen. Keep these concerns in mind when evaluating options.

APPLY THE SKILL

With a partner or group, identify a problem at your school. Follow the process steps and fill out a chart like the one at right to evaluate possible solutions.

	Pro's	Con's
Solution 1		
Solution 2		
Solution 3		

Organize and Interpret Information

6.21.C organize and interpret information from outlines, reports, databases, and visuals, including graphs, charts, timelines, and maps

Information, or data, can be collected in charts, databases, graphs, photos, models, and maps. Regardless of its format, you can **organize and interpret information** to draw conclusions, make comparisons, and improve your understanding of the information. Follow the steps at right.

Step 1 Study the information source to understand how it is organized.

Step 2 Read headings and subheadings and other elements.

Step 3 Interpret the information.

GUIDED MODEL

A ECONOMIC INDICATORS OF SELECTED COUNTRIES

B COUNTRY	GDP PER CAPITA (U.S. $)	LITERACY RATE (percent)
B Afghanistan	366	28.0
Brazil	8,536	90.0
China	3,422	93.3
Ethiopia	321	35.9
Germany	44,525	99.0
Mexico	10,249	92.8
United States	47,210	99.0

Source: The World Bank and the United Nations

TIP To create charts, graphs, or databases of your own, follow the formats used in your textbook or in the GeoActivity pages your teacher provides. See also R26 for more on how to interpret information from visuals.

Step 1 Study the information source to understand how it is organized.

A *The title tells me the chart has data on the economies of countries. In a chart, columns go up and down and rows go from left to right.*

Data can be represented in ways other than charts. When analyzing a map or model, examine all of its elements. Important data may be found where you least expect it.

Step 2 Read headings and subheadings and other elements.

This chart gives two types of economic indicator data recorded for each country. B *The columns record the economic indicator data.* B *The rows list information for each country.*

Step 3 Interpret the information.

Using the data in this chart, I can compare the data in the literacy rate column to the data in the GDP per capita column. I can draw the conclusion that a high literacy rate is tied to a high GDP per capita.

APPLY THE SKILL

Turn to *Human & Physical Geography*, pages 36–37, "Earth's Complex Structure." Examine the "Tectonic Plate Movements" model. Then analyze the information in it to answer the following questions.

1. What type of data does this model provide?

2. What type of plates are shown?

3. What are the four types of plate movements?

4. What is subduction?

5. Compare divergence and convergence.

6. Based on your analysis, what conclusions can you draw about the movement of Earth's plates?

Develop Vocabulary

Social studies concepts and terms can be a challenge. This lesson will help you monitor reading, identify language structures, and **develop vocabulary** for better comprehension. Team up with a partner and follow the steps.

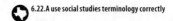 6.22.A use social studies terminology correctly

Step 1 Keep a list of words and phrases you'll read and use routinely in class.

Step 2 Break down sentences to understand them, and vary the kinds of sentences you use.

Step 3 Use strategies. Listen for context clues, create concept maps, and find or draw visuals to help you build vocabulary.

GUIDED MODEL

Building Schools

Ⓐ For more than 30 years, Afghanistan has endured armed <u>conflict</u>, <u>invasion</u>, and <u>political</u> instability. As a result, more than half of Afghan children do not attend school. Recognizing an immediate Ⓑ humanitarian need, multiple agencies are working with tribal leaders, military officials, and teachers to build and re-open schools.

<u>Education</u> is a key part of improving children's lives and futures. The number of years children spend in school is linked to their level of earnings as adults.

TIP As you add to you list over time, decide which words are more important to learn. Cross off ones you've gotten to know by sight. You can also add word parts such as prefixes and suffixes and what they mean.

Step 1 List words you'll use routinely.

Your goal is to get familiar with words for smoother, faster reading and better understanding of the text. List everyday classroom words as well as social studies terms. In the passage, frequently used social studies terms are underlined. What other words would you include on your list?

Step 2 Understand language structures.

Break down sentences to "unpack" the concepts they present. The paragraph marked with Ⓐ has three sentences with introductory phrases. Two sentences include lists. Who is doing the action? Identify the subjects of the sentences: 1) Afghanistan, 2) children, 3) agencies.

Step 3 Work with a partner to use vocabulary-building strategies.

Find the word *humanitarian*. Ⓑ Two context clues help show its meaning. It contains the word *human*, and it is paired with *need*, so it is a kind of human need. Also, the region has endured strife, so it is a need in response to problems caused by strife.

With a partner, create concept maps and include hints to help you remember meanings. "Test" one another with questions, and use terms often.

APPLY THE SKILL

Turn to *Europe Geography & History,* page 249. Read the "Exploration and Settlement" passage. With a partner, fill in a chart like the one at right to describe strategies you would use to monitor and improve your reading, and use to develop social studies vocabulary.

List social studies terms: location, continent, exploration, rulers empires, ports, bays, trade, industry, settlement
Find connecting words:
Create concept maps for:

Evaluate

When you read an informational text, you must **evaluate**, or assess, what you have read. You might evaluate whether the actions or contributions of people are positive or not, or what impact changes in culture have had. Follow the steps shown at right.

Step 1 Identify the action or event you want to evaluate.

Step 2 Gather evidence about the positive impact of the action or event.

Step 3 Gather evidence about the negative impact of the action or event.

Step 4 Decide if the evidence is adequate.

Step 5 Form your evaluation of the action.

GUIDED MODEL

(A) Eastern European countries have had mixed results since changing to a market economy. **(B)** Poland has had the greatest success. It has a fast-growing economy and exports goods throughout Europe. **(C)** Other countries have been slower to establish new businesses and become competitive. They have also experienced rises in prices and unemployment.

(B) The leaders of many eastern European countries wish to integrate with the rest of Europe. They want to join the European Union and NATO, a military alliance of democratic states in Europe and North America.

TIP Making a list of the positive and negative outcomes of a decision, event, or action can help you evaluate. Read the passage and list the positives and negatives. Then review your list and form your evaluation.

Step 1 Identify the action or event.

(A) the impact of Eastern Europe's adoption of a market economy

Step 2 Gather evidence about the positive impact of the action or event.

(B) Poland's economy has grown quickly. Poland now exports goods throughout Europe. It has caused many eastern European leaders to reach out to the rest of Europe.

Step 3 Gather evidence about the negative impact of the action or event.

(C) Some countries have been slow to establish new businesses and become competitive. They have experienced rises in prices and unemployment.

Step 4 Decide if the evidence is adequate.

There is evidence to support both the positive and negative effects of the action. The evidence seems factual.

Step 5 Form your evaluation of the action.

Changing to a market economy has had negative effects on some eastern European countries, However, it has been successful in others and has encouraged Eastern Europe to deepen connections with the rest of the world.

APPLY THE SKILL

Turn to *Europe Geography & History*, page 264, "Middle Ages and Christianity." Read "The Growth of Towns" passage. Record evidence from the passage and determine whether it is positive or negative using a chart like the one at right. Then write a brief evaluation of the impact of the growth of towns on Europe.

EVIDENCE	POSITIVE/NEGATIVE
Trade and business developed.	

Edit Drafts

After you have drafted a report, or even a single paragraph of writing, read it to be sure you have used correct spelling, grammar, sentence structures, and punctuation. Follow these steps to **edit**, or make corrections, to turn your draft into a final version.

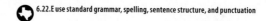 6.22.E use standard grammar, spelling, sentence structure, and punctuation

Step 1 Use an online or print dictionary. Look back at your sources, too, to check the spelling of names and places.

Step 2 Make sentences complete. Each must have a subject and verb, which should agree in number. Check your verb tenses.

Step 3 Use commas correctly. Use punctuation to avoid creating run-on sentences.

GUIDED MODEL

Ⓐ Machu Pichu

The Inca people built this place, which was a palace really. They cut large stones so Ⓐ perfect they didn't have to use cement. They moved giant stones to the location 8,000 feet up in the Ⓐ andes. Ⓑ No bulldozers and trucks. They used ropes. It is still Ⓐ their after 500 years Ⓒ even after earthquakes.

　　Ⓑ They did have Ⓐ an water system and a long-distance Ⓐ comunication system Ⓒ which were runners who ran relay Ⓒ and they could pass messages 140 miles in a day. Ⓑ Up and down mountains and across rivers.

TIP Professional writers create checklists for common writing mistakes they make. You can, too. Online sources list common misspellings such as *receive, occurred, definitely, resistance, until*—even *misspell*. If possible, print out such a list, or create your own.

Step 1 Use a dictionary. Check the spelling of names and places in your sources.

Misspelled words are marked with Ⓐ. "Spell-check" software would not have caught the incorrect spelling of *perfect* (which should be *perfectly*) or *their* (which should be *there*). In your drafts, look for homonyms, or words pronounced the same as other words but have different meanings. *(feet, feat; heard, herd)*

Step 2 Each sentence must have a subject and verb. Be sure verb tenses agree.

Sentences that need correction are marked with Ⓑ. Edit the second paragraph to have two correct sentence structures, instead of a run-on sentence and fragment.

Step 3 Use commas correctly. Use punctuation to avoid creating run-on sentences.

Punctuation mistakes are marked with Ⓒ. Two places need a comma. What punctuation would you use to edit the run-on sentence?

What other ways can you improve these two paragraphs?

APPLY THE SKILL

Turn to *Europe Geography & History*, pages 260–261, "The Republic of Rome." Read "The Roman Way" passage. Rewrite part or all of the section in your own words. Introduce errors in grammar, spelling, punctuation, and sentence structure. Trade your writing with a partner and make edits to correct the errors.

> ### The Roman Way
>
> Romans folowed a system of values called the Roman Way. You had to be loyalt to Rome. Work hard, do your dutys, and control yourself. Every citizen.

Use Primary and Secondary Sources

6.21.A differentiate between, locate, and use valid primary and secondary sources

Primary sources are materials written or provided by people who have had personal experience with an event. **Secondary sources** are materials written by people who did not witness or experience an event directly. Find and use these sources in reports and presentations.

Step 1 Locate source material for a topic.

Step 2 Identify whether the material is a primary or secondary source.

Step 3 Determine the main idea of the source.

Step 4 Determine the quality or credibility of source.

GUIDED MODEL

Mandela's Inspiration

Ⓐ Enlightenment thinkers asserted that Ⓑ people have natural rights, such as life, liberty, and property. They inspired Nelson Mandela in his struggle to end apartheid in South Africa. For his efforts, Mandela received the 1993 Nobel Peace Prize. The following is from his speech.

Ⓒ *The value of our shared reward will and must be measured by the joyful peace which will triumph.*

Thus shall we live, because we will have created a society which recognizes that all people are . . . entitled . . . to life, liberty, prosperity, human rights, and good governance.

—Nelson Mandela, 1993

TIP Primary sources give insights into societies and their history. Letters, speeches, songs, music, photographs, inventions, coins, and works of art are some primary source examples.

Step 1 Locate source material for a topic.

Find sources in your library. Museums and places such as the Library of Congress and the Smithsonian Institution have primary source collections. Ask your librarian to help you search the databases of these institutions.

Step 2 Identify whether the material is a primary or secondary source.

An observation from an expert or eyewitness is likely to be a primary source. The secondary source material in this textbook passage is marked with Ⓐ.

Step 3 Determine the main idea of the source.

MAIN IDEA Ⓑ People have natural rights that all humans should enjoy.

Step 4 Determine the quality or credibility of source.

The primary source in this passage is marked with Ⓒ. Ask yourself, "Is the author a reliable source of information?" *Nelson Mandela is a political activist and Nobel Peace Prize winner. He is a credible source. The secondary source is my textbook, which is also a reliable source.*

APPLY THE SKILL

Look back at pages 92 through 99. Identify images that show primary sources. Tell how you know each is a primary source. Describe how you could use these visual primary sources in a report or presentation.

Primary sources
1.
2.
3.

Interpret Information from Visuals

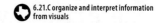
6.21.C organize and interpret information from visuals

Visuals, such as charts, graphs, maps, photos, artwork, and models, illustrate ideas within a text. When you **interpret visuals**, you determine what information is being presented and how it relates to other information about that topic. Follow the steps shown at right.

Step 1 Study the visual and determine what information it provides.

Step 2 Determine how the information in the visual relates to other information provided in a text.

Step 3 Analyze the information presented in the visual to enhance your understanding.

GUIDED MODEL

Solstices and Equinoxes

The moment at which summer and winter start is called a **B** solstice. June 20 or 21 is the summer solstice in the Northern Hemisphere. On December 21 or 22, the Northern Hemisphere has its winter solstice.

The beginning of spring and autumn is called an **B** equinox. In the Northern Hemisphere, the spring equinox occurs around March 21, and the autumn equinox occurs around September 23.

Step 1 Study the visual and determine what information it provides.

Examine any titles, labels, or captions for clues.

A *This diagram is titled "Earth's Four Seasons: Northern Hemisphere." The dates on the visual tell me the position of Earth in relationship to the sun throughout the year.*

Step 2 Determine how the information in the visual relates to other information provided in a text.

B *The summer and winter solstices and spring and autumn equinoxes are described in the text. The visual illustrates the information from the text.*

Step 3 Analyze the information presented in the visual to enhance your understanding.

Ask yourself: What information does the visual show? Why was this visual used? Does the visual represent information accurately? What does the visual show that is not explained in the text?

TIP Look for patterns and connections between items and information in a visual and the surrounding text. Study colors and symbols to understand what they represent.

A EARTH'S FOUR SEASONS: NORTHERN HEMISPHERE

B SPRING EQUINOX (March 21)
B WINTER SOLSTICE (December 21 or 22)
SUN
North Pole
24 hours
Northern Hemisphere
B SUMMER SOLSTICE (June 20 or 21)
365 days
B AUTUMN EQUINOX (September 23)
Southern Hemisphere
South Pole

APPLY THE SKILL

Turn to page 39, "Earth's Landforms." Interpret the information in "The Continental Margin":

1. What type of information does this visual provide?

2. Which text passage does this visual enhance?

3. Use the information in the related text passage and the visual to explain what the continental shelf is and where it is located.

4. What does the visual show you about continental rise that is not explained in the passage?

Interpret Physical Maps

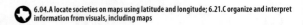

6.04.A locate societies on maps using latitude and longitude; 6.21.C organize and interpret information from visuals, including maps

Physical Maps provide information about the earth's physical features such as lakes, rivers, and mountains. You can learn about elevation, or relief, and absolute and relative location by studying physical maps. To read a physical map, follow the steps at right.

Step 1 Read the title of the map.

Step 2 Use the map legend.

Step 3 Use the map scale to measure distance.

Step 4 Use the compass rose or directional pointer to determine direction.

Step 5 Use the latitude and longitude gridlines to determine the region's location on Earth.

GUIDED MODEL

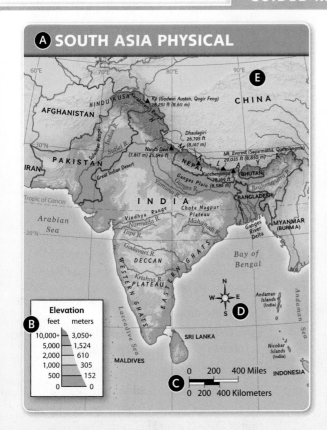

Step 1 Read the title of the map.

Ⓐ Read the title of the map to find out what type of map it is and what kind of information the map presents.

Step 2 Use the map legend.

Ⓑ A map legend explains the symbols used on the map. On a physical map, the legend usually provides information about physical features, such as mountains. The map also has a color-coded elevation scale to show how far above sea level each area is.

Step 3 Use the map scale.

Ⓒ Use the map scale to help you determine the distances between points on the map.

Step 4 Determine direction.

Ⓓ Use the compass rose or directional pointer to help you determine direction on the map.

Step 5 Determine latitude and longitude.

Ⓔ Examine the numbered gridlines on the map. The horizontal lines represent latitude. The vertical lines represent longitude.

TIP Making a chart is a good way to record important information from a physical map. Use a chart to record the map's title, legend information, scale information, latitude and longitude, and location.

APPLY THE SKILL

Turn to *Europe Geography & History*, Section 1.1, "Physical Geography." Interpret the map to answer the following questions.

1. What is the map about?

2. What type of map is this and what region does it represent?

3. What is the highest elevation in the country of Romania?

4. What is the approximate distance between the easternmost point in France and the westernmost point in Italy, in both miles and kilometers?

Interpret Political Maps

Political maps provide information about human-made features such as cities, capitals, and borders between countries. Unlike physical maps, political maps do not focus on the physical features of a country or region. To read a political map, follow the steps shown at right.

Step 1 Read the title of the map.

Step 2 Use the map legend.

Step 3 Use the map scale to measure distance.

Step 4 Use the compass rose or directional pointer to determine direction.

Step 5 Use the latitude and longitude gridlines to determine the region's location on Earth.

GUIDED MODEL

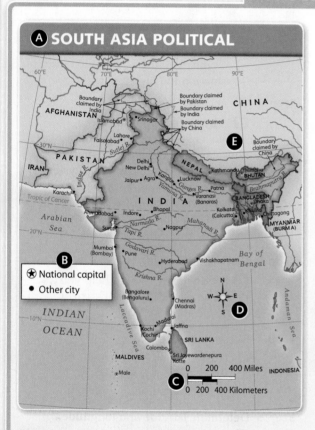

A SOUTH ASIA POLITICAL

★ National capital
• Other city

Step 1 Read the title of the map.

A Read the title of the map to find out what type of map it is and what information the map represents.

Step 2 Use the map legend.

B A map legend explains the symbols used on the map. Symbols for capital cities and major cities are usually found in the legend of a political map. On this map, New Delhi, India's capital, is represented by a star.

Step 3 Read the map scale.

C Use the map scale to help you determine the distances between cities or countries on the map.

Step 4 Determine direction.

D Use the compass rose or directional pointer to determine direction on the map.

Step 5 Determine latitude and longitude.

E Examine the numbered gridlines that intersect over the map. The horizontal lines represent latitude, and the vertical lines represent longitude. Latitude and longitude lines can help you establish the location of the countries or major cities shown.

TIP On many political maps, countries or states are shown in different colors. This makes it easy to distinguish their borders. Cities are often designated by a dot of varying sizes based on the city's population.

APPLY THE SKILL

Turn to the chapter introduction for *Europe Geography & History*. Locate the Europe Political map next to the Preview the Chapter page. Interpret the map and answer the following questions.

1. What type of map is this and what region does it represent?

2. What is the capital city of Spain?

3. What is the approximate distance between the easternmost and westernmost coasts of Iceland?

4. Where is Berlin located in relation to Warsaw?

Draw Sketch Maps

To better understand a place, whether a country or region, **draw a sketch map**. This can help show location in relation to other places or help you visualize political borders or physical features and their geographic importance.

6.04.E draw sketch maps that illustrate various places and regions

Step 1 Determine which map you are going to draw and give it a title.

Step 2 Sketch the outline of the location.

Step 3 Add important political and physical features to your map.

Step 4 Add a compass rose to your map.

Step 5 If appropriate, sketch and label surrounding countries or regions.

GUIDED MODEL

Ⓐ Map of Spain

N
W   Ⓒ   E
S

PORTUGAL

Ebro River

Ⓑ

Madrid

Ⓓ

SPAIN

TIP Sketching a map from memory is one way to check your understanding of a place. Drawing a region from memory can help you remember the location of countries, mountain ranges, large rivers, and other landmarks, which might cross boundaries or mark them.

Step 1 Determine which map you are going to draw and give it a title.

   Ⓐ Study existing maps and text describing that geographical location.

Step 2 Sketch the outline of the location.

   Ask yourself, "What shape is this location? What borders it?" Remember that sketch maps do not have to be perfect. Everyone's sketch map will look different.

Step 3 Add important political and physical features to your map.

   Ⓑ This student chose to draw and label the Ebro River in Spain.

Step 4 Add a compass rose to your map. Ⓒ

Step 5 If appropriate, sketch and label surrounding countries or regions.

   Ⓓ On this sketch map, the country of Portugal has been identified.

APPLY THE SKILL

Examine the Europe Political map next to the Preview the Chapter page in *Europe Geography & History*. Then examine the Europe Physical map and read the passage "A Peninsula of Peninsulas" in Section 1.1, "Physical Geography." Use a chart like the one at right to help you create a sketch map of Ireland.

| Map title: |
| Capital: |
| Major cities: |
| Surrounding countries: |

Create Charts and Graphs

🌐 6.03.D create graphs, charts depicting aspects of regions, countries

To organize information, it is useful to **create charts** and **graphs.** Charts simplify and summarize information. Graphs present numerical information. To create charts and graphs, follow the steps shown at right.

Step 1 Determine whether you should use a chart or graph to represent your data.

Step 2 Give your chart or graph a title to tell what kind of information it shows.

Step 3 Create your chart or graph using appropriate labels for the data.

GUIDED MODEL

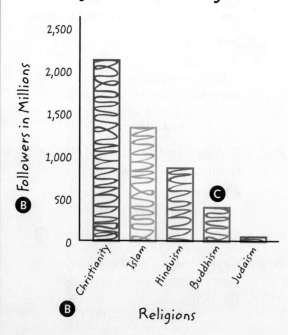

Ⓐ **Major World Religions**

Followers in Millions

Ⓑ

Ⓒ

Religions

Ⓑ

TIP Different visuals are used to represent different types of data. Line graphs are useful to compare changes over time. Bar graphs compare quantities. Pie graphs show percentages of a whole. Charts can be structured in many different ways, but they always simplify and organize information.

Step 1 Determine whether you should use a chart or graph to represent your data.

I want to represent the number of people who practice the major world religions: Christianity, Islam, Hinduism, Buddhism, and Judaism. The data is numerical, so I will create a graph. I will use a bar graph to compare the data and show which religion has the most followers and which religion has the least.

Step 2 Give your chart or graph a title to tell what kind of information it shows.

Ⓐ *I will call the bar graph "Major World Religions."*

Step 3 Create your chart or graph using appropriate labels for the data.

Ⓑ *My horizontal axis will represent the five major world religions. My vertical axis will represent the number of followers in millions. I will label the axes accordingly.*

Ⓒ *I will record my data on the bar graph using a different color to represent each world religion.*

APPLY THE SKILL

Turn to *Europe Geography & History,* and locate the Chapter Review. Use the "Miles of Railway Track in Selected European Countries" chart to create a line graph. To simplify the graph, include only the four countries with the highest totals. A line graph representing 1840 is shown at right.

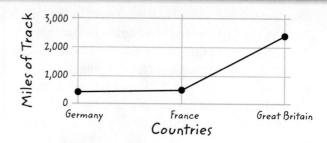

Miles of Track

Countries

Germany   France   Great Britain

Interpret Charts

A chart is a way to represent information or data visually. In a chart, information is organized, simplified, and summarized. As you examine data in a chart, pose and answer questions to find patterns or other connections and relationships. To **interpret charts,** follow the steps shown at right.

6.03.B pose and answer questions about geographic distributions on charts; 6.21.C interpret information from charts

Step 1 Read the title of the chart to find out what type of information the chart presents.

Step 2 Check the reliability of the source.

Step 3 Read any headings, subtitles, or labels to understand how the chart is organized.

Step 4 Examine the data in the chart.

Step 5 Pose and answer questions about the information.

GUIDED MODEL

A POPULATION OF MEDITERRANEAN CITIES (IN MILLIONS)

C City	1960	2011
C Athens, Greece	2.2	3.8
Barcelona, Spain	1.9	5.4
Istanbul, Turkey	1.74	11.0
Marseille, France	0.8	1.4
Rome, Italy	2.33	3.3

B Source: UN, 2013

TIP When you interpret a chart, compare the data and draw conclusions from the information. For example, in the chart above, you might conclude that Istanbul is the fastest-growing city on the Mediterranean. You might also conclude that, as a result, the city may face challenges in housing and employing its large population.

Step 1 Read the title of the chart to find out what type of information it represents.

TITLE A Population of Mediterranean Cities (in millions)

Step 2 Check the reliability of the source.

SOURCE B The UN, or United Nations, is a known and reliable source.

Step 3 Read any headings, subtitles, or labels to understand how the chart is organized.

C This chart is organized in columns and rows. The rows feature major Mediterranean cities, and the columns give data for 1960 and 2011.

Step 4 Examine the data in the chart.

The data tells how certain cities have grown over a period of 51 years. Its purpose is to report past data to compare with current data.

Step 5 Pose and answer questions about the information.

What is common to all the cities? Each grew. *Which city had the greatest growth?* Istanbul, Turkey. *What could account for this surge in growth?* I'll research this. I wonder what other cities in the world had similar growth.

APPLY THE SKILL

Turn to page 42, "Waters of the Earth." Interpret the "Longest World Rivers" chart to answer the following questions.

1. What information does the chart present?

2. How is the chart organized?

3. Where is the Amazon River located?

4. What is the length of the Mississippi-Missouri River?

5. What is the longest river in the world?

6. Of the two Asian rivers on the chart, which is longer?

Interpret Graphs

A graph is another way to represent information or data in picture form rather than written text. In a graph, data can be represented using numbers, symbols, or pictures. Common graphs include pie graphs, line graphs, and bar graphs. To **interpret graphs,** follow the steps shown at right.

6.21.C interpret information from graphs

Step 1 Read the title of the graph and identify what type of graph it is.

Step 2 Check the source of the data in the graph for reliability.

Step 3 Read the labels in the graph.

Step 4 Examine the data in the graph and look for patterns.

Step 5 Summarize the information in the graph.

GUIDED MODEL

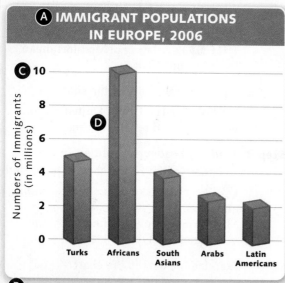

A IMMIGRANT POPULATIONS IN EUROPE, 2006

B Source: Council of Europe

TIP A pie graph is used to compare parts of a whole, and each "slice" represents a percentage. Remember that the percentages represented by the slices in a pie graph always add up to 100.

Step 1 Read the title of the graph and identify what type of graph it is.

TITLE **A** Immigrant Populations in Europe, 2006; This is a bar graph, which is often used to compare quantities.

Step 2 Check the source of the data in the graph for reliability.

SOURCE **B** Council of Europe, which is a reliable source on Europe.

Step 3 Read the labels in the graph.

C The vertical axis is labeled "Numbers of Immigrants." Its scale goes to ten million. The horizontal axis is labeled with five immigrant groups.

Step 4 Examine the data and look for patterns.

D The graph compares the numbers of immigrants to Europe from various regions in a single year.

Step 5 Summarize the information in the graph.

The graph shows that Africans made up the largest group of immigrants in Europe in 2006. The smallest group came from Latin America.

APPLY THE SKILL

Turn to "Compare Across Regions: World Languages" at the end of the Europe unit. Study the Number of Languages Spoken by Continent graph and use it to answer the following questions.

1. What do the colors of the bars represent?

2. What do the words written on the bars represent?

3. On which continent are the most languages spoken?

4. On which continent are the fewest languages spoken?

Create and Interpret Time Lines

6.21.C organize and interpret information from timelines

Another visual way to organize, represent, and review information is by creating a time line. When you **create a time line,** you record events and dates chronologically along an axis from left to right or from top to bottom. To create a time line, follow the steps at right.

Step 1 Decide what your time line will show and give your time line a title.

Step 2 Determine time line dates and place them in chronological order.

Step 3 Plot major events on the time line in the appropriate locations.

Step 4 Note the patterns that emerge on your time line.

GUIDED MODEL

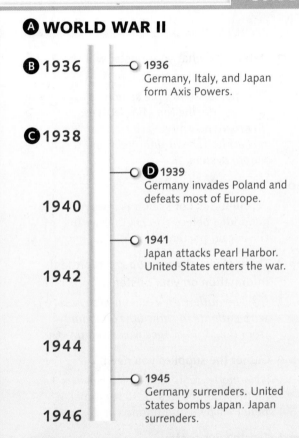

Ⓐ WORLD WAR II

Ⓑ 1936 — ○ 1936 Germany, Italy, and Japan form Axis Powers.

Ⓒ 1938

○ **Ⓓ 1939** Germany invades Poland and defeats most of Europe.

1940

○ 1941 Japan attacks Pearl Harbor. United States enters the war.

1942

1944

○ 1945 Germany surrenders. United States bombs Japan. Japan surrenders.

1946

TIP When you record B.C. dates on a time line, be careful to place them in the correct order. The higher the number, the further back in time it occurred. For example, 850 B.C. took place 350 years before 500 B.C. The year A.D. 1 took place immediately after 1 B.C. No zero year exists.

Step 1 Decide what your time line will show and give your time line a title.

Time lines often feature events that are thematically related.

I will create a time line to record the major events that led up to and took place during World War II.

TITLE Ⓐ World War II

Step 2 Determine time line dates and place them in chronological order.

Determine your start and end dates. Make sure the interval dates in between are regular.

Ⓑ *The events occur from 1936 to 1945. My start date will be 1936, and my end date will be 1946.* **Ⓒ** *I will put an interval date every two years.*

Step 3 Plot major events on the time line in the appropriate locations.

Ⓓ *For an event that occurs on a date that isn't labeled, I will draw a line from the time line and label the date.*

Step 4 Note the patterns that emerge.

On my time line, I see that Germany was powerful in the late 1930s and that the United States played an important role in the war.

APPLY THE SKILL

Turn to *Europe Geography & History*, Section 2.2, "Classical Greece." Study the time line and use it to answer the following questions.

1. What title might you give the time line?

2. What is the time span of the time line?

3. What are the intervals between major dates on the time line?

4. When did the Greeks defeat Persia?

5. What patterns do you see on the time line?

Create Models

You can **create models** to represent a geographic concept in two or three dimensions (length, width, depth). A three-dimensional scale model is a version of something much larger (such as a landform, building, battle, or space station) or something much smaller (such as a molecule or cell). Two-dimensional examples include diagrams and posters.

Step 1 Determine what your poster will show and research the topic.

Step 2 Brainstorm ideas for your poster and sketch them.

Step 3 Think of visual ways you can represent information on your poster.

Step 4 Gather the supplies you need.

Step 5 Create your poster.

GUIDED MODEL

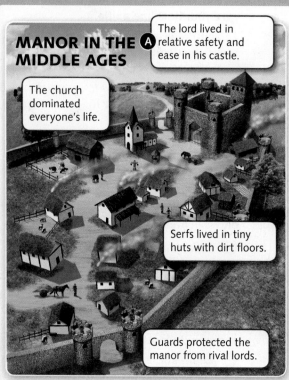

MANOR IN THE MIDDLE AGES

A The lord lived in relative safety and ease in his castle.

The church dominated everyone's life.

Serfs lived in tiny huts with dirt floors.

Guards protected the manor from rival lords.

TIP People build model clipper ships to get a sense of the history of sea transportation in previous centuries. For scale models, a 4:1 ratio means the model will be four times larger than the object; a 1:4 ratio means four times smaller. To draw a car on paper, your ratio might be 1:50—meaning your drawing would be 50 times smaller than the car.

Step 1 Determine what your poster will show and research the topic.

This poster shows the structure of a manor during the Middle Ages. To create this model, the author researched the Middle Ages and the feudal system.

Step 2 Sketch your ideas.

A rough draft or sketch is always a good idea before you begin drawing the actual poster.

Step 3 Think of visual ways you can represent information on your poster.

A *The author uses one large picture with callouts to show how a manor from the Middle Ages was structured.*

Step 4 Gather the supplies you need.

This model required some resources on the Middle Ages, drawing paper, a pencil or pen, and paint.

Step 5 Create your poster.

Work electronically or by hand. You can paste images onto your drawing if they help show what your model is to represent.

APPLY THE SKILL

Turn to pages 50–51, "Natural Resources." Read the "Earth's Resources" and "Categories of Resources" passages. Create a poster or other type of model to represent how Earth's natural resources are categorized and show examples of each type.

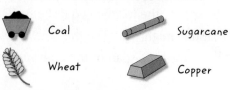

Earth's Natural Resources

Coal   Sugarcane

Wheat   Copper

Scientists and inventors create models to see how things work or to come up with ideas for improving people's lives. A cross-section diagram is a model that helps observers see what may not be visible in real life. Diagrams can also show parts that make up an object or system.

6.03.B pose and answer questions about distributions and patterns shown on models; 6.03.C compare regions, countries, using data from models; 6.03.D create models

Step 1 Determine what your diagram will show and research the topic.

Step 2 Brainstorm ideas for your diagram and sketch them.

Step 3 Think of visual ways you can represent information on your diagram.

Step 4 Gather the supplies you will need.

Step 5 Create your diagram.

GUIDED MODEL

EARTH'S STRUCTURE

A Crust

Upper Mantle

Lower Mantle

Outer Core

Inner Core

TIP Sketching a 2-D model is often the first step of building a 3-D model. Some artists and filmmakers use everyday materials to create realistic special effects on a small scale, which are photographed or filmed to appear larger than life.

Step 1 Determine what your diagram will show and research the topic.

This model shows the structure of Earth's layers. It is helpful because we cannot normally see them.

Step 2 Brainstorm ideas for your diagram and sketch them.

It is a good idea to determine and make a rough sketch of the approximate thicknesses of each layer ahead of time.

Step 3 Think of visual ways you can represent information on your diagram.

A *This model uses different colors for the layers, and labels each one.*

Step 4 Gather the supplies you will need.

This model probably required paints, markers, or colored pencils, as well as paper and a pen or pencil. Or the artist may have used a computer.

Step 5 Create your diagram.

Work electronically or by hand. If your idea turns out to be too complicated, simplify it.

APPLY THE SKILL

Posing and answering questions about what is shown in a model may help you notice things you might have missed. You can also pose and answer larger questions. Here are some examples:

- The model shown on pages 42–43 could apply to any world region or country. What does my model show in a larger sense?

- When I look at how the model applies to other places, are patterns apparent?

- Where else could what I've modeled be found in the world?

Create Databases

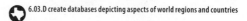
6.03.D create databases depicting aspects of world regions and countries

A database is a collection of information, or data, organized in a chart format so it can easily be viewed, used, and updated. You can use a computer program to **create databases** that allow you to search through the data to find only what you need. To create a database, follow these steps.

Step 1 Determine the information your database will contain and give it a title.

Step 2 Enter the column headings and/or row headings for your database.

Step 3 Enter the data in the appropriate columns and rows.

GUIDED MODEL

(A) FAMOUS EUROPEAN EXPLORERS

(B) Explorer's Name	Explorer's Country	Date of Exploration	Place Explored
(C) Bartolomeu Dias	Portugal	1488	Southern tip of Africa
Vasco de Gama	Portugal	1498	Southern tip of Africa; also reached India and opened up trade with Asia
Christopher Columbus	Italy (but he was working for Spain)	1492	Islands in the Caribbean; continents of North and South America
Jacques Cartier	France	1530s	Northern part of North America
Sir Francis Drake	England	1577	Sailed around the world

TIP Abbreviate headings. Be sure you enter consistent data under headings. If you had more information for a category, you could mark the place with an asterisk (*) and put additional information in a footnote.

Step 1 Determine the information your database will contain and give it a title.

(A) *This database includes data from a passage on European exploration. It records data about which explorers went to which regions. An appropriate title is "Famous European Explorers."*

Step 2 Enter the column headings and/or row headings for your database.

Remember, columns go up and down, and rows go from left to right. Database headings most commonly appear across the top or down the left side of the database, or in both places.

(B) *I have four categories of data, so I will use four columns, one per category. I will label each column with a heading that describes the data below it.*

Step 3 Enter the data in the appropriate columns and rows.

(C) *I will extract information from the text I have read and insert it in the appropriate column in the database. I will use a separate row to provide information on each explorer.*

APPLY THE SKILL

Turn to pages 46–47, "World Climate Regions." Read about the five climate regions featured in this section. Then create a database like the one at right to record the names of each climate region, a description of its weather and plant life, and a list of places that have that climate.

WORLD CLIMATE REGIONS			
CLIMATE REGION	WEATHER	PLANT LIFE	LOCATIONS

Create Graphic Organizers

6.22.D create visual material based on research (graphic organizers)

While you read, you can **create graphic organizers** such as charts, diagrams, and time lines to take notes and explore how the information is related. To create a graphic organizer, follow the steps shown at right.

Step 1 Determine your needs.

Step 2 Determine what type of graphic organizer you need.

Step 3 Draw your graphic organizer.

Step 4 Use information from the passage, plus any relevant maps or other features, to fill in your graphic organizer.

GUIDED MODEL

A PROBLEM
Earthquakes can cause severe damage and endanger people's lives.

↓

B CONTRIBUTING FACTORS
In some areas where earthquakes occur, buildings cannot withstand the intense shaking.

↓

C SOLUTION
Scientists are working hard to predict earthquakes. Engineers try to design buildings that keep people safe and minimize damage.

TIP You can use a cause-and-effect chain to help you understand the results of a particular event. Note that the chain can contain a single cause and multiple effects, or it can have many causes and only one effect.

Step 1 Determine your needs.

First, think about the type of information you are recording. Then determine what you will be doing with the information. Are you gathering facts, comparing two things, or recording a series of events?

Step 2 Determine what type of graphic organizer you need.

A chart can be used to record facts. A Venn diagram helps compare and contrast two things. A time line records a series of events over time. For this example, a problem-solution chart was created to identify a problem and understand how people are trying to solve it.

Step 2 Draw your graphic organizer.

Step 4 Use information from the passage, plus any relevant maps or other features to fill in your graphic organizer.

This student identified:

A the problem, in this case, the dangers posed by earthquakes;

B contributing factors, the situations that add to the problem;

C a possible solution to the problem.

APPLY THE SKILL

Turn to *Europe Geography & History,* Section 3.2, "The Industrial Revolution." Read "The Revolution Begins" passage. Then create a main idea and details graphic organizer like the one at right and use it to record important information from the text.

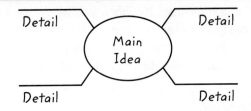

Conduct Internet Research

As you probably know, the World Wide Web (or "www") is part of the Internet and allows you access to online information and data. You can also locate on the Web primary and secondary sources for your reports and projects. To **conduct Internet research**, follow the steps shown at right.

Step 1 Choose and access a search engine.

Step 2 Type key words or phrases into the search field.

Step 3 Examine the search results.

Step 4 Visit the suggested Web sites and perform more specific searches for information.

Step 5 Keep track of sites that are helpful or that you might use later.

GUIDED MODEL

A

| "elephant habitat" | Search |

B

ELEPHANTS- Habitat & Distribution
ELEPHANTS- **Habitat** & Distribution...Discover animal, environmental, and zoological career facts as you explore in-depth topic coverage via SeaWorld, ...
www.seaworld.org/.../elephants- habitat & distribution.htm -

Elephant Facts - Defenders of Wildlife
Get the facts on **elephant**. **Elephants** are the largest land-dwelling mammals on earth. ... of **elephants' habitat** will become significantly hotter and drier, ...
www.defenders.org › Wildlife and Habitat -

African Elephants, African Elephant Pic ...
African **elephants** are the largest of Earth's **land** mammals. Their enormous ears help them to keep cool in the hot African climate. ...
animals.nationalgeographic.com/animals/.../african-**elephant**/ -

Elephants Habitat | Animal Habitats
A quick look into the **elephant's habitat**. In studying an **elephant's habitat**, the first thing one encounters is the fact that there are several species of ...
www.animalhabitats.org/**elephants_habitat**/**elephants_habitat**.htm -

TIP Copy and paste the Web addresses for the Web sites you have found helpful. To avoid plagiarism, the addresses will be part of your citations to give credit to your sources. (See page R4 for information on citing sources.)

Step 1 Choose and access a search engine.

Step 2 Type key words into the search field.
Be as specific as possible to narrow your search and yield better results.

A *I typed "elephant habitat" into the search field and clicked "Search."*

Step 3 Examine the search results.
Remember that Web addresses that end with .edu, .gov, and .org are often more reliable than .com sites. Review the addresses and summaries of each Web site and decide which ones to use.

B *This Web site's domain is .org, which is usually a reliable source, and the information is relevant to my topic, so I will go to this Web site.*

Step 4 Visit the suggested Web sites and perform more specific searches for information.
Once I'm on the site, I will search "elephant habitat preservation" to find more specific information.

Step 5 Keep track of sites that are helpful or that you might use later.
I've noted Web addresses I'll go back to often, such as the National Geographic Web site, the Library of Congress countries database, and an online encyclopedia.

APPLY THE SKILL

Think of a topic from this book you would like to research. Brainstorm key words to use on a search engine. Then, with your teacher's permission, use a Web browser to conduct Internet research on your topic. If possible, print copies of the information you find. Write a brief paragraph explaining your search process and results.

| "Ancient Greece" | Search |

Evaluate Internet Sources

Use only the most reliable and credible information as a resource. Limit the scope of Web searches to save time. Use quotation marks around key phrases. Or type site:gov or site:org at the end of your search request. To evaluate Internet sources follow these steps.

Step 1 Examine the Web site's Internet address.

Step 2 Identify the Web site's author.

Step 3 Identify when the Web site was created or last updated.

Step 4 Verify the information from the Web site using other reliable sources.

Step 5 Evaluate the Internet source.

GUIDED MODEL

Step 1 Examine the Web site's Internet address.

Ⓐ *This Web site's address is www.cia.gov. A government agency created the site, which makes it reliable.*

Step 2 Identify the Web site's author.

Sites that clearly name the author are more reliable than anonymous Web sites.

Ⓑ *The author of this Web site is the Central Intelligence Agency, or CIA. It is expert at collecting data.*

Step 3 Identify when the Web site was created or last updated.

Ⓒ *This Web site is updated every week, so the information is current.*

Step 4 Verify the information from the Web site using other reliable sources.

I found the same information in a print encyclopedia and on the National Geographic Web site.

Step 5 Evaluate the Internet source.

I believe this is a reliable source because it is created by the government, updated frequently, and has the same information as other reliable sources.

TIP Another way to evaluate an Internet source is to determine its intended audience. Ask yourself to whom the author is writing, and study the writing style, vocabulary, and tone. Does the author wish to inform, explain, persuade, or entertain? Does the author provide sufficient evidence for claims made or information provided? Note that many sites are solely for giving opinions, which appear valid but are not factually accurate.

Create Multimedia Presentations

6.22.C express ideas orally based on research or experiences; 6.22.D create written and visual material based on research

You can **create multimedia presentations** on any topic using media such as photographs, video clips, and audio recordings, and your own writing and research. To create a multimedia presentation, follow the steps shown at right.

Step 1 Determine the topic you will be presenting and the types of media you will use.

Step 2 Research your topic and organize your ideas.

Step 3 Write and edit your presentation to fit the amount of time you will have.

GUIDED MODEL

Ⓐ

Unlike many species of crab, the one shown here can swim as well as walk.

TIP Your presentation can be based on your experiences. Conduct research to provide a context or background for the experience you intend to share. For any presentation, search the **Magazine Maker CD-ROM** for images and information, which you can import. Be sure to rehearse your presentation a few times to identify and correct any problems.

Step 1 Determine the topic you will be presenting and the types of media you will use.

Certain types of media enhance topics more effectively than others. Once you have determined your topic, decide which media work best with it. Would your topic be enhanced by images, or would audio clips or music be more relevant? Would a video clip add meaning to your presentation? What about a map or graph? You decide.

Ⓐ This student used a photo from the **Digital Library** and wrote her own caption for it.

Step 2 Research your topic and organize your ideas.

Use reliable library and online sources. Take notes and then organize your material into a beginning (interesting fact or appealing idea), middle (images and ideas that tell a story), and ending (a close that sums up the ideas or refers back to your beginning).

Step 3 Put your presentation together.

Draft a script. Keep captions short and avoid putting into words what is obvious in the images. Time your presentation before you give it. If it is too long, edit parts that are the least necessary for your idea.

APPLY THE SKILL

Select a topic from this text and create a multimedia presentation about it by following the steps above. Use the **Digital Library** and **Magazine Maker CD-ROM** to create your presentation.

ANCIENT ROME

HANDBOOK
ECONOMICS & GOVERNMENT

································ **PART I ECONOMICS** ································

agriculture *n., the development of plants and animals to provide food.* Agricultural products include crops such as wheat, corn, and barley. Agriculture also includes animals that have been domesticated, or tamed. These animals are often called livestock, and they include cattle, sheep, pigs, and horses.

business cycle *n., a period during which a country's economic activities increase and then decrease in a relatively predictable pattern.* A business cycle has four phases. During expansion, businesses do well. At the peak of the cycle, economic activity begins to slow. During a contraction, economic activity continues to decrease. A contraction is also called a recession. The trough is the lowest level of economic activity. Then business starts to improve, and a new business cycle begins.

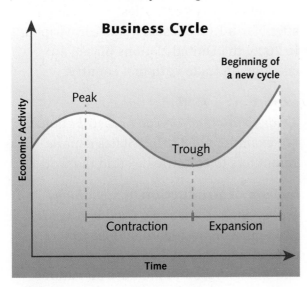

Business Cycle

capitalism *n., an economic system in which private individuals or groups own the resources and produce goods for a profit.* In capitalism, private individuals or groups decide to produce goods or

offer services. They offer those goods and services for sale in markets, which are places where people buy and sell. Businesses raise capital, or money, to create new products and hire workers. Capitalism is also called free enterprise because people are free to start businesses.

Bookstore, Los Angeles, California

command economy *n., an economic system in which the government controls a country's economic activities.* The government owns and controls the factories, farms, and stores in a country.

communism *n., an economic and political system in which the government owns and controls economic activities.* Communism is a type of command economy. In a Communist system, the government owns and operates factories, farms, and other types of economic activities. For example, in the steel industry, government officials decide what kind of steel and how much steel will be produced. North Korea, Vietnam, and Cuba have Communist systems. Communist economies have been much less efficient than free enterprise economies in producing goods and services. See **Part II Government** for the definition of communism as a political system.

corporation *n., a company in which people own shares, or parts of the company.* A corporation sells stock, or shares of the company, to raise money to create products and services. Shareholders often receive a dividend, which is a share of the profits. Multinational corporations are corporations that operate in several countries. People purchase shares of a corporation on a stock exchange.

depression *n., a deep and long-lasting contraction of economic activities.* During a depression, business activity falls dramatically. Businesses hire few workers. The unemployment rate, or percent of people without work, rises. In the United States, the Great Depression lasted from 1929 until the early 1940s. A recession is also a contraction in business. It is less severe and shorter than a depression.

A church in New York City distributes food in a breadline during the Great Depression.

developed nation *n., a country with highly-developed industries, a high standard of living, and private ownership of most businesses.* Developed nations have industries that make products like automobiles and computers. Less developed countries have fewer industries and rely on agriculture. They also have lower standards of living. The United States is a developed nation. Many countries in Africa, Asia, and Latin America are less developed countries.

economy *n., a country's system for producing and exchanging goods and services.* A country's economic development is based on its level of economic activity. If a country has a great deal of industry, it has a high level of economic development.

Economic Systems

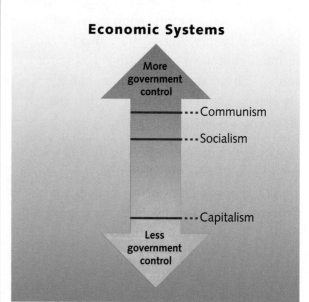

embargo *n., a government ban on trade with another country.* Countries set embargoes to show their disapproval of another country's activities. For example, after North Korea tested a nuclear weapon in 2006, the United Nations placed an embargo on trade with that country.

export *n., a good that one country sends to another for sale or distribution.* For example, the United States exports computers to countries around the world.

factors of production *n., the things that go into producing a good or a service.* Economists have identified four factors of production: land, labor, capital, and entrepreneurs. Land includes all natural resources, such as oil and silver. Labor is the work that people do. Capital is the machinery and other tools that are used to create a good or service. Entrepreneurs are people who start businesses.

free enterprise *n., an economic system in which businesses are privately owned, people buy and sell goods in free markets, and individuals freely make decisions whether to buy or sell.* The system is also called capitalism. The United States has a free enterprise system.

In a free enterprise system, producers are motivated by self-interest. To meet consumers' demand, producers decide to manufacture a good, such as an automobile, or offer a service. By doing so, they hope to make a profit. Consumers are also motivated by self-interest. They try to buy the best goods and services they can at the lowest price offered in a market.

Government makes sure that businesses compete fairly. It also ensures that food, medicines, and other products are safe. It provides services, such as defense, that are important to a country. The government also builds infrastructure, such as transportation facilities and roads.

Free Enterprise System

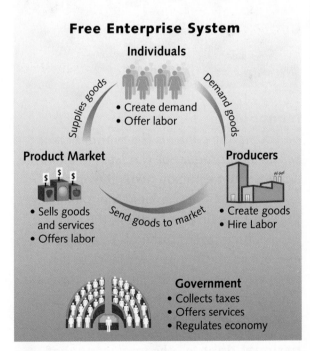

gross domestic product (GDP) *n., the total value of all the goods and services that a country produces in a specific time period, such as a year.* The GDP is an important measure of an economy's strength. Economists measure the GDP by adding together four kinds of goods and services. One is the goods and services that consumers buy. Another is the machines and other items that companies buy for their businesses. A third is goods and services that government buys. Fourth is the goods and services that a country exports to other countries.

GDP per capita is a country's GDP divided by the country's population. It shows how much the country produces per person.

Gross Domestic Product

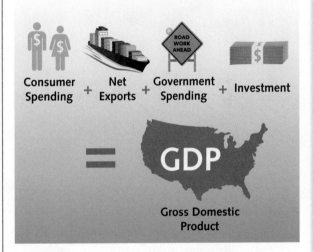

import *n., a good that one country receives from another for sale or distribution.* For example, the United States imports many cars and trucks from automobile manufacturers in Japan. Japan in turn, imports oil from Saudi Arabia.

industry *n., a group of businesses that produce a similar product or service.* For example, the film industry produces feature films. Common industries in the United States include construction, computers, pharmaceuticals, and electronics. In many industries, businesses take a raw material and turn it into a finished product. For example, in the clothing industry, businesses turn cotton, wool, and other materials into clothes.

inflation *n., an increase in the price of goods and services in a country.* In any given year, the average price of goods and services may go up. This is called an increase in the price level. The rate of increase is called the inflation rate. In 1980, for example, the United States had an inflation rate of about 14 percent. This means that the average prices that year were about 14 percent higher than in 1979.

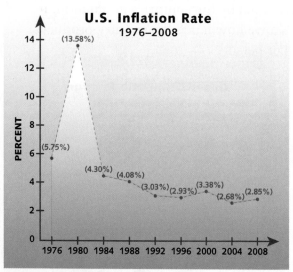

U.S. Inflation Rate
1976–2008

Source: U.S. Bureau of Labor Statistics

manufacturing *n., the production of physical products to be sold.* Manufacturing creates a wide variety of products, such as automobiles, steamships, airplanes, computers, and furniture. The term refers to the creation of items by machine and by hand. Light manufacturing means the creation of relatively small things, such as the circuits in computers. Heavy manufacturing means the creation of large objects, such as diesel engines for railroads. In 2010, manufacturing employed about 17 million workers in the United States and Canada.

market economy *n., an economic system in which people and businesses choose freely to buy and sell in markets.* A market is a place where people buy and sell goods and services. In a market economy, individuals make choices to buy and sell.

For example, an individual might decide to earn a living by making and selling T-shirts. After making them, the person would try to interest stores in selling the T-shirts. A store is a common type of market. The government establishes rules, such as the rule that stores should be safe and clean.

mechanization *n., the use of machines instead of humans or animals to perform tasks.* For example, in 1764, the Englishman James Hargreaves invented the spinning jenny. It was a machine that could spin yarn from wool. The machine allowed operators to create yarn much faster than they could by hand.

Spinning jenny

monopoly *n., the situation in which one company controls the production or selling of a product or service.* For example, suppose that a person owns the only grocery store in an isolated town. Because the store has no competition, the owner can set high prices on food. If someone else opens another grocery store in town, competition results. Because the stores are competing, they will have to lower prices and improve quality.

national debt *n., the total amount of money that the federal government owes.* If a government spends more money than it receives in taxes, it uses deficit spending. It must borrow money from individuals, companies, or other governments. As a government uses deficit spending, its national debt grows.

The national debt of the United States has grown rapidly since 1980. Critics say that the government should raise taxes, cut spending, or do a combination of the two to balance its budget.

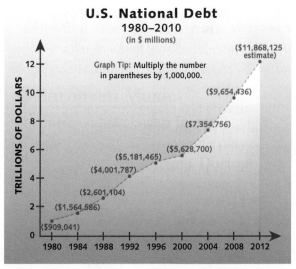

U.S. National Debt
1980–2010
(in $ millions)

Graph Tip: Multiply the number in parentheses by 1,000,000.

TRILLIONS OF DOLLARS

($11,868,125 estimate)
($9,654,436)
($7,354,756)
($5,628,700)
($5,181,465)
($4,001,787)
($2,601,104)
($1,564,586)
($909,041)

Source: U.S. Office of Management and Budget

natural resources *n., resources such as oil, coal, timber, and water that exist naturally in a place.* Having ample natural resources can help a country to develop its economy. For example, the United States has numerous natural resources, including timber and fresh water. On the other hand, Japan has become wealthy even though it has few energy resources like oil. It has developed its wealth by inventing new technologies and building quality products.

Oil pump

opportunity cost *n., the opportunity that a person gives up when he or she chooses to buy one item instead of another.* For example, suppose that Benita must decide between buying a new flat-screen television or taking a vacation. If she chooses the television, her opportunity cost is the vacation she did not take.

poverty *n., the lack of enough money to buy necessary things like food, clothing, and shelter.* Poverty is a worldwide problem. It causes disease and hunger. Poor people often do not have adequate shelter and suffer greatly during cold or hot weather. Economists say that more than one billion people in the world are poor. The U.S. government measures the percentage of its population that is poor. The graph below shows how the rate has changed over the past several years.

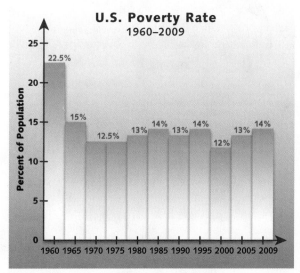

U.S. Poverty Rate
1960–2009

Percent of Population

22.5%
15%
12.5%
13%
14%
13%
14%
12%
13%
14%

1960 1965 1970 1975 1980 1985 1990 1995 2000 2005 2009

Source: U.S. Census Bureaus

raw materials *n., the materials that are used in manufacturing a final product.* Raw materials often come from natural resources, such as wood, oil, and iron ore. For example, the basic raw material in creating a table is wood. Cotton and wool are raw materials used in clothing.

retail goods *n., goods that are sold directly to consumers.* When you go to a store and purchase a DVD, you are buying a retail good. Today, merchants sell retail goods in a variety of ways. They sell them in stores, through vending machines, over the telephone, or on the Internet.

service industries *n., companies, nonprofit organizations, and government organizations that provide services rather than products.* Services include many activities, such as health care, education, financial operations, retail selling, and legal advice. In the United States, more than 75 percent of people work in service industries. Less developed countries, on the other hand, have fewer people working in service industries.

Comparing Industrial Sectors

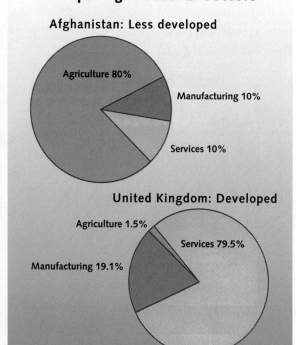

Afghanistan: Less developed

Agriculture 80%
Manufacturing 10%
Services 10%

United Kingdom: Developed

Agriculture 1.5%
Services 79.5%
Manufacturing 19.1%

Source: www.NationMaster.com

socialism *n., an economic system in which the government owns and operates most businesses.* Socialism first developed in Europe in the early 1800s. Socialists wanted to eliminate poverty and improve working conditions. During the 1840s, a German socialist named Karl Marx said that the government should own all businesses. His ideas gave rise to communism.

Today, Sweden and some other European countries are often called democratic socialist countries. This means the government owns fewer businesses than in Communist countries, but it does provide many services, such as health care. In addition, taxes are high. Many economists claim that socialism is less efficient than free enterprise.

specialization *n., the situation in which people focus on doing tasks at which they have the most skill.* By specializing, people and countries provide goods and services efficiently. South Korea, for example, specializes in building large ships. It exchanges the revenue from selling the ships for oil produced in Saudi Arabia. Both countries benefit by doing what they do best.

standard of living *n., the level of economic well-being that people in a country have.* In a country with a high standard of living, people have the income to purchase such items as automobiles. In a country with a low standard of living, most of the population struggles to have enough food, clothing, and shelter.

stock market or stock exchange *n., a market where people buy and sell stocks and bonds.* Companies are able to raise money in one of two ways. They can sell stocks, which are shares of ownership in the company, or they can issue bonds. A bond is a written agreement to borrow money, and the company pays the money back with interest.

People may want to sell stocks or bonds to raise money or make a profit. The sale of stocks and bonds takes place on a stock exchange or a stock market. Brokers handle both the buying and selling of stocks and bonds. The largest stock market in the United States is the New York Stock Exchange on Wall Street in Manhattan.

strike *n., a situation in which workers stop working in order to win higher wages or benefits.* Strikes are most often called by unions. A union is an organization that represents workers in a certain industry. If a union's workers believe that wages are not high enough, they may go on strike. The strike brings the company's operations to a halt. A wildcat strike occurs when workers go on strike without the union's support.

Auto workers on strike, Naperville, Illinois, 2007

supply and demand *n., the economic forces that decide the price and amount of a product or service.* The supply of a good or service is the amount that a business is willing and able to offer for sale. If the company can get a higher price, it will create more of the product or service. The demand is the amount of a good or service that consumers are willing and able to buy at a given price. Usually, the demand for a good or service goes down as the price rises. The price at which supply equals demand is called the equilibrium price.

The graph shows how supply and demand work. The gray line stands for demand. The green line stands for supply. The lines meet at equilibrium, when supply equals demand. At prices above equilibrium, demand for the product goes down. At prices below equilibrium, consumer demand rises.

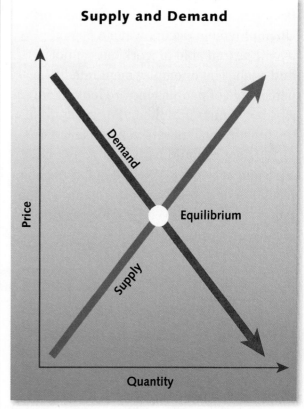

Supply and Demand

Demand

Supply

Price

Quantity

Equilibrium

tariff *n., a tax that a country places on goods imported from another country.* Countries use tariffs to protect their own companies from competition with other countries. For example, to protect auto manufacturers, a country might place tariffs on cars from other countries. The country's own manufacturers would thrive. However, consumers might pay more for their cars because there is less price competition.

trade *n., the exchange of services and goods.* Trade occurs when people cannot make things themselves but can get them from other people. For example, Chile grows asparagus. It exports the vegetable to countries around the world. With the money it earns, it imports automobiles from the United States, oil from Saudi Arabia, and so forth. This is an example of international trade. The trade within a country is called domestic trade.

unemployment rate *n., the percentage of people in a society who cannot find work.* Unemployment occurs when a person is willing and able to work but cannot find a job. The unemployment rate is the percentage of people who are looking for jobs but cannot find them. For example, if the unemployment rate is 8 percent, 8 out of 100 people could work, but do not have a job and are not able to find one. During a recession or depression, the unemployment rate rises. Unemployed people sometimes receive government aid.

wholesale goods *n., goods that producers sell to other business firms, such as stores.* Wholesalers buy goods in large quantities. They then sell those goods to retailers, who sell them to customers. For example, a factory in China might produce thousands of toys for children. A wholesaler buys the toys from the factory and ships the toys to retail stores around the world. Then the retailer sells them to you, the consumer. Without wholesalers, the modern economy would not work efficiently.

PART II GOVERNMENT

citizenship *n., membership in a state or a nation, with full rights and responsibilities.* A citizen of a country owes loyalty to that country. He or she is expected to perform certain duties, such as obeying the laws and paying taxes. In return, a citizen has certain rights, such as the right to vote. Civic participation is the way in which citizens participate in their government and society. Citizens let their representatives know what they think about important issues and participate in other ways.

Responsibilities of U.S. Citizens

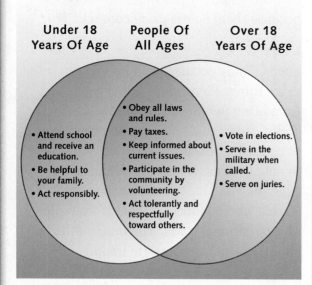

Under 18 Years Of Age
- Attend school and receive an education.
- Be helpful to your family.
- Act responsibly.

People Of All Ages
- Obey all laws and rules.
- Pay taxes.
- Keep informed about current issues.
- Participate in the community by volunteering.
- Act tolerantly and respectfully toward others.

Over 18 Years Of Age
- Vote in elections.
- Serve in the military when called.
- Serve on juries.

communism *n., an economic and political system in which the government owns and controls economic activities.* A communist government exerts great power over its people. This type of government is called totalitarian because it totally controls its people's lives. In the Soviet Union (1917–1991), the Communist Party outlawed all other parties, and the population had no freedom of speech, religion, or other rights.

constitution *n., a statement that explains the basic principles and rules of an organization.* The constitution of a government explains how leaders are selected, how laws are passed, and how laws are interpreted and enforced. The U.S. Constitution was ratified, or agreed to, by the states in 1789. In 1791, the states approved of the first 10 amendments, which are known as the Bill of Rights. These amendments guarantee rights, such as the right to speak freely. The U.S. Constitution can be changed, but doing so requires significant majorities to propose amendments, and an even greater majority of states to ratify the change.

democracy *n., a form of government in which the citizens of a nation or state hold the power to pass laws and select leaders.* The United States is a representative democracy in which people elect fellow citizens to serve in a legislature and pass laws. They also elect their leaders, such as the President of the United States. Representative democracies are also known as democratic republics or federal republics (see definition on this page). Democracy had its origins in Greek city-states.

dictatorship *n., a form of government in which a ruler holds total power.* A dictator usually comes to power through force. One of the most brutal dictators was Adolf Hitler of Nazi Germany, who ruled from 1933 to 1945. He created the policy that led to the Holocaust, or the murder of 6 million Jews and other people during World War II.

Adolf Hitler

executive branch *n., the branch of the federal government that implements and enforces laws.* In the United States, the president is the leader of the executive branch. He or she is the commander-in-chief of the armed forces. The president signs bills from Congress into law. The executive branch then makes sure that the laws are applied. To help enforce the laws, the president has a cabinet, and each member of the cabinet is responsible for a specific area of the federal government.

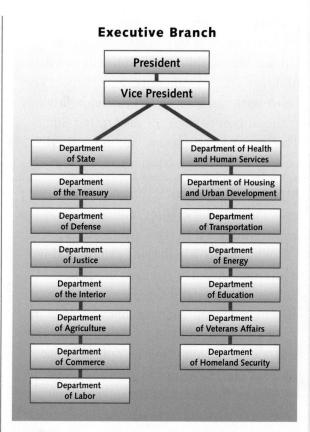

Executive Branch

President

Vice President

Department of State	Department of Health and Human Services
Department of the Treasury	Department of Housing and Urban Development
Department of Defense	Department of Transportation
Department of Justice	Department of Energy
Department of the Interior	Department of Education
Department of Agriculture	Department of Veterans Affairs
Department of Commerce	Department of Homeland Security
Department of Labor	

fascism *n., a form of government that has a dictator and controls political, economic, and other activities.* The two most well-known examples of fascism in the 20th century were Italy under Benito Mussolini (1922–1943) and Germany under Adolf Hitler (1933–1945). Mussolini came to power in Italy in 1922. He promised to solve the economic crisis that Italy faced after World War I. He soon became the country's dictator. Fascism in Italy ended in 1943 when the country surrendered during World War II.

federal republic *n., a form of government in which the population elects representatives to pass and carry out laws.* Many Western countries, including the United States and Canada, are federal republics. In federalism, a national, or federal, government shares power with states or provinces. The federal government has certain powers, such as national defense. The states or provinces control other activities, such as education.

judicial branch *n., the branch of government that interprets laws.* In the United States, the judicial branch consists of dozens of federal courts and judges. The court with the highest authority on laws is the Supreme Court of the United States. The judicial branch also includes district courts, which oversee cases at local levels.

legislative branch *n., the branch of government that creates, changes, or eliminates laws.* In the United States, Congress is the legislative branch, and it is divided into two Houses: the House of Representatives and the Senate. The states also have legislative branches, called state legislatures. In addition to passing laws, the U.S. Congress has other responsibilities. The Senate, for example, must approve of treaties with other countries. Democracies around the world have legislative branches. In the United Kingdom, for example, the Parliament passes laws.

Parliament, United Kingdom

limited government; unlimited government *n., a limited government places limits on governmental powers. An unlimited government does not place limits on governmental powers.* The United States has a limited government. The Constitution places limits on its powers. For example, the First Amendment states that the government does not have the power to limit people's free speech.

In unlimited government, the power of the government is not limited by a constitution or other document. Absolute monarchies and dictatorships are unlimited governments. From 1917 until 1991, the Soviet Union had an unlimited government.

monarchy *n., a form of government in which a king or a queen rules a country.* A monarch inherits the throne, or position, from his or her parent. Until the 1700s, monarchy was a common form of government. Britain, France, and Russia all had monarchs. In Russia, kings were known as czars. Then, in 1789, the French Revolution limited the powers of the French king, King Louis XVI. In 1793, the revolutionary government executed Louis and formed a republic. Through the 1800s and early 1900s, governments around the world became more democratic. They either abolished the monarchies completely or limited the powers of kings and queens.

oligarchy *n., a kind of government in which a small group of people holds power.* In an oligarchy, the rulers usually are either the military or the wealthy classes. Oligarchies usually rule for their own interests, not for the interests of people in lower classes. Myanmar (also known as Burma) is an oligarchy. It is ruled by a small group of military officers.

totalitarian *adj., a form of government in which a dictator or small group holds total control over the lives of the people in a country.* In a totalitarian country, the party in power is usually intolerant of other viewpoints and ideas. For example, in the 1930s, the Nazi Party rose to power in Germany by promising to bring back prosperity and return Germany to glory. The Nazi Party shut down all other parties, stating they were obstacles to these goals.

6.15.D analyze the experiences of diverse groups to multicultural societies; 6.15.E analyze similarities and differences among various world societies; 6.16.A identify institutions basic to all societies (religious); 6.17.A identify and describe how culture traits spread; 6.19.A explain significance of religious holidays and observances; 6.22.C express ideas orally based on research and experiences

From the beginning of human history, people have asked questions about what life means. What will happen after I die? What is the right way to act? Religion helps people find answers to questions like those.

World Religions
OVERVIEW

Religious institutions are basic to all societies. A religion is an organized system of beliefs and practices. Thousands of religions exist in the world. Most teach that one or more gods, or supreme powers, exist. To help people relate to the divine power, most religions teach a set of beliefs and a moral or ethical code. These codes of conduct also teach people how to treat each other. Groups of people who share beliefs often gather together to worship and celebrate important events, such as holidays or observances that honor the birth of a deity or that are times of remembrance or hope.

WORLD POPULATION'S RELIGIOUS AFFILIATIONS

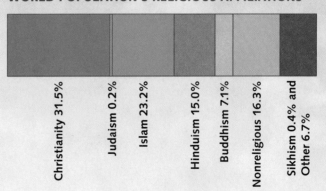

Christianity 31.5%
Judaism 0.2%
Islam 23.2%
Hinduism 15.0%
Buddhism 7.1%
Nonreligious 16.3%
Sikhism 0.4% and Other 6.7%

Source: PEW Forum on Religion and Public Life

✝CHRISTIANITY

Historical Origins

Christianity is based on the life and teachings of Jesus of Nazareth, also called Jesus Christ by Christians. Christians believe he was the son of God who died to save humanity from sin. He was a Jew who lived in the first century near Jerusalem, which was then part of the Roman Empire. Roman rulers put him to death fearing he might lead a revolt. The life of Jesus is recorded in the New Testament of the Christian Bible, which also contains stories of his followers and letters outlining Christian beliefs.

Detail of Jesus in Leonardo DaVinci's *The Last Supper*

Central Beliefs

The New Testament teaches that after Jesus was executed, he rose from the dead and ascended to heaven. Easter is the Christian holiday that observes Jesus' resurrection. Christians believe they gain salvation by believing in Jesus and following his teachings. Christians worship in churches. Their religious leaders are called either priests or ministers.

Spread of Christianity

Jesus' followers, called disciples, carried their faith around the Mediterranean world. In the A.D. 300s, Christianity became the official religion of the Roman Empire. Later, during the period of colonization, Europeans spread Christianity around the globe. It is now the largest and most widespread religion.

Christians wave palm fronds in Managua, Nicaragua, as they celebrate Palm Sunday, the first day of Holy Week, before Easter.

☪ISLAM

Historical Origins

Islam teaches that in the year 610, an Arab trader named Muhammad was visited by the angel Gabriel. The angel told Muhammad that he was God's messenger. Muslims believe that through a series of these visits, Muhammad received the words of the Qur'an, or sacred book. According to Islam, Muhammad was the last prophet that Allah, the Muslim name for God, sent to humanity. Muslims believe he is a direct descendant of Abraham, who is also the founder of Judaism.

A 17th-century Turkish ceramic tile from a mosque

Central Beliefs

Muslims, or followers of Islam, believe there is only one God, the same God worshipped by Jews and Christians. The word *Islam* means surrender, and the goal of Islam is to surrender to the will of Allah. Muslims do this by practicing the Five Pillars of Islam. These are professing faith, praying five times a day, giving to charity, fasting, and making a journey to Mecca. Muslims worship in mosques.

Spread of Islam

In the centuries after Muhammad's death, Muslims spread their religion by conquest, through trade, and through missionary work. Islamic rulers took control of Southwest Asia, Central Asia, North Africa, and parts of India and Spain. Today Islam continues to spread around the world through migration and conversion. It is the world's second largest religion.

Muslims engage in prayer at a mosque in Delhi, India, during Ramadan, a holy month of fasting.

✡ JUDAISM

Historical Origins

Judaism, the religion of the Jewish people, dates back more than 4,000 years. Its founder was Abraham, who lived in Mesopotamia. According to the Hebrew Bible, God told Abraham to move to Canaan in present-day Israel and Lebanon. God made an agreement with Abraham to bless his descendants. They later became known as Hebrews or Israelites. The Hebrew Bible contains books of law, history, and prophecy. Another important work is the Talmud, a collection of scholarly writings. The painting to the right, *Moses Rescued from the River Nile by Pharaoh's Daughter,* by Orazio Gentileschi, shows a famous scene from the Bible.

Moses, a descendant of Abraham, is rescued from the Nile.

Central Beliefs

Judaism was the first major religion to teach monotheism, or the belief in one God. Jews believe God is the creator of the whole universe. Traditional Judaism emphasizes rituals and ethics, such as observing the Sabbath, daily prayer, and study, as well as giving to charity, treating others well, and pursuing justice. Judaism's holiest day is Yom Kippur, a day of fasting, prayer, and looking back on the year. Today, Jews worship in synagogues, and their leaders are called rabbis.

A worshipper holds up a Torah scroll during a Passover blessing at the Western Wall in Jerusalem, Israel.

Spread of Judaism

For centuries, Judaism was practiced primarily in what is present-day Israel. Several times in history, empires conquered the region and drove many Jews from the area. The last major event occurred in A.D. 135 when Rome punished Jewish rebels attempting to regain independence. As Jews spread out around the world, Judaism spread with them.

☸ BUDDHISM

Historical Origins

Buddhism is based on the teachings of Siddhartha Gautama, known as the Buddha or "enlightened one." He was born a prince in India in the 400s or 500s B.C. Siddhartha was protected from seeing sickness, death, poverty, or old age until he was 29. However, after he learned about suffering, he left his palace to lead a religious life. While he was meditating several years later, Buddhists believe he received enlightenment about the meaning of life.

A 14th-century painting of Buddha

Central Beliefs

Buddhists believe that a law of cause and effect called karma controls the universe. Buddhists teach that suffering occurs because people desire what they do not have. A person who gives up desire and other negative emotions will achieve a state called nirvana, or the end of suffering. The basic beliefs of Buddhism are summarized in the Four Noble Truths. The actions that help people achieve nirvana are called the Eightfold Path.

Spread of Buddhism

During its first century, Buddhism spread across northern India. Over time, missionaries and travelers carried it to the Himalayas, Central Asia, and China. China spread Buddhism to Japan and Korea. In the 1800s, immigrants introduced Buddhism to the United States. In the late 20th century, the religion gained popularity in the United States and other Western countries.

FOUR NOBLE TRUTHS

- Suffering is a part of life.
- Desire is the cause of suffering.
- It is possible to move beyond suffering.
- There is a path that leads to the end of suffering.

Buddhist monks in Siem Reap, Cambodia, celebrate the birthday of Buddha.

ॐ HINDUISM

Historical Origins

Hinduism, one of the world's oldest religions, originated in India in about 1500 B.C. Scholars believe that it developed from the beliefs of a group of Indo-European people who spoke Sanskrit. The sacred writings of Hindus include the Vedas, which are poems and hymns, and the Puranas, which are sacred stories. Other Hindu texts such as the *Mahabharata*, of which the Bhagavad Gita is a part, teach Hindu beliefs in the form of epic poems.

Scene from the Bhagavad Gita, a sacred Hindu text

Central Beliefs

In general, Hindus believe in one eternal force called Brahman. This divine spirit takes the form of many gods and goddesses. The most important deities are Brahma, the creator; Vishnu, the preserver; and Shiva, the destroyer. Hindus believe that souls are constantly being reborn. Karma, the negative or positive effect of one's actions, determines if the soul moves to a higher or lower state of being. Hindu religious practice includes worship, study, and rituals such as bathing in the Ganges River.

Spread of Hinduism

Hinduism spread from India through parts of Southeast Asia, but now is practiced by few people in that region. In general, Hinduism has remained mainly a religion of the Indian people. Nearly 80 percent of Indians are Hindus. Indian immigrants have brought Hinduism to the United States.

Women light candles in observance of Diwali, the Hindu Festival of Lights, in Jaipur, India.

☬ SIKHISM

Historical Origins

Followers of Sikhism are called Sikhs, which means "student." Sikhism emerged in 1469 in Punjab, rising from the religious experience and teachings of Guru Nanak, Sikhism's first prophet. Nine gurus followed. The tenth, Guru Gobind Singh, vested his authority in the Sikh scripture—the Guru Granth Sahib—and the Khalsa—the community of initiated Sikhs. This led to the creation of a highly democratic religious community that practiced social justice.

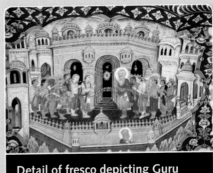

Detail of fresco depicting Guru Nanak Sikh, Sikhism's first prophet

Central Beliefs

Sikhs believe in one God who is formless, all-powerful, all-loving, and without fear or hate toward anyone. One can achieve unity with God through service to humanity, meditation, and honest labor. Sikhs do not use tobacco or alcohol, and they often follow a strict dress code, which includes never cutting their hair.

Vaisakhi is a significant holiday during which Sikhs celebrate their history, community, and values. Celebrated every April, it marks the day in the late 17th century when the tenth prophet of the Sikhs, Guru Gobind Singh, formalized the community of committed Sikhs (Khalsa). By accepting initiation into the Khalsa, one agrees to live a life in accordance with Sikh values and discipline.

Spread of Sikhism

Sikhism is practiced by nearly 27 million people, most of whom live in the Punjab region of northwest India. However, Sikhs have immigrated all over the world, and now large numbers of Sikhs live in the United States, Canada, and the United Kingdom.

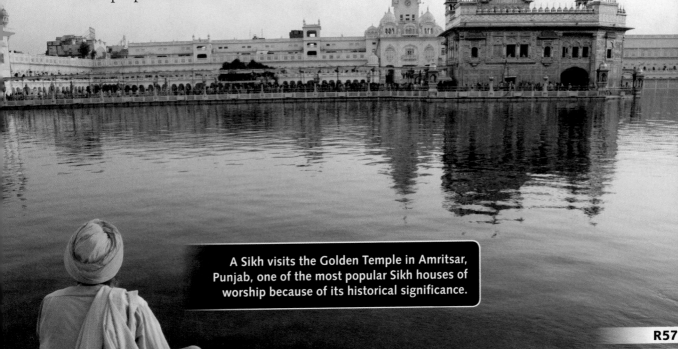

A Sikh visits the Golden Temple in Amritsar, Punjab, one of the most popular Sikh houses of worship because of its historical significance.

☯ CONFUCIANISM

6.15.D analyze experiences of diverse groups; 6.19.B explain significance of religious holidays; 6.22.C express ideas based on experiences

Historical Origins

Confucianism is an ethical system and philosophy based on the teachings of a Chinese public official and teacher named Kongfuzi. He is called Confucius in Western countries. He lived from 551 to 479 B.C. His goals were to revive traditional values and establish education as a way to improve society. The sayings and writings of Confucius were collected in a work called the *Analects*.

A 12th-century Chinese painting portrays Confucian filial piety.

Central Beliefs

One of the most important things in Confucianism is the concept of filial piety, in which children obey and honor their parents. Confucius applied this idea to other areas. For example, subjects should obey their rulers. Confucius taught that education, right relationships, and moral behavior would create an orderly society.

Spread of Confucianism

Confucianism became a way of life in China. Because China had a major influence on East Asia and Southeast Asia, Confucianism spread throughout these regions. It continues to be a strong cultural force in China and other Asian countries such as South Korea, Japan, and Singapore.

Celebrants participate in a festival in Qufu City, Shandong Province, China, the birthplace of Confucius.

FORMATIVE ASSESSMENT

RESEARCH LAB GeoJournal

Religious Understanding Day Organize a celebration of the world's religions.

Step 1 Talk in a group to analyze what the major religions have in common. Discuss what individuals or groups might experience in a society of one dominant religion or in a multicultural society. Your contribution to the discussion may be based on your own experiences or what you have read in essays or memoirs.

Step 2 Feature holidays of the religions. To gather information, go to **Connect to NG** for research links (Units 1, 9, and 10, for example). What images, symbols, or objects help explain a holiday's significance?

Step 3 Decide together what form the celebration can take. Talk about how to show respect for belief systems that are not your own.

GLOSSARY

A

abolition *n.*, the movement to end slavery, before and during the Civil War in the United States

Aborigine (AB uh RIHJ uh nee) *n.*, Australia's first developed culture

absolute location *n.*, the exact point where a place is located, identified by latitude and longitude coordinates

abstract *adj.*, an artistic style that stresses form and color over realism

accommodate *v.*, to make room for

acknowledge *v.*, to recognize

Acropolis *n.*, a rocky hill in Athens, Greece, that served as a fortress for the ancient city's most important buildings

adapt *v.*, to adjust or modify to fit

adherent *n.*, a follower of a religion, cause, or person

adventure tourism *n.*, a type of tourism in which travelers engage in physical activities such as mountain climbing, water sports, or hiking

aerodynamic *adj.*, designed to move with little wind resistance

African National Congress (ANC) *n.*, founded in the early 20th century, an organization of black South Africans, including Nelson Mandela, who protested discriminatory treatment

African Union *n.*, an organization of African countries that work toward economic progress

aging population *n.*, a demographic trend that occurs as the average age of a population rises

agricultural revolution *n.*, a period in which humans began to grow crops instead of gathering plants

Aguinaldo, Emilio *n.*, a leader in the movement for Filipino independence in the 1890s

al-Qaeda *n.*, a terrorist group based in Southwest Asia

Alamo *n.*, a fort in Texas where 200 Texans lost a battle during the U.S.-Mexican War

Alexander the Great *n.*, the conqueror who extended the Macedonian Empire and spread Greek culture throughout Eurasia from 334–323 B.C.

alliance *n.*, a partnership between countries

alluvial (a LOO vee ahl) *adj.*, describing the sediment deposited by a river

alluvial plain *n.*, a flat area of land next to a stream or river that floods

alluvium *n.*, the soil, or silt, carried by flowing water, which is ideal for farming

Alps *n.*, a European mountain chain

amendment *n.*, a formal change to a law

ancestry *n.*, the family one is descended from, going back in time; heritage

Amazon River Basin *n.*, located in South America, the largest river basin on Earth

Andes Mountains *n.*, mountain range extending 5,500 miles along the western side of South America

Angel Falls *n.*, the highest waterfall in the world, located in Venezuela

Angkor Wat *n.*, a large temple built in Cambodia in the 1100s dedicated to the Hindu deity Vishnu

animal-borne *adj.*, carried by animals

anime *n.*, a style of animation or cartoon developed in Japan

animism *n.*, a belief that everything, including objects in nature, has a soul

annexation *n.*, the adding of territory to a country

Antarctic Treaty *n.*, a 1959 agreement by 12 countries to use Antarctica for peaceful purposes and to share scientific discoveries

apartheid (uh PAHRT hyt) *n.*, the legal separation of the races; a system that denied black South Africans their rights

aqueduct *n.*, a transport system for carrying water long distances, sometimes raised on a bridge

aquifer *n.*, a layer of rock beneath Earth that contains water

arable *adj.*, fertile; suitable for farming

Aral Sea *n.*, a saltwater lake in Central Asia that has been greatly reduced in size due to diversion for irrigation of the rivers that flow into it

archipelago (ahr kuh PEH lug goh) *n.*, a chain of islands

arid *adj.*, very dry, having almost no rainfall

aristocrat *n.*, a member of the upper class

armistice *n.*, an agreement to stop fighting

artifact *n.*, an object made by humans from a past culture

Aryans (AIR ee uhnz) *n.*, nomads who migrated from Central Asia into the Indus Valley around 2000 B.C.

Asia-Pacific Economic Cooperation (APEC) *n.*, a global partnership founded in 1989 to strengthen economic ties among countries in the Pacific

Asoka *n.*, the leader at the height of the Mauryan Empire, around 250 B.C.

◻ GLOSSARY

assimilate *v.*, to be absorbed into a society's culture

assimilation *n.*, a process in which a minority group adopts the culture of the majority

assisted migration *n.*, a program set up in 1831 in which the British gave people money to move to Australia

Aswan High Dam *n.*, a dam on the Nile River completed in 1970

Atacama Desert *n.*, a desert located on the western side of the Andes Mountains

Atahualpa (AH tah WAHL pah) *n.*, the last emperor of the Incas before they were conquered by the Spanish in 1533

atoll *n.*, a ring-shaped reef, island, or chain of islands made of coral

attribute *n.*, a specific quality

Augustus *n.*, the first emperor of Rome in 27 B.C.

autonomy *n.*, a country or people's self-governance

Aymara (eye MAHR uh) *n.*, an indigenous culture who lives in the Andes Mountains of Peru and Bolivia

Aztec *n.*, a people who settled in the area of modern Mexico City, A.D. 1325–1525

B

ban *v.*, to outlaw or forbid

Bantu *n.*, an African group who moved from west Central Africa south and east across sub-Saharan Africa from 2000–1000 B.C.

barbarian *n.*, a soldier or warrior considered to be culturally less developed than those being fought; the term originally comes from the German tribes who invaded the Roman Empire in A.D. 235

Baroque period *n.*, a period from 1600–1750 in which music had complicated patterns and themes

barter *v.*, to trade or exchange goods without using money

bas-relief *n.*, a sculpture that is slightly raised from a flat background

basin *n.*, a region drained by a river system

bauxite *n.*, the raw material used to make aluminum

bay *n.*, a body of water surrounded on three sides by land

Bedouin (BEHD u ihn) *n.*, a nomadic Arabic-speaking people of Southwest Asia

benefit *v.*, to be useful to

Berlin Conference *n.*, a meeting of European nations in 1884 to settle disputes over their colonial claims in Africa

Berlin Wall *n.*, wall that divided Communist East Berlin from democratic West Berlin; it was torn down in 1989

Bhutto, Benazir *n.*, the female prime minister of Pakistan, 1988–1999

Biko, Stephen *n.*, the president of a student protest organization in South Africa who was arrested and killed in 1977

Bill of Rights *n.*, the first ten amendments to the U.S. Constitution

biodiversity *n.*, the variety of species in an ecosystem

biofuel *n.*, an alternative fuel that is a mixture of ethanol and gasoline

Black Sea *n.*, an inland sea bounded by Europe, Russia, Georgia, and Turkey

Blue Mosque *n.*, an historic mosque built in Istanbul by Sultan Ahmed I, completed in 1617

Bollywood *n.*, India's film industry in Mumbai

Bolshevik *n.*, a political party in Russia led by Lenin that overthrew the czar in 1917

Borobudur *n.*, a Buddhist temple complex in central Java

Bosporus Strait *n.*, the waterway that passes through Istanbul and connects the Black Sea and the Sea of Marmara

breakwater *n.*, a barrier built to protect a harbor

Buddhism *n.*, a religion founded in 525 B.C. in India by Siddhartha Gautama

bullet train *n.*, a train that travels more than 125 miles per hour, and is shaped like a bullet

butte *n.*, a hill or mountain with steep sides and a flat top

Byrd, Richard *n.*, an American who explored Antarctica by land and air in the 1940s

Byzantine Empire *n.*, the eastern part of the Roman Empire after A.D. 395 that lasted about 1,000 years

C

Caesar, Julius *n.*, a general who became the ruler of Rome, 46–44 B.C.

Calypso *n.*, a type of folk music that started in Trinidad

canal *n.*, a human-made waterway through land for boats and ships

Candomblé *n.*, a Brazilian religion that combines African spiritualism and Catholicism

canopy *n.*, a roof over a rain forest created by treetops

capital *n.*, a country's wealth and infrastructure

carapace *n.*, the hard shell of an animal such as a turtle

caravan *n.*, a group of merchants traveling together for safety

Cardamom Mountains *n.*, mountain range in Cambodia

Caribbean Sea *n.*, a tropical sea in the Western Hemisphere bounded by Mexico, Central America, the Greater Antilles, and the Lesser Antilles

cartographer *n.*, a mapmaker

cash crop *n.*, a farm crop sold for profit

Caspian Sea *n.*, the largest enclosed body of water on Earth, bounded by Russia, Kazakhstan, Turkmenistan, Azerbaijan, and Iran

caste system *n.*, a social structure in India composed of four main levels, which was started by the Aryans

categorize *v.*, to group information; to classify

Catherine the Great *n.*, the empress of Russia from 1762 to 1796

celadon *adj.*, green-glazed, describing pottery made by Korean artists

cenote (se NO tay) *n.*, an underground pool of water

Chang Jiang (chahng jyahng) *n.*, the longest river in Asia, which flows through China; also known as the Yangtze

Chang Jiang Plain *n.*, the plains along the Chang Jiang River

Chao Phraya River *n.*, a river that flows through Thailand

Chernobyl *n.*, a city in the Ukraine in which a nuclear reactor exploded in 1986

Choson *n.*, a dynasty in Korea that lasted from 1392 to 1910

Christian Bible *n.*, the sacred book of Christianity

Christianity *n.*, a religion based on the life and teachings of Jesus of Nazareth

citizen *n.*, a person living within a territory who has rights and responsibilities granted by the government

city-state *n.*, an independent state made up of a city and the territories depending on it

civil disobedience *n.*, the nonviolent disobeying of laws

civil war *n.*, a war between opposing groups of citizens in the same country

civilization *n.*, a society with a highly developed culture, politics, and technology

clan *n.*, a large family-based unit with loyalty to the group

Classical period *n.*, a period from 1750 to 1900 in which music followed the standard rules of form and complexity, such as sonatas or symphonies

climate *n.*, the average condition of the atmosphere of an area over a long period of time, including temperature, precipitation, and seasonal changes

climograph *n.*, a graph showing a region's climate through average precipitation and temperature

coalition *n.*, an alliance

coastal plains *n.*, the lowlands next to the seacoast

Cold War *n.*, a long period of political tension without fighting between the United States and the Soviet Union, roughly from 1948 to 1991

collective farm *n.*, in the Soviet Union, a large farm where workers grew food to be distributed to the entire population.

collide *v.*, to crash together

colonialism *n.*, the practice of one country directly ruling and developing trade in a foreign territory for its own benefit

colonize *v.*, to build settlements and develop trade in lands that a country controls

colony *n.*, an area controlled by a distant country

Columbian Exchange *n.*, the exchange of plants, animals, and disease between the Americas, Europe, and Africa that began in the 1500s

commerce *n.*, the business of trading goods and services

commercial agriculture *n.*, the business of producing crops to sell

commodity *n.*, a material or good that can be bought, sold, or traded

Common Market *n.*, the European Economic Community formed in 1957

commonwealth *n.*, a nation that governs itself but is part of a larger country

Commonwealth of Australia *n.*, the country of Australia that became part of the British Commonwealth in 1901

communal *adj.*, shared

communism *n.*, a system of government in which a single political party controls the government and the economy

competitive *adj.*, able to try to win a contest or race

complex *n.*, a connected set of buildings

comply *v.*, to follow a rule or an order

concentrated *adj.*, gathered in one central area

concentration camp *n.*, an area where Jews and others were held during World War II and murdered by the Nazis

GLOSSARY

condensation *n.,* the process of water vapor turning into liquid droplets due to cooling in the hydrologic cycle

Confucianism *n.,* an ethical system based on the teachings of Confucius

Congo River *n.,* a major river in Central Africa that ends in the Atlantic Ocean

conquistador *n.,* a Spanish soldier and leader that explored the newly discovered territories of North America, South America, Central America, and the Caribbean beginning in the 1500s, primarily in search of gold and silver

conservation *n.,* the protection of the environment

Constantine *n.,* Roman Emperor, 306–337 B.C., who made Christianity the official religion of the empire

constitution *n.,* a document that organizes a government and states its powers

consumer *n.,* a person who buys goods

contaminated *adj.,* infected; unfit for use because of the presence of unsafe elements

contiguous *adj.,* connected in one block

continent *n.,* a large landmass on Earth's surface; Earth has seven continents

continental drift *n.,* the slow movement of continents on tectonic plates

continental shelf *n.,* the edge of a continent that extends under water into the sea

controversy *n.,* a debate or quarrel

convert *v.,* to persuade someone to change religious beliefs

convey *v.,* to communicate

convict *n.,* a person sentenced to prison for committing a crime

Cook Islands *n.,* a country near New Zealand in the South Pacific made up of 15 small islands

Cook, James *n.,* a British navigator who explored and mapped the Pacific Islands in the 1770s

coral island *n.,* an island created by a gradual buildup of coral skeletons

coral reef *n.,* a rock-like structure built by layers of coral organisms

cordillera *n.,* a system of several parallel mountain ranges

Cortés, Hernán *n.,* the Spanish conquistador who defeated the Aztecs in 1525

cosmopolitan *adj.,* bringing together many different cultures and influences

Counter-Reformation *n.,* a movement within the Roman Catholic Church to reform its own practices

coup (KOO) *n.,* a sudden, illegal takeover of government by force

Creole *n.,* a blended language of European and non-European languages

crevasse *n.,* a deep, open crack in a glacier

cricket *n.,* a team game similar to baseball

critical *adj.,* extremely important, needed for survival

Crusades *n.,* military expeditions of the Roman Catholic Church to take back holy lands in the Middle East from Muslim control, 1096–1291

cuisine *n.,* the food and cooking traditions common to a certain region

cultural hearth *n.,* center of civilization from which ideas and technology spread

Cultural Revolution *n.,* social plan in China that lasted from 1966 to 1969 in which the government attempted to remove any capitalistic and anti-Communist elements from society

culture *n.,* a group's way of life, including types of food, shelter, clothing, language, behavior, and ideas

culture region *n.,* an area that is unified by common cultural traits

cuneiform (kyoo NEE uh form) *n.,* the earliest known form of writing, from Sumeria

currency *n.,* a form of money

current *n.,* the continuous movement of air or water in the same direction

cyclone *n.,* a storm with rotating winds, called a typhoon in the Eastern Hemisphere; a hurricane in other parts of the world

czar *n.,* term used for an emperor in Russia

D

dam *n.,* a barrier that controls the flow of water

Danube River *n.,* a river that starts in Germany and ends at the Black Sea

Daoism *n.,* an ethical system that emphasizes the harmony between people and nature; also called Taoism

Declaration of Independence *n.,* the document declaring U.S. independence from the British Empire, adopted July 4, 1776

deforestation *n.,* the practice of cutting down forests for crops or urban use

deity *n.,* a god or goddess

delta *n.,* an area where a river deposits sediment as it empties into a larger body of water

GLOSSARY

demilitarized zone (DMZ) *n.*, a neutral area between enemy countries, specifically between North Korea and South Korea

democracy *n.*, a form of government by the people, in which citizens often elect representatives to govern them

democratization *n.*, the process of becoming a democracy

demographics *n.*, the characteristics of a human population, such as age, income, and education

deny *v.*, to refuse to recognize

deplete *v.*, to drain or diminish a resource so as to make it no longer available or able to function as planned

descendants *n.*, future generations; relatives of a past family member

desertification *n.*, a gradual transition from fertile to less productive land

developed nations *n.*, countries with a high per capita gross domestic product

developing nations *n.*, countries with a low per capita gross domestic product

dialect *n.*, a regional variation of a main language

Diaspora *n.*, the movement of Jews away from Israel

dictator *n.*, a ruler with complete control

diffusion *n.*, a spreading out

diplomacy *n.*, discussion between groups or countries to resolve disputes or disagreements

discrimination *n.*, unfair treatment of an individual or group based on factors other than ability

displace *v.*, to force a people to leave their homes

disregard *v.*, to ignore

dissolve *v.*, to break up

distinct *adj.*, easily recognized

distort *v.*, to change the usual shape or appearance; twist out of shape

distribute *v.*, to spread an asset or resource amongst a larger group

diversify *v.*, to give variety to

diversity *n.*, variety

domestic policy *n.*, a government's plan for running affairs within its own borders

domesticate *v.*, to keep and use animals as a source of labor and food

dormant *adj.*, inactive, referring to a volcano

drought *n.*, a long period with little or no precipitation

Dry Pampas *n.*, dry grasslands in western Argentina

Dubai *n.*, a young and wealthy city and state in United Arab Emirates on the Persian Gulf

due process *n.*, in the United States, rules that authorities must follow in dealing with citizens

Dutch East India Company *n.*, a Netherlands company that dominated the spice trade in Southeast Asia

dynamic *adj.*, continuously changing

dynastic cycle *n.*, a pattern in the rise and fall of dynasties in Chinese history

dynasty *n.*, a series of rulers from the same family

E

earthquake *n.*, a shaking of Earth's crust generally caused by the collision or sliding of tectonic plates

Eastern Hemisphere *n.*, the half of Earth east of the prime meridian

ecologist *n.*, a scientist who studies the relationships between living things and their environment

economic globalization *n.*, the practice of economic activities being conducted across national borders

economic sector *n.*, a subdivision or smaller part of an economy, such as industry and agriculture

economy *n.*, a system in which people produce, sell, and buy things

ecosystem *n.*, a community of living organisms and their natural environment, or habitat

ecotourism *n.*, a way of visiting natural areas that conserves the natural resources of the region

El Niño (ehl NEEN yoh) *n.*, a reversal of usual wind and ocean currents

elevation *n.*, the height of a physical feature above sea level

eliminate *v.*, to get rid of

elite *adj.*, superior

Emancipation Proclamation *n.*, an 1863 document that freed all slaves living in Confederate held territory during the U.S. Civil War

emergence *n.*, the development and widespread use of something new

emigrate *v.*, to leave one's home country to live in another country

emirate *n.*, a state in the country of the United Arab Emirates

empire *n.*, a group of peoples or states ruled by a strong single ruler

Enduring Voices Project *n.*, a National Geographic project to study and preserve languages at risk of dying out

enhance *v.*, to improve the quality of something

Enlightenment *n.*, a social movement of the 1700s that worked for the education and rights of the individual

enlist *v.*, to volunteer for military service

entrepreneur *n.*, a person who starts up a new business

entrepreneurship *n.*, the characteristics of creativity and risk existing in a person or society

epic poem *n.*, a long poem that tells of a hero's adventures

epidemic *n.*, an outbreak of a disease affecting a great number of the population in a particular community

equator *n.*, an imaginary circle around Earth that is the same distance from the North and South Poles and divides Earth in half; the center or 0° line of latitude

equinox *n.*, when day and night are of equal length; occurs twice each year on March 21 or 22 and September 21 or 22

erode *v.*, to wear away

erosion *n.*, the process by which rocks and soil slowly break apart and are worn away

erratic *adj.*, inconsistent or irregular

eruption *n.*, a blast or explosion

escarpment *n.*, a steep slope

essential *adj.*, necessary

establish *v.*, to put into place

ethanol *n.*, a liquid alcohol removed from sugarcane or corn that can be used as a fuel alone or blended with gasoline

ethical system *n.*, a belief system that teaches moral behavior

ethnic group *n.*, a group of people who share a common culture, language, and sometimes racial heritage

ethnobotanist *n.*, a scientist who studies the relationship between cultures and plants

euro *n.*, the common currency of the European Union

European Union (EU) *n.*, an economic organization composed of 27 European member countries (2011)

eurozone *n.*, the countries that have adopted the euro as money

evaporation *n.*, the process of water turning into vapor and rising into the atmosphere due to the sun's heating; part of the hydrologic cycle

evident *adj.*, clearly present or observable

excavate *v.*, to carefully uncover or dig up

exchange *v.*, to convert money into another currency

exile *n.*, a state of absence from one's home country

exile *v.*, to force to leave a country

exoskeleton *n.*, a hard external covering that protects corals and other sea animals

expand *v.*, to make larger

expedition *n.*, a journey or voyage of some length, usually to other lands

exploit *v.*, to take advantage of; to use selfishly or unfairly for one's own profit

export revenue *n.*, money or income received for goods sold to another country

export *v.*, to send to another country for aid or profit

extent *n.*, the distance or degree to which something spreads

extinct *adj.*, completely gone, such as a species of animal or plant

extinction *n.*, the dying out of a species or type of living thing

extremist *n.*, a person with religious or political views that are outside the range of majority opinion

F

factory system *n.*, a way of working in which each person works on only one part of a product

failed state *n.*, a country in which government, economic institutions, and order have broken down

fallout *n.*, radioactive particles from a nuclear explosion that fall through the atmosphere

famine *n.*, a long period of food shortage

fault *n.*, a fracture in Earth's crust

federal republic *n.*, a democratic form of government in which voters elect representatives and the central government shares power with the states

federal system *n.*, a system of government with a strong central government and local government units

feral *adj.*, wild, having gone wild after it was once domesticated

fertile *adj.*, able to produce a great deal of fruit, crops, or offspring

Fertile Crescent *n.*, the area around the Tigris and Euphrates rivers

fertility rate *n.*, the average number of children born per woman at a certain period of time

fertilizer *n.*, a substance added to soil to enrich it

feudal system *n.*, a social structure during the Middle Ages consisting of a king, lords, vassals, and serfs

fiber optics *n.*, glass fibers used to send digital code quickly across great distances

first language *n.*, the language learned by the children of a people

fjord (fee ORD) *n.*, a deep, narrow bay

floodplain *n.*, the low-lying land next to rivers, formed by sediment left by flooding

Foja Mountains *n.*, a mountain range on the island of New Guinea in eastern Indonesia

food security *n.*, easy access to enough food

foremost *adj.*, first in rank or importance, leading

fortify *v.*, to strengthen

fossil *n.*, the preserved remains of ancient animals and plants

fragmented country *n.*, a country that is physically divided into separate parts, such as a chain of islands, and/or politically or culturally divided

free enterprise economy *n.*, a system in which privately-owned businesses create goods and services; also called a market economy or capitalism

free trade agreement *n.*, a treaty between countries that improves trade by limiting taxes on that trade

free trade *n.*, trade that does not impose taxes on imports

French Indochina *n.*, France's combined colonies of Vietnam, Cambodia, Laos, and others in Southeast Asia from 1887 through 1955

fuel cell *n.*, a small unit that, like a battery, combines chemicals to make energy

fuse *v.*, to blend

G

Gadsden Purchase *n.*, a sale in 1853 from Mexico to the United States that established the current U.S. southwestern border

Gandhi (GAHN dee), **Mohandas** *n.*, Indian leader who pushed for India's independence from the British through civil disobedience in the 1930s; considered the father of modern India

Ganges Delta *n.*, fertile area where the Ganges River flows into the Bay of Bengal

gaucho *n.*, a cowboy of South America

gauge *n.*, the measurement of the width of railroad tracks

generation *n.*, a group of individuals who are born and live about the same time

Genghis Khan (JEHNG-gihs KAHN) *n.*, the Mongol ruler who established an empire in Central Asia in the early 1200s

genre *n.*, a form of literature such as poem, play, or novel

geoglyph *n.*, a large geometric design or animal shape drawn on the ground

Geographic Information Systems (GIS) *n.*, computer-based devices that show data about specific locations

geographic pattern *n.*, a similarity among places

geothermal energy *n.*, heat energy from within the earth that can be turned into electricity

ger *n.*, a portable tent made of felt

Gettysburg Address *n.*, the speech Abraham Lincoln made in 1863 honoring soldiers who died at the Battle of Gettysburg during the U.S. Civil War

Giza *n.*, a city on the Nile where ten pyramids were built in ancient Egypt

glacier *n.*, a large mass of ice and packed snow

glasnost (GLAHS-nuhst) *n.*, the Soviet Union's policy of openness that encouraged people to speak openly about government, introduced by Mikhail Gorbachev in the 1980s

global *adj.*, worldwide

Global Positioning System (GPS) *n.*, a satellite system based in space that finds absolute location and time anywhere on Earth

global warming *n.*, the increase in Earth's average temperature since the mid-20th century

globalization *n.*, the development of a world economy based on free trade and the use of foreign labor

globe *n.*, a three-dimensional, or spherical, model of Earth

Gobi desert *n.*, the largest desert in Asia, covering much of southern Mongolia and extending into China

golden age *n.*, a period of great wealth, culture, and democracy in Greece

Golden Quadrilateral (GQ) *n.*, a superhighway that connects four major cities in India

Gorbachev, Mikhail (mih KYL GAWR buh chawf) *n.*, a leader in the Soviet Union 1985–1991; President from 1990 until it was dissolved in 1991

gorge *n.*, a deep, narrow passage surrounded by steep cliffs

government *n.*, an organization that keeps order, sets rules, and provides services for a society

GLOSSARY

Grand Bazaar *n.*, a center of shops and trading in Istanbul, Turkey

Grand Canyon *n.*, rock formation in southwestern United States that has been cut deeply by the Colorado River over millions of years

grasslands *n.*, wide open areas used for grazing and crops

Great Barrier Reef *n.*, a huge ecosystem off the coast of Australia made up of coral reefs

Great Depression *n.*, worldwide economic downturn in the 1930s, marked by poverty and high unemployment

Great Escarpment *n.*, the steep slope from the plateau of Southern Africa to the coastal plains

Great Lakes *n.*, five large freshwater lakes between Canada and the United States

Great Leap Forward *n.*, Mao Zedong's plan to make China's economy grow faster, 1958–1961

Great Plains *n.*, a flat area of land east of the Rocky Mountains

Great Pyramid of Khufu *n.*, the oldest and tallest pyramid in Egypt, built at Giza around 2550 B.C.

Great Recession *n.*, a downturn in the economies of the United States, Canada, and other countries, beginning in 2007

Great Rift Valley *n.*, a wide valley in East Africa, part of a chain of valleys formed when tectonic plates separated

Great Wall of China *n.*, a stone wall in northern China over 4,500 miles long, built to repel invaders from the north

Great Zimbabwe (zim BAH bwe) *n.*, a walled city of stone that the Shona people built in Southern Africa between 1200 and 1450

greenhouse gas *n.*, a gas that traps the sun's heat over Earth

griot (GREE oh) *n.*, a traditional African storyteller

gross domestic product (GDP) *n.*, the total value of all goods and services produced in a country in a given year

Guaraní (GWAH rah NEE) *n.*, an indigenous people who live in the lowlands on the Paraguay and Paraná rivers in South America

guest worker *n.*, a temporary laborer who migrates to work in another country

guillotine (GHEE uh teen) *n.*, a machine used to execute people during the French Revolution

Gutenberg, Johannes *n.*, a German printer who invented the printing press in 1450

H

habitat *n.*, the natural environment of a living plant or animal

Hagia Sophia *n.*, a museum in Istanbul, Turkey, that was originally built as a church during the Roman Empire and later served as a mosque.

half-life *n.*, the time needed for half the atoms in a radioactive substance to decay

Hammurabi *n.*, the king who developed a code of law in Babylonia in the 1700s B.C.

Han *n.*, a Chinese dynasty that lasted from 206 B.C. to A.D. 220

Harappan *adj.*, related to the first urban civilization in South Asia along the Indus River around 2600 B.C.

harbor *n.*, a place where ships can land protected from the open sea

Hatshepsut (hat SHEHP soot) *n.*, a female pharaoh in Egypt around 1500 B.C.

Hebrew Bible *n.*, the sacred book of Judaism

hemisphere *n.*, one-half of Earth

henna *n.*, a reddish powder used to create designs on skin

hereditary *adj.*, passed on through the family

heritage *n.*, a tradition passed down from ancestors

Hermitage Museum *n.*, a museum of art and culture in St. Petersburg, Russia

Hidalgo, Miguel *n.*, a Catholic priest who led a revolt in Mexico in 1810

hieroglyphics (HY ruh GLIHF ihks) *n.*, an ancient system of writing that uses pictures and symbols

highlands *n.*, areas of high mountainous land

Himalaya Mountains *n.*, the highest mountain range in the world, located in South Asia

Hinduism *n.*, religion practiced by more than 60 percent of the population of South Asia

Hitler, Adolf *n.*, German head of state from 1933 to 1945

Ho Chi Minh *n.*, the leader of North Vietnam who wanted to unify North and South Vietnam under communism; these efforts started the Vietnam War

Holocaust *n.*, the mass slaughter by the Nazis of six million Jews and others during World War II

homelands *n.*, during Apartheid, separate areas within South Africa where black South Africans were forced to live

hotspot *n.*, an unusually hot part of Earth's mantle

Huang He (hwahng huh) *n.*, China's second largest river, also called the Yellow River

Human Development Index (HDI) *n.*, a set of data used by geographers to compare quality of life in different countries including health, education, and standard of living

human rights *n.*, the political, economic, and cultural rights that all people should have

hunter-gatherer *n.*, a person who hunts animals and gathers plants and fruits for food

hurricane *n.*, a strong storm with swirling winds and heavy rainfall

Hussein, Saddam *n.*, the president of Iraq from 1979 to 2003

hybrid *n.*, a vehicle that can use either electricity or gas to run

hydroelectric power *n.*, a source of energy that uses flowing water to produce electricity

I

ice shelf *n.*, a floating sheet of ice attached to a landmass

immigrant *n.*, a person who takes up permanent residence in another country

immigrate *v.*, to move to a new country or region

immigration *n.*, the permanent movement of a person to a different country

impact *n.*, an effect that produces change

imperialism *n.*, the practice of extending a nation's influence by controlling other territories

Impressionism *n.*, an artistic style in which artists used light and color in short strokes to capture a moment in time

incentive *n.*, the reason or motive to do something

incorporate *v.*, to include; to combine with something already formed

indigenous *adj.*, native to the area in which something is found

indulgence *n.*, a fee paid to the church to relax the penalty for a sin during the Middle Ages

Indus River *n.*, a river in the western part of South Asia

Industrial Revolution *n.*, a period in the 1700s and 1800s in which workers in factories began to use machines and power tools for large-scale industry

industrialization *n.*, the shift to large-scale production using machines

industrialize *v.*, to develop manufacturing

infectious *adj.*, capable of spreading rapidly to others

infrastructure *n.*, the basic systems of a society such as roads, bridges, sewers, and electricity

inner islands *n.*, islands in Indonesia that include Java, Madura, and Bali

Institutional Revolutionary Party (PRI) *n.*, a political party that controlled Mexico's government from 1929 to 2000

interact *v.*, to affect other people and be affected by them

interior *n.*, the land that is away from a seacoast

Internet *n.*, a communications network

intersection *n.*, a place where people meet or paths cross

intifada *n.*, an uprising or rebellion, usually meant to reference the Palestinian revolt against Israel

invader *n.*, an enemy who enters a country by force

invasive species *n.*, non-native plants or animals introduced to a new area, intentionally or unintentionally, that disturb habitats of native life forms

Iron Curtain *n.*, an imaginary boundary that separated Communist and non-Communist countries in Europe during the Cold War

Irrawaddy River *n.*, a river that flows through Myanmar

irrigation *n.*, the process of redirecting water to crops through channels and ditches

Isis *n.*, an important Egyptian goddess

Islam *n.*, religion founded in Saudi Arabia in the early A.D. 600s

isolated *adj.*, cut off from others

isolation *n.*, separation or being set apart from others

isthmus *n.*, a narrow strip connecting two large land areas

J

Jainism *n.*, a religion in northwest India started in the late A.D. 500s

Java *n.*, one of the inner islands located in Southeast Asia

Jerusalem *n.*, the capital city of Israel

Jiang Jieshi (jee ahng jee shee) *n.*, a Chinese nationalist leader who fought Communists

Jinnah, Mohammed Ali *n.*, a leader of the All-India-Muslim League who helped found Pakistan and was Pakistan's first Governor-General from 1947–1948

Judaism *n.* a monotheistic religion founded in Israel

GLOSSARY

K

Kalahari *n.*, a major desert in southern Africa

Kanto Plain *n.*, flat area good for agriculture and industry located east of the Japanese Alps

karma *n.*, in Hinduism, the negative or positive effect one receives as a result of his or her actions

Kenyatta, Jomo (JOH moh ken YAA taa) *n.*, an African leader who helped gain Kenya's independence and became its first elected leader in 1963

Khmer Empire *n.*, the largest and longest-lasting empire in Cambodia from the 800s to 1430

Kievan Rus *n.*, the state established by the Varangian Russes in 882 that became part of modern Russia

Kilimanjaro *n.*, an inactive volcano in Tanzania that is 19,340 feet tall

kimono *n.*, traditional Japanese women's clothing

Kingman Reef *n.*, an unspoiled coral reef in the Line Islands between Hawaii and American Samoa

kinship *n.*, blood or family relationship

Knesset (kuh NEH set) *n.*, the Israeli parliament

Koguryo (koh gur YOO) *n.*, a kingdom in northern Korea in 37 B.C.

Kongo *n.*, a state founded in 1390 in Central Africa

Koryo *n.*, a dynasty that ruled Korea from 935 to 1392

Kremlin *n.*, a historic complex of palaces, armories, and churches in Moscow and the seat of Russian government

Krishna *n.*, in Hinduism, a deity in the bodily form of Vishnu

Kunlun Mountains *n.*, a mountain range in East Asia

Kurd *n.*, a member of a non-Arab ethnic group in Southwest Asia

L

labor force *n.*, the number of people available to work

land bridge *n.*, a strip of land connecting two landmasses

land reform *n.*, the breaking up of large estates to give land to the poor

landlocked *adj.*, surrounded by land on all sides, with no direct access to a seacoast

landmass *n.*, a very large area of land

language diffusion *n.*, the spread of languages from their original home

language family *n.*, a group of related languages

latitude *n.*, an imaginary line around Earth that runs east to west, showing location relative to the equator

launch *v.*, to start

legume *n.*, peas or beans

Lenin, V.I. *n.*, the Bolshevik leader who overthrew the czar in the Russian Revolution of 1917 and led the new government

liberate *v.*, to set someone or something free

lingua franca (LEEN gwa FRAWN kah) *n.*, the common language among several groups of people

linguist *n.*, a language scientist

literacy rate *n.*, the percentage of people who can read and write

literate *adj.*, able to read and write

Llanos *n.*, grasslands in northern South America

Locke, John *n.*, an English philosopher of the late 1600s who helped inspire the American Revolution and the Enlightenment

locks *n.*, devices in canals used to raise or lower ships between the waterways being connected

loess (less) *n.*, a yellow silt or sediment that forms thick deposits

longitude *n.*, an imaginary line running north to south from the North Pole to the South Pole that shows location relative to the prime meridian

Lost Boys of Sudan *n.*, a group of young men of Sudan who were orphaned by civil war and stuck together to escape the violence

Lost Decade *n.*, the 1990s in Japan, when production declined because businesses were deeply in debt

Louisiana Purchase *n.*, the land Thomas Jefferson bought in 1803, doubling the size of the United States

L'Ouverture, Toussaint (too SAN loh ver CHOOR) *n.*, a former slave who led Haiti's successful revolt for independence from France

lowland *n.*, a low-lying area

lucrative *adj.*, making money, or profitable

Luther, Martin *n.*, a German monk whose actions in 1517 led to the Reformation to address corruption in the Roman Catholic Church

M

Machu Picchu (MAH choo PEE choo) *n.*, a complex city built on a mountain by the Incas in the 1400s

Madura *n.*, one of the inner islands located in Southeast Asia

GLOSSARY

magnetic levitation (Maglev) *adj.*, type of train that rides on a cushion of air over tracks laid with many powerful magnets

mainland *n.*, the land connected to a continent, usually in reference to countries with both continental land and islands.

maintain *v.*, to preserve and carry on

Malay Peninsula *n.*, a peninsula in Southeast Asia that includes parts of Thailand, Myanmar, and the mainland section of Malaysia

Malaysia *n.*, a country in Southeast Asia at the bottom of the Malay Peninsula and the island of Borneo

malnutrition *n.*, the lack of enough food or nourishment

Mandela, Nelson *n.*, a leader of the African National Congress who was jailed for fighting apartheid, but who became the president of South Africa in 1994

manga *n.*, a type of Japanese comic book

Manifest Destiny *n.*, the idea that the United States had the right to expand its territory to the Pacific Ocean

Manila *n.*, the capital of the Philippines

manufacturing *n.*, the use of machines to make raw materials into usable products

Mao Zedong (MOW dzuh dahng) *n.*, the chairman of the Communist Party who led China from 1949–1976

Maori (MOW ree) *n.*, the native people of New Zealand

map *n.*, a two-dimensional, flat representation of Earth

marine *adj.*, sea-based

marine life *n.*, the plants and animals living in the ocean

marine reserve *n.*, an ocean area set aside to protect ocean life from humans

maritime *adj.*, related to the sea

marketing *n.*, advertising and promotion for a product or business

marsupial *n.*, a mammal whose females carry their babies in a pouch

martial law *n.*, government maintained by military power

mass media *n.*, communication from a single source with the potential to reach large audiences

Maya *n.*, a civilization that lived in the Yucatán and northern Central America from 100 B.C. to A.D. 900

medicinal plant *n.*, plant used to treat illness

meditation *n.*, the practice of using concentration to quiet and control thoughts

Mediterranean climate *n.*, a climate that has hot, dry summers and mild, rainy winters

megacity *n.*, a large city with more than 10 million people

Mekong River *n.*, the longest river in Southeast Asia; flows through Myanmar, Laos, and Thailand

Mesa Central *n.*, in Mexico, the southern area of the Mexican Plateau

messiah *n.*, a leader or savior

mestizo *n.*, a person who has mixed European and Native American ancestry

methane *n.*, a colorless, odorless natural gas released from carbon

metropolitan area *adj.*, populated place around a city that includes the city limits and the surrounding communities

Mexican Cession *n.*, the land ranging from Texas to California given by Mexico to the United States in the 1848 Treaty of Guadalupe Hidalgo

Mexican Plateau *n.*, a flat area of land that lies between the two ranges of the Sierra Madre Mountains in Mexico

microcredit *n.*, a small loan of money

microlending *n.*, the practice of making small loans to people starting their own businesses

Middle Ages *n.*, a period in Western Europe after the fall of the Roman Empire, from about 500 to 1500

Middle Passage *n.*, the months-long trip across the Atlantic Ocean in which enslaved Africans were brought to European colonies in the Americas

migrate *v.*, to move from one place to another

migration *n.*, the movement from one place to another

military dictatorship *n.*, a form of government in which the army runs the government

mineral *n.*, a solid natural substance found in rocks and Earth that is inorganic and has its own set of properties

missionary *n.*, a person sent by a religious organization to convert others to that religion

mobile *adj.*, movable

modernization *n.*, policies and actions designed to bring a country up to date in technology and other areas

modify *v.*, to change, or make less extreme

Mongol Empire *n.*, an empire established in Central Asia in the early 1200s by Genghis Khan

monk *n.*, a man who devotes himself to religious work

GLOSSARY

monopoly *n.*, the complete control of the market for a service or product

monotheism (MAHN uh thee ihz uhm) *n.*, a belief in one god

monotheistic *adj.*, related to a religious belief in one god

monotheistic religion *n.*, a system of belief in one god or deity

monsoon *n.*, a seasonal wind that brings intense rainfall during part of the year

Montezuma *n.*, an Aztec ruler who was killed by the Spanish conquistador Hernán Cortés

moral *adj.*, right and good, describing human behavior

mosque *n.*, a Muslim place of worship

mouth *n.*, the place where a river empties into a sea

movable type *n.*, a printing invention in which individual characters can be moved to create different pages of text

multinational corporation *n.*, a large company based in one country that establishes branches in several others

multi-party democracy *n.*, a political system in which elections include candidates from more than one party

multitudes *n.*, large numbers

Mundurukú (moon doo ROO koo) *n.*, an indigenous people of Brazil

mural *n.*, a large painting on a wall

mythology *n.*, a set of stories, traditions, and beliefs

N

Nairobi (ny ROE bee) *n.*, Kenya's capital city

Napoleon *n.*, Napoleon Bonaparte, the leader of France who conquered other European countries to build an empire, 1804–1815

National Action Party (PAN) *n.*, a political party in Mexico that won election in 2000

nationalism *n.*, a strong sense of loyalty to one's country

nationalize *v.*, to place a private industry under government control

natural rights *n.*, rights such as life, liberty, and property that people possess at birth

naturalization *n.*, the process that someone born in another country follows to become a citizen

navigable *adj.*, wide or deep enough to be traveled easily by boats and ships

navigation *n.*, the science of finding position and planning routes

Nazi Germany *n.*, Germany as led by the Nazi party from 1933–1945

N'Dour, Youssou *n.*, a famous griot from West Africa who plays Mbalax music

Nebuchadnezzar (nehb buh kuhd NEHZ uhr) *n.*, king of Babylonia, 605–562 B.C.

neutrality *n.*, the refusal to take sides or become involved

New Guinea *n.*, the world's second largest island, located in the southwest Pacific

New South Wales *n.*, in Australia, a colony built by convicts in 1788

Nile River *n.*, the longest river in the world; flows through Egypt and Africa for 4,000 miles

Nkrumah, Kwame (KWAA may en KROO mah) *n.*, an African leader in the 1950s and 1960s who helped Ghana gain independence

nocturnal *adj.*, active at night rather than during the day

nomad *n.*, a person who moves from place to place

nonrenewable *adj.*, cannot reproduce quickly enough to keep up with its use

nonrenewable fossil fuel *n.*, a source of energy such as oil, natural gas, or coal that is in limited supply

nonrenewable resource *n.*, a source of energy that is limited and cannot be replaced, such as oil

North American Free Trade Agreement (NAFTA) *n.*, a 1994 agreement that made trade and investment easier among Canada, Mexico, and the United States

North Anatolian Fault *n.*, a fracture in Earth's crust that runs east and west, just south of the Black Sea

North Atlantic Drift *n.*, a warm ocean current that warms the waters around the northwest part of Russia

North China Plain *n.*, the plain along the Huang He River

North Pole *n.*, the northernmost point on Earth, opposite the South Pole, where all lines of longitude meet

Northern European Plain *n.*, a vast lowland that stretches from France to Russia

Northern Hemisphere *n.*, the half of Earth north of the equator

novel *n.*, a long work of fiction with complex characters and plot

GLOSSARY

O

oasis *n.,* a fertile place with water in a dry desert area

occupy *v.,* to take over

Okavango Delta (oh kuh VAANG oh) *n.,* an inland delta in Botswana, where the Okavango River empties into a swamp

Olmec *n.,* an organized society who lived along the southern coast of the Gulf of Mexico in 1000 B.C.

one-child policy *n.,* the Chinese law of 1979 limiting families living in urban areas to one child

opera *n.,* a performance that tells a story through words and music

oppose *v.,* to object to

oral tradition *n.,* the passing of stories or histories by word of mouth from one generation to the next

Orange Revolution *n.,* the Ukraine's peaceful removal of its prime minister in 2004

Osman *n.,* the first leader of the Turks in the 1300s, for whom the Ottomans were named

Ottoman Empire *n.,* a large, wealthy empire from 1453 to 1923 centered in what is now Turkey

outer islands *n.,* islands in Indonesia that include Sumatra, Borneo, New Guinea, and others

outrigger canoe *n.,* a boat with an attached float that helps it balance

outsourcing *n.,* the shifting of jobs to workers outside of a company, often to a foreign country

overpopulation *n.,* the condition of too many people living in one place

P

Paekche (PAHK CHAY) *n.,* a kingdom in southwest Korea in 18 B.C.

pagoda *n.,* multistoried religious structure found in Asian countries, usually used for religious purposes

Palestine Liberation Organization (PLO) *n.,* an organization created by Palestinian leaders

Pampas *n.,* the grassy plain in Argentina

Pan-Africanism *n.,* a movement in the early 1900s to unite African people

Panama Canal Zone *n.,* the area in which the Panama Canal was built

pandemic *n.,* an outbreak of a disease that spreads over a wide geographic area

Papua New Guinea *n.,* a country in the South Pacific that is the eastern half of the island of New Guinea and includes nearby islands

papyrus *n.,* a paper-like material invented in ancient Egypt

Parliament *n.,* the legislative branch of India's government

parliamentary democracy *n.,* a government system in which the chief executive is the prime minister, chosen by the party with the most seats in Parliament

Partition *n.,* refers to the division of South Asia into the independent countries of India and Pakistan

patrician *n.,* a wealthy landowner in ancient Rome

Pearl Harbor *n.,* a U.S. naval base in Hawaii that the Japanese bombed in 1941 and that brought about U.S. entry into World War II

peat *n.,* the material from very old decayed plants that burns like coal

peninsula *n.,* a body of land surrounded on three sides by water

perestroika (pehr ih STORY kuh) *n.,* reform in the structure of the economy introduced by Mikhail Gorbachev in the Soviet Union in 1985

permafrost *n.,* permanently frozen ground

perspective *n.* an artistic way of showing objects as they appear to people in terms of relative distance or depth, as if in three dimensions

pesticide *n.,* a chemical that kills harmful insects and weeds

Peter the Great *n.,* Peter Romanov, who ruled Russia as czar from 1682 to 1725

petrochemicals *n.,* products made from petroleum, or oil

petroleum *n.,* raw material used to produce oil

pharaoh *n.,* a king in ancient Egypt

philosopher *n.,* a person who examines questions about the universe and searches for the truth

pictograph *n.,* a painted picture used to communicate

pilgrimage *n.,* a religious journey

pioneer *n.,* a settler of new land

pipeline *n.,* a series of connected pipes used to transport liquids or gases

Pizarro, Francisco *n.,* a Spanish conquistador who in 1533 overthrew the Incan emperor and founded the city of Lima, Peru

plain *n.*, a level area on Earth's surface

plantation *n.*, a large farm that grows crops for profit

plate *n.*, a rigid section of Earth's crust that can move independently

plateau *n.*, a plain high above sea level that usually has a cliff on all sides

plebeian *n.*, a farmer or lower class person in ancient Rome

poach *v.*, to hunt or fish illegally

poacher *n.*, a person who hunts or fishes illegally

poaching *n.*, illegal hunting or fishing

polder *n.*, land in the Netherlands that has been reclaimed from the sea for farming

policy *n.*, the official guidelines and procedures of an organization or government

pollution *n.*, chemical or physical waste that creates an unclean or dirty environment

Polynesian Triangle *n.*, a large area in the South Pacific that includes many islands

polytheism (PAHL ee thee ihz uhm) *n.*, the belief in more than one god

polytheistic religion *n.*, a system of belief in many deities or gods

popular culture *n.*, the arts, music, and other elements of everyday life in a region

porcelain *n.*, a type of strong ceramic pottery

port *n.*, a harbor for ships where goods are exchanged

Port-au-Prince *n.*, the capital city of Haiti

potential *n.*, possibility

precipitation *n.*, the process of water falling to Earth as rain, snow, or hail

predominant *adj.*, main, most common, superior to others

prehistoric *adj.*, before written history

preserve *v.*, to protect

pride *n.*, a group of lions that live together

prime meridian *n.*, the line of 0° longitude that runs from the North to the South Pole, and passes through Greenwich, England

privatization *n.*, the process of government-owned businesses becoming privately owned

profitable *adj.*, making money, financially successful

projection *n.*, a way of showing Earth's curved surface on a flat map

promote *v.*, to encourage

propaganda *n.*, information made to influence people's opinions or advance an organization or party's ideas

proportional representation *n.*, a system in which a political party gets the same percentage of seats as its percentage of votes

prosperous *adj.*, economically strong

protest *v.*, to object to

province *n.*, a smaller part of a larger country, especially in Canada

push-pull factors *n.*, reasons why people migrate; "push" factors cause them to leave; "pull" factors make them come to a place

pyramid *n.*, a stone monument built as a tomb in ancient Egypt

Q

qanat (kuh NOT) *n.*, a human-made underground tunnel on the Iranian Plateau, used for carrying water from the mountains

Qin (chihn) *n.*, the dynasty that ruled China from 221–206 B.C.

Qur'an *n.*, the sacred book of Islam

Quechua (KEHCH wah) *n.*, a people who live in the Andes Mountains of Peru, Ecuador, and Bolivia

R

radical *n.*, a person who wants an extreme change or holds an extreme political position

radioactive *adj.*, giving off energy caused by the breakdown of atoms

rain forest *n.*, a forest with warm temperatures, high humidity, and thick vegetation that receives more than 100 inches of rain per year

rain shadow *n.*, a dry region on one side of a mountain range

rainshadow effect *n.*, process in which moist air rises up a mountain range and then cools and falls as precipitation, leaving the other side of the range mostly dry

Ramses II *n.*, Egyptian pharaoh who reigned around 1185 B.C. and expanded Egypt's empire

raw materials *n.*, unfinished or natural materials such as minerals, oil, or coal used to make finished products

Re *n.*, the sun god of the ancient Egyptians

rebellion *n.*, a revolt or resistance to authority

recession *n.*, a slowdown in economic growth

reclaim *v.*, to take back

Reconstruction *n.*, the effort to rebuild and reunite the United States following the Civil War

reform *n.*, change aimed at correcting a problem

Reformation *n.*, the movement in the 1500s to reform Christianity

refuge *n.*, a safe place

refugee *n.*, a person who flees a place to find safety

region *n.*, a group of places with common traits

regulate *v.*, to control

reign *n.*, the period of rule for a king, queen, emperor, or empress

Reign of Terror *n.*, a movement in France led by Maximilien Robespierre in which 40,000 people were beheaded in 1793–94

reincarnation *n.*, the birth of the soul into another physical life

relative location *n.*, the position of a place in relation to other places

reliable *adj.*, dependable or trustworthy

relief *n.*, the change in elevation from one place to another

religious tolerance *n.*, the acceptance of different religions to be practiced at the same time, without prejudice

relocate *v.*, to move

remittance *n.*, money sent to a person in another place

remote *adj.*, hard to reach, isolated

Renaissance *n.*, meaning "rebirth," a period in the 1300–1500s in which culture and the arts flourished

renewable energy *n.*, energy from sources that do not run out, such as wind, sun, and water

renewable resource *n.*, a raw material or energy source that replaces itself over time

reparation *n.*, after a war, money paid as punishment, usually by the aggressors in the conflict

republic *n.*, a form of government in which officials are elected by the people to govern

reserve *n.*, land set aside for a special purpose such as farming, preserving habitats, or housing specific groups of people; a future supply (of oil)

reservoir *n.*, a large artificial lake that stores water

resistance *n.*, opposition

restore *v.*, to bring back

retreat *v.*, to go backward, not forward

revenue *n.*, income

reverse *v.*, to go in the opposite direction

revolution *n.*, an action to overthrow a government by citizens or colonists

Rhine River *n.*, a river that starts in Switzerland and ends in the North Sea

rift valley *n.*, a deep valley formed when Earth's crust separated, as in East Africa

Ring of Fire *n.*, an area along the rim of the Pacific Ocean where tectonic plates meet, causing many active volcanoes and earthquakes

Rio de Janeiro *n.*, a city in Brazil that will host the 2016 Olympic Games

ritual *n.*, a formal action that is regularly repeated

rivalry *n.*, competition or opposition between people

river basin *n.*, a low area drained by a river

Romantic Period *n.*, an artistic period in the early 1800s when artists painted landscapes and natural scenes to convey emotions

roots *n.*, cultural origins

Rub al Khali *n.*, a large desert in southern Saudi Arabia

Russian Revolution *n.*, the revolution in Russia in 1917 that overthrew the czar and put the Bolsheviks in power

Russification *n.*, the policy of putting Russians in charge of Soviet republics during the 1970s and 1980s

ruthless *adj.*, cruel

S

Sahara Desert *n.*, the largest hot desert in the world, covering most of North Africa

Sahel (saa HEL) *n.*, in Sub-Saharan Africa, a semiarid grassland that separates the Sahara in the north from tropical grasslands in the south

salinization *n.*, the building up of salt in soil

Samoa *n.*, a country governing the western Samoan islands in the South Pacific Ocean

samurai (SAM uh ry) *n.*, a skilled Japanese warrior

GLOSSARY

sanitation *n.*, measures such as sewers to protect public health

Sanskrit *n.*, the language of the Aryans, which became the basis for many languages in South Asia

Santa Anna *n.*, the Mexican president and general who won the battle of the Alamo but lost the U.S.-Mexican War

São Paolo *n.*, the largest city in Brazil

sarcophagus *n.*, a coffin

sari *n.*, a traditional Indian garment for women worn wrapped around the body

saturate *v.*, to soak thoroughly

savanna *n.*, grassland, as in the south of Sub-Saharan Africa

scale *n.*, the part of a map that indicates how big an area of Earth is shown

scarcity *n.*, a shortage of something

scientific station *n.*, a place to carry out research

scorched earth policy *n.*, in 1812, practice in which Russian troops, as they retreated from Napoleon's army, burned crops and resources that could supply the enemy

seafarer *n.*, a sea traveler

secede *v.*, to formally withdraw

secular *adj.*, worldly, not connected to a religion

segregation *n.*, separation by race

seismic *adj.*, having to do with earthquake activity or movement

seize *v.*, to take control of

self-rule *n.*, the government of a country by its own people

semiarid *adj.*, somewhat dry, with very little rainfall

serf *n.*, from the 1500s to the 1800s, a poor Russian or European peasant farmer who rented land from a landlord and had few rights

shalwar-kameez *n.*, a long shirt with loose-fitting pants worn in India and Southwest Asia

Shang *n.*, a family whose dynasty ruled China from 1766–1050 B.C.

sheikh *n.*, an Arab leader

Shi Huangdi (shee hwahng dee) *n.*, the ruler of the Qin dynasty, who became China's first emperor in 221 B.C.

Shi'ite (SHEE eyt) *adj.*, a branch of Muslims who believe that religious leaders should be descendants of Muhammad

Shinto *n.*, a native religion of Japan that is similar to animism

shogun *n.*, a military governor of Japan

Siberia *n.*, a huge region in central and eastern Russia

significant *adj.*, important

Sikhism *n.*, a religion in India started in the late A.D. 1400s

Silk Roads *n.*, ancient trade routes that connected Southwest and Central Asia with China

Silla (SIHL uh) *n.*, a kingdom in southeastern Korea in 57 B.C.

silt *n.*, fine particles of soil deposited along riverbanks

slash-and-burn *n.*, a farming method of clearing land by cutting down and burning forest and vegetation

Slavs *n.*, people who came from around the Black Sea or Poland and settled in the Ukraine and western Russia around A.D. 800

slum *n.*, an area in a city that is crowded, with poor housing and bad living conditions

smartphone *n.*, a handheld device that combines communication and software applications

socialism *n.*, a system of government in which the government controls economic resources

solstice *n.*, the point at which the sun is farthest north or farthest south of the Equator; the beginning of summer and winter

South Pole *n.*, the southernmost point on Earth, opposite the North Pole, where all lines of longitude meet

Southern Alps *n.*, a mountain range in New Zealand

Southern Hemisphere *n.*, the half of Earth south of the equator

sovereignty *n.*, a country's control over its own affairs

Soviet Union *n.*, the Union of Soviet Socialist Republics, a country made up of Russia and other Eurasian states, from 1922 to 1991

soybean *n.*, a type of bean grown for food and industrial products

spatial thinking *n.*, a way of thinking about space on Earth's surface, including where places are located and why they are there

GLOSSARY

Special Economic Zone *n.*, an area in China that was allowed to develop a market economy with less government control of business

sprawl *v.*, to spread out

standard of living *n.*, the level of goods, services, and material comforts of people in a country

staple *n.*, a basic part of people's diets

state *n.*, a defined territory with its own government

steel *n.*, a strong metal made from iron combined with other metals

steppe *n.*, a very large plain of dry grassland

strait *n.*, a narrow waterway that connects two bodies of water

strike *n.*, a work stoppage by employees who refuse to work

subcontinent *n.*, separate region of a continent

subsistence farmers *n.*, farmers who grow food for their families to eat, not to sell

subsistence farming *n.*, farming to grow only enough food for families to eat, not to sell

subsistence fishing *n.*, fishing for enough food to live on, not for profit

suffrage *n.*, the right to vote

Suleyman I *n.*, the emperor of the Ottoman Empire in the mid-1500s

sultan *n.*, a leader or ruler of the Ottoman Empire

Sumatra *n.*, one of the outer islands in Southeast Asia

Sunni (SOO nee) *adj.*, a branch of Islam that believes the religious leaders should be chosen from those most qualified, as opposed to being descendants of Muhammad

surplus *n.*, extra

suspension bridge *n.*, a bridge that is hung from two or more cables

sustainable *adj.*, capable of being continued without damaging the environment or using up resources permanently

Swahili *n.*, the Bantu language that is mainly spoken in East Africa, also knows as Kiswahwali

Sydney *n.*, the largest city in Australia and the state capital of New South Wales

symbol *n.*, an object or idea that can be used to represent another object or idea

T

taiga (TY guh) *n.*, the large forest area that stretches through northern Russia, Canada, and other northern countries

Taino (TY noh) *n.*, the native people of the Caribbean

Taj Mahal *n.*, a famous building built as a tomb for Shah Jahan's wife in India in the 1600s; now a UNESCO World Heritage site

Taliban *n.*, a group of Pashtuns in Afghanistan who began ruling Afghanistan in 1996

Taman Negara National Park *n.*, a national park in Malaysia within one of the world's oldest rain forests

tariff *n.*, a tax on imports and exports

tax *n.*, a fee paid to a government for public services

tectonic plate *n.*, a section of Earth's crust that floats on Earth's mantle

temperate *adj.*, mild, in terms of climate

terra cotta *n.*, baked clay

terrace *n.*, a flat surface that is built into a hillside

terraced *adj.*, flat fields cut into slopes or mountainsides

terrain *n.*, the physical features of the land

terrorism *n.*, a type of warfare using violence to achieve political results, typically carried out by individuals or small groups

terrorist *n.*, a person who uses violence to achieve political results

textile *adj.*, related to cloth or clothing

theme *n.*, topic

thirty-eighth parallel *n.*, the border along the 38° north latitude that separates North and South Korea, created in 1945

Three Gorges Dam *n.*, the largest dam in the world, located on the Chang Jiang River in China

Tibetan Plateau *n.*, a vast high plateau in Central Asia

Timbuktu *n.*, a city in West Africa that was a center of education in the 1200s

tolerance *n.*, acceptance of others' beliefs

tomb *n.*, a burial place

topography *n.*, physical features of land

tornado *n.*, a storm with powerful winds that follows an unpredictable path

GLOSSARY

totalitarian *adj.*, relating to a government ruled by a dictator that requires complete obedience to the state

tourism *n.*, the travel business or industry

Trail of Tears *n.*, the route the Cherokees took during their forced migration from the southeast United States to Oklahoma in the 1830s

trans-Atlantic slave trade *n.*, the business of trading slaves taken from Africa across the Atlantic Ocean to the Americas starting in the 1500s

trans-Saharan *adj.*, across the Sahara desert

Trans-Siberian Railroad *n.*, the world's longest continuous railroad, linking Moscow with eastern Russia across Siberia

transcontinental *adj.*, across an entire continent

transform *v.*, to remake or change

transition *n.*, a change from one activity or stage to another

transition zone *n.*, an area between two geographic regions that has characteristics of both

transpiration *n.*, a process by which plants and trees release water vapor into the air

transport *v.*, to send from one place to another

transportation corridor *n.*, a land or water route to move people and goods from place to place easily

treaty *n.*, an agreement between two or more countries

Treaty of Guadalupe Hidalgo *n.*, the agreement in 1848 in which Mexico gave up the area from Texas to California to the United States

Treaty of Tordesillas (tor duh SEE uhs) *n.*, a treaty in 1494 that divided South American land between the Spanish and Portuguese

Treaty of Versailles *n.*, a peace treaty that ended World War I in 1919

trench *n.*, a long ditch that protects soldiers from enemy gunfire

trend *n.*, a change over time in a specific direction

triangular trade *n.*, trade among three continents: the Americas, Europe, and Africa

tributary *n.*, a small river that drains into a larger river

tribute *n.*, fees paid to another ruler or country for protection or as a token of submission

troubadour *n.*, a singer during the Middle Ages who performed songs about knights and love

tsunami (soo NAH mee) *n.*, a large, powerful ocean wave

Tuareg (TWAH rehg) *n.*, a semi-nomadic people who travel across the Sahara in caravans, trading salt

tundra *n.*, flat treeless land found in arctic and subarctic regions

Tupinambá (too pee NAAM baa) *n.*, a people who lived near the mouth of the Amazon River and along the Atlantic Coast around 3000 B.C.

typhoon *n.*, a dangerous tropical storm with heavy rains and high winds, known as a hurricane in the Western Hemisphere

tyranny *n.*, a harsh government

U

United Arab Emirates *n.*, a country located on the Arabian Peninsula at the Persian Gulf

United Nations (UN) *n.*, an organization of countries formed in 1945 to keep peace among countries and protect human rights

Universal Declaration of Human Rights *n.*, an agreement approved by the United Nations that defines the rights that people all over the world should have

uplands *n.*, hills, mountains, and plateaus

Ur *n.*, an important Sumerian city-state, 2800–1850 B.C.

Ural Mountains *n.*, a mountain range that separates the Northern European Plain from the West Siberian Plain in Russia

urban *adj.*, describing or related to the city or suburbs

utilize *v.*, to make practical use of

V

vaccine *n.*, a treatment to increase immunity to a particular disease

vegetation *n.*, plant life

venue *n.*, the location for an organized event

veto *v.*, to reject a decision made by another government body

viceroy *n.*, a governor of Spain's colonies in the Americas who represented the Spanish king and queen

vocational *adj.*, related to job skills

volcano *n.*, a mountain that erupts in an explosion of molten rock, gases, and ash

vulnerable *adj.*, open, able to be hurt by outside forces

W

wallaby *n.*, a marsupial animal that is smaller than a kangaroo

wat *n.*, a Buddhist temple in Southeast Asia

waterway *n.*, a navigable route for traveling and transport

weapon of mass destruction (WMD) *n.*, a weapon that causes great harm to large numbers of people

weather *n.*, the condition of the atmosphere at a particular time, including temperature, precipitation, and humidity for a particular day or week

Western Hemisphere *n.*, the half of Earth west of the prime meridian

Wet Pampas *n.*, humid grasslands in eastern Argentina

Wilkes, Charles *n.*, an American who surveyed the coastline of Antarctica in the late 1830s

wind turbine *n.*, an engine powered by wind to generate electricity

Y

Yanomami (yaa noh MAA mee) *n.*, an indigenous people who still live in the Amazon River Basin as hunter-gatherers

yurt *n.*, a traditional felt tent of Central Asia

Z

zaibatsu (zeye BAHT sue) *n.*, family–run organizations in Japan that owned several businesses

Zambezi River *n.*, a river in Southern Africa that flows through many south-central countries to the Indian Ocean

Zheng He (jung huh) *n.*, an admiral in the Chinese navy who led seven naval voyages exploring lands outside China; his last voyage began in A.D. 1431

Zhou (joh) *n.*, the dynasty that ruled China from 1050–221 B.C.

zoologist *n.*, a scientist who studies animals

GLOSARIO

A

abolition [abolicionismo] *s.*, movimiento para terminar con la esclavitud, antes y después de la Guerra Civil en los Estados Unidos

Aborigine [aborigen] *s.*, primera cultura desarrollada de Australia

absolute location [ubicación absoluta] *s.*, punto exacto donde está ubicado un lugar, identificado por medio de las coordenadas de latitud y longitud

abstract [abstracto] *adj.*, estilo artístico que enfatiza la forma y el color por sobre el realismo

accommodate [albergar] *v.*, alojar

acknowledge [reconocer] *v.*, admitir, agradecer

Acropolis [Acrópolis] *s.*, colina rocosa ubicada en Atenas, Grecia, que servía de fortaleza para los edificios más importantes de la ciudad antigua

adapt [adaptar] *v.*, ajustar o modificar para que sea apropiado

adherent [partidario] *s.*, seguidor de una religión, causa o persona

adventure tourism [turismo aventura] *s.*, tipo de turismo en el cual los viajeros realizan actividades físicas, como montañismo, deportes acuáticos o senderismo

aerodynamic [aerodinámico] *adj.*, diseñado para moverse con poca resistencia del viento

African National Congress (ANC) [Congreso Nacional Africano (CNA)] *s.*, organización de sudafricanos negros (entre ellos, Nelson Mandela) que protestaron en contra del trato discriminatorio a principios del siglo XX

African Union [Unión Africana] *s.*, organización de países africanos que trabajan para lograr el progreso económico

aging population [envejecimiento de la población] *s.*, tendencia demográfica que ocurre cuando aumenta la edad media de una población

agricultural revolution [revolución agrícola] *n.*, período en el cual los seres humanos comenzaron a cultivar en lugar de recolectar plantas

Aguinaldo, Emilio [Aguinaldo, Emilio] *s.*, líder del movimiento por la independencia filipina en la década de 1890

Alamo [El Álamo] *s.*, fuerte ubicado en Texas donde 200 texanos perdieron una batalla durante la guerra entre Estados Unidos y México

Alexander the Great [Alejandro Magno] *s.*, conquistador que extendió el Imperio Macedónico y difundió la cultura griega por Eurasia desde 334–323 A.C.

alliance [alianza] *s.*, sociedad entre países

alluvial [aluvial] *adj.*, dicho del sedimento depositado por un río

alluvial plain [llanura aluvial] *s.*, área de tierra plana ubicada junto a un arroyo o río que se desborda

alluvium [aluvión] *s.*, suelo o cieno arrastrado por el agua que fluye, que es ideal para los cultivos

Alps [Alpes] *s.*, cadena montañosa europea

al-Qaeda [Al Qaeda] *s.*, grupo terrorista con sede en el suroeste de Asia

Amazon River Basin [cuenca del río Amazonas] *s.*, la cuenca fluvial más grande de la Tierra, ubicada en América del Sur

amendment [enmienda] *s.*, cambio formal que se hace a una ley

ancestry [ascendencia] *s.*, familia de la cual se desciende, remontándose al pasado; herencia

Andes Mountains [cordillera de los Andes] *s.*, cordillera que se extiende 5,500 millas a lo largo del costado occidental de América del Sur

Angel Falls [Salto Ángel] *s.*, el salto de agua más alto del mundo, ubicado en Venezuela

Angkor Wat [Angkor Wat] *s.*, templo grande construido en Camboya en el siglo XII, dedicado a la deidad hindú Vishnú

animal-borne [de tracción animal] *adj.*, transportado por animales

anime [anime] *s.*, estilo de animación o historieta desarrollado en Japón

animism [animismo] *s.*, creencia de que todas las cosas, incluidos los objetos naturales, tienen alma

annexation [anexión] *s.*, acción de añadir territorio a un país

Antarctic Treaty [Tratado Antártico] *s.*, acuerdo de 1959 entre 12 países para usar la Antártida con fines pacíficos y para compartir los descubrimientos científicos

apartheid [apartheid] *s.*, separación legal de las razas; sistema que privaba de sus derechos a los sudafricanos negros

aqueduct [acueducto] *s.*, sistema de transporte para llevar agua a grandes distancias, a veces elevado sobre un puente

aquifer [acuífero] *s.*, capa de roca subterránea que contiene agua

arable [cultivable] *adj.*, fértil; apropiado para la agricultura

Aral Sea [mar Aral] *s.*, lago de agua salada ubicado en el centro de Asia, cuyo tamaño se ha reducido mucho como consecuencia del desvío para irrigación de los ríos que desembocan en él

archipelago [archipiélago] *s.*, cadena de islas

arid [árido] *adj.*, muy seco, que casi no recibe lluvia

aristocrat [aristócrata] *s.*, miembro de la clase alta

armistice [armisticio] *s.*, acuerdo para dejar de luchar

artifact [artefacto] s., objeto hecho por seres humanos de una cultura pasada

Aryans [arios] s., nómades que migraron desde el centro de Asia al valle del Indo alrededor del año 2000 A.C.

Asia-Pacific Economic Cooperation (APEC) [Foro de Cooperación Económica Asia-Pacífico] s., asociación global fundada en 1989 para fortalecer los vínculos económicos entre los países del Pacífico

Asoka [Asoka] s., líder durante el apogeo del Imperio Maurya, alrededor del año 250 A.C.

assimilate [asimilarse] v., incorporarse en la cultura de una sociedad

assimilation [asimilación] s., proceso en el cual un grupo minoritario adopta la cultura de la mayoría

assisted migration [migración asistida] s., programa establecido en 1831 en el cual los británicos ofrecían dinero a la gente para que se mudara a Australia

Aswan High Dam [Presa Alta de Asuán] s., presa ubicada en el río Nilo, terminada en 1970

Atacama Desert [desierto de Atacama] s., desierto ubicado en el lado occidental de la cordillera de los Andes

Atahualpa [Atahualpa] s., el último emperador de los incas antes de ser conquistados por los españoles en 1533

atoll [atolón] s., isla, arrecife o cadena de islas con forma de anillo hechas de coral

attribute [atributo] s., cualidad específica

Augustus [Augusto] s., primer emperador de Roma, en 27 A.C.

autonomy [autonomía] s., auto-gobierno de un país o pueblo

Aymara [aimara] s., cultura indígena que habita en la cordillera de los Andes de Perú y Bolivia

Aztec [aztecas] s., pueblo que se estableció en el área de la actual ciudad de México, 1325–1525 D.C.

B

ban [proscribir] v., declarar fuera de la ley o prohibir

Bantu [bantúes] s., grupo africano que se trasladó desde el oeste de África central hacia el sur y hacia el este, a través del África subsahariana, entre 2000 y 1000 A.C.

barbarian [bárbaro] s., soldado o guerrero considerado culturalmente menos desarrollado que aquellos contra los que luchaba; el término proviene originalmente de las tribus germanas que invadieron el Imperio Romano en el año 235 D.C.

Baroque period [Barroco] s., período entre 1600 y 1750 en el cual la música presentaba esquemas y temas complicados

barter [canjear] v., comerciar o intercambiar bienes sin utilizar dinero

basin [cuenca] s., región bañada por un sistema fluvial

bas-relief [bajorrelieve] s., escultura que sobresale ligeramente de un fondo plano

bauxite [bauxita] s., materia prima que se utiliza para fabricar aluminio

bay [bahía] s., masa de agua rodeada por tierra en tres de sus lados

Bedouin [beduinos] s., pueblo nómade de habla árabe del suroeste de Asia

benefit [beneficiar] v., hacer bien

Berlin Conference [Conferencia de Berlín] s., encuentro de las naciones europeas en 1884 para resolver los conflictos sobre sus reclamos coloniales en África

Berlin Wall [Muro de Berlín] n., muro que dividía Berlín Este communista de Berlín Oeste demucrático

Bhutto, Benazir [Bhutto, Benazir] s., primera ministra mujer de Pakistán, 1988–1999

Biko, Stephen [Biko, Stephen] s., presidente de una organización sudafricana de protesta estudiantil que fue arrestado y asesinado en 1977

Bill of Rights [Declaración de Derechos] s., primeras diez enmiendas a la Constitución estadounidense

biodiversity [biodiversidad] s., variedad de especies que viven en un ecosistema

biofuel [biocombustible] s., combustible alternativo que es una mezcla de etanol y gasolina

Black Sea [mar Negro] s., mar interior que limita con Europa, Rusia, Georgia y Turquía

Blue Mosque [Mezquita Azul] s., mezquita histórica construida en Estambul por el Sultán Ahmed I, terminada en 1617

Bollywood [Bollywood] s., industria cinematográfica de la India, ubicada en Bombay

Bolshevik [bolchevique] s., partido político de Rusia liderado por Lenin que derrocó al zar en 1917

Borobudur [Borobudur] s., complejo de templos budistas ubicado en el centro de Java

Bosporus Strait [estrecho de Bósforo] s., paso que atraviesa Estambul y conecta el mar Negro y el mar de de Mármara

breakwater [rompeolas] s., barrera construida para proteger un puerto

Buddhism [budismo] s., religión fundada por Siddhartha Gautama en 525 A.C. en India

bullet train [tren bala] s., tren que viaja a más de 125 millas por hora y cuya forma es similar a una bala

butte [cerro testigo] s., colina o montaña con laderas escarpadas y cima plana

Byrd, Richard [Byrd, Richard] *s.*, estadounidense que exploró la Antártida por cielo y tierra durante la década de 1940

Byzantine Empire [Imperio Bizantino] *s.*, parte oriental del Imperio Romano después de 395 D.C. que duró aproximadamente 1,000 años

C

Caesar, Julius [César, Julio] *s.*, general que se convirtió en gobernante de Roma, 46–44 A.C.

Calypso [calipso] *s.*, tipo de música folclórica que se inició en Trinidad

canal [canal] *s.*, vía fluvial construida por el hombre a través de la tierra para botes y barcos

Candomblé [candomblé] *s.*, religión brasileña que combina el espiritualismo africano y el catolicismo

canopy [enramada] *s.*, techo creado sobre un bosque tropical por las copas de los árboles

capital [capital] *s.*, riqueza e infraestructura de un país

carapace [caparazón] *s.*, cubierta dura de ciertos animales, como la tortuga

caravan [caravana] *s.*, grupo de mercaderes que viajan juntos por razones de seguridad

Cardamom Mountains [colinas Cardamom] *s.*, cadena de montañas ubicada en Camboya

Caribbean Sea [mar Caribe] *s.*, mar tropical ubicado en el Hemisferio Occidental, que limita con México, América Central, las Antillas Mayores y las Antillas Menores

cartographer [cartógrafo] *s.*, persona que hace mapas

cash crop [cultivo comercial] *s.*, cultivo que se vende para obtener una ganancia

Caspian Sea [mar Caspio] *s.*, la masa de agua endorreica más grande de la Tierra, que limita con Rusia, Kazajistán, Turkmenistán, Azerbaiyán e Irán

caste system [sistema de castas] *s.*, en India, estructura social compuesta por cuatro niveles principales, que fue instaurada por los arios

categorize [categorizar] *v.*, agrupar información; clasificar

Catherine the Great [Catalina la Grande] *s.*, emperadora de Rusia desde 1762 hasta 1796

celadon [celadón] *adj.*, con barniz vítreo de color verde, referido a la cerámica realizada por los artistas coreanos

cenote [cenote] *s.*, un depósito de agua subterránea

Chang Jiang [Chang Jiang] *s.*, el río más largo de Asia, que fluye a través de China; también llamado Yangtsé

Chang Jiang Plain [llanura de Chang Jiang] *s.*, llanuras ubicadas junto al río Chang Jiang

Chao Phraya River [río Chao Phraya] *s.*, río que fluye a través de Tailandia

Chernobyl [Chernóbil] *s.*, ciudad ubicada en Ucrania, en la cual un reactor nuclear explotó en 1986

Choson [Choson] *s.*, dinastía coreana que duró desde 1392 hasta 1910

Christian Bible [Biblia cristiana] *s.*, libro sagrado del cristianismo

Christianity [cristianismo] *s.*, religión basada en la vida y en las enseñanzas de Jesús de Nazaret

citizen [ciudadano] *s.*, persona que vive dentro de un territorio y tiene derechos y responsabilidades garantizadas por el gobierno

city-state [ciudad estado] *s.*, estado independiente compuesto por una ciudad y los territorios que dependen de ella

civil disobedience [desobediencia civil] *s.*, desobediencia no violenta de las leyes

civil war [guerra civil] *s.*, guerra entre grupos opuestos de ciudadanos del mismo país

civilization [civilización] *s.*, sociedad con cultura, política y tecnología altamente desarrolladas

clan [clan] *s.*, unidad grande basada en la familia con lealtad hacia el grupo

Classical period [Clasicismo] *s.*, período comprendido entre 1750 y 1900 en el cual la música seguía las reglas establecidas para la forma y la complejidad, como en el caso de las sonatas o las sinfonías

climate [clima] *s.*, el promedio de las condiciones de la atmósfera de un área durante un largo período de tiempo, incluidas la temperatura, la precipitación y los cambios estacionales

climograph [gráfica del clima] *s.*, gráfica que muestra el clima de una región a través de la precipitación y la temperatura medias

coalition [coalición] *s.*, alianza

coastal plains [llanuras costeras] *s.*, tierras bajas ubicadas junto a la orilla del mar

Cold War [Guerra Fría] *s.*, largo período de tensión política sin lucha armada entre los Estados Unidos y la Unión Soviética, desde aproximadamente 1948 hasta 1991

collective farm [granja colectiva] *s.*, en la Unión Soviética, una granja grande donde los trabajadores cultivaban alimentos para distribuirlos a toda la población

collide [colisionar] *v.*, chocar

colonialism [colonialismo] *s.*, práctica de un país que directamente gobierna y desarrolla el comercio en un territorio extranjero para su propio beneficio

colonize [colonizar] *v.*, construir asentamientos y desarrollar el comercio en tierras que controla un país

colony [colonia] *s.*, área controlada por un país lejano

Columbian Exchange [Intercambio Colombino] *s.*, intercambio de plantas, animales y enfermedades entre las Américas, Europa y África que comenzó en el siglo XVI

commerce [comercio] *s.*, negocio de comprar y vender bienes y servicios

commercial agriculture [agricultura comercial] *s.*, negocio de producir cultivos para vender

commodity [mercancía] *s.*, material u objeto que se puede comprar, vender o comerciar

Common Market [Mercado Común] *s.*, Comunidad Económica Europea formada en 1957

commonwealth [mancomunidad] *s.*, nación que se gobierna a sí misma pero es parte de un país mayor

Commonwealth of Australia [Mancomunidad de Australia] *s.*, la nación de Australia, que entró a formar parte de la Mancomunidad Británica de Naciones en 1901

communal [comunal] *adj.*, compartido

communism [comunismo] *s.*, sistema de gobierno en el cual un único partido político controla el gobierno y la economía

competitive [competitivo] *adj.*, capaz de intentar ganar un concurso o una carrera

complex [complejo] *s.*, conjunto de edificios vinculados

comply [acatar] *v.*, seguir una regla o una orden

concentrated [concentrado] *adj.*, reunido en un área central

concentration camp [campo de concentración] *s.*, área donde los judíos y otras personas fueron detenidos durante la Segunda Guerra Mundial y asesinados por los nazis

condensation [condensación] *s.*, proceso por el cual el vapor de agua se convierte en gotitas de líquido debido al enfriamiento durante el ciclo hidrológico

Confucianism [confucianismo] *s.*, sistema ético basado en las enseñanzas de Confucio

Congo River [río Congo] *s.*, río principal ubicado en África Central que desemboca en el océano Atlántico

conquistador [conquistador] *s.*, soldado y líder español que exploraba los territorios recientemente descubiertos de América del Norte, América del Sur, América Central y el Caribe a partir del siglo XVI, fundamentalmente en busca de oro y plata

conservation [conservación] *s.*, protección del medio ambiente

Constantine [Constantino] *s.*, emperador romano, 306–337 A.C., que hizo del cristianismo la religión oficial del imperio

constitution [constitución] *s.*, documento que organiza un gobierno y enuncia sus poderes

consumer [consumidor] *s.*, persona que compra bienes

contaminated [contaminado] *adj.*, infectado; inapropiado para el uso debido a la presencia de elementos peligrosos

contiguous [contiguo] *adj.*, conectado en un bloque

continent [continente] *s.*, gran masa de tierra sobre la superficie de la Tierra; la Tierra tiene siete continentes

continental drift [deriva continental] *s.*, movimiento lento de los continentes sobre las placas tectónicas

continental shelf [plataforma continental] *s.*, borde de un continente que se extiende bajo el agua y se adentra en el mar

controversy [controversia] *s.*, debate o disputa

convert [convertir] *v.*, persuadir a alguien para que cambie sus creencias religiosas

convey [transmitir] *v.*, comunicar

convict [convicto] *s.*, persona sentenciada a prisión por cometer un crimen

Cook Islands [islas Cook] *s.*, país ubicado cerca de Nueva Zelanda, en el Pacífico Sur, formado por 15 islas pequeñas

Cook, James [Cook, James] *s.*, navegante británico que exploró y cartografió las Islas del Pacífico en la década de 1770

coral island [isla de coral] *s.*, isla creada por la acumulación gradual de esqueletos de coral

coral reef [arrecife de coral] *s.*, estructura parecida a una roca construida por capas de organismos de coral

cordillera [cordillera] *s.*, sistema de varias cadenas de montañas paralelas

Cortés, Hernán [Cortés, Hernán] *s.*, conquistador español que derrotó a los aztecas en 1525

cosmopolitan [cosmopolita] *adj.*, que reúne muchas culturas e influencias diferentes

Counter-Reformation [Contrarreforma] *s.*, movimiento dentro de la Iglesia Católica Romana para reformar sus propias prácticas

coup [golpe de estado] *s.*, toma repentina e ilegal del gobierno por medio de la fuerza

Creole [criollo] *s.*, lengua que mezcla elementos de idiomas europeos y no europeos

crevasse [grieta] *s.*, abertura profunda en un glaciar

cricket [cricket] *s.*, juego de equipo similar al béisbol

critical [crítico] *adj.*, extremadamente importante, necesario para sobrevivir

Crusades [Cruzadas] *s.*, expediciones militares de la Iglesia Católica Romana para recuperar las tierras santas ubicadas en Medio Oriente que estaban bajo control musulmán, 1096–1291

cuisine [cocina] *s.*, alimentos y tradiciones culinarias comunes a cierta región

cultural hearth [centro cultural] *s.*, centro de civilización desde el cual se difunden las ideas y la tecnología

GLOSARIO

Cultural Revolution [Revolución Cultural] *s.*, en China, plan social que duró desde 1966 hasta 1969, en el cual el gobierno intentó eliminar todos los elementos capitalistas y anticomunistas de la sociedad

culture [cultura] *s.*, modo de vida de un grupo, que incluye el tipo de alimentación, vivienda, vestido, idioma, comportamiento e ideas

culture region [región cultural] *s.*, área que está unificada por rasgos culturales comunes

cuneiform [cuneiforme] *s.*, primera forma de escritura conocida, proveniente de Sumeria

currency [moneda] *s.*, forma de dinero

current [corriente] *s.*, movimiento continuo de aire o agua que fluye en la misma dirección

cyclone [ciclón] *s.*, tormenta con vientos giratorios, llamada tifón en el Hemisferio Oriental; denominada huracán en otras partes del mundo

czar [zar] *s.*, término utilizado en Rusia para designar al emperador

D

dam [presa] *s.*, barrera que controla el flujo de agua

Danube River [río Danubio] *s.*, río que nace en Alemania y desemboca en el mar Negro

Daoism [taoísmo] *s.*, sistema ético que enfatiza la armonía entre las personas y la naturaleza

Declaration of Independence [Declaración de Independencia] *s.*, documento que declara que los Estados Unidos son independientes del Imperio Británico, adoptado el 4 de julio de 1776

deforestation [deforestación] *s.*, práctica de talar bosques para despejar la tierra y utilizarla para cultivos o uso urbano

deity [deidad] *s.*, dios o diosa

delta [delta] *s.*, área donde un río deposita sedimentos cuando desemboca en una masa de agua más grande

demilitarized zone (DMZ) [zona desmilitarizada] *s.*, área neutral entre países enemigos, específicamente entre Corea del Norte y Corea del Sur

democracy [democracia] *s.*, forma de gobierno del pueblo, en la cual los ciudadanos suelen elegir representantes para que los gobiernen

democratization [democratización] *s.*, proceso de convertirse en una democracia

demographics [demografía] *s.*, características de una población humana, tales como la edad, el ingreso y la educación

deny [negar] *v.*, no reconocer

deplete [agotar] *v.*, extraer o disminuir un recurso hasta que no esté disponible o no sea capaz de funcionar como planeado

descendants [descendientes] *s.*, generaciones futuras; parientes de un miembro de la familia que vivió en el pasado

desertification [desertificación] *s.*, transición gradual de la tierra fértil a tierra menos productiva

developed nations [naciones desarrolladas] *s.*, países con un alto producto interno bruto per cápita

developing nations [naciones en vías de desarrollo] *s.*, países con un bajo producto interno bruto per cápita

dialect [dialecto] *s.*, variante regional de un idioma principal

Diaspora [Diáspora] *s.*, dispersión de los judíos por todo el mundo

dictator [dictador] *s.*, gobernante con control total

diffusion [difusión] *s.*, propagación

diplomacy [diplomacia] *s.*, discusión entre grupos o países para resolver disputas o desacuerdos

discrimination [discriminación] *s.*, trato injusto de un individuo o grupo en base a factores distintos de la habilidad

displace [desplazar] *v.*, obligar a un pueblo a dejar su hogar

disregard [desconocer] *v.*, ignorar

dissolve [disolver] *v.*, deshacer

distinct [definido] *adj.*, fácilmente reconocible

distort [distorsionar] *v.*, modificar la forma o apariencia usual; deformar

distribute [distribuir] *v.*, repartir un bien o recurso entre un grupo mayor

diversify [diversificar] *v.*, dar variedad a algo

diversity [diversidad] *s.*, variedad

domestic policy [política interna] *s.*, plan de un gobierno para manejar los asuntos dentro de sus propias fronteras

domesticate [domesticar] *v.*, criar y usar animales como fuente de mano de obra y alimento

dormant [inactivo] *adj.*, latente, referido a un volcán

drought [sequía] *s.*, largo período con escasa o ninguna precipitación

Dry Pampas [Pampa seca] *s.*, región árida ubicada en el oeste de Argentina

Dubai [Dubái] *s.*, ciudad y estado joven y rico de los Emiratos Árabes Unidos, en el golfo Pérsico

due process [debido proceso] *s.*, en los Estados Unidos, reglas que las autoridades deben seguir al tratar con los ciudadanos

Dutch East India Company [Compañía Neerlandesa de las Indias Orientales] *s.*, compañía de los Países Bajos que dominaba el comercio de especias en el sureste de Asia

dynamic [dinámico] *adj.*, que cambia continuamente

dynastic cycle [ciclo dinástico] *s.*, patrón de ascenso y caída de las dinastías en la historia china

dynasty [dinastía] *s.*, serie de gobernantes de la misma familia

E

earthquake [terremoto] *s.*, sacudida de la corteza de la Tierra generalmente causada por el choque o el deslizamiento de las placas tectónicas

Eastern Hemisphere [Hemisferio Oriental] *s.*, la mitad de la Tierra ubicada al este del primer meridiano

ecologist [ecologista] *s.*, científico que estudia las relaciones entre los seres vivos y su medio ambiente

economic globalization [globalización económica] *s.*, práctica de actividades económicas que se realizan a través de las fronteras nacionales

economic sector [sector económico] *s.*, subdivisión o parte más pequeña de una economía, tal como la industria y la agricultura

economy [economía] *s.*, sistema en el cual las personas producen, venden y compran cosas

ecosystem [ecosistema] *s.*, comunidad de organismos vivos y su medio ambiente o hábitat natural

ecotourism [ecoturismo] *s.*, manera de visitar las áreas naturales que conserva los recursos naturales de la región

El Niño [El Niño] *s.*, inversión del viento y las corrientes oceánicas usuales

elevation [elevación] *s.*, altura de un accidente geográfico sobre el nivel del mar

eliminate [eliminar] *v.*, deshacerse de

elite [elite] *s.*, clase superior

Emancipation Proclamation [Proclama de Emancipación] *s.*, documento de 1863 que liberó a todos los esclavos que vivían en el territorio en poder de los Confederados durante la Guerra Civil estadounidense

emergence [aparición] *s.*, desarrollo y uso extendido de algo nuevo

emigrate [emigrar] *v.*, dejar el país natal para vivir en otro país

emirate [emirato] *s.*, estado del país de los Emiratos Árabes Unidos

empire [imperio] *s.*, grupo de pueblos o estados gobernados por un único gobernante fuerte

Enduring Voices Project [Proyecto Voces Perdurables] *s.*, proyecto de National Geographic para estudiar y conservar las lenguas que están en riesgo de desaparición

enhance [realzar] *v.*, mejorar la calidad de algo

Enlightenment [Ilustración] *s.*, movimiento social del siglo XVIII que trabajó a favor de la educación y de los derechos del individuo

enlist [alistarse] *v.*, presentarse como voluntario para el servicio militar

entrepreneur [empresario] *s.*, persona que comienza un negocio nuevo

entrepreneurship [espíritu empresarial] *s.*, características de creatividad y riesgo que existen en una persona o sociedad

epic poem [poema épico] *s.*, poema largo que relata las aventuras de un héroe

epidemic [epidemia] *s.*, brote de una enfermedad que afecta a una gran parte de la población de una comunidad en particular

equator [ecuador] *s.*, círculo imaginario alrededor de la Tierra que está a la misma distancia del Polo Norte y del Polo Sur y divide la Tierra por la mitad; la línea central o de 0° de latitud

equinox [equinoccio] *s.*, momento en que el día y la noche tienen la misma duración; ocurre dos veces al año, el 21 o 22 de marzo y el 21 o 22 de septiembre

erode [erosionar] *v.*, desgastar

erosion [erosión] *s.*, proceso por el cual las rocas y el suelo se rompen lentamente y se desgastan

erratic [errático] *adj.*, inconsistente o irregular

eruption [erupción] *s.*, estallido o explosión

escarpment [escarpe] *s.*, pendiente pronunciada

essential [esencial] *adj.*, necesario

establish [establecer] *v.*, instituir

ethanol [etanol] *s.*, alcohol líquido extraído de la caña de azúcar o del maíz que se puede usar como combustible, solo o mezclado con gasolina

ethical system [sistema ético] *s.*, sistema de creencias que enseña conductas morales

ethnic group [grupo étnico] *s.*, grupo de personas que tienen una cultura y una lengua en común y a veces comparten la misma herencia racial

ethnobotanist [etnobotánico] *s.*, científico que estudia la relación entre las culturas y las plantas

euro [euro] *s.*, moneda común de la Unión Europea

European Union (EU) [Unión Europea (UE)] *s.*, organización económica compuesta por 27 países miembros europeos (2011)

eurozone [eurozona] *s.*, países que han adoptado el euro como moneda

evaporation [evaporación] *s.*, proceso por el cual el agua se convierte en vapor y sube a la atmósfera debido al calentamiento del Sol; una parte del ciclo hidrológico

evident [evidente] *adj.*, claramente presente u observable

excavate [excavar] *v.*, quitar la tierra cuidadosamente o hacer un hoyo

exchange [cambiar] *v.*, convertir el dinero en otra moneda

exile [exilar] *v.*, obligar a alguien a dejar un país

exile [exilio] *s.*, situación en la que se está ausente del propio país natal

exoskeleton [exoesqueleto] *s.*, cubierta externa dura que protege a los corales y a otros animales marinos

expand [ampliar] *v.*, hacer más grande

expedition [expedición] *s.*, travesía o viaje de cierta extensión, usualmente a otras tierras

exploit [explotar] *v.*, aprovecharse de algo; usar de manera egoísta o injusta para beneficio propio

export [exportar] *v.*, enviar a otro país para obtener ayuda o un beneficio

export revenue [ingresos por exportaciones] *s.*, dinero o ingresos recibidos por los bienes vendidos a otro país

extent [extensión] *s.*, distancia o grado hasta el cual se difunde algo

extinct [extinto] *adj.*, completamente desaparecido, tal como una especie animal o vegetal

extinction [extinción] *s.*, desaparición de una especie o de un tipo de ser vivo

extremist [extremista] *s.*, persona con opiniones religiosas o políticas que están fuera del rango de la opinión de la mayoría

F

factory system [sistema fabril] *s.*, modo de trabajar en el cual cada persona trabaja en solo una parte de un producto

failed state [estado fallido] *s.*, país en el cual el gobierno, las instituciones económicas y el orden han colapsado

fallout [lluvia radiactiva] *s.*, partículas radiactivas provenientes de una explosión nuclear que caen a través de la atmósfera

famine [hambruna] *s.*, largo período de escasez de alimentos

fault [falla] *s.*, fractura en la corteza de la Tierra

federal republic [república federal] *s.*, forma democrática de gobierno en la cual los votantes eligen representantes y el gobierno central comparte el poder con los estados

federal system [sistema federal] *s.*, sistema de gobierno con un gobierno central fuerte y unidades gubernamentales locales

feral [asilvestrado] *adj.*, salvaje, que se ha convertido en salvaje después de haber sido domesticado

fertile [fértil] *adj.*, capaz de producir una gran abundancia de frutos, cultivos o crías

Fertile Crescent [Creciente Fértil] *s.*, área alrededor de los ríos Tigris y Éufrates

fertility rate [tasa de fertilidad] *s.*, promedio de niños nacidos por cada mujer en un cierto período de tiempo

fertilizer [fertilizante] *s.*, sustancia añadida al suelo para enriquecerlo

feudal system [sistema feudal] *s.*, durante la Edad Media, estructura social que consistía en un rey, señores, vasallos y siervos

fiber optics [fibra óptica] *s.*, fibras de vidrio utilizadas para enviar un código digital rápidamente a través de grandes distancias

first language [lengua materna] *s.*, idioma que aprenden los niños de un pueblo

fjord [fiordo] *s.*, bahía angosta y profunda ubicada

floodplain [planicie aluvial] *s.*, terreno bajo a la orilla de los ríos, formado por el sedimento dejado por la inundación

Foja Mountains [montañas Foja] *s.*, cadena de montañas ubicada en la isla de Nueva Guinea, en el este de Indonesia

food security [seguridad alimentaria] *s.*, fácil acceso a alimentos suficientes

foremost [principal] *adj.*, primero en rango o importancia, que lidera

fortify [fortificar] *v.*, fortalecer

fossil [fósil] *s.*, restos conservados de plantas y animales antiguos

fragmented country [país fragmentado] *s.*, país que está físicamente dividido en partes separadas, tales como una cadena de islas, y/o política o culturalmente dividido

free enterprise economy [economía de libre empresa] *s.*, sistema en el cual las empresas de propiedad privada producen bienes y servicios, también llamada economía de mercado o capitalismo

free trade [libre comercio] *s.*, comercio que no grava las importaciones con impuestos

free trade agreement [acuerdo de libre comercio] *s.*, tratado entre países que mejora el comercio al limitar los impuestos a dicho comercio

French Indochina [Indochina Francesa] *s.*, grupo de colonias pertenecientes a Francia, formado por Vietnam, Camboya, Laos y otras, ubicadas en el sureste de Asia, desde 1887 hasta 1955

fuel cell [celda de combustible] *s.*, unidad pequeña que, al igual que una pila o batería, combina sustancias químicas para producir energía

fuse [fusionar] *v.*, mezclar

■ GLOSARIO

G

Gadsden Purchase [Compra de Gadsden] *s.*, venta de territorio realizada en 1853 por México a los Estados Unidos que estableció la frontera suroccidental estadounidense actual

Gandhi, Mohandas [Gandhi, Mahatma] *s.*, líder indio que impulsó la independencia de la India respecto del Reino Unido mediante la desobediencia civil, en la década de 1930; considerado el padre de la India moderna

Ganges Delta [delta del Ganges] *s.*, área fértil donde el río Ganges desemboca en la bahía de Bengala

gaucho [gaucho] *s.*, vaquero de América del Sur

gauge [trocha] *s.*, medida del ancho de las vías del ferrocarril

generation [generación] *s.*, grupo de individuos que nacen y viven aproximadamente en la misma época

Genghis Khan [Gengis Kan] *s.*, gobernante mongol que estableció un imperio en el centro de Asia, a principios del siglo XIII

genre [género] *s.*, forma literaria, como un poema, una obra de teatro o una novela

geoglyph [geoglifo] *s.*, figura geométrica grande o forma de animal dibujada sobre el suelo

Geographic Information Systems (GIS) [Sistemas de Información Geográfica (SIG)] *s.*, aparatos computarizados que presentan datos sobre lugares específicos

geographic pattern [patrón geográfico] *s.*, similitud entre lugares

geothermal energy [energía geotérmica] *s.*, energía térmica proveniente del interior de la Tierra que se puede convertir en electricidad

ger [ger] *s.*, tienda portátil hecha de fieltro

Gettysburg Address [Discurso de Gettysburg] *s.*, discurso que Abraham Lincoln pronunció en 1863 en honor a los soldados que murieron en la batalla de Gettysburg durante la Guerra Civil estadounidense

Giza [Giza] *s.*, ciudad ubicada junto al Nilo, donde se construyeron diez pirámides en el antiguo Egipto

Glacier [glaciar] *s.*, masa grande de hielo y nieve acumulada

glasnost [glásnost] *s.*, política de la Unión Soviética de apertura que animó al pueblo a hablar abiertamente acerca del gobierno, introducida por Mijaíl Gorbachov en la década de 1980

global [global] *adj.*, mundial

Global Positioning System (GPS) [Sistema de Posicionamiento Global (GPS)] *s.*, sistema de satélites con base en el espacio que encuentra la ubicación absoluta y la hora de cualquier lugar de la Tierra

global warming [calentamiento global] *s.*, aumento de la temperatura media de la Tierra desde mediados del siglo XX

globalization [globalización] *s.*, desarrollo de una economía mundial basada en el libre comercio y el uso de mano de obra extranjera

globe [globo terráqueo] *s.*, modelo tridimensional, o esférico, de la Tierra

Gobi desert [desierto de Gobi] *s.*, el desierto más grande de Asia, que cubre gran parte del sur de Mongolia y se extiende hasta el interior de China

golden age [edad dorada] *s.*, período de gran riqueza, cultura y democracia en Grecia

Golden Quadrilateral (GQ) [Cuadrilátero de Oro] *s.*, superautopista que conecta cuatro ciudades importantes de la India

Gorbachev, Mikhail [Gorbachov, Mijaíl] *s.*, líder de la Unión Soviética, 1985–1991; presidente desde 1990 hasta que fue disuelta en 1991

gorge [desfiladero] *s.*, paso profundo y angosto rodeado por acantilados empinados

government [gobierno] *s.*, organización que mantiene el orden, establece reglas y proporciona servicios para una sociedad

Grand Bazaar [Gran Bazar] *s.*, centro de tiendas y comercios en Estambul, Turquía

Grand Canyon [Gran Cañón] *s.*, formación rocosa ubicada en el suroeste de los Estados Unidos que el río Colorado ha excavado profundamente durante millones de años

grasslands [praderas] *s.*, áreas abiertas y amplias apropiadas para el pastoreo y los cultivos

Great Barrier Reef [Gran Barrera de Coral] *s.*, ecosistema inmenso, ubicado cerca de la costa de Australia, hecho de arrecifes de coral

Great Depression [Gran Depresión] *s.*, descenso económico mundial ocurrido en la década de 1930, marcado por la pobreza y una alta tasa de desempleo

Great Escarpment [Gran Escarpe] *s.*, pendiente pronunciada que se extiende desde la meseta del sur de África hasta las llanuras costeras

Great Lakes [Grandes Lagos] *s.*, cinco lagos grandes de agua dulce ubicados entre Canadá y los Estados Unidos

Great Leap Forward [Gran Salto Adelante] *s.*, plan de Mao Zedong para hacer que la economía de China creciera más rápidamente, 1958–1961

Great Plains [Grandes Llanuras] *s.*, área de tierra baja y llana ubicada al este de las montañas Rocosas

Great Pyramid of Khufu [Gran Pirámide de Keops] *s.*, la pirámide más antigua y más alta de Egipto, construida en Guiza alrededor de 2550 A.C.

GLOSARIO

Great Recession [Gran Recesión] s., descenso de las economías de los Estados Unidos, Canadá y otros países, que comenzó en 2007

Great Rift Valley [Gran Valle del Rift] s., valle ancho ubicado en África Oriental, parte de una cadena de valles formados cuando las placas tectónicas se separaron

Great Wall of China [Gran Muralla China] s., muro de piedra ubicado en el norte de China de más de 4,500 millas de largo, construido para rechazar a los invasores provenientes del norte

Great Zimbabwe [Gran Zimbabue] s., ciudad amurallada de piedra que el pueblo shona construyó en el sur de África entre 1200 y 1450

greenhouse gas [gas invernadero] s., gas que atrapa el calor del Sol sobre la Tierra

griot [griot] s., narrador africano tradicional

gross domestic product (GDP) [producto interno bruto (PIB)] s., valor total de todos los bienes y servicios producidos en un país en un año dado

Guaraní [guaraníes] s., pueblo indígena que vive en los valles de los ríos Paraguay y Paraná, en América del Sur

guest worker [trabajador huésped] s., trabajador temporal que migra para trabajar en otro país

Guillotine [guillotina] s., máquina utilizada para ejecutar a las personas durante la Revolución Francesa

Gutenberg, Johannes [Gutenberg, Johannes] s., impresor alemán que inventó la imprenta en 1450

H

habitat [hábitat] s., medio ambiente natural de una planta o animal vivo

Hagia Sophia [Santa Sofía] s., museo ubicado en Estambul, Turquía, que se construyó originalmente como iglesia, durante el Imperio Romano, y luego sirvió de mezquita

half-life [vida media] s., tiempo necesario para que la mitad de los átomos de una sustancia radiactiva se desintegren

Hammurabi [Hammurabi] s., rey que desarrolló un código de leyes en Babilonia, en el siglo XVIII A.C.

Han [Han] s., dinastía china que duró desde 206 A.C. hasta 220 D.C.

Harappan [Harappa] s., primera civilización urbana del sur de Asia, desarrollada junto al río Indo alrededor de 2600 A.C.

harbor [embarcadero] s., lugar donde los barcos pueden atracar protegidos del mar abierto

Hatshepsut [Hatshepsut] s., mujer que fue faraón de Egipto alrededor de 1500 A.C.

Hebrew Bible [Biblia hebrea] s., libro sagrado del judaísmo

hemisphere [hemisferio] s., una mitad de la Tierra

henna [alheña] s., polvo rojizo usado para crear diseños sobre la piel

hereditary [hereditario] adj., que se transmite de padres a hijos

heritage [herencia] s., tradición que se transmite de los ancestros a los descendientes

Hermitage Museum [museo Hermitage] s., museo de arte y cultura ubicado en San Petersburgo, Rusia

Hidalgo, Miguel [Hidalgo, Miguel] s., sacerdote católico que lideró una revuelta en México en 1810

hieroglyphics [jeroglíficos] s., sistema antiguo de escritura que emplea imágenes y símbolos

highlands [tierras altas] s., áreas de terreno montañoso alto

Himalaya Mountains [Himalaya] s., la cordillera más alta del mundo, ubicada en el sur de Asia

Hinduism [hinduismo] s., religión practicada por más del 60 por ciento de la población de Asia del Sur

Hitler, Adolf [Hitler, Adolf] s., jefe de estado alemán desde 1933 hasta 1945

Ho Chi Minh [Ho Chi Minh] s., líder de Vietnam del Norte que quería unificar Vietnam del Norte y Vietnam del Sur bajo el comunismo; estos intentos dieron comienzo a la Guerra de Vietnam

Holocaust [Holocausto] s., asesinato masivo cometido por los nazis contra seis millones de judíos y otras personas durante la Segunda Guerra Mundial

homelands [terruños] s., durante el apartheid, áreas separadas dentro de Sudáfrica donde se obligaba a vivir a los sudafricanos negros

hotspot [punto caliente] s., parte inusualmente caliente del manto de la Tierra

Huang He [Huang He] s., el segundo río más largo de China, también llamado río Amarillo

Human Development Index (HDI) [Índice de Desarrollo Humano (IDH)] s., conjunto de datos utilizados por los geógrafos para comparar la calidad de vida en diferentes países, incluyendo salud, educación y estándar de vida

human rights [derechos humanos] s., derechos políticos, económicos y culturales que todas las personas deben tener

hunter-gatherer [cazador-recolector] s., persona que caza animales y recolecta plantas y frutos para alimentarse

hurricane [huracán] s., tormenta fuerte con vientos giratorios y lluvia intensa

Hussein, Saddam [Hussein, Saddam] s., presidente de Iraq desde 1979 hasta 2003

hybrid [híbrido] s., vehículo que puede funcionar a electricidad o gasolina

GLOSARIO

hydroelectric power [energía hidroeléctrica] *s.*, fuente de energía que emplea agua en movimiento para producir electricidad

I

ice shelf [capa de hielo] *s.*, lámina flotante de hielo adherida a una masa de tierra

immigrate [inmigrar] *v.*, mudarse a otro país o región

immigration [inmigración] *s.*, mudanza permanente de una persona a otro país

impact [impacto] *s.*, efecto que produce un cambio

imperialism [imperialismo] *s.*, práctica de extender la influencia de una nación controlando otros territorios

Impressionism [Impresionismo] *s.*, estilo artístico en el cual los artistas usaban la luz y el color en pinceladas cortas para capturar un momento de tiempo

incentive [incentivo] *s.*, razón o motivo para hacer algo

incorporate [incorporar] *v.*, incluir; combinar con algo ya formado

indigenous [indígena] *adj.*, originario del área donde algo se encuentra

indulgence [indulgencia] *s.*, durante la Edad Media, tarifa pagada a la iglesia para disminuir el castigo por un pecado

Indus River [río Indo] *s.*, río ubicado en la parte occidental de Asia del Sur

Industrial Revolution [Revolución Industrial] *s.*, período de los siglos XVIII y XIX durante el cual los trabajadores de las fábricas comenzaron a usar máquinas y herramientas eléctricas para producir a gran escala

industrialization [industrialización] *s.*, paso a una producción a gran escala mediante el uso de máquinas

industrialize [industrializar] *v.*, desarrollar la manufactura

infectious [infeccioso] *adj.*, capaz de propagarse rápidamente a otros

infrastructure [infraestructura] *s.*, sistemas básicos de una sociedad, tales como las carreteras, los puentes, las cloacas y el tendido eléctrico

inner islands [islas interiores] *s.*, islas de Indonesia entre las que se incluyen Java, Madura y Bali

Institutional Revolutionary Party (PRI) [Partido Revolucionario Institucional (PRI)] *s.*, partido político que controló el gobierno de México desde 1929 hasta 2000

interact [interactuar] *v.*, afectar a otras personas y verse afectado por ellas

interior [interior] *s.*, tierra que está lejos de la costa del mar

Internet *n.*, una red de comunicación

intersection [encrucijada] *s.*, lugar donde se encuentran las personas o se cruzan los caminos

intifada [intifada] *s.*, levantamiento o rebelión, usualmente se utiliza para referirse a la revuelta palestina en contra de Israel

invader [invasor] *s.*, enemigo que entra a un país por la fuerza

invasive species [especies invasoras] *s.*, plantas o animales no nativos introducidos en un área nueva, intencionalmente o no, que alteran los hábitats de los seres vivos nativos

Iron Curtain [Cortina de Hierro] *s.*, en Europa, frontera imaginaria que separaba los países comunistas de los no comunistas durante la Guerra Fría

Irrawaddy River [río Irawadi] *s.*, río que fluye a través de Myanmar

irrigation [irrigación] *s.*, proceso de redirigir el agua hacia los cultivos a través de canales y zanjas

Isis [Isis] *s.*, diosa egipcia importante

Islam [islamismo] *s.*, religión fundada en Arabia Saudita a principios del siglo VII D.C.

isolated [aislado] *adj.*, separado de los demás

isolation [aislamiento] *s.*, separarse o ser colocado aparte de los demás

isthmus [istmo] *s.*, franja estrecha de tierra que une dos áreas grandes de tierra

J

Jainism [jainismo] *s.*, religión del noroeste de India que se inició a fines del siglo VI D.C.

Java [Java] *s.*, una de las islas interiores del Sureste Asiático

Jerusalem [Jerusalén] *s.*, ciudad capital de Israel

Jiang Jieshi [Chiang Kai-shek] *s.*, líder nacionalista chino que combatió contra los comunistas

Jinnah, Mohammed Ali [Jinnah, Mohammed Ali] *s.*, líder de la Liga Musulmana Pan India que ayudó a fundar Pakistán y fue el primer gobernador general de Pakistán desde 1947–1948

K

Kalahari [Kalahari] *s.*, desierto importante del sur de África

Kanto Plain [llanura de Kanto] *s.*, área llana y propicia para la agricultura e industria ubicada en el este de los Alpes japoneses

karma [karma] *s.*, en el hinduismo, efecto positivo o negativo que una persona recibe como consecuencia de sus actos

Kenyatta, Jomo [Kenyatta, Jomo] *s.*, líder africano que ayudó a obtener la independencia de Kenia y en 1963 se convirtió en su primer gobernante electo

GLOSARIO

Khmer Empire [Imperio Jemer] *s.*, el imperio más vasto y duradero de Camboya, que se extendió desde inicios del siglo IX hasta 1430

Kievan Rus [Rus de Kiev] *s.*, estado fundado por los rusos Varegos en 882, que pasó a formar parte de la Rusia moderna

Kilimanjaro [Kilimanyaro] *s.*, volcán inactivo de Tanzania, de 19,340 pies de altura

kimono [kimono] *s.*, vestimenta femenina tradicional del Japón

Kingman Reef [arrecife Kingman] *s.*, arrecife de coral impoluto que forma parte de las Islas de la Línea, ubicadas entre Hawái y Samoa Americana

kinship [parentesco] *s.*, vínculo por consanguinidad o relación familiar

Knesset [Knéset] *s.*, parlamento del Estado de Israel

Koguryo [Goguryeo] *s.*, reino ubicado en el norte de Corea, en el año 37 A.C.

Kongo [Congo] *s.*, estado del centro de África, fundado en 1390

Koryo [Goryeo] *s.*, dinastía que gobernó Corea de 935 a 1392

Kremlin [Kremlin] *s.*, complejo histórico de palacios, arsenales e iglesias ubicado en Moscú, sede del gobierno ruso

Krishna [Krishna] *s.*, en el hinduismo, deidad encarnada en Visnú

Kunlun Mountains [montañas de Kunlun] *s.*, cordillera del este de Asia

Kurd [kurdo] *s.*, miembro de un grupo étnico no árabe del sudoeste de Asia

L

L'Ouverture, Toussaint [L'Ouverture, Toussaint] *s.*, ex esclavo que lideró la exitosa revuelta haitiana para lograr independizarse de Francia

labor force [fuerza laboral] *s.*, cantidad de personas disponibles para trabajar

land bridge [puente de tierra] *s.*, franja de tierra que conecta dos grandes masas de tierra

land reform [reforma agraria] *s.*, división de las fincas de gran extensión para dar tierras a los pobres

landlocked [sin litoral] *adj.*, rodeado de tierras, sin acceso directo al mar

landmass [masa de tierra] *s.*, área muy extensa de tierra

language diffusion [difusión de la lengua] *s.*, la expansión de una lengua desde su lugar de origen

language family [familia de lenguas] *s.*, grupo de lenguas relacionadas

latitude [latitud] *s.*, línea imaginaria que se extiende de este a oeste alrededor de la Tierra y que indica la ubicación en relación con el ecuador

launch [lanzamiento] *v.*, para empezar

legume [legumbre] *s.*, arvejas o frijoles

Lenin, V.I. [Lenin, V.I.] *s.*, líder bolchevique que destituyó al zar en la Revolución Rusa de 1917 y tomó el mando del gobierno nuevo

liberate [liberar] *v.*, conceder la libertad a algo o a alguien

lingua franca [lengua franca] *s.*, lengua común a varios grupos de personas

linguist [lingüista] *s.*, científico del lenguaje

literacy rate [alfabetismo] *s.*, porcentaje de personas que saben leer y escribir

literate [alfabetizado] *adj.*, que puede leer y escribir

Llanos [llanos] *s.*, praderas del norte de Sudamérica

Locke, John [Locke, John] *s.*, filósofo inglés de fines del siglo XVII que contribuyó a inspirar la Revolución Norteamericana y la Ilustración

locks [esclusas] *s.*, compartimentos que se usan en los canales para subir o bajar los barcos entre vías fluviales conectadas

loess [loes] *s.*, sedimento o limo de color amarillo que forma depósitos de gran espesor

longitude [longitud] *s.*, línea imaginaria que corre del Polo Norte al Polo Sur y que indica la ubicación en relación con el primer meridiano

Lost Decade [Década Perdida] *s.*, en Japón, la década de 1990, en la que disminuyó la producción porque las empresas estaban fuertemente endeudadas

Lost Boys of Sudan [Niños Perdidos de Sudán] *s.*, grupo de jóvenes de Sudán que quedaron huérfanos como consecuencia de la guerra civil y se mantuvieron unidos para escapar de la violencia

Louisiana Purchase [Compra de la Luisiana] *s.*, tierras compradas por Thomas Jefferson en 1803 que duplicaron el tamaño de los Estados Unidos

lowland [tierras bajas] *s.*, área de poca altura

lucrative [lucrativo] *adj.*, que hace ganar dinero o produce ganancia

Luther, Martin [Lutero, Martín] *s.*, monje alemán cuyos actos condujeron, en 1517, a la Reforma para enfrentar la corrupción de la Iglesia Católica

M

Machu Picchu [Machu Picchu] *s.*, ciudad compleja construida por los Incas sobre una montaña en el siglo XV

Madura [Madura] *s.*, una de las islas interiores ubicadas en el sudeste de Asia

magnetic levitation (Maglev) [levitación magnética] *adj.*, tipo de tren que se desliza sobre un colchón de aire por encima de vías dotadas de muchos imanes potentes

mainland [masa territorial] *s.*, tierra unida a un continente; usualmente se utiliza en relación con los países que poseen tanto un sector continental como islas

maintain [mantener] *v.*, conservar y continuar

Malay Peninsula [Península Malaya] *s.*, península del Sureste Asiático que abarca partes de Tailandia, Myanmar y la parte continental de Malasia

Malaysia [Malasia] *s.*, país del Sureste Asiático, situado en el extremo inferior de la península malaya y en la isla de Borneo

malnutrition [desnutrición] *s.*, insuficiencia de alimentos o nutrientes

Mandela, Nelson [Mandela, Nelson] *s.*, líder del Congreso Nacional Africano, encarcelado por luchar contra el apartheid, elegido presidente de Sudáfrica en 1994

manga [manga] *s.*, tipo de libro de historietas japonés

Manifest Destiny [Destino Manifiesto] *s.*, idea de que Estados Unidos tiene el derecho de expandir su territorio hacia el océano Pacífico

Manila [Manila] *s.*, capital de las Filipinas

manufacturing [manufactura] *s.*, uso de máquinas para convertir las materias primas en productos útiles

Mao Zedong [Mao Zedong] *s.*, presidente del Partido Comunista que gobernó China de 1949 a 1976

Maori [maoríes] *s.*, pueblo nativo de Nueva Zelanda

map [mapa] *s.*, representación plana, bidimensional, de la Tierra

marine [marino] *adj.*, perteneciente al mar

marine life [vida marina] *s.*, plantas y animales que viven en el océano

marine reserve [reserva marina] *s.*, área del océano resguardada para proteger a los animales marinos de los seres humanos

maritime [marítimo] *adj.*, relacionado con el mar

marketing [marketing] *s.*, publicidad y promoción de un producto o negocio

marsupial [marsupial] *s.*, mamífero cuyas hembras transportan a las crías en una bolsa abdominal

martial law [ley marcial] *s.*, gobierno que se mantiene por el poder militar

mass media [medios masivos de comunicación] *s.*, comunicación proveniente de una única fuente, con el potencial de llegar a grandes audiencias

Maya [maya] *s.*, civilización que vivió en el Yucatán y en la parte norte de Centroamérica de 100 A.C. a 900 D.C.

medicinal plant [planta medicinal] *s.*, planta que se usa para tratar enfermedades

meditation [meditación] *s.*, práctica de usar la concentración para calmar los pensamientos y controlarlos

Mediterranean climate [clima mediterráneo] *s.*, clima de veranos calurosos y secos e inviernos templados y lluviosos

megacity [megalópolis] *s.*, ciudad grande, que tiene más de 10 millones de habitantes

Mekong River [río Mekong] *s.*, el río más largo del Sureste Asiático; fluye a través de Myanmar, Laos y Tailandia

Mesa Central [Mesa Central] *s.*, en México, la parte sur de la meseta mexicana

messiah [mesías] *s.*, líder o salvador

mestizo [mestizo] *s.*, persona que tiene una mezcla de ancestros europeos y americanos nativos

methane [metano] *s.*, gas natural incoloro que se libera a partir del carbono

metropolitan area [área metropolitana] *adj.*, sitio poblado alrededor de una ciudad que incluye los límites de la ciudad y las comunidades que la rodean

Mexican Cession [Cesión Mexicana] *s.*, tierras que abarcan desde Texas hasta California, entregadas por México a los Estados Unidos en 1848, de acuerdo con el tratado de Guadalupe Hidalgo

Mexican Plateau [Meseta Mexicana] *s.*, área de tierras llanas que se encuentran entre las dos cordilleras montañosas de Sierra Madre, en México

microcredit [microcrédito] *s.*, préstamo de una suma pequeña de dinero

microlending [micropréstamo] *s.*, práctica de otorgar préstamos de sumas pequeñas de dinero a las personas que inician sus propios negocios

Middle Ages [Edad Media] *s.*, período en Europa occidental posterior a la caída del Imperio Romano, desde aproximadamente 500 a 1500

Middle Passage [Pasaje del Medio] *s.*, viaje para cruzar el océano Atlántico, que tomaba meses, en el cual los africanos esclavizados eran llevados a las colonias europeas en América

migrate [emigrar] *v.*, trasladarse de un lugar a otro

migration [migración] *s.*, traslado de un lugar a otro

military dictatorship [dictadura militar] *s.*, forma de gobierno en la que el ejército ejerce el control del gobierno

mineral [mineral] *s.*, sustancia sólida y natural que se encuentra en las rocas y en la Tierra; es inorgánica y tiene un conjunto propio de propiedades

missionary [misionero] *s.*, persona enviada por una iglesia a convertir a otras personas a esa religión

mobile [móvil] *adj.*, que se puede mover

modernization [modernización] *s.*, políticas y acciones diseñadas para que un país se actualice tanto tecnológicamente como en otras áreas

modify [modificar] *v.*, cambiar o hacer menos extremo

Mongol Empire [Imperio Mongol] *s.*, imperio establecido en Asia Central por Gengis Kan a comienzos del siglo XIII

monk [monje] *s.*, persona que dedica su vida a tareas religiosas

monopoly [monopolio] *s.*, control total del mercado para un servicio o producto

monotheism [monoteísmo] *s.*, creencia en un solo dios

monotheistic [monoteísta] *adj.*, relativo a la creencia religiosa en un solo dios

monotheistic religion [religión monoteísta] *s.*, sistema de creencias basadas en un solo dios o deidad

monsoon [monzón] *s.*, viento estacional que trae lluvias intensas durante parte del año

Montezuma [Moctezuma] *s.*, líder azteca asesinado por el conquistador español Hernán Cortés

moral [moral] *adj.*, correcto y bueno, referido al comportamiento humano

mosque [mezquita] *s.*, templo musulmán

mouth [desembocadura] *s.*, lugar donde un río desemboca en el mar

movable type [tipo móvil] *s.*, invento de aplicación en la imprenta, que permite mover los carácteres individuales para crear distintas páginas de texto

multinational corporation [corporación multinacional] *s.*, empresa grande que tiene su base en un país y que abre sucursales en muchos otros países

multi-party democracy [democracia multipartidaria] *s.*, sistema político en el cual las elecciones incluyen candidatos de más de un partido

multitudes [multitudes] *s.*, grandes cantidades

Mundurukú [mundurukú] *s.*, pueblo indígena de Brasil

mural [mural] *s.*, pintura de gran tamaño realizada sobre una pared

mythology [mitología] *s.*, conjunto de relatos, tradiciones y creencias

N

N'Dour, Youssou [N'Dour, Youssou] *s.*, famoso griot de África occidental que interpreta música Mbalax

Nairobi [Nairobi] *s.*, capital de Kenia

Napoleon [Napoleón] *s.*, emperador de Francia que conquistó otros países europeos y formó un imperio, 1804–1815

National Action Party (PAN) [Partido Acción Nacional (PAN)] *s.*, partido político mexicano que ganó las elecciones del año 2000

nationalism [nacionalismo] *s.*, profundo sentimiento de lealtad al propio país

nationalize [nacionalizar] *v.*, dar al gobierno el control de una empresa privada

natural rights [derechos naturales] *s.*, derechos como la vida, la libertad y la propiedad, que las personas poseen desde su nacimiento

naturalization [naturalización] *s.*, proceso que permite que una persona nacida en otro país se convierta en ciudadano

navigable [navegable] *adj.*, suficientemente ancho o profundo para que los barcos o botes puedan navegar sin inconvenientes

navigation [navegación] *s.*, ciencia de averiguar la posición y planear rutas marítimas

Nazi Germany [Alemania nazi] *s.*, Alemania bajo el régimen del partido nazi, de 1933 a 1945

Nebuchadnezzar [Nabucodonosor] *s.*, rey de Babilonia, 605–562 A.C.

neutrality [neutralidad] *s.*, negativa a tomar partido o a involucrarse

New Guinea [Nueva Guinea] *s.*, la segunda isla más grande del mundo, ubicada en el sudoeste del océano Pacífico

New South Wales [Nueva Gales del Sur] *s.*, colonia construida por convictos en Australia, en 1788

Nile River [río Nilo] *s.*, el río más largo del mundo; fluye 4,000 millas a través de Egipto y África

Nkrumah, Kwame [Nkrumah, Kwame] *s.*, líder africano de las décadas de 1950 y 1960, que contribuyó a lograr la independencia de Ghana

nocturnal [nocturno] *adj.*, activo de noche en lugar de durante el día

nomad [nómada] *s.*, persona que se desplaza de un lugar a otro

nonrenewable [no renovable] *adj.*, que no se puede reproducir con la misma rapidez con que se lo usa

nonrenewable fossil fuel [combustible fósil no renovable] *s.*, fuente de energía, como el petróleo, el gas natural o el carbón, cuya provisión es limitada

nonrenewable resource [recurso no renovable] *s.*, fuente de energía que es limitada, y no se puede reemplazar, como el petróleo

North American Free Trade Agreement (NAFTA) [Tratado de Libre Comercio de América del Norte (NAFTA)] *s.*, acuerdo firmado en 1994 que facilitó el comercio y la inversión entre Canadá, México y los Estados Unidos

North Anatolian Fault [Falla del Norte de Anatolia] *s.*, fractura de la corteza terrestre que se extiende al este y al oeste, justo al sur del mar Negro

North Atlantic Drift [Corriente del Atlántico Norte] *s.*, corriente marina cálida que calienta las aguas que bañan la parte noroeste de Rusia

North China Plain [Llanura del Norte de China] *s.*, llanura que se extiende a lo largo del río Huang He

North Pole [Polo Norte] *s.*, punto ubicado en el extremo norte de la Tierra, opuesto al Polo Sur, donde convergen todas las líneas de longitud

Northern European Plain [Llanura del Norte de Europa] *s.*, vastas tierras bajas que se extienden desde Francia hasta Rusia

Northern Hemisphere [Hemisferio Norte] *s.*, la mitad de la Tierra que se encuentra al norte del ecuador

novel [novela] *s.*, extensa obra de ficción, con trama y personajes complejos

O

oasis [oasis] *s.*, sitio fértil con agua ubicado en un área seca y desértica

occupy [ocupar] *v.*, apoderarse

Okavango Delta [delta del Okavango] *s.*, delta del interior de Botsuana, donde el río Okavango desemboca en un pantano

Olmec [olmecas] *s.*, sociedad organizada que vivió junto a la costa sur del golfo de México en 1000 A.C.

one-child policy [política de hijo único] *s.*, ley china de 1979 que limitaba a las familias que vivían en áreas urbanas a tener solamente un hijo

opera [ópera] *s.*, representación que cuenta una historia mediante música y palabras

oppose [oponerse] *v.*, objetar

oral tradition [tradición oral] *s.*, transmisión verbal de historias o relatos de una generación a la siguiente

Orange Revolution [Revolución Naranja] *s.*, destitución pacífica del primer ministro de Ucrania en 2004

Osman [Osman] *s.*, primer líder de los turcos en el siglo XIV, por cuyo nombre pasaron a ser llamados otomanos

Ottoman Empire [Imperio Otomano] *s.*, vasto y rico imperio que existió desde 1453 hasta 1923, centrado en el territorio actual de Turquía

outer islands [islas exteriores] *s.*, islas de Indonesia que incluyen a Sumatra, Borneo, Nueva Guinea y otras

outrigger canoe [canoa hawaiana] *s.*, bote que tiene adosado un flotador que le da estabilidad

outsourcing [subcontratar] *s.*, transferir empleos a trabajadores que no pertenecen a la compañía, que a menudo se encuentran en un país extranjero

overpopulation [superpoblación] *s.*, situación en la que demasiadas personas viven en un mismo lugar

P

Paekche [Baekje] *s.*, reino del sudoeste de Corea, en el año 18 A.C.

pagoda [pagoda] *s.*, estructura religiosa de varios pisos que se encuentra en los países asiáticos, a menudo utilizada con fines religiosos

Palestine Liberation Organization (PLO) [Organización para la Liberación de Palestina (OLP)] *s.*, organización creada por líderes palestinos

Pampas [Pampa] *s.*, llanuras cubiertas de pasto de la Argentina

Pan-Africanism [Panafricanismo] *s.*, movimiento surgido en los inicios del siglo XX para unir a los pueblos africanos

Panama Canal Zone [Zona del Canal de Panamá] *s.*, área en la que se construyó el canal de Panamá

pandemic [pandemia] *s.*, brote de una enfermedad que se propaga por una vasta área geográfica

Papua New Guinea [Papúa Nueva Guinea] *s.*, país del Pacífico Sur que abarca la mitad oriental de la isla de Nueva Guinea y las islas cercanas

papyrus [papiro] *s.*, material similar al papel inventado en el antiguo Egipto

Parliament [Parlamento] *s.*, poder legislativo del gobierno de la India

parliamentary democracy [democracia parlamentaria] *s.*, sistema de gobierno en el cual el poder ejecutivo está presidido por el primer ministro, que es elegido por el partido que posee la mayoría de los escaños del Parlamento

Partition [Partición] *s.*, se refiere a la división del sur de Asia en los países independientes de India y Paquistán

patrician [patricio] *s.*, rico terrateniente de la antigua Roma

Pearl Harbor [Pearl Harbor] *s.*, base naval de los EE.UU. ubicada en Hawái, bombardeada por los japoneses en 1941, lo cual provocó el ingreso de EE.UU. en la Segunda Guerra Mundial

peat [turba] *s.*, material que se forma a partir de la descomposición de plantas muy antiguas y que arde como el carbón

peninsula [península] *s.*, masa de tierra rodeada por agua en tres de sus lados

perestroika [perestroika] *s.*, reformas en la estructura económica de la Unión Soviética introducidas por Mijaíl Gorbachov en 1985

permafrost [permafrost] *s.*, suelo que está permanentemente congelado

perspective [perspectiva] *s. modo artístico de mostrar los objetos de la manera en que son vistos por las personas*, en términos de distancia o profundidad relativa, como si estuvieran en tres dimensiones

pesticide [pesticida] *s.*, sustancia química que mata insectos y malezas nocivas

Peter the Great [Pedro el Grande] *s.*, Pedro Romanov, zar que gobernó Rusia desde 1682 hasta 1725

petrochemicals [petroquímicos] *s.*, productos elaborados a partir del petróleo

petroleum [petróleo] *s.*, materia prima que se usa para producir combustibles

pharaoh [faraón] *s.*, rey en el antiguo Egipto

philosopher [filósofo] *s.*, persona que examina las preguntas sobre el universo y busca la verdad

pictograph [pictograma] *s.*, imagen pintada usada para comunicar

pilgrimage [peregrinaje] *s.*, viaje religioso

pioneer [pionero] *s.*, colono de tierras nuevas

pipeline [tubería] *s.*, serie de tubos o caños conectados para transportar líquidos o gases

Pizarro, Francisco [Pizarro, Francisco] *s.*, conquistador español que en 1533 derrocó al emperador y fundó la ciudad de Lima, Perú

plain [llanura] *s.*, área plana de la superficie terrestre

plantation [plantación] *s.*, granja de gran tamaño que produce cultivos para obtener ganancias

plate [placa] *s.*, sección rígida de la corteza terrestre que se puede mover de manera independiente

plateau [meseta] *s.*, llanura ubicada a gran altura sobre el nivel del mar que a menudo tiene un precipicio en todos sus lados

plebeian [plebeyo] *s.*, agricultor o persona de clase baja de la antigua Roma

poach [caza o pesca furtiva] *v.*, cazar o pescar ilegalmente

poacher [cazador o pescador furtivo] *s.*, persona que caza o pesca de manera ilegal

poaching [cazar o pescar furtivamente] *s.*, caza o pesca ilegal

polder [pólder] *s.*, tierras de los Países Bajos ganadas al mar que se destinan a la agricultura

policy [política] *s.*, pautas y procedimientos oficiales de una organización o gobierno

pollution [contaminación] *s.*, desechos químicos o físicos que generan un medio ambiente sucio o poco limpio

Polynesian Triangle [Triángulo Polinésico] *s.*, vasta área del Pacífico Sur que abarca muchas islas

polytheism [politeísmo] *s.*, creencia en más de un dios

polytheistic religion [religión politeísta] *s.*, sistema de creencias basadas en varios dioses o deidades

popular culture [cultura popular] *s.*, artes, música y otros elementos de la vida cotidiana de una región

porcelain [porcelana] *s.*, tipo de cerámica dura

port [puerto] *s.*, embarcadero para barcos donde se intercambian mercancías

Port-au-Prince [Puerto Príncipe] *s.*, capital de Haití

potential [potencial] *s.*, posibilidad

precipitation [precipitación] *s.*, proceso que hace caer agua sobre la Tierra, en forma de lluvia, nieve o granizo

predominant [predominante] *adj.*, principal, más común, superior a los demás

prehistoric [prehistórico] *adj.*, anterior a la historia escrita

preserve [preservar] *v.*, proteger

pride [manada] *s.*, grupo de leones que viven en comunidad

prime meridian [primer meridiano] *s.*, línea de longitud de 0° que se extiende desde Polo Norte al Polo Sur y que pasa por Greenwich, Inglaterra

privatization [privatización] *s.*, proceso por el que las empresas que eran propiedad del gobierno pasan a manos privadas

profitable [rentable] *adj.*, que hace ganar dinero, financieramente exitoso

projection [proyección] *s.*, modo de mostrar la superficie curva de la Tierra sobre un mapa plano

promote [fomentar] *v.*, animar, estimular

propaganda [propaganda] *s.*, información que se difunde para influir sobre la opinión de las personas o para promover las ideas de un partido u organización

proportional representation [representación proporcional] *s.*, sistema en el cual un partido político consigue un porcentaje de escaños igual al porcentaje de votos que obtuvo

prosperous [próspero] *adj.*, económicamente fuerte

protest [protestar] *v.*, objetar

province [provincia] *s.*, parte más pequeña en que se divide un país, especialmente Canadá

push-pull factors [factores de atracción y repulsión] *s.*, motivos por los que las personas emigran; los factores de "repulsión" las hacen partir de un sitio, los factores de "atracción" las hacen ir hacia otro sitio

pyramid [pirámide] *s.*, monumento construido en roca que servía de tumba en el antiguo Egipto

Q

qanat [qanat] *s.*, túnel subterráneo construido por el hombre en la meseta de Irán, usado para transportar agua desde las montañas

Qin [Qin] *s.*, dinastía que gobernó China durante el período 221–206 a.c.

Quechua [quechuas] *s.*, pueblo que vive en la cordillera de los Andes de Perú, Ecuador y Bolivia

Qur'an [Corán] *s.*, libro sagrado del islamismo

R

radical [radical] *s.*, persona que busca un cambio extremo o sostiene una posición política extrema

radioactive [radiactivo] *adj.*, que emite energía producida por la ruptura de un átomo

rain forest [bosque tropical] *s.*, bosque de temperatura cálida, humedad elevada y vegetación espesa que recibe más de 100 pulgadas de lluvia al año

rain shadow [sombra orográfica] *s.*, región seca ubicada sobre uno de los lados de una cordillera

rainshadow effect [efecto de la sombra orográfica] *s.*, proceso en el cual el aire húmedo asciende por una ladera de la cordillera y luego se enfría y cae en forma de precipitación, dejando el otro lado de la cordillera mayormente seco

Ramses II [Ramsés II] *s.*, faraón egipcio que reinó alrededor del año 1185 A.C. y expandió los límites del imperio egipcio

raw materials [materias primas] *s.*, materiales naturales o sin terminar, como minerales, petróleo o carbón, que se usan para elaborar productos terminados

Re [Ra] *s.*, dios solar de los antiguos egipcios

rebellion [rebelión] *s.*, revuelta o resistencia a la autoridad

recession [recesión] *s.*, desaceleración del crecimiento económico

reclaim [reclamar] *v.*, volver a tomar

Reconstruction [Reconstrucción] *s.*, esfuerzo realizado para reconstruir y unificar a los Estados Unidos después de la guerra civil

reform [reforma] *s.*, cambio que apunta a corregir un problema

Reformation [Reforma] *s.*, movimiento que surgió en el siglo XVI para reformar el cristianismo

refuge [refugio] *s.*, lugar seguro

refugee [refugiado] *s.*, persona que huye de un lugar para estar a salvo

region [región] *s.*, conjunto de sitios con características comunes

regulate [regular] *v.*, controlar

reign [reinado] *s.*, período de mando de un rey, reina, emperador o emperadora

Reign of Terror [El Terror] *s.*, movimiento francés liderado por Maximilien Robespierre, en el cual fueron decapitadas 40,000 personas, durante el período 1793–94

reincarnation [reencarnación] *n.*, el nacimiento de un alma en otra vida

relative location [ubicación relativa] *s.*, la posición de un lugar en relación con otros

reliable [confiable] *adj.*, fiable o de confianza

relief [relieve] *s.*, cambio en la elevación de un lugar a otro

religious tolerance [tolerancia religiosa] *s.*, aceptación de distintas religiones para que sean profesadas al mismo tiempo, sin prejuicios

relocate [relocalizar] *v.*, trasladar

remittance [remesa] *s.*, dinero enviado a una persona que se encuentra en otro lugar

remote [remoto] *adj.*, difícil de llegar, aislado

Renaissance [Renacimiento] *s.*, período que se desarrolló entre los siglos XIV y XVI, donde florecieron el arte y la cultura

renewable energy [energía renovable] *s.*, energía obtenida a partir de fuentes que no se agotan, como el viento, el Sol y el agua

renewable resource [recurso renovable] *s.*, materia prima o fuente de energía que se reemplaza a sí misma con el paso del tiempo

reparation [reparación] *s.*, dinero que, después de una guerra, pagan como castigo normalmente los agresores que iniciaron el conflicto

republic [república] *s.*, forma de gobierno en la cual las personas eligen funcionarios para que gobiernen

reserve [reserva] *s.*, tierras destinadas a propósitos especiales, como la agricultura, la preservación de los hábitats o para ser usadas como vivienda por determinados grupos de personas; futuro suministro (de petróleo)

reservoir [embalse] *s.*, lago artificial de gran tamaño para almacenar agua

resistance [resistencia] *n.*, oposición

restore [restaurar] *v.*, recuperar

retreat [retirarse] *v.*, ir hacia atrás, no hacia adelante

revenue [rentas] *s.*, ingresos

reverse [retroceder] *v.*, ir en la dirección opuesta

Revolution [revolución] *s.*, acción de ciudadanos o colonos cuyo objetivo es derrocar un gobierno

Rhine River [río Rin] *s.*, río que nace en Suiza y desemboca en el mar del Norte

rift valley [valle de fisura] *s.*, valle profundo que se formó al separarse la corteza terrestre, como en África Oriental

Ring of Fire [Anillo de Fuego] *s.*, área que se extiende a lo largo de las riberas del océano Pacífico, donde chocan las placas tectónicas, lo que genera terremotos y una gran actividad volcánica

Rio de Janeiro [Río de Janeiro] *s.*, ciudad de Brasil que albergará los juegos olímpicos de 2016

ritual [ritual] *s.*, acto formal que se repite regularmente

rivalry [rivalidad] *s.*, competencia u oposición entre personas

GLOSARIO

river basin [cuenca de un río] s., área baja por la que fluye un río

Romantic Period [Romanticismo] s., período artístico de comienzos del siglo XIX, en el cual los artistas pintaban paisajes y escenas de la naturaleza para transmitir emociones

roots [raíces] s., orígenes culturales

Rub al Khali [Rub al-Jali] s., vasto desierto ubicado al sur de Arabia Saudita

Russian Revolution [Revolución Rusa] s., revolución que tuvo lugar en Rusia en 1917, en la cual el zar fue depuesto y los bolcheviques tomaron el poder

Russification [rusificación] s., política de designar ciudadanos rusos a cargo de las repúblicas soviéticas durante las décadas de 1970 y 1980

ruthless [despiadado] adj., cruel

S

Sahara Desert [desierto de Sahara] s., el desierto más grande del mundo, que cubre la mayor parte del norte de África

Sahel [Sahel] s., pradera semiárida del África subsahariana, limitada al norte por el Sahara y al sur por las praderas tropicales

salinization [salinización] s., acumulación de sal en el suelo

Samoa [Samoa] s., país que comprende las islas occidentales de Samoa, ubicadas al sur del océano Pacífico

samurai [samurái] s., diestro guerrero japonés

sanitation [sanidad] s., medidas tomadas para proteger la salud pública, como la red cloacal

Sanskrit [sánscrito] s., idioma de los arios, que se convirtió en la base de numerosas lenguas del sur de Asia

Santa Anna [Santa Anna] s., presidente y general mexicano, que venció en la batalla de El Álamo, pero perdió la guerra entre los Estados Unidos y México

São Paolo [San Pablo] s., la ciudad más grande de Brasil

sarcophagus [sarcófago] s., ataúd

sari [sari] s., vestido tradicional femenino de la India, que se enrolla alrededor del cuerpo

saturate [saturar] v., remojar completamente

savanna [sabana] s., pradera, como la del sur del África subsahariana

scale [escala] s., parte de un mapa que indica el tamaño en el que se muestra un área de la Tierra

scarcity [escasez] s., falta o carencia de algo

scientific station [estación científica] s., sitio para desarrollar una investigación

scorched earth policy [táctica de tierra quemada] s., práctica llevada adelante por las tropas rusas en 1812, quienes, a medida que retrocedían ante el avance del ejército de Napoleón, quemaban los cultivos y todos los recursos que pudieran servir al enemigo para abastecerse

seafarer [navegante] s., persona que viaja por el mar

secede [separarse] v., retirarse formalmente, dejar de ser parte

secular [secular] adj., terrenal, sin vínculo con una religión

segregation [segregación] s., separación por raza

seismic [sísmico] adj., relacionado con la actividad o movimiento producidos por los terremotos

seize [apoderarse] v., tomar el control

self-rule [autonomía] s., gobierno ejercido por los propios habitantes de un país

semiarid [semiárido] adj., algo seco, con muy poca lluvia

serf [siervo] s., campesino ruso o europeo, pobre y con pocos derechos, que alquilaba tierras a un terrateniente entre los siglos XVI y XIX

shalwar-kameez [shalwar-kameez] s., camisa larga con pantalones holgados que se usa en la India y en el suroeste de Asia

Shang [Shang] s., familia cuya dinastía gobernó China desde 1766 hasta 1050 A.C.

sheikh [jeque] s., líder árabe

Shi Huangdi [Qin Shi Huang] s., líder de la dinastía Qin, que se convirtió en el primer emperador de la China en 221 A.C.

Shi'ite [chiita] adj., rama de musulmanes que considera que los líderes religiosos deben ser descendientes de Mahoma

Shinto [sintoísmo] s., religión nativa del Japón, similar al animismo

shogun [sogún] s., gobernador militar japonés

Siberia [Siberia] s., enorme región del centro y este de Rusia

significant [significativo] adj., importante

Sikhism [sijismo] s., religión que surgió a fines del siglo XV en la India

Silk Roads [rutas de la seda] s., antiguas rutas comerciales que unían el sudoeste y el centro de Asia con China

Silla [Silla] s., reino ubicado en el sudeste de Corea en el año 57 A.C.

silt [limo] s., partículas finas de suelo que se depositan a lo largo de las márgenes de los ríos

slash-and-burn [tala y quema] s., método agrícola que consiste en despejar las tierras talando y quemando el bosque y la vegetación

Slavs [eslavos] *s.*, pueblo originario de los alrededores del mar Negro o Polonia, que se instaló en Ucrania y el oeste de Rusia alrededor del año 800 D.C.

slum [barriada] *s.*, área densamente poblada de una ciudad, con viviendas precarias y malas condiciones de vida

smartphone [teléfono inteligente] *s.*, dispositivo portátil que combina la comunicación con aplicaciones de software

socialism [socialismo] *s.*, sistema de gobierno en el que el gobierno controla los recursos económicos

solstice [solsticio] *s.*, punto en que el Sol se encuentra a la distancia máxima, al sur o al norte, del ecuador; inicio del invierno y del verano

South Pole [Polo Sur] *s.*, punto más austral de la Tierra, opuesto al Polo Norte, donde convergen todas las líneas de longitud

Southern Alps [Alpes del Sur] *s.*, cordillera situada en Nueva Zelanda

Southern Hemisphere [Hemisferio Sur] *s.*, la mitad de la Tierra que se encuentra al sur del ecuador

sovereignty [soberanía] *s.*, control de un país sobre sus propios asuntos

Soviet Union [Unión Soviética] *s.*, Unión de las Repúblicas Socialistas Soviéticas, país formado por Rusia y otros estados euroasiáticos, que existió desde 1922 hasta 1991

soybean [soja] *s.*, tipo de frijol que se cultiva como alimento y para elaborar productos industriales

spatial thinking [pensamiento espacial] *s.*, manera de pensar en el espacio que está sobre la superficie de la Tierra, incluyendo la ubicación de los distintos lugares y por qué se encuentran allí

Special Economic Zone [Zona Económica Especial] *s.*, área de China en la que se permitió el desarrollo de una economía de mercado, con menor control de los negocios por parte del gobierno

sprawl [expandirse] *v.*, extenderse

standard of living [nivel de vida] *s.*, nivel de acceso de los habitantes de un país a bienes, servicios y comodidades materiales

staple [alimento básico] *s.*, constituyente básico de la dieta de las personas

state [estado] *s.*, territorio determinado que posee un gobierno propio

steel [acero] *s.*, metal de gran dureza elaborado a partir del hierro combinado con otros metales

steppe [estepa] *s.*, llanura muy extensa de praderas secas

strait [estrecho] *s.*, vía fluvial angosta que conecta dos masas de agua

strike [huelga] *s.*, interrupción del trabajo por parte de empleados que se niegan a trabajar

subcontinent [subcontinente] *s.*, región separada de un continente

subsistence farmers [agricultores de subsistencia] *s.*, agricultores que producen cultivos para alimentar a sus familias, no para vender

subsistence farming [agricultura de subsistencia] *s.*, agricultura que solamente produce cultivos para que las familias se alimenten, no para vender

subsistence fishing [pesca de subsistencia] *s.*, pescar para tener comida para poder vivir, no para obtener ganancias

suffrage [sufragio] *s.*, derecho al voto

Suleyman I [Suleyman I] *s.*, emperador del Imperio Otomano a mediados del siglo XVI

sultan [sultán] *s.*, líder o gobernante del Imperio Otomano

Sumatra [Sumatra] *s.*, una de las islas exteriores del sudeste de Asia

Sunni [sunita] *adj.*, rama del islamismo que sostiene que los líderes religiosos deben ser escogidos entre los candidatos más capacitados, a diferencia de hacerlo entre los descendientes de Mahoma

surplus [excedente] *s.*, extra

suspension bridge [puente colgante] *n.*, colgados de un puente que se cuelga de dos o más cables

sustainable [sustentable] *adj.*, capaz de ser continuado sin dañar el medio ambiente o sin agotar los recursos de manera permanente

Swahili [suajili] *s.*, lengua bantú hablada mayormente en África Oriental, también llamada kiswahili

Sydney [Sídney] *s.*, la ciudad más grande de Australia, capital del estado de Nueva Gales del Sur

symbol [símbolo] *s.*, objeto o idea que se puede usar para representar otro objeto o idea

T

taiga [taiga] *s.*, extensa área de bosques que se extiende a través del norte de Rusia, Canadá y otros países del norte

Taino [taínos] *s.*, pueblo nativo del Caribe

Taj Mahal [Taj Mahal] *s.*, famoso edificio construido en la India en el siglo XVII, para servir como tumba de la esposa de Shah Jahan; actualmente reconocido por la UNESCO como patrimonio de la humanidad

Taliban [talibán] *s.*, grupo de pashtunes de Afganistán que comenzaron a gobernar el país en 1996

Taman Negara National Park [Parque Nacional Taman Negara] *s.*, parque nacional de Malasia situado dentro de uno de los bosques tropicales más antiguos del mundo

tariff [arancel] *s.*, impuesto sobre las importaciones y exportaciones

GLOSARIO

tax [impuesto] *s.*, suma que se paga al gobierno para contar con servicios públicos

tectonic plate [placa tectónica] *s.*, sección de la corteza terrestre que flota sobre el manto terrestre

temperate [templado] *adj.*, benigno, en términos del clima

terra cotta [terracota] *s.*, arcilla endurecida al horno

terrace [terraza] *s.*, superficie llana construida sobre la ladera de un monte

terraced [abancalado] *adj.*, campo llano excavado en la pendiente o ladera de una montaña

terrain [terreno] *s.*, características físicas de la tierra

terrorism [terrorismo] *s.*, tipo de guerra que se vale de la violencia para obtener resultados políticos; es normalmente empleada por grupos reducidos o individuos

terrorist [terrorista] *s.*, persona que emplea la violencia para obtener resultados políticos

textile [textil] *adj.*, relativo a la tela o ropa

theme [tema] *s.*, tópico

thirty-eighth parallel [paralelo treinta y ocho] *s.*, frontera que separa Corea del Norte y Corea del Sur, establecida en 1945 a lo largo del paralelo de 38° de latitud norte

Three Gorges Dam [presa de las Tres Gargantas] *s.*, la presa más grande del mundo, emplazada sobre el río Chang Jiang, en China

Tibetan Plateau [meseta tibetana] *s.*, meseta vasta y de gran elevación situada en Asia Central

Timbuktu [Tombuctú] *s.*, ciudad de África Occidental que fue un centro educativo en el siglo XIII

tolerance [tolerancia] *s.*, aceptación de las creencias de los demás

tomb [tumba] *s.*, lugar donde se realiza un entierro

topography [topografía] *s.*, características físicas de la tierra

tornado [tornado] *s.*, tormenta de vientos muy fuertes que sigue una trayectoria impredecible

totalitarian [totalitario] *adj.*, relacionado con un gobierno dirigido por un dictador que exige obediencia absoluta al estado

tourism [turismo] *s.*, industria o negocio de los viajes

Trail of Tears [Sendero de Lágrimas] *s.*, ruta que siguieron los cheroquis durante su forzada emigración desde el sudeste de los Estados Unidos hasta Oklahoma, en la década de 1830

trans-Atlantic slave trade [tráfico transatlántico de esclavos] *s.*, negocio de traficar a América, a través del océano Atlántico, esclavos originarios de África, que se inició en el siglo XVI

transcontinental [transcontinental] *adj.*, que atraviesa todo un continente

transform [transformar] *v.*, rehacer o cambiar

transition [transición] *s.*, cambio de una actividad o etapa a otra

transition zone [zona de transición] *s.*, área situada entre dos regiones geográficas y que posee características de ambas

transpiration [transpiración] *s.*, proceso mediante el cual las plantas y los árboles liberan vapor de agua en el aire

transport [transportar] *v.*, enviar de un lugar a otro

transportation corridor [corredor de transporte] *s.*, ruta terrestre o marítima para trasladar personas o mercancías de un lugar a otro con facilidad

trans-Saharan [transahariano] *adj.*, que atraviesa el desierto del Sahara

Trans-Siberian Railroad [ferrocarril transiberiano] *n.*, el ferrocarril de servicio continuo más largo del mundo, que une Moscú con el este de Rusia, atravesando Siberia

treaty [tratado] *s.*, acuerdo entre dos o más países

Treaty of Guadalupe Hidalgo [Tratado de Guadalupe Hidalgo] *s.*, acuerdo firmado en 1848, por el cual México cedió a los Estados Unidos el área que se extiende desde Texas hasta California

Treaty of Tordesillas [Tratado de Tordesillas] *s.*, tratado firmado entre españoles y portugueses en 1494, a través del cual se dividieron la posesión de las tierras de Sudamérica

Treaty of Versailles [Tratado de Versalles] *s.*, tratado de paz que puso fin, en 1919, a la Primera Guerra Mundial

trench [trinchera] *s.*, zanja extensa que protege a los soldados del fuego enemigo

trend [tendencia] *s.*, cambio que se produce en determinada dirección con el paso del tiempo

triangular trade [comercio triangular] *s.*, comercio entre tres continentes: América, Europa y África

tributary [tributario] *s.*, río pequeño que fluye hacia un río más grande

tribute [tributo] *s.*, sumas pagadas a otro país o gobernante a cambio de protección o como muestra de sumisión

troubadour [trovador] *s.*, cantante de la Edad Media que interpretaba canciones sobre caballeros y el amor

tsunami [tsunami] *s.*, ola enorme y muy potente que se forma en el océano

Tuareg [tuareg] *s.*, pueblo semi nómada que se desplaza en caravanas a través del Sahara, comerciando sal

tundra [tundra] *s.*, tierras llanas y sin árboles que se encuentran en las regiones árticas y subárticas

GLOSARIO

Tupinambá [tupinambás] *s.*, pueblo que vivió cerca de la desembocadura del río Amazonas y a lo largo de la costa atlántica hacia el año 3000 A.C.

typhoon [tifón] *s.*, tormenta tropical peligrosa, que trae lluvias copiosas y vientos muy fuertes, que en el Hemisferio Occidental se denomina huracán

tyranny [tiranía] *s.*, gobierno duro o severo

U

United Arab Emirates [Emiratos Árabes Unidos] *s.*, país situado en la península arábiga, en el golfo pérsico

United Nations (UN) [Naciones Unidas (ONU)] *s.*, organización de países formada en 1945, con el objetivo de mantener la paz entre los países y proteger los derechos humanos

Universal Declaration of Human Rights [Declaración Universal de los Derechos Humanos] *s.*, acuerdo aprobado por las Naciones Unidas que define los derechos que deben tener todas las personas del mundo

uplands [tierras altas] *s.*, colinas, montañas y mesetas

Ur [Ur] *s.*, importante ciudad estado sumeria, 2800–1850 A.C.

Ural Mountains [montes Urales] *s.*, cordillera que separa la Llanura del Norte de Europa de la Llanura de Siberia Occidental, en Rusia

urban [urbano] *adj.*, que describe o está relacionado con la ciudad o los suburbios

utilize [utilizar] *v.*, hacer uso práctico de algo

V

vaccine [vacuna] *s.*, tratamiento para incrementar la inmunidad a una enfermedad determinada

vegetation [vegetación] *s.*, formas de vida vegetal

venue [sede] *s.*, ubicación donde tiene lugar un suceso programado

veto [veto] *v.*, rechazar una decisión tomada por otro órgano de gobierno

viceroy [virrey] *s.*, gobernador de las colonias españolas en América, en representación del rey y la reina de España

vocational [profesional] *adj.*, relacionado con las destrezas laborales

volcano [volcán] *s.*, montaña que, al entrar en erupción, explota y lanza roca derretida, gases y ceniza

vulnerable [vulnerable] *adj.*, abierto, que puede ser lastimado por fuerzas externas

W

wallaby [walabí] *s.*, marsupial más pequeño que un canguro

wat [wat] *s.*, templo budista del Sureste Asiático

waterway [vía fluvial] *s.*, ruta navegable que se usa para los viajes y el transporte

weapon of mass destruction (WMD) [arma de destrucción masiva] *s.*, arma que produce un daño inmenso a grandes cantidades de personas

weather [tiempo atmosférico] *s.*, condiciones de la atmósfera en un momento determinado, incluyendo la temperatura, precipitación y humedad de un día o una semana determinada

Western Hemisphere [Hemisferio Occidental] *s.*, la mitad de la Tierra que se encuentra al oeste del primer meridiano

Wet Pampas [Pampa húmeda] *s.*, región húmeda en el este de la Argentina

Wilkes, Charles [Wilkes, Charles] *s.*, estadounidense que exploró la costa de la Antártida a fines de la década de 1830

wind turbine [aerogenerador] *s.*, motor propulsado por el viento para generar electricidad

Y

Yanomami [yanomamis] *s.*, pueblo indígena cuyos habitantes son cazadores recolectores y continúan viviendo en la cuenca del río Amazonas

yurt [yurta] *s.*, carpa tradicional de fieltro de Asia Central

Z

zaibatsu [zaibatsu] *s.*, organizaciones dirigidas por familias japonesas, propietarias de numerosos negocios

Zambezi River [río Zambeze] *s.*, río del sur de África, que fluye hacia el océano Índico atravesando varios países situados en el sur del centro de África

Zheng He [Zheng He] *s.*, almirante de la marina china que lideró siete expediciones navales para explorar las tierras situadas más allá de China; su último viaje se inició en 1431 D.C.

Zhou [Zhou] *s.*, dinastía que gobernó China en el período 1050–221 A.C.

zoologist [zoólogo] *s.*, científico que estudia los animales

INDEX

A

abolition, 98
Aboriginal Land Rights Act, 1976, 678
Aborigines, 656–657, 678
  land taken by Britain, 661, 678
absolute location,
  defined, 14
  finding, 19, 85, 235, 531, 640
Acropolis, Greece, 256v
Adamawa Highlands, Nigeria, 362, 364
adaptation, human, 192
  examples of, 44, 88, 192, 201, 318, 335, 441, 472, 476, 534–535, 624
Adulis, Ethiopia, 372
adventure tourism, 680–681
Afghanistan, 412–413m, 414m, 451m, 456–457, 456m
  economic indicators of, 63v
  mineral resources in, 314
  political conflicts, 456
  schools and education in, 458–459
  Soviet invasion of, 456
  U.S. invasion of, 101, 457
Africa
  climate of, 47m
  Congo River Basin, 199
  independence movements in, 376–377
  religions of, 61m
  slave markets in, 208
  slave trade, 374–375
    and spread of African culture, 166, 216, 375
  trading in, early empires, 372–373
  in triangular trade, 152–153
  wildlife in, 368–369
  see also Southwest Asia and North Africa; Sub-Saharan Africa
African National Congress (ANC), 403
African Union (AU), 377, 385, 401
Afrikaners, 402
Age of Exploration, 268–269
agricultural revolution, 370, 422
agriculture, R41
  in Africa, 396–397
  as an economic sector, 128, 133
  in Argentina, 224–225
  in Caribbean, 152–153
  in Central America, 174–175, 174v
  in Central Asia, 318
  in Chile, 226–227
  climate and, 70, 312, 313, 604
  in the Great Plains, 80, 81m
  in Mexico, 84
  in Nile River Valley, 430, 431
  in Pacific islands, 652–653
  in Peru, 228
  in rain forests, 146
  slash-and-burn, 204–205, 205v
  in South America, 204–205
  in South Asia, 476–477, 477v
  in Southern Africa, 367
  in the steppes region, 334–335

  sustainable, in South Asia, 476
  terracing, 16v, 201
  see also cash crops; farming; subsistence farming
Aguinaldo, Emilio, 613
air masses, 45
Akbar the Great, Mughal ruler, 484
Aksum Empire, 372
al-Qadhafi, Colonel Mu'ammar, 449
al-Qaeda, 456
Alamo, Texas, 108
Albania, 245m, 246m, 279m, 293m
Alexander II, 326
Alexander the Great, 259, 423, 433
  empire of, 259m
Algeria, 412–413m, 414m, 451m
Ali, Ben, Tunisian president, 448
Allende, Salvador, 223
Allies (in World War I), 100, 278
alluvial gold, 372
alluvial plain, 417
alluvium, 528
Alps, 242v, 247, 250
alternative energy, 26–27v, 26m, 122–123, 350
  in India, 505
altitude zones, South America, 192v, 193
Amazon rain forest, 194, 198–199, 240
Amazon River, South America, 43v, 186v, 194–195, 195m
Amazon River Basin, 190m, 191, 193, 194, 195m
amendments, constitutional, 94, 125
American Indian tribes, 88, 89m, 90, 91, 91m
  see also Native Americans
American Revolution, 92–93
  French Revolution and, 272
American Samoa, 646m, 654m, 659m, 672–673v
Amorites, 423
Amsterdam-Rhine Canal, 182
Amundsen, Roald, 674
Analects (of Confucius), 542, 543
Anatolian Plateau, 420–421, 421m, 428
ancient Greece, 256–257, 420–421
Anderson, Greg, 662–663
Andes Mountains, South America, 190–191, 193, 194
  Inca empire, 200
  indigenous culture in, 217
  rain shadow of, 196
Angel Falls, Venezuela, 191
Angkor Wat, Cambodia, 594v, 608, 609
Angola, 357m, 358m, 367, 367m, 377m, 392v, 393m
Angostura Address, 210

anime, 570–571, 589
animism, 562, 563, 620
annexation, 108
Antarctic Treaty, 1959, 675
Antarctica, 646m, 647, 654m, 659m, 674–675, 674–675v, 675m
  adventure tourism in, 680
  defined as region, 17, 17m
  exploration of, 674–675
  research stations in, 674–675
Anthony, Katey Walter, 316–317
Antigua and Barbuda, 141m, 142m, 143m, 145m, 157m
Antilles. See Lesser Antilles
apartheid, 275, 402–403
Apennines, 250
aqueducts, 263
aquifers, 86–87, 481
Arab-Israeli Wars, 452, 453
Arabian Peninsula, 415, 418–419, 419m, 461m
  see also Dubai; Kuwait; Saudi Arabia; United Arab Emirates
Arabian Sea, 469m, 470m, 471m, 475m, 477m, 487m, 516m
arable land, 476
Arab Spring, 449
Aral Sea, 318–319
Archduke Franz Ferdinand, 276
archipelago, 142v, 143, 530
architecture
  ancient Greek, 257v, 258
  ancient Roman, 242v, 260
  Buddhist temples, 608, 609
  in Delhi, India, 504v
  in Dubai, 411v, 446v, 447v
  as expression of culture, 127, 201, 339
  and Inca engineering, 201
  in Istanbul, 442–443v
  Louvre pyramid, 243
  Peterhof Palace, St. Petersburg, 322
  in Prague, 283v
  pyramids, Egypt, 434–435
  religious, 72, 88v, 126v, 215v, 304v, 307v, 320v, 339v, 410v, 426v, 427v, 608v, 621v, 622v
  Renaissance, 266, 304v
  in Shanghai, 568–569v
  in Thailand, 622
  Western, in Russia, 322–323, 338, 339
Arctic Circle, 311
Arctic Ocean, 40, 42
Argentina, 189m, 190m, 191m, 193m, 205m
  agriculture and economy of, 224–225
  in Antarctica, 675m
  cuisine in, 221
  government changes in, 222
  indigenous populations in, 217v
  land use in, 225m, 687m
  ranching in, 686–687
arid land, 318, 415
  see also deserts
Armenia, 309m, 310m, 311, 311m, 313m, 315m, 345m

INDEX

INDEX

INDEX

INDEX

INDEX

INDEX

SKILLS INDEX

◻ ACKNOWLEDGMENTS

Text Acknowledgments

210: Excerpts from *El Libertador: Writings of Simón Bolívar* by Simón Bolívar, edited by David Bushness, translated by Fred Fornoff. Copyright © 2003 by Oxford University Press. Reprinted by permission of Oxford University Press. All rights reserved.

490: Excerpts from *The Illustrated Bhagavad Gita*, translated by Ranchor Prime. Copyright © 2003 by Godsfield Press, text © by Ranchor Prime. Reprinted by permission of Godsfield Press.

542: Excerpts from *The Analects of Confucius*, translated by Simon Leys. Copyright © 1997 by Pierre Ryckmans. Used by permission of W. W. Norton & Company, Inc.

639: Data from the International Union for Conservation of Nature (IUCN) Red List of Threatened Species by IUCN. Data copyright © 2008 by the IUCN Red List of Threatened Species. Reprinted by kind permission of IUCN.

◻ National Geographic School Publishing

National Geographic School Publishing gratefully acknowledges the contributions of the following National Geographic Explorers to our program and to our planet:

Greg Anderson, National Geographic Fellow
Katey Walter Anthony, 2009 National Geographic Emerging Explorer
Ken Banks, 2010 National Geographic Emerging Explorer
Katy Croff Bell, 2006 National Geographic Emerging Explorer
Christina Conlee, National Geographic Grantee
Alexandra Cousteau, 2008 National Geographic Emerging Explorer
Thomas Taha Rassam (TH) Culhane, 2009 National Geographic Emerging Explorer
Jenny Daltry, 2005 National Geographic Emerging Explorer
Wade Davis, National Geographic Explorer-in-Residence
Sylvia Earle, National Geographic Explorer-in-Residence
Grace Gobbo, 2010 National Geographic Emerging Explorer
Beverly Goodman, 2009 National Geographic Emerging Explorer
David Harrison, National Geographic Fellow
Kristofer Helgen, 2009 National Geographic Emerging Explorer
Fredrik Hiebert, National Geographic Fellow
Zeb Hogan, National Geographic Fellow
Shafqat Hussain, 2009 National Geographic Emerging Explorer
Beverly and Dereck Joubert, National Geographic Explorers-in-Residence
Albert Lin, 2010 National Geographic Emerging Explorer
Elizabeth Kapu'uwailani Lindsey, National Geographic Fellow
Sam Meacham, National Geographic Grantee
Kakenya Ntaiya, 2010 National Geographic Emerging Explorer
Johan Reinhard, National Geographic Explorer-in-Residence

Enric Sala, National Geographic Explorer-in-Residence
Kira Salak, 2005 National Geographic Emerging Explorer
Katsufumi Sato, 2009 National Geographic Emerging Explorer
Cid Simoes and Paola Segura, 2008 National Geographic Emerging Explorers
Beth Shapiro, 2010 National Geographic Emerging Explorer
José Urteaga, 2010 National Geographic Emerging Explorer
Spencer Wells, National Geographic Explorer-in-Residence

Photographic Credits

iii (l) ©Innovative Images/National Geographic School Publishing (c) ©Mary Lynne Ashley/National Geographic School Publishing (r) ©Martin Photography/National Geographic School Publishing. iv (l) ©Aesthetic Life Studio/National Geographic School Publishing (c) ©Gary Donnelly/National Geographic School Publishing (r) ©Cliento Photography/National Geographic School Publishing. vi Top to Bottom Left Side: ©Chris Ranier ©Gemma Atwal ©Ken Banks ©Rebecca Hale/National Geographic Stock ©Christina Conlee ©The Ocean Foundation/National Geographic Stock. Top to Bottom Right Side: ©Sybille Frütel Culhane ©Kevin Krug ©Mark Theissen/National Geographic Stock ©Tyrone Turner/National Geographic Stock ©Adrian Jackson ©G. Anker ©Courtesy of the Jane Goodall Institute. vii Top to Bottom Left Side: ©Chris Ranier ©Rebecca Hale, National Geographic Stock ©Brant Allen ©Rolex Awards ©Beverly Joubert/National Geographic Stock. Top to Bottom Right Side: ©Beverly Joubert/National Geographic Stock ©Calit2, Erik Jepsen ©Ka'uila Barber ©National Geographic Society, Explorer Programs and Strategic Initiatives ©Sharon Farmer ©Mark Thiessen/National Geographic Stock. viii Top to Bottom Left Side: ©Rebecca Hale/National Geographic Stock ©Lana Eklund ©Katsufumi Sato ©Victor Sanchez de Fuentes. Top to Bottom Right Side: ©Beth Shapiro ©Victor Sanchez de Fuentes ©Rachel Etherington ©David Evans/National Geographic Society. ix ©Richard Barnes/National Geographic Stock. x ©John Burcham, National Geographic Stock. xi ©Raul Touzon, National Geographic Stock. xii ©Rod Smith/National Geographic My Shot/National Geographic Stock. xiii ©Richard List, Corbis. xiv ©Photolibrary. xv ©David Alan Harvey/National Geographic Stock. xvi ©Smar Jodha/National Geographic My Shot/National Geographic Stock. xvii ©Kenji Kondo/epa/Corbis. xvii ©Gavin Hellier/Alamy. xix ©Nigel Pavitt, Corbis. xx ©R. Wallace/Stock Photos/Corbis. A1 ©Michael Dunning/Photographer's Choice/Getty Images. A6 (bl) ©Mark Hamblin/Photolibrary (br) ©Thomas Marent/Minden Pictures/National Geographic Stock (c) ©Gerard Soury/Photolibrary (t) ©John Cancalosi/Photolibrary. A7 (bl) ©Adam Jones/Getty Images (br) ©Klaus Nigge/National Geographic Stock (c) ©DLILLC/Corbis (t) ©Thomas Marent/Minden Pictures/National Geographic Stock. 1 (bkg) ©Franck Guiziou/Hemis/Corbis (b, l, r) ©Mark Thiessen/National Geographic Society. 2 (bl) ©Sharon Farmer (br) ©Ka'uila Barber (cl) ©G. Anker (cr) ©Rolex Awards (tl) ©National Geographic Stock (tr) ©Calit2, Erik Jepsen. 3 (b) ©Mark Thiessen/National Geographic Stock (c) ©Ken Banks (tl)

©Gemma Atwal (tr) ©Tyrone Turner/National Geographic Stock. 4 (bkg) ©Suman Bajpeyi/National Geographic My Shot/National Geographic Stock (l) ©Jennifer Shaffer/National Geographic School Publishing (t) ©Fresco JLinga/National Geographic My Shot/National Geographic Stock. 5 ©Scott S. Warren/National Geographic Stock. 6 (l) ©Susan Byrd/National Geographic My Shot/National Geographic Stock (r) ©Mitchell Funk/Photographer's Choice /Getty Images. 7 ©Nigel Pavitt, Corbis. 8 (bkg) ©Richard Barnes/National Geographic Stock (bl) ©Mitchell Funk/Photographer's Choice/Getty Images (cl) ©NASA Goddard Space Flight Center. (tl) ©David Evans/National Geographic Society. 10 ©Stephen Alvarez/National Geographic Stock. 11 ©Sunpix Travel/Alamy. 12 (bc) ©Mike Theiss/National Geographic Stock (cl) ©Blakeley/Alamy (cr) ©Michael S. Yamashita/National Geographic Stock 13 (tl) ©John Wark/Wark Photography, Inc. (tr) ©Mark Remaley/Precision Aerial Photo. 15 (b) ©Michael S. Yamashita/National Geographic Stock (t) ©Ma Wenxiao/Sinopictures/Photolibrary. 16 ©Susan Byrd/National Geographic My Shot/National Geographic Stock. 20 ©Stephen Alvarez/National Geographic Stock. 23 ©PictureLake/Alamy. 26 ©Brooks Kraft/Corbis. 28 (bc) ©James Forte/National Geographic Stock (bl) ©Kenneth Garrett/National Geographic Stock (br) ©Michael Poliza/National Geographic Stock (bkg) ©National Geographic Maps. 29 (bcl) ©N.C. Wyeth/National Geographic Stock (bcr) ©Justin Guarlglia/National Geographic Stock (bl) ©Kenneth Garrett/National Geographic Stock (br) ©Abraham Nowitz/National Geographic Stock 33 (b) ©David Trood/Getty Images (tr) ©Peter Carsten/National Geographic Stock. 34 ©Andrew Hasson/Alamy. 38 ©George H.H. Huey/Corbis. 41 (tc) ©Images & Volcans/Photo Researchers, Inc. (tr) ©Chris Cheadle/Getty Images. 44 ©Bill Hatcher/National Geographic Stock. 46 (bc) ©Michael Doolittle/Alamy (cl) ©Daniel Dempster Photography/Alamy (tl) ©Tom Bean/Alamy. 47 (tl) ©Frank Krahmer/Corbis (tr) ©imagebroker/Alamy. 50 ©Panoramic Images/Getty Images. 52 ©Michael Nichols/National Geographic Stock. 53 ©Russ Bishop/Alamy. 54 ©Kip Evans Photography. 55 ©NASA Goddard Space Flight Center. 56 (bc) ©Gordon Wiltsie/National Geographic Stock (bl) ©Ralph Lee Hopkins/National Geographic Stock (bkg) ©George Grall/National Geographic Stock (br) ©Paul Nicklen/National Geographic Stock 57 (bcl) ©Norbert Rosing/National Geographic Stock (bcr) ©William Albert Allard/National Geographic Stock (bl) ©Stuart Franklin/National Geographic Stock (br) ©Priit Vesilind/National Geographic Stock. 58 (b) ©David R. Frazier Photolibrary, Inc./Alamy (cl) ©Olivier Asselin/Alamy. 59 ©Greg Elms/Lonely Planet Images. 63 ©John Stanmeyer/National Geographic Stock. 64 ©Nic Bothma/epa/Corbis. 65 ©Alain Nogues/Corbis. 67 ©Michael Dunning/Photographer's Choice/Getty Images. 72 ©Romeo Gacad/AFP/Getty Images. 73 (b) ©Gordon Gahan/National Geographic Creative. 74 (b) ©Tetra Images/Corbis (bkg) ©John Burcham, National Geographic Stock (c) ©Walter Meayers Edwards, National Geographic Stock (t) ©Beth Shapiro. 77 ©Petra Engle/National Geographic Stock. 78 (b) ©Phil Schermeister/National Geographic Stock (bkg) ©Menno Boermans/Aurora Photos/Corbis (t) ©SeBuKi/Alamy. 80 ©Mike Grandmaison/Corbis. 82 ©Bill Hatcher/National Geographic Stock. 84 ©Daniel H. Bailey/Corbis. 86 (bkg) ©Jean-Pierre Lescourret/Corbis (cr) ©Mauricio Ramos. 88 ©Jon Arnold Images Ltd/Alamy. 89 ©American School Private Collection/Peter Newark American Pictures/The Bridgeman Art Library Nationality. 90 ©Thomas Sbampato/Photolibrary. 91

©The Granger Collection. 92 (l) ©The Granger Collection (r) ©photostock1/Alamy. 93 ©Visions LLC/Photolibrary. 95 ©William Manning/Corbis. 96 ©Bettmann/Corbis. 98 (l) ©Corbis (r) ©American School Private Collection/Courtesy of Swann Auction Galleries/ The Bridgeman Art Library. 99 ©Corbis. 100 ©Bettmann/Corbis. 101 ©Lynn Johnson/National Geographic Stock. 102 ©The Art Archive/Museo Ciudad Mexico/Gianni Dagli Orti. 103 (l) ©Kenneth Garrett/National Geographic Stock (r) ©David R. Frazier Photolibrary, Inc./Alamy. 104 ©The Stapleton Collection/The Bridgeman Art Library. 105 ©The Stapleton Collection/The Bridgeman Art Library. 106 ©The Granger Collection. 107 (b) ©The Granger Collection (t) ©Look and Learn Magazine Ltd/The Bridgeman Art Library. 108 (l) ©North Wind Picture Archives/Alamy (r) ©Randy Faris/Corbis. 109 (l) ©Corbis (r) ©Charles & Josette Lenars/Corbis. 110 ©North Wind Picture Archives/Alamy. 111 ©Hulton Archive/Getty Images. 114 ©Joe McNally/National Geographic Stock. 116 ©Jennifer Shaffer/National Geographic School Publishing. 117 ©Mike Theiss/National Geographic Society Image Sales. 118 ©Jennifer Shaffer/National Geographic School Publishing/Art Institute of Chicago. 120 ©Car Culture/Corbis. 123 (c) ©James Forte/National Geographic Stock (tr) ©Michael Dunning/Photographer's Choice/Getty Images. 124 ©Marjorie Kamys Cotera/Daemmrich Photography/The Image Works. 125 (tr) ©gubh83/Shutterstock. (cr) ©gubh83/Shutterstock. 126 ©Tono Labra/Photolibrary. 127 ©Keith Dannemiller/Alamy. 128 ©STR/Reuters/Corbis. 130 ©Alfredo Guerrero/epa/Corbis. 131 ©Blaine Harrington III/Alamy. 136 ©Corbis Premium RF/Alamy. 137 (b) ©Holly Wilmeth/Getty Images. 138 (b) ©Georgios Kollidas/Alamy (bkg) ©Raul Touzon, National Geographic Stock (c) ©Stephen Alvarez, National Geographic Stock. 141 ©Konrad Wothe/Minden Pictures. 142 (b) ©Jon Arnold Images Ltd/Alamy (bkg) ©Menno Boermans/Aurora Photos/Corbis (t) ©Danny Lehman/Corbis. 144 ©Dr. Richard Roscoe/Visuals Unlimited, Inc. 147 ©Stuart Westmorland/Corbis. 148 (b) ©Paul Hoekman (t) ©Bryan Wallace. 150 (bc) ©Roy Toft/National Geographic Stock (bl) ©Michael Nichols/National Geographic Stock (bkg) ©Paul Sutherland/National Geographic Stock (br) ©Steve Winter/National Geographic Society Image Sales. 151 (bcl) ©Michael Melford/National Geographic Stock (bcr) ©Bobby Haas/National Geographic Stock (bl) ©Christian Ziegler/National Geographic Stock (br) ©Roy Toft/National Geographic Stock. 152 ©Steve Winter/National Geographic Stock. 155 ©The Bridgeman Art Library. 156 (br) ©Georgios Kollidas/Alamy (r) ©Hemis/Alamy. 157 ©Stuwdamdorp/Alamy. 158 (bl) ©Creativ Studio Heinemann/Westend61/Corbis (c) ©Interfoto/Alamy. 159 (br) ©Reuters/Corbis (tl) ©Bettmann/Corbis (tl) ©Creativ Studio Heinemann/Westend61/Corbis. 162 ©Walter Bibikow/JAI/Corbis. 164 ©Martin Gray/National Geographic Stock. 165 ©Danita Delimont/Alamy. 166 ©Nico Tondini/Photolibrary. 167 ©Rick Gerharter/Lonely Planet Images. 168 ©National Geographic Stock. 169 ©Frans Lanting/Corbis. 170 ©Photolibrary. 172 ©Yuan Man/Xinhua Press/Corbis. 173 ©Logan Abassi/UN Handout/Corbis. 174 ©JS Callahan/tropicalpix/Alamy. 175 ©Michael Dunning/Photographer's Choice/Getty Images. 176 ©Lonely Planet Images /Alamy. 178 (bkg) ©Christian Heeb/Aurora Photos (c) ©Roy Toft/National Geographic Stock (r) ©Micahel & Patricia Fogden/Minden Pictures/National Geographic Stock. 179 ©Arterra Picture Library/Alamy. 183 (l) ©Jacques Marais/Getty Images (r) ©Danny Lehman/Corbis. 184 ©Christian Zeigler/National Geographic Stock. 185 (b) ©REUTERS/Olivia Harris. 186 (b) ©Frans Lanting/Corbis (bkg) ©Rod

Smith/National Geographic My Shot/National Geographic Stock (cl) ©David R. Frazier Photolibrary, Inc./Alamy (tl) ©Photograph by Victor Sanchez de Fuentes. 189 ©Nick Gordon/Oxford Scientific (OSF)/Photolibrary. 190 (bkg) ©Menno Boermans/Aurora Photos/Corbis (bl) ©Colin Monteath/Minden Pictures/National Geographic Stock (br) ©John Eastcott and Yva Momatiuk/National Geographic Stock. 192 ©Ivan Kashinsk/National Geographic Stock. 196 (bkg) ©Melissa Farlow/National Geographic Stock (br) ©Aldo Sessa/Tango Stock/Getty Images. 199 (br) ©Michael Nichols/National Geographic Stock (tr) ©Michael Dunning/Photographer's Choice/Getty Images. 200 ©Ethan Welty/Aurora Photos/Alamy. 201 ©Gnter Wamser/F1online digitale Bildagentur GmbH/Alamy. 202 ©Christina Conlee. 203 (b) ©Christina Conlee (t) ©Robert Clark/National Geographic Stock. 206 (bc) ©Maria Stenzel/National Geographic Stock (c) ©Peruvian School/Museo Arqueologia, Lima, Peru/Boltin Picture Library/The Bridgeman Art Library International (tr) ©McConnell, James Edwin/Private Collection /Look and Learn/The Bridgeman Art Library International. 207 ©Cro Magnon/Alamy. 208 (bc) ©The Art Archive/Bibliothéque des Arts Décoratifs Paris/Gianni Dagli Orti (tr) ©The Art Archive/Bibliothéque des Arts Décoratifs Paris/Gianni Dagli Orti. 209 ©The Art Archive/Kharbine-Tapabor. 211 ©Luis Marden/National Geographic Stock. 215 ©Florian Kopp/imagebroker/Alamy. 216 ©Paolo Aguilar/epa/Corbis. 219 ©Corey Wise/Lonely Planet Images/Getty Images. 220 ©Mike Theiss/National Geographic Stock. 221 ©Richard Nowitz/National Geographic Stock. 223 ©Ivan Alvarado/Reuters/Corbis. 224 ©Jeremy Hoare/Alamy. 225 (b) ©James P. Blair/National Geographic Stock (c) ©Nicolas Misculin/Reuters (t) ©Kit Houghton/Corbis. 226 ©Jennifer Shaffer/National Geographic School Publishing. 228 ©Keren Su/Corbis. 229 (t) ©Imaginechina/Corbis. 231 ©Robert Clark/National Geographic Stock. 232 ©Sebastiao Moreira/epa/Corbis. 234 (b) ©Mike Theiss/National Geographic Stock (bl) ©Charles Dharapak/Pool/Reuters. 240 ©Pete McBride/National Geographic Stock. 241 (b) ©Peter Tsai Photography/Alamy. 242 (b) ©Bob Krist/National Geographic Stock (bkg) ©Richard List/Corbis (c) ©Anne Keiser/National Geographic Stock. 245 ©Atlantide Phototravel/Corbis. 246 (b) ©Yann Arthus-Bertrand/Corbis (bkg) ©Menno Boermans/Aurora Photos/Corbis (t) ©Douglas Pearson/Corbis. 248 ©Owi-Diasign/Photolibrary. 250 ©National Geographic Stock. 252 ©Octavio Aburto. 254 (bc) ©Anne Keiser/National Geographic Stock (bl) ©Agnieszka Pruszek/National Geographic My Shot/National Geographic Stock (bkg) ©Jim Richardson/National Geographic Stock (br) ©Steve Raymer/National Geographic Stock. 255 (bcl) ©Greg Dale/National Geographic Stock (bcr) ©James P. Blair/National Geographic Stock (bl) ©Richard Nowitz/National Geographic Stock (br) ©James L. Stanfield/National Geographic Stock. 256 ©Panoramic Images/National Geographic Stock. 258 (l) ©Richard Nowitz/National Geographic Stock (r) ©The Art Gallery Collection/Alamy. 259 ©PoodlesRock/Corbis. 260 ©Jean-Pierre Lescourret/Corbis. 262 (l) ©Hoberman Collection/Corbis (r) ©The Bridgeman Art Library International. 263 ©North Wind Picture Archives/Alamy. 266 (bl) ©The Bridgeman Art Library (br) ©Underwood & Underwood/Corbis. 267 (bl) ©Doug Taylor/Alamy (br) ©The Bridgeman Art Library (t) ©The Bridgeman Art Library. 268 ©Richard Schlect/National Geographic Stock. 270 ©Paul Thompson/Corbis. 272 (l) ©The Bridgeman Art Library (r) ©The Gallery Collection/Corbis. 273 (b) ©Peter Horree/Alamy (t) ©The Bridgeman

Art Library. 274 ©The Bridgeman Art Library. 275 ©Scanfoto/X00729/Reuters/Corbis. 276 (l) ©Stefano Bianchetti/Corbis (r) ©Clynt Garnham/Alamy. 277 (l) ©Michael Nicholson/Corbis (r) ©Michael Nicholson/Corbis. 279 ©DC Premiumstock/Alamy. 282 ©Rudy Sulgan/Corbis. 284 ©MARKA/Alamy. 286 (l) ©Leonardo da Vinci (1452-1519) Louvre, Paris, France/ Giraudon/The Bridgeman Art Library (r) Claude Monet (1840-1926) Musee Marmottan, Paris, France/Giraudon/The Bridgeman Art Library Nationality. 287 ©Arnaud Chicurel/Hemis/Corbis. 288 ©The Gallery Collection/Corbis. 289 ©Columbia/The Kobal Collection. 290 ©Jon Arnold/JAI/Corbis. 291 ©Sergiy Koshevarov/StockPhotoPro. 292 ©Photolibrary. 294 ©Paul Seheult/Eye Ubiquitous/Corbis. 295 ©Perutskyi Petro/Shutterstock Photos. 296 ©Gregory Wrona/Alamy. 299 ©Michael Dunning/Photographer's Choice/Getty Images. 304 ©Grand Tour/Corbis. 305 (b) ©mangostock/age fotostock. 306 (b) ©Gerd Ludwig/Corbis (bkg) ©Photolibrary (c) ©Gordon Wiltsie, National Geographic Stock (t) ©Rebecca Hale, National Geographic Stock. 309 ©Klaus Nigge/National Geographic Stock. 310 (bkg) ©Menno Boermans/Aurora Photos/Corbis (br) ©Bruno Morandi/Robert Harding World Imagery/Corbis (tl) ©Maxim Toporskiy/Alamy. 312 ©Denis Sinyakov/Reuters/Corbis. 314 ©Cary Wolinsky/National Geographic Stock. 316 ©National Geographic Stock. 318 ©Gerd Ludwig/National Geographic Stock. 319 (tl) ©U.S. Geological Survey (tr) ©NASA. 320 (l) ©Sisse Brimberg/National Geographic Society (r) ©James L. Stanfield/National Geographic Society. 321 (l) ©Massimo Pizzotti/Getty (r) ©Dallas and John Heaton/Photolibrary. 322 ©Richard Klune/Corbis. 323 ©imagebroker/Alamy. 324 ©The Bridgeman Art Library (r) ©Cary Wolinsky/National Geographic Society. 325 (l) ©The Bridgeman Art Library. 326 ©North Wind Picture Archives/Alamy. 328 (l) ©Bettmann/Corbis (r) ©The Art Archive. 329 (b) ©Bettmann/Corbis (t) ©Thomas Johnson/Sygma/Corbis. 332 ©Paul Harris/JAI/Corbis. 334 ©Arne Hodalic/Corbis. 335 (tc) ©Michael Runkel/Robert Harding World Imagery/Corbis (tr) ©Maria Stenzel/National Geographic Stock (tr) ©Sean Sprague/Photolibrary. 336 ©Olaf Meinhardt/Visum/Fotofinder. 339 ©Kristel Richard/Grand Tour/Corbis. 340 ©Shepard Sherbell/Corbis Saba. 342 ©Imagesource/Photolibrary. 344 ©Oleg Nikishin/Stringer/Getty Images. 347 (c) ©iStockphoto ©Michael Dunning/Photographer's Choice/Getty Images. 352 ©iStockphoto. 353 (b) ©Yi Chan/Flickr/Getty Images. 354 (b) ©Ingo Arndt/Minden Pictures/National Geographic Stock (bkg) ©David Alan Harvey/National Geographic Stock (c) ©Mitsuaki Iwago/Minden Pictures/National Geographic Stock (t) ©Kakenya Ntaiya. 357 ©Top-Pics TBK/Alamy. 358 (bkg) ©Menno Boermans/Aurora Photos/Corbis (bl) ©tbkmedia/Alamy (tr) ©Michael Poliza/National Geographic Stock. 360 ©Michael Nichols/National Geographic Stock. 362 ©Philippe Bourseiller/Getty Images. 364 ©Ian Nichols/National Geographic Stock. 366 ©Mike Hutchings/Reuters. 368 (bc) ©Beverly Joubert/National Geographic Stock (bl) ©Beverly Joubert/National Geographic Stock. 370 ©Gerald Hoberman/Hoberman Collection UK/Photolibrary. 372 (bl) ©The Trustees of the British Museum/Art Resource (br) ©ADB Travel/dbimages/Alamy. 373 ©HIP/Art Resource. 376 ©Private Collection/Look and Learn/The Bridgeman Art Library International. 377 (bl) ©Mary Evans Picture Library/The Image Works (br) ©Bruce Dale/National Geographic Stock. 378 (bc) ©James L. Stanfield/National Geographic Stock (bl) ©Tim Laman/National Geographic Stock (bkg) ©George Steinmetz/National Geographic Stock (br)

©Annie Griffiths/National Geographic Stock. 379 (bcl) ©Roy Toft/National Geographic Stock (bcr) ©Tino Soriano/National Geographic Stock (bl) ©Jodi Cobb/ National Geographic Stock (br) ©Ed Kashi/National Geographic Stock. 382 ©Ralph Lee Hopkins/National Geographic Stock. 384 ©Vanessa Burger/Images of Africa Photobank Alamy. 386 ©Paul Gilham–FIFA/FIFA via Getty Images. 387 ©David Alan Harvey/National Geographic Stock. 388 (bc) ©Nigel Pavitt/John Warburton-Lee Photography/Alamy (bl) ©Sean Sprague/ Still Pictures/Photolibrary. 389 (cl) ©Michael Nichols/ National Geographic Stock (tr) ©Suzi Eszterhas/Minden Pictures/National Geographic Stock. 390 ©Jane Goodall Institute. 391 (bkg) ©Gerry Ellis/ Minden Pictures/ National Geographic Stock (br) ©Wade Davis/Ryan Hill. 392 ©Finbarr O'Reilly/Reuters. 394 ©George Steinmetz/ Corbis. 396 (b) ©Pascal Maitre/National Geographic Stock (tr) ©Joerg Boethling/Alamy. 398 ©Louise Gubb/ Corbis. 399 ©Michael Dunning/Photographer's Choice/ Getty Images. 400 ©Frederic Courbet/Still Pictures/ Photolibrary. 402 ©Ulrich Doering/Alamy. 403 ©Trinity Mirror/Mirrorpix/Alamy. 406 (bl) ©Chris Stenger/FN/ Minden Pictures/National Geographic Stock (br) ©Walker, Lewis W./National Geographic Stock. 407 (bkg) ©Clement Philippe/Arterra Picture Library/Alamy (bkg) ©Tim Fitzharris/Minden Pictures/National Geographic Stock (cf) ©Mattias Klum /National Geographic Stock (l) ©Tom Vezo/Minden Pictures/National Geographic Stock (rbkg) ©Ted Wood/Aurora Photos (rf) ©Thomas Lehne/ Alamy. 408 ©Anup Shah/Corbis. 409 (b) ©Heiner Heine/ Imagebroker/Alamy. 410 (b) ©Martin Gray/National Geographic Stock (bkg) ©Smar Jodha/National Geographic My Shot/National Geographic Stock (c) ©David Boyer/National Geographic Stock (t) ©Thomas Culhane. 413 ©Vanessa Lefort/National Geographic My Shot/National Geographic Stock. 414 (bkg) ©Menno Boermans/Aurora Photos/Corbis (cl) ©Gary Cook/Alamy (cr) ©Peter Adams/Getty Images. 416 ©Ed Kashi/National Geographic Stock. 418 ©Fischer Gunter/WoodyStock/ Alamy. 420 ©Chris Bradley/Axiom/photolibrary. 422 (bl) ©Victor R. Boswell, Jr/National Geographic Stock (br) ©Scala/Art Resource 423 (bl) ©Erich Lessing/Art Resource (br) ©Corbis. 424 ©Richard Nowitz/National Geographic Stock. 425 ©Oliver Weiken/epa/Corbis. 426 ©Bachmann Bachmann/F1 Online/photolibrary. 427 (bl) ©James Brunker/Alamy (tr) ©Kordcom Kordcom/age fotostock/photolibrary. 428 ©Yann Arthus-Bertrand/ Corbis. 429 ©The Art Archive/Topkapi Museum Istanbul/ Dagli Orti. 430 ©Gwill Owen/Sylvia Cordaiy Photo Library Ltd /Alamy. 431 ©NASA/JSC/Gateway to Astronaut Photography of Earth. 432 (bl) ©Paul Sutcliffe/ Alamy. (br) ©Erich Lessing/Art Resource. 433 (bc) ©Mary Jelliffe/Ancient Art & Architecture Collection Ltd./Alamy (tr) ©Kenneth Garrett/National Geographic Stock. 434 ©Kenneth Garrett/National Geographic Stock. 438 ©Keren Su/Corbis. 440 ©Alberto Arzoz/Axiom/Aurora Photos. 441 ©Walter Bibikow/Jon Arnold Images Ltd./ Alamy. 442 ©Gavin Hellier/Alamy. 443 ©David Bathgate/ Corbis. 444 (b) ©Radius Images/Corbis (bl) ©G. Anker. 445 ©Hanan Isachar/Corbis. 446 ©NASA/Science Faction/Corbis. 447 ©Matthias Seifert/Reuters/Corbis. 449 (tr) ©Umit Bektas/Reuters/Corbis ©Felipe Trueba/epa european pressphoto agency. 450 ©Mohammad Berno/ Document Iran/Corbis. 452 ©David Rubinger/Time & Life Pictures/Getty Images. 454 ©Sabah Arar/AFP/Getty Images. 457 ©Tim Gurney/Alamy. 459 ©Shehzad Noorani/Stillpictures/Aurora Photos. 463 ©Mark Thiessen/National Geographic Stock. 464 ©Bildarchiv Preussischer Kulturbesitz/Art Resource. 465 (bl) ©O. Louis Mazzatenta/National Geographic Creative. 466 (b)

©Peter Adams/Corbis (bkg) ©Tibor Bognar/agefotostock (c) ©Kenji Kondo/epa/Corbis (t) ©Hussain RAE photos. 469 ©Lynn M. Stone/Nature Picture Library. 470 (bkg) ©Menno Boermans/Aurora Photos/Corbis (bl) ©Tiziana and Gianni Baldizzone/Corbis (l) ©Dinodia Images/ Alamy (tc) ©Stephen Sharnoff/National Geographic Stock. 472 (bkg) ©Bobby Model/National Geographic Stock (l) ©James L. Stanfield/National Geographic Stock. 474 ©Frederic Soltan/Sygma/Corbis. 476 ©Lynsey Addario/National Geographic Image Collection. 478 ©Prakash Singh/AFP/Getty Image. 479 ©Blue Legacy International. 481 ©Michael Dunning/Photographer's Choice/Getty Images. 482 ©Luca Tettoni/Corbis. 483 (b) ©The Schoyen Collection (t) ©The Schoyen Collection. 484 (l) ©Silvio Fiore/SuperStock (r) ©The Trustees of the British Museum. 485 ©Thomas Retterath/Getty Images. 488 ©Jeremy Horner/Corbis. 489 ©Lineair/Photolibrary. 490 ©Bettmann/Corbis. 491 ©Art Directors & TRIP/ Alamy. 494 ©Harish Tyagi/epa/Corbis. 496 ©Louise Batalla Duran/Alamy. 497 ©Bruce Dale/National Geographic Stock. 498 (bkg) ©Ed Kashi/National Geographic Stock (l) ©Jodi Cobb/National Geographic Stock. 500 ©Ajay Verma/Reuters/Corbis. 501 (b) ©Foodfolio–StockFood Munich (t) ©Abraham Nowitz/ National Geographic Stock. 502 (bkg) ©David Cumming/ Eye Ubiquitous/Corbis (bl) ©Robert Wallis/Corbis (bc) ©Stephen Romilly/Alamy. 503 (b) ©Dharma Productions/ The Kobal Collection (t) ©Frazer Harrison/Getty Images. 504 ©Eric Feferberg/Pool/Reuters. 506 ©Fredrik Renander/Alamy. 507 (t1) ©Ed Kashi/National Geographic Stock (t2) ©Ed Kashi/National Geographic Stock (t2) ©Fridmar Damm/Corbis (t3) ©Akhtar Soomro/ Deanpictures/The Image Works (t4) ©Akhtar Soomro/ Deanpictures/The Image Works (t5) ©Andrew Holbrooke/ Corbis (t7) ©National Geographic Maps (t8) ©National Geographic Maps. 508 ©Ed Kashi/National Geographic Image Collection. 510 ©Sajjad Hussain/AFP/Getty Images. 511 ©Dinodia Photo Library. 512 ©Akhtar Soomro/ Deanpictures/The Image Works. 514 ©Andrew Holbrooke/Corbis. 521 (b) ©David H. Wells/age fotostock/ SuperStock. 522 (b) ©Michael Nichols/National Geographic Stock (bkg) ©George Steinmetz/National Geographic Stock (c) ©Gavin Hellier/Alamy (t) ©Albert Lin. 525 ©Mitsuaki Iwago/Minden Pictures/National Geographic Stock. 526 (b) ©Chun Ki Leung/National Geographic My Shot /National Geographic Stock (bkg) ©Menno Boermans/Aurora Photos/Corbis (t) ©Wang Jianjun/TAO Images Limited/Alamy. 528 ©Fritz Hoffmann/National Geographic Stock. 530 ©Reuters/ Mainichi Shimbun. 532 ©Toby Adamson/Axiom Photographic Agency/Getty Images. 534 ©Alison Wright/ National Geographic Stock. 536 (b) ©Unterthiner, Stefano/National Geographic Stock (cl) ©Katsufumi Sato/ National Geographic Society. 538 (bl) ©Richard Swiecki/ Royal Ontario Museum/Corbis (br) ©Ira Block/National Geographic Stock. 539 (bc) ©O. Louis Mazzatenta/ National Geographic Stock (tc) ©Atlantide Phototravel/ Corbis. 540 (bc) ©Michael S. Yamashita/National Geographic Stock (bl) ©Justin Guariglia/National Geographic Stock (bkg) ©O. Louis Mazzatenta/National Geographic Stock (br) ©Michael S. Yamashita/National Geographic Stock. 541 (bcl) ©Kenneth Ginn/National Geographic Stock (bcr) ©Kate Staszczak/National Geographic My Shot/National Geographic Stock (bl) ©Michael S. Yamashita/National Geographic Stock (br) ©Ira Block/National Geographic Stock. 542 ©Shiwei/Best View Stock/photolibrary. 544 ©Redlink/Corbis. 546 (bkg) ©Gregory A. Harlin/National Geographic Stock (b) ©National Geographic Maps. 548 ©Wendy Connett/ Alamy. 549 ©Rob Howard/Corbis. 550 ©Ira Block/

National Geographic Stock. 551 ©Ira Block/National Geographic Stock. 552 ©Asian Art & Archaeology, Inc./ Corbis. 553 (b) ©Private Collection/Peter Newark Military Pictures/The Bridgeman Art Library International. 554 (bl) ©H. Edward Kim/National Geographic Stock (br) ©Korea News Service/Reuters/Corbis. 555 (bl) ©John Van Hasselt/Sygma/Corbis ©(br) ©The Trustees of The British Museum/Art Resource. 556 (bl) ©Bettmann/Corbis. 557 (l) ©Bruce Burkhardt/Corbis (r) ©Michael S. Yamashita/ National Geographic Stock. 560 ©B.S.P.I./Corbis. 562 ©Buena Vista Images/Getty Images. 564 (bl) ©The Trustees of the British Museum/Art Resource. 565 ©View Stock/Alamy. 566 ©Justin Guariglia/National Geographic Stock. 568 (bc) ©Mark Leong/National Geographic Stock (bl) ©Richard Nowitz/National Geographic Stock (bkg) ©Scott S. Warren/National Geographic Stock (br) ©Jason Teale/National Geographic My Shot/National Geographic Stock. 569 (bcl) ©Pete Ryan/National Geographic Stock (bl) ©Michael S. Yamashita/National Geographic Stock (bcr) ©Thomas J. Abercrombie/National Geographic Stock (br) ©Jodi Cobb/National Geographic Stock. 570 (bl) ©Everett Kennedy Brown/epa/Corbis (cl) ©Everett Kennedy Brown/epa/Corbis. 571 ©Studio Ghibli/Tokuma Shoten/The Kobal Collection. 572 (b) ©Jose Fuste Raga/ Corbis. 574 (b) ©Jianan Yu/Reuters/Corbis. 577 ©Michael Dunning/Photographer's Choice/Getty Images. 578 ©epa/ Corbis. 580 (bl) ©Nicky LohReuters/Corbis (bkg) ©Justin Guariglia/National Geographic Stock. 582 ©Asia File/ Alamy. 585 (bkg) ©SJ. Kim/Flickr/Getty Images (tr) ©Jane Sweeney/JAI/Corbis. 586 (bc) ©Phil Iossifidis/National Geographic My Shot/National Geographic Stock (bl) ©Paul Chesley/National Geographic Stock (bkg) ©Alicia Pudsey/National Geographic My Shot/National Geographic Stock (br) ©Arkadiusz Dudzinski/National Geographic My Shot/National Geographic Stock. 587 (bcl) ©Winfield Parks/National Geographic Stock (bcr) ©Paul Chesley/National Geographic Stock (bl) ©Martin Gray/National Geographic Stock (br) ©Justin Guariglia/ National Geographic Stock. 591 (t) ©Feng Li/Getty Images. 592 ©John Woodcock/iStock Vectors/Getty Images. 593 (b) ©Stan Rohrer/Alamy. 594 (b) ©Paul Chesley/National Geographic Stock (bkg) ©Nigel Pavitt/Corbis (c) ©John Stanmeyer LLC, National Geographic Stock (t) ©Kevin Krug. 597 ©Tui De Roy/ Minden Pictures/National Geographic Society Image Sales. 598 (bkg) ©Menno Boermans/Aurora Photos/Corbis (bl) ©NASA (tr) ©Mary Plage/Photolibrary. 600 ©Brant Allen. 602 (bkg) ©Neil Rabinowitz/Corbis (bl) ©James P. Blair/National Geographic Society Image Sales. 604 ©John Stanmeyer/ National Geographic Society Image Sales. 606 ©Tim Laman/National Geographic Society Image Sales. 607 (bkg) ©Tim Laman/National Geographic Society Image Sales (cl) ©Tim Laman/National Geographic Society Image Sales (cr) ©Tim Laman/National Geographic Society Image Sales. 608 (c) ©Robert Clark/National Geographic Society Image Sales (cb) ©Robert Harding Picture Library Ltd/Alamy. 609 (br) ©View Stock/Alamy. 612 (bl) ©Stringer/Indonesia/Reuters/Corbis (r) ©Lindsay Hebberd/Corbis. 613 ©FPG/Hulton Archive/Getty Images. 615 ©W.E. Garrett/National Geographic Stock. 618 ©Jose Fuste Raga/Corbis. 620 (b) ©James Nachtwey VII/National Geographic Society Image Sales. 621 (tl) ©Friedrich Stark/Alamy (tr) ©Robert Clark/National Geographic Society Image Sales. 622 (bkg) ©Danita Delimont/Gallo Images/Getty Images (bl) ©Jon Arnold Images Ltd/ Alamy. 623 (cr) ©WoodyStock/Alamy. 624 ©Photolibrary. 625 ©National Geographic School Publishing. 626 (b) ©Ulet Ifansasti/Getty Images. 627 (tl) ©Buddy Mays/Alamy. 628 ©Imagemore Co., Ltd./Corbis. ©AFP/Getty Images 629 ©AFP/Getty Images. 630 ©Peter Adams/JAI/Corbis. 631 ©John Stanmeyer/National Geographic Society Image Sales. 633 (c)© Lauca Images/Alamy (t) ©Michael Dunning/Photographer's Choice/Getty Images. 634 ©Tengku Mohd Yusof/Alamy. 639 (b) ©Theo Aloffs/ Minden Pictures/National Geographic Stock (cl) ©Suzi Eszterhas/Minden Pictures/National Geographic Stock (cr) ©John Cancalosi/Photolibrary (tl) ©Tom Brakefield/ Photolibrary (tr) ©Top-Pics TBK/Alamy. 641 (b) ©Vladislav Kochelaevskiy/Alamy. 642 (b) ©R. Wallace/ Stock Photos /Corbis (bkg) ©Yva Momatiuk & John Eastcott/Minden Pictures/National Geographic Stock (c) ©Pixtal Images/Photolibrary (t) ©Ka'uila Barber. 645 ©Mitsuaki Iwago/Minden Pictures/National Geographic Stock. 646 (bkg) ©Menno Boermans/Aurora Photos/ Corbis (bl) ©Fred Bavendam/Minden Pictures/National Geographic Stock (tr) ©Michel Renaudeau/Photolibrary. 648 ©Kevin Schafer/Alamy. 649 ©Look Die Bildagentur der Fotografen GmbH/Alamy. 650 (b) ©Martin Harvey/ Corbis (t) ©John Carnemolla/Corbis. 652 ©Brian Skerry/ National Geographic Society Image Sales. 655 (t) ©Michael Dunning/Photographer's Choice/Getty Images (c) ©Jeff Hunter/Getty Images. 656 ©Catherine Karnow/ Corbis. 657 ©Belinda Wright/National Geographic Society Image Sales. 658 (b) ©Rob Howard/Corbis (t) ©Walter Meayers Edwards/National Geographic Society Image Sales. 659 (c) ©Jean Leo Dugast/Sygma/Corbis (t) ©Image Source/Corbis. 660 ©Patrick Eden/Alamy. 661 (bl) ©Corbis (l) ©Caro/Alamy (t) ©The Bridgeman Art Library. 662 ©Chris Ranier. 663 ©Chris Ranier. 666 ©Massimo Ripani/Grand Tour/Corbis. 668 ©Amy Toensing/National Geographic Stock. 669 ©David Ball/Alamy. 670 ©Stringer/Australia/X01245/Reuters/Corbis. 672 ©Randy Olson/National Geographic Stock. 674 ©George F. Mobley, National Geographic Stock. 676 ©Bates Littlehales/National Geographic Stock. 678 ©POOL/ Reuters/Corbis. 679 ©Phil Walter/Getty Images. 681 (bkg) ©David Doubilet/National Geographic Stock (tl) ©David McLain/National Geographic Stock (tr) ©David Wall/ Alamy. 682 ©David L. Moore/Alamy. 683 ©Tui De Roy/ Minden Pictures/National Geographic Stock. 688 ©Paul Nicklen/National Geographic Stock. R39 ©Fresco JLinga/ National Geographic My Shot/National Geographic Stock. R40 ©George Grall/National Geographic Stock. R41 ©SERDAR/Alamy. R42 ©Bettmann/Corbis. R44 ©Hulton Archive/Getty Images. R45 ©Svabo/Alamy. R47 ©Scott Olson/Getty Images. R49 ©Lordprice Collection/ Alamy. R50 ©Parbul TV via Reuters TV/Reuters/Corbis. R51 ©Markus Altmann/Corbis. R52 (b) ©Mario Lopez/ epa/Corbis (t) ©Alinari Archives/Corbis. R53 (b) ©Anindito Mukherjee/epa/Corbis (t) ©Werner Forman/ Art Resource. R54 (b) ©Ronen Zvulun/Reuters/Corbis (t) ©The Art Archive/Museo del Prado Madrid. R55 (b) ©Mak Remissa/epa/Corbis (t) ©Rubin Museum of Art/Art Resource. R56 (b) ©Joe McNally/National Geographic Stock (t) ©Biju/Alamy. R57 (b) ©Robert Harding World Imagery/Corbis (t) ©Art Directors & TRIP/Alamy. R58 (b) ©Christian Kober/Photolibrary (t) ©National Palace Museum Taiwan/The Art Archive.

Map Credits

Mapping Specialists, LTD., Madison, WI.
National Geographic Maps, National Geographic Society
Note: Culturally and economically, Cyprus is considered a European country. Geographically, many consider it to be part of Asia.

Illustrator Credits

Precision Graphics

AFRICA

SOUTHEAST ASIA

AUSTRALIA,
THE PACIFIC REALM
& ANTARCTICA

East

Asia

SOUTH
AMERICA

SOUTHWEST ASIA
& NORTH AFRICA

EUROPE

EUROPE

EUROPE

SOUTHWEST ASIA

Southeast Asia

SUB-SAHARAN
AFRICA

Central America
& the Caribbean

SOUTH
AMERICA

RUSSIA
& THE EURASIAN REPUBLICS

East
Asia

AUSTRALIA,
THE PACIFIC REALM
& ANTARCTICA

AUSTRALIA,
THE PACIFIC REALM
& ANTARCTICA

South Asia

Southeast Asia

Central America
& the Caribbean

South
Asia

East
Asia

NORTH
AMERICA

SOUTHWEST ASIA
& NORTH AFRICA

NORTH AM

North America

Russia & the Eurasian Republics

Southeast Asia

Central America & the Caribbean

Australia, the Pacific Realm & Antarctica

South Asia

Southeast Asia

Central America & the Caribbean

NATIONAL GEOGRAPHIC LEARNING

CENGAGE Learning®

Southwest Asia & North Africa

North America